TENTH EDITION

# Our Sexuality

## Robert Crooks

## Karla Baur

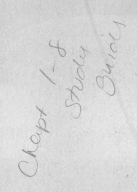

*Chapt 1-8 Study Guide*

*Prayer for Baby*

**WADSWORTH**
CENGAGE Learning™

Australia • Brazil • Japan • Korea • Mexico • Singapore • Spain • United Kingdom • United States

WADSWORTH
CENGAGE Learning™

**Our Sexuality, Tenth Edition**
Robert Crooks, Karla Baur

Publisher: Michele Sordi

Development Editor: Kirk Bomont

Assistant Editor: Magnolia Molcan

Editorial Assistant: Rachel Guzman

Senior Technology Project Manager:
Bessie Weiss

Executive Marketing Manager:
Kimberly Russell

Marketing Communications Manager:
Linda Yip

Project Manager, Editorial Production:
Mary Noel

Creative Director: Rob Hugel

Art Director: Vernon T. Boes

Print Buyer: Rebecca Cross

Permissions Editor: Roberta Broyer

Production Service: Mandy Hetrick,
Lachina Publishing Services

Text Designer: Liz Harasymczuk

Photo Researcher: Eric Schrader

Copy Editor: Robert Green,
Lachina Publishing Services

Illustrator: Adam Miller

Cover Designer: Irene Morris

Cover Image: Barnaby Hall/Getty Images

Compositor: Lachina Publishing Services

For product information and technology assistance, contact us at
**Cengage Learning Customer & Sales Support, 1-800-354-9706**

For permission to use material from this text or product,
submit all requests online at **cengage.com/permissions**
Further permissions questions can be emailed to
**permissionrequest@cengage.com**

Library of Congress Control Number: 2006940179

Student Edition
ISBN-13: 978-0-495-09554-5
ISBN-10: 0-495-09554-0

Paper Edition
ISBN-13: 978-0-495-80426-0
ISBN-10: 0-495-80426-6

Loose-leaf Edition
ISBN-13: 978-0-495-60508-9
ISBN-10: 0-495-60508-5

**Wadsworth**
10 Davis Drive
Belmont, CA 94002-3098
USA

Cengage Learning is a leading provider of customized learning solutions with office locations around the globe, including Singapore, the United Kingdom, Australia, Mexico, Brazil, and Japan. Locate your local office at:
**international.cengage.com/region**

Cengage Learning products are represented in Canada by Nelson Education, Ltd.

For your course and learning solutions, visit a**cademic.cengage.com**

Purchase any of our products at your local college store or at our preferred online store **www.ichapters.com**

Printed in Canada
4  5  6  7  11  10  09  08

*For our loving spouses, Sami Tucker and Jim Hicks, and the staff of Act Now—a community-based organization implementing an HIV/AIDS intervention program for southeastern Kenya.*

Bob Crooks, Sami Tucker, and senior peer educator staff of Act Now.

The integration of psychological, social, and biological components of human sexuality in this text is facilitated by the blending of the authors' academic and professional backgrounds. Robert Crooks has a Ph.D. in psychology. His graduate training stressed clinical and physiological psychology. In addition, he has considerable background in sociology, which served as his minor throughout his graduate training. His involvement with teaching human sexuality classes at the university, college, and medical school levels spans over two decades. Recently Bob and his wife, Sami Tucker, have been involved in the establishment and implementation of an HIV/AIDS education and intervention program in Kenya. Their work with this project includes designing a research strategy for assessing behavior change, developing a peer educator-based educational strategy, and conducting training sessions for Kenyan peer educator staff. Over the last four years they have traveled to Africa several times and devoted many months to the evolving Kenya program.

Karla Baur has a master's degree in social work; her advanced academic work stressed clinical training. She is a licensed clinical social worker in private practice, specializing in couples and sex therapy with adults. Karla has been certified as a sex educator, therapist, and sex therapy supervisor by the American Association of Sex Educators, Counselors, and Therapists. She has instructed sexuality classes at a medical school and several colleges and universities and has provided clinical training for other mental health professionals. Karla has also found a way to combine her clinical skills with her love of horses by providing performance enhancement training for equestrians. Furthermore, Karla has been involved in the HIV/AIDS program in Kenya, and in 2004 she joined Bob and Sami to train peer educators.

The authors have a combined total of over 60 years of teaching, counseling, and research in the field of sexology. Together they taught college sexuality courses for a number of years. They present workshops and guest lectures to a wide variety of professional and community groups, and they counsel individuals, couples, and families on sexual concerns. Their combined teaching, clinical, and research experiences, together with their graduate training, have provided them with an appreciation and sensitive understanding of the highly complex and personal nature of human sexuality.

It is the authors' belief that a truly sensitive understanding of our sexuality must be grounded in both the female and the male perspectives and experiences. In this sense, their courses, their students, and this text have benefited from a well-balanced perception and a deep appreciation of human sexual behavior.

# BRIEF CONTENTS

# CONTENTS

## PART THREE

### ● SEXUAL BEHAVIOR

#### 7 Love and Communication in Intimate Relationships 165

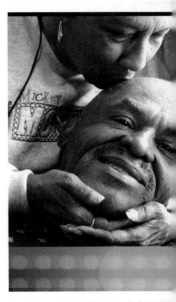

#### 8 Sexual Behaviors 212

# PART FOUR
## ► SEXUALITY AND
## THE LIFE CYCLE

## 11 Conceiving Children: Process and Choice   293

## 12 Sexuality During Childhood and Adolescence   322

## 13 Sexuality and the Adult Years   349

# PART FIVE
# ◗ SEXUAL PROBLEMS

## 14 Sexual Difficulties and Solutions   376

## 15 Sexually Transmitted Diseases   409

# PART SIX
# ◗ SOCIAL ISSUES

## 16 Atypical Sexual Behavior   461

# SPECIAL INTEREST FEATURES

## Sexual Orientation Coverage

Throughout the text, discussion is meant to be inclusive of all sexual orientations; however, places where special issues that concern sexual orientation are highlighted include:

### Chapter 1: Perspectives on Sexuality
- Model of sex for procreation (9)
- Medieval Christian attitudes of sex as sinful (11)
- Changing attitudes from the late 1960s to the present (16–17)
- Online LBGT community (16–17)

### Chapter 2: Sex Research: Methods and Problems
- Findings of the Kinsey reports (32)
- Lobbying by conservative groups against research on gays (33)

### Chapter 3: Gender Issues
- Variant gender identity and sexual orientation (62–63)
- Gender role expectations (71)

### Chapter 4: Female Sexual Anatomy and Physiology
- Sexual activity and the menstrual cycle (93)
- Need for routine mammograms for lesbians (104–105)

### Chapter 6: Sexual Arousal and Response
- Hypothalamus response to human pheromones, 144–145

### Chapter 7: Love and Communication in Intimate Relationships
- Do heterosexuals, gay men, and lesbians have different views of love and sex? (181–182)

### Chapter 8: Sexual Behaviors
- Erotic fantasies (214)
- Range of sexual expression compared to heterosexual relationships (223)
- Sexual expression in gay men (226–228)
- Touching in gay and lesbian relationships (224)

### Chapter 9: Sexual Orientations
- Basic definitions (234)
- Prevalence of homosexuality (235)
- Bisexuality (235–237)
- Psychosocial theories of sexual orientation (238)
- Biological theories of sexual orientation (239–241)
- Societal attitudes (241–245)
- Homophobia and hate crimes (245–248)
- Homosexuality and the media (248–249)
- Lifestyles (249)
- Coming out (249–253)
- Homosexual relationships (254–256)
- The gay rights movement (256–259)

### Chapter 11: Conceiving Children: Process and Choice
- Reproductive alternatives (298)
- Attitudes toward homosexuality of women who are anti-abortion (308)

### Chapter 12: Sexuality During Childhood and Adolescence
- Same-sex play during childhood (327–328)
- Gays and lesbians as "technical virgins" (332)
- Gay–straight alliances in high schools (337)
- Adolescent homosexuality (337–338)

### Chapter 13: Sexuality and the Adult Years
- Domestic partnerships (351)
- Legal marriage for gays and lesbians (362–364)
- Homosexual relationships in later years (372)

### Chapter 14: Sexual Difficulties and Solutions
- Faking orgasms (382)
- Sexual abuse in childhood (392)
- Lack of satisfaction in some heterosexual relationships due to homosexual desires (394)

### Chapter 15: Sexually Transmitted Diseases
- Gonorrhea resistance to antibiotics among gay men (419)
- Recent increased incidence of syphilis among gay men (420)
- Homosexual or bisexual men at high risk for hepatitis A or hepatitis B (429)
- HIV transmission via oral sex in gay men (441)
- HIV resistance among gay men (441)
- Increased involvement in risky sex in connection to availability of HAART (447)
- Nondisclosure of HIV status to partners (456)

### Chapter 16: Atypical Sexual Behavior
- Gay men "going in drag" as one form of cross-dressing (465)

### Chapter 17: Sexual Coercion
- Rape of men by men (492–493)
- Same-sex sexual harassment in the workplace (505)

# Coverage of Cultural Diversity

Comparisons across cultures and among members of ethnic groups within North America are infused throughout the text. Highlights include:

*Our Sexuality*, now in its tenth edition, provides students with an engaging, personally relevant, politically astute, and academically sound introduction to human sexuality. The text's comprehensive integration of biological, psychological, behavioral, political, and cultural aspects of sexuality has been consistently well received in each previous edition.

## ◗ New in This Edition

- This edition of *Our Sexuality* is breaking new ground in human sexuality textbooks by being the first book to emphasize in-depth coverage on the influence of politics on sexual issues. Professionals in the sexology field have become increasingly concerned about the often adverse impact of politics on sexuality. We believe that awareness of this influence is a crucial component of students' education in sexuality courses. Accordingly, we have added a new feature in the tenth edition titled **Sex and Politics**. In this feature, we seek to broaden understanding of the influence on sexuality by advocacy groups and government bodies—local, state, federal, and international. We present a range of topics where sex and politics meet:

  1. Efforts by well-organized groups and politicians that have impeded important research on human sexuality.
  2. States that have passed laws making it illegal to sell vibrators.
  3. Increases in federal funding for abstinence-only sex education in public schools, even though comprehensive sex education has been shown to be more effective in preventing pregnancy and the spread of sexually transmitted diseases.
  4. Controversy about whether lesbians, gay men, and bisexual and transgendered individuals should have the same civil rights as heterosexual individuals.
  5. President George W. Bush's decisions to withhold funds authorized by Congress for maternal and child health services in developing countries.
  6. U.S. policy's disregard of public health research findings, indicated by reducing condom promotion as an integral aspect of HIV/AIDS prevention in Africa.

  All of these critical issues and the political forces that influence the outcomes are discussed in specific

Sex and Politics boxes throughout the text. **Sex and Politics** margin icons call out material contained within the text.

- Another new feature incorporated in the tenth edition is the concept of **Sexual Intelligence,** introduced in Chapter 1 and integrated where appropriate in other chapters. We define sexual intelligence as being composed of four integral features, including understanding oneself sexually; having interpersonal sexual skills and integrity; knowing accurate, fact-based sexual information; and understanding the role that politics plays in the diverse arenas of sexuality. *Our Sexuality* endeavors to help professors who teach human sexuality courses to promote increased sexual intelligence among their students.
- The tenth edition of *Our Sexuality* has benefited from careful streamlining of content, resulting in a significant **reduction in text length**. While we have presented all essential topics in sufficient depth, the reduced length will increase students' access to the material.
- More than **1,000 new citations,** reflecting the most recent research, have been added, most from studies reported in the last two years.
- Several **new Sexuality and Diversity discussions** have been added throughout the text, dealing with topics such as the marriage crisis around the globe, cross-national data on sexual behavior of adolescents, and China's Mosuo culture, in which only women initiate intimate relationships. Many other Sexuality and Diversity discussions have been revised, expanded, and updated for the tenth edition.
- A wealth of **new and significantly updated information** in every chapter, highlights of which are described below.

## Chapter 1: Perspectives on Sexuality

- Explanation of our definition of "sexual intelligence."
- Discussion of pharmacists' use of the "conscience clause" with contraception prescriptions.
- Expanded information about Islam.
- Sexual consequences of China's openness to the West.
- Updated data on the media and sexuality.
- New information about sexuality and wireless technology.
- Legal status of non-procreative sexual behaviors.
- Supreme Court decisions affecting contraception and abortion.

## Chapter 2: Sex Research: Methods and Problems

- New Sex and Politics box: "Sex Research Under Siege."
- New example of random versus representative sample research.
- Major revision and update of "Sex Research in Cyberspace" section.

## Chapter 3: Gender Issues

- New discussion of a gender-egalitarian society on Vanatinai Island, in chapter opening section.
- Streamlined and updated discussion of "Sex Differentiation of the Brain."
- Major reorganization and streamlining of "Disorders Affecting Prenatal Hormonal Processes."
- Added discussion of a second circumcision accident twin study with a different outcome from that of the famous John/Joan case out of Johns Hopkins.
- Streamlined and updated "Gender Role" section.
- Major rewrite and update of discussion of the impact of television on gender-role stereotypes.

## Chapter 4: Female Sexual Anatomy and Physiology

- New information about alterations of the vulva by removing pubic hair, plastic surgery, and piercings.
- Legal and international attempts to eradicate female genital cutting.
- Condensed and streamlined information about the physiology of menstruation.
- Updated findings about hormone therapy after menopause.
- Clarification of research findings from the Women's Health Initiative.
- Updated breast cancer information and statistics.

## Chapter 5: Male Sexual Anatomy and Physiology

- Major rewrite and update of "Circumcision" section.
- Update and rewrite of prostate cancer content, including latest research, and two boxes from the ninth edition (PSA test and Prostate Cancer Treatment) omitted with content streamlined and incorporated into text.
- Updated On the Edge box: "Penile Augmentation."

## Chapter 6: Sexual Arousal and Response

- New Spotlight on Research box: "Monitoring Brain Function During Sexual Arousal with Magnetic Resonance Imaging."
- Update of pheromones content with latest research findings.
- New On the Edge box: "Sexual Arousal in a Nasal Spray" (a discussion of bremelanotide, also known as PT-141).
- Major reorganization and streamlining of "Sexual Response" section.
- Streamlined revision of Spotlight on Research box: "Monitoring Genital Changes During Sexual Arousal with Magnetic Resonance Imaging."

## Chapter 7: Love and Communication in Intimate Relationships

- This chapter represents a major updating, streamlining, and combining of material contained in chapters 7 and 8, ninth edition.
- Added important recent study dealing with MRI screening of brain dopamine levels to the "Chemistry of Love" section.
- Included discussion of "hooking up" and "friends-with-benefits relationships" to the section "What Is the Relationship Between Love and Sex?"
- New On the Edge box: "Internet Relationships."
- Streamlined and significantly shortened content dealing with sexual communication, primarily through selective modification of numerous authors' files and other examples that focus on communication strategies.

## Chapter 8: Sexual Behaviors

- New Sex and Politics box: "If Vibrators Are Outlawed, Only Outlaws Will Have Vibrators."
- New data on erotic dreams.
- Technology for sharing sexual fantasies.
- New table on frequency of masturbation by college students.
- Discussion of new technology in sex toys.
- Changes in the meaning and role of oral sex in sexual expression.
- Worldwide rates of anal intercourse.
- Nine new drawings depicting sexual behaviors.

## Chapter 9: Sexual Orientations

- New Sex and Politics box: "Goals of the Gay Rights Movement."
- Characteristics of "generation Q."
- Unique characteristics of bisexuality in women worldwide.
- Increase in the rate of bisexuality among women.
- Married homosexual males in China.
- New section discussing asexuality.
- States with nondiscrimination laws for sexual orientation.
- Updated information about discrimination toward versus acceptance of homosexuality around the globe.

- Anti-gay activism from closeted religious leaders.
- New statistics about same-sex partner households with children.
- Updated information about homosexuality and the media.
- Improvement in domestic partnership benefits and protection from discrimination in the workplace.
- Consequences of "don't ask, don't tell" policy for gay and lesbian troops in Iraq.
- Updated poll results on attitudes toward homosexuality.

## Chapter 10: Contraception

- Updated discussion of the benefits of using contraception.
- Four new Sex and Politics boxes: "The Power of Pro-Life Anti-Contraception Politics," "How Far-Right Politics in the United States Deprive Contraception to People in the Developing World," "Condoms: The Politics of Protection," and "Opposition to Emergency Contraception."
- Impact of the pro-life anti-contraception movement on access to birth control in the United States and across the globe.
- The George W. Bush administration's impact on the maternal/child death rates in the developing world.
- Revised tables outlining advantages and disadvantages of contraceptive methods.
- Pro-life's activism against condoms in the United States and Africa.
- Latest information and statistics dealing with the use of IUDs in the United States and worldwide.
- New table listing oral contraceptives that can be used for emergency contraception.
- Discussion of global access to emergency contraception and of a program to promote emergency contraception established by the American College of Obstetricians and Gynecologists.
- New guidelines for post-vasectomy fertility testing.
- Update on male contraceptive pill and injection.
- Non-hormonal contraceptive vaccine for women.

## Chapter 11: Conceiving Children: Process and Choice

- New Sex and Politics box: "*Roe v. Wade* and Beyond."
- Statistics on number of childless adults.
- Updated information about American attitudes toward parenthood.
- Financial and social costs of sex selection.
- Updated discussion of infertility, including lack of knowledge about it and marital benefits from it.
- Latest information pertaining to the relationship of maternal age to infertility.
- Updated information regarding assisted reproductive technologies.

- Discussion of the relationship between economic status and access to contraception and medical abortion.
- How other nations reduce abortion rates.
- Latest information on risks and effectiveness of medical abortion techniques.
- Current state restrictions on legal abortion and legal status of late-term abortion.
- Global maternal deaths resulting from illegal abortions.
- Characteristics of social services in states that have the most abortion restrictions.
- Religious beliefs and world views of pro-life and pro-choice individuals.
- Pregnancy and depression.
- Risk of dying from pregnancy or childbirth in Africa and Asia.
- Increased births among women over 45.
- Cesarean sections: controversy and rates.

## Chapter 12: Sexuality During Childhood and Adolescence

- New Sex and Politics box: "Abstinence-Only Sex Education."
- New Sexuality and Diversity discussion: "Cross-National Data on Sexual Behavior of Adolescents."
- New research findings regarding teenage oral sex behavior.
- Streamlined and updated material on adolescent coitus, incorporating recent research data.
- Major rewrite, update, and streamlining of "Adolescent Pregnancy" section.

## Chapter 13: Sexuality and the Adult Years

- Two new Sex and Politics boxes: "Marriage in Crisis Around the Globe" and "Legal Marriage for Same-Sex Couples".
- New statistics pertaining to marital status.
- Updated information about women's education level and likelihood of marrying.
- Discussion of single adults' use of Internet dating sites.
- New information about cohabitation.
- Governments that provide incentives for couples to have more children.
- Causes and consequences of higher male birth rates in China and India.
- Efforts in developing countries to reduce childbirth among girls younger than 13.
- Expanded section dealing with polygamy.
- New Sexuality and Diversity box, "Walking Marriage," describing the initiation of sexual relationships by Mosuo women in China.

- Updated discussion of the benefits of marriage.
- Updated discussion of the impact of birth of a child on marital satisfaction.
- Attitudes toward same-sex marriage and countries that offer legal marriage or civil unions for same-sex couples.
- State laws regarding same-sex marriage or civil union.
- Discussion of the controversy surrounding efforts to establish a constitutional ban on same-sex marriage in the United States.
- Punishments for women in Pakistan for extramarital relationships.
- Expanded information about the impact of extramarital affairs and characteristics of marriages involving infidelity.
- Global Sex Survey of rates of extramarital sex around the world.
- Extramarital affairs and the Internet.
- Updated divorce statistics and relationship between education level and divorce rates.
- Older adults, dating, and participation in unprotected sex.

## Chapter 14: Sexual Difficulties and Solutions

- This chapter represents a major updating, streamlining, and combining of material contained in chapters 15 and 16, ninth edition.
- New definition of *sexual health*.
- Impact of sexual problems on well-being and life satisfaction.
- Percentage of men with erection problems who ejaculate quickly.
- Role of adequate physical and psychological stimulation in defining a sexual disorder and the lack of a clear distinction between "normal" and "disordered."
- New criteria for hypoactive sexual desire disorder.
- Average percentage of men and women across the globe who want to be sexual more often.
- Expanded categories for female sexual arousal disorder and expanded definition of *female arousal disorder*.
- Addition of discussion on persistent sexual arousal disorder.
- Percentage of women who identify lack of orgasm during intercourse as a problem.
- Characteristics of sexual arousal of men with premature ejaculation problems.
- Primary precipitating event for vaginismus.
- Variations in sensitivity to stimulation involving premature orgasm and female arousal.
- New section on health habits and sexual functioning.
- Erectile disorder as a predictor of high blood pressure, heart disease, and diabetes.
- Percentages of people with spinal cord injuries who experience arousal and orgasm.

- Brain-imaging techniques and identification of vagus nerve pathway for orgasm.
- Global research showing association between equality of gender roles and sexual satisfaction.
- Male/female differences in likelihood of distraction by performance anxiety during sexual encounters.
- Impact of Viagra use on men's self-esteem and partners' sexual satisfaction.
- The media's influence on men's satisfaction with their bodies.
- Men's and women's satisfaction with penis size.
- Characteristics of masculinity that men value.
- New Sex and Diversity box: "Suffering for 'Beauty.'"
- Sexual consequences of teenage girls having unwanted sex.
- Role of atypical patterns of masturbation in ejaculatory inhibition and female orgasm with a partner.
- New medications under study for rapid ejaculation and female low-desire and arousal.

## Chapter 15: Sexually Transmitted Diseases

- New Sex and Politics box: "U.S. Policy Reduces Condom Promotion in Africa."
- Major updating throughout, with streamlined coverage in many sections.
- Latest data pertaining to new developments in, incidence of, and treatment of sexually transmitted diseases (STDs).
- New information on antibiotic-resistant gonorrhea.
- Discussion of increased incidence of syphilis among men who have sex with men.
- New material on *human papillomavirus* (HPV) vaccines.
- Discussion of recent developments in an HIV/AIDS prevention program in Kenya partially funded by royalties from this textbook.
- New Spotlight on Research box: "Circumcision as a Strategy for Preventing HIV Infection."
- Updates regarding highly active antiretroviral therapy (HAART) for HIV/AIDS, including recent availability of a single-pill, once-a-day HAART medication.
- Latest data on efforts to reduce mother-to-child-transmission (MTCT) of HIV in developing nations.
- New material on post-exposure prophylaxis (PEP)— the use of antiretroviral drugs to prevent HIV infection after unanticipated exposure to HIV.
- Discussion of pre-exposure prophylaxis (PREP) for preventing HIV infection in a new On the Edge box: "A Daily Pill to Prevent HJIV Infection."
- Latest research on vaginal microbicides.
- Discussion of recent advent of Web sites in San Francisco and Los Angeles to help inform partner(s) of STD exposure.

## Chapter 16: Atypical Sexual Behavior

- New information on Internet influences on sado-masochistic (SM) behavior.
- Discussion of recent Internet study of zoophilia.
- Updated discussion of sexual addiction.
- Major revision of On the Edge box: "Cyberspace Addiction and Compulsivity: Harmless Sexual Outlet or Problematic Sexual Behavior?"
- Significant revision and update of On the Edge box: "Video Voyeurism."

## Chapter 17: Sexual Coercion

- Updated statistics, rape prevalence.
- Revised and updated discussion of sexual coercion in dating situations.
- New information on date rape drugs.
- Discussion of wartime rape expanded to include the African nations of Sudan and Congo.
- Latest findings pertaining to rape and sexual assault of males.
- Streamlined and updated information dealing with sexual abuse of children.
- Updated statistics on the incidence of sexual harassment in the workplace.
- Recent developments pertaining to sexual harassment in academic settings, including court decisions establishing that educational institutions are liable for negligence in dealing with sexual harassment complaints.

## Chapter 18: Sex for Sale

- New Sex and Politics box: "Contemporary Censorship and Free Speech Controversies."
- New information about child pornography.
- Teens and Web cam pornography.
- Research indicating decrease in rape with increase in Internet access.
- Increase in indecency prosecution by the Federal Communications Commission.
- Increase in the public's use of sexually explicit media.
- New information about positive and negative effects of use of pornography.
- X-rated content's integration into mobile wireless technology.
- New On the Edge box: "The 'Pornification' of U.S. Culture."
- "Raunch Culture" and erotic role models for women.
- Percentage of men who have paid for sex.
- Female sex tourism.
- Percentage of sex workers who want to leave the "profession."
- New data from a nine-country study on prostitution.
- Percentage of sex workers younger than 18.
- Increase in Internet-facilitated sex work.
- Income generated by sex workers.

- Financial need as compelling motivation for entry into sex work.
- Childhood sex abuse history and sex workers.
- Post Traumatic Stress Syndrome and sex work.
- Financial incentives for sex workers to have unsafe sex.
- Impact of U.S. occupation of Iraq and sex trafficking.
- Lack of U.S. support for anti-trafficking measures.
- Depenalization of sex workers.
- Myth of sex work as a victimless crime.

## Continuing Features

- A **personal approach**. Users of the text have responded favorably to our attempts to make the subject human and personal, and in this tenth edition we have retained and strengthened the elements that contribute to this approach and expanded coverage of the impact that political decisions and policies have on individuals and groups.
- **Authors' files.** One of the most popular features of *Our Sexuality* has been the incorporation of voices of real people through the use of authors' files. These quotations—taken from the experiences and observations of students, clients, and colleagues—are woven into the text but highlighted by a color screen. Each chapter opens with an authors' file quotation illustrating an important concept pertinent to that chapter.
- **Nonjudgmental perspective.** Consistent with our personal focus, we have avoided a prescriptive stance on most issues introduced in the text. We have attempted to provide information in a sensitive, nonsexist, inclusive, nonjudgmental manner that assumes the reader is best qualified to determine what is most valid and applicable in her or his life.
- **Psychosocial orientation.** We focus on the roles of psychological and social factors in human sexual expression, reflecting our belief that human sexuality is governed more by psychosocial factors than by biological determinants. At the same time, we provide the reader with a solid basis in the anatomy and physiology of human sexuality and explore new research pertaining to the interplay of biology, psychology, and social learning.
- **Critical Thinking Questions,** some of which are new to this edition, appear in the margin. These questions are designed to help students apply their knowledge and experience while developing their own outlook. Each question encourages students to stop and think about what they are reading, in an attempt to facilitate higher-order processing of information and learning.

- **Spotlight on Research** boxes cover recent important research studies. Examples of this feature include "Monitoring Genital Changes During Sexual Arousal With Magnetic Resonance Imaging," "Sex Differences in Desire for Sexual Variety," and "Circumcision as a Strategy for Preventing HIV Infection."
- **At a Glance** tables designed to present important information in summary form. Examples of this feature include tables that outline factors involved in typical and atypical prenatal sex differentiation, factors to consider when choosing a birth control method, and common sexually transmitted diseases.
- **InfoTrac search terms** are suggested several times in each chapter—called out by a margin icon. The InfoTrac College Edition online **searchable** library (infotrac.cengage.com) includes a multitude of journals, many of which are specific to human sexuality. A four-month subscription to InfoTrac College Edition is available free to purchasers of the tenth edition, if the professor elects to use it.
- **Pedagogy.** Individuals learn in different ways. We therefore provide a variety of pedagogical aids to be used as the student chooses. Each chapter opens with an **outline** of major topic headings, complete with **chapter opening questions** that focus attention on important topics. **Key words** are boldfaced within the text, and a pronunciation guide follows selected key words. A **running glossary** in the text margin provides a helpful learning tool. Each chapter concludes with a **Summary** in outline form for student reference, annotated **Suggested Readings,** and annotated **Web Resources**. A complete **Glossary** as well as a complete **Bibliography** are provided at the end of the book.

## Organization

This book has been organized in a logical progression of topics. We begin, in **Part One—Introduction,** with the social and cultural legacy of sexuality in our society. We then describe how sex research is conducted and discuss the difficulties of gathering information in this sensitive area of human behavior. We conclude the opening unit with a detailed exploration of a variety of gender issues.

The three chapters of **Part Two—Biological Basis** present the biological foundations of sexuality, with separate chapters on male and female sexual anatomy followed by coverage of sexual arousal and sexual response patterns integrated into one chapter.

In **Part Three—Sexual Behavior,** a variety of relationship issues and sexual behaviors are discussed.

In **Part Four—Sexuality and the Life Cycle,** we discuss contraception, pregnancy, and issues pertaining to sexuality throughout the life cycle.

Sexual problems and their treatment and a detailed discussion of sexually transmitted diseases constitute the two chapters of **Part Five—Sexual Problems**.

The final section, **Part Six—Social Issues,** includes discussions of atypical sexuality, sexual coercion, pornography, and prostitution.

## Integrated Teaching and Learning Aids

### The Safer Sex and Contraception Kit (ISBN 0495104094)

Available to qualified adopters in the United States only. This kit is intended for classroom demonstrations of various forms of contraceptives. It includes the new O-ring, the patch, the diaphragm, contraceptive jelly, birth control pills, and more. (A Virtual Safer Sex and Contraception kit that includes photos of all of these devices is available to all adopters on the Instructor's Resource CD-ROM in PowerPoint®.)

### Study Guide (ISBN 0495104086)

Written by Rod Fowers of Highline Community College, each chapter of the *Study Guide* includes an Introduction, Learning Objectives, a Concept Map, a list of Key Terms, a Concept Check (fill-in-the-blank exercises with page references), a crossword puzzle, and a Practice Test.

### CengageNOW (access packaged with text, ISBN 0495427810)

Providing proven ease of use and efficient paths to success, CengageNOW is the powerful online study and assessment program that delivers the results you want—now—through a wide range of services and resources, including course management, homework, automatic grading, and diagnostics. Includes assessment tests written by Beverly Drinnin of Des Moines Area Community College. Includes animations of biological processes, video panels of gay, bisexual, and transgendered individuals, and sex workers.

### Multimedia Manager Instructor's Resource CD-ROM (ISBN 0495104442)

Multimedia Manager is the fastest way to build powerful, customized, media-rich lectures. Includes PowerPoint® lecture outlines written by Paz Galupo of Towson University. Also includes the Virtual Safer Sex kit for PC or Mac, Sex Toys with their descriptions,

Sexually Transmitted Disease photos from the Centers for Disease Control and the Instructor's Resource Manual, Test Bank, and RIG, along with images from the text and video clips.

## Test Bank (ISBN 0495104116)

Written by Rod Fowers of Highline Community College, the *Test Bank* includes over 100 multiple-choice questions per chapter, labeled with the correct answer, type of question, learning objective, and page reference. The *Test Bank* also includes more than 25 true-or-false questions per chapter and 15 short-answer questions per chapter that are tied to the Learning Objectives. Questions on the Web are marked with *www*. Fifteen to twenty-five questions per chapter come from the Study Guide.

## ExamView® Computerized Testing (Windows/Mac) (ISBN 0495104124)

Create, deliver, and customize tests and study guides (both print and online) in minutes with this easy-to-use assessment and tutorial system. You can build tests of up to 250 questions, using up to 12 question types. Using ExamView's complete word-processing capabilities, you can enter an unlimited number of new questions or edit existing questions.

## Instructor's Manual (ISBN 0495104132)

Written by Jennifer Musick of Long Beach City College. The introduction includes instructions on using the manual, teaching techniques, and generic handouts. Each chapter includes Learning Objectives, Teaching Ideas, Handouts, Discussion Questions, suggested videos or films, and recommended Web sites.

## WebTutor Toolbox on Web CT and Blackboard (on Web CT, ISBN for text when bundled with the book: 0495417408; on Blackboard, ISBN for text when bundled with the book: 0495417394)

This online supplement helps students succeed by taking them into an environment rich with study and mastery tools, communication aids, and additional course content. For students, WebTutor offers real-time access to a full array of study tools, including flashcards (with audio), practice quizzes and tests, online tutorials, exercises, asynchronous discussion, a whiteboard, and an integrated e-mail system.

Professors can use WebTutor Toolbox to offer virtual office hours, to post syllabi, to set up threaded discussions, to track student progress on quizzes, and more. You can customize the content of WebTutor in any way you choose, including uploading images and other resources, adding Web links, and creating course-specific practice materials.

## ABC Video—Human Sexuality (ISBN 0495006521)

Instructor Description: Our ABC videos feature short, high-interest clips from current news events as well as historic raw footage going back 40 years. Clips are drawn from such programs as *World News Tonight*, *Good Morning America*, *This Week*, *PrimeTime Live*, *20/20*, and *Nightline*, as well as numerous ABC News specials and material from the Associated Press Television News and British Movietone News collections.

## JoinIn on TurningPoint (ISBN 0495104140)

The easiest Audience Response System to use, JoinIn on TurningPoint features instant classroom assessment and learning, including questions on the Virtual Safer Sex kit, sex toys, reproductive technologies, Centers for Disease Control slides of sexually transmitted diseases, and questions that surround the video supplements.

## Web Site (academic.cengage.com/psychology/Crooks)

When you adopt *Our Sexuality*, you and your students will have access to a rich array of teaching and learning resources that you won't find anywhere else. This outstanding site features chapter-by-chapter online tutorial quizzes, chapter-by-chapter Web links, flashcards, and more!

The quality and longevity of *Our Sexuality* are due to talents and insights that extend beyond those of the authors. We are especially indebted to the staff of Wadsworth, the reviewers, and our students, who have added immeasurably to the merit of our book.

We owe special gratitude to reviewers and contributors to the tenth edition. Professors and specialty reviewers who lent their expertise at various stages in revising this and previous editions are listed on the following pages. We are especially indebted to Jim Strandberg, who lent his incisive gifts of nuance and clarity to the new Sex and Politics boxes.

Of all the members of the highly professional, competent, and supportive staff of Wadsworth who contributed to this and previous editions, we particularly appreciate the contributions of developmental editor Kirk Bomont, who worked tirelessly to ensure that the tenth edition of *Our Sexuality* would be the best yet. Kirk's sharp eye for detail and critical analysis of content was extremely beneficial to this edition. Consistent with our goal to reduce the overall length of the tenth edition, Kirk offered numerous valued suggestions for ways to reorganize and streamline content. Our sponsoring editor, Marianne Taflinger, again demonstrated the benefits of knowledgeable oversight in a project of this magnitude. Marianne's ability to creatively resolve issues proved invaluable as she guided the birth of this our tenth baby from beginning to end. Editorial assistants Lucy Faridany and Rachel Guzman competently took care of a myriad of details. Mary Noel, production editor, efficiently and competently managed the often complicated and hectic production schedule. Vernon Boes put his heart into helping artist Adam Miller develop the tone and content of the 12 entirely new drawings of sexual behavior and interaction. Vernon, together with Liz Harasymczuk, managed in exemplary fashion the demanding job of designing and implementing the new design elements of this edition. Magnolia Molcan adeptly supervised the development of the excellent supplements package and helped make CengageNOW a product rich with assets, from the Virtual Safer Sex kit to sex toys. Several freelance professionals added their talents at various stages of this edition. Research assistant Sami Tucker again demonstrated how invaluable her services are to the authors and to the academic strength of this book. The extremely current nature of the tenth edition is due largely to Sami's exhaustive search of the recent journal literature in a wide range of academic disciplines. Justin and Jim Hicks generously offered technical computer assistance that expedited the revision. Mandy Hetrick of Lachina Publishing Services provided production services in an accomplished and professional manner. We are also indebted to Robert Green, who performed superlatively as copy editor on this edition, and to photo researcher Eric Schrader, whose efforts have made the photo program of the tenth edition the best of any edition.

An outstanding marketing team at Wadsworth promoted this revision with consummate professionalism. We offer special thanks to our marketing manager, Kim Russell, and to Natasha Coats, marketing assistant.

We would also like to extend our thanks to the many reviewers who provided guidance, support, and insight for the current edition:

**Elizabeth Calamidas**
Richard Stockton College

**Mary Devitt**
Jamestown College

**Ann Stidham**
Presbyterian College

**Theodore Wagenaar**
Miami University

**Linda Zaitchik**
Newbury College

We also extend our continued thanks to reviewers of the previous nine editions:

**Daniel Adame**
Emory University

**Sylvester Allred**
Northern Arizona University

**Malinde Althaus**
University of Minnesota

**Linda Anderson**
University of North Carolina

**Veanne Anderson**
Indiana State University

**Wayne Anderson**
University of Missouri, Columbia

**Ann Auleb**
San Francisco State University

**Janice Baldwin**
University of California–Santa Barbara

Tommy Begay
University of Arizona

Jim Belcher
Valencia Community College

Betty Sue Benison
Texas Christian University

M. Betsy Bergen
Kansas State University

Thomas E. Billimek
San Antonio College

Linda Bilsborough
California State University–Chico

Jane Blackwell
Washington State University

John Blakemore
Monterey Peninsula College

Marvin J. Branstrom
Cañada College

Tom Britton, M.D.
Planned Parenthood, Portland,
   Oregon

Elizabeth Calamidas
Richard Stockton College

Anthony Cantrell
University of Colorado

Charles Carroll
Ball State University

Nick Chittester
Washington State University

Joan Cirone
California Polytechnic State
   University

Bruce Clear
The First Unitarian Church,
   Portland

David R. Cleveland
Honolulu Community College

Gretchen Clum
University of Missouri, St. Louis

Rosemary Cogan
Texas Tech University

Ellen Cole
Alaska Pacific University

Jeff Cornelius
New Mexico State University

Laurel Cox
Ventura College

John Creech
Collin Community College,
   Preston Ridge Campus

Susan Dalterio
University of Texas, San Antonio

Joseph Darden
Kean College

Deborah Davis
University of Nevada, Reno

Brenda M. DeVellis
University of North Carolina

Lewis Diana
Virginia Commonwealth
   University

Richard Dienstbier
University of Nebraska–Lincoln

Mary Doyle
Arizona State University

Beverly Drinnin
Des Moines Area Community
   College

Judy Drolet
Southern Illinois University,
   Carbondale

Andrea Parrot Eggleston
Cornell University

John P. Elia
San Francisco State University

Carol Ellison
Clinical Psychologist

Karen Eso
Bakersfield College

Peter Fabian
Edgewood College

April Few
Virginia Poly and State University

Catherine Fitchen
Dawson College

Karen Lee Fontaine
Purdue University, Calumet

Rod Fowers
Highline Community College

Lin S. Fox
Kean College of New Jersey

Gene Fulton
University of Toledo

David W. Gallagher
Pima Community College

Carol Galletly
Ohio State University

Kenneth George
University of Pennsylvania

David A. Gershaw
Arizona Western College

Glen G. Gilbert
Portland State University

Brian A. Gladue
University of Cincinnati

Mike Godsey
College of Marin

Gordon Hammerle
Adrian College

Debra Hansen
College of the Sequoias

Stephen Harmon
University of Utah

Claudette Hastie-Beahrs
Clinical Social Worker

Pearl A. Hawe
New Mexico State University

Bob Hensley
Iowa State University

Graham Higgs
Columbia College

Timothy Hulsey
Southwest Texas State University

Rosemary Iconis
York College

Barbara Ilardi
University of Rochester

Thomas Johns
American River College

David Johnson
Portland State University

James A. Johnson
Sam Houston State University

Kathleen Kendall-Tackett
University of New Hampshire

Al Kielwasser
San Francisco State

Sally Klein
Dutchess Community College

Peggy Kleinplatz
University of Ottawa

Patricia B. Koch
Pennsylvania State University

Kris Koehne
University of Tennessee

Robin Kowalski
Western Carolina University

Virginia Kreisworth
San Diego State University

Eric Krenz
California State University–Fresno

Vickie Krenz
California State University–Fresno

Lauren Kuhn
Portland Community College

Luciana Lagana
California State University–
Northridge

Miriam LeGare
California State University–
Sacramento

Sandra Leiblum
University of Medicine and
Dentistry/Robert Wood Johnson

Sanford Lopater
Christopher Newport University

Joseph LoPiccolo
University of Missouri

Laura Madson
New Mexico State University

Peter Maneno
Normandale College

Milton Mankoff
Queens College

Christel J. Manning
Hollins College

Jerald J. Marshall
University of Central Florida

Rhonda Martin
University of Tulsa

Donald Matlosz
California State University–Fresno

Leslie McBride
Portland State University

Deborah McDonald
New Mexico State University

Sue McKenzie
Dawson College

Brian McNaught
Gloucester, Massachusetts

Gilbert Meyer
Illinois Valley Community College

Deborah Miller
College of Charleston

John Money
Johns Hopkins University

Denis Moore
Honolulu Metropolitan
Community Church

Charlene Muehlenhard
University of Kansas

Louis Munch
Ithaca College

Ronald Murdoff
San Joaquin Delta College

Kay Murphy
Oklahoma State University

James Nash
California Polytechnic State
University

Jean L. Nash
Family Nurse Practitioner,
Portland, Oregon

Teri Nicoll-Johnson
Modesto Junior College

William O'Donohue
University of Nevada, Reno

Roberta Ogletree
Southern Illinois University,
Carbondale

Shirley Ogletree
Texas State University–San Marcos

Al Ono, M.D.
Obstetrician/Gynecologist

D. Kim Openshaw
Utah State University

Bruce Palmer
Washington State University

Monroe Pasternak
Diablo Valley College

Calvin D. Payne
University of Arizona

J. Mark Perrin
University of Wisconsin, River
Falls

John W. Petras
Central Michigan University

Valerie Pinhas
Nassau Community College

Ollie Pocs
Illinois State University

Robert Pollack
University of Georgia

Benjamin G. Rader
University of Nebraska, Lincoln

Patty Reagan
University of Utah

Deborah Richardson
University of Georgia

Barbara Rienzo
University of Florida

Barbara Safriet
Lewis and Clark Law School

Nancy Salisbury, M.D.
Portland, Oregon

Sadie Sanders
University of Florida

Marga Sarriugarte
Portland Rape Victim Advocate
Project

Dan Schrinsky, M.D.
Portland, Oregon

Cynthia Schuetz
San Francisco State University

Lois Shofer
Essex Community College

Jennifer Siciliani
University of Missouri–St. Louis

Sherman K. Sowby
California State University–Fresno

Lee Spencer
Arizona State University

Susan Sprecher
Illinois State University

Howard Starr
Austin College

Wendy Stock
Texas A&M University

Diana Taylor
Oregon Health Sciences University

Veronica Tonay
University of California–Santa Cruz

Perry Treadwell
Decatur, Georgia

Thomas Tutko
San Jose State University

James E. Urban
Kansas State University

Robert Valois
University of South Carolina

Jaye F. Van Kirk
San Diego Mesa College

Peter Vennewitz
Portland Planned Parenthood

Margaret Vernallis
California State University,
Northridge

John P. Vincent
University of Houston

**Laurie Volm**
Lake Grove Women's Clinic,
   Tualatin, Oregon

**David Ward**
Arkansas Tech

**Mary Ann Watson**
Metropolitan State College
   of Denver

**Paul Weikert**
Grand Valley State University

**Marianne Whatley**
University of Wisconsin–Madison

**Josephine Wilson**
Wittenberg University

**David Winchester, M.D.**
Urologist

**Deborah R. Winters**
New Mexico State University

**Michelle Wolf**
San Francisco State

**William Yarber**
Indiana University

Finally, we wish to thank our family and friends who, once again, were faced with the often unenviable task of keeping life moving positively while we were often buried (and sometimes a little grumpy). We are deeply grateful for their patience, resiliency, support, and encouragement.

*Robert Crooks*
*Karla Baur*

Throughout this textbook we discuss sexual attitudes, ideals, and behaviors of the past and present. We highlight similarities and differences in the Western world and beyond and emphasize the controversies inherent in sexual issues.

Finding one's way through the complex and conflicting perspectives related to human sexuality is both a personal and a societal challenge. We would like to open *Our Sexuality* with the Declaration of Sexual Rights, adopted by the World Association of Sexology,* as possible unifying guidelines:

Sexuality is an integral part of the personality of every human being. Its full development depends upon the satisfaction of basic human needs such as the desire for contact, intimacy, emotional expression, pleasure, tenderness and love.

Sexuality is constructed through the interaction between the individual and social structures. Full development of sexuality is essential for individual, interpersonal, and societal well-being.

Sexual rights are universal human rights based on the inherent freedom, dignity, and equality of all human beings. Since health is a fundamental human right, so must sexual health be a basic human right. In order to assure that human beings and societies develop healthy sexuality, the following sexual rights must be recognized, promoted, respected, and defended by all societies through all means.

Sexual health is the result of an environment that recognizes, respects and exercises these sexual rights:

1. **The right to sexual freedom.** Sexual freedom encompasses the possibility for individuals to express their full sexual potential. However, this excludes all forms of sexual coercion, exploitation and abuse at any time and situations in life.
2. **The right to sexual autonomy, sexual integrity, and safety of the sexual body.** This right involves the ability to make autonomous decisions about one's sexual life within a context of one's own personal and social ethics. It also encompasses control and enjoyment of our own bodies free from torture, mutilation and violence of any sort.
3. **The right to sexual privacy.** This involves the right for individual decisions and behaviors about intimacy as long as they do not intrude on the sexual rights of others.
4. **The right to sexual equity.** This refers to freedom from all forms of discrimination regardless of sex, gender, sexual orientation, age, race, social class, religion, or physical and emotional disability.
5. **The right to sexual pleasure.** Sexual pleasure, including autoeroticism, is a source of physical, psychological, intellectual and spiritual well-being.
6. **The right to emotional sexual expression.** Sexual expression is more than erotic pleasure or sexual acts. Individuals have a right to express their sexuality through communication, touch, emotional expression and love.
7. **The right to sexually associate freely.** This means the possibility to marry or not, to divorce, and to establish other types of responsible sexual associations.
8. **The right to make free and responsible reproductive choices.** This encompasses the right to decide whether or not to have children, the number and spacing of children, and the right to full access to the means of fertility regulation.
9. **The right to sexual information based upon scientific inquiry.** This right implies that sexual information should be generated through the process of unencumbered and yet scientifically ethical inquiry, and disseminated in appropriate ways at all societal levels.
10. **The right to comprehensive sexuality education.** This is a lifelong process from birth throughout the life cycle and should involve all social institutions.
11. **The right to sexual health care.** Sexual health care should be available for prevention and treatment of all sexual concerns, problems and disorders.

*Originally declared at the 13th World Congress of Sexology, 1997, Valencia, Spain. Revised and approved by the General Assembly of the World Association for Sexology (WAS) on August 26, 1999, during the 14th World Congress of Sexology, Hong Kong, and People's Republic of China. Reprinted with permission.

# Perspectives on Sexuality

© Chad Ehlers/Getty Images

*I wish I'd had this course and read this book when I was younger. It could have saved me some unnecessary grief. It would have helped me feel less confused about sexuality and more confident in making decisions that were in my best interest. (Authors' files)*

**Sexual intelligence** Sexual intelligence involves self-understanding, interpersonal sexual skills, scientific knowledge, and consideration of the cultural context of sexuality.

Sex and Politics

The multiple dimensions of sexuality affect us throughout our lives, and most students take this course, at least in part, to enhance their understanding of themselves sexually and their ability to relate well in a sexual relationship. Understanding oneself sexually and having interpersonal sexual skills and integrity are two characteristics we consider to be part of **sexual intelligence**, and these abilities help us make responsible decisions about our sexual behavior based on our personal values.

Sexual intelligence also depends on having accurate scientific knowledge about sexuality. Sexual science is a relatively young field. However, great leaps in research-based knowledge over the last century allow us to know, for example, about what happens to our bodies during sexual arousal and how to enhance pleasure, about biological components to sexual orientation, and about how to best protect ourselves and others from sexually transmitted diseases.

The fourth component of sexual intelligence is the critical consideration of the broader cultural, political, and legal contexts of sexual issues. When it comes to sexuality, the phrase "the personal is political" is apropos. For example, the conflict between women's ability to fill prescriptions from their doctors and pharmacists' religious beliefs has escalated. Some pharmacists have defied doctors' orders by refusing to fill prescriptions for birth control and emergency contraception. They may also refuse to refer a woman to another pharmacist or to return the prescription to her (Johnsen, 2005). Many "pro-life" organizations have lauded these pharmacists' obstruction of the contraceptive decisions of others as virtuous acts of conscience. A woman's access to prescription birth control depends on the "conscious clause" laws in the state in which she lives. Some states have established laws that forbid pharmacists from refusing to fill prescriptions, but others have laws making pharmacists' refusals legal (Sonfield, 2004).

The Museum of Sex opened its doors in New York City in September 2002 with an exhibit about the history of sex ⊙ in that city. The museum's mission is to preserve and present the history and cultural significance of human sexuality.

As of this writing, bipartisan members of Congress have introduced the Access to Legal Pharmaceuticals Act to ensure that women have their prescriptions filled. The bill requires a pharmacist who does object on religious grounds to refer a woman to a pharmacist who will fill the prescription (Epstein, 2005). However, pro-life leaders in Congress are blocking a vote on the legislation—in spite of the fact that 80% of adults in the United States believe pharmacists who oppose birth control for religious reasons should not refuse to fill women's prescriptions—leaving the variations in state laws to determine whether a pharmacist can refuse to fill a birth control prescription (CBS News and New York Times Poll, 2004). ■

Throughout this text, we strive to provide opportunities to support and develop the four aspects of sexual intelligence for our readers, understanding that the final expert on your sexuality is *you*. We welcome you to this book and your human sexuality class.

# Controversy and Diversity in Human Sexuality

Few topics generate as much attention and evoke as much pleasure and distress as the expression and control of human sexuality. In a sexuality class, students represent a

## A Child/Parent Sex Talk

To expand your understanding of your attitudes and experiences related to sexuality, you might consider interviewing your parents about their experiences and beliefs.

"WHAT?!? Talk to *my* parents about *sex*?!?"

The following ideas and suggestions may make this endeavor seem less daunting.

"But my mom and dad would *never* answer any questions about sex."

You might be quite surprised by how open your parents are to your interest. The tell-the-children-when-they-ask parenting approach is common. Plus, you can test the waters first: Start with a low-key question, and if they respond with a direct or an indirect "I don't want to talk about it," stop the interview and change the subject.

The first step is to pick your interviewee.* You may feel most comfortable beginning with a grandparent or another relative instead of a parent. Find a time when you will not be rushed and a place that will be private. (Alternatively, you can use e-mail, a phone call, or a letter; you might also find that several shorter conversations work best for you.) A possible way to begin is, "I'm taking a human sexuality class this term, and it made me wonder if you had any sex education in school." Now you have broken the ice, and if you have had a good reception, you can ask specifics about your interviewee's sexual education. Be sure to encourage elaboration after each question and not to rush to the next one: "What types of things did you learn about sex in school? What did you learn outside of school—from friends, your parents, books? What did your religion teach you? What sorts of bad information did you get about sex? What do you wish someone had told you?"

If things are rolling along, you might take a more personal bent: "How did you feel about your body changing from a child to a teenager? How quickly did you mature compared with your classmates? Did you know about menstruation/

The father–son "sex talk" scenes in the film American Pie depict the awkwardness that parents and children often experience when they discuss sexuality.

ejaculation before you experienced it? Who was your first crush? What do you wish you knew as a child or young adult that you know now? What do you think was easier, and what was more difficult, about sexuality for your generation than for mine?"

If your interview has come this far, you probably have a greater understanding and appreciation for the important aspects of your interviewee's life and, hopefully, of your own. So, who's next?

*Do not choose someone to interview unless there is a lot of goodwill in the relationship.

diversity of ages, ethnic and religious backgrounds, life experiences, and liberal and conservative attitudes. Students' sexual experiences vary; most students who have had sexual experiences relate sexually only with the other sex,* while some seek sexual relationships with members of the same sex, and still others seek sexual contact with both sexes. Some students have had no sexual partners; others have had many partners; still others have had one partner; and some have had long-term partnerships and marriages. Students' sexual choices and experiences also vary greatly in the degree of pleasure or distress that accompanies each situation. There are virtually no universals in sexual attitudes and experiences. With this in mind, we have attempted to bring an inclusive philosophy to our book. We begin this chapter with an overview of the diversity within the United States.

*We use the term *other sex* instead of *opposite sex* to emphasize that men and women are more alike than opposite.

# Diversity Within the United States

*Our Sexuality* explores the sexual attitudes and behaviors of people in many places around the globe, including the United States. Individuals of many ethnic and religious groups have made their homes in the United States, resulting in a wide range of sexual values and behaviors here (South-Paul, 2003). An ethnic group typically shares a common historical ancestry, religion, and language (Simon, 2006). We must also note that there is fluidity within the same ethnic group. Educational level and socioeconomic status are crucial in influencing sexual attitudes and behaviors. For instance, people with more education masturbate more often than less-educated people do (Kinsey et al., 1948; Michael et al., 1994). Another group-related difference has to do with oral–genital sex, which tends to be most common among young, college-educated whites and least common among African Americans and individuals with less education (Michael et al., 1994).

It should be stressed that differences between groups are generalities, not universal truths; even within groups, great diversity exists (Agbayani-Siewert, 2004). For example, Asian Americans include the descendants of Chinese laborers brought to the United States in the 19th century to build railroads, refugees from the Vietnam and Korean Wars, and individuals from Hong Kong, Japan, the Pacific islands, and many other Asian places (Brotto et al., 2005). Similarly, Muslims in the United States originate from more than 60 countries, and the Hispanic population comes from 22 different countries. Many of these subgroups within the Muslim, Asian American, and Hispanic population consider themselves culturally distinct from one another (Acosta-Belen & Bose, 2003; Hodge, 2005). However, in spite of the intra-group differences, when research looks at patterns, some inter-group differences emerge. For example, Asian Americans, *on the whole*, are less likely to engage in premarital intercourse than are Hispanic Americans, African Americans, or Americans of European descent (Cochran et al., 1991). Again, Hispanic culture, *on the whole*, often endorses sexual exploration for males but places a high value on chastity before marriage for women (Comas-Diaz & Greene, 1994).

The degree of *acculturation*—that is, replacing traditional beliefs and behavior patterns with those of the dominant subculture—also creates differences within subcultures. Recent immigrants tend to be close to the traditional values of their places of origin, but most individuals whose families have lived in North America for several generations are well assimilated (Barkley & Mosher, 1995). Films such as *My Big Fat Greek Wedding*, *American Desi*, and *Monsoon Wedding* depict the conflicts that can arise in immigrant families when the younger generation becomes more Americanized.

A factor that blurs differences between ethnic groups is that a significant, and ever-increasing, proportion of the U.S. population is *multiracial*; that is, some people have descended from two or more racial groups. Race and ethnicity are rarely simple, nonoverlapping classifications. "People all over the world have engaged in various degrees of mixing, particularly in the United States. . . . There is no way to look at every person and determine their exact racial background" (Wyatt, 1997, p. xv). The merging of ethnicity will likely increase over time in the United States because of the level of mixed-ethnic dating by young people. Almost 25% of teens have partners from ethnic groups other than their own (Ford et al., 2002).

Sexual attitudes and behaviors often vary widely even within the same religious group. For example, although Pope John Paul II maintained the traditional Roman

Stand-up comic and second-generation Korean American Margaret Cho shatters stereotypes of the submissive, reticent Asian female in her act. She takes provocative topics—such as bisexuality, what it would be like if men menstruated, and needing foreplay to have an orgasm—over the top.

Catholic view condemning all sexual activity that does not potentially lead to procreation, the views of American Catholics have run the gamut on issues such as contraception, abortion, and homosexuality In fact, 70% of churchgoing Catholics in the United States believe the pope should permit Catholics to use birth control devices (Miller & Dickey, 2005). Similarly, Orthodox Jews have much more conservative views regarding sexuality and gender roles than do Reform Jews. For example, Orthodox Judaism forbids sexual intercourse during menstruation, whereas Reform Judaism allows for individual preferences. Furthermore, fundamentalist Christians, who claim to interpret the Bible literally, differ greatly in views about sexuality from Christians who do not (Ostling, 2000). For example, fundamentalist Christianity typically holds that sexual intercourse before marriage is sinful, and it may oppose the use of birth control, whereas liberal Christianity might emphasize caring in a relationship and appreciate how contraception can enhance sexual intimacy.

Fundamentalists—whether Christian, Muslim, or Jewish—are far more restrictive of sexual behavior and roles for men and women than their more-liberal counterparts (Sullivan, 2006). Researchers have found that from "Afghanistan to Arkansas . . . the subordination of women is often a significant . . . objective" (Phillips, 2006, p. 370). A key desire of fundamentalists is to impose their sole concept of truth on a diverse and plural world (White, 2006). Over the last decade, extreme fundamentalism in these religions has increased and has engaged in political activism in conflicts surrounding sexual and gender-role issues (Carter, 2005; Phillips, 2006). ■

These similarities and differences in sexual beliefs, values, and behaviors are part of the *psychosocial* orientation of this textbook.

# ⊙ A Psychosocial Orientation

This book has a **psychosocial** orientation, reflecting our view that psychological factors (emotions, attitudes, motivations) and social conditioning (the process by which we learn our social groups' expectations and norms) have a crucial impact on sexual attitudes, values, and behaviors. *Our Sexuality* also covers the crucial biological foundations of human sexuality, including the roles of hormones and the nervous system, the biological components of sexual orientation, theories about the role of genetic selection through thousands of years of human evolution, and the impact of specific genetic variables on an individual. The term *biopsychosocial* describes the integration of the three dimensions.

**Psychosocial** Refers to a combination of psychological and social factors.

We may not always be aware of the extent to which our sexual attitudes and behaviors are strongly shaped by our society in general and by the particular social groups to which we belong (Laumann et al., 1994). The subtle ways we learn society's expectations regarding sexuality often lead us to assume that our behaviors or feelings are biologically innate, or natural. However, an examination of sexuality in other periods of Western history or in other societies (or even in different ethnic, socioeconomic, and age groups within our own society) reveals a broad range of acceptable behavior. What we regard as natural is clearly relative.

The diversity of sexual expression throughout the world tends to mask a fundamental generalization that can be applied without exception to all social orders: All societies have rules regulating the conduct of sexual behavior. "Every society shapes, structures, and constrains the development and expression of sexuality in all of its members" (Beach, 1978, p. 116). In addition, most people around the world say that sex is important in their overall lives, as we see in ⊙ **Figure 1.1**.

Knowledge about the impact of culture and individual experience can make it easier to understand and make decisions about our own sexuality. Therefore the major emphasis in *Our Sexuality* will be on the psychosocial aspects of human sexuality.

**Figure 1.1** Pfizer Global Study of Sexual Attitudes and Behaviors: How important is sex in your overall life? The study surveyed more than 26,000 people in 28 countries.

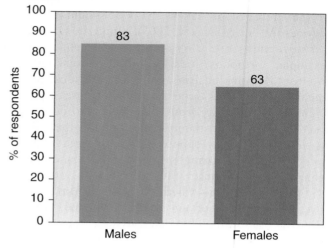

(a) **Percentage of men and women who said that sex was very/extremely/moderately important in their lives.**

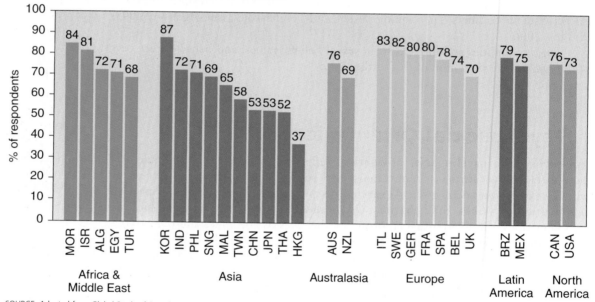

(b) **Percentage of people in each country who said that sex was very/extremely/moderately important to them.**

SOURCE: Adapted from Global Study of Sexual Attitudes and Behaviors funded by Pfizer, Inc. Copyright 2002 Pfizer, Inc.

# Cross-Cultural Perspectives

To elaborate on the cultural relativity of sexuality, we next discuss sexuality in the Islamic Middle East and in China.

## The Islamic Middle East

Islam is the world's fastest-growing religion, and its followers are called Muslims. Islam predominates in the Middle East, yet it is present in many other parts of the world: one-fifth of the world's population is Muslim, and an estimated four to six million Muslims live in the United States (Hodge, 2005). Muslims adhere to the teachings of the prophet Muhammad (c. 570–632 CE), which are recorded in the Qur'an. Muhammad opposed intercourse before marriage but valued intercourse within marriage as the highest good in human life, to be enjoyed by men and women alike; and he encouraged husbands to be "slow and delaying" (Abbott, 2000). Women are considered inherently sexual. Muhammad's son-in-law proclaimed, "Almighty God created sexual desire in ten parts: then he gave nine parts to women and one to men." The Qur'an requires both men and women to show modesty in public by wearing loose-fitting, body-covering clothing. A woman in Islamic dress is said to be like "a pearl in a shell" (Jehl, 1998).

Before Islam's development, *polygamy* (one man having multiple wives at the same time) was a common practice. When war led to a disproportionately higher number of women than men, polygamy provided husbands for widows and fathers for orphans. The Qur'an did not subsequently prohibit polygamy. It allows a man to have up to four wives, provided that the husband is fair to each of them.

The Qu'ran contains many passages that reconcile Islam with women's rights, religious pluralism, and homosexuality, and moderate Muslims do not share the prejudices of radical fundamentalists (Manji, 2006). Oppression of women and many of the extreme sexually related restrictions and punishments in Islamic countries do not stem from religion and the Qur'an but from Middle Eastern patriarchal cultural traditions and the emergence of fundamentalist sects (Ebadi, 2006; Hays, 2004). For example, Muslim fundamentalists are not following the Qur'an when they require girls to be genitally cut, insist that women be completely covered by clothing in public, or sanction "honor killing" (murdering a woman who has "dishonored" her husband and family by having been raped or having sex outside of marriage) (Chigbo, 2003; Power, 1998a).

Muslims' anger at the Bush Administrations' invasion and occupation of Iraq has fueled the growth and strength of radical fundamentalism, which condemns homosexuality. Under Saddam Hussein's rule, homosexuals in Iraq received a small degree of tolerance. However, since the removal of Saddam, radical fundamentalist religious leaders have called for homosexuals to be found and murdered (Ireland, 2006a; Lisotta, 2006). Further, the Iranian president who was elected in 2005 ran on a platform of "moral cleansing," which is enacted by religious police who entrap and torture gays and lesbians, and publicly execute them by hanging or stoning (Ireland, 2006b). ■

The top photo shows the doll, Fulla, that has replaced Barbie dolls in many Middle Eastern toy stores due to the recent increase in religious fundamentalism. Dressed in a black abaya and a head scarf, television commercials show her praying before sunrise on her pink prayer rug. The second photo shows a young Middle Eastern couple in Saudi Arabia.

## China

China's ancient history is rich in erotic literature and art. Indeed, the earliest known sex manuals, produced in China sometime around 2500 BCE, portrayed sexual techniques and a great variety of intercourse positions. In ancient China, Taoism (dating from around the second century BCE) actively promoted sexual activity—oral sex, sensual touching, and intercourse—for spiritual growth and harmony in addition to procreation (Brotto et al., 2005). The sexual connection of man and woman during intercourse was believed to join the opposing energies of yin (female) and yang (male), thereby balancing the essences of the two in each individual. Men were encouraged to ejaculate infrequently to conserve yang energy; orgasm for women helped create more yin energy and was sought after.

These liberal Taoist attitudes were replaced by a much stricter sexual propriety that emerged during a renaissance of Confucianism around 1000 CE. Sexual conservatism increased further after the Communist victory in 1949, and the government attempted to eliminate "decadent" Western sexual behaviors of pornography and prostitution. Under Communist rule, romantic gestures—even holding hands in public—put people at risk of persecution (Fan, 2006). Sex outside marriage was considered a bourgeois transgression, and sex within marriage more than once a week was deemed a counterproductive diversion of energy. A positive result of these measures and attitudes was that China all but eradicated sexually transmitted diseases (Wehrfritz, 1996).

**Sex and Politics**

© Gustavo Tomsich/CORBIS

China's government has since eased its control over individual lifestyle choices. As the government has grown more permissive toward sexuality, people's attitudes and behaviors have changed, including a slightly more open attitude towards homosexuality (Cui, 2006; Wong & Tang, 2004). Sexual behaviors prior to marriage have increased significantly. In 2005, 70% of residents in Bejing reported having had sexual relations before marriage, in contrast to 15.5% in 1989. In a study of seven major Chinese cities, the average age at which people aged 14 to 20 first had intercourse was 17.4 years old. In contrast, individuals aged 31 to 40 were on average more than six years older when they first had intercourse. Unfortunately, sexual knowledge and safe-sex skills have not kept up with the loosening of restrictions on sexual behavior, as shown by an increase in the number of single women obtaining abortions and rapidly growing rates of HIV infection, especially among Chinese 15 to 24 years old (Beech, 2005). The increase in HIV infections is especially problematic, because the social stigma for having AIDS is extreme, and Chinese doctors have only recently been trained to treat these conditions (X. Chen et al., 2000; Liu & Meyer, 2000). ∎

Detail of a 19th-century Chinese illustration, part of a rich cultural history of erotic art.

## ◗ Our Cultural Legacy: Sex for Procreation and Rigid Gender Roles

In the discussion of the Islamic Middle East and China, we saw that sexual pleasure for both men and women was more highly valued in earlier times than in the contemporary era. In the Western world the opposite is generally true, due to cultural changes regarding the purpose of sexual behavior and societal expectations for male and female sexuality. The patterns, conflicts, and changes stem from two themes: the belief that procreation is the only legitimate reason for sexual expression and the value of rigid distinctions between male and female roles. We will review these themes in the following two sections.

### Sex for Procreation

Historically in North America the idea that procreation was the only legitimate reason for sexual activity was prevalent (Francouer, 2001). Contemporary Roman Catholic doctrine and pro-life organizations continue to hold the belief that the only moral sexual expression occurs within marriage for purposes of procreation. For example, the American Life League maintains that people should not use contraception because "birth control leads to a state of mind that treats sexual activity as if it has nothing to do with babies" (American Life League, 2006, p. 1). In this view, when a couple has sexual intercourse, they have committed themselves to any resultant pregnancy: "The right to reproduce begins and ends with the decision to engage in intercourse." Therefore, the only moral choice for single people is abstaining from sex, and "if you are married, be faithful to your spouse, trusting in the Lord and His Will" (American Life League, 2006, p. 3). In general, this element of the pro-life movement hopes to end the lifestyle of having sex just for pleasure (Page, 2006).

Sexual behaviors that provide pleasure without the possibility of procreation—such as masturbation, oral sex, anal intercourse, and sex between same-sex partners—have been defined at various times as immoral, sinful, perverted, or illegal (Roffman, 2005). In fact, oral sex and anal sex were illegal in 10 states until 2003, when the Supreme Court overturned the laws forbidding those behaviors. The Court determined that private sexual contact between consenting adults is protected by the constitutional right to privacy. ■

Although most North Americans today do not believe that sexual activity is only for procreation, a residual effect of this belief is that many in our society often think of *sex* and *intercourse* as synonymous. Therefore, anything other than a penis in a vagina is not "sex." In the scandal involving President Bill Clinton and Monica Lewinsky, which began in 1998, Clinton's initial declaration that he did not have "sex with that woman" was true if "sex" is restricted to mean "intercourse," excluding kissing, oral sex, and genital petting. This line of thinking is rather common; in fact, a study of college students found that 60% did not consider engaging in oral sex as "having sex" (Sanders & Reinisch, 1999).

Certainly penile–vaginal intercourse can be a fulfilling part of heterosexual sexual expression, but excessive emphasis on intercourse can have negative consequences, as the following situation that brought a young couple to sex therapy illustrates:

*When we started going out, we decided to wait a while before having intercourse, but we had lots of hot sex together—orgasms and all. After we started having intercourse, all the other great stuff went by the wayside and sex became very routine and not much fun. (Authors' files)*

Thinking of intercourse as "real sex" perpetuates the notions that a man's penis is the primary source of satisfaction for his partner and that her sexual response and orgasm are supposed to occur during penetration. Such a narrow focus places tremendous performance pressures on both women and men and can create unrealistic expectations of coitus itself. This view can also result in devaluing nonintercourse sexual intimacy, which is often relegated to the secondary status of *foreplay* (usually considered as any activity before intercourse), implying that such activity is not important in and of itself and is to be followed by the "real sex" of coitus. In addition, sexual activity between members of the same sex does not fit the model of sex for procreation, causing people unfamiliar with gay and lesbian sexual practices, knowing that they do not involve penile–vaginal intercourse, to wonder, "What do they actually do during sex?"

**? Critical Thinking Question**

If you overheard someone say, "I had sex last night," what *specific behaviors* would you think had happened?

## Male and Female Gender Roles in Sexuality

The second theme and legacy of great significance is a rigid distinction between male and female roles. The gender-role legacy is based on far more than the physiological differences between the sexes. Although research has found physiological differences between males and females that create gender characteristics and inclinations in each sex, socialization limits, shapes, and exaggerates our biological tendencies. Rigid gender-role conditioning can limit each person's potential and can harm their sexuality. For example, gender-role expectations of "appropriate" behavior for men and women might contribute to the notion that the man must always initiate sexual activity while the woman must either set limits or comply. These patterns can place tremendous responsibility on a man and severely limit a woman's likelihood of discovering her own needs (Berman & Berman, 2001).

Across most cultures, women face more restrictions on, and experience greater sanctions against, their sexuality than men (Murphy, 2003). In the United States, for

Reuters/CORBIS

Musical performer Pink exudes explicit sexual energy, and in her "Stupid Girl" lyrics, she denigrates gender stereotypes that value women for their appearance instead of their brains and ambition.

example, the word *slut* remains predominantly an indictment of females. A recent survey found this idea to be prevalent among today's teens: 90% of boys and 92% of girls stated that girls get bad reputations for having sex. In contrast, only 40% of boys and 43% of girls said that boys get bad reputations for the same behavior (Kaiser Family Foundation, 2003). We hope that our discussion of gender roles and sexuality will help you navigate the challenges they present. To better understand the influence of contemporary social beliefs on sexuality in the Western world, we must examine their historical roots, particularly those that pertain to the legacies of sex for procreation and rigid gender roles. Where did these ideas come from, and how relevant are they to us today?

# ◗ Sexuality in the Western World: A Historical Perspective

## Judaic and Christian Traditions

By the time Hebraic culture was established, gender roles were highly specialized. The book of Proverbs, in the Hebrew Bible, lists the duties of a good wife: She must instruct servants, care for her family, keep household accounts, and obey her husband. Procreation and bearing children (especially sons) were essential; the Hebrews' history of being subjugated, persecuted, and enslaved made them determined to preserve their people—to "be fruitful, and multiply, and replenish the earth" (Genesis 1:28).

Yet sex within marriage was believed to be more than a reproductive necessity. To "know" a partner sexually, within marriage, was recognized in the Old Testament of the Bible and in tradition as a profound physical and emotional experience (Haffner, 2004). The Song of Songs in the Bible (also known as the Song of Solomon) contains sensuous love poetry. In this small excerpt, the bridegroom speaks:

> *How fair is thy love, . . . my bride!*
> *How much better is thy love than wine!*
> *And the smell of thine ointments than all manner of spices!*
> *Thy lips, oh my bride, drop honey—honey and milk are under thy tongue.*
> (Song of Songs 4:10–11)

And the bride:

> *I am my beloved's and his desire is toward me.*
> *Come, my beloved, let us go forth into the field; Let us lodge in the villages . . . .*
> *There will I give thee my love.*
> (Song of Songs 7:10–12)

The joyful appreciation of sexuality displayed in these lines is part of the Judaic tradition. This view was overshadowed, however, by teachings of Christianity. To understand why this happened, we have to remember that Christianity developed during the later years of the Roman Empire, a period of social instability. Many exotic cults had been imported from Greece, Persia, and other parts of the empire to provide sexual entertainment and amusement. Early Christians separated themselves from these practices by associating sex with sin.

We know little about Jesus' specific views on sexuality, but the principles of love and tolerance were the foundation of his teachings. However, Paul of Tarsus, a follower of Christianity, had a crucial influence on the early church. (He died in 66 CE, and many of his writings were incorporated into the Christian Bible, in the New Testament.) Paul emphasized the importance of overcoming "desires of the flesh"—including anger, selfishness, hatred, and nonmarital sex—in order to inherit the Kingdom of God. He associated spirituality with sexual abstinence and saw **celibacy** (SEH-luh-buh-see), the state of being unmarried and therefore abstaining from sexual intercourse, as superior to marriage. Hence, sex, which is essential for reproduction, was a necessary but religiously denigrated act.

**? Critical Thinking Question**

How do your religious views influence your decision making with regard to sexuality?

**Celibacy** Historically defined as the state of being unmarried; currently defined as not engaging in sexual behavior.

## Sex as Sinful

Later church fathers expanded on the theme of sex as sin. The bishop Augustine (354–430) declared that lust was the original sin of Adam and Eve; his writings formalized the notion that intercourse could rightly take place only within marriage, for the purpose of procreation (Bullough, 2001). Augustine also believed that female subordination was intrinsic to God's creation, which led to the idea that any intercourse position other than the one with the man on top was "unnatural" (Wiesner-Hanks, 2000).

During the Middle Ages (the period of European history from the fall of the Western Roman Empire in 476 to the beginning of the Renaissance in about 1400), attitudes toward sex varied from era to era and place to place, but the belief that sex was sinful persisted throughout. Theologian Thomas Aquinas (1224–1274) further refined this idea in a small section of his *Summa Theologica*. Aquinas maintained that human sexual organs were designed for procreation and that any other use—as in homosexual acts, oral–genital sex, anal intercourse, or sex with animals—was against God's will, heretical, and a "crime against nature." Local priests relied on handbooks called Penitentials, catalogs of sins with corresponding penances, to guide them in responding to confessions. Using withdrawal to avoid pregnancy was the most serious sin and could require a penance of fasting on bread and water for years. "Unnatural acts" of oral or anal sex were also viewed as gravely sinful and drew more severe penances than murder (Fox, 1995). Of course, homosexual relations precluded the possibility of reproduction and consisted of many "unnatural acts." From Aquinas's time on, homosexuals were to find neither refuge nor tolerance anywhere in the Western world (Boswell, 1980).

The teachings of Jesus Christ emphasized love, compassion, and forgiveness. Death by stoning was the prescribed punishment for a woman who committed adultery, but Jesus admonished the men who had brought her to him for judgment: "He that is without sin among you, let him first cast a stone at her" (John 8:7). After all the men left without throwing any stones, Jesus told the woman, "Neither do I condemn thee: go, and sin no more" (John 8:11).

## Eve Versus Mary

During the Middle Ages two contradictory images of women crystallized, and each image had its own impact on society's view of female sexuality and on women's place in society. The first image is the Virgin Mary; the second image is Eve as an evil temptress.

Initially, Mary was a figure of secondary importance in the Western Church. Her status was elevated and she became more prominent when the Crusaders returned from Constantinople, the seat of the Eastern Church. They brought to the West a view of Mary as a gracious, compassionate protector and an exalted focus of religious devotion.

The practice of *courtly love*, which evolved at about this time, reflected a compatible image of woman as pure and above reproach. Ideally, a young knight would fall in love with a married woman of higher rank. After a lengthy pursuit, he would find favor, but his love would remain unconsummated because her marriage vows ultimately proved inviolable. This paradigm caught the medieval imagination, and troubadours performed ballads of courtly love in courts throughout Europe.

The medieval image of Eve as the temptress in the Garden of Eden provided a counterpoint to the unattainable, compassionate Virgin Mary. This image, promoted

Interpretations of Adam and Eve's transgressions in the Garden of Eden have influenced values about sexuality.

Antagonism toward women reached a climax during the witch hunts of the 15th century.

by the Church, reflected an increasing emphasis on Eve's sin and ultimately resulted in heightened antagonism toward women. This antagonism reached its climax in the witch hunts led by the Catholic Church in continental Europe and the British Isles. They began in the late 15th century—after the Renaissance was well under way—and lasted for close to 200 years (Morgan, 2006). Witchcraft was blamed on carnal lust, and most "witches" were accused of engaging in sexual orgies with the devil (Wiesner-Hanks, 2000). Ironically, while Queen Elizabeth I (1533–1603) brought England to new heights, an estimated 50,000 women were executed as witches in Europe during and after her reign (Barstow, 1994).

## A Sex-Positive Shift

The prevailing view of nonreproductive sex as sinful was modified by Protestant reformers of the 16th century. Both Martin Luther (1483–1546) and John Calvin (1509–1564) recognized the value of sex in marriage (Berman & Berman, 2001). According to Calvin, marital sex was permissible if it stemmed "from a desire for children, or to avoid fornication, or to lighten and ease the cares and sadnesses of household affairs, or to endear each other" (Taylor, 1971, p. 62). The Puritans, often maligned for having rigid views about sex, also shared an appreciation of sexual expression within marriage (D'Emilio & Freedman, 1988; Wiesner-Hanks, 2000). In fact, one man was expelled from Puritan Boston when, among other offenses, "he denied . . . conjugal . . . fellowship unto his wife for the space of 2 years" (Morgan, 1978, p. 364).

The 18th-century Enlightenment was partly an outgrowth of the new scientific rationalism: Ideas reflected facts that could be objectively observed, rather than subjective beliefs and superstition. Women were to enjoy increased respect, at least for a short time. Some women, such as Mary Wollstonecraft of England, were acknowledged for their intelligence, wit, and vivacity. Wollstonecraft's book *The Vindication of the Rights of Women* (1792) attacked the limited gender roles for females, such as the prevailing practice of giving young girls dolls rather than schoolbooks. Wollstonecraft also asserted that sexual satisfaction was as important to women as to men and that premarital and extramarital sex was not sinful.

## The Victorian Era

Unfortunately, these progressive views did not prevail. The Victorian era, which took its name from the queen who ascended the British throne in 1837 and ruled for over 60 years, brought a sharp turnaround. The sexes had highly defined roles. Women's sexuality was polarized between the images of Madonna and Eve (which evolved in the vernacular into the "Madonna-whore" dichotomy). Upper- and middle-class Victorian women in Europe and the United States were valued for their delicacy and ladylike manners—and consequently were constrained by such restrictive devices as corsets, hoops, and bustles. Their presumed fragility and limited roles resulted in marginalization through idealization (Glick & Fisk, 2001; Real, 2002). Popular opinion of female sexuality was reflected by the widely quoted physician William Acton, who wrote, "The majority of women are not very much troubled with sexual feelings of any kind" (Degler, 1980, p. 250). Women's duties centered on fulfilling their families' spiritual needs and providing a comfortable home for their husbands to retreat to after working all day. The world of women was clearly separated from that of men. Consequently, intensely passionate friendships sometimes developed between women, providing the support and comfort that were often absent in marriage.

In general, Victorians encouraged self-restraint in all aspects of their lives, and Victorian men were expected to conform to the strict propriety of the age (Radar, 2003). However, prostitution flourished during this period because Victorian men often set morality aside in the pursuit of sexual companionship. The gender-role separation between the worlds of husbands and wives created a sexual and emotional distance in many Victorian marriages. Victorian men could smoke, drink, joke, and find

**? Critical Thinking Question**

How does the Madonna-whore dichotomy affect your sexuality today?

sexual companionship with the women who had turned to prostitution out of economic necessity, whereas their wives were caught in the constraints of propriety and sexual repression.

Despite the prevailing notions of the asexual Victorian woman, Celia Mosher, a physician born in 1863, conducted the only known research about the sexuality of women of that era. Over a span of 30 years, 47 married women completed her questionnaire. The information gathered from the research revealed a picture of female sexuality different from the one commonly described (perhaps even prescribed) by "experts" of the time. Mosher found that most of the women experienced sexual desire, enjoyed intercourse, and experienced orgasm (Ellison, 2000).

Nineteenth-century U.S. culture was full of sexual contradictions. Women's sexuality was polarized between the opposing images of Madonna and whore, and men were trapped between the ideal of purity and the frank pleasures of sexual expression. Gender-role beliefs about sexuality were taken to even greater extremes in the cases of African American men and women under slavery. Furthermore, the oppressive myths about African American men and women were used to justify slavery, as examined in the following Sexuality and Diversity discussion. Unfortunately, shades of these myths have persisted and play a role in contemporary racial tensions.

In the Victorian era the marriageable woman possessed morals that were as tightly laced as her corset. Ironically, prostitution flourished at this time.

## SEXUALITY AND DIVERSITY

### Slavery's Assault on Sexuality and Gender Roles

An extreme manifestation of gender roles and sexuality was imposed on black slaves in the United States; stereotypes of black sexuality provided a justification for the institution of slavery and white power.* Europeans' ethnocentric reactions in their first encounters with black Africans set the stage for the denigration of black sexuality during slavery. Europeans reacted to African customs with disgust and fear, comparing the sexual habits of Africans to those of apes. Dehumanizing blacks as animalistic, oversexed "heathens" gave many white slave owners a rationale for exploitation and domination (Moran, 2001).

The Madonna-whore dichotomy was drastically exaggerated in the case of female slaves. The dominant image of black womanhood was the Jezebel—a treacherous seductress with an insatiable sexual appetite. White men (including some Union soldiers who raped slave women as they plundered towns and plantations) used these prejudices to exempt their sexual abuse and exploitation of black women from questions of their own immorality (Guy-Sheftall, 2003). Enslaved women lacked clothing to cover their bodies "properly," and their work in the fields and the house often required them to raise their dresses above their knees—nothing a "decent" woman would do. Slaves had no rights to their own bodies. During slave sales they were stripped naked so that prospective buyers could closely examine their bodies, including their genitals, as if they were cattle. The irrational logic that no self-respecting woman would allow herself to be put on such display was used by whites to confirm black women's wanton nature. Slave owners publicly discussed female slaves' reproductive capacity and managed their "breeding" (often by the slave owner and his

*Adapted from Douglas (1999) and Wyatt (1997).

sons), forcing promiscuity on them (Solinger, 2005). The economic benefit of rapid births of slave children was clearly expressed by Thomas Jefferson: "I consider a woman who brings a child every two years as more profitable than the best man on the farm; what she produces is an addition to capital" (Davis, 2002, p. 109).

The stereotype of "Mammy" provided slave owners with a counterbalance to the Jezebel and represented the slave owners' successful civilizing of black women, including their sexuality. Mammy was supposed to be loyal, obedient, and asexual. She cooked, cleaned, and cared for white children, often even nursing infants. Her labors enabled many white women to maintain their delicate, ladylike images.

The male complement to the Jezebel was the stereotype of the highly sexual, potentially violent "buck." Whites considered him a powerful animal and exploited his ability to work and to produce offspring with his mythical, larger-than-white-sized penis. On the one hand, slave owners depended economically on black men's physical strength and sexual virility. On the other hand, they feared those same qualities. The fabricated threat of sexual seduction of white women and racist logic sanctioned the tools necessary to control black men and to assuage the slave owners' insecurities that their own stereotypes created. During the slavery era, black men were beaten, whipped, castrated, and lynched with impunity. After emancipation, people freed from slavery had greater opportunities to shape their own lives, but the lynching of black men and raping of black women continued as a means of maintaining social control over those who challenged the norms of white supremacy (Douglas, 1999; Wyatt, 1997).

The historical events and surrounding controversies discussed in the previous sections show that the sex-for-procreation and gender-role issues are legacies of the Hebrew and Christian Bibles, of Augustine and Thomas Aquinas, of the Victorian era, and of slavery. These legacies are with us still, found in the complex conflicts between the values of personal pleasure, practicality, and tradition in 20th-century Western life (Jakobsen & Pellegrini, 2003).

## The 20th Century*

Sigmund Freud (1856–1939) led in changing perspectives about sexuality in the 20th century with the first of several books, *The Interpretation of Dreams* (1900). Freud's belief that sexuality was innate in women as well as in men helped expand Victorian concepts about sexuality. The physician Havelock Ellis (1859–1939), in his book *On Life and Sex* (1920), emphasized "the love-rights of women," and his seven-volume

---

*Our primary sources for this material are Czuczka (2000) and Glennon (1999).

*Studies in the Psychology of Sex* regarded any sexual practice—including masturbation and homosexuality, previously considered "perversions"—as healthy so long as no one was harmed. Theodore Van de Velde (1873–1937) stressed the importance of sexual pleasure in his popular marriage manuals.

While ideas about the "proper" role of female sexuality were changing, the women's suffrage movement began in the late 19th century. Its goal of giving women the right to vote grew out of several related developments, such as the abolition of slavery and the demand that women be permitted to attend universities and hold property. The passage in 1920 of the 19th Amendment to the U.S. Constitution guaranteed women the right to vote but did not usher in a new era of equality.

Many women in the 1920s broke out of traditional "at home" roles and enjoyed the independence the automobile provided. The clothing styles of the "flapper" expressed women's rejection of Victorian moral standards.

However, subsequent historical events and technology brought new sexual perspectives and possibilities. U.S. involvement in World War I created an environment for increased equality and flexibility of gender roles, as thousands of women left the traditional homemaker role and took paying jobs for the first time. American men serving as soldiers in Europe were introduced to the more open sexuality there. Soon after they returned home from the war, Henry Ford's mass-produced automobiles of the 1920s provided increased independence and privacy for young people's sexual explorations. The advent of movies presented romance and sex symbols for public entertainment. The "flappers"—young, urban, single, middle-class women—rejected the ideals of Victorian restraint for short slinky dresses and the exuberant, close-contact dancing of the Roaring Twenties. The changes in sexual mores consisted mainly of the prevalence of kissing and "petting" (sex play short of intercourse) among young unmarried people that went beyond acceptable Victorian standards, but women usually avoided premarital intercourse to prevent pregnancy and jeopardizing their reputations (Radar, 2001).

A return to more restrained behavior came with the Great Depression in the 1930s. Conversely, the hardships of the time also led to new laws mandating the right of women to have access to contraceptive information and devices. Before the development of penicillin in the 1940s, no effective treatment existed for life-threatening sexually transmitted diseases. Once penicillin became available, another feared consequence of sex became less harmful. During World War II, housewives once again filled the gaps in the workplace left by men who were fighting overseas and encountering more open European sexuality.

During World Wars I and II, U.S. soldiers who socialized with European women were influenced by more cosmopolitan sexual mores.

## After World War II

After World War II, living in the suburbs became the ideal and goal of middle-class families, financed by the father as breadwinner. Women returned the workplace to men and devoted themselves to their homes, children, and husbands. Popular psychology of the era claimed that women who worked outside the home were neurotic and suffered from "penis envy." The fashion industry's ideal "refeminized" women with clothing that emphasized the bustline, small waist, and full skirts (Radar, 2001). During the postwar retreat into traditional gender roles, Alfred Kinsey and associates' *Sexual Behavior in the Human Male* (1948) and *Sexual Behavior in the Human Female* (1953) were best sellers in spite of (or possibly because of) denunciations of his work by medical professionals, clergy, politicians, and the press (Brown & Fee, 2003). Kinsey's data pertaining to the prevalence of women's sexual interest and response were particularly shocking to both professionals and the public. The surprising statistics on same-sex behavior, masturbation, and novel acts in the bedroom contributed to the growing acceptance of a variety of sexual behaviors.

In the 1950s, television, which emphasized suburban social conformity and featured sitcoms portraying married couples in separate beds, entered American homes at the same time as the first issue of *Playboy*, which emphasized sex as recreation. Together, these media represented a dichotomy that played out through the 1950s.

## The Times Are a-Changin'

It was not until the 1960s—after the flurry of post–World War II marriages, the baby boom, and widespread disappointment in the resulting domesticity of women—that a new movement for gender-role equality began. In the 1960s and throughout the 1970s, feminism and the "sexual revolution" confronted the norms of previous decades. The oral contraceptive pill, introduced in the 1960s, and later the intrauterine device (IUD), morning-after pills, and spermicides gave women newfound security in pursuing sexual pleasure with greatly reduced fear of pregnancy (Ofman, 2000).

By 1965 the Supreme Court had made contraceptive use by married couples legal, and by 1972 contraceptive use by unmarried individuals was legal. The widespread acceptance of contraceptives and the subsequent availability of legal abortion by Supreme Court mandate in 1973 permitted sexuality to be separated from procreation as never before in Western cultures. The world had changed, too, so that many people were concerned with the ecological and economic costs of bearing children—costs that were not as relevant in the pre-industrial world.

Masters and Johnson's *Human Sexual Response* (1966) and *Human Sexual Inadequacy* (1970) illuminated women's capacity for orgasm and propelled sex therapy into a legitimate endeavor. Sexual self-help books appeared, such as *Our Bodies, Ourselves* (Boston Women's Health Collective, 1971), and *For Yourself: The Fulfillment of Female Sexuality* (Barbach, 1975). These books emphasized women's sexual self-awareness, whereas *The Joy of Sex* (Comfort, 1972) highlighted varied, experimental sexual behavior for couples.

In the increasingly tolerant atmosphere of the late 1960s and the 1970s, attitudes began to change toward a long-standing taboo, homosexuality. Gays and lesbians began to openly declare their sexual orientation and to argue that such a personal matter should not affect their rights and responsibilities as citizens. In 1973 the American Psychiatric Association removed homosexuality from its

© Spencer Grant/PhotoEdit

Each square of the 54-ton AIDS Quilt was made by the partner, friends, or family of a person who died from AIDS.

diagnostic categories of mental disorders. Then, the early 1980s brought the first AIDS diagnosis. The so-called "gay plague" dramatically increased the visibility of homosexual individuals and amplified both negative and positive public sentiments toward homosexuality.

Unfortunately, increased violence against gays highlighted the extreme beliefs of some. For others, homosexuality continued to remain a scapegoat for society's ills, as demonstrated by the Reverend Jerry Falwell's comments about the cause of the September 11 attacks: "The pagans and the abortionists and the feminists and the gays and the lesbians . . . all of them who have tried to secularize America, I point the finger in their face and say, 'You helped this happen'" (Falwell, 2001, p. 61).

In contrast, the media, most notably television, reflected positive changing attitudes about homosexuality. Mainly as a result of gay activism, by the mid-1990s, television began to incorporate gays and lesbians into programming. Gay and lesbian characters appeared on shows such as *ER*, *Sex and the City*, *Roseanne*, and *Friends*. Ellen DeGeneres's coming-out show on *Ellen* was an event of the 1997 season (Marin & Miller, 1997). In the footsteps of *Ellen*'s trailblazing lesbian lead character, *Will and Grace* had gay and lesbian story lines for eight seasons, with main characters who were likable and well-rounded (Colucci, 2006). Changes in the media's portrayal of homosexuality illustrate how the media simultaneously reflect and influence sexual information, attitudes, and behaviors (Gross, 2001). What do the media say to us about sexuality? The following sections explore that very question.

Courtesy of Faith In America, Inc.

A media campaign based on Christian values hopes to break-down anti-homosexual prejudice.

## The Media and Sexuality

The phenomenon that we know as mass media began less than 600 years ago. The invention of typesetting in 1450 meant that books could be mechanically printed instead of laboriously handwritten, which made them available to the common woman

Photofest/Universal

The winner of many awards, *Brokeback Mountain* was the first same-sex romance film to be number one at the box office.

and man. Black-and-white silent movies first played for a paying audience in 1895, and in 1896, *The Kiss*, the first film in cinematic history of a couple kissing, was criticized as scandalous and brought demands for censorship (Dirks, 2006). The first black-and-white television sets arrived in the 1940s (initially so fascinating that families would sit in the living room watching test patterns on the screen). By 1972 the number of color television sets in U.S. homes finally exceeded the number of black-and-white TVs. The explosion of media technology since then has flooded us with exposure to sexual words and images. Increased amounts and explicitness of sexual content have accompanied the huge technological advances. For example, only 50 years ago a Hollywood movie would not be released to the public if it showed a husband and wife in the same bed (Lapham, 1997).

## Television

The impact of the Internet may soon surpass that of television, but to date, television has likely had the most significant effect on sexual attitudes and behaviors, given the amount of time people spend watching it. By the time we are 18 years old, each of us has watched TV for an average of 20,000 hours—certainly enough time for it to have some influence on our perspectives about sexuality (Folb, 2000). The number of sexual scenes on standard network programs has nearly doubled since 1998, and ○ **Figure 1.2** shows when various types of sexual content first appeared on television. However, fewer young people are shown engaging in sexual activity: one in ten depictions of sexual intercourse involves teens and young adults, compared with one in four in 1998. Among the 20 most-watched shows by teens, 70% include sexual content (talking about sex, sexual innuendo), and 45% include sexual behavior (Kaiser Family Foundation, 2006). Many critics are concerned that such material presents a far too cavalier approach to sex, encouraging youth to be sexually active too early, but most studies on the subject have been inconclusive (Escobar-Chaves et al., 2005). However, a recent study established a sexual media diet (SMD) by weighing the amount of sexual content in the TV shows, movies, music, and magazines that the teens consumed regularly, along with the amount of time teens spent using the four forms of media. The study found that white teens whose SMD was in the top 20% were 2.2 times more likely to have had sexual intercourse by age 16 than those whose SMD was in the lowest 20% (Brown, 2006).

○ **Figure 1.2** The evolution of broken taboos on TV.

SOURCE: Modified from TV Guide, August 2, 2003.

At times, the ways sexual issues are presented on television have beneficial effects—promoting greater knowledge, tolerance, and positive social change. Television advice and educational programs can offer constructive guidance. For example, *Loveline* host Drew Pinsky discusses young people's concerns about relationships and sex and gives advice. *Berman and Berman*, a show hosted by psychologist and physician sisters, provides sex education for women. In addition, network and cable programs on child abuse, rape, and transgender concerns have helped to increase knowledge and to reduce the stigma associated with such topics (American Academy of Pediatrics, 2001b). Although many daytime talk shows have taken a sensational approach to sex, presenting topics such as "Cousins in Love" or "Immortalized on Video in Compromising Positions," other talk shows have helped to break down cultural taboos and have revealed the enormous diversity of human sexual expression. *The Phil Donahue Show* (which began airing in the late 1960s and ended in 1996) and *Oprah* (which began airing in 1986) have provided a forum for people to learn about and discuss many aspects of human sexuality (Gross, 2001).

Television news reporting broke new ground on several sexual issues in the 1990s. Anita Hill's televised testimony accusing Supreme Court nominee Clarence Thomas of sexual harassment brought this issue to the public's attention. Consequently, workplace policies about sexual harassment were implemented across the country. In a different example, the Clinton-Lewinsky scandal raised numerous issues, including the definition of *sex*, what a wife's response should be to infidelity, and whether words such as *penis* and *oral sex* should be on the evening news.

Information about the potentially harmful physical and emotional consequences of sex has increased in programming. In 2005, 27% of television shows depicting or discussing intercourse referred to the risks and responsibilities of sex—twice the rate in 1998. Shows popular with teens have had an even greater increase in safe-sex content (Kaiser Family Foundation, 2006). One organization, called The Media Project, works with the television industry to incorporate realistic information about sexuality and responsibility into programming. The Project's accomplishments include episodes on *Felicity* about date rape, safe sex, and condom use, including a scene showing the correct way to use a condom. The Media Project also sponsors the annual SHINE Awards (Sexual Health in Entertainment) to recognize television programs that constructively portray sexual health issues (Folb, 2000).

The media can play a significant role in countries where sexual information has been taboo. For example, Egypt and China have recently allowed the first sex education programs to be presented via public media. In 2006 an Egyptian sex therapist began the first television sex education program. "Serious Talk" attempts to correct rampant sexual misinformation and ignorance in a culturally acceptable manner by melding Islam with modern sexual knowledge (El-Noshakaty, 2006). In China "Tonight's Whisperings" radio program began in 1998 to address the gap between sexual ignorance from the repression of sexual information during Cultural Revolution and today's increases in teen sexual behavior. The show's hosts respond to questions viewers send via email and text message, many of which reveal a lack of basic sexual facts (Fan, 2006).

However, many depictions of sexuality in the media may trivialize the complexity of sexuality and create unrealistic expectations regarding sexual experiences. Daytime soaps were the first type of program to emphasize more explicit sexual content, usually involving sexual intrigue based on infidelity, revenge, or exploitation (Greenberg & Woods, 1999). Shows such as *Desperate Housewives*, *Everwood*, and *The OC* depict all manner of couplings—one involving a woman and her teenage gardener, another involving adultery with a married ex-boyfriend (Streisand, 2005). Cable TV and satellite TV offer programs containing far more sexual explicitness than network programs—as shown by *Sex in the City*, in which four New York women talk with each other about faking orgasm, disappointment with penis size and rapid ejaculation, "funky spunk" (bad-tasting ejaculate), and an uncircumcised penis. Reality TV programs—*Real World*, *Temptation Island*, *The Bachelor*, and the like—are fueled by sexual themes. Videos and DVDs offer films of varying sexual explicitness for consumers to watch in the privacy of their own homes.

Music videos bridge television and the music industry. Up to 50% of music videos (depending on the type of music) have sexual content, some portraying sexual coercion.

That raises the question of how such content might interfere with young people's learning about healthy relationships (Brown, 2002; Wyatt, 1997). Increasingly, music videos are being watched via cell phone, so watching them on TV may decline.

## Advertising

**? Critical Thinking Question**

Can you think of an advertisement that helped reshape sexual sterotypes? How did the advertisement achieve that?

Advertising is present in most forms of media or stands alone, as on the ubiquitous billboard. Sexual images, often blatant but sometimes subtle, are designed to help attract attention to and sell products. An ad that has high sexual appeal can be a powerful marketing tool. For example, jeans sales doubled following the 1980s ad in which a young Brooke Shields promised that nothing came between her and her Calvin Klein jeans (Kuriansky, 1996). Advertising relies on the false promises that love or sex or both will come with the acquisition of a certain beauty product, brand of liquor, brand of clothing, sound system, or car. Most sexual content in advertising trivializes sex and reinforces the idea that only young, hard male and female bodies merit attraction, with the exception of advertising aimed at the large consumer group of aging baby boomers. Occasionally, advertising helps to break down taboos. For example, presidential candidate Bob Dole's advertisements for Viagra helped bring erectile dysfunction into public discourse.

## Magazines

**? Critical Thinking Question**

Do you think that most young women's main interest in sex is having "kinky" sexual variety?

Popular magazines contain a range of sexually related articles—from excellent information about self-help and relationship skills to articles that promote stereotypical gender roles, body-image insecurity, superficiality, and manipulation in relationships. At the checkout stand, the front pages of the tabloids try to titillate us with headlines such as "Cops Probe Daddy's Secret Porn Life." Magazines designed for young men emphasize two themes: information about "what women want" and how to promote "kinky" sexual variety with partners (Taylor, 2005).

Women's magazines often contain excellent self-help information. For example, the October 2005 *Seventeen* magazine's "Vagina 101: What's Healthy and What's Not" answered many questions women often have. (Incidentally, Albertson's grocery store corporation found the facts and photos objectionable and removed that issue from their stores.) Articles about sexual interaction may provide positive support for sexual exploration and assertiveness; such an article in *Cosmopolitan* encouraged its readers to stimulate their clitoris during intercourse to enhance arousal and help them reach orgasm. Conversely, articles like "Do You Make Men M-E-L-T?" may reinforce gender-role stereotypes and performance pressure. The ubiquitous information telling readers how to make themselves prettier, skinnier, and sexier ("Boy Magnet Beauty" and "Mega Makeovers: Go from So-So to Supersexy") may contribute to body-image insecurity.

Advertisers increasingly use group sex scenes to market their products.

Image courtesy of The Advertising Archives

## The Internet

The best research study about sexuality in the United States, the National Health and Social Life Survey (NHSLS), concluded that our attitudes and behaviors are dramatically influenced by the people in our social groups (Laumann et al., 1994). This research was conducted before the 1990s explosion in cyberspace communication. By 2006 there were over one billion Internet users worldwide. The current usage rate consists of about 17% of the worldwide population, leaving enormous growth potential (Internet World Stats, 2006). The number of social networking sites, whose purpose is to facilitate communication between people, has increased dramatically in a very short time. A favorite of young people, MySpace.com was launched in 2003 and had 70 million users by 2006 (Romano, 2006). The impact of this communication revolution on sexual attitudes and behaviors is potentially epic. Now people in disparate social groups—different age groups, races, religions, ethnic groups, and economic groups—can communicate more easily than ever before. Distance and cultural barriers are becoming less and less of an obstacle, which presents "(t)he possibility for the kinds of quantum leaps that human minds can make when they share ideas" (Shernoff, 2006, p. 20). Conversely, people with stigmatized sexual interests shared by few can connect with like-minded individuals, given that sexuality in its myriad forms has made its presence known on the Internet (Ross, 2005). The Internet has been especially revolutionary for LBGT (lesbian, bisexual, gay, and transgendered) users. The online LBGT community has blossomed in the last decade, and chat rooms have replaced bars as the primary place to meet others (Umstead, 2005).

The Internet can provide quick access to useful information related to sexuality. "Dear Abby"–type sex columnists answer online questions, and the abundance of self-help information ranges from Web sites for breast and prostate cancer to message boards posting wig-care tips for transsexuals. In contrast to self-help and general sexuality education, the approximately 72 million people who visit adult sites each month in the United States are looking for something else in the consumer-driven interactive sexual supermarket. Some use chat rooms to talk about their wildest fantasies or participate in multiplayer interactive adult games, often experimenting by assuming different personae and sexes (Ross, 2005). Others engage in real-time chat, via instant messaging, and use audio devices and video cameras for online interaction. Many users seek sexually explicit images or webcam live-action "cyberstrippers" for arousal during masturbation. Remote interactive technology, dubbed "teledildonics," provides interactive, rather than solo, stimulation. Teledildonics allows one person to control another's sex toy over the Internet. Users manipulate a control panel that varies the intensity of motion of the other person's sleeve-style vibrator or dildo with an attached vibrating bunny for clitoral stimulation.

Most of the Internet's technological developments have been advanced by the sex industry. Adult programming continues to be a revenue source for recent developments in cell phones, iPod "pod porn," PDAs, PSP game handhelds, and broadband video streaming platforms (Alexander, 2006). Experts expect further developments in remote-control sexual stimulation (Crowe, 2005: Summers, 2005; Umstead, 2005). Animated computer graphics with sexual content is another rapidly developing technology.

The Internet has also become a huge dating service, an interactive personal-ad opportunity people can use for online conversations to see if they want to meet in person. Although it has risks, Internet dating can have the advantages of clarifying one's agenda for a relationship up front, whether one is seeking casual sex or a soul-mate life partner. For some, the level of self-disclosure online may actually establish more intimacy before beginning a physical relationship than meeting face-to-face without prior e-mail communication.

Research has found that most people use adult Web sites for benign recreational activity. However, almost 9% of the study's participants spent *at least* 11 hours a week online, resulting in problems in their lives when they became so involved with sex online that their personal sexual relationships and other life responsibilities suffered (Cooper et al., 1999). Even more problematic is that some sexual predators use the Internet to sexually exploit others, and a site like MySpace.com is a sexual predator's dream come true (Romano, 2006). Further, the easily available extreme sexual material on the Internet is not developmentally appropriate for young people, but it can be difficult to avoid. The constructive and destructive possibilities of cyberspace sexuality appear as unlimited as those potentials in human nature. The Internet's sexual content is highly salient because about 69% of North America's population has Internet access (Internet World Stats, 2006), and we will discuss various elements of this topic throughout the text.

## Sexuality: Where the Personal Is Political

Sex and Politics

The personal and political (laws, policies, and norms) are truly merged when it comes to sexuality. The historical, cross-cultural, and intra-cultural perspectives that we have examined in this chapter clearly show the impact of social norms on sexuality and may help us to appreciate the unique position in which we currently find ourselves. We can define our own sexuality on the basis of personal choices to a far greater degree than was possible for the ancient Hebrews, the early Christians, the Europeans of the Middle Ages, the Victorian Europeans and North Americans of the 19th century—and to a far greater degree than is possible for many contemporary non-Western societies. With the increased understanding and acceptance of diversity in human sexuality that developed during the 20th century, we have greater freedoms and responsibilities today. Although some would argue that increased tolerance of diversity creates more problems than it solves, in general we agree with the idea that "the sexual health of an individual or society is enriched with the understanding, tolerance, and compassion for the diversity of sexual identities and sexual expressions that are a part of the human condition" (Coleman, 2000, p. 4). ■

And yet, the exponential changes in the last century have left us with many unresolved questions. Consequently, in the 21st century we face controversies about social

policies, laws, and ethics in almost every area related to human sexuality—many of which are decided by voters, school boards, state and federal courts, and the U.S. Supreme Court (Bernstein & Schaffner, 2005). We have seen throughout this chapter that social norms, sometimes codified into law, can support or interfere with the individual's right to privacy and personal choice (Kaiser, 2004; Wildman, 2001). Controversies pertaining to sexuality that we will continue to face include the following:

- Should public schools provide abstinence-only or comprehensive sex education?
- Should same-sex couples be able to legally marry?
- Should health insurance be required to cover costs for contraception?
- Should state and federal laws limit access to abortion?

- Should teens be able to obtain contraceptive services without parental consent?
- Should a person's HIV status be part of the public record?
- Should prostitution be legal?

We hope that your experience grappling with today's challenges related to sexuality contributes to your sexual intelligence and your personal ability to navigate all the different topics that make up our sexuality.

**? Critical Thinking Question**

How do these current controversies relate to our sex-for-procreation and rigid gender-role legacies?

# SUMMARY

## Controversy and Diversity in Human Sexuality
- Few topics generate as much attention and controversy as issues surrounding sexuality.

## Diversity Within the United States
- Variations in acculturation, religious belief, and socioeconomic status create sexual diversity within ethnic groups of the United States.

## A Psychosocial Orientation
- This book stresses the role of psychological factors and social conditioning in shaping human sexuality.

## Cross-Cultural Perspectives
- To better appreciate the importance of social conditioning, we can compare sexual attitudes and behaviors in other cultures.
- Followers of Islam, or Muslims, believe enjoyment of sex in marriage is important for men and women. Female sexuality is seen as powerful, and in some parts of the Islamic Middle East, veils, female genital cutting, and segregation of the sexes until marriage are considered necessary to contain women's sexuality.
- In ancient China sexual activity was a means to spiritual growth.
- Communist China's government attempted to isolate its people from Western sexual attitudes and practices, and its sexual norms were conservative until recent loosening of government restrictions.

## Our Cultural Legacy: Sex for Procreation and Rigid Gender Roles
- This book critically explores the effects of two pervasive themes related to sexuality: sex limited to reproduction (procreation) and inflexible gender roles.

## Sexuality in the Western World: A Historical Perspective
- The ancient Hebrews stressed the importance of childbearing and also had an appreciation of sexuality within marriage.

- Gender-role differences between men and women were well established in ancient Hebraic culture. Women's most important roles were to manage the household and bear children, especially sons.
- Christian writers such as Paul of Tarsus, Augustine, and Thomas Aquinas contributed to the view of sex as sinful, justifiable only in marriage for the purpose of procreation.
- Two contradictory images of women developed in the Middle Ages: the pure and unattainable woman on a pedestal, manifested in the cult of the Virgin Mary and in courtly love; and the evil temptress, represented by Eve and by women persecuted as witches.
- Leaders of the Reformation of the 16th century challenged the requirement that clergy remain celibate and recognized sexual expression as an important aspect of marriage.
- Women were viewed as asexual in the Victorian era, and the lives of "proper" Victorian men and women were largely separate. Men often visited prostitutes for companionship as well as sexual relations.
- The theories of Freud, research findings, and feminism changed the Victorian notion of women being asexual.
- U.S. involvement in World Wars I and II exposed American men to the more open sexuality of Europe and placed American women in the workforce (temporarily).
- Technical advances in contraception in the 20th century have permitted people to separate sexuality from procreation to a degree not previously possible.
- Dramatic changes in understanding and acceptance of homosexuality began in the 1960s.

## The Media and Sexuality
- Mass media as we know it have existed a short time relative to the greater human experience.
- The explosion of mass media—radio, movies, television, VCRs and DVDs, and the Internet—presents a vast array of sexual information and misinformation that at least highlights the diversity in human sexuality.
- Sexual explicitness in all popular media continues to increase.
- The impact of the Internet on sexual attitudes, knowledge, and behavior has both constructive and problematic possibilities.

## Sexuality: Where the Personal Is Political

- The scientific, psychological, and social changes in the 20th century have led to the contemporary individual's increased ability to make personal decisions regarding sexuality.
- Laws, social policies, and norms related to sexuality merge this personal subject with "politics."

## ◑ Suggested Readings

**Barstow, Anne** (1994). *Witchcraze*. San Francisco: Pandora. A compelling, comprehensive account of the witch hunts and gender-based violence.

**D'Emilio, John, and Estelle Freedman** (1988). *Intimate Matters*. New York: Harper & Row. A full-length examination of the history of sexuality and how the meaning and place of sexuality in the United States have changed.

**Kilbourne, Jean** (2000). *Can't Buy My Love: How Advertising Changes the Way We Think and Feel*. New York: Simon & Schuster. An illuminating look at the messages about sex, power, and relationships in advertising.

**Klein, Marty** (2006). *America's War on Sex: The Attack on Law, Lust, and Liberty*. Westport, CT: Praeger Publishers. An expose of religious conservatives systematic undermining of reproductive and sexual rights.

**Klein, Marty**. Sexual Intelligence Newsletter at www .sexualintelligence.org. Challengest sex negativity and government hypocrisy.

**Reichert, Tom** (2003). *The Erotic History of Advertising*. New York: Prometheus Books. A detailed history of the use of the erotic in advertising.

## ◑ Web Resources

**CengageNOW Web Site**
Go to **academic.cengage.com** to link to practice quiz questions, interactive activities, Internet links, critical thinking exercises, discussion forums, and more. You can also access sites from the Wadsworth Psychology Study Center (**academic .cengage.com/psychology**) or you can connect directly to the following sites:

**Human Sexuality Web**
Designed, maintained, and updated by graduate students at the University of Missouri, Kansas City, this site contains information concerning sex education, sexual counseling, sexual health issues, and related topics on sexuality.

**SIECUS**
SIECUS, the Sexuality Information and Education Council of the United States, is a well-respected nonprofit organization specializing in sex education and sexuality. Its Web site provides current and reliable information.

**Ask NOAH About Sexuality**
NOAH (New York Online Access to Health) offers detailed and relevant resources on sexual issues in both English and Spanish on its Web site.

**Variations in Sex Laws**
This Web site provides an interesting collection of direct links to laws pertaining to sexuality in Australia, Canada, various U.S. states, and traditional Islamic nations.

*Our Sexuality* **Book Companion Web Site academic.cengage.com/psychology/ crooks** Visit your book companion Web site where you will find flash cards, practice quizzes, Internet links, and more to help you study.

**Just what you need to know NOW!**
Spend time on what you need to master rather than on information you already have learned. Take a pretest for this chapter, and CengageNOW will generate a personalized study plan based on your results. The study plan will identify the topics you need to review and direct you to online resources to help you master those topics. You can then take a post-test to help you determine the concepts you have mastered and what you will still need to work on. Try it out! Go to **academic.cengage.com/login** to sign in with an access code or to purchase access to this product.

**InfoTrac College Edition Online Library**
Sign in to **academic.cengage.com/login** or visit your free book companion Web site at **academic.cengage.com/psychology/crooks** to access InfoTrac College Edition, an online searchable library that includes a multitude of journals, many specific to human sexuality. These journals include *Archives of Sexual Behavior; Archives of Sexual Health Behavior; Canadian Journal of Human Sexuality; Hispanic Journal of the Behavioral Sciences; Journal of Cross-Cultural Psychology; Journal of Physical Education, Recreation, and Dance; Journal of Sex Research;* and *Sex Roles.*

# Sex Research: Methods and Problems

Rob Melnychuk/Getty Images

- A number of social observers have suggested that men who are active consumers of sexually violent films, magazines, and other pornography are likely to adopt abusive attitudes toward women. As a result, they show an increased tendency to commit rape and other abusive acts toward women.
- Many people believe that a few drinks make sex more enjoyable. After imbibing a little alcohol, they say that their inhibitions relax; they feel more sensual and more friendly toward the person they are with.
- Early in the last century, Sigmund Freud asserted that women's orgasms resulting from vaginal penetration are more "mature" than those resulting from clitoral stimulation alone. A common assumption today is that "vaginal" orgasms are superior to clitoral orgasms.

You have probably heard these three assertions before, and you may agree with one or even all of them. But if you were called on to prove that they were true or untrue, how would you go about compiling evidence? Or, as the quotation at the top of this page asks, How do you study sex?

**Sexology** The study of sexuality.

The role of **sexology**, the study of sexuality, is to test such assumptions in a scientific way, to find out whether they are true or false and to document what underlying relationships, if any, they reveal. This task is not easy. Although intrinsically interesting to most of us, human sexual behavior is also inherently difficult to study because it occupies an intensely private area in our lives that few of us are comfortable discussing with others. People often feel embarrassed or even threatened when asked to disclose details about their sexual attitudes or behavior to another person, especially to a sex researcher who is a stranger to them (Turner, 1999). In addition, the subject matter of sexology abounds with myth, exaggeration, secrecy, and value judgments.

Despite these problems, sex researchers are accumulating a growing body of knowledge about human sexual behaviors and attitudes—including the three assumptions with which we began this chapter: Does violent pornography lead to abusive behaviors such as rape? Does alcohol increase sexual pleasure? What are the differences between vaginal and clitoral orgasms? We will revisit these and other questions in this chapter as we discuss the methods used to study sexuality, the kinds of questions appropriate to each method, and the problems inherent in each method. In the process, we will also learn something about evaluating published research.

We hope that in the following pages you will begin to appreciate what we know and what we do not know and how confident we can be about the available knowledge. You may also begin to sense the steps we can take to further expand our scientific knowledge of sexual behavior. Perhaps you will contribute to our understanding of this important area of human experience. We invite you to do so.

**InfoTrac Search Words**

- Sexology

## ● The Goals of Sexology

People who study human sexuality share certain goals with scientists in other disciplines. These goals include *understanding, predicting,* and *controlling* or influencing the events that are the subject matter of their respective fields.

The first two scientific goals—understanding and predicting behavior—are not difficult to comprehend. For example, a pharmacologist who knows how blood pressure medications interfere with sexual functioning can use this knowledge to predict what dosage of a drug could be tolerated by a patient with a particular health condition without experiencing impaired sexual functioning. Similarly, a psychologist who knows something about the way certain behavior patterns influence the quality of couples' interactions can help a couple predict whether they will have a happy marriage.

The third goal, using scientifically acquired knowledge to control behavior, is a more difficult concept to comprehend. Understandably, many people express concern about the legitimacy of applying scientific knowledge to control people's behavior. A certain amount of skepticism in this area is probably healthy, and it would be inaccurate to suggest that all knowledge acquired through research leads directly to behavior control. Nevertheless, sexologists have been able to influence, to some degree, a large body of phenomena. For example, understanding how adolescents make decisions about contraceptive use has resulted in the development of school-based sex-education programs, many of which are linked to family planning clinic services. These innovative programs have often resulted in positive behavioral changes, such as increased contraceptive use among sexually active teenagers. Similarly, knowledge about the psychobiological causes of certain sexual problems, such as premature ejaculation and lack of vaginal lubrication, has enabled specialists to develop therapies aimed at controlling such disruptive symptoms, as we will see in Chapter 14.

Most of us would not object to the goal of controlling or influencing events in the examples just described. However, sexologists, like other scientists, must also contend with situations in which the application of this goal raises important questions. For instance, is it appropriate for fertility specialists to use their knowledge to help a couple conceive a child of a desired biological sex? Is it appropriate for a sex therapist to subject imprisoned sex offenders to aversive stimuli (such as putrid odors) in an effort to control deviant sexual urges? Clearly, the goal of controlling or influencing human behavior should be carefully evaluated within a framework of ethical consideration.

Compared with many other disciplines, sexology is an infant science, having originated largely in the 20th century. The pioneering work of Alfred Kinsey, the first researcher to conduct an extensive general survey of American sexual behaviors, took place only in the late 1940s and early 1950s. Many questions remain unanswered, although a considerable body of knowledge is accumulating. In the remainder of this chapter, we examine some of the research methods that have been used to explore human sexuality.

# ● Nonexperimental Research Methods

We began this chapter with three common notions about human sexual behavior: that exposure to violent pornography can increase a man's tolerance of, and willingness to commit, sexually violent acts, such as rape; that alcohol can enhance sexual responsiveness; and that vaginal orgasms are superior to clitoral orgasms. How do researchers go about investigating hypotheses such as these? In this section, we will look at three nonexperimental methods: (1) the case study, (2) the survey, and (3) direct observation. Later in the chapter, we will learn about a fourth method, experimental research. ● **Table 2.1** summarizes these four major methods of studying sexual behavior. As we will see, not every research method is appropriate to every type of research question.

## Case Studies

A **case study** examines either a single subject or a small group of subjects, each of whom is studied individually and in depth. Data are gathered using a variety of means, including direct observation, questionnaires, testing, and even experimentation.

People often become subjects for case studies because they behave in an atypical way or have a physical or emotional disorder. Thus a large portion of our information about sexual response difficulties (such as erectile disorder in men and lack of orgasmic response in women) comes from case studies of individuals seeking treatment for these problems. Also, much of what we know about sex offenders, transsexuals, incest victims, and the like has been learned from case studies.

Not surprisingly, a number of case studies have investigated the relationship between sexually violent media and rape. In many of these studies, rapists report high levels of exposure to sexually violent films, magazines, and books (Marshall, 1988). However, it is unclear whether violent attitudes toward women and behaviors such as rape result directly from exposure to sexually violent media. The mere fact that rapists seem more inclined than nonrapists to consume pornography does not necessarily imply a cause-and-effect relationship. Perhaps there are other plausible explanations. For example, the types of environments that tend to socialize men to be violent

**Case study** A nonexperimental research method that examines either a single subject or a small group of subjects individually and in depth.

| Method | Brief Description | Advantages | Disadvantages |
|---|---|---|---|
| Case study | Examines a single subject or a small group of subjects, each of whom is studied individually and in depth. | Flexibility in data-gathering procedures.<br><br>In-depth explorations of behaviors, thoughts, and feelings. | Limited generalizability of findings.<br><br>Accuracy of data limited by fallibility of human memory. Not suitable for many kinds of research questions. |
| Survey | Data pertaining to sexual attitudes and behaviors derived from relatively large groups of people by means of questionnaires or interviews. | Relatively cheap and quick method for obtaining large amounts of data.<br><br>Can obtain data from more people than is practical to study in the laboratory or through case studies. | Problems of:<br>  Nonresponse<br>  Demographic bias<br>  Inaccurate information |
| Direct observation | Researchers observe and record responses of participating subjects. | Virtually eliminates the possibility of data falsification.<br><br>Behavioral record can be kept indefinitely on videotapes or films. | Subjects' behavior can be influenced by presence of observer(s) or the artificial nature of the environment where observations are made. |
| Experimental method | Subjects presented with certain events (stimuli) under managed conditions that allow for reliable measurement of their reactions. | Provides a controlled environment for managing relevant variables.<br><br>Suited to discovering causal relationships between variables. | Artificiality of laboratory settings can adversely influence or bias subjects' responses. |

toward women might also be characterized by accessibility to violent pornography. Alternatively, men who have abusive proclivities directed toward women may be inclined to consume sexually violent pornography. Thus, although the case-study method shows that this media exposure is often associated with rape, it cannot tell us the exact nature of the relationship.

The case-study method has also been used to investigate the common assertion that alcohol enhances sexual responsiveness and pleasure. In fact, evidence from some case studies suggests just the reverse, at least among chronic alcoholics. Case studies of alcoholic subjects have shown decreased arousability and lowered sexual interest, although it is possible that this effect is due to the general physical deterioration that accompanies heavy, long-term alcohol use.

The case-study approach offers some advantages to researchers. One advantage is the flexibility of data-gathering procedures. Although the open-ended format of the case study offers little opportunity for investigative control, it often provides opportunities to acquire insight into specific behaviors. The highly personal, subjective information about what individuals actually think and feel about their behavior is an important step beyond simply recording activities. This case-study method sacrifices some control, but it offers opportunities to explore specific behaviors, thoughts, and feelings in depth and can add considerable dimension to our information.

The case-study method does have some limitations, however. Because case studies typically focus on individuals or small samples of especially interesting or atypical cases, it is often difficult to generalize findings accurately to broader populations. A second limitation of case studies is that a person's past history, especially the person's childhood and adolescence, usually does not become a target of research until the individual manifests some unusual behavior later in life, as an adult. People often have trouble accurately remembering events from years ago. Furthermore, memory is also subject to intentional efforts to distort or repress facts.

A third limitation of the case study is that it is not suitable for many kinds of research questions. For instance, a case study might not be the best method for testing the third assumption on this chapter's opening page—that vaginal orgasms are superior to clitoral orgasms. And because personal accounts can be influenced by factors such as emotions, values, and the vagaries of memory, the reliability of the case-study method can also be in doubt. As we will see shortly, this type of research problem is better suited to the direct-observation method.

**? Critical Thinking Question**

Many studies have reported an association between abnormally low levels of testosterone and decreased sexual desire in both sexes. Can case-study research clarify whether this association reflects a cause-and-effect relationship? If so, how? If not, why not?

## Surveys

Most of our information about human sexuality has been obtained from a second important research method, the **survey**, in which people are asked about their sexual experiences or attitudes. The survey method enables researchers to collect data from a large number of people, usually more than can be studied in a clinical setting or in the laboratory. Surveys can be conducted orally, through face-to-face or telephone interviews, or through paper-and-pencil questionnaires. Recently, computerized interviews have been used to gather information about sexual behaviors and other sensitive topics. We will discuss this technological aid to sex research later in this chapter.

Although the methods of conducting written and oral surveys are somewhat different, their intent is the same. Each tries to use a relatively small group, called the *survey sample*, to draw inferences or conclusions about a much larger group with a particular characteristic (called a *target population*). Examples of target populations are married adults and high school adolescents.

Most information about human sexual behavior has been obtained through questionnaire or interview surveys.

### Choosing the Sample

The questions asked by sexologists often apply to populations that are too large to study in their entirety. For example, if you wanted to obtain information about the sexual practices of American married couples in their later years, your population would include all married couples in the United States over a given age, say 65. Clearly, it would be impossible to question everyone in this group. Sex researchers resolve this problem by obtaining data from a relatively small sample of the target population. The confidence with which conclusions about the larger population can be drawn depends on the technique used to select this sample.

Typically, researchers strive to select a **representative sample** (sometimes called a *probability sample*)—that is, a sample in which various subgroups are represented proportionately to their incidence in the target population. Target populations can be subdivided into smaller subgroups by such criteria as age, economic status, geographic locale, and religious affiliation. In a representative sample, every individual in the larger target population has a chance of being included.

What procedures would you use to select a representative sample that could be surveyed to assess the sexual practices of older American married couples? How would you ensure the representativeness of your selected sample? A good beginning would be to obtain U.S. Census Bureau statistics on the number of married couples whose partners are age 65 and older who reside in major geographic regions of the United States (East, South, and so on). Next, you would select subgroups of your sample according to the actual distribution of the larger population. Thus, if 25% of older married couples live in the East, 25% of your sample would be drawn from this region. Similarly, if 15% of older married couples in the East fall into an upper socioeconomic status category, 15% of those subjects selected from the East would be drawn from this group.

Once you had systematically compiled your lists of potential subjects, your final step would be to select your actual subjects from these lists. To ensure that all members of each subgroup had an equal chance of being included, you might use a table of random numbers to generate random selections from your lists. If these procedures were correctly applied, and if your final sample was large enough, you could be reasonably confident that your findings could be generalized to all married American couples age 65 or older.

Another kind of sample, the **random sample**, is selected from a larger population, using randomization procedures. A random sample may or may not be the same as a representative sample. For example, assume that you are a social scientist on the faculty of a rural university in the Midwest whose students are inclined to hold relatively

**Survey** A research method in which a sample of people are questioned about their behaviors and/or attitudes.

**Representative sample** A type of limited research sample that provides an accurate representation of a larger target population of interest.

**Random sample** A randomly chosen subset of a population.

conservative social views. You wish to conduct a survey to assess American university students' experience with "hook-ups" (short-term or one-time loveless sexual encounters between strangers or casual acquaintances). Since it is convenient to draw your subjects from the student population enrolled at your university, you randomly select your survey sample from a roster of all enrolled students.

A substantial majority of your sample respond to your well-designed, anonymously administered questionnaire. Can you now be relatively confident that your results reflect the propensity of students to engage in hook-ups—if not in the greater United States, at least in your geographic region? Unfortunately, you cannot, because you have selected subjects from a sample that is not necessarily representative of the broader community of university students. Students at your university tend to have conservative social views, a trait that may both influence their likelihood of engaging in hook-ups and render them atypical of large segments of American university students, especially those enrolled in urban universities on the East and West Coasts, whose student populations tend to hold more-liberal social views.

Thus, even though randomization is often a valid selection tool, a study sample cannot be truly representative unless it reflects all the important subgroups in the target population. All things considered, representative samples generally allow for more-accurate generalizations to the entire target population than do random samples. However, random samples are often quite adequate and thus are used widely.

**? Critical Thinking Question**

What procedures would you use to select a representative sample of American college students age 18 to 22, to assess the effect of alcohol consumption on sexual functioning?

**InfoTrac Search Words**

- Survey sexual
- Random sample sexual

## Questionnaires and Interviews

Once selected, subjects in a sample can be surveyed through either a written questionnaire or an interview. Both procedures involve asking the participants a set of questions, which might range from a few to over 1,000. These questions can be multiple-choice, true-or-false, or discussion questions; subjects can respond alone, in the privacy of their homes, or in the presence of a researcher.

Each survey method has advantages and disadvantages. Questionnaires tend to be quicker and cheaper to administer than interview surveys. In addition, because filling out a form affords greater anonymity than facing an interviewer, subjects might be considerably more likely to answer questions honestly, with minimal distortion. Sexual behavior is highly personal, and in interviews subjects might be tempted to describe their behaviors or attitudes in a more favorable light. Finally, because most written questionnaires can be evaluated objectively, their data are less subject to researcher bias than are interviews.

On the other hand, interviews have some advantages that questionnaires do not have. First, the format of an interview is more flexible. If a particular question is confusing to the subject, the interviewer can clarify it. In addition, interviewers have the option of varying the sequence of questions if it seems appropriate for a particular respondent. And finally, skillful interviewers can establish excellent rapport with subjects, and the resulting sense of trust may produce more revealing responses than is possible with paper-and-pencil questionnaires. Some sex researchers have found that combining face-to-face interviews (to establish rapport) with written questionnaires (to tap sensitive information) is an especially effective survey method (Laumann et al., 1994; Siegel et al., 1994).

## Problems of Sex Survey Research: Nonresponse, Inaccuracy, and Demographic Bias

Regardless of the survey strategy used, sex researchers find that it is difficult to secure a representative sample. This is because many people do not want to participate in sex studies. For instance, assuming that you used proper sampling procedures to choose your sample of older married couples in the example discussed earlier, what proportion of your representative sample would actually be willing to answer your questions? **Nonresponse**, the refusal to participate in a research study, is a common problem that consistently plagues sex survey research (Turner, 1999).

**Nonresponse** The refusal to participate in a research study.

No one has ever conducted a major sex survey in which 100% of the selected subjects voluntarily participated. In fact, some studies include results obtained from samples in which only a small minority responded. This raises an important question: Are people who agree to take part in sex surveys any different from those who refuse?

Perhaps volunteer subjects in sex research are a representative cross section of the population, but we have no theoretical or statistical basis for that conclusion. As a matter of fact, the opposite might well be true. People who volunteer to participate may be the ones who are the most eager to share their experiences, who have explored a wide range of activities, or who feel most comfortable with their sexuality. (Or it may be that the most experienced people are those who are least willing to respond because they feel that their behaviors are atypical or extreme.) A preponderance of experienced, inexperienced, liberal, or conservative individuals can bias any sample.

Research suggests that **self-selection**, or volunteer bias, is an important concern for sex researchers (Plaud et al., 1999; Wiederman, 2001). Studies strongly suggest that volunteers for sex research are more sexually experienced and hold more positive attitudes toward sexuality and sex research than do nonvolunteers (Boynton, 2003; Plaud et al., 1999; Wiederman, 1999). In addition, research indicates that women are less likely than men to volunteer for sex research (Boynton, 2003; Plaud et al., 1999), a finding that suggests female sex research samples are more highly selected than male samples.

**Self-selection** The bias introduced into research study results because of participants' willingness to respond.

Another problem inherent in sex survey research has to do with the accuracy of subjects' responses. Most data about human sexual behavior are obtained from respondents' own reports of their experiences, and people's actual behavior can be quite different from what they report (Catania, 1999b; Ochs & Binik, 1999). How many people accurately remember when they first masturbated, and with what frequency, or at what age they first experienced orgasm? Some people may also distort or falsify their self-disclosures to maintain or even enhance their social image (Catania, 1999b). This tendency to provide *socially desirable* responses can involve people who consciously or unconsciously conceal certain facts about their sexual histories because they view them as abnormal, foolish, or painful to remember. People can also feel pressure to deny or minimize their experiences regarding behaviors for which strong taboos exist, such as incest, homosexuality, and masturbation. In other cases, people can purposely inflate their experience, perhaps out of a desire to appear more liberal, experienced, or proficient.

A third type of problem that affects sex surveys is **demographic bias**. Most of the data available from sex research in the United States have come from samples weighted heavily toward white middle-class volunteers. Typically, college students and educated white-collar workers are overrepresented. Ethnic and racial minorities and less educated individuals are underrepresented.

**Demographic bias** A kind of sampling bias in which certain segments of society (such as white, middle-class, white-collar workers) are disproportionately represented in a study population.

How much of an effect do nonresponse and demographic bias have on sex research findings? We cannot say for sure. But so long as elements of society, including the less educated and ethnic and racial minorities, are underrepresented, we must be cautious in generalizing findings to the population at large. The informational deficit pertaining to sexual behaviors of American racial and ethnic minorities is lessening with the recent emergence of several studies that included members of various ethnic minority groups in the United States. These studies demonstrate that ethnicity often exerts considerable influence on sexual attitudes and behaviors (Laumann et al., 1994; Okazaki, 2002; Wiederman et al., 1996). Throughout this textbook, we describe results from several studies as we discuss ethnicity in relation to a variety of topics.

 InfoTrac Search Words

- Demographic bias
- Self-selection bias

## The Kinsey Reports

The studies of Alfred Kinsey are perhaps the best known and most widely cited example of survey research. With his associates Kinsey published two large volumes in the decade following World War II: One, on male sexuality, was published in 1948; the follow-up report on female sexuality was published in 1953. These volumes contain the results of extensive survey interviews, the aim of which was to determine patterns of sexual behavior in American males and females.

The Kinsey sample consisted of 5,300 white males and 5,940 white females. Respondents came from both rural and urban areas in each state and represented a range of ages, marital status, occupations, educational levels, and religions. However, the sample had a disproportionately greater number of better-educated city-dwelling Protestants, whereas older people, rural dwellers, and those with less education were underrepresented. African Americans and other racial minorities were completely omitted from the sample. And, finally, all subjects were volunteers. Thus in no way can Kinsey's study population be viewed as a representative sample of the American population.

Although published over 50 years ago, many of Kinsey's data are relevant today (Reinisch & Beasley, 1990). The passage of time has not altered the validity of certain findings—for example, that sexual behavior is influenced by educational level and that heterosexuality or homosexuality is often not an all-or-none proposition. However, certain other areas—such as coital rates among unmarried people—are more influenced by changing societal norms. Therefore we might expect the Kinsey data to be less predictive of contemporary practices in these areas. Nevertheless, even here the data are still relevant; they provide one possible basis for estimating the degree of behavioral change over the years.

## The National Health and Social Life Survey

The outbreak of the devastating AIDS epidemic in the 1980s occurred at a time when the U.S. public health community was ill informed about the contemporary sexual practices of the citizenry. To fill this informational void with data that could be used to predict and prevent the spread of AIDS, an agency within the U.S. Department of Health and Human Services called in 1987 for proposals to study the sexual attitudes and practices of American adults. A team of distinguished researchers at the University of Chicago answered this call with a plan for a national survey to assess the prevalence of a broad array of sexual practices and attitudes and to place them in their social contexts within the U.S. population. The research team—Edward Laumann and his colleagues John Gagnon, Robert Michael, and Stuart Michaels—were initially heartened by the acceptance of their proposal in 1988 and by the provision of government funds adequate to support a survey of 20,000 people.

A sample size this large would have allowed the investigators to draw reliable conclusions about various subpopulations in America, such as diverse ethnic minorities and homosexuals. However, after more than two years of extensive planning, the research team's efforts were dealt a crushing blow when federal funding for their study was withdrawn. In 1991, conservative members of Congress, offended by the prospect of government funding of sex research, introduced legislation that effectively eliminated federal funding for such studies. Unfortunately, legitimate sexuality research remains under fire, largely from conservative organizations and politicians who continue to feel threatened by this type of research (Clark, 2005). (See the box titled "Sex Research under Siege.") ∎

Undaunted by this setback, Laumann and his colleagues secured funding from several private foundations that enabled them to proceed with their project, albeit with a much smaller sample. The research team, working with the National Opinion Research Center at the University of Chicago, used sophisticated sampling techniques to select a representative sample of 4,369 Americans age 18 to 59. An amazing 79% of the sample subjects agreed to participate, yielding a final study group of 3,432 respondents. This high response rate dramatically demonstrates that a broad array of people will participate in a highly personal sex survey when they are assured that the societal benefits of the research are important and that the confidentiality of their responses is guaranteed. Furthermore, this unusually high participation rate, together with the fact that the study population closely approximated many known demographic characteristics of the general U.S. population, yielded data that most social scientists believe reliably indicate the sexual practices of most American adults age 18 to 59.

© Wallace Kirkland/Time Life Pictures/Getty Images

Alfred Kinsey, a pioneer sex researcher, conducted one of the most comprehensive surveys on human sexuality.

 InfoTrac Search Words

- National Health and Social Life Survey

 Sex and Politics

? Critical Thinking Question

Should the federal government fund sex research? Are there potential benefits for the American people that justify such expenditures?

## Sex Research Under Siege

Conservative organizations and politicians have made a concerted effort to pressure federal agencies (a major funding source) to withdraw or minimize financial support for sexuality research (Clark, 2005; Kaplan, 2004, Leshner, 2003). Christian fundamentalist groups, such as the Traditional Values Coalition, have zealously lobbied Congress to block funding for a variety of sex research projects, especially research aimed at study populations deemed inappropriate, such as gay men and prostitutes (Kaiser, 2003). During a 2003 committee meeting in the U.S. House of Representatives, Mike Ferguson (Republican from New Jersey) presented a list of sex research projects compiled by the Traditional Values Coalition that he claimed had no value in protecting public health and thus were a waste of money. Among projects on this hit list were a study of sexual arousal patterns by the Kinsey Institute and an investigation of HIV risk behaviors among women sex workers in San Francisco (Clark, 2003).

Fortunately, some members of Congress, most notably Representative Henry Waxman (Democrat from California), have defended federal funding for sex research while decrying efforts by the Traditional Values Coalition and similar organizations to block valuable scientific investigations. Support for continued funding of sexuality research was barely sufficient to thwart a measure to block funding of five specific grants that was introduced by Representative Patrick Toomey (Republican from Pennsylvania) in 2003. This measure, dubbed the Toomey amendment, was defeated by just two votes.

This "rattling of the sabers" by conservative forces has had a chilling impact on sexuality research in America. A prime example of fallout from such pressure was the closure of the Boston University Sexuality and Research

Treatment program in 2004, which ended a 20-year-old program and valuable research into human sexual arousal and response (Clark, 2005). The threat of funding cuts has caused some sex researchers to seek financial support from drug companies whose primary interest is in developing pharmaceutical treatments for sexual difficulties. A direct consequence of this shift in funding sources has been a de-emphasis on the psychosocial aspects of human sexual functioning and a diversion of sex research "from its original mission—deepening our understanding of this critical aspect of human behavior in a way that benefits all of society" (Clark, 2005, p. 18).

Compounding the problem of sex research under siege is that "the Bush administration, with the aid of a Republican-controlled Congress, has launched an unprecedented assault on sexual and reproductive health and rights in the U.S. and abroad" (Kempner, 2004, p. 3). At the heart of this repressive sexuality agenda "is an all-out war on condoms and safer sex" (Kaplan, 2004, p. 4). An example of the impact of this sex-negative political atmosphere was a forced audit of publicly funded studies of sexual risk taking in San Francisco that was spearheaded by conservative members of Congress in 2003 (Clark, 2005).

This is a difficult time for sex research in America. The scientific community is united in the belief that allowing the political clout of organized extremist groups to influence or control research funding would set a very dangerous precedent. It is hoped that opposition to political meddling in scientific research will sustain the integrity of scientific peer review and thus leave decisions on what constitutes legitimate research in the hands of competent professionals, not elected officials.

---

Forced to limit their sample size, Laumann and his associates had to forgo sampling a broad range of subpopulations and instead oversampled African Americans and Hispanic Americans to secure valid information about these two largest ethnic minorities in America. Thus, although the study population was representative of white Americans, African Americans, and Hispanic Americans, too few members of other racial and ethnic minorities (such as Jews, Asian Americans, and Native Americans) were included to provide useful information about these groups.

Laumann and his colleagues trained 220 professionals with prior interviewing experience to interview all 3,432 respondents face to face. They designed the questionnaire to be easily understood and to flow naturally across various topics. Using trained, experienced interviewers ensured that respondents understood all the questions posed. In addition, the questionnaire contained internal checks to measure the consistency of answers, to validate the overall responses.

This study, titled the National Health and Social Life Survey (NHSLS), provided the most comprehensive information about adult sexual behavior in America since Kinsey's research. In fact, because Laumann and his associates used far better sampling techniques than did the Kinsey group, the NHSLS study stands alone as the most representative U.S. sex survey and as one that reliably reflects the sexual practices of the

The NHSLS research team (left to right): Robert Michael, John Gagnon, Stuart Michaels, and Edward Laumann.

© Bruce Powell

general U.S. adult population in the 1990s. An analysis of the NHSLS findings was published in two books. The first book is a detailed and scholarly text titled *The Social Organization of Sexuality: Sexual Practices in the United States* (Laumann et al., 1994). Michael, Gagnon, Laumann, and Gina Kolata—a respected *New York Times* science author—wrote a less technical companion volume for the general public titled *Sex in America: A Definitive Study*. This book, also published in 1994, emerged as a popular trade book.

Like all sex research, the NHSLS has its share of critics. However, most sexologists, including us, are impressed with the excellent research design and scope of the study and generally accept the findings as representing the most accurate data available. Not surprisingly, publication of the two descriptive books created a storm of media attention. This was especially true because the NHSLS findings contradicted conventional wisdom—promulgated by magazine surveys and mass media images— that envisioned a "sex crazy" American populace madly pursuing excessive indulgence in all kinds of conventional and unconventional sexual practices. In reality, the results of the NHSLS reflect an American people who are more content with their erotic lives, less sexually active, and more sexually conservative than was widely believed. These findings are especially ironic in view of the judgmental opposition by conservative legislators to the Laumann study, who feared it would provide a mandate for excessive sexual expression.

As previously mentioned, our understanding of the impact of ethnic diversity on sexual behavior has been improving as a result of several research studies. The NHSLS is a good example of this expanding knowledge base. In the following Sexuality and Diversity discussion, we describe a few pertinent findings from this landmark study that add to our awareness of the association between ethnicity and sexuality.

**InfoTrac Search Words**

- Sexuality and diversity

## SEXUALITY AND DIVERSITY

### *Pertinent Findings From the NHSLS*

Of the 3,432 American adult respondents to the NHSLS, approximately 75% were white Americans, 12% were African Americans, 8% were Hispanic Americans, and the balance was drawn from other ethnic and racial groups, notably Asian Americans and Native Americans (Laumann et al., 1994). The following information provides a brief overview of some important ethnicity findings of this study.

The NHSLS revealed the effect of ethnicity on several sexual behaviors, including the number of sexual partners, the likelihood of choosing sex partners from the same ethnic group, oral sex, anal sex, masturbation, and experience with coercive sex. A larger percentage of African Americans (27.1%) reported having more than one sex partner in the past year than both Hispanic Americans (19.9%) and white Americans (15.1%). However, ethnic differences in the number of sex partners are less pronounced when assessed over a longer time span. The relevant statistics for a five-year span are 48.0% for African Americans, 36.6% for Hispanic Americans, and 37.2% for white Americans.

One finding of interest was that the percentage of noncohabitational sexual partnerships from the same ethnic group was very high, more than 90%, for both African Americans and white Americans. In marked contrast, Hispanic American respondents reported that only about 50% of their noncohabitational sexual partnerships were with members of their ethnic group. ⬤ **Table 2.2** outlines several other notable ethnic variations in sexuality. Two of the most pronounced differences were in the areas of oral sex and masturbation. African Americans reported markedly lower rates of involvement in both these sexual practices than either white Americans or Hispanic Americans.

⬤ **TABLE 2.2**   **Ethnicity and Sexual Practices**

| Sexual Practice | White Americans | | African Americans | | Hispanic Americans | |
|---|---|---|---|---|---|---|
| | Men | Women | Men | Women | Men | Women |
| Experience with giving oral sex (%) | 81.4 | 75.3 | 50.5 | 34.4 | 70.7 | 59.7 |
| Experience with receiving oral sex (%) | 81.4 | 78.9 | 66.3 | 48.9 | 73.2 | 63.7 |
| Experience with anal sex (%) | 25.8 | 23.2 | 23.4 | 9.6 | 34.2 | 17.0 |
| Did not masturbate at all in last year (%) | 33.4 | 55.7 | 60.3 | 67.8 | 33.3 | 65.5 |
| Masturbated at least once per week in last year (%) | 28.3 | 7.3 | 16.9 | 10.7 | 24.4 | 4.7 |
| Women ever sexually forced by a man (%) | | 23.0 | | 19.0 | | 14.0 |

SOURCE: Laumann et al. (1994).

## Survey Findings Regarding Two Issues: Violent Pornography and Alcohol Use

How might the survey method be used to clarify the three assertions with which we began this chapter? The first assertion, concerning violent media and men's likelihood to develop abusive attitudes and behaviors toward women, has been the subject of a number of surveys in the last decade or so.

One of the most notable studies involved 222 male nonoffender college students who were administered a questionnaire regarding their use of pornography and their self-reported likelihood of committing rape or using sexual force. Of these men, 81% had used nonviolent pornography during the previous year, whereas 35% had used sexually violent pornography. Of the subjects who had used sexually violent pornography, many more indicated a likelihood of raping or using sexual force against a woman than did subjects who used only nonviolent pornography (Démare et al., 1988). Other surveys of different populations of men (including some imprisoned rapists) have provided further indications that exposure to sexually violent media can lead to increased tolerance for sexually aggressive behavior, greater acceptance of the myth that women want to be raped, reduced sensitivity to rape victims, desensitization to violence against women, and, in some cases, an increased probability of committing a rape (Donnerstein & Linz, 1984; Rosen & Beck, 1988).

The second assertion, concerning the effect of alcohol on sexual responsiveness, has also been the subject of survey research. One study conducted in 1970 asked 20,000 middle- and upper-middle-class Americans whether drinking enhanced their sexual pleasure (Athanasiou et al., 1970). Most respondents answered yes—60% stating that alcohol helped put them "in the mood" for sex, with a significantly higher proportion of women providing this response. This finding should be interpreted with some caution, however, because people's memories of events can differ considerably from their actual behaviors. For the third assertion, regarding the superiority of vaginal orgasms, any survey results would also need to be interpreted with caution, for the same reasons. A more appropriate method for studying this question is direct observation, to which we turn next.

## Direct Observations

**Direct observation**
A method of research in which subjects are observed as they go about their activities.

A third method for studying human sexual behavior is **direct observation**. In this method, researchers observe and record responses of participating subjects. Although observational research is quite common in the social sciences, such as anthropology, sociology, and psychology, little research of this nature occurs in sexology because of the highly personal and private nature of human sexual expression.

The most famous example of direct observational research is the widely acclaimed work of William Masters and Virginia Johnson. Along with the Kinsey research, Masters and Johnson's study of human sexual response is probably the most often mentioned sex research, and it is cited frequently in this textbook. Masters and Johnson used direct observation in a laboratory setting to learn about physiological changes during sexual arousal. The result, *Human Sexual Response* (1966), was based on laboratory observations of 10,000 completed sexual response cycles. Results of these observations are presented in Chapter 6.

The Masters and Johnson research sample consisted of sexually responsive volunteers (382 women and 312 men), drawn largely from an academic community of above-average intelligence and socioeconomic background—obviously not a representative sample of the entire U.S. population. However, the physical signs of sexual arousal, the subject of their study, appear to be rather stable across a wide range of people with diverse backgrounds.

Masters and Johnson used a number of techniques to record physiological sexual responses. These included the use of photographic equipment and instruments to measure and record muscular and vascular changes throughout the body. They also used direct observation as well as ingenious measurement devices to record changes in sex organs. (Electronic devices for measuring sexual arousal will be described later in this chapter.) Masters and Johnson recorded responses to a variety of stimulus situations in their laboratory: masturbation, coitus with a partner, and stimulation of the breasts alone. As a follow-up to all recorded observations, each participant was extensively interviewed.

Masters and Johnson's observational approach provided a wealth of information about the manner in which women and men respond physiologically to sexual stimulation. Among other findings, they observed no biological difference between clitoral and vaginal orgasms. This observation will be discussed at greater length in Chapter 6.

William Masters and Virginia Johnson used direct observation to study the physiological sexual responses of women and men.

© Bettmann/CORBIS

Direct observation has clear advantages as a research method. For studying sexual response patterns, seeing and measuring sexual behavior firsthand is clearly superior to relying on subjective reports of past experiences. Direct observation virtually eliminates the possibility of data falsification through memory deficits, boastful inflation, or guilt-induced repression. Furthermore, records of such behaviors can be kept indefinitely on videotape or film. But this approach also has disadvantages. A major problem lies in the often unanswerable question of just how much a subject's behavior is influenced by the presence of even the most discreet observer. This question has been asked often since the publication of Masters and Johnson's research. Researchers using direct observation attempt to minimize this potential complication by being as unobtrusive as possible, remaining in a fringe location, observing through one-way glass, or perhaps using remotely activated video cameras. But the subject is still aware that he or she is being observed.

Although there is merit to criticisms of the direct-observation method, Masters and Johnson's research has demonstrated that it can withstand the test of time. Their findings are still applied in many areas—including infertility counseling, conception control, sex therapy, and sex education—with beneficial results.

## ◑ The Experimental Method

A fourth method, **experimental research**, is being used with increasing frequency to investigate human sexual behavior. This method involves presenting subjects with certain events (stimuli) under managed conditions that allow for reliable measurement of their reactions.

**Experimental research** Research conducted in precisely controlled laboratory conditions so that subjects' reactions can be reliably measured.

Experimental research, as typically conducted in a laboratory environment, has a major advantage over other methods because it provides a controlled environment in which all possible influences on subjects' responses, other than the factors that are being investigated, can be ruled out. A researcher using the experimental method manipulates a particular set of conditions, or variables, and observes the effect of this manipulation on subjects' behavior. The experimental method is particularly suited to discovering causal relationships between variables.

There are two types of *variables* (behaviors or conditions that can have varied values) in any experimental research design: independent and dependent. An **independent variable** is a condition or component of the experiment that is under the control of the researcher, who manipulates or determines its value. Conversely, a **dependent variable** is an outcome or resulting behavior that the experimenter observes and records but does not control.

**Independent variable** In an experimental research design, a condition or component that is under the control of the researcher, who manipulates or determines its value.

**Dependent variable** In an experimental research design, an outcome or resulting behavior that the experimenter observes and records but does not control.

With this brief summary of the experimental method in mind, let us consider how this technique might clarify the relationship between sexually violent media and rape attitudes and behavior. A number of research studies have provided compelling evidence that sexually violent media can cause attitudes to shift toward greater tolerance of sexually aggressive behavior and can actually contribute to some rapists' assaultive behaviors. We consider three experiments, the first involving college men and the other two using convicted rapists as subjects.

The first study was conducted with 271 college men who were divided into two groups. Subjects in the first group were exposed to movies with nonviolent sexual themes, whereas subjects in the second group saw R-rated films in which men were shown committing sexual violence against women (who eventually experienced a transformation from victim to willing partner). A few days after viewing the movies, all subjects completed an attitude questionnaire. The results demonstrated that the men who viewed the violent films were generally much more accepting of sexual violence toward women than those subjects who were exposed to movies with consensual, nonviolent erotic themes (Malamuth & Check, 1981).

**? Critical Thinking Question**

What are the independent and dependent variables in this study? (See p. 44 for the answer).

Two other research studies, with comparable research designs, compared the erectile responses (dependent variable) of matched groups of rapists and nonrapists to two different taped descriptions of sexual activity (independent variable)—one involving rape and the other, mutually consenting sexual activity (Abel et al., 1977; Barbaree et al., 1979). While subjects listened to the tapes, penile tumescence (engorgement) was measured with a penile strain gauge, which is described in the next section of this chapter. In both experiments rapists experienced erections while listening to violent descriptions of rape, whereas their nonrapist counterparts did not. Descriptions of consenting sexual activity produced similar levels of arousal in both groups of men. These findings suggest that exposure to sexually violent media not only encourages attitudes of violence toward women but also influences at least some men who rape to "sexualize" violence.

The experimental method has also been used to study the relationship between alcohol use and sexual responsiveness (although it has not been used to study vaginal orgasms). In one study of 48 male college students, a penile strain gauge was used to measure engorgement as subjects watched a sexually explicit film, first while not under the influence of alcohol and then several days later, after the subjects had consumed controlled amounts of alcohol. Findings showed that sexual arousal was reduced by drinking alcohol and that the more alcohol consumed, the greater the reduction (Briddell & Wilson, 1976). A similar experiment tested the relationship between arousal and alcohol intake in women, with consistent results (Wilson & Lawson, 1976).

**Critical Thinking Question**

Of the four research techniques discussed (case study, survey, direct observation, and experimental study), which method do you think would be most helpful for investigating the effect of chronic pain on sexual functioning? Why?

**InfoTrac Search Words**

- Experimental sex research

These studies illustrate one of the primary advantages of the experimental method. Because researchers can control variables precisely, they are able to draw conclusions about causal relationships to a degree not possible with other research methods. However, this method also has disadvantages. One of the most important limitations has to do with the artificiality of laboratory settings, which can adversely influence or bias subjects' responses. As in direct-observation research, the fact that people know they are in an experiment can alter their responses from those that might occur outside the laboratory.

Before concluding this chapter, we turn our attention to several additional areas of concern regarding how we acquire information about sexual practices. First, we examine three technologies used in sex research. Next, we discuss ethical guidelines for conducting human sex research. Finally, we end this chapter by describing a process for evaluating research.

# ◉ Technologies in Sex Research

Sex researchers have benefited from the development of three distinct technologies for collecting data. The first technology we will discuss—electronic devices for measuring sexual arousal—has been around for several decades. The other technologies—computerized assessment of sexual behavior and sex research in cyberspace—are both relatively new.

## Electronic Devices for Measuring Sexual Arousal

Experimental research and direct-observation studies of human sexual responses often use measures of sexual arousal. In the early years of sex research, investigators had to rely largely on subjective reports of these responses. However, advances in technology over the last few decades have produced several devices for electronically measuring arousal (see ◉ **Figure 2.1**).

The penile strain gauge is a flexible loop that looks something like a rubber band with a wire attached. It is actually a thin rubber tube filled with a fine strand of mercury. A tiny electrical current from the attached wire flows through the mercury continuously. The gauge is placed around the base of the penis. As an erection occurs, the rubber tube stretches, and the strand of mercury becomes thinner, changing the flow of the current. These changes are registered by a recording device. The penile strain gauge can measure even the slightest changes in penis size and is so sensitive that it can even record every pulse of blood into the penis. In the interests of privacy a subject can attach the gauge to his own penis. Researchers can also measure male sexual arousal with a penile plethysmograph or a metal-band gauge, devices that also fit around the penis and reflect small changes in its circumference.

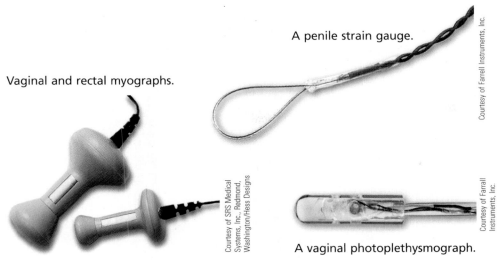

Vaginal and rectal myographs.

A penile strain gauge.

Courtesy of Farrell Instruments, Inc.

Courtesy of SRS Medical Systems, Inc., Redmond, Washington/Hess Designs

Courtesy of Farrall Instruments, Inc.

A vaginal photoplethysmograph.

**Figure 2.1** Devices for electronically measuring sexual arousal.

When a woman is sexually aroused, her vaginal walls fill with blood in a manner comparable to the engorgement of a man's penis. The vaginal photoplethysmograph is a device designed to measure this increased vaginal blood volume. It consists of an acrylic cylinder, about the size and shape of a tampon, that is inserted into the vagina. The cylinder contains a light that is reflected off the vaginal walls and a photocell that is sensitive to the reflected light. When the vaginal walls fill with blood during sexual arousal, less light is reflected to the photocell. These changes in light intensity, continuously recorded by an electronic device, provide a measure of sexual arousal comparable to that provided by the penile strain gauge. Like the male device, the vaginal photoplethysmograph can be inserted in privacy by the research subject. In addition to the vaginal photoplethysmograph, two other devices are used to measure sexual response; the vaginal myograph and the rectal myograph are implements inserted into the vagina or rectum that measure muscular activity in the pelvic area.

## Computerized Assessment of Sexual Behavior

When an interviewer-administered questionnaire (IAQ) is used in sex research, the human element involved in a face-to-face encounter can influence the respondent to underreport certain sensitive behaviors and to overreport more normative or socially acceptable behaviors (Gribble et al., 1999; Potdar & Koenig, 2005). A written or self-administered questionnaire (SAQ) provides an alternative survey method that can overcome some of the difficulties of an IAQ by providing a more private and potentially less threatening means of reporting sensitive behavior. However, SAQs can also be limited by the reading ability or literacy of respondents (Couper & Stinson, 1999). Failure to understand written survey questions can be a significant limiting factor when people with relatively low literacy are surveyed.

The recent advent of computer-assisted self-interview (CASI) technology for surveying children, adolescents, and adults has provided an excellent tool for overcoming these barriers to successful sex research. With CASI technologies literacy problems and the potentially negative effect of a human interviewer are minimized. Furthermore, researchers can be confident that key elements of questions' presentation and measurement are standardized for all respondents.

Two varieties of CASI technology are currently used. In video CASI technology, respondents view questions on a computer screen and enter their answers by pressing labeled keys on the computer keyboard. Audio CASI offers a somewhat more advanced technology in which respondents listen to questions through headphones (which may also be simultaneously displayed by on-screen print) and enter their answers by keystrokes. The audio component has voice-quality sound. Unlike video CASI and more traditional survey methods, audio CASI does not require respondents to be literate. Furthermore, because questions are prerecorded, this technology allows multilingual administration without requiring researchers to be multilingual.

Teenagers are more willing to share sensitive information on sexual behavior when they are working with a computer.

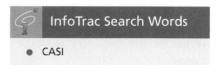

InfoTrac Search Words

● CASI

The application of CASI technology is becoming more widespread, and numerous studies have demonstrated that this method is an effective tool for collecting sensitive information on a variety of topics (Couper et al., 2003; Potdar & Koenig, 2005; van Griensven et al., 2006). For example, a recent study demonstrated that male adolescents were more likely to report engaging in risky sexual behavior via audio CASI than when interviewed face to face (Potkar & Koenig, 2005).

## Sex Research in Cyberspace

As the Internet has rapidly evolved into a common household technology, opportunities have emerged to conduct sex research using this technology (Mustanski, 2001; Parks et al., 2006: Rhodes et al., 2003). Traditionally, the Internet has been used by scientists to distribute research information rather than to collect data. Today, the Internet provides access to a diverse and growing population of potential research participants and is becoming an important medium for conducting research. In this section we will describe the advantages and disadvantages of sex research in cyberspace and examine some of the ethical issues posed by this technology.

Almost any kind of survey questionnaire can be posted on the Internet, and these survey instruments can be visually and functionally similar or identical to conventional questionnaires (Rhodes et al., 2003). So what are the advantages of Internet-based surveys over conventional instruments? Cyberspace questionnaires are considerably cheaper than traditional paper-and-pencil questionnaires because they eliminate printing costs, decrease the need for data collection staff, and do not require distribution and collection costs, such as for postage and envelopes. Online surveys can save 20–80% of the total costs associated with traditional questionnaires (Parks et al., 2006; Rhodes et al., 2003). In comparison with mailed, self-administered questionnaires, time can also be saved with Internet-based surveys (Pealer & Weiler, 2000). Research also indicates that people responding to electronic surveys are less influenced by social desirability and more inclined to share information that they might not disclose through traditional written questionnaires or interviews. Perhaps this is because they believe that their responses are more anonymous and secure (Bowen, 2005; Parks et al., 2006).

The collection and management of data are also typically more efficient with Internet-based surveys. For example, survey data can be automatically inserted via e-mail into a corresponding database. Furthermore, researchers can make adjustments to Internet-based surveys as unforeseen problems related to item comprehension are discovered (Rhodes et al., 2003). In addition to the ease of revising items, new follow-up queries, based on preliminary data analysis, can be added as desired.

With hundreds of millions of people worldwide accessing the Internet daily, the World Wide Web provides "nearly limitless numbers of potential study respondents across geographical and cultural boundaries" (Rhodes et al., 2003, p. 68). Researchers conducting sex research in cyberspace can also recruit hidden populations of geographically isolated participants or those who might otherwise be difficult to find locally (Bowen, 2005).

A final advantage of this approach to sex research is that online data collection can yield information that is more usable or accurate than data obtained through other methods (Rhodes et al., 2003). This is accomplished by reducing errors in two ways. First, errors are minimized by including prompts, menus, and clearly stated explanations designed to guide a respondent to complete the entire survey accurately. Problems commonly encountered with paper-and-pencil questionnaires include unanswered questions and multiple responses to questions asking for a single answer. Internet surveys can make completion of all items a requirement for questionnaire submission and acceptance, and multiple responses can be eliminated by appropriate prompts. Second, Internet surveys that standardize respondents' interactions with the survey document eliminate errors associated with incorrect data entry and problems that stem from variations in how traditional surveys are administered or in how interviewers interpret responses (Rhodes et al., 2003).

A significant disadvantage of Internet-based sex surveys is their association with considerable sample-selection bias (Wallis et al., 2003). At present, a "digital divide" exists, meaning that Internet users are still not representative of the general U.S. population. Internet users tend to be younger, better educated, and more affluent than nonusers (Rhodes et al., 2003). Because of this demographic bias, findings from Internet surveys must be cautiously interpreted. However, as the popularity of the Internet attracts an increasingly diverse population of users, we can expect that Internet-user demographics will mirror the general population more closely.

Other challenges and disadvantages of this approach to sex research include low response rates for Internet-based surveys and multiple survey submissions (Pealer & Weiler, 2000; Rhodes et al., 2003). Response rates are incalculable because Web counters that allow researchers to document the number of visits to a Web site cannot differentiate between respondents and nonrespondents. Thus the problem of nonresponse or volunteer bias that plagues all sex survey research is a concern for online investigators as well. Although multiple submissions have yet to surface as a major problem in cyberspace research (Rhodes et al., 2003), the potentially damaging effect of multiple submissions remains a concern. Internet researchers are using several methods to minimize this problem; these include using identifying information (zip code, date of birth, and so on) to detect multiple or duplicate responses and embedding a question within the survey, asking if the respondent has previously completed the same survey (Rhodes et al., 2001a, 2001b).

Privacy issues are especially acute when doing sex research in cyberspace. Unfortunately, "promises of anonymity on the Internet can rarely, if ever, be given with 100% certainty, since a persistent hacker or an official with a court order may be able to discover the identity of research participants" (Binik et al., 1999, p. 86). Risks of exposure are small, but a few incidents have been reported. To minimize participants' risks, Internet researchers are increasingly using special techniques to provide anonymity.

**? Critical Thinking Question**

In a time of widespread media reports of unauthorized access to personal files by Internet hackers, is it ethical for sexologists to conduct sex research online? Why or why not?

**InfoTrac Search Words**

- Internet sex research

# ● Ethical Guidelines for Human Sex Research

Researchers in a range of investigative fields, including sexology, share a common commitment to maintaining the welfare, dignity, rights, well-being, and safety of their human subjects. Detailed lists of ethical guidelines have been prepared by a number of professional organizations, including the American Psychological Association (APA), the American Medical Association (AMA), and the Society for the Scientific Study of Sex (SSSS).

The ethical guidelines require, among other things, that no pressure or coercion be applied to ensure the participation of volunteers in research and that researchers avoid procedures that might cause physical or psychological harm to human subjects. Researchers need to obtain informed consent from participants before conducting an experiment. Obtaining informed consent involves explaining the general purpose of the study and each participant's rights as a subject, including the voluntary nature of participation and the potential costs and benefits of participation (Seal et al., 2000). Researchers must also respect a subject's right to refuse to participate at any time during the course of a study. In addition, special steps must be taken to protect the confidentiality of the data and to maintain participants' anonymity unless they agree to be identified (Margolis, 2000).

The issue of deception in research remains controversial. Some studies would lose their effectiveness if participating subjects knew in advance exactly what the experimenter was studying. The ethical guideline generally applied to this issue is that if deception must be used, a postexperiment debriefing must thoroughly explain to participants why the deception was necessary. At that time, subjects must be allowed to request that their data be removed from the study and destroyed.

Sometimes it is hard for researchers to weigh objectively the potential benefits of a study against the possibility of harming subjects. Recognizing this difficulty, virtually every institution conducting research in the United States has established an ethics committee that reviews all proposed studies. If committee members perceive that the subjects' welfare is insufficiently safeguarded, the proposal must be modified or the research cannot be conducted. In addition, federal funding for research is denied to any institution that fails to conduct an adequate ethics committee review before data collection begins.

InfoTrac Search Words

• Sex research ethical

# ◐ Evaluating Research: Some Questions to Ask

We hope that the material presented here and elsewhere in our book will help differentiate legitimate scientific sex research from the many frivolous nonscientific polls and opinion surveys that are widespread in the contemporary media. Even when you are exposed to the results of serious investigations, it is wise to maintain a critical eye and to avoid the understandable tendency to accept something as factual just because it is presented as being "scientific." The following list of questions may prove useful as you evaluate the legitimacy of any research, sex or otherwise, that you are exposed to.

1. What are the researchers' credentials? Are the investigators professionally trained? Are they affiliated with reputable institutions (research centers, academic institutions, or the like)? Are they associated with any special-interest groups that may favor a particular research finding or conclusion?
2. Through what type of media were the results published: reputable scientific journals, scholarly textbooks, popular magazines, newspapers, the Internet?
3. What approach or type of research method was used, and were proper scientific procedures adhered to?
4. Were a sufficient number of subjects used, and is there any reason to suspect bias in the selection method?
5. Is it reasonable to apply the research findings to a larger population beyond the sample group? To what extent can legitimate generalizations be made?
6. Is there any reason to believe that the research methods could have biased the findings? (Did the presence of an interviewer encourage false responses? Did cameras place limitations on the response potentials?)
7. Are there any other published research findings that support or refute the study in question?

## The Goals of Sexology

- The goals of sexology include understanding, predicting, and controlling behavior.
- Pursuit of the goal of controlling behavior is often modified or tempered by ethical issues.

## Nonexperimental Research Methods

- Nonexperimental methods for studying sexuality include case studies, surveys, and direct observation.
- Case studies typically produce a great deal of information about one or a few individuals. They have two advantages: flexibility and the opportunity to explore specific behaviors and feelings in depth. Disadvantages include lack of investigative control, possible subjective bias on the researcher's part, and poor sampling techniques, which often limit the possibility of making generalizations to broad populations.
- Most information about human sexual behavior has been obtained through questionnaire or interview surveys of relatively large populations of respondents. Questionnaires have the advantage of being anonymous, inexpensive, and quickly administered. Interviews are more flexible and allow for more rapport between researcher and subject.
- Sex researchers who use surveys face certain common problems. These include the following:
    - The virtual impossibility of getting 100% participation of randomly selected subjects, making it difficult to obtain a representative sample. Self-selection of samples, or volunteer bias, is a common problem.
    - Biases created by nonresponse: Do volunteer participants have significantly different attitudes and behaviors from nonparticipants?
    - The problem of accuracy: Respondents' self-reports may be less than accurate because of limitations of memory, boastfulness, guilt, or simple misunderstandings.
    - Demographic biases: Most samples are heavily weighted toward white, middle-class, better-educated participants.
- Research has demonstrated that ethnicity often exerts considerable influence on sexual attitudes and behaviors.
- The Kinsey surveys were broad-scale studies of human sexual behavior that were somewhat limited by sampling techniques that overrepresented young, educated, city dwellers.
- The National Health and Social Life Survey (NHSLS) stands alone as the single most representative sex survey ever conducted in the United States. It has provided a reliable view of the sexual practices of the general U.S. adult population in the 1990s.
- There is little direct-observation sex research because of the highly personal nature of sexual expression. When direct observation can be used, the possibility of data falsification is significantly reduced. However, subjects' behavior might be altered by the presence of an observer. Furthermore, the reliability of recorded observations can sometimes be compromised by preexisting researcher biases.

## The Experimental Method

- In experimental research, subjects are presented with events (stimuli) under managed conditions that allow for reliable measurement of their reactions.
- The purpose of the experimental method is to discover causal relationships between independent and dependent variables.
- An independent variable is a condition or component of an experiment that is controlled or manipulated by the experimenter.
- A dependent variable is an outcome or resulting behavior that the experimenter observes and records but does not control.
- Experimental research offers two advantages: control over the relevant variables and direct analysis of possible causal factors. However, the artificiality of the experimental laboratory setting can alter subject responses from those that might occur in a natural setting.

## Technologies in Sex Research

- The penile strain gauge, vaginal photoplethysmograph, vaginal myograph, and rectal myograph are devices used for electronically measuring human sexual response.
- Video CASI and audio CASI are two versions of computer-assisted self-interview technology that are increasingly being effectively used to collect sensitive information from children, adolescents, and adults.
- The Internet has become an important medium for conducting sex research. The collection and management of data are more efficient with Internet-based surveys and are also cheaper, faster, and more error free than traditional survey methods. Disadvantages of Internet-based sex surveys include sample-selection bias, low response rates, and multiple survey submissions.

## Ethical Guidelines for Human Sex Research

- Sexologists and other researchers operate under ethical guidelines that seek to ensure the welfare, dignity, rights, well-being, and safety of their human subjects.
- These ethical guidelines require that researchers obtain informed consent from participants, avoid procedures that might cause physical or psychological harm to subjects, and maintain confidentiality of both data and participants.

## Evaluating Research: Some Questions to Ask

- In evaluating any study of sexual behavior, it is helpful to consider who conducted the research, examine the methods and sampling techniques, and compare the results with those of other reputable studies.

## Suggested Readings

**Bancroft, John** (Ed.) (2000). *The Role of Theory in Sex Research*. Bloomington, IN: Indiana University Press. A scholarly book that presents the proceedings from a workshop, hosted at the Kinsey Institute, that focused on the role of theory in sex research.

**Bland, Lucy, and Laura Doan** (Eds.) (1998). *Sexology in Culture: Labelling Bodies and Desires*. Chicago, IL: University of Chicago Press. An informative collection of writings contributed by 13 scholars who discuss the historical emergence of sexology within the context of cultural influences.

**Brannigan, Gary, Elizabeth Allgeier, and Albert Allgeier** (1998). *The Sex Researchers*. New York: Longman. An interesting and illuminating discussion of a diverse group of contemporary sex researchers and some of the issues and concerns that have influenced their research.

**Laumann, Edward, John Gagnon, Robert Michael, and Stuart Michaels** (1994). *The Social Organization of Sexuality*. Chicago: University of Chicago Press. An informative report on the most comprehensive and representative survey of sexual practices and attitudes in the American population.

**Wiederman, Michael** (2001). *Understanding Sexuality Research*. Belmont, CA: Wadsworth. A helpful guide to thinking critically about research in human sexuality.

**Wiederman, Michael, and Bernard Whitley** (Eds.) (2002). *Handbook for Conducting Research on Human Sexuality*. Mahwah, NJ: Lawrence Erlbaum Associates. An excellent overview of the methodological and ethical issues associated with sex research.

## Web Resources

### CengageNOW Web Site
Go to **academic.cengage.com** to link to practice quiz questions, interactive activities, Internet links, critical thinking exercises, discussion forums, and more. You can also access sites from the Wadsworth Psychology Study Center (**academic.cengage.com/psychology**) or you can connect directly to the following sites:

### Kinsey Institute for Research in Sex, Gender, and Reproduction
The Kinsey Institute, founded by the pioneer sexologist Alfred Kinsey, sponsors a Web site dedicated to supporting interdisciplinary research in human sexuality. The Research and Publications section describes the center's most recent studies.

### The Society for the Scientific Study of Sexuality (SSSS)
Meetings and research sponsored by the SSSS, a respected organization of scholars and professionals dedicated to the advancement of knowledge about sexuality, are announced on its Web site.

### Society for the Psychological Study of Lesbian, Gay, and Bisexual Issues
One of more than 50 divisions of the American Psychological Association, Division 44 focuses on sexual orientation issues, and its Web site provides information on recent research in this field.

### Centers for Disease Control and Prevention
Many of the issues addressed by the Centers for Disease Control and Prevention (CDC) deal with aspects of human sexuality, including such topics as adolescent sexuality, contraception and pregnancy, and sexually transmitted diseases. The Web site contains a wealth of recent research information about sexual behavior and related health issues.

### The U.S. Census Bureau
Census data as they relate to human sexuality are cited frequently in our textbook. This Web site can be accessed to obtain accurate research data pertaining to a range of issues involving sexuality, such as recent trends in marriages and divorces, family composition, single living, and cohabitation.

### The National Health and Social Life Survey
This Web site provides an overview and summary of this important survey research study.

### Electronic Journal of Human Sexuality
This Web site contains a collection of articles and papers dealing with a diverse range of sexuality topics.

### Answer to Question on p. 37
The independent variable in this experiment was the degree of violence in the movies observed by the participants. The dependent variable was the subjects' responses to the questionnaire.

### *Our Sexuality* Book Companion Web Site academic.cengage.com/psychology/crooks
Visit your book companion Web site where you will find flash cards, practice quizzes, Internet links, and more to help you study.

### Just what you need to know NOW!
Spend time on what you need to master rather than on information you already have learned. Take a pretest for this chapter, and CengageNOW will generate a personalized study plan based on your results. The study plan will identify the topics you need to review and direct you to online resources to help you master those topics. You can then take a post-test to help you determine the concepts you have mastered and what you will still need to work on. Try it out! Go to **academic.cengage.com/login** to sign in with an access code or to purchase access to this product.

### InfoTrac College Edition Online Library
Sign in to **academic.cengage.com/login** or visit your free book companion Web site at **academic.cengage.com/psychology/crooks** to access InfoTrac College Edition, an online searchable library that includes a multitude of journals, many specific to human sexuality. These journals include *Archives of Sexual Behavior; Archives of Sexual Health Behavior; Canadian Journal of Human Sexuality; Hispanic Journal of the Behavioral Sciences; Journal of Cross-Cultural Psychology; Journal of Physical Education, Recreation, and Dance; Journal of Sex Research;* and *Sex Roles.*

# Gender Issues

AP

*I was taught early on what appropriate gender behavior was. I remember thinking how unfair it was that I had to do weekly cleaning duties while all my brother had to do was take out the garbage. When I asked my mom why, she said, "Because he is a boy and that is man's work, and you are a girl and you do woman's work." (Authors' files)*

Among the residents of a small island near New Guinea, awareness of gender-appropriate behavior, as described in the above anecdote, is virtually nonexistent. Research by anthropologist Maria Lepowsky (1994) revealed that inhabitants of Vanatinai Island, known locally as "the motherland," behave in a truly gender-egalitarian manner. Men and women are considered equal, and there are no separate gender ideologies in this culture. Women have the same access as men to power and prestige. Both sexes are involved in important decision making, and both appear to enjoy the same freedom to explore their sexuality. Furthermore, the Vanatinai language contains no feminine or masculine pronouns. This pronounced difference between egalitarian roles for men and women in Vanatinai society and gender-based behavior expectations that predominate in American culture raises certain fundamental questions: What constitutes maleness and femaleness? How can the expectations and assumptions for each sex differ so greatly from one society to another? If some gender-related behaviors are learned, do any of the behavioral differences between men and women have a biological basis? How do gender-role expectations affect sexual interactions? These are questions that we will address in this chapter.

## ◗ Male and Female, Masculine and Feminine

Through the ages people have held to the belief that we are born males or females and just naturally grow up doing what men or women do. The only explanation required has been a reference to "nature taking its course." This viewpoint has a simplicity that helps make the world seem like an orderly place. However, closer examination reveals a much greater complexity in the way our maleness or femaleness is determined and in the way our behavior, sexual and otherwise, is influenced by this aspect of our identity. This fascinating complexity is our focus in the pages that follow. But first it will be helpful to clarify a few important terms.

### Sex and Gender

**Sex** Biological maleness and femaleness.

**Gender** The psychological and sociocultural characteristics associated with our sex.

**Gender assumptions** Assumptions about how people are likely to behave based on their maleness or femaleness.

Many writers use the terms *sex* and *gender* interchangeably. However, each word has a specific meaning. **Sex** refers to our biological femaleness or maleness. There are two aspects of biological sex: *genetic sex*, which is determined by our sex chromosomes, and *anatomical sex*, the obvious physical differences between males and females. **Gender** is a concept that encompasses the special psychosocial meanings added to biological maleness or femaleness. Thus, although our sex is linked to various physical attributes (chromosomes, penis, vulva, and so forth), our gender refers to the psychological and sociocultural characteristics associated with our sex—in other words, our femininity or masculinity. In this chapter we use the terms *masculine* and *feminine* to characterize the behaviors that are typically attributed to males and females. One undesirable aspect of these labels is that they can limit the range of behaviors that people are comfortable expressing. For example, a man might hesitate to be nurturing lest he be labeled feminine, and a woman might be reticent to act assertively for fear of being considered masculine. It is not our intention to perpetuate the stereotypes often associated with these labels. However, we find it necessary to use these terms when discussing gender issues.

When we meet people for the first time, most of us quickly note their sex and make assumptions about how they are likely to behave based on their maleness or femaleness. These are **gender assumptions**. For most people gender assumptions are an important part of routine social interaction. We identify people as being either the same sex as we are or the other sex. (We have avoided using the term *opposite sex* because we believe it overstates the differences between males and females.) In fact, many of us find it hard to interact with a person whose gender is ambiguous. When we are unsure of our identification of someone's gender, we may become confused and uncomfortable.

## Gender Identity and Gender Role

**Gender identity** refers to each individual's subjective sense of being male or female. Most of us realize in the first few years of life that we are either male or female. However, there is no guarantee that a person's gender identity will be consistent with his or her biological sex, and some people experience considerable confusion in their efforts to identify their own maleness or femaleness. We will look into this area in more detail later in this chapter.

**Gender role** (sometimes called *sex role*) refers to a collection of attitudes and behaviors that are considered normal and appropriate in a specific culture for people of a particular sex. Gender roles establish sex-related behavioral expectations that people are expected to fulfill. Behavior thought to be socially appropriate for a male is called masculine; for a female, feminine. When we use the terms *masculine* and *feminine* in subsequent discussions, we are referring to these socialized notions.

Gender-role expectations are culturally defined and vary from society to society. For example, a kiss on the cheek is considered a feminine act and therefore inappropriate between men in American society. In contrast, such behavior is consistent with masculine role expectations in many European and Middle Eastern societies.

**Gender identity** How one psychologically perceives oneself as either male or female.

**Gender role** A collection of attitudes and behaviors that a specific culture considers normal and appropriate for people of a particular sex.

 **InfoTrac Search Words**

- Gender identity
- Gender role

# ⊙ Gender-Identity Formation

Like the knowledge that we have a particular color hair or eyes, gender is an aspect of our identity that most people take for granted. Certainly, gender identity usually—but not always—comes with the territory of having certain biological parts. But there is more to it than simply looking like a female or a male. As we will see in the following paragraphs, the question of how we come to think of ourselves as either male or female has two answers. The first explanation centers on biological processes that begin shortly after conception and are completed before birth. But a second important explanation has to do with social-learning theory, which looks to cultural influences during early childhood to explain both the nuances of gender identity and the personal significance of being either male or female. We explore first the biological processes involved in gender-identity formation, summarized in ⊙ **Table 3.1**.

## Gender Identity as a Biological Process: Typical Prenatal Differentiation

From the moment of conception many biological factors contribute to the differentiation of male or female sex. In the following paragraphs, we explore how biological sex differentiation occurs during prenatal development. Our discussion follows a chronological sequence. We begin at conception, looking at chromosomal differences between male and female, and then continue with the development of gonads, the production of hormones, the development of internal and external reproductive structures, and, finally, sex differentiation of the brain.

## Chromosomal Sex

Our biological sex is determined at conception by the chromosomal makeup of the **sperm** (male reproductive cell) that fertilizes an **ovum,** or egg (female reproductive cell). Except for the reproductive cells, human body cells contain 46 chromosomes, arranged in 23 pairs (see ⊙ **Figure 3.1**). Twenty-two of these pairs are matched; that is, the two chromosomes of each pair look almost identical. These matched sets, called **auto-somes** (AW-tuh-sohmes), are the same in males and females and do not significantly

**Sperm** The male reproductive cell.

**Ovum** The female reproductive cell.

**Autosomes** The 22 pairs of human chromosomes that do not significantly influence sex differentiation.

| Characteristic | Female | Male |
|---|---|---|
| Chromosomal sex | XX | XY |
| Gonadal sex | Ovaries | Testes |
| Hormonal sex | Estrogens | Androgens |
| | Progestational compounds | |
| Internal reproductive structures | Fallopian tubes | Vas deferens |
| | Uterus | Seminal vesicles |
| | Inner portions of vagina | Ejaculatory ducts |
| External genitals | Clitoris | Penis |
| | Inner vaginal lips | Scrotum |
| | Outer vaginal lips | |
| Sex differentiation of the brain | Hypothalamus becomes estrogen sensitive, influencing cyclic release of hormones. | Estrogen-insensitive male hypothalamus directs steady production of hormones. |
| | Two hypothalamic areas are smaller in the female brain. | Two hypothalamic areas are larger in the male brain. |
| | Cerebral cortex of right hemisphere is thinner in the female brain. | Cerebral cortex of right hemisphere is thicker in the male brain. |
| | Corpus callosum is thicker in the female brain. | Corpus callosum is thinner in the male brain. |
| | Less lateralization of function in the female brain compared to the male brain. | More lateralization of function in the male brain compared to the female brain. |

**Sex chromosomes** A single set of chromosomes that influences biological sex determination.

influence sex differentiation. One chromosome pair, however—the **sex chromosomes**—differs in females from that in males. Females have two similar chromosomes, labeled XX, whereas males have dissimilar chromosomes, labeled XY.

As noted, the reproductive cells are an exception to the 23-pair rule. As a result of a biological process known as *meiosis*, mature reproductive cells contain only half the usual complement of chromosomes—one member of each pair. (This process is necessary to avoid doubling the chromosome total when sex cells merge at conception.) A normal female ovum (or egg) contains 22 autosomes plus an X chromosome. A normal male sperm cell contains 22 autosomes plus either an X or a Y chromosome. If the ovum is fertilized by a sperm carrying a Y chromosome, the resulting XY combination will produce a male child. In contrast, if an X-chromosome–bearing sperm fertilizes the ovum, the result will be an XX combination and a female child. Two X chromosomes are necessary for internal and external female structures to develop completely. But if one Y chromosome is present, male sexual and reproductive organs will develop (Harley et al., 1992; Page et al., 1987).

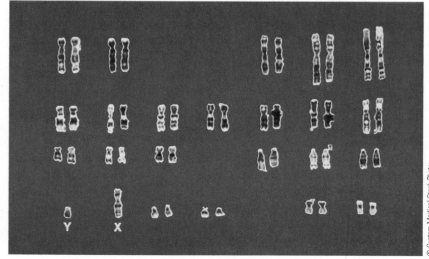

○ **Figure 3.1** Human cells contain 22 pairs of matched autosomes and 1 pair of sex chromosomes. A normal female has two X chromosomes, and a normal male has an X and a Y chromosome.

© Custom Medical Stock Photo

Researchers have located a single gene on the short arm of the human Y chromosome that seems to play a crucial role in initiating the sequence of events that leads to the development of the male gonads, or **testes**. This maleness-determining gene is called *SRY* (Bancroft, 2002; Jegalian & Lahn, 2001b).

Findings from a study conducted by scientists from Italy and the United States suggest that a gene or genes for femaleness also exist. These researchers studied four cases of chromosomal males with feminized external genitals. All these individuals were found to have XY chromosomes and a working *SRY* (maleness) gene. Three of the four individuals exhibited clearly identifiable female external genitals; the fourth had ambiguous genitals. If the maleness gene was the dominant determinant of biological sex, the external genitals of these individuals would have developed in a typical male pattern. What, then, triggered this variation from the expected developmental sequence? Examination of these individuals' DNA revealed that a tiny bit of genetic material on the short arm of the X chromosome had been duplicated. As a result, each of the subjects had a double dose of a gene designated as *DSS*. This condition resulted in feminization of an otherwise chromosomally normal male fetus (Bardoni et al., 1994).

These findings suggest that a gene (or genes) on the X chromosome helps to push the undifferentiated gonads in a female direction just as the *SRY* gene helps to start construction of male sex structures. Such observations contradict the long-held belief that the human fetus is inherently female and that, unlike male prenatal differentiation, no gene triggers are necessary for female differentiation.

## Gonadal Sex

In the first weeks after conception the structures that will become the reproductive organs, or **gonads**, are the same in males and females (see **Figure 3.2a**). Differentiation begins about 6 weeks after conception. Genetic signals determine whether the mass of undifferentiated sexual tissue develops into male or female gonads (Bancroft, 2002; Hiort and Holterhus, 2000). At this time an *SRY* gene product (or products) in a male fetus triggers the transformation of embryonic gonads into testes. In the absence of *SRY*, and perhaps under the influence of the *DSS* or other femaleness gene, the undifferentiated gonadal tissue develops into **ovaries** (see **Figure 3.2b**).

Once the testes or ovaries develop, these gonads begin releasing their own sex hormones. As we will see next, these hormones become the critical factor in further sex differentiation, and genetic influence ceases.

## Hormonal Sex

The gonads produce hormones and secrete them directly into the bloodstream. Ovaries produce two classes of hormones: **estrogens** (ES-troh-jens) and **progestational compounds**. Estrogens, the most important of which is *estradiol*, influence the

**Testes** Male gonads inside the scrotum that produce sperm and sex hormones.

**Gonads** The male and female sex glands: ovaries and testes.

**Ovaries** Female gonads that produce ova and sex hormones.

**Estrogens** A class of hormones that produce female secondary sex characteristics and affect the menstrual cycle.

**Progestational compounds** A class of hormones, including progesterone, that are produced by the ovaries.

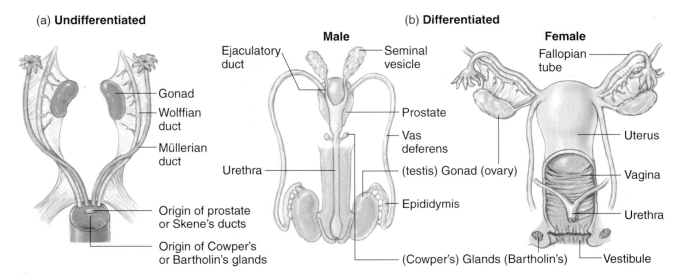

**Figure 3.2** Prenatal development of male and female internal duct systems from (a) undifferentiated (before 6th week) to (b) differentiated.

development of female physical sex characteristics and help regulate the menstrual cycle. Of the progestational compounds, only *progesterone* is known to be physiologically important. It helps to regulate the menstrual cycle and to stimulate development of the uterine lining in preparation for pregnancy. The primary hormone products of the testes are **androgens** (AN-droh-jens). The most important androgen is *testosterone*, which influences both the development of male physical sex characteristics and sexual motivation. In both sexes the adrenal glands also secrete sex hormones, including small amounts of estrogen and greater quantities of androgen.

## Sex of the Internal Reproductive Structures

By about 8 weeks after conception the sex hormones begin to play an important role in sex differentiation. The two duct systems shown in Figure 3.2a—the *Wolffian ducts* and the *Müllerian ducts*—begin to differentiate into those internal structures shown in Figure 3.2b. In a male fetus, androgens secreted by the testes stimulate the Wolffian ducts to develop into the vas deferens, seminal vesicles, and ejaculatory ducts. Another substance released by the testes is known as *Müllerian-inhibiting substance* (MIS). MIS causes the Müllerian duct system to shrink and disappear in males (Bancroft, 2002; Lee et al., 1997). In the absence of androgens the fetus develops female structures (Clarnette et al., 1997). The Müllerian ducts develop into the fallopian tubes, the uterus, and the inner third of the vagina; and the Wolffian duct system degenerates.

## Sex of the External Genitals

The external genitals develop according to a similar pattern. Until the gonads begin releasing hormones during the 6th week, the external genital tissues of male and female fetuses are undifferentiated (**◐ Figure 3.3**). These tissues will develop into either male or female external genitals, depending on the presence or absence of a testosterone product known as *dihydrotestosterone* (DHT). DHT stimulates the *labioscrotal swelling* to become the scrotum and the *genital tubercle* and *genital folds* to differentiate into the glans and shaft of the penis, respectively. The genital folds fuse around the urethra to form the shaft of the penis, and the two sides of the labioscrotal swelling fuse to form the scrotum; these fusions do not occur in females. In the absence of testosterone (and possibly under the influence of a substance or substances triggered by the *DSS*, or femaleness gene), the genital tubercle becomes the clitoris, the genital folds become the inner vaginal lips (labia minora), and the two sides of the labioscrotal swelling differentiate into the outer vaginal lips (labia majora). By the 12th week the differentiation process is complete: The penis and scrotum are recognizable in males; the clitoris and labia can be identified in females.

Because the external genitals, gonads, and some internal structures of males and females originate from the same embryonic tissues, it is not surprising that they have corresponding, or homologous, parts. **◐ Table 3.2** summarizes these female and male counterparts. We will look at the form and function of human sex organs in more detail in Chapters 4 and 5.

| **◐ TABLE 3.2** | Homologous Sex Organs |
| --- | --- |
| **Female** | **Male** |
| Clitoris | Glans of penis |
| Hood of clitoris | Foreskin of penis |
| Labia minora | Shaft of penis |
| Labia majora | Scrotal sac |
| Ovaries | Testes |
| Skene's ducts | Prostate gland |
| Bartholin's glands | Cowper's glands |

## Sex Differentiation of the Brain

Important structural and functional differences in the brains of human females and males are in part a result of prenatal sex-differentiation processes (Dennis, 2004; Hines, 2004; Wisniewski et al., 2005). Many areas of the developing prenatal brain are significantly affected by circulating hormones (both testosterone and estrogen), which contribute to the development of these sex differences (Arnold, 2003, 2004; Dennis, 2004; Hines, 2004).

At the broadest level, there is a significant sex difference in overall brain size. By age 6, when human brains reach full adult size, male brains are approximately 15% larger than female brains (Gibbons, 1991). Researchers believe that this size difference results from the influence of androgens, which stimulate faster growth in boys' brains

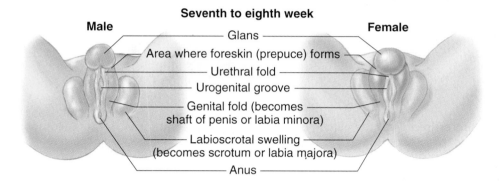

**Undifferentiated before sixth week**

Genital tubercle
Urethral fold
Urethral groove
Genital fold
Anal pit

Figure 3.3 Prenatal development of male and female external genitals from undifferentiated to fully differentiated.

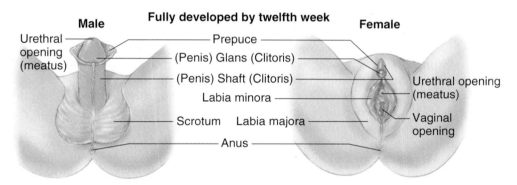

**Seventh to eighth week**

Male                                                  Female

Glans
Area where foreskin (prepuce) forms
Urethral fold
Urogenital groove
Genital fold (becomes shaft of penis or labia minora)
Labioscrotal swelling (becomes scrotum or labia majora)
Anus

**Fully developed by twelfth week**

Male                                                  Female

Urethral opening (meatus)
Prepuce
(Penis) Glans (Clitoris)
(Penis) Shaft (Clitoris)
Labia minora
Scrotum    Labia majora
Anus
Urethral opening (meatus)
Vaginal opening

(Wilson, 2003). Other specific human brain sex differences involve at least three major areas: the *hypothalamus* (hy-poh-THAL-uh-mus), the left and right *cerebral hemispheres,* and the *corpus callosum* (◗ **Figure 3.4**).

A number of studies link marked differences between the male and female **hypothalamus** to the presence or absence of circulating testosterone during prenatal differentiation (McEwen, 2001; Reiner, 1997a, 1997b). In the absence of circulating testosterone the female hypothalamus develops specialized receptor cells that are sensitive to estrogen in the bloodstream. In fetal males the presence of testosterone prevents these cells from developing sensitivity to estrogen. This prenatal differentiation is critical for events that take place later. During puberty the estrogen-sensitive female hypothalamus directs the pituitary gland to release hormones in cyclic fashion, initiating the menstrual cycle. In males the estrogen-insensitive hypothalamus directs a relatively steady production of sex hormones.

Research has uncovered several intriguing findings pertaining to sex differences in one tiny hypothalamic region called the *bed nucleus of the stria terminalis* (BST) (Chung et al., 2002; Gu et al., 2003). The BST contains androgen and estrogen receptors and appears to exert a significant influence on human sex differences and human sexual functioning. One central area of the BST is much larger in men than in women (Zhou et al., 1995), and a posterior region of the BST is more than twice as large in men as in women (Allen & Gorski, 1990). Researchers have also reported sex differences in an anterior region of the hypothalamus, called the *preoptic area* (POA). One specific site in the POA is significantly larger in adult men than in adult women (Allen et al., 1989; Swaab et al., 1995). Evidence from these and other studies has led some theorists to hypothesize that sex differences in both human sexual behavior and gender-biased

**Hypothalamus** A small structure in the central core of the brain that controls the pituitary gland and regulates motivated behavior and emotional expression.

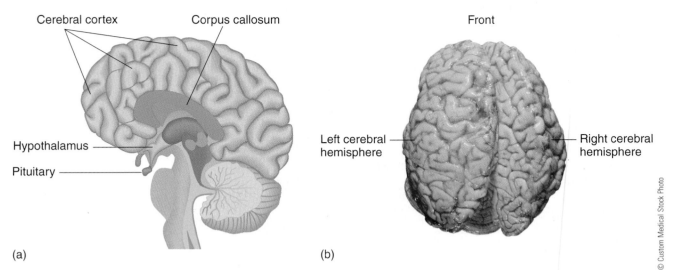

Cerebral cortex     Corpus callosum           Front

Hypothalamus

Pituitary

Left cerebral hemisphere          Right cerebral hemisphere

(a)                        (b)

© Custom Medical Stock Photo

⊙ **Figure 3.4** Parts of the brain: (a) cross section of the human brain showing the cerebral cortex, corpus callosum, hypothalamus, and pituitary gland; (b) top view showing the left and right cerebral hemispheres. Only the cerebral cortex covering of the two hemispheres is visible.

**Cerebrum** The largest part of the brain, consisting of two cerebral hemispheres.

**Cerebral hemispheres** The two sides (right and left) of the cerebrum.

**Cerebral cortex** Outer layer of the cerebral hemispheres that is responsible for higher mental processes.

**Corpus callosum** The broad band of nerve fibers that connects the left and right cerebral hemispheres.

behavior in children and adults result, in part, from a generalized sex-hormone-induced masculinization or feminization of the brain during prenatal development (Bancroft, 2002; Cohen-Kettenis, 2005; Lerman et al., 2000).

Other key differences between male and female brains have been demonstrated in the function and structure of the cerebral hemispheres and the corpus callosum. The **cerebrum**, consisting of two **cerebral hemispheres** and the interconnection between them, is the largest part of the human brain. The two hemispheres, although not precisely identical, are almost mirror images of each other (see Figure 3.4b). Both cerebral hemispheres are covered by an outer layer, called the **cerebral cortex**, which is a major brain structure responsible for higher mental processes, such as memory, perception, and thinking. Without a cortex we would cease to exist as unique, functioning individuals.

As Figure 3.4b illustrates, the two hemispheres are approximately symmetric, with areas on the left side roughly matched by areas on the right side. A variety of functions, such as speech, hearing, vision, and body movement, are localized in various regions of the cortical hemispheres. Furthermore, each hemisphere tends to be specialized for certain functions. For example, in most people verbal abilities, such as the expression and understanding of speech, are governed more by the left hemisphere than by the right. In contrast, the right hemisphere seems to be more specialized for spatial orientation, including the ability to recognize objects and shapes and to perceive relationships between them.

The term *lateralization of function* is used to describe the degree to which a particular function is controlled by one rather than both hemispheres. If, for example, a person's ability to deal with spatial tasks is controlled exclusively by the right hemisphere, we could say that this ability in this person is highly lateralized. In contrast, if both hemispheres contribute equally to this function, the person would be considered bilateral for spatial ability.

Even though each cerebral hemisphere tends to be specialized to handle different functions, the hemispheres are not entirely separate systems. Rather, our brain functions mostly as an integrated whole. The two hemispheres constantly communicate with each other through a broad band of millions of connecting nerve fibers, called the **corpus callosum** (Smith et al., 2005) (see Figure 3.4a). In most people a complex function such as language is controlled primarily by regions in the left hemisphere, but interaction and communication with the right hemisphere also play a role. Furthermore, if a hemisphere primarily responsible for a particular function is damaged, the remaining intact hemisphere might take over the function (Ogden, 1989).

Keeping in mind this general overview of brain lateralization, we note that research has revealed some important differences between male and female brains in the structure of the cerebrum. First, studies of the fetal brains of both humans and rats have found that the cerebral cortex in the right hemisphere tends to be thicker in male brains than in female brains (de Lacoste et al., 1990; Diamond, 1991b). Perhaps of even greater significance is the finding of differences between male and female brains in the overall size of the corpus callosum in a number of animals, including humans (Coe et al., 2002). Several studies have demonstrated that this structure is significantly thicker in women's brains than in men's brains (Smith et al., 2005). This greater thickness of the corpus callosum allows for more intercommunication between the two hemispheres, which could account for why female brains are less lateralized for function and male brains have larger asymmetries in function (Kimura, 1992; Wilson, 2003).

Research has clearly demonstrated differences between male and female brains in the degree of hemispheric specialization for verbal and spatial cognitive skills. Women tend to use both brain hemispheres when performing verbal and spatial tasks, whereas men are more likely to exhibit patterns of hemispheric asymmetry by using only one hemisphere for each of these functions (Lambe,1999; Wisniewski et al., 2005). The stronger communication network between the two halves of a female's brain might explain why women typically exhibit less impairment of brain function than men do after comparable neurological damage to one hemisphere (Majewska, 1996).

Researchers and theorists are debating whether these structural differences between male and female cerebrums can explain differences between the sexes in cognitive functioning. Females often score somewhat higher than males on tests of verbal skills, whereas the reverse is often true for spatial tests (Beller & Gafni, 2000; Gron et al., 2000; Halpern & LaMay, 2000). Some researchers suggest that differences between male and female hemispheric and corpus callosum structures indicate a possible biological basis for such differences between the sexes in cognition (Geer & Manguno-Mire, 1997; Gur et al., 1995; Leibenluft, 1996). However, many theorists argue that reported differences between males and females in cognitive skills are largely due to psychosocial factors (Fausto-Sterling, 2000; Green et al., 1999). They cite substantial evidence that such differences have declined sharply in recent years (Carter, 2000; Fausto-Sterling, 2000; Hyde, 2004. Finally, to put the question of sex differences in proper perspective, we acknowledge the informed observation of eminent psychologist Carol Tavris (2005), who recently stated that "the similarities between the sexes in behavior and aptitude are far greater than the differences" (p. 12).

**InfoTrac Search Words**

- Sex differentiation

## Atypical Prenatal Differentiation

Thus far we have considered only typical prenatal differentiation. However, much of what is known about the impact of biological sex differentiation on the development of gender identities comes from studies of atypical differentiation.

We have seen that the differentiation of internal and external sex structures occurs under the influence of biological cues. When these signals deviate from normal patterns, the result can be ambiguous biological sex. A person with ambiguous or contradictory sex characteristics is sometimes called a *hermaphrodite* (her-MAF-roh-dite), a term derived from the mythical Greek deity Hermaphroditus, who was thought to possess biological attributes of both sexes. It is becoming more common to refer to such people as **intersexed** rather than as hermaphroditic (Morris, 2003).

When discussing the condition of being intersexed, it is important to distinguish between **true hermaphrodites** and **pseudohermaphrodites**. True hermaphrodites, who have both ovarian and testicular tissue in their bodies, are exceedingly rare (Blackless et al., 2000; Parker, 1998). Their external genitals are often a mixture of female and male structures. Pseudohermaphrodites are much more common, occurring with an approximate frequency of 1 in every 2,000 births (Colapinto, 2000; Diamond, 2004). These individuals also possess ambiguous internal and external reproductive anatomy, but unlike true hermaphrodites, pseudohermaphrodites are born with gonads that match their chromosomal sex. Studies of pseudohermaphrodites have helped to clarify the relative roles of biology and social learning in the formation of gender identity. This intersex condition can occur because of an atypical combination of sex chromosomes or as a result of prenatal hormonal irregularities. In this section, we consider evidence from five varieties of pseudohermaphrodites, summarized in ○ **Table 3.3**.

**Intersexed** A term applied to people who possess biological attributes of both sexes.

**True hermaphrodites** Exceedingly rare individuals who have both ovarian and testicular tissue in their bodies; their external genitals are often a mixture of male and female structures.

**Pseudohermaphrodites** Individuals whose gonads match their chromosomal sex but whose internal and external reproductive anatomy has a mixture of male and female structures or structures that are incompletely male or female.

**InfoTrac Search Words**

- Intersex(ed)
- Hermaphrodite
- Transgender

| Syndrome | Chromosomal Sex | Gonadal Sex | Reproductive Internal Structures | External Genitals | Fertility | Secondary Sex Characteristics | Gender Identity |
|---|---|---|---|---|---|---|---|
| Turner's syndrome | 45, XO | Fibrous streaks of ovarian tissue | Uterus and fallopian tubes | Normal female | Sterile | Undeveloped; no breasts | Female |
| Klinefelter's syndrome | 47, XXY | Small testes | Normal male | Undersized penis and testes | Sterile | Some feminization of secondary sex characteristics; may have breast development and rounded body contours. | Usually male, although higher than usual incidence of gender identity confusion. |
| Androgen insensitivity syndrome | 46, XY | Undescended testes | Lacks a normal set of either male or female internal structures | Normal female genitals and a shallow vagina | Sterile | At puberty, breast development and other signs of normal female sexual maturation appear, but menstruation does not occur. | Female |
| Fetally androgenized females | 46, XX | Ovaries | Normal female | Ambiguous (typically more male than female) | Fertile | Normal female (individuals with adrenal malfunction must be treated with cortisone to avoid masculinization). | Usually female, but significant level of dissatisfaction with female gender identity; oriented toward traditional male activities. |
| DHT-deficient males | 46, XY | Undescended testes at birth; testes descend at puberty | Vas deferens, seminal vesicles, and ejaculatory ducts but no prostate; partially formed vagina | Ambiguous at birth (more female than male); at puberty, genitals are masculinized. | Sterile | Female before puberty; become masculinized at puberty. | Female prior to puberty; majority assume traditional male identity at puberty. |

## Sex-Chromosome Disorders

Errors occasionally occur at the first level of biological sex determination, and individuals are born with one or more extra sex chromosomes or missing one sex chromosome. More than 70 atypical conditions of the sex chromosomes have been identified (Nielson & Wohlert, 1991). These irregularities are associated with various physical, health, and behavioral effects. We consider two of the most widely researched of these conditions: Turner's syndrome and Klinefelter's syndrome.

**Turner's syndrome**
A rare condition, characterized by the presence of one unmatched X chromosome (XO), in which affected individuals have normal female external genitals but their internal reproductive structures do not develop fully.

**Turner's Syndrome Turner's syndrome** is a relatively rare condition characterized by the presence of only one sex chromosome, an X. This condition is estimated to occur in about 1 in every 1700–2500 live female births (Intersex Society of North America, 2006). The number of chromosomes in the fertilized egg is 45 rather than the typical 46; the sex-chromosome combination is designated XO. People with this combination develop normal external female genitals and consequently are classified as females. However, their internal reproductive structures do not develop fully; ovaries are absent or represented only by fibrous streaks of tissue. Females with

Turner's syndrome do not develop breasts at puberty (unless given hormone treatment), do not menstruate, and are sterile. As adults, women with this condition tend to be unusually short (Gravholt et al., 1998).

Because the gonads are absent or poorly developed, and because the hormones are consequently deficient, Turner's syndrome permits gender identity to be formed in the absence of gonadal and hormonal influences (the second and third levels of biological sex determination). Individuals with Turner's syndrome identify themselves as female, and as a group they are not distinguishable from biologically normal females in their interests and behavior (Kagan-Krieger, 1998). This characteristic strongly suggests that a feminine gender identity can be established in the absence of ovaries and their products.

**Klinefelter's Syndrome** A more common sex-chromosome error in humans is **Klinefelter's syndrome**. This condition, estimated to occur once in about every 1,000 live male births (Intersex Society of North America, 2006), results when an atypical ovum containing 22 autosomes and 2 X chromosomes is fertilized by a Y-chromosome-bearing sperm, creating an XXY individual. Despite the presence of both the XY combination characteristic of normal males and the XX pattern of normal females, individuals with Klinefelter's syndrome are anatomically male. This condition supports the view that the presence of a Y chromosome triggers the formation of male structures. However, the presence of an extra female sex chromosome impedes the continued development of these structures, and males with Klinefelter's syndrome typically are sterile and have undersized penises and testes. Furthermore, these individuals often have little or no interest in sexual activity (Money, 1968; Rabock et al., 1979). Presumably, this low sex drive is related, at least in part, to deficient production of hormones from the testes.

Males with Klinefelter's syndrome tend to be tall and somewhat feminized in their physical characteristics; they might exhibit breast development and rounded body contours (Looy & Bouma, 2005). Testosterone treatments during adolescence and adulthood can enhance the development of male secondary sexual characteristics and can increase sexual interest (Kolodny et al., 1979). These individuals usually identify themselves as male; however, they often manifest some degree of gender-identity confusion (Mandoki et al., 1991).

## Disorders Affecting Prenatal Hormonal Processes

The ambiguous sex characteristics associated with pseudohermaphroditism can also result from genetically induced biological errors that produce variations in prenatal hormonal processes. We consider three examples of disorders caused by hormonal errors: androgen insensitivity syndrome, fetally androgenized females, and DHT-deficient males.

**Androgen Insensitivity Syndrome** A rare genetic defect causes a condition known as **androgen insensitivity syndrome (AIS)**, wherein the body cells of a chromosomally normal male fetus are insensitive to androgens (Mazur, 2005). The result is feminization of prenatal development, so that the baby is born with normal-looking female genitals and a shallow vagina. Not surprisingly, babies with AIS are identified as female and reared accordingly. The anomaly is often discovered only in late adolescence, when a physician is consulted to find out why menstruation has not started. A recent review of many AIS studies revealed that these individuals acquire a clear female gender identity and behave accordingly (Mazur, 2005). In one study, investigators compared psychological outcomes and gender development in a group of 22 women with AIS and a control group of 22 women without AIS. No significant differences were found between the women with AIS and the matched control subjects for any psychological outcome measures, including gender identity, sexual orientation, gender-role behaviors, and overall quality of life (Hines et al., 2003).

At first glance these observations seem to support the importance of social learning in shaping gender-identity formation. However, a case can also be made that these findings indicate the strong impact of biological factors in gender-identity formation. The lack of receptivity to androgen in individuals with AIS might prevent the masculinization

**Klinefelter's syndrome** A condition characterized by the presence of two X chromosomes and one Y chromosome (XXY) in which affected individuals have undersized external male genitals.

**Androgen insensitivity syndrome (AIS)** A condition resulting from a genetic defect that causes chromosomally normal males to be insensitive to the action of testosterone and other androgens. These individuals develop female external genitals of normal appearance.

of their brains necessary to develop a male identity, just as it results in failure to develop male genitals.

**Fetally Androgenized Females** In a second type of rare atypical sex differentiation, chromosomally normal females are prenatally masculinized by exposure to excessive androgens—the excess usually caused by a genetically induced malfunctioning of their own adrenal glands (*adrenogenital syndrome*) (Dessens et al., 2005; Hines et al., 2004). As a result, such babies are born with masculine-looking external genitals: An enlarged clitoris can look like a penis, and fused labia can resemble a scrotum (❯ **Figure 3.5**). These babies are usually identified as female by medical tests, treated with minor surgery or hormone therapy to eliminate their genital ambiguity, and reared as girls.

Numerous studies have revealed that even though a substantial majority of **fetally androgenized females** develop a female gender identity, many engage in traditionally male activities and reject behavior and attitudes commonly associated with a female gender identity (Dessens et al., 2005; Hines et al., 2004). A small number of these individuals experience such discomfort with the female sex of assignment that they eventually assume a male gender identity with commensurate male gender-role behaviors (Meyer-Bahlburg et al., 1996; Slijper et al., 1998). These various studies of fetally androgenized females appear to reflect the significant impact of biological factors in gender-identity formation.

**DHT-Deficient Males** A third variety of atypical prenatal differentiation is caused by a genetic defect that prevents conversion of testosterone into the hormone dihydrotestosterone (DHT), which is essential for normal development of external genitals in a male fetus. The testes of males with this disorder do not descend before birth, the penis and scrotum remain undeveloped so that they resemble a clitoris and labia, and a shallow vagina is partially formed. Because their genitals look more female than male, **DHT-deficient males** are typically identified as female and reared as girls. However, because their testes are still functional, an amazing change occurs at puberty as accelerated testosterone production reverses the DHT deficiency. This causes the testes to descend and the clitorislike organs to enlarge into penises. In short, these DHT-deficient males undergo rapid transformation, from apparently female to male! How do they respond?

Research has shown that a majority of DHT-deficient males make a switch from a female gender identity to a male gender identity, usually in adolescence or early adulthood (Cohen-Kettenis, 2005; Imperato-McGinley et al., 1979). These findings challenge the widely held belief that once gender identity is formed in the first few years of life, it cannot be changed.

These examples of atypical sex differentiation appear to provide contradictory evidence. In the first example of males with AIS, chromosomal males insensitive to their own androgens acquire a female gender identity consistent with the way they are reared. In the second example, prenatally masculinized chromosomal females tend to behave in a typically masculine manner even though they are reared female. Finally, in the third example, chromosomal males whose biological maleness is not apparent until puberty are able to switch their gender identity to male, despite early socialization as girls. Are these results at odds with one another, or is there a plausible explanation for their seeming inconsistencies?

As described earlier, some data suggest that prenatal androgens influence sex differentiation of the brain just as they trigger masculinization of the sex structures. The same gene defect that prevents masculinization of the genitals of males with AIS might also block masculinization of their brains, thus influencing the development of

**Fetally androgenized female** A chromosomally normal (XX) female who, as a result of excessive exposure to androgens during prenatal sex differentiation, develops external genitalia resembling those of a male.

**DHT-deficient male** A chromosomally normal (XY) male who develops external genitalia resembling those of a female as a result of a genetic defect that prevents the prenatal conversion of testosterone into dihydrotestosterone (DHT).

❯ **Figure 3.5** Masculinized external genitals of a fetally androgenized female baby.

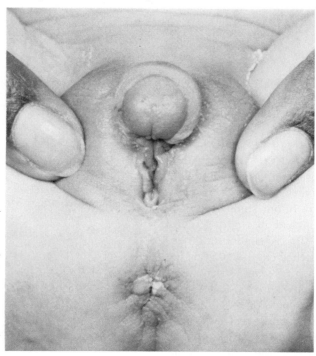

a female gender identity. Similarly, the masculinizing influence of prenatal androgens on the brain might also account for the tomboyish behaviors of fetally androgenized females. But what about DHT-deficient males who appear to make a relatively smooth transition from a female to a male gender identity? Perhaps these boys' brains were prenatally programmed along male lines. Presumably, they had normal levels of androgens and, except for genital development, could respond appropriately to these hormones at critical stages of prenatal development. We cannot state with certainty that prenatal androgens masculinize the brain. However, this interpretation offers a plausible explanation for how DHT-deficient individuals, already hormonally predisposed toward a male gender identity despite being identified as female, can change to a male identity at adolescence in response to changes in their bodies.

These fascinating studies underscore the complexity of biological sex determination. We have seen that many steps, each susceptible to errors, are involved in sex differentiation before birth. There is substantial research evidence that biological factors, especially prenatal brain exposure to androgens, contribute to gender-identity formation. But there is more to the question: Just what makes us female or male? To further amplify this question, we now turn to the role of social-learning factors in influencing gender-identity formation *after* birth.

## Social-Learning Influences on Gender Identity

Thus far we have considered only the biological factors involved in the determination of gender identity. Our sense of femaleness or maleness is not based exclusively on biological conditions, however. Social-learning theory suggests that our identification with either masculine or feminine roles or a combination thereof (androgyny) results primarily from the social and cultural models and influences that we are exposed to during our early development (Lips, 1997; Lorber, 1995).

Even before their baby is born, parents (and other adults involved in child rearing) have preconceived notions about how boys and girls differ. And through a multitude of subtle and not so subtle means, they communicate these ideas to their children (Witt, 1997). Gender-role expectations influence the environments in which children are raised, from the choice of room color to the selection of toys. They also influence the way parents think of their children. For example, in one study parents were asked to describe their newborn infants. Parents of boys described them as "strong," "active," and "robust," whereas parents of girls used words such as "soft" and "delicate"—even though all their babies were of similar size and muscle tone (Rubin et al., 1974). Not surprisingly, gender-role expectations also influence the way parents respond to their children: A boy might be encouraged to suppress his tears if he scrapes a knee and to show other "manly" qualities, such as independence and aggressiveness, whereas girls might be encouraged to be nurturing and cooperative (Hyde, 2004; Mosher & Tomkins, 1988).

By age 3, most children have developed a firm gender identity (DeLamater & Friedrich, 2002). From this point, gender-identity reinforcement typically becomes somewhat self-perpetuating, as most children actively seek to behave in ways that they are taught are appropriate to their own sex (DeLamater & Friedrich, 2002). It is not

**cathy®**          **by Cathy Guisewite**

Although parents are becoming more sensitive to the kinds of toys children play with, many still choose one set of toys and play activities for boys and another set for girls.

unusual for little girls to go through a period of insisting that they wear fancy dresses or practice baking in the kitchen—sometimes to the dismay of their own mothers, who have themselves adopted more-practical wardrobes and have abandoned the kitchen for a career! Likewise, young boys may develop a fascination for superheroes, policemen, and other cultural role models and try to adopt behaviors appropriate to these roles.

Anthropological studies of other cultures also lend support to the social-learning interpretation of gender-identity formation. In several societies the differences between males and females that we often assume to be innate are simply not evident. In fact, Margaret Mead's classic book *Sex and Temperament in Three Primitive Societies* (1963) reveals that other societies may have different views about what is considered feminine or masculine. In this widely quoted report of her fieldwork in New Guinea, Mead discusses two societies that minimize differences between the sexes. She notes that among the Mundugumor both sexes exhibit aggressive, insensitive, uncooperative, and non-nurturing behaviors that would be considered masculine by our society's norms. In contrast, among the Arapesh both males and females exhibit gentleness, sensitivity, cooperation, nurturing, and nonaggressive behaviors that would be judged feminine in our society. And, in a third society studied by Mead, the Tchambuli, masculine and feminine gender roles are actually the reverse of what Americans view as typical. Because there is no evidence that people in these societies are biologically different from Americans, their often diametrically different interpretations of what is masculine and what is feminine seem to result from different processes of social learning.

Finally, proponents of the social-learning interpretation of gender-identity formation refer to various studies of intersexed children born with ambiguous external genitals who are assigned a particular sex and reared accordingly. Much of the early work in this area was performed at Johns Hopkins University Hospital by a team headed by John Money. When these treatment approaches were being implemented, Money and his colleagues believed that a person is psychosexually neutral or undifferentiated at birth and that social-learning experiences are the essential determinants of gender identity and gender-role behavior (Money, 1961, 1963; Money & Ehrhardt, 1972).

Therefore, little attention was paid to matching external genitals with sex chromosomes. Rather, because the guiding principle was how natural the genitals could be made to look, many of these intersexed infants were assigned to the female sex, because surgical reconstruction of ambiguous genitalia to those of a female form is mechanically easier and aesthetically and functionally superior to constructing a penis (Diamond, 2004; Diamond & Sigmundson, 1997; Nussbaum, 2000).

Money and his colleagues followed these surgically altered children over a period of years and reported that in most cases children whose assigned sex did not match their chromosomal sex developed a gender identity consistent with the way they were reared (Money, 1965; Money & Ehrhardt, 1972). Additional evidence supporting these findings was recently published. Researchers surveyed 39 adult participants who had undergone surgical alteration as infants at Johns Hopkins. All of these individuals are genetic males who were born with a micropenis with a urethral opening on its underside. Some of the individuals were altered to be anatomical females and others to be anatomical males, with gender assigned accordingly. Most of these respondents (78% of women and 76% of men) reported being satisfied with the gender chosen for them and with their body image, sexual functioning, and sexual orientation. However, 2 of the 39 switched gender as adults (Migeon et al., 2002).

Research has revealed that at least some intersexed children may not be as psychosexually neutral at birth as originally believed. Long-term follow-ups of several intersexed children treated under the Johns Hopkins protocol revealed that some of these individuals have had serious problems adjusting to the gender assigned to them (Diamond, 1997; Diamond & Sigmundson, 1997). One especially compelling account involved two identical twin boys, one of whom experienced a circumcision accident that destroyed most of his penile tissue. Because no amount of plastic surgery could adequately reconstruct the severely damaged penis, it was recommended that the child be raised as a female and receive appropriate sex-change surgery. A few months later the parents decided to begin raising him as a girl. Shortly thereafter, castration and initial genital surgery were performed to facilitate feminization. Follow-up analyses of these twins during their early childhood years revealed that, despite possessing identical genetic materials, they responded to their separate social-learning experiences by developing opposite gender identities. Furthermore, the child reassigned to the female gender was described as developing into a normally functioning female child.

If the story of these twins ended here, we would have strong evidence of the dominant role of social learning in gender-identity formation. However, a later follow-up (Diamond & Sigmundson, 1997) found that, beginning at age 14, still unaware of the XY chromosome status and against the recommendations of family and treating clinicians, this person decided to stop living as a female. This adamant rejection of living as a female, together with a much improved emotional state when living as a male, convinced therapists of the appropriateness of sexual reassignment. His postsurgical adjustment was excellent and, aided by testosterone treatments, he "emerged" as an attractive young man. At the age of 25 he married a woman, adopted her children, and comfortably assumed his role as father and husband. This remarkable story is told in a book by John Colapinto (2000) titled *As Nature Made Him: The Boy Who Was Raised as a Girl.*

This case study illustrates the critical importance of long-term longitudinal studies of children whose sex has been reassigned. The early childhood phase of the follow-up of this person was widely reported in the press and the academic and medical communities as providing clear evidence that gender identity is psychologically neutral at birth, as yet uninfluenced by social-learning experiences. Now, after many years during which this viewpoint predominated, we have found out how wrong this interpretation may be. Even John Money, formerly a major proponent of this perspective, moderated his position in later years (see Money, 1994b).

As a footnote to this famous case of apparent misapplication of the Johns Hopkins protocol, we mention another, underreported case with a different outcome. It concerns a boy whose penis was burned off during a circumcision procedure. This individual, also raised as a girl from infancy, was interviewed by professionals at ages 16 and 26. Although tomboyish as a child and bisexual as an adult, this person has maintained

# Treatment Strategies for Intersexed People: Debate and Controversy

People born with ambiguous external genitals are often viewed as biological accidents that need to be fixed. John Money and his colleagues at Johns Hopkins were the primary architects of a treatment protocol for intersexed individuals that became standard practice by the early 1960s and persists to the present. According to this protocol, a team of professionals, in consultation with the parents, choose which gender to assign an intersexed child. To reduce the possibility of future adjustment problems or gender confusion, the physicians usually provide surgical and/or hormonal treatments. Money and his associates reported that most intersexed individuals treated according to this protocol develop into relatively well-adjusted people with gender identities consistent with the way they were reared (Money, 1965; Money and Ehrhardt, 1972).

But serious questions have emerged about both the long-term benefits and the ethical appropriateness of this standard treatment protocol (Dreger, 2003; Fausto-Sterling, 2000; Kessler, 1998). Milton Diamond, an outspoken critic of John Money's treatment strategies, has conducted long-term follow-ups of a number of intersexed individuals treated under this standard protocol. His research has revealed that some of these individuals experience significant adjustment problems that they attribute to the biosocial "management" of their intersexed conditions (Diamond, 1997, 1998, 2004; Diamond & Sigmundson, 1997; Vilain, 2001).

The research of Diamond and others, and the testimony of people who have been harmed by treatment they have received via the standard protocol, has triggered an intense debate among intersexed people, researchers, and health-care professionals about what constitutes proper treatment of intersexed infants (Meyer-Bahlburg, 2005). Many specialists still support Money's protocol and argue that intersexed infants should be unambiguously assigned a gender at the earliest possible age, certainly before the emergence of gender identity in the second year of life. This position endorses surgical and/or hormonal intervention to minimize gender confusion. An alternative viewpoint, championed by Diamond and others, suggests a threefold approach to treating intersexed people. First, health-care professionals should make an informed best guess about the intersexed infant's eventual gender identity and then counsel parents to rear the child in this identity. Second, genital-altering surgeries (which later might need to be reversed) should be avoided during the early years of development. And third, quality counseling and accurate information should be provided to both the child and his or her parents during the developmental years to ensure that the child is eventually able to make an informed decision about any additional treatment steps, such as surgery and/or hormone treatments. A distinguished group of intersex researchers has strongly advocated delaying medical intervention until a child is old enough to

## ? Critical Thinking Question

Assume that you are the leader of a team of health professionals who must decide the best treatment for an intersexed infant. Would you assign a gender identity and perform the surgical and/or hormonal treatments consistent with the assigned gender? If so, what gender would you select? Why? If you would decide not to assign a gender, what kind of follow-up or management strategy would you suggest during the child's developmental years?

a female gender identity, unlike the more famous example of the twin who assumed a male gender identity as an adult (Bradley et al., 1998).

Another study has raised questions about the common practice of surgically assigning a sex to a child with ambiguous external genitals. This investigation reported on the development of 27 children born without penises (a condition known as *cloacal exstrophy*) but who were otherwise males with normal testes, chromosomes, and hormones. Twenty-five of the 27 underwent sex reassignment shortly after birth, by means of castration, and their parents raised them as females. All 25 exhibited play activities typical of males, and 14 eventually declared themselves boys. The two boys who were not reassigned and thus were raised as boys seemed to be better adjusted than their reassigned counterparts. These results led William Reiner, lead researcher on this investigation, to conclude that "with time and age, children may well know what their gender is, regardless of any and all information and child rearing to the contrary" (Reiner, 2000, p. 1).

Several prominent researchers now argue that prevailing assumptions about gender neutrality at birth and the efficacy of sex reassignment of children may be wrong. In fact, more and more evidence has shown that, despite great care in rearing chromosomal males sex-reassigned as females, some—perhaps many—of them manifest strong male tendencies in their developmental years and may even change their assigned sex after they reach puberty (Colapinto, 2000; Diamond & Sigmundson, 1997; Reiner, 1997, 2000). Concerns about the benefits and ethics of standard treatment practices used with intersexed individuals have instigated a lively debate have developed a male or female gender identity (Caldwell, 2005).

Both Diamond's treatment strategy and the standard protocol raise important questions. Does genital-altering surgery performed on mere babies violate their rights as humans to give informed consent? Would intersexed children left with ambiguous genitals have problems functioning in schools or other settings where their condition might become known to others? Might society eventually evolve beyond the two-sex model and embrace the legitimacy of a third, intersexed condition located somewhere on the spectrum between male and female?

A number of case studies have reported instances of people who comfortably adjusted to their untreated intersexed condition (Fausto-Sterling, 1993, 2000; Laurent, 1995). Furthermore, in recent years a number of intersexed people treated under the standard protocol have expressed strong resentment over being subjected to medical intervention as infants (Goodrum, 2000; Looy & Bouma, 2005; Morris, 2003). In fact, "many intersexed people, now adults, are advocating for an end to the way intersexed children are seen as 'damaged goods' needing to be fixed" (Goodrum, 2000, p. 2).

Intersex activists, who have established many advocacy organizations, such as Bodies Like Ourselves and the Intersex Society of North America (ISNA), argue that intersexed people are cases of genital variability, not genital abnormality. The ISNA advocates a noninterventionist, child-centered approach in which an intersexed child is not subjected to genital-altering surgery; he or she may choose such procedures later in life (Caldwell, 2005; Melby, 2002a; Nussbaum, 2000). Furthermore, intersex activists and many medical ethicists believe that violations of medical ethics occur (1) when genital-altering surgery is performed on babies unable to provide informed consent, (2) when intersexed people are denied the right to remain intersexed people with their own identity, and (3) when parents are encouraged to withhold information from their children about their intersex condition.

Intersex activists have also strongly denounced one aspect of intersex treatment that previously was largely ignored. Genital-altering surgery can impair an individual's capacity for sexual pleasure (Chase, 2003; Creighton & Liao, 2004; Morris, 2003). For example, surgical reduction of an enlarged clitoris in a fetally androgenized female can result in reduced erotic sensation and thus can interfere with genital pleasure and orgasmic capacity (Minto, 2003; Morris, 2003).

More questions than answers exist about the most appropriate treatment strategy for intersexed infants. This uncertainty is due largely to a scarcity of long-term outcome studies on intersexed individuals (Meyer-Bahlburg, 2005). We hope that time and research will eventually resolve this dilemma.

among intersexed individuals, researchers, and practitioners, described in the boxed discussion "Treatment Strategies for Intersexed People: Debate and Controversy."

## The Interactional Model

Scientists have argued for decades about the relative importance of nature (biological determinants) versus nurture (social learning and the environment) in shaping human development. Today it seems clear that gender identity is a product of both biological factors and social learning. The evidence is simply too overwhelming to conclude that normal infants are psychosexually neutral at birth. We have seen that human infants possess a complex and yet to be fully understood biological substrate that predisposes them to interact with their social environment in either a masculine or a feminine mode. However, few researchers believe that human gender identity has an exclusively biological basis. There is simply too much evidence supporting the important role of life experiences in shaping the way we think about ourselves—not only as masculine or feminine but in all aspects of how we relate to those around us. Consequently, most theorists and researchers support an *interactional model*, which acknowledges both biology and experience in the development of gender identity (Golombok & Fivush, 1995; Looy & Bouma, 2005; Ridley, 2003). Let us hope that as we acquire more data from further research, especially from long-term longitudinal analyses, we will gain a clearer understanding of the relative impact of these two powerful forces on gender-identity formation and gender-role behavior.

# Transsexualism and Transgenderism

We have learned that gender-identity formation is a complex process influenced by many factors, with congruity between biological sex and gender identity by no means guaranteed. We have become increasingly aware of the rich diversity in gender identities and roles. Many people fall somewhere within a range of variant gender identities. The community of gender-variant people, composed of *transsexual* and *transgendered* individuals, has acquired considerable voice in both the professional literature and the popular media.

A **transsexual** is a person whose gender identity is opposite to his or her biological sex (Cole et al., 1997). Such people feel trapped in a body of the "wrong" sex, a condition known as **gender dysphoria**. Thus an anatomically male transsexual feels that *she* is a woman who, by some quirk of fate, has been provided with male genitals but who wishes to be socially identified as female. Many transsexuals undergo sex-reassignment procedures involving extensive screening, hormone therapy, and genital-altering surgery. However, not all gender-dysphoric people want complete sex reassignment. Instead, they may want only the physical body, gender role, or sexuality of the other sex. Many gender-dysphoric individuals, including most transsexuals, want all three of these aspects of the other sex, but some are content to take on only one or two (Carroll, 1999). Furthermore, some transgendered people who manifest variant gender-role behaviors experience little or no gender dysphoria.

The term **transgendered** is generally applied to individuals whose appearance and/or behaviors do not conform to traditional gender roles. In other words, trans-gendered people, "to varying degrees, 'transgress' cultural norms as to what a man or woman 'should be'" (Goodrum, 2000, p. 1). These "transgressions" often involve cross-dressing, either occasionally or full-time. Nontranssexual cross-dressers used to be labeled *transvestites*. This term is now generally applied only to people who cross-dress to achieve sexual arousal (see the discussion of *transvestic fetishism* in Chapter 16). Transgendered people who cross-dress typically do so to obtain psychosocial rather than sexual gratification.

Some intersexed people, who were born exhibiting a mixture of male and female external genitals, also consider themselves members of the transgendered community. This group can include intersexed individuals who have undergone surgical and/or hormonal treatments to establish congruence between their anatomical sex structures and their gender identity (Goodrum, 2000).

The primary difference between a transsexual and a transgenderist is that the transgenderist does not want to change his or her physical body to create a better fit with personal or societal role expectations. Transsexuals often undergo major surgeries to make their physical bodies congruent with their gender identity. In contrast, most transgendered people have no wish to undergo anatomical alterations but do occasionally or frequently dress like and take on the mannerisms of the other sex. Some transgenderists live full-time manifesting gender-role behaviors opposite to those ascribed by society to someone of their biological sex (Bolin, 1997).

**Transsexual** A person whose gender identity is opposite to his or her biological sex.

**Gender dysphoria** Unhappiness with one's biological sex or gender role.

**Transgendered** A term applied to people whose appearance and/or behaviors do not conform to traditional gender roles.

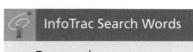

InfoTrac Search Words

- Transsexual
- Transgender

## Variant Gender Identity and Sexual Orientation

Many people are confused about the difference between gender identity (especially variant gender identity) and sexual orientation. Simply stated, gender identity is who we are—our own subjective sense of being male, female, or some combination of the two. Sexual orientation refers to which of the sexes we are emotionally and sexually attracted to (see Chapter 9).

Before sex reassignment, most transsexuals are attracted to people who match them anatomically but not in gender identity. Thus a transsexual with a female gender identity, feeling trapped in a man's body (and probably identified as a male by society), is likely to be attracted to men. In other words, she has a heterosexual orientation based on her own self-identification as female. If she acts on her sexual desires before undergoing sex reassignment, she may be falsely labeled as homosexual. In terms of postsurgical sexual orientation almost all female-to-male transsexuals desire female

## Respectful Communication With a Transsexual or Transgendered Individual

Alexander John Goodrum (2000) wrote an informative article on transsexualism and transgenderism in which he discussed how people should communicate or interact with individuals with variant gender identities and/or behaviors. We summarize his suggestions as follows:

- It is important to refer to transsexual or transgendered individuals appropriately. If someone identifies himself as male, refer to him as *he;* if she identifies herself as female, refer to her as *she.* If you are not sure, it is all right to ask what this person prefers or expects. Once you know, try to be consistent. If you occasionally forget and use the wrong pronoun, make the correction. Most transsexual or transgendered people will understand slipups and appreciate your efforts.
- Never "out" someone by telling others, without permission, that he or she is transsexual or transgendered. Furthermore, do not assume that other people know about

a person's variant gender identity. Many transgendered and transsexual individuals pass very well, and the only way others would know about their variant gender status would be by being told. Clearly, the decision whether to communicate gender status should be made only by the individual, and failure to honor this right would be highly disrespectful.
- Common sense and good taste mandate that we never ask transsexual or transgendered people what their genital anatomy looks like or how they relate sexually to others.
- Finally, make no assumptions about whether a person has a homosexual, bisexual, or heterosexual orientation. A person who believes that it is appropriate to reveal information about sexual orientation may elect to communicate this to you.

sexual partners, whereas male-to-female transsexuals can be sexually oriented to either sex, with most preferring male sex partners (Zhou et al., 1995). It is important to note that most transsexuals who pursue sex reassignment are motivated primarily by a desire to alleviate a gender identity conflict rather than to increase their sexual attractiveness to desired partners (Bockting, 2005).

Although transsexuals are predominantly heterosexual, the transgendered community is more eclectic, consisting of gay men, lesbians, bisexuals, and heterosexuals (Goodrum, 2000).

## Transsexualism: Etiology, Sex-Reassignment Procedures, and Outcomes

In the 1960s and early 1970s, when medical procedures for altering sex were first being developed in the United States, approximately three out of every four people requesting a sex change were biological males who wished to be females (Green, 1974). Although most health professionals believe that males seeking sex reassignment still outnumber females, evidence indicates that the ratio has narrowed appreciably (Landen et al., 1998; Olsson & Moller, 2003).

A vast accumulation of clinical literature has focused on the characteristics, causes (etiology), and treatment of transsexualism. Certain factors are well established. We know that most transsexuals are biologically normal individuals with healthy sex organs, intact internal reproductive structures, and the usual complement of XX or XY chromosomes (Meyer-Bahlburg, 2005). Furthermore, transsexualism is usually an isolated condition, not part of any general psychopathology, such as schizophrenia or major depression (Cohen-Kettenis & Gooren, 1999). What is less understood is why these individuals reject their anatomies.

Many transsexuals develop a sense of being at odds with their genital anatomy in early childhood; some recall identifying strongly with characteristics of the other sex at as early as 5, 6, or 7 years of age. In some cases these children's discomfort is partially relieved by imagining themselves to be members of the other sex, but many of them eventually progress beyond mere imagining to actual cross-dressing. Less commonly, a strong identity with the other sex may not emerge until adolescence or adulthood.

The etiology of transsexualism is not clearly understood. Moreover, considerable controversy exists regarding the most appropriate clinical strategies for dealing with this condition. Keeping this debate in mind, we will summarize the tenuous state of knowledge about this highly unusual variant gender identity.

## Etiology

Many theories have tried to explain transsexualism, but the evidence is inconclusive (Cole et al., 2000; Money, 1994a). Some writers maintain that biological factors play a decisive role. One theory suggests that prenatal exposure to inappropriate amounts of hormones of the other sex causes improper brain differentiation (Dessens et al., 1999; Zhou et al., 1995). Some evidence indicates that in transsexuals, sexual differentiation of the brain and the genitals occurs discordantly (Krujiver et al., 2000; Meyer-Bahlburg, 2005). It has also been suggested that transsexualism can be induced by abnormal levels of adult sex hormones. However, this explanation is contradicted by numerous indications that sex hormone levels are normal in adult transsexuals (Meyer et al., 1986; Zhou et al., 1995).

Another theory, which has some supporting evidence, holds that social-learning experiences contribute significantly to the development of transsexualism. A child may be exposed to a variety of conditioning experiences that support behaving in a manner traditionally attributed to the other sex (Bradley & Zucker, 1997; Cohen-Kettenis & Gooren, 1999). Such cross-gender behaviors may be so exclusively rewarded that it may be difficult or impossible for the individual to develop the appropriate gender identity.

## Options for Transsexuals

The mental health field has traditionally considered only two possible solutions for overcoming the gender dysphoria of transsexuals: changing gender identity to match the physical body or changing the body to match gender identity (Carroll, 1999). Other options exist, however, and clinical evidence has indicated that some preoperative transsexuals have discovered that it may be psychologically sufficient to express themselves through such activities as cross-dressing (Carroll, 1999). Nevertheless, in most cases, psychotherapy, without accompanying biological alterations, has generally been inadequate to help transsexuals adjust to their bodies and gender identities. For such individuals the best course of action might be to change their bodies to match their minds, through surgical and hormonal alteration of genital anatomy and body physiology. However, medical alteration is not a simple solution, because it is both time-consuming and costly.

## Sex-Reassignment Procedures

The initial step of a sex change involves extensive screening interviews, during which a person's motivations for undergoing the change are thoroughly evaluated. Individuals with real conflicts and confusion about their gender identity are not considered for surgical alteration. Individuals with an apparently genuine incongruence between their gender identity and their biological sex are then instructed to adopt a lifestyle consistent with their gender identity (i.e., dress style and behavior patterns). If, after several months to a year or longer, it appears that the individual has successfully adjusted to that lifestyle, the next step is hormone therapy, a process designed to accentuate latent traits of the desired sex. Thus males wishing to be females are given drugs that inhibit testosterone production together with doses of estrogen that induce some breast growth, soften the skin, reduce facial and body hair, and help to feminize body contours. Muscle strength diminishes, as does sexual interest, but there is no alteration of vocal pitch. Women who want to become men are treated with testosterone, which helps to increase growth of body and facial hair and produces a deepening of the voice and a slight reduction in breast size. Testosterone also suppresses menstruation. Most health professionals who provide sex-change procedures require a candidate to live for at least 1 year as a member of the other sex while undergoing hormone therapy, before surgery. At any time during this phase the process can be reversed, although few transsexuals choose this option.

The final step of a sex change is surgery (● **Figure 3.6**). Surgical procedures are most effective for men wishing to be women. The scrotum and penis are removed, and a vagina is created through reconstruction of pelvic tissue (see Figure 3.6a). During this surgical procedure, great care is taken to maintain the sensory nerves that serve the skin of the penis, and this sensitive skin tissue is relocated to the inside of the newly fashioned vagina. Intercourse is possible, although use of a lubricant may be necessary, and many male-to-female transsexuals report postsurgical capacity to experience sexual arousal and orgasm (Lawrence, 2005; Schroder & Carroll, 1999). Hormone treatments can produce sufficient breast development, but some individuals also receive implants. Body and facial hair, which were reduced by hormone treatments, can be further removed by electrolysis. Finally, if desired, an additional surgical procedure can be performed to raise the pitch of the voice in male-to-female transsexuals (Brown et al., 2000).

A biological female who desires to be male generally has her breasts, uterus, and ovaries surgically removed and her vagina sealed off. Constructing a penis is much more difficult than constructing a vagina. In general, the penis is fashioned from abdominal skin or from tissue from the labia and perineum (see Figure 3.6b). This constructed organ cannot achieve a natural erection in response to sexual arousal. However, several options are available that can provide a rigid penis for intercourse. One involves fashioning a small hollow skin tube on the underside of the penile shaft into which a rigid silicone rod can be inserted. Another option is an implanted inflatable device, which will be described in Chapter 14. If erotically sensitive tissue from the clitoris is left embedded at the base of the surgically constructed penis, erotic feelings and orgasm are sometimes possible (Lief & Hubschman, 1993).

### Outcomes of Sex Reassignment

Numerous studies of the psychosocial outcome of gender reassignment provide a basis for optimism about the success of sex-reassignment procedures. The single most consistent finding of these investigations is that most people who have undergone these procedures experience significant improvement in their overall adjustment to life (Campo et al., 2003; De Cuypere et al., 2005; Lawrence, 2003).

## ● Gender Roles

We have seen that social learning is an important influence on the formation of gender identity early in life, so that even by the age of 2 or 3 years, most children have no doubt about whether they are boys or girls. This influence continues throughout our

● **Figure 3.6** The genitals following sex-change surgery: (a) Male-to-female sex-change surgery is generally more effective than (b) female-to-male sex-change surgery.

(a)

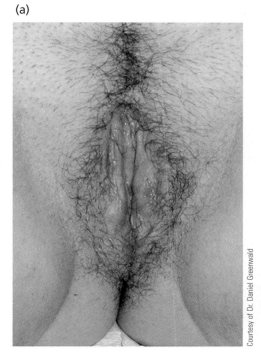

Courtesy of Dr. Daniel Greenwald

(b)

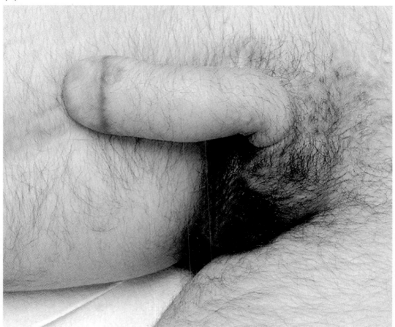

Courtesy of Dr. Daniel Greenwald

lives, because we are influenced by *gender roles* (or *sex roles*)—that is, behaviors that are considered appropriate and normal for men and women in a society.

The ascribing of gender roles leads naturally to certain assumptions about how people will behave. For example, men in North American society have traditionally been expected to be independent and aggressive, whereas women were supposed to be dependent and submissive. Once these expectations are widely accepted, they may begin to function as stereotypes. A **stereotype** is a generalized notion of what a person is like based only on that person's sex, race, religion, ethnic background, or similar category. Stereotypes do not take individuality into account.

Many common gender-based stereotypes are widely accepted in our society. Some of the prevailing notions about men maintain that they are aggressive (or at least assertive), logical, unemotional, independent, dominant, competitive, objective, athletic, active, and above all, competent. Conversely, women are frequently viewed as nonassertive, illogical, emotional, subordinate, warm, and nurturing.

Not all people accept these gender-role stereotypes, and we have seen a trend away from strict adherence to gender-typed behavior, especially among younger people (Ben-David & Schneider, 2005; Menvielle, 2004). Research suggests that women are less entrenched than men in rigid gender-role stereotypes and are more inclined to embrace positions of equality with men (Ben-David & Schneider, 2005). In spite of these positive changes in American culture, stereotypical gender roles still pervade our society (Hyde, 2004; Rider, 2000). Indeed, many individuals are comfortable fulfilling a traditional masculine or feminine role, and we do not wish to demean or question the validity of their lifestyles. Rather, we are concerned with finding out why gender roles are so prevalent in society. We turn to this question next.

**Stereotype** A generalized notion of what a person is like based only on that person's sex, race, religion, ethnic background, or similar criteria.

**InfoTrac Search Words**

- Gender stereotype
- Gender role

## How Do We Learn Gender Roles?

You have probably heard the argument that behavioral differences between men and women are biologically determined, at least to some degree. Men cannot bear or nurse children. Likewise, biological differences in hormones, muscle mass, and brain structure and function can influence some aspects of behavior. However, most theorists explain gender roles as largely a product of **socialization**—that is, the process by which individuals learn, and adopt, society's expectations for behavior. In the following Sexuality and Diversity discussion, we see how cultural and ethnic groups within a society have varying expectations of men's and women's behavior.

**Socialization** The process by which our society conveys behavioral expectations to the individual.

### SEXUALITY AND DIVERSITY

#### Ethnic Variations in Gender Roles

Throughout this textbook we have focused primarily on gender assumptions that prevail in the traditional mainstream—white Americans of European origin. Here we look briefly at gender roles among three different ethnic groups: Hispanic Americans, African Americans, and Asian Americans.

Traditional Hispanic American gender roles are epitomized by the cultural stereotypes of *marianismo* and *machismo*. Marianismo derives from the Roman Catholic notion that women should be pure and self-giving—like the Virgin Mary. It ascribes to women the primary role of mothers who are faithful, virtuous, passive, and subordinate to their husbands and who act as the primary preserver of the family and tradition (McNeill et al., 2001; Raffaelli & Ontai, 2004; Reid & Bing, 2000). The concept of machismo projects an image of the Hispanic American male as strong, independent, virile, and dominant—the head of the household and major decision maker in the family (McNeill et al., 2001; Raffaelli & Ontai, 2004; Torres, 1998). Machismo also embodies the notion that it is acceptable to be sexually aggressive and to seek conquests outside the marriage. Thus Hispanic culture often expresses a double standard in which wives are to remain faithful to one man and husbands can have outside affairs (McNeill et al., 2001). This double standard has its origins in the early socialization of Hispanic youth that encourages boys to be sexually adventurous and girls to be virtuous and virginal (Raffaelli & Ontai, 2004).

Of course, marianismo and machismo are just stereotypes, and many Hispanic Americans do not embrace these gender-role assumptions (Vasquez, 1994). Furthermore, assimilation, urbanization, and upward mobility of Hispanic Americans are combining to diminish the impact of these cultural stereotypes as they reduce gender-role inequities (McNeill et al., 2001; Sanchez, 1997).

In a second ethnic group, African Americans, women play a central role in families that tends to differ from the traditional nuclear family model of mother, father, and children (Bulcroft et al., 1996; Greene, 1994; Reid & Bing, 2000). African American women have traditionally been a bulwark of strength in their communities since the days of slavery. Because women could not depend economically on men under the system of slavery, African American men did not typically assume the dominant role in the family. This accounts, in part, for why relationships between African American women and men have tended more toward egalitarianism and economic parity than has been true of other cultural groups, including the dominant white culture (Blee & Tickamyer, 1995; Bulcroft et al., 1996). The historical absence of economic dependence also helps explain why so many African American households are headed by women who define their own status.

Another factor is the high unemployment rate among African American males—more than double the rate for whites (Bureau of Labor Statistics, 2005). The realities of unemployment and the American welfare system undoubtedly contribute to some African American men's avoidance of marriage and to absence from the home. Consequently, African American women often assume gender-role behaviors that reflect a reversal of the gender patterns traditional among white Americans.

A third minority group, Asian Americans, represents great diversity both in heritage and country of origin (China, the Philippines, Japan, India, Korea, Vietnam, Cambodia, Thailand, and others). Asian Americans tend to place more value on family, group solidarity, and interdependence than do white Americans (Bradshaw, 1994; Okazaki, 2002). Like her Hispanic counterparts, the Asian American woman expects her family obligations to take higher priority than her own individual aspirations (Pyke & Johnson, 2003). Thus, although more Asian American women work outside the home than women in any other American ethnic group, many spend their lives supporting others and subordinating their needs to the family (Bradshaw, 1994; Cole, 1992). As a result, achievement-oriented Asian women are often caught in a double bind, torn between contemporary American values of individuality and independence and the traditional gender roles of Asian culture.

Although no typical pattern exists, the diverse Asian cultures still tend to allow greater sexual freedom for men than for women while perpetuating the gender-role assumption of male dominance (Ishii-Kuntz, 1997a, 1997b; Pyke & Johnson, 2003). However, Asian culture tends to promote a higher level of sexual conservatism in both sexes than is typical of other U.S. ethnic groups, including whites (Okazaki, 2002).

As these accounts illustrate, social learning and cultural traditions influence gender-role behaviors within American society. How does society convey these expectations? In the following sections we look at five agents of socialization: parents, peers, schools, television, and religion.

## Parents as Shapers of Gender Roles

Many social scientists view parents as influential agents of gender-role socialization (Iervolino et al., 2005; Kane, 2006; Leaper et al., 1998). A child's earliest exposure to what it means to be female or male is typically provided by parents (Witt, 1997). As we saw earlier, in the discussion of gender-identity formation, parents often have different expectations for girls and boys, and they demonstrate these expectations in their interactions. In general, parents tend to be more protective and restrictive of girl babies and provide less intervention and more freedom for boys (Skolnick, 1992). Furthermore, research has found that sons are more likely than daughters to receive parental encouragement for self-assertion behaviors and for controlling or limiting their emotional expression, whereas girls receive more encouragement for expressing social-engagement behavior (Block, 1983; Leaper et al., 1998).

Although an increasing number of parents are becoming sensitive to the gender-role implications of a child's playthings, many others encourage their children to play with toys that help prepare them for specific adult gender roles. Girls are often given dolls, tea sets, and miniature ovens. Boys frequently receive things like trucks, cars, balls, and toy weapons. Children who play with toys thought appropriate only for the other sex are often rebuked by their parents. Because children are sensitive to these expressions of displeasure, they usually develop toy preferences consistent with their parents' gender-role expectations.

That there are significant toy preferences throughout childhood, usually evident by age 2 or 3, is well established by evidence and not a subject of debate among social scientists (Iervolino et al, 2005; Tavris, 2005). However, the causes of these preferences are a source of varied opinions. Many writers, including us, believe that social learning significantly influences toy selection. Another perspective is offered by the developing field of *evolutionary psychology*. Evolutionary psychology maintains that many of our behaviors, even some that appear to be exclusively a product of social learning, have been molded by a long period of biological evolution. This evolution has favored the selection of genes that predispose individuals to certain sex-specific behaviors and thus assist in the survival and reproduction of the species (Bjorklund & Pellegrini, 2000).

Gerianne Alexander (2003) has proposed an evolutionary perspective on the origin of sex-typed toy preferences. Briefly stated, Alexander argues that boys' preferences for "masculine" toys, such as trucks and balls, which can be used actively and observed moving in space, reflect the adaptive significance of acquiring spatial abilities useful in such species-survival tasks as hunting and killing wild game for food. Similarly, girls' preferences for "feminine" toys, such as dolls, might reflect the adaptive benefit of acquired gender-role behaviors that are useful for taking care of infants and for child rearing. From this evolutionary perspective the association between toy preferences and gender-role behaviors evolved from the social roles of early males and

The establishment of stereotypical masculine or feminine roles can be influenced by traditional child-rearing practices.

© Stephen Simpson/Getty Images

© Ian Shaw/Getty Images

females, and "preferences for objects such as toys may indicate a biological preparedness for a 'masculine' or 'feminine' gender role" (G. Alexander, 2003, p. 7).

Although more and more parents try to avoid teaching their children gender stereotypes, many still encourage their children to engage in gender-typed play activities and household chores (Lytton & Romney, 1991; Menvielle, 2004). Even when parents do make a conscious effort not to teach gender roles, some behaviors may seem so natural that they occur unconsciously. Thus a boy's father may invite him to play catch, change the oil in the family car, or mow the lawn, whereas a girl may receive frequent reminders to keep her room tidy or invitations to help prepare meals. This differential treatment has the effect of guiding children toward specific and different adult roles (Fisher-Thompson, 1990).

## The Peer Group

A second important influence in the socialization of gender roles is the peer group (Fagot, 1995). One element of peer-group influence that begins early in life is a voluntary segregation of the sexes (Maccoby, 1988, 1990, 1998; Powlishta et al., 1993). This begins during the preschool years, and by first grade, children select members of their own sex as playmates about 95% of the time (Maccoby, 1998; Maccoby & Jacklin, 1987). Segregation of the sexes, which continues into the school years, contributes to sex typing in play activities that help prepare children for adult gender roles (Moller et al., 1992). Girls often play together with dolls and tea sets, and boys frequently engage in athletic competitions and play with toy guns. Such peer influences contribute to the socialization of women who are inclined to be nurturing and nonassertive and of men who are comfortable being competitive and assertive.

One aspect of peer-group structure among American children that helps to perpetuate traditional gender roles is the tendency to select same-sex playmates most of the time.

By late childhood and adolescence the influence of peers becomes even stronger (Doyle & Paludi, 1991; Hyde, 2004). Children of this age tend to view conformity as important, and adhering to traditional gender roles promotes social acceptance by their peers (Absi-Semaan et al., 1993; Moller et al., 1992). Most individuals who do not behave in ways appropriate to their own sex are subjected to pressure in the form of ostracism or ridicule.

## Schools, Textbooks, and Gender Roles

Studies indicate that girls and boys receive quite different treatment in the classroom, a process that strongly influences gender-role socialization (AAUW, 1992; Duffy et al., 2001; Eccles et al., 1999; Kantrowitz, 1992; Keller, 2002; Sadker & Sadker, 1994). Among other findings, these studies reported that

- Teachers call on and encourage boys more than girls.
- Boys who call out answers without being recognized are generally not penalized, whereas girls tend to be reprimanded for the same behavior.
- Teachers tolerate inappropriate behavior from elementary school boys more than from girls.
- Boys are more likely than girls to receive attention, remedial help, and praise from their teachers.
- Teachers pay more attention to girls who act dependently, but they are more likely to respond to boys who behave in independent or aggressive ways.
- Girls frequently lose confidence in their math and science abilities in the middle school years.

Fortunately, schools in the United States are now acting to reduce classroom perpetuation of stereotypical gender roles (Meyerhoff, 2004). An influx of younger teachers who are products of a more gender-aware generation has aided in this gradual transformation of classroom environments. One of the most striking examples of this change has been a concerted effort by American schools to ensure equal educational opportunities for both sexes in math and science and to create educational environments in which girls as well as boys are encouraged to participate in these subjects.

School textbooks have also perpetuated gender-role stereotypes. In the early 1970s two major studies of children's textbooks found that girls were typically portrayed as dependent, unambitious, and not very successful or clever, whereas boys were shown to have just the opposite characteristics (Saario et al., 1973; Women on Words and Images, 1972). In the early 1980s, men played the dominant roles in about two out of every three stories in American reading texts—an improvement from four out of every five stories in the early 1970s (Britton & Lumpkin, 1984). Textbook publishers in the 1990s and early 2000s have continued to improve markedly in their efforts to avoid gender stereotypes. However, like the culture they represent, textbooks are still not completely free of stereotyped gender roles.

## Television and Gender-Role Stereotypes

Another powerful agent of gender-role socialization is television. Depictions of men and women in TV dramas are often blatantly stereotypical. Men are considerably more likely than women to appear as active, intelligent, and adventurous, and to take positions of leadership. However, these stereotypes are beginning to break down due to an increasing number of TV dramas, such as *Commander in Chief*, *ER*, *The West Wing*, and *Bones*, that feature multidimensional and competent women characters. Nevertheless, prime-time television remains largely a male-dominated medium. In television news and political talk programs, men also continue to be disproportionately represented as the authoritative sources on most topics. A recent analysis of Sunday morning political talk shows on television conducted by the National Organization for Women (2006) found that women are dramatically underrepresented as knowledgeable experts on a range of topics (only 11% of guests were female).

Television commercials also tend to further gender stereotypes. Commercials aimed at children typically portray girls and boys in stereotypical gender roles (Pike & Jennings, 2005). In commercials for nonhousehold products aimed at adult consumers, men are more likely than women to appear as the authoritative source of information (Furnham & Mak, 1999). However, one significant shift has occurred in television commercials promoting household products. When men appear in these ads, they are often depicted as fumbling incompetents (Berkowitz, 2006). Furthermore, bumbling fathers are now the norm in network sitcoms, where they are considerably more likely than mothers to be portrayed negatively (Tierney, 2005). This shift toward featuring doofus dads in television comedies may be attributed to the fact that "four out of five viewers of network sitcoms are women, and they apparently like to see Mom smarter that Dad" (Tierney, 2005, p. 1).

It is safe to assume that the sexist stereotypes depicted by television programming have some impact as agents of socialization, considering that most American children spend hours in front of the TV each day. Fortunately, the television industry is gradually reducing gender biases in its programming, partly because of the influence of media advocacy groups who have worked tirelessly to reduce the portrayal of traditional stereotypes of male and female roles.

## Religion and Gender Roles

Organized religion plays an important role in the lives of many Americans. Despite differences in doctrines, most religions exhibit a common trend in their views about gender roles (Eitzen & Zinn, 2000). Children who receive religious instruction are likely to be socialized to accept certain gender stereotypes, and people who are religious are inclined to endorse gender stereotypes (Basow, 1992; Robinson et al., 2004). In Jewish, Christian, and Islamic traditions these stereotypes commonly embrace an emphasis on male supremacy, with God presented as male through language such as *Father*, *He*, or *King*. The biblical conceptualization of Eve as created from Adam's rib provides a clear endorsement of the gender assumption that females are meant to be secondary to males.

The composition of the leadership of most religious organizations in the United States provides additional evidence of male dominance and of the circumscription of female gender roles. Until 1970 no women were ordained as clergy in any American Protestant denomination. No female rabbis existed until 1972, and the Roman Catholic Church still does not allow female priests.

Movements are afoot to change the traditional patriarchal nature of organized religion in America, as evidenced by several recent trends. In 2006 Katherine Jefferts Schori was elected presiding bishop of the Episcopal Church in America—the first woman to lead a church in the history of the worldwide Anglican Communion (Banerjee, 2006). Female enrollment in seminaries and divinity schools has increased dramatically, the number of ordained women in Protestant ministries has more than doubled, and the number of female rabbis has also increased significantly (Eitzen & Zinn, 1994; Renzetti & Curran, 1992; Ribadeneira, 1998). Efforts are also under way to reduce sexist language in church proceedings and religious writings (Gorski, 2002).

We see, then, that family, friends, schools and textbooks, television (and other media, such as movies, magazines, and popular music), and religion frequently help to develop and reinforce traditional gender-role assumptions and behaviors in our lives. We are all affected by gender-role conditioning to some degree, and we could discuss at great length how this process discourages development of each person's full potential. However, this textbook deals with our sexuality, so it is the impact of gender-role conditioning on this aspect of our lives that we examine in the next section.

The number of women ordained as clergy has increased dramatically.

## Gender-Role Expectations: Their Impact on Our Sexuality

Gender-role expectations exert a profound impact on our sexuality. Our beliefs about males and females, together with our assumptions about what constitutes appropriate behaviors for each, can affect many aspects of sexual experience. Our assessment of ourselves as sexual beings, the expectations we have for intimate relationships, our perception of the quality of such experiences, and the responses of others to our sexuality are all significantly influenced by our identification as male or female.

In the following pages we examine some of our gender-role assumptions and their potential effects on relations between the sexes. We do not mean to imply that only heterosexual couples are limited by these assumptions. Gender-role stereotypes can influence people regardless of their sexual orientation, although homosexual couples might be affected somewhat differently by them.

### Women as Undersexed, Men as Oversexed

A long-standing, mistaken assumption in many Western societies is that women are inherently less sexually inclined than men. Such gender stereotypes can result in women being subjected to years of negative socialization during which they are taught to suppress or deny their natural sexual feelings. Although these stereotypes are beginning to fade as people strive to throw off some of the behavior constraints of generations of socialization, many women are still influenced by such views. How can a woman express interest in being sexual or actively seek her own pleasure if she believes that women are not supposed to have sexual needs? Some women, believing that it is not appropriate to be easily aroused sexually, direct their energies to blocking or hiding these normal responses.

Males can be harmed by being stereotyped as supersexual. A man who is not immediately aroused by a person he perceives as attractive and/or available can feel somehow inadequate. After all, are not all men supposed to be instantly eager when confronted with a sexual opportunity? We believe that such an assumption is demeaning and reduces men to insensitive machines that respond automatically when the correct button is pushed. Male students in our classes frequently express their frustration and ambivalence over this issue. The following account is typical of these observations:

> When I take a woman out for the first time, I am often confused over how the sex issue should be handled. I feel pressured to make a move, even when I am not all that inclined to hop into the sack. Isn't this what women expect? If I don't even try, they may think there is something wrong with me. I almost feel like I would have to explain myself if I acted uninterested in having sex. Usually it's just easier to make the move and let them decide what they want to do with it. (Authors' files)

Clearly, this man believes that he is expected to pursue sex, even when he does not want to, as part of his masculine role. This stereotypical view of men as the initiators of sex in developing relationships can be distressing for both sexes, as we see in the next section.

## Men as Initiators, Women as Recipients

In our society traditional gender roles establish the expectation that men will initiate intimate relationships (from the opening invitation for an evening out to the first overture toward sexual activity) and that women will respond with permission or denial (Dworkin & O'Sullivan, 2005). As the following comment reveals, this can make men feel burdened and pressured:

> Women should experience how anxiety-provoking it can be. I get tired of always being the one to make the suggestion, since there's always the potential of being turned down. (Authors' files)

A woman who feels compelled to accept a passive female role can have a difficult time initiating sex. It could be even harder for her to assume an active role during sexual activity. Many women are frustrated, regretful, and understandably angry that such cultural expectations are so deeply ingrained in our society. The following comments, expressed by women talking together, reflect some of these thoughts:

> I like to ask men out and have often done so. But it's frustrating when many of the men I ask out automatically assume that I want to jump in bed with them just because I take the initiative to make a date. (Authors' files)

> It is hard for me to let my man know what I like during lovemaking. After all, he is supposed to know, isn't he? If I tell him, it's like I am usurping his role as the all-knowing one. (Authors' files)

## Women as Controllers, Men as Movers

Many women grow up believing that men always have sex on their minds. For such a woman it may be a logical next step to become the controller of what takes place during sexual interaction. By this we do not mean actively initiating certain activities, which she sees as the prerogative of men, the movers. Rather, a woman may see her role as controlling her male partner's rampant lust by making certain he does not coerce her into unacceptable activities. Thus, instead of enjoying how good it feels to have her breasts caressed, she may concentrate on how to keep his hand off her genitals. This concern with control can be particularly pronounced during the adolescent dating years. It is not surprising that a woman who spends a great deal of time and energy regulating sexual intimacy might have difficulty experiencing sexual feelings when she finally allows herself to relinquish her controlling role.

Conversely, men are often conditioned to see women as sexual challenges and to go as far as they can during sexual encounters. They too may have difficulty appreciating the good feelings of being close to and touching someone when all they are thinking about is what they will do next. Men who routinely experience this pattern can have a hard time relinquishing the mover role and being receptive rather than active during sexual interaction. They might be confused or even threatened by a woman who switches roles from controller to active initiator.

## Men as Unemotional and Strong, Women as Nurturing and Supportive

Perhaps one of the most undesirable of all gender-role stereotypes is the notion that being emotionally expressive, tender, and nurturing is appropriate only for women (Plant et al., 2000). We have already seen that men are often socialized to be unemotional. A man who is trying to appear strong might find it difficult to express vulnerability, deep feelings, and doubts. This conditioning can make it exceedingly difficult for a man to develop emotionally satisfying intimate relationships.

For example, a man who accepts the assumption of nonemotionality might approach sex as a purely physical act, during which expressions of feelings have no place. This results in a limited kind of experience that can leave both parties feeling dissatisfied. Women often have a negative reaction when they encounter this characteristic in men, because women tend to place great importance on openness and willingness to express feelings in a relationship. However, we need to remember that many men must struggle against a lifetime of "macho" conditioning when they try to express long-suppressed emotions. Women, on the other hand, can grow tired of their role as nurturers, particularly when their efforts are greeted with little or no reciprocity.

We have discussed how strict adherence to traditional gender roles can limit and restrict the ways we express our sexuality. These cultural legacies are often expressed more subtly today than in the past, but rigid gender-role expectations linger on, inhibiting our growth as multidimensional people and our capacity to be fully ourselves with others. Although many people are breaking away from stereotyped gender roles and are learning to accept and express themselves more fully, we cannot underestimate the extent of gender-role learning that still occurs in our society.

Many people are now striving to integrate both masculine and feminine behaviors into their lifestyles. This trend, often referred to as androgyny, is the focus of the final section of this chapter.

## Transcending Gender Roles: Androgyny

The word **androgyny** (an-DRAW-ji-nee), meaning "having characteristics of both sexes," is derived from the Greek roots *andr*, meaning "man," and *gyne-*, meaning "woman." The term is used to describe flexibility in gender role. Androgynous individuals have integrated aspects of masculinity and femininity into their personalities and behavior. Androgyny offers the option of expressing whatever behavior seems appropriate in a given situation instead of limiting responses to those considered gender appropriate. Thus androgynous men and women might be assertive on the job but nurturing with friends, family members, and lovers. Many men and women possess characteristics consistent with traditional gender assumptions but also have interests and behavioral tendencies typically ascribed to the other sex. Actually, people can range from being very masculine or feminine to being *both* masculine and feminine—that is, androgynous.

The social psychologist Sandra Bem (1974, 1993) developed a paper-and-pencil inventory for measuring the degree to which individuals are identified with masculine or feminine behaviors or a combination thereof. Similar devices have been developed since Bem's pioneering work (Spence & Helmreich, 1978). Armed with these devices for measuring androgyny, a number of researchers have investigated how androgynous individuals compare with strongly gender-typed people.

A number of studies indicate that androgynous people are more flexible in their behaviors, are less limited by rigid gender-role assumptions, have higher levels of self-esteem, make better decisions in group settings, have better communication skills, and exhibit more social competence and motivation to achieve than do people who are strongly gender typed or those who score low in both areas (Hirokawa et al., 2004;

**Androgyny** A blending of typical male and female behaviors in one individual.

Katz & Ksansnak, 1994; Kirchmeyer, 1996; Shimonaka et al., 1997). Research also demonstrates that masculine and androgynous people of both sexes are more independent and less likely to have their opinions swayed than are individuals who are strongly identified with the feminine role (Bem, 1975). In fact, both androgyny and high masculinity appear to be adaptive for both sexes at all ages (Sinnott, 1986). However, feminine and androgynous people of both sexes appear to be significantly more nurturing than those who adhere to the masculine role (Bem, 1993; Coleman & Ganong, 1985; Ray & Gold, 1996).

We need to be cautious about concluding that androgyny is an ideal state, free of potential problems (Sampson, 1985). One study found that masculine-typed males demonstrated better overall emotional adjustment than did androgynous males (Jones et al., 1978). Another study, of college professors in their early careers, found that androgynous individuals exhibited greater personal satisfaction but more job-related stress than those who were strongly gender typed (Rotheram & Weiner, 1983). In a large sample of college students masculine personality characteristics were also more closely associated with being versatile and adaptable than was the trait of androgyny (Lee & Scheurer, 1983). Other studies have also indicated that it may be masculinity, not femininity or androgyny, that is most closely associated with successful adjustment and positive self-esteem (Basoff & Glass, 1982; Unger & Crawford, 1992; Williams & D'Alessandro, 1994). This may be "because masculine attributes are viewed more positively and consequently lead to greater social rewards" (Burn et al., 1996, p. 420). Thus, although androgyny is often associated with emotional, social, and behavioral competence, more information is necessary for a complete picture of its effect on personal adjustment and satisfaction.

Androgynous individuals, both male and female, seem to have more positive attitudes toward sexuality and are more aware of and expressive of feelings of love than are individuals who are traditionally gender typed (Ganong & Coleman, 1987; Walfish & Myerson, 1980). Androgynous people also appear to be more tolerant and less likely to judge or criticize the sexual behaviors of others (Garcia, 1982). Studies have found that androgynous women are more orgasmic and experience more sexual satisfaction than do feminine-typed women (Kimlicka et al., 1983; Radlove, 1983). However, two separate investigations have revealed that masculine males are significantly more comfortable with sex than are androgynous females, indicating that biological sex may still exert a stronger effect than gender typing (Allgeier, 1981; Walfish & Myerson, 1980).

Our own guess is that androgynous people tend to be flexible and comfortable in their sexuality. We would expect such people, whether men or women, to have great capacity to enjoy both the emotional and the physical aspects of sexual intimacy. Androgynous lovers are probably comfortable both initiating and responding to invitations for sexual sharing, and they are probably not significantly limited by preconceived notions of who must do what—and how—during their lovemaking. These observations are supported by research indicating that androgynous couples experience more emotional and sexual satisfaction and personal commitment in their relationships than do gender-typed couples (Rosenzweig & Daily, 1989; Stephen & Harrison, 1985).

Research on androgyny continues, and we certainly have good reasons to be cautious about an unequivocally enthusiastic endorsement of this behavioral style. Nevertheless, evidence collected thus far suggests that people who can transcend traditional gender roles are able to function more comfortably and effectively in a wider range of situations. Androgynous individuals can select from a broad repertoire of feminine and masculine behaviors. They can choose to be independent, assertive, nurturing, or tender, based not on gender-role norms but rather on what provides them and others with optimum personal satisfaction in a given situation.

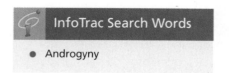
InfoTrac Search Words

● Androgyny

## Male and Female, Masculine and Feminine

- The processes by which our maleness and femaleness are determined and the manner in which they influence our behavior, sexual and otherwise, are highly complex.
- Sex refers to our biological maleness or femaleness, as reflected in various physical attributes (chromosomes, reproductive organs, genitals, and so forth).
- Gender encompasses the special psychosocial meanings added to biological maleness or femaleness—in other words, our masculinity or femininity. Our ideas of masculinity and femininity involve gender assumptions about behavior based on a person's sex.
- Gender identity refers to each person's subjective sense of being male or female.
- Gender role refers to a collection of attitudes and behaviors a specific culture considers normal and appropriate for people of a particular sex.
- Gender roles establish sex-related behavioral expectations, which are culturally defined and therefore vary from society to society and from era to era.

## Gender-Identity Formation

- Research efforts to isolate the many biological factors that influence a person's gender identity have resulted in the identification of six biological categories, or levels: chromosomal sex, gonadal sex, hormonal sex, sex of the internal reproductive structures, sex of the external genitals, and sex differentiation of the brain.
- Under normal conditions these six biological variables interact harmoniously to determine our biological sex. However, errors can occur at any of the six levels. The resulting irregularities in the development of a person's biological sex can seriously complicate acquisition of a gender identity.
- The social-learning interpretation of gender-identity formation suggests that our identification with either masculine or feminine roles results primarily from the social and cultural models and influences to which we are exposed.
- Most theorists embrace an interactional model in which gender identity is seen as a result of a complex interplay of biological and social-learning factors.

## Transsexualism and Transgenderism

- A transsexual is a person whose gender identity is opposite to his or her biological sex.
- The term *transgendered* is generally applied to individuals whose appearance and behaviors do not conform to the gender roles society ascribes to people of a particular sex.
- Most transsexuals are heterosexually oriented. The transgendered community has a more eclectic composition of gay men, lesbians, bisexuals, and heterosexuals.
- The scientific community has not reached a consensus about the causes and best treatment for transsexualism. Some transsexuals have successfully undergone sex-reassignment procedures in which their bodies are altered to match their gender identities.

## Gender Roles

- Widely accepted gender-role assumptions can begin to function as stereotypes, which are notions about what people are like based not on their individuality but on their inclusion in a general category, such as age or sex.
- Many common gender-based stereotypes in our society encourage us to prejudge others and restrict our opportunities.
- Socialization is the process by which society conveys its behavioral expectations to us.
- Ethnic variations in gender roles are observed among Hispanic Americans, African Americans, and Asian Americans.
- Parents, peers, schools, textbooks, television, and religion all act as agents in the socialization of gender roles.
- Gender-role expectations can have a profound effect on our sexuality. Our assessment of ourselves as sexual beings, the expectations we have for intimate relationships, our perception of the quality of such experiences, and the responses of others to our sexuality are all significantly influenced by our own perceptions of our gender roles.
- Androgynous individuals are people who have moved beyond traditional gender roles by integrating aspects associated with both masculinity and femininity into their lifestyles.

## ⏵ Suggested Readings

**Dreger, Alice** (1998). *Hermaphrodites and the Medical Invention of Sex.* Cambridge, MA: Harvard University Press. A fascinating discussion of how medical and social scientists have historically construed the sex, gender, and sexuality of intersexed people and why. An epilogue contains informative narratives of several intersexed individuals treated according to the still-standard protocol developed in the 1950s.

**Fausto-Sterling, Anne** (2000). *Sexing the Body: Gender Politics and the Construction of Sexuality.* New York: Basic Books. This book provides information about how the scientific community has historically politicized the human body. Three chapters describe how intersexed people have traditionally been dealt with as "damaged goods" and why such individuals should not be coerced into compromising their differences to fit a flawed societal definition of normality.

**Hines, Melissa** (2004). *Brain Gender.* New York: Oxford University Press. A scholarly review of current research and theory pertaining to the brain's role in shaping gender identity and gender-role behaviors.

**Lips, Hilary** (2001). *Sex and Gender* (4th ed.). Mountain View, CA: Mayfield. An informative text that provides a thorough review of the professional literature pertaining to sex differences in social behavior and experiences. Lips presents information suggesting that gender differences are relatively small and, when present, stem largely from the socialization of gender-role expectations.

**Preves, Sharon** (2002). *Intersex and Identity.* Piscataway, NJ: Rutgers University Press. An illuminating and informative book that gives voice to people with intersex conditions. Preves, a sociologist, provides insights into intersexuality through her analyses of life-history interviews with 37 adults who were treated for this condition as children.

## ● Web Resources

### CengageNOW Web Site
Go to **academic.cengage.com** to link to practice quiz questions, interactive activities, Internet links, critical thinking exercises, discussion forums, and more. You can also access sites from the Wadsworth Psychology Study Center (**academic.cengage.com/psychology**) or you can connect directly to the following sites:

### Gender Talk
Detailed explanations and challenges to conventional attitudes about gender issues, gender identity, and transgenderism in particular are explored on this Web site.

### Intersex Society of North America
The ISNA is an advocacy organization devoted to educating the public about issues related to intersexed individuals.

### Ingersoll Gender Center
The Ingersoll Center is a nonprofit agency for the transsexual, transvestite, and transgender community. Among the highlights of its Web site are a catalog of publications, opinion pieces, and links to related organizations.

### Bodies Like Ours
Valuable Web resource that provides information about the intersex condition and support for intersexed people.

### International Foundation for Gender Education
A good source of information about gender issues, including transgenderism and transsexualism.

### Gender Inn
This Web site lists many valuable resources for further information about gender, including lists of books, articles, and other Web sites.

### Harry Benjamin International Gender Dysphoria Association
This Web site provides information designed to increase the public's understanding of gender-identity disorders.

*Our Sexuality* **Book Companion Web Site academic.cengage.com/psychology/ crooks** Visit your book companion Web site where you will find flash cards, practice quizzes, Internet links, and more to help you study.

### Just what you need to know NOW!
Spend time on what you need to master rather than on information you already have learned. Take a pretest for this chapter, and CengageNOW will generate a personalized study plan based on your results. The study plan will identify the topics you need to review and direct you to online resources to help you master those topics. You can then take a post-test to help you determine the concepts you have mastered and what you will still need to work on. Try it out! Go to **academic.cengage.com/login** to sign in with an access code or to purchase access to this product.

### InfoTrac College Edition Online Library
Sign in to **academic.cengage.com/login** or visit your free book companion Web site at **academic.cengage.com/psychology/crooks** to access InfoTrac College Edition, an online searchable library that includes a multitude of journals, many specific to human sexuality. These journals include *Archives of Sexual Behavior; Archives of Sexual Health Behavior; Canadian Journal of Human Sexuality; Hispanic Journal of the Behavioral Sciences; Journal of Cross-Cultural Psychology; Journal of Physical Education, Recreation, and Dance; Journal of Sex Research;* and *Sex Roles.*

# Female Sexual Anatomy and Physiology

## ❯ The Vulva

What are two reasons to do a genital self-exam?

Does the clitoris serve any purpose other than sexual pleasure?

What are some myths about the hymen?

## ❯ Underlying Structures

What is the function of the bulbs and glands that underlie the vulval tissue?

What are Kegel exercises, and how can they affect a woman's sexual responsiveness?

## ❯ Internal Structures

How (and why) does vaginal lubrication occur?

Which internal structure produces the most hormones?

## ❯ Menstruation

Are there physiological signs that a woman is ovulating and therefore at the most fertile point in her menstrual cycle?

What are the symptoms of premenstrual syndrome and dysmenorrhea?

What can a woman do to minimize these symptoms?

## ❯ Menopause

What are some positive effects of menopause?

What are the potential benefits and risks of hormone replacement therapy?

## ❯ Gynecological Health Concerns

Why do vaginal infections and urinary tract problems occur?

How effective is the Pap smear in detecting cervical cancer?

## ❯ The Breasts

What are the steps for a breast exam?

What percentage of breast cancers is attributed to a genetic flaw?

Many women are as unacquainted with their genitals as this woman was. However, gaining knowledge and understanding of her body can be an important aspect of a woman's sexual well-being and her sexual intelligence. In this chapter we present a detailed description of all female genital structures, external and internal. The discussion is intended to be easy to use for reference, and we encourage women readers to do a self-exam as part of reading it (see the Your Sexual Health box on page 80). We begin with a discussion of the external structures, then discuss the underlying structures and the internal organs. The chapter continues with information about menstruation, menopause, and breasts and then closes with women's health information.

## ◐ The Vulva

**Vulva** The external genitals of the female, including the pubic hair, mons veneris, labia majora, labia minora, clitoris, and urinary and vaginal openings.

The **vulva** encompasses all female external genital structures: the hair, the folds of skin, and the urinary and vaginal openings. *Vulva* is the term we use most frequently in this textbook to refer to the external genitals of the female. The vulva is sometimes mistakenly referred to as the vagina, an internal structure with only the opening a part of the vulva. For reference, see ◐ **Figure 4.1**. The appearance of the vulva, which

◐ **Figure 4.1** The structures and variations of the vulva: (a) external structures and (b–d) different colors and shapes. External female genitals have many common variations.

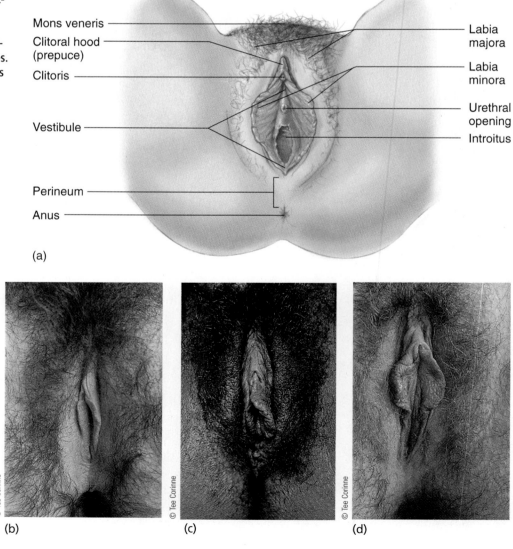

Mons veneris

Clitoral hood (prepuce)

Clitoris

Vestibule

Perineum

Anus

Labia majora

Labia minora

Urethral opening

Introitus

(a)

© Tee Corinne

(b)          (c)          (d)

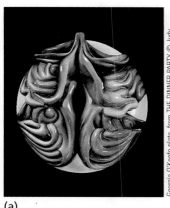
(a)

(b)

Vulva shapes in art and nature:
(a) one of the plates in Judy Chicago's *Dinner Party*, a permanent exhibit symbolizing women in history at the Brooklyn Museum of Art;
(b) the vulvalike beauty of a flower.

Georgia O'Keefe plate, from THE DINNER PARTY © Judy Chicago, 1979. China paint on porcelain, 14" diameter. Photo © Through the Flower Archives.

© Charles Marden Fitch/SuperStock

varies from person to person, has been likened to that of certain flowers, seashells, and other forms found in nature. Transformed vulvalike shapes have been used in artwork, including *The Dinner Party* by Judy Chicago. This work consists of 39 ceramic plates symbolizing significant women in history.

## The Mons Veneris

Translated from Latin, **mons veneris** means "the mound of Venus." Venus was the Roman goddess of love and beauty. The mons veneris, or mons, is the area covering the pubic bone. It consists of pads of fatty tissue between the pubic bone and the skin. Touch and pressure on the mons can be sexually pleasurable because of the presence of numerous nerve endings. At puberty the mons becomes covered with hair that varies in color, texture, and thickness from woman to woman. Sometimes women are concerned about these differences:

**Mons veneris** A triangular mound over the pubic bone above the vulva.

> I always felt uncomfortable in college physical education classes because I had very thick, dark pubic hair, more so than most other women. One day my best friend and I were talking and she mentioned that she felt self-conscious in the showers after P.E. class because her pubic hair was light-colored and sparse. I told her my concerns. We laughed and both decided to stop worrying about it. (Authors' files)

During sexual arousal the scent that accompanies vaginal secretions is held by the pubic hair and can add to sensory erotic pleasure. Pubic hair also prevents uncomfortable friction and provides cushioning during intercourse. Most women and their partners enjoy the lush sensuality of their pubic hair.

Removing pubic hair has primarily been the practice of porn stars and exotic dancers, but it has become a grooming trend some mainstream women practice. Women remove their pubic hair by trimming, shaving, waxing, or using a depilatory; some remove it permanently by laser or cut designs into it, such as a heart or a lightning bolt, for a unique aesthetic effect (Speer, 2005). Others trim the bikini line to prevent pubic hair from peeking out of a bathing suit or thong underwear (Singer, 2005). Some keep only a "landing strip," a triangle or small strip on the mons, while a few remove all pubic hair and go "bald" (Merkin, 2006).

## The Labia Majora

The **labia majora** (LAY-bee-uh muh-JOR-uh), or outer lips, extend downward from the mons on each side of the vulva. They begin next to the thigh and extend inward, surrounding the labia minora and the urethral and vaginal openings. Next to the thigh the outer lips are covered with pubic hair; their inner parts, next to the labia minora, are hairless. The skin of the labia majora is usually darker than the skin of the thighs. The nerve endings and underlying fatty tissue are similar to those in the mons.

**Labia majora** The outer lips of the vulva.

## Genital Self-Exam for Women

Women are born with curiosity about their bodies. In fact, physical self-awareness and exploration are important steps in a child's development. Unfortunately, many women receive negative conditioning about the sexual parts of their bodies from earliest childhood. They learn to think of their genitals as "privates" or "down there"—parts of their body not to be looked at, touched, or enjoyed. It is common for women to react with discomfort to the suggestion of examining their genitals.

This self-exploration exercise provides an opportunity to learn about yourself—your body and your feelings. Like many other exercises and information throughout this textbook that are aimed at helping students improve their self-knowledge or sexual health, some female readers may choose to read about this exercise but not do it, or do only a few steps. To begin the self-exam, use a hand mirror, perhaps in combination with a full-length mirror, to look at your genitals from different angles and postures—standing, sitting, lying down. You may find it helpful to draw a picture of your genitals and label the parts (identified in Figure 4.1). All women have the same parts, but the shades of color, the shapes, and the textures vary from woman to woman. As you are looking, try to become aware of whatever feelings you have about your genital anatomy. Women have different kinds of reactions to looking at their genitals:

*I don't find it to be an attractive part of my body. I wouldn't go as far as to call it ugly. I think it would be easier to accept if it was something you weren't taught to hide and think was dirty, but I've never been able to understand why men find the vulva so intriguing. (Authors' files)*

*I think it looks very sensuous; the tissues look soft and tender. (Authors' files)*

*I was told by a previous partner that my vulva was very beautiful. His comment made me feel good about my body. (Authors' files)*

Besides examining yourself visually, use your fingers to explore the various surfaces of your genitals. Focus on the sensations produced by the different kinds of touching. Note which areas are most sensitive and how the nature of stimulation varies from place to place. The primary purpose of doing this exercise is to explore, not to become sexually aroused. However, if you do become sexually excited during this self-exploration, you may be able to notice changes in the sensitivity of different skin areas that occur with arousal.

Routine self-examination is an aspect of preventive health care.

The genital self-exam serves another purpose besides helping women feel more comfortable with their anatomy and sexuality. Monthly self-examinations of the genitals can augment routine medical care. Women who know what is normal for their own bodies can often detect small changes and seek medical attention promptly. Problems usually require less extensive treatment when they are detected early. If you discover any changes, consult a health practitioner immediately. **Gynecology** (guy-nuh-KOL-uh-jee) is the medical specialty for female sexual and reproductive anatomy.

**Gynecology** The medical practice specializing in women's health and in diseases of the female reproductive and sexual organs.

## The Labia Minora

**Labia minora** The inner lips of the vulva, one on each side of the vaginal opening.

**Prepuce** The foreskin or fold of skin over the clitoris.

The **labia minora** (LAY-bee-uh muh-NOR-uh), or inner lips, are located within the outer lips and often protrude between them. The inner lips are hairless folds of skin that join at the **prepuce** (PREE-pyoos), or clitoral hood, and extend downward past the urinary and vaginal openings. They contain sweat and oil glands, extensive blood vessels, and nerve endings. They vary considerably in size, shape, length, and color from woman to woman, as Figure 4.1 shows. During pregnancy the inner lips become darker in color.

Although there is no universal standard for what labia should look like, some women have had their labia minora altered by labiaplasty (cosmetic surgery to change their size and shape). Women have the surgeon make their labia more symmetrical, small, or plump. (In contrast, pendulous labia are considered beautiful in the Hottentot culture of Africa, and women start pulling on them early in childhood to enlarge them.) Increased exposure to Internet, magazine, and film pornography where female genitals are center stage may contribute to women's belief that they should look different from the way they do naturally (Kobrin, 2006; Navarro, 2004). Plastic surgeons who do this procedure report that the motivation to have it done comes from the women themselves rather than their male partners. Men who persuade their partners to have labiaplasty typically want their partners' labia to conform to the vulva appearance they like most when watching pornography (Douglas et al., 2005). Risks to labiaplasty include painful scarring or nerve damage that can result in hypersensitivity or sensation loss that impairs sexual arousal and pleasure.

Piercing and wearing jewelry on vulva tissues is another way some alter the appearance of their genitals. Prior to the 1990s, in the Western world, body piercing was associated with exotic, faraway peoples seen in *National Geographic*. Now both men and women in the West have extended this form of "body art" to their genitals. The most common sites for female genital piercings are the clitoral hood or body and the labia minora or majora. Rings and barbells are placed through the piercings. Body piercings that are visible to the public are often meant to express individuality and identity with a subculture; genital piercings are personal body decorations to be shared with a sexual partner. It is unknown to what extent piercings genuinely improve erotic stimulation. Risks from the piercing procedure include contracting HIV, Hepatitis B, and bacterial infections. Subsequent to the piercing, local and systemic infections, abscess formation, allergic reactions, torn flesh, and problematic scarring can result. The rings and barbells can also damage the genital tissue of the sexual partner (Kreahling, 2005; Meltzer, 2005).

## The Clitoris

The **clitoris** (KLIT-uh-rus) comprises the external **shaft** and **glans** and the internal **crura** (KROO-ra), or roots, that project inward from each side of the clitoral shaft. The shaft and glans are located just below the mons area, where the inner lips converge. They are covered by the clitoral hood, or prepuce. Genital secretions, skin cells, and bacteria combine to form **smegma**, which can accumulate under the hood and occasionally form lumps and cause pain during sexual arousal or activity. Smegma can be prevented from collecting in this area by drawing back the hood when washing the vulva. If the smegma is already formed, a health-care practitioner can remove it.

If you look at ⊙ **Figure 4.2** on the following page, which shows the clitoris with the hood removed, you can see that the glans is supported by the shaft. The shaft itself cannot be seen, but it can be felt and its shape can be seen through the hood. The shaft contains two small spongy structures called the **cavernous bodies**, which engorge with blood during sexual arousal (Hamilton, 2002). These become the crura (internal leglike stalks) where they connect to the pubic bones in the pelvic cavity. The glans is often not visible under the clitoral hood, but it can be seen if a woman gently parts the labia minora and retracts the hood. The glans looks smooth, rounded, and slightly translucent. The size, shape, and position of the clitoris vary from woman to woman. These normal differences have no known relation to sexual arousal and functioning.

Initially, it may be easier for a woman to locate her clitoris by touch rather than sight because of its sensitive nerve endings. The external part of the clitoris, although tiny, has about the same number of nerve endings as the head of the penis. The clitoral glans in particular is highly sensitive, and women usually stimulate this area with the hood covering it to avoid direct stimulation, which may be too intense. Research into female masturbation patterns has found that clitoral stimulation, not vaginal insertion, is the most common way women achieve arousal and orgasm when masturbating. Although all other sexual organs, male and female, have additional functions in reproduction or

**Clitoris** A highly sensitive structure of the female external genitals, the only function of which is sexual pleasure.

**Shaft** The length of the clitoris between the glans and the body.

**Glans** The head of the clitoris, which is richly endowed with nerve endings.

**Crura** The innermost tips of the cavernous bodies that connect to the pubic bones.

**Smegma** A cheesy substance of glandular secretions and skin cells that sometimes accumulates under the hood of the clitoris.

**Cavernous bodies** The structures in the shaft of the clitoris that engorge with blood during sexual arousal.

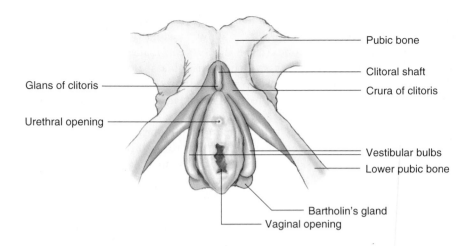

**Figure 4.2** The underlying structures of the vulva.

Pubic bone

Clitoral shaft

Glans of clitoris

Crura of clitoris

Urethral opening

Vestibular bulbs

Lower pubic bone

Bartholin's gland

Vaginal opening

**? Critical Thinking Question**

What should parents tell their daughters about their clitorises?

waste elimination, the only purpose of the clitoris is sexual pleasure and arousal.

In some parts of the world the sexual role of the clitoris is so troubling that the structure is removed during female genital cutting, as described in the following Sexuality and Diversity discussion.

## SEXUALITY AND DIVERSITY

### *Female Genital Cutting: Torture or Tradition?*

Various forms of female genital cutting have been practiced at some time in almost all parts of the world, including the United States from 1890 through the late 1930s to "cure" masturbation (Hamilton, 2002). Genital cutting still occurs in the United States when girls are born with a larger than normal clitoris—a topic of increasing controversy (Coventry, 2000). Each year approximately 2 million girls and women in more than 40 countries in Africa, the Middle East, and Asia undergo one of several types of genital cutting, usually as part of an initiation from childhood to womanhood and to become eligible for marriage (Leye, 2006). "Female genital mutilation" is another term for female genital cutting, but many women who have undergone these procedures believe that their genitals are made more appealing rather than "mutilated" (Nour, 2006). The village midwife or a health worker performs the procedures, which are usually arranged by the girl's mother (Mwai, 2006; Prince-Gibson, 2000). The simplest procedure, circumcision, consists of cutting off the clitoral hood. Another common practice is the removal of the clitoris itself, called clitoridectomy. In the most extreme practice, genital infibulation, the clitoris and the labia are cut off. Then both sides of the vulva are scraped raw and stitched up (sometimes with thorns) while the girl is held down. Razor blades or broken glass are used to cut the tissue, and the procedure is done without anesthetics, disinfectants, or sterile instruments (Rosenthal, 2006). The girl's legs are bound closed around the ankles and thighs for about a week (Nour, 2000). The tissue then grows together, leaving only a small opening for urine and menstrual flow to pass through. It is estimated that 130 million women and girls now living have undergone one of these forms of genital cutting, and 96 percent of married women in Egypt have been circumsized (El-Zanaty & Way, 2006; Nour, 2006).

© Marie Dorigny/Sipa Press

A baby girl is about to undergo female genital cutting in Ethiopia, where both Muslims and Christians still continue this practice despite a constitutional ban.

The main objective of genital cutting is to ensure virginity before marriage. Young girls are considered unmarriageable if they do not have the prescribed excision. Because marriage is usually the only role for a woman in these cultures, her future and her family's pride depend on upholding this tradition. About 60 percent of Egyptian women believe that husbands prefer a wife to be circumcised (El-Zanaty & Way, 2006). The social stigma for remaining uncircumcised is severe. For example, in Sudan one of the most vile invectives a man can be called is "the son of an uncircumcised mother" (Al-Krenawi & Weisel-Lev, 1999).

The most serious gynecological and obstetric complications often arise from genital infibulation. These include bleeding and pain that lead to shock and death, prolonged bleeding that leads to anemia, and infection that causes delayed healing, tetanus, and gangrene. Long-term consequences include urinary obstruction, blockage of menstrual flow, and recurrent reproductive tract infections. Infertility rates are higher among women whose labia were removed (Ball, 2005). Extensive vaginal scarring can cause serious difficulties during childbirth; 50% more women who have undergone genital cutting die from delivery complications (along with their babies) than women who have not been cut (Eke & Nkanginieme, 2006). Because of recent immigration patterns, U.S. obstetricians and gynecologists are encountering some of the estimated 168,000 girls and women now living in the United States who have undergone genital cutting (Elwood, 2005; Sugar & Graham, 2006).

The outcry over female genital cutting has pushed the United Nations to suspend its policy of nonintervention in the cultural practices of individual nations. The United Nations Fourth World Conference on Women in 1995 also condemned female genital cutting. Unfortunately, the strength of cultural tradition in many societies remains difficult to overcome, and even where the practice is illegal, the laws are difficult to enforce (Nour, 2006). This issue has raised complex legal and ethical questions. Canada was the first nation to recognize female genital cutting as a basis for granting refugee status. In 1996 the highest U.S. immigration court granted asylum to a West African teenager for protection against female genital cutting (Superville, 1996). ■

- Female genital cutting

A good deal of controversy has surrounded the role of the clitoris in sexual arousal and orgasm. Despite long-existing scientific knowledge about the highly concentrated nerve endings in the clitoris, the erroneous belief has persisted that vaginal rather than clitoral stimulation is—or should be—exclusively responsible for female sexual arousal and orgasm. However, the clitoris is far more sensitive to touch than the vagina. The interior of the vagina does contain nerve endings, but not the type that respond to light touch (Pauls et al., 2006). (This is why women do not feel tampons or diaphragms when they are correctly in place.) Nevertheless, many women find internal pressure and stretching sensations inside the vagina during manual stimulation or intercourse highly pleasurable. Some women experience more intense arousal from vaginal stimulation than from clitoral stimulation, especially after they are aroused and the vaginal tissues are fully engorged. Research using brain-imaging technology has found that women (with and without spinal cord injury) can experience orgasm using cervical self-stimulation (Whipple & Komisaruk, 2006). As more and more scientific research is done, a wider range of individual variation becomes apparent (Ellison, 2000).

**? Critical Thinking Question**

How are the genital piercing and cosmetic labiaplasty done for women in the Western world similar to and different from the genital cutting done to women in Africa, the Middle East, and Asia?

## The Vestibule

The **vestibule** (VES-ti-byool) is the area of the vulva inside the labia minora. It is rich in blood vessels and nerve endings, and its tissues are sensitive to touch. (In architectural terminology the word *vestibule* refers to the entryway of a house.) Both the urinary and the vaginal openings are located within the vestibule.

**Vestibule** The area of the vulva inside the labia minora.

## The Urethral Opening

Urine collected in the bladder passes out of a woman's body through the urethral opening. The **urethra** (yoo-REE-thruh) is the short tube connecting the bladder to the urinary opening, located between the clitoris and the vaginal opening.

**Urethra** The tube through which urine passes from the bladder.

## The Introitus and the Hymen

**Introitus** The opening to the vagina.

**Hymen** Tissue that partially covers the vaginal opening.

The opening of the vagina, called the **introitus** (in-TROH-i-tus), is located between the urinary opening and the anus. Partially covering the introitus is a fold of tissue called the **hymen** (HIGH-men), which is typically present at birth and usually remains intact until initial coitus. The hymen opening is usually large enough to insert tampons. Occasionally, this tissue is too thick to break easily during intercourse; a medical practitioner might then be needed to make a minor incision. In rare cases an *imperforate hymen*, tissue that completely seals the vaginal opening, causes menstrual flow to collect inside the vagina. When this condition is discovered, a medical practitioner can open the hymen with an incision. Although it is rare, it is possible for a woman to become pregnant even if her hymen is still intact and she has not experienced penile penetration. If semen is placed on the labia minora, the sperm can swim into the vagina. Unless pregnancy is desired, sexual play involving rubbing the penis and vulva together should be avoided without contraception.

Although the hymen can protect the vaginal tissues early in life, it has no other known function. Nevertheless, many societies, including our own, have placed great significance on its presence or absence. Euphemisms such as *cherry* or *maidenhead* have been used to describe the hymen. In our society and many others, people have long believed that a woman's virginity can be proved by the pain and bleeding that can occur with initial coitus, or "deflowering." At different times in various cultures blood-stained wedding-night bed sheets were seen as proof that the groom had wed "intact goods" and that the marriage had been consummated. Even today, some women, particularly women from Japan and the Middle East, undergo *hymenalplasty*, surgical reconstruction of the hymen, to conceal the loss of their virginity (Alexander, 2005).

Although pain or bleeding sometimes occurs during initial coitus, the hymen can be partial, flexible, or thin enough for no discomfort or bleeding to occur; it may even remain intact after intercourse. If a woman manually stretches her hymen before initial intercourse, she may be able to minimize the discomfort that sometimes occurs. To do this, first insert a lubricated finger (using saliva or a water-soluble sterile lubricant) into the vaginal opening and press downward toward the anus until you feel some stretching. After a few seconds, release the pressure and relax. Repeat this step several times. Next, insert two fingers into the vagina and stretch the sides of the vagina by opening the fingers. Repeat the downward stretching with two fingers as well. ■

**Sexual Health**

## The Perineum

**Perineum** The area between the vagina and anus of the female and the scrotum and anus of the male.

The **perineum** (per-uh-NEE-um) is the area of smooth skin between the vaginal opening and the anus (the sphincter through which bowel movements pass). The perineal tissue is endowed with nerve endings and is sensitive to touch. During childbirth, an incision called an *episiotomy* is sometimes made in the perineum to prevent the ragged tearing of tissues that can occur when the newborn passes through the birth canal. We will discuss this in more detail in Chapter 11.

## ◐ Underlying Structures

If the hair, skin, and fatty pads were removed from the vulva, several underlying structures could be seen (see Figure 4.2). The shaft of the clitoris would be visible, no longer concealed by the hood, as would the crura. These bodies are part of the vast network of bulbs and vessels that engorge with blood during sexual arousal. The **vestibular** (veh-STIB-yoo-ler) **bulbs** alongside the vagina also fill with blood during sexual excitement, causing the vagina to lengthen and the vulvar area to swell. These bulbs are similar in structure and function to the spongy tissue in the penis that engorges during arousal and causes erection (Bartlik & Goldberg, 2000). Compression of these tissues by the penis during intercourse causes internal sensations that some women find pleasurable (Ellison, 2000).

**Vestibular bulbs** Two bulbs, one on each side of the vaginal opening, that engorge with blood during sexual arousal.

**Bartholin's glands** Two small glands slightly inside the vaginal opening that secrete a few drops of fluid during sexual arousal.

**Bartholin's glands**, one on each side of the vaginal opening, were once believed to be the source of vaginal lubrication during sexual arousal; however, they typically produce only a drop or two of fluid just before orgasm. The glands are usually not

## Kegel Exercises

The pelvic floor muscles squeeze involuntarily at orgasm; they can also be trained to contract voluntarily through a series of exercises known as **Kegel** (KAY-gul) **exercises**. These exercises were developed by Arnold Kegel in 1952 to help women regain urinary control after childbirth. (Because of excessive stretching and tearing of perineal muscles during childbirth, women who have recently given birth commonly lose urine when they cough or sneeze.) Kegel exercises have been shown to have other effects besides restoring muscle tone (Beji, 2003). After about 6 weeks of regular exercise, many women report increased sensation during intercourse and a general increase in genital sensitivity. This seems to be associated with their increased awareness of their sex organs and their improved muscle tone.

The steps for the Kegel exercises are as follows:

1. Locate the muscles surrounding the vagina. This can be done by stopping the flow of urine to feel which muscles contract. An even more effective way of contracting the pelvic floor muscles is to contract the anal sphincter as if to hold back gas.
2. Insert a finger into the opening of your vagina and contract the muscles you located in Step 1. Feel the muscles squeeze your finger.
3. Squeeze the same muscles for 10 seconds. Relax. Repeat 10 times.
4. Squeeze and release as rapidly as possible, 10 to 25 times. Repeat.
5. Imagine trying to suck something into your vagina. Hold for 3 seconds.
6. This exercise series should be done three times a day.

---

noticeable, but sometimes the duct from a Bartholin's gland becomes clogged, and the fluid that is normally secreted remains inside and causes enlargement. If this occurs and the swelling does not subside within a few days, it is best to see a health-care practitioner. Besides the glands and network of vessels, a complex musculature underlies the genital area, as seen in ❿ **Figure 4.3**. The *pelvic floor muscles* have a multidirectional design that allows the vaginal opening to expand greatly during childbirth and to contract afterward.

**Kegel exercises** A series of exercises that strengthen the muscles underlying the external female or male genitals.

## ❿ Internal Structures

Internal female sexual anatomy consists of the vagina, cervix, uterus, and ovaries. These are discussed in the following sections. Refer to ❿ **Figure 4.4** for cross-section and front views of the female pelvis.

### The Vagina

The **vagina** is a canal that opens between the labia minora and extends into the body, angling upward toward the small of the back, to the cervix and uterus. Most women

**Vagina** A stretchable canal in the female that opens at the vulva and extends about 4 inches into the pelvis.

❿ **Figure 4.3** The underlying muscles of the vulva. These muscles can be strengthened by using the Kegel exercises described in the Your Sexual Health box.

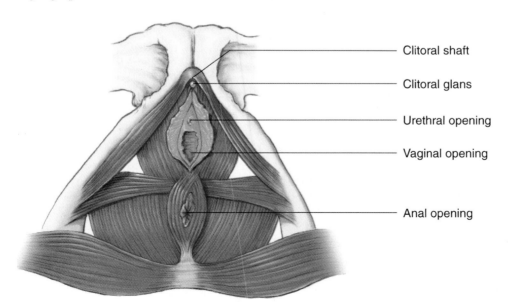

Clitoral shaft

Clitoral glans

Urethral opening

Vaginal opening

Anal opening

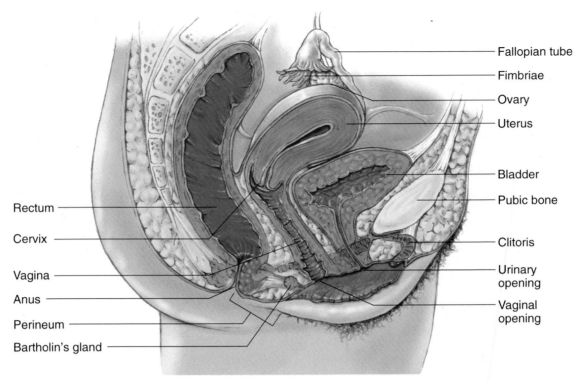

Fallopian tube
Fimbriae
Ovary
Uterus

Bladder
Pubic bone

Clitoris
Urinary opening
Vaginal opening

Rectum
Cervix
Vagina
Anus
Perineum
Bartholin's gland

(a) **Side view**

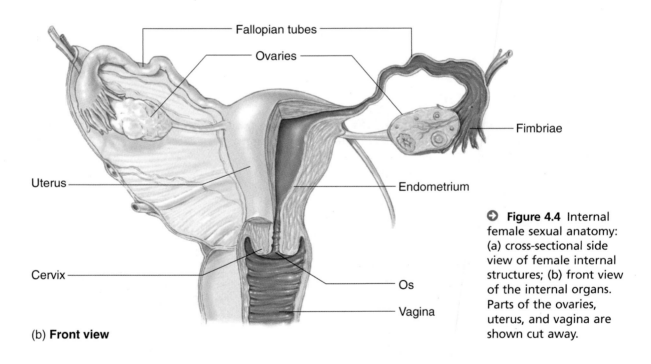

Fallopian tubes
Ovaries

Fimbriae

Uterus

Endometrium

Cervix

Os
Vagina

(b) **Front view**

⬡ **Figure 4.4** Internal female sexual anatomy: (a) cross-sectional side view of female internal structures; (b) front view of the internal organs. Parts of the ovaries, uterus, and vagina are shown cut away.

have never seen inside their own vaginas, but it is possible to do so during their regular pelvic exams. The health-care practitioner can use a mirror to show a woman her vagina after the speculum is holding the vaginal walls open. Women who are unfamiliar with their anatomy can have a difficult time when they first try inserting a tampon into the vagina:

> *No matter how hard I tried, I couldn't get a tampon in until I inserted a finger and realized that my vagina slanted backward. I had been pushing straight up onto the upper wall. (Authors' files)*

The unaroused vagina is approximately 3 to 5 inches long. The analogy of a glove is often used to illustrate the vagina as a potential rather than an actual space, with its walls able to expand enough to serve as a birth passage. In addition, the vagina changes in size and shape during sexual arousal, as we will discuss in Chapter 6.

The vagina contains three layers of tissue: mucous, muscle, and fibrous tissue. All these layers are richly endowed with blood vessels. The **mucosa** (myoo-KOH-suh) is the layer of mucous membrane that a woman feels when she inserts a finger inside her vagina. The folded walls, or **rugae** (ROO-jee), feel soft, moist, and warm, resembling the inside of one's mouth. The walls normally produce secretions that help maintain the chemical balance of the vagina. During sexual arousal, a lubricating substance exudes through the mucosa.

Most of the second layer, composed of muscle tissue, is concentrated around the vaginal opening. Because of the concentration of musculature in the outer third and the expansive ability of the inner two thirds of the vagina, a situation often develops that can be at best funny and at worst embarrassing. During headstands and certain yoga or coital positions with the pelvis elevated, gravity causes the inner two thirds to expand and draw air into the vagina. The outer muscles tighten, and the trapped air is forced back out through the tightened muscles, creating a sound we usually associate with a different orifice. One student has suggested calling this phenomenon "varting," because the sound is similar to that of a fart (fortunately, there is no unpleasant smell). Surrounding the muscular layer is the innermost vaginal layer, composed of fibrous tissue. This layer aids in vaginal contraction and expansion and acts as connective tissue to other structures in the pelvic cavity.

## Arousal and Vaginal Lubrication

So far in this chapter, we have described the parts of the female sexual anatomy, but we have said relatively little about how these structures function. Because lubrication is a unique feature of the vagina, the process is explained here. Other physiological aspects of female arousal will be discussed in Chapter 6.

During sexual arousal, a clear, slippery fluid begins to appear on the vaginal mucosa within 10 to 30 seconds after effective physical or psychological stimulation begins. This lubrication is a result of **vasocongestion**, caused by the extensive network of blood vessels in the tissues surrounding the vagina engorging with blood. Clear fluid seeps from the congested tissues to the inside of the vaginal walls to form the characteristic slippery coating of the sexually aroused vagina.

Vaginal lubrication serves two functions. First, it enhances the possibility of conception by helping to alkalinize the normally acidic vaginal chemical balance. Vaginal pH level changes from 4.5 to 6.0–6.5 with sexual arousal (Meston, 2000). Sperm travel faster and survive longer in an alkaline environment than in an acidic one. (The seminal fluid of the male also helps alkalinize the vagina.) Second, vaginal lubrication can increase sexual enjoyment. During manual genital stimulation, the slippery wetness can increase the sensuousness and pleasure of touching. During oral–genital sex, some women's partners enjoy the erotic scent and taste of the vaginal lubrication. During intercourse, vaginal lubrication makes the walls of the vagina slippery, which facilitates entry of the penis into the vagina. Lubrication also helps make the thrusting of intercourse pleasurable. Without adequate lubrication, entry of the penis and subsequent thrusting can be uncomfortable for the woman—and often for the man. Irritation and small tears of the vaginal tissue can result.

Insufficient vaginal lubrication can be remedied in several ways, depending on the source of the difficulty. Changing any anxiety-producing circumstances and engaging in effective stimulation are important. Saliva, lubricated condoms, or a nonirritating water-soluble jelly can be used to provide additional lubrication. Occasionally, hormone treatment is necessary. ■

## The Grafenberg Spot

The **Grafenberg spot** is an area within the anterior (or front) wall of the vagina, about 1 centimeter from the skin's surface and one third to one half the way in from the vaginal opening. It consists of a system of glands (Skene's glands) and ducts that

**Mucosa** Collective term for the mucous membranes; moist tissue that lines certain body areas such as the penile urethra, vagina, and mouth.

**Rugae** The folds of tissue in the vagina.

**Vasocongestion** The engorgement of blood vessels in particular body parts in response to sexual arousal.

Sexual Health

**Grafenberg spot** Glands and ducts in the anterior wall of the vagina. Some women experience sexual pleasure, arousal, orgasm, and an ejaculation of fluids from stimulation of the Grafenberg spot.

surround the urethra. This area is believed to be the female counterpart to the male prostate gland, developed from the same embryonic tissue (Heath, 1984).

The Grafenberg spot has generated considerable interest because of reports that some women experience sexual arousal, orgasm, and perhaps even an ejaculation of fluid when stimulated there (Darling et al., 1990), although many women do not have such an area of increased sensation. We will further discuss the role of the Grafenberg spot in female sexual response in Chapter 6.

## Vaginal Secretions and Chemical Balance of the Vagina

Both the vaginal walls and the cervix (discussed on p. 89) produce white or yellowish secretions. These secretions are normal and are a sign of vaginal health. They vary in appearance according to hormone level changes during the menstrual cycle. (Keeping track of these variations is the basis for one method of birth control, discussed in Chapter 10.) The taste and scent of vaginal secretions can also vary with the time of a woman's cycle and her level of arousal.

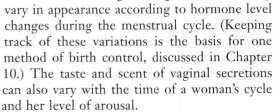

Eve Ensler's one-woman play *The Vagina Monologues* answers the question, "If your vagina could talk, what would it say?" Ensler's play has spurred a global grassroots movement, called V-Day, to stop violence against women and girls.

**Douching** Rinsing out the vagina with plain water or a variety of solutions. It is usually unnecessary for hygiene, and douching too often can result in vaginal irritation.

The vagina's natural chemical and bacterial balance helps promote healthy mucosa. The chemical balance is normally rather acidic (pH 4.5*—the same as in red wine [Angier, 1999]). A variety of factors can alter this balance, resulting in vaginal problems. Among these are **douching** (rinsing out the inside of the vagina) and using feminine-hygiene sprays. Douching is definitely *not* necessary for routine hygiene and can alter the natural chemical balance of the vagina. Douching can increase a woman's susceptibility to infections and other health risks, although most women mistakenly believe douching is healthy (Ness et al., 2003). Various studies have found that douching increases the risk of pelvic inflammatory disease, endometriosis (discussed on p. 94), transmission of HIV, ectopic pregnancy (discussed on p. 89), and decreased fertility. Furthermore, douching during pregnancy increases the likelihood of preterm births (Cottrell, 2003). Feminine-hygiene sprays can cause irritation, allergic reactions, burns, infections, dermatitis of the thighs, and numerous other problems. In fact, genital deodorant sprays and body powders have been associated with an increased risk of ovarian cancer (Cook et al., 1997). Furthermore, deodorant tampons are unnecessary: Menstrual fluid has virtually no odor until it is outside the body. Regular bathing with a mild soap and washing between the folds of the vulva are all that are necessary for proper hygiene.

Advertising has turned our cultural negativity about female sexual organs into extremely profitable businesses. Women grow up hearing slogans such as "Unfortunately, the trickiest deodorant problem a girl has isn't under her pretty little arms," and "Our product eliminates the moist, uncomfortable feeling most women normally have just because they're women."

Consequently, women in the United States spend about $500 million each year on over-the-counter douches. Minorities and educationally and economically disadvantaged women appear more vulnerable to this misinformation: Twice as many African American women douche than white women, and regardless of race, the prevalence of douching is higher in women who have less education and income (Cottrell, 2003).

---

*pH is a measure of acidity or alkalinity. A neutral substance (neither acidic nor alkaline) has a pH of 7. A lower number means a substance is more acidic; a higher number means it is more alkaline.

## The Cervix

The **cervix** (SER-viks), located at the back of the vagina, is the small end of the pear-shaped uterus (see Figure 4.4). The cervix contains mucus-secreting glands. Sperm pass through the vagina into the uterus through the **os**, the opening in the center of the cervix.

A woman can see her own cervix if she learns to insert a **speculum** into her vagina. She can also ask for a mirror when she has her pelvic exam. A woman can feel her own cervix by inserting one or two fingers into the vagina and reaching to the end of the canal. (Sometimes squatting and bearing down brings the cervix closer to the vaginal entrance.) The cervix feels somewhat like the end of a nose, firm and round in contrast to the soft vaginal walls.

Saturn Stills/Photo Researchers, Inc.

## The Uterus

The **uterus** (YOO-tuh-rus), or womb, is a hollow, thick, pear-shaped organ, approximately 3 inches long and 2 inches wide in a woman who has never had a child. (It is somewhat larger after pregnancy.) The uterus is suspended in the pelvic cavity by ligaments; in different women its position can vary from *anteflexed* (tipped forward toward the abdomen) to *retroflexed* (tipped back toward the spine). Women with retroflexed uteri are more likely to experience menstrual discomfort or have difficulty inserting a diaphragm. Although it was once thought that a retroflexed uterus interfered with conception, it does not impair fertility.

The walls of the uterus consist of three layers. The external layer is a thin membrane called the **perimetrium** (pear-ee-MEE-tree-um). The middle layer, or **myometrium** (my-oh-MEE-tree-um), is made of longitudinal and circular muscle fibers that interweave like the fibers of a basket; this enables the uterus to stretch during pregnancy and contract during labor and orgasm. At the top of the uterus, an area called the *fundus*, the uterine walls are especially thick. The inner lining of the uterus is called the **endometrium** (en-doh-MEE-treeum). Rich in blood vessels, the endometrium nourishes the *zygote* (united sperm and egg), which travels down to the uterus from the fallopian tubes after fertilization. In preparation for this event, the endometrium thickens in response to hormone changes during the monthly menstrual cycle, discussed later in this chapter. The endometrium is also a source of hormone production.

## The Fallopian Tubes

Each of the two 4-inch **fallopian** (fuh-LOH-pee-un) **tubes** extends from the uterus toward an ovary, at the left or the right side of the pelvic cavity (see Figure 4.4). The outside end of each tube is shaped like a funnel, with fringelike projections called **fimbriae** (FIM-bree-eye) that hover over the ovary. When the egg leaves the ovary, it is drawn into the tube by the fimbriae.

Once the egg is inside the fallopian tube, the movements of tiny hairlike cilia and the contractions of the tube walls move it along at a rate of approximately 1 inch every 24 hours. The egg remains viable for fertilization for about 24 to 48 hours. Therefore fertilization occurs while the egg is still close to the ovary. After fertilization the zygote begins developing as it continues traveling down the tube to the uterus.

An **ectopic pregnancy** occurs when a fertilized ovum implants in tissue outside of the uterus, most commonly in the fallopian tube (Ramarkrishnan & Scheid, 2006). This implantation can rupture the tube and cause uncontrolled bleeding, which is a serious medical emergency. The most common symptoms of ectopic pregnancy are

The speculum opens the walls of the vaginal canal.

**Cervix** The small end of the uterus, located at the back of the vagina.

**Os** The opening in the cervix that leads to the interior of the uterus.

**Speculum** An instrument used to open the vaginal walls during a gynecological exam. The speculum opens the walls of the vaginal canal.

**Uterus** A pear-shaped organ inside the female pelvis, within which the fetus develops.

**Perimetrium** The thin membrane covering the outside of the uterus.

**Myometrium** The smooth muscle layer of the uterine wall.

**Endometrium** The tissue that lines the inside of the uterine wall.

**Fallopian tubes** Two tubes, extending from the sides of the uterus, in which the egg and sperm travel.

**Fimbriae** Fringelike ends of the fallopian tubes, into which the released ovum enters.

**Ectopic pregnancy** A pregnancy that occurs when a fertilized ovum implants outside the uterus, most commonly in a fallopian tube.

abdominal pain and spotting that occur 6 to 8 weeks after the last menstrual period. Diagnostic tests can establish the presence of an ectopic pregnancy, and medical and surgical procedures are used to treat it (Scott, 2006).

### The Ovaries

**Ovaries** Female gonads that produce ova and sex hormones.

The two **ovaries**, which are about the size and shape of almonds, are at the ends of the fallopian tubes, one on each side of the uterus. They are connected to the pelvic wall and the uterus by ligaments. The ovaries are endocrine glands that produce three classes of sex hormones. The estrogens, as mentioned in Chapter 3, influence development of female physical sex characteristics and help regulate the menstrual cycle. The progestational compounds also help regulate the menstrual cycle and promote maturity of the uterine lining in preparation for pregnancy. The ovaries also produce about half of a woman's testosterone (Lemonick, 2004). Around the onset of puberty the female sex hormones play a critical role in initiating maturation of the uterus, ovaries, and vagina and in developing the secondary sex characteristics, such as pubic hair and breasts.

**Ovulation** The release of a mature ovum from the ovary.

The ovaries contain about 1 million immature ova at birth and between 400,000 and 500,000 at menarche (Federman, 2006). During the years between puberty and menopause, one or the other ovary typically releases an egg during each cycle. Only 400 ova are destined for full maturation during a woman's reproductive years (Macklon & Fauser, 2000). **Ovulation** (ahv-yoo-LAY-shun), or egg maturation and release, occurs as the result of the complex chain of events we know as the menstrual cycle, discussed in the next section.

## ● Menstruation

**Menstruation** The sloughing off of the built-up uterine lining that takes place if conception has not occurred.

**Menstruation** (men-stroo-A-shun), the sloughing off of uterine lining that takes place if conception has not occurred, is a sign of normal physical functioning. Negative attitudes about it persist in contemporary American society; however, young women typically have more positive attitudes about menstruation than do women in older generations (Maravan et al., 2005).

### Attitudes About Menstruation

American folklore reveals many interesting ideas about menstruation and raises the question whether negative beliefs about menstruation are meant to constrain women and reinforce their lower social status (Forbes et al., 2003). Myths include the belief that it is harmful for a woman to be physically active during menstruation, that a corsage worn by a menstruating woman will wilt, and that a tooth filling done during menstruation will fall out (Milow, 1983). Contemporary Orthodox Jews adhere to the Bible concerning sexual contact during menstruation: "And if a woman have an issue and her issue in her flesh be blood, she shall be apart seven days: and whosoever toucheth her shall be unclean until the even" (Leviticus 15:19). In practice, an Orthodox Jewish woman avoids sexual activity until after a ceremonial cleansing bath following the end of her period. One intention of this monthly abstinence is to help keep the couple's sexual desire for one another strong (Rothbaum & Jackson, 1990).

Native American women retreated to special huts during menstruation.

The meanings of menstrual rituals in other cultures are often ambiguous, and little is actually known about the significance of menstrual taboos. In some societies a menstruating woman is isolated from the community and remains in a "menstrual hut." Researchers have rarely asked about the meaning of and experiences in the menstrual huts. Do women feel resentful and diminished or honored and pleased by the break from normal labor? Scattered reports suggest considerable variability, with positive meanings being fairly common. Menstrual customs can provide women with a means of solidarity, influence, and autonomy. For example, in some Native American traditions, women were believed to be at their most powerful during menstruation. They would retreat to a "moon lodge" to be free of mundane daily chores. Blood flow was believed to purify women and to enable them to gather spiritual wisdom to benefit the entire tribe. Most Native American tribes also had celebrations for a girl's first menstruation (Angier, 1999; Owen, 1993). For the Inca Indians in South America, shedding blood symbolized the transformation into adulthood; boys bled when elders pierced the boys' ears and inserted large ear spools as part of their coming-of-age ceremony (Wiesner-Hanks, 2000).

**InfoTrac Search Words**

- Menstruation

In a few cultures menstruation is described in lyrical words and positive images. The Japanese expression for a girl's first menstruation is "the year of the cleavage of the melon," and one East Indian description of menstruation is the "flower growing in the house of the god of love" (Delaney et al., 1976). In some contemporary Hindu and Muslim Indian families, a religious ceremony is held after a girl begins menstruation (Marvan et al., 2006).

Despite negative myths and societal attitudes toward menstruation, most women associate regular menstrual cycles with healthy functioning and femininity. Further, research has found that women who have positive attitudes toward, and are comfortable with, menstruation are less likely to take sexual risks and more likely to be more comfortable with their bodies and with being sexually assertive than are women who have negative attitudes toward menstruation (Schooler, 2005). In addition, women who had been sexual with their partner during their periods were particularly comfortable with menstruation and were more aroused by sexual activities (Rempel & Baumgartner, 2003).

**Critical Thinking Question**

What messages about menstruation do you observe in advertising and television programs?

Some women and families are redefining menstruation from a more positive perspective. For example, some may have a celebration or give a gift to a young woman when she has her first menstrual period (Kissling, 2002). One aspect of the menstrual cycle that people often see as positive is its cyclic pattern, typical of many natural phenomena.

The poet May Sarton describes the analogy between the menstrual cycle and nature in this 1937 poem:*

> There were seeds  
> within her  
> that burst at intervals  
> and for a little while  
> she would come back  
> to heaviness,

> and then before a surging miracle  
> of blood,  
> relax, and re-identify herself,  
> each time more closely  
> with the heart of life.

## Menarche

The menstrual cycle usually begins in the early teens, between the ages of 11 and 15, although some girls begin earlier or later. The first menstrual bleeding is called **menarche** (MEH-nar-kee). The timing of menarche appears to be related to heredity, general health, and altitude (average menarche is earlier in lower altitudes) and occurs during a time of other changes in body size and development (Forbes, 1992). Menstrual cycles end at menopause, which in most women occurs between the ages of 45 and 55. Differences in the age of menarche are often a concern for young women, especially those who begin earlier or later than the norm. Many young women, and most young men, are not fully informed about the developments and changes that accompany the onset of menstruation, and that lack of knowledge can result in confusion and apprehension.

**Menarche** The initial onset of menstrual periods in a young woman.

## Menstrual Physiology

During the menstrual cycle the uterine lining is prepared for the implantation of a fertilized ovum. If conception does not occur, the lining sloughs off and is discharged

---

*" 'She Shall Be Called Woman' Part 5" from *Collected Poems 1930–1933* by May Sarton. Copyright © 1998, 1984, 1993, 1980, 1974 by May Sarton. Reprinted by permission of W. W. Norton & Company, Inc.

as menstrual flow. The length of the menstrual cycle is usually measured from the beginning of the first day of flow to the day before the next flow begins. The menstrual period itself typically lasts 2 to 6 days. It is normal for the volume of the menstrual flow (usually 6 to 8 ounces) to vary. The cycle length varies from woman to woman; it can be anywhere from 24 to 42 days, but higher fertility may be associated with the length of cycle. One study found that women who menstruated every 30 to 31 days had higher rates of pregnancy than did women with shorter or longer cycles (Small et al., 2006). (This is *not* to say that women with shorter and longer cycles are protected from pregnancy).

Regardless of the total cycle length, the interval between ovulation and the onset of menstruation is 14 days, plus or minus 2 days, even when there is several weeks' difference in the total length of the cycle, as shown in ➲ **Figure 4.5**. Some women experience a twinge, cramp, or pressure in the lower abdomen, called Mittelschmerz (German for middle pain), at ovulation. Mittelschmerz is caused by the swelling and bursting of the follicle or by a little fluid or blood from the ruptured follicle that irritates the sensitive abdominal lining. The released ovum then travels to the fallopian tube. Occasionally, more than one ovum is released. If two ova are fertilized, nonidentical twins will develop. When one egg is fertilized and then divides into two separate zygotes, identical twins result.

Around the time of ovulation, secretions of cervical mucus increase because of increased levels of estrogen. The mucus also changes, becoming clear, slippery, and stretchy. The pH of this mucus is more alkaline; as noted earlier, a more alkaline vaginal environment contributes to sperm motility and longevity. This is the time in the cycle when a woman can most easily become pregnant.

## Menstrual Synchrony

An interesting phenomenon known as **menstrual synchrony** sometimes occurs among women who live together and have considerable contact with one another: They develop similar menstrual cycles (Cutler, 1999). The function of the uniform cycles is unknown, but the sense of smell is believed to be the trigger.

To test this hypothesis, researchers had subjects with normal menstrual cycles swab their upper lips with either perspiration extract from another woman or with plain alcohol. Within three menstrual cycles 80% of the subjects who had received the perspiration extract were menstruating in sync with their perspiration donors. The control group showed no menstrual cycle changes (Cutler et al., 1986).

**Menstrual synchrony**
Simultaneous menstrual cycles that sometimes occur among women who live in close proximity.

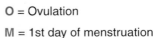

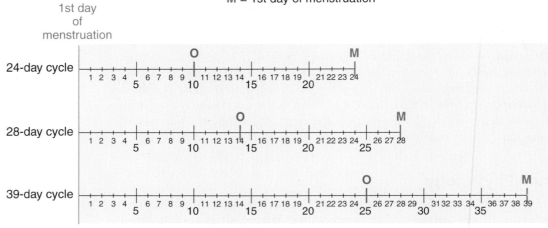

➲ **Figure 4.5** Ovulation timing and cycle length. Regardless of the length of the cycle, ovulation occurs 14 days before menstruation.

## The Menstrual Cycle

The menstrual cycle is regulated by intricate relationships between the hypothalamus and various endocrine glands, including the pituitary gland, the adrenal glands, and the ovaries and uterus. The hypothalamus monitors hormone levels in the bloodstream throughout the cycle, releasing chemicals that stimulate the pituitary to produce two hormones that affect the ovaries: **follicle-stimulating hormone (FSH)** and **luteinizing** (LOO-te-uh-ny-zing) **hormone (LH)**. FSH stimulates the ovaries to produce estrogen and also causes ova to mature in follicles (small sacs) within the ovaries. LH causes the ovary to release a mature ovum. LH also stimulates the development of the **corpus luteum** (the portion of the follicle that remains after the matured egg has been released), which produces the hormone progesterone.

The menstrual cycle is a self-regulating and dynamic process. Each hormone is secreted until the organ it acts on is stimulated; at that point the organ releases a substance that circulates back through the system to reduce hormonal activity in the initiating gland. This *negative-feedback mechanism* provides an internal control that regulates hormone fluctuation throughout the phases of the menstrual cycle.

## Sexual Activity and the Menstrual Cycle

A number of studies have tried to determine whether sexual interest is affected by the menstrual cycle. The findings vary from no change to increased interest at ovulation, during menstruation, or a few days prior to menstruation. In an attempt to control for external variables such as contraceptive use, fear of pregnancy, and male influence, one research group examined the relationship between cycle phase and sexual response and activity in a sample of lesbians. In this sample, partner- and self-initiated sexual activity increased in frequency at mid-cycle, as did orgasm, but sexual thoughts and fantasies peaked in the first 3 days after the onset of menstruation (Matteo & Rissman, 1984). Great individual variation appears to exist.

Couples often avoid sexual activity and intercourse during menstruation (Barnhart et al., 1995). Although from a medical point of view there are no health reasons to avoid intercourse during menstruation (except in the case of excessive bleeding or other menstrual problems), many couples do so. Reasons for avoiding sex during a woman's period vary. Uncomfortable physical symptoms of breast tenderness and menstruation can reduce sexual desire or pleasure, and the messiness can inhibit sexual playfulness. Religious beliefs can also be a factor. Some women and men avoid sexual activity because of culturally induced shame about menstruation. If people do prefer to abstain from coitus during menstruation, the remaining repertoire of sexual activities is still available:

> When I'm on my period, I leave my tampon inside and push the string in, too. My husband and I have manual and oral stimulation, and a great time! (Authors' files)

Some women use a diaphragm or cervical cap to hold back the menstrual flow during coitus. Orgasm by any means of stimulation can be beneficial to a menstruating woman. The uterine contractions and release of vasocongestion often reduce backache, feelings of pelvic fullness, and cramping.

## Menstrual Cycle Problems

Most women undergo some physical or mood changes, or both, during their menstrual cycles. In many cases the changes are minor; for others the symptoms interfere with their daily lives (Nelson, 2006). In some cases women experience heightened pleasant moods during ovulation or menstruation (McFarlane et al., 1988). Popular culture, as reflected by the media, tends to put forth negative and distorted perspectives about the menstrual cycle, particularly about premenstrual syndrome (PMS). An analysis of 78 magazine articles showed the perpetuation of the stereotype of the maladjusted woman, listing 131 different symptoms of PMS. Titles included, "The Taming of the Shrew Inside of You" and "Premenstrual Frenzy" (Chrisler & Levy, 1990).

**Follicle-stimulating hormone (FSH)** A pituitary hormone secreted by a female during the secretory phase of the menstrual cycle. FSH stimulates the development of ovarian follicles. In males it stimulates sperm production.

**Luteinizing hormone (LH)** The hormone secreted by the pituitary gland that stimulates ovulation in the female. In males it is called the interstitial cell hormone (ISCH) and stimulates production of androgens by the testes.

**Corpus luteum** A yellowish body that forms on the ovary at the site of the ruptured follicle and secretes progesterone.

Most scientific research about menstruation has focused on negative effects. However, one study compared women's responses to the Menstrual Joy Questionnaire (MJQ) with those of a commonly used research tool, the Menstrual Distress Questionnaire. The MJQ's questions about such positive qualities as increased sexual desire, high spirits, feelings of affection, and self-confidence did result in subjects later reporting more-positive attitudes and fewer negative symptoms about menstruation. The researchers concluded that the way menstruation is portrayed by research and popular culture affects how women think about their menstrual cycles (Chrisler et al., 1994).

## Premenstrual Syndrome

**Premenstrual syndrome (PMS)** Symptoms of physical discomfort and emotional irritability that occur 2 to 12 days before menstruation.

**Premenstrual syndrome (PMS)** is a catchall term used to identify myriad physical and psychological symptoms that can occur before each menstrual period. As many as 200 premenstrual symptoms are listed in medical and research literature (O'Brien et al., 2000). Typical symptoms include bloating, breast swelling, and pain. (Fat layers in the waist and thighs become slightly thicker before menstruation—hence the period-related tight-jeans syndrome [Pearson, 2000].) Psychological symptoms include irritability, tension, depression, mood swings, and a feeling of a lack of emotional control. Some of these PMS symptoms can be disruptive to close relationships and result in increased conflict and withdrawal (Pearlstein et al., 2000).

InfoTrac Search Words

• PMDD

Approximately 80–95% of women experience mild discomfort premenstrually, and only 5% have no PMS symptoms before menstruation. Five percent of women have symptoms severe enough for a diagnosis of **premenstrual dysphoric disorder (PMDD)**, with symptoms significantly affecting their normal functioning (Steiner et al., 2006).

**Premenstrual dysphoric disorder (PMDD)** Premenstrual symptoms severe enough to significantly disrupt a woman's functioning.

The causes of PMS and PMDD are unknown (Girman et al., 2003). Placebo-controlled studies have shown that medications used for depression, called SSRIs, alleviate physical and psychological symptoms and improve quality of life and interpersonal functioning (Steiner et al., 2006). Oral contraceptives can also help some women (Doheny, 2006).

## Dysmenorrhea

**Dysmenorrhea** Pain or discomfort before or during menstruation.

**Prostaglandins** Hormones that induce uterine contractions.

Painful menstruation is called **dysmenorrhea** (dis-meh-nuh-REE-uh). *Primary dysmenorrhea* occurs during menstruation and is usually caused by the overproduction of **prostaglandins**, chemicals that cause the muscles of the uterus to contract. Problems with primary dysmenorrhea usually appear with the onset of menstruation at adolescence. The symptoms are generally most noticeable during the first few days of a woman's period and include abdominal aching and/or cramping. Some women also experience nausea, vomiting, diarrhea, headache, dizziness, fatigue, irritability, or nervousness.

*Secondary dysmenorrhea* occurs before or during menstruation and is characterized by constant and often spasmodic lower abdominal pain that typically extends to the back and thighs. The symptoms are often similar to those of primary dysmenorrhea and are caused by factors other than prostaglandin production; possible causes include the presence of an intrauterine device (IUD), pelvic inflammatory disease (chronic infection of the reproductive organs), benign uterine tumors, obstruction of the cervical opening, and **endometriosis** (en-doh-mee-tree-OH-sis). Endometriosis, which affects up to 15% of premenopausal women (including adolescents), occurs when endometrial-like tissue implants in the abdominal cavity. The implanted tissue often adheres to other tissue in the pelvic cavity, reducing mobility of the internal structures while engorging with blood. The engorged tissues and adhesions can cause painful menstruation, lower backache, and pain from pressure and movement during intercourse. Once the cause of secondary dysmenorrhea has been diagnosed, appropriate treatment can begin (Propst & Laufer, 1999).

**Endometriosis** A condition in which uterine tissue grows on various parts of the abdominal cavity.

## Amenorrhea

**Amenorrhea** The absence of menstruation.

Besides discomfort or pain, another fairly common menstrual difficulty is **amenorrhea** (ay-meh-nuh-REE-uh), the absence of menstruation. Two types of amenorrhea exist: primary and secondary. *Primary amenorrhea* is the failure to begin to menstruate at puberty. It can be caused by problems with the reproductive organs, hormonal imbalances, poor health, or an imperforate hymen. *Secondary amenorrhea* involves the disruption of an established menstrual cycle, with the absence of menstruation for 3 months or more. This is a normal condition during pregnancy and breast-feeding. It is also common in women who have just begun menstruating and in women approaching menopause. Women who discontinue birth control pills occasionally do not menstruate for several months, but this situation is usually temporary and resolves spontaneously.

Amenorrhea is more common among athletes than among the general population (Colino, 2006). Women who experience athletic amenorrhea also have decreased estrogen levels. This reduction in estrogen can place them at increased risk for developing serious health problems, such as decreased bone mineral density, with a resultant increased incidence of bone fractures and atrophy of the genital tissues. Athletic amenorrhea can be reversed by improving diet, gaining weight, or in some cases, decreasing training intensity (Epp, 1997). Anabolic steroid use to attempt to enhance athletic performance will, among more dangerous side effects, cause amenorrhea (Kuipers, 1988). Medical or hormonal problems can produce amenorrhea (Hagan & Knott, 1998; Stener-Victorin et al., 2000). Women with *anorexia nervosa*, an eating disorder that often results in extreme weight loss, frequently stop menstruating because of hormonal changes that accompany emaciation (Ghizzani & Montomoli, 2000).

Planned amenorrhea can be desirable at times; most women would prefer not to be menstruating on their honeymoons, while camping, at a swim competition, or in many other situations. Since the standard oral contraceptive pill was introduced, many women have skipped the last seven dummy pills and begun a new pack to avoid a period (Miller, 2001). An oral contraceptive pill called Seasonale, designed so that women have only four periods a year, became available in 2003 (Kalb, 2003a).

## Self-Help for Menstrual Problems

Women may be able to alleviate some of the unpleasant symptoms before and during menstruation by their own actions. Moderate exercise throughout the month as well as proper diet can contribute to improvement of menstrual difficulties (Stearns, 2001). For example, increasing fluids and fiber helps with the constipation that sometimes occurs before and during menstruation. Decreasing salt intake and avoiding foods high in salt (salad dressing, potato chips, bacon, pickles, to name a few) can help reduce swelling and bloating caused by water retention. Food supplements such as calcium, magnesium, B vitamins, and 200 IU of vitamin E twice a day can also help relieve cramps and bloating (Gaby, 2005; Girman et al., 2003). Oral contraceptives usually decrease menstrual cramps and the amount of flow, and some women use them for those reasons alone (Nelson, 2006).

!  Sexual Health

A woman who experiences menstrual pain may find it useful to keep a diary to track symptoms, stresses, and daily habits, such as exercise, diet, and sleep. She may be able to note a relationship between symptoms and habits and modify her activities accordingly. The information can also be helpful for specific diagnosis if she consults a health-care practitioner. If a woman notices changes in her cycle that last for three months, she should consult her health-care provider (Colino, 2006). ■

## Toxic Shock Syndrome

In May 1980 the Centers for Disease Control (CDC) published the first report of **toxic shock syndrome (TSS)** in menstruating women. Symptoms of TSS, which is caused by toxins produced by the bacterium Staphylococcus aureus, include fever, sore throat, nausea, vomiting, diarrhea, red skin flush, dizziness, and low blood pressure (Hanrahan, 1994). Because TSS progresses rapidly and can cause death, a person with several of the symptoms of TSS should consult a physician immediately.

TSS is rare, and the number of reported TSS cases has fallen sharply since the peak in 1980, most likely as a result of removing highly absorbent tampons from the market (Petitti & Reingold, 1988). Some guidelines have been developed that can help to prevent toxic shock. One suggestion has been to use sanitary napkins instead

**Toxic shock syndrome (TSS)** A disease that occurs most commonly in menstruating women and that can cause a person to go into shock.

of tampons. For women who want to continue using tampons, it is advisable to use regular instead of super-absorbent tampons, to change tampons three to four times during the day, and to use napkins for some time during each 24 hours of menstrual flow.

# Menopause

**Climacteric** Physiological changes that occur during the transition period from fertility to infertility in both sexes.

**Perimenopause** The time period before menopause when estrogen is decreasing.

**Menopause** Cessation of menstruation as a result of the aging process or surgical removal of the ovaries.

**InfoTrac Search Words**

• Menopause

The term **climacteric** (kli-MAK-tuh-rik) refers to the physiological changes that occur during the transition period from fertility to infertility in both sexes. In women around 40 years of age, the ovaries begin to slow the production of estrogen. This period before complete cessation of menstruation is called **perimenopause**, and it can last for up to 10 years. Menstruation continues but cycles can become irregular, with erratic and absent or heavy bleeding as menopause approaches (Bastian et al., 2003). Up to 90% of women experience a change in menstrual patterns and sexual response during perimenopause. Also, by age 40 a woman's level of circulating testosterone is half what it was when she was 20 years old, and supplementation might be appropriate (S. Davis, 2000). Some women experience similar symptoms described in the following menopause section (Torpy, 2003). Low-dose birth control pills are sometimes prescribed to alleviate the perimenopausal symptoms and to prevent bone loss (Seibert et al., 2003).

**Menopause**, one of the events of the female climacteric, is the permanent cessation of menstruation. Menopause occurs as a result of certain physiological changes and takes place at a mean age of 51 but can occur in the 30s or as late as the 60s (Andrews, 2006). About 10% of women reach menopause by age 45 (Speroff & Fritz, 2005). Research indicates that women who experience earlier menopause smoke tobacco, began their periods by age 11, had shorter cycles, had fewer pregnancies, and had less time of oral contraceptive use than women who experience menopause later (Palmer et al., 2003).

The general public and the medical community have begun to focus more on menopause because of the great increase in the number of women who live many years after menopause. In 1900 the average life expectancy of a woman in the United States was 51 years. Today the average life expectancy for U.S. women is 82 years. Currently, almost 42 million women in the United States are over age 50 (Watt et al., 2003). By 2020 there will be 60 million postmenopausal women. In practical terms, this means that millions of women will experience the second half of their adult life following menopause; menopause can be seen as the gateway to a second adulthood (Brewster et al., 1999). Signs indicate that the baby boom generation will encourage the health-care system to deal with menopause more thoroughly than before (Hudson, 2006).

The experience of menopause varies greatly from woman to woman. Some women experience few physical symptoms other than cessation of menstruation. For these women menopause is surprisingly uneventful:

*After hearing comments for years about how menopause was so traumatic, I was ready for the worst. I was sure surprised when I realized I had hardly noticed it happening. (Authors' files)*

In addition, most women feel relieved that they no longer need to be concerned about pregnancy, contraception, and menstruation. They may experience an increased sense of freedom in sexual intimacy as a result (Andrews, 2006).

However, for many women, menopause brings a range of symptoms that can vary from mild to severe (Pinkerton & Zion, 2006). The most acute menopausal symptoms occur in the 2 years before and the 2 years following the last menstrual period. Hot flashes and night sweats are common difficulties. Hot flashes can range from a mild feeling of warmth to a feeling of intense heat and profuse perspiration, especially around the chest, neck, and face. A severe hot flash can soak clothing or sheets in perspiration. The flashes usually last for 1 to 5 minutes. Hot flashes can occur several times a day and during sleep. About 75% of women experience hot flashes, and women smokers experience hot flashes more frequently than nonsmokers (C. Shaw, 1997; Staropoli et al., 1997). For unknown reasons, African American women experience more hot flashes and women of Asian descent have fewer hot flashes than other racial and ethnic groups (Avis et al., 2001). Researchers have studied the physiology of hot flashes for over 30 years and still do not know how hot flashes occur (Schatz & Robb-Nicholson, 2006).

Other symptoms can significantly affect a woman's daily life, and indirectly, her sexuality (Dennerstein & Goldstein, 2005). Thinning of the vaginal walls and less lubrication from the decline in estrogen can make intercourse uncomfortable or painful (Goldstein & Alexander, 2005). Sleep disturbance can increase during menopause and can easily result in fatigue and irritability during the day (Kantrowitz, 2006). Menopausal symptoms can also include dizziness, difficulty with balance, diminished pleasure from touch, itchy or burning skin, sensitivity to clothing or touch, and numbness or tingling in hands and feet. In addition, estrogen deficiency can cause severe headaches, short-term memory loss, difficulty concentrating, and increased anxiety (Richards et al., 2006). Depression may also occur during menopause, due to other troubling symptoms or hormonal changes (Cohen et al., 2006; Freeman et al., 2006).

## Hormone Therapy

**Hormone therapy (HT)*** for women involves using supplemental hormones—estrogen, progesterone, and/or testosterone—to alleviate problems that can arise from the decrease in natural hormone production that occurs during the female climacteric. Also, younger women with hormone deficiencies following removal of their ovaries often use HT. ○ **Table 4.1** summarizes the benefits and risks of each of these hormones.

Hormones used in HT come from three main sources. Estrogen and progesterone can be derived from plants or made from synthetic chemicals, some of which are bioidentical to human estrogen (i.e., they have the same chemical structure). Testosterone is made from synthetic chemicals. The most widely used estrogen in the United States, conjugated equine estrogen (CEE), is made from pregnant mares' urine. (Some oppose this practice because of the treatment the mares and foals endure

**Hormone therapy (HT)**
The use of supplemental hormones during and after menopause or following surgical removal of the ovaries.

○ **TABLE 4.1**    **Benefits and Risks of Hormone Therapy**

| Hormone | Benefits | Problems |
|---|---|---|
| Estrogen | Maintains thickness and vascularity of vaginal and urethral tissue for comfort and lubrication during sexual interaction. | Increases the incidence of endometrial, ovarian, and breast cancer. |
| | Help prevent unrinary tract problems. | Increases risk of blood clots. |
| | Reduces hot flashes and sleep disturbance from night sweats. | |
| | Protects against osteoporosis (abnormal bone loss) and resultant fractures, particularly of the hip. | |
| | May protect from heart disease. | |
| | Reduces risk of colon cancer and Altzheimers. | |
| Progesterone | Eliminates the estrogen-caused increase in endometrial and ovarian cancer. | Alters the type of fats in the bloodstream and increases the risk of cardiovascular disease. |
| | | Increases the incidence of breast cancer. |
| Testosterone | Helps maintain or restore sexual interest. | Side effects include increase in hair growth and acne. |
| | Increases overall energy. | |

SOURCE: Speroff & Fritz (2005).

---

*Another abbreviation commonly seen for hormone therapy is HRT, or hormone replacement therapy. In the past, treatment with hormones was intended to replace the hormone levels after menopause to premenopause levels. Currently, the smallest dose of hormone therapies that alleviates symptoms associated with menopause is the usual treatment approach.

in order for the urine to be harvested (Love & Rochman, 2006). The CEE used in the HT products Premarin (estrogen only) and Prempro (estrogen and progesterone) is not bioidentical to human estrogen, and it contains impurities with unknown medical properties (Food and Drug Administration, 1997). However, most of the hormone therapy research in the United States has used conjugated equine estrogen (Love & Rochman, 2006)

## Controversy in Hormone Therapy Research

Choosing whether or not to use menopausal hormone therapy is one of the most complicated health decisions women must make. Few medical topics are in such a state of flux and controversy as hormone therapy for menopause, despite over 50 years of published research (Hudson, 2006). The most contradictory and confusing concerns relate to heart disease and breast cancer.

Regarding heart disease, most studies have found that the estrogen in HT significantly lowers the risk of cardiovascular problems in women. However, in 2002, the Women's Health Initiative (WHI) research reported findings that HT increased the risk of heart disease (Women's Health Initiative, 2002). Upon further analysis, the discrepant findings are likely due to the difference in the average ages of the study populations and the relative health of blood vessels in younger and older women (Hodson, 2006). The subjects in the studies that found HT had a protective effect against heart disease began HT at around age 50, at the onset of menopause. In contrast, women in the WHI study were, on average, 18 years past menopause when they began HT for the study (Grodstein et al., 2006). The cardiovascular system of a 50-year-old woman has healthier tissue than that of a 68-year-old woman, and HT appears to help maintain the younger cardiovascular tissue's health. In contrast, advanced plaque begins to form by age 60, and once plaques have formed, estrogen may make them so fragile they rupture, forming clots and causing heart attacks (Manson & Bassuk, 2006). Therefore, for women who begin HT at menopause, "hormone therapy can have a beneficial role in the primary prevention of coronary heart disease" (Speroff & Fritz, 2005, p. 733).

An in-depth analysis of research regarding the impact of hormone therapy on breast cancer makes the following conclusions. First, women using combined estrogen and progesterone HT have a slightly increased risk of breast cancer. (This increased risk is eliminated after HT is discontinued [Cockey, 2003]). Second, the women on HT who do develop breast cancer have a lower risk of dying from the cancer than women who have breast cancer but are not taking HT. The significant decrease in fatal breast cancer in women taking HT is likely due to two factors: These women may have more-frequent breast cancer screening, and the hormones in HT seem to effect cancerous tumors so they are detectable and can be treated at an earlier, less aggressive stage of malignancy (Speroff & Fritz, 2005). Even more recent research has found that hormone therapy that combines estrogen with testosterone has an increased risk of breast cancer (Tamimi et al., 2006). Women who have had a hysterectomy and are taking only estrogen do not have an increase in breast cancer risk until after 15 years of use (Chen et al., 2006).

## A Challenging Decision

A menopausal woman should weigh the potential benefits and risks of HT against the symptoms of hormone deficiency. For many women the benefits far outweigh the risks, and for other women the opposite is true (Hodson, 2006). New research results emerge continuously, and although they can be contradictory, it is this information that women and their health-care providers have available to make the important decision of whether to use HT (Larson, 2006; Reddy et al., 2006). Unfortunately, data are currently insufficient to support the effectiveness of complementary and alternative therapies such as soy, herbs, acupuncture, and naturopathy for treating menopausal symptoms (Nedrow et al., 2006). We recommend that women thoroughly discuss the available evidence and their individual health history and lifestyle with a health-care practitioner specializing in menopause and HT. ■

**! Sexual Health**

# Gynecological Health Concerns

Gynecological health problems range from minor infections to cancer. In this section, we provide information and self-help suggestions on several topics.

## Urinary Tract Infections

Women often develop infections of the urinary tract, the organ system that includes the urethra, bladder, and kidneys. If the infection progresses all the way to the kidneys, severe illness can result (Pace, 2000). About 15% of women will have a urinary tract infection in their lifetimes; many have more than one (Delzell & Lefevre, 2000; Mayo Clinic Health Oasis, 1999). The symptoms of urinary tract infections include a frequent need to urinate, a burning sensation when urinating, blood or pus in the urine, and sometimes lower pelvic pain (D'Epiro, 1997). A conclusive diagnosis of a urinary tract infection requires laboratory analysis of a urine sample. Such an infection generally responds to short-term antibiotic treatment (Uehling et al., 1997).

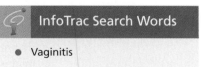

Bacteria that enter the urethral opening typically are the cause of urinary tract infections (Raz et al., 2000). Observing a few routine precautions can help prevent urinary tract infections. Coitus is the most frequent means by which bacteria enter the urinary tract; the bacteria are massaged into the urethra by the thrusting motions of intercourse. For those who have frequent problems with such infections, it is important that both partners wash their hands and genitals before and after intercourse. Using intercourse positions that cause less friction against the urethra can also help. Women can also use water-soluble lubricants (not petroleum jelly) when vaginal lubrication is insufficient, because irritated tissue is more susceptible to infection. Urinating immediately after intercourse helps wash out bacteria (Leiner, 1997). Careful wiping from front to back after both urination and bowel movements helps keep bacteria away from the urethra. Urinating as soon as you feel the urge also reduces the likelihood of infection. It can also be helpful to drink plenty of liquids, especially cranberry juice (Kiel & Nashelsky, 2003), and to avoid substances such as coffee, tea, and alcohol, which have an irritating effect on the bladder. ■

## Vaginal Infections

When the natural balance of the vagina is disturbed or when a nonnative organism is introduced, a vaginal infection, or **vaginitis** (va-juh-NYE-tus), can result. Usually the woman herself first notices symptoms of vaginitis: irritation or itching of the vagina and vulva, redness of the introitus and labia, unusual discharge, and sometimes a disagreeable odor. (An unpleasant odor can also be due to a forgotten tampon or diaphragm.) Types of vaginal infections include yeast infections, bacterial infections, and trichomoniasis, discussed in detail in Chapter 15.

**Vaginitis** Inflammation of the vaginal walls caused by a variety of vaginal infections.

It is important for vaginitis to be treated and cured. Chronic irritation from long-term infections can play a part in predisposing a woman to cervical cell changes that can lead to cancer. The following suggestions may help prevent vaginitis from occurring in the first place (Solimini, 1991):

1. Eat a well-balanced diet low in sugar and refined carbohydrates.
2. Maintain general good health with adequate sleep, exercise, and emotional release.
3. Use good hygiene, including (a) bathing regularly with mild soap; (b) wiping from front to back, vulva to anus, after urinating and having bowel movements; (c) wearing clean cotton underpants (nylon holds in heat and moisture that encourages bacterial growth); (d) avoiding the use of feminine-hygiene sprays and douching, colored toilet paper, bubble bath, and other people's washcloths or towels to wash or wipe your genitals; and (e) ensuring that your sexual partner's hands and genitals are clean before beginning sexual activity.
4. Be sure that you have adequate lubrication before coitus: natural lubrication or a water-soluble lubricant. Do not use petroleum-based lubricants (such as Vaseline),

because they are not water soluble and are likely to remain in the vagina and harbor bacteria. Petroleum-based lubricants can also weaken, and will eventually degrade, latex condoms or diaphragms.

5. Use condoms if you or your partner is non-monogamous. ■

## The Pap Smear

**Pap smear** A screening test for cancer of the cervix.

The **Pap smear** is an essential part of routine preventative health care for all women, including sexually active adolescents and postmenopausal women. During this screening test for cervical cancer, cells are taken from the cervix. The vaginal walls are held open with a speculum, and a few cells are removed with a cervical brush or a small wooden spatula; these cells are put on a glass slide and sent to a laboratory to be examined. The cells for a Pap smear are taken from the *transition zone*, the part of the cervix where long, column-shaped cells called *columnar cells* meet flat-shaped cells called *squamous cells*. A Pap smear is not painful, because there are so few nerve endings on the cervix. A vaginal Pap smear is done when the woman's cervix has been removed, although the incidence of vaginal cancer is low.

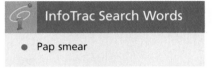

InfoTrac Search Words

• Pap smear

Since the widespread use of Pap smears began in the 1950s, the death rate from cervical cancer has decreased dramatically (Boen, 2006). Because of access to early detection and follow-up treatment, women in the United States have a 70% chance of surviving cervical cancer. In contrast, an average of only 41% of women across the developing world survive cervical cancer; for Thailand the survival rate is 58%, but for sub-Saharan Africa it is only 21% (Parry, 2006). Each year about 250,000 women in the developing world die of cervical cancer (Kalb & Springen, 2006). Women throughout the world who are economically disadvantaged and do not participate in screening programs are far more likely to die from cervical cancer than other women (Moore, 2006).

Sexual Health

Women should have their first Pap smear no more than 3 years after becoming sexually active, or by age 21. Depending on a health-care provider's recommendation, a woman may have this test once every 2 years, every year, twice a year, or even more frequently. Pap smears are not always accurate in detecting cervical cancer, so regular testing increases the likelihood of discovering it (Felix, 2003). Several factors increase the risk of developing cervical cancer. These include having sexual intercourse early, having multiple sexual partners, smoking tobacco, inhaling secondary smoke, and having had a virus called human papillomavirus (HPV) (Wyand & Arrindell, 2005). ■

New technologies for detecting cervical cancer are being developed, and a vaccine to prevent some types of cervical cancer has been approved by the FDA (Parry, 2006). To be most effective, the vaccine must be given to girls 10 to 12 years old before they are sexually active (Dailard, 2006). Extremist Christian groups like Focus on the Family vigorously oppose vaccinating school-age girls, believing it will undermine abstinence and promote promiscuity (Noller, 2006), an issue that we will discuss further in Chapter 15.

## Surgical Removal of the Uterus and Ovaries

**Hysterectomy** Surgical removal of the uterus.

**Oophorectomy** Surgical removal of the ovaries.

Some medical problems may require a woman to undergo a **hysterectomy** (his-tuh-REK-tuh-mee), surgical removal of the uterus, or an **oophorectomy** (oh-uh-fuh-REK-tuh-mee), surgical removal of the ovaries, or both. Such problems include bleeding disorders, severe pelvic infections, and the presence of benign (noncancerous) tumors (Kilbourne & Richards, 2001). Cancer of the cervix, uterus, or ovaries is also cause for hysterectomy or oophorectomy. Of these three cancers, ovarian cancer is by far the deadliest (Eheman et al., 2006; Tingulstad et al., 2003). Victims of ovarian cancer have about a 40% survival rate for 5 years from diagnosis because the cancer is difficult to detect in its early stages (Werness & Eltabbakh, 2001). In about 80% of women with ovarian cancer, the disease is advanced when diagnosed (Kaelin et al., 2006). New technology is needed to detect this cancer early.

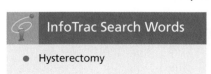

InfoTrac Search Words

• Hysterectomy

An estimated 33% of women have a hysterectomy by age 65, making it the second most frequently performed major operation for women in the United States. Hysterectomy rates are higher among low-income women, women with less than a high-school education, and women who live in the South. Researchers suspect that a lack of preventive health care in these groups allows problems to advance to the point where other treatments are not viable (Palmer et al., 1999). Before consenting to undergo a hysterectomy or similar surgery, it is important for a woman to obtain a second opinion; to fully inform herself of the benefits, risks, and alternatives to surgery; and to arrange for thorough preoperative and postoperative information and counseling (Wade et al., 2000).

The effects of hysterectomy on a woman's sexuality vary. First of all, hysterectomy does not affect the sensitivity of the clitoris. Some women find that the elimination of medical problems and painful intercourse, assured protection from unwanted pregnancy, and lack of menstruation enhance their quality of life in general and their sexual functioning and enjoyment (Flory et al., 2006; Rannestad et al., 2001). However, other women experience an alteration or decrease in their sexual response after removal of the uterus. Sensations from uterine vasocongestion and elevation during arousal as well as uterine contractions during orgasm are absent and can change the physical experience of sexual response. Some changes result from damage to the nerves in the pelvis. The exact locations of nerves vital to female sexual function have not been identified, and no nerve-sparing procedures are done during pelvic surgeries in women (Berman & Berman, 2000). Scar tissue or alterations to the vagina can also have an effect. When ovaries are removed, symptoms common to menopause will occur unless hormone therapy is undertaken. An important variable in postsurgical sexual adjustment is the quality of the partner relationship and how the woman and her partner perceive the surgery (Helstrom et al., 1995).

## The Breasts

Breasts are not part of the internal or external female genitalia. Instead, they are **secondary sex characteristics** (physical characteristics other than genitals that distinguish males from females). In a physically mature woman the breasts consist internally of fatty tissue and **mammary** (MAM-uh-ree), or milk, **glands** (**Figure 4.6**). The

**Secondary sex characteristics** The physical characteristics other than genitals that indicate sexual maturity, such as body hair, breasts, and deepened voice.

**Mammary glands** Glands in the female breast that produce milk.

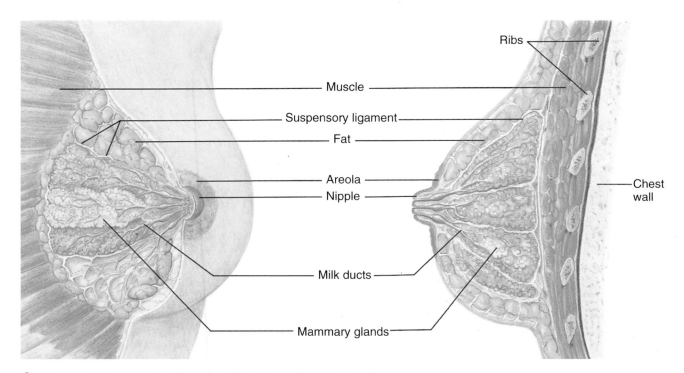

**Figure 4.6** Cross-section front and side views of the female breast.

glandular tissue in the breasts responds to sex hormones. During adolescence, both the fatty and the glandular tissue develop markedly. Breasts show some size and texture variations at different phases of the menstrual cycle and when influenced by pregnancy, nursing, or birth control pills (Robb-Nicholson, 2006). The amount of glandular tissue in the breasts varies little from woman to woman, despite differences in size. Consequently, the amount of milk produced after childbirth does not correlate with the size of the breasts. Variation in breast size is due primarily to the amount of fatty tissue distributed around the glands. It is common for one breast to be slightly larger than the other.

The *nipple* is in the center of the *areola* (ah-REE-oh-luh), the darker area of the external breast. The areola contains sebaceous (oil-producing) glands that help lubricate the nipples during breast-feeding. The openings of the mammary glands are in the nipples. Some nipples point outward from the breast, others are flush with the breast, and still others sink into the breast. The nipples become erect when small muscles at their base contract in response to touch, sexual arousal, or cold. For many women breast and nipple stimulation is an important source of pleasure and arousal during masturbation or sexual interaction. Some find that such stimulation helps build the sexual intensity that leads to orgasm; others enjoy it for its own sake. Other women find breast and nipple touching a neutral or unpleasant experience.

Breasts come in a multitude of sizes and shapes. One writer explained, "On real women, I've seen breasts as varied as faces: breasts shaped like tubes, breasts shaped like tears, breasts that flop down, breasts that point up, breasts that are dominated by thick, dark nipples and areola, breasts with nipples so small and pale they look airbrushed" (Angier, 1999, p. 128).

Breast size is a source of considerable preoccupation for many women and men in our society:

> In talking with my friends about how we feel about our breasts, I discovered that not one of us feels really comfortable about how she looks. I've always been envious of women with large breasts because mine are small. But my friends with large breasts talk about feeling self-conscious about their breasts too. (Authors' files)

Surgeries to enlarge or reduce breasts reflect the dissatisfaction many women feel because their breasts do not fit the cultural ideal. Each year over 200,000 women in the United States have cosmetic breast implant surgery (Springen, 2003). Since the late 1980s increasing numbers of young women are receiving breast augmentation (Farr, 2000). Many women who have cosmetic breast augmentation are pleased with the results. Others experience painful or disfiguring complications and poor results, such as loss of breast sensation, asymmetric breasts, and capsular contraction (hardening of scar tissue around the implant, pressing the soft capsule into a hard disk). One study found that 73% of women with breast implants experienced side effects, and 27% of women had their implants removed within 3 years because of infection, painful scar tissue, or a broken or leaking implant (about 15% rupture by 10 years) (Springen, 2003).

**? Critical Thinking Question**

Should adolescents be allowed to have breast enlargement surgery? Why or why not?

Breast size and shape vary from woman to woman.

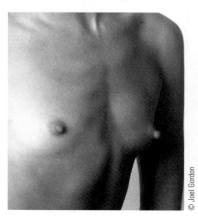
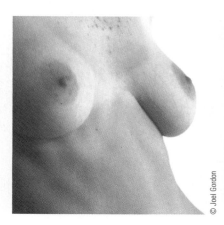

© Joel Gordon

## Breast Self-Exam

A breast self-examination (BSE) is an important part of self–health care for women. This exam can help a woman know what is normal for her own breasts. She can do the breast exam herself and can also teach her partner to do it. As of 2003 the American Cancer Society stopped recommending monthly breast self-exams for early cancer detection because large, rigorous studies have shown that BSE does not decrease deaths from breast cancer. Women find most cancerous tumors accidentally, by routine touching in the shower or while dressing, or when their partners notice a lump. Therefore the American Cancer Society recommends that women use BSE occasionally for self-awareness in order to know how their breasts normally feel so that they can detect changes (Smith et al., 2003). The steps of a breast exam are illustrated in the box "How to Examine Your Breasts." It is helpful to fill out a chart, such as the one shown in ❯ **Figure 4.7**, to keep track of lumps in the breasts. Many breasts normally feel lumpy. Once a woman becomes familiar with her own breasts, she can notice any changes. If there is a change, she should consult a health-care practitioner, who might recommend further diagnostic testing. Ninety percent of breast lumps, most of which are benign, are found by women themselves. ■

Fill out a chart, like the one shown here, when you examine your breasts. For any lump you find, mark

1. its location
2. its size (BB, pea, raisin, grape)
3. its shape (rounded or elongated)

Compare each record with the last one, and consult your health practitioner regarding any changes. A new or changing lump should be checked as soon as possible. Most such lumps will prove to be benign.

Today's date _____

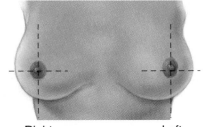

Right          Left

SOURCE: Reprinted with permission from Kaiser Foundation Health Plan of Oregon.

❯ **Figure 4.7** It is helpful to use a chart similar to this one to keep track of lumps in the breasts.

## Breast Cancer Screening

Breast self-examination and routine breast exams by your health-care provider are important screening tools. Another such tool is **mammography** (ma-MAWG-ruh-fee), a highly sensitive X-ray screening test to help detect cancerous breast cells and lumps. Mammography uses low levels of radiation to create an image of the breast, called a *mammogram*, on film or paper. Mammography can often detect a breast lump up to several years before it can be felt manually; it can also sometimes find cancerous cell changes that occur even before a lump develops (Aldridge et al., 2006). With earlier detection of breast cancer, a decrease in mortality (❯ **Table 4.2**) and an increase in breast-conserving treatments are possible (Hamilton et al., 2003).

**Mammography** A highly sensitive X-ray test for the detection of breast cancer.

❯ **TABLE 4.2** | Five Year Survival Rate for U.S. Women by Stage of Cancer at Diagnosis

| Stage of Cancer | Percentage of Cancer Diagnosed at This Stage | Survival Rate at 5 Years (%) |
|---|---|---|
| Local (confined to breast) | 60 | 98 |
| Regional (spread to lymph nodes) | 31 | 76 |
| Distant (spread to other organs) | 6 | 16 |

In North America one woman dies of breast cancer approximately *every 12 minutes*.

SOURCE: American Cancer Society (2003).

# How to Examine Your Breasts

1. **In the shower**: Examine your breasts during a bath or shower; hands glide more easily over wet skin. With fingers flat, move your hands gently over every part of each breast. Use your right hand to examine your left breast and your left hand to examine your right breast. Check for any lump, hard knot, or thickening.

2. **Before a mirror**: Inspect your breasts with your arms at your sides. Next, raise your arms high overhead. Look for any changes in the contour of each breast: a swelling, a dimpling of the skin, or changes in the nipple. Then rest your palms on your hips and press down firmly to flex your chest muscles. Left and right breasts will not match exactly—few women's breasts do.

3. **Lying down**: To examine your right breast, put a pillow or folded towel under your right shoulder. Place your right hand behind your head (this distributes breast tissue

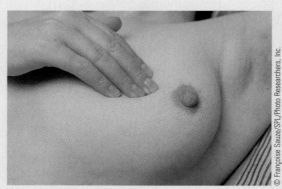

more evenly on the chest). With your left hand, fingers flat, press gently in small circular motions around an imaginary clock face. Begin at the outermost top of your right breast for 12 o'clock, then move to 1 o'clock, and so on around the circle back to 12. A ridge of firm tissue in the lower curve of each breast is normal. Then move in an inch, toward the nipple, and keep circling to examine every part of your breast, including the nipple. This requires at least three more circles. Now slowly repeat this procedure on your left breast.

Finally, squeeze the nipple of each breast gently between thumb and index finger. Any discharge, clear or bloody, should be reported to your doctor immediately—as should the discovery of any unusual lump, swelling, or thickening anywhere in the breast.

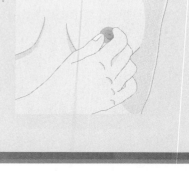

**Figure 4.8** Breast self-exam.

Mammography is less effective for detecting breast cancer in women from 40 to 49 years of age than in those older than 50, mainly because of the greater density of the breast tissue, which makes it more difficult for the mammogram to illuminate potential problem areas (Mitka, 2003b). However, almost 6,000 women in their 40s die each year from breast cancer, and the American Medical Association, the American Cancer Society, and the National Cancer Institute recommend yearly mammograms for this age group (Kaelin et al., 2006; Pace, 2001).

Although mammography is an effective screening test, it can miss a significant number of tumors or result in a false-positive test (Cardenas & Frisch, 2003). Research is exploring better breast-screening technology (Flobbe et al., 2003). Currently, the best method for early detection of breast cancer is a combination of monthly manual self-exams, routine exams by a health-care practitioner, and mammography as recommended (Caplan et al., 2000). ■

It is especially important for lesbians to be conscientious about scheduling regular exams and mammograms; they tend to be screened less often than heterosexual

women because they do not have birth control medical appointments. Lesbians may also avoid health-care services rather than confront the insensitivity and ignorance of some medical practitioners (Hammond, 2006; Heck et al., 2006). Many lesbians report that past negative experiences have made them less likely to seek services when they have a problem (Makadon, 2006).

In 5–10% of women breast cancer can develop from flaws in a gene that is now detectable (Burke et al., 1997). Women with this gene flaw have up to an 80% chance of developing breast cancer and may have an increased risk for ovarian cancer (Humphries & Gill, 2003). Women now have the opportunity to decide whether to use drugs for cancer prevention or to have a preventive mastectomy (Armstrong et al., 2000).

## Breast Lumps

Three types of lumps can occur in the breasts. The two most common are *cysts*, which are fluid-filled sacs, and *fibroadenomas*, which are solid, rounded tumors. Both are benign (not cancerous or harmful) tumors, and together they account for approximately 80% of breast lumps. In some women the lumps create breast tenderness that ranges from mild to severe discomfort, which is called *fibrocystic disease* (Deckers & Ricci, 1992). The causes of fibrocystic disease are unknown but may be hormonally related. Caffeine in coffee, tea, cola drinks, and chocolate might contribute to the development of benign breast lumps. Dietary changes that have helped some women reduce their symptoms include eating more fish, chicken, and grains and less red meat, salt, and fats.

The third kind of breast lump is a *malignant tumor* (a tumor made up of cancer cells). Breast cancer affects approximately 1 in 7 women in the United States. In 2005 breast cancer killed about 40,000 U.S. women and 410,000 women worldwide (Evans, 2006; Prentice, 2003). The risk of breast cancer rises with age; half of all breast cancer is diagnosed in women age 65 and older (Nattinger, 2000). Although breast cancer is less common in women in their 20s and 30s, cancers that occur in young women are often more aggressive and result in a higher mortality rate (Fraunfelder, 2000). Breast cancer in men is relatively rare, accounting for 1% of all cases (Fentimen et al., 2006).

The good news is that overall mortality from breast cancer is at its lowest since 1950, most likely because of earlier detection. Unfortunately, the survival rate for African American women (71%) is lower than for white women (82%) (Boyd & Wilmoth, 2006; Simon, 2006). Socioeconomic characteristics of lower income, lack of health-care coverage, and apprehension about using health and medical services lead to differences in preventive health care (such as breast exams and mammograms). As a result, African American women tend to have more-advanced breast cancer prior to detection (Aldridge et al., 2006; Bullock & McGraw, 2006). That physicians are less likely to refer women of lower socioeconomic status for mammograms also contributes to the problem (Lukwago et al., 2003).

Certain risk factors that increase or decrease a woman's chances of developing breast cancer are outlined in ⊙ **Table 4.3**. However, compelling scientific evidence indicates that environmental exposure to toxic chemicals may contribute to as much as 50% of breast cancer (Evans, 2006). The environment's significance has been validated by research indicating that adopted children whose adoptive parents died of cancer had five times the risk of the average person of developing the same disease (D. Davis, 2000). Exposure to environmental pollution, pesticides, radiation, and synthetic chemicals found in plastics, detergents, and pharmaceutical drugs can mimic estrogen's effects on the body and can cause cells to grow out of control and form tumors (Steingraber, 2005). Some breast cancer scientists and activist groups are attempting to have a greater percentage of cancer research funds allocated to investigations into environmental causes of cancer to assist advances in prevention (Lyman, 2006; McCormick, 2002). ■

**Risk Factors for Breast Cancer**
85% of women who develop breast cancer have no known risk factors

| Higher Risk | Lower Risk |
| --- | --- |
| Inherited breast cancer gene | No inherited breast cancer gene |
| Higher lifetime cumulative estrogen exposure | Lower lifetime estrogen exposure |
|   Menstruation onset before age 12 |   Menstruation onset after age 12 |
|   No pregnancies |   One or more pregnancies |
|   First child after age 30 and subsequent children later in life |   First child before age 30 and subsequent children early in life |
|   Never breast-fed a child |   Breast-fed a child[a] |
|   Menopause after age 55 |   Menopause prior to age 54 |
|   Obesity |   Slenderness |
|   Intact ovaries |   Both ovaries removed early in life |
| Two or more first-degree relatives with breast cancer | No family history of breast cancer |
| Over age 65 | Below age 65 |
| Sedentary lifestyle | Regular exercise |
| One or more alcoholic drinks a day | Less than 1 alcoholic drink a day |
| High-fat diet | Low-fat diet |
| Normal dose of aspirin or ibuprofen (Advil) less than 3 times per week | Normal dose of aspirin or ibuprofen (Advil) 3 times per week |

[a] An analysis of 50 worldwide epidemiologic studies suggests that the longer women breast-feed, the more they are protected against breast cancer (Collaborative Group on Hormonal Factors in Breast Cancer, 2002).

SOURCES: Cain (2000), Cardenas & Frisch (2003), Higa (2000), Marchioni (2003), Verloop et al. (2000).

# Breast Cancer

In 1974 Betty Ford and Happy Rockefeller were the first public figures to openly discuss their breast cancer and mastectomies. Before their courageous actions most women kept their breast cancer and its treatment as private as possible. In the ensuing years extensive resources have arisen to help women and their loved ones better manage a diagnosis of breast cancer. Political activism has also increased the previous disproportionately small percentage of research funding for breast cancer (Thorne & Murray, 2000).

Once breast cancer has been diagnosed, several forms of treatment can be used, and others are being developed (E. Cohen, 2001; Fischman, 2001; Voelker, 2000). Radiation therapy, chemotherapy, hormone therapy, immunotherapy, *lumpectomy* (surgical removal of the lump and small amounts of surrounding tissue only), **mastectomy** (surgical removal of all or part of the breast), or a combination of these procedures can be performed. If the cancer is small, localized, and in an early stage, lumpectomy with chemotherapy or radiation can provide as good a chance of a cure as a mastectomy. Breakthroughs in treatment are improving survival rates (Kaelin et al., 2006).

Breast cancer and its treatments can adversely affect a woman's sexuality (Henson, 2002). Research indicates that approximately 50% of women who have had breast cancer experience sexual problems resulting from the physical effects of chemotherapy and radiation and hormone therapy (Fleming & Kleinbart, 2001). The loss of one or both breasts is usually significant to women. Breasts symbolize many aspects of femininity and can be an important aspect of self-image (Potter & Ship, 2001). The stimulation of a woman's breasts during lovemaking, by massaging, licking, or sucking—and the stimulation her partner receives from doing these things and from simply looking at her breasts—is often an important component of sexual arousal for both the woman and her partner. Consequently, surgical removal of

**Mastectomy** Surgical removal of the breast(s).

InfoTrac Search Words

- Breast cancer

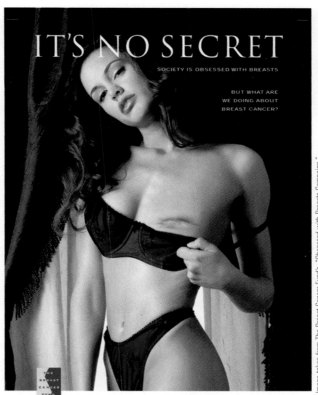

The Breast Cancer Fund's "Obsessed with Breasts" campaign used this attention-getting image to promote breast cancer education.

Image taken from The Breast Cancer Fund's, "Obsessed with Breasts Campaign." www.breastcancerfund.org. Photographer: Heward Jue

one or both breasts can create challenges of sexual adjustment for the couple (Polinsky, 1995).

Reconstructive breast surgery can enhance a woman's emotional and sexual adjustment following a mastectomy. In many cases a new breast can be made with a silicone pouch containing silicone gel or saline water that is placed under the woman's own skin and chest muscle. In 2002 about 70,000 women in the United States had implants following mastectomy (Healy, 2003).

The American Cancer Society's Reach to Recovery program provides an important service to women with breast cancer. Volunteers in the program, who have all had surgery and other treatments, meet with women who have recently been diagnosed or had treatment and offer them emotional support and encouragement. They also provide positive models of women who have successfully adjusted to dealing with breast cancer. In fact, a growing body of evidence suggests that many breast cancer survivors, like many survivors of other cancers, report positive changes in personal relationships, appreciation of life, and their life priorities (Bellizzi & Blank, 2006).

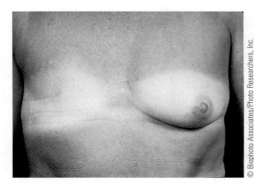 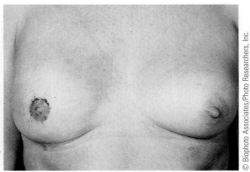

© Biophoto Associates/Photo Researchers, Inc.

Reconstructive surgery following a mastectomy can enhance a woman's general and sexual adjustment.

## The Vulva

- Genital self-exploration is a good way for a woman to learn about her own body and to notice any changes that may require medical attention.
- The female external genitals, also called the vulva, comprise the mons veneris, labia majora, labia minora, clitoris, and urethral and vaginal openings. Each woman's vulva is unique in shape, color, and texture.
- The mons veneris and labia majora have underlying pads of fatty tissue and are covered by pubic hair beginning at adolescence.
- The labia minora are folds of sensitive skin that begin at the hood over the clitoris and extend downward to below the vaginal opening, or introitus. The area between them is called the vestibule.
- The clitoris is composed of the external glans and shaft and the internal crura. The glans contains densely concentrated nerve endings. The only function of the clitoris is sexual pleasure.
- The urethral opening is located between the clitoris and the vaginal introitus.
- Many cultures have placed great importance on the hymen as proof of virginity. However, there are various sizes, shapes, and thicknesses of hymens, and many women can have initial intercourse without pain or bleeding. Also, women who have decided to have coitus can learn how to stretch their hymens to help make their first experience comfortable.

## Underlying Structures

- Below the surface of the vulva are the vestibular bulbs and the pelvic floor muscles.

## Internal Structures

- The vagina, with its three layers of tissue, extends about 3 to 5 inches into the pelvic cavity. It is a potential rather than an actual space and increases in size during sexual arousal, coitus, and childbirth. The other internal reproductive structures are the cervix, uterus, fallopian tubes, and ovaries.
- Kegel exercises are voluntary contractions of the vaginal muscles.
- Vaginal lubrication, the secretion of alkaline fluid through the vaginal walls during arousal, is important both in enhancing the longevity and motility of sperm cells and in increasing the pleasure and comfort of intercourse.
- The Grafenberg spot occupies about 1 centimeter along the surface of the top wall of the vagina. Many women report erotic sensitivity to pressure in some area of their vaginas.
- The vaginal walls and cervix produce normal secretions.

## Menstruation

- The menstrual cycle results from a complex interplay of hormones. Although negative social attitudes have historically been attached to menstruation, some people are redefining it in a more positive fashion.
- There are usually no medical reasons to abstain from intercourse during menstruation. However, many people do limit their sexual activity during this time.
- Some women have difficulties with PMS (premenstrual syndrome), PMDD (premenstrual dysphoric disorder), or primary or secondary dysmenorrhea. Knowledge about the physiological factors that contribute to these problems is increasing, and some of the problems can be treated.
- Amenorrhea occurs normally during pregnancy, while breastfeeding, and after menopause. It can also be due to medical problems or poor health. A pill that prevents menstruation for three months has been developed.
- Toxic shock syndrome (TSS) is a rare condition that occurs most often in menstruating women. Its symptoms include fever, sore throat, nausea, red skin flush, dizziness, and low blood pressure. If untreated, it can be fatal.

## Menopause

- Menopause is the cessation of menstruation, and it signals the end of female fertility. The average age of menopause is 51. Because of increases in life expectancy, women can expect to live half their adult lives following menopause.
- Most women experience few uncomfortable symptoms during the aging process and maintain sexual interest and response. Others experience symptoms such as hot flashes, sleep disturbance, depression or anxiety, headaches, and sensitivity to touch as a result of declining estrogen levels.
- Hormone therapy (HT) is a medical treatment for menopausal symptoms and helps to protect against osteoporosis and heart disease. Potential side effects necessitate careful use of such therapy.

## Gynecological Health Concerns

- About 15% of women will experience a urinary tract infection caused by bacteria that enter the urethra.
- Occasionally, a vaginal infection occurs that results in irritation, unusual discharge, or a disagreeable odor.
- The Pap smear has significantly reduced deaths from cervical cancer. A woman can use her own speculum to examine her cervix.
- There is considerable medical controversy about the appropriate use of hysterectomy. Hysterectomy or oophorectomy can affect—either positively or negatively—a woman's sexuality.

## The Breasts

- The breasts are composed of fatty tissue and milk-producing glands. Self-examination of the breasts is an important part of health care.
- Three types of lumps can appear in the breasts: cysts, fibroadenomas, and malignant tumors. Careful diagnosis of a breast lump is important. Mammography and other tests can help detect and diagnose breast cancer. A lumpectomy is often as effective as more-severe procedures.

## ◑ Suggested Readings

Bouris, Karen (1993). *The First Time*. Berkeley, CA: Conari Press. A collection of personal stories about "losing virginity" as a pivotal female experience.

Ellison, Carol (2000). *Women's Sexualities*. Oakland, CA: New Harbinger Publications. Illuminating information and analysis based on in-depth interviews with women age 23 to 90, emphasizing the challenges and triumphs of sexual development.

Love, Susan (2005). *Dr. Susan Love's Breast Book*. New York: De Capo Lifelong Books. Discussions of every aspect of the breast, including the importance of political awareness and action for breast-health issues.

Silver, Marc (2004). *Breast Cancer Husband: How to Help Your Wife (and Yourself) during Diagnosis, Treatment, and Beyond*. Emmaus, PA: Rodale Press. A tender, funny, and rock-solid guide to providing support, written by an editor at *US News & World Report*.

Stewart, Elizabeth, and Paula Spencer (2002). *The V Book: A Doctor's Guide to Complete Vulvovaginal Health*. New York: Bantam Books. This book draws on the latest medical research and clinical gynecological experience to provide extensive information about women's genital health.

## ◑ Web Resources

### CengageNOW Web Site

Go to **academic.cengage.com** to link to practice quiz questions, interactive activities, Internet links, critical thinking exercises, discussion forums, and more. You can also access sites from the Wadsworth Psychology Study Center (**academic.cengage.com/psychology**) or you can connect directly to the following sites:

### Gyn101

A visit to this Web site walks you through a first visit to a gynecologist. Among the resources available are how to choose a gynecologist, what to expect in a gynecological exam, and suggested questions to ask your health-care provider.

### OBGYN.net Women and Patients

This site includes valuable reference information on gynecological health, including links to recent research articles on a host of topics.

### National Vaginitis Association

This site spells out the differences in symptoms and treatment of various vaginal infections.

### National Women's Information Center

This Web site serves as a wide-ranging resource center on women's health issues and is sponsored by the Office on Women's Health of the U.S. Department of Health and Human Services.

### North American Menopause Society

The resources available at this Web site include basic facts about menopause, a helpful FAQ, and information about educational materials available to both consumers and health-care providers.

***Our Sexuality* Book Companion Web Site** academic.cengage.com/psychology/crooks Visit your book companion Web site where you will find flash cards, practice quizzes, Internet links, and more to help you study.

**Just what you need to know NOW!**
Spend time on what you need to master rather than on information you already have learned. Take a pretest for this chapter, and CengageNOW will generate a personalized study plan based on your results. The study plan will identify the topics you need to review and direct you to online resources to help you master those topics. You can then take a post-test to help you determine the concepts you have mastered and what you will still need to work on. Try it out! Go to academic.cengage.com/login to sign in with an access code or to purchase access to this product.

**InfoTrac College Edition Online Library**
Sign in to **academic.cengage.com/login** or visit your free book companion Web site at **academic.cengage.com/psychology/crooks** to access InfoTrac College Edition, an online searchable library that includes a multitude of journals, many specific to human sexuality. These journals include *Archives of Sexual Behavior; Archives of Sexual Health Behavior; Canadian Journal of Human Sexuality; Hispanic Journal of the Behavioral Sciences; Journal of Cross-Cultural Psychology; Journal of Physical Education, Recreation, and Dance; Journal of Sex Research;* and *Sex Roles.*

# Male Sexual Anatomy and Physiology

© Erich Lessing, Art Resource/NY

*Who needs a lecture on male anatomy? Certainly not the men in this class. It's hanging out there all our lives. We handle and look at it each time we pee or bathe. So what's the mystery? Now the female body—that's a different story. That's why I'm in the class. Let's learn something that isn't so obvious. (Authors' files)*

This statement, from a student in a sexuality class, illustrates two common assumptions. The first is that male sexual anatomy is simple. All you need to know is "hanging out there." The second, perhaps more subtle implication is that female genital structures are considerably more complicated and mysterious than men's.

These assumptions call for some rethinking, for a few reasons. One is that there is more than meets the eye. The sexual anatomy of men and women is complex and varies widely from one individual to another. Another reason is that knowing about our own sexual anatomy and functioning, although it does not guarantee sexual satisfaction, at least provides a degree of comfort with our bodies and perhaps a greater ability to communicate with a partner. Equally important, an understanding of our own bodies provides a crucial basis for detecting potential health problems. In this chapter, we provide information that every man should know regarding self-exams and health care. Expanding knowledge and understanding of his genital anatomy and physiology can be an important aspect of a man's sexual well-being and his sexual intelligence. As in Chapter 4, we encourage readers to use the pages that follow as a reference for their own self-knowledge and improved health.

# Sexual Anatomy

We begin with discussions of the various structures of the male sexual anatomy. Descriptive accounts are organized according to parts of the genital system for easy reference. Later in this chapter (and in Chapter 6) we will look more closely at the way the entire system functions during sexual arousal.

## The Penis

The **penis** consists of nerves, blood vessels, fibrous tissue, and three parallel cylinders of spongy tissue. It does not contain a bone or an abundance of muscular tissue, contrary to some people's beliefs. However, an extensive network of muscles are present at the base of the penis. These muscles help eject both semen and urine through the urethra.

A portion of the penis extends internally into the pelvic cavity. This part, including its attachment to the pubic bones, is referred to as the **root**. When a man's penis is erect, he can feel this inward projection by pressing a finger up between his anus and scrotum. The external, pendulous portion of the penis, excluding the head, is known as the **shaft**. The smooth, acorn-shaped head is called the **glans**.

Running the entire length of the penis are the three cylinders referred to earlier. The two larger ones, the **cavernous bodies** (*corpora cavernosa*), lie side by side above the smaller, third cylinder, the **spongy body** (*corpus spongiosum*). At the root of the penis the innermost tips of the cavernous bodies, or *crura*, are connected to the pubic bones. At the head of the penis the spongy body expands to form the glans. These structures are shown in **Figure 5.1**.

All these cylinders are similar in structure. As the terms *cavernous* and *spongy* imply, the cylinders are made of spongelike irregular spaces and cavities. Each cylinder is also richly supplied with blood vessels. When a male is sexually excited, the cylinders become engorged with blood, resulting in penile erection. During sexual arousal the spongy body may stand out as a distinct ridge along the underside of the penis.

The skin covering the penile shaft is usually hairless and quite loose, which allows for expansion when the penis becomes erect. Although the skin is connected to the shaft at the neck (the portion just behind the glans), some of it folds over and forms a cuff, or hood, over the glans. This loose covering is called the **foreskin**, or *prepuce*. In

**Penis** A male sexual organ consisting of the internal root and the external shaft and glans.

**Root** The portion of the penis that extends internally into the pelvic cavity.

**Shaft** The length of the penis between the glans and the body.

**Glans** The head of the penis; it is richly endowed with nerve endings.

**Cavernous bodies** The structures in the shaft of the penis that engorge with blood during sexual arousal.

**Spongy body** A cylinder that forms a bulb at the base of the penis, extends up into the penile shaft, and forms the penile glans.

**Foreskin** A covering of skin over the penile glans.

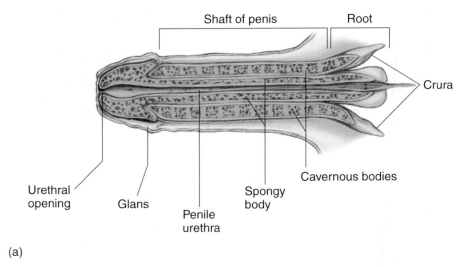

**Figure 5.1** Interior structure of the penis: (a) view from above and (b) cross section of the penis.

Shaft of penis

Root

Crura

Cavernous bodies

Spongy body

Penile urethra

Glans

Urethral opening

(a)

**Top of penis**

Cavernous bodies

Penile urethra

Spongy body

Skin

**Underside of penis**

(b)

some males the foreskin covers the entire head, whereas in other males only a portion of the head is covered. Typically, the foreskin can be retracted (drawn back from the glans) quite easily. *Circumcision* involves the surgical removal of this sleeve of skin. Although familiar in our culture, circumcision is only one of many procedures for altering male genitalia that are practiced around the world, as described in the following Sexuality and Diversity discussion on male genital modification and mutilation.

## SEXUALITY AND DIVERSITY

### *Male Genital Modification: Cultural Beliefs and Practices*

Throughout the world, people hold strong beliefs about the importance and implications of altering male genitals through a variety of procedures. These rituals and customs have been chronicled through the ages. (Female genital modification is also widespread, as discussed in Chapter 4.)

The most common genital alteration is *circumcision*, the surgical removal of the foreskin. Circumcision is practiced in many societies for religious, ritual, or hygienic reasons. Historically, circumcision is an old practice. Examinations of ancient Egyptian mummies have revealed evidence of circumcision as far back as 6000 BCE, and Egyptian records at least 5,000 years old depict circumcised men. Australian aborigines, Muslims, and some African tribes have also used male circumcision to mark a rite of passage or to signify a covenant with God (Melby, 2002b).

For thousands of years Jews have practiced circumcision according to scripture (Genesis 17:9–27), as a religious rite. The ceremony, called a *bris*, takes place on the eighth day after birth. Similarly, the followers of Islam have a long-standing tradition of circumcision. Although circumcision is widespread among Middle Eastern and African societies, it is relatively uncommon in Europe today.

A variation of circumcision, called *superincision* (in which the foreskin, instead of being removed, is split lengthwise along its top portion), is practiced among certain

South Pacific cultures as a kind of rite of passage or initiation ritual into sexual maturity (Gregersen, 1996). Mangaia and the Marquesas Islands are two societies that perform this procedure when a boy reaches adolescence (Marshall, 1971; Suggs, 1962).

*Castration*, removal of the testes, is a more extreme male genital mutilation that also has its roots in antiquity. This practice has been justified for a variety of reasons: to prevent sexual activity between harem guards (eunuchs) and their charges, to render war captives docile, to preserve the soprano voices of European choirboys during the Middle Ages, and as part of religious ceremonies (in ancient Egypt hundreds of young boys were castrated in a single ceremony). In the United States in the mid-19th century castration was sometimes performed as a purported cure for the evils of masturbation (Melby, 2002b). During this same time period American medical journals also reported that castration was often a successful treatment for "insanity."

In more modern times castrations have occasionally been performed for legal reasons, either as a method of eugenic selection (e.g., to prevent a mentally disabled person from having offspring) or as an alleged deterrent to sex offenders (see Chapter 6). The ethical basis of these operations is highly controversial. Finally, castration is sometimes performed as medical treatment for diseases, such as prostate cancer and genital tuberculosis (Parker & Dearnaley, 2003; Pickett et al., 2000).

The entire penis is sensitive to touch, but the greatest concentration of nerve endings is found in the glans. Although the entire glans area is extremely sensitive, many men find that two specific locations are particularly responsive to stimulation. One is the rim, or crown, which marks the area where the glans rises abruptly from the shaft. This distinct ridge is called the **corona** (kuh-ROH-nuh). The other is the **frenulum** (FREN-yoo-lum), a thin strip of skin connecting the glans to the shaft on the underside of the penis. The location of these two areas is shown in ❯ **Figure 5.2**.

Most men enjoy having the glans stimulated, particularly the two areas just mentioned, but individuals vary in their preferences. Some men occasionally or routinely prefer being stimulated in genital areas other than the glans of the penis. The mode of stimulation, either manual (by self or partner) or oral, can influence the choice of preferred sites. Some of these variations and individual preferences are noted in the following accounts:

**Corona** The rim of the penile glans.

**Frenulum** A highly sensitive thin strip of skin that connects the glans to the shaft on the underside of the penis.

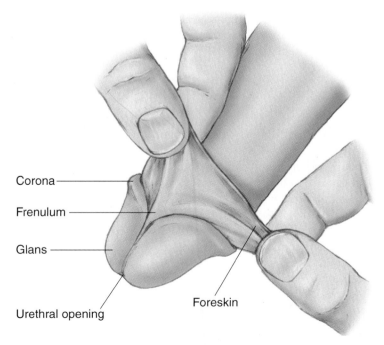

❯ **Figure 5.2** The underside of the uncircumcised penis, showing the location of the corona and frenulum—two areas on the penis that harbor a high concentration of sensitive nerve endings.

Corona

Frenulum

Glans

Urethral opening

Foreskin

*When I masturbate I frequently avoid the head of my penis, concentrating instead on stroking the shaft. The stimulation is not so intense, which allows a longer time for buildup to orgasm. The result is that the climax is generally more intense than if I focus only on the glans. (Authors' files)*

*During oral sex with my girlfriend, I sometimes have to put my hand around my penis, leaving just the head sticking out, so she will get the idea what part feels best. Otherwise, she spends a lot of time running her tongue up and down the shaft, which just doesn't do it for me. (Authors' files)*

## Strengthening Musculature Around the Penis

As previously mentioned, the internal extension of the penis is surrounded by an elaborate network of muscles. This musculature is comparable to that in the female body, and strengthening these muscles by doing Kegel exercises can produce benefits for men similar to those experienced by women. In most men these muscles are quite weak because they are usually only contracted during ejaculation. The following description, adapted from *Male Sexuality* (Zilbergeld, 1978, p. 109), is a brief outline of how these muscles can be located and strengthened:

1. Locate the muscles by stopping the flow of urine several times while urinating. The muscles you squeeze to accomplish this are the ones on which you will concentrate. If you do a correct Kegel while not urinating, you will notice your penis move slightly. Kegels done when you have an erection will cause your penis to move up and down.
2. Begin the exercise program by squeezing and relaxing the muscles 15 times, twice daily. Do not hold the contraction at this stage. (These are called "short Kegels.")
3. Gradually increase the number of Kegels until you can comfortably do 60 at a time, twice daily.
4. Now practice "long Kegels" by holding each contraction for a count of 3.
5. Combine the short and long Kegels in each daily exercise routine, doing a set of 60 of each, once or twice a day.
6. Continue with the Kegel exercises for at least several weeks. You may not notice results until a month or more has passed. By this time the exercises will probably have become automatic, requiring no particular effort.

Some of the positive changes men have reported after doing the male Kegel exercises include stronger and more pleasurable orgasms, better ejaculatory control, and increased pelvic sensation during sexual arousal. ■

○ **Figure 5.3** The scrotum and the testes. The spermatic cord can be located by palpating the scrotal sac above either testis with the thumb and forefinger.

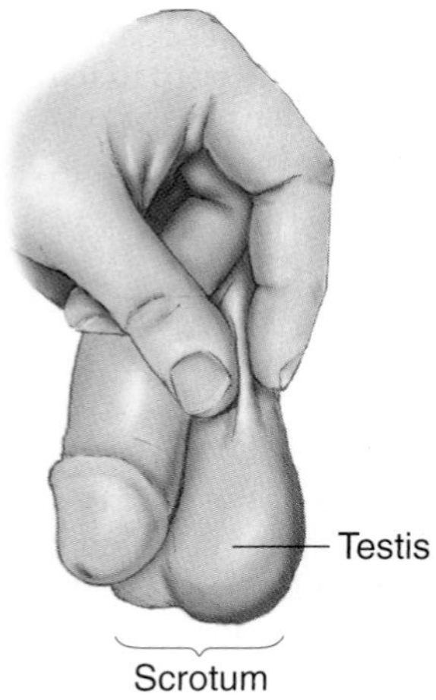

— Testis

Scrotum

## The Scrotum

The **scrotum** (SKROH-tum), or scrotal sac, is a loose pouch of skin that is an outpocket of the abdominal wall in the groin area directly underneath the penis (○ **Figure 5.3**). Normally, it hangs loosely from the body wall, although cold temperatures or sexual stimulation can cause it to move closer to the body.

The scrotal sac consists of two layers. The outermost layer is a covering of thin skin that is darker in color than other body skin. It typically becomes sparsely covered with hair at adolescence. The second layer, known as the *tunica dartos*, is composed of smooth muscle fibers and fibrous connective tissue.

Within the scrotal sac are two separate compartments, each of which houses a single **testis** (plural *testes*), or *testicle*. (For a diagram of the testes within the scrotal sac, see ○ **Figure 5.4**.) Each testis is suspended in its compartment by the **spermatic** (spur-MAT-ik) **cord**. The spermatic cord contains the sperm-carrying tube, or

**Scrotum** The pouch of skin of the external male genitals that encloses the testes.

**Testis** Male gonad inside the scrotum that produces sperm and sex hormones.

**Spermatic cord** A cord attached to the testis that contains the vas deferens, blood vessels, nerves, and cremasteric muscle fibers

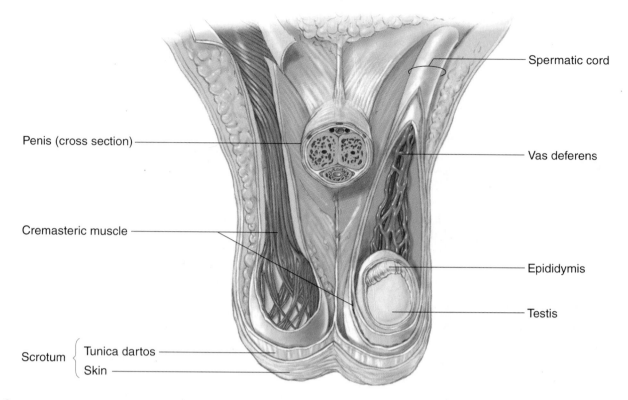

Penis (cross section)

Cremasteric muscle

Scrotum {
Tunica dartos
Skin

Spermatic cord

Vas deferens

Epididymis

Testis

**⊙ Figure 5.4** Underlying structures of the scrotum. This illustration shows portions of the scrotum cut away to reveal the cremasteric muscle, spermatic cord, vas deferens, and a testis within the scrotal sac.

*vas deferens*, and blood vessels, nerves, and *cremasteric muscle* fibers, which influence the position of the testis in the scrotal sac. These muscles can be voluntarily contracted, causing the testes to move upward. Most males find that they can produce this effect with practice; this exercise is one way for a man to become more familiar with his body. As shown in Figure 5.3, the spermatic cord can be located by palpating the scrotal sac above either testis with the thumb and forefinger. The cord is a firm, rubbery tube that is generally quite pronounced.

The scrotum is sensitive to any temperature change, and numerous sensory receptors in its skin provide information that prevents the testes from becoming either too warm or too cold. When the scrotum is cooled, the tunica dartos contracts, wrinkling the outer skin layer and pulling the testes up closer to the warmth of the body. This process is involuntary, and the reaction sometimes has amusing ramifications:

> When I took swimming classes in high school, the trip back to the locker room was always a bit traumatic. After peeling off my swimsuit, it seemed like I had to search around for my balls. The other guys seemed to have the same problem, since they were also frantically tugging and pulling to get everything back in place. (Authors' files)

Another kind of stimulation that causes the scrotum to draw closer to the body is sexual arousal. One of the clearest external indications of impending male orgasm is the drawing up of the testes to a position of maximum elevation. The major scrotal muscle involved in this response is the cremasteric muscle. Sudden fear can also cause strong contractions of this muscle, and it is also possible to initiate contractions by stroking the inner thighs. This response is known as the *cremasteric reflex*.

## The Testes

The testes, or testicles, have two major functions: the secretion of sex hormones and the production of sperm. The testes form inside the abdominal cavity, and late in fetal development they migrate through the *inguinal canal* from the abdomen to the scrotum (Ferrer & McKenna, 2000).

At birth the testes are normally in the scrotum, but in some cases one or both fail to descend. This condition, known as **cryptorchidism** (krip-TOR-kuh-di-zum) (meaning "hidden testis"), affects 3–5% of male infants (Kollin et al., 2006). Undescended testes often move into place spontaneously sometime after birth. However, if they have not descended by age 6 months, the likelihood of spontaneous descent is small (Kelsberg et al., 2006).

Parents should watch out for cryptorchidism, especially when both testes are affected. Sperm production is affected by temperature. Average scrotal temperature is several degrees lower than body temperature, and sperm production appears to be optimal at this lower temperature. Undescended testes remain at internal body temperature, which is too high for normal sperm production, and infertility could result (Kelsberg et al., 2006; Kollin et al., 2006). Cryptorchidism is also associated with an increased risk for developing testicular cancer (Dunleavey, 2006; Kollin et al., 2006). Surgical or hormonal treatment is sometimes necessary to correct this condition (Kollin et al., 2006; Vinardi et al., 2001). ■

In most men the testes are asymmetric. Note in Figure 5.3 that the left testis hangs lower than the right testis. This is usually the case because the left spermatic cord is generally longer than the right. Although this difference has often been attributed to excessive masturbation, there is no truth to this assertion. It is no more unusual than a woman having one breast that is larger than the other. Our bodies simply are not perfectly symmetric.

It is important for men to become familiar with their testes and to examine them regularly. The testes can be affected by a variety of diseases, including cancer, sexually transmitted diseases, and an assortment of infections. (Diseases of the male sex organs are discussed at the end of this chapter and in Chapter 15.) Most of these conditions have observable symptoms, and early detection allows for rapid treatment; early detection can also prevent far more serious complications. ■

Unfortunately, most men do not regularly examine their testes. Research suggests that among high-school-age males the percentage is extremely low, perhaps 2% at most. Even among male college students the percentage is very low, probably less than 10% (Adelman & Joffe, 2000; Best & Davis, 1997). Furthermore, one study indicates that instruction about testicular self-examination in high-school health classes is also relatively uncommon (Wohl & Kane, 1997). Yet this simple, painless, and potentially lifesaving process, which takes only a few minutes, is an excellent method for detecting early signs of disease. This procedure is described and illustrated in the boxed discussion "Male Genital Self-Examination."

### The Seminiferous Tubules

Within the testes are two separate areas involved in the production and storage of sperm. The first of these, the **seminiferous** (seh-muh-NI-fuh-rus) **tubules** (sperm-bearing tubules), are thin, highly coiled structures located in the approximately 250 cone-shaped lobes that make up the interior of each testis (⊙ **Figure 5.5**). Sperm production takes place in these tubules, usually beginning sometime after the onset of puberty. Men continue to produce viable sperm well into their old age, often until death, although the production rate diminishes with aging. The **interstitial** (in-ter-STI-shul) **cells**, or *Leydig's cells*, are located between the seminiferous tubules. These cells are the major source of androgen, and their proximity to blood vessels allows direct secretion of their hormone products into the bloodstream. (We will discuss the role of hormones in sexual behavior in Chapter 6.)

### The Epididymis

The second important area for sperm processing is the **epididymis** (eh-puh-DID-uh-mus) (literally, "over the testes"). Sperm produced in the seminiferous tubules

**Cryptorchidism** A condition in which the testes fail to descend from the abdominal cavity to the scrotal sac.

**! Sexual Health**

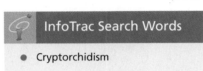

**InfoTrac Search Words**

- Cryptorchidism

**! Sexual Health**

**Seminiferous tubules** Thin, coiled structures in the testes in which sperm are produced.

**Interstitial cells** Cells located between the seminiferous tubules that are the major source of androgen in males.

**Epididymis** The structure along the back of each testis in which sperm maturation occurs.

## Male Genital Self-Examination

Our male readers can conduct a self-examination of their genitals standing, reclining against a backrest, or in a sitting position (see photo). A good time to do this is after a hot shower or bath, because heat causes the scrotal skin to relax and the testes to descend. This relaxed, accessible state of the testes can make detecting any unusual condition easier.

First, notice the cremasteric cycle of contraction and relaxation, and experiment with initiating the cremasteric reflex. Then explore the testes one at a time. Place the thumbs of both hands on top of a testis and the index and middle fingers on the underside. Then apply a small amount of pressure and roll the testis between your fingertips. The surface should be fairly smooth and firm in consistency. The contour and texture of male testes varies from individual to individual, and it is important to know your own anatomy so that you can note changes. Having two testes allows for direct comparison, which is helpful in spotting abnormalities (although it is common for the two testes to vary slightly in size). Areas that appear swollen or feel painful to the touch can indicate the presence of an infection. The epididymis, which lies along the back of each testis, occasionally becomes infected, sometimes causing an irregular area to become tender to the touch. Also, be aware of any mass

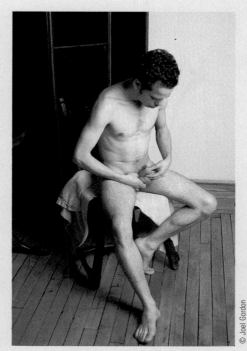

© Joel Gordon

Self-examination can increase a man's familiarity with his genitals. Any irregularity, such as a lump or tender area in the scrotum, should be examined immediately by a physician.

within the testis that feels hard or irregular to the fingertips but that can be painless to touch. This mass, which may be no larger than a BB shot or small pea, could be an indication of early-stage testicular cancer. This cancer, although relatively rare, can progress rapidly. Early detection and prompt treatment are essential to successful recovery. Testicular cancer is discussed further at the end of this chapter.

While examining your genitals, also be aware of any unusual changes in your penis. A sore or an unusual growth anywhere on its surface can be a symptom of an infection, a sexually transmitted disease, or in rare cases, penile cancer. Although cancer of the penis is among the rarest of cancers, it is also one of the most traumatic and, unless diagnosed and treated early, deadly (Gordon et al., 1997). Penile cancer usually begins as a small, painless sore on the glans or, in the case of uncircumcised men, the foreskin. The sore can remain the same for weeks, months, or even years until it changes into a cauliflowerlike mass that is chronically inflamed and tender. Clearly, the time to first seek medical attention is immediately after first noticing the sore, when the prospect for a cure remains good.

---

moves through a maze of tiny ducts into this C-shaped structure that adheres to the back and upper surface of each testis (see Figure 5.5). Evidence suggests that the epididymis serves primarily as a storage chamber where sperm cells undergo additional maturing, or ripening, for a period of several weeks. During this time they are completely inactive. Researchers theorize that a selection process also occurs in the epididymis, in which abnormal sperm cells are eliminated by the body's waste removal system.

## The Vas Deferens

Sperm held in the epididymis eventually drain into the **vas deferens** (vas DEH-fuh-renz), a long, thin duct that travels up through the scrotum inside the spermatic cord. The vas deferens is close to the surface of the scrotum along this route, which makes the common male sterilization procedure, **vasectomy** (vuh-SEK-tuh-mee), relatively simple. (Vasectomy is described in Chapter 10.)

**Vas deferens** A sperm-carrying tube that begins at the testis and ends at the urethra.

**Vasectomy** Male sterilization procedure that involves removing a section from each vas deferens.

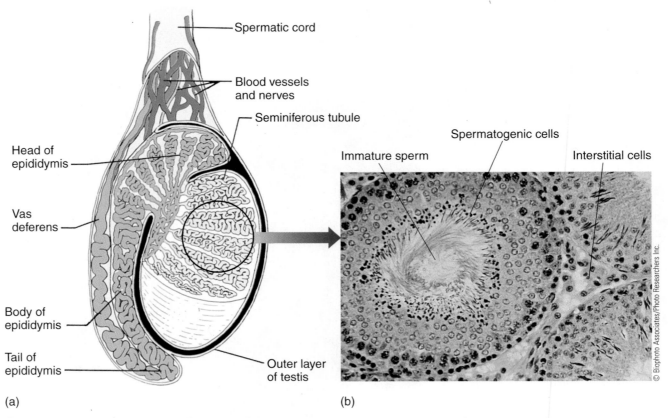

Spermatic cord

Blood vessels
and nerves

Seminiferous tubule

Spermatogenic cells

Immature sperm

Interstitial cells

Head of
epididymis

Vas
deferens

Body of
epididymis

Tail of
epididymis

Outer layer
of testis

© Biophoto Associates/Photo Researchers Inc.

(a)

(b)

○ **Figure 5.5** (a) Internal structure of a testis. Sperm are produced in the seminiferous tubules and transported to the epididymis, which serves as a storage chamber. (b) The cross-section enlargement view of the seminiferous tubules shows spermatogenic (sperm-making) cells and the interstitial cells.

**Ejaculatory ducts**
Two short ducts located within the prostate gland.

**Urethra** The tube through which urine passes from the bladder to the outside of the body.

**Seminal vesicles** Small glands adjacent to the terminals of the vas deferens that secrete an alkaline fluid (conducive to sperm motility) that constitutes the greatest portion of the volume of seminal fluid released during ejaculation.

**Prostate gland** A gland located at the base of the bladder that produces about 30% of the seminal fluid released during ejaculation.

The spermatic cord exits the scrotal sac through the inguinal canal, an opening that leads directly into the abdominal cavity. From this point the vas deferens continues its upward journey along the top of the bladder and loops around the ureter, as shown in ○ **Figure 5.6**. (This pathway is essentially the reverse of the route taken by the testis during its prenatal descent.) Turning downward, the vas deferens reaches the base of the bladder, where it is joined by the excretory duct of the *seminal vesicle*, forming the **ejaculatory duct**. The two ejaculatory ducts (one from each side) are very short, running their entire course within the prostate gland. At their ends they open into the prostatic portion of the **urethra** (yoo-REE-thruh), the tube through which urine passes from the bladder.)

## The Seminal Vesicles

The **seminal vesicles** (SEH-muh-nul VEH-si-kuls) are two small glands adjacent to the terminals of the vas deferens (see Figure 5.6). Their role in sexual physiology is not completely understood. It was once assumed that they functioned primarily as storage centers for sperm. However, we now know that they secrete an alkaline fluid that is rich in fructose. This secretion constitutes a major portion of the seminal fluid, perhaps as much as 70%, and its sugar component seems to contribute to sperm nutrition and motility (Spring-Mills & Hafez, 1980). Up to this point in its journey from the testis, a sperm cell is transmitted through the elaborate system of ducts by the continuous movement of *cilia*, tiny hairlike structures that line the inner walls of these tubes. Once stimulated by energy-giving secretions of the seminal vesicles, however, sperm propel themselves by the whiplike action of their own tails.

## The Prostate Gland

The **prostate** (PROS-tayt) **gland** is a structure about the size and shape of a walnut, located at the base of the bladder (see Figure 5.6). As described earlier, both ejaculatory

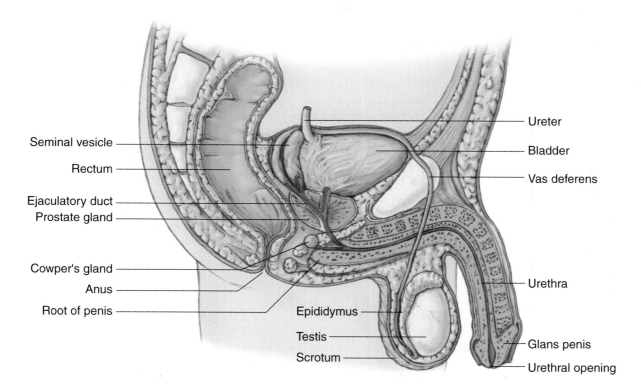

Seminal vesicle
Rectum
Ejaculatory duct
Prostate gland
Cowper's gland
Anus
Root of penis
Epididymus
Testis
Scrotum
Ureter
Bladder
Vas deferens
Urethra
Glans penis
Urethral opening

**Figure 5.6** Male sexual anatomy: A cross-section side view of the male reproductive organs.

ducts and the urethra pass through this gland. The prostate is made up of smooth muscle fibers and glandular tissue, whose secretions account for about 30% of the seminal fluid released during ejaculation.

Although the prostate is continually active in a mature male, it accelerates its output during sexual arousal. Its secretions flow into the urethra through a system of sievelike ducts, and here the secretions combine with sperm and the seminal vesicle secretions to form the seminal fluid. The prostatic secretions are thin, milky, and alkaline. This alkalinity helps counteract the unfavorable acidity of the male urethra and the female vaginal tract, making a more hospitable environment for sperm. We will discuss some prostate gland health concerns at the end of this chapter.

## The Cowper's Glands

The **Cowper's glands**, or *bulbourethral glands*, are two small structures, each about the size of a pea, located one on each side of the urethra just below where the urethra emerges from the prostate gland (see Figure 5.6). Tiny ducts connect both glands directly to the urethra. When a man is sexually aroused, these organs often secrete a slippery, mucuslike substance that appears as a droplet at the tip of the penis. Like the prostate's secretions, this fluid is alkaline and helps buffer the acidity of the urethra; it is also thought to lubricate the flow of seminal fluid through the urethra. Contrary to some reports, though, this droplet has virtually no function as a vaginal lubricant during coitus. In many men this secretion does not appear until well after the beginning of arousal, often just before orgasm. Other men report that the droplet appears immediately after they get an erection, and still others rarely or never produce these preejaculatory droplets. All these experiences are normal variations of male sexual functioning.

The fluid from the Cowper's glands should not be confused with semen; however, it does occasionally contain active, healthy sperm. This is one reason among many why the withdrawal method of birth control is not highly effective. (Withdrawal and other methods of birth control are discussed in Chapter 10.)

**Cowper's glands** Two pea-sized glands located alongside the base of the urethra in the male that secrete an alkaline fluid during sexual arousal.

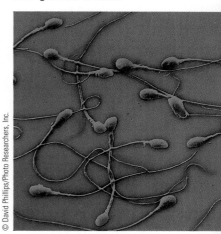

Sperm, as seen under a microscope.

## Semen

**Semen or seminal fluid**
A viscous fluid ejaculated through the penis that contains sperm and fluids from the prostate, seminal vesicles, and Cowper's glands.

As we have seen, the **semen** or **seminal fluid** ejaculated through the opening of the penis comes from a variety of sources. Fluids are supplied by the seminal vesicles, the prostate gland, and Cowper's glands, with the seminal vesicles providing the greatest portion (Eliasson & Lindholmer, 1976; Spring-Mills & Hafez, 1980). The amount of seminal fluid that a man ejaculates—roughly 1 teaspoon on average—is influenced by a number of factors, including the length of time since the last ejaculation, the duration of arousal before ejaculation, and age (older men tend to produce less fluid). The semen of a single ejaculation typically contains between 200 and 500 million sperm, which account for only about 1% of the fluid's total volume. Chemical analysis shows that semen is also made up of ascorbic and citric acids, water, enzymes, fructose, bases (phosphate and bicarbonate buffers), and a variety of other substances. None of these materials is harmful if swallowed during oral sex. However, semen of an HIV-infected man can transmit the virus to the man's partner if the recipient has open sores or bleeding gums in his or her mouth (see Chapter 15).

## ◗ Male Sexual Functions

Up to this point in the chapter we have looked at the various *parts* of the male sexual system, but we have not described their *functioning* in much detail. In the following pages, we examine two of these functions: erection and ejaculation.

## Erection

**Erection** The process by which the penis or clitoris engorges with blood and increases in size.

An **erection** is a process coordinated by the autonomic nervous system (Manecke & Mulhall, 1999). When a male becomes sexually excited, the nervous system sends out messages that cause expansion of the arteries leading to the three erectile cylinders in the penis. As a result, the rate of blood flow into these parallel cylinders increases rapidly. Because blood flowing out of the penis through veins cannot keep up with the inflow, it accumulates in the spongelike tissues of the three erectile cylinders, causing erection. The penis remains erect until the messages from the nervous system stop and the inflow of blood returns to normal.

The capacity for erection is present at birth. It is common and quite natural for infant boys to experience erections during sleep or diapering, from stimulation by clothing, and later by touching themselves. Nighttime erections occur during the rapid eye movement (REM), or dreaming, stage of sleep (Chung & Choi, 1990). Erotic dreams can play a role, but the primary mechanism seems to be physiological, and erections often occur even when the dream content is clearly not sexual. Often a man awakens in the morning just after completing a REM cycle. This explains the phenomenon of morning erections, which were once erroneously attributed to a full bladder.

Although an erection is basically a physiological response, it also involves psychological components. In fact, some writers distinguish between psychogenic (from the mind) and physiogenic (from the body) erections, although in most cases of sexual arousal, inputs come simultaneously from both thoughts and physical stimulation.

How great an influence does the mind have on erections? We know that it can inhibit the response: When a man becomes troubled by erection difficulties, the problem might be psychological, as we will discuss in Chapter 14. Also, extensive evidence shows that men can enhance their erection (as reflected in increased penile tumescence) by forming vivid mental images or fantasies of sexual activity (Dekker et al., 1985; Smith & Over, 1987).

## Ejaculation

**Ejaculation** The process by which semen is expelled from the body through the penis.

The second basic male sexual function is **ejaculation**—the process by which semen is expelled through the penis to the outside of the body. Many people equate male orgasm with ejaculation. However, these two processes do not always take place simultaneously. Before puberty a boy might experience hundreds of "dry orgasms"—

orgasms without any ejaculation of fluid. Occasionally, a man may have more than one orgasm in a given sexual encounter, with the second or third orgasm producing little or no expelled semen. Thus, although male orgasm is generally associated with ejaculation, these two processes are not one and the same and they do not necessarily occur together.

From a neurophysiological point of view, ejaculation—like erection—is basically a spinal reflex (Truitt & Coolen, 2002). Effective sexual stimulation of the penis (manual, oral, or coital) results in the buildup of neural excitation to a critical level. When a threshold is reached, several internal physical events are triggered.

The actual ejaculation occurs in two stages (⊙ **Figure 5.7**). During the first stage, sometimes called the **emission phase**, the prostate, seminal vesicles, and *ampulla* (upper portions of the vas deferens) undergo contractions. These contractions force various secretions into the ejaculatory ducts and prostatic urethra. At the same time, both internal and external *urethral sphincters* (two muscles, one located where the urethra exits the bladder and the other below the prostate) close, trapping seminal fluid in the *urethral bulb* (the prostatic portion of the urethra, between these two muscles). The urethral bulb expands like a balloon. A man typically experiences this first stage as a subjective sense that orgasm is inevitable, the "point of no return" or "ejaculatory inevitability."

In the second stage, sometimes called the **expulsion phase**, the collected semen is expelled out of the penis by strong, rhythmic contractions of muscles that surround the urethral bulb and root of the penis. In addition, contractions occur along the entire urethral route. The external urethral sphincter relaxes, allowing fluid to pass through, while the internal sphincter remains contracted to prevent the escape of urine. The first two or three muscle contractions around the base of the penis are quite strong and occur at close intervals. Most of the seminal fluid is expelled in

**Emission phase** The first stage of male orgasm, in which the seminal fluid is gathered in the urethral bulb.

**Expulsion phase** The second stage of male orgasm, during which the semen is expelled from the penis by muscular contractions.

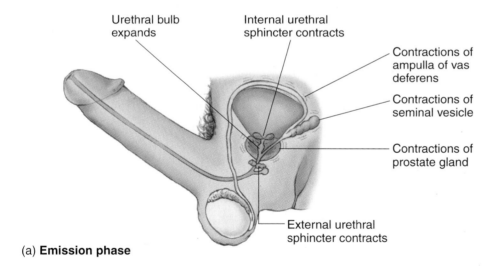

Urethral bulb expands

Internal urethral sphincter contracts

Contractions of ampulla of vas deferens

Contractions of seminal vesicle

Contractions of prostate gland

External urethral sphincter contracts

(a) **Emission phase**

⊙ **Figure 5.7** Male sexual anatomy during ejaculation: (a) the emission phase and (b) the expulsion phase.

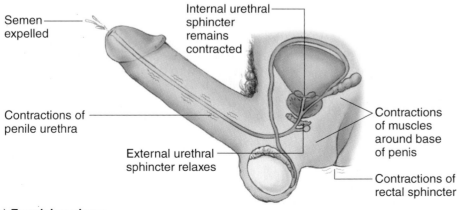

Semen expelled

Internal urethral sphincter remains contracted

Contractions of penile urethra

Contractions of muscles around base of penis

External urethral sphincter relaxes

Contractions of rectal sphincter

(b) **Expulsion phase**

spurts corresponding to these contractions. Several more muscle responses typically occur, with a gradual diminishing of intensity and lengthening of time intervals between contractions. The entire expulsion stage usually occurs in 3 to 10 seconds.

Some men have an experience known as **retrograde ejaculation**, in which semen is expelled into the bladder rather than through the penis. This results from a reversed functioning of the two urethral sphincters (the internal sphincter relaxes while the external sphincter contracts). The condition sometimes occurs in men who have undergone prostate surgery (Kassabian, 2003). In addition, illness, congenital anomaly, and certain drugs (most notably, tranquilizers), can induce this reaction. Retrograde ejaculation itself is not harmful (the seminal fluid is later eliminated with the urine). However, a man who consistently experiences this response would be wise to seek medical attention, not only because the effective result is sterility but also because retrograde ejaculation could be a sign of an underlying health problem. ■

Sometimes a man experiences orgasm without direct genital stimulation. The most familiar of these occurrences are **nocturnal emissions**, which are commonly known as wet dreams. The exact mechanism that produces this response is not fully understood. (Women also experience orgasm during sleep.) The possibility of a man using fantasy alone to reach orgasm in a waking state is exceedingly remote, and we have never heard a firsthand account of this phenomenon. Kinsey and his associates (1948) stated that only 3 or 4 of the males in their sample of over 5,000 reported this experience. In contrast, significantly greater numbers of women in Kinsey's sample (roughly 2%) reported orgasms from fantasy alone (Kinsey et al., 1953). Another kind of nongenitally induced ejaculation that men sometimes report is reaching orgasm during sex play (activities such as mutual kissing or manual or oral stimulation of his partner) when there is no penile stimulation.

**Retrograde ejaculation**
The process by which semen is expelled into the bladder instead of out of the penis.

**Nocturnal emission**
Involuntary ejaculation during sleep; also known as a wet dream.

## ◑ Concerns About Sexual Functioning

Men frequently voice a variety of concerns about sexual functioning. Several of these are addressed throughout this textbook. At this point we want to discuss two areas that receive considerable attention: the significance of penis size and the necessity and impact of circumcision. Claims are frequently made that one or both of these physical characteristics can influence the sexual pleasure of a man or his partner. In the following sections we examine the available evidence.

### Penis Size

*When I was a kid, my friends were unmerciful in their comments about my small size. They would say things like, "I have a penis, John has a penis, but you have a pee-pee." Needless to say, I grew up with a very poor self-image in this area. Later it was translated into anxiety-ridden sexual encounters where I would insist that the room be completely dark before I would undress. Even now, when I realize that size is irrelevant in giving sexual pleasure, I still worry that new partners will comment unfavorably about my natural endowment. (Authors' files)*

*All my life I have been distressed about the size of my penis. I have always avoided places such as community showers where I would be exposed to others. When my penis is hard it is about five inches long; but when it is flaccid, it is rarely longer than an inch or inch and a half, and thin as well. I don't like to be nude in front of the girls I sleep with, and that feeling of uneasiness is often reflected during sex. (Authors' files)*

These men are not alone in their discomfort. Their feelings are echoed in more accounts than we can remember. Penis size has occupied the attention of most men and many women at one time or another. In general, it is more than idle curiosity that stimulates interest in this topic. For many it is a matter of real concern, perhaps even cause for apprehension or anguish.

## Penile Augmentation

Concern over penis size has contributed to a recent surge in cosmetic surgery to enlarge this body part. Penis enlargement ads have become a ubiquitous portion of e-mail spam, and in the United Kingdom, penile augmentation has become the number one cosmetic surgery elected by British men (Reuters, 2003). Introduced in the United States over a decade ago, *phalloplasty*, or *penis augmentation*, involves lengthening the penis, increasing its girth, or a combination of both. To increase length, a surgeon makes an incision at the base of the penis and severs the ligaments that attach the penile root to the pelvic bone. This allows the portion of the penis normally inside the body cavity to drop down to the exterior, increasing its visible length by an inch or more. Additional thickness or girth can be added by tissue grafts or by injections of fat taken by liposuction from other body areas, usually the abdomen (Austoni & Guarneri, 1999; Taylor, 1995).

Although there have been no controlled clinical studies of penile augmentation to date, a number of anecdotal reports suggest that the results of these procedures are rarely impressive and can be disconcerting, disfiguring, and even dangerous (Collins, 2002; Fraser, 1999; Shuit, 1996). Ligament-cutting surgery can result in some loss of sensation, scarring, and a changed angle of erection (the erect penis may point down instead of up). Sometimes scar tissue reconnects the severed ligaments to the pelvic bone; this can result in more retrac-

tion of the penis into the body cavity than was the case before surgery. Portions of injected fat are often rejected by the body, and this can leave the penis with a lumpy, misshapen appearance. Many men who have undergone these procedures have reported being dissatisfied, embarrassed, and embittered by the results (Shuit, 1996; Wessells et al., 1996).

Men who elect to have penis augmentation often have penises that would not be judged small by any standards (Alexander, 1994). This fact, combined with the rising incidence of this cosmetic surgery, adds further evidence to how widespread men's concerns are about the acceptability of their penises. Anyone contemplating this potentially dangerous or disfiguring procedure should be extremely cautious. Currently, there is little good evidence about the procedure's efficacy. Furthermore, neither the American Urological Association nor the American Society of Plastic and Reconstructive Surgeons has endorsed penile augmentation.

Advertisements for penis-enlargement creams and pills have appeared in men's magazines and e-mail spam. These alleged penis enlargers generally comprise concoctions of herbs and reported aphrodisiacs, such as yohimbine. While these products may increase blood flow via vasodilatation of veins, thereby enhancing erection, there is absolutely no evidence that they increase penis size (McQuire, 2005; Reid, 2003).

---

It does not take much imagination to understand why penis size often seems so important. As a society, we tend to be overly impressed with size and quantity. Bigger cars are better than compacts, the bigger the house the better it is, and by implication, big penises provide more pleasure than smaller ones. Certainly, the various art forms, such as literature, painting, sculpture, and movies, do much to perpetuate this obsession with big penises. The concern some men feel over perceived size inadequacy has led them to seek a surgical solution, as described in the box titled "Penile Augmentation."

The result of all this attention to penis size is that men often come to view size in and of itself as an important attribute in defining their masculinity or their worth as lovers. Such a concept of virility can contribute to a poor self-image. Furthermore, if either a man or his partner views his penis as being smaller than it should be, this can decrease sexual satisfaction for one or both of them—not because of physical limitations but rather as a self-fulfilling prophecy.

As we learned in Chapter 4, the greatest sensitivity in the vaginal canal is concentrated in its outer portion. (We focus here on heterosexual penile–vaginal intercourse because concerns about penis size often relate to this kind of sexual activity.) Although some women do find pressure and stretching deep within the vagina to be pleasurable, this is not usually required for female sexual gratification. In fact, some women find deep penetration painful, particularly if it is quite vigorous:

Preoccupation with penis size is evident in a variety of cultures and art forms.

© Erich Lessing/Art Resource, NY

*You asked if size was important to my pleasure. Yes, but not in the way you might imagine. If a man is quite large, I worry that he might hurt me. Actually, I prefer that he be average or even to the smaller side. (Authors' files)*

A physiological explanation exists for the pain or discomfort some women feel during deep penetration. Because the female ovaries and male testes originate from

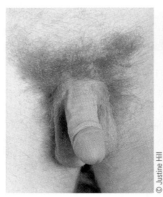  

⊙ **Figure 5.8** Many variations exist in the shape and size of the male genitals. The penis in the right-hand photo is uncircumcised.

**? Critical Thinking Question**

Assume that you are assigned to debate whether a cause-and-effect relationship exists between penis size and sexual satisfaction of women during penile–vaginal intercourse. Which position would you argue? What evidence would you use to support your position?

the same embryonic tissue source, they share some of the same sensitivity. If the penis bangs into the cervix and causes the uterus to be slightly displaced, this action can in turn jar an ovary. The resulting sensation is somewhat like a male's experience of getting hit in the testes. Fast stretching of the uterine ligaments has also been implicated in deep-penetration pain. However, some women find slow stretching of these same ligaments pleasurable.

These observations indicate the importance of being gentle and considerate during intercourse. If one or both partners want deeper or more vigorous thrusting, they can experiment by gradually adding these components to their coital movements. It might also be helpful for the woman to be in an intercourse position other than underneath her partner (see Figure 8.7), so that she has more control over the depth and vigor of penetration.

⊙ **Figure 5.8** shows several flaccid (nonerect) penises of different sizes, all well within the normal range. It is worth noting that penis size is not related to body shape, height, length of fingers, race, or anything else (Money et al., 1984). It should also be mentioned that small flaccid penises tend to increase more in size during erection than do penises that are larger in the flaccid state (Jamison & Gebhard, 1988; Masters & Johnson, 1966). It is also important to note that, even though physiological evidence indicates that large penises are not necessary for female sexual pleasure during coitus, some women do have subjective preferences regarding penis size and shape, just as some men have such preferences about breasts. Research indicates, however, that women are no more sexually aroused by depictions of large penises than by portrayals of medium or small penises (Fisher et al., 1983).

Finally, as we close this section, we take a look at another interesting cultural phenomenon that reflects a rather unusual, even bizarre, concern about penises that some men in other cultures experience in epidemic proportions: koro.

## SEXUALITY AND DIVERSITY

### *Koro: The Genital Retraction Syndrome*

**Genital retraction syndrome (GRS)** Unusual, culture-bound phenomenon in which a male believes his penis is shrinking and retracting into his body.

**Koro** A widely used term for the genital retraction syndrome.

**Genital retraction syndrome (GRS)** is an unusual culture-bound phenomenon that has attracted considerable attention in many areas of the world community, especially Asia and Africa. GRS, known under a variety of local names or phrases that mean "shrinking penis," is most widely referred to as **koro**. A man afflicted with koro typically believes that he is the victim of a contagious disease that causes his penis to shrink and retract into his body, an alarming prospect made worse by local traditions or folklore that adds the warning that this condition is usually fatal (Kovacs & Osvath, 2006; Ritts, 2003; Vaughn, 2003). The belief in koro is thousands of years old, and numerous accounts of its existence have surfaced in Malaysia, Indonesia, China, India, and several countries in West Africa. The term *koro* is believed to derive from the Malaysian word for tortoise, the association being the capacity of the tortoise to retract its head and legs into its body (carapace). In Malaysia the word for tortoise is often used as a local slang word for penis (Vaughn, 2003).

Although koro is sometimes manifested as an isolated anomaly in a single individual (Ritts, 2003), it is most commonly expressed as a fast-spreading social belief that affects hundreds or even thousands of males, causing widespread panic and hysteria. One such instance took place in Singapore in 1967 (Vaughn, 2003). A rapidly spread rumor that contaminated pork was causing penis shrinkage resulted in Singapore hospitals being swamped with thousands of men who were convinced that their penises were shrinking and retracting. Many of these men had used mechanical means—clamps made from chopsticks, weights hung from their penises, and even relatives or friends grabbing firmly on to their "disappearing" anatomy—to keep their penises from slipping away. A coordinated public education program initiated by local physicians resulted in the eventual dissipation of this mass hysteria with no fatalities or lost penises, although many bruised private parts were undoubtedly left in its wake.

The mass-hysteria nature of GRS was also reflected in an epidemic of koro in northeastern India in 1982. It was caused by a fast-moving rumor that the penises of boys were shrinking. Thousands of panicked parents brought their sons to hospitals, usually with their penises bound up or otherwise restrained to prevent further shrinkage. This epidemic was quelled by medical authorities, who toured the region with loudspeakers to reassure anxious citizens. The authorities also conducted large-scale public measuring of penises at regular intervals to demonstrate that no shrinking was taking place (Nixin, 2003).

In countries along the west coast of Africa, from Cameroon to Nigeria, koro is commonly associated with black magic and sorcerers and typically involves penis theft rather than retraction (Vaughn, 2003). Recent outbreaks of "penis thievery" have been reported in Nigeria, Cameroon, Ghana, and Ivory Coast. These episodes usually involve public accusations of penis theft, usually as the result of an unexpected or unwelcome touch from a stranger (Huyghe, 2003; Trull, 2003). Accused perpetrators of penis snatching are often physically assaulted and sometimes killed by angry victims and other concerned citizens (Huyghe, 2003).

Epidemics of koro are best explained as anxiety-based delusions that are modeled and communicated among vulnerable men (Huyghe, 2003). GRS appears to have much in common with the Western phenomenon of panic attacks, with the added dimension of sexual overlay. In some Asian and African cultures where sexual anxiety is high and stories of genital retraction are common, it is not surprising that a man might panic in response to widespread rumors of genital retraction or thievery, especially when such rumors are reinforced by his own observations of the natural process of genital shrinking in response to cold or anxiety (Mclaren & Ringe, 2006). Furthermore, when a man's guilt and/or anxiety arise out of real or imagined sexual excesses, he can be easily transformed into a prime candidate for irrational beliefs and receptivity to the seemingly bizarre syndrome of koro (Ritts, 2003).

## Circumcision

**Circumcision** (ser-kum-SI-zhun), the surgical removal of the foreskin (● **Figure 5.9**), is widely practiced throughout the world for religious, ritual, or health reasons. Each year slightly more than half of U.S. newborn males, about one million, are circumcised (Fauntleroy, 2005; McGinnis, 2005). Although the procedure is quite common, it is also quite controversial.

Proponents of routine circumcision have maintained that the procedure has significant health benefits. The area under the foreskin, if not routinely cleaned, can harbor a variety of infection-causing organisms. Numerous studies indicate that circumcision decreases the incidence of childhood urinary tract infections (Kinkade et al., 2005) and adult penile cancer (Kinkade et al., 2005; Loughlin, 2005). There is also strong evidence that circumcision

**Circumcision** Surgical removal of the foreskin of the penis.

InfoTrac Search Words

- Circumcision

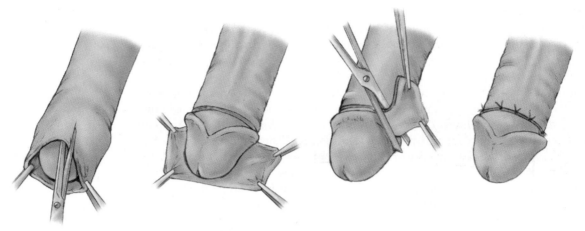

Figure 5.9 Circumcision, the surgical removal of the foreskin.

provides increased protection against HIV, the virus that causes AIDS (Auvert et al., 2005; Baeten et al., 2005; Reynolds et al., 2004). (See Chapter 15 for a discussion of the relationship between circumcision status and vulnerability to HIV infection.) Evidence also suggests that circumcision reduces the risk of genital warts infection but may provide no protection against other sexually transmitted diseases, including genital herpes, gonorrhea, and syphilis (MacLean, 2005; Reynolds et al., 2004).

Opponents of routine circumcision have, with increasing frequency, leveled several arguments against it. First, the foreskin could serve some important function yet to be determined. Second, some investigators have expressed concern that sexual function may be altered by excising the foreskin; we consider this question shortly. Finally, some health professionals think that performing this procedure on a newborn is unnecessarily traumatic and invites possible surgical complications.

Despite recommendations for the use of pain relief analgesia for circumcision by the American Academy of Pediatrics and the American Society of Anesthesiologists, less than half the number of infant boys undergoing this procedure receive any analgesia at all (Boschert, 2004; Horton, 2005). However, infants undergoing circumcison without analgesia feel and respond to pain (Boschert, 2004; Howard et al., 1998), and pain associated with circumcision can have long-lasting negative effects on future infant behavior (Taddio et al., 1997b). Some health risks of circumcision include hemorrhage, infections, mutilation, shock, and psychological trauma (Fauntleroy, 2005; Meldrum & Rink, 2005).

Because the circumcision issue has so many pros and cons, it is not surprising that the medical profession in the United States has been somewhat indecisive in its position regarding circumcision. In 1989 the American Academy of Pediatrics (AAP) assumed a neutral stance by suggesting that circumcision has both medical advantages and some risks (Shoen et al., 1989). More recently the AAP modified its position on circumcision by shifting from neutrality to a position of moderate opposition to this medical procedure (Task Force on Circumcision, 1999).

Clearly, the debate about the potential health benefits of infant circumcision will continue, and future editions of this textbook may present still other modifications of the AAP position on the issue. However, to put this continuing debate and current medical evidence into proper perspective, we note that in most cases good personal genital hygiene practices allow uncircumcised boys to grow into adulthood without encountering significant health problems (Gange, 1999; Van Howe, 1998).

Beyond the issue of hygiene, another question has often come up about circumcision: Do circumcised men enjoy any erotic or functional advantages over uncircumcised men (or vice versa)?

Some people assume that circumcised men respond more quickly during penile–vaginal intercourse because of the fully exposed glans. However, except when a

> **? Critical Thinking Question**
>
> Which of the research methods described in Chapter 2 might effectively demonstrate whether being circumcised affects a man's sexual response and pleasure? What kind of research design would you use in such a study?

condition known as **phimosis** (an extremely tight foreskin) exists, there is no difference in contact during intercourse. The foreskin of an uncircumcised man is retracted during coitus, so the glans is fully exposed. It might be assumed, in fact, that the glans of a circumcised man is less sensitive, because of the toughening effect of constant exposure to chafing surfaces.

Masters and Johnson (1966) investigated both of these questions and found no evidence of differences in responsiveness. However, the Masters and Johnson data failed to include the all-important dimension of subjective assessment by men who have experienced both conditions after achieving sexual maturity. Anecdotal reports in the medical literature testify that some men experience less sexual satisfaction after undergoing adult circumcision (Gange, 1999; Melby 2002b; Task Force on Circumcision, 1999). One study of men who were circumcised as adults to alleviate medical conditions such as phimosis found that many reported experiencing improved sexual satisfaction subsequent to the surgical procedure (Carson, 2003). It would seem that questions about the relationship between circumcision and male sexual arousal remain to be answered, and "little consensus exists regarding the role of the foreskin in sexual performance and satisfaction" (Laumann et al., 1997, p. 1052).

**Phimosis** A condition characterized by an extremely tight penile foreskin.

**? Critical Thinking Question**

If you had a newborn son, would you have him circumcised? Why or why not?

# ◗ Male Genital Health Concerns

The male genital and internal reproductive structures can be adversely affected by a variety of injuries and diseases. We describe some of these health concerns in the following pages. Should any of our male readers become affected by one of these conditions, we urge immediate consultation with a physician. **Urology** (yoo-ROL-oh-jee) is the medical specialty that focuses on the male reproductive structures.

**Urology** The medical specialty dealing with reproductive health and genital diseases of the male and urinary tract diseases in both sexes.

## The Penis: Health-Care Issues

Caring for the penis is an important aspect of sexual self-health. Washing the penis regularly with soap and water, at least once a day, is an excellent self-health practice. (There is also evidence, discussed in Chapter 15, that washing the genitals before and after sex can reduce the chances of exchanging infectious organisms with one's partner.) Uncircumcised males should pay particular attention to drawing the foreskin back from the glans and washing all surfaces, especially the underside of the foreskin. A number of small glands located in the foreskin secrete an oily, lubricating substance. If these secretions are allowed to accumulate under the foreskin, they combine with sloughed-off dead skin cells to form a cheesy substance called **smegma**. When smegma builds up over time, it generally develops an unpleasant odor, becomes grainy and irritating, and can serve as a breeding ground for infection-causing organisms. Sometimes the glans or shaft of the penis can develop an eczemalike reaction—"weepy" and sore—that results from an allergic reaction to the vaginal secretions of the man's partner. Using a condom can help to alleviate this condition, but it is important to consult a physician to clarify the condition's origin and treatment.

**! Sexual Health**

**Smegma** A cheesy substance of glandular secretions and skin cells that sometimes accumulates under the foreskin of the penis or hood of the clitoris.

Men can protect their penises by using a condom during all sexual encounters with individuals whose health status is unknown to them. This affords improved protection against the transmission of sexually transmitted diseases for both partners. Other strategies for preventing disease transmission are described in Chapter 15.

Some sexual gadgets can also be hazardous to penile health. For example, a "cock ring" (a tight-fitting ring that encircles the base of the penis) may accomplish its intended purpose of sustaining erections, but it can also destroy penile tissue by cutting off the blood supply. In the past, sexually oriented magazines published testimonials attesting to the pleasure of masturbating with a vacuum cleaner. This is not a good idea! Research suggests that severe penile injuries (including decapitation of the glans) resulting from masturbating with vacuum cleaners and electric brooms are much more common than reported (Benson, 1985; Grisell, 1988).

On rare occasions, the penis can be fractured (Adducci & Ross, 1991; Hargreaves & Plail, 1994). This injury involves a rupture of the cavernous bodies when the penis is erect. This injury most commonly occurs during coitus. A student reported his encounter with this painful injury:

> I was having intercourse with my girlfriend in a sitting position. She was straddling my legs using the arms of the chair and her legs to move her body up and down on my penis. In the heat of passion, she raised up a little too far, and I slipped out. She sat back down hard, expecting me to repenetrate her. Unfortunately, I was off target and all of her weight came down on my penis. I heard a cracking sound and experienced excruciating pain. I bled quite a bit inside my penis, and I was real sore for quite a long time. (Authors' files)

This account suggests that taking precautions during coitus is wise. This injury usually happens in the heat of passion and often involves putting too much weight on the penis when attempting to gain or regain vaginal penetration. When the woman is on top, the risk increases. Communicating the need to go slow at these times can avert a painful injury. Treatment of penile fractures varies from splinting and ice packs to surgery. Most men injured in this fashion regain normal sexual function. ■

## Penile Cancer

As stated earlier in this chapter, men can be afflicted with penile cancer, a rare malignancy that can be deadly if not diagnosed and treated in its earliest stages. Of the approximately 1,300 men in the United States who develop penile cancer in a given year, only half will be alive 5 years later. However, if the cancer is caught early and if it has not spread to lymph nodes, the 5-year survival rate is about 90% (Gordon et al., 1997). Such startling figures argue eloquently for the critical importance of seeking medical attention for any sore on the penis (see the boxed discussion "Male Genital Self-Examination" earlier in this chapter for a description of the early symptoms of penile cancer). Risk factors associated with penile cancer include being over age 50; a history of multiple sexual partners and sexually transmitted diseases, especially genital herpes; poor genital hygiene, which contributes to smegma-induced inflammation of the glans; being uncircumcised (see earlier discussion of circumcision); and a long history of tobacco use (Fair et al., 1993; Gordon et al., 1997). Penile cancer, left untreated, will ultimately destroy the entire penis and spread to lymph nodes and beyond.

InfoTrac Search Words

- Penile cancer
- Testicular cancer

## Testicular Cancer

Testicular cancer accounts for only about 1% of all cancers that occur in males; however, it is the most common malignancy that occurs in young men age 15 to 35 (Dunleavey, 2006; Wagner & Kavoussi, 2005). Furthermore, the incidence of testicular cancer seems to be on the increase in many Western countries (Srivastava & Krieger, 2000; Whiteford & Wordley, 2003). During the early stages of testicular cancer, there are usually no symptoms beyond a mass within the testis. The mass feels hard or irregular to the fingertips and is distinguishable from surrounding healthy tissue. It may be painless to touch, but some men do report tenderness in the area of the growth. Occasionally, other symptoms are reported; these include fever, a dull ache in the groin area, sensation of dragging or heaviness in a testis, tender breasts and nipples, and painful accumulation of fluid or swelling in the scrotum. Some types of testicular cancers tend to grow more rapidly than any other tumors that have been studied. Therefore, for successful treatment, it is important to detect the mass as soon as possible and to seek medical attention immediately. Improved therapeutic procedures have consistently yielded a survival rate better than 90% among men treated for early-detected testicular cancer (Dunleavey, 2006; Whiteford & Wordley, 2003). Some men procrastinate in seeking medical treatment because they are afraid that such procedures will create erectile problems or reduce their capacity to enjoy sexual pleasure. In fact, these problems occur in only a small minority of men treated for testicular cancer (Hartmann et al., 1999).

## Diseases of the Prostate

As you will recall from our earlier discussion, the prostate gland is a walnut-sized structure at the base of the bladder that contributes secretions to the seminal fluid. The prostate is a focal point of some of the more common "male problems," which range from inflammation and enlargement to cancer.

### Prostatitis

One of the most frequent disorders of the prostate gland, *prostatitis*, occurs when the prostate becomes enlarged and inflamed, often as a result of an infectious agent, such as the gonococcus bacterium (responsible for gonorrhea) or the protozoan *Trichomonas*. (These agents are discussed in Chapter 15.) Prostatitis can occur in a man of any age. About half of all men will experience prostatitis at some time (Diaz-Parker & Bratslavsky, 2005). Its symptoms include pain in the pelvic area or base of the penis, lower abdominal ache, backache, aching testes, the urgent need to urinate frequently, a burning sensation while urinating, a cloudy discharge from the penis, and difficulties with sexual functions, such as painful erections or ejaculations and reduced sexual interest. Prostatitis can be effectively treated with a variety of prescription drugs—most commonly, antibiotics. Other medications, such as anti-inflammatory agents and alpha-blockers, have also proved to be beneficial in some instances (Jack & Zeitlin, 2005).

### Benign Prostatic Hyperplasia

As men grow older, the prostate gland tends to increase in size, a condition known as *benign prostatic hyperplasia* (BPH). About 50% of men between the ages of 50 and 70, and close to 90% of men over age 80, experience this problem (Gacci et al., 2003; Gaynor, 2003). The enlarged gland tends to put pressure on the urethra, thus decreasing urine flow. If this problem is severe, surgery or medications can help (Carson et al., 2005; Gacci et al., 2003).

### Prostate Cancer

Among U.S. males cancer of the prostate is the most frequently diagnosed cancer (other than that of the skin) and is currently the second leading cause of cancer death after lung cancer (Lam et al., 2004; Wallace, 2004). Factors known to be associated with the development of prostate cancer include old age, family history of prostate cancer, being African American, and high fat consumption (Pomerantz & Kantoff, 2006; Rapp & Gerber, 2005; Wallace, 2004). The incidence of prostate cancer is 70% higher among African American men than among white men, and black men have a lower survival rate than white men for comparable stages of prostate cancer (Wallace, 2004; U.S. Preventive Services Task Force, 2003b). The reasons for the increased risk and lower survival rate among African American men are not known, but genetic, hormonal, and nutritional factors have been implicated (Eastman & Kattan, 2000).

Symptoms of prostate cancer include many of those previously listed for prostatitis, especially pain in the pelvis and lower back and urinary complications. However, prostate cancer often lacks easily detectable symptoms in its early stages. A physical examination and a blood test may be performed in an effort to make an early diagnosis. In the physical examination, a physician inserts a finger into the rectum, a procedure called a digital rectal examination (DRE). Under normal conditions, this exam is only mildly uncomfortable. The discovery of a marker for prostate cancer—*prostate-specific antigen* (PSA)—detectable by a blood test, has added another tool for physicians to use in diagnosing early prostate cancer. A normal PSA level is less than 4 nanograms PSA per milliliter of blood (Rapp & Gerber, 2005; Zepf, 2005). Some cancer specialists have suggested that a lower cutoff for normal would increase sensitivity of cancer detection

© Doug Pensinger/Getty Images

American cyclist Lance Armstrong won the 1999, 2000, 2001, 2002, 2003, 2004, and 2005 Tour de France cycling races after undergoing successful treatment for testicular cancer.

**InfoTrac Search Words**

- Prostate cancer
- PSA

(Catalona et al., 2006; Zepf, 2005). In one recent study prostate cancer was found, via tissue biopsies, in 449 men (15.2%) of 2,950 men with PSA values below 4.0 ng per mL (Zepf, 2005).

Efforts to detect prostate cancer using the DRE and PSA level as screening tools are far from precise (Hoffman, 2006; Schwartz et al., 2005). Many tumors are not detected by DRE. Both benign and malignant tumors can cause elevations in PSA levels (Woodrum et al., 1998). The U.S. government sponsors a task force of medical experts who regularly issue statements that address preventive health services for use in primary care clinical settings, including screening tests, counseling of patients, and treatment strategies. This task force, called the U.S. Preventive Services Task Force (USPSTF), released its latest recommendations for prostate cancer screening in 2003. The report concluded that "the evidence is insufficient to recommend for or against routine screening for prostate cancer using prostate-specific antigen (PSA) testing or digital rectal examination (DRE)" (U.S. Preventive Services Task Force, 2003b, p. 787). The USPSTF based this recommendation on research data indicating that the balance of potential benefits (reduced disease-related suffering and mortality) and harms (false-positive results, unnecessary biopsies, and treatment complications) remain uncertain. Furthermore, to date no conclusive evidence has emerged that PSA screening reduces the mortality associated with prostate cancer (Rapp & Gerber, 2005). This finding adds considerable fuel to a growing controversy among practitioners and researchers as to whether PSA screening is even advisable or beneficial in most cases. A recent review of evidence published since 2000 concluded "that data supporting the efficacy of PSA screening remain unconvincing" (Hoffman, 2006, p. 438).

Once prostate cancer has been diagnosed, it can be treated in a number of ways, including just monitoring the cancer to determine whether its rate of progression poses a serious health threat. Medical practitioners often recommend medical intervention (usually surgery or radiation) for men with a life expectancy of at least 10 years (Bhatnagar & Kaplan, 2005). Among treatment options are radical prostatectomy (removal of the entire prostate gland), cryotherapy, in which the cancerous cells are destroyed by freezing, and two forms of radiation—external-beam radiotherapy and internal radiotherapy by means of implanted radioactive iodine or palladium seeds (Lam et al., 2005; Hocht & Hinkelbein, 2005). Because growth of prostatic cancer tumors is stimulated by androgen, another treatment option is either orchidectomy (surgical removal of the testes) or the use of androgen-blocking drugs or hormones (Shahinian et al., 2006; Waxman & Mazhar, 2003). Finally, because the dangers or complications of surgery, radiation therapy, or hormone therapy can outweigh potential benefits, especially for older men, an approach called expectant management, which involves "watchful waiting" with deferred treatment, is sometimes most appropriate (Bhatnagar & Kaplan, 2005; Jani & Hellman, 2003).

Considerable controversy exists about the optimal approach to treating early-detected prostate cancer. Furthermore, a debate rages over whether the benefits outweigh the health risks of treatment. Medical experts differ widely as to whether treatment should be immediate or deferred. Arguments for immediate treatment, especially for young men, include longer survival time, significantly less pain, and prevention of metastatic disease (the spread of cancer to other areas). Support for watchful waiting comes from studies indicating that most men die from unrelated causes before experiencing serious complications from untreated prostate cancer; furthermore, surgical, radiation, or hormonal treatments can result in a variety of complications, including incontinence, bowel problems, erection difficulties, and inability to experience orgasm (Bhatnagar & Kaplan, 2005; Harris et al., 2004; Schwartz et al., 2005).

Until well-controlled long-term studies of treatment outcomes provide clear evidence supporting a specific prostate cancer treatment, both clinicians and patients will continue to struggle with the dilemma of treatment choice. For now, good medical management of prostate cancer involves extensive counseling about treatment options and active involvement of the patient in decisions about treatment. We hope that by the time our young male readers reach middle age, better treatment options and more powerful diagnostic tools will be available.

## Sexual Anatomy

- The penis consists of an internal root within the body cavity; an external, pendulous portion known as its body, or shaft; and the smooth, acorn-shaped head, called the glans. Running the length of the penis are three internal cylinders filled with spongelike tissue that becomes engorged with blood during sexual arousal.
- The scrotum is a loose outpocket of the lower abdominal wall, consisting of an outer skin layer and an inner muscle layer. Housed within the scrotum are the two testes, or testicles, each suspended within its respective compartment by the spermatic cord.
- Human testes have two major functions: sperm production and secretion of sex hormones.
- Sperm development requires a scrotal temperature slightly lower than normal body temperature.
- The interior of each testis is divided into a large number of chambers that contain the thin, highly coiled seminiferous tubules, in which sperm production occurs.
- Adhering to the back and upper surface of each testis is a C-shaped structure, the epididymis, within which sperm cells mature.
- Sperm travel from the epididymis of each testis through a long, thin tube, the vas deferens, which eventually terminates at the base of the bladder, where it is joined by the ejaculatory duct of the seminal vesicle.
- The seminal vesicles are two small glands, each near the terminal of a vas deferens. They secrete an alkaline fluid that makes up about 70% of semen and appears to nourish and stimulate sperm cells.
- The prostate gland, located at the base of the bladder and traversed by the urethra, provides about 30% of the seminal fluid released during ejaculation.
- Two pea-sized structures, the Cowper's glands, are connected by tiny ducts to the urethra just below the prostate gland. During sexual arousal, the Cowper's glands often produce a few drops of slippery alkaline fluid, which appear at the tip of the penis.
- Semen consists of sperm cells and secretions from the prostate, seminal vesicles, and Cowper's glands. The sperm component is only a tiny portion of the total fluid expelled during ejaculation.

## Male Sexual Functions

- Penile erection is an involuntary process that results from adequate sexual stimulation—physiological, psychological, or both.
- Ejaculation is the process by which semen is transported out through the penis. It occurs in two stages: the emission phase, when seminal fluid is collected in the urethral bulb, and the expulsion phase, when strong muscle contractions expel the semen. In retrograde ejaculation semen is expelled into the bladder.

## Concerns About Sexual Functioning

- Penis size does not significantly influence the ability to give or receive pleasure during penile–vaginal intercourse. Nor is it correlated with other physical variables, such as body shape or height.
- Circumcision, the surgical removal of the foreskin, is widely practiced in the United States. The potential medical benefits of circumcision include reduced risks of penile cancer, HIV infection, and urinary tract infection. Data concerning the effect of circumcision on erotic function are limited and inconclusive.

## Male Genital Health Concerns

- The male genital and internal reproductive structures can be adversely affected by a variety of diseases and injuries.
- Injuries to the penis can be avoided by not using various sexual gadgets and by taking precautions during coitus.
- Penile cancer is a rare malignancy that can be deadly if not diagnosed and treated in its earliest stage. Testicular cancer is more common than penile cancer, especially in young men. If detected in its early stages, testicular cancer is also highly curable.
- The prostate gland is a focal point of some of the more common male problems, including prostatitis, benign prostatic hyperplasia, and prostate cancer. A variety of drugs and surgical procedures are used to treat these conditions. Considerable controversy exists about what constitutes the best treatment strategy for prostate cancer.

## ◗ Suggested Readings

**Alan Guttmacher Institute** (2002). *In Their Own Right: Addressing the Sexual and Reproductive Health Needs of Men.* New York: Alan Guttmacher Institute. Important issues related to men's sexual health are addressed in this valuable book published by a highly respected organization.

**Kinsey, Alfred C., Wardell B. Pomeroy, and Clyde E. Martin** (1948). *Sexual Behavior in the Human Male.* Philadelphia: Saunders. An abundance of details about male sexual anatomy, the way males respond physiologically to sexual stimulation, and extensive data on male sexual behaviors.

**Zilbergeld, Bernie** (1999). *The New Male Sexuality: A Guide to Sexual Fulfillment.* New York: Bantam. An exceptionally well-written and informative treatment of male sexuality, including such topics as sexual functioning, self-awareness, and overcoming difficulties.

# ⓸ Web Resources

## CengageNOW Web Site
Go to **academic.cengage.com** to link to practice quiz questions, interactive activities, Internet links, critical thinking exercises, discussion forums, and more. You can also access sites from the Wadsworth Psychology Study Center (**academic.cengage.com/psychology**) or you can connect directly to the following sites:

### Male Health Center
An array of information is offered on this Web site, much of it related to male genital health, birth control from the male perspective, and sexual functioning.

### Circumcision Information and Resource Pages
Although this Web site provides general information about the pros and cons of circumcision and articles written by those with various opinions on the subject, it takes the point of view that, other than for religious or cultural reasons, in most cases male circumcision is an unnecessary surgery.

### The Journal of Urology
This Web site for a leading American medical journal provides content often related to genital health concerns of both men and women. Free access is provided to tables of contents and article abstracts.

### Prostate Cancer
This Web site, sponsored by the Prostate Cancer Research and Education Foundation, is devoted to providing current information on prostate cancer and its treatment. The numerous resources available here include journal abstracts, discussion forums, and descriptions of various treatment strategies.

### Testicular Cancer Resource Center
Testicular self-examinations, treatment options for testicular cancer, and issues involved in the post-treatment period—including an e-mail support group—are described and discussed on this Web site.

### Lance Armstrong Foundation
This Web site is an excellent resource for information about testicular cancer, including topics such as prevention and awareness, treatment, caregiver resources, and survivor stories.

## *Our Sexuality* Book Companion Web Site academic.cengage.com/psychology/crooks
Visit your book companion Web site where you will find flash cards, practice quizzes, Internet links, and more to help you study.

## Just what you need to know NOW!
Spend time on what you need to master rather than on information you already have learned. Take a pretest for this chapter, and CengageNOW will generate a personalized study plan based on your results. The study plan will identify the topics you need to review and direct you to online resources to help you master those topics. You can then take a post-test to help you determine the concepts you have mastered and what you will still need to work on. Try it out! Go to **academic.cengage.com/login** to sign in with an access code or to purchase access to this product.

## InfoTrac College Edition Online Library
Sign in to **academic.cengage.com/login** or visit your free book companion Web site at **academic.cengage.com/psychology/crooks** to access InfoTrac College Edition, an online searchable library that includes a multitude of journals, many specific to human sexuality. These journals include *Archives of Sexual Behavior; Archives of Sexual Health Behavior; Canadian Journal of Human Sexuality; Hispanic Journal of the Behavioral Sciences; Journal of Cross-Cultural Psychology; Journal of Physical Education, Recreation, and Dance; Journal of Sex Research;* and *Sex Roles.*

# CHAPTER 6

# Sexual Arousal and Response

Royalty Free/CORBIS

*There was never any heat or passion in my five-year relationship with Doug. He was a nice man, but I could never bridge the gap between us, which was due, in large part, to his unwillingness or inability to let go and express his feelings and vulnerability. Our lovemaking was like that too—kind of mechanical, as though he was there physically but not emotionally. I seldom felt any sexual desire for Doug, and sometimes my body barely responded during sex. How different it is with Matt, my current and, hopefully, lifetime partner. There was an almost instant closeness and intimacy at the beginning of our relationship. The first time we made love I felt like I was on fire. It was like we were melded together, both physically and emotionally. Sometimes just hearing his voice or the slightest touch arouses me intensely. (Authors' files)*

Sexual arousal and sexual response in humans are influenced by many factors: hormones, our brain's capacity to create images and fantasies, our emotions, various sensory processes, the level of intimacy between two people, and a host of other influences. We begin this chapter by discussing some of the things that influence sexual arousal. We then turn our attention to ways our bodies respond to sexual stimulation. We concentrate primarily on biological factors and events associated with human sexual arousal and response, but by focusing on physiology we do not mean to minimize the importance of psychological and cultural influences. In fact, psychosocial factors probably play a greater role than biological factors do in the extremely varied patterns of human sexual response, as we will discover in later chapters. However, it is always difficult, if not impossible, to differentiate between the complementary roles of psychological and biological factors as they influence our sexuality. How do you separate the rich diversity of psychological influences from where they are collected, interpreted, and stored in the human nervous system? Clearly, the expression of our sexuality is determined by a complex interplay or interaction between social, emotional, and cognitive factors; hormones; brain neurons; and spinal reflexes. Furthermore, an improved understanding of the various influences that help to shape our individual patterns of sexual arousal and response can add an important dimension to our expanding sexual intelligence.

# The Role of Hormones in Sexual Behavior

A number of hormones influence sexuality, sensuality, and interpersonal attraction in humans. Among the most widely discussed are androgens and estrogens, commonly referred to as sex hormones. These substances belong to the general class of **steroid hormones** that are secreted by the gonadal glands (testes and ovaries) and the adrenal glands.

**Steroid hormones** The sex hormones and the hormones of the adrenal cortex.

No doubt you have heard the common descriptive expressions *male sex hormones* and *female sex hormones*. As we will see, linking specific hormones to one or the other sex is somewhat misleading—*both* sexes produce male and female sex hormones. As discussed in Chapter 3, the general term for male sex hormones is *androgens*. In males about 95% of total androgens are produced by the testes. Most of the remaining 5% are produced by the outer portions of the adrenal glands (called the adrenal cortex). A woman's ovaries and adrenal glands also produce androgens in approximately equal amounts (Davis, 1999; Rako, 1996). The dominant androgen in both males and females is testosterone. Men's bodies typically produce 20 to 40 times more testosterone than women's bodies (Rako, 1999; Worthman, 1999). Female sex hormones, estrogens, are produced predominantly by the ovaries in females. Male testes also produce estrogens, but in quantities much smaller than what occurs in female bodies.

**Neuropeptide hormones** Chemicals produced in the brain that influence sexuality and other behavioral functions.

**Oxytocin** A neuropeptide produced in the hypothalamus that influences sexual response and interpersonal attraction.

The arousal, attraction, and response components of human sexuality are also influenced by **neuropeptide hormones**, which are produced in the brain. One of the most important neuropeptide hormones, **oxytocin**, is sometimes referred to as a "love hormone"; it appears to influence our erotic and emotional attraction to one another. In the following sections, we discuss research findings that link oxytocin to human sexual attraction, arousal, and behavior. But first we consider the evidence linking testosterone to sexual functioning in both sexes and examine the role of estrogens in female sexuality.

# Sex Hormones in Male Sexual Behavior

A number of research studies have linked testosterone with male sexuality (Dabbs, 2000; Freeman et al., 2001; McNicholas et al., 2003). This research indicates that testosterone generally has a greater effect on male sexual desire (libido) than on sexual functioning (Crenshaw, 1996). Thus a man with a low testosterone level might have little interest in sexual activity but nevertheless be fully capable of erection and orgasms. However, testosterone does influence sensitivity of the genitals, and thus a testosterone deficiency can decrease sexual pleasure (Crenshaw, 1996; Rako, 1996). Furthermore, some men experience erectile difficulties that are associated with testosterone deficiency.

One source of information about testosterone's effect on male sexual function is studies of men who have undergone **castration**. This operation, called **orchidectomy** in medical language, involves removal of the testes, and it is sometimes performed as medical treatment for such diseases as genital tuberculosis and prostate cancer (Parker & Dearnaley, 2003; Pickett et al., 2000). Two European studies reported that surgically castrated men experience significantly reduced sexual interest and activity within the first year after undergoing this operation (Bremer, 1959; Heim, 1981). Other researchers have recorded incidences of continued sexual desire and functioning for as long as 30 years following castration, without supplementary testosterone treatment (Ford & Beach, 1951; Greenstein et al., 1995). However, even when sexual behavior persists following castration, the levels of sexual interest and activity generally diminish, often markedly (Bradford, 1998; Rosler & Witztum, 1998). That this reduction occurs so frequently indicates that testosterone is an important biological instigator of sexual desire.

**Castration** Surgical removal of the testes.

**Orchidectomy** The surgical procedure for removing the testes.

A second line of research investigating links between hormones and male sexual functioning involves androgen-blocking drugs. A class of drugs known as *antiandrogens* has been used in Europe and America to treat sex offenders as well as certain medical conditions, such as prostate cancer (Bradford, 1998; Waxman & Mazhar, 2003). Antiandrogens drastically reduce the amount of testosterone circulating in the bloodstream (Waxman & Mazhar, 2003). One of these drugs, medroxyprogesterone acetate (MPA; also known by its trade name, Depo-Provera), has received a great deal of media attention in the United States. A number of studies have found that MPA and other antiandrogens are often effective in reducing both sexual interest and sexual activity in human males (and females) (Crenshaw, 1996; Crenshaw & Goldberg, 1996). However, altering testosterone levels is not a completely effective treatment for sex offenders, especially in cases where sexual assaults stem from nonsexual motives, such as anger or the wish to exert power and control over another person.

A third source of evidence linking testosterone to sexual motivation in males is research on **hypogonadism**, a state of testosterone deficiency that results from certain diseases of the endocrine system. (Hypogonadism is also associated with the aging process in some older men.) If this condition occurs before puberty, maturation of the primary and secondary sex characteristics is retarded, and the individual may never develop an active sexual interest. The results are more variable if testosterone deficiency occurs in adulthood. Extensive studies of hypogonadal men provide strong evidence that testosterone plays an important role in male sexual desire (McNicholas et al., 2003; Nusbaum et al., 2005; Yassin et al., 2005). For example, hypogonadal men who receive hormone treatments to replace testosterone often experience a return of normal sexual interest and activity (McNicholas et al., 2003; Nusbaum et al., 2005).

**Hypogonadism** Impaired hormone production in the testes that results in testosterone deficiency.

# Sex Hormones in Female Sexual Behavior

Although we know that estrogens contribute to a general sense of well-being, help maintain the thickness and elasticity of the vaginal lining, and contribute to vaginal lubrication (Kingsberg, 2002; Traish et al., 2002a), the role of estrogens in female sexual behavior is still unclear. Some researchers have reported that when postmenopausal women (menopause is associated with marked reduction in estrogen production) or women who have had their ovaries removed for medical reasons receive estrogen therapy (ET), they experience not only heightened vaginal lubrication but also somewhat increased sexual desire, pleasure, and orgasmic capacity (Dow et al., 1983; Kingsberg, 2002). The sexual benefits that often result from ET occur because estrogen provides "mood-mellowing" benefits and thus creates an emotional atmosphere receptive to sexual involvement (Crenshaw, 1996; Wilson, 2003). In addition, estrogen might play a somewhat subtle yet facilitating role in sexual arousal "in that the feminizing effects of estrogen on breasts, skin, and genitals may improve self-confidence and, indirectly, sexual desire" (Bartlik et al., 1999, p. 51). See Chapter 4 for a more detailed discussion of ET, including the link between ET and breast cancer.

Other investigators have found that ET has no discernible impact on sexual desire, and, when estrogen is administered in relatively high doses, it can even decrease libido (Levin, 2002; Redmond, 1999). In view of these contradictory findings, the role of estrogens in female sexual motivation and functioning remains unclear.

There is far less ambiguity about the role of testosterone in female sexuality. Considerable evidence leaves little doubt that testosterone plays an important role as the major libido hormone in females (Apperloo et al., 2003; Levin, 2002; Tucker, 2004). Numerous experimental evaluations of the effects of testosterone on female sexuality provide evidence of a clear causal relationship between levels of circulating testosterone and sexual desire, genital sensitivity, and frequency of sexual activity. For instance, many studies have shown that testosterone replacement therapy enhances sexual desire and arousal in postmenopausal women (Apperloo et al., 2003; Gelfand, 2000).

Other investigations have found that women who received testosterone or estrogen-testosterone therapy after natural menopause or surgical removal of their ovaries (ovariectomy) experience remarkably greater levels of sexual desire, sexual arousal, and sexual fantasies than women who received estrogen alone or no hormone therapy after surgery (Apperloo et al., 2003; Nusbaum et al., 2005; Shifen et al., 2000; Tucker, 2004).

Most of the evidence indicating the importance of testosterone in female sexual functioning has come from studies of women with low levels of this hormone because of ovariectomy, adrenalectomy, or natural menopause. One study of considerable interest sought to determine the effects of supplemental testosterone on the physiological and subjective sexual arousal in a group of sexually functional women with

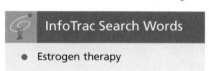

InfoTrac Search Words

• Estrogen therapy

normal hormone levels. The investigators found that sublingually administered testosterone (under-the-tongue tablets) caused a significant increase in genital responsiveness within a few hours and that there was a strong and significant association between the increase in genital arousal and subjective reports of "genital sensation" and "sexual lust" (Tuiten et al., 2000).

Other studies have found that when testosterone is administered to women with a history of low sex drive and inhibited sexual arousal, the reported frequencies of sexual fantasies, masturbation, and sexual interaction with a partner typically increase (S. Davis, 2000; Shifen et al., 2000). Furthermore, when researchers compared testosterone levels in a group of healthy, sexually functional women with levels in a group of women with a reported lifetime history of low sex drive, they found evidence linking low libido with reduced testosterone levels. Women in the low-libido group were found to have significantly lower levels of testosterone than those in the sexually functional group (Riley & Riley, 2000).

## How Much Testosterone Is Necessary for Normal Sexual Functioning?

Now that we have learned that testosterone plays a critical role in maintaining sexual desire in both sexes, we might ask, How much testosterone is necessary to ensure normal sexual arousability? The answer to this question is complex and is influenced by several factors.

Testosterone in the bodies of both sexes comes in two forms: attached (bound) and unattached (free). About 95% of the testosterone circulating in a man's blood is bound on a protein molecule (either albumin or globulin), where it is inactive or metabolically ineffective. The remaining 5% is the unattached version of testosterone, which is metabolically active and influences male libido (Crenshaw, 1996; Donnelly & White, 2000). Comparable figures for women are 97–99% bound testosterone and only 1–3% free testosterone to produce effects on bodily tissues (Rako, 1996). The sum of free and bound testosterone in each man or woman is total testosterone. The normal range of total testosterone in the blood of a man is 300–1,200 ng/dL (nanograms per deciliter; a nanogram is one-billionth of a gram). In women the normal range of total testosterone is 20–50 ng/dL (Rako, 1996; Winters, 1999). The essential amount, or critical mass, of testosterone necessary for adequate functioning varies from person to person in both sexes (Crenshaw, 1996; Rako, 1996). That women normally have much smaller amounts of testosterone than men do does not mean that women have lower or weaker sex drives than men. Rather, women's body cells seem more sensitive to testosterone than men's body cells. Therefore only a little testosterone is necessary to stimulate female libido (Bancroft, 2002; Crenshaw, 1996).

Too much testosterone can have adverse effects on both sexes (Redmond, 1999). Excess testosterone supplements in men can cause a variety of problems, including disruption of natural hormone cycles, salt retention, fluid retention, and hair loss. Furthermore, although no evidence suggests that testosterone causes prostate cancer, excess testosterone can stimulate growth of preexisting prostate cancer (Bain, 2001; Nusbaum et al., 2005). In women excess testosterone can stimulate significant growth of facial and body hair, increase muscle mass, reduce breast size, and enlarge the clitoris (Kingsberg, 2002). However, in most instances only the use of irresponsibly high doses of testosterone over a sustained period of time results in the development of adverse side effects in either sex (Rako, 1999). Furthermore, as we have seen, supplementary testosterone can help restore sexual desire to men and women with deficient levels of this libido hormone.

A normal level of total testosterone in either sex does not necessarily rule out a biological basis for a flagging sex drive, because the key hormonal component in libido—free testosterone—can be abnormally low even though the total testosterone level is within normal limits. Consequently, should you find yourself experiencing testosterone deficiency (see next section), it is important that, as an informed consumer of health care, you have your free testosterone levels assessed in addition to your total testosterone level. Until recently, most physicians ordered testing of only total testosterone. Even today, this improper and incomplete testing procedure is still followed by some medical practitioners. ■

! Sexual Health

Finally, the rate at which testosterone production diminishes with aging differs markedly in men and women. As commonly happens, when a woman's ovaries begin to shut down at menopause, her total testosterone may fall quickly in just a matter of months. For other women the onset of testosterone deficiency is more gradual, taking place over a period of several years (Gelfand, 2000; Kingsberg, 2002). (Women who have their ovaries surgically removed are more likely to experience an abrupt or precipitous loss of testosterone.) When a woman's ovaries are no longer producing normal levels of testosterone, even though her adrenal glands continue to produce testosterone, their output also diminishes (Rako, 1999).

In contrast, in men the decline in testosterone with aging is usually much less precipitous. Although testosterone production in both the testes and the adrenal glands diminishes with aging, the changes are generally gradual rather than abrupt and typically take place over an extended number of years (McNicholas et al., 2003; Sadovsky, 2005). This is probably due in large part to the continued functioning of the testes, which, unlike the ovaries, do not undergo a fairly rapid shutdown in the middle of life.

The general signs of testosterone deficiency are similar in both sexes, even though they have a more rapid onset in women than in men. The most obvious symptoms of testosterone deficiency are listed in ◐ **Table 6.1**.

## Testosterone Replacement Therapy

If you find yourself experiencing some of the symptoms listed in Table 6.1, you might want to seek medical advice regarding possible testosterone replacement therapy (TRT). At present, men generally find it much easier than women to secure medical advice about TRT. The use of testosterone supplements to treat male sexual difficulties is relatively common. In marked contrast, the medical community is often reluctant to

- Decrease in one's customary level of sexual desire.
- Reduced sensitivity of the genitals and the nipples to sexual stimulation.
- Overall reduction in general levels of sexual arousability, possibly accompanied by decreased orgasmic capacity and/or less intense orgasms.
- Diminished energy levels and possibly depressed mood.
- Increased fat mass.
- Decreased bone mineral density, which can result in osteoporosis in both sexes.
- Reduced body hair.
- Decreased muscle mass and strength.

SOURCES: Bain (2001), Kingsberg (2002), McNicholas et al. (2003), Nusbaum et al. (2005), and Sadovsky (2005).

prescribe supplementary testosterone for women who manifest symptoms of deficiency. However, a gradual awakening to the benefits of testosterone supplement therapy is under way. In fact, several leading authorities on gynecology and menopause stress the need for educating medical practitioners as well as health-care consumers, especially postmenopausal women, about the use of supplementary testosterone (Gelfand, 2000; Johnson, 2002).

Because of the highly individualized way that both men and women respond to hormones, there is no clear-cut right or wrong approach to TRT. Furthermore, TRT is not necessary for every person whose testosterone levels are lower than normal. Ideally, a person will seek the counsel of an informed physician who will both determine the appropriateness of TRT and work with him or her to find the best dosage and method of administration to effectively alleviate the symptoms of testosterone deficiency.

Testosterone supplements can be administered to men or women orally (swallowing), sublingually (under-the-tongue tablets), by injection, by implantation of a pellet, or by direct application to the skin, using either a testosterone gel formulation or a transdermal skin patch (McNicholas et al., 2003; Morales, 2003; Sinclair & Kligman, 2005). Testosterone can also be applied to women by means of vaginal creams and gels. Experts on TRT caution against taking too much testosterone. Taking a dose greater than necessary to eliminate deprivation symptoms is not likely to improve libido and general energy level and could result in adverse side effects. Furthermore, as discussed in Chapter 4, one recent study suggests that women undergoing testosterone therapy may have an increased risk of breast cancer (Tamimi, 2006).

## Oxytocin in Male and Female Sexual Behavior

The neuropeptide hormone *oxytocin*, which is produced in the hypothalamus, exerts significant influence on sexual response, sensuality, and interpersonal erotic and emotional attraction (Blaicher et al., 1999; Love, 2001; Wilson, 2003). A well-known biological function of oxytocin is to facilitate ejection of milk from the nipple during breastfeeding (Wilson, 2003). Some refer to oxytocin as the snuggle chemical because its release during breast-feeding facilitates mother-child bonding (Love, 2001). The release of oxytocin during sexual arousal and response may have a similar bonding effect on sexual partners.

Oxytocin is secreted during cuddling and physical intimacy, and touch is an especially powerful triggering mechanism for its release. Increased levels of circulating oxytocin have been shown to stimulate sexual activity in a variety of animals, including humans (Anderson-Hunt & Dennerstein, 1994; Wilson, 2003). This hormone increases skin sensitivity to touch and thus encourages or facilitates affectionate behavior (Love, 2001; McEwen, 1997). In humans oxytocin levels increase as a person moves through a sexual response cycle from initial excitement to orgasm, and high levels of oxytocin are associated with orgasmic release in both sexes (Anderson-Hunt & Dennerstein, 1994; Wilson, 2003). Oxytocin also stimulates contractions of the uterine wall during orgasm (Wilson, 2003).

The significant escalation of oxytocin release at the point of orgasm, together with the elevated levels of this hormone that remain in the blood for a time afterward, could contribute to the emotional and erotic bonding of sexual partners and to a sense of shared attraction (Love, 2001; Pedersen, 1992). Research with human subjects indicates that oxytocin plays an important role in facilitating social attachment with others and in the development and fostering of feelings of being in love (Carter, 1998; Wilson, 2003). Autistic children, who commonly exhibit a reduced ability to form social attachments and express love, often have significantly reduced levels of oxytocin (Green et al., 2001). This finding provides further evidence of the association between oxytocin levels and the capacity to form attachments and loving interactions.

## The Brain and Sexual Arousal

From our experience we know that the brain plays an important role in our sexuality. Our thoughts, emotions, and memories are all mediated through the brain's complex mechanisms. Sexual arousal can occur without any sensory stimulation; it can result from *fantasy* (in this case, thinking of erotic images or sexual interludes). Some individuals can even reach orgasm during a fantasy experience without any physical stimulation (Whipple & Komisaruk, 1999; Whipple et al., 1992).

We know that specific events can cause us to become aroused. Less apparent is the role of individual experience and cultural influence, both of which are mediated by our brains. Clearly, we do not all respond similarly to the same stimuli. Some people can become highly aroused if their partners use explicit sexual language; others find such words threatening or a sexual turnoff. Cultural influences also play an important role. For example, the smell of genital secretions may be more arousing to many Europeans than to members of our own deodorant-conscious society. Before turning to a more detailed discussion of the brain and sexual arousal, we take a brief look at cultural influences on sexual arousal in the following Sexuality and Diversity discussion.

## SEXUALITY AND DIVERSITY

### Cultural Variations in Sexual Arousal

Although the biological mechanisms underlying human sexual arousal and response are essentially universal, the particular sexual stimuli and/or behaviors that people find arousing are greatly influenced by cultural conditioning. For example, in Western societies, in which the emphasis during sexual activity tends to be heavily weighted toward achieving orgasm, genitally focused activities are frequently defined as optimally arousing. In contrast, in some Asian societies sexual practices are interwoven with spiritual traditions of Hinduism, Buddhism, and Taoism, in which the *primary* goal of sexual interaction is not the mere achievement of orgasm but an extension of sexual arousal for long periods of time, often several hours (Stubbs, 1992). Devotees of Eastern Tantric traditions often achieve optimal pleasure by emphasizing the sensual and spiritual aspects of shared intimacy rather than orgasmic release (Devi, 1977; Richard, 2002).

In many non-Western societies, especially some African cultures, female orgasm is either rare or completely unknown (Ecker, 1993). Furthermore, in some of these societies, vaginal lubrication is negatively evaluated and male partners may complain about it (Ecker, 1993). This societal attitude provides an impetus for the practice of "dry sex," described in Chapter 15.

Even in American society, ethnicity influences sexual response, and its effect is evident in female orgasm rates reported in the National Health and Social Life Survey (NHSLS). In this study 38% of African American women reported that they always have an orgasm during sexual interaction with their primary partner, compared with 26% of white American women and 34% of Hispanic women (Laumann et al., 1994). In the following paragraphs, we provide brief examples of some other facets of cultural diversity in human sexual arousal.

Kissing on the mouth, a universal source of sexual arousal in Western society, is rare or absent in many other parts of the world. Certain North American Inuit people and inhabitants of the Trobriand Islands would rather rub noses than lips, and among the Thonga of South Africa kissing is viewed as odious behavior. Hindu people of India are also disinclined to kiss because they believe that such contact symbolically contaminates the act of sexual intercourse. In their survey of 190 societies, Clellan Ford and Frank Beach (1951) found that mouth kissing was acknowledged in only 21 societies and was practiced as a prelude or accompaniment to coitus in only 13.

Oral sex (both cunnilingus and fellatio) is a common source of sexual arousal among island societies of the South Pacific, in industrialized nations of Asia, and in much of the Western world. In contrast, in Africa (with the exception of northern regions), such practices are likely to be viewed as unnatural or disgusting.

Foreplay in general, whether it be oral sex, sensual touching, or passionate kissing, is subject to wide cultural variation. In some societies, most notably those with Eastern traditions, couples strive to prolong intense states of sexual arousal for several hours (Devi, 1977). Although varied patterns of foreplay are common in Western cultures, these activities are often of short duration, as lovers move rapidly toward the "main event" of coitus. In still other societies foreplay is either sharply curtailed or absent altogether. For example, the Lepcha farmers of the southeastern Himalayas limit foreplay to men briefly caressing their partners' breasts, and among the Irish inhabitants of Inis Beag, precoital sexual activity is reported to be limited to mouth kissing and rough fondling of the woman's lower body by her partner (Messenger, 1971).

Another indicator of cultural diversity is the wide variety in standards of attractiveness. Although physical qualities exert a profound influence on human sexual arousal in virtually every culture, standards of attractiveness vary widely, as can be seen in the accompanying photos of women and men from around the world who are considered attractive in their own cultures. What may be attractive or a source of erotic arousal in one culture may seem strange or unattractive in others. For instance, although some island societies attach erotic significance to the shape and textures of female genitals, most Western societies do not. To cite a final example, in many societies, bare female breasts are not generally viewed as erotic stimuli, as they are in the United States.

Our standards of physical attractiveness vary widely, as can be seen in these six photos of women and men from around the world who are considered attractive in their cultures.

**Cerebral cortex** The outer layer of the brain's cerebrum that controls higher mental processes.

**Limbic system** A subcortical brain system composed of several interrelated structures that influences the sexual behavior of humans and other animals.

The brain is the storehouse of our memories and cultural values, and consequently its influence over our sexual arousability is profound. Strictly mental events, such as fantasies, are the product of the **cerebral cortex**, the thinking center of the brain that controls such functions as reasoning, language, and imagination. The cerebral cortex represents only one level of functioning at which the brain influences human sexual arousal and response. At a subcortical level the **limbic system** seems to play an important part in determining sexual behavior, both in humans and in other animals.

**Figure 6.1** shows some key structures in the limbic system. These include the *cingulate gyrus*, the *amygdala*, the *hippocampus*, and parts of the *hypothalamus*,

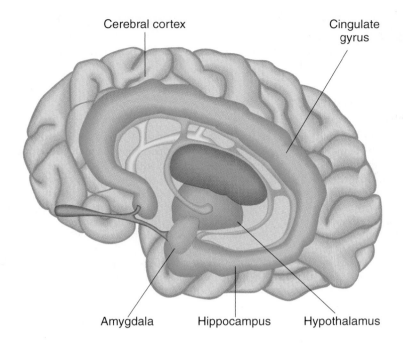

Cerebral cortex

Cingulate gyrus

Amygdala    Hippocampus    Hypothalamus

Figure 6.1 The limbic system, a region of the brain associated with emotion and motivation, is important in human sexual function. Key structures, shaded in color, include the cingulate gyrus, portions of the hypothalamus, the amygdala, and the hippocampus.

which plays a regulating role. Research links various sites in the limbic system with sexual behavior (Arnow et al., 2002; Karamaeta, 2002; Stark, 2005). Investigators have begun to use magnetic resonance imaging (MRI) technology to record brain activity during sexual arousal. This research, described in the Spotlight on Research box, has provided further evidence of the involvement of the limbic system in sexual responding.

Evidence indicates that electrical stimulation of the hypothalamus in human subjects produces sexual arousal, sometimes culminating in orgasm (Sem-Jacobsen, 1968). Furthermore, cases have been recorded in which therapeutic electrical and chemical brain stimulation of humans has had a similar impact.

Medical researcher Robert Heath (1972) experimented with limbic system stimulation in patients suffering from various disorders. He theorized that stimulation-induced pleasure would prove to have some therapeutic value. One patient, a man with an emotional disorder, was provided with a self-stimulation device that he used up to 1,500 times per hour to administer stimulation to an area in his limbic system. He described the stimulation as producing intense sexual pleasure, protesting each time the unit was taken away from him. Another patient, a woman with an epileptic disorder, reported intense sexual pleasure and experienced multiple orgasmic responses as a direct result of brain stimulation.

Several studies have implicated the hypothalamus in sexual functioning. For instance, researchers have reported increased sexual activity in rats, including erections and ejaculations, triggered by stimulation in both anterior and posterior regions of the hypothalamus (Paredes & Baum, 1997). When certain parts of the hypothalamus are surgically destroyed, the sexual behavior of both males and females of several species can be dramatically reduced (Hitt et al., 1970; Paredes & Baum, 1997). One region in the preoptic area of the hypothalamus, the *medial preoptic area* (MPOA), has been implicated in sexual arousal and sexual behavior. Electrical stimulation of the MPOA increases sexual behavior, and damage to this area reduces or eliminates sexual activity in males of a wide variety of species (Stark, 2005; Wilson, 2003). Opiate drugs, such as heroin and morphine, have a suppressive effect on the MPOA and are known to inhibit sexual performance in both sexes (Argiolas, 1999).

Certain naturally occurring brain substances, called *neurotransmitters* (chemicals that transmit messages in the nervous system) are also known to influence sexual arousal and response by their effect on the MPOA. One of these transmitter substances, **dopamine**, has both an excitatory effect on the MPOA and a facilitatory effect on sexual arousal and response in males of many species (Giargiari et al., 2005; Wilson, 2003). Furthermore, testosterone is known to stimulate the release of

InfoTrac Search Words

● Limbic system

**Dopamine** A neurotransmitter that facilitates sexual arousal and activity.

## Monitoring Brain Function During Sexual Arousal With Magnetic Resonance Imaging

Cutting-edge research has demonstrated the benefits of using a powerful technology to map or record brain activity during sexual arousal. *Magnetic resonance imaging (MRI)* is a research and diagnostic device that uses magnetic fields and radiowave pulses to construct extremely detailed three-dimensional images of the brain and other areas of the body. This technology can provide images of the soft tissues of the brain, blood flow in various brain regions, and indications of which regions of the brain activate or "light up" (via accelerated neuron firing) during various mental processes, such as thinking or emoting. Researchers have demonstrated that MRI can be used to record brain activity during sexual arousal of either sex (Arnow et al., 2002; Holstege et al., 2003, Karama et al., 2002; Whipple & Komisaruk, 2005).

In one study, male and female subjects viewed erotic video clips while undergoing MRI scanning (Karama et al., 2002). Brain activation in regions of the limbic system, espe-cially pronounced in the amygdala, was observed in both sexes. In another experiment, men viewed erotic video clips while being scanned in an MRI machine. Brain activation during sexual arousal was observed in these research subjects, especially in the hypothalamus and cingulate gyrus, both limbic system structures (Arnow et al., 2002). Another study used MRI scanning to record brain activity during women's orgasmic responses. Heightened levels of brain activation was observed in several areas of the limbic system, including the hypothalamus, amygdala, hippocampus, and cingulate gyrus (Whipple & Komisaruk, 2005).

The results of these and similar studies demonstrate that MRI technology offers an excellent tool for monitoring the brain during sexual arousal and response. Clearly this technique holds great promise for advancing our understanding of the role of the brain in our sexuality.

---

dopamine in the MPOA in both males and females (Wilson, 2003). This finding indicates one possible mechanism by which testosterone stimulates libido in both sexes.

**Serotonin** A neurotransmitter that inhibits sexual arousal and activity.

In contrast to the facilitatory impact of dopamine on sexual behavior, the neurotransmitter **serotonin** appears to inhibit sexual activity. Male ejaculation causes a release of serotonin in both the MPOA and the *lateral hypothalamus*, an area on the sides of the hypothalamus. This released serotonin temporarily reduces sex drive and behavior by inhibiting the release of dopamine (Hull et al., 1999). Serotonin also suppresses sexual arousal by blocking the action of oxytocin (Wilson, 2003). Humans who suffer from depression are often provided antidepressant medications called *selective serotonin reuptake inhibitors* (SSRIs). These drugs, whose effect is to increase serotonin levels in the brain, often interfere with libido and sexual response. Research has shown that SSRIs diminish genital sensitivity and reduce orgasmic capacity in both sexes (Michelson et al., 2002; Wilson, 2003).

Collectively these various findings provide strong evidence that dopamine facilitates sexual arousal and activity in women and men, whereas serotonin appears to provide an inhibitory effect on both sexes.

It is doubtful that researchers will ever find one specific "sex center" in the brain. However, it is clear that both the cerebral cortex and the limbic system play important roles in initiating, organizing, and controlling human sexual arousal and response. In addition, the brain interprets a variety of sensory inputs that often exert a profound influence on sexual arousal. We examine this topic in the next section.

## ❿ The Senses and Sexual Arousal

It has been said that the brain is the most important sense organ for human sexual arousal. This observation implies that any sensory event, if so interpreted by the brain, can serve as an effective sexual stimulus. The resulting variety in the sources of erotic stimulation helps explain the tremendous sexual complexity of humans.

Of the major senses, touch tends to predominate during sexual intimacy. However, all the senses have the potential to become involved, and sights, smells, sounds, and tastes can all be important contributors to erotic arousal. There are no blueprints for the what and how of sensory stimulation. Each of us is unique; we have our own individual triggers of arousal.

## Touch

Stimulation of the various skin surfaces is probably a more frequent source of human sexual arousal than any other type of sensory stimulus. The nerve endings that respond to touch are distributed unevenly throughout the body, which explains why certain areas are more sensitive than others. Those locations that are most responsive to tactile pleasuring are commonly referred to as the **erogenous zones**. A distinction is often made between primary erogenous zones (those areas that contain dense concentrations of nerve endings) and secondary erogenous zones (other areas of the body that have become endowed with erotic significance through sexual conditioning).

A list of **primary erogenous zones** generally includes the genitals, buttocks, anus, perineum, breasts (particularly the nipples), inner surfaces of the thighs, armpits, navel, neck, ears (especially the lobes), and the mouth (lips, tongue, and the entire oral cavity). It is important to remember, however, that just because a given area qualifies as a primary erogenous zone, does not guarantee that stimulating it will produce arousal in a sexual partner. What is intensely arousing for one person may produce no reaction—or even irritation—in another.

The **secondary erogenous zones** include virtually all other regions of the body. For example, if your lover tenderly kissed and stroked your upper back during each sexual interlude, this area could be transformed into an erogenous zone. Such secondary locations become eroticized because they are touched within the context of sexual intimacies. A man and a woman describe how touch enhances their sexual experiences:

*I love being touched all over, particularly on my back. Each touch helps to develop trust and a sense of security. (Authors' files)*

*Soft touches, not necessarily genital, arouse me most. When he lightly traces my neck and back with his fingers, my nerves become highly sensitive, and my entire body starts tingling with arousal. (Authors' files)*

**Erogenous zones** Areas of the body that are particularly responsive to sexual stimulation.

**Primary erogenous zones** Areas of the body that contain dense concentrations of nerve endings.

**Secondary erogenous zones** Areas of the body that have become erotically sensitive through learning and experience.

© Deborah Egan

Sensual touching is one of the most frequent sources of erotic stimulation.

## Vision

In our society visual stimuli appear to be of great importance. Prime evidence is the emphasis we often place on physical appearance, including such activities as personal grooming, wearing the right clothes, and the extensive use of cosmetics. Therefore it is not surprising that vision is second only to touch in the hierarchy of stimuli that most people view as sexually arousing.

The popularity of sexually explicit men's magazines in our society suggests that the human male is more aroused by visual stimuli than is the female. Early research seemed to support this conclusion. Kinsey found that more men than women reported being sexually excited by visual stimuli, such as pinup erotica and stag shows (Kinsey et al., 1948, 1953). However, this finding reflects several social influences, including the greater cultural inhibitions attached to such behavior in women at the time of his research and the simple fact that men had been provided with far more opportunities to develop an appetite for such stimuli. Furthermore, many women found the old-style porn films and videos, which were made to appeal exclusively to men, to be offensive and insensitive and thus not something they would acknowledge as a source of sexual arousal (Striar & Bartlik, 2000). This interpretation is supported by later research that used physiological recording devices (see Chapter 2) to measure sexual arousal under controlled laboratory conditions. These studies have demonstrated strong similarities in the physical responses of males and females to visual erotica (Murnen & Stockton, 1997; Rubinsky et al., 1987). Most women display physiologically measurable arousal while watching erotic films, even those who report no feelings

**InfoTrac Search Words**

- Erogenous zones

**? Critical Thinking Question**

It has been said that women enjoy hugging and touching more than genital sex, whereas men have little interest in the "preliminaries," preferring to "get down to the real thing." Do you believe this statement reflects a genuine difference between the sexes? If so, is it learned or biologically determined?

of being aroused (Laan & Everaerd, 1996). Research findings suggest that when sexual arousal is measured by self-reports rather than by physiological devices, women are less inclined than men to report being sexually aroused by visual erotica (Koukounas & McCabe, 1997; Mosher & MacIan, 1994). This finding could reflect the persistence of cultural influences that make women reluctant to acknowledge being aroused by filmed erotica, or it could indicate that females have greater difficulty than males identifying signs of sexual arousal in their bodies, or it could be a combination of these factors.

## Smell

A person's sexual history and cultural conditioning often influence what smells he or she finds arousing. We typically learn through experience to view certain odors as erotic and others as offensive. From this perspective there may be nothing intrinsic to the fragrance of genital secretions that causes them to be perceived as either arousing or distasteful. We might also argue the contrary—that the smell of genital secretions would be universally exciting to humans were it not for conditioning that taught some people to view them as offensive. This latter interpretation is supported by the fact that some societies openly recognize the value of genital smells as a sexual stimulant. For example, in areas of Europe where the deodorant industry is less pervasive, some women use the natural bouquet of their genital secretions, strategically placed behind an ear or in the nape of the neck, to arouse their sexual partners.

Two people describe the impact of smell on their sexuality:

*Sometimes my partner exudes a sex smell that makes me instantly aroused. (Authors' files)*

*There is really something stimulating about the scent of a woman, and I enjoy both the smell and taste of a woman's skin. (Authors' files)*

The near obsession many people in our society have with masking natural body odors makes it difficult to study the effects of these smells. Any natural odors that might trigger arousal tend to be well disguised by frequent bathing, perfumes, deodorants, and antiperspirants. Nevertheless, each person's unique experiences allow certain smells to acquire erotic significance, as the following anecdote reveals:

*I love the smells after making love. They trigger little flashes of erotic memories and often keep my arousal level in high gear, inducing me to go on to additional sexual activities. (Authors' files)*

In a society that is often concerned about natural odors, it is nice to see that some people appreciate scents associated with sexual intimacy and their lovers' bodies.

**Pheromones** Certain odors produced by the body that relate to reproductive functions.

The females of many species secrete certain substances, called **pheromones** (FARE-oh-mones), during their fertile periods (Rako & Friebely, 2004; Wyatt, 2003). Two anatomically distinct sites in the human nose may be involved in pheromonal receptivity. These two sites are the *vomeronsal organ* (VMO) and the *olfactory epithelium* (OE). Both of these areas transmit neural messages to the brain. A number of studies indicate that these sites in human noses can detect and respond to pheromones (McCoy & Pitino, 2002; Rako & Friebely, 2004; Savic et al., 2005). In one recent study, Swedish researchers isolated two substances suspected of being human pheromones: *Estratetraenol* (EST), an estrogenlike chemical found in female urine, and *androstadienone* (AND), a derivative of testosterone found in men's sweat. Using MRI and PET (positron emission tomography) brain scans, these scientists found that exposure to EST activated ("lit up") the hypothalamuses of heterosexual men but not heterosexual women, whereas smelling AND activated this brain structure in women but not men. (As described earlier in this chapter, the hypothalamus is implicated in sexual functioning.) One additional finding of interest in this study is that when the brains of gay men were scanned, their hypothalamuses responded to AND and EST in a similar way to those of the heterosexual female subjects (Savic, et al., 2005).

Although mounting evidence suggests that humans do indeed secrete pheromones, there is insufficient evidence to determine whether these substances act as sexual attractants. Undaunted by the inconclusive nature of the available data, a number of American and international corporations have invested in the commercial development and marketing of perfumes and colognes allegedly containing substances that possess human pheromone properties (Cutler, 1999; Kohl, 2002; Small, 1999). However, the jury is still out on whether these products contain genuine sexual-attractant pheromones.

Contrary to what the marketers of commercial scents would like us to believe, Alan Hirsch, a researcher at the Smell and Taste Treatment and Research Foundation in Chicago, recently found that the odors reported to be most sexually arousing for either sex were not colognes or perfumes. In Hirsch's study, which used measures of penile tumescence and vaginal blood flow as physiological markers of arousal, women were most stimulated by the scents of licorice, cucumbers, and banana nut bread. Men reacted most strongly to the smells of lavender, pumpkin pie, and doughnuts. Although none of the tested odors inhibited the arousal of men, some smells did inhibit vaginal blood engorgement in women, including the odor of barbecued meat, cherries, and men's colognes (Adamson, 2003)!

### InfoTrac Search Words

- Pheromones

## Taste

Taste, which has yet to be fully investigated, seems to play a relatively minor role in human sexual arousal. This is no doubt at least partly influenced by industry advertisements that promote breath mints and flavored vaginal douches. Besides making many individuals extremely self-conscious about how they taste or smell, such commercial products can mask any natural tastes that relate to sexual activity. Nevertheless, some people can still detect and appreciate certain tastes that they learn to associate with sexual intimacy, such as the taste of vaginal secretions or semen.

## Hearing

Whether people make sounds during sexual activity is highly variable, as is a partner's response. Some people find words, intimate or erotic conversation, moans, and orgasmic cries to be highly arousing; others prefer that their lovers keep silent during sex play. Some people, out of fear or embarrassment, make a conscious effort to suppress spontaneous noises during sexual interaction. Because of the silent, stoic image accepted by many males, it may be exceedingly difficult for men in particular to talk, cry out, or groan during arousal. Yet in one research study, many women reported that their male partners' silence hindered their own sexual arousal (DeMartino, 1970). Female reluctance to emit sounds during sex play might be influenced by the notion that "nice" women are not supposed to be so passionate that they make noises.

Besides being sexually arousing, talking to each other during a sexual interlude can be informative and helpful ("I like it when you touch me that way," "A little softer," and so on). If you happen to be a person who enjoys noisemaking and verbalizations during sex, your partner may respond this way if you discuss the matter beforehand. We will discuss talking about sexual preferences in Chapter 7.

Two people describe how sounds affect their lovemaking:

### Critical Thinking Question

In your opinion, which of the senses has the greatest impact on sexual arousal and sexual interaction? Why? Do men and women differ in terms of which senses predominate during sexual intimacy?

*It is very important for me to hear that my partner is enjoying the experience. A woman who doesn't mind moaning is a pleasure to be with. It is good to be with someone who does not mind opening up and letting you know she is enjoying you. If my partner doesn't provide enough voice communication with sex, forget it. (Authors' files)*

*I like to hear our bodies slapping together as we make love and to hear him moan and groan for more. I also like to hear my name being called, and I like to say his. (Authors' files)*

# Aphrodisiacs and Anaphrodisiacs in Sexual Arousal

Up to this point, we have considered the impact of hormones, brain processes, and sensory input on human sexual arousal. Several other factors can also affect a person's arousability in a particular situation. Some of these directly affect the physiology of arousal; others can have a strong impact on a person's sexuality through the power of belief. In the pages that follow we examine the effects of a number of products that people use to attempt to heighten or reduce sexual arousal.

## Aphrodisiacs: Do They Work?

**Aphrodisiac** A substance that allegedly arouses sexual desire and increases the capacity for sexual activity.

An **aphrodisiac** (a-fruh-DEE-zee-ak) (named after Aphrodite, the Greek goddess of love and beauty) is a substance that supposedly arouses sexual desire or increases a person's capacity for sexual activities. Almost from the beginning of time, people have searched for magic potions and other agents to revive flagging erotic interest or to produce Olympian sexual performances. That many have reported finding such sexual stimulants bears testimony, once again, to the powerful role of the mind in human sexual activity. We first consider a variety of foods that have been held to possess aphrodisiac qualities, and then we turn our attention to other alleged sexual stimulants, including alcohol and an assortment of chemical substances.

InfoTrac Search Words

• Aphrodisiac

Almost any food that resembles the male external genitals has at one time or another been viewed as an aphrodisiac (Eskeland et al., 1997; Foley, 2006). Many of us have heard the jokes about oysters, although for some a belief in the special properties of this particular shellfish is no joking matter. One wonders to what extent the oyster industry profits from this pervasive myth. Other foods sometimes considered aphrodisiacs include bananas, asparagus, cucumbers, tomatoes, ginseng root, and potatoes (Castleman, 1997). Particularly in Asian countries, a widespread belief persists that the ground-up horns of animals such as rhinoceros and reindeer are powerful sexual stimulants (Foley, 2006). (Have you ever used the term *horny* to describe a sexual state? Now you know its origin.) Unfortunately, the rhinoceros population in Africa has dwindled to the point of near extinction, largely as a result of the erroneous belief that rhinoceros horn is an effective aphrodisiac (Tudge, 1991).

A number of drugs are also commonly thought to have aphrodisiac properties. Of these drugs, perhaps more has been written about the supposed stimulant properties of alcohol than about any other presumed aphrodisiac substance. In our culture the belief in the erotic enhancement properties of alcoholic beverages is widespread:

*I am a great believer in the sexual benefits of drinking wine. After a couple glasses I become a real "hound in bed." I can always tell my partner is in the mood when she brings out a bottle of chilled rosé. (Authors' files)*

Far from being a stimulant, alcohol has a depressing effect on higher brain centers and thus reduces cortical inhibitions, such as fear and guilt, that often block sexual expression (Cocores & Gold, 1989; McKay, 2005). Alcohol can also impair our ability to cognitively process information (e.g., values and expectations for behavioral consequences) that might otherwise put the brakes on sexual impulses (MacDonald et al., 2000). In addition, alcohol can facilitate sexual activity by providing a convenient rationalization for behavior that might normally conflict with one's values ("I just couldn't help myself, with my mind fogged by booze").

Consumption of significant amounts of alcohol, however, can have serious negative effects on sexual functioning (McKay, 2005). Research has demonstrated that with increasing levels of intoxication both men and women experience reduced sexual arousal (as measured physiologically), decreased pleasurability and intensity of orgasm, and increased difficulty in attaining orgasm (McKay, 2005; Rosen & Ashton, 1993). Heavy alcohol use can also result in general physical deterioration, which commonly reduces a person's interest in and capacity for sexual activity.

Alcohol use can have even more serious potential consequences in conjunction with sexual activity. Research has demonstrated a strong association between alcohol use and an inclination to participate in sexual practices that have a high risk for contracting a life-threatening disease, such as AIDS (Dittman, 2003; MacDonald et al., 2000). (Other mind-altering drugs, such as marijuana and cocaine, have also been implicated in high-risk sexual behavior.) ■

In addition to alcohol, several other drugs have also been ascribed aphrodisiac qualities. Some of the substances included in this category are amphetamines, such as methylene-dioxymethamphetamine (MDMA), commonly known as ecstasy; methamphetamine, often referred to as crystal meth; barbiturates; cantharides, also known as Spanish fly; cocaine; LSD and other psychedelic drugs; marijuana; amyl nitrite (a drug used to treat heart pain), also known as poppers; and L-dopa (a medication used in the treatment of Parkinson's disease). As you can see in the summary provided in ⊙ **Table 6.2**, not one of these drugs possesses attributes that qualify it as a true sexual stimulant.

⊙ **TABLE 6.2**   **Some Alleged Aphrodisiacs and Their Effects**

| Name (and Street Name) | Reputed Effect | Actual Effect |
| --- | --- | --- |
| Alcohol | Enhances arousal; stimulates sexual activity. | Can reduce inhibitions to make sexual behaviors less stressful. Alcohol is actually a depressant and in quantity can impair erectile ability, arousal, and orgasm. |
| Amphetamines ("speed," "uppers") | Elevate mood; enhance sexual experience and abilities. | Central nervous system stimulants; amphetamines reduce inhibitions. High doses or long-term use can cause erectile disorder, delayed ejaculation, and inhibition of orgasm in both sexes and can reduce vaginal lubrication in women. |
| Amyl nitrite ("snappers," "poppers") | Intensifies orgasms and arousal. | Dilates arteries to brain and also to genital area; produces time distortion and warmth in pelvic area. Can decrease sexual arousal, delay orgasm, and inhibit or block erection. |
| Barbiturates ("barbs," "downers") | Enhance arousal; stimulate sexual activity. | Reduce inhibitions in similar fashion to alcohol and may decrease sexual desire, impair erection, and inhibit ejaculation. |
| Cantharides ("Spanish fly") | Stimulates genital area, causing person to desire coitus. | Not effective as a sexual stimulant. Cantharides acts as a powerful irritant that can cause inflammation to the lining of the bladder and urethra. |
| Cocaine ("coke") | Increases frequency and intensity of orgasm; heightens arousal. | Central nervous system stimulant; cocaine loosens inhibitions and enhances sense of well-being; may impair ability to enjoy sex, reduce sexual desire, inhibit erection, or cause spontaneous or delayed ejaculation. |
| LSD and other psychedelic drugs (including mescaline, psilocybin) | Enhance sexual response. | No direct physiological enhancement of sexual response. Can produce altered perception of sexual activity; frequently associated with unsatisfactory erotic experiences. |
| L-dopa | Sexually rejuvenates older males. | No documented benefits to sexual ability. L-dopa occasionally produces a painful condition known as priapism (constant, unwanted erection). |
| Marijuana | Elevates mood and arousal; stimulates sexual activity. | Enhances mood and reduces inhibitions in a way similar to alcohol. Can inhibit sexual response and may distort the time sense, with the resulting illusion of prolonged arousal and orgasm. |
| Yohimbine | Induces sexual arousal and enhances sexual performance. | Appears to have genuine aphrodisiac effect on rats. Recent evidence suggests it may enhance sexual desire or performance in some humans. |

SOURCES: Crenshaw (1996), Crenshaw & Goldberg (1996), Eisner et al. (1990), Finger et al. (1997), McKay (2005), Rosen & Ashton (1993), Rowland et al. (1997), and Yates & Wolman (1991).

Researchers are currently studying one drug that may eventually be shown to have aphrodisiac qualities for at least some people. Since the 1920s, reports have touted the aphrodisiac properties of yohimbine hydrochloride, or yohimbine, a crystalline alkaloid derived from the sap of the yohimbe tree, which grows in West Africa. Experiments conducted by Stanford University researchers with male rats have found that injections of yohimbine induce intense sexual arousal and performance in these animals (Clark et al., 1984). The data suggest that this drug is a true aphrodisiac, at least for rats. Several recent studies with male humans suggest that yohimbine treatment has the capacity to positively affect sexual desire or performance, at least in men with erectile disorders (Ernst & Pittler, 1998; Vermani et al., 2005; Rowland et al., 1997). Another study also demonstrated that yohimbine increases physiologically measured sexual arousal in postmenopausal women who report below-normal levels of sexual desire (Meston & Worcel, 2002).

**? Critical Thinking Question**

Assume that research eventually reveals that yohimbine or some other substance has genuine aphrodisiac qualities. What possible benefits might be associated with its use? What possible abuses might arise? Would you consider using an aphrodisiac? If so, under what conditions?

Three prescription drugs used to treat male erectile dysfunction—Viagra, Levitra, and Cialis—may technically be classified as aphrodisiacs in that they increase capacity for sexual activity by facilitating genital vasoscongestion and erection (see Chapter 14). None of these drugs increase sexual desire. In contrast, the drug bremelanotide, currently undergoing clinical trials, may prove to be a genuine aphrodisiac that directly increases sexual desire. We discuss this possibility in the box titled "Sexual Arousal in a Nasal Spray."

In view of the widespread inclination of humans to seek out substances with aphrodisiac qualities, and in light of escalating advances in the realm of sexual medicine, it seems likely that a variety of genuine aphrodisiacs will be available in the future. At present, people continue to use various substances despite clear-cut evidence that they lack true aphrodisiac qualities. Why do so many people around the world swear by the effects of a little powdered rhino horn, that special meal of oysters and banana salad, or the marijuana cigarette before an evening's dalliance? The answer lies in faith and suggestion; these are the ingredients frequently present when aphrodisiac claims are made. If a person believes that something will improve his or her sex life, this faith is often translated into the subjective enhancement of sexual pleasure. From this perspective, literally anything has the potential of serving as a sexual stimulant. Consistent with this perspective is Theresa Crenshaw's (1996) cogent observation that "love, however you define it, seems to be the best aphrodisiac of all" (p. 89).

## Anaphrodisiacs

Several drugs are known to inhibit sexual behavior. Substances that have this effect are called **anaphrodisiacs** (an-a-fruh-DEE-zee-aks). Common drugs with anaphrodisiac potential include previously discussed antiandrogens, opiates, tranquilizers, anticoagulants, antihypertensives (blood pressure medicine), antidepressants, antipsychotics, nicotine, birth control pills, sedatives, ulcer drugs, appetite suppressants, steroids, anticonvulsants used for treating epilepsy, cardiovascular medications, cholesterol reducers, over-the-counter allergy medicines that cause drowsiness, and drugs for treating cancer, heart disease, fluid retention, and fungus infections (Crenshaw & Goldberg, 1996; DeLamater & Sill, 2005; Finger et al., 1997).

**Anaphrodisiac** A substance that inhibits sexual desire and behavior.

A great deal of evidence indicates that regular use of opiates, such as heroin, morphine, and methadone, often produces a significant—and sometimes dramatic—decrease in sexual interest and activity in both sexes (Ackerman et al., 1994; Finger et al., 1997). Serious impairment of sexual functioning associated with opiate use can include erectile problems and inhibited ejaculation in males, and reduced capacity to experience orgasm in females.

Tranquilizers, used widely in the treatment of a variety of emotional disorders, have been shown sometimes to reduce sexual motivation, impair erection, and delay or inhibit orgasm in both sexes (Crenshaw & Goldberg, 1996; Olivera, 1994).

Many antihypertensives, drugs used for treating high blood pressure, have been experimentally demonstrated to seriously inhibit erection and ejaculation, reduce the intensity of orgasm in male subjects, and reduce sexual interest in both sexes (DeLamater & Sill, 2005; Finger et al., 1997).

Another class of commonly prescribed psychiatric medications, antidepressants, almost without exception cause adverse changes in sexual response. These changes

## Sexual Arousal in a Nasal Spray

A new drug for treating sexual dysfunction in both men and women is currently undergoing clinical trials. This medication, generically labeled bremelanotide, is a synthetic chemical also referred to as PT-141 in the scientific literature. Bremelanotide may prove to be the first genuine aphrodisiac that directly increases sexual desire and arousal. A number of clinical studies have demonstrated that bremelanotide, delivered as a nasal spray, has been an effective treatment for erectile dysfunction and desire disorders in both sexes (Dibbell, 2005; Diamond, 2005, 2004; Rosen, 2004).

The discovery of the potential aphrodisiac/arousal effects of bremelanotide was a serendipitous (accidental) event. The peptide Melanotan II, from which bremelanotide was derived, was originally tested as a sunless tanning agent. In a clinical test Melatonin II was shown to induce both tanning and, unexpectedly, sexual arousal and spontaneous erection in volunteer subjects. The developer of Melatonin II, Palatin Technologies, then commenced clinical trials designed to achieve FDA approval of bremelanotide for treatment of male and female sexual dysfunction. Almost 1,000 human subjects have reported experiencing enhanced sexual desire and arousal under the influence of this drug (Dibbell, 2005). The mechanism whereby bremelanotide achieves its arousal effect is not fully understood, but it is believed to result from a direct effect on the brain (as opposed to a Viagra-like effect on the external genitals) (Dibbell, 2005). Bremelanotide could be on the prescription drug market as early as 2008, depending on the results of the ongoing clinical trials.

include decreased desire in both sexes, erectile disorder in men, and delayed or absent orgasmic response in both sexes (Gregorian et al., 2002; Michelson et al., 2002).

Antipsychotic drugs are also likely to disrupt sexual response. Potential adverse reactions include erectile disorder and delay of ejaculation in men and orgasm difficulties and reduced sexual desire in both sexes (Finger et al., 1997).

Many people are surprised to hear that birth control pills are also commonly associated with reduced sexual desire. A recent study of the effects of four different oral contraceptives on various sex hormones found that all four produced a marked reduction in the blood levels of free testosterone (Wiegratz et al., 2003). As we learned earlier, free testosterone influences both female and male libido. A recent study found that erotic video-induced sexual arousal in young women, as measured by vaginal photoplethysmography, was inhibited by oral contraceptive use (Seal et al., 2005).

Perhaps the most widely used and least recognized anaphrodisiac is nicotine. There is evidence that smoking can significantly retard sexual motivation and function by constricting the blood vessels (thereby retarding vasocongestive response of the body to sexual stimulation) and perhaps by reducing testosterone levels in the blood (McKay, 2005; Mannino et al., 1994). However, the evidence linking nicotine to reduced testosterone levels is inconclusive (Kapoor & Jones, 2005).

# ⊙ Sexual Response

Human sexual response is a highly individual physical, emotional, and mental process. Nevertheless, there are a number of common physiological changes that allow us to outline some general patterns of the sexual response cycle. Masters and Johnson (1966) and Helen Singer Kaplan (1979), a noted sex therapist and author, have described these patterns. We briefly outline Kaplan's ideas before turning to a detailed analysis of Masters and Johnson's work.

## Kaplan's Three-Stage Model

Kaplan's model of sexual response, an outgrowth of her extensive experience as a sex therapist, contains three stages: *desire*, *excitement*, and *orgasm* (see ⊙ **Figure 6.2**). Kaplan suggested that sexual difficulties tend to fall into one of these three categories and that it is possible for a person to have difficulty in one while continuing to function normally in the other two.

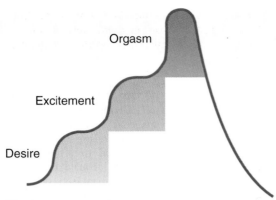

**Figure 6.2** Kaplan's three-stage model of the sexual response cycle. This model is distinguished by its identification of desire as a prelude to sexual response.

SOURCE: Kaplan (1979).

One of the most distinctive features of Kaplan's model is that it includes desire as a distinct stage of the sexual response cycle. Many other writers, including Masters and Johnson, do not discuss aspects of sexual response that are separate from genital changes. Kaplan's description of desire as a prelude to physical sexual response stands as a welcome addition to the literature. Kaplan's model was initially widely embraced as one that rectified a perceived deficiency in the Masters and Johnson model. However, it is now realized that simply adding a desire phase does not necessarily provide a complete model of human sexual arousal and response. One problem with assuming that desire belongs in such a model is that perhaps as much as 30% of sexually experienced, orgasmic women rarely or never experience spontaneous sexual desire (Levin, 2002). Fewer men appear to be included in this category. For example, in the NHSLS, 33% of women reported being uninterested in sex compared with 16.5% of men (Laumann et al., 1994).

It is clear, then, that not all sexual expression is preceded by desire. For example, a couple might agree to engage in sexual activity even though they are not feeling sexually inclined at the time. Frequently, they may find that their bodies begin to respond sexually to the ensuing activity, despite their lack of initial desire.

## Masters and Johnson's Four-Phase Model

Masters and Johnson distinguish four phases in the sexual response patterns of both men and women: *excitement, plateau, orgasm,* and *resolution.* ⟳ **Figures 6.3** and **6.4** illustrate these four phases of sexual response. These charts provide basic maps of common patterns characterized by strong similarities in the responses of men and women to sexual stimuli. Masters and Johnson did, however, note one significant difference between the sexes: the presence of a *refractory period* (a recovery stage in which there is a temporary inability to reach orgasm) in the male resolution phase.

The simplified nature of these diagrams can easily obscure the richness of individual variation that does occur. Masters and Johnson were charting only the physiological responses to sexual stimulation. Biological reactions might follow a relatively predictable course, but the variability in individual responses to sexual arousal is considerable. These variations are suggested in the several individual reports of arousal, orgasm, and resolution included later in this chapter.

Two fundamental physiological responses to effective sexual stimulation occur in both women and men. These are *vasocongestion* and *myotonia.* These two basic reac-

**Figure 6.3** Female sexual response cycle. Masters and Johnson identified three basic patterns in female sexual response. Pattern A most closely resembles the male pattern, except that a woman can have one or more orgasms without dropping below the plateau level of sexual arousal. Variations of this response include an extended plateau with no orgasm (pattern B) and a rapid rise to orgasm with no definitive plateau and a quick resolution (pattern C).

SOURCE: Masters & Johnson (1966).

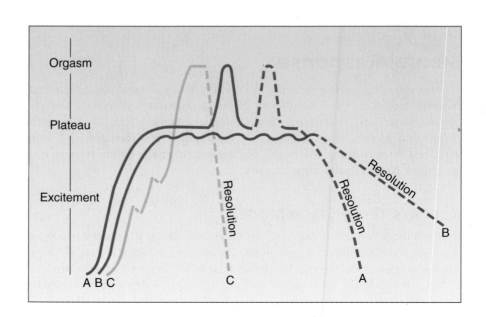

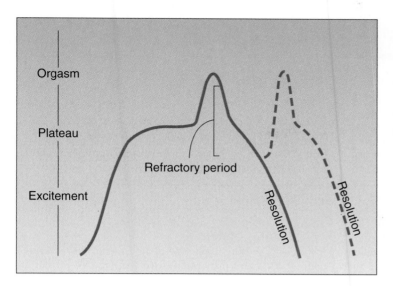

**Figure 6.4** Male sexual response cycle. Only one male response pattern was identified by Masters and Johnson. However, men do report considerable variation in their response pattern. Note the refractory period; males do not have a second orgasm immediately after the first.

SOURCE: Masters & Johnson (1966).

tions are the primary underlying sources for almost all biological responses that take place during sexual arousal.

**Vasocongestion** is the engorgement with blood of body tissues that respond to sexual excitation. Usually the blood flow into organs and tissues through the arteries is balanced by an equal outflow through the veins. During sexual arousal, however, the arteries dilate, increasing the inflow beyond the capacity of the veins to carry blood away. This results in widespread vasocongestion in both superficial and deep tissues. The visible congested areas might feel warm and appear swollen and red as a result of increased blood content. The most obvious manifestations of this vasocongestive response are the erection of the penis in men and lubrication of the vagina in women. In addition, other body areas can become engorged—the labia, testes, clitoris, nipples, and even the earlobes.

As described in Chapter 2, Masters and Johnson and other researchers have used devices such as the vaginal photoplethysmograph and the penile strain gauge to electronically measure vasocongestion during sexual arousal. Investigators have also begun to explore the benefits of using magnetic resonance imaging (MRI) technology to study sexual response. This new approach to assessing the physiology of sexual arousal is described in the Spotlight on Research box on the following page.

The second basic physiological response is **myotonia** (my-uh-TOH-nee-uh), the increased muscle tension that occurs throughout the body during sexual arousal. Myotonia is evident in both voluntary flexing and involuntary contractions. Its most dramatic manifestations are facial grimaces, spasmodic contractions of the hands and feet, and the muscular spasms that occur during orgasm.

The phases of the response cycle follow the same general patterns, regardless of the method of stimulation. Masturbation, manual stimulation by one's partner, oral pleasuring, penile–vaginal intercourse, dreaming, fantasy, and, in some women, breast stimulation can all result in completion of the response cycle. Often the intensity and rapidity of response vary according to the kind of stimulation.

**Table 6.3** on the following page summarizes the major physiological changes that occur in women and men during the four phases of the sexual response cycle. Note the similarities in the sexual response patterns of men and women. We discuss some important differences in greater detail at the conclusion of this chapter. In the following paragraphs we provide a few observations regarding each of the four phases of sexual response and some personal reports.

During the **excitement phase** both sexes experience an increase in myotonia, vasocongestion, heart rate, and blood pressure. While the appearance of a **sex flush** (a pink or red rash on the chest or breasts) can occur in either sex, it is more common in females. The length of this phase is highly variable in both sexes, ranging from less than a minute to several hours, and the degree of arousal can fluctuate between low and high. The following two reports, the first by a woman and the second by a man, give some indication of subjective variations in how people describe their sexual arousal.

**Vasocongestion** The engorgement of blood vessels in particular body parts in response to sexual arousal.

**Myotonia** Muscle tension.

**Excitement phase** Masters and Johnson's term for the first phase of the sexual response cycle, in which engorgement of the sexual organs and increases in muscle tension, heart rate, and blood pressure occur.

**Sex flush** A pink or red rash that can appear on the chest or breasts during sexual arousal.

## Monitoring Genital Changes During Sexual Arousal With Magnetic Resonance Imaging

Earlier in this chapter we discussed the use of magnetic resonance imaging (MRI) to monitor the brain during sexual arousal. MRI technology can also provide images of the soft tissues of the genitals. These images can be used to monitor changes in blood engorgement of the genital tissues as demonstrated in several recent studies of female sexual arousal (Deliganis et al., 2000; Maravilla et al., 2000, 2003).

An excellent example of this technological advance is research conducted by Kenneth Maravilla and his colleagues (2003). These investigators recruited a number of sexually functional women to participate in a series of three studies in which genital tissues were monitored using MRI while the women viewed videos of erotic content and video segments of nonerotic, neutral images. Participants also rated their subjective levels of sexual arousal by completing questionnaires. All three investigations yielded similar results. All subjects reported sexual arousal on the subjective questionnaires that was closely associated with increased clitoral blood volume and size. Maravilla and his colleagues found

that the magnetic resonance images provided excellent visualization of the genital anatomic structures of the participants, including major blood vessels involved in vasocongestion. In addition, the images allowed precise calculation of changes in clitoral size and in blood volume of the genital tissues during sexual arousal. Among the findings was an increase in both the degree of blood engorgement and overall size of the clitoris during the erotic video segment compared with its state during the neutral segment. On average, clitoral size more than doubled from the unaroused state to the aroused state for all subjects.

These investigations and similar studies demonstrate that MRI is an excellent method for observing and quantitatively measuring genital changes during sexual arousal. Application of this technology offers an advanced alternative to the use of electronic devices for measuring sexual arousal, such as the vaginal photoplethysmograph and the penile strain gauge, described in Chapter 2.

**TABLE 6.3  Major Physiological Changes During Each of the Four Phases of the Sexual Response Cycle**

| Phase | Reactions Common to Both Sexes | Female Responses | Male Responses |
|---|---|---|---|
| Excitement | • Increase in myotonia, heart rate, and blood pressure.<br>• Sex flush and nipple erections occur (more common in females). | • Clitoris swells.<br>• Labia majora separate away from vaginal opening.<br>• Labia minora swell and darken in color.<br>• Lubrication begins.<br>• Uterus elevates.<br>• Breasts enlarge. | • Penis becomes erect.<br>• Testes elevate and engorge.<br>• Scrotal skin thickens and tenses. |
| Plateau | • Myotonia becomes pronounced, and involuntary muscular contractions may occur in hands and feet.<br>• Heart rate, blood pressure, and breathing increase. | • Orgasmic platform (engorement of outer third of the vagina) forms.<br>• Clitoris withdraws under its hood.<br>• Uterus becomes fully elevated.<br>• Areola becomes more swollen. | • Engorgement and elevation of testes becomes more pronounced.<br>• Cowper's gland secretions may occur. |
| Orgasm | • Involuntary muscle spasms throughout body.<br>• Blood pressure, breathing, and heart rates at maximum levels.<br>• Involuntary contractions of rectal sphincter. | • Orgasmic platform contracts rhythmically 3 to 15 times.<br>• Uterine contractions occur.<br>• Clitoris remains retracted under its hood.<br>• No further changes in breasts or nipples. | • During emission phase, internal sex structures undergo contractions, causing pooling of seminal fluid in urethral bulb.<br>• During expulsion phase, semen expelled by contractions of muscles around base of penis. |
| Resolution | • Myotonia subsides, and heart rate, blood pressure, and breathing rates return to normal immediately after orgasm.<br>• Sex flush disappears rapidly.<br>• Nipple erection subsides slowly. | • Clitoris descends and engorgement slowly subsides.<br>• Labia return to unaroused size.<br>• Uterus descends to normal position.<br>• Lack of orgasm after period of high arousal may dramatically slow resolution. | • Erection subsides over a period of a few minutes.<br>• Testes descend and return to their normal size. Scrotum resumes wrinkled appearance.<br>• Resolution quite rapid in most men. |

AT A GLANCE

*When I am aroused, I get warm all over, and I like a lot of holding and massaging of other areas of my body besides my genitals. After time passes with that particular stimulation, I prefer more direct manual stroking if I want orgasm. (Authors' files)*

*When I am sexually aroused, my whole body feels energized. Sometimes my mouth gets dry, and I may feel a little light-headed. I want to have all of my body touched and stroked, not just my genitals. I particularly like the sensation of feeling that orgasm is just around the corner, waiting and tantalizing me to begin the final journey. Sometimes a quick rush to climax is nice, but usually I prefer making the arousal period last as long as I can stand it, until my penis feels like it is dying for the final strokes of ecstasy. (Authors' files)*

The term **plateau phase** is somewhat of a misnomer in that in the behavioral sciences the term *plateau* is typically used to describe a leveling-off period during which no observable changes in behavior can be detected. For example, it might refer to a flat spot in a learning curve where no new behaviors occur for a certain period of time. The plateau stage has been diagrammed in just this manner in the male chart (Figure 6.4) and in pattern A of the female chart (Figure 6.3). In actuality, the plateau level of sexual arousal involves a powerful surge of sexual tension in both sexes (e.g., increase in blood pressure and heart and breathing rates) that continues to mount until it reaches the peak that leads to orgasm.

The plateau phase is often brief, typically lasting a few seconds to several minutes. However, many people find that prolonging sexual tensions at this high level produces greater arousal and ultimately more-intense orgasms. This is reported in the following subjective accounts:

**Plateau phase** Masters and Johnson's term for the second phase of the sexual response cycle, in which muscle tension, heart rate, blood pressure, and vasocongestion increase.

*When I get up there, almost on the verge of coming, I try to hang in as long as possible. If my partner cooperates, stopping or slowing when necessary, I can stay right on the edge for several minutes, sometimes even longer. I know that all it would take is one more stroke and I'm over the top. Sometimes my whole body gets to shaking and quivering, and I can feel incredible sensations shooting through me like electric charges. The longer I can make this supercharged period last, the better the orgasm. (Authors' files)*

*When I masturbate, I like to take myself almost to the point of climaxing and then back off. I can tell when orgasm is about to happen because my vagina tightens up around the opening, and sometimes I can feel the muscles contract. I love the sensations of balancing myself on the brink, part of me wanting to come and the other part holding out for more. The longer I maintain this delicate balance, the more shattering the climax. Sometimes the pleasure is almost beyond bearing. (Authors' files)*

As effective stimulation continues, many people move from plateau to **orgasm**. This is especially true for men, who almost always experience orgasm after reaching the plateau level of sexual response. In contrast to men, women sometimes obtain plateau levels of arousal without the release of sexual climax. This is often the case during penile–vaginal intercourse when the man reaches orgasm first or when effective manual or oral stimulation is replaced with penetration as the female approaches orgasm. Orgasm is the shortest phase of the sexual response cycle, typically lasting only a few seconds.

For both sexes the experience of orgasm can be an intense mixture of highly pleasurable sensations, but whether that experience differs from male to female has been the subject of considerable debate. This question was evaluated in two separate experimental analyses of orgasm descriptions provided by college students (Wiest, 1977; Wiest et al., 1995). When compared using a standard psychological rating scale, women's and men's subjective

**Orgasm** A series of muscular contractions of the pelvic floor muscles occurring at the peak of sexual arousal.

**? Critical Thinking Question**

Do you believe that men and women differ in the importance they attach to experiencing orgasm during sexual sharing? Why or why not?

descriptions of orgasm were indistinguishable in both investigations. Similar results were obtained in an earlier study, in which a group of 70 expert judges were unable to distinguish reliably between the written orgasm reports of men and women (Proctor et al., 1974). A more recent investigation found that when men and women were asked to use adjectives to describe their subjective experience of orgasm, similarities in description significantly outweighed differences (Mah & Binik, 2002).

Beyond the question of sex differences in orgasmic experiences, it is clear that great individual variation exists in how people, both men and women, describe orgasms. The following Sexuality and Diversity discussion provides some indication of the varied ways people experience and describe their orgasmic experiences.

## SEXUALITY AND DIVERSITY

### Subjective Descriptions of Orgasm

The following accounts, selected from our files, illustrate the diversity of orgasmic descriptions. The first account is by a woman and the second by a man. The final three descriptions—labeled Reports A, B, and C—contain no specific references that identify the sex of the describers. Perhaps you would like to try to determine whether they were reported by a man or a woman. The answers follow the summary at the end of the chapter.

*Female: When I'm about to reach orgasm, my face feels very hot. I close my eyes and open my mouth. It centers in my clitoris, and it feels like electric wires igniting from there and radiating up my torso and down my legs to my feet. I sometimes feel like I need to urinate. My vagina contracts anywhere from 5 to 12 times. My vulva area feels heavy and swollen. There isn't another feeling like it—it's fantastic!*

*Male: Orgasm for me draws all my energy in toward a core in my body. Then, all of a sudden, there is a release of this energy out through my penis. My body becomes warm and numb before orgasm; after, it gradually relaxes and I feel extremely serene.*

*Report A: It's like an Almond Joy, "indescribably delicious." The feeling runs from the top of my head to the tips of my toes as I feel a powerful surge of pleasure. It raises me beyond my physical self into another level of consciousness, and yet the feeling seems purely physical. What a paradox! It strokes all over, inside and out. I love it simply because it's mine and mine alone.*

*Report B: An orgasm to me is like heaven. All my tensions and anxieties are released. You get to the point of no return, and it's like an uncontrollable desire that makes things start happening. I think that sex and orgasm are one of the greatest phenomena that we have today. It's a great sharing experience for me.*

*Report C: Having an orgasm is like the ultimate time I have for myself. I am not excluding my partner, but it's like I can't hear anything, and all I feel is a spectacular release accompanied with more pleasure than I've ever felt doing anything else. (Authors' files)*

Although the physiology of female orgasmic response is relatively well understood, misinformation about its nature has prevailed in our culture. Sigmund Freud (1905) developed a theory of the vaginal versus clitoral orgasm that has adversely affected people's thinking about female sexual response. Freud viewed the vaginal orgasm as more mature than the clitoral orgasm and thus preferable. The physiological basis for this theory was the assumption that the clitoris is a stunted penis. This led to the conclusion that erotic sensations, arousal, and orgasm resulting from direct stimulation of the clitoris were expressions of "masculine" rather than "feminine" sexuality (Sherfey, 1972). Unfortunately, this theory led many women to believe, incorrectly, that they were sexually maladjusted. Our knowledge of embryology has established the falseness of the theory that the clitoris is a masculine organ, as we have seen in our discussion of the genital differentiation process in Chapter 3.

Contrary to Freud's theory, the research of Masters and Johnson suggests that there is one kind of orgasm in females, physiologically speaking, regardless of the method of stimulation. Most female orgasms result from direct or indirect stimulation of the clitoris. However, as we note elsewhere, females can experience orgasm from fantasy alone, during sleep (nocturnal orgasms), or by stimulation of other body areas such as the nipples or the *Grafenberg spot.*

**The Grafenberg Spot** A number of studies have reported that some women are capable of experiencing orgasm, and perhaps ejaculation, when an area along the anterior wall of the vagina is vigorously stimulated (Levin, 2003; Whipple & Komisaruk, 1999). This area of erotic sensitivity, briefly mentioned in Chapter 4, has been named the Grafenberg spot (or *G spot*) in honor of Ernest Grafenberg (1950), a gynecologist who first noted the erotic significance of this location in the vagina almost 60 years ago. It has been suggested that the Grafenberg spot is not a point that can be touched by the tip of one finger but rather is a fairly large area composed of the lower anterior wall of the vagina and the underlying urethra and surrounding glands (Skene's glands) (Heath, 1984).

The Grafenberg spot can be located by "systematic palpation of the entire anterior wall of the vagina between the posterior side of the pubic bone and the cervix. Two fingers are usually used, and it is often necessary to press deeply into the tissue to reach the spot" (Perry & Whipple, 1981, p. 29). This exploration can be conducted by a woman's partner, as shown in ● **Figure 6.5**. Some women are able to locate their Grafenberg spots through self-exploration.

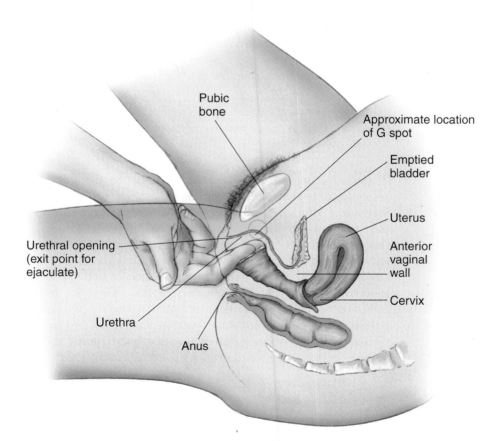

● **Figure 6.5** Locating the Grafenberg spot. Usually two fingers are used, and it is often necessary to press deeply into the anterior wall of the vagina to reach the spot.

Perhaps the most amazing thing about Grafenberg spot orgasms is that they are sometimes accompanied by the ejaculation of fluid from the urethral opening (Schubach, 1996; Whipple, 2000). Research indicates that the source of this fluid may be the "female prostate," discussed in Chapter 4. The ducts from this system empty directly into the urethra. In some women, Grafenberg spot orgasms result in fluid being forced through these ducts and out the urethra. In view of the homologous nature of Grafenberg spot tissue and the male prostate, we can speculate that the female ejaculate is similar to the prostatic component of male seminal fluid (Zaviacic & Whipple, 1993). This notion has been supported by research in which specimens of female ejaculate were chemically analyzed and found to contain high levels of an enzyme, prostatic acid phosphatase (PAP), characteristic of the prostatic component of semen (Addiego et al., 1981; Belzer et al., 1984). Some women report that the fluid has a mild semenlike scent. However, other research suggests that the ejaculated fluid is chemically closer to urine than to male semen (Alzate, 1990; Schubach, 1996). A final note of interest was provided by a report of a biochemical analysis of "female prostate" glandular tissue that revealed the presence of prostate-specific antigen (PSA), a substance secreted by the male prostate (Zaviacic, 2000).

Although the existence of Grafenberg spot orgasms, sometimes accompanied by ejaculation, has been reported with some degree of reliability, our understanding of this phenomenon is far from complete. For example, how common are these responses? (A survey of 2,350 U.S. and Canadian professional women revealed that 40% of the respondents reported sometimes experiencing a fluid-release ejaculation at the moment of orgasm [Darling et al., 1990].) Is the female Grafenberg area a genuine homologue of the male prostate? Clearly, more research is necessary before conclusive answers can be obtained for these and other questions.

**Resolution phase** The fourth phase of the sexual response cycle, as outlined by Masters and Johnson, in which the sexual systems return to their nonexcited state.

During the final phase of the sexual response cycle, **resolution**, the sexual systems return to their nonexcited state. If no additional stimulation occurs, the resolution begins immediately after orgasm. Some of the changes back to a nonexcited state take place rapidly, whereas others occur more slowly. The following two self-reports, the first by a man and the second by a woman, provide some indication of how people vary in their feelings after orgasm:

*After orgasm I feel relaxed and usually very content. Sometimes I feel like sleeping, and other times I feel like I want to touch my partner if she is willing. I like to hold her and just be there. (Authors' files)*

*After orgasm I feel very relaxed. My moods do vary—sometimes I'm ready to start all over; other times I can jump up and really get busy; and at other times I just want to sleep. (Authors' files)*

**Refractory period** The period of time following orgasm in the male, during which he cannot experience another orgasm.

These subjective reports sound similar. But one significant difference exists in the responses of women and men during this phase: their physiological readiness for further sexual stimulation. After orgasm the male typically enters a **refractory period**—a time when no amount of additional stimulation will result in orgasm. The length of this period ranges from minutes to days, depending on a variety of factors, such as age, frequency of previous sexual activity, and the degree of the man's emotional closeness to and sexual desire for his partner. In contrast to men, women generally experience no comparable refractory period. They are physiologically capable of returning to another orgasmic peak from anywhere in the resolution phase. However, a woman may or may not want to do so. In the last two sections of this chapter, we discuss the effects of aging on sexual arousal and response and then consider some differences between men's and women's patterns of sexual response.

# Aging and the Sexual Response Cycle

As people grow older, they will notice changes in sexual arousal and response patterns. In this section we briefly summarize some of the more common variations that occur in the sexual response cycles of women and men.

# The Sexual Response Cycle of Older Women

In general, all phases of the response cycle continue to occur for older women but with somewhat decreased intensity (Masters & Johnson, 1966; Segraves & Segraves, 1995).

## Excitement Phase

The first physiological response to sexual arousal, vaginal lubrication, typically begins more slowly in an older woman. Instead of taking 10 to 30 seconds, it may take several minutes or longer before vaginal lubrication is observed. In most cases the amount of lubrication is reduced (Kingsberg, 2002; Nusbaum et al., 2005). Research using the vaginal photoplethysmograph found that postmenopausal women's vaginal blood-volume increase during sexual arousal is smaller than in premenopausal women. However, women in both groups reported similar levels of sexual activity and enjoyment, indicating that the somewhat lowered vasocongestion response is within the range necessary for normal function (Morrell et al., 1984). Another study found that older women who engage in sexual relations once or twice weekly lubricate more readily than women who experience infrequent sexual relations (Brackett et al., 1994).

When lubrication and vaginal expansion during sexual response is considerably diminished, uncomfortable or painful intercourse can result (Mansfield et al., 1995). In addition, some women report decreased sexual desire and sensitivity of the clitoris, both of which interfere with sexual excitement. Hormone therapy, estrogen creams applied to the vagina, and vaginal lubricants can often help these symptoms (Kingsberg, 2002). ■

**! Sexual Health**

## Plateau Phase

During the plateau phase, the vaginal orgasmic platform develops, and the uterus elevates. In a postmenopausal woman these changes occur to a somewhat lesser degree than before menopause (Masters & Johnson, 1966).

## Orgasm Phase

Contractions of the orgasmic platform and the uterus continue to occur at orgasm, although the number of these contractions is typically reduced in older women. Older women remain capable of multiple orgasms and may continue to experience them (Nusbaum et al., 2005). However, many older women require a longer period of stimulation to reach orgasm, and some experience a reduced capacity to have an orgasm (Nusbaum et al., 2005; Sarrel, 1988).

Orgasm appears to be an important aspect of sexual activity to older women. One survey found that 69% of women age 60 to 91 listed "orgasm" first in response to the question "What do you consider a good sexual experience?" (Starr & Weiner, 1981). Only 17% of the women answered "intercourse" to the same question. In addition, "orgasm" was the most frequent response to the question "What in the sex act is most important to you?" Sixty-five percent of the women reported that their frequency of orgasm was the same as when they were younger.

## Resolution Phase

The resolution phase typically occurs more rapidly in postmenopausal women (Nusbaum et al., 2005). Labia color change, vaginal expansion, orgasmic platform formation, and clitoral retraction all disappear soon after orgasm. This is most likely due to the overall reduced amount of pelvic vasocongestion during arousal.

In summary, the effects of aging on female sexuality vary considerably. Most women experience minor changes, and some find their sexual interest, excitement, and orgasmic capacity seriously affected. An active sex life helps maintain vaginal health, and a functional and interested partner as well as good couple communication contribute to gratifying sexual relations for the older woman. Hormone therapy can also resolve many of the problems that interfere with enjoyable sexual response.

# The Sexual Response Cycle of Older Men

Most changes in the sexual response cycle of older men involve alterations in the intensity and duration of response (Masters & Johnson, 1966; Segraves & Segraves, 1995).

### Excitement Phase

During youth, many males can experience an erection in a few seconds. This ability is typically altered with the aging process. Instead of requiring 8 to 10 seconds, a man might require several minutes of effective stimulation to develop an erect penis. Furthermore, an older man's erection may be less firm than was typical of his younger days. More direct physical stimulation, such as hand caressing or oral stimulation, may also be desirable or necessary. This slowed rate of erectile response can cause alarm, stimulating a fear of impotence in some men:

> I guess it was the little things adding up that finally made me realize it was taking me longer to get a hard-on—the fact that I could go to bed with an extremely desirable woman and still be flaccid; that kissing and hugging often wasn't enough to get me started. At first I was shaken up at this discovery, thinking that maybe I would lose my potency. However, I received some good advice from my physician, who assured me that while things may slow down a bit, they continue to remain functional. (Authors' files)

Fortunately, this man received good advice. Most men retain their erectile capacities throughout their lifetimes. When a man and his partner understand that a slowed rate of obtaining an erection is normal, the altered pattern has little or no effect on their enjoyment of sexual expression.

### Plateau Phase

Older men do not typically experience as much myotonia (muscle tension) during the plateau phase as when they were younger. Complete penile erection is frequently not obtained until late in the plateau phase, just before orgasm. One result of these changes is that an older man is often able to sustain the plateau phase much longer than he did when he was younger, which can significantly enhance his pleasure. Many men and their partners appreciate this prolonged opportunity to enjoy other sensations of sexual response besides ejaculation. When a man engages in intercourse, his partner also may appreciate his greater ejaculatory control.

### Orgasm Phase

Most aging males continue to experience considerable pleasure from their orgasmic responses. In fact, 73% of older men in one study reported that orgasm was "very important" in their sexual experiences (Starr & Weiner, 1981). However, they may note a decline in intensity. Frequently absent are the sensations of ejaculatory inevitability that correspond with the emission phase of ejaculation. The number of muscular contractions occurring during the expulsion phase are typically reduced and so is the force of ejaculation (Nusbaum et al., 2005).

### Resolution Phase

Resolution typically occurs more rapidly in older men (Nusbaum et al., 2005). Loss of erection is usually quite rapid, especially compared with that of younger men. Resolution becomes faster with aging, and the refractory period between orgasm and the next excitement phase gradually lengthens (DeLamater & Friedrich, 2002). Men may begin to notice this as early as their 30s or 40s. Often, by age 60 the refractory period lasts for several hours, even days in some cases.

⊙ **Table 6.4** summarizes the common changes in the sexual response cycles of older women and men.

## ⊙ Differences Between the Sexes in Sexual Response

More and more, writers are emphasizing the basic similarities of sexual response in men and women. We see this as a positive trend away from the once-popular notion

**◯ TABLE 6.4**    Typical Age-Related Changes in the Sexual Response Cycles of Older Men and Women

| Phase | Typical Changes in Women | Typical Changes in Men |
|---|---|---|
| Excitement | • Vaginal lubrication is somewhat delayed and occurs with less volume.<br>• Vaginal mucosa thins, and length and width of vagina decrease. | • Longer time required to obtain an erection.<br>• Erection may be less firm. |
| Plateau | • Vaginal orgasmic platform less pronounced.<br>• Less elevation of uterus. | • Less overall muscle tension.<br>• Less elevation of testes.<br>• This phase often elongated in time. |
| Orgasm | • Fewer orgasmic contractions.<br>• Occasionally uterine contractions may be painful. | • Number of muscular contractions decrease, and force of ejaculation is lessened.<br>• Sensations of ejaculatory inevitability may be absent. |
| Resolution | • Typically occurs more rapidly as vaginal expansion, orgasmic platform, and clitoral retraction disappears soon after orgasm. | • Occurs more quickly with rapid loss of erection.<br>• Refractory period between orgasm and the next excitement phase gradually lengthens. |

that great differences exist between the sexes—an opinion that undoubtedly helped create a big market for many "love manuals" designed to inform readers about the mysteries and complexities of the "opposite sex." Now we know that much can be learned about our partners by carefully observing our own sexual patterns. Nevertheless, there are some real and important primary differences. In the following pages we outline and discuss some of them.

## Greater Variability in Female Response

One major difference between the sexes is the range of variations in the sexual response cycle. Although the graphs in Figures 6.3 and 6.4 do not reflect individual differences, they do demonstrate a wider range in the female response. One pattern is outlined for the male, and three patterns are drawn for the female.

In the female chart the sexual response pattern represented by line A is most similar to the male pattern (see Figure 6.3). It differs in an important way, however, in its potential for additional orgasms without dropping below the plateau level. Line B represents quite a different female pattern: a smooth advance through excitement to the level of plateau, where the responding woman may remain for some time without experiencing orgasm. The consequent resolution phase is more drawn out. Line C portrays a rapid rise in excitement, followed by one intense orgasm and a quick resolution.

Although it appears that women often have more variable sexual response patterns than men, this does not imply that all males experience the response cycle in exactly the same way. Men report considerable variation from the Masters and Johnson standard, including several mild orgasmic peaks followed by ejaculation, prolonged pelvic contractions after the expulsion of semen, and extended periods of intense excitement before ejaculation that feel like one long orgasm (Zilbergeld, 1978). In other words, there is no single pattern of sexual response, nor is there one "correct way." All patterns and variations—including one person's different reactions to sexual stimuli at different times or in different situations—are completely normal.

## The Male Refractory Period

The refractory period in the male cycle is certainly one of the most significant differences in sexual responses between the sexes. Men typically find that a certain minimum time must elapse after an orgasm before they can experience another climax. Most women have no such physiologically imposed shutdown phase.

Speculation about why only men have a refractory period is considerable. It seems plausible that some kind of short-term neurological inhibitory mechanism is triggered by ejaculation. This notion is supported by some fascinating research conducted by British scientists (Barfield et al., 1975). These researchers speculated that certain chemical pathways between the midbrain and the hypothalamus—pathways known to be involved in regulating sleep—might have something to do with post-orgasm inhibition in males. To test their hypothesis, the researchers destroyed a specific site, the *ventral medial lemniscus*, along these pathways in rats. For comparison they surgically eliminated three other areas in hypothalamic and midbrain locations in different rats. Later observations of sexual behavior revealed that the elimination of the ventral medial lemniscus had a dramatic effect on refractory periods, cutting their duration in half.

Some people believe that the answer to the riddle of refractory periods is somehow connected with the loss of seminal fluid during orgasm. Most researchers have been skeptical of this idea because there is no known substance in the expelled semen to account for an energy drain, marked hormone reduction, or any of the other implied biochemical explanations.

Still another explanation suggests that *prolactin*, a pituitary hormone secreted copiously following orgasm in both sexes, may be the biological "off switch" that induces the male refractory period (Kruger et al., 2002; Levin, 2003). This interpretation, while provocative, fails to account for the absence of a female refractory period. Whatever the reason for it, the refractory period is common not just to human males but to males of virtually all other species for which data exist, including rats, dogs, and chimpanzees.

## Multiple Orgasms

**Multiple orgasms** More than one orgasm experienced within a short time period.

Differences between the sexes occur in still a third area of sexual response patterns: the ability to experience **multiple orgasms**. Technically speaking, the term *multiple orgasms* refers to having more than one orgasmic experience within a short time interval.

Although researchers differ in their views of what constitutes a multiple orgasmic experience, for our own purposes we can say that if a man or woman has two or more sexual climaxes within a short period, that person has experienced multiple orgasms. There is, however, a distinction between males and females that is often obscured by such a definition. It is not uncommon for a woman to have several sequential orgasms, separated in time by the briefest of intervals (perhaps only seconds). In contrast, the spacing of male orgasms is typically more protracted.

How many women experience multiple orgasms? Kinsey and colleagues (1953) reported that about 14% of their female study subjects regularly had multiple orgasms. In 1970 a survey of *Psychology Today* readers revealed a 16% figure (Athanasiou et al., 1970).

On the surface it might seem that the capacity for multiple orgasms is limited to a minority of women. However, the research of Masters and Johnson showed that this assumption is false:

> If a female who is capable of having regular orgasms is properly stimulated within a short period after her first climax, she will in most instances be capable of having a second, third, fourth, and even a fifth and a sixth orgasm before she is fully satiated. As contrasted with the male's usual inability to have more than one orgasm in a short period, many females, especially when clitorally stimulated, can regularly have five or six full orgasms within a matter of minutes. (Masters and Johnson, 1961, p. 792)

**?** Critical Thinking Question

Women collectively appear to have a greater capacity for orgasm, to experience orgasm from a wider range of stimulation, and to have more problems experiencing orgasm than men. To what factors do you attribute this greater variation in female orgasmic response patterns?

Thus we find that most women have the capacity for multiple orgasms, but apparently only a small portion of the female population experiences them. Why does this large gap exist between capacity and experience? The answer may lie in the source of stimulation. The Kinsey report and the *Psychology Today* survey were based on orgasm rates during penile–vaginal intercourse. For a variety of reasons—not the least of which is the male's tendency to stop after his orgasm—women are not likely to continue coitus beyond their initial orgasm. In sharp contrast, several researchers have demonstrated that women who masturbate and those who relate sexually to other women are considerably more likely both to reach initial orgasm and to continue to additional orgasms (Athanasiou et al., 1970; Masters & Johnson, 1966).

We do not mean to imply that all women should be experiencing multiple orgasms. On the contrary, many women prefer sexual experiences during which they have a single orgasm or perhaps no orgasm at all. The data on multiple orgasmic capacities of women are not meant to be interpreted as the way women "should" respond. This could lead to a new kind of arbitrary sexual standard. The following quote illustrates the tendency to set such standards:

> When I was growing up, people considered any young, unmarried woman who enjoyed and sought active sexual involvements to be disturbed or promiscuous. Now I am told that I must have several orgasms each time I make love in order to be considered "normal." What a switch in our definitions of normal or healthy—from the straightlaced, noninvolved person to this incredible creature who is supposed to get it off multiply at the drop of a hat. (Authors' files)

As suggested earlier, multiple orgasms are considerably less common among males. They are most often reported by very young men, and their frequency declines with age. It is unusual to find men, even those of college age, who routinely experience more than one orgasm during a single sexual encounter. However, we agree with Alex Comfort (1972), who asserted that most men are probably more capable of multiple orgasms than they realize. Many have been conditioned by years of masturbation to get it over with as quickly as possible to avoid detection. Such a mental set hardly encourages an adolescent to continue experimenting after the initial orgasm. Through later experimentation, though, many men make discoveries similar to the one described in the following personal reflection of a middle-aged man:

> Somehow it never occurred to me that I might continue making love after experiencing orgasm. For 30 years of my life, this always signaled endpoint for me. I guess I responded this way for all the reasons you stated in class and a few more you didn't cover. My wife was with me the night you discussed refractory periods. We talked about it all the way home, and the next day gave it a try. Man, am I mad at myself now for missing out on something really nice all of these years. I discovered that I could have more than one orgasm in one session, and while it may take me a long time to come again, the getting there is a very nice part. My wife likes it, too! (Authors' files)

Evidence suggests that some men actually can experience multiple orgasms. In one study, 21 men (age 25 to 69) were interviewed, and all of them stated that they were usually but not always multiply orgasmic. For this investigation, male multiple orgasms were defined as "two or more orgasms with or without ejaculation and without, or with only very limited, detumescence [loss of erection] during one and the same sexual encounter" (Dunn & Trost, 1989, p. 379). The men's patterns varied, with some men experiencing ejaculation with the first orgasm, followed by more "dry" orgasms. Other men reported having several orgasms without ejaculation followed by a final ejaculatory orgasm. Still others reported variations on these two themes.

It is not necessary for lovemaking always to end with ejaculation. Many men find it pleasurable to continue sexual activity after a climax:

> One of the best parts of sex for me is having intercourse again shortly after my first orgasm. I find it is relatively easy to get another erection, even though I seldom experience another climax during the same session. The second time round I can concentrate fully on my partner's reactions without being distracted by my own building excitement. The pace is generally mellow and relaxed, and it is a real high for me psychologically. (Authors' files)

Thus multiple orgasms can be seen not as an ultimate goal to be sought above all else but rather as a possible area to explore. A relaxed approach to this possibility can give interested women and men an opportunity to experience more of the full range of their sexual potentials.

## The Role of Hormones in Sexual Behavior

- Both sexes produce so-called male sex hormones and female sex hormones. In men the testes produce about 95% of total androgens and some estrogens. A woman's ovaries and adrenal glands produce androgens in roughly equal amounts, and estrogens are produced predominantly by her ovaries.
- The dominant androgen in both sexes is testosterone. Men's bodies typically produce 20 to 40 times as much testosterone as women's bodies, but women's body cells are more sensitive to testosterone than men's are.
- Although it is difficult to distinguish the effects of sex hormones from those of psychological processes on sexual arousal, research strongly indicates that testosterone plays a critical role in maintaining sexual desire in both sexes.
- A major symptom of testosterone deficiency in both sexes—a decrease in one's customary level of sexual desire—can be eliminated by testosterone replacement therapy. However, raising the level of testosterone above a normal range can have adverse effects on both sexes.
- The neuropeptide hormone oxytocin, produced in the hypothalamus, exerts significant influence on sexual responses, sensuality, and interpersonal erotic and emotional attraction.

## The Brain and Sexual Arousal

- The brain plays an important role in human sexual arousal by mediating our thoughts, emotions, memories, and fantasies.
- Evidence links stimulation and surgical alteration of various brain sites with sexual arousal in humans and other animals.
- The limbic system, particularly the hypothalamus, plays an important part in sexual function.
- Certain neurotransmitter substances in the brain are known to influence sexual arousal and response. Dopamine facilitates sexual arousal and activity in women and men, and serotonin provides an inhibitory effect on both sexes.

## The Senses and Sexual Arousal

- Touch tends to predominate among the senses that stimulate human sexual arousal. Locations on the body that are highly responsive to tactile pleasuring are called erogenous zones. Primary erogenous zones are areas with dense concentrations of nerve endings; secondary erogenous zones are other areas of the body that take on erotic significance through sexual conditioning.
- Vision is second only to touch in providing stimuli that most people find sexually arousing. Recent evidence suggests that women respond to visual erotica as much as men do.

- Research has yet to clearly demonstrate whether smell and taste play a biologically determined role in human sexual arousal, but our own unique individual experiences may allow certain smells and tastes to acquire erotic significance. However, our culture's obsession with personal hygiene tends to mask natural smells and tastes that relate to sexual activity.
- Research on nonhuman animals has isolated a variety of pheromones (sexual odors) that are strongly associated with reproductive sexual activities.
- Studies have provided tentative evidence that humans also produce pheromones that act as sexual attractants.
- Some individuals find sounds during lovemaking to be highly arousing, whereas others prefer that their lovers be silent during love play. Communication during a sexual interlude, besides being sexually stimulating to some, can also be informative.

## Aphrodisiacs and Anaphrodisiacs in Sexual Arousal

- No clear evidence indicates that any substance we eat, drink, smoke, or inject has genuine aphrodisiac qualities. Faith and suggestion account for the apparent successes of a variety of alleged aphrodisiacs.
- Certain substances are known to have an inhibitory effect on sexual behavior. These anaphrodisiacs include drugs such as opiates, tranquilizers, antihypertensives, antidepressants, antipsychotics, nicotine, birth control pills, and sedatives.

## Sexual Response

- Kaplan's model of sexual response contains three stages: desire, excitement, and orgasm. This model is distinguished by its inclusion of desire as a distinct stage of the sexual response cycle separate from genital changes.
- Masters and Johnson describe four phases in the sexual response patterns of both women and men: excitement, plateau, orgasm, and resolution.
- During the excitement phase, both sexes experience increased myotonia (muscle tension), heart rate, and blood pressure. Sex flush and nipple erection often occur, especially among women. Female responses include engorgement of the clitoris, the labia, and the vagina (with vaginal lubrication), elevation and enlargement of the uterus, and breast enlargement. Males experience penile erection, enlargement and elevation of the testes, and sometimes Cowper's gland secretions.
- The plateau phase is marked by dramatic accelerations of myotonia, hyperventilation, heart rate, and blood pressure. In females the clitoris withdraws under its hood, the labia minora deepen in color, the orgasmic platform forms in the vagina, the uterus is fully elevated, and the areolas become swollen. In males the corona becomes fully engorged, the testes continue both elevation and enlargement, and Cowper's glands are active.

- Orgasm is marked by involuntary muscle spasms throughout the body. Blood pressure, heart rate, and respiration rate peak. Orgasm lasts slightly longer in females. Male orgasm typically occurs in two stages: emission and expulsion. It is difficult to distinguish subjective descriptions of female and male orgasms.
- Masters and Johnson suggest that one kind of physiological orgasm occurs in females, regardless of the method of stimulation.
- Some women can experience orgasm and perhaps ejaculation when the Grafenberg spot, an area along the anterior wall of the vagina, is vigorously stimulated.
- During the resolution phase, sexual systems return to their nonexcited state, a process that can take several hours, depending on a number of factors. Erection loss occurs in two stages, the first rapid and the second more protracted.

## Aging and the Sexual Response Cycle

- As women and men grow older, they notice changes in their sexual arousal and response patterns. For both sexes all phases of the response cycle generally continue to occur but with somewhat decreased intensity.
- An older woman typically requires more time to achieve vaginal lubrication. The sexual response cycle of the older woman is also characterized by less vaginal expansion, diminished orgasmic intensity, and a more rapid resolution.
- Less commonly, women can experience a decrease in sexual desire, clitoral sensitivity, and/or the capacity for orgasm.
- Older men typically require longer periods of time to achieve erection and reach orgasm. Greater ejaculatory control may enhance sexual pleasure for both their partners and themselves.
- The sexual response cycle of the aging male is also characterized by less myotonia, reduced orgasmic intensity, more rapid resolution, and longer refractory periods.

## Differences Between the Sexes in Sexual Response

- Many writers now emphasize the fundamental similarities in the sexual responses of men and women. However, certain important primary differences exist between the sexes.
- As a group, females demonstrate a wider variability in their sexual response patterns than do men.
- The presence of a refractory period in the male is one of the most significant differences in the response cycles of the two sexes. No cause for this period has been clearly demonstrated, but evidence suggests that ejaculation activates neurological inhibitory mechanisms.
- Multiple orgasms occur more often in females than in males.
- Women are more likely to experience multiple orgasms while masturbating than during coitus. Evidence suggests that some men can also experience a series of orgasms in a short time period.

Answer to Sexuality and Diversity Quiz on p. 154
   Report A: Male; Report B: Female; Report C: Female

## ◗ Suggested Readings

**Crenshaw, Theresa, and James Goldberg** (1996). *Sexual Pharmacology: Drugs That Inhibit Sexual Function*. New York: Norton. A must-read for anyone wishing to expand his or her knowledge about a broad array of prescription medications that have adverse sexual side effects.

**Jaffe, Maurice, and Elizabeth Fenwick** (1995). *Sexual Happiness for Women: A Practical Approach* and *Sexual Happiness for Men: A Practical Approach*. New York: Holt. Two companion books that provide valuable information and serve as helpful resource guides to enhanced sexual responsiveness and pleasure. Each book is recommended for both sexes.

**Maines, Rachel** (1999). *The Technology of Orgasm: Hysteria, the Vibrator, and Women's Sexual Satisfaction*. Baltimore: Johns Hopkins University Press. A fascinating, enlightening, and comprehensive discussion of many aspects of sexuality, with especially valuable information about female sexual response, including an informative look at the history of the female orgasm.

**Masters, William, and Virginia Johnson** (1966). *Human Sexual Response*. Boston: Little, Brown. A highly technical book that outlines the authors' major contributions to the understanding of the physiology of human sexual response. It is a good source for readers who would like more detailed information about physiological responses to sexual stimulation.

**Rako, Susan** (1996). *The Hormone of Desire*. New York: Harmony Books. A moving, often profound gem of a book that began as one woman physician's search for answers to her own personal and sexual discomfort associated with menopause-induced testosterone deficiency. Meticulously researched and packed with valuable facts, this book is an excellent source of information about testosterone-replacement therapy.

**Wyatt, Tristram** (2003). *Pheromones in Animal Behavior*. New York: Cambridge University Press. An informative book that provides a thorough and illuminating discussion of pheromone research.

## ◗ Resource

North American Menopause Society, P.O. Box 94527, Cleveland, OH 44101. This organization will provide a referral list of member physicians, grouped by states, who can provide informed medical advice about testosterone replacement therapy.

## ◗ Web Resources

**CengageNOW Web Site**
Go to **academic.cengage.com** to link to practice quiz questions, interactive activities, Internet links, critical thinking exercises, discussion forums, and more. You can also access sites from the Wadsworth Psychology Study Center (**academic.cengage.com/psychology**) or you can connect directly to the following sites:

**The Facts About Aphrodisiacs**
   On this page from the U.S. Food and Drug Administration's Web site, claims of traditional aphrodisiacs are described and shot down.

**Mysteries of Odor in Human Sexuality**
This Web site serves as a comprehensive information resource for general and scientific knowledge about human pheromones. Access to free abstracts of journal publications is provided.

### *Our Sexuality* Book Companion Web Site academic.cengage.com/psychology/crooks

Visit your book companion Web site where you will find flash cards, practice quizzes, Internet links, and more to help you study.

### Just what you need to know NOW!

Spend time on what you need to master rather than on information you already have learned. Take a pretest for this chapter, and CengageNOW will generate a personalized study plan based on your results. The study plan will identify the topics you need to review and direct you to online resources to help you master those topics. You can then take a post-test to help you determine the concepts you have mastered and what you will still need to work on. Try it out! Go to **academic.cengage.com/login** to sign in with an access code or to purchase access to this product.

### InfoTrac College Edition Online Library

Sign in to **academic.cengage.com/login** or visit your free book companion Web site at **academic.cengage.com/psychology/crooks** to access InfoTrac College Edition, an online searchable library that includes a multitude of journals, many specific to human sexuality. These journals include *Archives of Sexual Behavior; Archives of Sexual Health Behavior; Canadian Journal of Human Sexuality; Hispanic Journal of the Behavioral Sciences; Journal of Cross-Cultural Psychology; Journal of Physical Education, Recreation, and Dance; Journal of Sex Research;* and *Sex Roles.*

# Love and Communication in Intimate Relationships

Peter Byron/PhotoEdit, Inc.

*For me, the potential for falling in love begins with a physical attraction. But looks only count for so much. I need an intimate friendship and closeness in order to possibly fall in love. Trust is another important part of a relationship that can lead to love. A prospective partner would also need to share some of my interests, and I would need to share some of his. Finally, and perhaps most important, good communication in a relationship is essential for me to be truly in love. (Authors' files)*

Love, attraction, attachment, and sexual communication in intimate relationships are important and complex aspects of people's lives. In this chapter, we look at these interactions from various perspectives and examine some of the research dealing with them. We consider a number of questions: What is love? What kinds of love are there? What determines why we fall in love with one person and not another? How do various styles of attraction influence our relationships with others? How does sex fit into relationships? How does love relate to jealousy? What qualities or behaviors help to maintain relationship satisfaction over many years? And finally, how does sexual communication contribute to the satisfaction of intimate relationships?

## ⊙ What Is Love?

*O Love is the crooked thing,*
*There is nobody wise enough*
*To find out all that is in it*
*For he would be thinking of love*
*Till the stars had run away*
*And the shadows eaten the moon.*

William Butler Yeats, "Brown Penny"

Love has intrigued people throughout history. Its joys and sorrows have inspired artists and poets, novelists, filmmakers, and other students of human interaction. Indeed, love is one of the most pervasive themes in the art and literature of many cultures. Each of our own lives has been influenced in significant ways by love, beginning with the love we received as infants and children. Our best and worst moments in life can be tied to a love relationship.

But what is love? How do we define it?

Love is a special kind of attitude, with strong emotional and behavioral components. It is also a phenomenon that eludes easy definition or explanation. As the following definitions suggest, love can mean different things to different people:

> Love is patient and kind; love is not jealous or boastful; it is not arrogant or rude. Love does not insist on its own way; it is not irritable or resentful; it does not rejoice at wrong, but rejoices in the right. Love bears all things, believes all things, hopes all things, endures all things. (I Corinthians 13:4–7)

> Love is a temporary insanity curable by marriage or by removal of the patient from the influences under which he incurred the disorder. (Bierce, 1943, p. 202)

> Love is that condition in which the happiness of another person is essential to your own. (Heinlein, 1961, p. 345)

As difficult as love is to define, can it be meaningfully measured? Some social scientists have attempted to do so, with varied results (Davis & Latty-Mann, 1987; Hatfield & Sprecher, 1986a). Perhaps the most ambitious attempt to measure love was undertaken years ago by psychologist Zick Rubin (1970, 1973), who developed a 13-item questionnaire (the Love Scale) designed

Love has been the inspiration for some of our greatest works of literature, art, and music.

Rolf Konow/Sygma/Corbis

to assess a person's desire for intimacy with, and caring and attachment for, another. Some evidence supporting the validity of the Love Scale was obtained in an investigation of the popular belief that lovers spend a great deal of time looking into one another's eyes (Rubin, 1970). Couples were observed through a one-way mirror while they waited to participate in a psychological experiment. The findings revealed that weak lovers (couples who scored below average on the Love Scale) made significantly less eye contact than did strong lovers (those with above-average scores).

Perhaps in the years ahead we will have access to a variety of new perspectives on the question of what love is, largely because of a marked increase in the number of scientists, especially social psychologists, who have begun to study love (Neto, 2001).

# Types of Love

Love takes many forms. Love exists between parent and child and between family members. Love between friends, known to the ancient Greeks as *philia*, involves concern for the other's well-being. Lovers may experience two additional types of love: passionate love and companionate love. In this section we look more closely at these two widely discussed types of love and then present two contemporary models or theories of love.

## Passionate Love

**Passionate love,** also known as romantic love or infatuation, is a state of extreme absorption with and desire for another. It is characterized by intense feelings of tenderness, elation, anxiety, sexual desire, and ecstasy. Generalized physiological arousal, including increased heartbeat, perspiration, blushing, and stomach churning along with a feeling of great excitement, often accompanies this form of love.

**Passionate love** State of extreme absorption in another person. Also known as romantic love.

Intense passionate love typically occurs early in a relationship. It sometimes seems as though the less one knows the other person, the more intense the passionate love is. In passionate love, people often overlook faults and avoid conflicts. Logic and reasoned consideration are swept away by the excitement. One perceives the object of one's passionate love as providing complete personal fulfillment.

Not surprisingly, passionate love is often short-lived, typically measured in months rather than years. Love that is based on ignorance of a person's full character is likely to change with increased familiarity. However, this temporary aspect of passionate love is often overlooked, especially by young people who lack experience with long-term love relationships. Many couples, convinced of the permanence of their passionate feelings, choose to make some kind of commitment to each other (becoming engaged, moving in together, getting married, etc.) while still fired by the fuel of passionate love—only to become disillusioned later. When ecstasy gives way to routine, and the annoyances and conflicts typical of ongoing relationships surface, lovers may begin to have some doubts about their partners.

*The first weeks and months of my relationship with Bob were incredible. I felt like I had found the perfect partner, someone who filled all that was missing in my life. Then, suddenly, he started to get on my nerves, and we started fighting every time we saw each other. It took a while to realize that we were finally seeing each other as real people instead of dream companions. (Authors' files)*

Some couples can work through this period to ultimately find a solid basis on which to build a lasting relationship of mutual love. Others discover, often to their dismay, that the only thing they ever really shared was passion. Unfortunately, many people who experience diminishing passion believe that this is the end of love rather than a possible transition to a different kind of love.

 InfoTrac Search Words

- Passionate love
- Companionate love

## Companionate Love

**Companionate love**
A type of love characterized by friendly affection and deep attachment based on extensive familiarity with the loved one.

**Companionate love** is a less intense emotion than passionate love. It is characterized by friendly affection and a deep attachment that is based on extensive familiarity with the loved one. It involves a thoughtful appreciation of one's partner. Companionate love often encompasses a tolerance for another's shortcomings along with a desire to overcome difficulties and conflicts in a relationship. This kind of love is committed to ongoing nurturing of a partnership. In short, companionate love is often enduring, whereas passionate love is almost always transitory.

Sex in a companionate relationship typically reflects feelings associated with familiarity, especially the security of knowing what pleases the other. This foundation of knowledge and sexual trust can encourage experimentation and subtle communication. Sexual pleasure strengthens the overall bond of a companionate relationship. Although sex is usually less exciting than in passionate love, it is often experienced as richer, more meaningful, and more deeply satisfying, as the following statement reveals:

> ? **Critical Thinking Question**
>
> What do you think are the key differences between passionate love and companionate love? How do these characteristics fit into a list of things that you believe are essential to a successful, lasting love relationship?

*Between my first and second marriages, I really enjoyed the excitement of new sexual relationships, especially after so much sexual frustration in my first marriage. Even though I sometimes miss the excitement of those times, I would never trade it for the easy comfort, pleasure, and depth of sexual intimacy I now experience in my 17-year marriage. (Authors' files)*

## Sternberg's Triangular Theory of Love

The distinction between passionate and companionate love has been further refined by psychologist Robert Sternberg (1986, 1988), who has proposed an interesting theoretical framework for conceptualizing what people experience when they report being in love. According to Sternberg, love has three dimensions or components: passion, intimacy, and commitment (◑ **Figure 7.1**):

**Passion** The motivational component of Sternberg's triangular love theory.

- **Passion** is the motivational component that fuels romantic feelings, physical attraction, and desire for sexual interaction. Passion instills a deep desire to be united with the loved one. In a sense, passion is like an addiction, because its capacity to provide intense stimulation and pleasure can exert a powerful craving in a person.

◑ **Figure 7.1** In Sternberg's love triangle, various combinations of the three components of love (passion, intimacy, and commitment) make up the different kinds of love. Note that nonlove is the absence of all three components.

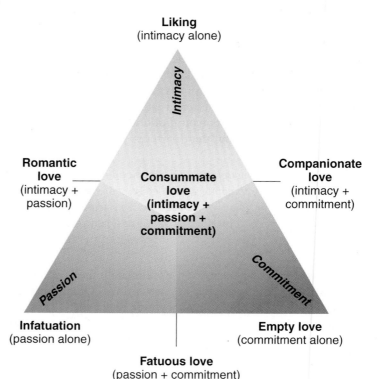

- **Intimacy** is the emotional component of love that encompasses the sense of being bonded with another person. It includes feelings of warmth, sharing, and emotional closeness. Intimacy also embraces a willingness to help the other and an openness to sharing private thoughts and feelings with the beloved.
- **Commitment** is the thinking or cognitive aspect of love. It refers to the conscious decision to love another and to maintain a relationship over time despite difficulties that may arise.

**Intimacy** The emotional component of Sternberg's triangular love theory.

**Commitment** The thinking component of Sternberg's triangular love theory.

Sternberg maintains that passion tends to develop rapidly and intensely in the early stages of a love relationship and then declines as the relationship progresses. In contrast, intimacy and commitment continue to build gradually over time, although at different rates (○ **Figure 7.2**). Thus Sternberg's theory provides a conceptual basis for the transition from passionate to companionate love. Passionate love, consisting mainly of romantic feelings and physical attraction, peaks early and quickly subsides. However, as passion weakens, many couples experience a growth in both intimacy and commitment as their relationship evolves into one of companionate love (Sprecher & Regan, 1998). If intimacy does not flourish and if a couple does not make a mutual decision to commit to each other, their relationship will be on shaky ground when passion fades and conflicts surface. In contrast, commitment and a sense of bondedness and mutual concern can sustain a relationship during periods of dissatisfaction and conflict.

All three of Sternberg's love components are important dimensions of a loving relationship, but they typically exist in different patterns and to varying degrees in different relationships. Moreover, they often change over time within the same relationship. Sternberg suggests that such variations yield different kinds of love—or at least differences in how people experience love (see Figure 7.1). For instance, the absence of all three components yields what Sternberg calls *nonlove* (what most of us feel for casual acquaintances). When only intimacy is present, the experience is one of *friendship* or liking. If only passion exists, without intimacy or commitment, one experiences *infatuation*. The presence of commitment without passion and intimacy yields *empty love* (such as might be experienced in a long-term, static relationship). If intimacy and commitment exist without passion, one experiences *companionate love* (often characteristic of happy couples who have shared many years together). When passion and commitment are present but without intimacy, the experience is *fatuous love*, a kind of foolish involvement characteristic of whirlwind courtships or situations in which one worships and longs for another person from afar. Love characterized by passion and intimacy but no commitment is described by Sternberg as *romantic love*. Finally, when all three components are present, the experience is *consummate love*, the fullest kind of love, which people often strive for but find difficult to achieve and sustain.

Empirical research has provided some support for Sternberg's love model. One study of dating couples reported that the presence of two of Sternberg's love components—intimacy and commitment—was predictive of relationship stability and longevity (Hendrick et al., 1988). Another investigation found that married people demonstrated higher levels of commitment to their relationships than unmarried people did, a finding

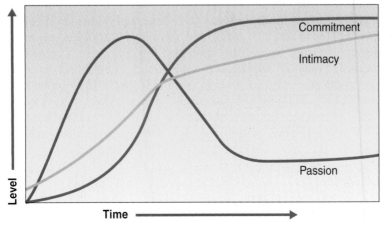

○ **Figure 7.2** Sternberg theorizes that the passion component of love peaks early in a relationship and then declines, whereas the other two components, intimacy and commitment, continue to build gradually over time.

consistent with Sternberg's model (Acker & Davis, 1992). This same study found that, although intimacy continued to rise in longer relationships, passion declined for both sexes but more sharply for women than for men. Further investigations of Sternberg's triangular theory found that lovers' definition and communication of the three components of love remained relatively stable over time (Reeder, 1996) and that compatibility of a couple is enhanced if both partners possess similar levels of passion, intimacy, and commitment (Drigotas et al., 1999).

## Lee's Styles of Loving

Instead of attempting to describe different patterns or *types* of love, John Allan Lee (1974, 1988, 1998) proposed a theory that describes six different *styles of loving* that characterize intimate human relationships: romantic, game playing, possessive, companionate, altruistic, and pragmatic.

- People with a *romantic* love style (*eros*) tend to place their emphasis on physical beauty as they search for ideal mates. Romantic, erotic lovers delight in the visual beauty and tactile and sensual pleasures provided by their lover's body, and they tend to be very affectionate and openly communicative with their partner.
- People with a *game-playing* love style (*ludus*) like to play the field and acquire many sexual "conquests" with little or no commitment. Love is for fun, the act of seduction is to be enjoyed, and relationships are to remain casual and transitory.
- People with a *possessive* love style (*mania*) tend to seek obsessive love relationships, which are often characterized by turmoil and jealousy. These people live a roller-coaster style of love, in which each display of affection from the lover brings ecstasy and the mildest slight produces painful agitation.
- People with a *companionate* love style (*storge* [STOR-gay]) are slow to develop affection and commitment but tend to experience relationships that endure. This style is love without fever or turmoil, a peaceful and quiet kind of relating that usually begins as friendship and develops over time into affection and love.
- People with an *altruistic* love style (*agape*) are characterized by selflessness and a caring, compassionate desire to give to another without expectation of reciprocity. Such love is patient and never demanding or jealous.
- People with a *pragmatic* love style (*pragma*) tend to select lovers based on rational, practical criteria (such as shared interests) that are likely to lead to mutual satisfaction. These individuals approach love in a businesslike fashion, trying to get the best "romantic deal" by seeking partners with social, educational, religious, and interest patterns that are compatible with their own.

What happens when two different people in a relationship naturally tend toward different styles of loving? For Lee this is a critical question. He suggests that loving relationships frequently fail to thrive over time because "too often people are speaking different languages when they speak of love" (Lee, 1974, p. 44). Even though both partners try to build a lasting involvement, their efforts can be undermined by a losing struggle to integrate incompatible loving styles. In contrast, satisfaction and success in loving relationships often depend on finding a mate who "shares the same approach to loving, the same definition of love" (Lee, 1974, p. 44).

An inventory called the Love Attitude Scale has been developed to measure Lee's six loving styles (Hendrick & Hendrick, 2003, 1986), and this research tool has generated some empirical studies of his theory. Studies that have used this scale provide some support for Lee's hypothesis that relationship success is influenced by compatibility in styles of loving (Davis & Latty-Mann, 1987; Hendrick & Hendrick, 2003). College students prefer to date people with love styles similar to their own (Hahn & Blass, 1997; Hendrick & Hendrick, 2003). Evidence also exists of sex differences in college students' styles of love. One investigation revealed that college women are more likely than men to embrace companionate, pragmatic, and possessive love styles, whereas college men are more likely to manifest romantic or game-playing love styles (Hendrick & Hendrick, 2003). Another study also found sex differences in love styles among college students, with women more likely to manifest companionate, pragmatic, and romantic styles, and men more likely to embrace game-playing and altruistic styles (Lacey et al., 2004).

One study used the Love Attitude Scale to investigate the relationship between styles of loving and relationship satisfaction at different stages of life (Montgomery & Sorell, 1997). The study sample included 250 adults in four groups: college-age single youths; young, childless married adults; married adults with children living at home; and married adults whose grown-up children had left home. Two loving styles, *eros* and *agape*, were positively associated with relationship satisfaction for all life stages. Predictably, *ludus* was negatively associated with satisfaction for all three groups of married adults. *Storge* was significantly related to relationship satisfaction only for the married couples with children at home. *Mania* and, surprisingly, *pragma* were not significantly related to relationship satisfaction for any life-stage group. These findings are supported by other research demonstrating that *ludus* is a strong predictor of relationship dissatisfaction and that individuals who score high on the love styles of *eros, storge,* or *agape* experience greater relationship satisfaction than individuals with other love styles (Meeks et al., 1998).

# ❿ Falling in Love: Why and With Whom?

What determines why people fall in love and with whom they fall in love? These questions are exceedingly complex. Some writers believe that people fall in love to overcome a sense of aloneness and separateness. Psychoanalyst Erich Fromm (1965) suggested that union with another person is the deepest need of humans. Another psychoanalyst and writer, Rollo May, author of *Love and Will* (1969), also believed that as people experience their own solitariness, they long for the refuge of union with another through love. Other observers see loneliness as a by-product of our individualistic and highly mobile society rather than as an inherent part of the human condition. This view emphasizes the connectedness that we all have with the people around us—through all our social relationships, language, and culture. According to this view, love relationships are one aspect of a person's social network rather than a cure for the "disease" of loneliness (Solomon, 1981).

We have seen that love is a complex human emotion that can be explained, at least in part, by various psychosocial interpretations of its origins. However, the answer to why we fall in love also encompasses, to some degree, complex neurochemical processes that occur in our brains when we are attracted to another person. We discuss findings about the chemistry of love in the next section.

## The Chemistry of Love

People caught up in the intense passion of blooming love often report feeling swept away or feeling a kind of natural high. Such reactions might have a basis, at least in part, in brain chemistry, according to researchers Michael Liebowitz, author of *The Chemistry of Love* (1983), and Anthony Walsh, author of *The Science of Love* (1991). These investigators contend that the initial elation and the energizing "high" of excitement, giddiness, and euphoria characteristic of passionate love result from surging levels of three key brain chemicals: norepinephrine, dopamine, and especially phenylethylamine (PEA). These chemicals, called *neurotransmitters*, allow brain cells to communicate with each other, and they are chemically similar to amphetamine drugs; thus they produce amphetamine-like effects, such as euphoria, giddiness, and elation. As Walsh noted, "When we meet someone who is attractive to us, the whistle blows at the PEA factory" (quoted in Toufexis, 1993, p. 50). Furthermore, as we learned in Chapter 6, oxytocin and dopamine both contribute to sexual arousal, which adds further fire to passionate love.

Oxytocin, secreted by the hypothalamus during cuddling and physical intimacy, plays an important role in facilitating social attachment and in fostering feelings of being in love (Carter, 1998; Lucentini, 2005; Love, 2001). Results of a recent study provide further evidence of the role of dopamine in the chemistry of love. In this investigation, researchers used magnetic resonance imaging (MRI) to scan the brains of men and women while they viewed photos of a loved romantic partner and of a close friend. It was the photos of lovers, not friends, that caused areas of the brain rich in dopamine to "light up" (Bartels & Zeki, 2004).

The amphetamine-like highs and elevated sexual arousal associated with new love typically do not last—perhaps in part because the body eventually develops a tolerance to PEA and related neurotransmitters, just as it does to amphetamines. With time, our brains simply become unable to keep up with the demand for more and more PEA to produce love's special kick. Thus the highs that we feel at the beginning of a relationship eventually diminish. This observation provides a plausible biological explanation for why passionate or romantic love is short-lived.

Liebowitz points out another parallel to amphetamine use. He notes that the anxiety, despair, and pain that follow the loss—or even potential loss—of a romantic love relationship are similar to what a person addicted to amphetamines experiences during drug withdrawal. In both cases the loss of mood-lifting chemicals results in a sometimes protracted period of emotional pain.

Do other brain chemicals exist that help to explain why some relationships endure beyond the initial highs of passionate love? According to both Walsh and Liebowitz, the answer is yes. The continued progression from infatuation to the deep attachment characteristic of long-term loving relationships results, at least in part, from the brain gradually stepping up production of another set of neurotransmitters called *endorphins*. These morphinelike, pain-blunting chemicals are soothing substances that help produce a sense of euphoria, security, tranquility, and peace. Thus they can cause us to feel good when we are with a loved partner. This could be another reason why abandoned lovers feel so terrible after their loss: they are deprived of their daily dose of feel-good chemicals.

Just as we know little about why people fall in love, we have no simple explanation for why they fall in love with one person instead of another. A number of factors are often important: proximity, similarity, reciprocity, and physical attractiveness.

**InfoTrac Search Words**

- Interpersonal attraction

## Proximity

**Proximity** The geographic nearness of one person to another, which is an important factor in interpersonal attraction.

Although people often overlook **proximity,** or geographic nearness, in listing factors that attracted them to a particular person, proximity is one of the most important variables. We often develop close relationships with people whom we see frequently in our neighborhood, in school, at work, or at our place of worship.

Why is proximity such a powerful factor in interpersonal attraction? Social psychologists have offered a number of plausible explanations. One is simply that familiarity breeds liking or loving. Research has shown that when we are repeatedly exposed to novel stimuli—unfamiliar musical selections, works of art, human faces, and so on—our liking for such stimuli increases (Bornstein, 1989; Brooks & Watkins, 1989; Nuttin, 1987). This phenomenon, called the **mere exposure effect,** explains in part why we are attracted to people in close proximity to us.

**Mere exposure effect** A phenomenon in which repeated exposure to novel stimuli tends to increase an individual's liking for such stimuli.

Another reason that proximity influences whom we are attracted to is that people often meet each other in locations where they are engaging in activities that reflect common interests. This observation is supported by the National Health and Social Life Survey (NHSLS) (see Chapter 2), which included questions about where people are most likely to meet their intimate partners. Laumann and his associates (1994) sorted their data into high and low preselection locales. High preselection meant that people were together in locations where they shared common interests, such as physical health and fitness (working out at the local fitness center) or topics of study (taking the same classes at school). Low preselection locales included places that bring a diverse group of people together, such as bars and vacation sites. Predictably, Laumann and colleagues found that places with high levels of preselection were more likely to yield sex-partner connections than locales with low preselection values.

Work and school were especially prevalent as places where people connect with future intimate partners. This finding reflects both the amount of time people spend in these locations and the possible effect of shared common interests. In addition, working with or taking classes with potential partners provides opportunities for repeated contacts. Many of us are reluctant to initiate a relationship the first time or two we meet or interact with another person. However, at work or in class, we come into contact with a desired person day after day. This allows us to get to know this

**Percentage of Couples in Various Types of Relationships That Are Homophilous for Age, Educational Status, and Religion**

| Type of Homophily | Marriage (%) | Cohabitation (%) | Long-Term Partnership (%) | Short-Term Partnership (%) |
|---|---|---|---|---|
| | | Type of Relationship | | |
| Age (defined as difference of no more than 5 years in partners' ages) | 78 | 75 | 76 | 83 |
| Educational status (defined as difference of no more than one educational category[a]) | 82 | 87 | 83 | 87 |
| Religion (defined as having same affiliation) | 72 | 53 | 56 | 60 |

[a]Categories: Less than high school, high school graduate, vocational training, 4-year college degree, postgraduate
SOURCE: Adapted from Laumann et al.

person better, to become more comfortable interacting with him or her, and eventually to muster the motivation to ask for a first date.

## Similarity

**Similarity** is also influential in determining whom we fall in love with. Contrary to the old adage that opposites attract, people who fall in love often share common beliefs, values, attitudes, interests, and intellectual abilities (Amodio & Showers, 2005; Byrne, 1997; Sherman & Jones, 1994). We also tend to pair romantically with people whose level of physical attractiveness is similar to our own (Feingold, 1988; Folkes, 1982). This tendency to match physical attractiveness with a partner might be related to our fear of being rejected if we approach someone whom we perceive to be much more attractive than ourselves (Bernstein et al., 1983).

We also tend to be attracted to people who are similar to us in age, educational status, and religious affiliation. Similarity in personal characteristics is referred to as *homophily*, or the tendency to form relationships with people of similar or equal status in various social and personal attributes. Data from the NHSLS reflecting homophily in age, educational status, and religion for various types of relationships appear in ○ **Table 7.1**.

© Duomo/CORBIS

People who fall in love often share common interests.

The NHSLS also revealed that people generally tend to form partnerships with people of similar race and ethnicity. The following Sexuality and Diversity discussion describes this dimension of attraction.

## SEXUALITY AND DIVERSITY

### Partner Choice and Race

The NHSLS provided data about the extent to which people form intimate relationships with members of the same race. As described in Chapter 2, a lack of funds forced Edward Laumann and his associates (1994) to include adequate numbers of only the two largest ethnic minorities in America. Consequently, ○ **Table 7.2** contains data pertaining only to white Americans, African Americans, and Hispanic

Americans. These data summarize a sample of almost 2,000 nonmarital, noncohabitational heterosexual partnerships.

As you can see by examining the values in Table 7.2, the percentages of same-race noncohabitational partnerships are very high for both sexes among whites and African Americans. In contrast, the percentage of same-race noncohabitational partnerships is considerably lower among Hispanic respondents. Thus it would appear that "Hispanics as a group are less exclusive with respect to sexual partnering than are whites or blacks" (Laumann et al., 1994, p. 246).

Another study examined partner choice and race among 75,000 cohabiting couples and 480,000 married couples in the United States (Blackwell & Lichter, 2000). In contrast to the findings of the NHSLS, Blackwell & Lichter found that the inclination to select same-race partners was less pronounced among white Americans than among other racial groups. Specifically, the incidence of same-race partnerships among both cohabiting and married couples was highest among African Americans, followed in order by Asian Americans, Hispanic Americans, and whites.

○ **TABLE 7.2**    **Noncohabitational Sexual Partnerships by Race and Sex**

| Race | Percentage of Same-Race Partnerships | |
| --- | --- | --- |
| | Men (%) | Women (%) |
| White | 92 | 87 |
| African American | 82 | 97 |
| Hispanic American | 54 | 65 |

SOURCE: Laumann et al. (1994).

Why are we drawn to people who are like us? For one thing, people with similar attitudes and interests are often inclined to participate in the same kinds of leisure activities. Even more important, we are more likely to communicate well with people whose ideas and opinions are similar to ours, and communication is an important aspect of enduring relationships. It is also reassuring to be with similar people, because they confirm our view of the world, validate our own experiences, and support our opinions and beliefs (Amodio & Showers, 2005; Byrne et al., 1986).

Perceived similarity in others could be especially attractive to us because we have strong expectations of being accepted and appreciated by people who are like us (Sprecher & McKinney, 1993). That these expectations are often fulfilled is reflected in research findings indicating that people who are similar in a variety of social and personal traits are more likely to stay together than people who are less similar (Weber, 1998).

## Reciprocity

**Reciprocity** The principle that when we are recipients of expressions of liking or loving, we tend to respond in kind.

Still another factor drawing us to a particular individual is our perception that that person is interested in us. People tend to react positively to flattery, compliments, and other expressions of liking and affection. In the study of interpersonal attraction, this concept is reflected in the principle of **reciprocity,** which holds that when we receive expressions of liking or loving, we tend to respond in kind (Byrne & Murnen, 1988). In turn, reciprocal responses can set in motion a further escalation of the relationship: By responding warmly to people who we believe feel positively toward us, we often induce them to like us even more (Curtis & Miller, 1988). Furthermore, our sense of self-esteem is affected by the extent to which we feel attached to and liked by others. Knowing that someone likes us increases our sense of belonging or being socially integrated in a relationship and hence bolsters our self-esteem (Baumeister & Leary, 1995).

## Physical Attractiveness

**Physical attractiveness** Physical beauty, which is a powerful factor in attracting lovers to each other.

As you might expect, **physical attractiveness** often plays a dominant role in drawing lovers together. Despite the saying that beauty is only skin deep, experiments have shown that physically attractive people are more likely to be sought as friends and lovers and to be perceived as more likable, interesting, sensitive, poised, happy, sexy, competent, and socially skilled than people of average or unattractive appearance (Baron et al., 2006; Marcus & Miller, 2003; Sangrador & Yela, 2000).

Why is physical beauty such a powerful factor in attracting us to others? One answer has to do with aesthetics. We all enjoy looking at something or someone whom we consider beautiful. Another factor is that many people apparently believe that beautiful people have more to offer in terms of desirable personal qualities than those who are less attractive. We might also be attracted to beautiful people because they offer us the possibility of status by association. And perhaps beautiful people, by virtue of having been treated well by others over the course of their lives, are secure and comfortable with themselves, a fact that can translate into especially satisfying relationships with others. Finally, evidence shows that people consider physical beauty an indicator of health and that, other things being equal, we are attracted to healthy people (Kalick et al., 1998; Marcus & Miller, 2003).

Researchers have sought to determine whether both sexes are equally influenced by physical attractiveness in forming impressions of people they meet. Several studies have found that male college students place significantly greater emphasis on physical appearance in selecting a partner for a sexual or long-term relationship than do college women, who tend to place greater emphasis on such traits as ambition, status, interpersonal warmth, and personality characteristics (Nevid, 1984; Townsend & Wasserman, 1998). Other studies have found that American men place a greater emphasis on physical attractiveness than do American women (Bailey et al., 1994; Sprecher et al., 1994). Is this difference typical of men and women in other cultures as well?

A cross-cultural study of sex differences in heterosexual mate preferences provided strong evidence that men worldwide place greater value than do women on mates who are both young and physically attractive. In this study, conducted by psychologist David Buss (1994), subjects from 37 samples drawn from Africa, Asia, Europe, North and South America, Australia, and New Zealand were asked to rate the importance of a wide range of personal attributes in potential mates. These attributes included dependability, attractiveness, age, good financial prospects, intelligence, sociability, and chastity.

Without exception, men in all the surveyed cultures placed greater emphasis on a potential mate's youth and attractiveness than women did (Buss, 1994). In contrast, women placed greater value on potential mates who were somewhat older, had good financial prospects, and were dependable and industrious. This is not to say that physical attractiveness was unimportant to women of these varied cultures. In fact, many women considered physical attractiveness important—although less so than financial responsibility and dependability.

What accounts for the apparent consistency across so many cultures in what appeals to men and to women in a potential mate? And what accounts for the differences between men and women? Buss provides a *sociobiological* explanation—that is, he explains a species' behavior in terms of its evolutionary needs. According to Buss (1994), evolution has biased mate preferences in humans, as it has in other animals. Males are attracted to young, physically attractive females because these characteristics are good predictors of reproductive success. Simply put, a young woman has more reproductive years remaining than does an older woman. Furthermore, smooth, unblemished skin, good muscle tone, lustrous hair, and similar features of physical attractiveness are indicators of good health—and thus are strong signs of reproductive value. On the other hand, women tend to find older, established men more attractive because characteristics such as wealth and high social rank are predictors of security for their offspring. Youth and physical attractiveness are less important to females, because fertility is less related to age for males than it is for females.

Studies have also revealed that American women typically consider traits such as ambition and being a good provider more important in mate selection than do their male counterparts (Buss & Schmitt, 1993). Differences between American men and women in other aspects of mate selection are described in the following Sexuality and Diversity discussion.

## Differences Between American Men and Women in Mate Selection Preferences

Researchers Susan Sprecher, Quintin Sullivan, and Elaine Hatfield (1994) surveyed a national representative sample of more than 13,000 English- or Spanish-speaking people in the United States, age 19 or older. ● **Figure 7.3** shows the average response rating of men and women to several items on a questionnaire used in the survey. One part of the questionnaire contained several items that asked respondents how willing they would be to marry someone who had more or less education, was older or younger, was not likely to hold a steady job, and so on. Subjects indicated their level of agreement with each item on a scale from 1 ("not at all") to 7 ("very willing").

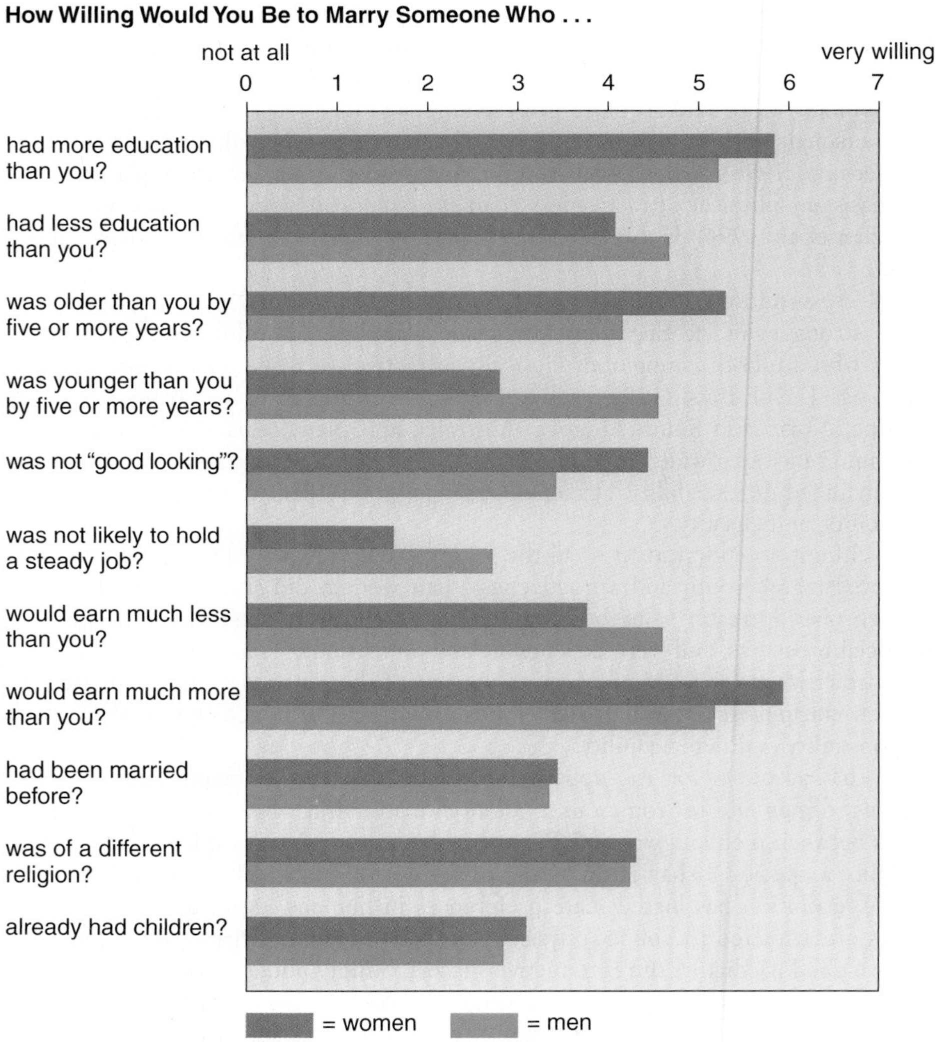

**How Willing Would You Be to Marry Someone Who . . .**

● **Figure 7.3** Differences between American men and women in aspects of mate selection.

The results indicate that women respondents were significantly more willing than men to marry someone who was better educated, older, would earn more, and was not good looking. Conversely, women were significantly less willing than men to marry someone who had less education, was younger, was not likely to hold a steady job, and would earn less. There were only minor differences between the sexes on items related to prior marriages, religion, and already having children.

# Love and Styles of Attachment

**Attachment** is a term for the intense emotional tie that develops between two individuals, such as the tie between an infant and a parent or between adult lovers (Rholes et al., 2006). It is possible to experience attachment without love, but it is unlikely that love of one person for another can exist in the absence of attachment. Although love itself is difficult to measure and study, researchers have had considerable success in investigating various aspects of attachment, including how it forms, effects of attachment deprivation, and styles of attachment. The last of these dimensions, styles of attachment, is of particular interest to social scientists. In the following pages, we examine key research findings pertaining to attachment and human relationships.

**Attachment** Intense emotional tie between two individuals, such as an infant and a parent or adult lovers.

## Attachment Styles

The way we form attachments, which has its roots in infancy, has a great impact on how we relate to loved partners. Much of our scientific knowledge about how attachment styles are established and how they later affect us comes from the work of developmental psychologist Mary Ainsworth (Ainsworth 1979, 1989; Ainsworth et al., 1978). Ainsworth used a laboratory procedure that she labeled the "strange situation." In this procedure a 1-year-old infant's behavior in an unfamiliar environment is assessed under various circumstances: with the mother present, with the mother and a stranger present, with only a stranger present, and totally alone.

Ainsworth discovered that infants react differently to these strange situations. Some, whom she labeled *securely attached*, used their mothers as a safe base for happily exploring the new environment and playing with the toys in the room. When separated from their mothers, the securely attached infants appeared to feel safe, expressed only moderate distress over their mothers' absence, and seemed confident that their mothers would return to provide care and protection. When reunited with their mothers, these infants sought contact and often resumed exploring their environments. *Insecurely attached* infants reacted differently. They showed more apprehension and less of a tendency to leave their mothers' sides to explore. They were severely distressed when their mothers left, often crying loudly, and when their mothers returned, they often seemed angry, expressing hostility or indifference.

Analysis of the data from Ainsworth's strange-situation research allowed subdivision of the category of insecurely attached infants into those expressing *anxious-ambivalent attachment* (infants manifesting extreme separation anxiety when their mothers left) and those expressing *avoidant attachment* (infants seeming to want close bodily contact with their mothers but to be reluctant to seek this, apparently because they could sense their mothers' detachment or indifference).

What accounts for these differences in attachment styles? The answer probably lies in a combination of inborn differences between infants and of parenting practices. Some infants are innately predisposed to form more secure attachments than others, just as some newborns seem to respond more positively to being held and cuddled than others. A second factor contributing to differences in babies' reactions to the strange situation was the way their mothers responded to them at home. Mothers of securely attached infants were inclined to be sensitive and responsive to their infants. For example, some mothers fed their babies when they were hungry rather than following a set schedule. They

According to research on attachment, the quality of cuddling and snuggling behaviors that occur between babies and parents influences comparable interactions between adult lovers.

also tended to cuddle their babies at times other than during feeding or diapering. In contrast, mothers of infants classified in one of the two insecurely attached categories tended to be less sensitive and responsive and were inconsistent in their reactions to their babies. For example, they fed their infants when they felt like it and sometimes ignored their babies' cries of hunger at other times. These mothers also tended to avoid close physical contact with their babies.

The establishment of a trusting, secure attachment between a child and a parent appears to have demonstrable effects on a child's later development. Several studies have shown that securely attached children, who learn that parents are a source of security and trustworthiness, are likely to demonstrate much greater social competence than children in either category of insecure attachment (Aspelmeier & Kerns, 2003; Sroufe, 1985; Sroufe et al., 1983). Anxious-ambivalent children, who have learned that parents respond inconsistently to their needs, are often plagued with uncertainty in new situations, and they frequently exhibit negative reactions to life situations, such as angry outbursts, an obsessive need to be near their parents, and an inconsistency in responses to others that reflects ambivalence about how to respond. Avoidant children, whose parents often neglect them, develop negative views of others and are reluctant to let others get close to them.

These various attachment styles, developed during infancy, tend to continue throughout our lives and to exert considerable influence on both our capacity to form loving attachments and the way we relate to significant others.

## Adult Intimate Relationships as an Attachment Process

A number of social scientists have conceptualized adults' close or romantic relationships as an attachment process (e.g., Aspelmeier & Kerns, 2003; Feeney & Noller, 1996). From this perspective, individuals transfer attachment styles and patterns acquired from parent-child relationships to peers with whom they become emotionally and sexually involved. In this sense, romantic partners come to serve as attachment figures (Aspelmeier & Kerns, 2003; Collins et al., 2006; Hazan & Zeifman, 1999).

Adult attachments between lovers or partners can be one of the three varieties we described. Securely attached adults seem to be best equipped to establish stable, satisfying relationships. These individuals find it relatively easy to get close to others and feel comfortable with others being close to them. They feel secure in relationships and do not fear being abandoned. In contrast, adults with an anxious-ambivalent attachment style often have a poor self-image and feel insecure in relationships. These individuals might want to get close to a partner very much but feel ambivalent about getting close because they fear that their partner does not want to be close to them. They may try to overcome their ambivalence by making desperate attempts to get close to a partner, often relinquishing much of their independence in the process. Reflecting the third attachment style, avoidant adults feel uncomfortable with any degree of closeness to a partner. These individuals often have difficulty trusting or depending on a partner. They frequently view others negatively and thus find it hard to let others get close to them and share intimacy. Avoidant adults desire a great deal of independence. Research reveals that slightly more than half of U.S. adults are securely attached, about one fourth are avoidant, and one fifth are anxious-ambivalent (Hazan & Shaver, 1987). ◉ **Table 7.3** outlines some of the common ways the three attachment styles influence interpersonal relationships.

Research indicates that people who form couples commonly have the same style of attachment—further evidence of how influential similarity is in determining whom we fall in love with (Gallo & Smith, 2001; Latty-Mann & Davis, 1996). The most common pairing was comprised of people who both had a secure attachment style (Chappell & Davis, 1998). This is not surprising, because secure people tend to respond positively to others and feel comfortable with closeness; their attachment style thus makes them more desirable as love partners than people with any other attachment style. In one study of 354 couples, over half comprised people who both had a secure attachment style. Predictably, no pairings comprised people who both had an anxious-ambivalent or an avoidant attachment style—no doubt because such

| Securely Attached Adults | Anxious-Ambivalent Adults | Avoidant Adults |
|---|---|---|
| Find it relatively easy to get close to others. Comfortable having others close to them. | Want to be close to others but believe that others may not want to be close to them. | Very uncomfortable with being close to others. |
| Feel secure in relationships and do not fear abandonment. | Worry that partners do not really love them and thus may leave them. | Believe that love is only transitory and that their partner will inevitably leave at some point in time. |
| Comfortable with both depending on partner and being depended upon. | May want to merge completely and be engulfed by partner. | Worry about becoming dependent on another and distrustful of someone depending on them. |
| Love relationships typically characterized by happiness, satisfaction, trust, and reciprocal emotional support. | Relationships characterized by roller-coaster emotional shifts and obsessive sexual attraction and jealousy. | Generally want less closeness than their partners seem to desire. Fear intimacy and experience emotional shifts from highs to lows. |
| Relationship duration averages 10 years. | Relationship duration averages about 5 years. | Relationship duration averages 6 years. |

SOURCE: Adapted from Ainsworth (1989), Ainsworth et al. (1978), and Shaver et al. (1988).

people would be quite incompatible with each other. People with a secure attachment style reported the highest level of relationship satisfaction, especially if their partner also had that style (Kirkpatrick & Davis, 1994).

Still another study of 128 couples found that attachment style influences how partners in a relationship interact. Securely attached individuals reported dealing constructively and effectively with relationship conflicts and/or their partner's potentially damaging behavior. When problems surfaced, they opened lines of communication for discussing and resolving the problems. In contrast, people with either of the two insecure attachment styles tended to respond to problems or conflicts with avoidance or withdrawal (Scharfe & Bartholomew, 1995).

These various findings, considered collectively, provide strong evidence of the impact of attachment styles on liking, loving, and relationship satisfaction.

# ◗ Issues in Loving Relationships

In the following paragraphs, we explore dynamics that cause complications in intimate relationships, focusing on two questions in particular. First we discuss the relationship between love and sex. Next we explore how jealousy affects relationships and what, if anything, can be done to keep it under control.

## What Is the Relationship Between Love and Sex?

Although we tend to associate sex with love, the connection is not always clear. It is certainly true that some people engage in sexual relations without being in love. One example of sex without love is the relatively common practice of **hook-ups** (or "hooking up"), which are short-term, loveless, sexual liaisons that occur during a brief interval (e.g., spring break, an ocean cruise, or a "one-nighter") (Lambert et al., 2003). Another example of loveless sex is the phenomenon of **"friends with benefits" relationships (FWBRs)**, which encompass sexual interaction between people who consider each other friends but not partners in a romantic relationship (Hughes et al., 2005). Researchers find it intriguing that such involvements combine the dual benefits of friendship and sexual gratification while avoiding the responsibilities and commitment associated with romantic love relationships (Hughes et al., 2005). Evidence suggests that FWBRs are quite common on college campuses. On three separate campuses the percentage of students reporting their involvement in FWBRs was 48.5%, 54%, and 61.7% (Afifi & Faulkner, 2000; Mongeau et al., 2003).

Love can also exist independently of any sexual attraction or expression. However, the ideal intimate relationship for most of us is one replete with feelings of both mutual love and mutual sexual gratification.

**Hook-ups** Short-term, loveless sexual liaisons that occur during a brief interval.

**"Friends with benefits" relationships (FWBRs)** Sexual interaction between friends who do not define their relationship as romantic.

Feelings of being in love with and sexually attracted to another person are frequently intertwined, and these feelings are especially pronounced in the early stages of a relationship. Research on college students indicates that both women and men consider sexual desire and attraction an important ingredient of romantic love (Regan, 1998). The complex interplay between love and sex gives rise to many questions: Does sexual intimacy deepen a love relationship? Do men and women have different views of the relationship between sex and love? And is sex without love appropriate? Here, we attempt to shed light on these and related questions.

## Does Sexual Intimacy Deepen a Love Relationship?

*I had known Chris for some time and thought I was ready to be sexual with him. So, after an evening out together, I asked him if I could stay at his place, and he said yes. I felt really aroused as we got in bed. I really enjoyed exploring the shapes and textures of his body. As we started to touch each other's genitals, though, I felt uncomfortable. If we proceeded in the direction we were headed, we would be going beyond the level of emotional intimacy I felt. It seemed that I would have to shut out the closeness I felt in order to go further. I had to choose between intimacy and genital contact. Our closeness was more important to me, and I told him that I wanted us to know each other more before going further sexually. (Authors' files)*

The woman just quoted made the decision to postpone further sexual involvement until she became more comfortable in her relationship. Many individuals take a different course, moving quickly to sexual intimacy. In some cases this can deepen a relationship. However, this result is certainly not assured. In fact, when a relationship becomes sexual before a couple has established a more generalized bond of intimacy—fostered by a growing awareness, understanding, and appreciation of each other—the individuals involved can actually feel farther apart emotionally.

It is reasonable to suspect that people sometimes attempt to justify their sexual behavior by deciding they are in love. Indeed, it is likely that some couples enter into premature commitments (such as going steady, moving in together, becoming engaged, or even getting married) to convince themselves of the depth of their love and thus of the legitimacy of their sexual involvement.

## Do Men and Women View Sex and Love Differently?

In general, men and women tend to view the relationship between sex and love somewhat differently (Hendrick & Hendrick, 1995; Regan & Berscheid, 1995). For instance, men are more likely than women to define being in love, and to assess the quality of the romantic involvement, in terms of sexual satisfaction (Fischer & Heesacker, 1995; McCabe, 1999). Studies also indicate that it is easier for men than for women to have sexual intercourse for pleasure and physical release without an emotional commitment (Buss, 1999; Townsend, 1995). However, this difference between men and women diminishes somewhat with age; older women are more likely than younger women to list desire for physical pleasure as an important motivation for sex (Murstein & Tuerkheim, 1998).

Despite these apparent differences, both men and women value love and affection in sexual relationships. Furthermore, two nationwide surveys of large representative samples of American men and women, conducted in 1984 and 1994, revealed a trend toward convergence of male and female attitudes about the relationship between love and sex. In the 1984 study, 59% of men and 86% of women reported that it was difficult to have sex without love (Ubell, 1984). However, 10 years later, 71% of the men indicated it was difficult to relate sexually to someone without love, whereas the percentage of women expressing this viewpoint did not change (86%) (Clements, 1994).

Other studies have confirmed that, despite differences in how men and women view the association between love and sex, both sexes are similar in what they consider important ingredients of successful and rewarding loving relationships (Regan, 1998; Sprecher et al., 1995). Among attributes ranked as very important by both men and women are good communication, commitment, and a high quality of emotional and physical intimacy (Byers & Demmons, 1999; Fischer & Heesacker, 1995; McCabe, 1999).

## Do Heterosexuals, Gay Men, and Lesbians View Love and Sex Differently?

*I would not consider myself to be biased against homosexuals. However, I do feel some degree of disapproval of the gay lifestyle, which often seems to involve casual affairs based more on sex than genuine caring. Some gay men I know have had more partners in the last couple of years than I have had in a lifetime. (Authors' files)*

This opinion reflects a belief widespread among heterosexuals that homosexuals, especially gay men, form liaisons with same-sex partners that are based primarily on sexual interaction and that are often devoid of genuine attachment, love, commitment, and overall satisfaction. A number of researchers have revealed the essential fallacy of this thinking by demonstrating that homosexuals, like heterosexuals, generally seek out loving, trusting, caring relationships that embrace many dimensions of sharing in addition to sexual intimacy (Adler et al., 1989; Kurdek, 1995b; Zak & McDonald, 1997). Lesbians and gay men differ in the degree to which they associate emotional closeness or love with sex, consistent with overall differences between men and women in their views of sex and love. Whereas men in general are more likely than women to separate sex and love, gay men have shown a particularly strong inclination to make this separation. Some gay men have engaged in frequent casual sexual encounters without love or caring attachment; such activity was especially common before the AIDS epidemic (Bell & Weinberg, 1978; Gross, 2003a). Rather than indicating that gay men do not value love, this finding merely reveals that some gay men value sex as an end itself. In contrast, most lesbians postpone sexual involvement until they have developed emotional intimacy with a partner (Leigh, 1989; Zak & McDonald, 1997). A number of researchers have suggested that such differences between gay men and lesbians result from patterns of gender-role socialization that make casual sex more permissible for males than for females. Furthermore, they argue that heterosexual men would be as likely as gay men to engage in loveless, casual sex if women were equally interested, and if most heterosexual couples did not assume that their relationship was exclusive (Foa et al., 1987; Leigh, 1989).

Finally, love plays a prominent role in the lives of homosexual people as a nexus for establishing a self-imposed identity as either a lesbian or a gay man. Many heterosexually oriented people have had sexual contact with same-sex partners. This is especially true during late childhood and during adolescence, when same-sex contact can be either experimental and transitory or an expression of a lifelong orientation (see Chapter 12). These same-sex sexual activities are not sufficient in and of themselves to establish an identity as a homosexually oriented person. Rather, it is falling in love with a person of the same sex that often supplies the key element necessary to establish a gay or lesbian identity (Troiden, 1988).

## Jealousy in Relationships

*Jealousy* has been defined as an aversive emotional reaction evoked by a real or imagined relationship involving one's partner and a third person (Bringle & Buunk, 1991). Many people think that jealousy is a measure of devotion and that the absence of jealous feelings implies a lack of love (Buss, 2000). People commonly have ambivalent attitudes toward jealousy, "seeing it sometimes as a sign of insecurity, sometimes as a sign of love, and sometimes as both simultaneously" (Puente & Cohen, 2003, p. 458). Jealousy is related more to injured pride, or to people's fear of losing what they want to control or possess, than to love. For example, a person who finds that a spouse enjoys someone else's company might feel inadequate and therefore jealous. As described in our discussion of reciprocity, we often enter into and remain in relationships because they provide a sense of belongingness and bolster our self-esteem. We often rely on our partner to validate our positive sense of self. Consequently, we can feel threatened and sense a potential loss of both reciprocity and a positive self-image if we perceive that our partner is considering a replacement for us (Boekhout et al., 1999).

The intense emotions of jealousy are therefore often due to our imagining and fearing being abandoned by our partner for someone else (Sharpsteen & Kirkpatrick,

● Jealousy

1997). Jealous feelings can be further heightened by envy of certain characteristics of the rival, because we are more likely to be jealous of individuals who have qualities that we desire. In general, traits over which women show the most envy are attractiveness and popularity, whereas men are more envious of wealth and fame (Barker, 1987; Salovey & Rodin, 1985).

Some people are more prone to feeling jealousy than others. Individuals who have a low opinion of themselves, reflected in feelings of insecurity and inadequacy, are more likely to feel jealousy in a relationship (Brehm et al., 2002; Buss, 1994, 1999). This relates to a point we have already made—that a healthy self-esteem is the foundation for building intimate relationships. Second, people who see a large discrepancy between who they are and who they would like to be are also prone to jealousy. Not surprisingly, such individuals also are likely to have low self-esteem. And third, people who place a high value on traits such as wealth, fame, popularity, and physical attractiveness might be more likely to feel jealousy in a relationship (Salovey & Rodin, 1985).

Jealousy is frequently a factor in precipitating violence in marriages and dating relationships (Buss, 1999; Puente & Cohen, 2003; Vandello & Cohen, 2003). Research demonstrates that jealousy-precipitated violence is more commonly directed toward one's partner or lover than toward a third-party rival (Mathes & Verstrate, 1993; Paul & Galloway, 1994).

Jealousy is an uncomfortable feeling that can stifle the development of a relationship and the pleasure of being together. For both men and women the emotions and thoughts associated with jealousy are negative; they include feeling anxious, depressed, or angry and having a sense of being less valued by and attractive to one's partner (Bush et al., 1988). Jealousy can also have a paradoxical effect, because although a jealous person wishes to maintain both the relationship and his or her self-image, both of these desires are likely to be damaged when jealous feelings are expressed (Buunk & Bringle, 1987).

Although it is clear that jealousy has many negative effects, it is not always clear how jealous feelings should be handled when they occur in a relationship. The box titled "Coping with the Green-Eyed Monster" offers suggestions to people who want to decrease feelings of jealousy, either in themselves or in their partners.

## The Sexes' Differing Experiences of Jealousy

Not everyone responds to jealousy in the same way, and a number of studies have found differences in the ways women and men respond. In general, women are more likely than men to acknowledge feeling jealous (Barker, 1987; Clanton & Smith,

**Critical Thinking Question**

Research indicates that women are more likely than men to acknowledge feeling jealous. What do you think accounts for this difference between the sexes?

1977). Furthermore, several studies have suggested that a woman's jealousy tends to focus on her partner's emotional involvement with another person, whereas a man's jealousy tends to focus on his partner's sexual involvement with another (Fisher, 1999; Shackelford et al., 2002). However, a review of various evidence found little support for this suggested difference between the sexes (Harris, 2003). One study of heterosexual and homosexual men and women found that both sexes were more concerned about a partner's emotional involvement with another person than about sexual involvement (Harris, 2002).

Another difference between women's and men's jealousy patterns is that women often blame themselves when a conflict over jealousy arises, whereas men typically attribute their jealousy to a third party or to their partner's behavior (Barker, 1987; Daly et al., 1982). Women have also been shown to be more inclined than men to deliberately provoke jealousy in their partners (Sheets et al., 1997; White & Helbick, 1988). This difference in the sexes' jealousy patterns might stem from the fact that women experiencing jealousy often suffer simultaneously from feelings of inadequacy and worthlessness. Consequently, a woman's efforts to arouse jealousy in a partner can

## Coping with the Green-Eyed Monster

It is common for the green-eyed monster, jealousy, to raise its ugly head at least sometime during a relationship. Dealing with jealousy can be difficult, because such feelings often stem from a deep sense of inadequacy within the jealous individual rather than within the relationship. A person threatened by insecurity-induced feelings of jealousy often withdraws from his or her partner or goes on the attack with accusations or threats. These ineffective coping behaviors often provoke a similar reaction in the nonjealous partner: withdrawal or counterattack. A more effective approach for the jealous person is to acknowledge his or her own feelings of jealousy and to clarify their source. Thus a jealous person might initiate discussion by saying something like "Mary, I am afraid for us and a little bit crazy over all the time you spend working late with your coworkers, especially with that guy Bill!" Such an open acknowledgment of feelings without threats or accusations might prompt Mary to respond with reassurances, and a positive dialogue might ensue.

Jealousy is an uncomfortable feeling that often harms a relationship and stifles the pleasure of being together.

In many situations, a jealous person will not acknowledge that a problem exists and will not express a desire to work on it. If so, the essential first step to resolving the problem is to motivate that person to begin working to eliminate the painful jealousy feelings and the destructive behaviors that such feelings often induce. Robert Barker (1987), a marital therapist, provides valuable guidelines for accomplishing this in his book *The Green-Eyed Marriage: Surviving Jealous Relationships.* Barker maintains that a jealous person is most likely to become motivated to work on the problem and to permit help from others when he or she is

- *confident that there is no danger of losing the valued partner.* Direct reassurance that the relationship is not in danger is often ineffective and sometimes can even be counterproductive. A more effective strategy is to refer, at various times, to being together in the future. Consequently, a nonjealous partner planning to initiate a discussion about jealousy might first pick a few opportune times to say such things as "It will be great when the children are all grown and we have more time just for us."
- *assured that the problem comes from the relationship rather than from defects in his or her character.* A jealous person is much more likely to begin dealing with the jealousy when both partners acknowledge that it is a shared problem.

The nonjealous partner can move thinking in this direction by stating, "This is a problem we share, and we both have to work equally to overcome it."
- *confident about being genuinely loved and respected.* Because jealousy often stems from feelings of inadequacy and insecurity, the nonjealous partner can help minimize these negative emotions and bolster self-esteem and confidence by "regularly reaffirming affection for the jealous person verbally, emotionally, and physically" (Barker, 1987, p. 100).
- *not provoked into feeling shame or guilt.* Understandably, many people who are undeservedly targets of jealousy become angry and inclined to strike back with sarcasm, ridicule, or put-downs to shame their jealous partners into abandoning their unfounded accusations. Unfortunately, such negative counterattacks are likely to have the opposite effect, promoting more anger and defensiveness. Worse yet, the jealous person might be even less willing to acknowledge a need for change.
- *is able to empathize with the person who has been hurt by the jealous behavior.* When jealous people can understand and empathize with the pain their behavior has caused their partner, the incentive to change may increase. The challenge for the nonjealous partner is to foster empathy rather than guilt. This can be accomplished by verbalizing the pain but not blaming the jealous partner. Thus, Mary might say to her jealous partner, "I love you, Mike, and I feel really bad when I have to work late and I know you are at home wishing we could be together. It is really painful to think that my work situation sometimes seems more important than our relationship."

Once the motivation for change is established, and once a couple begins a dialogue to deal with jealousy, several of the communication strategies outlined in this chapter can help them work on the problem. Suggestions for self-disclosure, listening, feedback, and asking questions can help to clearly establish what each partner wants and expects of the relationship. For example, after disclosing his fears, Mike might tell Mary that he would worry less if she would spend less time working with Bill after hours or maybe just include others from the office when working late.

actually be an attempt to bolster self-worth by eliciting increased attention from a partner concerned about her actions. Men also often attach feelings of inadequacy to jealousy. However, the relationship is frequently reversed in men, with awareness of jealousy occurring first, followed by feeling inadequate (White & Helbick, 1988).

One investigation assessed the relationship between perceived parenthood quality and jealousy. Women respondents in this study were more likely to become jealous over infidelity if they perceived their partner as bad parent material, because an inadequate parent who abandons their relationship would be less likely than a good parent to continue supporting their children. In sharp contrast, male respondents were more likely to become jealous if they perceived their partner as good parent material, because they might lose an ideal partner for producing and caring for their children (Sharpsteen, 1995).

# ❿ Maintaining Relationship Satisfaction

Human relationships present many challenges. One challenge involves building positive feelings about ourselves. Another involves establishing satisfying and enjoyable relationships with family, peers, teachers, coworkers, employers, and other people in our social network. A third challenge involves developing special intimate relationships with friends and, when we want them, sexual relationships. Finally, many people confront the challenge of maintaining satisfaction and love within an ongoing committed relationship. In this section, we present factors that contribute to ongoing satisfaction in relationships. We also discuss the value of sexual variety within a relationship.

## Ingredients in a Lasting Love Relationship

Ingredients commonly present in a lasting love relationship include self-acceptance, acceptance by one's partner, appreciation of one another, commitment, good communication, realistic expectations, shared interests, equality in decision making, and the ability to face conflict effectively. These characteristics are not static; they evolve and change and influence one another over time. Often they need to be deliberately cultivated.

One review of the research on marital satisfaction reported that successful marriages that remain strong over the long haul often exhibit certain other characteristics (Karney & Bradbury, 1995):

- Parents of both spouses had successful, happy marriages.
- Spouses have similar attitudes, interests, and personality styles.
- Both spouses are satisfied with their sexual sharing.
- The couple has an adequate and steady income.
- The woman was not pregnant when the couple married.

In another study, researchers asked a sample of 560 women and men to judge the importance of a number of different elements to the success of a marriage or a long-term committed relationship. Elements judged to be important for high-quality relationships included the following (Sprecher et al., 1995):

- Supportive communication: Open and honest communication and a willingness to talk about difficult issues and concerns.
- Companionship: Sharing mutual interests and enjoying many activities together.
- Sexual expression: Spontaneity and variety in sexual sharing, and feeling sexually attractive to one's partner.

In still another study of 300 happily married couples, the most frequently named reason for an enduring and happy marriage was seeing one's partner as one's best friend. Qualities that individuals especially appreciated in a partner were caring, giving, having integrity, and having a sense of humor. These couples were aware of flaws in their mates, but they believed that the likable qualities were more important. Many said that their mates had become more interesting to them over time. They preferred shared rather than separate activities, which appeared to reflect the richness in the relationship. Most couples were generally satisfied with their sex lives, and for some the sexual passion had become more intense over time (Lauer & Lauer, 1985).

Maintaining frequent positive interactions is crucial to continued satisfaction in a relationship. The saying "It's the little things that count" is especially meaningful here. When one partner says to the other, "You do not love me anymore," that often means, "You are not doing as many of the things as you used to do that show me you love me." These behaviors are often so small that the partners may not really notice them. However, when couples do fewer things to make one another feel loved (or when they stop doing them entirely), the deficit is often experienced as a lack of love. Continuing affectionate and considerate interaction helps maintain a feeling of love:

> The kinds of things that enhance my feeling that my partner still loves me may seem quite inconsequential, but to me they aren't. When he gets up to greet me when I come home, when he takes my arm crossing the street, when he asks, "Can I help you with that," when he tells me I look great, when he holds me in the middle of the night, when he thanks me for doing a routine chore—I feel loved by him. Those little things—all added up—make a tremendous difference to me. (Authors' files)

An older couple's intimacy and affection develop from years of shared experiences.

It is also useful to talk with our partners, to communicate what is especially enjoyable, or to suggest new ideas. The golden rule ("Do unto others as you would have them do unto you") does not always apply in relationships, because people's preferences are often quite different. One partner may not know what the other partner wants unless that person expresses it. Enjoyment with and appreciation of one another in nonsexual areas typically enhance sexual interest and interactions. Often couples report a lack of desire for sexual intimacy when they are not feeling emotionally intimate.

## Sexual Variety: An Important Ingredient

> There is a special little restaurant with great steaks and a cozy, intimate atmosphere that I love to visit once every few months. Good companionship, a favorite bottle of wine, a tasty dinner, and I am living. Let a friend invite me back the next day, and it is still good, but not quite so stimulating. Given an invitation for a third trip in as many days, and I might just as soon stop off for a McDonald's quarter-pounder. (Authors' files)

Many people have a strong desire to seek variety in life's experiences. They might acquire an assortment of friends, each of whom provides a unique enrichment to their lives. Likewise, they might read different kinds of books, pursue a variety of recreational activities, eat different kinds of foods, and take a variety of classes. Yet many of these same people settle for routine in their sex lives.

Unfortunately, many people enter into a committed relationship thinking that intense sexual excitement will always follow naturally when two people are in love. But, as we have seen in this chapter, the initial excitement must eventually be replaced by realistic and committed efforts to maintain the vitality and rewards of a working relationship. Once a person is committed to a primary partner, the variety offered by a succession of relationships is no longer available. Some individuals may need to seek variety in other ways.

Not every couple feels the need for sexual variety. Many people are quite comfortable with established routines and have no desire to change them. However, if you prefer to develop more variety in your sexual relationship, the following paragraphs may be helpful.

Communication is critical. Talk to your partner about your needs and feelings. Share with him or her your desire to try something different. Perhaps some of the guidelines for sexual communication discussed in the following sections will help you make requests and exchange information.

Even though time inevitably erodes the novelty of a relationship, the resulting decline of passion can be countered by introducing novelty into patterns of sexual sharing. This can be accomplished by avoiding routine times and places. Make love in places other than the bed (on the laundry room floor, in the shower, alongside a mountain trail) and at various times ("birdsong in the morning," a "nooner," or in the middle of the night when you wake up feeling sexually aroused).

Some of the most exciting sexual experiences take place on the spur of the moment, with little or no planning. It is easy to see how such experiences might occur frequently during courtship. It is equally apparent how they can become distant memories after a couple settles into the demanding daily schedule of living together. Nevertheless, you may find that striving to maintain this spontaneity will stand you in good stead as your relationship is nurtured over months or years together.

On the other hand, planning for intimate time—sexual and nonsexual—can also help maintain closeness. Make dates with one another and consciously continue the romantic gestures that came naturally early in the relationship. Commit your energy and time to your sexual relationship.

Do not let questions of what is "normal" get in the way of an enriched and varied erotic life. Too often, people refrain from experiencing something new because they believe that different activities are "abnormal." In reality, only you can judge what is normal for you. Sexologists concur that any sexual activity is normal so long as it gives pleasure and does not cause emotional or physical discomfort or harm to either partner. Emotional comfort is important because "discomfort and conflict rather than intimacy and satisfaction can result if behaviors are tried which are too divergent from personal values and attitudes" (Barbach, 1982, p. 282).

We do not mean to imply that all people must have active, varied sex lives to be truly happy; this is not the case. As we have already seen, some partners find comfort and contentment in repeating familiar patterns of sexual interaction. Others consider sex relatively unimportant compared with other aspects of their lives and choose not to exert special efforts in pursuing its pleasures. However, if your sexuality is an important source of pleasure in your life, perhaps these suggestions and others in this textbook will be important to you. ■

Do men and women differ in their desire for sexual variety? The cross-cultural research described in the Spotlight on Research box provides strong evidence that the sexes do differ in the desire for sexual variety.

In the remainder of this chapter, we discuss sexual communication: the ways people express their feelings and convey their needs and desires to sexual partners. We consider the reasons that such attempts are sometimes unsuccessful; we also explore ways to enhance this important aspect of our sexual lives.

## ◉ The Importance of Sexual Communication

Sexual communication can contribute greatly to the satisfaction of an intimate relationship. Good communication about sexual desires and concerns has frequently been identified as a valuable asset to the development and maintenance of a satisfying and enduring sexual relationship (Byers, 2005; Byers & Demmons, 1999; Ferroni & Jaffee, 1997). We do not mean that extensive verbal dialogue is essential to all sexual sharing; there are times when spoken communication is more disruptive than constructive. Nevertheless, partners who never talk about the sexual aspects of their relationship are denying themselves an opportunity to increase their closeness and pleasure through learning about each other's needs and desires.

**Mutual empathy** The underlying knowledge that each partner in a relationship cares for the other and knows that the care is reciprocated.

Central to this discussion is our belief that the basis for effective sexual communication is **mutual empathy**—the underlying knowledge that each partner in a relationship cares for the other and knows that the care is reciprocated. With this perspective in mind we discuss various approaches to sexual communication that have proved helpful in the lives of many people. We do not claim to have the final word on the many nuances of human communication; nor do we suggest that the ideas offered here will work for everyone. Communication strategies often need to be individually modified; and sometimes the differences between two people are so profound that

## Differences in Men's and Women's Desire for Sexual Variety

A number of evolutionary psychologists have hypothesized that the mating strategies of men and women have evolved differentially; a difference is especially pronounced in the motivations underlying the pursuit of short-term sexual relationships. According to this perspective, men seeking short-term mates are often motivated by a desire for sexual variety, which is reflected in their inclinations both to pursue numerous sex partners and to consent to sex relatively quickly. In contrast, women's underlying motivations for seeking short-term relationships seem to be focused on selectively obtaining men of higher status and/or excellent genetic quality (Gangestad & Simpson, 2000; Schmitt, 2003; Schmitt et al., 2001).

Support for this interpretation was recently provided by a cross-cultural survey of 16,288 people selected from 10 major world regions: North America, South America, western Europe, eastern Europe, southern Europe, the Middle East, Africa, Oceania, South and Southeast Asia, and eastern Asia. This investigation was conducted by evolutionary psychologist David Schmitt (2003). Schmitt used an anonymous nine-page survey questionnaire, translated into local languages, to assess three primary variables: (1) the number of sexual partners desired at differing time intervals ("Number of Partners" measure), (2) relationship duration before experiencing sexual intercourse ("Time Known" measure), and

(3) the extent to which participants were actively seeking short-term mating partners ("Short-Term Seeking" measure).

The results of this comprehensive investigation provided strong evidence that men and women differ fundamentally in their short-term mating psychology, especially in the desire for sexual variety, and that these differences appear to be culturally universal throughout the sampled world regions. Schmitt's findings revealed that "men not only possess a greater desire than women do for a variety of sexual partners, men also require less time to elapse than women do before consenting to sexual intercourse, and men tend to more actively seek short-term mateships than women do" (Schmitt, 2003, p. 101). Schmitt concluded that his investigation strongly supported the evolutionary psychology viewpoint that men's evolved short-term mating strategies are rooted in a desire for sexual variety. For example, even among women participants who responded that they were "strongly seeking" a short-term partner, less than 20% desired more than one partner in the next month. In contrast, among men in the "strongly seeking" category, over 50% desired more than one partner in the next month. This percentage increased to 69% and 75% for the next 6 months and 1 year, respectively. For women respondents the percentage increases for the same time periods were minimal.

even the best communication cannot ensure a mutually satisfying relationship. We hope, though, that some of these shared experiences and suggestions can be helpful in your own life.

## Reasons That Sexual Communication Is Difficult

Some of the most important reasons that sexual communication is difficult lie in our socialization, the language available for talking about sex, and the fears many people have about self-expression.

## Socialization and Sexual Communication

The way we were reared as children often contributes to later difficulties in talking about sexual needs. The lack of communication about sexual matters in many American homes is detrimental in a number of ways. Not talking about sex at home deprives a young child of one valuable source of a vocabulary for talking about sex later in life. This lack of communication can also imply that sex is not an acceptable topic for conversation. Furthermore, children acquire communication skills most effectively when they are provided with models of verbal interaction followed by the opportunity to express their own thoughts in an accepting atmosphere. None of these elements is typically available in a home where people simply do not talk about sex.

Lack of positive models frequently extends beyond the home. Few people have access to classroom or textbook sources that portray how couples talk about sex. Neither peer groups nor the popular media fill the gap by providing realistic or positive information. Widely viewed movies rarely depict any meaningful verbal communication between on-screen lovers and, when dialogue does occur, it is typically ambiguous and insensitive (Striar & Bartlik, 2000).

## Language and Sexual Communication

Another obstacle to effective communication is the lack of a suitable language for sex. By the time we are grown up and eager to communicate sexual needs and feelings, many of us do not know how to go about it. The very words we have learned to describe sex might have become associated with negative rather than positive emotions. Many of us have learned to snicker over taboo sex words or to use them in an angry, aggressive, or insulting manner. Consequently, it can be uncomfortable to use those same words to describe an activity with someone for whom we really care.

Thus, when we want to begin engaging in sexual communication, we find ourselves struggling to find the right language for this most intimate kind of dialogue. The range of words commonly used to describe genital anatomy gives some indication of our society's mixed messages about sexuality. Two extremes tend to predominate: street language at one end and clinical terminology at the other.

Within the context of our culture it is natural—or at least common—to feel shy or embarrassed when talking about sexuality with friends and lovers. However, this awkwardness can often be avoided or overcome, and people certainly find ways of learning to live with the vocabulary. Some people give their own or their partners' genitals nicknames, such as Fuzzylove, Slurpy, Artesia, Pokey, Peter, or Moby, in an attempt to avoid negative associations with much of the existing terminology. When both partners in a couple choose personal names for their genitalia—ones that are easy to say and have positive connotations—it can "open up their communication by fostering playfulness" (*Contemporary Sexuality*, 1999d, p. 1). Couples who are experiencing sexual problems in their relationship have been shown to benefit from using playful names for their genitals (Godow, 1999). A key element in the success of using personal or playful names for sexual anatomy and sexual interaction is that both partners are comfortable with the terms used.

Many benefits and joys are associated with talking to our lovers while we touch their bodies. This is a wonderful time to develop intimacy while learning about each other's needs and preferences. It is a particularly good way to discover what words are mutually acceptable.

Ethnic variations in communication styles also significantly affect how people talk about sex. The following Sexuality and Diversity discussion examines such variations.

## SEXUALITY AND DIVERSITY

### *Ethnic Variations in Intimate Communication*

Textbooks, lectures, and general media sources that portray how couples can effectively communicate about intimate matters, especially sex, are not plentiful. Thus it should come as no surprise that data on ethnic variations in intimate communication are also limited. In this discussion, we draw on a sparse database to offer a few generalizations about variations in styles of communicating about sexual intimacy that occur among white Americans, African Americans, Hispanic Americans, and Asian Americans.

The belief that good communication is the heart and soul of healthy intimate relationships is rather common among white Americans (especially white women) and, to a lesser extent, African Americans; however, among Hispanic American and Asian American couples, "working on" communication competence is generally much less emphasized (Bradshaw, 1994; Chang & Holt, 1991; Hecht et al., 1993; Ting-Toomey & Korzenny, 1991). Thus, although white Americans and African Americans may openly discuss sex with a partner, the general assumption among Hispanic American couples is that they will not discuss their sexual relationship (Guerrero-Pavich, 1986; Van Oss Marin & Gomez, 1994). Asian American couples are also less inclined to discuss sex, consistent with a general tendency to value nonverbal, indirect, and intuitive communication over explicit verbal interaction (Bradshaw, 1994; Del Carmen, 1990).

White Americans and, to a lesser extent, African Americans tend to be more self-oriented in intimate relationships than either Hispanic Americans or Asian Americans (Gudykunst et al., 1996; Hecht et al., 1990, 1993; Trafimow et al., 1991). This stress on *individualism*—an ideology that places greater emphasis on the individual than on the couple or group—is perhaps best reflected by the statement "I'm doing something with you, and I will get my needs met (and you might as well)" (Hecht et al., 1993, p. 155). In contrast, Hispanic Americans and Asian Americans are more likely to stress *collectivism*—an ideology that focuses on the couple or group rather than on the individual (Hecht et al., 1993; Parks & Vu, 1994). This perspective on intimate relationships is reflected by the statement "We are doing something together that we are both getting something out of" (Hecht et al., 1993, p. 155).

Perhaps because of the emphasis on individualism in white American relationships, overt conflict is considered natural and something to be dealt with and resolved. African American couples are less comfortable dealing with conflict, and Hispanic American couples tend to view conflicts as a negative indicator that a relationship is disharmonious or unbalanced (Collier, 1991; Ting-Toomey & Korzenny, 1991). Because harmonious relationships and the collective good of the group are valued over individualism and rewards for oneself, Asian Americans are also strongly inclined to avoid conflicts that involve direct confrontation with a primary partner (Del Carmen, 1990).

From these general differences between ethnic groups in the United States, it follows that, although Asian and Hispanic American couples may not necessarily encounter more relational sexual problems than white or African Americans, they are certainly less inclined to acknowledge or discuss such concerns. Furthermore, it is unlikely that members of either the Asian or the Hispanic ethnic groups would be inclined to seek professional help for relationship problems, especially those of a sexual nature.

Ethnic variations also exist in nonverbal sexual communication. Hispanic Americans rely heavily on nonverbal communication to reveal sexual information, and they place particular emphasis on the use of touching to convey love, a desire for intimacy, or sexual intent (Hecht et al., 1990). Touching also plays a major role among African Americans, who touch more than white Americans, who in turn touch more than Asian Americans (Butts, 1981; Hecht et al., 1990; Parham et al., 1999).

Interpersonal distance—another important aspect of nonverbal sexual communication discussed later in this chapter—is much more contracted among Hispanic Americans than among white Americans. This fact can lead to misunderstandings when members of these two ethnic groups interact. Thus a white American may misinterpret a close-standing Hispanic person as issuing an invitation for intimacy when, in actuality, the close proximity to another is typical of Hispanic culture (Bryjak & Soroka, 1994; Sluzki, 1982). African Americans also tend to establish smaller interpersonal distances than white Americans (Halberstadt, 1985).

## Gender-Based Communication Styles

Still another factor that can hinder communication between heterosexual partners is the difference in women's and men's styles of relating to other people (Canary & Dindia, 1998; James & Cinelli, 2003; Greene & Faulkner, 2005; Tannen, 1994, 2001). According to Deborah Tannen (1990, 1994), a professor of linguistics at Georgetown University, men and women often have different communication goals. Men use language to convey information, to achieve status in a group, to challenge others, and to prevent being pushed around. Men often enter into conversations concerned about who is one-up and who is one-down. From this perspective, communication becomes something of a contest to avoid being put in a one-down position. A man operating within this framework might be overly sensitive about asking for advice or for suggestions about how to respond in a particular situation (sexual or otherwise), about being told to do something, or about engaging in any other behavior that even remotely resembles being in a one-down or pushed-around position.

In contrast, Tannen maintains that women use language to achieve and share intimacy, to promote closeness, and to prevent others from pushing them away. Women are not typically socialized to use language as a defensive weapon to avoid being dominated or controlled. Rather, their concern is often to use dialogue as a way to get

Communication between heterosexual partners can be hindered by differences between women's and men's styles of relating to other people.

close to another person—and to judge how close to or distant from a valued partner they are.

A woman's goal in talking about her concerns is often to foster a sense of sharing and rapport and to achieve the feeling that she is not alone. She wants a response that says, "I understand; I have been there too." That response puts both communicators on equal footing, allowing intimacy to be built around equality. A woman may be looking only for understanding or a willingness to talk openly about a concern, but her male partner is often likely to respond with advice or solutions. This response frames him "as more knowledgeable, more reasonable, more in control—in a word, one-up. And this contributes to the distancing effect" (Tannen, 1990, p. 53). Women can minimize this relationship-eroding influence by clearly telling their male partner that, when dealing with intimacy or emotional troubles, they do not want to hear quickly offered solutions. Instead, they want their partner to listen to their concerns and be willing to openly discuss and share viewpoints about problems on an equal footing.

Since the publication of Tannen's research, many investigations have looked at gender differences in communication styles. A recent review of a large number of these studies concluded that the differences between men's and women's styles of communicating are, in general, relatively small (Canary & Dindia, 1998). Clearly, the gender differences described by Tannen and others do exist, as verified by this literature review. However, the differences are not so large as to suggest that the two sexes are from different cultures. In fact, research indicates that similarities outweigh differences in women's and men's communication styles (MacGeorge et al., 2004). Men and women can communicate effectively about a broad array of topics, including sexual intimacy. Being aware of and responsive to the gender differences outlined by Tannen can only improve communication between the sexes.

## Anxieties About Sexual Communication

Beyond the handicaps imposed by socialization and language limitations, difficulties in sexual communication for some people can also be rooted in anxieties about exposing themselves. Any sexual communication involves a certain amount of risk: By talking, people place themselves in a position vulnerable to judgment, criticism, and even rejection. The willingness to take risks can be related to the amount of trust that exists within a relationship. Some couples lack this mutual trust, and for them the risks of openly expressing sexual needs are too great to overcome. Others have a high degree of reciprocal caring and trust; for them the first hesitant steps into sexual dialogue can be considerably easier.

Even when a climate of goodwill prevails, however, it still can be difficult to establish a satisfying pattern of sexual dialogue. In such circumstances a couple might be frustrated in their efforts to resolve their communication problems strictly on their own. Instead, they should probably seek professional counseling. (In Chapter 14 we provide some guidelines for seeking professional assistance.)

We have outlined reasons that many people find it difficult to engage in meaningful and effective sexual communication. Despite these difficulties, communication is an important part of sexual sharing, just as it is an important part of many other aspects of a relationship. The potential rewards are enhanced sexual experiences and enriched relationships.

## ● Talking: Getting Started

How does one begin communicating about sex? In this section we explore a few of the many ways of breaking the ice. These suggestions may be useful not just at the beginning of a relationship but throughout its course.

### Talking About Talking

When people feel uneasy about a topic, often the best place to start is to talk about talking. Discussing *why* it is hard to talk about sex can be a good place to begin. Each of us has our own reasons for finding this difficult, and understanding those reasons can help set a relationship on a solid foundation. Perhaps you can share experiences about earlier efforts to discuss sexual topics with parents, teachers, physicians, friends, or lovers. It might be helpful to move gradually into the arena of sexual communication by directing your initial discussions to nonthreatening, less personal topics (such as new birth control methods, pornography laws, etc.). Later, as your mutual comfort increases, you may be able to talk about more personal feelings and concerns.

### Reading and Discussing

Because many people find it easier to read about sex than to talk about it, articles and books dealing with the subject can provide the stimulus for personal conversations. Partners can read the material separately, then discuss it together; or a couple can read it jointly and discuss their individual reactions. Often it is easier to make the transition from a book or article to personal feelings than to begin by talking about highly personal concerns.

### Sharing Sexual Histories

Another way to start talking is to share sexual histories. There may be many questions that you would feel comfortable discussing with your partner. For instance, how was sex education handled in your home or at school? How did your parents relate to each other—were you aware of any sexuality in their relationship? When did you first learn about sex, and what were your reactions? Many other items could be added to this brief list; the questions depend on the feelings and needs of each individual.

Reading together about sensitive matters can foster discussion.

## ● Listening and Feedback

Communication, sexual or otherwise, is most successful when it is two-sided, involving both an effective communicator and an active listener. In this section, we focus on the listening side of this process.

Have you ever wondered why certain people seem to draw others to themselves like iron to a magnet? With some thought, you will probably conclude that, among other things, these individuals are often good listeners. What special skills do they possess that make us feel that they really care about what we have to say? The next time you are with such a person, observe closely. Make a study of his or her listening habits. Perhaps your list of good listening traits will include several of the following: being an active listener, maintaining eye contact, providing feedback, supporting one's partner's communication efforts, and expressing unconditional positive regard.

### Be an Active Listener

Some people are *passive* listeners. They stare blankly into space as their companion talks, perhaps grunting uh-huh now and then. Such responses make us, the talker, think that the listener is indifferent, even when this is not the case, and we may soon grow tired of trying to share important thoughts with someone who does not seem to be receptive:

> When I talk to my husband about anything really important, he just stares at me with a blank expression. It is like I am talking to a piece of stone. I think he hears the message, at least sometimes, but he rarely shows any response. Sometimes I feel like shaking him and screaming, "Are you still alive?" Needless to say, I don't try communicating with him very much anymore. (Authors' files)

Being an *active* listener means actively communicating that you are both listening to and genuinely interested in what your partner is saying (Cole & Cole, 1999; Gottman et al., 1998). You can communicate this through attentive body language, appropriate and sympathetic facial expressions, nodding your head, asking questions ("Could you give me an example?"), or making brief comments ("I see your point"). Sometimes it is helpful to reciprocate in the conversation. For example, as your partner relates a feeling or incident, you may be reminded of a similar point in your own life. Making such associations and candidly expressing them—provided that you do not sidetrack the conversation to your own needs—can encourage your partner to continue voicing important concerns.

## Maintain Eye Contact

Maintaining eye contact is one of the most vital aspects of good face-to-face communication. Our eyes are wondrously expressive of feelings. When our partners maintain eye contact with us while we are sharing important thoughts or feelings with them, the message is clear: They care about what we have to say. When we fail to maintain eye contact, we deny our partners valuable feedback about how we are perceiving their messages.

## Provide Feedback

The purpose of communication is to provide a message that has some effect on the listener. However, a message's impact is not always the same as its intent, because communications can be (and often are) misunderstood. This is particularly true with a topic such as sexuality, where language is often roundabout or awkward. Therefore, giving our partners *feedback*, or reaction to their message, *in words* can be helpful. Besides clarifying how we have perceived our partners' comments, such verbal feedback reinforces that we are actively listening.

We can also benefit by asking our partners to respond to a message we think is important. A question such as "What do you think about what I have just said?" can encourage feedback that can help us determine the impact of our message on our partners.

## Support Your Partner's Communication Efforts

Many of us can feel vulnerable when communicating important messages to our partners. Support for our efforts can help alleviate our fears and anxieties and can encourage us to continue building the communication skills so important for a viable relationship. Think how good it can feel, after struggling to voice an important concern, to have a partner say, "I'm glad you told me how you really feel," or "Thanks for caring enough to tell me what was on your mind." Such supportive comments can help foster mutual empathy while ensuring that we will continue to communicate our thoughts and feelings candidly.

## Express Unconditional Positive Regard

The concept of unconditional positive regard is borrowed from the immensely popular *Client-Centered Therapy*, by Carl Rogers (1951). In personal relationships unconditional positive regard means conveying to our partners the sense that we will continue to value and care for them regardless of what they do or say. Unconditional positive regard encourages a person to talk about even the most embarrassing or painful concerns. The following anecdote reveals one person's response to this valued attribute:

*I know that my wife will continue to love me no matter what I say or reveal. In an earlier marriage, I could never express any serious concerns without my wife getting defensive or just plain mean. As a consequence, I quit talking about the things that really mattered. What a relief it is to be with someone who I can tell what is on my mind without worrying about the consequences. (Authors' files)*

# Discovering Your Partner's Needs

Discovering what is pleasurable to your partner is an important part of sexual intimacy. Many couples want to know each other's preferences but are uncertain how to find out. In this section, we look at some effective ways of learning about our partners' wants and needs.

## Asking Questions

One of the best ways to discover your partner's needs is simply to ask. However, there are several ways of asking: Some can be helpful, whereas others may be ineffective or even counterproductive. We review a few of the most common ways of asking questions and the effect each is likely to have.

### Yes/No Questions

Imagine being asked one or more of the following questions in the context of a sexual interlude with your partner:

1. Was it good for you?
2. Do you like oral sex?
3. Do you like it when I touch you this way?

At first glance these questions seem reasonably worded. However, they all share one characteristic that reduces their effectiveness: They are **yes/no questions**. Each asks for a one-word answer, even though people's thoughts and feelings are rarely so simple.

For example, consider question 2, "Do you like oral sex?" Either answer—"Yes, I do," or "No, I don't"—gives the couple little opportunity to discuss the issue. Certainly, the potential for discussion exists. Nevertheless, in a world where sexual communication is often difficult under the best of circumstances, the asker may get no more than the specific information requested. In some situations, of course, a brief yes or no is all that is necessary. But the person responding might have mixed feelings about oral sex (for example), and the phrasing of the question leads to oversimplification. **Open-ended questions,** or questions that allow the respondent to state a preference, can make it easier for your partner to give accurate replies.

**Yes/no question** A question that asks for a one-word answer (yes or no) and thus provides little opportunity for discussing an issue.

**Open-ended question** A question that allows a respondent to share any feelings or information she or he thinks is relevant.

## Open-Ended Questions

Some people find that asking open-ended questions is a particularly helpful way to discover their partners' desires. The following list gives some examples of open-ended questions:

1. What gives you the most pleasure when we make love?
2. What things about our sexual relationship would you most like us to change?
3. What are your feelings about oral sex?

A primary advantage of open-ended questions is that they allow your partner freedom to share any feelings or information she or he thinks is relevant. With no limitations or restrictions attached, you can learn much more than a simple yes/no answer could provide.

One possible drawback of the open-ended approach is that your partner may not know where to begin when asked such general questions. Consider being asked something like "What do you like best about our lovemaking ?" Some people might welcome the unstructuredness of this question, but others might have difficulty responding to such a broad query, particularly if they are not accustomed to openly discussing sex. If this is the case, a more structured approach may have a better chance of encouraging talk. There are several ways of structuring your approach; one is the use of either/or questions.

### Either/Or Questions

Either/or question
A question that allows statement of a preference.

The following list gives examples of **either/or questions**:

1. Would you like the light on when we make love, or should we turn it off?
2. Is this the way you want to be touched, or should we experiment with a different kind of caress?
3. Do you want to talk now or later?

Either/or questions offer more structure than do open-ended questions, and they encourage more participation than simple yes/no queries. People often appreciate the opportunity to consider a few alternatives.

Besides asking questions, we can discover the sexual needs of our partners in other ways. Here, we discuss three other communication techniques: self-disclosure, comparing notes, and giving permission.

## Self-Disclosure

Direct questions often put people on the spot. Whether you have been asked, "Do you enjoy oral sex?" or "How do you feel about oral sex?" it may be difficult to respond candidly, simply because you do not know your partner's feelings on the subject. If the topic has strong emotional overtones, it may be difficult to reply—no matter how thoughtfully the question has been phrased. It is the content, not the communication technique, that causes the problem.

One way to broach potentially loaded topics is to start with a self-disclosure:

Discovering what is pleasurable to your partner is an important part of sexual intimacy.

*For the longest time, I avoided the topic of oral sex with my lover. I didn't have the slightest idea what she felt about it. I was afraid to bring it up for fear she would think I was some kind of pervert. Eventually I could no longer tolerate not knowing her feelings. I brought it up by first talking about my mixed emotions, like feeling that maybe it wasn't natural but at the same time really wanting to try it out. As it turned out, she had similar feelings but was afraid to bring them up. Afterward we laughed about how we had both been afraid to break the ice. Once we could talk freely, it was easy to add this form of stimulation to our sex life. (Authors' files)*

Personal disclosures require give and take. It is much easier to share feelings about strongly emotional topics when a partner is willing to make similar disclosures. Admittedly, such an approach has risks, and occasionally one can feel vulnerable sharing personal thoughts and feelings. Nevertheless, the increased possibility for open, honest dialogue may be worth the discomfort a person may feel about making the first disclosure. Research clearly reveals that self-disclosure of sexual desires and needs is positively associated with obtaining sexual satisfaction in intimate relationships (Byers & Demmons, 1999; Greene & Faulkner, 2005). Research also indicates that when one partner openly discusses his or her own

© Bruce Ayres/Getty Images

feelings, the other partner is likely to do the same (Derlego et al., 1993; Hendrick & Hendrick, 1992).

It is becoming more and more common for people to engage in intimate communication online. The lack of face-to-face monitoring may increase both the rapidity and emotional intensity of self-disclosures (Ben-Ze'ev, 2003). Thus a potential drawback of online sex talk is that it may induce premature and perhaps ill-advised disclosures. However, the relative anonymity of cyberspace may empower people to disclose personal feelings about sexual issues. This may be especially true for men, who often find it difficult to discuss their feelings (Basow & Rubenfeld, 2003; Levant, 1997). We consider relating on the Web in more detail in the box titled "Internet Relationships" on the following page.

**? Critical Thinking Question**

Do partners benefit from discussing their sexual likes and dislikes with each other, or should they be more selective in what they share? Would your opinion about the appropriate level of disclosure be influenced by the nature of the relationship (i.e., dating, cohabiting, or married)?

## Discussing Sexual Preferences

While planning an evening out, many couples consider it natural to discuss each other's preferences: "Would you like to go to a concert, or would you rather go to the movies?" "How close do you like to sit?" "Do you prefer vegetarian, Italian, or meat and potatoes?" Afterward they may candidly evaluate the evening's events: "The drummer was great." "I think we should sit farther from the speakers next time." "Boy, I wouldn't order the scampi again." Yet many of the same couples never think of sharing thoughts about mutual sexual enjoyment.

Admittedly, discussing sexual preferences and evaluating specific sexual encounters are a big step up from discussing an evening out. Nevertheless, people do engage in this type of sexual dialogue. Some people feel comfortable discussing sexual preferences with a new lover before progressing to lovemaking. They might talk about what areas of their bodies are most responsive, how they like to be touched, what intercourse positions are particularly desirable, the easiest or most satisfying way to reach orgasm, time and location preferences, special turn-ons and turn-offs, and a variety of other likes and dislikes.

The appeal of this open, frank approach is that it allows a couple to focus on particularly pleasurable activities rather than discovering them by slow trial and error. However, some people feel that such dialogues are far too clinical, perhaps even robbing the sexual experience of the excitement of experimentation and mutual discovery. Furthermore, what a person finds desirable might differ with different partners, so it might be difficult to assess one's own preferences in advance.

Couples might also find it helpful to discuss their feelings after having sex. They can offer reactions about what was good and what could be better. They can use this time to reinforce the things they found particularly satisfying in their partner's lovemaking ("I loved the way you touched me on the insides of my thighs"). A mutual feedback session can be extremely informative; it can also contribute to a deeper intimacy between two people.

## Giving Permission

Discovering your partner's needs can be made immeasurably easier by the practice we call **giving permission**. Basically, giving permission means providing encouragement and reassurance. One partner tells the other that it is okay to talk about specific feelings or needs—indeed, that he or she wants very much to know how the other feels about the subject.

**Giving permission** Providing reassurance to one's partner that it is okay to talk about specific feelings or needs.

**He:** I'm not sure how you like me to touch you when we make love.
**She:** Any way you want to is good.
**He:** Well, I want to know what you like best, and you can help me by saying what feels good while I touch you.

Many of us have felt rebuffed in our efforts to communicate our needs to others. It is no wonder that people often remain silent even when they want to share personal feelings. Giving and receiving permission to express needs freely can contribute to the exchange of valuable information.

## Internet Relationships

The Internet has created a virtual community that has radically expanded options for meeting potential intimate partners and for communicating about sex (Philaretou, 2005; Waskul, 2004). Earlier in this chapter, we described how proximity, or geographical nearness, influences whom we are attracted to. Cyberspace has created a world of virtual proximity, in which people can be electronically close while being separated by hundreds or thousands of miles (Wright, 2004).

People may be drawn to various relationship-oriented Web sites because of a perceived commonality of interest with others who visit the site. Some may be surfing the Web looking for meaningful romantic connections (Benotsch et al., 2002). Others may be motivated by a desire to discuss sexual fantasies or to share online sexual behavior (Ross, 2005). The absence of relationship constraints posed by face-to-face (FTF) interaction may help explain the growing popularity of computer-mediated relating (CMR). For people who have difficulty relating to others FTF, the anonymity of online relationships may allow them to express themselves more easily, which can lead to an improved sense of social connectedness and the formation of strong online attachments (Fleming & Rickwood, 2004).

Online communication may contribute to the development of romantic relationships by eliminating the role that physical attractiveness plays in the development of attraction. In the absence of this dimension of interpersonal attraction, formed impressions of another may be strongly influenced by imagination, which can create a powerful attraction to another (Ben-Ze'ev, 2004). Freed from the influence of visual cues, romantic/erotic connections may evolve from emotional intimacy rather than physical attraction. CMR may also be less constrained by the gender-role assumptions that frequently influence FTF interactions between the sexes.

These relative advantages of CMR are counterbalanced by potential drawbacks of relating on the Internet. For example, erotic/intimate connections may develop with such rapidity that the tempering influence of good judgment may not be applied (Benotsch et al., 2002; Genuis & Genuis, 2005). This rapid escalation of relationship intensity may be triggered by a reduction in feelings of vulnerability when disclosing personal information in the relative anonymity of cyberspace and by the psychological comfort of revealing private thoughts while in a safe, cozy home environment. Rapidly developing Internet relationships may become eroticized prematurely, without forming the knowledge-based foundation of trust so essential to relationship satisfaction. This "eroticized pseudointimacy" may prove difficult to sustain if online romances progress to FTF relating (Cooper & Sportolari, 1997).

Another potential disadvantage of communicating online is that people may be untruthful when disclosing such topics as personal interests, occupation, marital status, and age. In addition, FTF meetings with online partners carry considerable risk. The media is replete with accounts of Web relationships that result in abuse, violence, stalking, or harassment. Furthermore, research indicates that the chances of engaging in risky, condomless sex during an initial FTF meeting with an online partner are quite high (Chiasson et al., 2003; Genuis & Genuis, 2005; McFarlane et al., 2002).

The phenomenon of Internet relationships is rapidly evolving, and future research will no doubt provide a better understanding of the impact of the Web on people's intimate lives. Perhaps the best advice we can offer readers who are exploring relationships via the Internet is to take it slow, communicate honestly and encourage your partner to do the same, disclose carefully, and by all means, if you choose to meet FTF, do so in a safe public place and without expectations of a sexual encounter.

## ◗ Learning to Make Requests

People are not mind readers. Nevertheless, many lovers seem to assume that their partners know (perhaps by intuition?) just what they need. People who approach sex with this attitude are not taking full responsibility for their own pleasure. If sexual encounters are unsatisfactory, it is often more convenient to blame a partner—"You don't care about my needs"—than to admit that one's own reluctance to express needs may be the problem. Expecting partners to somehow know what is wanted without telling them places a heavy burden on them. Many people think that they shouldn't have to ask. But in fact, asking a partner to do something can be an affirmative, responsible action that helps both people.

### Taking Responsibility for Our Own Pleasure

*When two people are really in harmony with each other, you don't have to talk about your sexual wants. You each sense and respond to the other's desires. Talking just tends to spoil these magical moments. (Authors' files)*

The situation this person describes seems to exist more in the fantasyland of idealized sex than in the real world. As we just noted, people are not mind readers, and intuition leaves much to be desired as a substitute for genuine communication. A person who expects another to know his or her needs by intuition is saying, "It's not my business to let you know my needs, but it is yours to know what they are," and by inference, "If my needs are not fulfilled, it is your fault, not mine." Needless to say, this is a potentially destructive approach that can lead to blaming, misunderstandings, and unsatisfying sex.

The best way to get our needs met is to speak up. Two individuals willing to communicate their desires and take responsibility for their own pleasure create an excellent framework for effective, fulfilling sexual intimacy. Deciding to assume responsibility for our own satisfaction is an important step. Just as important are the methods we select for expressing our needs. The way a request is made has a decided effect on the reaction it draws. Suggestions are listed in the next two sections.

## Making Requests Specific

The more specific a request is, the more likely it is to be understood and heeded. Lovers often ask for changes in the sexual aspects of their relationships in the vaguest language. It can be uncomfortable, even anxiety provoking, to be on the receiving end of an ill-defined request. Just how does one respond? Probably by doing little, if anything.

The key to preventing unnecessary stress for both partners is delivering requests as clearly and concisely as possible. Thus an alternative to the vague request "I'd like you to try touching me differently" might be "I would like you to touch me gently around my clitoris but not directly on it." Other examples of specific requests follow:

1. I would like you to spend more time touching and caressing me all over before we have intercourse.
2. I really enjoy it when you keep on kissing and caressing me after you're inside me.
3. I would like you to stroke my penis with your hand.

## Using "I" Language

Counselors encourage their clients to use "I" language when stating their needs to others (Worden & Worden, 1998). This forthright approach brings the desired response more often than does a general statement. For example, saying "I would like to be on top" is considerably more likely to produce that result than "What would you think about changing positions?"

Expressing requests directly may not always be effective. Some people want to make all the decisions, and they may not take kindly to requests from their partners during lovemaking. A partner's assertiveness might offend them. You might want to determine whether this is your partner's attitude before a sexual encounter, because doing so can help you avoid an awkward situation. One way to determine this is to ask the open-ended question "How do you feel about asking for things during lovemaking?" Or you might choose to wait and find out during sex play. At any rate, if a person appears closed to direct requests, you may wish to reevaluate your strategy. Perhaps making your needs known at some time other than during sexual interaction will give your partner a more relaxed opportunity to consider your desires. Nevertheless, we strongly encourage you to use "I" language in whatever context you make your requests.

## ⊙ Expressing and Receiving Complaints

Contrary to the popular romantic image, no two people can fill all of each other's needs all the time. It seems inevitable that people in an intimate relationship will sometimes need to register complaints and request changes. Accomplishing this may not be easy for caring individuals whose relationship is characterized by mutual empathy. The most effective way to voice a concern is to complain rather than to criticize (Gottman, 1994). Complaining involves constructively expressing relationship concerns rather than criticizing (and is by no means synonymous with whining). Occasional constructive complaining actually benefits a relationship because it helps partners identify problems that need to be discussed and resolved. Complaining involves several of the strategies outlined in the following sections, such as being sensitive about when to express a complaint, using "I" language, and tempering complaints with praise. Complaints are voiced in the expectation that constructive change beneficial to both partners will occur. In contrast, criticisms are often leveled to hurt, downgrade, express contempt, get even, or gain dominant status over a partner. Criticism often involves "attacking someone's personality or character—rather than a specific behavior—usually with blame" (Gottman, 1994, p. 73). Couple communication patterns tainted by expressions of denigration, criticism, and contempt can deeply harm a relationship. We discuss the effects of such negative communication tactics in more detail later in this chapter. When complaints pertain to the emotionally intense area of sexual intimacy, they can be doubly difficult to express and receive. Partners will want to think carefully about appropriate strategies and potential obstacles to accomplishing these delicate tasks.

## Constructive Strategies for Expressing Complaints

One important consideration for effectively verbalizing a complaint to your partner is to pick the right time and place.

### Choose the Right Time and Place

*Whenever my lover brings up something that is bothering her about our sex life, it inevitably is just after we have made love. Here I am, relaxed, holding her in my arms, thinking good thoughts, and she destroys the mood with some criticism. It's not that I don't want her to express her concerns, but her timing is terrible. The last thing I want to hear after lovemaking is that it could have been better. (Authors' files)*

*"If something is bothering you about our relationship, Lorraine, why don't you just spell it out."*

This man's dismay is obvious. His partner's decision to voice her concerns during the afterglow of lovemaking works against her purpose. He may feel vulnerable, and he clearly resents having his good mood following sex broken by the prospect of a potentially difficult conversation. Of course, other couples find this time, when they are exceedingly close to each other, a good occasion to air their concerns.

Many people, like the woman in the example, do not choose the best time to confront their lovers. Rather, the time chooses them: They jump right in when the problem is uppermost in their mind. Although dealing with an issue immediately can have benefits, it is not always the best strategy. Negative emotions, such as disappointment, resentment, or anger, when running at full tide, can easily hinder constructive interaction. We should avoid expressing complaints when anger is at its peak. Although we may have every intention of making our complaint constructive, anger has a way of disrupting a search for solutions. Sometimes, however, it is necessary to express anger; at the end of this section we consider how to do so appropriately.

In most cases it is unwise to tackle a problem when either you or your partner has limited time or is tired, stressed, preoccupied, or under the influence of drugs or alcohol. Rather, try to select an interval when both of you have plenty of time and feel relaxed and close to each other.

A pragmatic approach to timing is simply to tell your lover, "I really value our sexual relationship, but there are some concerns I would like to talk over with you. Is this a good time, or would you rather we talked later?" Be prepared for some anxiety-induced stalling. If your partner is hesitant to talk now, support his or her right to pick another time or place. However, it is important to agree on a time, particularly if you sense that your partner might prefer to let the matter go.

Choosing the right place for expressing sexual concerns can be as important as timing. Some people find sitting at the kitchen table while sharing a pot of coffee a more comfortable setting than the place where they make love; others might prefer the familiarity of their bed. A walk through a park or a quiet drive in the country, far removed from the potential interferences of a busy lifestyle, may prove best for you. Try to sense your partner's needs. When and where is she or he most likely to be receptive to your requests for change?

Picking the right time and place to deliver a complaint does not ensure a harmonious outcome, but it certainly improves the prospects of your partner's responding favorably to your message. Using other constructive strategies can also increase the likelihood of beneficial interaction. One of these is to combine a complaint with praise.

Choosing the right time and place to express sexual concerns can facilitate communication.

© Peter M. Fisher/CORBIS

## Temper Complaints With Praise

The strategy of tempering complaints with praise is based largely on common sense. All of us tend to respond well to a compliment, but we tend to find a harsh complaint or criticism difficult to accept, especially by itself. The gentler approach of combining compliment and complaint is a good way to reduce the negative impact of the complaint. It also gives your partner a broader perspective from which to evaluate the complaint, reducing the likelihood that he or she will respond defensively or angrily. Consider how you might react differently to the following complaints, depending on whether they are accompanied by praise:

| COMPLAINT ALONE | COMPLAINT WITH PRAISE |
|---|---|
| 1. When we make love, I feel that you are inhibited. | 1. I like it when you respond to me while we make love. I think it could be even better if you would take the initiative-sometimes. Does this seem like a reasonable request? |
| 2. I am really getting tired of your turning off the lights every time we make love | 2. I enjoy hearing and feeling you react when we make love. I also want to watch you respond. How would you feel about leaving the lights on sometimes? |
| 3. I think our lovemaking is far too infrequent. It almost seems like sex is not as important to you as it is to me. | 3. I love having sex with you, and it has been bothering me that we don't seem to have much time for it recently. What do you think about this? |

Sadly, just about all of us have been on the receiving end of complaints like those in the left column. Common reactions are anger, humiliation, anxiety, and resentment. Although some people respond to such harsh complaints by resolving to make things better, that response is unlikely. On the other hand, affirmative complaints, such as the examples in the right-hand column, are more likely to encourage efforts to change. A good deal of wisdom lies in the saying "People are usually more motivated to make a good thing better than to make a bad thing good." This applies as much to sexual activity as to any other area of human interaction.

When delivering complaints, it is also a good idea to ask for feedback. Regardless of how much warmth and goodwill we put into this difficult process, the possibility always exists that our partners will become silent or change the subject. Asking them how they feel about our requests for change helps reduce this possibility. (Note that all the preceding "Complaint With Praise" examples end with a request for feedback.)

 **Critical Thinking Question**

Some people think that combining praise with a complaint is a manipulative technique designed to coerce behavior changes by tempering requests with insincere praise. Do you agree with this point of view? Why or why not?

## Avoid "Why" Questions

People frequently use "why" questions as thinly veiled efforts to criticize or attack their partners while avoiding full responsibility for what is said. Have you ever asked or been asked any of the following questions?

1. Why don't you make love to me more frequently?
2. Why don't you show more interest in me?
3. Why don't you get turned on by me anymore?

Such questions have no place in a loving relationship; they are hurtful and destructive. Rather than conveying simple requests for information, they typically convey hidden messages of anger that the speaker is unwilling to communicate honestly. These are hit-and-run tactics that cause defensiveness and seldom induce positive changes.

## Express Negative Emotions Appropriately

Earlier we noted that it is wise to avoid confronting our partners when resentment or anger is riding high. However, there probably will be times when we feel compelled to express negative feelings. If so, certain guiding principles can help defuse a potentially explosive situation.

Avoid focusing your anger on the character of your partner ("You are an insensitive person"). Instead, try directing your dissatisfaction toward his or her behaviors ("When you don't listen to my concerns, I think they are unimportant to you and I feel sad"). At the same time, express appreciation for your partner as a person ("You are very important to me, and I don't like feeling this way"). This acknowledges that we can feel distressed by our partners' behaviors yet still feel loving toward them—an often overlooked but important truth.

Negative feelings are probably best expressed with clear, honest "I" statements rather than with accusatory and potentially inflammatory "you" statements. Consider the following:

| "YOU" STATEMENTS | "I" STATEMENTS |
|---|---|
| 1. You don't give a damn about me. | 1. Sometimes I feel ignored, and this makes me afraid for us. |
| 2. You always blame me for our problems. | 2. I don't like being blamed. |
| 3. You don't love me. | 3. I feel unloved. |

"I" statements are self-revelations, expressing how we feel without placing blame or attacking our partners' character. In contrast, "you" statements frequently come across as attacks on our partners' character or as attempts to fix blame. When we express a concern with a statement that begins with *I* instead of *you*, our partners are less likely to feel criticized and thus to become defensive. Furthermore, using "I" statements to express emotions such as sadness, hurt, or fear conveys a sense of our vulnerability to our partners. They may find it easier to respond to these "softer" emotional expressions than to accusations expressing resentment, anger, or disgust.

## Limit Complaints to One per Discussion

Many of us tend to avoid confrontations with our partners. This understandable reluctance to deal with negative issues can result in an accumulation of unspoken complaints. Consequently, when we finally reach the point where we need to say something, it may be difficult to avoid unleashing a barrage of complaints that includes everything on our current list of grievances. Such a response, although understandable, only serves to magnify rather than resolve conflicts between lovers, as reflected in the following account:

My wife lets things eat on her without letting me know when I do something that she disapproves of. She remembers every imagined shortcoming and blows it way out of proportion. But I never learn about it until she has accumulated a long list of complaints. Then she hits me with all of them at once, dredging them up like weapons in her arsenal, all designed to make me feel like an insensitive creep. I sometimes hear about things that happened years ago. She wonders why I don't have anything to say when she is done haranguing me. But what do you say when somebody has just given you 10 or 20 reasons why your relationship with her is lousy? Which one do you respond to? And how can you avoid being angry when somebody rubs your face in all your shortcomings, real or imagined? (Authors' files)

You can reduce the likelihood of creating such a counterproductive situation in your own relationships by limiting your complaints to one per discussion. Even if you have half a dozen complaints you want to talk about, it will probably serve your relationship better to pick one and relegate the rest to later conversations.

Most of us find a complaint that goes on and on hard to listen to, even when it is about just one thing. When delivering a complaint, be concise. Just briefly describe the concern, limit examples to one or two, and then stop.

## Receiving Complaints

Delivering complaints to a partner is difficult; likewise, receiving complaints from someone you love can be an emotionally rending experience. However, people involved in an intimate, loving relationship inevitably need to register complaints on occasion. How you respond to a complaint can significantly affect not only your partner's inclination to openly share concerns in the future but also the probability of resolving the complaint in a manner that strengthens rather than weakens the relationship.

When your partner delivers a complaint, take a few moments to gather your thoughts. A few deep breaths are probably a much better initial response than blurting out, "Yeah, well, what about the time that you . . . !" Ask yourself, Is this person trying to give me information that may be helpful? In a loving relationship where mutual empathy prevails, perhaps you will be able to see the potential for positive consequences, even though you have just received a painful message. You can respond to such a communication in several ways. We hope one or more of the following suggestions will help in such circumstances.

Responding appropriately to a complaint can help strengthen a relationship.

## Acknowledge a Complaint and Find Something to Agree With

Perhaps if you allow yourself to be open to a complaint, you will see a basis for it. Suppose that your partner feels angry about your busy schedule and complains that you are not devoting enough time to the relationship. Maybe you think he or she is overreacting or forgetting all the time you have spent together. However, you also know that this concern has some basis. It can be helpful to acknowledge that basis by saying something like "I can understand how you might feel neglected because I have been so preoccupied with my new job." Such constructive acknowledgment can occur even if you think the complaint is largely unjustified. By reacting in an accepting and supportive manner, you are conveying the message that you hear, understand, and appreciate the basis for your partner's concern.

## Ask Clarifying Questions

Your partner may deliver a complaint so vaguely that you need clarification. If this happens, ask questions. Suppose your partner complains that you do not take enough time in your lovemaking. You might respond by asking, "Do you mean that we should spend more time touching before we have intercourse, or that I should wait longer before coming, or that you want me to hold you for a longer time after we have sex?"

## Express Your Feelings

It can be helpful to talk about your feelings in response to a complaint rather than letting those feelings dictate your response. Your partner's complaint may cause you to feel angry, hurt, or dejected. Putting your feelings into words is probably more effective than acting them out. Responses such as yelling, stomping out of the room, crying, or retreating into a shell of despair are unlikely to lead to productive dialogue. Instead, it may be helpful to tell your partner, "That was really hard to hear, and I feel hurt" or "Right now I feel angry, so I need to stop and take a few breaths and figure out what I am thinking and feeling."

## Focus on Future Changes You Can Make

An excellent way to close discussion of a complaint is to focus on what the two of you can do to make things better. Perhaps this is the time to say, "My new job is really important to me, but our relationship is much more important. Maybe we can set aside special times each week when we will keep outside concerns from intruding on our time together."

Sometimes people agree to make things better but neglect to discuss concrete changes that will resolve what triggered the complaint. Taking the time to identify and agree on specific changes is crucial.

## ❶ Saying No

Many of us have difficulty saying no to others. Our discomfort in communicating this direct message is perhaps most pronounced when it applies to intimate areas of relationships. This is reflected in the following anecdotes:

> Sometimes my partner wants to be sexual when I only want to be close. The trouble is, I can't say no. I am afraid she would be hurt or angry. Unfortunately, I am the one who ends up angry at myself for not being able to express my true feelings. Under these circumstances, sex isn't very good. (Authors' files)

> *It is so hard to say no to a man who suggests having sex at the end of a date. This is especially true if we have had a good time together. You never know if they are going to get that hangdog hurt look or become belligerent and angry. (Authors' files)*

These accounts reveal common concerns that inhibit us from saying no. We might believe that a rejection will hurt the other person or make him or her angry or even combative. Laboring under such fears, we might decide that it is less stressful simply to comply. Unfortunately, this reluctant acquiescence can create such negative feelings that the resulting shared activity may be less than pleasurable for both parties.

Many of us have not learned that it is okay to say no. Perhaps more importantly, we may not have learned strategies for saying this. In the following section we consider some potentially useful ways to say no.

## A Three-Step Approach to Saying No

Many people have found it helpful to have a definite plan or strategy in mind for saying no to invitations for intimate involvements. Having such a strategy can help you prevent being caught off guard, not knowing how to handle a potentially unpleasant interaction with tact. One approach you may find helpful involves three distinct steps, or phases:

1. Express appreciation for the invitation (e.g., "Thanks for thinking of me" or "It's nice to know that you like me enough to invite me"). You may also wish to validate the other person ("You are a good person").
2. Say no in a clear, unequivocal fashion ("I would prefer not to make love / go dancing / get involved in a dating relationship").
3. Offer an alternative, if applicable ("However, I would like to have lunch sometime / give you a back rub").

The positive aspects of this approach are readily apparent. We first indicate our appreciation for the expressed interest in us. At the same time, we clearly state our wish not to comply with the request. Finally, we end the exchange on a positive note by offering an alternative. Of course, this last step will not always be an option (e.g., when turning down a request from someone with whom we wish to have no further contact). Between lovers, however, a mutually acceptable alternative often exists.

## Avoiding Sending Mixed Messages

Saying no in clear, unmistakable language is essential to the success of the strategy just outlined. Nevertheless, when it comes to sexual intimacy, many of us sometimes send mixed messages about what we do and do not want. Consider, for example, someone who responds positively to a partner's request for sexual intimacy but then spends an inordinate amount of time soaking in the bathtub while the patiently waiting partner falls asleep. Or consider a person who expresses a desire to have sex but instead becomes engrossed in a late-night talk show. Both of these people are sending mixed messages that may reflect their own ambivalence about engaging in sexual relations.

As described in the next section, many of the messages we send about our sexual desires are conveyed nonverbally. When our nonverbal messages seem to contradict our verbal messages, our partners can have difficulty grasping our true intention. For example, we might say we are not interested in being sexual but then touch our partner in an intimate manner, or we might express willingness to engage in intercourse but then not be very responsive. In such circumstances, when our verbal and nonverbal messages seem discordant, our partners are likely to have difficulty determining what we are actually communicating. Furthermore, when the verbal and nonverbal components of communication are inconsistent with each other, the nonverbal component usually prevails (Preston, 2005).

The effect of such mixed messages is usually less than desirable. The recipient is often confused about the other person's intent. He or she may feel uncertain or even inadequate ("Why can't I figure out what you really want?"), and such feelings may turn to anger ("Why do I have to guess?") or withdrawal. These reactions are understandable under the circumstances. Faced with contradictory messages, most of us are unsure what to do: act on the first message or on the second one? Consider the following:

> It really bothers me when my partner says we will make love when I get home from night school and then she is too busy studying to take a break. Even though it was her suggestion, sometimes I wonder if she had any intention to make love. (Authors' files)

All of us can benefit from occasionally considering whether we are sending mixed messages. Try looking for inconsistencies between your verbal messages and your subsequent actions. Does your partner seem confused or uncertain when interacting with you? If you do spot yourself sending a double message, decide which one you really mean, then state it in unmistakable language. It can also be helpful to consider why you sent contradictory messages.

If you are on the receiving end of such messages, it may be helpful to discuss your confusion and ask your partner which of the two messages you should act on. Perhaps your partner will recognize your dilemma and act to resolve it. If she or he seems unwilling to acknowledge the inconsistency, it may be helpful to express your feelings of discomfort and confusion as the recipient of the conflicting messages.

## ◑ Nonverbal Sexual Communication

Sexual communication is not confined to words. Sometimes a touch or a smile can convey a great deal of information. Tone of voice, gestures, facial expressions, and changes in breathing are also important elements of such communication:

> I can usually tell when my sweetheart is in the mood for some loving. There is a certain softness about her face and a huskiness that comes into her voice. She touches me more with her hands, and it almost seems like she presents her body as more open and vulnerable. There is some truth to all this stuff about body language. She rarely needs to verbalize her desire for sex because I usually get the message. (Authors' files)

> Sometimes when I want my lover to touch me in a certain place, I move that portion of my body closer to his hands or just shift my position to make the area more accessible. Occasionally, I will guide his hand with mine to show him just what kind of stimulation I want. (Authors' files)

These examples reveal some of the varieties of nonverbal communication that have particular significance for our sexuality. In this section we direct our attention to four important components of nonverbal sexual communication: facial expressions, interpersonal distance, touching, and sounds.

Facial expressions of emotion are often a powerful component of nonverbal communication.

© Adamsmith/Getty Images

### Facial Expressions

Facial expressions often communicate the feelings a person is experiencing. Although people's expressions certainly vary, most of us have learned to accurately identify particular emotions from facial expressions. The rapport and intimacy between lovers can further increase the reliability of this skill.

Looking at our lovers' faces during sexual activity often gives us a quick reading of their level of pleasure. If we see a look of complete rapture, we are likely to continue providing the same type of stimulation. However, if the look conveys something less than ecstasy, we may decide to try something different or ask our partners for verbal direction.

Facial expressions can also provide helpful cues when talking over sexual concerns with a partner. If a lover's face reflects anger, anxiety, or some other disruptive emotion, it might be wise to deal with this emotion immediately ("I can tell you are angry. Can we talk about it?"). Conversely, a face that shows interest, enthusiasm, or appreciation can encourage us to continue expressing a particular feeling or concern. It is also a good idea to be aware of the nonverbal messages you are giving when your partner is sharing thoughts or feelings with you. Sometimes we inadvertently shut down potentially helpful dialogue by tightening our jaws or frowning at an inappropriate time.

## Interpersonal Distance

Social psychologists and communication specialists have much to say about *personal space*. The essence of this idea is that we tend to maintain different distances between ourselves and the people with whom we have contact, depending on our relationship (actual or desired) to them. The intimate space to which we admit close friends and lovers restricts contact much less than the distance we maintain between ourselves and people we do not know or like.

When someone attempts to decrease interpersonal distance, it is generally interpreted as a nonverbal sign that she or he is attracted to the other person or would like more intimate contact. Conversely, if someone withdraws when another person moves close, this action can usually be interpreted as a lack of interest or a gentle kind of rejection.

Lovers, whose interpersonal distance is generally at a minimum, can use such spatial cues to signal desire for intimacy. When your lover moves in close, making his or her body available for your touches or caresses, the message of wanting physical intimacy (not necessarily sex) is apparent. Similarly, when he or she curls up on the other side of the bed, it may be a way of saying, "Please don't come too close tonight."

## Touching

Touch is a powerful vehicle for nonverbal sexual communication between lovers. Hands can convey special messages. For example, increasing or decreasing the tempo with which you rub your lover's back can signal a desire for more-intense or less-intense reciprocated stimulation. Reaching out and drawing your partner closer can indicate your readiness for more intimate contact. In the early stages of a relationship, touch can also be used to express a desire to become closer.

Decreased interpersonal space often indicates attraction and perhaps a desire for more-intimate contact.

*When I meet a man and find myself attracted to him, I use touch to convey my feelings. Touching him on the arm to emphasize a point or letting my fingers lightly graze across his hand on the table generally lets my feelings be known. (Authors' files)*

Touch can also defuse anger and heal rifts between temporarily alienated lovers. As one man stated:

*I have found that a gentle touch, lovingly administered to my partner, does wonders in bringing us back together after we have exchanged angry words. Touching her is my way of reestablishing connection. (Authors' files)*

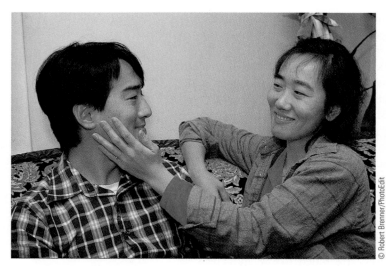

Touch is a powerful vehicle for nonverbal sexual communication.

## Sounds

Many people like making and hearing sounds during sexual activity. Some individuals find increased breathing, moans, groans, and orgasmic cries extremely arousing. Also, such sounds can be helpful indicators of how a partner is responding to lovemaking. Some people find the absence of sounds frustrating:

*My man rarely makes any sounds when we make love. I find this to be very disturbing. In fact, it is a real turn-off. Sometimes I can't even tell if he has come or not. If he wasn't moving, I'd think I was making love to a corpse. (Authors' files)*

Some people make a conscious effort to suppress spontaneous noises during sex play. In doing so, they deprive themselves of a potentially powerful and enjoyable form of nonverbal sexual communication. Not uncommonly, their deliberate silence also hinders their partners' sexual arousal, as the foregoing example illustrated.

In this section on nonverbal sexual communication, we have acknowledged that not everything has to be spoken between lovers. However, facial expressions, interpersonal distance, touching, and sounds cannot convey all our complex needs and emotions in a close relationship; words are needed, too. One writer observed, "As a supplement to verbal communication, acts and gestures are fine. As a substitute, they don't quite make it" (Zilbergeld, 1978, p. 158).

## ◗ Communication Patterns in Successful and Unsuccessful Relationships

What does research reveal about the communication patterns in successful, satisfying, long-lasting relationships versus the communication patterns in unhappy relationships that usually fail in the long run? The most informative research on communication patterns in relationships has been conducted by psychologist John Gottman and his colleagues (Gottman, 1994; Gottman & Silver, 2000; Gottman et al., 1998, 1999, 2003). They used a multimethod research model for building an extensive database drawn from many studies of married couples (see Chapter 13 for a description of Gottman's research methods). Gottman identified a number of communication patterns that are predictive of marital happiness or unhappiness. Happily married couples resolve conflicts by using a variety of *constructive* communicative tactics, which are described in the following section.

### Gottman's Constructive Communication Tactics

Gottman identified a number of constructive communication tactics. These tactics include leveling and editing, validating, and volatile dialogue.

### Leveling and Editing

*Leveling* involves stating our thoughts and feelings clearly, simply, and honestly—preferably while using "I" language. For example, Gary is distressed because his partner, Susan, seldom initiates sex. Gary might say, "I love having sex with you, and I am concerned that most of the time it seems to be my idea that we make love. I am not sure what this means." When we begin to level with our partners, we might also need to do some editing of what we say. *Editing* means that we do not say things that we know would be hurtful to our partners, and that we limit our comments to information relevant to the issue at hand. Even though Gary might feel anger toward Susan, it would be counterproductive for him to say something like "Your seeming indifference to having sex with me ticks me off and makes me wonder what your problem is." It would also be unhelpful to add comments irrelevant to the issues, such as "And I get real tired having to be the one who does all the shopping and makes all the decisions about what we are going to eat."

## Validating

*Validating* involves telling our partners that, given their point of view, we can understand why they think or feel the way they do. Validating a partner's viewpoint does not mean that we invalidate our own position regarding the issue at hand. Rather, we are simply facilitating constructive dialogue by acknowledging the reasonableness of our partner's concern. For example, Susan might respond to Gary by saying, "I really enjoy our lovemaking, and I can see why you might think differently since I usually let you take the lead."

## Volatile Dialogue

Even happily paired couples occasionally butt heads on certain issues, and Gottman's research suggests that some degree of conflict is actually essential to the long-term happiness of a relationship. While studying couples' interaction patterns and reported levels of satisfaction over time, Gottman and his colleagues made a rather startling discovery. Couples in the early stages of a relationship who experienced some conflicts and arguments reported less satisfaction than early-stage couples who rarely or never argued. However, after 3 years the situation reversed itself, and couples who occasionally argued reported significantly more relationship satisfaction than those who avoided arguments.

What accounts for this seemingly paradoxical finding? Gottman suggests that couples who do not argue are likely ignoring important issues that should be addressed rather than left to fester and erode happiness. When problems are never discussed and resolved, both partners can harbor feelings of resentment and frustration that, when allowed to build over time, can drive a wedge between them. In contrast, conflict in a relationship fulfills the crucial role of identifying issues that need to be discussed for the relationship to thrive. Gottman found that some of his long-term happy couples actually used rather passionate or volatile dialogue to resolve conflicts.

# Gottman's Destructive Communication Tactics

From his observations of hundreds of couples, Gottman also identified destructive communication tactics. These tactics include criticism, contempt, defensiveness, stonewalling, and belligerence.

## Criticism

As described earlier, *criticism* is different from complaining. Criticism that involves expression of contempt and denigration can harm a relationship. In contrast, complaining can be healthy because it allows expression of frustration and identifies issues that need to be discussed and resolved. Complaints are effectively registered with "I" language that focuses on the issue, whereas criticisms usually involve attacking someone's character with "you" statements. Receiving a complaint stated as "I feel frustrated that our lovemaking has become somewhat predictable and routine" can feel very different from receiving a criticism stated as "You always want to make love in the same old way." The latter statement is likely to be taken as a personal attack, which puts the recipient in a defensive position that clearly does not encourage constructive dialogue.

## Contempt

*Contempt* is similar to criticism, but it degrades communication to an even more intense level of negativity by adding insults, sarcasm, and even name-calling to the critical commentary. For example, someone might say, "You are so narrow and limited in your approach to lovemaking and life in general. How did I ever connect with such a stilted, boring person?" Contempt can also be expressed nonverbally by sneering, rolling one's eyes, or ignoring a partner's messages. This negative communication tactic causes emotional pain, does nothing to remedy or resolve issues, creates new problems in the form of defensiveness, anger, and resentment, and thereby erodes the quality of a relationship.

### Defensiveness

A person who feels personally attacked or victimized by a partner's criticism or contempt is likely to respond with *defensiveness*. This involves constructing a defense rather than attempting to discuss and resolve an issue. Defensiveness can take the form of self-protective responses, such as making excuses, denying responsibility, or replying with a criticism of one's own. Thus the recipient of the contemptuous criticism described earlier might respond by saying, "You think I'm a boring lover? Take a long look at yourself. All you ever care about is your own pleasure, and you never give me a chance to say what I want!" In this situation one partner attacks and the other defends and counterattacks. Will a relationship that involves such tactics survive? Not likely.

### Stonewalling

*Stonewalling* occurs when a person concludes that any response to a partner's criticism or complaint will not be helpful or productive and therefore decides not to respond at all. The stonewaller simply puts up a wall and refuses to communicate, responding instead with silence, by walking out of the room, by turning on the TV, by picking up a book, or the like. This silent-treatment tactic communicates disapproval, distancing, and the belief that nothing one can do will improve the situation, so one might as well say nothing. A person who stonewalls a partner may have found that previous efforts to defuse the partner's critical attacks have been ineffective and that it is therefore no longer productive to engage in seemingly futile dialogue.

### Belligerence

The fifth destructive communication tactic involves a confrontational, "in your face" type of interaction that is likely to emerge as a relationship suffers from prolonged patterns of poor communication. *Belligerence* often entails a purposely provoking style of interaction intended to diminish or challenge a partner's right to influence patterns of interaction in the relationship. For example, a belligerent person might say to his or her partner, "So what if I always want to be on top when we have intercourse. What are you going to do about it?"

Clearly, all five of these destructive tactics erode and interfere with rather than improve a couple's communication. Such styles of communication are likely to increase conflict and negativity, diminish positive exchanges between partners, and cause an escalation of hostility rather than solve problems. People in a relationship characterized by these negative, harmful exchanges may eventually decide that they would be better off ending the relationship—a conclusion supported by Gottman's research finding that long-term relationship survival rates are low for such couples.

We can conclude from the research on couple communication that partners who have satisfying, long-lasting relationships communicate in ways that differ markedly from those used by partners who have unhappy, often short-lived relationships. Positive communication strategies are not limited to those discussed in this section. Many of the strategies outlined in this chapter, when incorporated into a couple's communication about sex and other relationship issues, are predictive of satisfying and enduring partnerships.

# SUMMARY

## What Is Love?

- Zick Rubin developed a 13-item questionnaire for measuring love.

## Types of Love

- Passionate love is characterized by intense, vibrant feelings that tend to be relatively short-lived.

- Companionate love is characterized by deep affection and attachment.
- Robert Sternberg's triangular theory maintains that love has three components: passion (the motivational component), intimacy (the emotional component), and commitment (the cognitive component). Various combinations of these three components yield eight different kinds of love.
- John Allan Lee proposed a theory that describes six different styles of loving: romantic, game playing, possessive, companionate, altruistic, and pragmatic.

## Falling in Love: Why and With Whom?

- Falling in love has been explained as resulting from the need to overcome a sense of aloneness, the desire to justify sexual involvement, or sexual attraction.
- The intense feelings of being passionately in love might have a basis in surging levels of the brain chemicals norepinephrine, dopamine, and especially phenylethylamine (PEA). The progression from passion to deep attraction might result from the gradual increase of endorphins in the brain.
- Factors known to contribute strongly to interpersonal attraction and falling in love include proximity, similarity, reciprocity, and physical attractiveness. We often develop loving relationships with people whom we see frequently, who share similar beliefs, who seem to like us, and whom we perceive as physically attractive.

## Love and Styles of Attachment

- The way we form attachments, which has its roots in infancy, greatly affects how we relate to loved partners.
- Securely attached children, who learn that parents are a source of security and trust, demonstrate much greater social competence than insecurely attached children, who are classified as either anxious-ambivalent or avoidant.
- Attachment styles developed during infancy continue throughout life to considerably influence a person's capacity to form loving attachments and the way the person relates to significant others.
- Securely attached adults are best equipped to establish stable, satisfying relationships. They are comfortable being close to others, feel secure in relationships, and do not fear being abandoned.
- Anxious-ambivalent adults often have a poor self-image, are insecure in relationships, and struggle with ambivalence about achieving closeness with others.
- Avoidant adults are uncomfortable with any degree of closeness, have problems trusting or depending on a partner, and often view others negatively.
- People who become couples often have similar styles of attachment. The most common pairing comprises partners who both have a secure attachment style.
- People with a secure attachment style report the highest levels of relationship satisfaction, especially if both partners in a relationship have a secure attachment style.

## Issues in Loving Relationships

- Various perspectives exist on the connections between love and sex. Most students in our surveys report that love enriches sexual relations but is not necessary for enjoyment of sex.
- Women consistently link love with sexual behavior more than men do, but research indicates that men and women are becoming more similar on this issue.

- Gay men and lesbians, like heterosexuals, generally seek out loving, trusting, caring relationships that embrace many dimensions of sharing in addition to sexual intimacy.
- Some people consider jealousy a sign of love, but it might actually reflect fear of losing possession or control of another.
- Jealousy is frequently a factor in precipitating violence in marriages and dating relationships.
- Research indicates that men and women react differently to jealousy.

## Maintaining Relationship Satisfaction

- Ingredients often present in a lasting love relationship include self-acceptance, acceptance of one's partner, appreciation of one another, commitment, good communication, realistic expectations, shared interests, equality in decision making, and the ability to face conflict effectively.
- Variety is often an important ingredient of enjoyable sex in a long-term relationship. For some couples, however, the security of routine is more satisfying.

## The Importance of Sexual Communication

- Sexual communication often contributes to the contentment and enjoyment of a sexual relationship; infrequent or ineffective sexual communication is a common reason that people feel dissatisfied with their sex lives.
- An excellent basis for effective sexual communication is mutual empathy—the underlying knowledge that each partner in a relationship cares for the other and knows that care is reciprocated.
- Childhood socialization, characterized by lack of communication about sexual matters, can contribute to later difficulties in sexual communication with a partner.
- Our language is characterized by a conspicuous absence of an effective, comfortable sexual vocabulary.
- Differences between women's and men's styles of relating to other people can hinder communication. Men often use language to convey advice and information and to maintain a one-up status. In contrast, women typically use language to promote closeness and to achieve and share intimacy.
- Some people object to sexual communication on the grounds that it disrupts spontaneity or that it may place one in a position of increased vulnerability to judgment, criticism, or rejection.

## Talking: Getting Started

- It is often difficult to start talking about sex. Suggestions for getting started include talking about talking, reading about sex and discussing the material, and sharing sexual histories.

## Listening and Feedback

- Communication is most successful between an active listener and an effective speaker.
- The listener can facilitate communication by maintaining eye contact with the speaker, providing feedback, expressing appreciation for communication efforts, and maintaining an attitude of unconditional positive regard.

## Discovering Your Partner's Needs

- Efforts to communicate with sexual partners are often hindered by yes/no questions, which encourage limited replies. Effective alternatives include open-ended and either/or questions.
- Self-disclosure can make it easier for a partner to communicate her or his own needs. Sharing fantasies, beginning with mild desires, can be a particularly valuable kind of exchange.
- Discussing sexual preferences either before or after a sexual encounter can be beneficial.
- Giving permission encourages partners to share feelings freely.

## Learning to Make Requests

- Making requests is facilitated by (1) taking responsibility for one's own pleasure, (2) making sure requests are specific, and (3) using "I" language.

## Expressing and Receiving Complaints

- It is important to select the right time and place for expressing sexual concerns. Avoid registering complaints when anger is at its peak.
- Complaints are generally most effective when tempered with praise. People are usually more motivated to make changes when they are praised for their strengths as well as made aware of things that need improvement.
- "Why" questions that blame a partner do not further the registering of constructive complaints.
- It is wise to direct anger toward behavior rather than toward a person's character. Anger is probably best expressed with clear, honest "I" statements rather than with accusatory "you" statements.
- Relationships are better served when complaints are limited to one per discussion.
- Acknowledging an understanding of the basis for a partner's complaint can help establish a sense of empathy and lead to constructive dialogue.
- It can be helpful to ask clarifying questions when complaints are vague. Calmly verbalizing the feelings aroused when one receives a complaint often avoids nonproductive, heated exchanges.
- An excellent closure to receiving a complaint is to focus on what can be done to rectify the problem in a relationship.

## Saying No

- A three-step strategy for saying no to invitations for intimate involvements is expressing appreciation for the invitation, saying no clearly and unequivocally, and offering an alternative, if applicable.
- To avoid sending mixed messages, occasionally check for inconsistencies between verbal messages and subsequent actions. Recipients of mixed messages might find it helpful to express their confusion and to ask which of the conflicting messages they are expected to act on.

## Nonverbal Sexual Communication

- Sexual communication is not confined to words alone. Facial expressions, interpersonal distance, touching, and sounds also convey a great deal of information.
- The value of nonverbal communication lies primarily in its ability to supplement, not replace, verbal communication.

## Communication Patterns in Successful and Unsuccessful Relationships

- Constructive communication tactics that contribute to relationship satisfaction and longevity include leveling and editing, validating, and volatile dialogue.
- Destructive communication tactics include criticism, contempt, defensiveness, stonewalling, and belligerence. Such tactics lead to increased conflict and negativity, cause an escalation of hostility, and frequently result in relationship failure.

## ◗ Suggested Readings

**Ackerman, Diane** (1994). *A Natural History of Love.* New York: Random House. A highly praised book that provides a readable, entertaining, and informative exploration of the historical, cultural, and biological roots of love.

**Gottman, John, and Nan Silver** (2000). *The Seven Principles for Making Marriage Work.* New York: Crown Publishers. A practical and informative discussion of how research on patterns of marital interaction can be applied to strengthening couple relationships.

**Hendrick, Clyde, and Susan Hendrick** (2000). *Close Relationships: A Sourcebook.* Thousand Oaks, CA: Sage. An informative overview of research on the related topics of attraction, love, intimacy, and the development and maintenance of relationships.

**Tannen, Deborah** (2001). *You Just Don't Understand: Women and Men in Conversation.* New York: Quill. A highly readable book that uses vivid examples to outline the distinctly different conversational styles of males and females.

**Weber, Ann, and John Harvey** (Eds.) (1994). *Perspectives on Close Relationships.* Boston: Allyn & Bacon. A collection of scholarly articles that deal with a variety of relationship issues, including attraction, attachment, love, sexual intimacy, and jealousy.

## ◗ Web Resources

**CengageNOW Web Site**
Go to **academic.cengage.com** to link to practice quiz questions, interactive activities, Internet links, critical thinking exercises, discussion forums, and more. You can also access sites from the Wadsworth Psychology Study Center (**academic .cengage.com/psychology**) or you can connect directly to the following sites:

**Relationship Issues**
Although aimed at teenagers, this short series of Web pages on the Planned Parenthood Web site addresses questions about relationships and sexual activity that many young adults ask.

**Sexual Communication**
This page from the Web site of the Counseling Center at SUNY–Buffalo provides helpful tips on building positive communication within a relationship.

**Communicating About Sex**
A slide show presentation on communicating about sex and intimacy is accessible at the Houghton College Web site.

### The Human Awareness Institute

The Human Awareness Institute is one of many private groups that offer workshops to help couples communicate more effectively and improve relationships. Information on these workshops is available at this Web site.

### The Couples Place

This Web site provides information that can help strengthen intimate relationships.

### American Association for Marriage and Family Therapy

This professional organization's Web site provides referrals to various sources (books, articles, therapists) that can help resolve problems in intimate relationships.

**Our Sexuality Book Companion Web Site** academic.cengage.com/psychology/crooks Visit your book companion Web site where you will find flash cards, practice quizzes, Internet links, and more to help you study.

**Just what you need to know NOW!** Spend time on what you need to master rather than on information you already have learned. Take a pretest for this chapter, and CengageNOW will generate a personalized study plan based on your results. The study plan will identify the topics you need to review and direct you to online resources to help you master those topics. You can then take a post-test to help you determine the concepts you have mastered and what you will still need to work on. Try it out! Go to academic.cengage.com/login to sign in with an access code or to purchase access to this product.

**InfoTrac College Edition Online Library** Sign in to academic.cengage.com/login or visit your free book companion Web site at academic.cengage.com/psychology/crooks to access InfoTrac College Edition, an online searchable library that includes a multitude of journals, many specific to human sexuality. These journals include *Archives of Sexual Behavior; Archives of Sexual Health Behavior; Canadian Journal of Human Sexuality; Hispanic Journal of the Behavioral Sciences; Journal of Cross-Cultural Psychology; Journal of Physical Education, Recreation, and Dance; Journal of Sex Research;* and *Sex Roles.*

# Sexual Behaviors

Stuart Pearce/A.G.E. Foto Stock/FirstLight

*My sexuality has had many different dimensions during my life. My childhood mastur-*
*bation was a secret desire and guilt that I never did admit to the priest in the confes-*
*sional. "Playing doctor" was intriguing and exciting in its "naughtiness." The hours of*
*hot kissing and petting of my teenage and early college years developed my sexual*
*awareness. My first intercourse experience was with a loved and trusted boyfriend. It*
*was a profound physical and emotional experience; 30 years later the memory still*
*brings me deep pleasure. As a young adult in the 1960s and 1970s my sexual expres-*
*sion alternated between periods of recreational sex and celibacy. Within marriage the*
*comforts and challenges of commitment; combining sex with an intense desire to*
*become pregnant; the primal experience of pregnancy, childbirth, and nursing greatly*
*expanded the parameters of my sexuality. Now, balancing family, career, personal*
*interests, and regular hair appointments, my sexuality is a quiet hum in the back-*
*ground. I'm looking forward to retirement and time and energy for more than coffee*
*and a kiss in the morning. (Authors' files)*

People express their sexuality in many ways. The emotions and meanings that they attach to sexual behavior also vary widely. In this chapter, we discuss the importance of context in sexual expression and describe a variety of sexual behaviors. We consider individuals first and later look at couples' sexual behavior. We begin with a discussion of celibacy.

## ◑ Celibacy

A physically mature person who does not engage in sexual behavior is said to be *celi-bate*. In **complete celibacy** a person neither masturbates nor has sexual contact with another person. In **partial celibacy** an individual masturbates but does not have inter-personal sexual contact. Celibacy is not commonly thought of as a form of sexual expression. However, when it represents a conscious decision not to engage in sexual behavior, this decision in itself is an expression of one's sexuality, and it may manifest a person's sexual intelligence. Celibacy, or abstinence, can be a viable option until the context for a sexual relationship is appropriate and positive for a given individual.

Celibacy is most commonly associated with religious devotion; joining a religious order or becoming a priest or nun often includes a vow of celibacy. The ideal of reli-gious celibacy is to transform sexual energy into service to humanity (Abbott, 2000). Mother Teresa of Calcutta and Mahatma Gandhi of India exemplified this ideal, and they are admired for their moral leadership (Sipe, 1990).

Historically, some women embraced celibacy to free themselves from the limita-tions of the expected gender roles of marriage and motherhood. In the Middle Ages a woman could obtain an education if she became a nun. In a convent, nuns had access to libraries and could correspond with learned theologians. Lay women were prohib-ited such privileges. Elizabeth I, England's Virgin Queen, avoided marriage to main-tain her political power, but she had several unconsummated love affairs during her rule. She entertained proposals from numerous well-connected suitors for her own political purposes, subjecting herself to repeated courtly inspections to confirm her virginity (Abbott, 2002).

Today many factors can lead a person to be celibate. Some people choose to be celibate until marriage because of religious or moral beliefs. Others maintain celibacy until their personal criteria for a good sexual relationship have been met. Some choose celibacy because they have experienced confusion or disappointment in past sexual relationships and they want to spend some time establishing new relationships without the complicating factor of sexual interaction (Elliott & Brantley, 1997). A 28-year-old man explained:

*There was a period not too long ago in my life where I had been abstinent for about*
*four years. I had been on both sides of the cheating fence and began to realize that*
*sex wasn't just something that I wanted to take, or could take, lightly. The feelings*
*that can be created out of a physical relationship are simply too powerful to toy*

**Complete celibacy** An expression of sexuality in which an individual does not engage in either masturba-tion or interpersonal sexual contact.

**Partial celibacy** An expression of sexuality in which an individual does not engage in interpersonal sex-ual contact but continues to engage in masturbation.

*around with. I was terribly afraid of being hurt again, or of perhaps hurting someone else, so I chose not to get sexual with anyone. (Authors' files)*

At times a person can be so caught up in other aspects of life that sex is simply not a priority. Health considerations, such as concerns about pregnancy or sexually transmitted diseases, can also prompt a decision not to have sexual intercourse.

Some people find that a period of celibacy can be rewarding. They can often refocus on themselves during such a period—exploring self-pleasuring; learning to value their aloneness, autonomy, and privacy; or giving priority to work and nonsexual relationship commitments. Friendships can gain new dimensions and fulfillment. Of the many options for sexual expression, celibacy is one that people sometimes have considerable trouble understanding. However, celibacy can be a personally valuable choice.

# ❶ Erotic Dreams and Fantasy

Some forms of sexual experience occur within a person's mind, with or without sexual behavior. These are erotic dreams and fantasy—mental experiences that arise from our imagination or life experience or that are stimulated by books, drawings, photographs, or movies.

## Erotic Dreams

Erotic dreams, and occasionally orgasm, can occur during sleep without a person's conscious direction. One study found that 93% of men and 86% of women reported having erotic dreams (Schredl et al., 2004). A person might waken during such a dream and notice signs of sexual arousal: erection, vaginal lubrication, or pelvic movements. Orgasm can also occur during sleep; this is called **nocturnal orgasm**. When orgasm occurs, males usually notice the ejaculate—hence the term *wet dream* or *nocturnal emission*. Women also experience orgasm during sleep, but female orgasm may be more difficult to determine because of the absence of visible evidence. Women who are most likely to have orgasms during sleep also report a higher frequency of sexual intercourse and of orgasm from masturbation than women who are less likely to have nocturnal orgasms (Wells, 1983).

**Nocturnal orgasm** Involuntary orgasm during sleep.

## Erotic Fantasy

Erotic waking fantasies commonly occur during daydreams, masturbation, or sexual encounters with a partner. A review of research about fantasy found that about 95% of men and women reported having experienced sexual fantasies (Leitenberg & Henning, 1995). Comparing the content of homosexuals' and heterosexuals' fantasies revealed more similarities than differences, leaving aside the sex of the imagined partner (Leitenberg & Henning, 1995).

### Functions of Fantasy

Erotic fantasies serve many functions. First, they can be a source of pleasure and arousal. Erotic thoughts typically serve to enhance sexual arousal during masturbation and partners' sexual activities. Sexual fantasies can also help people overcome anxiety and facilitate sexual functioning or compensate for a somewhat negative sexual situation. Fantasies can be a way to mentally rehearse and anticipate new sexual experiences. Imagining seductive glances, that first kiss, or a novel intercourse position may help a person implement such activities more comfortably (Leitenberg & Henning, 1995).

Sexual fantasies can allow tolerable expression of "forbidden wishes." That a sexual activity in a fantasy is forbidden can make it more exciting. People in sexually exclusive relationships can fantasize about past lovers or others to whom they feel attracted, even though they are committed to a single sexual partner. In a fantasy, a person can

MOMMA by Mell Lazarus. By permission of Mell Lazarus and Creators Syndicate, Inc.

experience lustful group sex, cross-orientation sexual liaisons, brief sexual encounters with strangers, erotic relations with friends and acquaintances, incestuous experiences, sex with animals, or any other sexual activity imaginable—all without actually engaging in them.

Another function of erotic fantasy can be to provide relief from gender-role expectations (Pinhas, 1985). Women's fantasies of being the sexual aggressor and men's fantasies of being forced to have sex can offer alternatives to stereotypical roles. In her first book about male sexual fantasy, Nancy Friday reported that one of the major themes is men's abdication of control in favor of passivity:

> It may seem lusty and dashing always to be the one who chooses the woman, who decides when, where, and how the bedroom scene will be played. But isn't her role safer? The man is like someone who has suggested a new restaurant to friends. What if it doesn't live up to expectations he has aroused? The macho stance makes the male the star performer. The hidden cost is that it puts the woman in the role of critic. (Friday, 1980, p. 274)

Research indicates that almost twice as many women as men fantasize about being forced to have sex (Knafo & Jaffe, 1984; Maltz & Boss, 1997). Although the fantasy of being forced to have sex provides an alternative to gender-role expectations for men, the same type of fantasy has other meanings for women. For women, who often learn to have mixed feelings about being sexual, this type of fantasy offers sexual adventures free from the responsibility and guilt of personal choice. One study found that women who reported having fantasies of being forced to have sex had more positive feelings about sex in general than women who did not have such fantasies. The research also showed that forced-sex fantasies are not usually an indication of having had past abusive experiences. It is important to emphasize that enjoyment of forced-sex fantasies does not mean women really want to be raped (Gold et al., 1991). A woman is in charge of her fantasies, but as a victim of sexual aggression she is not in control.

## Male/Female Similarities and Differences in Sexual Fantasy

Men's and women's fantasy lives have some aspects in common. First, the frequency of fantasy is similar for both sexes during sexual activity with a partner (Leitenberg & Henning, 1995). Second, both men and women indicate a wide range of fantasy content. A research summary of heterosexual male/female content of sexual fantasy (Leitenberg & Henning, 1995) found notable differences:

- Men's fantasies are more active and focus more on a woman's body and on what they want to do to it, whereas women's fantasies are more passive and focus more on men's interest in their bodies.
- Men's sexual fantasies focus more on explicit sexual acts, nude bodies, and physical gratification; whereas women use more emotional context and romance in their sexual fantasies.
- Men are more likely to fantasize about multiple partners and group sex than are women.
- Men are more likely to have dominance fantasies, whereas women are more likely to have submission fantasies.

## Fantasies: Help or Hindrance?

Erotic fantasies are generally considered a healthy and helpful aspect of sexuality (Renaud & Byers, 2001). People who feel less guilty about sexual fantasies during intercourse reported higher levels of sexual satisfaction and functioning than did others who felt more guilty about having sexual fantasies (Cado & Leitenberg, 1990). Sexual fantasies help many women experience arousal and orgasm during sexual activity, and a deficit of erotic fantasy often occurs along with problems of low sexual desire and arousal (Boss & Maltz, 2001). Many sex therapists encourage their clients to use sexual fantasies as a source of stimulation to help them increase interest and arousal.

Although most of the available research supports erotic imagining as helpful, sexual fantasy has also been considered symptomatic of poor sexual relationships or other personal problems (Perel, 2003). Some men have difficulty experiencing orgasm during intercourse because the idiosyncratic sexual fantasies they require for intense arousal are discordant with partner sexual behavior (Perleman, 2001). Fantasizing privately during sex with a partner can erode intimacy in the relationship. One study found that college students had a double standard about their own sexual fantasies versus their partners'. Study participants of both sexes thought that fantasizing about someone other than their partner was normal and did not jeopardize the exclusivity of the relationship. However, the idea that their partner fantasized about someone else made the participants feel jealous and threatened, as though the fantasy was a kind of unfaithfulness. The most threatening fantasy a partner could have was about a mutual friend or classmate rather than a fantasy about someone who in reality was an unlikely rival, such as a movie star (Yarab & Allgeier, 1998).

Individuals who have experienced sexual abuse as children are sometimes troubled by intrusive, unwanted sexual fantasies. Developing new fantasies based on self-acceptance and loving relationships can be a part of healing for these individuals (Boss & Maltz, 2001). As with most other aspects of sexuality, what determines whether fantasizing is helpful or disturbing to a relationship is its meaning and purpose for the individuals concerned.

Some people decide to incorporate a particular fantasy into their actual sexual behavior with a partner. Acting out a fantasy can be pleasurable; however, if it is uncomfortable for a partner, counter to one's value system, or has possible negative consequences, one should consider the advantages and disadvantages of acting it out. For some people, fantasies are more exciting when they remain imaginary and are disappointing when acted out.

Several Internet activities and technologies present an intermediate step between private fantasy and actual behavior. Sharing and developing one's sexual fantasies online—in chat rooms, during online multiplayer erotic games, and with webcam technology—involve revealing the fantasies, usually to strangers. Interestingly, talking about fantasies online with strangers does help some individuals take the step of expressing their previously private sexual imaginings and interests to their actual partners.

In some cases fantasy can influence a person to act in a way that harms others. This is of particular concern in the case of people who sexually assault children or adults. A person who thinks that he or she is in danger of committing such an act should seek professional psychological assistance. ■

# Masturbation

In this textbook the word **masturbation** is used to describe self-stimulation of one's genitals for sexual pleasure. *Autoeroticism* is another term used for masturbation. We discuss some perspectives on and purposes of masturbation and specific techniques used in masturbation.

**Masturbation** Stimulation of one's own genitals to create sexual pleasure.

## Perspectives on Masturbation

Masturbation has been a source of social concern and censure throughout Judeo-Christian history. This state of affairs has resulted in both misinformation and considerable personal shame and fear. Many of the negative attitudes toward masturbation are rooted in early Jewish and Christian views that procreation was the only legitimate purpose of sexual behavior. Because masturbation obviously could not result in conception, it was condemned (Wiesner-Hanks, 2000). During the mid-18th century, the "evils" of masturbation received a great deal of publicity in the name of science, largely because of the writings of a European physician named Samuel Tissot. He believed that semen was made from blood and that the loss of semen was debilitating to health, and he wrote vividly about the mind- and body-damaging effects of "self-abuse." This view of masturbation influenced social and medical attitudes in Europe and North America for generations, as reflected by an "encyclopedia" of health published in 1918, which describes the following "symptoms" of masturbation:

> The health soon becomes noticeably impaired; there will be general debility.... Next come sore eyes, blindness, stupidity, consumption, spinal affliction, emaciation, involuntary seminal emissions, loss of all energy or spirit, insanity and idiocy—the hopeless ruin of both body and mind. (Wood & Ruddock, 1918, p. 812)

In the 1800s, sexual abstinence, simple foods, and fitness were lauded as crucial to health. The Reverend Sylvester Graham, who promoted the use of whole-grain flours and whose name is still attached to graham crackers, wrote that ejaculation reduced precious "vital fluids." He beseeched men to abstain from masturbation and even marital intercourse to avoid moral and physical degeneracy. John Harvey Kellogg, a physician, carried Graham's work further and developed the cornflake to help prevent masturbation and sexual desire. (Kellogg believed that bland food dampened sexual desires). Other techniques to control masturbation included bandaging the genitals, tying one's hands at night, clitoridectomy, applying carbolic acid to the clitoris, and suturing foreskins shut, as well as employing mechanical devices (Planned Parenthood Federation of America, 2003a).

Freud and most other early psychoanalysts recognized that masturbation does not harm physical health, and they saw it as normal during childhood. However, they believed that masturbation in adulthood could result in "immature" sexual development and the inability to form good sexual relationships. In contrast, contemporary research indicates that masturbation is not harmful to sexual adjustment in young adulthood (Leitenberg et al., 1993).

Views today reflect conflicting beliefs about masturbation; some of the traditional condemnation still exists. In 1976 the Vatican issued a "Declaration on Certain Questions Concerning Sexual Ethics," which described masturbation as an "intrinsically and seriously disordered act." This perspective was maintained in 1993 by Pope John Paul II's condemnation of masturbation as morally unacceptable. Many fundamentalist Christians share this view of masturbation. Indeed, some individuals abstain from masturbation because of their religious beliefs.

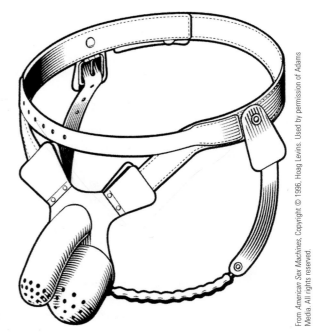

This lockable metal genital pouch with leather straps, patented in 1910, was designed to prevent masturbation by patients in mental hospitals.

*I don't masturbate, because I've learned from my church and my parents that sexual love in marriage is an expression of God's love. Any other kind of sex diminishes the meaning I will find with my wife. (Authors' files)*

**? Critical Thinking Question**

Why are laws against the sale of sex toys an example of a lack of sexual intelligence?

Condemnation of masturbation also intrudes into public policy, as described in the Sex and Politics box, "If Vibrators Are Outlawed, Only Outlaws Will Have Vibrators." In contrast, many view masturbation as a healthy and positive aspect of sexuality. For example, Betty Dodson, author of *Liberating Masturbation*, writes:

Masturbation, of course, is our first natural sexual activity. It's the way we discover our eroticism, the way we learn to respond sexually, the way we learn to love ourselves and build self-esteem. (Dodson, 1974, p. 13)

## Purposes of Masturbation

**! Sexual Health**

People masturbate for a variety of reasons, not the least of which is the pleasure of arousal and orgasm. The most commonly reported reason is to relieve sexual tension (Michael et al., 1994). Masturbation is also valuable as a means of self-exploration. Sex educator Eleanor Hamilton recommends masturbation to adolescents as a way to release tension and to become "pleasantly at home with your own sexual organs" (1978, p. 33). Indeed, people can learn a great deal about their sexual responses from masturbation. Self-stimulation is often helpful for women learning to experience orgasms and for men experimenting with their response patterns to increase ejaculatory control. (We discuss masturbation as a tool for increasing sexual satisfaction in Chapter 14.) Finally, some people find that masturbation helps them get to sleep at night, because the same generalized feelings of relaxation that often follow a sexual encounter can also accompany self-pleasuring (Ellison, 2000). ■

**? Critical Thinking Question**

What do you think parents should tell their children about masturbation?

At times the satisfaction from an autoerotic session can be more rewarding than an interpersonal sexual encounter, as the following quote illustrates:

*I had always assumed that masturbation was a second-best sexual expression. One time, after reflecting back on the previous day's activities of a really enjoyable morning masturbatory experience and an unsatisfying experience that evening with a partner, I realized that first- and second-rate were very relative. (Authors' files)*

Some people find that the independent sexual release available through masturbation can help them make better decisions about relating sexually with other people. Furthermore, within a relationship masturbation can help to even out the effects of dissimilar sexual interest. Masturbation can also be a shared experience:

*When I am feeling sexual and my partner is not, he holds me and kisses me while I masturbate. Also, sometimes after making love I like to touch myself while he embraces me. It is so much better than sneaking off to the bathroom alone. (Authors' files)*

**! Sexual Health**

A common concern about masturbation is "doing it too much." ⊙ **Table 8.1** shows the range in frequency of masturbation among college students. Even in writings where masturbation is said to be normal, masturbating "to excess" is often presented as unhealthy. A definition of excess rarely follows. If a person were masturbating so much that it significantly interfered with any aspect of his or her life, there might be cause for concern. However, in that case masturbation would be a symptom or manifestation of some underlying problem rather than the problem itself. For example, someone who is experiencing intense emotional anxiety might use masturbation as a way to relieve anxiety or as a form of self-comforting. The problem in this case is the intense emotional anxiety, not the masturbation. ■

## If Vibrators Are Outlawed, Only Outlaws Will Have Vibrators

The belief that self-stimulation is immoral enough to be worthy of governmental control is currently seen in the states that have made the display or sale of sex toys illegal: Alabama, Georgia, Indiana, Louisiana, Mississippi, and Virginia (Babcock, 2006). Alabama's attorney general argued that there is "a legitimate legislative interest in discouraging prurient interests in autonomous sex" (ACLU, 2006, p. 1). The maximum penalty for selling a sex toy is a $10,000 fine and a year of hard labor. Ironically, in all these states, people can legally sell semiautomatic assault weapons like the AK47 or Uzi, but not vibrators (Davidson, 2006; Klein, 2000). The legal arguments about the sale of sex toys are based on whether devices for sexual gratification are protected under the constitutional right to personal autonomy, privacy, and free speech (Hobbs, 2006). "It should not be a matter of what someone thinks about sex toys based on their personal religious beliefs. . . . They should be protected under the same grounds that protect our right to privacy in any adult's own bedroom" (Lawless, 2006, p. 1).

Courtesy of Dee Boyles, February 10, 2007.

| ○ TABLE 8.1 | Two Thousand College Students Answer the Question "How Often Do You Masturbate?" | |
|---|---|---|
| | Men (%) | Women (%) |
| Two or more times a week | 50 | 16 |
| Less than two times a week but more than never | 38 | 44 |
| Never | 12 | 40 |

SOURCE: Elliott & Brantley (1997).

Most men and women, both married and unmarried, masturbate on occasion. Women tend to masturbate more after they reach their 20s than they did in their teens. Kinsey hypothesized that this was due to increased erotic responsiveness, opportunities for learning about the possibility of self-stimulation through sex play with a partner, and a reduction in sexual inhibitions. Masturbation is often considered inappropriate when a person has a sexual partner or is married. Some people believe that they should not engage in a sexual activity that excludes their partners, or that experiencing sexual pleasure by masturbation deprives their partners of pleasure. Others mistakenly interpret their partner's desire to masturbate as a sign that something is wrong with their relationship. But unless it interferes with mutually enjoyable sexual intimacy in the relationship, masturbation can be considered a normal part of each partner's sexual repertoire. It is common for people to continue masturbation after they marry. In fact, individuals who engage in sexual activity with their partners more frequently than other individuals also masturbate more often (Laumann et al., 1994). Moreover, one study found that married women who masturbated to orgasm had greater marital and sexual satisfaction than women who did not masturbate (Hurlbert & Whittaker, 1991).

## Ethnicity and Masturbation

Adults who are most likely to masturbate, and most likely to masturbate more frequently than others, have several characteristics in common—indicating that even this

**Figure 8.1** Male masturbation.

private sexual behavior is strongly influenced by a person's social group (Laumann et al., 1994). They have liberal views, are college-educated, and are living with a sexual partner. White men and women masturbate more than African American men and women. Among white, African, and Hispanic Americans, Hispanic women have the lowest rate of masturbation.

## Self-Pleasuring Techniques

In this section we offer descriptions of self-pleasuring techniques. Specific techniques for masturbation vary. Males commonly grasp the penile shaft with one hand, as shown in ○ **Figure 8.1**. Some men prefer to use lotion; others like the natural friction of a dry hand. Up-and-down motions of differing pressures and tempos provide stimulation. A man can also stroke the glans and frenulum or caress or tug the scrotum. Or, rather than using his hands, a man can rub his penis against a mattress or pillow.

Women enjoy a variety of stimulation techniques. Typically, the hand provides circular, back-and-forth, or up-and-down movements against the mons and clitoral area (see ○ **Figure 8.2**).

The glans of the clitoris is rarely stimulated directly, although it can be stimulated indirectly when covered by the hood. Some women thrust the clitoral area against an object such as bedding or a pillow. Others masturbate by pressing their thighs together and tensing the pelvic floor muscles that underlie the vulva. Contrary to what is often portrayed in pornography, only some women use vaginal insertion to reach orgasm during masturbation. Only 1.5% of women in Shere Hite's survey (1976) used vaginal insertion of a finger or penis-shaped object; over half of this small group had also used clitoral stimulation before insertion.

Some individuals also use vibrators and other sex toys for added enjoyment or variation in self-stimulation. Although some men enjoy using a vibrator on their genitals, women tend to be more enthusiastic about such devices. Many women have also discovered that hand-held showerheads provide pleasurable sensations when directed to their vulvas. Surveys find that 46 to 60% of women in the United States use vibrators, and over 75% are in a sexual relationship (Berman, 2004; Springen, 2005). Ninety percent of women who masturbate with a vibrator are comfortable talking to their partner about it, and many couples incorporate vibrators into their sex play (Berman, 2004). Sociologist Pepper Schwartz encourages men not to feel threatened by including a vibrator with their partners, "Gentlemen, this is not your competition, it's your colleague" (Schwartz, 2006). Several different types of vibrators are available, and people's preferences vary. *Good Vibrations: The New Complete Guide to Vibrators*, by Joani Blank (2000), has a detailed discussion of vibrators.

The vibrator is only one kind of sex toy for self-pleasuring and enhancing sexual interaction with one's partner. Throughout history the *dildo*, or artificial penis, has been used to enhance sexual arousal. Small dildos are also used for anal stimulation. For several thousand years women in China and Japan have used ben-wa balls

**Figure 8.2** Female masturbation.

for pleasure. Two balls, one hollow and one filled with a heavy liquid, are inserted into the vagina while the woman lies on a hammock or sits in a swing in order for the

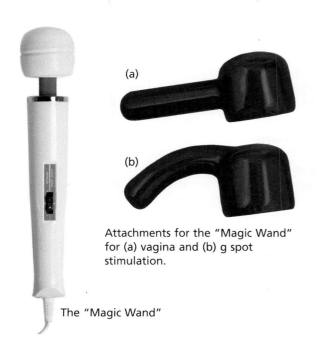

The "Magic Wand"

Attachments for the "Magic Wand" for (a) vagina and (b) g spot stimulation.

The ring fits at the base of the penis, and the ball stimulates the clitoris.

Vibrators come in many forms. The TV show "Sex and the City" brought the rabbit to the public's attention.

Photos: Courtesy of Vibratex, Inc.; www.vibratex.com

motion to move the balls and create inner sensations. Men can use latex or rubber simulations of female genitals for masturbation. More elaborate sex toys that stimulate several genital sites at once are also available, and high-tech varieties are under development (Otto, 1999). The iBuzz—a small, capsule-shaped device that vibrates in sync with the music played on an iPod or MP3 player—is worn inside underwear or inside the vagina. The intensity of the vibrations varies with the volume setting.

Although masturbating is valuable for many people in various situations, not everyone wants to do it. Sometimes, in our attempts to help people who would like to eradicate their negative feelings about self-stimulation, it may sound as if the message is that people *should* masturbate. This is not the case. Masturbation is an option for sexual expression, not a mandate.

# ▶ Sexual Expression: The Importance of Context

Up to this point in the chapter, we have been looking at ways that people express themselves sexually as individuals. However, many of the sexual behaviors with which we are concerned take place as interactions between people. In the sections that follow we discuss some of the more common forms of shared sexual behavior.

## The Context of Sexual Expression

Although the following sections include discussions of sexual techniques, a sexual interaction cannot stand on its own; it exists within the context of motivation and meanings of the individuals involved and the relationship as a whole. One writer explained:

> Sex can be motivated by excitement or boredom, physical need or affection, desire or duty, loneliness or complacency. It can be a bid for power or an egalitarian exchange, a purely mechanical release of tension or a highly emotional fusion, a way to wear oneself out for sleep or a way to revitalize oneself. Sex can be granted as a reward or inducement, an altruistic offering or a favor; it can also be an act of selfishness, insecurity, or narcissism. Sex can express almost anything and mean almost anything (Fillion, 1996, p. 41).

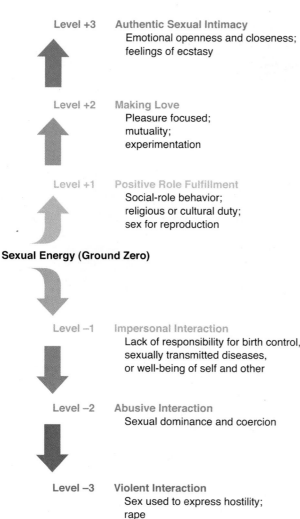

Level +3　Authentic Sexual Intimacy
Emotional openness and closeness;
feelings of ecstasy

Level +2　Making Love
Pleasure focused;
mutuality;
experimentation

Level +1　Positive Role Fulfillment
Social-role behavior;
religious or cultural duty;
sex for reproduction

**Sexual Energy (Ground Zero)**

Level –1　Impersonal Interaction
Lack of responsibility for birth control,
sexually transmitted diseases,
or well-being of self and other

Level –2　Abusive Interaction
Sexual dominance and coercion

Level –3　Violent Interaction
Sex used to express hostility;
rape

**○ Figure 8.3** The Maltz hierarchy of sexual interactions (Maltz, 2001c).

# The Maltz Hierarchy

The context within which sexual experiences occur is critically important in determining whether they are positive for individuals and relationships. Author and sex therapist Wendy Maltz developed a model of sexual expression that describes levels of constructive and destructive sexual experiences (Maltz, 2001c). Maltz sees sexual energy as a neutral force; however, the intent and consequences of sexual behavior can lead in negative or positive directions. For example, marital intercourse may be intensely passionate; alternatively, it may be spousal rape.

The three positive levels of sexual interaction are built on mutual choice, caring, respect, and safety. As shown in **○ Figure 8.3**, Level +1 (Positive Role Fulfillment) reflects well-defined gender roles, established by social or religious custom, in which (in heterosexual relationships) the man is the initiator and the woman is the receiver. Sexual interactions at this level are characterized by mutual respect, a lack of coercion and resentment, and a strong sense of safety and predictability. Pregnancy and reduction of sexual tension are common goals for sex.

Level +2 (Making Love) emphasizes mutual pleasure through individual sexual creativity and experimentation. Traditional gender-role behavior is set aside, and sex expands to an erotic recreational experience. Partners reveal themselves more deeply through sexual self-expression and communication that create greater intimacy.

Level +3 (Authentic Sexual Intimacy) brings a shared sense of deep connection both to oneself and to one's partner, with reverence toward the body in the erotic experience. The enjoyment of sensual pleasure includes a profound expression of love for one another. Emotional honesty and openness are of paramount importance, and each partner gains a deeper sense of wholeness. Authentic sexual intimacy can be a momentary peak experience, or it can characterize an entire lovemaking experience.

Maltz points out that sexual interactions can also be upsetting or traumatic ordeals, often imposed on one person by another. On the negative side of her hierarchy, each level becomes increasingly destructive and abusive. Level –1 (Impersonal Interaction) is marked by a lack of respect and responsibility toward oneself and the other person. Here, individuals disregard possible negative consequences for themselves and their partners, including unwanted pregnancy and exposure to sexually transmitted diseases. Enduring unpleasant sex and being dishonest about issues relevant to the partner (health status or meaning of the sexual experience) occur at this level. These experiences result in uncomfortable, uneasy feelings. Alcohol and drug use are often elements in sexual experiences that individuals later regret (Kaiser Family Foundation, 2003a).

Level –2 (Abusive Interaction) involves one person's conscious domination of another by psychological coercion. Examples include nonviolent acquaintance rape and incest, and degrading coercive communication. Distorted thinking allows the exploitative person to rationalize or deny the harm he or she is inflicting on the other person. The experience usually damages the exploited person's self-esteem.

Level –3 (Violent Interaction) occurs when sexual energy is used purposefully to express hostility. Sex organs are weapons and targets. Rape is the most extreme example.

## Frequency of Sexual Activity

The results of a 1998 survey of 10,000 people in the United States found that the national average of frequency of sexual activity is once a week, each episode lasting about half an hour (Robinson & Godbey, 1998). The survey did not inquire about satisfaction or specific behaviors that occurred during the sexual activity. Most other research has found that people with more formal education are more likely to engage in a wider variety of behaviors during a sexual episode than are those with less formal education. However, what is meaningful and satisfying to a given individual and couple is most important.

The following discussions of shared sexual behaviors, except for coitus and gay and lesbian sexual expression, are directed toward all individuals, regardless of their sexual orientation. In fact, because sex between same-sex partners does not duplicate the pervasive heterosexual model's emphasis on penile–vaginal intercourse, gays' and lesbians' sexual repertoire is often more expansive and creative than heterosexuals' (Nichols, 2000; Sanders, 2000).

The sequence in which the following sexual behaviors are presented does not mean that such a progression is best in a particular sexual relationship or encounter; for example, a heterosexual couple may desire oral–genital stimulation *after* coitus rather than before. Nor is any one of these activities necessary in a given relationship or encounter: Complete sexual experience can consist of any or all of them, with or without orgasm. A sex therapist explained: "Once you've begun to think of sex as creating mutual erotic pleasure rather than as manufacturing orgasms, sex is a continuum of possibilities. You may find, for example, that low-key genital—or even non-genital—stimulation can be surprisingly erotic and relaxing" (Ellison, 2000, p. 317). In addition, because sexuality is influenced by the relationship as a whole, it may be best to think of foreplay as how partners have treated each other since their last sexual experience together (Joannides, 1996).

## Kissing and Touching

*i like my body when it is with your*
*body. It is so quite new a thing.*
*Muscles better and nerves more.*
*i like your body. i like what it does,*
*i like its hows. i like to feel the spine*
*of your body and its bones, and the trembling*
*-firm-smoothness and which i will*
*again and again and again*
*kiss, i like kissing this and that of you,*

*i like, slowly stroking the, shocking fuzz*
*of your electric fur, and what-is-it comes*
*over parting flesh. . . . And eyes big love-*
    *crumbs,*

*and possibly i like the thrill*

*of under me you so quite new*

    e. e. cummings\*

### Kissing

Many of us can remember our first romantic kiss; most likely it was combined with feelings of awkwardness. Kissing can be an intense, erotic, profound experience, well suggested by the poet Tennyson: "Once he drew, with one long kiss, my whole soul through my lips."

The lips and mouth are generously endowed with sensitive, pleasure-producing nerve endings that make it feel good to kiss and to be kissed in infinite variations. Seventeen kinds of kisses are described in the *Kama Sutra*, the classical Indian text on eroticism (Ards, 2000). Kissing with closed mouths tends to be more tender and affectionate, whereas open-mouth, or deep, or French kissing is usually more sexually intense. Kissing can also run the gamut of oral activities, such as licking, sucking, and mild biting. All places on the body are possibilities for kissing.

Western practices and attitudes about kissing are by no means universal. Mouth-to-mouth kissing is completely absent in the highly explicit erotic art of ancient Chinese and Japanese civilizations. In Japan in the 1920s mouth kissing was viewed so negatively that Rodin's famous sculpture *The Kiss* was concealed from public view when it was displayed there as part of an exhibit of European art. Other cultures—the Lepcha of Eurasia, the Chewa and Thonga of Africa, and the Siriono of South America—consider kissing unhealthy and disgusting (Tiefer, 1995).

---

"i like my body when it is with your . . ." Copyright 1923, 1925, 1951, 1953 © 1991 by the Trustees for the E. E. Cummings Trust. Copyright © 1976 by George James Firmage, from *Complete Poems: 1904–1962* by E. E. Cummings, edited by George J. Firmage. Used by permission of Liveright Publishing Corporation.

## Touching

Touch is one of the first and most important senses that we experience when we emerge in this world. Infants who have been fed but deprived of this basic stimulation have died for lack of it. A classic animal study showed that when baby monkeys' and other primates' physical needs were met but they were denied their mothers' touch, they grew up to be extremely maladjusted (Harlow & Harlow, 1962).

Touch forms the cornerstone of human sexuality shared with another (Kluger, 2004). In Masters and Johnson's evaluation:

Touch is an end in itself. It is a primary form of communication, a silent voice that avoids the pitfall of words while expressing the feelings of the moment. It bridges the physical separateness from which no human being is spared, literally establishing a sense of solidarity between two individuals. Touching is sensual pleasure, exploring the textures of skin, the suppleness of muscle, the contours of the body, with no further goal than enjoyment of tactile perceptions. (Masters & Johnson, 1976, p. 253)

The body's erogenous zones are especially responsive to touch. For example, about 81 percent of women and 51 percent of men reported that stimulation of their breasts and nipples caused and/or enhanced their arousal (Levin & Meston, 2006). However, touch does not need to be directed to an erogenous area to be sexual. The entire body surface is a sensory organ, and touching—almost anywhere—can enhance intimacy and sexual arousal. Different people like different types and intensities of touch, and the same person can find a certain touch highly arousing one time and unpleasant the next. It is helpful for couples to communicate openly about touching.

In lesbian sexual relationships the mutual desire for and appreciation of touching can result in increased sexual arousal and orgasm compared to women in heterosexual relationships. Female sexuality expert Shere Hite stated that greater sexual satisfaction between women occurs because "lesbian sexual relations tend to be longer and involve more all-over body sensuality" (1976, p. 413). ◗ **Table 8.2** compares sexual behaviors and responses of lesbian and heterosexual women.

Touch can be pleasurable for both the giver and the receiver.

◗ **TABLE 8.2** Comparison of Lesbian and Heterosexual Women's Last Sexual Experience

| Experience During Last Sexual Contact | Lesbians (%) | Heterosexual Women (%) |
|---|---|---|
| Had more than one orgasm | 32 | 19 |
| Received oral sex | 48 | 20 |
| Lasted 15 minutes or less | 4 | 14 |
| Lasted more than 1 hour | 39 | 15 |

SOURCES: Lesbian statistics from *Advocate* magazine survey (Lever, 1994); heterosexual statistics from the National Health and Social Life Survey (Laumann et al., 1994).

Contrary to the stereotype that sexual experiences of gay men are completely genitally focused, extragenital eroticism and affection are important aspects of sexual contact for many male couples. "Compared to other men, gay men are often able to have more diversity, self-expression, and personal enjoyment in their sexual contact" (Sanders, 2000, p. 253). Hugging, kissing, snuggling, and total-body caressing are important. A survey of gay men found that 85% liked such interactions more than any other category of sexual behavior (Lever, 1994).

Rubbing genitals together or against other parts of a partner's body can be included in any couple's sexual interaction and is common in lesbian lovemaking. Rubbing one's genitals against someone else's body or genital area is called **tribadism**. Many lesbians like this form of sexual play because it involves all-over body contact and a generalized sensuality. Some women find the thrusting exciting; others straddle a partner's leg and rub gently. Some rub the clitoris on the partner's pubic bone (Loulan, 1984).

**Tribadism** Rubbing one's genitals against another's body or genitals.

## Manual Stimulation of the Female Genitals

The kinds of genital touches that induce arousal vary from one woman to another. Even the same woman might vary in her preference from one moment to the next. Women can prefer gentle or firm movements on different areas of the vulva. Direct stimulation of the clitoris is uncomfortable for some women; touches above or along the sides are sometimes preferable. Insertion of a finger into the vagina can enhance arousal. Most women approaching orgasm commonly need steady, consistent rhythm and pressure of touch through orgasm (Ellison, 2000).

The vulval tissues are delicate and sensitive. If not enough lubrication exists to make the vulva slippery, it can easily become irritated. A lubricant such as Astroglide, a lotion without alcohol or perfume, or saliva can be used to moisten the fingers and vulva to make the touch more pleasurable. Anal stimulation or penetration is erotic to some women but not to others. It is important not to touch the vulva or vagina with the same finger used for anal stimulation, because if bacteria in the rectum are introduced into the vagina, they can cause infections. ■

## Manual Stimulation of the Male Genitals

Men also have individual preferences for manual stimulation, and like women, they might desire a firmer or softer touch—and faster or slower strokes—as their arousal increases. Gentle or firm stroking of the penile shaft and glans and light touches or tugging on the scrotum may be desired, as shown in ⊙ **Figure 8.4**. Some men find that lubrication with a lotion or saliva increases pleasure. (For heterosexual couples, if intercourse might follow, lotion should be nonirritating to the woman's genital tissues.) Immediately following orgasm the glans of the penis may be too sensitive to stimulate. Some men also enjoy manual stimulation or penetration of the anus.

⊙ **Figure 8.4** Manual stimulation can be a highly pleasurable way for partners to explore each other's sensations.

## ⊙ Oral–Genital Stimulation

Both the mouth and the genitals are primary biological erogenous zones, areas of the body generously endowed with sensory nerve endings. Thus couples that are psychologically comfortable with oral–genital stimulation often find both giving and receiving it to be highly pleasurable. Oral–genital contact can produce pleasure, arousal, or orgasm. As one woman stated:

> I think that men put too much emphasis on a woman coming from "regular sex." A lot of women I know, including myself, have only experienced orgasm (aside from masturbation) through oral sex. I thoroughly enjoy getting and giving oral sex. I love the sounds, sights, smells, and tastes. (Authors' files)

Oral–genital stimulation can be done individually (by one partner to the other) or simultaneously. Some people prefer oral sex individually, because they can focus on either giving or receiving, as in ⊙ **Figure 8.5**. Others especially enjoy the mutuality of simultaneous oral–genital sex. Simultaneous stimulation is sometimes referred to as 69 because of the body positions suggested by that number (⊙ **Figure 8.6**). Besides the position illustrated in the figure, a variety of

⊙ **Figure 8.5** During oral sex one partner can give full attention to the experience of giving while the other can enjoy receiving.

○ **Figure 8.6** Simultaneous oral–genital stimulation in the 69 position.

**Cunnilingus** Oral stimulation of the vulva.

**Fellatio** Oral stimulation of the penis.

! Sexual Health

other positions can be used, such as lying side-by-side and using a thigh for a pillow. Because arousal becomes intense during mutual oral–genital stimulation, partners need to be careful not to suck or bite too hard.

Different terminology is used to describe oral–genital stimulation of women and oral–genital stimulation of men. **Cunnilingus** (kuh-ni-LIN-gus) is oral stimulation of the vulva: the clitoris, labia minora, vestibule, and vaginal opening. Many women find the warmth, softness, and moistness of the partner's lips and tongue highly pleasurable and effective in producing sexual arousal or orgasm. Variations of stimulation include rapid or slow circular or back-and-forth tongue movement on the clitoral area, sucking the clitoris or labia minora, and thrusting the tongue into the vaginal opening. Some women are especially aroused by simultaneous manual stimulation of the vagina and oral stimulation of the clitoral area.

**Fellatio** (fuh-LAY-shee-oh) is oral stimulation of the penis and scrotum. Options for oral stimulation of the male genitals include gently or vigorously licking and sucking the glans, the frenulum, and the penile shaft; and licking or enclosing a testicle in the mouth. Some men enjoy combined oral stimulation of the glans and manual stroking of the penile shaft, testes, or anus. Among homosexual men fellatio is the most common mode of sexual expression (Lever, 1994).

It is usually best for the partner performing fellatio to control the other's movements by grasping the penis manually below her or his lips to prevent it from going farther into the mouth than is comfortable. This helps avoid a gag reflex. Also, too vigorous thrusting could result in lacerations of the partner's lips as he or she attempts to protect the penis from his or her teeth.

Couples differ in their preference for including ejaculation into the mouth as a part of male oral–genital stimulation. Many find it acceptable, and some find it exciting. For those who do not want oral sex to include ejaculation into the mouth, a couple can agree beforehand that the one being stimulated will indicate when he is close to orgasm and withdraw from his partner's mouth. For couples who are comfortable with ejaculating into the mouth, the ejaculate can be swallowed or not, according to one's preference. The flavor of ejaculate varies from person to person and is influenced by the factors described in ○ **Table 8.3**. ■

In the United States, differences in oral sex experience and attitudes

○ **TABLE 8.3**    **Factors Affecting Taste of Ejaculate**

| Taste | Source of Taste |
| --- | --- |
| Bitter | Coffee, alcohol, cigarettes, and marijuana (can also be due to urinary or prostate infections). |
| Sharp | Red meats, greasy foods, dairy products, chocolate, asparagus, broccoli, or spinach. |
| Moderate | Having none of the bitter factors and only one or two factors from the Sharp group. |
| Mild | A vegetarian diet. Fruit (especially pineapple and apples), parsley, celery, spearmint, and peppermint. |
| Sweet | Naturally fermented beverages or someone who is diabetic or borderline diabetic. |

SOURCE: Hamilton (2002).

exist among population segments, as shown in the following Sexuality and Diversity discussion.

## SEXUALITY AND DIVERSITY

### Oral Sex Experiences Among American Men and Women

The National Health and Social Life Survey (Laumann et al., 1994) questioned men and women of different ethnic, educational, and religious backgrounds to compare their experiences of oral sex. The findings are summarized in ○ **Table 8.4**. In general, white Americans (both men and women) have the highest level of experience with oral sex, followed by Hispanic Americans; African Americans having the lowest rate of oral sex. However, socioeconomic level is more important than race. A study comparing African American and white American men of matched socioeconomic status found similar rates of oral sex experience (Samuels, 1997).

**○ TABLE 8.4** — Oral Sex Experiences from the National Health and Social Life Survey

| | Performed Oral Sex (%)[a] | | Received Oral Sex (%)[a] | |
|---|---|---|---|---|
| | Men | Women | Men | Women |
| **Race** | | | | |
| White | 81 | 75 | 81 | 78 |
| African American | 51 | 34 | 66 | 49 |
| Hispanic American | 71 | 60 | 73 | 64 |
| **Education** | | | | |
| Less than high school | 59 | 41 | 61 | 50 |
| High school graduate | 75 | 60 | 77 | 67 |
| Any college | 81 | 78 | 84 | 82 |
| **Religion** | | | | |
| Conservative Protestant | 67 | 56 | 70 | 65 |
| Other Protestant | 82 | 74 | 83 | 77 |
| Catholic | 82 | 74 | 82 | 77 |
| Other or none | 79 | 78 | 83 | 83 |

[a]Rounded to nearest percentage point.

SOURCE: Laumann et al. (1994, p. 141).

Education level usually relates to socioeconomic status, and from Kinsey's research to that of today, it is clear that people with more formal education are considerably more likely than less-educated people to have oral sex. Higher education makes a greater difference in the percentage of women who have had oral sex than it is does for men. Another study noted attitudinal differences between women regarding oral sex: Career women were more likely than homemakers to consider oral sex a "normal" act (65% to 43%) (Janus & Janus, 1993).

Some people have qualms about oral–genital stimulation. They may believe that their own or the partner's genitals are unattractive. Although routine thorough washing of the genitals with soap and water is adequate for cleanliness, some people think the genitals are unsanitary because they are close to the urinary opening and anus. Another reason some heterosexual people object to oral sex stems from the belief that it is a homosexual act—even when experienced by heterosexual couples. Although many gays and lesbians engage in oral sex, the activity is not homosexual by nature. Rather, its homosexuality or heterosexuality depends on the sexes of the partners involved.

Despite these negative attitudes, oral–genital contact is quite common and has become even more so since Kinsey's studies. A recent study found that the meaning and role of oral–genital sex have also changed greatly over time. For example, most adults believe that oral sex is more intimate than intercourse, whereas most teens believe the opposite (Gelperin, 2005). Furthermore, women born before 1950 almost never experienced oral sex in high school or before marriage. Oral sex occurred after considerable commitment and after the couple had been engaging in intercourse for some time. Recent research of high school students has found that about 50% of teenagers have had oral sex—with young men and women giving and receiving equally (Mosher et al., 2005). In fact, teens are more likely to have oral sex than intercourse and have had more oral sex partners than intercourse partners (Halpern-Felsher et al., 2006). Frequently, teens use oral sex as a strategy to avoid intercourse and technically maintain their virginity (Ellison, 2000).

Some individuals may engage in oral sex instead of intercourse because they believe they cannot contract HIV (the virus that causes AIDS) through oral sex. However, because oral–genital contact often involves an exchange of bodily fluids, it does pose the risk of transmitting or contracting HIV. This virus can enter the bloodstream through small breaks in the skin of the mouth or genitals. Although the risk of transmitting HIV through oral–genital contact is low, only monogamous partners who are both free of the virus are completely safe when engaging in such behavior. (We discuss further precautions against transmitting HIV in Chapter 15.) ■

## ❿ Anal Stimulation

An estimated 25% of all adults have experienced anal intercourse at least once (Seidman & Rieder, 1994), and anal intercourse may be growing more common among young people. A study of 813 women enrolled in a college women's health course found that 32% had engaged in anal intercourse (Flannery et al., 2003). Among gay men, anal stimulation is less common than oral sex and mutual masturbation (Lever, 1994).

The anus has dense groups of nerve endings that can respond erotically. Some women report orgasmic response from anal intercourse (Masters & Johnson, 1970), and heterosexual and homosexual men often experience orgasm from stimulation during penetration. Individuals and couples also use anal stimulation for arousal and variety during other sexual behaviors. Manually stroking the outside of the anal opening or inserting one or more fingers into the anus can be pleasurable for some people during masturbation or partner sex.

Because the anus contains delicate tissues, special care needs to be taken during anal stimulation. A nonirritating lubricant and gentle penetration are necessary to avoid discomfort or injury. It is helpful to use lubrication on both the anus and the penis or whatever object is being inserted. The partner receiving anal insertion can bear down (as for a bowel movement) to relax the sphincter. The partner inserting needs to go slowly and gently, keeping the penis or other object tilted to follow the direction of the colon (Morin, 1981). It is essential for sex toys or other objects used for anal stimulation to have a larger base than tip; otherwise an object can slip past the anal opening and become trapped by the anal sphincter, requiring a trip to the emergency room to remove the object.

Important health risks are associated with anal intercourse. Heterosexual couples should never have vaginal intercourse directly following anal intercourse, because bacteria in the anus can cause vaginal infections. Oral stimulation of the anus, known as **anilingus** (or, in slang, "rimming"), is extremely risky; various intestinal infections, hepatitis, and sexually transmitted diseases can be contracted or spread through oral–anal contact, even with precautions of thorough washing. Careful use of a dental dam helps prevent transmission of bacteria and viruses.

**Anilingus** Oral stimulation of the anus.

Anal intercourse is one of the riskiest of all sexual behaviors associated with transmission of HIV, particularly for the receptive partner. For women the risk of contracting this virus through unprotected anal intercourse is greater than the risk of contraction through unprotected vaginal intercourse (Silverman & Gross, 1997). Heterosexual and gay male couples who wish to reduce their risk of transmitting or contracting this deadly virus should refrain from anal intercourse or use a condom and practice withdrawal before ejaculation. In Chapter 15 we more fully discuss precautions to avoid transmission of HIV. ■

Figure 8.7 Man-above, face-to-face intercourse position.

## Coitus and Coital Positions

A heterosexual couple can choose a wide range of positions for penile–vaginal intercourse, or coitus. ⊙ Table 8.5 on page 230 shows college students' three favorite positions. Many people have a favorite position yet enjoy others, as shown in ⊙ Figures 8.7 through 8.10. A 30-year-old man stated:

> Different intercourse positions usually express and evoke particular emotions for me. Being on top, I enjoy feeling aggressive; when on the bottom, I experience a special kind of receptive sensuality. In the side-by-side position, I easily feel gentle and intimate. I like sharing all these dimensions of myself with my lover. (Authors' files)

Each position provides various opportunities for physical and emotional expression. Changes in health, age, weight, pregnancy, or partners can create different preferences. In some positions, one person has greater freedom to initiate and control the tempo, angle, and style of movement to create arousing stimulation. In other positions, mutual control of the rhythm of thrusting works well. Some positions—

⊙ Figure 8.8 The woman-above intercourse position.

**Figure 8.9** Face-to-face, side-lying inter-course position.

such as the woman above, sitting upright—lend themselves to manual stimulation of the clitoris during intercourse. Many couples like a position that allows partners to make eye contact and see each other's bodies. The face-to-face, side-lying position can provide a particularly relaxed connection, with each partner having one hand free to caress the other's body. Rear entry can be a good position during pregnancy, when pressure against the woman's abdomen is uncomfortable. Intercourse can occur with or without orgasm for one or both partners.

Beyond options for position, cooperation and consideration are important, particularly at **intromission** (entry of the penis into the vagina). Often the woman can best guide her partner's penis into her vagina by moving her body or using her hand. If the penis slips out of the vagina, which can occur fairly easily in some positions, it is usually easiest for the woman to lend a helping hand to guide the penis back into the vagina.

**Intromission** Insertion of the penis into the vagina

**TABLE 8.5** — College Students Answer the Question "What Is Your Favorite Intercourse Position?"

|  | Men (%) | Women (%) |
|---|---|---|
| Man on top | 25 | 48 |
| Woman on top | 45 | 33 |
| Doggie style | 25 | 15 |

Source: Elliott & Brantley (1997).

## Intercourse the Tantric Way

The concept of male orgasm as the ultimate point of heterosexual intercourse is alien to concepts and practices of Tantric sex (Yarian & Anders, 2006). Margo Anand, in her book *The Art of Sexual Ecstasy* (1991), explains that Tantra was an ancient Eastern path of spiritual enlightenment, begun in India around 5000 BCE. Tantric thought holds that an erotic act of love between a god and a goddess created the world. According to this viewpoint, sexual expression can become a form of spiritual meditation and a path of deep connection (Kuriansky & Simonson, 2005).

In Tantric sex the male learns to control and delay his own orgasm and to redirect the sexual energy throughout his and his partner's body. Before intercourse, lovers usually slowly and erotically stimulate each other. When both partners are ready for intercourse, the woman guides gentle, relaxed penetration. The couple initially keeps thrusting to a minimum, generating energy by subtle inner movements, such as contractions of the muscles surrounding the opening of the vagina. The couple

**Figure 8.10** The rear-entry intercourse position can be a comfortable option during pregnancy.

Tantric sex: the Infinite cycle.

harmonize their breathing, finding a common rhythm of inhaling and exhaling, while visualizing the warmth, arousal, and energy in the genitals moving upward in their bodies. Movements can become active and playful, always slowing or stopping to relax before the man experiences orgasm. The partners welcome feelings of profound intimacy and ecstasy, often looking into each other's eyes, creating a "deep relaxation of the heart" (Anand, 1991).

# SUMMARY

## Celibacy

- Celibacy means not engaging in sexual activities. Celibacy can be complete (avoiding masturbation and interpersonal sexual contact) or partial (including masturbation). In many circumstances celibacy is a positive way of expressing one's sexuality.

## Erotic Dreams and Fantasy

- Erotic dreams often accompany sexual arousal and orgasm during sleep. Erotic fantasies serve many functions: They can enhance sexual arousal, help overcome anxiety or compensate for a negative situation, allow rehearsal of new sexual experiences, permit tolerable expression of forbidden wishes, and provide relief from gender-role expectations.

## Masturbation

- Masturbation is self-stimulation of the genitals, intended to produce sexual pleasure.
- Past attitudes toward masturbation have been highly condemnatory. However, the meaning and purposes of masturbation are currently being more positively reevaluated.
- Masturbation is a behavior that tends to continue throughout adulthood, although its frequency varies with age and sex.

## Sexual Expression: The Importance of Context

- The meaning of sexual expression can vary from a profound sense of love for self and other to exploitation and abuse. The Maltz hierarchy delineates six levels.

## Kissing and Touching

- The entire body's surface is a sensory organ, and kissing and touching are basic forms of communication and shared intimacy.
- Preferences as to the tempo, pressure, and location of manual genital stimulation vary from person to person. A lubricant, a nonirritating lotion, or saliva on the genitals can enhance pleasure.

## Oral–Genital Stimulation

- Oral–genital contact has become more common in recent years. Qualms about oral–genital stimulation usually stem from false ideas that it is unsanitary or solely a homosexual act or from religious beliefs that it is immoral.
- Cunnilingus is oral stimulation of the vulva; fellatio is oral stimulation of the male genitals.

## Anal Stimulation

- Couples engage in anal stimulation for arousal, orgasm, and variety. Careful hygiene is necessary to avoid introducing anal bacteria into the vagina. To reduce the chances of transmitting the AIDS virus, couples should avoid anal intercourse or use a condom and practice withdrawal before ejaculation.

## Coitus and Coital Positions

- The diversity of coital positions offers potential variety during intercourse. The man-above, woman-above, side-by-side, and rear-entry positions are common.
- Tantric sex emphasizes intense, prolonged sexual intimacy.

## ◗ Suggested Readings

**Abbott, Elizabeth** (2000). *A History of Celibacy: From Athena to Elizabeth I, Leonardo da Vinci, Florence Nightingale, Gandhi, and Cher*. New York: Scribner. An illuminating and witty account of the potential and significance of celibacy.

**Anand, Margo** (1991). *The Art of Sexual Ecstasy*. Los Angeles: Tarcher. A comprehensive exploration of principles and practice of Tantric sex.

**Boss, Suzie, and Wendy Maltz** (2001). *Private Thoughts: Exploring the Power of Women's Sexual Fantasies*. Novato, CA: New World Library. A description of women's fantasy styles, the functions of fantasy, and steps to understanding and overcoming troubling fantasies.

**Joannides, Paul** (1996). *The Guide to Getting It On!* Waldport, OR: Goofy Foot Press. A humorous and instructive guide emphasizing nitty-gritty techniques and the perspective that "it doesn't matter what you've got in your pants if there's nothing in your brain to connect it to" (p. 1).

**Newman, Felice** (1999). *The Whole Lesbian Sex Book: A Passionate Guide for All of Us*. San Francisco: Cleis Press. A comprehensive sex manual designed for lesbians and suitable for heterosexual women who want to enhance their sexuality.

**Silverstein, Charles, and Felice Picano** (1993). *The New Joy of Gay Sex*. New York: Perennial. An uninhibited sex manual, including safer-sex practices.

## ◗ Web Resources

**CengageNOW Web Site**
Go to **academic.cengage.com** to link to practice quiz questions, interactive activities, Internet links, critical thinking exercises, discussion forums, and more. You can also access sites from the Wadsworth Psychology Study Center (**academic.cengage.com/psychology**) or you can connect directly to the following sites:

**The Celibate FAQ**
Frequently asked questions (FAQs) and answers about choosing a celibate lifestyle are offered at this site. Examples include how to tell people you are celibate and the advantages and disadvantages of celibacy.

**Healthy Sex**
This Web site, developed by the respected author and sex therapist Wendy Maltz, promotes a healthy attitude toward sex based on caring, respect, and safety. Partner communication, sexual intimacy, and sexual fantasy are among the topics explored.

**Good Vibrations**
This is the Web site for the Good Vibrations Store, which sells sex toys, videos, and books.

**Go Ask Alice**
This Web site provides lots of information about sexual behavior.

**Fallwell**
This site confronts homophobic religious dogma.

***Our Sexuality* Book Companion Web Site** academic.cengage.com/psychology/crooks Visit your book companion Web site where you will find flash cards, practice quizzes, Internet links, and more to help you study.

**Just what you need to know NOW!**
Spend time on what you need to master rather than on information you already have learned. Take a pretest for this chapter, and CengageNOW will generate a personalized study plan based on your results. The study plan will identify the topics you need to review and direct you to online resources to help you master those topics. You can then take a post-test to help you determine the concepts you have mastered and what you will still need to work on. Try it out! Go to **academic.cengage.com/login** to sign in with an access code or to purchase access to this product.

**InfoTrac College Edition Online Library**
Sign in to **academic.cengage.com/login** or visit your free book companion Web site at **academic.cengage.com/psychology/crooks** to access InfoTrac College Edition, an online searchable library that includes a multitude of journals, many specific to human sexuality. These journals include *Archives of Sexual Behavior; Archives of Sexual Health Behavior; Canadian Journal of Human Sexuality; Hispanic Journal of the Behavioral Sciences; Journal of Cross-Cultural Psychology; Journal of Physical Education, Recreation, and Dance; Journal of Sex Research;* and *Sex Roles*.

# Sexual Orientations

- **A Continuum of Sexual Orientations**

  Approximately what percentage of men and women are exclusively homosexual? What percentage have had sex with another member of the same sex?

  What are the four different types of bisexuality?

  What percentage of people are asexual?

- **What Determines Sexual Orientation?**

  What psychosocial theories have been advanced to explain sexual orientation?

  What biological factors influence sexual orientation?

- **Societal Attitudes**

  How have Western religious views and the views of medical and psychological professionals changed concerning homosexuality?

  What are some of the indications of homophobia?

  What causes homophobia and hate crimes?

- **Lifestyles**

  What is the "gay lifestyle"?

  What has research shown to be the effects on children of being reared by lesbian mothers?

  What steps are involved in coming out as a lesbian or a gay man?

- **The Gay Rights Movement**

  What was the Stonewall incident, and what impact did it have on the gay community?

  What are some of the decriminalization, antidiscrimination, and positive rights successes and goals of the gay rights movement?

*My life as a young lesbian was very different from the lesbian youth I see today. No one I knew talked about homosexuality, and I dated boys because my friends did. I was in my early thirties before my first sexual experience with a woman, but even that blissful experience didn't make me think of myself as a lesbian. It was several more years before I identified myself as a lesbian and had gay friends other than my partner. Today young lesbians have lots of positive information and images to help them understand and accept themselves. But they also face intense negativity from conservative reactions to gay rights. In my era the fact that homosexuality was so "hush-hush" gave us considerable privacy and protection by being overlooked. We never confronted the harassment, violence, or antigay activism that is now part of the picture. (Authors' files)*

**Homosexual** A person whose primary erotic, psychological, emotional, and social orientation is toward members of the same sex.

**Gay** A homosexual person, typically a homosexual male.

**Lesbian** A homosexual female.

Many people think of homosexuality as sexual contact between individuals of the same sex. However, this definition is incomplete. It does not take into account two important dimensions: the context within which the sexual contact is experienced and the feelings and perceptions of the people involved. Nor does it encompass all the meanings of the word **homosexual,** which can refer to erotic attraction, sexual behavior, emotional attachment, and a definition of self (Diamond, 2003b; Eliason & Morgan, 1998). The following definition incorporates a broader spectrum of elements: A homosexual person is an individual "whose primary erotic, psychological, emotional, and social interest is in a member of the same sex, even though those interests may not be overtly expressed" (Martin & Lyon, 1972, p. 1). ⊙ **Figure 9.1** indicates at what age individuals first feel same-sex attraction.

A common synonym for homosexual is **gay.** Gay was initially used as a code word between homosexuals, and it has moved into popular usage to describe homosexual men and women as well as the social and political concerns related to homosexual orientation. It has also come to be used, mainly by teens, as a negative label, as in "That is so gay!" (Caldwell, 2003b). Homosexual women are often referred to as **lesbians**. Pejorative words such as *faggot, fairy, homo, queer, lezzie,* and *dyke* have traditionally been used to demean homosexuality. However, in certain gay and lesbian subcultures, some people use these terms with each other in positive or humorous ways (Bryant & Demian, 1998).

Many men and women born after 1970 call themselves *queer* and refer to *queer culture* to diffuse the negativity of the word and to blur the boundaries between subgroups of gay men, lesbians, bisexuals, and all variations of transgendered people belonging to the "queer nation" (Vary, 2006). Members of "Generation Q" see themselves as different, even alienated, from lesbians and gay men over 30, partly because of their unique history of coming of age during AIDS activism (Nichols, 2000).

In this chapter, we begin with a discussion of the continuum of homosexuality and heterosexuality.

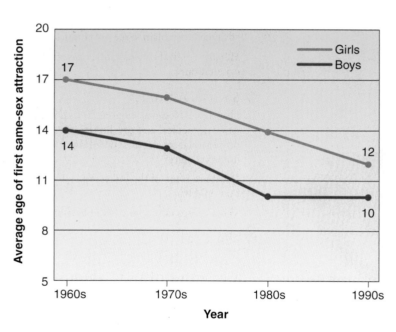

⊙ **Figure 9.1** Gay and lesbian teens today recall first feeling attraction to the same sex 4 or 5 years earlier than teens in the 1960s.

**Sexual orientation** Sexual attraction to one's own sex (homosexual), to the other sex (heterosexual), to both sexes (bisexual), or lack of sexual interest to either sex (asexual).

## ⊙ A Continuum of Sexual Orientations

*Homosexuality, bisexuality, heterosexuality,* and *asexuality* are words that identify one's **sexual orientation**—that is, to which of the sexes one is attracted. Attraction to same-sex partners is a homosexual orientation, and attraction to other-sex partners is a heterosexual orientation, also referred to as *straight*. **Bisexuality** refers to degrees of attraction to both same- and other-sex partners. Because sexual orientation is only one aspect of a person's life, we use these three terms as descriptive adjectives rather than as nouns that label one's total identity.

**Bisexuality** Sexual attraction to both men and women.

In our society we tend to make clear-cut distinctions between homosexuality and heterosexuality. Actually, the delineation is not so precise. A relatively small percentage of people consider themselves exclusively homosexual, and over 90% of people in the United States think of themselves as exclusively heterosexual. These groups represent the opposite ends of a broad spectrum. Individuals between the ends of the spectrum exhibit various mixtures of feelings and/or experience. For example, a person who sometimes fantasizes about same-sex partners during masturbation, has pleasurable sexual dreams about same-sex partners, but has only had sexual experiences with other-sex partners is somewhere between the ends of the spectrum (Epstein, 2006).

○ **InfoTrac Search Words**

● Bisexuality

○ **Figure 9.2** shows a seven-point continuum that Alfred Kinsey devised in his analysis of sexual orientations in American society (Kinsey et al., 1948). The scale ranges from 0 (exclusive contact with and erotic attraction to the other sex) to 6 (exclusive contact with and attraction to the same sex). In between are various degrees of homosexual and heterosexual orientation; Category 3 represents equal homosexual and heterosexual attraction and experience.

○ **Figure 9.2** Kinsey's continuum of sexual orientation, based on both feelings of attraction and sexual behavior.

| 0 | 1 | 2 | 3 | 4 | 5 | 6 |
|---|---|---|---|---|---|---|
| Exclusively heterosexual with no homosexual | Predominantly heterosexual, only incidentally homosexual | Predominantly heterosexual but more than incidentally homosexual | Equally homosexual and heterosexual | Predominantly homosexual but more than incidentally heterosexual | Predominantly homosexual but incidentally heterosexual | Exclusively homosexual with no heterosexual |

SOURCE: Adapted from Kinsey et al. (1948, p. 638).

**? Critical Thinking Question**

Where would you place yourself on the Kinsey scale?

The patterns in which people fall on the Kinsey scale vary by biological sex. Men, both homosexual and heterosexual, typically occupy the far ends of the scale. Women also occupy the ends but are more likely than men to be found on the scale between Categories 2 and 5. Recent research has found that women who identify themselves as heterosexual are 27 times more likely than heterosexual men to express moderate or higher attraction to their own sex (Lippa, 2006).

A limitation of the Kinsey scale is the impression it gives of a fixed, static sexual orientation, when in fact people's placement on the scale can vary at different times in their lives. For example, because the scale is based on both feelings of attraction and behavior, someone who is bisexual would be on different sides of the center of the scale, depending on whether his or her current partner was male or female. Sexual orientation is best evaluated by observing patterns over a life span rather than at any given time (Fox, 1990).

## Homosexuality

According to the Kinsey data, the exclusively homosexual category comprises 2% of women and 4% of men. Kinsey's estimates were made some time ago, however, and they have been criticized because of the way the data were collected. The more recent National Health and Social Life Survey (NHSLS) found somewhat lower statistics: 1.4% of women and 2.8% of men identify themselves as homosexual. However, another question that asked subjects if they had had sex with another person of the same sex since age 18 found that about 5% of men and 4% of women had done so (Laumann et al., 1994). In The Global Sex Survey, an average of 12% of respondents from 41 countries said they had had at least one same-sex experience (Durex, 2006).

## Bisexuality

A useful definition of bisexuality is that a bisexual person can "enjoy and engage in sexual activity with members of both sexes, or recognizes a desire to do so" (MacDonald, 1981). As stated earlier, more women than men are bisexual, and women with

**?** Critical Thinking Question

Why, do you think, are women more likely to be bisexual than men?

high sex drives are most likely to be bisexual. Data from over 3,600 research participants found that high sex drive in heterosexual women is associated with increased sexual attraction to both men and women (Lippa, 2006). The higher a woman's sex drive is, the more she feels sexual desire for both sexes. In contrast, high sex drive in straight men, gay men, and lesbians is associated with increased sexual attraction only to one sex or the other. These findings are consistent across age groups and have been replicated across many regions of the world, including Latin America, Australia, India, and western Europe. The universality of the results indicates a likely biological contribution to the differences.

Many societies' greater tolerance for same-sex affection between women than between men may also be a factor. When female celebrities such as Angelina Jolie and Madonna have same-sex experiences, it typically enhances their fame and marketability (Owen, 2006). For male celebrities to disclose having such experiences would most likely damage their career.

## Types of Bisexuality

Several different types of bisexuality exist: a real orientation, a transitory orientation, a transitional orientation, and homosexual denial (Fox, 1990; Ross et al., 2003). Bisexuality as a real orientation means that some people feel attracted to both sexes. An individual with this orientation might or might not be sexually active with more than one partner at a time but would continue to be capable of feeling attracted to both sexes (Kinnish et al., 2005).

Rates of bisexuality among U.S. women have nearly tripled in the past decade: 11% of women reported having had at least one sexual experience with another woman in their lifetime, up from 4% a decade earlier. Some college women view their same-sex experiences as temporary sexual experiments before they graduate and marry men; this pattern is common enough to have its own label, *LUG*s, or lesbians until graduation (Kennedy, 2006). In contrast, men have not shown much change: 6% of men reported having had at least one sexual experience with another man, only 1% more than did 10 years ago (Jones, 2006). Men tend to consider themselves dichotomously as gay or straight, but women are somewhat more apt to say, "It depends on who I'm with" (Bailey et al., 1993b). One study found that 58% of women in lesbian couples reported choosing the orientation of their current sexual relationship. Although they could enjoy sex with men, they preferred lesbian relationships and characterized them as less gender-role stereotyped and more intimate (Rosenbluth, 1997).

Bisexual behavior can also be transitory—a temporary involvement by people who are actually heterosexual or homosexual (Dykes, 2000). Transitory same-sex behavior can occur in single-sex boarding schools and prisons. However, the people involved consider themselves heterosexual even when involved in same-sex behavior, and they resume heterosexual relationships when opportunities for such are again available (Kalb & Murr, 2006). Furthermore, some prostitutes and male hustlers may do business with either sex and yet be exclusively involved in heterosexual or homosexual relationships in their personal lives.

Bisexuality can also be a transitional state, in which a person is changing from one orientation to another. This person will remain in the new orientation, as illustrated in the following account:

*I had led a traditional life with a husband, two kids, and community activities. My best friend and I were very active in the PTA together. Much to our surprise, we fell in love.*

Britney Spears and Madonna include erotic kisses in their 2003 MTV Video Music Awards performance.

*We were initially secretive about our sexual relationship and continued our marital lives, but then we both divorced our husbands and moved away to start a life together. The best way I can describe being with her is that life is now like a color TV, instead of a black-and-white. (Authors' files)*

The transition from bisexuality to homosexuality may be most common during adolescence. One study found that about half of youths who initially identified themselves as bisexual considered themselves gay or lesbian 5 years later. In contrast, young people who identified themselves as gay or lesbian maintained that identity over time (Rosario et al., 2006).

Less often, people initially identify themselves as lesbian or gay, then become involved in other-sex relationships. It can sometimes be challenging to develop a heterosexual relationship after having had a gay or lesbian identity. For example, JoAnn Loulan, a longtime lesbian activist and author of *Lesbian Sex*, received a great deal of negative reaction from other lesbians, including being branded a "hasbian," when she fell in love with and became involved with a man (White, 2003). The transition from same-sex to other-sex relationships most often occurs with women. In one study of 80 women age 18 to 25, the subjects were sexually involved with other women when the research began. Within 5 years, 25% of the women were in heterosexual relationships. Although their identity and choice of sex of partners had changed, their feelings of attraction to other women remained the same (Diamond, 2003a).

Finally, bisexuality can be an attempt to deny exclusive homosexual interests and to avoid the full stigma of homosexual identity (MacDonald, 1981). For example, a number of people marry to maintain a facade of heterosexuality but continue to have strong homosexual desires and secretive homosexual contacts, as exemplified in the heartbreak of the men and their wives in the movie *Brokeback Mountain* (Butler, 2006). Marrying despite having a homosexual orientation is likely to be much more common the more stigmatized and taboo homosexuality is. For example, although prejudice against homosexuality has lessened slightly in China, nearly 80% of homosexual males there are either married or intend to marry (Cui, 2005).

Gay men and lesbians sometimes view the bisexual person as someone who really is homosexual but lacks the courage to identify himself or herself as such (McBride, 2005). Self-identified bisexual individuals are sometimes met with ambivalence and suspicion and are often pressured by heterosexual or homosexual people to adhere to one orientation (Diamond, 2003a; Grannis, 2005).

## Asexuality

Asexuality, feeling no sexual attraction to either sex, has rarely been studied. One national probability study of 18,000 people in Britain found that 1% of individuals were asexual (Bogaert, 2004). Most asexual men and women have been asexual throughout their lives.. Although more women than men were identified as asexual, the study found several factors associated with both sexes. These factors include short stature and health problems. Also, asexual women had their first menstrual period later than other women. Such factors could indicate a biological basis for asexuality. However, asexual individuals of both sexes scored lower than other individuals on demographic variables of education level and socioeconomic status, and the short stature as well as health problems could be consequences of disadvantaged economic conditions.

According to the Asexual Visibility and Education Network, asexuality is a sexual orientation, not a choice. Asexual individuals lack sexual attraction toward others, but they have a range of interest in friendships, affection, and partnerships. Some masturbate but feel no interest in partnered sexual expression (Jay, 2005).

## ▶ What Determines Sexual Orientation?

A variety of theories have attempted to explain the origins of sexual orientation, particularly homosexuality. Considerable research has been done over the years, much of the findings are contradictory, and still no definitive scientific answers exist. In the next few pages, we consider common notions about the causes of homosexuality and evaluate research that has attempted to substantiate these notions.

## Psychosocial Theories

Psychosocial explanations of the development of a homosexual orientation relate to life incidents, parenting patterns, or psychological attributes of the individual. Bell and his colleagues (1981) conducted the most comprehensive study about the development of sexual orientation. They used a sample of 979 homosexual men and women matched to a control group of 477 heterosexual people. All research subjects were asked questions about their childhood, adolescence, and sexual practices during 4-hour face-to-face interviews. Bell then used sophisticated statistical techniques to analyze possible causal factors in the development of homosexuality or heterosexuality. We cite this research frequently throughout this section because of its excellent methodology.

### The "By Default" Myth

Some people believe that unhappy heterosexual experiences cause a person to become homosexual. Statements such as "All a lesbian needs is a good lay" or "He just needs to find the right woman" reflect the notion that homosexuality is a default choice for people who have not had satisfactory heterosexual experiences and relationships. Contrary to this myth, Bell's analysis of the data indicated that homosexual orientation reflects neither a lack of heterosexual experience nor a history of negative heterosexual experiences (Bell et al., 1981). Bell and his colleagues found that homosexual and heterosexual groups did not differ in their frequency of dating during high school, but fewer homosexual subjects reported that they enjoyed heterosexual dating. Lesbianism is sometimes assumed to be due to fear or distrust of men rather than to an attraction toward women. The illogic of this argument is clear if we turn it around and say that female heterosexuality is caused by a fear and distrust of women.

### The Seduction Myth

Some people believe that young women and men become homosexual because they have been seduced by older homosexual people or because they have "caught" it from someone else—particularly a well-liked and respected teacher who is homosexual. People who believe that gay men and lesbians should not teach in schools—about 36% of Americans—probably believe in the seduction and contagion myths (Leland, 2000b). Contrary to these myths, research indicates that sexual orientation is most often established before school age and that most homosexual people have their first sexual experiences with someone close to their own age (Bell et al., 1981).

### Freud's Theory

Another prevalent theory has to do with certain patterns in a person's family background. Psychoanalytic theory implicated both childhood experiences and relationships with parents. Sigmund Freud (1953 [1905]) maintained that one's relationship with one's father and mother was crucial. He believed that in "normal" development, we all pass through a "homoerotic" phase. Boys, he argued, could become fixated at this homosexual phase if they had a poor relationship with their father and an overly close relationship with their mother; the same thing might happen to a woman if she developed envy for the penis (Black, 1994). Later clinical research attempted to confirm this hypothesis (Bieber et al., 1962). Although some gays and lesbians have this dynamic in their family backgrounds, many homosexual individuals do not, and plenty of heterosexual people were reared in families where this pattern prevailed. Bell and his colleagues (1981) concluded that no particular phenomenon of family life could be singled out as "especially consequential for either homosexual or heterosexual development" (p. 190)—a conclusion supported by additional research (Epstein, 2006; Savin-Williams, 2000).

## Biological Theories

Researchers have explored a number of areas to establish biological causes for sexual orientation, and the most convincing evidence has to do with genetic factors and prenatal hormonal influences.

## Genetic Factors

One line of research has examined the possibility that genetic factors contribute to homosexuality. Several studies have found that male and female homosexuality is strongly *familial*, which is to say that it appears to run in families (Bailey & Bell, 1993; Bailey & Benishay, 1993; Pattatucci & Hamer, 1995). The mere fact that homosexuality tends to be familial does not necessarily mean genetic factors are the cause; the psychosocial influences of a common family environment could just as easily be involved.

Researchers often use twin studies to gain a better understanding of the relative influences of social environment (nurture) and genetic makeup (nature). Identical twins originate from a single fertilized ovum that divides into two separate fetuses with identical genetic codes. Therefore, any differences between the twins must be due to environmental influences. In contrast, fraternal twins occur when a woman's ovaries release two ova and each ovum is fertilized by a different sperm cell. Because fraternal twins result from the fertilization of two separate eggs, their genetic makeup is no more alike than that of any other siblings. Physical and behavioral differences between fraternal twins may be due to genetic factors, environmental influences, or a combination of the two. When identical twins are more alike (*concordant*) than same-sex fraternal twins in a particular trait, we can assume that the trait has a strong genetic basis. Conversely, when a trait shows a comparable degree of concordance in both types of twins, we can reasonably assume that environment is exerting the greater influence.

The most recent twin study recruited subjects from a twin registry in Australia (Bailey et al., 2000). Over 1,500 same-sex identical and fraternal male and female twin pairs were included in this study. Each participant completed an anonymous questionnaire that addressed broad areas of sexuality, including items pertaining to sexual orientation. Using a strict criterion for determining homosexual orientation, the researchers found a concordance rate (the percentage of pairs in which both twins are homosexual) of 20% among identical male twins and 0% among pairs of male fraternal twins. The corresponding concordance rates for female identical and fraternal pairs were 24% and 10.5%, respectively (Bailey et al., 2000). The markedly higher concordance rates for identical twin pairs provide strong evidence of a genetic component to sexual orientation in some individuals. In the Spotlight on Research box on the next page, we discuss research that indicates the influence of various factors during the prenatal period of development.

## Gender Nonconformity

Other evidence for a biological predisposition toward homosexuality comes from the strong link between adult homosexuality and **gender nonconformity** as a child (Bailey et al., 2000; Ellis et al., 2005). Gender nonconformity is the extent to which an individual differs from stereotypical characteristics of masculinity or femininity during childhood; it is measured by asking respondents how traditionally masculine or feminine they were as children and how much they enjoyed conventional boys' or girls' activities.

Researchers have found that male and female homosexual adults are more likely to have experienced gender nonconformity during childhood than heterosexual adults are (Bailey & Zucker, 1995; Green, 1987; Lippa, 2002). Half of homosexual males and only one quarter of heterosexual males did not conform to a typical "masculine" identity pattern, whereas about four fifths of homosexual females and two thirds of heterosexual females were not highly "feminine" during childhood (Bell et al., 1981). Similar patterns have been documented cross-culturally. Bell and his colleagues speculated, "If there is a biological basis for homosexuality, it probably accounts for gender nonconformity as well as for sexual orientation" (1981, p. 217).

Marinethemes.com/Stephen Wong

Two male whales rub their penises together as one example of homosexual behavior in animals. The world's first museum exhibition about homosexuality among animals opened in 2006 at the Oslo Natural History Museum in Norway. Male and female homosexuality has been observed in more than 1,500 animal species and is well documented for 500 animals. Giraffes, parrots, penguins, beetles, or hyenas exhibit some of the bisexual behaviors of the bonobo, a type of chimpanzee, that has sexual interactions with both males and females as a means of social bonding (Doyle, 2006).

**Gender nonconformity**
A lack of conformity to stereotypical masculine and feminine behaviors.

# Prenatal Influences

Some researchers have speculated that adult hormone levels contribute to sexual orientation. However, no well-controlled study has found a difference in circulating levels of sex hormones in adult homosexual or heterosexual men and women. Instead, scientists have looked at the influences that hormones and other factors may have during the prenatal period of development. As we saw in Chapter 3, prenatal levels of sex hormones have a masculinizing or feminizing influence on the developing fetal brain. Laboratory research on animals has demonstrated that hormones given prenatally can masculinize female fetuses and feminize male fetuses, which results in same-sex social and mating behavior when the animals mature (Vandenberg, 2003). Other prenatal conditions besides hormone levels probably influence development of sexual orientation (Lippa, 2003; Rahman & Wilson, 2003).

Research on prenatal factors and human attributes associated with a homosexual orientation are described in the following sections. It is important to keep in mind that research results in several areas are inconsistent. For example, some studies looking at cognitive abilities and sexual orientation have reported that gay men show cognitive abilities more like those of heterosexual women than those of heterosexual men: superior verbal skills and poorer performance on spatial processing. But other studies have found no difference in cognitive patterns between homosexual and heterosexual men (Rachman & Wilson, 2003). Studies with small sample sizes most often find differences, but larger, more rigorous investi-

gations tend to find no differences. Furthermore, studies that find differences are much more likely to be published than those that do not.

Some areas of research indicate possible differences in prenatal influences between men and women. For example, the onset of puberty is typically 12 months later for boys than for girls. However, numerous studies have found that gay and bisexual men begin puberty earlier than heterosexual men. In contrast, no such differences have been found to correlate with women's sexual orientation (Bogaert et al., 2002).

Birth order and the sex of siblings is another area in which research has found a correlation with male homosexuality but not with female homosexuality (Zucker et al., 2003). Research using samples of self-identified homosexuals and heterosexuals has found that homosexual men tended to have more older brothers than did heterosexual men, and each additional older brother increased the odds of same-sex attraction (Blanchard & Bogaert, 1996; Bogaert, 2005; Lauman et al., 1994; Wellings et al., 1994). No correlation was found between male homosexuality and having older or younger sisters of any number, and no correlation was evident between female homosexuality and sibling constellations of any kind. These studies found no evidence of sexual interaction between older and younger brothers or of any other environmental factors that might have contributed to younger brothers' feelings of attraction to other men.

## Implications If Biology Is Destiny

The evidence for biological causation of homosexuality raises important issues. If homosexuality is biologically based, people who assume that homosexuality is unnatural or immoral might reevaluate their beliefs. Society might thus become more accepting of homosexuality (Stein, 1999; Wood, 2000). However, research findings are inconsistent concerning how people who believe that homosexuals are "born that way" view homosexuality. Some studies report increases in antigay attitudes and others indicate more positive, accepting attitudes about issues such as homosexual teachers and equal rights in employment (Haslalm & Levy, 2006; Levy, 2006; Wolfe, 1998). How common is the belief that homosexuality is innate? It depends on whom you ask: Approximately 49% of the general population, compared with 75% of gays, think that homosexuality is something people are born with (Kitch, 2006; Leland, 2000b).

Other people raise concerns about the potential negative consequences if homosexuality is proven to have biological causes. If homosexuality is then labeled as biologically "defective," biological engineering to prevent or change homosexuality during pregnancy, screening techniques to prevent the birth of gay people, or medical techniques to change a person's sexual orientation might be developed and implemented (Stein, 1999; Gore, 1998). Furthermore, some maintain that the "We're born that way, so don't discriminate against us" justification for equal rights and protections under the law leads only to sympathy and tolerance for having a "defective" orientation (Woodson, 2005).

In conclusion, research suggests that a biological predisposition to exclusive homosexuality does exist. However, in general, the causes of sexual orientation remain a matter of speculation; most likely they involve multiple developmental pathways. Rather than thinking in terms of a single cause for sexual orientation, it seems more

Researchers hypothesize that the correlation between older brothers and male homosexual orientation is due to an increasing maternal immune response to successive pregnancies of males. Some mothers develop antibodies to H-Y antigen produced by a gene on the Y chromosome. This antigen influences prenatal sexual differentiation of the brain. More maternal antibodies develop with each pregnancy, resulting in an increased effect on younger brothers. In contrast, female fetuses are the same sex as the mother; thus they have the same XX chromosomes as the mother, making an immune response unlikely (Bogaert, 2003a).

Patterns of finger length show differences between heterosexual and homosexual individuals. Heterosexual women's index fingers tend to be about the same length as their ring fingers, but heterosexual men's ring fingers are often considerably longer than their index fingers. Research has found that lesbians' finger lengths follow the typical male pattern. Homosexual men had finger length ratios that exaggerated the heterosexual male pattern (ring finger longer than index finger). Researchers point to the increased masculinization of finger length patterns in homosexual women and men as evidence of exposure to increased levels of prenatal androgen (Rahman & Wilson, 2003; Williams et al., 2000). The role of higher levels of prenatal androgens in the development of some homosexual men may also be indicated by the finding that homosexual men tended to have larger penises than did heterosexual men (Bogaert & Hershberger, 1999).

Research in sexual orientation and left- or right-handedness shows both similarity and difference in characteristics of male and female homosexuality (Lippa, 2003b; Mustanski et al., 2002). Handedness appears to be established before birth; when observed by ultrasound, a fetus indicates right- or left-handedness by thumb-sucking choice and greater movement of one arm. In a meta-analysis of studies with a combined total of almost 25,000 subjects, homosexual participants had 39% greater odds of being left-handed than heterosexuals (Lalumiere et al., 2000). Later research found that gay men had far greater odds of being left-handed than did lesbians (Lippa, 2003).

All these research findings, considered collectively, strongly suggest the importance of prenatal influences—hormonal and other—and brain development on sexual orientation. Research on human subjects indicates that higher levels of masculinizing prenatal hormones in female fetuses are associated with lesbianism. It further indicates that, depending on the characteristic, higher levels of prenatal masculinizing or feminizing hormones in male fetuses are associated with male homosexuality (Lippa, 2003a; Rahman & Wilson, 2003). However, no studies have taken direct measures of prenatal hormones to compare with various characteristics over the life span to provide more-definitive information (Rahman & Wilson, 2003).

appropriate to consider the continuum of sexual orientation as being influenced by an interaction of various psychosocial and biological factors, which are unique to each person.

# ◗ Societal Attitudes

Around the world societal attitudes toward homosexuality vary considerably, as we discuss in the following Sexuality and Diversity box.

## SEXUALITY AND DIVERSITY

### Homosexuality in Cross-Cultural Perspective

Attitudes toward homosexuality vary considerably across cultures. A number of studies of other cultures, including ancient ones, have revealed widespread acceptance of homosexual behaviors. For example, in ancient Greece homosexual relationships between men were considered a superior intellectual and spiritual expression of love, whereas heterosexuality provided the more pragmatic benefits of children and a family unit. In addition, over 50% of 225 Native American tribes accepted male homosexuality, and 17% accepted female homosexuality (Pomeroy, 1965).

Some societies *require* their members to engage in homosexual activities. For example, all male members of the Sambia society in the mountains of New Guinea engage in exclusively homosexual behaviors from approximately 7 years of age until the late teens or early 20s, when men marry. Sambian men believe that a prepubertal boy becomes a strong warrior and hunter by drinking as much semen as possible from postpubertal boys' penises. Once a boy reaches puberty, he must no longer fellate other boys but can experience erotic pleasure from fellatio by boys who cannot yet ejaculate. From the start of their erotic lives and during the years of peak orgasmic capacity, young men engage in frequent obligatory and gratifying homoeroticism. During the same period, looking at or touching females is taboo. Yet as they approach marriage, these youths create powerful erotic daydreams about women. During the first weeks of marriage, they experience only fellatio with their wives: thereafter they make intercourse part of their heterosexual activity. After marriage they stop homosexual activity, experience great sexual desire for women, and engage exclusively in heterosexual activity for the rest of their lives (Stoller & Herdt, 1985).

Events in Cuba demonstrate how a society can make rapid changes regarding homosexuality. During the first 35 years of the Communist revolution, lesbians and gay men were seen as deviant antirevolutionaries and were expelled from the Communist Party and state and university jobs. Some were sent to labor camps. In 1992 Cuban leader Fidel Castro blamed the previous homophobia on ingrained attitudes of *machismo*. He expressed support for gay rights and described homosexuality as a natural human tendency that must be respected. Since then, gay men and lesbians have been able to walk down the street holding hands and join one of several gay organizations without fear of reprisal (Otis, 1994). Castro's niece, Mariela Castro, has been instrumental in working through a government-funded organization to promote acceptance of lesbians, gay men, and transgendered individuals (Israel, 2006).

However, extreme violation of basic human rights for gays and lesbians is a common experience in many places around the globe, as shown in ● **Figure 9.3**. Amnesty International USA has increased its attention to this problem. This group has documented such abuses as the decapitation murder of a bisexual politician in Brazil, "social cleansing" death squads in Colombia, the death penalty for homosexual individuals in Iran and Iraq, and persecution of gay and AIDS activists in many countries (Amnesty International, 2003; El-Rouayheb; 2006; Rose 2006). In the United States before 1990 the Immigration and Naturalization Service deemed homosexuality legal grounds for exclusion from this country, but it now grants political asylum to people fleeing persecution based on sexual orientation (Burr, 1996a).

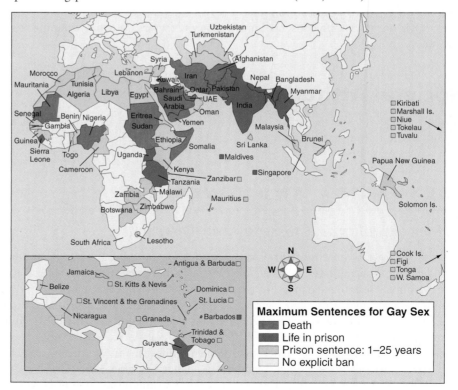

● **Figure 9.3** Punishment for gay sex.

In other places, equal rights are increasing. Fourteen countries, mostly European, have established national laws that protect gay men, lesbians, and bisexuals from discrimination (see 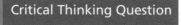 **Table 9.1**). South Africa has the most comprehensive legal protection, which was included in its constitution in 1996. (Notice that the United States does not appear on this list of countries because it

| ⊙ TABLE 9.1 | Fourteen Countries With National Laws That Protect Gays, Lesbians, and Bisexuals From Discrimination | |
| --- | --- | --- |
| Canada | Ireland | Slovenia |
| Denmark | Israel | South Africa |
| Finland | The Netherlands | Spain |
| France | New Zealand | Sweden |
| Iceland | Norway | |

SOURCE: Siecus (1999b).

has yet to pass a federal law against discrimination for sexual orientation.) Domestic partnerships have legal status in Canada, Denmark, Sweden, Switzerland, Norway, Spain, Iceland, Belgium, France, two cities in Italy, and Brazil (the first Latin American country to grant such status) (Brooke, 2000; Henry, 2000; Power, 1998b). South Africa, the Netherlands, Belgium, Spain, and Canada give same-sex couples the unprecedented right to marry (Wines, 2005). In the Netherlands gays and lesbians can legally adopt children (Deutsch, 2000). In 2000, Great Britain joined Australia, Canada, and New Zealand in eliminating its ban on gays in the military (Wang, 2000). ■

## Judeo-Christian Attitudes Toward Homosexuality

According to the Judeo-Christian tradition that predominates in our own North American culture, homosexuality has been viewed negatively. Many religious scholars believe that the condemnation of homosexuality increased during a Jewish reform movement beginning in the 7th century BCE, through which Jewish religious leaders wanted to develop a distinct closed community. Homosexual activities were a part of the religious practices of many peoples in that era, and rejecting such practices was one way of keeping the Jewish religion unique (Fone, 2000; Kosnik et al., 1977). The Old Testament included strong prohibitive statements: "You shall not lie with a man as one lies with a female; it is an abomination" (Leviticus 18:22). (Leviticus also calls the eating of shellfish [Lev. 11:10] and the cutting of men's hair [Lev. 19:27] abominations.) Today Jewish people are divided over their religious stance toward homosexuality. In Israel in 2002 the first openly gay man was appointed to the Knesset, or parliament, drawing dissent from Orthodox Jews (Landsberg, 2002). Reform Judaism sanctioned same-sex marriages in 2000, and conservative Jewish leaders are reexamining their ban on same-sex marriages and the ordination of openly gay and lesbian clergy (Friess, 2003).

Laws against homosexual behaviors, which stem from biblical injunctions against same-sex contact, have historically been exceedingly punitive. People with homosexual orientations have been tortured and put to death throughout Western history. In the American colonies homosexual people were condemned to death by drowning and burning. In the late 1770s, Thomas Jefferson was among the political leaders who suggested reducing the punishment from death to castration for men who committed homosexual acts (Fone, 2000; Katz, 1976).

Current Christian theological positions toward homosexuality express a great range of convictions (Haffner, 2004). Different denominations, and different groups within the same denomination, have taken different stances. In many mainstream denominations, groups are working to open their churches to gay and lesbian parishioners and clergy, while fundamentalists in the same denominations oppose such inclusion. Conflicts between these two positions are likely to increase as denominations attempt to establish clear positions and policies about homosexuality (Soukup, 2006; Johnson & Nelson, 2003).

The Unitarian Universalist Association and the United Church of Christ are the only Christian denominations that officially sanction the blessing of gay and lesbian unions (Haffner, 2000). Although many churches' official policies do not allow church bonding ceremonies for gays and lesbians, some clergy support and perform these

**? Critical Thinking Question**

How do your religious beliefs, or absence of beliefs, influence your attitudes toward homosexuality?

**Sex and Politics**

ceremonies for homosexual couples (Dotinga, 1998). The first major American denomination to ordain an openly gay candidate was the United Church of Christ in 1972. In 2003 the Right Reverend V. Gene Robinson was consecrated as a bishop in the Episcopal Church, becoming the first openly gay bishop in any mainstream denomination (Freiberg, 2003). Moving in the opposite direction, in 2005 the pope barred gays from being priests in the Roman Catholic Church (Sullivan, 2005). Many gay rights activists believe that the support of churches is crucial if the civil rights movement for gay men and lesbians is to be fully successful (Sullivan, 1997). ∎

## From Sin to Sickness

In the early to mid-1900s, societal attitudes toward homosexuality shifted. The belief that homosexual people were sinners was replaced to some degree by the belief that they were mentally ill. The medical and psychological professions have used drastic treatments in attempting to cure the "illness" of homosexuality. Surgical procedures such as castration were performed in the 1800s. As late as 1951, lobotomy (surgery that severs nerve fibers in the frontal lobe of the brain) was performed as a cure for homosexuality. Psychotherapy, drugs, hormones, hypnosis, shock treatments, and aversion therapy (pairing nausea-inducing drugs or electrical shock with homosexual stimuli) have all been used to the same end (Fone, 2000).

Actually, the research of several decades contradicts the notion that homosexual people are mentally ill. Although some research has found that gay men have a slightly increased rate of depression and anxiety compared with heterosexual men (Mills et al., 2004; Rochman, 2003), this difference is probably due to the stigma attached to gay men and the losses and stresses of coping with the AIDS epidemic. Alan Bell and Martin Weinberg concluded that "homosexual adults who have come to terms with their homosexuality, who do not regret their sexual orientation, and who can function effectively sexually and socially, are no more distressed psychologically than are heterosexual men and women" (1978, p. 216).

In 1973, after great internal conflict, the American Psychiatric Association removed homosexuality from its diagnostic categories of mental disorders. In light of contemporary research on homosexuality—and the fact that both the American Psychiatric Association and the American Psychological Association no longer categorize homosexuality as a mental illness—most therapists and counselors have changed the focus of therapy. Rather than attempting to "cure" homosexual clients by changing their sexual orientation, therapists provide **gay-affirmative therapy** to help them live in a society that harbors considerable hostility toward them (Crisp, 2006). This change in therapeutic practice is significant because it defines the problem as society's negativity toward homosexuality rather than as homosexuality itself (Kort, 2004). However, heterosexist bias still occurs in mental health and family therapy due to psychotherapists' lack of knowledge about issues unique to gays and lesbians (Long & Serovich, 2003).

Some mental health practitioners and religious groups advocate therapy to help dissatisfied homosexual individuals control, lessen, or eliminate their homosexual feelings and behavior through **conversion therapy** or **sexual reorientation therapy** (Kemena, 2000; Nicolosi et al., 2000a). Ministry groups such as Exodus International, a nondenominational Christian organization, blends religious teachings with group counseling to focus on childhood traumas believed to have caused the participants' homosexuality: abandonment by fathers, absent mothers, sexual abuse, or violent parents. The conversion process attempts to develop heterosexual desire in participants and, failing that, to enable them to abstain from same-sex sexual contact. Different studies of conversion therapy have reported varied results: from 4% to 45% of participants report no longer struggling with homosexual desires or behavior and having success in being completely heterosexual, being in a heterosexual relationship, or at least being more heterosexual than homosexual (Nicolosi et al., 2000b; Shidlo et al., 2001). (The higher success rates come from studies done by conversion therapists.)

Among those whose sexual orientation was not altered by conversion therapy are two of the founders of Exodus International, Michael Bussee and Garry Cooper, who left their marriages for each other in 1979 (Goldberg, 2006). Other individuals who

Sex and Politics

**Gay-affirmative therapy** Therapy to help homosexual clients cope with negative societal attitudes.

**Conversion therapy/sexual reorientation therapy** Therapy to help homosexual men and women change their sexual orientation.

failed at conversion therapy report that they lied to their therapist about continuing homosexual behavior during their treatment, and that the treatment had contributed to their self-hatred (Nguyen, 2006; Shidlo et al., 2001). For many people who cannot make the changes they wish for, the belief that one can only "be with God or be gay" presents irreconcilable choices. Such a dilemma can drive people to suicide (Clementson, 2000b; M. Miller, 2000). ■

## Homophobia

The term **homophobia** describes anti-homosexual attitudes, irrational fears of homosexual people, or fear and loathing of homosexual feelings in oneself. Homophobia can be best thought of as a prejudice similar to racism, anti-Semitism, or sexism. *Heterosexism* is a variation of homophobia; it is defined by beliefs that stigmatize and denigrate any behaviors, identities, relationships, and communities that are not heterosexual (Berkman & Zinberg, 1997; Van Voorhis & Wagner, 2002). The recognition of homophobia and heterosexism as the problem represents a significant shift from the view that homosexuality itself was the problem.

Unfortunately, homophobia is still common and often plays a big role in the lives of many gay men, lesbians, and bisexuals. It is expressed in many ways (LaSala, 2006). For example, Republican senator Rick Santorum, in a 2003 Associated Press interview, claimed that removing antisodomy laws and creating privacy protection for gay and lesbian sex is tantamount to protecting bigamy, polygamy, and incest (Mondics, 2003). A few years earlier, Senate majority leader Trent Lott compared homosexuality to kleptomania and alcoholism and led the opposition to antidiscrimination laws in employment because gays are "dangerous, unhealthy, or just plain wrong" (Fuller, 2000, p. E7). Such expressions contribute to the ongoing daily harassment and discrimination of anyone outside "acceptable" heterosexual parameters, and they legitimize the mindset of people who commit *hate crimes* directed at gays. Hate crimes include assault, robbery, and murder, and they are committed because the victim belongs to a certain race, religion, or ethnic group or has a certain sexual orientation (Ghent, 2003; Herek et al., 1999). The film *Soldier's Girl*, based on a murder in 1999, depicts the dynamics of hate crimes. ■

**Homophobia** Irrational fears of homosexuality, the fear of the possibility of homosexuality in oneself, or loathing toward one's own homosexuality.

- Homophobia

## Hate Crimes

Hate crimes are subject to severer sentences than other crimes. About 33 states now have hate crime laws that include proscriptions against antigay violence (❯ **Figure 9.4**)

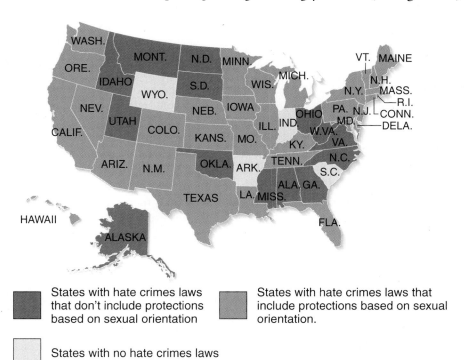

■ States with hate crimes laws that don't include protections based on sexual orientation

☐ States with hate crimes laws that include protections based on sexual orientation.

☐ States with no hate crimes laws

❯ **Figure 9.4** Types of hate crime laws by state.

Public awareness of hate crimes against gays rose sharply after the 1998 death of Matthew Shepard. Shepard was an openly gay 21-year-old University of Wyoming student who hoped for a career in diplomacy and human rights. After two 21-year-old high school dropouts pistol-whipped Shepard, crushing his skull, they tied him to a fence outside town and left him to die. Most people were horrified by this crime; 700 mourners came to his funeral. But outside the church, other people carried signs with such messages as "No tears for queers" and "No fags in heaven."

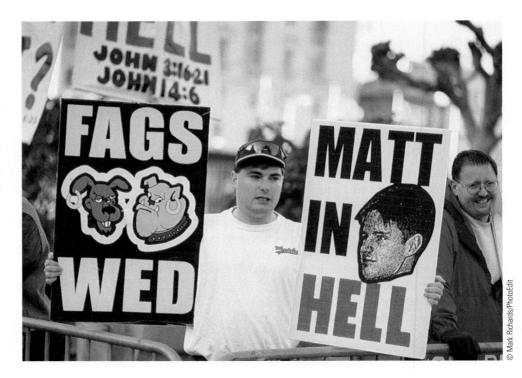

"If an openly gay man touches your arm in a public place and you feel uncomfortable, that doesn't make him a pervert. That makes you homophobic."
—Jimmy Kimmel on *Jimmy Kimmel Live,* 2003.

(Gay and Lesbian Task Force, 2005). More than one third of gay men and lesbians have been victims of violence (Parrott & Zeichner, 2006). However, hate crimes are less likely to be reported than other crimes, because survivors expect nonsupportive responses from authorities (Herek et al., 1999). ■

## Causes of Homophobia and Hate Crimes

Murdering a gay man, voting to allow discrimination against homosexual people in employment and the right to marry, and calling a lesbian a dyke to insult her may seem unrelated, but they have some key elements in common. First, they reflect at the most fundamental level humankind's poor record of accepting and valuing differences between people. The lack of acceptance of racial, religious, and ethnic differences has fueled vicious, inhuman events such as ethnic cleansing, the Holocaust, and the Inquisition. The many religions that define homosexuality negatively also predispose groups and individuals to assume the same view. Research shows that individuals who are more religiously conservative have more negative attitudes toward homosexuality than people who are less conservative in their beliefs (Kite & Whitley, 1998a; Kyes & Tumbelaka, 1994; Negy & Eisenman, 2006).

Second, homophobia and hate crimes are related to traditional gender-role identification: Individuals who hold traditional gender-role stereotypes tend to have more-negative feelings about homosexuality than do others (Herek & Gonzalez-Rivera, 2006; Louderback & Whitley, 1997). Furthermore, men typically have more-negative attitudes toward homosexuality than do women—reflecting, perhaps, the more rigid gender-role parameters for boys and men compared with girls and women in our culture (Kite & Whitley, 1998b; Herek & Capitanio, 1999). Research in Australia found that young men between the ages of 14 and 17 had more-negative attitudes about homosexuality than any other grouping based on sex and age (Plummer, 2005). Lesbians do not evoke as negative feelings in heterosexual men as gay men do (Mahaffey et al., 2005). This may be, in part, because heterosexual men do not feel uncomfortable about their sexual feelings toward women in general.

Researchers have found that most perpetrators of antigay hate crimes—only males, to date—claim that homosexuality's violation of male gender norms is the primary motivation for their violence. Perpetrators, often acting in pairs or in larger groups, try to reassure themselves and their friends of their "masculinity" by assaulting a man who has stepped outside the rigid boundaries of male gender roles. The same motivation makes transgendered individuals frequent targets of violence (Maurer, 1999). Increased collaboration for social change between transgendered individuals and groups and gay rights organizations evolved, in part, from understanding the importance of gender diversity (Coleman, 1999; Denny, 1999).

Another element involved in homophobia and hate crimes is an attempt to deny or suppress homosexual feelings in oneself. Uncomfortable with his or her own sexuality, the homophobic person focuses on what is "wrong" with the sexuality of other people (Kantor, 1998). One study found that men with strong negative attitudes toward gay men actually have erotic feelings toward other men but deny being aware of their arousal (Adams et al., 1996). The study had men watch sexually explicit videotapes of heterosexual people, lesbians, and gay men while wearing a penile plethysmograph to measure the increase in erection in response to each scenario. Without knowing the results from the plethysmograph, subjects rated how sexually aroused they felt while watching each video. Men who were not homophobic said that they did not feel aroused by the gay male video, and the plethysmograph confirmed their report. In contrast, homophobic men also denied feeling sexually aroused while watching the gay male video, but the plethysmograph recorded physical arousal (Kantor, 1998). These findings suggest that homophobic men are not aware of, or are unwilling to acknowledge, their homoerotic

Homophobia is infrequently directed toward lesbians. Female same-sex sexual behavior is sexually arousing to many people, and ads suggesting lesbian sex are common in advertising.

arousal. Aggression toward gays may be a defensive reaction to homophobic men's discomfort with their own unwanted feelings (Kite & Whitley, 1998a).

Some of the most virulent antigay rhetoric has come from deeply closeted men in positions of religious leadership. For example, the Reverend Ted Haggard promoted antigay sentiments and policy as president of the 30 million National Association of Evangelicals and senior pastor of the 14,000 member New Life Church in Colorado Springs. A regular consultant to President G. W. Bush, the married father of five children admitted to "sexually immoral conduct" and left both leadership positions after a man claimed that Haggard had paid him for sex nearly every month for 3 years (Elliott, 2006). The Reverend Lonnie Latham, a minister from Oklahoma and an executive committee member of the strongly antigay Southern Baptist Convention, was arrested for sexually propositioning a male undercover police officer. John Paulk, a former chairman of Exodus International who claimed to have succeeded in becoming heterosexual, was photographed in a gay bar buying drinks for patrons. The Reverend Steven Baines, an elder in the Christian Church (Disciples of Christ) explains, "when religion is used to bring repression and darkness rather than liberation and light, it is toxic to both leaders and followers" (Baines 2006, p. 2).

## Homophobia's Impact on Heterosexuals

The careful avoidance of any behavior that might be interpreted as homosexual can restrict the lives of heterosexual people. For example, during lovemaking, heterosexual men may be unable to enjoy having their nipples stimulated or may be reluctant to allow their female partners to take the lead if they believe that their enjoyment of these behaviors demonstrates homosexual "tendencies" (Wells, 1991). Same-sex friends or family members may refrain from spontaneous embraces, people may shun "unfeminine" or "unmasculine" clothing, or a woman may decide not to identify herself as a feminist because she fears being called a lesbian. Homophobia can have an

Gay and straight men laughing and getting along? Nonthreatening gay flirtation with straight men? *Queer Eye for the Straight Guy*'s funny, kind-hearted makeovers for heterosexual men may increase viewers' acceptance of homosexuality.

especially significant effect on the depth of intimacy in male friendships (Plummer, 1999). Men's fear of same-sex attraction often keeps them from allowing themselves the emotional vulnerability required for deep friendship, thus limiting their relationships largely to competition and "buddyship" (Nelson, 1985).

## Increasing Acceptance

Individuals' homophobic attitudes can change with deliberate effort, experience, or education. In fact, people who personally know someone who is gay are usually more accepting of homosexuality (Leland, 2000b; Span & Vidal, 2003). Individual acts of courage can also make an impact; the college student who invites people regardless of sexual orientation to his party, the accountant who has his partner's photo on his desk at work, or the straight doctor with a lesbian sister who confronts someone making a derogatory gay joke all help make a difference (Solmonese, 2005). We do see a positive trend in acceptance of homosexuality when attitudes toward homosexuality are compared by age group. Young adults (18–29 years old) are significantly more accepting of gay rights than people over 30, who are still more tolerant than those over 50. The increased acceptance may have to do with the fact that 65% of people younger than 50 have a homosexual friend or acquaintance, whereas 45% of people older than 50 do (Leland, 2000b).

## Homosexuality and the Media

Since the mid-1960s, daytime talk shows—*The Phil Donahue Show* and *Oprah*, in particular—have brought previously unknown visibility to gays, lesbians, and bisexual people. Donahue's arrival in the national media coincided with lesbian and gay activism, and his focus on controversial topics gave homosexual guests unprecedented opportunities to represent their own lives and issues. Oprah Winfrey began her talk show in 1986, contributing her empathic style to discussions with guests belonging to sexual minorities (Gross, 2001).

The new Batwoman in DC Comics' "52" series is an out lesbian with an active love life and a detective ex-girlfriend (Ferber, 2006).

Homosexuality became more visible—and was portrayed in a more positive light—in the 1990s cinema. The 1993 film *Philadelphia*, starring Tom Hanks, was the first major Hollywood feature to confront homophobia and AIDS and was a box-office success. Robin Williams played the role of a partner in a longtime gay relationship in *The Birdcage*, a popular movie about two families with opposing social and sexual points of view. These films showed the exotic and tragic sides of homosexuality. In the later 1990s, movies such as

*My Best Friend's Wedding* and *In and Out* began to portray homosexuals in more-ordinary roles. The movie *Brokeback Mountain*, a love story of two Wyoming cowboys won numerous awards and was the first same-sex romance to be number one at the box office (Vary, 2006).

On cable TV *Queer Eye for the Straight Guy* challenged prejudices about relationships between straight and gay men, and *Six Feet Under* and *The L Word* portrayed complex gay and lesbian characters (Archer, 2006). *Queer as Folk*, which presented a no-holds-barred picture of gay life received criticism from gay viewers for its portrayals of recreational sex and drug use (Shelton, 2003; Tipton, 2003). *South of Nowhere*, the only TV show to have a lesbian teenage girl as the main character, explores her new same-sex relationship and the reactions of friends and family members (Kennedy, 2006).

Making gays more commonly known in the mainstream media provides an opportunity for greater familiarity with and understanding of homosexuality. GLAAD (Gay and Lesbian Alliance Against Defamation) honors each year's outstanding representations of lesbian, gay, bisexual, and transgendered people in the media and recognizes members of the media who have promoted equal rights for sexual minorities. For example, a January 2006 episode of ABC's soap opera *General Hospital* spoke out strongly against homophobic violence against the gay character, Lucas, and included a public service announcement about resources (Grant, 2006). Five months later a press release announced that an upcoming episode of the CBS soap *As the World Turns* would feature the character Luke's coming out and would include a public service announcement encouraging viewers to make a difference in combating the "rejection, prejudice, and violence" gay people face every day. In response, The Traditional Values Coalition attacked the "antireligious bigotry" of the announcement and unsuccessfully attempted to coerce CBS to eliminate the public service announcement, branding GLAAD as "one of the most dangerous organizations in America" (Romine, 2006, p. 3). ■

**InfoTrac Search Words**

● Homosexuality and the media

**Sex and Politics**

The Acadamy of Motion Pictures Arts and Sciences hired Ellen DeGeneres to host the 2007 Oscars.

**Coming out** The process of becoming aware of and disclosing one's homosexual identity.

# ⊙ Lifestyles

We sometimes hear references to the "gay lifestyle" in popular vernacular. What is the gay lifestyle exactly? The term probably does not imply that all gays engage in the same work, recreation, and spiritual activities. The word *lifestyle* seems to be a euphemism for sexual conduct between same-sex partners (Howey & Samuels, 2000). In this discussion, we will see that homosexual lifestyles are as varied as heterosexual lifestyles. All social classes, occupations, races, religions, and political persuasions are represented among homosexual people. The only characteristics that homosexual people necessarily have in common are their desire for emotional and sexual fulfillment with someone of the same sex and their experiences of oppression from a hostile social environment. We look first at issues related to coming out and to how being secretive or open about their sexual orientation affects the lives of gays and lesbians.

## Coming Out

The extent to which homosexual individuals decide to be secretive or open about their sexual orientation significantly affects their lifestyle. There are various degrees of being "in the closet," and several steps are involved in **coming out**—acknowledging, accepting, and openly expressing one's homosexuality (Patterson, 1995). Gays, lesbians, and bisexual people base decisions about coming out on issues of safety and acceptance for themselves and others. Being openly lesbian, gay, or bisexual can be personally liberating but may not be adaptive in every situation (Anderson & Holliday, 2003; Oswald & Culton, 2003). Passing as heterosexual can help an individual avoid negative social consequences but exacts its toll in the stresses of maintaining secrecy (Berger, 1996). Individual circumstances significantly affect decisions about coming out. Historical context also influences coming out, as indicated in a study of three different generations of lesbians:

1. Lesbians who became adults before the gay rights era began in the 1970s
2. Lesbians who became adults during the gay rights era, between 1970 and 1985
3. Lesbians who became adults after 1985

Vince Bucci/Getty Images

New Jersey governor, democrat James McGreevey, was married when he resigned from office after his lover attempted to extort money from him in exchange for maintaining secrecy about his homosexual relationship.

With each consecutive age group, women's awareness of their sexual orientation, initial same-sex sexual experience, labeling of themselves as lesbian, and disclosing to others occurred earlier in life. For example, women in the youngest group were, on average, 20 years old when they identified themselves as lesbian, whereas women in the oldest group were 32 years old. The most significant change over time was that more and more women had sexual experiences with other women before having such experiences with men. This was true for most women in the youngest group, whereas the opposite was true for most women in both older groups (Parks, 1999).

Although coming-out decisions are unique to each individual and situation, many have common elements: self-acknowledgment, self-acceptance, and disclosure. We look at each of these in the following sections.

### Self-Acknowledgment

The initial step in coming out is usually a person's realization that she or he feels different from the mainstream heterosexual model (Meyer & Schwitzer, 1999). Some people report knowing that they were attracted to the same sex when they were small children. Many realize during adolescence that something is missing in their heterosexual involvements and that they find same-sex peers sexually attractive (Cloud, 2005; Mallon, 1996).

Once individuals recognize homosexual feelings, they must usually confront their own internalized homophobia as they deal with the reality that they belong to a stigmatized minority group (Katz, 1995). Some homosexual men and women attempt to suppress their sexual orientation, even from their own awareness, and often they succeed. These people actively seek sexual encounters with members of the other sex, and it is not uncommon for them to marry in an attempt to convince themselves of their "normalcy" (Dubé, 2000). Some homosexual individuals who have been married (one third of the women and one fifth of the men in Bell and Weinberg's 1978 study) did so to avoid openly confronting their sexual orientation.

### Self-Acceptance

Accepting one's homosexuality is the next important step after realizing it. Self-acceptance is often difficult, because it involves overcoming the internalized negative and homophobic societal view of homosexuality:

> Initially a homosexual person often has difficulty from the pervasive condemnatory attitudes toward homosexuality. . . . His prejudice against himself is an almost exact parallel to the prejudice against homosexuals held in the larger culture. (Weinberg, 1973, p. 74)

When individuals belong to a socially stigmatized group, self-acceptance becomes a difficult but essential challenge (Ryan & Futterman, 2001).

Coming out can be especially problematic for teenagers (Kitts, 2005). Most gay and lesbian teens experience confusion about their feelings and have few places to go for support and guidance (Rosario et al., 2002; Russell, 2001). In fact, they usually encounter considerable hostility and harassment (Satterly & Dyson, 2005). At a stage of development when a sense of belonging to their peer group is especially important, almost half of gay and lesbian teens lost at least one friend after they came out (Ryan & Futterman, 1997). Judgment from their own families is another source of stress for gay and lesbian adolescents (Ueno, 2005). Some parents throw their gay children out of the house or stop support for schooling.

Despite the discrimination that homosexual adolescents face, many of them can cope effectively and develop an integrated and positive identity (Savin-Williams, 2005). It is helpful for gay and lesbian adolescents to find at least one supportive, nonjudgmental adult with whom to talk. The Internet provides teens with connections to others to help reduce their isolation. Support groups and gay teen organizations are emerging to help teens deal with the difficulties they face. The first accredited public high school for gay students, Harvey Milk School, in New York City, opened its doors in fall 2003 to provide students with a safe and supportive learning environment (Henneman, 2003).

## Disclosure

Following acknowledgment and self-acceptance is the decision to be secretive or open. Occasionally, a gay or lesbian will find others abruptly opening the closet door for them. *Outing* is the term for the public disclosure of someone's secret homosexual orientation by someone else. Otherwise, being homosexual usually requires ongoing decisions about whether to be in or out of the closet as new relationships and situations unfold (Kelly, 1998). **Passing** is a term sometimes used for maintaining the false image of heterosexuality (Lynch, 1992). Passing as heterosexual is usually easy because most people assume that everyone is heterosexual. Heterosexual people sometimes do not understand disclosure issues, as exemplified by the following comment:

> *I don't see any reason why they have to tell anyone. They can just lead their lives without making such a big deal out of it. (Authors' files)*

**Passing** Presenting a false image of being heterosexual.

In some daily interactions, sexual orientation is irrelevant, but homosexuality and heterosexuality are strong undercurrents that touch many parts of life. Imagine being a closeted homosexual person and hearing a friend make a derogatory reference to "fags" or "dykes," being asked, "When are you going to settle down and get married?" or being invited to bring a date to an office party. In one writer's words, "Because of its devalued status, affirmation of homosexuality (or disclaiming it) becomes a more significant act than the same would be for a heterosexual, with significant consequences for a lifestyle" (Gagnon, 1977, p. 248). In the Let's Talk About It box titled "Guidelines for Coming Out to Friends" we offer some suggestions for coming out.

With some exceptions, the more within "the system" one is or desires to be, the more risk there is in being open about one's sexual orientation. Jobs, social position, and friends can all be placed in jeopardy (Druzin et al., 1998; Horvath & Ryan, 2003). The conservativeness of the surrounding community or time in history can further affect one's decisions about whether to come out and to whom (Stein, 2001). Coming out is a particularly difficult issue for homosexual adults who are parents. Approximately 60% of homosexual men and women who have been married have at least one child (Bell & Weinberg, 1978). It is not unusual for gay parents to lose custody or visitation rights strictly on the basis of their sexual orientation, regardless of their fitness as parents (Schwartz, 1990).

## Telling the Family

Disclosing one's homosexuality to family can be more difficult than disclosing it to others. Coming out to one's family is a particularly significant step, as the following account by a 35-year-old man illustrates:

> *Most of my vacation at home went well, but the ending was indeed difficult. Gay people kept cropping up in conversation. My mother was very down on them (us), and I of course was disagreeing with her. Finally she asked me if I was "one of them." I said yes. It was very difficult for her to deal with. She asked a lot of questions, which I answered as calmly, honestly, and rationally as I could. We spent a rather strained day together. It was so painful for me to see her suffering so much heartache over this and not even having a clue that the issue is the oppression of gay people. I just wish my mother didn't have to suffer so much from all this. (Authors' files)*

Parents may react with anger or guilt about what they "did wrong" (Woog, 1997). Research does indicate that as societal attitudes become more positive about homosexuality, parents react more receptively to disclosure (Pearlman, 2005). Families that are less rigid and authoritarian and more cohesive are more likely to react with less stress to disclosure of homosexuality (Willoughby et al, 2006). ○ **Table 9.2**

○ **TABLE 9.2** Readers of the Newsmagazine *The Advocate* Answer the Question "Have You Come Out to Your Parents?"

| Answer | Percentage |
|---|---|
| Yes, and they took the news well. | 63 |
| Yes, and they rejected me. | 11 |
| No. | 26 |

SOURCE: *The Advocate* (January 20, 1998, p. 22).

## Guidelines for Coming Out to Friends

If you are a gay or lesbian, the unexpected is to be expected when you come out to a friend. A friend who is "liberal" may have more difficulty than a more "conservative" person. It is essential to remember that your friend's reactions say something about his or her own strengths and weaknesses rather than anything about you. The following guidelines are meant to help you begin devising your own plan of disclosure. They are adapted from the book *Outing Yourself*, by Michelangelo Signorile (1995).

1. *Support network.* You should have a support network of gays in place, especially those who have come out to lots of different people in their lives. Their experiences and support will give you a solid base from which to act.

2. *First choice.* Try to make your first disclosure to a heterosexual person an easy one. You might not choose your best straight friend, because the stakes are high. Pick someone whom you would expect to be accepting. The person also needs to be trustworthy and capable of keeping your news private for a while as you come out to others.

3. *Mental practice.* Practice imagining yourself coming out in realistic detail. Picture yourself in a familiar setting where both you and your friend will be comfortable. Envision feeling pleased with yourself for sharing something you feel good about (not something you have to apologize for). Practice saying, "There's something I want to tell you about myself, because our friendship is important to me. I trust you, and you're close to me. I am a lesbian/I am gay."

4. *Advance planning.* Plan the time: be sure to allow enough time to talk at length if things go well. Plan the place: be sure it is somewhere both of you will be comfortable. Arrange to have at least one of your gay friends available for support afterward and to debrief. Be prepared to calmly answer such questions as, How do you know you're gay? How long have you known? What caused it? Can you change? Do you have AIDS?

5. *Rely on patience.* Remember that you are telling your friend something he or she has not had a chance to prepare for, whereas you have had a lot of time to prepare. Many people are surprised, shocked, and confused and need some time to think or ask questions. An initial negative reaction does not necessarily mean the friend will not accept it. If a friend reacts negatively but shows respect, stay and talk things over. Sympathize with his or her shock and confusion: "I can see this news upsets you."

6. *Control your anger.* If the person becomes hostile or insulting, politely end the meeting: "I'm sorry you aren't accepting my news well, and it's best for me to go now." Don't give your friend a real reason to be mad at you by being mean or rude or flying off the handle. As you come out to people, you will find that some are not capable or willing to maintain their friendship with you. With others, letting them know you more fully will allow the meaning and closeness in the relationship to grow. Over time you will create a network of friends with whom you can enjoy the freedom of being your full self.

shows how many readers of *The Advocate*, a gay newsmagazine, have come out to their parents, and their parents' reactions. Potentially more problematic than coming out to one's parents is coming out to one's spouse and children. A gay or lesbian closeted in a heterosexual marriage may have grave concerns about the reactions of his or her spouse and children, who indeed tend to struggle with the disclosure (Sanders, 2000).

**DOONESBURY**
by Garry Trudeau

To a greater extent than white homosexual people, gay, lesbian, and bisexual people from other racial and ethnic groups are more likely to stay in the closet with their families and community than to be open and face alienation, not only from their families but also from their heritage (Span & Vidal, 2003; Zea et al., 2003). For example, traditional Asian cultures place greater significance on loyalty and conformity to one's family than on individual needs and desires. Being openly homosexual is seen as shaming the family, and not marrying and creating heirs to carry on the family name is a failure for the whole extended family. In addition, lesbianism is an affront to the traditions of an ethnic group that expects virginity for unmarried women and views "good women" as primarily nonsexual. The organization Parents, Families, and Friends of Lesbians and Gays (PFLAG), which has over 400 chapters nationwide, helps parents and others develop understanding, acceptance, and support.

In general, the African American community has stronger negative views of homosexuals than does white society. The executive director of Gay Men of African Descent in New York stated, "Holding hands walking down the street? That's not something I'd do in Harlem" (Leland, 2000b). The expression, "on the down-low" refers to African American men secretly having sex with men while appearing to be heterosexual by having girlfriends or wives (Kalb & Murr, 2006). One study found that African American lesbians and gay men had a greater incidence of depressive distress than white homosexual people, most likely as a result of the doubly stigmatized status of race and sexual orientation (Cochran & Mays, 1994). The emphasis on masculinity as the ideal gender norm in the lower socioeconomic segment of the African American community—and the emphasis on *machismo* for Hispanic men—creates particular difficulty for gender-nonconforming gays.

Unfortunately, antigay prejudice has gravely hindered African American communities from proactively addressing the AIDS crisis (Cose, 2006; Bond 2006). Although leaders such as the Reverend Al Sharpton, Coretta Scott King, and the Reverend Jesse Jackson have supported gay civil rights, the influence of strong fundamentalist Christian beliefs contributes to the higher degree of intolerance in the general black community (Gallagher, 1997a; Monroe, 1997). A study of college students found that higher religiosity in African American students was a significant variable associated with greater negative attitudes toward homosexuality (Negy & Eisenman, 2005).

## Involvement in the Gay Community

The need to belong is a deeply felt human trait. For many homosexual individuals a sense of community helps provide a sense of belonging and the affirmation and acceptance that are missing in the larger culture (Russell & Richards, 2003). Social and political involvement with other homosexual people is another step in coming out. Homosexual people have helped found service organizations, educational centers, and professional organizations, such as the Gay and Lesbian Medical Association and Gay and Lesbian Criminal Justice Professionals (Hayden & Peraino, 1999). Gay fraternities have formed on college campuses across the United States (DeQuine, 2003). Homosexual retirement communities provide alternatives to traditional retirement communities, in which older gays and lesbians may have to be on their guard against negative attitudes of other residents (Rosenberg, 2001). Religious organizations for homosexual people have been established, including the 40,000-member Metropolitan Community Church, with 400 congregations in 19 countries, and denominational groups such as Dignity for Roman Catholics and Integrity for Episcopalians (Gallagher, 1994; Michael et al., 1994). In addition, the Internet has provided a gay virtual community in ways never before possible (Shernoff, 2006).

The AIDS crisis precipitated increased community involvement and coherence (Fineman, 1993). The gay and lesbian communities mobilized educational efforts, developed innovative programs for caring for AIDS patients, created an impressive network of volunteers to provide needed support for persons with AIDS, and lobbied—often quite visibly—for increased AIDS awareness and medical research funding.

© Reuters/CORBIS

The Reverend Al Sharpton, addressing the Justice Coalition Summit in Atlanta, Georgia, said, "In 2004, the religious right was concerned about re-electing George W. Bush. They couldn't come to black churches to talk about the war, about health care, about poverty. So they did what they always do and reached for the bigotry against gay and lesbian people."

## Homosexual Relationships

Some people mistakenly think that homosexual partners always enact the stereotypically active "male" and passive "female" roles. Because this model of male/female role-playing has historically predominated in our culture, both heterosexual and homosexual intimate relationships have been patterned after it (O'Sullivan, 1999). However, more-egalitarian relationships are being followed by both heterosexual and homosexual couples today. In regard to gender roles, a homosexual relationship may well be more flexible than a heterosexual one in our society.

Gay and lesbian couples face challenges similar to those heterosexual couples face in creating satisfying relationships. In addition, they have distinctive concerns as members of a stigmatized minority. In the absence of social acceptance, couples face challenges regarding disclosing their relationship in their personal and work lives and coping with the stress from antigay discrimination and prejudice (Otis et al., 2006).

### Aspects of Gay and Lesbian Relationships

One study that compared characteristics of homosexual and heterosexual relationships found a major difference: Heterosexual couples were likely to adhere more closely to traditional gender-role expectations than were homosexual couples (Peplau, 1981). Most of the homosexual relationships studied resembled "best friendships" combined with romantic and erotic attraction.

This study also found many similarities between homosexual and heterosexual relationships. Matched samples of homosexual and heterosexual women and men indicated that being able to talk about one's most intimate feelings with a partner was most important in a love relationship. In addition, partners in a love relationship, regardless of sexual orientation, must reconcile desires for togetherness and independence. For many individuals, these desires were not mutually exclusive; some people wanted both a secure love relationship and meaningful activities and friendships separate from the relationship.

Responses from homosexual and heterosexual women were distinct in some ways from those of homosexual and heterosexual men. Women gave higher ratings to the importance of having an egalitarian relationship and having similar attitudes and political beliefs. Women also placed greater importance on emotional expressiveness within a relationship than did men. Compared with heterosexual women's sexual interactions, lesbian sexual interactions tend to have more of the characteristics often associated with greater sexual enjoyment. A review of the research comparing lesbian and heterosexual women's sexual experiences found that lesbian couples had more nongenital sexual interaction before genital contact, took more time in a sexual encounter, felt more comfortable using erotic language with each other, were more assertive sexually, and had lower rates of problems with orgasm (Iasenza, 2000).

Another study used a marital satisfaction inventory to compare relationship functioning of gay and lesbian couples with that of cohabiting heterosexual couples (Means-Christensen et al., 2003). The study found that cohabiting same-sex and other-sex couples have more similarities than differences in areas such as problem-solving communication, control over finances, and verbal and physical aggression. However, one difference between the groups was that lesbians and heterosexual men reported higher levels of satisfaction with the quality of emotional expressiveness and shared leisure time than did gay men and heterosexual women.

### Differences Between Gays and Lesbians in Sexual Attitude and Behavior

Homosexual men and women differ in the average number of their sexual partners. Lesbians are likely to have had far fewer sexual partners, and lesbian couples are much more likely than male couples to have monogamous relationships (Dubé, 2000; Roth-

Comedian Rosie O'Donnell developed R Family Vacations, which offers a cruise package especially designed for gay and lesbian families.

© Katy Winn/CORBIS

blum, 2000). Lesbians associate emotional closeness with sex more than do gay men, a finding consistent with the male/female heterosexual patterns discussed in Chapter 7. One study found that most lesbians waited to have sex with a partner until they had developed emotional intimacy. Although 46% of gay men had become friends with their partners before having sex, as a group they were more likely than lesbians to have had sexual experiences with casual acquaintances or people they had just met (Sanders, 2000). Gender-role socialization gives men more permission, even encouragement, to have casual sex than it gives women.

Beginning in the 1980s a lesbian "radical sex" subculture began to develop that was unparalleled among heterosexual women. Involvement in recreational sex, anonymous sex, "kinky" sex, group sex, sadomasochistic sex, and role-polarized sex went beyond the typical boundaries of female sexuality. Organizations sprang up for lesbians who pursue these sexual expressions, and this subculture continues to grow (Bonet et al., 2006; Nichols, 2000).

Before the AIDS epidemic some homosexual men had frequent casual sexual encounters—sometimes hundreds or more (Bell & Weinberg, 1978; Kinsey et al., 1948). These encounters were sometimes exceedingly brief, occurring in bathhouses, public restrooms, or in film booths in pornography shops. This type of brief recreational sexual contact is on the rise again, as AIDS has become less of a death sentence (Jefferson, 2005). However, sexual involvement with many partners is not universal among homosexual men (Isay, 1989; Kurdek, 1995a). Some men want to have a strong emotional relationship before becoming sexually involved. And for some men, being involved in an ongoing relationship eliminates sexual interest in other men.

## Family Life

Traditionally, a family has been considered to consist of a heterosexual couple and their children, but many forms of family life exist in contemporary society. Surveys indicate that between 45% and 80% of lesbians and between 40% and 60% of gay men are currently in a steady relationship, and many have long-term cohabiting relationships (National Gay and Lesbian Task Force, 2003). Homosexual people also form family units, either as single parents or as couples, with children, who are included in the family through a variety of circumstances. Census data show that 33% of lesbian and female bisexual couples and 22% of gay and male bisexual couples are raising children (National Gay and Lesbian Task Force, 2003). These families live not only in urban, progressive areas: 96% of counties in the United States have homosexual-parented families (Johnson & Piore, 2004). Many have children who were born in previous heterosexual marriages. A gay man or couple may enlist the help of a surrogate to have a baby. Others become parents with adopted or foster children (Brooks & Goldberg, 2001; Sherman, 2002).

Most laws about adoption by homosexual parents are ambiguous, and in many cases homosexual people adopt as individuals rather than couples (Galst & Hilty, 2003; Ryan et al., 2004). In 1998 New Jersey became the first state to allow partners in gay and lesbian couples to jointly adopt children, and California, Connecticut, Illinois, Massachusetts, New York, Vermont, and the District of Columbia have since established laws to permit such adoptions. Five states—Florida, Nebraska, Oklahoma, Utah, and Mississippi—have laws banning adoption by homosexual couples (National Gay and Lesbian Task Force, 2006; Tate, 2001). ■

People have questioned the ability of homosexual parents to provide a positive family environment for children. However, research has found that children of lesbian mothers are essentially no different from other children in terms of general development, self-esteem, gender-related problems, gender roles, and sexual orientation (Golombok et al., 2003). Most children with gay or lesbian parents grow up as heterosexual (Bailey et al., 1995; Golombok & Tasker, 1996). After analyzing scientific research on gay and lesbian parenthood, the American Academy of Pediatrics decided to endorse adoption by gay and lesbian couples to provide children with the security of two legally recognized parents (Contemporary Sexuality, 2002a).

In support of same-sex marriage, actors Angelina Jolie and Brad Pitt have stated that they will not legally marry until gay men and lesbians are granted the right to marry.

STR/AFP/Getty Images

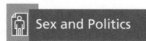

Sex and Politics

Unfortunately, children with gay or lesbian parents frequently face other people's prejudices (Barovick, 2002). They often have to learn to ignore name-calling, their friends' parents restricting their children from from visiting their homes, and others' ignorance (Howey & Samuels, 2000). For example, when a sixth-grade teacher asked for examples of different kinds of families, a girl who lived with her mother and her female partner raised her hand and offered, "Lesbian." The teacher replied, "This is such a nice town. There wouldn't be any lesbians living here" (Kantrowitz, 1996, p. 53).

The growing gay rights movement, which began in the 1960s, has provided support for many homosexual men and women and promoted greater knowledge and acceptance in the general community. In the following section, we describe some of the movement's activities.

# The Gay Rights Movement

InfoTrac Search Words

● Gay rights movement

Forty years before World War II the first organization promoting education about homosexuality and the abolition of laws against homosexuality was founded in Germany. However, the Nazis' rise to power ended the homosexual rights movement in Germany, and about 50,000 gay men were sent to death camps (Schoofs, 1997). Not until the 1950s did people in the United States found organizations for homosexual men and women, despite the conservative atmosphere of the times. The Mattachine Society had chapters in many cities and provided a national network for support and communication. The Daughters of Bilitis, an organization of lesbians, published a journal called *The Ladder*, which contained fiction, poetry, and political articles. The goals of both organizations were to educate homosexual and heterosexual people about homosexuality, increase understanding of homosexuality, and eliminate discriminatory laws toward homosexual individuals (Katz, 1976).

## The Stonewall Incident and Beyond

During the 1960s many people began to question traditional attitudes in American society in all areas, including the sexual. In this atmosphere, more and more homosexual people began to challenge the social problems they faced. The symbolic birth of homosexual activism occurred in 1969 in New York City when police raided a gay bar, the Stonewall. Police raids on gay bars were common, but this time the bar's patrons fought back. A riot ensued and did not end until the following day. The Stonewall incident served as a catalyst for the formation of gay rights groups, and activities such as Gay Pride Week and parades are held yearly to commemorate the Stonewall riot (Herrell, 1992). In 1994 more than 1 million people gathered in New York to celebrate the 25th anniversary of the incident. The following Sex and Politics box discusses goals of those who support gay rights.

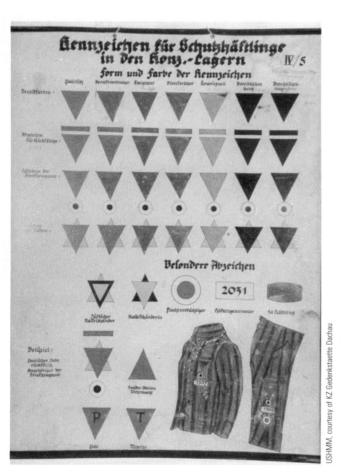

USHMM, courtesy of KZ Gedenkstaette Dachau

The Nazis linked homosexuality to a Jewish plot to weaken the masculinity of Aryan men. Nazi Germany decimated the base of the world's gay rights movement in Berlin. Forced to wear a pink triangle symbol on their sleeves, more than 100,000 gay men were arrested and about 50,000 were sent to death camps. The U.S. Holocaust Memorial Museum's exhibit The Nazi Persecution of Homosexuals, 1933–1945, illustrates this persecution of gay men (Karlin, 2003). In 2006 Berlin added a monument to gay victims of Nazi persecution to the city's Holocaust memorial.

# Goals of the Gay Rights Movement

Since the early 1970s various groups and individuals have worked to promote rights for lesbians, gays, and bisexual people while others have worked against these goals. Homosexual rights efforts fall into three general areas: decriminalization of private sexual behavior, antidiscrimination, and positive rights (Stein, 1999).

### Decriminalization of Private Sexual Behavior

The United States had a long history of laws declaring sodomy illegal. Sodomy was legally defined as oral and/or anal sex between heterosexuals and homosexuals. In 2003 the U.S. Supreme Court, basing its decision on the constitutional right to privacy, overturned a Texas sodomy law that made private sexual contact between homosexuals illegal. The *Lawrence et al. v. Texas* ruling also overturned laws in four other states that had banned sex between homosexuals and in another nine states that had banned "sodomy" (oral and/or anal sex) between partners of any sexual persuasion. Along with the majority of U.S. citizens who believe government should stay out of the bedrooms of consenting adults, gay rights supporters applauded the ruling because sodomy laws had been selectively enforced against homosexuals.

### Antidiscrimination

The National Gay Task Force was founded in 1973 to help meet the second goal of the gay rights movement, to end various kinds of discrimination toward homosexuals. A major legislative goal of gay rights advocates is an amendment to the 1964 Civil Rights Act that would broaden it to include "affectional or sexual orientation" along with race, creed, color, and sex (Wildman, 2001). This would make it illegal to discriminate in housing, employment, insurance, and public accommodations on the grounds of sexual orientation (Cohn, 1992). Further, International Day Against Homophobia, an organization based in Paris, has begun a global campaign to establish a United Nations resolution to decriminalize homosexuality worldwide (Tin, 2006).

Enormous progress ending discrimination in the workplace has occurred. In 1980 no company offered domestic partner benefits; currently more than 8,000 do. Further, 92.2% of Fortune 500 companies have anti-discrimination policies based on sexual orientation. The number of major companies that score 100% on the Human Rights Campaign's Corporate Equality Index increased from 13 to 103. The scoring is based on company practices and policies prohibiting discrimination based on sexual orientation and gender identity, diversity training, and providing benefits to employee partners (Solomonese, 2005). Seventeen states, the District of Columbia, and many city governments have also established laws and policies prohibiting anti-

| TABLE 9.3 | States With Nondiscrimination Laws for Sexual Orientation |
|---|---|
| California | Nevada |
| Connecticut | New Hampshire |
| District of Columbia | New Jersey |
| Hawaii | New Mexico |
| Illinois | New York |
| Maine | Rhode Island |
| Maryland | Vermont |
| Massachusetts | Washington |
| Minnesota | Wisconsin |

SOURCE: National Gay and Lesbian Task Force, State Nondiscrimination Laws in the U.S., May 2006, Washington, D.C.

gay discrimination (○ Table 9.3) (Abbott et al., 2006; Sullivan, 2003).

Almost 90% of Americans believe that homosexual people should have equal rights in employment, as seen in ○ Table 9.4 (Gallup Poll, 2006; Leland, 2000b). However, only 33% of the respondents in a survey of the general population believe that there is a lot of discrimination against homosexual people, and even fewer, 29%, said our government needs to do more to protect homosexual rights. These statistics contrast greatly with the survey of the homosexual population: 60% believe that there is a lot of discrimination, and 83% believe that the government needs to do more to protect their rights (Leland, 2000b).

Eliminating discrimination in the military has been far less successful than in employment and housing. Gays have always served in the U.S. military—and have always faced hostility. After Bill Clinton was elected president in 1992, Congress and Clinton implemented the "don't ask, don't tell" policy. According to this policy, homosexuals were allowed to

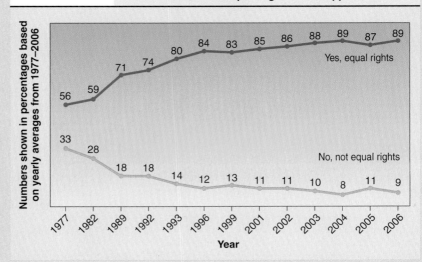

**TABLE 9.4** Percentage of Adults Who Think Homosexuals Should or Should Not Have an Equal Right to Job Opportunities

Numbers shown in percentages based on yearly averages from 1977–2006

Yes, equal rights: 1977: 56; 1982: 59; 1989: 71; 1992: 74; 1993: 80; 1996: 84; 1999: 83; 2001: 85; 2002: 86; 2003: 88; 2004: 89; 2005: 87; 2006: 89

No, not equal rights: 1977: 33; 1982: 28; 1989: 18; 1992: 18; 1993: 14; 1996: 12; 1999: 13; 2001: 11; 2002: 11; 2003: 10; 2004: 8; 2005: 11; 2006: 9

Year

FAMILY *Redefined.*

*For more information, visit* PETINSURANCE.COM/FAMILY

All family members deserve the best healthcare, including your pet. A VPI Pet Insurance policy can safeguard against the rising cost of veterinary care by helping pay for lab fees, medications, surgeries, X-rays, and more. VPI also offers coverage for routine care that includes vaccinations and prescription flea control. Best of all, you're free to use any licensed veterinarian, anywhere. Protecting your entire family just got easier.

**CALL TODAY TO SPEAK TO A LICENSED PET INSURANCE SPECIALIST. 800-874-0362**

*Courtesy of Veterinary Pet Insurance Co./DVM Insurance Agency (VPI)*

serve in the military—even though the military considered them unfit for service—provided that they kept their orientation secret (Hernandez, 2006).

Two linguists in the Army—one fluent in Korean, the other fluent in three languages and training to be an interrogator—were among the 322 linguists discharged from the military under the "don't ask, don't tell" policy (Curtis, 2005).

© Christopher Lane

Since implementation of the policy, an estimated 11,000 gays and lesbians—more than before the policy—have been expelled from the military (Mansfield, 2006). According to the Servicemembers Legal Defense Network, by the year 2000, discharges on the basis of sexual orientation were 73% higher than before the "don't ask, don't tell" policy (Fone, 2000). Lesbians are even more likely than gay men to be expelled; almost 33% of military personnel discharged because of their sexual orientation were women, although women make up only 14% of the armed forces (Biederman, 2003). This policy has been a disservice to the nation, as highlighted by the discharges of gay and lesbian translators of Arabic and other key languages, which may have seriously compromised U.S. diplomatic and counter-terrorism efforts by leaving critical counterintelligence material untranslated (Frank, 2005).

During the Iraq occupation, the need for secrecy has had adverse effects on closeted homosexual troops. Both partners in a relationship have to be circumspect when communicating with each other. Partners at home have no access to support services that the military provides families; consequently, they are unlikely to be the first to know if their loved ones are wounded, captured, or killed (Biederman, 2003). Ironically, closeted gay and lesbian U.S. troops are serving alongside openly homosexual troops from Great Britain and Australia, 2 of the 24 nations that welcome homosexual soldiers (Neff, 2004).

Sexual orientation has no known negative effect on the ability of troops to work together effectively (Bull, 2003). However, since 1994 an estimated $200 million has been spent to recruit and train troops later discharged for homosexuality—money that could have been better spent on providing troops with lifesaving equipment (Curtis, 2005). Furthermore, the "don't ask, don't tell" policy has not been supported by the majority of the general population. Gallup polls indicate that 63% of people support gays and lesbians serving openly in the military, compared with 32% who oppose it (Kiefer, 2006). In 2006, the Servicemembers Legal Defense Network organized over 100 bipartisan members of Congress to support a bill repealing the military's ban on homosexual people serving openly in the military (Osburn, 2006).

Beyond decriminalization of gay and lesbian sexual behavior and legal protection from discrimination, positive rights provide equal recognition and protection for gays' and lesbians' relationships and families. Legal adoption and marriage are positive rights issues. Earlier in this chapter, we discussed the benefits to children of having both their parents legally recognized as such, and we will discuss the debate about homosexual marriage in Chapter 13.

> **? Critical Thinking Question**
>
> If you had the power to decide whether gays and lesbians could serve openly in the U.S. military, what would you decide? Why?

The current homosexual rights situation is well stated by Kevin Jennings, founder of the Gay, Lesbian, and Straight Education Network: "It's the best and worst times to be gay. There's an unprecedented level of visibility and activism, but with that an unprecedented level of backlash and opposition" (Ritter, 2000, p. 3). We hope that progress will continue to be made and that homosexual men and women will be freer to love, work, and contribute to society.

# SUMMARY

## A Continuum of Sexual Orientations

- The word *homosexual* can represent an objective or subjective appraisal of sexual behavior, emotional affiliation, and/or self-definition.
- Kinsey's seven-point continuum ranges from exclusive heterosexuality to exclusive homosexuality. Kinsey based his ratings on a combination of erotic attraction and overt sexual behaviors.
- According to estimates from the National Health and Social Life Survey, approximately 2.8% of men and 1.4% of women identify themselves as homosexual.
- Bisexuality can be characterized by overt behaviors and/or erotic responses to both males and females. As with heterosexuality and homosexuality, a clear-cut definition of bisexuality is difficult to establish.
- Four types of bisexuality are real orientation, transitory orientation, transitional orientation, and homosexual denial.
- Asexuality is a lack of sexual attraction to either sex.

## What Determines Sexual Orientation?

- A number of psychosocial and biological theories have attempted to explain the development of homosexuality.
- Psychosocial theories relate to parenting patterns, life experiences, or psychological attributes of a person.
- Theories of biological causation look to prenatal or adult hormone differences as well as genetic factors. A biological predisposition toward homosexuality for some gays and lesbians is suggested by research on twins, finger length, handedness, and gender nonconformity.
- Sexual orientation, regardless of where it falls on the continuum, seems to form through a composite of factors unique to each person.

## Societal Attitudes

- Cross-cultural attitudes toward homosexuality range from condemnation to acceptance. Negative attitudes toward homosexuality still predominate in our society.
- Current Judeo-Christian positions toward homosexuality vary greatly.

- Homophobia is the irrational fear of homosexuality, the fear of homosexual feelings within oneself, or self-loathing because of one's own homosexuality. Young males often exhibit the most extreme homophobia, especially in perpetrating hate crimes.
- Since the early 1990s, the media have increasingly portrayed homosexuality in a positive light—a development that may help lead to increasing familiarity with and acceptance of homosexuality.

## Lifestyles

- Contrary to popular stereotypes, homosexual individuals exhibit a wide variety of lifestyles.
- The choice of coming out or being "in the closet" often has a significant effect on a homosexual person's lifestyle. The steps of coming out involve recognizing one's homosexual orientation, deciding how to view oneself, and being open about one's homosexuality.
- As gender-role stereotyping has decreased, many couples—both homosexual and heterosexual—have developed increasingly egalitarian relationships. Differences between homosexual men and homosexual women can be attributed to general gender-role differences between men and women. Lesbian "sex radicals" are moving past typical boundaries of female sexuality.

## The Gay Rights Movement

- Homosexual activism arose in the late 1960s. Its main goals are decriminalization of private sexual behavior, antidiscrimination in employment, housing, and the military, and positive rights, such as marriage and adoption. These goals are opposed by various individuals and groups.

## ◗ Suggested Readings

**Fone, Byrne** (2000). *Homophobia: A History*. New York: Metropolitan Books. A chronicle of the evolution of homophobia through the centuries and how it remains the last acceptable prejudice.

**Rust, Paula** (Ed.) (2000). *Bisexuality in the United States*. New York: Columbia University Press. A collection of important writings on theories of and research on bisexuality.

**Stein, Ed** (1999). *The Mismeasure of Desire: The Science, Theory, and Ethics of Sexual Orientation*. Oxford: Oxford University Press. An in-depth analysis of research on biological causes of homosexuality. Stein critiques the limitations and liabilities of the "we're born that way" rationale for homosexual rights.

**Sullivan, Andrew** (1995). *Virtually Normal*. New York: Knopf. A gay conservative deals with his sexual orientation and offers unique perspectives on other conservatives.

## ◗ Resources

**The National Gay and Lesbian Task Force**, 1325 Massachusetts Ave. NW, Washington, DC 20005; (202) 393-5177. A group that provides information about social, political, and educational organizations in particular locales.

**National Center for Lesbian Rights**, 870 Market Street, Suite 570, San Francisco, CA 94102; (415) 392-6257. A legal resource center working to eradicate discrimination against lesbians.

**Parents, Families, and Friends of Lesbians and Gays (PFLAG)**, 1726 M Street NW, Suite 400, Washington, DC 20036; (202) 467-8194. A group that provides support and counseling for parents, and public education on homosexual rights.

## ◗ Web Resources

**CengageNOW Web Site**

Go to **academic.cengage.com** to link to practice quiz questions, interactive activities, Internet links, critical thinking exercises, discussion forums, and more. You can also access sites from the Wadsworth Psychology Study Center (**academic.cengage.com/psychology**) or you can connect directly to the following sites:

**An Encyclopedia of Gay, Lesbian, Bisexual, and Queer Culture**

This Web site offers a free encyclopedia about homosexual and bisexual culture.

**Bisexual Resource Center**

This site presents a variety of information related to bisexuality, including feature articles, news updates, and links.

**Sexual Orientation: Science, Education, and Policy**

This Web site builds on the work of Gregory Herek at the University of California, Davis. Herek's research focuses on sexual orientation, anti-homosexual violence, homophobia, and other concerns of gay men, lesbians, and bisexual people.

**Sexual Orientation and Homosexuality**

This page on the Web site of the American Psychological Association provides detailed answers to commonly asked questions about what determines sexual orientation.

**Youth Talkline**

A free and confidential service staffed by young peer counselors to talk about issues of gay youth.

**Human Rights Campaign**

The Human Rights Campaign is an organization dedicated to securing equal rights for lesbians and gay men. The group's Web site provides news updates on legislation related to homosexual rights, descriptions of its public education programs, and information on such topics as coming out.

**The Advocate Online**

*The Advocate*, a weekly national newsmagazine covering issues of interest to lesbians and gay men, offers up-to-date news and feature articles on its Web site.

**Lesbian Mothers Support Society**

This Web site offers peer support and information on a range of topics related to becoming pregnant and being a lesbian parent.

**Our Sexuality Book Companion Web Site** academic.cengage.com/psychology/ **crooks** Visit your book companion Web site where you will find flash cards, practice quizzes, Internet links, and more to help you study.

## Just what you need to know NOW!

Spend time on what you need to master rather than on information you already have learned. Take a pretest for this chapter, and CengageNOW will generate a personalized study plan based on your results. The study plan will identify the topics you need to review and direct you to online resources to help you master those topics. You can then take a post-test to help you determine the concepts you have mastered and what you will still need to work on. Try it out! Go to **academic.cengage.com/login** to sign in with an access code or to purchase access to this product.

## InfoTrac College Edition Online Library

Sign in to **academic.cengage.com/login** or visit your free book companion Web site at **academic.cengage.com/psychology/crooks** to access InfoTrac College Edition, an online searchable library that includes a multitude of journals, many specific to human sexuality. These journals include *Archives of Sexual Behavior; Archives of Sexual Health Behavior; Canadian Journal of Human Sexuality; Hispanic Journal of the Behavioral Sciences; Journal of Cross-Cultural Psychology; Journal of Physical Education, Recreation, and Dance; Journal of Sex Research;* and *Sex Roles.*

# Contraception

© Deborah Gilbert/Getty Images

*It's a good thing that there are lots of birth control options, because I've used most of them at one time or another. I was able to be on the pill before my boyfriend and I first started having intercourse in college. That was before AIDS, so I didn't need to use anything else "embarrassing." I tried the combination pill and the minipill, then used an IUD for a while. After I was first married, we used natural family planning and the diaphragm or cervical cap successfully. After our children were born, foam and condoms filled in for us until my husband got a vasectomy. I never had any particular problems with any of the methods, and I'm very grateful to never have had an unwanted pregnancy, but it sure is nice to be free of needing to use contraceptives. (Authors' files)*

# Historical and Social Perspectives

People's concern with controlling conception goes back at least to the beginning of recorded history. In ancient Egypt women placed dried crocodile dung next to the cervix to prevent conception. In 6th-century Greece, eating the uterus, testis, or hoof paring of a mule was recommended. In more recent historical times the 18th-century Italian adventurer Giovanni Casanova was noted for his animal-membrane condoms tied with a ribbon at the base of the penis. In 17th-century western Europe vaginal sponges soaked in a variety of solutions were used for contraception (McLaren, 1990).

## Contraception in the United States

Although we may take for granted the variety of contraceptive, or birth control, methods available in the United States today, this situation is quite recent. Throughout American history both the methods available for contraception and the laws concerning their use have been restrictive. In the 1870s, Anthony Comstock, then secretary of the New York Society for the Suppression of Vice, succeeded in enacting national laws that prohibited the dissemination of contraceptive information through the U.S. mail on the grounds that such information was obscene; these laws were known as the Comstock Laws (Kreinen, 2002a). At that time, the only legitimate form of birth control was abstinence, and reproduction was viewed as the only acceptable reason for sexual intercourse.

Margaret Sanger was the person most instrumental in promoting changes in birth control legislation and availability in the United States. Sanger was horrified at the misery of women who had virtually no control over their fertility and bore child after child in desperate poverty. In 1915 she opened an illegal clinic where women could obtain and learn to use the diaphragms she had shipped from Europe. She also published birth control information in her newspaper, *The Woman Rebel*. As a result, Sanger was arraigned for violating the Comstock Laws. She fled to Europe to avoid prosecution but later returned to promote research on birth control hormones, a project financed by her wealthy friend Katherine Dexter McCormack.

Sanger and McCormack wanted to develop a reliable method by which women could control their own fertility (Tone, 2002). However, it was not until 1960 that the first birth control pills came on the U.S. market, after limited testing and research in Puerto Rico. Fertility control through contraception rather than abstinence was a profound shift that implied an acceptance of female sexual expression and broadened the roles that women might choose (D'Emilio & Freedman, 1988; Harer, 2001).

Prior to the 1965 U.S. Supreme Court ruling of *Griswold* v. *Connecticut*, states could prohibit the use of contraceptives by married people (381 U.S. 479). The Court based its decision to overrule states' prohibitions on the right to privacy of married couples. In 1972 the Supreme Court case *Eisenstadt* v. *Baird* extended the right to privacy to unmarried individuals by decriminalizing the use of contraception by single people (405 U.S. 438).

Margaret Sanger dedicated herself to helping women and families have every child be a wanted child.

Critical Thinking Question

How does the belief that abstinence is the only moral form of birth control play out today?

In the ensuing years other laws governing contraceptive availability have continued to change. In most states, laws now allow the dispensing of contraceptives to adolescents without parental consent and permit pharmacies to display condoms, spermicidal foam, and contraceptive sponges on shelves in the main store rather than behind the counter. Controversy continues on the national level about whether to require parental notification when minors receive contraceptive services from government-funded organizations. The concern, of course, is that teens who would otherwise choose not to have intercourse would have it if contraception were easily available. However, research indicates that the rate of sexual activity does not increase even when condoms are available at schools for no cost (Blake et al., 2003). ∎

## Contraception as a Contemporary Issue

Worldwide contraceptive use has increased dramatically in the last several decades: an estimated 60% of couples currently use contraception, compared with 10% in 1970 (David & Russo, 2003). In the Western world, 95% of women have used contraception at one time or another. Furthermore, the typical heterosexual woman may need some form of contraception for 30 or more years because she is only trying to become pregnant, or is pregnant, for a small percentage of her reproductive life (Reape, 2005). The increase in teenagers' contraceptive use is very positive news. As contrasted with an early 1990 survey, in 2006 about 20% more teens reported using condoms the last time they had sexual intercourse, and fewer are attempting to prevent pregnancy by using the ineffective approach of withdrawal (Santelli et al., 2006).

? Critical Thinking Question

What role, if any, did religion play in your parents' contraceptive use? In your birth control decisions?

The availability and use of reliable birth control is desirable for a variety of reasons. First and foremost, with contraception heterosexual couples can enjoy sexual intimacy with minimal risk of unwanted pregnancies. Children are more likely to be born to parents who are prepared for the responsibility of rearing them, and the ability to space children at least 18 months apart increases newborn health (Conde-Agudelo et al., 2006). Far fewer women than ever before have to decide to have an abortion. Effective birth control methods have also allowed women in the United States to become equal partners with men in modern society. As a result of the increased earning power of women, men have had opportunities unknown to their own fathers to expand their involvement with their children (Pope, 2006).

Many contemporary religious groups approve of and even favor the use of birth control. However, objections to contraception often stem from religious beliefs, and some individuals and couples do not use a birth control device because of their religion. Despite the fact that most Roman Catholics in the United States use contraception and want the Pope to approve its use for Catholics, the official doctrine of the Church still holds that all birth control methods other than abstinence and methods based on the menstrual cycle are immoral (Kissling, 2003; McClure, 2004; Shorto, 2006). Many far-right Christians, self-described as "pro-life," also oppose contraceptive use and include it along with comprehensive sex education and abortion in the "unholy trinity," which constitutes "a

Nirmala Palsamy was named "Heroine of the Planet" in honor of her work to educate women about family planning and birth control.

blasphemous mockery of God's plan for the family" (Human Life International, 2004, p. 2), as explained further in the following boxes "How Far-Right Politics in the United States Denies Contraception to People in the Developing World" and "The Power of Pro-Life Anti-Contraception Politics."

Making contraceptives available to the men and women throughout the world who desire to use them will help alleviate overpopulation. At the end of the 20th century,

## How Far-Right Politics in the United States Denies Contraception to People in the Developing World

Tragically, millions of women and couples around the world are unable to exercise their right to decide freely and responsibly whether and when to have children. UNFPA, the United Nations Population Fund, estimates that 561 million women and their partners around the globe do not have access to effective contraceptive methods, resulting in 22 million abortions, 1.4 million infant deaths, and 142,000 pregnancy-related deaths of mothers (Cohen, 2006; Illingsworth, 2006). In these countries the chances of dying from complications of pregnancy, childbirth, and abortion average 1 in 65. The African country Niger has the worst rate: 1 in 7 mothers there dies in childbirth (Page, 2006). In contrast, women in developed countries have a 1 in 2,125 chance of the same fate (Mulchahey, 2005).

The Bush administration has contributed to these problems by enacting its anti-contraception policies globally as well as domestically (Brazile, 2006). In fact, the United States is the only country that has international anti-contraceptive organi-zations. Every year since 2002, the Bush administration has refused to release $34 million that Congress appropriated for UNPFA to provide contraceptive and women's reproductive health services. The Pro-Life Caucus in Congress, the right-wing Population Research Institute (which considers providing voluntary contraceptive services a human rights abuse), and another 100 pro-life groups lobbied successfully to block release of the funds (Page, 2006). Furthermore, Bush proposed a severe funding cut in 2007 to another reproductive health organization, USAID, the U.S. Agency for International Development. USAID and UNFPA provide a significant proportion of contraceptive and maternal health services to developing nations. To attempt to counter the Bush administration's cuts and provide funding for these programs, a bipartisan group in Congress has developed the Ensuring Access to Contraceptives Act of 2006. It is unknown at the time of this writing whether this proposed legislation will be effective in restoring funds (Cohen, 2006).

worldwide population stood at 6.5 billion, compared with less than half that number—2.3 billion—in 1950. The United Nations projects an increase to 8.9 billion by 2050. Of that growth, 95% is expected to occur in poorer, developing countries, where the population already exceeds the availability of bare necessities: housing, food, and fuel. When impoverished families have many children, they cannot secure adequate food, health care, and education for each child (Page, 2006). Furthermore, overpopulation (and overconsumption of the world's resources by developed countries) poses a dire threat to the earth's environment.

An essential factor in controlling population levels is to expand women's access to education and economic opportunity (Douglas, 2006; Zlidar et al., 2004). Across the globe women with higher levels of education have fewer children (Morgan, 2003); and as **⊙ Figure 10.1** illustrates, this pattern also holds across ethnic lines in the United States.

> **? Critical Thinking Question**
>
> How are the limits to contraception access gained by pro-life religious groups compatible or incompatible with freedom of religion?

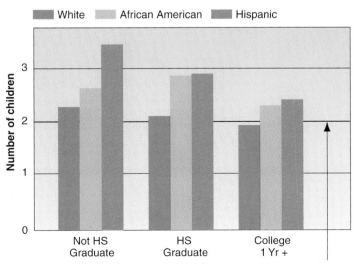

■ White ■ African American ■ Hispanic

As the education of women increases, the number of children they have decreases. Reproductive patterns among racial groups become more similiar the higher the education level (Grant, 1994).

**⊙ Figure 10.1** Average number of children by mother's education level and race or ethnicity in the United States. The more educated a woman is, the fewer children she is likely to have. Reproductive patterns among racial groups become more similar the higher the education level is (Grant, 1994).

## The Power of Pro-Life Anti-Contraception Politics

Although the vast majority of U.S. citizens think favorably toward birth control, much of the pro-life religious right opposes all contraceptive methods. They are zealous in their activism to prevent other people's access to it and have well-financed organizations. Their political influence has grown since George W. Bush became president. During his administration Bush has implemented many policies and laws concerning reproductive health, in support of the extreme right's goals. He has also appointed anti-birth control individuals to key reproductive health, judicial, and scientific positions in the government (Tummino, 2006). For example, in late 2006 president George W. Bush appointed Eric Keroack as head of family-planning programs in the Department of Health and Human Services, despite opposition from members of Congress and reproductive-rights groups. Keroak was formerly the medical director for "crisis pregnancy centers" that advise against the use of contraceptives and advocate abstinence to prevent pregnancy. His new position gives him authority over $283 million each year to provide contraceptive services, primarily to individuals with low incomes (Fox, 2006). Whether influenced by his own personal religious beliefs or his need to maintain the votes of his far-right supporters, Bush's leadership has resulted in keeping far more women in the United States and around the world from having access to contraception and from being able to prevent unwanted pregnancies (Page, 2006). We will discuss the influence of politics on condom education and use, contraception in the developing world, and emergency contraception in Sex and Politics boxes throughout this chapter.

Anti-contraception religious groups do not see contraceptives as a means of preventing abortion. Rather, they believe that "the dangerous practice of birth control is a gateway to abortion" (American Life League, 2006, p. 2). They attempt to justify their opposition to birth control by inaccurately claiming that oral contraceptives and emergency contraception cause abortion by preventing the fertilized egg (called the blastocyst, which contains 30 to 200 cells) from implanting on the uterine wall. However, birth control pills and emergency contraception work primarily by preventing ovulation, and altering the uterine lining to prevent implantation may be one of several infrequent secondary means by which these contraceptives prevent pregnancy. False claims about how methods work appear to be a thin veneer on pro-lifers' overall opposition to birth control, as clearly stated by the American Life League, "A.L.L. is opposed to all abortion, contraception and other threats to the human person and family" (American Life League, 2006). Even methods like condoms, spermicides, and diaphragms that prevent the egg and sperm from reaching one another are believed to offend God because they prevent the conception of a human being (Pope, 2006). In essence, this religious belief in the

prerogative of sperm and egg to join trumps every individuals' and couples' choice to use contraception (Phillips, 2006).

Many pro-life supporters embrace the traditional role of women staying at home and raising children as an ideal. Therefore, they view access to contraception, in its potential to help women expand their roles beyond obligatory reproduction into traditional male realms of work and politics, to be a threat they must defeat (Phillips, 2006; Quindlen, A., 2005; Scheidler, 2006). Of course, this thinking occurs elsewhere in the world. For example, gender-role expectations of those in political power in Japan were the reason birth control pills were illegal there until 1999. Government leaders opposed the pill because it gave women some independence in decisions about their fertility and sexuality, which was incongruent with the traditional ideal of the docile Japanese woman (*Contemporary Sexuality*, 1999b).

Belief in the vital role of contraception in women's health has led to lawsuits and legislative bills aimed at requiring health insurers to provide coverage for prescription contraceptives. In 1998, the Pro-Life Caucus of Congress succeeded in defeating federal legislation that would have required health insurance companies to pay for birth control. Since then, 23 states have passed legislation to require insurers that cover prescription drugs to include contraceptives in their coverage (Alan Guttmacher Institute, 2006).

In the United States, anti-contraception forces have worked to reduce federal and state funding for contraceptive services. Funding for community clinics that provide free or affordable birth control has declined 59% since 1980, leaving several million low-income women without access to contraception, in spite of the fact that 73% of Americans believe that access to birth control should not be limited by someone's inability to pay for it (Harris, 2006; Lindberg et al., 2006). At the state level, pro-life Christian groups have persuaded several state governments to put all family planning funds into "abortion alternative" programs. In Missouri, such a reallocation cast adrift 30,000 women who had relied on state-funded birth control (Pollitt, 2005).

The consequences of the funding and program cuts for low-income women are obvious: Since 1994, unplanned pregnancy rates among poor women have increased by 29% while the rates among higher-income women have decreased by 20% (Kristof, 2006). Furthermore, states with higher public family planning expenditures have reported lower rates of unplanned pregnancy and abortion and improved health of infants. Another result of restrictions to birth control is that the United States has one of the highest abortion rates of any Western country (Feldmann, 2006; Speroff & Fritz, 2005). These statistics indicate that opposing birth control, and the changes in gender roles and the meaning of sexual expression it supports, is a higher pro-life priority than preventing abortion.

# Sharing Responsibility and Choosing a Birth Control Method

Each birth control method has its advantages and disadvantages. An individual or a couple might find that one method suits a certain situation best. Sharing the responsibility enhances a particular method's use.

## It Takes Two

Research shows that more couples share contraceptive decision making now than in the past (Grady et al., 2000). Sharing the responsibility of contraception can enhance a relationship and can be a good way to practice discussing personal and sexual topics. Failing to talk about birth control can cause women to resent men for putting the entire responsibility on them. Furthermore, it is foolish for a man to assume that a woman has "taken care of herself." As one male student asked:

> If you have sex with a girl and she tells you she's on the pill, how do you know if she's telling the truth? (Authors' files)

Many women do not regularly practice birth control, especially if they are not in a long-term relationship, and some use methods inconsistently or incorrectly (Trussell et al., 1999). Not using contraception can negatively affect both partners' sexual experience and general feelings of well-being, and dealing with an unwanted pregnancy is difficult (Brooks, 2002). It is in the best interests of both partners to be actively involved in choosing and using contraception.

The first step in sharing contraceptive responsibility may be for one partner to ask the other about birth control before having intercourse for the first time. Research has found that both male and female college students need to develop skills to discuss contraception. Women need to become effective in obtaining contraceptives, and men need to learn to be assertive about refusing to engage in intercourse without effective contraception (Gilliam, 2006; Van den Bossche & Rubinson, 1997). Openness to using condoms or to engaging in noncoital sexual activities, whether as the contraceptive method of choice or as a backup or temporary method, is another way for partners to share responsibility for birth control.

**Would you be more careful if it was you that got pregnant?**

See your pharmacist for free information on family planning, venereal disease and other communicable diseases.

For the Clinic nearest you call your local Health Department or (800) 952-5250

Sponsored by Pharmacists Planning Service, Inc. in conjunction with La Clinica De La Raza, Oakland, California

Photography by DALE ALISON BARTON

## Choosing a Birth Control Method

Many forms of birth control are available to couples. However, an ideal method—one that is 100% effective, completely safe, with no side effects, reversible, separate from sexual activity, inexpensive, easy to obtain, usable by either sex, and not dependent on the user's memory—is unavailable now and in the foreseeable future (Mills & Barclay, 2006). Each current method has advantages and disadvantages with regard to effectiveness, side effects, cost, and convenience (as summarized in Tables 10.1 and 10.2). It is a good idea to be familiar with the various methods available because most people will use several of them during their active sex lives.

## Effectiveness

Contraceptive effectiveness is best evaluated by looking at the **failure rate** (the number of women out of 100 who become pregnant by the end of the first year of using a particular method). ○ **Table 10.1** shows the failure rate when contraceptive methods are used correctly and consistently; it also shows the rate of accidental pregnancies resulting from improper or inconsistent use. The most important variable of method

**Failure rate** The number of women out of 100 who become pregnant by the end of 1 year of using a particular contraceptive.

## ⊙ TABLE 10.1 Effectiveness of Various Birth Control Methods

| Method | Failure Rate[a] if Used Correctly and Consistently | Typical Number[a] Who Become Pregnant Accidentally |
|---|---|---|
| Outercourse | 0 | 0 |
| **Hormone-based methods** | | |
| Estrogen–progestin pills, including Seasonale | 0.1 | 8 |
| Progestin-only pills | 0.5 | 3 |
| Vaginal ring (NuvaRing) | 0.3 | 8 |
| Skin patch (Ortho Evra) | 0.3 | 8 |
| Depo-Provera injection | 0.3 | 0.3 |
| Lunelle | 0.05 | 0.2 |
| Implanon | 0.1 | 0.1 |
| Progesterone IUDs | | |
|     Progestasert T | 0.1 | 0.1 |
|     Mirena | 0.1 | 0.1 |
| **Barrier and spermicide methods** | | |
| Male condoms | 3 | 16 |
| Female condoms | 5 | 21 |
| Vaginal spermicides | 6 | 26 |
| Cervical barrier methods with spermicide | | |
|     Diaphragm with spermicide | 6 | 12 |
|     Cervical cap | | |
|       Woman has been pregnant | 20 | 40 |
|       Woman has never been pregnant | 9 | 20 |
|     Sponge | | |
|       Woman has been pregnant | 20 | 40 |
|       Woman has never been pregnant | 9 | 20 |
|     FemCap | 4 | 15 |
|     Lea's Shield | 6 | 18 |
| **Nonhormonal IUD** | | |
| Copper-T (Paragard) | 0.6 | 0.8 |
| **Sterilization** | | |
| Tubal sterilization | 0.05 | 0.5 |
| Vasectomy | 0.1 | 0.2 |
| **Fertility awareness** | | |
| Standard days method | 5 | 12 |
| Rhythm, calendar, basal temperature, and cervical mucus methods | 9 | 20 |
| **Withdrawal** | 4 | 24 |
| **No method** | 85 | 85 |

[a]Number of women out of 100 who become pregnant by the end of the first year of using a particular method.

SOURCES: Akert (2003), Alan Guttmacher Institute (2002), Hutti (2003), Long (2002), and Speroff & Fritz (2005).

effectiveness is human error. Ignorance of the correct use of a method, negative beliefs about using a method, lack of partner involvement, forgetfulness, or deciding that "this one time won't matter" all greatly reduce effectiveness and increase the chances of pregnancy. In addition, people who feel guilty about sex are less likely to use contraception effectively (Strassberg & Mahoney, 1988). Men and women who are uncomfortable with their sexuality are likely to take a passive role in contraceptive decision making, leaving themselves vulnerable to whatever their partners do, or do not do, about birth control. A woman may also be concerned about whether her partner sees her as a "nice girl" or as "easy." A simple way to appear as a "nice girl" is to be unprepared with birth control (Angier, 1999).

About half of all unintended pregnancies occur among women using contraceptives (Speroff & Fritz, 2005). Unmarried women younger than 30 years old are most likely to have a contraceptive failure, and married women older than 30 are least likely to do so. In addition, low-income women experience greater failure rates than more-affluent women, possibly because of limited availability of health care (Fu et al., 1999).

## Using Backup Methods to Increase Contraceptive Effectiveness

Under various circumstances, a couple may need or want to use **backup methods**—that is, more than one method of contraception used simultaneously. Condoms, contraceptive foam, and the diaphragm are possible backup methods that can be combined in many ways with other birth control methods for extra contraceptive protection. Circumstances in which a couple might use a backup method include the following:

**Backup methods** Contraceptive methods used simultaneously with another method to support it.

- During the first cycle of the pill.
- For the remainder of the cycle, after forgetting to take two or more birth control pills or after several days of diarrhea or vomiting while on the pill.
- The first month after changing to a new brand of pills.
- When taking medications, such as antibiotics, that reduce the effectiveness of the pill.
- During the initial 1 to 3 months after IUD insertion.
- When first learning to use a new method of birth control.
- When the couple wants to increase the effectiveness of contraception (for instance, using foam and a condom together offers effective protection).

## Which Contraceptive Method Is Right for You?

Effectiveness is not the only important factor in choosing a method of birth control. Many additional factors—including cost, ease of use, and potential side effects—influence individuals' and couples' decisions about whether to use a particular birth control method. ⊙ **Table 10.2** summarizes some of the most important factors: comparative expenses and advantages versus disadvantages of the most commonly used methods.

Beyond the variables listed in Table 10.2, the decision about which birth control method to use must take into account one more important factor: the individuals who will be using it (Ranjit et al., 2001). The statements presented in the boxed discussion "Which Contraceptive Method Is Best for You?" (page 272) are designed to help you take into account your own concerns, circumstances, physical condition, and personal qualities as you make this very individual decision. We discuss a number of commonly used contraceptive methods in the paragraphs that follow, and this more specific information may help you make your choice.

## "Outercourse"

This important method deserves special mention because it involves the decision to be sexual without engaging in penile–vaginal intercourse. Noncoital forms of sexual intimacy, which have been called **outercourse**, can be a viable form of birth control. Outercourse includes all avenues of sexual intimacy other than penile–vaginal intercourse, including kissing, touching, mutual masturbation, and oral and anal sex. The voluntary avoidance of coitus offers effective protection from pregnancy, provided that the male does not ejaculate near the vaginal opening. Outercourse can be used as a primary or temporary means of preventing pregnancy, and it can also be used when it is advisable not to have intercourse for other reasons—for example, following childbirth or abortion or during a herpes outbreak. This method has no undesirable contraceptive side effects. However, it does not eliminate the chances of spreading sexually transmitted diseases, especially if it involves oral or anal sex.

**Outercourse** Noncoital forms of sexual intimacy.

| Method | Cost per Year for 100 Occurrences of Intercourse | Advantages | Disadvantages |
|---|---|---|---|
| Outercourse | 0 | No medical side effects; helps develop nonintercourse sexual intimacy. | Risk of unplanned intercourse; no protection from STDs. |
| **Hormone-based methods** | | | |
| Estrogen–progestin pills, including Seasonale | $384–$516 ($32–$43 per cycle) | Very effective. No interruption of sexual experience. Reduces PMS, menstrual cramps, and flow. Improves acne. May reduce migraine headaches associated with menstrual cycle fluctuations. Reduced risk of ovarian, endometrial, and colon cancer. No increased risk of stroke in healthy, nonsmoking women under age 35. | No protection from STDs. Slightly increased risk of blood clot, especially in first 2 years of use. May increase migraine headaches. Possible side effects of nausea, fluid retention, irregular bleeding, decreased sexual interest. |
| Progestin-only pills | $384–$456 ($32–$38 per cycle) | Very effective; no interruption of sexual experience; no estrogen-related side effects; can be used during breast-feeding. | No protection from STDs. Breakthrough bleeding. May worsen acne. Must be taken same time each day to be effective. |
| Vaginal ring (NuvaRing) | $580 | Do not have to remember to take daily pill; consistent, low-dose release of hormone; no interruption of sexual experience. | No protection from STDs; increased vaginal discharge; expulsion of ring; not effective for women over 198 pounds. |
| Skin patch (Ortho Evra) | $420 | Same as vaginal ring. | Slightly higher breakthrough bleeding than oral contraceptives; skin irritation; no protection from STDs. |
| Depo-Provera injection | $196 ($70 per injection plus office visit) | Very effective; no interruption of sexual experience; do not have to remember to take on daily basis; no estrogen-related side effects; good choice during breast-feeding. | No protection from STDs; breakthrough bleeding; weight gain; headaches; mood change; clinic visit and injection every 3 months. |
| Lunelle | $420 ($35 per injection) | Same as for Depo-Provera; may have estrogen-related side effects; no breakthrough bleeding. | Same as for Depo-Provera, but clinic visit and injection required monthly. |
| Implanon | Currently unknown | Offers longer protection than any other hormonal contraceptive. Highly effective. No need to remember to use daily or monthly method. No estrogen-related side effects. | No protection from STDs. May cause irregular bleeding and spotting. Risks of progestin-related side effects. |
| **Progesterone IUDs** Progestasert T | $500 first year | Very effective; no interruption of sexual activity; don't have to remember to use; can be used during breast-feeding. | No protection from STDs; increased risk of pelvic inflammatory disease for women with multiple partners; increased menstrual flow and cramps; may be expelled; rare incidence of perforating the uterine wall. |
| Mirena | $700 1st year, $140 if used for 5 years | Same as Progestasert T, except lighter periods; can be used longer than the Progestasert T. | Same as Progestasert T. |
| **Barrier and spermicide methods** | | | |
| Male condoms | $100 ($1.00 each) | Some protection from STDs; available without a prescription. | Interruption of sexual experience; reduces sensation. |
| Female condoms | $300 ($3.00 each) | Same as male condoms. | Same as male condoms; higher cost than male condoms; difficulty inserting. |

| Method | Cost per Year for 100 Occurrences of Intercourse | Advantages | Disadvantages |
|---|---|---|---|
| Vaginal spermicides | $85 (85¢ per application) | No prescription necessary. | Interruption of sexual experience; skin irritation; no protection from STDs; not effective enough to be used without a condom. |
| **Cervical barrier methods with spermicide** | | | |
| Diaphragm | $50 diaphragm, $280 for fitting, $85 for spermicide | Some protection from bacterial STDs; can be put in before sexual experience; no side effects; decreased incidence of cervical cancer. | Limited protection from STDs. Increased urinary tract infections. Requires practice to use correctly; can cause vaginal or cervical irritation. |
| Cervical cap | Same as diaphragm. | Same as diaphragm; no increase in urinary tract infections. | Same as diaphragm. |
| Sponge | $200 ($2 each) | Same as diaphragm; no increase in urinary tract infections. | Same as diaphragm. |
| FemCap | $65, $32.50 if used for 2 years; $85 for spermicide | Same as diaphragm; does not need to be fitted by health-care practitioner; has a loop to assist removal. | Same as diaphragm. |
| Lea's Shield | $145 ($60 each, replaced every year); $85 for spermicide | Same as diaphragm; does not need to be fitted by health-care practitioner; has a loop to assist removal. | Same as diaphragm. |
| **Nonhormonal IUD** Copper-T (Paragard) | $550 first year; $55 if kept for 10 years | Can be kept for 10 years; don't have to remember to use; also used for emergency contraception; can be used during breast-feeding. | No protection from STDs; increased menstrual flow and cramps; may be expelled; increased risk of pelvic inflammatory disease for women with multiple partners; rare incidence of perforating the uterine wall. |
| **Sterilization** Tubal sterilization | $1,200–$2,500 | Highly effective and permanent; reduces risk of ovarian cancer; transcervical sterilization is safest and least expensive of female sterilization procedures. | No protection from STDs; not easy to reverse for fertility; discomfort after procedure. |
| Vasectomy | $250–$1,000 | Easier procedure, less expensive, and lower failure rate than female sterilization. | No protection from STDs; not easy to reverse for fertility; discomfort after procedure. |
| **Fertility awareness** Standard days method | 0 | Most effective of fertility awareness methods; acceptable to Catholic Church. | No protection from STDs; uncertainty of safe times; periods of abstinence from intercourse or use of other methods; requires careful observation and tracking. |
| Rhythm, calendar, basal temperature, and cervical mucus methods | 0 | Acceptable to Catholic Church; no medical side effects. | No protection from STDs; uncertainty of safe times; periods of abstinence from intercourse or use of other methods. |
| **Withdrawal** | 0 | No medical side effects. | No protection from STDs; interruption of intercourse. |
| **No method** | 0 | Acceptable only if pregnancy desired. | No protection from STDs. |

SOURCES: Akert (2003), Alan Guttmacher Institute (2002), Hutti (2003), Long (2002), Panzer et al., (2006), and Speroff & Fritz (2005).

## Which Contraceptive Method Is Best for You?

Answer yes or no to each statement as it applies to you and, if appropriate, your partner.

1. You have high blood pressure or cardiovascular disease.
2. You smoke cigarettes.
3. You have a new sexual partner.
4. An unwanted pregnancy would be devastating to you.
5. You have a good memory.
6. You or your partner has multiple sexual partners.
7. You prefer a method with little or no bother.
8. You have heavy, crampy periods.
9. You need protection against sexually transmitted diseases.
10. You are concerned about endometrial and ovarian cancer.
11. You are forgetful.
12. You need a method right away.
13. You are comfortable touching your genitals and your partner's.
14. You have a cooperative partner.
15. You like a little extra vaginal lubrication.
16. You have sex at unpredictable times and places.
17. You are in a monogamous relationship and have at least one child.

*Scoring*

Recommendations are based on *yes* answers to the following numbered statements: • Combination pill and Lunelle: 4, 5, 6, 8, 16 • Progestin-only pill: 1, 2, 5, 7, 16 • Condoms: 1, 2, 3, 6, 9, 12, 13, 14 • Depo-Provera: 1, 2, 4, 7, 11, 16 • Cervical barrier methods: 1, 2, 13, 14 • IUD: 1, 2, 7, 11, 13, 16, 17 • Spermicides and the sponge: 1, 2, 12, 13, 14, 15.

## ⊙ Hormone-Based Contraceptives

In this section, we look at the most popular hormone-based birth control methods: oral contraceptives, the vaginal ring, the transdermal patch, and injected contraception.

### Oral Contraceptives

Oral contraceptives have evolved during 40 years of developing variations in the chemical structure and dosage of hormones, resulting in a wide range of choices (Calderoni & Coupey, 2005). Oral contraceptives are the most commonly used reversible method of birth control by women in the United States, including college-age women. More than 100 million women worldwide use the pill (Blackburn et al., 2000). Four basic types of oral contraceptives are currently on the market: the constant-dose combination pill, the triphasic pill, the extended cycle pill, and the progestin-only pill.

For most women who use them, oral contraceptives improve overall health (Speroff & Fritz, 2005). However, women with a history of certain conditions should not use oral contraceptives; these conditions include blood clots, strokes, circulation problems, heart problems, jaundice, cancer of the breast or uterus, and undiagnosed genital bleeding. In addition, a woman who has a liver disease or who suspects or knows that she is pregnant should not take the pill. Women who smoke cigarettes or have migraine headaches, depression, high blood pressure, epilepsy, diabetes or prediabetes symptoms, asthma, or varicose veins should weigh the potential risks most carefully and use the pill only under close medical supervision. ⊙ **Table 10.3** describes rare but serious side effects of the birth control pill. ■

! Sexual Health

### The Pill: Four Basic Types

**Constant-dose combination pills** Birth control pills that contain a constant daily dose of estrogen and progestin.

The **constant-dose combination pill** has been available since the early 1960s and is the most commonly used oral contraceptive in the United States. It contains two hormones, synthetic estrogen and progestin (a progesteronelike substance). The dosage of these hormones remains constant throughout the menstrual cycle. There are more than 32 different varieties of combination pills, and each variety contains various amounts and ratios of the two hormones. The amount of estrogen in pills has decreased from as much as 175 micrograms in 1960 to an average of 25 micrograms (Ritter 2003).

| | | |
|---|---|---|
| **⊙ TABLE 10.3** | **Remember "ACHES" for the Pill: Symptoms of Possible Serious Problems With the Birth Control Pill** | |

| Initial | Symptoms | Possible Problem |
|---|---|---|
| A | Abdominal pain (severe) | Gallbladder disease, liver tumor, or blood clot |
| C | Chest pain (severe) or shortness of breath | Blood clot in lungs or heart attack |
| H | Headaches (severe) | Stroke, high blood pressure, or migraine headache |
| E | Eye problems: blurred vision, flashing lights, or blindness | Stroke, high blood pressure, or temporary vascular problems at many possible sites |
| S | Severe leg pain (calf or thigh) | Blood clot in legs |

SOURCE: Adapted from Hatcher & Guillebaud (1998).

The **triphasic pill**, which has been on the market since 1984, is another type of oral contraceptive. Unlike the constant-dose combination pill, the triphasic pill provides fluctuations of estrogen and progesterone levels during the menstrual cycle. The triphasic pill is designed to reduce the total hormone dosage and any side effects while maintaining contraceptive effectiveness.

Another constant-dose pill on the market is called an *extended cycle* contraceptive because it is taken continuously for 3 months without placebo pills. The only brand on the market, **Seasonale**, has a lower dose of estrogen and progestin than most other constant-dose or triphasic pills. Seasonale reduces the number of menstrual periods to 4 instead of 13 per year, which significantly benefits women who have uncomfortable menstrual symptoms during the placebo phase of using the combination pill (Kripke 2006).

The **progestin-only pill**, which has been on the market since 1973, contains only 0.35 milligrams of progestin—about one third the amount in an average-strength combination pill. Like the combination pill, the progestin-only pill has a constant-dose formula. The progestin-only pill contains no estrogen and is a good option for women who prefer or require a nonestrogen pill (Burkett & Hewitt, 2005).

**Triphasic pills** Birth control pills that vary the dosages of estrogen and progestin during the menstrual cycle.

**Seasonale** Birth control pills that reduce menstrual periods to four times a year.

**Progestin-only pills** Contraceptive pills that contain a small dose of progestin and no estrogen.

## How Oral Contraceptives Work

The estrogen in the combination, triphasic, and extended-release pills prevents conception primarily by inhibiting ovulation. The progestin in these pills provides secondary contraceptive protection by thickening and chemically altering the cervical mucus so that the passage of sperm into the uterus is hampered. Progestin also causes changes in the lining of the uterus, making it less receptive to implantation by a fertilized egg (Larimore & Stanford, 2000). In addition, progestin can inhibit ovulation. The progestin-only pill works somewhat differently. Most women who take the progestin-only pill probably continue to ovulate at least occasionally. The primary effect of this pill is to alter the cervical mucus to a thick and tacky consistency that effectively blocks sperm from entering the uterus. As with the combination pill, secondary contraceptive effects are provided by alterations in the uterine lining that make it unreceptive to implantation.

## How to Use Oral Contraceptives

Several ways exist to begin taking oral contraceptives; a woman who does so should carefully follow the instructions of her health-care practitioner. Unlike other oral contraceptives that are taken in 28-day cycles, Seasonale is taken daily for 3 months, followed by 7 days of inactive tablets before taking it for another 3 months. Some medications reduce the effectiveness of oral contraceptives; these are listed in ⊙ **Table 10.4**.

Forgetting to take one or more pills sharply reduces the effectiveness of oral contraceptives, as does taking the pill at a different time each day. Missing one or more pills can lower hormone levels and allow ovulation to occur. A significant number of women do forget to take the pill each day. However, women underestimate how often they forget their pills. A study that relied on electronic tracking of the time and date women took pills from the container, rather than on user self-report, found that up to 50% of users missed three or more pills per cycle, greatly reducing the contraceptive effectiveness of the method (Potter et al., 1996). To help prevent missing pills, a woman can use a pill case with a built-in clock and alarm to alert her the same time each day if she has not taken her pill.

! Sexual Health

| ○ **TABLE 10.4** | **Medications That Reduce Oral Contraceptive Effectiveness** | |
| --- | --- | --- |
| Some medications can reduce the effectiveness of birth control pills. Tell every physician who gives you medication that you are taking oral contraceptives. Use a backup method, such as foam or condoms, when you use any of the following medications or herbal remedies: | | |
| Barbiturates | Dilantin | |
| Ampicillin | Rifampin (for tuberculosis) | |
| Tetracycline | Phenylbutazone (for arthritis) | |
| Tegretol | St. John's Wort | |

SOURCE: Markowitz et al. (2003) and Zlidar (2000).

If you are using oral contraceptives and you miss a pill, you should take the missed pill as soon as you remember and then take your next pill at the regular time. If you forget more than one pill, it is best to consult your health-care practitioner. You should also use a backup method, such as contraceptive foam or condoms, for the remainder of your cycle. ■

## The Vaginal Ring and the Transdermal Patch

NuvaRing and Ortho Evra are two hormone-based contraceptive methods that do not require taking a pill each day. Both synthetic estrogen and progestin are embedded in either a 2-inch-diameter soft and transparent vaginal ring (NuvaRing) or a beige matchbook-size transdermal patch (Ortho Evra), as shown in ○ **Figure 10.2**.

### How the Ring and Patch Work

Both NuvaRing and Ortho Evra release the hormones embedded in them through the vaginal lining or skin into the bloodstream. The hormones then work in the same way as the pill to prevent pregnancy.

### How to Use the Ring and Patch

The ring is inserted into the vagina between day 1 and day 5 of a menstrual period. It is worn inside the vagina for 3 weeks, then removed for 1 week and replaced with a new ring. The ring can remain in place during intercourse, or it can be removed for up to 3 hours at a time without reducing its contraceptive effectiveness (Long, 2002).

In using the patch, a woman chooses a specific day of the week after a menstrual period starts and identifies that day as "patch change day." She replaces the old patch with a new patch on that same day each week for 3 weeks, followed by a patch-free 7-day interval. The patch can be placed on the buttock, abdomen, upper outer arm, or upper torso (P. Murphy, 2003).

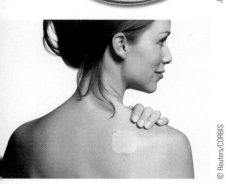

○ **Figure 10.2** The ring (top) and patch (bottom) eliminate the need to remember a birth control pill each day.

J. Darin Derstine

© Reuters/CORBIS

## Injected Contraceptives

Depo-Provera is an injectable hormone-based contraceptive. It was approved by the U.S. Food and Drug Administration (FDA) in 1992 (Kaunitz, 1994). Lunelle, another injected contraceptive, was approved in 2000 (Galewitz, 2000).

### How Injected Contraceptives Work

The active ingredient in Depo-Provera is progestin, which inhibits the secretion of gonadotropins and prevents follicular maturation and ovulation. These actions also cause the endometrial lining of the uterus to thin, preventing implantation of a fertilized egg. Progestin also alters the cervical mucus. Lunelle combines progestin and estrogen, as do combination pills.

### How to Use Injected Contraceptives

A health-care provider gives the Depo-Provera shot once every 12 weeks, ideally within 5 days of the beginning of menstruation. It usually takes 10 months after stopping Depo-Provera for a woman to get pregnant (Galewitz, 2000). Lunelle requires a monthly injection, and fertility returns immediately after stopping injections.

## Contraceptive Implant

Implanon is a matchstick-size slender rod $1\frac{1}{2}$ inches long. It is inserted under the skin of the upper arm and releases contraceptive hormones. Implanon had been sold in more than 30 countries since 1998 before it was approved by the FDA in 2006 for use in the United States (Bridges, 2006).

### How the Implant Works

Implanon releases a slow, steady dose of progestin, and it prevents pregnancy in the same ways as the progestin-only mini pill. It may not be effective for women more than 30% heavier than their medically ideal weight.

### How to Use the Implant

A medical practitioner inserts the rod in a quick surgical procedure that requires only a local anesthetic. It is effective for up to 3 years.

## Barrier and Spermicide Methods

Hormone-based methods cause changes in a woman's body that inhibit ovulation and implantation. Another group of contraceptive devices works in a different way—by preventing sperm from reaching an ovum. In this section, we look at condoms and four cervical barrier devices. In addition, we include vaginal spermicides in this section because their effect is also to prevent sperm from reaching an egg. Other than the condom, barrier methods do not protect against STDs, including AIDS and genital warts (Winer et al., 2006).

### Condoms

A **condom** is a sheath that fits over the erect penis. It has a long history. An illustration of a man wearing a condom was painted on a wall in a cave in France 12,000 to 15,000 years ago (Planned Parenthood, 2002). In 1564 an Italian anatomist, Fallopius, described a penile sheath made of linen. Mass production of inexpensive modern condoms began after the development of vulcanized rubber in the 1840s.

Condoms, also called prophylactics and rubbers, are the only temporary method of birth control available for men and the only form of contraception that effectively reduces transmission of sexually transmitted diseases, including AIDS. They are one of the most popular contraceptive methods used in the United States. A recent study found that education level is correlated with condom use in men. When unmarried men between ages 15 and 44 were asked if they had used a condom the last time they had had sexual intercourse, 38% of men who had a high school education or less and 58% of men who had some college education or a bachelor's degree or more reported having used a condom (Martinez, 2006). Worldwide, an estimated 6 to 9 billion condoms are used each year (Gardner et al., 1999). Despite condoms' widespread use and dual utility in preventing pregnancy and the spread of STDs, anti-contraception, abstinence-only groups have disseminated inaccurate information about them and worked to restrict correct information, as described in the Sex and Politics box on page 276.

Condoms are made of thin surgical latex, polyurethane, or natural membrane (from sheep intestines). Some condoms have special features and are colored or flavored. Trojan's Extended Pleasure condoms have a desensitizing agent on the inside to help delay ejaculation. Some condoms have a small nipple at the end, called a reservoir tip, and others have a contoured shape or textured surface. Most condoms come rolled up and wrapped in foil or plastic, and they are lubricated or nonlubricated (**◑ Figure 10.3**). Lubricated condoms are less likely to break than nonlubricated ones, and according to some men, they reduce penile sensation less during intercourse. Natural-membrane condoms cost more than latex condoms but tend to interfere less with sensation. However, natural-membrane condoms contain small pores that can permit passage of viruses associated with several STDs, including AIDs, genital herpes, and hepatitis.

Condoms are available without prescription at pharmacies and grocery stores, from family planning clinics, by mail order, in vending machines, and in school-based condom programs (Blake et al., 2003; Guttmacher et al., 1997). They have an average shelf life of about 5 years (not all packages are dated). Latex condoms should not be stored in hot places, such as the glove compartment of a car or a back pocket, because heat can cause the latex to deteriorate.

**Condom** A sheath that fits over the penis and is used for protection against unwanted pregnancy and sexually transmitted diseases.

## Condoms: The Politics of Protection

In 2001 the National Institutes of Health, the Department of Health and Human Services, and the National Institute of Allergy and Infectious Diseases jointly stated that research shows that consistent use of male condoms protects against the spread of HIV from one person to another (National Institute of Allergy and Infectious Diseases, 2001). Using a condom is 10,000 times safer than not using one (SIECUS, 2005). In spite of the enormous personal and public health benefits of condoms, pro-life individuals and organizations are engaged in a well-financed anti-condom campaign. The pro-life movement "finds fault with every kind of birth control, from the Pill, which revolutionized women's (and men's) lives, to the condom, which in our era is the last stand against the most virulent sexually transmitted diseases" (Pope, 2006, p. 3).

Anti-contraception, abstinence-only groups—including Pro-Life America, United for Life, Physicians for Life, American Life League, and the Vatican—falsely state on their Web sites and in

UCLA's Fowler Museum exhibit, *"Dress Up Against AIDS,"* hoped to destigmatize condoms and inspire their use to prevent AIDS. It featured 14 garments designed by Brazillian artist Adriana Bertini, made entirely of condoms rejected by industry quality tests.

J.P. Moczulski/Reuters/CORBIS

their printed materials that HIV and other infectious agents can pass through condoms, thereby spreading STDs (Pope, 2006). Furthermore, under the Bush administration, the U.S. government has allocated millions of tax dollars for abstinence-only sex education that misinforms students by claiming that condoms are ineffective in preventing pregnancy and STD transmission (Shorto, 2006). The pro-life, anti-condom campaign also discourages condom use in African countries where the world's highest rate of HIV has had devastating effects. Even the Centers for Disease Control (CDC) succumbed to pressure from anti-condom forces led by Senator Tom Coburn (Republican from Oklahoma) and removed information from its Web site about different types of condoms, how to use condoms correctly, and the effectiveness of condoms in preventing the spread of STDs and HIV (Platner, 2005). Subsequently, President Bush appointed Senator Coburn to co-chair the Presidential Advisory Council on HIV/AIDS (Platner, 2005).

## How the Condom Works

When a man uses a condom properly, both the ejaculate and the fluid from Cowper's gland secretions (sometimes called "precum" in slang) are contained in the tip. The condom thus serves as a mechanical barrier, effectively preventing any sperm from entering the vagina.

! Sexual Health

○ **Figure 10.3** Condoms come in many varieties.

## How to Use the Condom

Correct and consistent use of the condom is essential for its effectiveness, but studies of college students have found that user error is common. Putting a condom on after

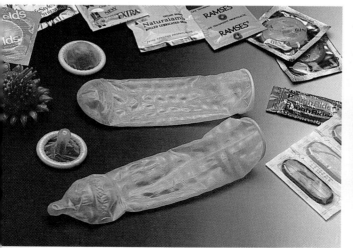

© Joel Gordon (both)

vaginal penetration but before ejaculation is a common error that increases the risk of pregnancy and STD transmission (Crosby et al., 2002). The Let's Talk About It box on page 278 discusses the importance of condom use and provides some suggestions for communicating more effectively about their use.

Most condoms are packaged rolled up. Correct use includes unrolling the condom over the erect penis before any contact between the penis and the vulva occurs. Sperm in the Cowper's gland secretions or in the ejaculate can travel from the labia into the vagina. For maximum comfort and sensation, an uncircumcised man can retract the foreskin before unrolling the condom over the penis (Bolus, 1994). When using a plain-end condom (without the reservoir tip), the end needs to be twisted before unrolling the condom over the penis, as shown in ● **Figure 10.4**. Doing this leaves some room at the end for the ejaculate and reduces the chances of the condom breaking. In the unusual case that a condom breaks or slips off during intercourse, contraceptive foam, cream, or jelly should be inserted into the vagina *immediately* (Walsh et al., 2004).

A condom breaks more easily without lubrication than with it, so if the condom is nonlubricated, put some saliva or water-based lubricant on the vulva and on the outside of the condom before inserting the penis into the vagina. Do *not* use oil-based lubricants, because they reduce the condom's integrity and increase the chances of breakage (Spruyt et al., 1998). See ● **Table 10.5** for a detailed list of safe and unsafe lubricants to use with condoms.

Because the penis begins to decrease in size and hardness soon after ejaculation, it is important to hold the condom at the base of the penis before withdrawing from the vagina. Otherwise the condom can slip off and spill semen inside the vagina. Condoms are best disposed of in the garbage rather than the toilet, because they can clog plumbing. ■

## The Female Condom

The female condom is made of polyurethane or latex. It resembles a male condom (● **Figure 10.5**) but is worn internally by the woman. A flexible plastic ring at the closed end of the sheath fits loosely against the cervix, rather like a diaphragm (discussed in the next section). Another ring encircles the labial area. Although the female condom fits the contours of the vagina, the penis moves freely inside the sheath,

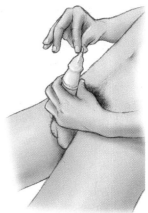

Courtesy of San Francisco AIDS Foundation

● **Figure 10.4** (top) The end of a plain-end condom needs to be twisted, leaving space at the tip, before it is unrolled over the penis. (bottom) A condom with a reservoir tip does not need to be twisted.

● **T A B L E  10.5**  **Which Lubricants Are Safe and Unsafe to Use With Condoms?**

| Safe | Unsafe |
| --- | --- |
| Water-based or silicone lubricants | Aldara cream |
| Aqualube | Baby oil or cold creams |
| Astroglide | Bag Balm |
| Cornhuskers Lotion | Edible oils (e.g., vegetable, olive, peanut, corn, sunflower) |
| Water and saliva | Body lotions |
| Glycerin | Massage oils |
| All ID lubricants (except ID Cream) | Mineral oil |
| Aloe-9 | Petroleum jelly |
| H-R Lubricating Jelly | Rubbing alcohol |
| K-Y Lubricating Jelly | Shortening |
| Prepair | Suntan oils and lotions |
| Probe | Whipped cream |
| ForPlay | Vaginal yeast infection creams and suppositories |
| Gynol II | |
| Wet (except Wet Oil) | |
| Silicone lubricant | |
| DeLube | |
| Vaginal spermicides | |

SOURCE: Adapted from Hatcher, R. et al. (2003). *A Pocket Guide to Managing Contraception*. Tiger, GA: Bridging the Gap Foundation.

## Don't Go Inside Without Your Rubbers On

The writers of a sex education book expressed their unequivocal perspectives on avoidance of effective condom use:

> If we hear any more whining about how condoms are annoying, uncomfortable deal breakers, we are going to *puke*. Could it be you've been using nonlubricated, inch-thick, five-cent prophylactics from a vending machine all your life? So condoms don't figure in your full-on, flesh-to-flesh fantasy world—we get it. We're also sure that oozing genital ulcers and child support payments don't pop up in that utopia either (Taylor & Sharkey, 2003, pp. 182–183).

Women purchase 50% of condoms sold today. One study found that refusing to have sex unless a partner used a condom was the most common approach used by college women to encourage condom use (De Bro et al., 1994). These facts represent good condom sense because, along with unwanted pregnancy, women have much more to lose than men when a couple does not use a condom. A woman is much more likely to get an STD (including HIV/AIDS) from one act of intercourse than is a man, and bacterial STDs do much more damage to a woman's reproductive tract than to a man's and can ruin her subsequent ability to have a baby.

The book *Before You Hit the Pillow, Talk* (Foley & Nechas, 1995) offers suggestions for communicating about condoms. Basically, be clear and assertive and do not get drawn into an argument. Deciding beforehand that you will not have intercourse without using a condom will give your position the strength it needs. Some examples of specific conversations follow.

| Partner's Statement | Your Response |
|---|---|
| "I'm on the pill. You don't need to use a rubber." | "I'd like to use one anyway, then we'll be doubly protected." |
| "It doesn't feel as good with a condom." | "It will still feel better than nothing." |
| "It's not very romantic." | "Neither is pregnancy or disease." |
| "I wouldn't do anything to hurt you." | "Great. Let me help you put it on." |
| "I'd rather not have sex if we have to use a condom." | "OK. What would you like to do instead?" |

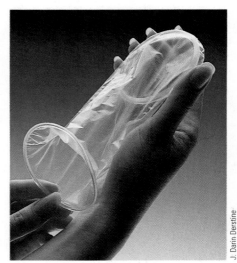

J. Darin Derstine

(a)

which is coated with a silicone-based lubricant. Used correctly, female condoms can substantially reduce the risk of transmission of some STDs (Minnis & Padian, 2001).

Reports vary about the user-friendliness of the female condom. Only 7% of women and 8% of men in FDA studies said that they disliked the female condom (F. Stewart, 1998c). Women in another study appreciated being able to insert the female condom before sexual activity, not needing to remove it immediately following ejaculation, and having sex be less messy than it would be without a condom. Others liked having an option they could use for protection from STDs and pregnancy instead of relying on male condom use. However, women reported frustration and difficulty with insertion, reduced pleasurable sensations, and problems with partner resistance to the method (Choi et al., 2003).

(b)

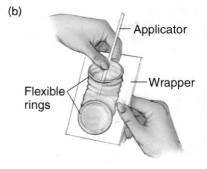
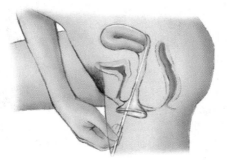
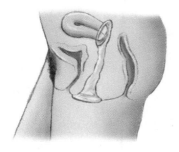

Applicator

Wrapper

Flexible rings

**Figure 10.5** (a) The female condom. (b) A female condom consists of two flexible polyurethane rings and a soft, loose-fitting polyurethane sheath.

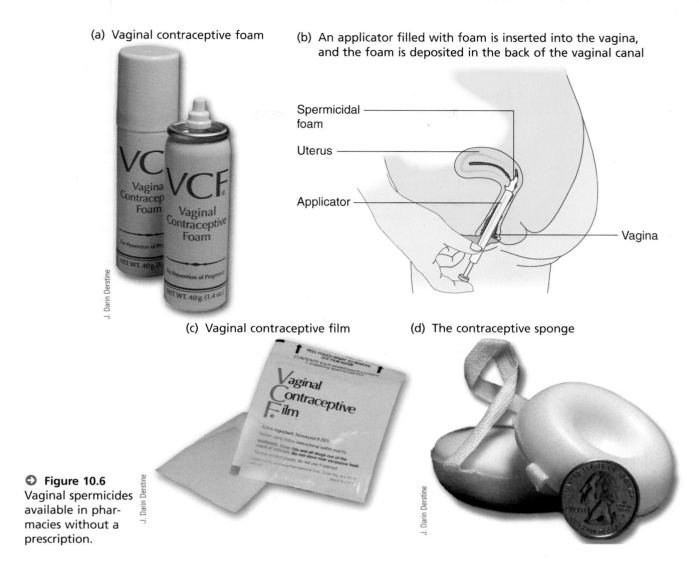

(a) Vaginal contraceptive foam

(b) An applicator filled with foam is inserted into the vagina, and the foam is deposited in the back of the vaginal canal

Spermicidal foam

Uterus

Applicator

Vagina

(c) Vaginal contraceptive film

(d) The contraceptive sponge

Vaginal Contraceptive Film

○ **Figure 10.6**
Vaginal spermicides available in pharmacies without a prescription.

J. Darin Derstine

## Vaginal Spermicides

Several types of **vaginal spermicides** are available without a prescription: foam, suppositories, the sponge, creams and jellies, and contraceptive film (○ **Figure 10.6**). *Foam* is a white substance that resembles shaving cream. It comes in a pressurized can and has a plastic applicator. *Vaginal suppositories* have an oval shape, and the *sponge* is a doughnut-shaped spermicide-containing device that absorbs and subsequently kills sperm. *VCF*, a vaginal contraceptive film, is a paper-thin, 2-by-2-inch sheet that is laced with spermicide. It is packaged in a matchbook-like container with 10 to 12 sheets.

**Vaginal spermicides**
Foam, cream, jelly, suppositories, and film that contain a chemical that kills sperm.

### How Spermicidal Methods Work

Foam, suppositories, the sponge, creams and jellies, and VCF all contain a *spermicide*, a chemical that kills sperm. When foam is inserted with the applicator, it rapidly covers the vaginal walls and the cervical os, or opening to the uterus (see Figure 10.6). Contraceptive vaginal suppositories take about 20 minutes to dissolve and cover the walls. One brand of suppository, Encare, effervesces and creates foam inside the vagina; other brands melt. Once VCF is inserted into the vagina, next to the cervix, it dissolves into a stay-in-place gel.

### How to Use Vaginal Spermicides

Spermicides are less effective in preventing pregnancy than most other methods, so they need to be used with condoms. Complete instructions for use come with each package of vaginal spermicide. For maximum protection, it is important to use the product as directed. Another application of spermicide is necessary before each additional act of intercourse. In contrast, the sponge is effective for repeated acts of intercourse and can be inserted up to 24 hours before intercourse. It is probably better to shower rather than take a bath after sex when using a spermicide, to prevent the spermicide from being rinsed out of the vagina.

## Cervical Barrier Devices

The practice of covering the cervix to provide protection from pregnancy has existed for centuries. In 18th-century Europe, Casanova promoted the idea of using a squeezed-out lemon half to cover the cervix, and European women shaped beeswax to cover the cervix. In 1838 a German gynecologist took wax impressions of each patient's cervix to make custom caps out of rubber (Seaman & Seaman, 1978).

As shown in ○ **Figure 10.7**, the diaphragm, cervical cap, FemCap, and Lea's Shield are four methods combining a physical barrier that covers the cervix with vaginal spermicide to protect the cervix from contact with viable sperm. These devices are dome shaped, with a rim around the open side. The diaphragm covers the upper vaginal wall from behind the cervix to underneath the pubic bone. The cervical cap fits over the cervix only. The FemCap and the Lea's Shield have rims that rest on the vaginal wall surrounding the cervix and have removal straps. Unlike the other devices, the Lea's Shield allows a one-way flow of fluid from the cervix to the vagina but prevents semen from contact with the cervix.

### How to Use Cervical Barrier Devices

The diaphragm and cervical cap are individually fitted by a skilled health-care practitioner. The practitioner should also teach women how to insert it properly so that they are confident about using it on their own (Hollander, 2006; McNaught & Jamieson, 2005). In contrast, the FemCap and Lea's Shield do not have to be fitted.

○ **Figure 10.7** Cervical barrier devices.

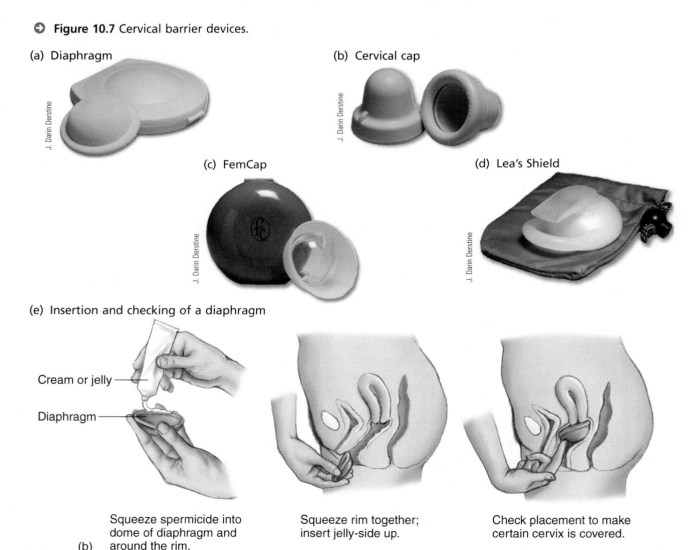

(a) Diaphragm

(b) Cervical cap

(c) FemCap

(d) Lea's Shield

(e) Insertion and checking of a diaphragm

Cream or jelly

Diaphragm

(b) Squeeze spermicide into dome of diaphragm and around the rim.

Squeeze rim together; insert jelly-side up.

Check placement to make certain cervix is covered.

However, unlike the case in several other countries, where they are available over the counter, they require a prescription in the United States. All barrier devices are used with spermicidal cream or jelly placed inside the dome of the cup and on the rim. Do *not* use oil-based lubricants with a diaphragm or cervical cap because these devices are made of latex and will deteriorate when used with oil-based lubricants. (The FemCap and Lea's Shield are made from silicone.)

To insert any of these barrier devices, squeeze the sides of the rim together with one hand, and use your other hand to open the lips of the vulva, as shown in Figure 10.7e. With the spermicide side up, push the device into the vagina. After you have inserted it, you or your partner need to feel inside the vagina to make sure the dome covers the cervix. Some women prefer to insert the dome ahead of time, in privacy, whereas others share the insertion with their partners. As one man explained:

> I have always hated "just-before" birth control devices like condoms and diaphragms. However, with my present partner, the diaphragm is part of our sexual excitement. We usually become quite stimulated before reaching for the jelly and diaphragm, and I often use manual clitoral stimulation while she inserts it. I have also learned to put it in while she continues to stimulate herself and me at the same time. Also, the leftover jelly is a good lubricant. The pause between being ready for intercourse and actually doing it seems to heighten the whole thing. (Authors' files)

All cervical barrier devices should remain in the vagina for at least 8 hours to provide time for the spermicide to kill sperm in the folds of the vagina. If intercourse occurs again before 8 hours elapse, leave the device in place and apply additional spermicide inside the vagina. Recommendations vary by method for the length of time before intercourse for insertion and after intercourse for removal:

|  | Hours Before Intercourse | Hours After Intercourse |
| --- | --- | --- |
| Diaphragm | up to 6 | at least 8, no more than 24 |
| Cervical cap | up to 6 | at least 8, no more than 24 |
| FemCap | up to 8 | at least 8, no more than 48 |
| Lea's Shield | up to 8 | at least 8, no more than 48 |

To remove the diaphragm or cervical cap, put a finger under the front rim to break the air seal, then pull the device out of the vagina. The FemCap and Lea's Shield have flexible loops for removal. After removal, wash the device with a mild soap and warm water and then dry it. The diaphragm and cervical cap can last for several years, but the FemCap and Lea's Shield are usable for only one year. Take the device with you to your annual exam and Pap smear so that your health-care practitioner can evaluate its fit and condition. A pregnancy (including a miscarriage or an abortion) or a weight change of more than 10 pounds may require a different diaphragm.

## ▶ Intrauterine Devices

**Intrauterine devices**, commonly referred to as IUDs, are small plastic objects that are inserted into the uterus. The three most common IUDs are the Copper-T (Para-Gard), Progestasert T, and Mirena (○ **Figure 10.8**). The Copper-T is a plastic T with a copper wire wrapped around its stem and copper sleeves on the side arms. The Progestasert T is a plastic T with slow-releasing progesterone in the plastic. Mirena, the newest IUD on the U.S. market, is a polyethylene T with a cylinder containing progesterone (Akert, 2003). All three IUDs have fine plastic threads attached; the threads are designed to hang slightly out of the cervix into the vagina.

The IUD is the most common reversible contraceptive used by women in the developing world (Salem 2006; Speroff & Fritz, 2005). Women in the United States who use the IUD are usually very pleased with the method, as indicated by its 80% continuation rate (how many women who start using a method are still using it one year later). This is a higher continuation rate than for pills, patches, rings, condoms, or Depo-Provera (Hatcher, 2006). In addition, serious complications are rare with the modern IUD, and are described in ○ **Table 10.6**.

**Intrauterine device (IUD)** A small, plastic device that is inserted into the uterus for contraception.

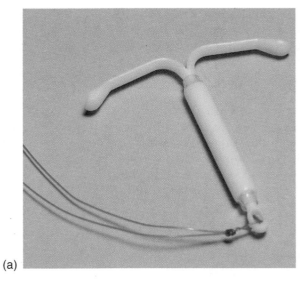

(a)

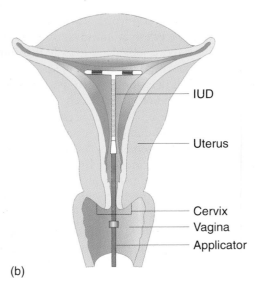

- IUD
- Uterus
- Cervix
- Vagina
- Applicator

(b)

⊙ **Figure 10.8** (a) The Mirena IUD. (b) Position of the IUD after insertion by a health-care practitioner.

## How the IUD Works

Both the copper and the progesterone in IUDs are effective in preventing fertilization. The Copper-T seems to alter the tubal and uterine fluids, which affects the sperm and egg so fertilization does not occur. The Progestasert T and Mirena have effects similar to those of hormonal contraceptive methods such as the pill and Depo-Provera. It disrupts ovulatory patterns, thickens cervical mucus, alters endometrial lining, and impairs tubal motility (G. Stewart, 1998).

⊙ **TABLE 10.6** Remember "PAINS" for the IUD: Symptoms of Possible Serious Problems With the IUD

| Initial | Symptoms |
| --- | --- |
| P | Period late, no period |
| A | Abdominal pain |
| I | Increased temperature, fever, chills |
| N | Nasty discharge, foul discharge |
| S | Spotting, bleeding, heavy periods, clots |

SOURCE: Adapted from G. Stewart (1998).

! Sexual Health

## How to Use the IUD

The IUD is inserted by a health-care professional using sterile instruments. The inserter and IUD are introduced through the cervical os into the uterus; the inserter is then withdrawn, leaving the IUD in place. The Copper-T can potentially be in place for 10 to 12 years, and the progesterone IUDs from 7 to 10 years (Speroff & Fritz, 2005). A woman should be screened for gonorrhea and chlamydia before IUD insertion because the procedure can carry bacteria associated with these STDs into the uterus. The use of the IUD is best limited to women who are in monogamous relationships and do not have other risk factors for sexually transmitted diseases (Speroff & Fritz, 2005).

While a woman is using an IUD, she or her partner needs to check each month after her menstrual period to see that the thread is the same length as when the device was inserted. To do this, one reaches into the vagina with a finger and finds the cervix. The thread should be felt in the middle of the cervix, protruding out of the small indentation in the center. Occasionally it curls up in the os and cannot be felt, but any time a woman or her partner cannot find it, she needs to check with her health-care specialist. She should also seek attention if the thread seems longer or if the plastic protrudes from the os; this probably means that her body is expelling the IUD. ■

## ⊙ Emergency Contraception

What if a condom slips off or a divorced couple is unexpectedly intimate (for "old time's sake") without birth control, or a couple runs out of condoms and uses only foam, or a woman is raped while trying to walk to her car after a night class, or a woman is two days late starting a new pack of pills, or a woman drinks too much at a party and has unprotected sex, or a woman leaves her NuvaRing in longer than 5 weeks, or a couple with a new baby have intercourse before they restart birth control?

Fortunately, in these and numerous other situations, a possible pregnancy can be prevented by using **emergency contraception (EC)**. After unprotected intercourse, administration of hormone pills or insertion of a Copper-T IUD are options for emergency contraception. Hormone pills are the most commonly used method. Taken within 24 hours after intercourse, they are 95% effective in preventing pregnancy; within 72 hours they are 75% effective; and even within 120 hours, they can provide some degree of protection from pregnancy, but sooner is better (Curtis et al., 2004; Kort, 2006; Yakush, 2005). Hormonal options include two products specifically made for EC: Preven (two doses of combined estrogen and progesterone ) and Plan B (two doses of 0.75 mg levonorgestrel, a progesterone). The first dose is taken as soon as possible, and the second dose is taken 12 hours later. The World Health Organization recommends Plan B as the most effective oral EC with the fewest side effects. It suggests taking both Plan B tablets at the same time, whereas the Preven doses are taken 12 hours apart (Curtis, 2004). As shown in ❍ **Table 10.7**, two or more oral contraceptives can be substituted if the emergency contraceptive treatment is not available. The Web site *http://ec.princeton.edu* and the telephone hotline 1-888-668-2528 provide information about how to obtain EC throughout the United States and Canada.

These hormone treatments work primarily by inhibiting ovulation (Population Council, 2005). They may also provide secondary protection by altering cervical mucus and the lining of the uterus. When a woman uses EC, she should also be aware of and watch for side effects similar to those related to birth control pills. Nausea and vomiting are the most common side effects of the estrogen-progestin EC but are unlikely to occur with Plan B.

If the Copper-T IUD is inserted up to five days after unprotected intercourse, it is over 99% effective in preventing pregnancy (Golden et al., 2001). Its failure rate of less than 1% makes the Copper-T IUD the most effective form of EC. It is appropriate for women who plan to use the IUD as an ongoing method of contraception, but its use is limited to women who are at low risk of PID and STDs (Long 2002).

Emergency contraception prevented about 51,000 abortions in the United States in 2000 (Jones et al., 2002b). Increased availability and use of EC could prevent an estimated 2.3 million unintended pregnancies each year in the United States. Studies at abortion clinics indicate that 50 to 60% of the patients would have been treatable with and would have wanted to use emergency contraception rather than have an abortion if they had known about it and had had access to it (Speroff & Fritz, 2005). A nationwide Harris Poll found that 58% of adults in the United States (incuding

❍ **TABLE 10.7**   **Oral Contraceptive Pills for Emergency Contraception**

| Instead of Progestin-Only Plan B | |
| --- | --- |
| Ovrette: 40 pills as soon as possible within 120 hours after unprotected intercourse | |
| **Instead of Estrogen-Progestin Preven[a]** | |
| 2 pills as soon as possible within 120 hours after unprotected intercourse and 2 more 12 hours later: | |
| Ogestrel | Ovral |
| 4 pills as soon as possible within 120 hours after unprotected intercourse and 4 more 12 hours later: | |
| Cryselle | Levlen |
| Levora | Lo/Ovral |
| Low-Ogestrel | Nordette |
| Portia | Seasonale |
| Seasonique | |
| 5 pills as soon as possible within 120 hours after unprotected intercourse and 5 more 12 hours later: | |
| Alesse | Aviane |
| Lessina | Levlite |
| Lutera | |

[a]In 28-day packs, only the first 21 pills can be used. The last 7 contain *no* hormones.

SOURCE: Adapted from Princeton University, Office of Population Research & Association of Reproductive Health Professionals (2006). *Answers to Frequently Asked Questions About Emergency Contraception in the United States of America.* Retrieved 2006 from The Emergency Contraception Web site: http://ec.princeton.edu/.

## Opposition to Emergency Contraception

Given that easy access to emergency contraception could cut the yearly abortion rate in the United States in half, one would assume that anti-abortion leaders and organizations would use their political influence to expedite women's access to emergency contraception. They could look to a program in France designed to reduce the country's abortion rate; in that program, nurses in middle schools and high schools provide students with free emergency contraception (Kristof, 2006). Other examples to emulate exist in the 38 developed and developing countries around the world (including Albania, Mexico, Peru, Portugal, the Republic of Congo, Tunisia, Canada, and the United Kingdom) that provide EC at no cost in government clinics or sell emergency contraception from store shelves along with other over-the-counter medications such as aspirin and eye drops (Barroso, 2006; Tummino, 2006). However, instead of adopting others' effective methods of preventing abortion, many pro-life activists and organizations believe that "the only 'emergency' in this case is the woman's fear of being pregnant" and apply political pressure to limit other citizens' access to emergency contraception (American Life League, 2006, p. 1).

As a result of the political pressure put on the FDA by pro-life groups, over 40 Republican Congresspeople, and President Bush in 2004, the FDA rejected its scientific advisory panel's recommendation that Plan B emergency contraception be made available to women over the counter without a prescription. The FDA claimed it needed more time to evaluate the impact of OTC availability of emergency contraception on young teenagers, despite research findings that OTC access to EC for teens does not increase frequency of unprotected sex or decrease the use of other contraceptives (Graham, 2006; Harper et al., 2005; Heavey, 2006; Marson et al., 2005). Ironically, religious teens are most likely to benefit from emergency contraception because teens who describe themselves as strongly religious are less likely to use contraception at first intercourse than other adolescents (Hillard, 2005; Graham, 2006).

The FDA's decision was highly unusual and cast doubt on the integrity of the agency as a scientific body immune to political and religious ideology. Critics of the decision concluded "that politics matters more to this administration than women's health" (Editorial Board, 2006, p. B4; Camp, 2006; Kerr, 2006). Plan B was the only drug over the last 10 years that has not been approved for OTC status following an FDA committee recommendation (Kort, 2006). Furthermore, the FDA staff, who normally sign nonapproval statements, refused to sign one in this case because they disagreed vehemently with the decision. In addition, the director of the Office of Women's Health at the FDA resigned due to the FDA's disregard for scientific and clinical evidence of the benefits of over-the-counter status for Plan B (Fennell, 2006).

The numerous medical societies and public health organizations that have attempted for many years to make emergency contraception available continued to advocate for the FDA to reverse its decision. Due to barriers that make emergency contraception largely inaccessible to women when they need it, in 2006 the American College of Obstetricians and Gynecologists initiated the "Ask Me" campaign to encourage their patients to obtain an advance prescription and have emergency contraception on hand in case it is necessary (Victory & Nilsson, 2006). Furthermore, pro-contraceptive activists filed lawsuits and Senators Hillary Clinton (Democrat from New York) and Patty Murray (Democrat from Washington) led three years of political advocacy that helped result in the 2006 FDA decision to allow pharmacists to sell EC to women age 18 and older. The FDA decision fell short of the desired outcome—making EC available to women of all ages on store shelves without having to ask a pharmacist for it—and advocates for that decision will continue to work toward achieving the easiest possible access for all women (Richards, 2006; Tummino, 2006).

53% of Catholics and 39% of born-again Christians) think that EC should be easily available in pharmacies (Harris Poll, 2006). However, as we discuss in the Sex and Politics box, politically powerful opposition to emergency contraception interferes with its availability to women who want to prevent an unplanned pregnancy.

## ◑ Fertility Awareness Methods

The birth control methods that we have discussed so far require the use of pills or devices. Some of these methods have side effects in some users, and there can be serious health risks associated with using oral contraceptives and the IUD. The barrier methods we have looked at—condoms, vaginal spermicides, and the diaphragm—have fewer side effects, but they require that the couple use them each time they have intercourse.

**Fertility awareness methods** Birth control methods that use the signs of cyclic fertility to prevent or plan conception.

Many couples are interested in a birth control method that has no side effects, is inexpensive, and does not interrupt spontaneity during sexual interaction (Fehring, 2004). In the next paragraphs, we look at methods of birth control based on changes during the menstrual cycle. These methods, which may answer some couples' needs, are sometimes referred to as *natural family planning* or **fertility awareness methods**.

They are based on the fact that a fertile woman's body reveals subtle and overt signs of cyclic fertility that can be used both to help prevent and to plan conception.

There are four different fertility awareness methods: the standard days method, the mucus method, the calendar method, and the basal body temperature method. Any of these can be used in combination to increase effectiveness. About 4% of women in the United States use natural family planning (Stanford et al., 1998). During the fertile period, couples using fertility awareness methods can abstain from intercourse and engage in other forms of sexual intimacy or can continue having intercourse and use other methods of birth control during the fertile time. Unfortunately, present research indicates that, other than the standard days method, fertility awareness methods are considerably less effective than most other birth control methods (Jennings et al., 1998).

## Standard Days Method

The **standard days method** is the newest approach to natural family planning. It is appropriate for women who have menstrual cycles between 26 and 32 days long. Couples avoid unprotected intercourse on days 8 through 19 of each menstrual cycle. This "fertile window" is 12 days long to take into account both the days around ovulation and the possible variations in timing of ovulation from one cycle to another. The standard days method has been clinically tested and shows the highest rate of effectiveness for natural family planning methods (Arevalo et al., 2002). A woman can keep track on a calendar or use the CycleBeads shown in ● **Figure 10.9** to help track the days.

**Standard days method** A birth control method that requires couples to avoid unprotected intercourse for a 12-day period in the middle of the menstrual cycle.

## Mucus Method

The **mucus method**, also called the *ovulation method*, is based on the cyclic changes of cervical mucus that reveal periods of fertility in a woman's cycle. To use this method, a woman learns to "read" the amounts and textures of vaginal secretions and to maintain a daily chart of the changes. A woman reads her mucus by putting her fingers inside her vagina and noting the consistency of the secretions:

**Mucus method** A birth control method based on determining the time of ovulation by means of the cyclical changes of the cervical mucus.

- After menstruation some "dry days" pass when no vaginal discharge appears on the vulva.
- When a yellow or white sticky discharge appears, unprotected coitus should be avoided.
- Several days later, the ovulatory mucus appears. It is clear, stringy, and stretchy in consistency, similar to egg white. A drop of this mucus will stretch between an open thumb and forefinger for at least $1^{1}/_{2}$ inches before breaking. A vaginal feeling of wetness and lubrication accompanies this discharge, which has a chemical balance and texture that help sperm enter the uterus.
- Approximately 4 days after the ovulatory mucus begins and 24 hours after a cloudy discharge resumes, it is considered safe to resume unprotected intercourse.

The fertile period usually totals 9 to 15 days out of each cycle. In many cities classes in the mucus method are offered at a hospital or clinic. Each woman's mucus patterns vary, and taking a class is the best way to learn how to interpret the changes.

J. Darin Derstine

● **Figure 10.9** Cycle-Beads, based on the standard days method, help a woman track her menstrual cycle and know when she can and cannot get pregnant. To use the CycleBeads, a woman moves a black ring each day onto the next of 32 color-coded beads, which represent fertile and low-fertility days.

## Calendar Method

**Calendar method**
A birth control method based on abstinence from intercourse during calendar-estimated fertile days.

Using the **calendar method**, also called the *rhythm method*, a woman estimates the calendar time during her cycle when she is ovulating and fertile. To use this method, a woman keeps a chart, preferably for 1 year, of the length of her cycles. (She cannot be using oral contraceptives during this time because they impose a cycle that may not be the same as her own.)

- The first day of menstruation is counted as day 1. The woman counts the number of days of her cycle, the last day being the one before the onset of menstruation.
- To determine high-risk days, on which she should avoid unprotected coitus, the woman subtracts 18 from the number of days of her shortest cycle. For example, if her shortest cycle was 26 days, day 8 would be the first high-risk day.
- To estimate when unprotected coitus can resume, the woman subtracts 10 from the number of days in her longest cycle. For example, if her longest cycle is 32 days, she would be able to resume intercourse on day 22.

## Basal Body Temperature Method

**Basal body temperature method** A birth control method based on body temperature changes before and after ovulation.

Another way of estimating high-fertility days is through temperature, using the **basal body temperature method**. Immediately before ovulation the basal body temperature (BBT, the body temperature in the resting state on waking in the morning) drops slightly. After ovulation the corpus luteum releases more progesterone, which causes the body temperature to rise slightly (0.2°F). Because these temperature changes are slight, a thermometer with easy-to-read gradations must be used. Special electronic thermometers have been developed for measuring BBT and are effective in indicating fertile times in the cycle.

# ❿ Sterilization

*Sterilization* is the most effective method of birth control except abstinence from sexual intercourse, and its safety and permanence appeal to many who want no more children or who prefer to remain childless. Sterilization is the leading method of birth control in the United States and around the world (Landry, 2002). Although research is investigating ways to reverse sterilization, current reversal procedures involve complicated surgery and their effectiveness is not guaranteed (Liang, 2000). Therefore, sterilization is recommended only to those who desire a permanent method of birth control (Sandlow et al., 2001).

Needless to say, sterilization should always be the decision of each individual or couple. Unfortunately, that has not always been the policy in the United States. In 1924 a Supreme Court decision, *Buck v. Bell*, legalized forced sterilization as part of the eugenics (good breeding) program in the United States. Continuing into the 1970s, more than 30 states participated in the forced or coerced sterilization of 70,000 U.S. citizens. Most victims were women, and more than 60% were African Americans. Some women were sterilized without their knowledge after giving birth. Others were forced to choose sterilization or termination of family welfare benefits. The state ordered some sterilizations for women it defined as lazy or promiscuous. To date, North Carolina is the only state to issue a formal apology and to establish a commission to make amends to the victims (Schoen, 2006; Sinderbrand, 2005). ■

## Female Sterilization

**Tubal sterilization**
Female sterilization accomplished by severing or tying the fallopian tubes.

Female sterilization has become a relatively safe, simple, and inexpensive procedure. **Tubal sterilization** can be accomplished by a variety of techniques that use small incisions and either local or general anesthesia. A *laparoscopy* is shown in ❿ **Figure 10.10.** One or two small incisions are made in the abdomen, usually at the navel and slightly below the pubic hairline. A narrow, lighted viewing instrument called a laparoscope is inserted into the abdomen to locate the fallopian tubes. The tubes are then tied off, cut, clipped, or cauterized to block passage of sperm and eggs. The incisions are

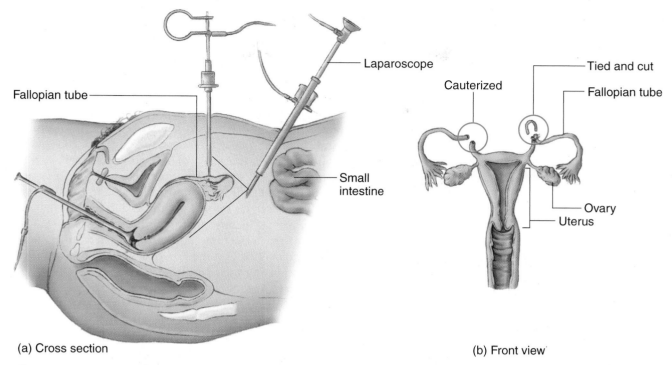

Fallopian tube

Laparoscope

Small intestine

Cauterized

Tied and cut

Fallopian tube

Ovary

Uterus

(a) Cross section

(b) Front view

⊙ **Figure 10.10** Female sterilization by laparoscopic ligation. Front view shows tubes after ligation.

generally so small that adhesive tape rather than stitches is used to close them after surgery. Sometimes, in a procedure called a *culpotomy*, the incision is made through the back of the vaginal wall.

A new technique does not require an operating room, general anesthesia, or as much recovery time (Kerin et al., 2003). The procedure takes half an hour and is performed using local anesthesia. During a **transcervical sterilization**, a physician inserts a tiny coil, called Essure (shown in ⊙ **Figure 10.11**), into the vagina, through the cervix, and into the opening of each fallopian tube in the uterus. When the coil is released, it expands and anchors itself in place. Essure is made of polyester fibers and nickel-titanium alloy, the same material used to make artificial heart valves. The coil promotes tissue growth that, after 3 months, blocks the fallopian tubes and prevents the ovum and sperm from meeting. Women and/or their partners should use another form of birth control during those 3 months (Ritter, 2003). The most common side effect is cramping; in rare cases the coil is expelled or perforates the fallopian tube.

Sterilization does not affect a woman's reproductive and sexual system. Until menopause her ovaries continue to release their eggs. The released eggs simply degenerate, as do millions of other cells daily. The woman's hormone levels and the timing of menopause remain unchanged. Her sexuality is not physiologically changed, but she may find that her interest and arousal increase because she is no longer concerned about pregnancy or birth control methods (Stewart & Carignan, 1998).

## Male Sterilization

Male sterilization is as effective as female sterilization and has the advantages of being safer and less expensive and having fewer complications following surgery. Although 500,000 men in the United States have vasectomies each year, three times more married women than married men in the United States have undergone sterilization (Baill et al., 2003).

**Vasectomy** is a 20-minute minor surgical procedure, usually done in a physician's office, that involves cutting and closing each vas deferens, the sperm-carrying duct, so that sperm are blocked from passing out the penis during sexual arousal and ejaculation (⊙ **Figure 10.12**).

**Transcervical sterilization** A method of female sterilization using a tiny coil that is inserted through the vagina, cervix, and uterus into the fallopian tubes.

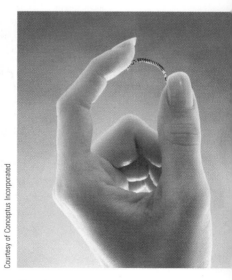

Courtesy of Conceptus Incorporated

⊙ **Figure 10.11** Essure, a tiny coil that is used in female sterilization.

**Vasectomy** Male sterilization accomplished by cutting and closing each vans deferens

(1) The vas deferens is located.

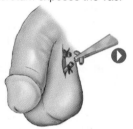

(2) A small incision in the scrotum exposes the vas.

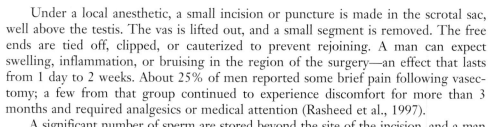

(3) A small section of the vas is removed, and the ends are cut and/or cauterized.

(4) The incision is closed.

(5) Steps 1–4 are repeated on the other side.

**Vasovasostomy** Surgical reconstruction of the vas deferens to reverse a vasectomy.

Under a local anesthetic, a small incision or puncture is made in the scrotal sac, well above the testis. The vas is lifted out, and a small segment is removed. The free ends are tied off, clipped, or cauterized to prevent rejoining. A man can expect swelling, inflammation, or bruising in the region of the surgery—an effect that lasts from 1 day to 2 weeks. About 25% of men reported some brief pain following vasectomy; a few from that group continued to experience discomfort for more than 3 months and required analgesics or medical attention (Rasheed et al., 1997).

A significant number of sperm are stored beyond the site of the incision, and a man remains fertile for some time after the operation. Therefore, effective alternative methods of birth control should be used until semen analysis reveals no sperm in the seminal fluid. Many physicians recommend that a vasectomized man have a test for sperm 3 months after the vasectomy (Shah & Fisch, 2006). In rare cases the two free ends of the severed vas grow back together (this is called *recanalization*) (Stewart & Carignan, 1998).

Vasectomy does not alter production of male sex hormone. In addition, a vasectomized man continues to produce sperm, which are absorbed and eliminated by his body. The consistency and odor of his semen remain the same, and his ejaculations contain almost as much volume as before, because sperm constitute less than 1% of the total ejaculate. Most men report that vasectomy does not negatively affect their sexual functioning (Stewart & Carignan, 1998). Some experience greater spontaneity and pleasure due to less fear of impregnating their partners.

Up to 3 men out of 1,000 who have had a vasectomy request a **vasovasostomy**, a reversal of a vasectomy (Liang, 2000). Approximately 80% of vasovasostomies are done for men in a second marriage following divorce (Fallon et al., 1981). The shorter the interval is between vasectomy and vasovasostomy, the better the outcome. The best measure of success is the partner's subsequent pregnancy; various studies report an average pregnancy rate of 50% (Matthews et al., 1997).

## ▶ Less-Than-Effective Methods

Besides the contraceptive methods we have been discussing, others exist that are far less effective and less commonly used. We mention some of them here because people may have misconceptions about their effectiveness. We discuss nursing, withdrawal, and douching as methods of birth control.

### Nursing

Nursing a baby delays a woman's return to fertility after childbirth when the baby is only breast-fed. However, breast-feeding is not a fully reliable method of birth control because there is no way of knowing when ovulation will resume. Amenorrhea (lack of menstruation) usually occurs during nursing, but it is not a reliable indication of inability to conceive. Nearly 80% of breast-feeding women ovulate before their first menstrual period. The longer a woman breast-feeds, the more likely it is that ovulation will occur (Kennedy & Trussell, 1998).

### Withdrawal

The practice of the man removing his penis from the vagina just before he ejaculates is known as *withdrawal*. It is ineffective because the preejaculatory Cowper's gland secretions can carry sperm that can fertilize an egg. Also, it may be difficult for the man to judge exactly when he must withdraw, and his tendency is to remain inside the vagina as long as possible, which may be too long. Any sperm deposited on the labia while the man withdraws his penis can swim into the vagina. Both partners may experience pleasure-reducing anxiety about whether he will withdraw in time.

### Douching

Although some women use *douching* after intercourse as a method of birth control, it is ineffective. After ejaculation some sperm reach the inside of the uterus in a matter of 1 or 2 minutes. In addition, the movement of the water from douching may actually help sperm reach the opening of the cervix. Furthermore, frequent douching is not recommended because it can irritate vaginal tissues.

# New Directions in Contraception

As we have seen in this chapter, potential health hazards and inconveniences are associated with available contraceptive methods. Unwanted pregnancies occur each year because of contraceptive and user failure. Further research is needed to improve the safety, reliability, and convenience of birth control (Nass & Strauss, 2004; Schwartz & Gabelnick, 2002).

However, research requires funding. Most clinical trials for contraception occur in foreign countries with the financial help of the United States (Benagiano & Cottingham, 1997). U.S. funds for international family planning programs to conduct clinical trials on contraception have been minimal. In addition, some pharmaceutical companies have dropped their contraceptive research programs because of the great expense of extensive clinical trials needed for product approval by the FDA and because of concern about product liability expenses (Tone, 2002). Given these limitations, we look at future possibilities for both men and women. ■

## New Directions for Men

Research has shown that most men would use a male contraceptive pill (Upadhyay, 2005). Because contraceptive failure has greater consequences for women than for men, whether women would trust their male partners to reliably use a male pill is a concern. Research has found that most women say they would trust their partners to use such a pill; only 2% said they would not trust their partners to do so. In addition, men and women think that a male pill is a good idea because the responsibility for contraception tends to fall too much to women (Nieschlag & Henke, 2005; Upadhyay, 2005).

At present, male contraception is limited to condoms, vasectomy, and withdrawal. Current research has concentrated on inhibiting sperm production, motility, or maturation. No easy solution exists because any drug aimed at inhibiting sperm production needs at least 10 weeks to work—the length of the sperm production cycle

Reuters/Miro Kuzmanovic/Landov

Other countries are more proactive with developing new versions of condoms. By 2008 Germany's Institute for Condom Consultancy hopes to offer a spray-on condom. The man inserts his penis into a can with interior nozzles that spray latex to enclose the penis in a perfect fit, non-slip condom. South Africa's Pronto condom is made so users put it on quickly. The package opens by bending it in half in both directions. The user holds on to each side of the packaging to pull it over the penis, then pulls the packaging off at the base of the penis.

Courtesy of Clifford Jay Snider

"First Man on the Pill" is a poster to recruit volunteers for clinical trials for the male birth control pill (Roots, 2004).

(N. Alexander, 2003). In addition, medications that affect sperm production usually impair sexual interest and function and may have other side effects.

The most promising possibility is using testosterone or a combination of progestin and testosterone in an implant or by injection. Some studies are finding a full return to fertility in 4 to 5 months after using male hormone contraception (Liu et al., 2006). Two sterilization methods in clinical trials are forms of reversible vasectomy. One involves injecting a blocking gel into the vas deferens; to reverse the procedure, the gel can be dissolved. The second method uses the Intra Vas Device, which consists of two plugs inserted into each vas deferens; the plugs can be removed later. Implantation and removal of this device can be done in 20 minutes each (Upadhyay, 2005).

## New Directions for Women

A nonhormonal contraceptive vaccine that would be a fundamentally new form of birth control is being studied (Williams et al., 2006). However, other new directions for women consist of variations on methods of delivery and formulations of hormones in existing methods. In the case of oral contraceptives, new progestins and extending the time a woman takes pills without stopping are being tested (Edelman, 2006; Miller, 2006). Researchers are also studying new designs for IUDs, and a spray-on contraceptive may be added to the choices of transdermal contraceptives. Second-generation female condoms and diaphragms are under development. Hoping to provide women with STD and HIV protection that is under their own control, researchers are studying spermicides that contain microbicides (substances that stop STD transmission) (Dhawan & Mayer, 2006).

Since the advent of the pill, contraceptive options have greatly increased. However, the ideal of 100% effective, reversible contraceptives for men and women—methods that also have no side effects and protect against sexually transmitted infections—will, unfortunately, not be available anytime in the foreseeable future.

**Critical Thinking Question**

Do you think women would be naive to believe men who say they are on the pill? Why or why not?

S U M M A R Y

## Historical and Social Perspectives

- From the beginning of recorded history, humankind has been concerned about birth control.
- Margaret Sanger opened the first birth control clinics in the United States at a time when it was illegal to provide birth control information and devices.
- Objections to contraception stem from Roman Catholic doctrine and far-right pro-life religious beliefs. However, most church members in the United States use some kind of artificial contraception.

## Sharing Responsibility and Choosing a Birth Control Method

- A man can share contraceptive responsibility with his female partner by getting informed, asking a new partner about birth control, accompanying his partner to her exam, using condoms and/or coital abstinence if the couple chooses, and sharing the expense of the exam and contraceptive method.
- Comparison of convenience, safety, cost, and effectiveness may influence the choice of contraception.
- People who feel guilty and have negative attitudes about sexuality are less likely to use contraception effectively than people who have positive attitudes about sexuality.

## Hormone-Based Contraceptives

- Four types of oral contraceptives are available. The constant-dose combination pill contains steady doses of estrogen and progestin. The triphasic pill provides fluctuations of estrogen and progesterone levels throughout the menstrual cycle. The extended cycle pill reduces menstrual cycles to four per year. The progestin-only pill consists of low-dose progestin.
- Advantages of oral contraceptives include high effectiveness and lack of interference with sexual activity. Birth control pills are also associated with lower incidences of uterine, ovarian, and colon cancer. An additional advantage is reduction of menstrual flow and cramps. The advantage of the progestin-only pill is the reduced chance of side effects from estrogen. The vaginal ring, NuvaRing; the transdermal patch, Ortho Evra, and the injectable Depo-Provera are hormone-based contraceptives that do not require remembering to take a pill each day.
- Disadvantages of hormone-based contraceptives include possible side effects such as a slight increase in the likelihood of blood clots, an increase in migraine headaches, nausea, fluid retention, irregular bleeding, and reduced sexual interest. Disadvantages of the progestin-only pill include irregular bleeding and the possibility of additional

side effects. In general, the health risks of oral contraceptives are far lower than those from pregnancy and birth.

- Depo-Provera is an injectable contraceptive that lasts for 3 months.

## Barrier and Spermicide Methods

- Condoms are available in a variety of styles. Advantages include protection from sexually transmitted diseases and availability as a backup method. Disadvantages include interruption of sexual activity and reduced penile sensation. A female condom has also been developed.
- Vaginal spermicides (including contraceptive foam, the sponge, vaginal suppositories, creams and jellies, and contraceptive film) are available without a prescription. Advantages of vaginal spermicides include lack of serious side effects and added lubrication. Disadvantages include low level of effectiveness unless used with a condom, possible irritation of genital tissues, and interruption of sexual activity.
- Advantages of cervical barrier methods include lack of side effects, high effectiveness with knowledgeable and consistent use, and possible promotion of vaginal health. Disadvantages include interruption of sexual activity, potential irritation from the spermicidal cream or jelly, and possible misplacement during insertion or intercourse.

## Intrauterine Devices

- The Copper-T, Progestasert T, and Mirena are the only intrauterine devices (IUDs) on the U.S. market. Advantages of the IUD include uninterrupted sexual interaction and simplicity of use. Disadvantages include the possibilities of increased cramping and spontaneous expulsion. Uterine perforation is rare. The IUD increases risk of pelvic inflammatory disease for women with multiple partners.

## Emergency Contraception

- Plan B, Preven, oral contraceptives and the Copper-T IUD can be used for emergency contraception when a woman has had unprotected intercourse.
- The FDA denied over-the-counter status to emergency contraception, against its committee's recommendation.

## Fertility Awareness Methods

- Contraceptive methods based on the menstrual cycle— including the standard days, mucus, calendar, and basal body temperature methods—help in planning coital activity to avoid a woman's fertile period.

## Sterilization

- At this time sterilization should be considered permanent. A decision to be sterilized should be carefully evaluated.
- Tubal ligation is the sterilization procedure most commonly performed for women. It does not alter a woman's hormone levels or menstrual cycle or the timing of menopause.
- Vasectomy, the sterilization procedure for men, is not effective for birth control immediately after surgery because sperm remain in the vas deferens above the incision.

## Less-Than-Effective Methods

- Breast-feeding, douching, and the withdrawal method are not reliable methods of contraception.

## New Directions in Contraception

- Possible contraceptive methods for men in the future include the use of hormones to reduce the production and motility of sperm.
- Possible future contraceptive methods for women include variations of the IUD, spermicides that contain microbicides effective against STDs, and new methods for delivering hormones.

## ⓞ Suggested Readings

**Hatcher, Robert, et al.** (2004). *Contraceptive Technology,* 18th edition. New York: Ardent Media. A comprehensive, up-to-date book about birth control—a must for anyone who wants the latest information about the technology and effects of contraception.

**Page, Christina** (2006). *How the Pro-Choice Movement Saved America: Freedom, Politics and the War on Sex.* New York: Basic Books. An in-depth analysis of how the pro-life movement has attacked birth control laws and policies that help prevent unwanted pregnancies and abortion.

**Schoen, Johanna** (2006). *Choice and Coercion: Birth Control, Sterilization, and Abortion in Public Health and Welfare.* Chapel Hill: University of North Carolina Press. An examination of the repressive and liberating potential of contraception on a local and global level.

**Tone, Andrea** (2002). *Devices and Desires: A History of Contraceptives in America.* New York: Hill and Wang. An intricate history of birth control in the United States, from Victorian pessaries to alleged racism in government policies.

## ⓞ Web Resources

**CengageNOW Web Site**
Go to **academic.cengage.com** to link to practice quiz questions, interactive activities, Internet links, critical thinking exercises, discussion forums, and more. You can also access sites from the Wadsworth Psychology Study Center (**academic .cengage.com/psychology**) or you can connect directly to the following sites:

**Margaret Sanger Papers Project**
The life, writings, and work of the American birth control pioneer Margaret Sanger are highlighted on this Web site. The site also includes an extensive list of links to related sites.

**Successful Contraception**
The Association of Reproductive Health Professionals provides this Web site. Along with excellent information about various methods of contraception, the site includes an interactive feature to help you choose the method of birth control most appropriate for you.

**International Planned Parenthood Federation**
The well-known organization promoting family planning and contraception provides this Web site, which features breaking news, press releases, journal articles, and other resources.

### Contraceptive Choices

A quick guide to the advantages and disadvantages of various types of contraception are included on this Web page, sponsored by the Planned Parenthood Federation of America.

### Emergency Contraception

Detailed information about emergency contraception, including how to use certain oral contraceptives for emergency contraception.

### When Timing Is Everything

A full array of birth control pill cases with alarm notification to help women remember when to take their pill.

### Condomania

Search through hundreds of different types of condoms.

*Our Sexuality* **Book Companion Web Site academic.cengage.com/psychology/ crooks** Visit your book companion Web site where you will find flash cards, practice quizzes, Internet links, and more to help you study.

**Just what you need to know NOW!**
Spend time on what you need to master rather than on information you already have learned. Take a pretest for this chapter, and CengageNOW will generate a personalized study plan based on your results. The study plan will identify the topics you need to review and direct you to online resources to help you master those topics. You can then take a post-test to help you determine the concepts you have mastered and what you will still need to work on. Try it out! Go to **academic.cengage.com/login** to sign in with an access code or to purchase access to this product.

**InfoTrac College Edition Online Library**
Sign in to **academic.cengage.com/login** or visit your free book companion Web site at **academic.cengage.com/psychology/crooks** to access InfoTrac College Edition, an online searchable library that includes a multitude of journals, many specific to human sexuality. These journals include *Archives of Sexual Behavior; Archives of Sexual Health Behavior; Canadian Journal of Human Sexuality; Hispanic Journal of the Behavioral Sciences; Journal of Cross-Cultural Psychology; Journal of Physical Education, Recreation, and Dance; Journal of Sex Research;* and *Sex Roles.*

# Conceiving Children: Process and Choice

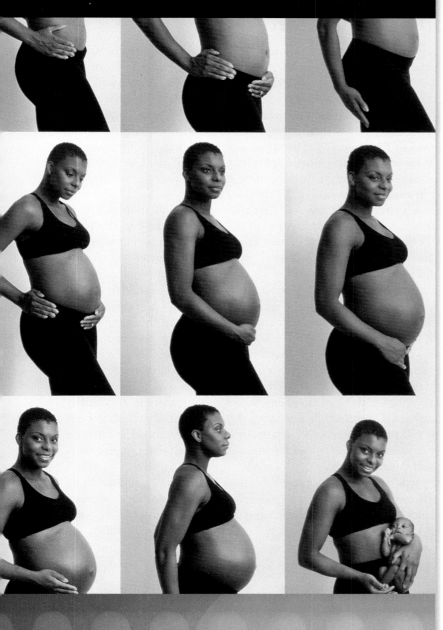

© Michael Krasowitz/Getty Images

*I've been an "expectant" father twice, but my role was drastically different the second time because of changes in obstetrical practices. During my first child's birth, it was the classic scene of Dad pacing the waiting room floor while my wife was in the delivery room. In my second marriage, the pregnancy was "our pregnancy" from the beginning. I went to doctor's appointments and saw our baby's ultrasound pictures. Seeing his heart beat so early in the pregnancy gave me a feeling of connection right from the start. We attended prepared childbirth classes together, and I was there from start to finish during labor and when she delivered our baby. I went with him to the nursery for all the weighing, measuring, and cleaning, then brought him back to his mother in the birthing suite. I wish I'd had those experiences with my first child's birth. (Authors' files)*

One of the most important decisions we will probably make in our lifetime is whether to become a parent. In this chapter we address the pros and cons of parenthood. We also discuss the processes of conception, pregnancy, and birth and some of the emotions that accompany them from the viewpoints of the parents. We encourage people who desire further information to seek more extensive references or to consult a health-care practitioner. As a starting point, we look at the option of parenthood and some of the alternatives that are available for people who want to become parents.

## ◗ Parenthood as an Option

More couples and individuals than in the past are choosing to be "kid-free," largely due to the availability of effective modern contraceptives. In 1975 about 9% of 40-year-old women did not have children; in 1997 almost 17% were childless (Clark, 2000). If we narrow the group to women executives over 40, 42% do not have children (Jeffrey, 2006). Remaining childless has many potential advantages. Individuals and couples have much more time for themselves, more financial resources, and more spontaneity with regard to their recreational, social, and work patterns. Nonparents can more fully pursue careers, creating more opportunity for fulfillment in their professional lives. At the same time, there is usually more time and energy for companionship and intimacy in an adult relationship (Carroll, 2000).

In general, childless marriages are less stressful; and some studies show that they are happier and more satisfying than marriages with children, especially in the years following a first child's birth (Crohan, 1996; Lavee et al., 1996). Not having to worry about providing for the physical and psychological needs of children can make a difference, because conflict about *who* does *what* for the children is a major source of disenchantment for many couples (Cowan & Cowan, 1992; Vehjar et al., 2006). Note, however, that the reduced marital satisfaction after children may be because many unhappily married couples remain together because they have young children.

Becoming parents of adopted or biological children also has many potential advantages. A national representative sample found that 98% of fathers and 97% of mothers agreed with the statement "The rewards of being a parent are worth it, despite the costs and work it takes" (Martinez et al., 2006, p. 28). Children give as well as receive love, and their presence can enhance the love between couples as they share in the experiences of raising their offspring. Successfully managing the challenges of parenthood can also build self-esteem and provide a sense of accomplishment. Parenthood is often an opportunity for discovering new and untapped dimensions of oneself that can give one's life greater meaning and satisfaction.

The potential rewards of either becoming parents or remaining childless can be romanticized or unrealistic for a given person or couple, and some people experience considerable ambivalence. As one writer put it, having children changes your life—but so does not having them (Cole, 1987).

## ◗ Becoming Pregnant

In the remainder of this chapter, we look at some of the developments, experiences, and feelings involved in the physiological process of becoming parents, starting with becoming pregnant. This first step can be difficult for some couples.

## Enhancing the Possibility of Conception

Picking the right time for intercourse is important in increasing the probability of conception. Conception is most likely to occur within the 6-day period ending on the day of ovulation (Wilcox et al., 1995). It is difficult to predict the exact time of ovulation, but several methods permit a reasonable approximation. Ovulation predictor tests, which measure the rise in luteinizing hormone (LH) in urine before ovulation, can accurately identify the best time for conception and can be purchased over the counter (Perris, 2000). Otherwise, the mucus method, body temperature, and the principles of the calendar method can also be used to estimate ovulation time, as discussed in Chapter 10. ■

Some individuals and couples are interested in enhancing the possibility of conceiving a child of a specific sex, as discussed in the Sexuality and Diversity section.

## SEXUALITY AND DIVERSITY

### Preselecting a Baby's Sex: Technology and Cross-Cultural Issues

The desire to have a child of a certain sex has existed since ancient times, when sex selection was done after the fact. For example, in ancient Roman society, infanticide was practiced against unwanted female babies (Faerman et al., 1997). Superstitions about determining the sex of a child during intercourse are part of Western folk tradition—for example, the belief that if a man wears a hat during intercourse, he will father a male child or that if a man hangs his trousers on the left bedpost, he will sire a girl.

In China, India, and South Korea, the preference for a son is particularly strong, and killing infant girls and selective abortion of female fetuses are common (Chung, 2006; Coontz, 2005). In India a woman can obtain an ultrasound for about $12 to determine the sex of the fetus, and if it is a girl have an abortion for about $35 (Power, 2006). The Bill and Melinda Gates Foundation funded a study in a rural area of India where there are 628 girls for every 1,000 boys under 6 years of age. Economic and cultural factors contribute to the importance of sons. Sons provide for parents through their old age, offering security in the absence of governmental social support. In Hindu and Confucian religious traditions in Asia, only sons can light their parents' funeral pyres and pray to release the souls of dead parents. Sons will bring future earnings to their parents, but daughters are a financial liability to their families when they require the expense of a dowry. Women's work will also contribute to the family into which they marry. China's one-child policy has greatly reduced the birthrate—from 4.8 children per family in 1970 to 1.8 today—but parents' desire to have that one child be male has also altered the natural birth ratio from 100 girls to 105 boys to 100 girls to 118 boys (Power, 2006; Robinson, 1999).

An effective technique for sex selection, pre-implantation genetic diagnosis (PGD), creates embryos in the laboratory. The sex of the embryos is tested, and a physician subsequently inserts the embryos of the desired sex into the woman's uterus. The approximately $20,000 procedure offers almost 100% certainty of the sex of the baby (Ulick, 2004). Less certain results occur with the more commonly used laboratory techniques that can separate X-chromosome–bearing sperm from Y-chromosome–bearing sperm. Once the laboratory separation process is complete, the desired X or Y fraction is introduced into the vagina by artificial insemination. Success rates are about 90% for female babies and 70% for male babies. However, the rather "unromantic" nature of semen collection and artificial insemination will probably limit the use of sex selection techniques unless parents have compelling reasons to conceive a child of a particular sex (Berkowitz, 2000). Sex preselection offers benefits to couples at risk for passing on X-chromosome–linked diseases to their children.

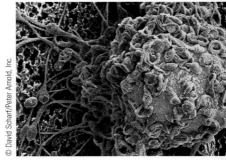

© David Scharf/Peter Arnold, Inc.

The first stage of pregnancy: only one of the sperm surrounding this ovum will fertilize it.

# Infertility

InfoTrac Search Words

● Infertility

Sixty percent of couples become pregnant within 3 months, but if attempts at impregnation are unsuccessful after 6 months, a couple should consult a physician. It has been estimated that about 10% of U.S. couples attempting pregnancy experience fertility problems, defined as not conceiving after at least 1 year (Oliwenstein, 2005). Because approximately 50% of infertility cases involve male factors, it is important that both partners be evaluated (Jegalian & Lahn, 2001b). We usually think of infertility as the inability to conceive any children, but secondary infertility—the inability to conceive a second child—occurs in 10% of couples (Diamond et al., 1999).

Infertility is a complex and distressing problem. It can have a demoralizing effect on the infertile individual's sense of self and on the couple's sense of their integrity as a healthy unit (Scharf & Weinshel, 2000). Its causes are sometimes difficult to determine and remain unidentified in as many as 15% of cases (Nilsson et al., 1994). In addition, most couples seeking treatment for infertility are ultimately unsuccessful in their efforts to conceive, despite trying various avenues of treatment (Toner, 2002). Furthermore, research has found that most women throughout the world in developed and developing countries are unknowledgeable about basic facts associated with their infertility, as reported by a survey of 17,500 women in 10 different countries (The American Fertility Association, 2006).

## Infertility and Sexuality

Most people grow up believing that they can conceive children when they decide to begin a family. Experiencing infertility is an unanticipated shock and crisis (Wilkes, 2006). As their infertility becomes more evident and undeniable, a couple may feel a great sense of isolation from others during social discussions of pregnancy, childbirth, and child rearing. As one woman who has been unable to conceive stated:

> Coffee breaks at work are the worst times; everyone brings out their pictures of their kids and discusses their latest parental trials and tribulations. When one of the women complains about having problems with something like child-care, I just want to shout at her and tell her how lucky she is to be able to have such a "problem." (Authors' files)

Problems with infertility can have profoundly negative effects on a couple's relationship and sexual functioning (Schmidt, 2006). Partners can also become isolated from each other and believe that the other does not really understand. Each partner might feel inadequate about his or her masculinity or femininity because of problems with conceiving. Each may feel anger and guilt and wonder, "Why me?" Finally, both may feel grief over life experiences they can never have—namely, pregnancy, birth, and conceiving and rearing their own biological children (Miller, 2003).

Intercourse itself can evoke these uncomfortable feelings and can become an emotionally painful rather than pleasurable experience, fraught with anxiety and sadness about failing to conceive (Salonia et al., 2006). Studies have found that most infertile couples experience some sexual dissatisfaction or dysfunction at one point or another (Zoldbrod, 1993). In addition, the medical procedures used in fertility diagnosis and treatment are disruptive to the couple's sexual spontaneity and privacy. Sex can become stressful and mechanical, resulting in performance anxiety that interferes with sexual arousal and emotional closeness (Pawson, 2003).

In contrast, 20% of men and 25% of women report that infertility helped their marriage. The determining characteristics were whether men actively communicated their feelings instead of avoiding conversations about pregnancy and burying themselves in work. In addition to increasing closeness in the relationship, couples who communicated with each other about the infertility also reduced their overall individual stress by doing so (Aaronson, 2006).

## Female Infertility

A woman can have difficulty conceiving or be unable to conceive for a number of reasons. Problems with ovulation account for approximately 20% of infertility (Urman &

Yakin, 2006). Increasing age reduces fertility significantly: A woman's fertility peaks between ages 20 and 24 and begins to decrease rapidly after age 30. Fertility rates in women ages 35 to 39 are up to 46% lower, and in ages 40 to 45 are 95% lower than women at their peak fertility (Speroff & Fritz, 2005).

Hormone imbalances, severe vitamin deficiencies, metabolic disturbances, poor nutrition, genetic factors, emotional stress, or medical conditions can contribute to ovulatory problems (Marx & Mehta, 2003). Ovulation, and thus pregnancy, can also be inhibited by a below-normal percentage of body fat, which results from excessive dieting or exercise. Being even 10–15% below normal weight is sufficient to inhibit ovulation. Women who smoke cigarettes are less fertile and take longer to become pregnant than nonsmokers. Alcohol and drug abuse reduces fertility in women, and environmental toxins can also impair female fertility (Isaacs, 2006). Ovulation problems can sometimes be treated with a variety of medications that stimulate ovulation. Although often successful and generally safe, these drugs can produce certain complications, including a greatly increased chance of multiple births (Filicori, 2003).

If tests indicate that the woman is ovulating and that her partner's semen quality is satisfactory, the next step often is a postcoital test to see whether the sperm remain viable and motile in the cervical mucus (Chretien, 2003). A woman's cervical mucus can contain antibodies that attack her partner's sperm, or it can form a plug that blocks their passage (Ginsburg et al., 1997). Intrauterine insemination, placing semen directly into the uterus, can be helpful in some cases.

Infections and abnormalities of the cervix, vagina, uterus, fallopian tubes, or ovaries can destroy sperm or prevent them from reaching the egg (Rebar, 2004). Scar tissue from old infections—in the fallopian tubes or in or around the ovaries—can block the passage of sperm and eggs. Sexually transmitted diseases (STDs) are a common cause of these problems. Tubal problems can sometimes be resolved by surgically removing the scar tissue around the fallopian tubes and ovaries.

Some fertility specialists think that celebrity moms who have babies later in life, such as Susan Sarandon, give the false impression that conception at any age is easy.

## Male Infertility

Most causes of male infertility are related to abnormalities in sperm number and/or motility (the vigor with which sperm cells propel themselves). A major cause of infertility in men is a damaged or enlarged vein in the testis or vas deferens, called a **varicocele** (Ehrenfeld, 2002). The varicocele causes blood to pool in the scrotum, which elevates temperature in the area, impairing sperm production (Stephenson, 2003b). Infectious diseases of the male reproductive tract can alter sperm production, viability, and transport (Villanueva-Diaz et al., 1999). For instance, mumps, when it occurs in adulthood, can affect the testes, lowering sperm output; and infection of the vas deferens can block the passage of sperm. Infections caused by STDs are another major cause of infertility. Smoking, alcohol, and drug use and abuse reduce fertility as well (Kunzle et al., 2003; Sandlow, 2000). Cocaine use decreases spermatogenesis, and marijuana impedes sperm motility (Leibowitz & Hoffman, 2000). Environmental toxins, such as chemicals, pollutants, and radiation, can also produce low sperm counts and abnormal sperm cells (Duty et al., 2003; Hampton, 2005). Sperm absorb and metabolize environmental toxins more easily than do other body cells, which can also result in birth defects (Tanenbaun, 1997).

When the sperm count is low, to increase the concentration of sperm, the optimal frequency of ejaculation during intercourse is usually every other day, beginning 6 days before ovulation and during the week that the woman is ovulating (Speroff et al., 1989). A man with a low sperm count might also want to avoid taking hot baths, wearing

**Varicocele** A damaged or enlarged vein in the testis or vas deferens.

! Sexual Health

**Intracytoplasmic sperm injection (ICSI)** Procedure in which a single sperm is injected into an egg.

**Artificial insemination** A medical procedure in which semen is placed in a woman's vagina, cervix, or uterus.

**Surrogate mother** A woman who is artificially inseminated by the male partner in a childless couple, carries the pregnancy to term, delivers the child, and gives it to the couple for adoption.

**Assisted reproductive technology (ART)** The techniques of extrauterine conception.

**In vitro fertilization (IVF)** Procedure in which mature eggs are removed from a woman's ovary and fertilized by sperm in a laboratory dish.

**Zygote intrafallopian transfer (ZIFT)** Procedure in which an egg is fertilized in the laboratory and then placed in a fallopian tube.

**Gamete intrafallopian transfer (GIFT)** Procedure in which the sperm and ovum are placed directly in a fallopian tube.

tight clothing and undershorts, and riding bicycles long distances, because these and similar environments subject the testes to higher than normal temperatures. ∎

For poor semen quality or quantity, **intracytoplasmic sperm injection (ICSI)** can result in pregnancy. ICSI involves injecting each harvested egg with a single sperm and is one of the advances in reproductive technology we discuss in the next section.

## Reproductive Alternatives

Various alternatives have been developed to help couples overcome the problem of infertility. **Artificial insemination** is one option to be considered in certain instances. In this procedure, semen is mechanically introduced into the woman's vagina or cervix or, in some cases, directly into her uterus, a procedure called *intrauterine insemination*. If the man is not producing adequate viable sperm or if a woman does not have a male partner, artificial insemination with a donor's semen is another option. Approximately 70,000 babies are born from sperm donor pregnancies each year in the United States, mainly to single women and lesbians (Noonan & Springen, 2001).

A **surrogate mother** is a woman who is willing to be artificially inseminated by the male partner of a childless heterosexual or gay couple or to undergo in vitro fertilization using eggs and sperm from a couple. She carries the pregnancy to term, delivers the child, and gives it to the couple for adoption. Surrogacy can be done anonymously through an attorney or privately by arrangement between the woman and the couple. In the few states that allow surrogate mothers to be paid, they typically receive a fee between $20,000 and $30,000. In the last 30 years, surrogate mothers in the United States have given birth to approximately 25,000 children (Glaser, 2006). Surrogacy is also "outsourced" to India, generating $400 million in yearly revenues. Childless individuals and couples pursue surrogacy in India due to the absence of laws and the low cost of surrogacy fees and medical expenses (Ghura, 2006).

Advances in reproductive technology are referred to as **assisted reproductive technology (ART)**. The world's first test-tube baby was born in England in 1978, and currently in the United States about 48,000 women each year deliver babies that began in a laboratory (King, 2006). In **in vitro fertilization (IVF)** the ovaries are stimulated by hormonal fertility drugs to produce multiple ova. The mature eggs are removed from the woman's ovary and are fertilized in a laboratory dish by her partner's sperm. After 2 or 3 days several fertilized eggs of two to eight cells each are then introduced into the woman's uterus. Excess embryos are often frozen so that if the first implantation does not take place, the procedure can be repeated (Fosas et al., 2003). If this procedure is successful, at least one egg will implant and develop. The success rate of live births from ART has increased to almost 30% after 30 years of medical development. Live births are more likely when the mother is under 30, and less likely when using frozen eggs or embryos (Kelley, 2005; King, 2006; Speroff & Fritz, 2005).

Variations on IVF involve transferring fertilized ova to a fallopian tube rather than to the uterus, a procedure known as **zygote intrafallopian transfer (ZIFT)**. In **gamete intrafallopian transfer (GIFT)**, the sperm and ova are placed directly in the fallopian tube, where fertilization normally occurs.

© Phillips Mitchell

Domestic partners Michael Meehan and Thomas Dysarz hold the year-old quadruplets born in 2002 to a surrogate mother and conceived through in vitro fertilization using Michael's sperm. Now active and healthy, the babies weighed about 3 pounds at birth and spent their first month of life in neonatal intensive care (DeLaMar, 2003).

Donated ova can be used for IVF when the woman does not have ovaries, does not produce her own ova, or has a heritable genetic disease. Donation of ova is analogous to donor artificial insemination. Donors are usually women in their 20s, a sister or friend of the infertile woman, or another woman undergoing IVF who donates her ova to another woman wanting the IVF procedure. In cases in which both partners are infertile, IVF can be done with both donated sperm and donated ova (Kingsberg et al., 2000).

Pre-implantation genetic testing is currently available, and genetic alteration prior to implantation might be implemented soon (Geary & Moon, 2006). Genetic alteration could give parents with a known genetic defect—predisposing them to developing Alzheimer's, breast cancer, cystic fibrosis, or another illness—the ability to have their eggs and sperm genetically altered to remove the illness-causing genetic material prior to in vitro fertilization and implantation (Begley, 2001). Nine months later the couple's baby, without the legacy of family genetic problems, is born. Many bioethicists support this development, which can shield children from disabling and life-threatening genetic problems. Others oppose this technology because it could be frivolously used to genetically engineer "designer babies" (Begley, 1998).

### InfoTrac Search Words

- Assisted reproductive technologies

## Financial and Health Costs of Assisted Reproductive Techniques

Assisted reproductive techniques are expensive. One IVF procedure costs between $12,000 and $14,000, and more than one attempt is often needed. Donor eggs or sperm, ICSI, and any other additional procedures add to the cost (King, 2006).

### ? Critical Thinking Question

Do you think children conceived by donor sperm and/or egg insemination should be told about this? Why or why not?

Multiple embryos are implanted during IVF to increase the chances of conception, and about 30% of pregnancies result in multiple births (Gorman, 2002). Multiple births often exceed twins or triplets, and news broadcasts periodically feature births with more than five babies. Any multiple pregnancy increases the danger to babies, with greater incidence of prenatal and postnatal death, prematurity, low birth weight, and birth defects (Cheung, 2006). In some cases one or more fetuses are reduced during the pregnancy to increase the likelihood that at least one or two others will survive. For mothers the risks of cesarean deliveries, high blood pressure, and other birth complications, including death, increase with multiple births (Dickey, 2003; MacKay et al., 2006). As a physician stated, "The human uterus is not meant to carry litters" (Heyl, 1997, p. 66). In the On the Edge box on page 300, we discuss other dilemmas presented by assisted reproductive technologies.

## Pregnancy Detection

The initial signs of pregnancy can provoke feelings from joy to dread, depending on the woman's desire to be pregnant, her partner's feelings, and a variety of surrounding circumstances. Although some women have either a light blood flow or spotting (irregular bleeding) after conception, usually the first indication of pregnancy is the absence of the menstrual period at the expected time. Breast tenderness, nausea, vomiting, or other nonspecific symptoms (such as extreme fatigue or change in appetite) can also accompany pregnancy in the first weeks or months.

Any of these clues might cause a woman to suspect that she is pregnant. Medical techniques such as blood or urine tests and pelvic exams can make the determination with greater certainty. The blood and hence urine of a pregnant woman contains the hormone **human chorionic gonadotropin** (cohr-ee-AH-nik goh-na-duh-TROH-pun) **(HCG)**, which is secreted by the placenta. Sensitive blood tests for HCG have been developed that can detect pregnancy as early as 7 days after conception (G. Stewart, 1998). Commercially available at-home pregnancy urine or saliva tests can detect pregnancy shortly after a missed menstrual period (Carmichael, 2002). Because elective home pregnancy tests can yield both false-positive and false-negative results, a health-care practitioner should confirm the results.

**Human chorionic gonadotropin (HCG)** A hormone that is detectable in the urine of a pregnant woman within 1 month of conception.

## ● Spontaneous and Elective Abortion

Not every pregnancy results in a birth. Many pregnancies end in spontaneous or elective abortion.

## Miscarriage

Even when pregnancy has been confirmed, complications can prevent full-term development of the fetus. A **miscarriage** is a **spontaneous abortion** that occurs in the first 20 weeks of pregnancy (Stephenson, 2006). At least one in seven known pregnancies ends in miscarriage (Springen, 2005). Most miscarriages occur in the first trimester

**Spontaneous abortion (miscarriage)** The spontaneous expulsion of the fetus from the uterus early in pregnancy, before it can survive on its own.

## Legal, Ethical, and Personal Dilemmas of Assisted Reproductive Technologies

Assisted reproductive technologies have presented our society with unprecedented ethical and legal dilemmas (Haynes & Miller, 2003). Extra embryos often result from the assisted reproductive process, and some couples generously put their surplus embryos up for adoption to be implanted in another woman (Stolberg, 2001). Other situations result in controversy, as when a divorcing couple disagrees about what to do with the embryos they froze before they ended their marriage. By the year 2000, more than 20,000 frozen embryos were in dispute (Silvertsen, 2000).

Reproductive technology has made it possible for women past the age of menopause to become pregnant, carry the pregnancy, and deliver their babies. To date, the oldest woman to have a baby by ART was almost 67 years old (Milbourne, 2006). The postmenopausal woman's own ova are not viable, so ova from a younger woman are fertilized in vitro, usually with the sperm from the older woman's husband. With hormonal assistance the woman's uterus can maintain a pregnancy.

Scientific and popular reactions to older men having children are quite different from attitudes about older women doing so. Only scattered criticism is directed at men who father in their 60s, 70s, and even 80s. However, although life expectancy in the Western world often enables a healthy woman who has a child in her 50s or early 60s to raise the child into adult–hood, attitudes toward the older woman becoming a mother are often negative. Doctors who provide reproductive assistance to postmenopausal women are accused of acting irresponsibly, tampering with nature, and playing God (Ethics Committee, American Society for

After trying to get pregnant for 16 years, this couple had a healthy infant daughter, named Cynthia, in 1996 through assisted reproductive technology. At the time, Cynthia's birth made her mother, at age 63, the oldest woman to give birth.

Reproductive Medicine, 1997). On the other hand, others believe that it is unethical to deny women conception on the basis of age alone (Paulson, 2000).

Fifty years ago assisted reproductive techniques were found in science fiction stories instead of at the approximately 340 assisted reproductive centers in the United States (Andrews & Elster, 2000). Scientific imagination and technological advancements will continue to expand the options for reproductive technologies as well as the legal, ethical, and personal quandaries that invariably accompany them (Gibbs, 2001).

---

○ **TABLE 11.1** **Prime Suspects: Possible Causes of Miscarriage**

| |
|---|
| Maternal age greater than 35 years |
| More than 5 alcoholic drinks per week |
| More than 375 mg of caffeine per day (2–3 cups of coffee) |
| Rejection of abnormal fetus |
| Cocaine use |
| Damaged cervix |
| Chronic kidney inflammation |
| Abnormal uterus |
| Infection |
| Underactive thyroid gland |
| Autoimmune reaction |
| Diabetes |
| Emotional shock |
| Aspirin and nonsteroidal anti-inflammatory drugs early in pregnancy |

SOURCES: D. Li et al. (2003), Rasch (2003), and Speroff & Fritz (2005).

(the first 13 weeks) of pregnancy; many occur before the woman knows she is pregnant. ○ **Table 11.1** gives the most common causes of miscarriage, but in many cases doctors are unable to determine the specific cause (Thompson, 2003a).

Early miscarriages can appear as a heavier than usual menstrual flow; later miscarriages might involve uncomfortable cramping and heavy bleeding. Fortunately for women who desire a child, one miscarriage rarely means that a later pregnancy will be unsuccessful.

However, miscarriage can be a significant loss for the woman or couple. If the expectant parents strongly desired the pregnancy, have been trying to conceive for some time, or have miscarried before, the emotional effect may be particularly painful. Couples may need to grieve the loss of this hoped-for pregnancy and baby for several months before pursuing another pregnancy (Salisbury, 1991). Some parents who lose an unborn child find it meaningful to name the baby or have a memorial service (Beck et al., 1988).

## Elective Abortion

In contrast to a spontaneous abortion, an **elective abortion** involves a decision to terminate a pregnancy by using medical procedures. Each year, 3 million women in the United States have unplanned pregnancies. Unfortunately, due to the erosion of government-funded contraceptive services since 1994, low-income women are now four times more likely to have an unplanned pregnancy than higher-income women (Wind, 2006). Many of the unplanned pregnancies become welcome and wanted; 21% of women and 25% of men considered the pregnancies in the last 5 years "mistimed" (National Survey of Family Growth, 2006). However, other unwanted pregnancies result in 1.3 million abortions each year in the United States, and an estimated 43% of women in the United States will have had an abortion by age 45 (Kaiser Family Foundation, 2002; Kristof, 2006).

Fifty-three percent of women who have abortions are age 25 or younger: 20% are younger than 19, and 33% are between 20 and 25. Young unmarried white women obtain the most abortions. Married women have approximately 20% of abortions in a given year. About 61% of women having abortions each year have previously given birth, and women with four or more children are more likely to have an abortion than women with fewer children. Among women having an abortion, 43% identify themselves as Protestant, and 27% as Catholic (Boonstra, 2006).

**Elective abortion** Medical procedure performed to terminate pregnancy.

## How Women Decide

After a woman confirms that she is pregnant (assuming that she was not trying to conceive), she must then decide whether to carry the pregnancy and keep the child, give the child up for adoption, or have an abortion. Abortion is a last resort for women who are faced with pregnancies they did not want (Wind, 2006). Research indicates that women rely on practical and emotional matters to make their decisions about their dilemma.

Concern and responsibility for others is a frequent reason for choosing to terminate the pregnancy. Younger women often say they are unprepared for motherhood, and older women cite the difficulties in meeting their responsibilities to their current children as their primary reason for needing an abortion. In the United States two-thirds of women who have abortions say their primary reason is that they cannot afford a child, and 60% of abortions occur among those with an annual income below $28,000 for a family of three (Boonstra et al., 2006; Finer et al., 2005).

The United States has one of the highest abortion rates in the developed world. Other developed countries that help mothers by providing maternity leave, health care, education and training, an adequate minimum wage, and other social services have lower rates of abortion than the United States. Germany, the Netherlands, and Belgium have abortion rates 66% lower; France's rate is 50% lower. All of the countries with lower abortion rates also provide comprehensive sex education in schools and easy access to inexpensive or free birth control and emergency contraception—government policies that the fundamentalist far-right and the George W. Bush administration oppose in the United States (Kristof, 2006).

Sex and Politics

Each year in the United States 21 out of every 10,000 women of reproductive age have an abortion. In contrast, the Netherlands has an abortion rate of 8 out of 10,000 women because the country places a high value on contraceptive use and provides comprehensive sex education, easy access to contraceptives, and extensive social and health services to women and children (Boonstra et al., 2006; Carter, 2005).

The very highest abortion rates are in countries that severely restrict abortion but do not provide the social services, sex education, and access to contraception that the Netherlands and other like-minded governments do. In the Netherlands each year 8 out of 10,000 women of childbearing age have abortions. In contrast, 56 out of 10,000 women in Peru have abortions each year (Boonstra et al., 2006). The number of women in the United States who have abortions each year is 21 out of 10,000, clearly reflecting its position between countries with progressive social policies and countries with conservative ones.

Simply providing access to effective contraception can have a dramatic effect on a country's abortion rate. The Soviet Union legalized abortion in 1955 because of the number of deaths and health problems resulting from illegal abortions, and it historically had one of the highest abortion rates in the world. Soviet men and women had access only to low-quality condoms and diaphragms; consequently, they used abortion as a primary means of birth control. It was common for a woman who wanted to limit the number of children in her family to have 10 or more abortions in her lifetime. As late as 1990, the Soviet Union's yearly abortion rate was over 100 per 10,000 women. This situation began to change in the late 1980s, when trade with the Western world opened, and modern contraceptives arrived in the Soviet Union. In 1992 the Russian government, seeing the initial decrease in abortions when people had access to modern contraceptive methods, began subsidizing family planning services and distributing free contraceptives. Consequently, more people used effective birth control, and the abortion rate declined by 53% between 1988 and 1998, as shown in ⊙ **Figure 11.1** (Boonstra et al., 2006: Westoff, 2006). ■

## Shared Responsibility

A couple can share responsibility for the decision whether to have an abortion and for the abortion itself, if that choice is made, in several ways. First, the man can help his partner clarify her feelings and can express his own regarding the unwanted pregnancy and how best to deal with it. Important topics for a couple to discuss include each person's life situation at the time; their feelings about the pregnancy and each other, pros and cons of choices, and their future plans as individuals and as a couple. If the man and woman disagree on what to do, the final decision rests with the woman: Male partners do not have a legal right to demand or deny abortion for the woman. ■

## Psychological Reactions to Abortion

Choosing abortion is usually a difficult decision for a woman and her partner. It means weighing and examining highly personal values and circumstances. When made, the decision is usually fraught with ambivalence. Even when the pregnancy is unwanted, one or both partners may feel loss and sadness. They may also feel regret, depression, anxiety, guilt, or anger about the abortion or why it was necessary.

A great many factors can affect either partner's emotional response to the abortion. The timing of the abortion is important; early abortions are medically and usually emotionally less stressful than later abortions. The reactions of close friends and family, the attitude of the medical staff and physician performing the abortion, the partners' personal views about abortion, pressure from others about the decision, and the nature and strength of the couple's relationship can all contribute to whether each partner's emotional response is positive or negative. Women who decide to have an abortion usually experience some anxiety or depression, but once the abortion is over, relief is the most common feeling. In

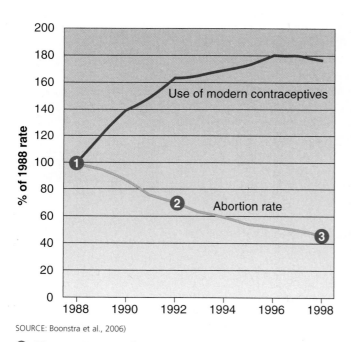

SOURCE: Boonstra et al., 2006)

⊙ **Figure 11.1** Decline in Soviet Union/Russia's abortion rate with increased access to contraception:

1. Trade opens with Western world.

2. Government subsidizes family planning clinics and contraceptives.

3. A 53% decline in abortion rate is achieved in one decade.

general, well-designed studies of psychological reactions following abortion have consistently found a low risk for problems (Adler et al., 2003), and most women experience a marked improvement in their quality of life after abortion (Westhoff et al., 2003).

## Pregnancy Risk Taking and Abortion

In many cases an unwanted pregnancy is clearly a matter of contraceptive failure. One study found that more than half of women who had an abortion were using contraception when they became pregnant (Hutti, 2003). For other women or couples seeking abortions the pregnancy can be traced to contraceptive risk taking—that is, not using contraceptives consistently or reliably, sometimes because of inconvenience, side effects of methods, or perceived low risk of pregnancy (Jones et al., 2002a). Being under the influence of alcohol or drugs reduces judgment and greatly increases contraceptive risk taking, unless the woman is using a method such as the pill or IUD.

Young women who feel a high degree of guilt about sex are less likely to use contraception effectively than those who do not feel guilty (Strassberg & Mahoney, 1988). Proactively using contraception acknowledges a woman's intent to engage in intercourse, and she may not want her partner to think that she is "that kind of girl." Women of any age may not be assertive about contraception because they fear alienating a partner by asking for his cooperation in planning and using birth control. For some women who lack strong self-esteem, the possibility of losing a relationship is more worrisome than the possibility of pregnancy. Unfortunately, such women are more likely to engage in intercourse with men who refuse to take precautions and who then walk away from responsibility if a pregnancy occurs (Malloy & Patterson, 1992).

Furthermore, women who have experienced psychological, physical, and/or sexual abuse in childhood are more than twice as likely to have an unintended pregnancy than women whose childhoods were free from abuse. Women whose mothers suffered frequent physical abuse from their partners are also more likely to have an unwanted first pregnancy. Apparently, these childhood traumas reduce a woman's ability to take the necessary steps to effectively prevent an unintended first pregnancy (Dietz, 1999).

**? Critical Thinking Question**

Why would childhood abuse increase the likelihood of having an unintended pregnancy?

## Procedures for Abortion

Several different abortion procedures are used at different stages of pregnancy. Ninety percent of abortions in the United States are done in the first 12 weeks of pregnancy (Wind, 2006). Early abortion is very safe. The risk of dying from a surgical abortion is 0.1 per 100,000 women, while the risk of pregnancy fatality is 11.8 per 100,000 (Zielinski, 2006). ○ **Figure 11.2** shows the stages of pregnancy when abortions take place. The most common procedures are *medical abortion, suction curettage, D and E,* and *prostaglandin induction.*

**Medical abortion** The use of medications to end a pregnancy of 7 weeks or less.

**Medical abortion** uses medications instead of surgery to end a pregnancy. A woman can have a medical abortion within days of a missed period and up to 7 weeks into a pregnancy. The medication mifepristone, commonly known as RU 486, became available in 2000 to women in the United States. Medical abortion has been available in European countries since 1980—20 years earlier than in the United States due to years of anti-abortion political action against the U.S. manufacture and distribution of medications for abortion (Jones & Henshaw, 2002). A medical abortion is 99% effective in ending pregnancies of less than 7 weeks and 91% effective in the 8th week of pregnancy (Speroff & Fritz, 2005). It is safer than the surgical procedures done later in pregnancy (Benson et al., 2003). In addition, a woman who opts for a medical abortion can see her family doctor at an office instead of going to another facility (Vason, 2003).

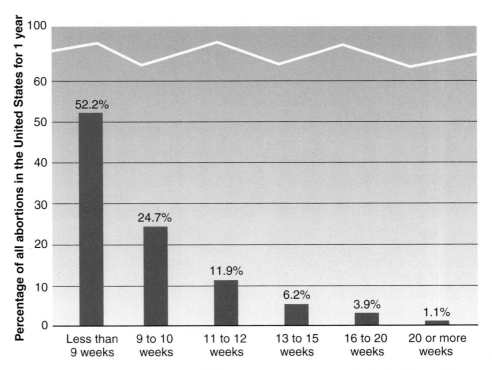

**Weeks into pregnancy (full-term pregnancy usually lasts 40 weeks)**

○ **Figure 11.2** When abortions are performed Eighty-eight percent of all abortions are done before 12 weeks. (Sontag, 1997, p. A8).

Medical abortion works by blocking the hormone progesterone, which causes the cervix to soften, the lining of the uterus to break down, and bleeding to begin. A few days later the woman takes a second medicine that makes the uterus contract and expel the grape-size embryonic sac (Jain et al., 2002). ● **Figure 11.3** shows how a medical abortion works. Side effects can include cramping, headaches, nausea, or vomiting, but many women experience no physical side effects (Hausknecht, 2003).

**Suction curettage** is a surgical technique used 7–13 weeks past the last menstrual period. A suction curettage is performed by physicians at clinics or hospitals and takes about 10 minutes. During the abortion local anesthetic is used and a small plastic tube is inserted through the cervical os into the uterus. The tube is attached to a vacuum aspirator, which draws the placenta, built-up uterine lining, and fetal tissue out of the uterus. Rare complications include uterine infection or perforation, hemorrhage, or incomplete removal of the uterine contents (Speroff & Fritz, 2005). Research data indicate that a first-trimester abortion has little effect on subsequent fertility or pregnancy, but research also shows that having two or more abortions can lead to a higher incidence of miscarriage or ectopic pregnancy in subsequent pregnancies (Tharaux-Deneux et al., 1998).

If a pregnancy progresses past approximately 12 weeks, the suction curettage procedure is no longer as safe, because the uterine walls have become thinner, making perforation and bleeding more likely. For pregnancy termination between 13 and 21 weeks, a **D and E**, or **dilation and evacuation**, is the safest and most widely used technique. A combination of suction equipment, special forceps, and a curette (a metal instrument used to scrape the walls of the uterus) is used. General anesthesia is usually required and the procedure is riskier. About 8.9 women out of 100,000 will die from an abortion after 20 weeks of pregnancy—still less than the rate of 11.8 out of 100,000 who die from a full-term pregnancy (Boonstra et al., Zielinski, 2006).

Second-trimester pregnancies can also be terminated by using compounds such as **prostaglandins**, hormones that cause uterine contractions. The prostaglandin is introduced into the vagina as a suppository or into the amniotic sac by inserting a needle through the abdominal wall; the fetus and placenta are usually expelled from the vagina within 24 hours. Complications from procedures that induce labor contractions include nausea, vomiting, and diarrhea; tearing of the cervix; excessive bleeding; and the possibility of shock and death.

**Suction curettage** A procedure in which the cervical os is dilated by using graduated metal dilators or a laminaria; then a small plastic tube, attached to a vacuum aspirator, is inserted into the uterus, drawing the fetal tissue, placenta, and built-up uterine lining out of the uterus.

**Dilation and evacuation (D and E)** An abortion procedure in which a curette and suction equipment are used.

**Prostaglandins** Hormones that are used to induce uterine contractions and fetal expulsion for second-trimester abortions.

● **Figure 11.3** How medical abortions work.

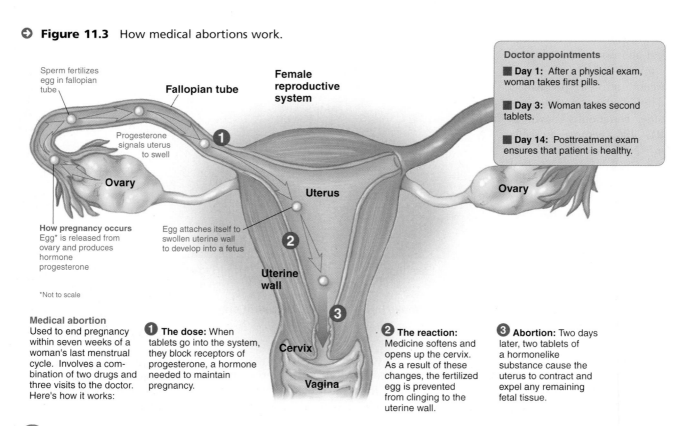

Female reproductive system

Sperm fertilizes egg in fallopian tube

Fallopian tube

Progesterone signals uterus to swell

Ovary

Uterus

Ovary

**How pregnancy occurs**
Egg* is released from ovary and produces hormone progesterone

Egg attaches itself to swollen uterine wall to develop into a fetus

Uterine wall

Cervix

Vagina

*Not to scale

**Medical abortion**
Used to end pregnancy within seven weeks of a woman's last menstrual cycle. Involves a combination of two drugs and three visits to the doctor. Here's how it works:

❶ **The dose:** When tablets go into the system, they block receptors of progesterone, a hormone needed to maintain pregnancy.

❷ **The reaction:** Medicine softens and opens up the cervix. As a result of these changes, the fertilized egg is prevented from clinging to the uterine wall.

❸ **Abortion:** Two days later, two tablets of a hormonelike substance cause the uterus to contract and expel any remaining fetal tissue.

**Doctor appointments**

■ **Day 1:** After a physical exam, woman takes first pills.

■ **Day 3:** Woman takes second tablets.

■ **Day 14:** Posttreatment exam ensures that patient is healthy.

**Late-term abortion** or **intact dilation and evacuation** is done after 20 weeks and before viability at 24 weeks' gestation. It is reserved for situations when serious health risks to the woman, or severe fetal abnormalities, exist. In this procedure the cervix is dilated, the fetus emerges feetfirst out of the uterus, and the fetal skull is collapsed to permit passage of the head through the cervix and vagina. Although late-term abortions after 21 weeks of pregnancy are rare, comprising less than 1% of all abortions in the United States, they continue to be the focus of intense political controversy (Rosenberg, 2003a). Opponents of abortion rights call this procedure partial-birth abortion, and the media has adopted this term instead of dilation and extraction despite its imprecise meaning and absence from medical texts (Pollitt, 2006). In 2003 Congress approved a ban on late-term abortion, and President George W. Bush signed the bill. However, several federal courts declared the ban unconstitutional and the ban was not enacted (Miller, 2006). In 2006 the Supreme Court agreed to hear the Bush administration's appeal of the federal courts' previous decision against a ban. Bush's appointment of anti-abortion Supreme Court justices has given hope to far-right anti-abortion forces that the Court will decide counter to all previous federal court decisions and uphold the first-ever federal ban on abortion (Miller, 2006). ■

## Illegal Abortions

About 25% of the women in the world live in countries where abortion is illegal. Desperate to end unwanted pregnancies, they attempt to self-induce abortions by using enemas, laxatives, pills, herbs, soap, and various other substances. Illegal abortionists typically insert a catheter or sharp instrument into the uterus to induce contractions. Such unsafe abortions cause 13% of all maternal deaths throughout the world (Boonstra et al., 2006; Thomas, 2006). In Brazil, a predominantly Roman Catholic country, illegal abortion is the fourth leading cause of death among women (Johnson, 2006). Brazil is one of the many countries in Latin America that is considering legalizing abortion (Barroso, 2006).

## The Abortion Controversy

Elective abortion continues to be a highly controversial political issue in the United States and many other countries. Beliefs regarding the beginning of life, the reproductive choices of women, and the role of law influence the stand one takes regarding elective termination of pregnancy.

### Abortion: Historical Overview

Laws regulating abortion have changed over time. In ancient China and Europe abortion early in pregnancy was legal. In the 13th century, St. Thomas Aquinas delineated the Catholic Church's view that the fetus developed a soul after conception—after 40 days for males and 90 days for females. Centuries later, in the late 1860s Pope Pius IX declared that human life begins at conception and is at any stage just as important as the mother's. The Roman Catholic Church still maintains this position (Jones & Crocklin, 2000).

Early American law, based on English common law, allowed abor-

Abortion supporters and opponents usually believe very strongly in their positions.

tion until the pregnant woman felt quickening, or movement of the fetus. During the 1860s, abortion became illegal in the United States, except when necessary to save the

## *Roe* v. *Wade* and Beyond

By the 1960s, advocacy groups of women and men were lobbying for change and began to win a few battles on the state level. In 1973, based on the right to privacy, the U.S. Supreme Court in *Roe. v. Wade* legalized a woman's right to terminate her pregnancy before the fetus has reached the age of viability. *Viability* is defined as the fetus's ability to survive independently of the woman's body—an ability that develops by the 6th or 7th month of pregnancy. *Roe v. Wade* voided the remaining state laws that treated abortion as a criminal act for both the doctor performing the abortion and the woman undergoing the procedure. ○ **Figure 11.4** shows the decline in deaths from abortion after some states liberalized their laws and following *Roe v. Wade*.

However, the legalization of abortion in 1973 did not end the controversy. Legislation in the late 1970s greatly curtailed the availability of medically safe abortions to low-income women, making abortion the only medical procedure for which the federal government restricts access. In 1977 Congress passed the Hyde Amendment, which restricted federal Medicaid funds for abortions, leaving 6 million low-income women of reproductive age, who obtain their health care through Medicaid, without this resource (Boonstra & Sonfield, 2000). States may use their own funds to provide abortions for low-income women, but by 2006 only 17 states were paying for abortions for low-income women. Consequently, many poor women sacrifice their rent, food, and clothing money for themselves and their children to pay for abortion. They are also more likely to have to have later abortions, with more risk and more expense, due to the time they need to acquire the necessary funds (Webster, 2006).

The Supreme Court has made additional rulings since the Hyde Amendment that allow states to place restrictions on abortion (Miller, 2006; Webster, 2006). These regulations impede, and often eliminate, women's access to abortion. The Clinton administration from 1993 to 2001 reversed a number of laws related to abortion, including the gag rule that had banned funds for family planning clinics that include abortion information and counseling in their services. Clinton also signed the Freedom of Access to Clinic Entrances Act, which

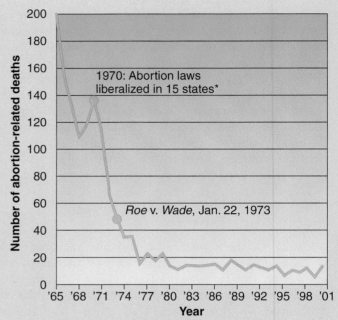

*By the end of 1970, four states had repealed their anti-abortion laws, and 11 states had reformed them.

○ **Figure 11.4** Deaths from abortion declined dramatically after legalization.

prohibited interference by protesters at clinics. Military hospitals overseas were permitted to perform abortions, provided that patients paid for them. Clinton also reversed the Global Gag Rule, the American policy established by the Reagan administration in 1984 that cut off aid to international family planning and maternal/child health programs involved in any abortion-related activities, including information and referral. However, George W. Bush reinstated the Global Gag Rule after gaining the presidency in 2001. His administration has supported implementing more restrictions at the state level. As of 2006, restrictions include the following:

**? Critical Thinking Question**

Why do states with the most restrictions on abortion typically provide the fewest resources for mothers and children, and why do states with the fewest restrictions on abortion provide the most resources for mothers and children?

**InfoTrac Search Words**

● Abortion

woman's life. Reasons for this change included the belief that population growth was important to the country's developing economy, and, perhaps, the male-dominated political system's unease about the emerging movement of middle-class white women seeking independence and equality (Sheeran, 1987). Consequently, women who had enough money would travel to a country where abortion was legal or persuade an American physician to perform a safe, illegal abortion. Women without the money to pursue such options may have been fortunate enough to find one of the skilled underground abortion providers working for free or for little compensation. Otherwise, they resorted to desperate measures: "back alley" abortions using unsafe, unskilled, and unsanitary procedures, or self-induced abortions, sometimes using a wire coat hanger, douching with bleach, or swallowing turpentine (Solinger, 2005). The momentum for legalizing abortion arose from these circumstances. We discuss the many legal changes and challenges in the Sex and Politics box.

- 29 states require a mandatory counseling session
- 24 states also require a 24-hour waiting period between the counseling and abortion
- 4 states restrict private insurance from covering abortion unless the woman purchases additional coverage for that purpose
- 21 states unnecessarily require an abortion to be done at a hospital instead of a clinic after a certain number of weeks of pregnancy—even though abortions performed at clinics are safe. For pregnancies past 16 weeks, Texas requires that abortions be done at hospitals, but no hospitals in Texas perform abortions—only clinics do (Pollitt, 2004).
- 34 states have parental consent laws that require a minor to obtain one or both parents' consent before she can have an abortion

Most adolescents do discuss their pregnancy options with their parents. However, laws that require parental notification and consent for abortion assume that all parents are loving, responsible, and capable of having their daughters' best interests at heart. Sadly, this is not the case for abusive and neglectful parents. For these and other reasons, many leading medical groups oppose mandatory parental consent requirements for abortion—groups such as the American Medical Association, the American Academy of Pediatrics, and the American Academy of Family Physicians. Research finds that increased rates of second-term abortions occur after parental notification laws are in place (Joyce et al., 2006). It is ironic that parental consent is not required for the pregnant young woman to have the baby and assume the responsibilities of parenthood, but it is required if she decides *not* to become a mother (Stotland, 1998).

It would seem logical to assume that states that restrict abortion would provide increased resources for the children who are born into difficult circumstances because abortion was not an option. However,

states with the most legal restrictions on abortion also provide the fewest resources to facilitate adoption, the least assistance to children in low-income families, and the lowest funds to educate children (Cassel, 2006; Schroedel, 2000). Past president Jimmy Carter states, "Many fervent pro-life activists do not extend their concern to the baby who is born, and are the least likely to support benevolent programs that they consider 'socialistic' " 2005, p. 94). Pro-life members of Congress commonly vote against initiatives that would help low-income pregnant women: maternal and child health care, child care, and job training (Miller, 2006).

How the present and future U.S. presidents, Congress, and the Supreme Court supports or opposes a woman's right to decide whether to continue an unwanted pregnancy remains a critical question. In 2006 several legislatures began drafting laws making abortion illegal in their states, in the hopes that the Supreme Court will reverse the *Roe v. Wade* decision, and thus allow each state to determine its own abortion laws (Black, 2006).

© Signe Wilkinson. The Washington Post Writers Group. Reprinted with permission.

## The Current Debate

Public opinion polls show that the majority of Americans—55 to 65%, depending on the poll—believe that women should have access to legal abortion, in spite of the reality that by 2006 only 13% of all counties in the United States had an abortion provider. Access is most severely limited for young, low-income, unmarried, African American women (Boonstra et al., 2006; Sotorbani et al., 2004).

The central tension in the abortion controversy is the debate between those arguing for the fetus's right to live and those arguing for the woman's right to choose when to become a mother. About 42% of people in the United States consider themselves to be pro-life and 53% to be pro-choice. Depth of religious belief shows the strongest difference: 59% of pro-life individuals versus 30% of pro-choice individuals say that religion is very important to them (Saad, 2006). People on both sides of the debate also tend to differ in their basic worldview, as shown in ● **Table 11.2**.

The religious anti-abortion, or pro-life, advocates argue that life begins at conception and that the fetus is a person who should have the right to live. "Because

| ⊙ TABLE 11.2 | Characteristics of Women Who Are Anti-Abortion and Pro-Choice |
|---|---|

**Anti-Abortion**

Believe procreation is primary purpose of sex

Have traditional attitudes about female role

Are full-time homemakers or have low-paying jobs

Have large families

Disapprove of non-marital sex

Disapprove of homosexuality

Are practicing Roman Catholics

**Pro-Choice**

Believe intimacy is primary purpose of sex

Have strong interest in work roles

Have well-paid careers

Have small families

Maintain few ties to organized religion

SOURCES: Deitch (1983), and Lynxwiler & Gay (1994).

every human life is precious in the eyes of God . . . it is clear that abortion is the wanton taking of human life" (National Pro-Life Alliance, 2006, p. 1). "The fetus is an immature, dependent form of human life which only needs time and protection to develop" (Callahan, 2002, p. 181). Consequently, abortion is seen as immoral. Anti-abortion groups want to "save every pre-born baby in this country" (National Pro-Life Alliance, 2006, p. 1) by reestablishing national legislation to make abortion illegal and by having Congress pass the Life at Conception Act, which establishes the unborn fetus as an independent being. Members of this minority are part of the 23% of the public that want to see *Roe* v. *Wade* overturned and that have been waging an active and effective battle against legal and available abortion (Saad, 2006). A primary tactic has been to lobby Congress to place restrictions on access to abortion and to prevent reelection of pro-choice Congress members.

Extreme anti-abortion activists have gone beyond legal means to restrict abortion—blocking clinic entrances; harassing patients, physicians, and staff; and burning or bombing clinics (Campo-Flores, 2006; Miller, 2005). Each year, 56% of abortion clinic providers deal with demonstrators picketing their clinics or homes or blocking clients' entrances, vandalism, and bomb threats (Henshaw & Finer, 2003; Palmer, 2000). Since 1993, pro-life extremists have resorted to killing physicians and staff who work in abortion clinics, believing that these murders are justified to save unborn babies (Henshaw & Finer, 2003). Doctors and clinics that provide abortions now must implement stringent security measures: metal detectors, alarms, and bullet-proof glass and vests.

In contrast to the anti-abortion view, pro-choice individuals and groups see abortion as a necessary last resort. Of the general public, 63% want *Roe* v. *Wade* to remain in place (Saad, 2006). Pro-choice advocates support a woman's choice *not* to have an abortion, but they strongly oppose government control over a woman's right to make her own reproductive decisions. They want women faced with the dilemma of an unwanted pregnancy who decide that terminating it is their best alternative to be able to do so (Willis, 2002). A columnist stated, "Mothering is so critical and so challenging that to force anyone into its service is immoral" (Quindlen, 2003b, p. 26). Many prestigious organizations, including many that are religious, have made public statements opposing anti-abortion legislation: Catholics for Choice, the National Academy of Sciences, the American Public Health Association, the American Medical Association, and the American College of Obstetricians and Gynecologists.

The abortion debate will remain passionate and bitter because of fundamental differences in beliefs and worldviews of people with strong commitments to one side or the other. However, most people experience considerable ambivalence about abortion (Connell, 1992). Many people who believe abortion is wrong also believe that any woman who wants an abortion should be able to obtain it legally (Stone & Waszak, 1992). As one woman stated:

> Part of my problem is that what I think and how I feel about this issue are two entirely different matters. . . . I cannot bring myself to say I am in favor of abortion. I don't want anyone to have one. I want people to use contraceptives and for those contraceptives to be foolproof. I want people to be responsible for their actions, mature in their decisions. I want children to be loved, wanted, well cared for. [At the same time,] I cannot bring myself to say I am against choice. I want women who are young, poor, single or all three to be able to direct the course of their lives. I want women who have had all the children they want or can afford or their bodies can withstand to be able to decide their future. I want women who are in bad marriages or destructive relationships to avoid being trapped by pregnancy. . . . Even as I refuse to pass judgment on other women's lives, I weep for the children who might have been. (Smith, 1985, p. 16)

# The Experience of Pregnancy

Pregnancy is a unique and significant experience for both a woman and her partner. In the following pages, we look at the experience and the effect it has on the individuals and the couple. Many of the experiences are encountered by heterosexual and lesbian couples alike. In this section the heterosexual couple is used as a frame of reference.

## The Woman's Experience

Each woman has different emotional and physical reactions to pregnancy, and the same woman may react differently to different pregnancies. Here are two reactions at the opposite ends of the continuum:

> *I loved being pregnant. My face glowed for nine months. I felt like a kindred spirit to all female mammals and discovered a new respect for my body and its ability to create life. The bigger I got, the better I liked it. (Authors' files)*

> *If I could have babies without the pregnancy part, I'd do it. Looking fat and slowed down is a huge drag. (Authors' files)*

Factors influencing a woman's emotional reactions can include how the decision for pregnancy was made, current and impending lifestyle changes, her relationship with others, her financial resources, her self-image, and hormonal changes. The woman's acquired attitudes and knowledge about childbearing and her hopes and fears about parenthood also contribute to her experience. Positive support and attention from her partner are helpful in creating a happy pregnancy.

Women sometimes feel that they should experience only positive emotions when they are pregnant. However, pregnancy often elicits an array of contradictory emotions. One study of 1,000 women found a wide range of feelings about pregnancy: 35% loved being pregnant, 40% had mixed feelings about it, 8% hated it, and the remainder had different experiences with each of their pregnancies. The researchers concluded that the degree of physical discomfort a woman experiences during the 9 months of pregnancy greatly influences her feelings about being pregnant (Genevie & Margolies, 1987). For some women pregnancy is a very difficult period; about 20% of women experience significant depression during pregnancy (Miller & Underwood, 2006).

## The Man's Experience

An expectant father obviously does not experience the same physical sensations that a pregnant woman does (although occasionally a "pregnant father" reports psychosympathetic symptoms, such as the nausea or tiredness his partner is experiencing). However, the experiences of pregnancy and birth are often profound for the father. What exactly does the "male pregnancy" involve? Like the woman, he often reacts with a great deal of ambivalence. He may feel ecstatic but also fearful about the woman's and the baby's well-being. It is common for men to feel frightened about the impending birth and whether he will be able to "keep it together." He may feel especially tender toward his partner and become more solicitous. At the same time, he may feel a sense of separateness from the woman because of the physical changes that only she is experiencing. However, prenatal ultrasonography allows fathers to see the fetus growing in the uterus and can create greater feelings of involvement (Sandelowski, 1994). Most men feel concern over the impending increase

Demi Moore's beautifully pregnant nude photo on the cover of *Vanity Fair* highlights the sensual richness of the pregnant woman's form.

in financial responsibility. In all, the expectant father has special needs, as does his partner, and it is important that the woman be aware of these needs and be willing to respond to them. One study of expectant fathers found that when men did share their feelings with their partners, the relationships deepened (Shapiro, 1987).

## Sexual Interaction During Pregnancy

In pregnancies with no risk factors, the woman and couple can continue sexual activity and orgasm as desired until the onset of labor (Schaffir, 2006). A woman's sexual interest and responsiveness will likely change throughout the course of her pregnancy. Nausea, breast tenderness, and fatigue can inhibit sexual interest during the first 3 months. A resurgence of sexual desire and arousal occurs for some women in the second trimester, but most research shows a progressive decline in sexual interest and activity over the 9 months of pregnancy (Bogren, 1991). Some of the most common reasons women give for decreasing sexual activity during pregnancy include physical discomfort, feelings of physical unattractiveness, and fear of injuring the unborn child (Colino, 1991).

For some women pregnancy can result in a heightened awareness of their bodies and an increased sensuality. Others feel intensely "womanly" and are less inhibited sexually. The increased vasocongestion of the genitals during pregnancy can heighten sexual desire and response for some women. Women who have positive attitudes about sexuality to begin with tend to maintain more sexual interest, activity, and satisfaction during pregnancy than do women with negative attitudes about sexuality (Fisher & Gray, 1988).

The partner's feelings also affect the sexual relationship during pregnancy. Reactions to the woman's changing body and to the need for adjustment in the couple's sexual repertoire can vary from increased excitement to inhibition for the partner. Especially late in pregnancy, awareness of the baby can make lovemaking seem like a crowded event:

> Sex during the third trimester requires a sense of humor. It doesn't seem to matter where you touch her anymore; the baby pops up everywhere. You can't escape the little kicks and jabs, and the thought of tiny feet and fists inches away (or closer) can be disconcerting. (Stern, 1987, p. 78)

During pregnancy a couple will need to modify intercourse positions. The side-by-side, woman-above, and rear-entry positions are generally more comfortable than the man-above position as pregnancy progresses. Oral and manual genital stimulation as well as total body touching and holding can continue as usual. In fact, pregnancy is a time when a couple can explore and develop these dimensions of lovemaking more fully; even if intercourse is not desired, intimacy, eroticism, and sexual satisfaction can continue. For most couples pregnancy is a time of significant emotional and physical changes. Open communication, accurate information, mutual support, and flexibility in sexual frequency and activities can help maintain and strengthen the bond between the partners. ■

! Sexual Health

## ◑ A Healthy Pregnancy

Once a woman becomes pregnant, her own health habits and care play an important part in the development of a healthy fetus.

### Fetal Development

The 9-month (40-week) span of pregnancy is customarily divided into three 13-week segments, called *trimesters*. Characteristic changes occur in each trimester.

### First-Trimester Development

As with all mammals, a human begins as a **zygote** (ZYE-goht), a united sperm cell and ovum. The sperm and egg unite in one of the fallopian tubes, where the egg's fin-

**Zygote** The single cell resulting from the union of sperm and egg cells.

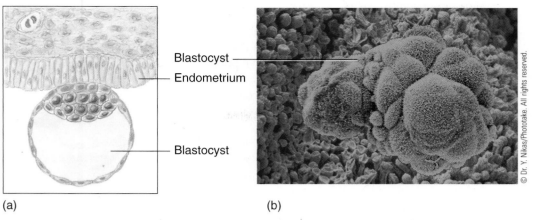

Blastocyst
Endometrium

Blastocyst

(a)                                                                (b)

○ **Figure 11.5** The blastocyst implanted on the uterine wall, shown (a) in diagram and (b) in photo taken by a scanning electron microscope.

gerlike microvilli draw the sperm to it (Begley, 1999). The zygote then develops into the multicelled **blastocyst** (BLAStuh-sist) that implants on the wall of the uterus about 1 week after fertilization (Fazleabas & Kim, 2003) (○ **Figure 11.5**). Growth progresses steadily. By 9–10 weeks after a woman's last menstrual period, the fetal heartbeat can be heard with a special ultrasound stethoscope known as the Doppler. By the beginning of the second month from the time of conception, the fetus is 0.5 to 1 inch long, grayish, and crescent shaped. During the second month, the spinal canal and rudimentary arms and legs form, as do the beginnings of recognizable eyes, fingers, and toes. During the third month, internal organs, such as the liver, kidneys, intestines, and lungs, begin limited functioning in the 3-inch fetus.

**Blastocyst** Multicellular descendant of the united sperm and ovum that implants on the wall of the uterus.

## Second-Trimester Development

The second trimester begins with the fourth month of pregnancy. By now the sex of the fetus can often be distinguished. External body parts, including fingernails, eyebrows, and eyelashes, are clearly formed. The fetus's skin is covered by fine downlike hair. Future development consists primarily of growth and refinement of the features that already exist. Fetal movements, or quickening, can be felt by the end of the fourth month. By the end of the fifth month the fetus's weight has increased to 1 pound. Head hair can appear at this time, and subcutaneous fat develops. By the end of the second trimester, the fetus has opened its eyes.

Fetal development at 9 weeks. The fetus is connected to the placenta by the umbilical cord.

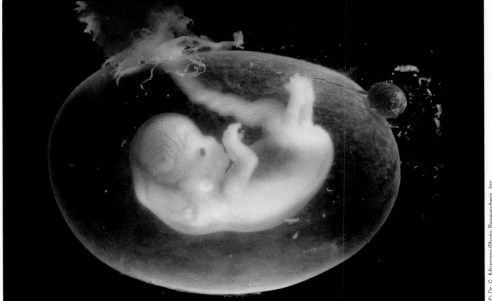

### Third-Trimester Development

In the third trimester, the fetus continues to grow, developing the size and strength it will need to live on its own (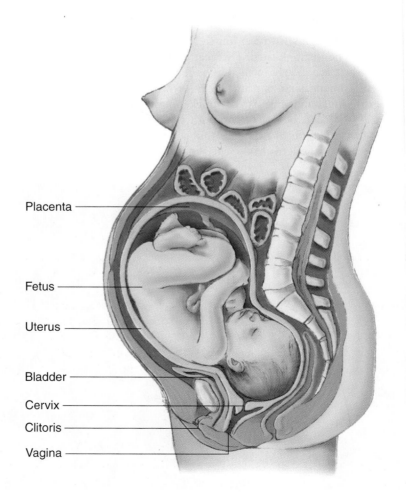 **Figure 11.6**). It increases in weight from 4 pounds in the seventh month to an average of over 7 pounds at birth. The downlike hair covering its body disappears, and head hair continues growing. The skin becomes smooth rather than wrinkled. The fetus is covered with a protective creamy, waxy substance called the **vernix caseosa** (VER-niks ka-see-OH-suh).

**Vernix caseosa** A waxy, protective substance on the fetus's skin.

### Prenatal Care

Some of the problems with fetal development are genetic and unpreventable, but the mother's own health and nutrition are crucial to providing the best environment for fetal development and for her own physical well-being during pregnancy and childbirth. This is one reason it is important for a woman to have a complete physical examination and health assessment before becoming pregnant. She should also have a test to determine her immunity to rubella (German measles), a disease that can cause severe fetal defects if the mother contracts it while she is pregnant. An HIV test should also be done before or during pregnancy, because HIV can be transmitted to the developing fetus during pregnancy, and therapies are available to help improve maternal and infant health (Krist, 2001).

Thorough prenatal care is essential for promoting the health of both the mother and the fetus. Components of optimal prenatal care include good nutrition, general good health, adequate rest, routine health care, exercise, and childbirth education (Thompson, 2003a). Unfortunately, many babies are born without adequate prenatal care, a situation that increases the chances of problems, including low birth weight, lung disorders, brain damage, and abnormal growth patterns. These problems can have lifelong effects (Hack, 2002).

**Figure 11.6** Pregnancy in the ninth month. The uterus and abdomen have increased in size to accommodate the fetus.

Placenta

Fetus

Uterus

Bladder

Cervix

Clitoris

Vagina

Women most likely to delay obtaining adequate prenatal care are unmarried African American or Hispanic individuals under age 20 who have not graduated from high school and are uninsured or on Medicaid. They typically live in low-income neighborhoods with crowded clinics and a shortage of doctors' offices (Bloche, 2004). Furthermore, statistics indicate that four times as many African American women as white women die from childbirth complications (Hoyert et al., 2000; Stolberg, 1999). Because of the poor access to health care for people without health insurance or adequate government-funded clinics, the United States compares unfavorably with nine other countries in maternal and infant mortality rates. Sweden has the lowest rate of maternal and infant deaths, and Switzerland, Canada, Australia, and the United Kingdom are among the nine other countries with fewer women and children dying from pregnancy and childbirth than in the United States (Cowley, 2003).

The fate of pregnant women in developing countries is severe (Imam, 2006). A North American woman's risk of dying from pregnancy or childbirth is 1 in 3,700, but an African woman's risk of a pregnancy-related death is 1 in 6; an Asian woman's risk is 1 in 65. Substandard services, poverty, women's underlying poor health, and gender-related factors resulting in women's lack of decision-making power in their families contribute to these high mortality rates (E. Murphy, 2003).

## Risks to Fetal Development

The rapidly developing fetus depends on the mother for nutrients, oxygen, and waste elimination as substances pass through the **placenta** (a disk-shaped organ attached to the wall of the uterus, shown in ○ **Figure 11.7**). The fetus is joined to the placenta by the umbilical cord. The fetal blood circulates independently within the closed system of the fetus and the inner part of the placenta. Maternal blood flows in the uterine walls and through the outer part of the placenta. Fetal blood and maternal blood do not normally intermingle. All exchanges between the fetal and maternal circulatory systems occur by passage of substances through the walls of the blood vessels. Nutrients and oxygen from the maternal blood pass into the fetal blood vessels; carbon dioxide and waste products from the fetus pass into the maternal blood vessels, to be removed by maternal circulation.

The placenta prevents some kinds of bacteria and viruses—but not all—from passing into the fetal circulatory system. Many bacteria and viruses, including HIV, do cross through the placenta. Certain prescription medications, legal drugs such as tobacco and alcohol, and illegal drugs are dangerous to the developing fetus. As many as one in three infants has been exposed to alcohol or other drugs in utero (Andrews & Patterson, 1995). Tobacco and alcohol affect a far greater number of babies each year, with more significant health consequences, than do illegal drugs (Pirie et al., 2000; Yuan et al., 2001).

A serious health hazard for the fetus is maternal cigarette smoking, which reduces the amount of oxygen in the bloodstream and increases the chances of miscarriage and of pregnancy complications that can result in fetal or infant death (Lain et al., 2006). Infants of mothers who smoked during pregnancy often weigh less, have more respiratory diseases, have a 50–70% greater chance of having a cleft lip or palate, and have significantly lower developmental scores and an increased incidence of reading disorders compared with matched children of nonsmokers (Olds et al., 1994; Williams, 2000). Approximately 25% of U.S. women are smokers when they learn they are pregnant, and 60–75% of them continue to smoke throughout their pregnancies (Zapka et al., 2000). It is not just smoking that is harmful; smokeless tobacco use has similar risks (Gupta & Subramoney, 2006).

Alcohol easily crosses the placental membranes into all fetal tissues, especially brain tissue. **Fetal alcohol syndrome (FAS)** is the leading cause of birth defects and developmental disabilities in the United States (Walling, 2005). Since 1981 the Food and Drug Administration has advised women to abstain *completely* from alcohol use during pregnancy to avoid the risk of damage to their babies. Any alcohol use can cause problems; even one drink per day has been associated with adverse birth effects.

© Leland Bobbe/Getty Images

Moderate exercise usually contributes to a healthy pregnancy and delivery. A pregnant woman should consult her health-care provider for guidelines specific to her situation.

**Placenta** A disk-shaped organ attached to the uterine wall and connected to the fetus by the umbilical cord. Nutrients, oxygen, and waste products pass between mother and fetus through the cell walls of the placenta.

**Fetal alcohol syndrome (FAS)** Syndrome in infants caused by heavy maternal prenatal alcohol use; characterized by congenital heart defects, damage to the brain and nervous system, numerous physical malformations of the fetus, and below-normal IQ.

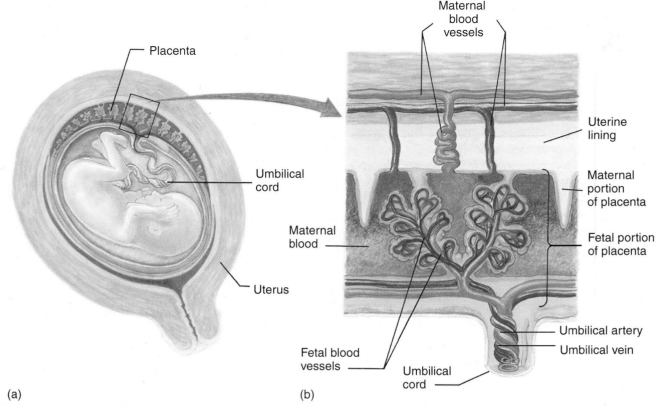

Placenta

Umbilical cord

Maternal blood

Uterus

(a)

Maternal blood vessels

Uterine lining

Maternal portion of placenta

Fetal portion of placenta

Umbilical artery

Umbilical vein

Fetal blood vessels

Umbilical cord

(b)

○ **Figure 11.7** The placenta exchanges nutrients, oxygen, and waste products between the maternal and fetal circulatory systems. (a) The placenta attached to the uterine wall. (b) Close-up detail of the placenta.

InfoTrac Search Words

● Fetal alcohol syndrome

One drink a day during the first three months of pregnancy is associated with an IQ of children at 10 years of age that is 2 points lower than the IQ of children whose mothers did not drink. Binge drinking (five or more drinks per occasion) is extremely toxic to the fetus. Alcohol use can cause intrauterine death and spontaneous abortion, premature birth, congenital heart defects, damage to the brain and nervous system, and numerous physical malformations of the fetus. Babies can be born addicted to alcohol and consequently experience alcohol withdrawal for several days after birth. The effects of FAS persist through childhood; children with FAS continue to be smaller than normal and developmentally delayed and to have behavior problems (Willford et al., 2006).

The babies of mothers who regularly used illegal addictive drugs, such as amphetamines and opiates, during pregnancy are often born premature and have low birth weight (Sprauve et al., 1997). In addition, after birth these babies experience withdrawal from the drug: They have tremors, disturbed feeding and sleep patterns, and abnormal muscle tension, and they often require hospitalization in neonatal intensive care units. These children can experience permanent birth defects and damage to sensory, motor, and cognitive abilities that continue past infancy (Zambrana & Scrimshaw, 1997).

In a number of tragic situations, children have been damaged by prescription and over-the-counter medications taken by their mothers during pregnancy. For example, the drug thalidomide, prescribed as a sedative to pregnant women in the early 1960s, caused severe deformities to the extremities. Some grown children of women who were given diethylstilbestrol (DES) while pregnant have developed genital tract abnormalities, including cancer (Mitka, 2003a). Antibiotics need to be prescribed selectively during pregnancy because tetracycline, a frequently used antibiotic, can damage an infant's teeth and cause stunted bone growth if it is taken after the 14th week of pregnancy (Lynch et al., 1991). Many over-the-counter medications, such as ibuprofen, aspirin, and histamines, can be detrimental to the fetus, and effects are unknown for many other nonprescription drugs and herbs (Glover et al., 2003). Toxic substances found in the polluted environment can also harm fetal development (Haney, 1994).

Our knowledge about the effects of most of the drugs and other substances consumed by pregnant women is limited (Janssen & Genta, 2000). But we are learning of more and more potential hazards. For this reason no medications should be used during pregnancy unless they are absolutely necessary and are taken under close medical supervision. ■

! Sexual Health

## Pregnancy After Age 35

An increasing number of women delay having children until after 35 years of age. Births in the United States to women between the ages of 45 and 49 nearly tripled from 1990 to 1999. In 2002, more than 5,000 women in that age range gave birth, and more than 200 women age 50 to 54 gave birth (Tyre, 2004). The greatest risk women and their partners face when they consider postponing having a child until the woman is in her mid-30s or older is that her fertility decreases with age.

Healthy older women have no higher risk than younger women of having a child with birth defects *not* related to abnormal chromosomes. However, the rate of fetal defects resulting from chromosomal abnormalities (such as Down syndrome) rises with maternal age. The estimated risk of such fetal defects is 2.6 per 1,000 before age 30, 5.6 at age 35, 15.8 at age 40, and 53.7 at age 45. For women between the ages of 35 and 44, prenatal testing for these birth defects and elective abortion reduce the risk of bearing an infant with a severe birth defect to a level comparable to that for younger women (Yuan et al., 2000).

Pregnancy in women over age 35 poses additional increased risks to the mother and fetus. Slightly higher rates of maternal death, premature delivery, cesarean sections, and low birth-weight babies occur (London, 2004). Most physicians find that pregnancy for a healthy woman over age 35 is safe and not difficult to manage medically (Schrinsky, 1988). Chronic illnesses such as diabetes and high blood pressure play a greater role than age itself in problems with labor, delivery, and infant health (Yuan et al., 2000).

# ◑ Childbirth

The full term of pregnancy usually lasts about 40 weeks from the last menstrual period, although there is some variation in length. Some women have longer pregnancies; others give birth to fully developed infants up to a few weeks before the 9-month term is over. The experience of childbirth also varies a good deal, depending on many factors: the woman's physiology, her emotional state, the baby's size and position, the kind of childbirth practices used, and the kind of support she receives.

**Prepared childbirth**
Birth following an education process that can involve information, exercises, breathing, and working with a labor coach.

## Contemporary Childbirth

Today's parents-to-be can expect to work as part of a team with their health-care provider in preparing and planning for the physical and emotional aspects of childbirth. Parents-to-be often participate in **prepared childbirth** classes that provide thorough information about medical interventions and the process of labor and birth. The classes also provide training for the pregnant woman and her labor coach (either her partner, family member, or a friend) in breathing and relaxation exercises designed to cope with the pain of childbirth. Research has found that women assisted by a birth attendant during labor had fewer cesarean sections, less pain medication, shorter length of labor, and greater satisfaction with the birth experience (Campbell et al., 2006; McNiven et al., 1992).

Approaches to contemporary childbirth began to develop when Grantly Dick-Read and Fernand Lamaze began presenting their ideas about childbirth in the late 1930s and early 1940s. They believed that most of the pain during childbirth stemmed from the muscle tension caused by fear. To reduce anxiety, they advocated education about the birth

© Jiang Jin/SuperStock

Prepared childbirth classes help prepare expectant mothers and fathers for childbirth.

process, relaxation and calm, consistent support during a woman's labor, breathing exercises, voluntarily relaxing abdominal and perineal muscles, and breathing exercises.

## Stages of Childbirth

Despite variations in childbirth, there are three generally recognizable stages in the process (see ◐ **Figure 11.8**). A woman can often tell that labor has begun when regular contractions of the uterus begin. Another indication of beginning **first-stage labor**, the gradual dilation of the cervix to 10 centimeters, is the "bloody show" (discharge of the mucus plug from the cervix). The amniotic sac can rupture in the first stage of labor, an occurrence sometimes called "breaking the bag of waters." Before the first stage begins, **effacement** (flattening and thinning) of the cervix has usually already occurred and the cervix has dilated slightly. The cervix continues to dilate throughout the first stage. The first stage is the longest of the three stages, usually lasting 10 to 16 hours for the first childbirth and 4 to 8 hours in subsequent births.

**Second-stage labor** begins when the cervix is fully dilated and the infant descends farther into the vaginal birth canal. Usually the descent is headfirst, as shown in Figure 11.8b. The second stage often lasts from half an hour to 2 hours—although it can be shorter or longer. During this time the woman can actively push to help the baby out, and many women report their active pushing to be the best part of labor:

*I knew what "labor" meant when I was finally ready to push. I have never worked so hard, so willingly. (Authors' files)*

The second stage ends when the infant is born.

**First-stage labor** The initial stage of childbirth in which regular contractions begin and the cervix dilates.

**Effacement** Flattening and thinning of the cervix that occurs before and during childbirth.

**Second-stage labor** The middle stage of labor, in which the infant descends through the vaginal canal.

◐ **Figure 11.8** The three stages of childbirth: (a) first-stage labor, (b) second-stage labor, and (c) third-stage labor.

(a) **First stage**
Dilation of cervix, followed by transition phase, when baby's head can start to pass through the cervix

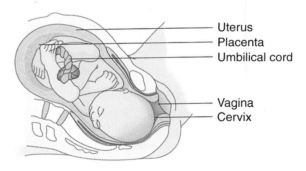

Uterus
Placenta
Umbilical cord

Vagina
Cervix

(b) **Second stage**
Passage of the baby through the birth canal, or vagina, and delivery into the world

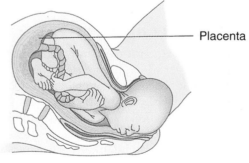

Placenta

(c) **Third stage**
Expulsion of the placenta, blood, and fluid ("afterbirth")

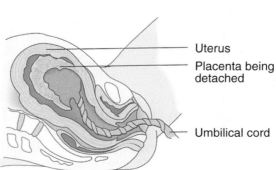

Uterus
Placenta being detached

Umbilical cord

**Third-stage labor** lasts from the time of birth until the delivery of the placenta, shown in Figure 11.8c. With one or two more uterine contractions, the placenta usually separates from the uterine wall and comes out of the vagina, generally within half an hour of the birth. The placenta is also called the **afterbirth**.

### Delivery by Cesarean Section

A **cesarean** (sih-ZEHR-ee-un) **section,** or **C-section**, in which the baby is removed through an incision made in the abdominal wall and uterus, can be a lifesaving surgery for the mother and child. Cesarean birth is recommended in a variety of situations, including when the fetal head is too large to pass through the mother's pelvic structure, when the mother is ill, or when there are indications of fetal distress during labor or birth complications, such as a breech presentation (feet or bottom coming out of the uterus first). Mothers who experience a C-section often have anesthesia that allows them to be awake to greet their baby when he or she is born. In many hospitals fathers remain with the mothers during cesarean births.

A woman can have more than one baby by C-section, although medical risks increase with each subsequent caesarean delivery (Getahun et al., 2006; Silver et al., 2006). Also, most women can have subsequent vaginal births, depending on the circumstances of the earlier cesarean birth(s) and of the subsequent birth (Crawford & Kaufmann, 2006). Although many women who have C-sections are less satisfied with their birth experiences than women who have vaginal births, adjustment following childbirth is similar in the two groups (Padawer et al., 1988).

In 1970, 5.5% of births in the United States were cesarean deliveries, increasing to over 29% by 2004 (Resnik, 2006). (In contrast, the caesarean rate for the poorest 20% of women in 20 developing countries is below 1%.) Some maintain that high rates reflect better use of medical technology. Others believe that cesarean sections are used too readily, and a 15% rate would better indicate medical necessity for the procedure (Ronsman et al., 2006). An analysis of birth data found that 11% of C-sections for a first pregnancy and 65% of repeat C-sections may not have been necessary (Kabir et al., 2005). Intensive fetal monitoring, aggressive malpractice lawsuits if serious problems follow a vaginal birth, and maternal and physician preference are three reasons for the increase (Stobbe, 2005). However, higher rates of caesarean delivery have not proportionally improved maternal and infant survival rates (Resnik, 2006; Robb-Nicholson, 2006).

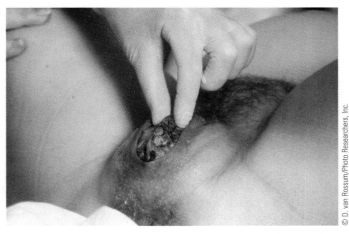
© D. van Rossum/Photo Researchers, Inc.

Second-stage labor is usually the highlight of the birth process.

**Third-stage labor** The last stage of childbirth, in which the placenta separates from the uterine wall and comes out of the vagina.

**Afterbirth** The placenta and amniotic sac following their expulsion through the vagina after childbirth.

**Cesarean section** A childbirth procedure in which the infant is removed through an incision in the abdomen and uterus.

## After Childbirth

The first several weeks following birth are referred to as the **postpartum period**. This is a time of both physical and psychological adjustment for each family member, and it is likely to be a time of intensified emotional highs and lows. The new baby affects the roles and interactions of all family members. The parents can experience an increased closeness to each other as well as some troublesome feelings. A partner might sometimes feel jealous of the close relationship between the mother and child. Both partners may want extra emotional support from each other, but each may have less than usual to give. The time and energy demands of caring for an infant can contribute to weariness and stress. Conflict about the division of household and child-care labor can become problematic in the early months and years of the child's life (Cowan & Cowan, 1992). A good support system for the new parents can be immensely helpful. Understanding that these feelings are a common response to adjustments to the new baby may help new parents cope with the stresses involved.

**Postpartum depression (PPD)** affects 15% of mothers (Routh, 2000). Unlike the more common "baby blues"—tearfulness and mood swings lasting up to 10 days that about 75% of new mothers feel—PPD involves classic symptoms of depression,

**Postpartum period** The first several weeks after childbirth.

**Postpartum depression (PPD)** Symptoms of depression and possibly obsessive thoughts of hurting the baby.

InfoTrac Search Words

• Breast-feeding

including insomnia, anxiety, panic attacks, and hopelessness. At its most extreme, women suffering from PPD lose interest in their babies or develop obsessive thoughts about harming themselves or their babies. Such reactions may be partly due to the sudden emotional, physical, and hormonal changes following birth. Sleep deprivation from waking many times in the night to care for the newborn also is stressful and diminishes emotional and physical reserves. Fortunately, PPD can be effectively treated (Beck, 2006).

## Breast-Feeding

**Colostrum** A thin fluid secreted by the breasts during later stages of pregnancy and the first few days after delivery.

After childbirth the mother's breasts first produce a yellowish liquid, called **colostrum**, which contains antibodies and protein. Lactation, or milk production, begins about 1 to 3 days after birth. Pituitary hormones stimulate milk production in the breasts in response to the stimulation of the infant suckling the nipples. If a new mother does not begin or continue to nurse, milk production subsides within a matter of days.

Breast-feeding has many practical and emotional advantages. Breast milk provides the infant with a digestible food filled with antibodies and other immunity-producing substances (Wold & Adlerberth, 1998). Research has revealed that babies who were breast-fed were less distressed than other infants when experiencing pain or stress (Shah et al., 2006). Nursing also induces uterine contractions that help speed the return of the uterus to its pre-pregnancy size. Breast-feeding can be a positive emotional and sensual experience for the mother. For women who nurse, breast-feeding is another opportunity for close physical contact with the baby.

© Erika Stone/Photo Researchers, Inc.

For a woman who decides to nurse, breast-feeding is another opportunity for close physical contact with her baby.

*I love seeing the contentment spread over my baby's face as she fills her tummy with milk from my breasts. It's an awe-inspiring continuation of our physical connection during pregnancy to see her growing chubby-cheeked from nourishment my body provides her. (Authors' files)*

Nursing can temporarily inhibit ovulation, particularly for women who feed their babies only breast milk (Perez et al., 1992). However, as we saw in Chapter 10, nursing is not a reliable method of birth control. Estrogen-containing birth control pills should not be used during nursing because the hormones reduce the amount of milk and affect milk quality. However, progesterone-only pills can be used because progesterone affects neither milk supply nor quality (Salisbury, 1991). Some couples prefer foam and condoms to avoid any extra hormones during nursing.

Nursing also has some short-term disadvantages. For one, nursing causes reduced levels of estrogen, which conditions and maintains vulvar tissue and promotes vaginal lubrication. As a result, the nursing mother may be less interested in sexual activity, and her genitals may become sore from intercourse (Barrett et al., 2000). The woman's breasts may also be tender and sore. Milk may be ejected involuntarily from her nipples during sexual stimulation—a source of potential amusement or embarrassment. It is often easier to share child-care responsibilities by bottle-feeding than by nursing; the father can have a greater role in holding and feeding the infant. However, a nursing mother can use a breast pump to extract her milk so that it is available to her partner or another caregiver for bottle-feeding the baby.

Although exclusive breast-feeding for the first 6 months is encouraged by the American Academy of Pediatrics and the World Health Organization, a nationally representative survey in the United States found that only 47% of 1-week-old children had been exclusively breast-fed and that only 10% of 6-month-old babies were breast-fed. Women most likely to have breast-fed were college graduates in the highest income level, and women least likely to have breast-fed were at the lowest education and income levels, residents of the South, teenage mothers, African American mothers, and smokers (Ruowei, 2002). Some mothers' lives are too demanding for the sole feeding responsibility of nursing, particularly if they return to work shortly after childbearing (Brandon, 2001). Breast-feeding rates in Sweden are significantly higher than in the United States, due in large part to generous maternity leave of a full year at 80% of their wages for most employees (Gibbs, 2002). Of all the industrialized countries, only the United States and Australia lack laws that require paid parental leave with a guaranteed return to work (Jeffery, 2006).

## Sexual Interaction After Childbirth

Couples are commonly advised that intercourse can resume after the flow of the reddish uterine discharge, called **lochia** (LOH-kee-uh), has stopped and after **episiotomy** incisions or vaginal tears have healed, usually in about 3–4 weeks. However, most couples wait to resume intercourse until 6–8 weeks after birth (Volm, 1997). An important factor to consider is when intercourse is physically comfortable for the woman. This depends on the type of birth, the size and presentation of the baby, the extent of episiotomy or lacerations, and the individual woman's rate of healing. The postpartum decrease in hormones, especially pronounced with breast-feeding, can cause discomfort during intercourse. After a cesarean birth the couple needs to wait until the incision has healed enough for intercourse to occur without discomfort. Other sexual and affectionate relations can be shared while waiting.

A new baby brings significant changes in daily life that can affect sexual intimacy (Botros et al., 2006). Research has found high levels of sexual difficulties after childbirth. Before pregnancy 38% of the study participants reported experiencing sexual problems, but 80% experienced one or more sexual problems in the first 3 months after delivery. At 6 months 64% were still having difficulty. The most common concerns were decreased sexual interest, vaginal dryness, and painful intercourse. A researcher, who has written books about pregnancy and the first year of motherhood, warns women and their partners to be prepared for their sex lives to be "downright crummy" for up to a year: "Mother Nature is using her entire arsenal of tricks, from hormones to humility, to keep you focused on your baby and not on getting pregnant again" (Iovine, 1997a, p. 158).

Fatigue is also a major factor affecting sexuality after childbirth. The demands of caring for a new baby on both the woman and her partner may mean that there is not much time or energy left for sexual expression (Gearhart & Robboy, 2005). Fitting lovemaking into the baby's and parents' schedules can be quite a challenge. Concern about the baby can also interfere:

> It seems that every time we start to make love, the baby cries. Even though I know he's been fed and is dry, I can't focus on my sexual feelings. And when he gets quiet, I worry that he's dead! My husband has the same reactions, so lots of times we don't get much going together. (Authors' files)

Women and their partners, whose sexual activity has been disrupted by pregnancy and birth, may feel out of practice in their sexual relationship. It is often helpful to resume sexual activity in an unhurried, exploratory manner. ■

**Lochia** A reddish uterine discharge that occurs after childbirth.

**Episiotomy** An incision in the perineum that is sometimes made during childbirth.

## Parenthood as an Option

- An increasing number of couples are choosing not to be parents.
- The realities of parenthood or child-free living are difficult to predict.

## Becoming Pregnant

- Timing intercourse to correspond to ovulation enhances the likelihood of conception.
- About 10% of couples in the United States have problems with infertility, and a cause is not found in as many as 15% of infertile couples.

- Failure to ovulate and blockage of the fallopian tubes are typical causes of female infertility. Low sperm count is the most common cause of male infertility.
- Alcohol, illegal drug use, cigarette smoking, and infections from sexually transmitted diseases reduce fertility in both women and men.
- The emotional stress and the disruption of a couple's sexual relationship from infertility can result in sexual problems.
- The legal and social issues related to artificial insemination, surrogate motherhood, and assisted reproductive technologies are complex and will continue to create controversy.
- Artificial insemination is done with donor semen when the husband is infertile.
- The first sign of a pregnancy is usually a missed menstrual period. Urine and blood tests and pelvic examinations are used to determine pregnancy.

## Spontaneous and Elective Abortion

- Spontaneous abortion, or miscarriage, occurs in approximately one in seven known pregnancies. Most miscarriages occur within the first 3 months of pregnancy.
- Elective abortion is a highly controversial social and political issue in the United States today. Medications, suction curettage, D and E, and prostaglandin induction are the medical techniques used to induce abortion.
- Contraceptive method failure is a major contributor to women's having repeat abortions.
- Contraceptive risk taking often precedes an unplanned pregnancy and consequent abortion.
- In 1973 the U.S. Supreme Court legalized a woman's right to decide to terminate her pregnancy before the fetus reaches the age of viability. In 1977 the Hyde Amendment restricted the use of federal Medicaid funds for abortion and limited low-income women's access to abortion. Since then, many state legislatures have imposed further limitations on the availability of abortion.
- Pro-choice and pro-life advocates have fundamental differences in their beliefs about many aspects of life.

## The Experience of Pregnancy

- Women have a wide range of psychological reactions to pregnancy, including 20% who experience significant depression.
- Men have become increasingly involved in the prenatal, childbirth, and child-rearing processes.
- Although changes of position may be necessary, sensual and sexual interaction can continue as desired during pregnancy, except in occasional cases of medical complications.

## A Healthy Pregnancy

- Pregnancy is divided into three trimesters, each of which is marked by fetal changes.
- Nutrient, oxygen, and waste exchange between the woman and her fetus occurs through the placenta. Substances harmful to the fetus can pass through the placenta from the mother's blood.
- Smoking, alcohol, illegal drugs, and certain medications can severely damage the developing fetus.
- More women are deciding to have children after age 35. These women have slightly decreased fertility and a somewhat higher risk of conceiving a fetus with chromosomal abnormalities. However, with careful monitoring of pregnancy and childbirth, their risks can be reduced to the level of those of younger women.

## Childbirth

- Prepared childbirth, popularized by Fernand Lamaze and Grantly Dick-Read, has changed childbirth practices. Most hospitals now support participation of the woman's partner and a team approach to decision making about the birth process.
- Second-stage labor is the descent of the infant into the birth canal, ending with birth. The placenta is delivered in the third stage.
- The rate of caesarean sections has increased significantly in the United States, with continuing debate about the procedure.

## After Childbirth

- Many physical, emotional, and family adjustments must be made following the birth of a baby. Postpartum depression affects up to 15% of new mothers.
- Both breast- and bottle-feeding have advantages and disadvantages.
- Intercourse after childbirth can usually resume once the flow of lochia has stopped and any vaginal tears or the episiotomy incision has healed. However, it may take longer for sexual interest and arousal to return to normal.

## ◗ Suggested Readings

**Cohen, John, and Sandra Carson** (2005). *Coming to Terms: Uncovering the Truth About Miscarriage.* Boston: Houghton Mifflin. After his wife experienced four miscarriages, this award-winning science writer wrote a comprehensive and enlightening book about miscarriage.

**Carroll, Laura** (2000). *Families of Two: Interviews With Happily Married Couples Without Children by Choice.* Philadelphia: Exlibris Corp. An inside look at couples who choose to live child-free.

**Eisenberg, Arlene, Heidi Murkoff, and Sandee Hathaway** (1991). *What to Expect When You're Expecting.* New York: Workman. A clear, comprehensive month-by-month guide that answers concerns of mothers- and fathers-to-be.

**Nilsson, Lennart** (1977). *A Child Is Born.* New York: Dell. A classic book of exquisite photographs of fetal development.

**Peoples, Debbie, and Harriett Ferguson** (2000). *Experiencing Infertility: An Essential Resource.* New York: Norton. A comprehensive presentation of the decision-making process and emotional roller coaster of infertility. Offers sound ideas and coping methods, from assessing infertility to shifting gears to adoption.

**Solinger, Rickie** (2005). *Pregnancy and Power: A Short History of Reproductive Politics in America.* New York: New York University Press. A deeply researched book about the historical context of today's "culture wars" pertaining to reproductive and sexual issues.

## ◗ Resources

**International Childbirth Education Association**, P.O. Box 20048, Minneapolis, MN 55420. Provides information and resources for childbirth education.

**Resolve: The National Infertility Association**, 1310 Broadway, Somerville, MA 02144; (888) 623-0744. A national nonprofit organization that provides support groups, education, and publications for couples struggling with infertility.

# ▶ Web Resources

**International Council on Infertility Information Dissemination (INCIID)**

For those seeking more information on infertility, this Web site provides especially helpful fact sheets on various types of fertility treatments and assisted reproductive techniques.

**Alan Guttmacher Institute**

This well-respected nonprofit organization sponsors a great deal of research on issues related to sexuality, contraception, and abortion. Among the features of its Web site are news updates and descriptions of recent research affecting reproductive health.

**NARAL Pro-Choice America**

An advocacy group for abortion rights, NARAL offers a Web site promoting legal and educational efforts to guarantee reproductive rights.

**Lamaze International**

Lamaze International provides information promoting healthy pregnancy and childbirth on their Web site.

# Sexuality During Childhood and Adolescence

© Paul Steel/CORBIS

*My earliest recollection of an experience that could be labeled as sexual in nature involved thrusting against the pillow in my crib and experiencing something that felt really good, which I now believe must have been an orgasm (actually, I remember doing this many times). I was probably around 2 at the time, give or take a few months. What is odd about these early experiences is that I distinctly remember sleeping in my parents' bedroom but never being reprimanded for this "self-abuse" behavior. Either my parents were very heavy sleepers, or they were very avant-garde in their view of sex. Knowing my parents, I presume the former is true. (Authors' files)*

In many Western societies, including the United States, it was once common to view the period between birth and puberty as a time when sexuality remains unexpressed. However, as many of you can no doubt attest to from your own experiences, the early years of life are by no means a period of sexual dormancy. Perhaps you can even recall sensual or sexual experiences similar to the quoted account that date from the early years of your life. In this chapter, we outline many of the common sexual experiences and behaviors that take place during the formative years from infancy through adolescence.

# Sexual Behavior During Infancy and Childhood

Research over the last several decades has clearly demonstrated that a variety of behaviors and body functions, including sexual eroticism, develop during infancy and childhood. In some ways sexuality is especially important during this period, because many experiences during these formative years have a great effect on the future expression of adult sexuality.

In this section we briefly outline some typical sexual and sensual behaviors that occur during infancy and childhood.

## Infant Sexuality

For most people the capacity for sexual response is present from birth (DeLamater & Friedrich, 2002; Thanasiu, 2004). In the first 2 years of life, a period generally referred to as infancy, many girls and boys discover the pleasures of genital stimulation (Lidster & Horsburgh, 1994; Yang et al., 2005). As reflected in the quotation from our files that opened this chapter, this activity often involves thrusting or rubbing the genital area against an object, such as a doll or a pillow. Pelvic thrusting and other signs of sexual arousal in infants, such as vaginal lubrication and penile erection, are often misinterpreted or unacknowledged. However, careful observers have noted these indicators of sexuality in the very young (Lively & Lively, 1991; Ryan, 2000; Thanasiu, 2004). In some cases both male and female infants have been observed experiencing what appears to be an orgasm. The infant, of course, cannot offer spoken confirmation of the sexual nature of such reactions, but the behavior is so remarkably similar to that exhibited by sexually responding adults that little doubt exists about its nature. Alfred Kinsey and his associates, in their book on female sexuality, detailed the observations of a mother who had frequently observed her 3-year-old daughter engaging in unmistakably masturbatory activity:

Lying face down on the bed, with her knees drawn up, she started rhythmic pelvic thrusts, about one second or less apart. The thrusts were primarily pelvic, with the legs tensed in a fixed position. The forward components of the thrusts were in a smooth and perfect rhythm which was unbroken except for momentary pauses during which the genitalia were readjusted against the doll on which they were pressed; the return from each thrust was convulsive, jerky. There were 44 thrusts in unbroken rhythm, a slight momentary pause, 87 thrusts followed by a slight momentary pause, concentration and intense breathing with abrupt jerks as orgasm approached. She was completely oblivious to everything during these later stages of the activity. Her eyes were glassy and fixed in a vacant stare. There was noticeable relief and relaxation after orgasm. (Kinsey et al., 1953, pp. 104–105)

Kinsey also detailed references to male infant sexuality:

> The orgasm in an infant or other young male is, except for lacking of ejaculation, a striking duplicate of orgasm in an older adult. The behavior involves a series of gradual physiologic changes, the development of rhythmic body movements with distinct penis throbs and pelvic thrusts, an obvious change in sensory capacities, a final tension of muscles, especially of the abdomen, hips, and back, a sudden release with convulsions, including rhythmic anal contractions—followed by the disappearance of all symptoms. A fretful baby quiets down under the initial sexual stimulation, is distracted from other activities, begins rhythmic pelvic thrusts, becomes tense as climax approaches, is thrown into convulsive action, often with violent arm and leg movements, sometimes with weeping at the moment of climax. (Kinsey et al., 1948, p. 177)

It is impossible to determine what such early sexual experiences mean to infants, but it is reasonably certain that these activities are gratifying. Many infants of both sexes engage quite naturally in self-pleasuring unless such behavior produces strong negative responses from parents or other caregivers.

Clearly, an infant is unable to differentiate sexual pleasure from other forms of sensual enjoyment. Many of the natural everyday activities involved in caring for an infant, such as breast-feeding and bathing, involve pleasurable tactile stimulation that, although essentially sensual in nature, stimulate a genital or sexual response (Frayser, 1994; Martinson, 1994).

## Childhood Sexuality

### InfoTrac Search Words

• Childhood sexuality

Enjoying sexual intimacy as an adult may be related to childhood experiences of warm, pleasurable contact, particularly with parents.

What constitutes normal and healthy sexual behavior in children? This is a difficult question for which we have no definitive answer; the data on childhood sexuality are scarce. Research in this area is limited by a number of factors, not the least of which is political squeamishness over what "might be interpreted as exploiting children or introducing sexual ideas to them" (*Contemporary Sexuality*, 1998, p. 1). It is difficult to obtain financial support for basic research on childhood sexuality, and federal guidelines in the United States either prohibit such studies or make them considerably difficult to conduct. Recently, a team of researchers surmounted some of these obstacles to research in the United States by interviewing a large sample of primary caregivers (all mothers) of children, ages 2 to 12. The results of this informative study are described in the boxed discussion "Normative Sexual Behavior in Children: A Contemporary Sample."

People show considerable variation in their sexual development during childhood, and diverse influences are involved (Bancroft, 2003). Despite these differences, however, certain common features in the developmental sequence tend to emerge. As we outline our somewhat limited knowledge of some of these typical behaviors, keep in mind that each person's unique sexual history can differ in some respects from the described behaviors. It is also important to realize that, other than reports from primary caregivers, most of what we know about childhood sexual behavior is based on recollections of adults who are asked to recall their childhood experiences. As we noted in Chapter 2, accurately remembering experiences that occurred many years earlier is quite difficult.

A child can learn to express her or his affectionate and sensual feelings through activities such as kissing and hugging. The responses the child receives to these expressions of intimacy can have a strong influence on the manner in which he or she expresses sexuality in later years. The inclinations we have as adults toward giving and receiving affection seem to be related to our early opportunities for warm, pleasurable contact with significant others, particularly parents (DeLamater & Friedrich, 2002; Hatfield, 1994; Singer, 2002). A number of researchers believe that children who are deprived

© Michael Newman/PhotoEdit

# Normative Sexual Behavior in Children: A Contemporary Sample

Psychologist William Friedrich and his colleagues (1998) at the Mayo Clinic interviewed a large sample of mothers regarding sexual behaviors they had observed in their children. Sexual behaviors were reported for 834 children, ages 2 to 12, who were screened for the absence of sexual abuse. The mother informants were asked how often they had seen their children displaying 38 different sexual behaviors over the past 6 months. When 20 or more mothers reported observing a specific behavior, Friedrich and his associates considered it a developmentally normal form of childhood sexual expression. We outline some of the key findings of this important study in the following paragraphs.

A wide range of sexual behaviors were observed at varying levels of frequency throughout the entire age range of children. As shown in ◗ Table 12.1, the most frequently observed sexual behaviors were self-stimulation, exhibitionism (often exposure of private body parts to another child or adult), and behavior related to personal boundaries, such as touching their mother's or other women's breasts. Sexually intrusive behavior—such as a child putting his or her hand on another child's genitals—were observed less frequently.

The frequency of observed sexual behaviors was inversely related to age, with overall frequency peaking at age 5 for both sexes and then declining over the next 7 years. Two-year-old children of both sexes were observed to be more overtly sexual than children in the 10- to 12-year-old age range. The amount of observable sexual behaviors increased among both boys and girls up to age 5 and then began to decline. The observed decline in sexual behaviors after age 5 does not necessarily suggest that children actually engage in fewer sexual behaviors as they grow older. Rather, Friedrich and his colleagues suggested that it is likely that children become more private about sexual expression as they mature. Furthermore, older children spend more time with their peers, and thus there are fewer opportunities for parental observation.

Ethnicity was not significantly related to the reported childhood sexual behaviors. There was, however, a positive association between maternal attitudes toward sexuality and frequency of observed sexual behaviors. Mothers who described themselves as having a "relaxed" approach to such things as family nudity and sleeping and/or bathing with their children reported higher levels of sexual activity in their children. The sexual behavior of children was also significantly related to maternal education level and to maternal attitude about the acceptability of sexual behavior in children. Mothers who had more years of education and who reported believing that sexual feelings and behaviors in children are normal reported observing more sexual behavior in their children.

Friedrich and his colleagues concluded that overt sexual behavior, particularly in young children, appears to be a normal part of development. This finding is especially important at a time when concern about childhood sexual abuse is understandably paramount in the minds of many parents, educators, and clinicians. In a concluding comment these researchers noted that it is important for parents (and other adults) to be aware that "simply because a 5-year-old boy touches his genitals occasionally, even after a weekend with his noncustodial parent, it does not mean he has been sexually abused. Rather, it is behavior that is seen in almost two-thirds of boys at that age" (Friedrich et al., 1998, pp. 11–12).

◗ **TABLE 12.1** **Percentage of Mothers Who Reported Observing Sexual Behavior in Their Children at Least Once in the Preceding 6-Month Period**

| Observed Behavior | Males, Age (in Years) | | | Females, Age (in Years) | | |
|---|---|---|---|---|---|---|
| | 2–5 | 6–9 | 10–12 | 2–5 | 6–9 | 10–12 |
| Touches sex parts in public | 26.5 | 13.8 | 1.2 | 15.1 | 6.5 | 2.2 |
| Touches sex parts at home | 60.2 | 39.8 | 8.7 | 43.8 | 20.7 | 11.6 |
| Touches other child's sex parts | 4.6 | 8.0 | 1.2 | 8.8 | 1.2 | 1.1 |
| Touches adult's sex parts | 7.8 | 1.6 | 0.0 | 4.2 | 1.2 | 0.0 |
| Touches breasts | 42.4 | 14.3 | 1.2 | 43.7 | 15.9 | 1.1 |
| Shows sex parts to children | 9.3 | 4.8 | 0.0 | 6.4 | 2.4 | 1.1 |
| Shows sex parts to adults | 15.4 | 6.4 | 2.5 | 13.8 | 5.4 | 2.2 |
| Masturbates with hand | 16.7 | 12.8 | 3.7 | 15.8 | 5.3 | 7.4 |
| Masturbates with toy/object | 3.5 | 2.7 | 1.2 | 6.0 | 2.9 | 4.3 |
| Talks about sex acts | 2.1 | 8.5 | 8.9 | 3.2 | 7.2 | 8.5 |
| Puts mouth on breasts | 5.7 | 0.5 | 0.0 | 4.3 | 2.4 | 0.0 |
| Knows more about sex | 5.3 | 13.3 | 11.4 | 5.3 | 15.5 | 17.9 |

SOURCE: Adapted with permission from "Normative Sexual Behavior in Children: A Contemporary Sample," by W. Friedrich et at., *Pediatrics*, Vol. 101, p. e9, Copyright 1998.

of "contact comfort" (being touched and held) during the first months and years of life can have difficulty establishing intimate relationships later in their lives (Harlow & Harlow, 1962; Montagu & Matson, 1979; Prescott, 1989). Furthermore, other research suggests that affection and physical violence are, to some extent, mutually exclusive. For example, a study of 49 separate societies found that in cultures where children are nurtured with physical affection, instances of adult violence are few. Conversely, high levels of adult violence are manifested in those cultures in which children are deprived of physical affection (Prescott, 1975).

## Childhood Masturbation

Infants fondle their genitals and masturbate by rubbing or thrusting their genital area against an object, such as a pillow or a doll, but the rhythmic manipulation of the genitals associated with adult masturbation generally does not occur until a child reaches the age of 2 and a half or 3 years old (DeLamater & Friedrich, 2002; Martinson, 1994).

Masturbation is one of the most common and natural forms of sexual expression during the childhood years (Thanasiu, 2004). The study described in the Spotlight on Research box reported that approximately 16% of mothers observed their 2- to 5-year-old children masturbating with their hands (Friedrich et al., 1998). Various other studies indicate that approximately one third of female respondents and two thirds of males reported having masturbated before adolescence (Elias & Gebhard, 1969; Friedrich et al., 1991; Hunt, 1974). In one recently reported study of college students, a slightly larger percentage of women respondents (40%) than men respondents (38%) reported masturbating before reaching puberty (Bancroft et al., 2003a).

Parental reactions to self-pleasuring can be an important influence on developing sexuality. Most parents and other primary caregivers in American society tend to discourage or prohibit such activities and may even describe them to other adults as unusual or problematic (Ryan, 2000). Comments about masturbation that pass from parent to child are typically either nonexistent or often negative. Think back to your youth. Did your parents ever express to you that they accepted this activity? Or did you have an intuitive sense that your parents were comfortable with self-pleasuring in their children? Probably not. Most often, a verbal message to "stop doing that," a disapproving look, or a slap on the hand is the response children receive to masturbation. These gestures may be noted even by a very young child who has not yet developed language capabilities.

How can adults convey their acceptance of this natural and normal form of self-exploration? One way to begin is by not reacting negatively to the genital fondling that is typical of infants and young children. Later, as we respond to children's questions about their bodies, it may be desirable to mention the potential for pleasure that exists in their genital anatomy ("It feels good when you touch it"). Respecting privacy—for example, knocking before entering a child's room—is another way to foster comfort with this very personal activity. Perhaps you may feel comfortable with making specific accepting responses to self-pleasuring activity in your children, as did the parent in the following account:

> One day my seven-year-old son joined me on the couch to watch a football game. He was still in the process of toweling off from a shower. While he appeared to be engrossed in the activity on the screen, I noticed one hand was busy stroking his penis. Suddenly his eyes caught mine observing him. An uneasy grin crossed his face. I wasn't sure how to respond, so I simply stated, "It feels good, doesn't it?" He didn't say anything, nor did he continue touching himself, but his smile grew a little wider. I must admit I had some initial hesitancy in openly indicating my approval for such behavior. I was afraid he might begin openly masturbating in the presence of others. However, my fears were demonstrated to be groundless in that he continues to be quite private about such activity. It is gratifying to know that he can experience the pleasures of his body without the unpleasant guilt feelings that his father grew up with. (Authors' files)

Another concern, voiced in the previous anecdote, is that children will begin masturbating openly in front of others if they are aware that their parents accept such behavior. This also is a reasonable concern. Few of us would be enthusiastic about needing to deal with Johnny or Suzy masturbating in front of Grandma. However, children are generally aware enough of social expectations to maintain a high degree of privacy in something as emotionally laden and personal as self-pleasuring. Most of them are much more capable of making important discriminations than parents sometimes acknowledge. In the event that children do masturbate in the presence of others, it would seem reasonable for parents to voice their concerns, taking care to label the choice of location and not the activity as inappropriate. An example of how this situation can be handled with sensitivity and tact is to say to the child, "I know that

**! Sexual Health**

feels good, but it is a private way to feel good. Let's find a place where you will have the privacy you need" (Planned Parenthood Federation of America, 2002, p. 12).

Many children masturbate. Telling them to stop this behavior rarely eliminates it, even if such requests are backed with threats of punishment or claims that masturbation causes mental or physical deterioration. Rather, these negative responses most likely succeed only in greatly magnifying the guilt and anxiety associated with this behavior (Singer, 2002). ■

## Childhood Sex Play

Besides self-stimulation, prepubertal children often engage in play that can be viewed as sexual (Ryan, 2000; Sandnabba et al., 2003; Thanasiu, 2004). Such play takes place with friends or siblings of the same or the other sex who are about the same age (Thanasiu, 2004). It can occur as early as the age of 2 or 3 years, but is more likely to take place between the ages of 4 and 7 (DeLamater & Friedrich, 2002). Alfred Kinsey and colleagues (1948, 1953) noted that 45% of the females and 57% of the males in their sample reported having these experiences by age 12. In other research 61% of a sample of American college students reported engaging in one or more forms of sex play with another child before age 13 (Greenwald & Leitenberg, 1989), 83% of Swedish high school seniors (81% males, 84% females) acknowledged engaging in childhood sex play prior to age 13 (Larsson & Svedin, 2002), and 56% of a group of adult professionals remembered engaging in activities perceived as sexual with other children before age 12 (Ryan et al., 1988). The activities ranged from exhibition and inspection of the genitals, often under the guise of playing doctor, to simulating intercourse by rubbing genital regions together. Although most adults, particularly parents, tend to react to the apparent sexual nature of this play, for many children the play aspects of the interaction are far more significant than any sexual overtones.

Curiosity about what is forbidden probably plays an important role in encouraging early sexual exploration. Curiosity about the sexual equipment of others, particularly the other sex, is quite normal (DeLamater & Friedrich, 2002; Thanasiu, 2004). Many day-care centers and nursery schools now have bathrooms open to both sexes so that children can learn about sexual differences in a natural, everyday way.

Besides showing interest in sexual behaviors, many children in the 5–7 age range begin to act in ways that mirror the predominant heterosexual marriage script in our society. This is apparent in the practice of playing house, which is typical of children of this age. Some of the sex play described earlier occurs within the context of this activity.

By the time children reach the age of 8 or 9, there is a pronounced tendency for boys and girls to begin to play separately, although romantic interest in the other sex may exist at the same time (DeLamater & Friedrich, 2002). Furthermore, despite an apparent decline in sex play with others, curiosity about sexual matters remains high. This is an age when many questions about reproduction and sexuality are asked (Gordon & Gordon, 1989; Parsons, 1983).

Most 10- and 11-year-olds are keenly interested in body changes, particularly those involving the genitals and secondary sex characteristics, such as underarm hair and breast development. They often wait in eager anticipation for these signs of approaching adolescence. Many prepubescent children become extremely self-conscious about their bodies and may be reticent about exposing them to the view of others. Separation from the other sex is still the general rule, and children of this age often strongly protest any suggestions of romantic interest in the other sex (Goldman & Goldman, 1982).

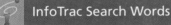

### ? Critical Thinking Question

Assume that you are a parent of a 7-year-old and that one day you find your child playing doctor with a playmate of the same age of the other sex. Both have lowered their pants, and they seem to be involved in visually exploring each other's bodies. How would you respond? Would you react differently according to the sex of your child?

### InfoTrac Search Words

- Childhood sexuality

Many children find the play aspects of interactions such as this one more important than any sexual overtones.

Sex play with friends of the same sex is common during the childhood years (DeLamater & Friedrich, 2002; Sandnabba et al., 2003). In fact, during this time, when the separation of the sexes is particularly strong, same-sex activity is probably more common than heterosexual encounters (DeLamater & Friedrich, 2002; Martinson, 1994). In most instances these childhood same-sex encounters are transitory, soon replaced by the heterosexual courting of adolescence (Reinisch & Beasley, 1990; Thornburg & Aras, 1986). Nevertheless, for some of these children sex play with friends of the same sex can reflect a homosexual or bisexual orientation that will develop more fully during adolescence and adulthood. However, youthful same-sex experiences in and of themselves rarely play a determinant role in establishing a homosexual orientation (Bell et al., 1981; Van Wyk, 1984). We encourage parents who become aware of these behaviors to avoid responding in an overly negative fashion or labeling such activity as homosexual in the adult sense.

It is clear that self-discovery and peer interactions are important during childhood development of sexuality. These factors continue to be influential during the adolescent years, as we will discover later in this chapter. But first we turn our attention to the physical changes that accompany the onset of adolescence.

# ◉ The Physical Changes of Adolescence

Adolescence is a time of dramatic physiological changes and social-role development. In Western societies it is the transition between childhood and adulthood that typically spans the period between ages 12 and 20. Most of the major physical changes of adolescence take place during the first few years of this period. However, important and often profound changes in behavior and role expectations occur throughout this phase of life. By cross-cultural standards, adolescence in our society is rather extended. In many cultures (and in Western society in preindustrial times) adult roles are assumed at a much earlier age. Rather than undergoing a protracted period of child-adult status, the child is often initiated into adulthood upon reaching puberty.

**Puberty** (from the Latin *pubescere*, "to be covered with hair") is a term frequently used to describe the period of rapid physical changes in early adolescence. The mechanisms that trigger the chain of developments are not fully understood. However, we do know that the hypothalamus plays a key role (Brook, 1999a; Caufriez, 1997). In general, when a child is between 8 and 14 years old, the hypothalamus increases secretions that cause the pituitary gland to release larger amounts of hormones known as **gonadotropins** into the bloodstream (Brook, 1999a). These hormones stimulate activity in the gonads, and they are chemically identical in boys and girls. However, in males they cause the testes to increase testosterone production, whereas in females they act on the ovaries to produce elevated estrogen levels. From the age of 9 or 10 years the levels of these gonadal steroid hormones begin to increase as the child approaches puberty (Bancroft, 2003).

In response to higher levels of male and female hormones, external signs of characteristic male and female sexual maturation begin to appear. The resulting developments—breasts; deepened voice; and facial, body, and pubic hair—are called **secondary sex characteristics**. Growth of pubic hair in both sexes and breast budding (slight protuberance under the nipple) in girls are usually the earliest signs of puberty. A growth spurt also follows, stimulated by an increase in sex hormones, growth hormone, and a third substance called insulin-like growth factor 1 (Caufriez, 1997). This spurt eventually terminates, again under the influence of sex hormones, which send signals to close the ends of the long bones. External genitals also undergo enlargement; the penis and testes increase in size in the male, and the labia become enlarged in the female (◉ **Figure 12.1**).

The only event of puberty that is clearly different in boys and girls is growth (Brook, 1999a). Because estrogen is a much better facilitator of growth hormone secretion by the pituitary gland than is testosterone, as soon as a girl starts to show pubertal development, she starts to grow more quickly (Brook, 1999a). Even though the magnitude of the pubertal growth spurt is roughly equal in both sexes, it begins

**InfoTrac Search Words**

- Puberty

**Puberty** A period of rapid physical changes in early adolescence during which the reproductive organs mature.

**Gonadotropins** Pituitary hormones that stimulate activity in the gonads (testes and ovaries).

**Secondary sex characteristics** The physical characteristics other than genital development that indicate sexual maturity, such as body hair, breasts, and deepened voice.

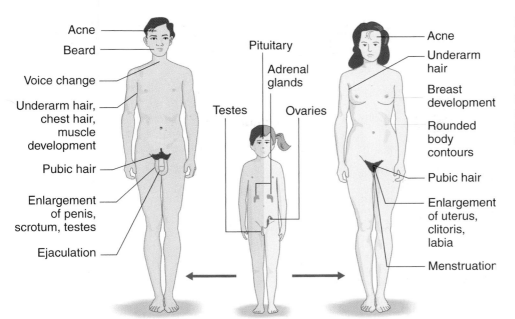

Figure 12.1 Hormonal changes during puberty, triggered by the influence of the hypothalamus over the pituitary gland, stimulate rapid growth and the development of secondary sex characteristics.

about 2 years earlier in girls. This is why the average 12-year-old girl is considerably taller than her male counterpart.

Under the influence of hormone stimulation the internal organs of both sexes undergo further development during puberty. In girls the vaginal walls become thicker, and the uterus becomes larger and more muscular. Vaginal pH changes from alkaline to acidic as vaginal and cervical secretions increase in response to the changing hormone status. Eventually, menstruation begins; the first menstrual period is called *menarche* (discussed in Chapter 4). Initial menstrual periods can be irregular and can occur without ovulation. Some adolescent girls experience irregular menstrual cycles for several years before their periods become regular and predictable. Consequently, methods of birth control based on the menstrual cycle can be particularly unreliable for females in this age group. Most girls begin menstruating around the age of 12 or 13, but there is widespread variation in the age at menarche (Chumlea et al., 2003).

The median age at menarche for all girls in the United States is 12.43 years (Chumlea et al., 2003). Only 10% of U.S. girls are menstruating by age 11.1 years, but by age 13.75 years 90% are menstruating (Chumlea et al., 2003). The age at which menarche occurs has fallen steadily since the beginning of the 20th century (Anderson et al., 2003; Midyett et al., 2003). However, the rate of decline has slowed considerably over the last few decades, and there has been a downward shift of only 4 months in the last 30 years (Chumlea et al., 2003). There are significant differences in the ages at menarche for different racial and ethnic groups in the United States, as described in the Sexuality and Diversity discussion.

## SEXUALITY AND DIVERSITY

### American Ethnic Diversity in Age at Menarche

A recent analysis of menstrual status data obtained from a nationally representative sample of 2,510 girls, age 8 to 20 years, found significant ethnic differences in age at menarche (Chumlea et al., 2003). This analysis provided estimates of the median ages at which 10%, 25%, 50%, 75%, and 90% of the population had attained menarche for each of three ethnic samples: white Americans, African Americans, and Hispanic Americans. The data, summarized in ○ **Table 12.2**, reveal that African American girls start to menstruate earlier than girls in the other two ethnic groups. This difference is significant when compared with white girls at the age levels at which 10%, 25%, and 50% of the girls had started menstruating. In terms of statistical significance, Hispanic American girls began menstruating earlier than white girls only at the 25% level.

| ⭘ TABLE 12.2 | Age at Menarche (in Years) for Selected Percentiles of U.S. Girls | | | | |
|---|---|---|---|---|---|
| | Percentile | | | | |
| | 10% | 25% | 50% | 75% | 90% |
| **Ages by race** | | | | | |
| White | 11.32 | 11.90 | 12.55 | 13.20 | 13.78 |
| African American | 10.52 | 11.25 | 12.06 | 12.87 | 13.60 |
| Hispanic American | 10.81 | 11.49 | 12.25 | 13.01 | 13.69 |
| **Overall median age** | 11.11 | 11.73 | 12.43 | 13.13 | 13.75 |

SOURCE: Adapted with permission from "Age and Menarche and Racial Comparisons in U.S. Girls," W. Chumlea et al., *Pediatrics*, Vol. III, pp.110–113, Copyright 2003.

In boys the prostate gland and seminal vesicles increase noticeably in size during puberty. Although boys can experience orgasms throughout childhood, ejaculation is not possible until the prostate and seminal vesicles begin functioning under the influence of increasing testosterone levels. Typically, the first ejaculation occurs a year after the growth spurt has begun, usually around age 13, but as with menstruation, the timing is highly variable (Stein & Reiser, 1994). The initial appearance of sperm in the ejaculate typically occurs at about age 14 (Kulin et al., 1989; Wheeler, 1991). There appears to be a period of early adolescent infertility in many girls and boys following initial menstruation or ejaculation. However, this should not be depended on for birth control. In some males sperm production occurs in the early stages of puberty, and even the first ejaculation can contain viable sperm (Abrahams, 1982).

Voice changes caused by growth of the voice box (larynx) occur in both sexes, but they are more dramatic in boys, who often experience an awkward time when their voice alternates between low and high pitches. Facial hair in boys and axillary (under-arm) hair in both sexes usually appear approximately 2 years after pubic hair does. Increased activity of oil-secreting glands in the skin can cause facial blemishes, or acne.

Many of these physical developments are sources of concern or pride to the adolescent and his or her family and friends. Feeling self-conscious is a common reaction, and individuals who mature early or late often feel particularly self-conscious.

Social changes also take place. Boy-girl friendships often change, and adolescents are likely to become—at least temporarily—more homosocial, relating socially primarily with members of the same sex. This phase does not last very long, however. The period of adolescence is marked not only by physical changes but also by important behavioral changes. In the following pages, we look at some important areas of adolescent sexual behavior.

# ⭘ Sexual Behavior During Adolescence

Adolescence is a period of exploration, when sexual behavior—both self-stimulation and partner-shared stimulation—generally increases. Although much of teenage sexuality is a progression from childhood behaviors, a new significance is attached to sexual expression. We will look at some areas in which important developments occur during adolescence, including the sexual double standard, masturbation, noncoital sex, development of ongoing relationships, intercourse, and homosexuality.

## The Sexual Double Standard

Although children have been learning gender-role stereotypes since infancy, the emphasis on gender-role differentiation often increases during adolescence. One way that gender-role expectations for males and females are revealed is through the existence of a sexual double standard: different standards of sexual permissiveness for women and men, with more restrictive standards almost always applied to women

(Crawford & Popp, 2003; Greene & Faulkner, 2005; Muehlenhard et al., 2003). As we will see in Chapter 14, the double standard can influence both male and female sexuality throughout our lives. Sexually emerging teenagers often receive the full brunt of this polarizing societal belief. A review of 30 studies published since 1980 found clear evidence that the sexual double standard continues to influence the sexuality of both adolescents and adults (Crawford & Popp, 2003). However, evidence gathered in recent years indicates that the sexual double standard is diminishing among adolescents and adults in North America, especially among women (Baumeister, 2000; Greene & Faulkner, 2005). Nevertheless, the double standard is still an influential factor in the lives of many males and females (Crawford & Popp, 2003; Milhausen & Herold, 1999).

Because the double standard continues to affect adolescent sexual behavior, let us briefly consider some of its potential influences. For males the focus of sexuality may be sexual conquest. Young men who are nonaggressive or sexually inexperienced are often labeled with highly negative terms such as *sissy*. On the other hand, peers often provide social reinforcement for stereotypically masculine attitudes and behaviors; for example, approval is given to aggressive and independent behaviors. For some young men, telling their peers about their sexual encounters is more important than the sexual act itself:

*My own self-image was at stake. There I was—good-looking, humorous, athletic, liked to party—but still a virgin. Everybody just assumed that I was an expert at making love. I played this role and, without a doubt, always implied, "Yes, we did, and boy, was it fun." (Authors' files)*

For females the message and the expectations are often very different. The following account illustrates one woman's view of both sides of the double standard:

*It always seemed so strange, how society encouraged virginity in girls but it was okay for boys to lose theirs. I came from a large family, with my brother being the oldest child. I remember when word got around how much of a playboy my brother was (he was about 18). My parents were not upset, but rather seemed kind of proud. But when my sisters and I were ready to go out, our parents became suspicious. I can always remember how I felt and how if I ever became a parent I wouldn't allow such an inequality and emphasis on female virginity. (Authors' files)*

Many girls face a dilemma. They may learn to appear sexy to attract males, yet they often experience ambivalence about overt sexual behavior. If a young woman refuses to have sex, she may worry that boyfriends will lose interest and stop dating her. But if she engages in sex, she may fear that she has gained a reputation for being "easy."

## Masturbation

Although a significant number of teenagers do not experience sexual intercourse by the age of 19, many masturbate. As we saw earlier in this chapter, masturbation is a common sexual expression during childhood. During adolescence the behavior tends to increase in frequency. Masturbation frequency rates among females are notably lower than among males for all age groups, including adolescents (Leitenberg et al., 1993; Simon & Gagnon, 1998). By the time they have reached the end of adolescence, almost all males and approximately three out of four females have masturbated (Coles & Stokes, 1985; Janus & Janus, 1993; Kolodny, 1980).

Masturbation can serve as an important avenue for sexual expression during adolescence. Besides providing an always available outlet for sexual tension, self-stimulation is an excellent way to learn about one's body and its sexual potential. Teenagers can experiment with different ways of pleasuring themselves, thereby increasing their self-knowledge. This information may later prove helpful during sexual interaction with a partner.

## Noncoital Sexual Expression

**Noncoital sex** Physical contact, including kissing, touching, and manual or oral–genital stimulation—but excluding coitus.

Noncoital sexual expression provides an important way for many couples to relate to one another, often as an alternative to intercourse. **Noncoital sex** refers to erotic physical contact that can include kissing, holding, touching, manual stimulation, or oral–genital stimulation—but not coitus. *Petting, making out,* and *messing around* are other expressions for noncoital sex. Perhaps one of the most noteworthy changes in the pattern of noncoital sexual adolescent behaviors involves oral sex. A number of recent surveys have shown that the incidence of oral–genital stimulation among teenagers has risen dramatically (Mosher, 2005; Halpern-Felsher et al., 2005). A national survey reported that more than one half of the adolescent respondents had engaged in oral sex, that about one in four who had not had coitus had experienced oral sex, and among those teenagers experienced in coitus, 83% of females and 88% of males reported oral sex encounters (CDC National Center for Health Statistics, 2006).

Many teenagers consider oral sex to be more acceptable in dating situations and significantly less risky than coitus in reference to health, social, and emotional consequences (Halpern-Felsher et al., 2005). Unfortunately, many teens seem to be unaware of the potential health risks associated with oral sex, including transmission of diseases like HIV/AIDS, genital herpes, and gonorrhea (see Chapter 15).

For some young people noncoital sex is highly valued because it provides perceived opportunities to experience sexual intimacy while technically maintaining virginity. However, the very notion of virginity is problematic for a number of reasons. Most important, defining virginity as the absence of a single act (coitus) perpetuates the twin beliefs that "real sex" equals penile–vaginal intercourse and that virginity involves only heterosexual coitus. What about lesbians, gay men, and heterosexuals who have not experienced coitus but who engage in other forms of sexual behavior, such as mutual masturbation, oral–genital, oral–anal, penile–anal, and genital–genital contact? Are these individuals all "technically virgins"? What about women whose only experience with penile intromission occurred during an act of rape? Are they no longer virgins despite their lack of consent?

The very idea that people can engage in virtually every conceivable form of sexual interaction but one and still remain virgins seems to be a questionable (antiquated?) concept. Perhaps it is time to begin de-emphasizing a term that is both value laden and exclusive.

Many adolescents form caring relationships with each other.

© Vincent Besnault/Getty Images

## Ongoing Sexual Relationships

Despite the lingering double standard, data indicate that early sexual experiences, both coital and noncoital, are now more likely to be shared within the context of an ongoing relationship than they were in Kinsey's time. Studies conducted in the United States have shown that from early to late adolescence the percentage of teens involved in romantic relationships approximately doubles from 30–36% in early adolescence to 67–72% in late adolescence (Overbeck et al., 2003). Furthermore, contemporary adolescents are most likely to be sexually intimate with someone they love or to whom they feel emotionally attached (Laumann et al., 1994; Overbeck et al., 2003). In addition, noteworthy changes in the attitudes and behaviors of both sexes are narrowing the gender gap. Teenage women seem to be more comfortable with having sex with someone for whom they feel affection rather than believing they must "save themselves" for a love relationship. At the same time, adolescent males are increasingly inclined to have sex within an affectionate or loving relationship rather than engaging in sex with a casual acquaintance or stranger, which was once typical for adolescent males (Laumann et al., 1994; Sprecher & McKinney, 1993). Nevertheless, casual sexual relationships via "hook-ups" (see Chapter 7) are also relatively common among adolescents (George et al., 2006).

## Sexual Intercourse

A frequently quoted statistic in sex research is the number of people in a given category who have engaged in "premarital sex." As a statistic in sex surveys, premarital sex is defined as penile–vaginal intercourse that takes place between partners before they are married. However, the term *premarital sex* is misleading for two reasons. First, as a measure that is frequently used to indicate the changing sexual or moral values of American youth, it excludes a broad array of noncoital heterosexual and homosexual activities. For some people, abstaining from coitus before marriage might not reflect a lack of sexual activity. Second, the term *premarital* has connotations that may seem highly inappropriate to some people:

*I really hate those survey questions that ask, "Have you engaged in premarital coitus?" What about those of us who plan to remain single? Does this mean we will be engaging in "premarital sex" all of our lives? I object to the connotation that marriage is the ultimate state that all are supposed to evolve into. (Authors' files)*

Because of these limitations, we avoid using the term *premarital sex* in subsequent discussions. We now turn to some of the available data on sexual intercourse during adolescence; then we look at two related areas, adolescent pregnancy and the use of contraceptives.

## Incidence of Adolescent Coitus

Even though many contemporary teenagers have not experienced sexual intercourse, the results of 11 nationwide surveys reveal a strong upward trend in adolescent coitus from the 1950s through the 1970s (○ **Table 12.3**). Results of the more recent of these surveys (and other surveys) suggest that this upward trend has leveled off and even decreased somewhat over the last 2 decades. Data from the National Youth Risk Behavior Surveys (YRBSs) for the years 1991, 1995, 1999, 2001 and 2005, presented in ○ **Table 12.4**, indicate that

○ **TABLE 12.3** Percentage of Adolescents Who Reported Experiencing Coitus by Age 19

| Study | Females (%) | Males (%) |
|---|---|---|
| Kinsey et al. (1948, 1953) | 20 | 45 |
| Sorenson (1973) | 45 | 59 |
| Zelnick & Kantner (1977) | 55 | No males in survey |
| Zelnick & Kantner (1980) | 69 | 77 |
| Mott & Haurin (1988) | 68 | 78 |
| Forrest & Singh (1990) | 74 | No males in survey |
| Sonenstein et al. (1991) | No females in survey | 79 |
| Centers for Disease Control (1996) | 66[a] | 67[a] |
| Centers for Disease Control (2000b) | 66[a] | 64[a] |
| Centers for Disease Control (2002c) | 60[a] | 61[a] |
| Centers for Disease Control (2006) | 62[a] | 64[a] |

[a]Percentages reporting having had intercourse by their senior year (usually age 17 or 18).

○ **TABLE 12.4** Percentage of U.S. High School Students Who Reported Sexually Risky Behaviors, 1991–2005

| Grade | Survey Year | Ever Had Sexual Intercourse (%) | Four or More Sexual Partners During Lifetime (%) | Currently Sexually Active (%) | Condom Use During Last Sexual Intercourse (%) |
|---|---|---|---|---|---|
| 9 | 1991 | 39.0 | 12.5 | 22.4 | 53.3 |
| | 1995 | 36.9 | 12.9 | 23.6 | 62.9 |
| | 1999 | 38.6 | 11.8 | 26.6 | 66.6 |
| | 2001 | 34.4 | 9.6 | 22.7 | 67.5 |
| | 2005 | 34.3 | 9.4 | 21.9 | 74.5 |
| 10 | 1991 | 48.2 | 15.1 | 33.2 | 46.3 |
| | 1995 | 48.0 | 15.6 | 33.7 | 59.7 |
| | 1999 | 46.8 | 15.6 | 33.0 | 62.6 |
| | 2001 | 40.8 | 12.6 | 29.7 | 60.1 |
| | 2005 | 42.8 | 11.5 | 29.2 | 65.3 |
| 11 | 1991 | 62.4 | 22.1 | 43.3 | 48.7 |
| | 1995 | 58.6 | 19.0 | 42.4 | 52.3 |
| | 1999 | 52.5 | 17.3 | 37.5 | 59.2 |
| | 2001 | 51.9 | 15.2 | 38.1 | 58.9 |
| | 2005 | 51.4 | 16.2 | 39.4 | 61.7 |
| 12 | 1991 | 66.7 | 25.0 | 50.6 | 41.4 |
| | 1995 | 66.4 | 22.9 | 49.7 | 49.5 |
| | 1999 | 64.9 | 20.6 | 50.6 | 47.9 |
| | 2001 | 60.5 | 21.6 | 47.9 | 49.3 |
| | 2005 | 63.1 | 21.4 | 49.4 | 55.4 |

SOURCE: Adapted from Centers for Disease Control (1998, 2000b, 2000c, 2002c, 2006).

from 1991 to 2005 the overall percentage of high school students in the United States who had ever had sexual intercourse declined somewhat for all grade levels. The prevalence of condom use among sexually active high school students increased somewhat during this 10-year period.

Evidence indicates that the leveling off in adolescent coital rates has not been as pronounced among young teenagers. Data from a number of studies indicate that over the last several decades there has been a trend toward experiencing first coitus at an earlier age in both sexes, and this trend is consistent across a diverse range of ethnic groups (Centers for Disease Control, 2002c, 2004; Cooksey et al., 2002; O'Donnell et al., 2003). However, different American ethnic groups vary in their experiences with adolescent sex. These differences are described in the following Sexuality and Diversity discussion.

## SEXUALITY AND DIVERSITY

### American Ethnic Diversity in Adolescent Sexual Experiences

A variety of studies have consistently reported that African American teenagers are more likely to engage in adolescent coitus than either white or Hispanic American teenagers (Centers for Disease Control, 2002c, 2006; McBride et al., 2003; O'Donnell et al., 2003). For example, a recent nationwide study reported that African American high school seniors were significantly more likely than Hispanic American seniors and white American seniors to have experienced sexual intercourse (Centers for Disease Control, 2006). The results of this study, summarized in ○ Table 12.5, also revealed that African American youth tend to have their initial experiences with intercourse at an earlier age than either Hispanic American or white youth.

○ TABLE 12.5    Ethnicity and Percentage of Adolescents Reporting Having Had Sexual Intercourse

|  | Males | | | Females | | | Males and Females Combined | | |
|---|---|---|---|---|---|---|---|---|---|
|  | White (%) | Black (%) | Hispanic (%) | White (%) | Black (%) | Hispanic (%) | White (%) | Black (%) | Hispanic (%) |
| By 12th grade | 42.2 | 74.6 | 57.6 | 43.7 | 61.2 | 44.4 | 43.0 | 67.6 | 51.0 |
| Before age 13 | 5.0 | 26.8 | 11.1 | 2.9 | 7.1 | 3.6 | 4.0 | 16.5 | 7.3 |

SOURCE: Centers for Disease Control (2006).

These ethnic differences in adolescent sexual experiences could be related more to economic status than to race or ethnicity. Poverty is a strong predictor of sexual activity among adolescents (Kissinger et al., 1997; Singh & Darroch, 2000). Teenagers from the least affluent segments of American society are more likely to engage in sexual activity than those from more affluent classes, and African Americans and Hispanic Americans are often less affluent than white Americans. Furthermore, recent studies indicate that African American adolescents raised in more affluent homes are significantly more likely to abstain from sexual intercourse than their poorer counterparts (Leadbeater & Way, 1995; Murry, 1996).

Just as America's ethnic groups vary in their experiences with adolescent sex, there are also noteworthy variations across nations as described in the following Sexuality and Diversity discussion.

## SEXUALITY AND DIVERSITY

### Adolescent Sexual Behavior in Developed Countries

In 2001 and 2002 the World Health Organization (WHO) sponsored the administration of the Health Behaviors in School-Aged Children (HBSC) survey, administered to national samples of adolescents in many countries. Data pertaining to teens' responses to four survey questions are shown in ⊙ **Table 12.6**. (For comparison, we have included comparable data obtained from the National Youth Risk Behavior Survey, a representative survey of adolescents in the United States.)

**⊙ TABLE 12.6** Cross-National Data on Sexual Behavior of Adolescents

| Nation | Ever had Sexual Intercourse: 15-Year-Olds (%) | | Mean Age First Intercourse: 15-Year-Olds (%) | | Condom Used Last Intercourse: 15-Year-Olds (%) | | Used Contraception Last Intercourse: 15-Year-Olds (%) | |
|---|---|---|---|---|---|---|---|---|
| | Boys | Girls | Boys | Girls | Boys | Girls | Boys | Girls |
| Austria | 22.1 | 19.1 | 13.5 | 13.6 | 84.8 | 78.9 | 90.2 | 93.0 |
| Belgium-Flemish | 26.3 | 23.7 | 14.0 | 14.2 | 81.3 | 59.7 | 90.5 | 89.6 |
| Belgium-French | 34.4 | 23.2 | 13.7 | 14.0 | 78.1 | 64.8 | 82.2 | 81.5 |
| Cananda | 24.7 | 24.0 | 13.9 | 14.2 | 79.8 | 71.7 | 86.8 | 85.5 |
| Croatia | 23.2 | 9.7 | 14.0 | 14.5 | 75.2 | 73.1 | 76.7 | 74.6 |
| England | 35.7 | 40.4 | 14.0 | 14.1 | 69.6 | 70.8 | 80.4 | 87.5 |
| Finland | 23.0 | 33.1 | 14.1 | 14.2 | 72.6 | 58.6 | 88.2 | 86.0 |
| France | 26.1 | 18.3 | 13.5 | 13.9 | 87.0 | 77.0 | 92.1 | 92.6 |
| Germany | 22.5 | 33.5 | 13.7 | 14.2 | 75.6 | 64.4 | 87.8 | 94.9 |
| Greece | 33.6 | 9.6 | 14.3 | 14.6 | 91.2 | 82.5 | 91.2 | 82.5 |
| Hungary | 25.5 | 16.4 | 14.1 | 14.4 | 84.5 | 71.8 | 84.5 | 72.5 |
| Israel | 32.4 | 9.7 | 14.3 | 14.7 | 89.3 | 73.6 | 91.7 | 77.4 |
| Latvia | 21.8 | 14.1 | 14.2 | 14.4 | 81.0 | 77.3 | 86.9 | 84.0 |
| Lithuania | 26.4 | 10.8 | 13.5 | 13.6 | 82.2 | 70.4 | 88.1 | 81.6 |
| Netherlands | 24.2 | 21.6 | 13.8 | 14.0 | 83.3 | 72.4 | 92.4 | 97.0 |
| Poland | 20.9 | 9.2 | 14.1 | 14.7 | 73.4 | 72.5 | 73.4 | 72.5 |
| Portugal | 30.2 | 20.3 | 13.7 | 14.8 | 68.5 | 77.8 | 74.8 | 82.7 |
| Scotland | 32.9 | 34.6 | 14.0 | 14.0 | 76.2 | 63.4 | 81.2 | 73.8 |
| Slovenia | 30.8 | 21.6 | 14.1 | 14.4 | 80.4 | 67.6 | 89.2 | 83.3 |
| Spain | 18.0 | 14.8 | 14.2 | 14.5 | 89.1 | 89.1 | 89.8 | 90.6 |
| Sweden | 25.3 | 30.9 | 13.7 | 13.8 | 72.9 | 57.6 | 92.2 | 90.5 |
| Switzerland | 25.1 | 20.6 | 14.0 | 14.5 | 78.3 | 83.0 | 87.3 | 95.2 |
| Ukraine | 47.2 | 24.0 | 14.5 | 14.9 | 83.7 | 59.2 | 85.0 | 62.5 |
| USA | 36.5 | 30.6 | 13.7 | 14.1 | 69.0 | 60.2 | 89.3 | 83.0 |
| Wales | 28.7 | 40.1 | 14.3 | 14.3 | 75.2 | 63.6 | 82.4 | 84.8 |

SOURCE: Adapted from Ross et al. (2004).

The percentages of 15-year-old boys who reported having had sexual intercourse ranged from 18% (Spain) to 47.2% (Ukraine). Comparable percentages for 15-year-old girls ranged from 9.2% (Poland) to 40.4% (England). The mean (average) age of first intercourse among 15-year-old boys who reported ever having had sexual intercourse ranged from 13.5 (Austria, France, and Lithuania) to 14.5 (Ukraine). Comparable figures for girls ranged from 13.6 (Austria and Lithuania) to 14.9 (Ukraine).

The percentages of sexually active boys who reported that a condom was used the last time they had sexual intercourse ranged from 68.5% (Portugal) to 91.2% (Greece); for girls the percentages ranged from a low of 58.6% (Finland) to a high of 89.1% (Spain). Finally, the proportion of sexually active boys reporting the use of at least one method of contraception (including but no limited to condoms and oral contraceptives) during their most recent intercourse ranged from 73.4% (Poland) to 92.4% (Netherlands); for girls the percentages ranged from 62.5% (Ukraine) to 95.2% (Switzerland).

The trend in both sexes toward having intercourse at an earlier age is a source of considerable concern for many social scientists and health practitioners. Numerous studies have linked early sexual intercourse with increased risk for adverse health outcomes, including unintended pregnancy, increased probability of exposure to HIV and other sexually transmitted diseases (STDs), and increased number of lifetime sexual partners (Ashby et al., 2006; Donenberg et al., 2003; Sieving et al., 2006).

## Reasons for Engaging in Adolescent Coitus

A number of conditions motivate teenagers to engage in sexual intercourse. An accelerated output of sex hormones, especially testosterone, increases sexual desire and arousability in both sexes. Some adolescents are motivated by curiosity and a sense of readiness to experience intercourse. About half the men and one fourth of the women in the NHSLS reported that their primary reason for engaging in their initial coital experience was curiosity and feeling ready for sex (Laumann et al., 1994). Many teenagers consider sexual intercourse a natural expression of affection or love (Sprecher & McKinney, 1993). Almost half the women and one fourth of the men who responded in the NHSLS reported that affection for their partner was the primary reason for engaging in first intercourse (Laumann et al., 1994). A push toward "adult" behaviors, peer pressure, pressure from dating partners, and a sense of obligation to a loyal partner are other reasons that adolescents engage in coitus (Lammers et al., 2000; Rosenthal et al., 1999).

## Factors That Predispose Teenagers to Early or Late Onset of Coitus

Researchers have identified several factors that appear to predispose young adolescents to engage in sexual intercourse while very young or to delay coitus until they are older. Various psychosocial factors have been shown to be potentially powerful predisposing conditions for early onset of coitus. These include poverty, family conflict or marital disruption, teens living in single-parent or reconstituted families, parents' lack of education, lack of parental supervision, substance abuse (especially alcohol), low self-esteem, and a sense of hopelessness (Hingson et al., 2003; McBride et al., 2003; O'Donnell et al., 2006; Regnerus & Luchies, 2006). Other predisposing factors that have been identified include poor academic performance and low educational expectations (Lammers et al., 2000; Steele, 1999), tolerance for antisocial behavior and association with delinquent peers (French & Dishion, 2003; Rosenthal et al., 1999), exposure to a diet of television high in sexual content (Ashby et al., 2006; Collins et al., 2005), and having been sexually victimized (molested or raped) (Boyer & Fine, 1992; Lammers et al., 2000). Adolescent females who are involved with a partner who is several years older are much more likely to experience coitus than females with same-age partners (Kaestle et al., 2002).

**? Critical Thinking Question**

Assume that you are a parent of a teenager who asks, "How do I know when I should have sex?" What would you answer, and why?

Research has also provided insights into the characteristics and experiences of adolescents who choose to delay onset of sexual intercourse. A few studies suggest that strong religious beliefs, regular religious service attendance, and spiritual interconnectedness with friends lessen the likelihood of early sexual intercourse (Bancroft et al., 2003; Holder et al., 2000). Other researchers have found that adolescents' perception of maternal disapproval of teenage coitus and satisfaction with the relationship with their mothers are positively associated with adolescent sexual abstinence or less sexual activity (Althaus, 1994; Jaccard et al., 1996). Findings from a nationwide survey revealed that late onset of puberty, parental disapproval of teenage intercourse, good grades, and strong religious beliefs were all associated with delayed onset of coitus (Resnick et al., 1997). Another survey of 26,000 students in grades 7–12 found that factors significantly associated with postponing coitus included higher socioeconomic status, good school performance, high parental expectations, and adolescents' belief that they had one or more adults in their lives who cared about them (Lammers et al., 2000). Several other studies have also found a positive link between delayed onset of teenage sexual activity and high-quality parent-child relationships and communication (Dittus & Jaccard, 2000; Karofsky et al., 2000; Regnerus & Luchies, 2006). Finally, an analysis of data obtained from a national study of 12,000 teenagers in grades 7–12 found a strong association between higher intelligence and delayed coital experience (Halpern et al., 2000).

# Homosexuality

Various studies indicate that 6–11% of girls and 11–14% of boys report having experienced same-sex contact during their adolescent years (Haffner, 1993; Hass, 1979). Most of these contacts took place not with older adults but between peers. These data, or the behaviors they describe, do not entirely reflect later orientation. Same-sex contact with the intent of sexual arousal can be either experimental and transitory or an expression of a lifelong sexual orientation. Many gay and lesbian adolescents do not act on their sexual feelings until adulthood, and many people with heterosexual orientations have one or more early homosexual experiences.

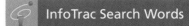

**InfoTrac Search Words**

- Adolescent homosexuality

Gay, lesbian, and bisexual teenagers frequently encounter adverse societal reactions to their sexual orientation. Consequently, they may find it especially difficult to become comfortable with their developing sexuality. Unlike many other cultures in the world community, American society is not noted for embracing the fact of adolescent sexuality, even the often assumed heterosexuality of its young people. American teenagers who are at variance with the dominant heterosexual script can therefore experience a double societal rebuke of both their sexual orientation and the fact that they are sexually active.

For most gay, lesbian, and bisexual adolescents the process of reconciling their sexuality with the expectations of their peers and parents can be a difficult and often painful process that can create severe problems, including unusually high incidences of depression, substance abuse, and suicide attempts (Harrison, 2003; Rienzo et al., 2006). Not being "part of the crowd" can be emotionally painful for teenagers, who often find themselves scorned by their peers. Adolescents who are suspected of being homosexual are sometimes bullied, sexually harassed, or physically assaulted (Harrison, 2003; Williams et al., 2005). Many lesbian and gay adolescents are unable to talk openly with their parents about their sexual orientation. Those who do are frequently emotionally (if not physically) forsaken by their families (Dempsey, 1994; Frankowski, 2004), and they may eventually leave home, voluntarily or otherwise, because their parents cannot accept their sexuality. Some gay, lesbian, and bisexual teenagers even experience antigay violence at the hands of family members (Hunter, 1990; Safren & Heimberg, 1999). In addition to being victims of violence, young people with a homosexual orientation can find it difficult to find confidants with whom they can share their concerns or find guidance (Safren & Heimberg, 1999). Parents, ministers, physicians, and teachers often are unable to offer constructive help or support. In addition, a society that generally fears and rebukes same-sex orientations has traditionally provided few positive role models for gay, lesbian, or bisexual teenagers.

It is apparent from this brief discussion that American gay, lesbian, and bisexual adolescents often must achieve self-acceptance of their sexual orientation within the context of powerful societal pressures not to accept and/or act on that orientation—not an enviable task. Fortunately, people in the United States have gradually become more accepting of behaviors that vary from the dominant scripts for sexual and gender behaviors. Information about homosexuality is becoming increasingly available, as is support for people with same-sex orientations. Many colleges and some high schools in the United States now provide a more accepting environment for the establishment of support groups for gay and lesbian students. Nationwide, there are hundreds of Gay-Straight Alliances (GSAs) on high school campuses. GSAs are clubs composed of both homosexual and heterosexual students who meet to exchange information, provide support to one another, and devise strategies for changing anti-homosexual attitudes in their schools (Ness, 2000a). While the establishment of these support groups is a welcome development, research indicates that public school districts across the United States are still largely remiss in addressing the needs of gay, lesbian, and bisexual students (Rienzo et al., 2006).

Internet chat rooms and message boards can be especially helpful sources of support and constructive information for gay, lesbian, and bisexual teenagers. In addition, in recent years homosexuality has become more visible and has been portrayed in a more positive light in the media. Several prominent entertainment and sports celebrities who have openly acknowledged their homosexuality are now available as potential role models. (See Chapter 9 for more-detailed information about homosexuality and the media and the gay Internet community.) We hope that increasing

Teenagers march in the sixth annual Gay/Straight Youth Pride March in Boston. Several thousand young people took part in the rally, demanding respect and declaring that their sexuality is their own business.

societal acceptance of homosexuality, together with more positive role models and media portrayals, will help make this time of life easier for adolescents with homosexual orientations.

## The Effect of AIDS on Teenage Sexual Behavior

Many health professionals are concerned that American teens are particularly at risk for becoming infected with HIV, the virus that causes AIDS (Feroli & Burstein, 2003; Murphy et al., 2003; Rosengard et al., 2005). The largest percentage of AIDS cases in the United States occurs among people in their 20s and 30s who were infected with HIV in their teens or 20s (Centers for Disease Control, 2006a). People younger than age 25 account for one half of new HIV infections (Adams & Rust, 2006; Nguyen et al., 2006).

Various surveys have shown that most adolescents in the United States are familiar with the basic facts about AIDS and are aware that high-risk activities can lead to transmission of HIV. Unfortunately, even though most teens know the basic facts about AIDS, this knowledge has not resulted in behavior changes in many teenagers. Several studies of high school–age and college-age youths suggest that because most teenagers do not believe that they are at risk for contracting HIV, most do not significantly alter their sexual behavior to avoid infection (Feroli & Burstein, 2003; Lynch et al., 2000).

The notion of the "personal fable" (Elkind, 1967) is relevant to a consideration of adolescent risk taking and sexual behavior. Adolescents are particularly susceptible to a kind of cognitive egocentrism, an illusionary belief pattern in which they view themselves as somehow invulnerable and immune to the consequences of dangerous and risky behavior (Feroli & Burstein, 2003; Hillis, 1994; Murstein & Mercy, 1994). Thus many adolescents continue to engage in high-risk sexual behaviors, not because they are ignorant about AIDS and other STDs but because they falsely view themselves as being at very low (or no) risk of suffering negative consequences (Feroli & Burstein, 2003; Ku et al., 1993).

Behaviors that put young people at risk for HIV infection include engaging in intercourse without condoms; using alcohol, cocaine, and other drugs that impair judgment, reduce impulse control, and thus increase the likelihood of hazardous sexual activity; sharing needles with other intravenous drug users; exposing themselves to multiple sexual partners; and choosing sexual partners indiscriminately (Dittman,

! Sexual Health

2003; Dunn et al., 2003; Hingson et al., 2003). The continuing trend toward a younger age of first intercourse is disturbing because people who begin sexual activity by age 15 tend to have significantly more lifetime sexual partners than those who begin having sexual intercourse at an older age (McBride et al., 2003; O'Donnell et al., 2003). (Exposure to multiple sexual partners is a high-risk sexual behavior, as discussed in Chapter 15.) ■

With the growing awareness that teenage women are at risk for HIV infection (and other STDs), most family clinic counselors now encourage clients, even those on birth control pills, to regularly use condoms to protect themselves against STDs. Unfortunately, this advice is often unheeded, for a variety of reasons. Many young women and their partners are unwilling to deal with the minor inconvenience of condoms when they believe that they are already adequately protected from an unwanted pregnancy (Ott et al., 2002). A recent study of 436 sexually active adolescents found that condom use among teenagers who used birth control pills was much lower than condom use among adolescents who did not use oral contraceptives (Ott et al., 2002).

Finally, many heterosexual adolescents who may use condoms when engaging in vaginal intercourse usually do not use condoms during anal intercourse (Baldwin & Baldwin, 2000). As we describe in Chapter 15, anal intercourse is one of the riskiest of all sexual behaviors associated with HIV transmission.

# Adolescent Pregnancy

The incidence of adolescent pregnancy in the United States has declined somewhat (American Academy of Pediatrics, 2006; CDC National Center for Health Statistics, 2005). However, the still alarmingly high rate of teenage pregnancies in America continues to be an urgent social concern. Among Western industrialized nations, the United States has the highest rate of teen pregnancy (American Academy of Pediatrics, 2006). Approximately 900,000 unmarried American adolescents—that is, about 1 in 5 of all sexually active teenage women—become pregnant each year (American Academy of Pediatrics, 2006; Sieving et al., 2006). This adolescent pregnancy rate is roughly four times higher than in several western European nations, even though the age-specific levels of teenage sexual activity in these countries are comparable to those in the United States (Davtyan, 2000; SIECUS Fact Sheet, 2003). This finding raises the obvious question of whether contraception is either significantly underused or misused by adolescents in the United States. We address this issue in a later section of this chapter.

Of the nearly 1 million teenage pregnancies occurring annually in the United States, approximately 51% result in live births, 35% in induced abortion, and 14% in miscarriage or stillbirth (American Academy of Pediatrics, 2006).

## Negative Consequences of Teenage Pregnancy

The cited statistics on teenage pregnancy represent a great deal of human suffering. A pregnant teenager is more likely to have physical complications than a woman in her 20s. These complications include anemia, toxemia, hypertension, hemorrhage, miscarriage, and even death (American Academy of Pediatrics, 2006). Adolescent pregnancy is also associated with prenatal and infant mortality rates that are markedly higher than the rates among older pregnant women (American Academy of Pediatrics, 2006).

Pregnant teenagers are also at especially high risk for STDs because of a likely reduction in the use of condoms, which are no longer needed to prevent pregnancy. Research indicates that less than 30% and perhaps as few as 8% of sexually active pregnant adolescent women use condoms consistently during intercourse (Byrd et al., 1998; Niccolai et al., 2003). These findings are disturbing because the resultant

Approximately 900,000 unmarried American teenage women become pregnant each year. Many experience considerable hardship as a result of their pregnancy.

increase in susceptibility to STDs during pregnancy can have negative health consequences for both the youthful mother and her baby.

A teenager's unintended pregnancy and the decision to keep her child often have a serious negative effect on her education and on her financial resources (American Academy of Pediatrics, 2006; Shearer et al., 2002). Although it is now illegal to bar pregnant teenagers and teen mothers from public school, a large number of these young women drop out of school, and many do not return (Cassell, 2002; Marx & Hopper, 2005). Faced with the burden of child-care duties and the limitations of inadequate education, teenage mothers are often underemployed or unemployed and dependent on social service agencies (Paukku et al., 2003a; Shearer et al., 2002). Furthermore, low education levels and limited employment skills often thwart the efforts of these young mothers to obtain economic independence as they move beyond their teenage years.

The negative effect of adolescent pregnancy is further exhibited in the lives of the resulting children. Teenage mothers often provide parenting of a lower quality than adult mothers do (Coley & Chase-Lansdale, 1998; Stier et al., 1993). In addition, the children of teenage mothers are at greater risk of having physical, cognitive, and emotional problems than are the children of adult mothers (Meschke et al., 2000; Shearer et al., 2002). These children of young mothers are also more likely to demonstrate deficits in intellectual ability and school performance than children of older mothers (American Academy of Pediatrics, 2006; Shearer et al., 2002).

## Use of Contraceptives

Despite the physical, economic, lifestyle, and emotional stress of pregnancy and parenthood—and despite the availability of birth control today—many sexually active American teenagers do not use contraceptives consistently or effectively (CDC National Center for Health Statistics, 2005). Furthermore, many adolescents do not use any contraception at all the first few times they have sexual intercourse (CDC National Center for Health Statistics, 2005; Lance, 2004). Almost one half of sexually active teenage respondents to a recent national survey reported not using a condom during their last intercourse experience (American Academy of Pediatrics, 2006).

On a more positive note, a recent survey of a nationally representative sample of American youth and adults, the National Survey of Family Growth (NSFG), found that adolescents today are more likely to use contraception than their counterparts a decade or two ago (CDC National Center for Health Statistics, 2005). While it is encouraging to see a trend toward increased use of contraception among teens, it is disturbing that the NSFG also revealed that many adolescents are uninformed about birth control choices. The problem of ignorance is compounded by the wide proliferation of abstinence-only sex education programs in U.S. schools, which teach teens that abstinence is the only option for avoiding pregnancy while failing to present any positive information about effective contraceptive methods (Alan Guttmacher Institute, 2006). A third of teens responding to the NSFG survey reported receiving no formal instruction about birth control from any source. Clearly a lack of knowledge or misconceptions about the safety, effectiveness, and side-effects of various contraception methods can significantly reduce an adolescent's inclination to use birth control. We discuss abstinence-only school sex education in a later section of this chapter.

Many teenagers wait months after becoming sexually active to seek birth control advice, and some never seek counsel. Misconceptions about possible health risks associated with some contraceptive methods, fear of the pelvic exam, embarrassment associated with seeking out and/or purchasing contraceptive devices, and concerns about confidentiality keep many teenagers from seeking birth control advice (Alan Guttmacher Institute, 2006; Iuliano et al., 2006; Jones et al., 2005). Confidentiality can be a major issue for adolescents, who are often willing to discuss their sexuality and contraception needs with their health-care provider only when they know these discussions will remain confidential. Many teens do not use family planning clinics because they fear parental discovery. A recent analysis of data obtained from 79 family planning clinics across America revealed that 1 in 5 teenagers would have unsafe sex (use rhythm, withdrawal, or no method of contraception) if it were legally mandated that their parents had to be notified before they could receive birth control prescriptions (Jones et al., 2005). Among those adolescents whose parents were unaware of their clinic visits, 70% said they would stop using the clinic services if parental notification was required.

Several factors or personal attributes have been found to be associated with adolescents' use or nonuse of birth control. Teenage women in less stable relationships and those who experience infrequent intercourse are likely to be ineffective contraception users (Glei, 1999; Klein, 2005). Furthermore, teenage women age 17 or younger whose partners are more than 3 years older are significantly less likely to use birth control than are their peers who have partners closer in age (Manlove et al., 2004; Marin et al., 2006). Being involved with an older partner may result in "reduced power in a sexual relationship and reduced control over contraceptive decision-making" (Manlove et al., 2004, p. 265). Adolescents who experience intercourse at an early age are less likely to use contraception than their peers who delay intercourse onset, and research has revealed an inverse relationship between pregnancy rate and age at first intercourse (Lagana, 1999). Sexually active adolescents are also more likely to have unprotected sex if intercourse occurs after they have consumed alcohol (Hingson et al., 2003; LaBrie et al., 2005). Finally, many sexually active young women believe that they lack the right to communicate about and/or control aspects of their sexual interaction with men, and thus lack of sexual assertiveness is often associated with inconsistent contraceptive use (Rickert et al., 2002).

Research has shown that adolescents involved in stable, long-term relationships, in which they communicate with their partners about contraception and other issues, tend to consistently use birth control effectively (Klein, 2005; Stone & Ingham, 2002). Parent-child communication about contraception has also been positively linked to adolescent contraceptive use (Halpern-Felsher et al., 2004; Stone & Ingham, 2002). Academic success in school and having well-educated parents are also associated with effective use of contraception (Klein, 2005; Manlove et al., 2004). Research also indicates that adolescents raised in families that stress personal responsibility for behavior tend to be effective users of birth control (Whitaker et al., 1999; Wilson et al., 1994). Finally and perhaps most obviously, adolescents who are the most knowledgeable about contraceptives are the most likely to use them consistently and effectively (Lagana, 1999).

 **Critical Thinking Question**

Should parents provide birth control devices to their teenage children who are actively dating or going steady? Why or why not?

## Strategies for Reducing Teenage Pregnancy

Many authorities on adolescent sexuality agree that educational efforts designed to increase teenagers' awareness of contraception and other aspects of sexuality would be much more effective if they treated sexuality as a positive aspect of our humanity rather than something that is wrong or shameful. Teenagers who have a positive and accepting attitude toward their sexuality are more likely to use contraceptives effectively (Lagana, 1999; Meschke et al., 2000). In many western European countries, where teenage birthrates are dramatically lower than in the United States even though levels of adolescent sexual activity are equal to or greater than those in America, sex is viewed as natural and healthy and teenage sexual activity is widely accepted. This stands in sharp contrast to the United States, where sex is often romanticized and flaunted but also frequently portrayed as something sinful or dirty that should be hidden.

We offer a list of suggestions for reducing teenage pregnancy rates in the United States. These suggestions were gleaned from a large body of research on adolescent sexuality.

1. The American family planning clinic system and school-based health clinics need to be upgraded and expanded to provide free or low-cost contraceptive services to all adolescents who want them. Schools and the media should become more involved in publicizing that these services are not limited to poor people. Of equal importance is the need to publicize that clinics maintain the confidentiality of their clients.
2. The United States should follow the lead of several European nations in establishing a compulsory national sex education curriculum that is extended to all

grade levels. Safe expression of adolescent sexuality should be treated as a health issue rather than as a political or religious issue. Research clearly reveals that teenagers who are valued, respected, and expected to act responsibly often do so (Kelly & McGee, 1999). Research also indicates that teenagers who have been exposed to comprehensive sex education are considerably less likely to become pregnant than those who have had no such education, especially if exposure to sex education occurs before the young people become sexually active (Kirby, 2000; Lagana, 1999; Philliber et al., 2002).

3. Efforts to educate teenagers to prevent unwanted pregnancies must recognize that male attitudes are important for the practice and effectiveness of birth control (Goodyear et al., 2000). Adolescent boys often consider birth control to be their partners' responsibility (Braverman & Strasburger, 1993b; Lagana, 1999). Sex education programs should stress that responsibility for contraception is shared. A survey of several thousand American teenagers revealed that respondents who believed that responsibility for pregnancy prevention should be shared were more likely to have used contraception effectively than those who felt that the responsibility belonged to one partner or the other (Zabin et al., 1984). A preponderance of research on teen pregnancy has focused largely or exclusively on the young women who become pregnant rather than on the teenage men who contribute to this outcome (Goodyear et al., 2000). This has limited our understanding of the varied causes of teen pregnancy, and future research efforts should focus more on the sexual attitudes and behaviors of adolescent males that contribute to high teenage pregnancy rates in the United States.

4. Condoms should be made readily available in middle schools and high schools (Crosby & Lawrence, 2000; Kirby, 2000). One study assessed the rate of condom use and sexual activity among 7,119 students in New York City public high schools, where condoms are available in school, and compared these rates with those exhibited by 5,738 high school students in Chicago, where condoms were not made available in school. The results: The availability of condoms in schools significantly increased condom use by sexually active teenage subjects but did not contribute to an increase in rates of sexual activity (Guttmacher et al., 1997). Another recent survey of a representative sample of more than 4,000 teenagers enrolled in Massachusetts high schools with and without condom availability programs found that students in schools where condoms were available were more likely to receive instruction on proper condom use and less likely to report lifetime or recent sexual intercourse experiences than adolescents whose schools lacked condom availability programs (Blake et al., 2003). The results of these two studies suggest that school-based condom availability can reduce teenage pregnancy and lower the risk of contracting STDs, including HIV/AIDS.

## ⚪ Sex Education

Many parents today want to contribute to the sex education of their children. Societal values about sex are rapidly changing, and we all are exposed to contrasting opinions. How much should children see, or how much should they be told? Many parents—even some who are comfortable with their own sexuality—have difficulty judging the "best" way to react to their children's sexuality.

Perhaps the information that we offer in the following paragraphs will help modify some of this uncertainty. We do not profess to have the last word on raising sexually healthy children, so we advise you to read this material with a critical eye. Along the way, however, you may acquire some new insights that will aid you in your efforts to provide meaningful sex education for your children, either now or in the future.

### Answering Children's Questions About Sex

Parents often ask us when they should start telling their children about sex. One answer is, when the child begins to ask questions. It seems typical for children to inquire about sex along with myriad other questions they ask about the world around them. Research has indicated that by about age 4, most children begin asking questions about how babies are made (Martinson, 1994). What is more natural than to ask where you came from? Yet this curiosity is often stopped short by parental response. A flushed face and a few stammering words, a cursory "Wait till your mother (or father) comes home to ask that question," or "You're not old enough to learn about such things" are a few of the common ways that communication in this vital area is blocked before it has a chance to begin. Putting off questions at this early age means that you may be confronted with the potentially awkward task of starting a dialogue on sexual matters at a later point in your children's development.

It can be helpful for parents to include information about sex (when appropriate) in everyday conversations that their children either observe or participate in. Accomplishing this with a sense of ease and naturalness can increase the comfort with which the children introduce their own questions or observations about sex.

If a child's questions either do not arise spontaneously or get sidetracked at an early age, there might be a point when you as a parent will feel it is important to begin to talk about sex. Perhaps a good starting point is to share your true feelings with your child—that possibly you are a bit uneasy about discussing sex or that maybe you are confused about some of your own feelings or beliefs. By expressing your own indecision or vulnerability, you may actually make yourself more accessible. During this initial effort, simply indicating your feelings and leaving the door open to future discussions may be all that is needed. An incubation period is often valuable, allowing a child to interpret your willingness to talk about sexuality. If no questions follow this first effort, it might be wise to select a specific area for discussion. Some suggested open-ended questions for a low-key beginning include the following:

- What do you think sex is?
- What do you know about how babies are made?
- What are some of the things that your friends tell you about sex?
- How do you feel about the changes in your body? (for older children or early adolescents)

Understandably, parents sometimes tend to overload a child who expects a relatively brief, straightforward answer to his or her question. For example, 5-year-olds who inquire, "Where did I come from?" probably are not asking for a detailed treatise on the physiology of sexual intercourse and conception. It is probably more helpful to just briefly discuss the basics of sexual intercourse, perhaps including the idea of potential pleasure in such sharing. It is also a good idea to check to see whether your child has understood your answer to his or her question. In addition, you might wish to ask if you have provided the information that was desired and also to let the child know that you are open to more questions. When young children want more information, they will probably ask for it, provided that an adult has been responsive to their initial questions.

Some parents believe that it is inappropriate to tell their children that sexual interaction is pleasurable. Others conclude that there is value in discussing the joy of sex with their children, as revealed in the following account:

> One evening, while I was sitting on my daughter's bed talking about the day's events, she expressed some concern over her next-door playmate's announcement that her father was going to purchase a stud horse. Apparently, she had been told to have me build a higher fence to protect her mare. Even though she knew all about horses mating, she asked why this was necessary. I explained the facts to her, and then she asked the real question on her mind: "Do you and Mom do that?" to which I replied, "Yes." "Do my uncle and aunt do that?" Again, "Yes," which produced the final pronouncement, "I don't think I'll get married." Clearly, she felt some strong ambivalence about what this sexual behavior meant to her. It seemed very important that I make one more statement—namely that not only did we do this but that it is a beautiful and pleasurable kind of sharing and lots of fun! (Authors' files)

Reluctance to express the message that sex can be enjoyable can stem from parents' concern that their children will rush right out to find out what kind of good times they have been missing. There is little evidence to support such apprehension. There are, however, many unhappy lovers striving to overcome early messages about the dirtiness and immorality of sex.

## Initiating Conversations When Children Do Not Ask Questions

Some topics never get discussed, at least not at the proper time, unless parents are willing to take the initiative. We are referring to certain aspects of sexual maturation that a child may not consider until he or she experiences them. These include menstruation, first ejaculation, and nocturnal (nighttime) orgasms. Experience with first menstruation or ejaculation can come as quite a shock to the unprepared, as revealed in the following two anecdotes:

*I hadn't even heard of menstruation when I first started bleeding. No one was home. I was so frightened I called an ambulance. (Authors' files)*

*I remember the first time I ejaculated during masturbation. At first I couldn't believe it when something shot out of my penis. The only thing I could figure is that I had whipped up my urine. However, considering earlier lectures from my mother about the evils of "playing with yourself," I was afraid that God was punishing me for my sinful behavior. (Authors' files)*

It is important that youngsters be aware of these physiological changes before they actually happen. Children's natural curiosity about sex might cause them to discuss these topics with friends, who are usually not the most reliable sources of information. It is certainly better for parents to provide a more accurate description of these natural events.

Most young people prefer that their parents be the primary source of sex information and that their mothers and fathers share equally in this responsibility (Hutchinson & Cooney, 1998; Kreinin et al., 2001; Somers & Surmann, 2004). Research indicates that fewer than 20% of parents engage in meaningful dialogue about sex with their children (Davtyan, 2000; Howard & McCabe, 1990). This is unfortunate, because children and teenagers can benefit greatly from candid discussions with their parents about sex, as exemplified by the following anecdote provided by a young woman enrolled in a sexuality class:

*First my mother, and later my father, talked to me at separate times about sex. I was enlightened by these conversations, and they created a closer bond and increased confidentiality and trust among all of us. I was very thankful that both of my parents talked with me about sex. I realized that they really cared about my well-being, and I appreciated their efforts to say to me what their parents did not say to them. (Authors' files)*

To the extent that parents do take an active role in the sex education of their children, mothers are far more likely than fathers to fulfill this function (Ackard & Neumark-Sztainer, 2001; Hutchinson & Cooney, 1998). Unfortunately, most American parents do not provide adequate sex education to their children (Kreinin et al., 2001; Meschke et al., 2000). Research has revealed that even where there is close and open communication between parents and children, sex often is not discussed (Fisher, 1987). Several studies have shown that friends are the principal source of information about sex for young people in the United States (Kreinin et al., 2001; Starr, 1997). Thus the gap created by lack of information in the home is likely to be filled with incorrect information from peers and other sources (Whitaker & Miller, 2000). This can have serious consequences; for example, an adolescent may hear from friends that a girl will not get pregnant if she has intercourse only now and then. Peers may also encourage traditional gender-role behavior, and they often put pressure on each other to become sexually active. Thus the challenge for parents is whether they want to become actively involved in their children's sex education, minimizing some of the pitfalls faced by children and adolescents who turn to their peers for sex (mis)information.

Parents might hesitate to discuss sex with their children because they are concerned that such communication will encourage early sexual experimentation. However, there is no clear evidence that sex education in the home contributes to either irresponsible sexual activity or an increased likelihood of adolescent sexual behavior. Moreover, adolescent children who openly, positively, and frequently communicate with their parents about sex are more likely to have fewer sexual partners and later and less frequent sexual activity than teenagers who do not talk to their parents about sex (Jaccard et al., 2000; Meschke et al., 2000; K. Miller et al., 1999). Furthermore, positive parent-adolescent communication about sex has been linked to decreased risk of contracting STDs, more effective and consistent use of birth control, and decreased incidence of teenage pregnancies (Halpern-Felsher et al., 2004; Lehr et al., 2005; Stone & Ingham, 2002).

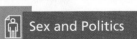

## Critical Thinking Question

Many people believe that sex education can itself cause problems, because they think that the more children learn about sex, the more likely they are to experiment sexually. Do you think this assumption is valid? If so, do you believe that it is a good reason not to teach children about sex?

## School-Based Sex Education

In response to the frequent lack (or insufficiency) of information from the home and the inaccuracy of much of what children hear from peers, other social institutions in the United States, especially schools, are attempting to provide sex education. A nationwide study of health education policies and programs in the nation's schools found that 43% of the states, 52% of school districts, and 57% of schools required sex education at the elementary school level (Kann et al., 2001). These results are far from encouraging, especially because an appreciable minority of American youth begin sexual activity before their teenage years. Sometime during middle or junior high school many young people's intentions to become sexually involved increase and thus "the upper elementary grades provide an ideal time to positively influence children's unanswered questions about sexual issues" (Price et al., 2003, p. 9).

The quality and extent of school-based sex education programs vary considerably. Various surveys reveal that even though an overwhelming majority of parents and other adults support including sex education in schools, only a minority of U.S. schools offer comprehensive sex education courses (Haffner & Wagoner, 1999; Trevor, 2002). A comprehensive poll of adults in the United States found that 93% of respondents supported sex education in high school and that 84% indicated support for sex education in middle or junior high school. Furthermore, the vast majority of polled respondents agreed that teenagers should be provided information to help them avoid STDs and unplanned pregnancies, and they collectively rejected the abstinence-only-until-marriage approach to sex education (Haffner & Wagoner, 1999). So how have U.S. schools responded to this public mandate for quality school-based sex education?

Public school sex education programs are often hampered by pressures from well-organized and highly vocal minorities opposed to such education. In response to these pressures, many school systems completely omit sex education from their curricula, and others attempt to avert controversy by allowing only discussion of "safe" topics, such as reproduction and anatomy. Consequently, important areas for discussion, such as interpersonal aspects of sexuality and preventing pregnancy, are entirely overlooked. We discuss the adverse impact of abstinence-based sex education in American public schools in the box titled "Abstinence-Only Sex Education." ■

Although opposition to sex education in the schools continues, a huge majority of parents support the idea.

Human Body

Poor Baby

© Will & Deni McIntyre/Photo Researchers, Inc.

Sex and Politics

## Abstinence-Only Sex Education

A survey of a nationally representative sample of 825 public school districts in America revealed that 35% of the districts taught "abstinence only" as their approach to preventing STDs and pregnancies in adolescents (Landry, 1999). Only 14% of the surveyed districts offered comprehensive sex education, which treats abstinence as merely one option for teenagers in a curriculum that provides broad-based information about such topics as sexual maturation, contraception, abortion, STDs, relationship issues, and sexual orientation. In abstinence-only programs discussions of contraception are either prohibited entirely or permitted only to emphasize the alleged shortcomings of birth control methods. Unfortunately, the trend toward adopting abstinence-only sex education in public schools has escalated in recent years, supported by numerous conservative social and political groups and fueled by the power of the federal purse.

In 1996 the U.S. Congress allocated $250 million to fund abstinence-only programs at a rate of $50 million per year for the period of 1998–2002 (Goodson et al., 2003). Recently federal government funding of abstinence-only sex education programs was increased to $135 million annually through 2007 (Schaalma et al., 2004). To date almost $900 million federal taxpayer dollars have been spent on such programs. While this approach to school-based sex education has continued to gain momentum, the federal government has provided zero funding for comprehensive sex education programs (Schaalma et al., 2004). What does research reveal about the efficacy of abstinence-only programs, largely funded by taxpayers?

A number of comprehensive investigations of abstinence-only programs have provided no substantial evidence that such programs either delay the onset of sexual intercourse (or other sexual behaviors) or significantly change adolescents' attitudes about engaging in sexual relations (Goodson et al., 2003; Kirby, 2002; Max & Hopper, 2005; Schaalma et al., 2004; Smith, 2005). Furthermore, programs that teach abstinence without also providing essential information about sexual health, contraception, and safer-sex strategies do little to reduce adolescent pregnancy and the spread of STDs (Sullivan, 2005; Tauber et al., 2005). Recent studies of adolescents in Texas—a state that has aggressively promoted an abstinence-only approach in its schools, pronouncements and policies—reveal that the pregnancy rate among Texas 15- to 19-year-olds is the highest of all 50 states and STD rates among adolescents are well above national averages (Zenilman, 2006). According to a congressional report issued in 2004, a majority of the federally funded abstinence-only programs are replete with inaccurate and misleading information and often fail to maintain a separation of science and religion (Tauber et al., 2005).

A scathing indictment of abstinence-only sex education was recently provided by Jonathan Zenilman (2006), a Johns Hopkins University physician scientist: "Promoting ineffective abstinence-only intervention, railing against condom efficacy, eliminating comprehensive reproductive health education, and not providing our children with the skills to protect themselves is *public health malpractice*" (p. 5).

In contrast to the dismal record of abstinence-only sex education, as outlined in the Sex and Politics box, numerous studies provide strong evidence that comprehensive sex education programs that stress safer sex and provide accurate information about various contraceptive methods actually increase the use of birth control, reduce teenage pregnancies, reduce high-risk sexual behavior, do not hasten the onset of intercourse (and in some cases actually delay onset), do not increase the frequency of intercourse, and do not increase the number of an adolescent's sexual partners (in some cases they reduce partner number) (Kirby 2001, 2002; Smith, 2005; Schaalma et al., 2004).

# SUMMARY

- The traditional view of infancy and childhood as a time when sexuality remains unexpressed is not supported by research findings.

## Sexual Behavior During Infancy and Childhood

- Infants of both sexes are born with the capacity for sexual pleasure and response, and some experience observable orgasm.

- Self-administered genital stimulation is common among both boys and girls during the first two years of life.
- The inclinations we have as adults toward giving and receiving affection seem to be related to our early opportunities for pleasurable contact with others, especially parents.
- Masturbation is one of the most common sexual expressions during the childhood years. Parental reactions can be an important influence on developing sexuality.
- Sex play with other children, which can occur as early as age 2 or 3, increases in frequency during the 5- to 7-year-old age range.
- Separation of the sexes tends to become pronounced by the age of 8 or 9. However, romantic interest in the other sex and curiosity about sexual matters are typically high during this stage of development.
- The ages of 10 and 11 are marked by keen interest in body changes, continued separation of the sexes, and a substantial incidence of homosexual encounters.

## The Physical Changes of Adolescence

- Puberty encompasses the physical changes that occur in response to increased hormone levels. These physical developments include maturation of the reproductive organs and consequent menstruation in girls and ejaculation in boys.

## Sexual Behavior During Adolescence

- The sexual double standard often pressures males to view sex as a conquest and places females in a double bind about saying yes or no.
- The percentage of adolescents who masturbate increases between the ages of 13 and 19.
- Noncoital sexual expression is a common sexual behavior among adolescents. *Noncoital sex* refers to erotic contact that might include kissing, touching, manual stimulation, or oral–genital stimulation—but not coitus.
- Adolescent sexual expression is now more likely to take place within the context of an ongoing relationship than it was during Kinsey's time.
- A significant increase in the number of both young men and young women who experience intercourse by age 19 has occurred over the last 5 decades. These increases have been considerably more pronounced among females.
- During the 1990s and 2000s adolescent coital rates leveled off and even decreased appreciably for all but young teenagers.
- Same-sex experiences during adolescence can be experiments or an expression of permanent sexual orientation.

## Adolescent Pregnancy

- The United States has the highest rate of adolescent pregnancy in the industrialized West. In recent years the incidence of adolescent pregnancy in the United States has fallen somewhat.
- Approximately 900,000 unmarried U.S. adolescent females become pregnant each year. Adolescent pregnancy is often associated with social, medical, educational, and financial difficulties.
- Many adolescents who have intercourse do not use contraceptives consistently or effectively.
- The low rate of contraceptive use among U.S. adolescents is related to a number of factors, including ignorance, false beliefs, inadequate home- or school-based sex education, misconceptions about health risks associated with some contraception methods, embarrassment over acquiring contraceptive devices, concerns about confidentiality, and lack of communication with partners about birth control.
- Strategies for reducing the teenage pregnancy rate in the United States include upgrading the family planning clinic system, establishing a compulsory national sex education curriculum, educating males about their contraceptive responsibility, and providing access to condoms in middle schools and high schools.

## Sex Education

- One answer to the question of when to start discussing sex with our children is, when they start asking questions. If communication does not spontaneously occur, it may be helpful for parents to initiate dialogue, perhaps by simply sharing their feelings or asking nonstressful, open-ended questions.
- Some important topics—particularly menstruation, first ejaculation, and nocturnal orgasms—are rarely discussed unless parents take the initiative.
- Although most adolescents prefer their parents to be the primary source of sex information, evidence indicates that peers are considerably more likely than parents to provide this information, often in a biased and inaccurate manner.
- Even though an overwhelming majority of parents and other adults support school sex education, only a minority of American schools offer comprehensive sex education programs.
- Research indicates that comprehensive school-based sex education programs increase the use of birth control, reduce teenage pregnancies, reduce high-risk sexual behavior, do not hasten the onset or frequency of coitus, and do not increase the number of an adolescent's sexual partners.

## ◗ Suggested Readings

**Bass, Ellen, and Kate Kaufman** (1996). *Free Your Mind: The Book for Gay, Lesbian, and Bisexual Youth and Their Allies.* Scranton, PA: HarperCollins. A thoughtful and informative book that provides young people with practical information about what it means to be homosexual and bisexual. The book also offers validation, reassurance, and advice.

**Kempner, Martha** (2001). *Toward a Sexually Healthy America: Abstinence-Only-Until-Marriage Programs That Try to Keep Our Youth "Scared Chaste."* New York: SIECUS. A review of the educational philosophy, common curriculum characteristics, and potential harm of abstinence-only programs that attempt to control young people's sexual behavior by instilling fear, shame, and guilt. (To purchase this publication, send $10 to SIECUS, 130 West 42nd Street, Suite 350, New York, NY 10036-7802.)

**Leight, Lynn** (1990). *Raising Sexually Healthy Children.* New York: Avon. A well-written, insightful book that provides a wealth of information to parents who wish to provide a conducive atmosphere for developing positive sexual attitudes and healthy sexual behavior in their children.

**Moglia, Ronald, and Jan Knowles** (Eds.) (1997). *All About Sex: A Family Resource on Sex and Sexuality.* Westminster, MD: Random House. A book that provides valuable information about sexuality to family members, both children and adults, to enhance family communication about sexual matters.

**Schwartz, Pepper** (2000). *Ten Talks Parents Must Have With Their Children About Sex and Character.* Boston: Time Warner Trade Publishing. An excellent resource for parents of children in grades 4 through 12 that offers helpful advice on how to initiate conversations about sexuality with children and what to say. Topics include family values clarification, safe sex, ethics and character, peer pressure, the media, and the Internet.

# ⊙ Web Resources

**CengageNOW Web Site**
Go to **academic.cengage.com** to link to practice quiz questions, interactive activities, Internet links, critical thinking exercises, discussion forums, and more. You can also access sites from the Wadsworth Psychology Study Center (**academic .cengage.com/psychology**) or you can connect directly to the following sites:

**All About Sex Discussion**
Information on this Web site is divided into sections for teens, preteens, and parents. For the teens and preteens, frank but sensitive explanations of such topics as sex and sexuality, masturbation, sexual orientation, and virginity are provided.

**Talk to Your Kids About Sex and Relationships**
Part of a larger initiative called "Talk to Your Kids About Tough Issues" (sponsored by Children Now and the Kaiser Family Foundation), this Web site offers parents practical advice and resources for talking to children about sexuality and related issues.

**A Web Page by Teens for Teens**
This Web site is dedicated to the discussion of sexuality and relationships for teens. Boasting an all-teen editorial board, this site also has content written by teens. It is sponsored by the Network for Family Life Education (School for Social Work, Rutgers University).

**The Alan Guttmacher Institute (AGI)**
A valuable source of information about a variety of topics dealing with reproductive health, including issues pertaining to adolescent pregnancy.

**Hetrick-Martin Institute (HMI)**
This Web site provides useful information and resources to gay, lesbian, bisexual, and transgendered youth.

**Sex, etc.**
This Web site provides youth with accurate and candid information about their sexuality.

**Teenwire**
Sponsored by the Planned Parenthood Federation of America, this Web site provides information about adolescent sexuality and relationships.

Two Web sites sponsored by the **American Social Health Association**
These Web sites provide answers to questions about teen sexual health and sexually transmitted diseases.

**Advocates for Youth**
Sections of this Web site provide information about topics important to youth, including emergency contraception, youths advocating for their right to sexual health information and services and comprehensive sex education, peer education programs, pregnancy and STD prevention, dating violence, and resources for gay, lesbian, and transgendered youth.

*Our Sexuality* **Book Companion Web Site academic.cengage.com/psychology/ crooks** Visit your book companion Web site where you will find flash cards, practice quizzes, Internet links, and more to help you study.

**Just what you need to know NOW!**
Spend time on what you need to master rather than on information you already have learned. Take a pretest for this chapter, and CengageNOW will generate a personalized study plan based on your results. The study plan will identify the topics you need to review and direct you to online resources to help you master those topics. You can then take a post-test to help you determine the concepts you have mastered and what you will still need to work on. Try it out! Go to **academic.cengage.com/login** to sign in with an access code or to purchase access to this product.

**InfoTrac College Edition Online Library**
Sign in to **academic.cengage.com/login** or visit your free book companion Web site at **academic.cengage.com/psychology/crooks** to access InfoTrac College Edition, an online searchable library that includes a multitude of journals, many specific to human sexuality. These journals include *Archives of Sexual Behavior; Archives of Sexual Health Behavior; Canadian Journal of Human Sexuality; Hispanic Journal of the Behavioral Sciences; Journal of Cross-Cultural Psychology; Journal of Physical Education, Recreation, and Dance; Journal of Sex Research;* and *Sex Roles.*

# Sexuality and the Adult Years

Thinkstock/Getty Images

*After 44 years of marriage, with our kids in homes of their own, we can really enjoy ourselves. We often go out to dinner, come back home, dance to music from the 1940s, talk, kiss, massage each other, and then maybe even have sexual intercourse. Our lovemaking can take several hours, and we're both completely satisfied. (Authors' files)*

Intimate relationships of several forms occupy a position of considerable significance in many adults' lives. An adult's relationship status—single, married, or living with someone—is an important element of one's identity to oneself and others. In this chapter, we examine several forms of adult relationships and the influences of aging on intimate relationships.

## ● Single Living

Remaining single as an alternative to marriage or following divorce has become an increasingly prominent lifestyle in the United States, and most single people are

happy with their non-married status, whether on a temporary or permanent basis (McGinn, 2006). Many adults will spend more years living single than married. Single adults age 15 and over comprise 44.4% of the population in the United States (U.S. Census Bureau, 2006). Unmarried Americans now make up 40% of homebuyers and 42% of the workforce. Furthermore, 33% of men and 25% of women between 30 and 34 years old have never been married—four times the percentage of the unmarried in 1970 (Straus, 2006).

Not long ago, women who pursued higher education were less likely to marry. However, today they are more likely to marry than are women with lower levels of education, although they marry later than the average woman. Women college graduates born since 1960 marry two years later, and women who obtain post-graduate degrees marry five years later than the average woman (Coontz, 2006).

Single living encompasses a range of sexual patterns and differing degrees of personal satisfaction. Some people who live alone remain celibate by choice or because of lack of available partners. Others are involved in a long-term, sexually exclusive relationship with one partner. Some practice *serial monogamy*, moving through a succession of sexually exclusive relationships. Some single people develop a primary relationship with one partner and have occasional sex with others. Still others prefer concurrent sexual and emotional involvements with a number of different partners. Levels of sexual activity among single people vary widely, just as they do among married people. In terms of how happy singles are about their sex lives, research suggests that married people experience higher levels of sexual activity and satisfaction than singles, but many singles claim that their sex lives are more exciting (Laumann et al., 1994).

### Singles and the Internet

The Internet sites designed for singles to connect with one another has greatly altered the "singles scene." Match.com was the first large singles site, started in 1995. Internet dating sites now make up 30% of all paid Internet content, and each month, over 40% of single adults in the United States visit dating sites. The largest demographic group using these sites consists of higher-income, college-educated individuals, but the fastest-growing segment of Internet dating traffic is the 50-and-older population (Juarez, 2006; Straus, 2006). Sites offer search engines to find matches based on a great diversity of characteristics and interests, including religion, race, age, political leanings, shyness, and vegetarianism (Katz, 2003).

Although being single has become more acceptable in our society, most people still choose to live with a partner or marry, and we examine these options next.

# Cohabitation

*When I was a college student in the early 1960s, the possibility of living with someone without the sanctity of marriage simply never entered my mind. The topic of unmarried people living together was never discussed, although I occasionally heard a hushed reference to someone "living in sin." (Authors' files)*

This account reflects a once prevalent societal attitude toward **cohabitation** (living together in a sexual relationship without being married). In the past few decades both the number of people choosing to cohabit and societal acceptance of what was once an unconventional practice have increased significantly, as shown in **Figure 13.1**. Census figures reveal that by 2000 the number of unmarried couples living together in the United States was 5.5 million (U.S. Bureau of the Census, 2003). Cohabitation is most common among adults in their mid-20s; about 25% of people in this age group cohabit (Waite & Joyner, 2001). Men with a high school education or less are more likely to live conjointly with women, as shown in **Figure 13.2**. Cohabitation is usually a short-term arrangement; only 33% of those who cohabit live together for 2 years, and only 10% do so for 5 or more years (Willetts, 2006).

**Domestic partnership** is a term applied to heterosexual and homosexual people who live with a partner in the same household in a committed relationship but who are not legally married. Many local, regional, and national governments and private businesses have provided established benefits such as health insurance for couples in domestic partnerships. In Sweden the 30% of couples who share a household and are not married have all the rights and obligations of married couples, unlike the legal vulnerabilities inherent in

**Cohabitation** Living together and having a sexual relationship without being married.

**Domestic partnership** An unmarried couple living in the same household in a committed relationship.

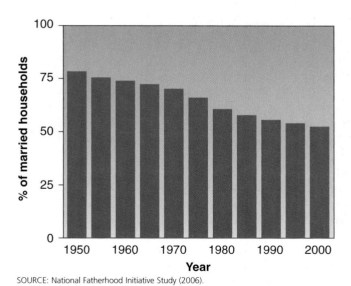

SOURCE: National Fatherhood Initiative Study (2006).

**Figure 13.1** The number of married households is down, suggesting that more people are living together without marrying.

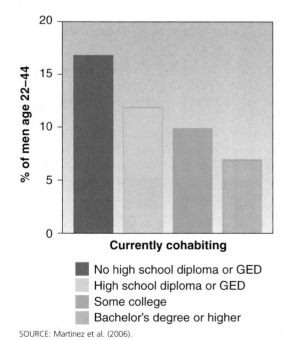

**Currently cohabiting**

- No high school diploma or GED
- High school diploma or GED
- Some college
- Bachelor's degree or higher

SOURCE: Martinez et al. (2006).

**Figure 13.2** Percentage of men ages 22–44 who are currently cohabiting, by level of education.

cohabitation in the United States. France is currently considering strengthening the legal rights for couples who register their unions, hoping to provide more stability to children (Mezin, 2006).

## Similarities and Differences Between Cohabitation and Marriage

Cohabitation has blurred the boundaries between marriage and single living, having similar and distinct characteristics. Research reports that people who live together initially have a frequency of conflict and level of relationship satisfaction similar to those of married people. Compared with their married counterparts, individuals who live together tend to have less traditional gender-role attitudes, less desire to have children, and more equity in doing household tasks (Blackwell & Lichter, 2000). However, research has shown that the longer people cohabit without getting married, the greater the instability, unhappiness, and lack of interaction the individuals say they experience in the relationship compared with what married couples say they experience (Brown, 2003; Willetts, 2006). Whether cohabiting or married, partners tend to be similar to each other in education and race, although cohabiting partners tend to differ from each other more than married partners differ. Cohabiting women tend to have partners who are less educated than, or as educated as, they are. In contrast, married women tend to have husbands who are better educated than they are. This difference between cohabiting women and married women indicates that the greater commitment between married partners may engender more restrictive requirements for a partner.

Most cohabiting partners expect their relationship to be sexually exclusive. However, data from a nationally representative survey indicates that cohabiting individuals are less likely than married people to be monogamous. The decreased sexual exclusivity is attributed to cohabiting individuals' lower investment in their relationship (Treas & Giesen, 2000).

Many people of an older generation have seen their children and grandchildren cohabit, and at this stage of their lives, some older people live together without marriage even though they would not have done so in their youth (Espinoza, 2003). For example, in 1999, 75% more couples comprising partners age 65 and older were cohabiting than in 1990. Older heterosexual couples often cohabit rather than marrying, because remarriage can mean higher income tax rates, the end of alimony payments, and the loss of spousal pension, military, and Social Security benefits.

## The Impact of Cohabitation Before Marriage

Most research indicates that people who lived together before getting married report more difficulty in their marriages and are at greater risk of getting divorced than people who did not live together prior to marriage (Amato et al., 2003; Cobb et al., 2003). It is unknown whether people who cohabit have personal characteristics that make them more prone to divorce or whether the experience of cohabitation generates greater risk of divorce. Nevertheless, marriages preceded by living together are 50% more likely to end in divorce, with one exception. Heterosexual couples in which the woman never had sex with or lived with a man other than the one she married do not have an increased risk of divorce (Teachman, 2003).

Research shows that marriage involves a higher degree of commitment and stability than does cohabitation (Binstock & Thornton, 2003), which may be one reason that marriage continues to enjoy widespread appeal. About 96% of adults in the United States marry, and many marry more than once (Bergman, 2006). A closer look at the institution of marriage might provide some insight into its continuing allure.

> **? Critical Thinking Question**
>
> Why, do you think, does living together before marriage not improve chances of a stable marriage?

## ❶ Marriage

Marriage is an ever-changing institution found in virtually every society (Kuzma, 2006). It has traditionally served several functions for society and individuals. It typically provides stable family units, in which children acquire knowledge about their society's rules and mores through the teachings of their married parents or kinship groups. Marriage functions as an economic partnership that integrates child rearing, performance of household tasks, and earning an income into one family unit. Marriage also defines inheritance rights to family property. For thousands of years, marriage has been about property and politics instead of personal happiness. Arranged marriage prevailed in Europe before the 19th century. Parents in elite classes arranged their children's marriages to develop alliances between families, consolidate wealth and political power, and even maintain peace between countries. Marriage in lower classes was also an economic arrangement; building a labor pool of children and combining skills, resources, and helpful in-laws were primary considerations (Coontz, 2005).

Many societies today are concerned about how marriage affects the social order and attempt to modify its impact, as discussed in the Sex and Politics box on page 354, "Marriage in Crisis."

## Marriage in Current Collectivist and Individualist Cultures

Scientists who study cultures have identified two opposing characteristics that differentiate cultures from each other: collectivism and individualism. Whether a culture is collectivist or individualist influences its views regarding the purpose of marriage. *Collectivist cultures*—such as those of contemporary India, Pakistan, Thailand, the Philippines, the Middle East, and other parts of Asia and Africa—emphasize group, or collective, goals over individual aspirations. In such cultures marriage serves the purpose of uniting families rather than just two people. Parents in collectivist cultures often arrange the marriages of their children. Individuals are not to put their own feelings for someone above the more important commitments to the needs of family, community, or religion. In fact, intense love between two individuals can be seen as a threat to the stability of the extended family. When collectivist cultures become more individualist, marriages may become less stable, as we see in China. The easing of government control over individual choices and an increase in Western influence contributed to a 21% increase in divorces in one year's time in 2004 (Beech, 2005).

In contrast to collectivist cultures, *individualist cultures*, such as those of present-day Canada, Europe, Australia, "European" Brazil, and the United States, stress individual desires and goals over family interests. People in individualist cultures place considerably more emphasis on feelings of love as a basis for marriage than do people in collectivist cultures (Levine et al., 1995). The importance of love in deciding to

On their wedding day, a groom in Kenya lifts the veil of his bride, whose face he may never have seen before.

## Marriage in Crisis

Many countries around the world consider the status and role of marriage to be in crisis, but the specific concerns vary greatly. For example, economic planners in Spain would like the 50% of women between ages 25 and 29 who are single to stimulate the country's economic growth by marrying earlier and having more children. The German, Austrian, French, Japanese, Russian, and Korean governments are also concerned about increasing the number of births, and some even provide financial incentives and preferential access to housing and child care for people who have children, regardless of marital status. For example, for a couple having a second child the Russian government offers payment of $9,200, longer paid maternity leave, and financial assistance for child care (Niedowski, 2006). In contrast, the Czech Republic encourages an increase in single living, hoping it will reduce the country's 50% divorce rate.

Several countries are concerned about various kinds of obstacles to marriage for men. Leaders in Saudi Arabia and the United Arab Emirates want families to lower high bride prices so young men can afford to marry. In Italy commentators criticize the 33% of single men between ages of 30 and 35 who still live at home, enjoying their mothers' cooking and housekeeping. The governments and people of India and China are worried about the millions of men who by 2020 will be without women to marry as a result of the imbalanced ratio of boys to girls (Hesketh & Xing, 2006). The Bill and Melinda Gates Foundation funded a study in a rural area of India where they found that, for children under 6 years of

age, there are 628 girls for every 1,000 boys. The greater number of boys than girls has occurred because female fetuses are often aborted and female infants are killed due to the strong cultural preference for boys (Chung, 2006; Coontz, 2005; Power, 2006). In India, according to Hindu tradition, sons have the important role of lighting their parents' funeral pyres. Sons will earn future wealth for the family, but the dowries daughters require in order to marry are a financial loss to their families. The Indian government has begun to offer families scholarships for girls' education to attempt to encourage births of female children. However, the many-centuries-old tradition of higher status for having male children will be very difficult to change (Power, 2006).

The United Nations and other organizations are campaigning in the Middle East and other parts of Africa and Asia to prevent girls age 13 and younger from being married. Around the world, about 51 million girls are married so young that they face special health risks and high rates of poverty (Stoparic, 2006). In a region of Ethiopia 50% of girls are married before age 15. Young wives whose bodies have not fully matured often experience traumatic childbirth: They can be in labor for days, which can result in a dead baby and a permanently damaged birth canal (Pathfinder International, 2006). Child and teen wives typically have much older husbands, who are often polygamous; and the husbands' age and polygamy increase the chances that they are already infected with HIV and will transmit it to their wives soon after marriage (Ali, 2006; Clark et al., 2006).

marry is a recent innovation in the long history of human existence. It was not until the end of the 1700s that personal choice based on love replaced family interests as the ideal basis of marriage in the Western world (Coontz, 2006).

### Polygamy

Collectivist cultures are likely to practice polygamy—a marriage between one man and several women. Although it is unfamiliar to much of the Western world, polygamy has been the most common form of marriage across the ages, and it remains prevalent today in the Middle East and other parts of Africa. The religion of Islam allows a man to have up to four wives; the man's personal wealth and his ability to provide for numerous wives usually determine how many he marries (Coontz, 2005).

In countries where polygamy is the norm, some people do oppose its practice. For example, in the African country Swaziland, a man's right to polygamy is part of the new constitution. However, despite the fact that the king has 13 wives, his 18-year-old daughter, Princess Sikhanyiso, is leading opposition to the tradition. The opponents—including women in both urban and rural areas—view polygamy as a cover for having extramarital affairs. Men make their girlfriends into short-term wives and soon discard them for new girlfriend-wives. Women's desire to have love and sexual satisfaction without sharing a man with other women is the primary motivation for the opposition and reflects a trend toward individualism in collectivist cultures. As a Swaziland attorney stated, "Polygamy is going to die a natural death because women want the devotion of a husband unfettered by other wives" (UN Office for the Coordination of Humanitarian Affairs, 2006, p. 2). Furthermore, the spread of HIV throughout the family of wives is of great concern in this country, which has one of the world's highest HIV rates. Research in India validates this concern, finding that most women in India who contract HIV are in polygamous marriages and obtain the disease from their husbands (The Hindu News Update Service, 2006).

In the United States' early history, Mormons practiced polygamy, but the Mormon Church disavowed the practice in 1890. However, fundamentalist sects that broke away from the Mormon Church continue to practice polygamy—despite the fact that it is against the law in all 50 states and is opposed, according to a poll, by 92% of adults in the United States. Experts believe that 30,000 to 50,000 polygamists live in the United States, including a growing number of Muslims and evangelical Christians (Peyser, 2006). Polygamy activist groups, including the Centennial Park Action Committee, Truth Bearer, and Principle Voices, are lobbying for decriminalization of the practice. They maintain that individuals should have the right to engage in the private conduct of polygamy without government interference, a view shared by a 2006 report commissioned by the Canadian Justice Department that recommended decriminalizing polygamy (Soukup, 2006).

Few cultures recognize unions between one woman and several men (polyandry), and even fewer permit sexual activity outside of marriage. A matriarchal culture in China turns common concepts of marriage upside down, as discussed in the Sexuality and Diversity box, "Where Women Choose."

HBO's *Big Love* portrays the tribulations and joys of a family with one husband, three wives, and their children. Viagra helps the devoutly religious and hardworking husband keep "up" with his marital duties. Typical family tensions are multiplied by the dynamics of one man and three women, and their attempt to keep their marital arrangement secret from their suburban neighbors.

## SEXUALITY AND DIVERSITY

### Where Women Choose

In a remote part of China, on the shore of a lake at a high altitude, surrounded by towering mountains, the Mosuo society has one of the most unusual marriage arrangements in the world. This ancient **matriarchal society** of about 50,000 people has lasted nearly 2,000 years and thrives today. Because of their isolated location, the Mosuo people have been successful in resisting the imposition of patriarchal family traditions common in other parts of China. Since the society is a matriarchy, women carry the family name and govern the economic and social affairs of the extended family. All of the sons and daughters of each woman live their entire lives together in their mother's house.

**Matriarchal society**
A society in which women carry the family name through the generations, and women govern the economic and social affairs of the community.

Each Mosuo house is usually a home for two to three generations of women and their sons and daughters.

Dressed for an annual festival, this Mosuo woman invites men of her choosing to spend the night with her in her room at her mother's home.

After an initiation ceremony into adulthood at age 13, each girl is given her own room in the family house. There she can welcome lovers of her choice to come in the evening and stay overnight with her. Each dawn, her lover returns to his own mother's home, where he lives. This tradition is called "walking marriage" because men walk to women's houses to be with them overnight. A woman initiates a walking marriage by a glance or a special touch on the palm of her chosen's hand. Men never initiate, but they can decline an invitation.

When a Mosuo woman becomes pregnant and bears a child, the child stays in the family house of the woman's mother. The woman's brothers help raise their sister's children. The biological father assumes no fathering role except for his sisters' children. The only reasons men and women get together are for love and sexual intimacy, not for child rearing. Therefore, walking marriages are easily begun and ended. Once love dies for either partner, the walking marriage is over: The woman might find that her lover's nightly visits stop, or her lover might arrive to find her door locked (Bennion, 2005).

## Marriage in the Western World

Marriage based on love promises regular companionship, sexual gratification, a loving and enduring involvement, and parenting options—all within the security of a legitimized social institution. And on the whole, married people are happier and healthier, both physically and psychologically, than unmarried people (Horwitz et al., 1996; Prior & Hayes, 2003). Married men move up the career ladder faster and earn more money than single men (Elder, 2005). However, such benefits hold only for certain marriages. Individuals in distressed marriages are in poorer health than those in nondistressed marriages, as found by a national longitudinal survey. In fact, they have greater health risks than divorced individuals. Furthermore, the adverse health effects of a distressed marriage have a cumulative effect, increasing with time in the marriage and therefore greater at older ages (Umberson et al., 2006).

## Interracial Marriage

As recently as 1967, interracial marriage was banned in more than a dozen states. *Miscegenation*—sex between members of different races, whether or not the people involved were married—was also illegal until the U.S. Supreme Court invalidated those laws in 1967 (Moran, 2001). Since the elimination of those discriminatory and racist laws, interracial marriage has increased dramatically—from less than 1% of all marriages in 1970 to over 5% in 2000, as ➋ **Figure 13.3** reflects (Pew Research Center, 2006). Twenty percent of married Asian Pacific islanders have a non-Asian spouse, and 6% of married African Americans are wedded to people outside their race (Leland & Beals, 1997). Interracial marriage rates are higher in California than in any other state; there 10% of marriages are mixed (O'Connor, 1998).

One of the few studies on relationship quality in interracial couples found that interracial and same-race couples were similar in conflict and attachment styles. However, interracial couples reported significantly higher relationship satisfaction than same-race couples. The researchers concluded that either interracial relationships are less burdened with problems than same-race relationships, or individuals in interracial relationships are more effective in coping with problems (Troy et al., 2006).

Lack of acceptance of interracial dating and marriage in the United States has been experienced by people of color as well as by white Americans (Cose, 2003; Teich, 2006). Ethnic and racial communities sometimes consider minority individuals who pair with white partners "race traitors" or "whitewashed" (Pan, 2000; Zia, 2003). Opinion polls show that about 30% of white Americans still oppose black-white marriages (Goodheart, 2004). However, such attitudes are less common among young adults, 60% of whom have dated someone of another race (O'Connor, 1998). In addition, 22% of U.S. adults have a close relative married to someone of a different race (Pew Research Center, 2006).

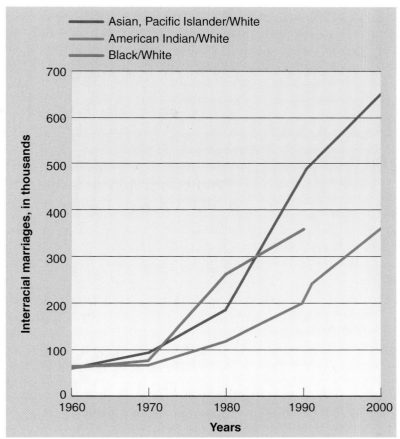

SOURCES: Leland & Beals (1997, p. 60), and Fields & Caspar (2001).

○ **Figure 13.3**
Increase in interracial marriages since 1960. Data for marriages between American Indians and whites were not gathered after 1990 because of small sample size.

Multiethnic superstars, such as singer Mariah Carey and golfer Tiger Woods, have helped familiarize our culture with ethnic mixing. One out of every 19 children born today—compared with 1 in 100 in 1970—is of mixed race. The standard racial and ethnic census categories of black, white, Asian, and Hispanic are too simplistic for today's population, and in 2000 the census provided, for the first time, the option of indicating mixed race (Clementson, 2000b).

## Changing Expectations and Marital Patterns

A large discrepancy exists between the American marriage ideal and actual marriage practices (Corliss & Steptoe, 2004). Although cohabitation, high divorce rates, and extramarital sexual involvement are all antithetical to the traditional ideal, they are widespread. In fact, the most politically conservative areas of the country—the so-called Bible Belt—have some of the highest rates of divorce and numbers of unwed mothers (Coontz, 2005). Some reasons for the contradictions between ideal marriage and actual marriage practices have to do with changes in both the expectations for marriage and the social framework of marriage.

Contemporary couples usually marry for love and enter marriage with expectations for fulfilling their sexual, emotional, spiritual, social, financial, and perhaps coparenting needs (T. Edwards, 2000; Gager & Sanchez, 2003). Furthermore, many people hope that happiness is at least a likely, if not guaranteed, outcome of marriage. Ironically, as people's expectations for marriage have risen, our society's support networks for marriage have declined. Extended families and small communities have become less close-knit and supportive, placing increased demands on marriage to meet a variety of needs. Couples are often hard-pressed to find outside resources for help with household tasks, child-care assistance, financial aid, and emotional support. Although the challenges of sharing everyday life in marriage can enrich and fulfill some couples, such challenges can disillusion others (Patz, 2000). Furthermore, people now live much longer than they did in the past, requiring marriages to keep pace with the ever-changing needs of each partner over many more years.

The arrival of children poses significant challenges to couples. An analysis of 90 studies found a 42% drop in marital satisfaction following the birth of a first child, and a slightly smaller drop with each additional child. Up to 50% of new-parent couples experience as much marital distress as couples who are in marital therapy to address their problems (Picker, 2005). Research also found that in marriages most likely to remain happy in parenthood, the husband understands his wife's inner life, admires her, and actively keeps romance alive (Gottman & Silver, 2000).

## Predicting Marital Satisfaction

Studies conducted by psychologist John Gottman and his colleagues have revealed surprisingly accurate criteria for predicting marital success. Their findings, described next, are summarized and discussed in Gottman's books *Why Marriages Succeed or Fail* (1994), *What Predicts Divorce* (1993), and *The Seven Principles for Making Marriage Work* (2000). Gottman did not study long-term cohabiting gay and lesbian couples. Some of his findings would apply to same-sex couples, but the patterns based on male/female relationships do not. His team used an extensive database drawn from 20 different studies of 2,000 couples. As spouses discussed a problem area in their marriage, they were videotaped and monitored for physiological changes (such as changes in heart rate and blood pressure). Using this information combined with follow-up questionnaires and interviews, Gottman and his associates identified a number of patterns that predict marital discord, unhappiness, and separation. Identifying such patterns has provided the basis for predicting with better than 90% accuracy whether a couple will separate within the first few years of marriage. These patterns included the following:

- The ratio of positive to negative interactions
- Facial expressions of disgust, fear, or misery
- High levels of heart rate
- Defensive behaviors, such as making excuses and denying responsibility for disagreement
- Verbal expressions of contempt by the wife
- Stonewalling by the husband (showing no response when his wife expresses her concerns)

A ratio of five positive interactions to one negative interaction is key. Gottman summarized, "It is the balance between positive and negative emotional interactions in a marriage that determines its well-being—whether the good moments of mutual pleasure, passion, humor, support, kindness, and generosity outweigh the bad moments of complaining, criticism, anger, disgust, contempt, defensiveness, and coldness" (1994, p. 44). The 5:1 ratio is more important than how much a couple fights or how compatible they are socially, financially, and sexually. When couples maintain or improve this ratio, they can have long-lasting, satisfying marriages regardless of their particular relationship style. Gottman's research found that both men and women say

Expressions of contempt can erode marital satisfaction and longevity.

Bliss © 1998. Reprinted with permission of Stephen Hersh.

## Know Your Partner

Test the strength of your relationship in this quiz prepared by John Gottman.

*True or False*

1. I can name my partner's best friends.
2. I can tell you what stresses my partner is currently facing.
3. I know the names of some of the people who have been irritating my partner lately.
4. I can tell you some of my partner's life dreams.
5. I can tell you about my partner's basic philosophy of life.
6. I can list the relatives my partner likes the least.
7. I feel that my partner knows me pretty well.
8. When we are apart, I often think fondly of my partner.
9. I often touch or kiss my partner affectionately.
10. My partner really respects me.
11. There is fire and passion in this relationship.
12. Romance is definitely still a part of our relationship.
13. My partner appreciates the things I do in this relationship.
14. My partner generally likes my personality.
15. Our sex life is mostly satisfying.
16. At the end of the day, my partner is glad to see me.
17. My partner is one of my best friends.
18. We just love talking to each other.
19. There is lots of give-and-take in our discussions (both partners have influence).
20. My partner listens respectfully, even when we disagree.
21. My partner is usually a great help as a problem solver.
22. We generally mesh well on basic values and goals in life.

**Scoring**: Give yourself 1 point for each true answer.

Above 12: You have a lot of strength in your relationship. Congratulations.

Below 12: Your relationship could stand some improvement and could probably benefit from some work on the basics, such as improving communication.

---

that the quality of the friendship with their spouse is the most important factor in marital satisfaction (Gottman & Silver, 2000). The Your Sexual Health box contains a quiz devised by Gottman.

Gottman found other critical patterns in newlyweds who wind up in stable and happy marriages (Gottman et al., 1998). These successful patterns are distinct for women and men. Women typically initiate discussions about concerns and problems in the marriage. To the extent that women use a "softened start-up," a calm, kind, diplomatic beginning to the discussion, they have stable and happy marriages. Conversely, men who accept influence from their wives end up in long-term good marriages. Husbands who reject their wives' requests and concerns—in essence, husbands who refuse to share their power with their wives—find themselves in unstable, unhappy marriages that are more likely to lead to divorce. A husband's ability to accept his wife's influence is unrelated to his age, income, occupation, or educational level. Although these patterns are unique for each sex, the positive interaction between them is evident: A wife will be more inclined to use a softened start-up if she knows her husband will be responsive to her, and a husband will be more likely to accept the influence of a wife who begins a conflict discussion in a diplomatic fashion.

© Mark Hanauer/CORBIS

## Sexual Behavior and Satisfaction in Marriage

Compared with Kinsey's research groups, married women and men in the United States today appear to be engaging in a wider repertoire of sexual behaviors and enjoying sexual interaction more. The frequency and duration of sexual play before intercourse have increased, with more people focusing on such play itself rather than viewing it as preparation for coitus. Oral stimulation of the breasts and manual stimulation of the genitals

Married couples are engaging in a wider variety of sexual behaviors and enjoying sexual interaction more often than in previous eras.

## TABLE 13.1 Relationship Status and Orgasm Experience

| | Always or Usually Have an Orgasm with Partner | |
|---|---|---|
| | Men (%) | Women (%) |
| Dating | 94 | 62 |
| Living together | 95 | 68 |
| Married | 95 | 75 |

SOURCE: Laumann et al. (1994).

have increased; so has oral–genital contact, both fellatio and cunnilingus (Clements, 1994; Laumann et al., 1994).

Sexual satisfaction and relationship quality in marriage are often found together—as in relationships other than marriage, in which sexual satisfaction is associated with relationship satisfaction, love commitment, and stability (Aponte & Machado, 2006; Sprecher, 2002). Data indicate slightly greater sexual satisfaction for married people than for single people, as shown in ◑ **Table 13.1**. In an extensive analysis of the National Health and Social Life Survey (NHSLS) data, couples reported that the quality of sex in marriage became slightly less with greater duration of marriage (Liu, 2003).

Men and women in marriages are not equally satisfied with their sexual lives. Research indicates that married women report lower levels of sexual satisfaction than do their husbands (Liu, 2003). This difference is a complicated issue, and the causes for it are unknown. Liu speculated that the lower satisfaction wives express stems from two factors. First, wives experience orgasm in fewer sexual experiences than their husbands do. Second, because women typically invest more time and energy in the general relationship than men, women may have greater expectations for the quality of the sexual relationship than men do.

Sexless unions are not uncommon in marriage. A psychologist who interviewed married people between the ages of 25 and 55, stated, "I was astonished at how many married couples said they hadn't had sex in years" (Murray, 1992, p. 64). Former U.S. labor secretary Robert Reich made a point about the pressures faced by overworked couples when he applied this acronym to them: DINS—dual income, no sex (Deveny, 2003). Demands of employment, doing laundry, fixing the lawn mower, socializing with two sets of relatives and friends, and countless other activities can reduce the time and energy a couple has for intimate sharing. It is important to note, however, that a lack of sexual interaction does not necessarily mean the marriage is bad. Sex is not, and perhaps never was, a high priority. And, as the psychologist previously mentioned observed, "There are many forms of human connection. These couples are not willing to sacrifice a marriage that is working on other levels" (Murray, 1992, p. 64).

*"No, but I do think there should be a law against no-sex marriage."*

As we have seen in this section, marriage is usually a challenge, and couples who marry find their hopes and plans disappointed often. Despite the difficulties in the institution of marriage, many same-sex couples hope to marry. Advocacy organizations, with the help of gay, lesbian, and heterosexual supporters, are vigorously attempting to secure for all couples—regardless of the partners' sex—the legal right to be married. This contentious issue is discussed in the Sex and Politics box on page 362, "Legal Marriage for Same-Sex Couples?"

## ◑ Extramarital Relationships

**Extramarital relationship** Sexual interaction by a married person with someone other than his or her spouse.

The term **extramarital relationship** refers to sexual interaction between a married person and someone other than her or his spouse. The term is a general one that makes no distinction between the many ways in which extramarital sexual activity occurs. Such activity can be secret or based on an agreement between the married partners. The extramarital relationship may be casual or may involve deep emotional attachment; it may last for a brief time or an extended one. Sometimes it occurs within the context of an alternative lifestyle, such as swinging or polyamory.

Most societies have restrictive norms pertaining to extramarital sex, norms typically more restrictive for women than for men. For example, historically women in Pakistan who were convicted of adultery were sentenced to death or given mandatory prison sentences. In 2006 Pakistani president Pervez Musharraf amended the law so the more than 6,000 women in prison on adultery charges could be released on bail (UN Office for the Coordination of Humanitarian Affairs, 2006). In contrast, some societies studied before 1970 have allowed extramarital sex, as described in the following Sexuality and Diversity discussion.

## SEXUALITY AND DIVERSITY

### Attitudes Toward Extramarital Sexuality in Other Cultures

The Aborigines of western Australia's Arnhem Land openly accept extramarital sexual relationships for both wives and husbands. They welcome the variety in experience and the break in monotony offered by extramarital involvements. Many report increased appreciation of, and attachment to, their spouse as a result of such experiences.

The Polynesian Marquesans, although not open advocates of extramarital affairs, nevertheless tacitly accept such activity. A Marquesan wife often takes young boys or her husband's friends or relatives as lovers. Conversely, her husband may have sexual relations with young unmarried girls or with his sisters-in-law. Marquesan culture openly endorses the practices of partner swapping and sexual hospitality, in which unaccompanied visitors are offered sexual access to the host of the other sex. Some Inuit groups also practiced sexual hospitality, in which a married female host had intercourse with a male visitor (Gebhard, 1971).

The Turu of central Tanzania regard marriage primarily as a cooperative economic and social bond. Affection between husband and wife is generally thought to be out of place; most members of this society believe that the marital relationship is endangered by the instability of love and affection. The Turu have evolved a system of romantic love, called *Mbuya*, which allows them to seek affection outside the home without threatening the stability of the primary marriage. Both husband and wife actively pursue these outside relationships (Gebhard, 1971).

## Consensual Extramarital Relationships

**Consensual extramarital relationships** occur in marriages where both partners know about and agree to sexual involvements outside the marriage. A variety of arrangements fall under the category of consensual extramarital involvements. We briefly examine three arrangements: swinging, open marriage, and polyamory.

**Consensual extramarital relationship** A sexual relationship that occurs outside the marriage bond with the consent of one's spouse.

### Swinging

**Swinging**, or comarital sex, refers to a form of consensual extramarital sex that a married couple shares (Atwood & Seifer, 1997). This activity was labeled wife swapping in the past, but swingers discarded this term because it implies male ownership. Husband and wife participate simultaneously and in the same location—usually in suburban homes, at clubs, or sometimes at "conventions" for "adventures into sensual living" with other couples. In contrast, sex clubs cater to singles or couples who pay for admission to watch others have sex or to engage in recreational sex with other club visitors.

A documentary released in 2000, *The Lifestyle: Group Sex in the Suburbs*, provided insight into the prevalence and nature of contemporary swinging. The filmmaker found that every state except North Dakota has at least one swinging club. The clubs provide contacts for the estimated 3 million swingers in North America (Chocano, 2000). The film features interviews of typical swingers: middle-class, middle-aged suburban married

**Swinging** The exchange of marital partners for sexual interaction.

# Legal Marriage for Same-Sex Couples?

Later in this chapter we will see that older heterosexual people are increasingly deciding to live together and forgo legal marriage, yet many gay and lesbian people, along with other gay-rights advocates, are striving to have the United States join South Africa, Spain, Canada, Denmark, Belgium, and the Netherlands in recognizing the legal right of homosexual people to marry (Human Rights Campaign, 2006). Why is securing this right important? First, it would end discrimination in marriage, a legal institution regulated by the government (Wolfson, 2005). Opponents of same-sex marriage tend to believe that homosexuality is immoral and that legal recognition of such marriage would confer government approval of relationships the opponents find objectionable. However, civil law does not take the right to marry away from other individuals whom many disapprove of and who are actual criminals, such as "tax cheats, dead-beat parents, and even murderers on death row" (Kitch, 2006, F2). In good conscience, how can a democratic country withhold the civil right of marriage from law-abiding, taxpaying same-sex partners? As a graduate student clarified this view, "I feel about marriage the same way I do about the military: It isn't an institution I wish to join, but if it exists, it ought to be open to everyone" (Gaboury, 2005, p. 30).

The U.S. government has changed marriage laws based on equal rights many times in its history. It ended the legal subordination of women in marriage by changing laws that prohibited married women from owning property and entering into contracts. It made marital rape illegal (Coontz, 2005a). Laws finally established the right of people of different races to marry. In addition, the principle of the right to privacy led to laws making it legal for married couples and single individuals to have access to contraceptives. Laws also changed to establish the right of couples, not the government, to decide to divorce.

Each time a law was changed to establish greater equality and privacy in marriage, opponents fought the change, claiming that it went against God's will and would ruin the institution of marriage. However, such changes have actually helped marriage to become a union of equals who are together because of love and a desire to make a commitment to build a life together (Coontz, 2005). In addition, U.S. democracy is based on the principle of separation of church and state. Freedom of religion guarantees the right of every church not to marry any specific couple for any reason. Conversely, no religion should dictate to our government which couples can obtain marriage licenses (Wolfson, 2005). However, religion is a common basis for opposition to same-sex marriage, as expressed by William Bennett, editor of the *Book of Virtues* and codirector of Empower America:

> The legal union of same-sex couples would shatter the conventional definition of marriage, change the rules which govern behavior, endorse practices which are completely antithetical to the tenets of all of the world's religions, send conflicting signals about marriage and sexuality, particularly to the young, and obscure marriage's enormous consequential function—procreation and child-rearing. (Bennett, 1996, p. 27)

Royal Canadian Mounted Police officers Jason Tree and David Connors were married in Canada on June 30, 2006. They began dating 8 years earlier, while in college (Hays, 2006).

In contrast, a proponent of gay marriage, Andrew Sullivan (formerly a senior editor of *The New Republic* and author of *Virtually Normal: An Argument About Homosexuality*), stated:

> What we seek is not some special place in America but merely to be a full and equal part of America. . . . Some of us are lucky enough to meet the person we truly love. And we want to commit to that person in front of our family and country for the rest of our lives. . . . Why indeed would any conservative seek to oppose those very family values for gay people that he or she supports for everybody else? (Sullivan, 1996, p. 26)

Without the legal right to marriage the estimated 600,000 gay and lesbian couples and their children in the United States lack the 1,000-plus federal benefits that married heterosexual couples have, including benefits regarding inheritance; Social Security; child custody; immigration rights; joint insurance policies for health, home, or auto; and status as next of kin for hospital visits or even for making funeral arrangements for a partner (Kitch, 2006). Psychological benefits also exist. A 2-year study of the impact of marriage on gay and lesbian couples in Denmark, where same-sex couples have had the legal right to marriage since 1989, found that a significant benefit for the married same-sex couples was an increased sense of security (Spedale & Eskridge, 2000).

As of 2006, 39% of the general population in the United States believed that same-sex marriage should be legal. Younger people and women tended to view same-sex marriage more favorably than other groups (Gallup Poll, 2006). Support for same-sex marriage has increased and is expected to continue doing so because of younger people's more accepting attitudes (Dickinson, T., 2006).

However, in 1996 the U.S. Congress passed, and President Clinton signed, the Defense of Marriage Act, which denied federal recognition of same-sex marriages and gave states the right not to recognize such marriages performed in other states. By 2006, 41 states had passed laws banning same-sex marriage (Taylor, 2006). Many are perplexed by the name "Defense of Marriage Act," wondering how preventing same-sex marriages "defends" heterosexual marriages. As conservative Republican Bob Hall states, "The anti-same-sex-marriage amendment isn't going to help my marriage by so much as a red whisker. If you think it will protect your marriage, that marriage is already shot" (Hall, 2006, p. 1). Ironically, in 2003 Massachusetts, where same-sex marriage is legal, had the lowest divorce rate in the United States: 5.7 divorces per 1,000 married people. In contrast, some of the states where strong opposition to same-sex marriage predominates have the highest rates: 10.8 divorces per 1,000 married people in Kentucky and 12.7 in Arkansas (Goldberg, 2006).

In 2003 a significant development in the same-sex marriage controversy involved an attempt in Congress to pass an amendment to the U.S. Constitution that would prohibit same-sex marriage. The marriage amendment would write overt discrimination against gays and lesbians into the Constitution (White, 2006). President George W. Bush supported the proposed amendment, but it failed to pass Congress in 2006. Some political analysts said that the Bush administration used the same-sex marriage controversy to motivate the religious right to go to the polls and increase the turnout of other voters who would vote for far-right political candidates (Dickinson, T., 2006).

In contrast to discriminatory measures, in 2004 Massachusetts affirmed a constitutional right to same-sex marriage, making it the first state to issue fully legal marriage licenses to gay and lesbian couples (Belluck & Zezima, 2004). Previously, the Vermont Supreme Court ruled that it is unconstitutional to deny same-sex couples the benefits of marriage, and the state legislature subsequently established a law enabling same-sex couples to form "civil unions" (Moats, 2004). Connecticut and California have also approved civil unions for gays and lesbians. The District of Columbia, Hawaii, Maine, and New Jersey have enacted laws that provide straight and same-sex

Scott Gries/Getty Images

In his HBO special *Never Scared*, Chris Rock said, "People always say we can't have gay marriage because marriage is a sacred institution. No, it's not! Not in America! Not with *Who Wants to Marry a Millionaire* and *The Bachelor* and *Who Wants to Marry a Midget*!"

unmarried couples with some rights previously restricted to married straight couples. State-sanctioned marriages and civil unions entitle couples to the approximately 300 rights, benefits, and responsibilities that states provide married heterosexual couples. However, state laws recognizing same-sex marriages or civil unions do not entitle couples to recognition in other states or to the previously described federal marriage benefits. One federal marriage benefit did become available to same-sex couples in mid-2006, when Congress passed, and President Bush signed into law, a new retirement benefit. The benefit had previously been available only to married couples. The Pension Protection Act allows any U.S. citizen to designate any other American (regardless of the marital status or sex of the individual) to inherit his or her 401(k) retirement plan without immediate taxation (Solomonese, 2006).

In 2005 a Pew Research Poll found that for the first time a majority of respondents in the United States—53%—favored providing same-sex couples with legal arrangements

Reprinted by permission of Peter Steiner, AARP Bulletin, May 2004, p. 34.

"Is the groom male or female?"

*continued*

| **⚫ TABLE 13.2** | Countries With Partnership Benefits* for Same-Sex Couples |
|---|---|
| Croatia | Denmark |
| Finland | France |
| Germany | Hungary |
| Iceland | Israel |
| New Zealand | Norway |
| Portugal | Slovenia |
| Sweden | Switzerland |
| United Kingdom | |

*Rights are more limited than rights in marriage.

SOURCE: Human Rights Campaign (2006).

that gave them the same rights as married couples (Pew Research Poll, 2005). Many countries around the world have already extended various types of partnership benefits to same-sex couples, as shown in ⚫ **Table 13.2**.

Controversy over legal civil marriage for gays and lesbians will play out at the state and national level for years to come. The conflict is about much more than two same-sex people marrying; it is also about what kind of country the United States will be: "Is America indeed to be a nation where we *all*, minorities as well as majorities, popular as well as unpopular, get to make important choices in our lives, or is it to be a land of liberty and justice for some?" (Wolfson, 2005, p. 18).

couples who look to the recreational sex of swinging for enhancement of the sex in their long-term marriages. The film shows that group sex and bisexual expression between women, but not men, are common in the swinger culture (Holden, 2000).

## Open Marriage and Polyamory

**Open marriage** A marriage in which spouses, with each other's permission, have intimate relationships with other people as well as with the marital partner.

The 1972 book *Open Marriage*, by George and Nena O'Neill, brought widespread public attention to the concept of **open marriage**, in which wife and husband agree to have intimate and sexual relationships outside their marriage. A more recent term, *managed monogamy*, refers to agreements primary partners negotiate with each other for sex outside their relationship (Hanus, 2006).

*Polyamory* has become the term many people use to describe multiple consensual sexual relationships. Polyamorists distinguish their relationships from other non-monogamous relationships by their emphasis on emotional commitment in multiple sexual relationships. Polyamorist literature emphasizes "responsible nonmonogamy, honest, ethical relationships that consist of trios, groups of couples, and intentionally created families (Wise, 2006). In 2005 the Dutch government recognized a three-person cohabitation contract between a married couple and another individual, who formed the first government-recognized polyamorous union. After signing the contract the three had a ceremony and a honeymoon (Hanus, 2006).

## Nonconsensual Extramarital Relationships

**Nonconsensual extramarital sex** Sexual interaction in which a married person engages in an outside sexual relationship without the consent (or presumably, the knowledge) of his or her spouse.

In **nonconsensual extramarital sex** a married person engages in a sexual relationship outside the marriage, without the consent (or presumably, the knowledge) of his or her spouse. Polls indicate that about 15% of women and 22% of men have had sex outside their marriages (Ali & Miller, 2004). This form of behavior has been given many labels, including *cheating, adultery, infidelity, having an affair*, and *fooling around*. These negative labels reflect the fact that more than 90% of the general U.S. public says that extramarital sex is "always" or "almost always" wrong (Treas & Giesen, 2000).

## How Common Are Extramarital Affairs?

The NHSLS, with its sample of 3,432 Americans ages 18 to 59, provides current rates of extramarital affairs. Although 94% of the married subjects indicated that they had been monogamous in the past year, the survey reported rates of extramarital involvement at some time during marriage at 25% of married men and 15% of married women (Laumann et al., 1994). More recent surveys have shown similar results

(Miller, 2004). ○ **Table 13.3** shows a global comparison of the percentage of adults who say they have had an extramarital affair.

## Why Do People Have Affairs?

Various complex theories abound on the reasons for nonconsensual extramarital sex. In part, intrinsic conflicts in human nature contribute. As author Erica Jong explained, "We are pair-bonding creatures—like swans or geese. We can also be as promiscuous as baboons or bonobos. Those are the two extremes of human sexuality, and there are all gradations of chastity and sensuality in between" (2003, p. 48). Sometimes nonconsensual extramarital relationships are motivated simply by a desire for excitement and variety, even when an individual has no particular complaints about his or her marriage and even says the marriage is happy (Straus, 2006).

Another possible motive is the person's desire to reestablish his or her sense of individuality and autonomy, which has been diminished within the context of marriage (Schnarch, 1991). An individual may not be developed enough emotionally to keep being true to him- or herself in the face of a partner's discomfort or disapproval, so that individual seeks a new, secret relationship to reestablish a sense of self (J. Shaw, 1997). For some people, the need to confirm that they are still desirable to members of the other sex can lead them into an affair. In other cases, people are highly dissatisfied with their marriages. If emotional needs are not being met within the marriage, having an "illicit lover" may seem particularly inviting (Friedman, 1994). In some situations, affairs also provide the impetus to end a marriage that is no longer satisfying (Brown, 1988). Occasionally, the reason for outside involvements is the unavailability of sex within the marriage. A lengthy separation, a debilitating illness, or a partner's inability or unwillingness to relate sexually can influence a person to look elsewhere for sexual fulfillment.

The secrecy of an illicit relationship often adds to its intensity. Researchers examined secrecy in relationships and found that the research subjects spent more time thinking about former lovers who were kept secret than about those their current partner knew about (Wegner et al., 1994). The researchers also set up a laboratory experiment involving male and female university students. Subjects were seated in mixed-sex pairs for card games, and couples were asked to touch feet under the table while playing cards with another couple. Sometimes this game of footsie was secret; other times it was not. Couples in the "secret footsie" group reported greater attraction to each other after the game than did couples whose foot touching was not secret. The researchers concluded that secrecy often intensifies attraction in relationships.

Are there differences between people who are sexually exclusive and those who have sex outside their primary relationship? Studies have found that most of the factors increasing the likelihood of affairs were characteristics of the person rather than of the relationship. First, age is important: Individuals between the ages of 18 and 30 were twice as likely to have an affair as people over 50. Men who had been involved in

○ **TABLE 13.3** Percentage of Population in 2005 Global Sex Survey That Say They Have Had at Least One Extramarital Affair

|  | Extramarital Affair (%) |
|---|---|
| Israel | 7 |
| Poland | 10 |
| Spain | 10 |
| Germany | 11 |
| Hong Kong | 11 |
| Ireland | 12 |
| Slovakia | 12 |
| Malaysia | 14 |
| United Kingdom | 14 |
| China | 15 |
| Greece | 15 |
| India | 15 |
| Taiwan | 15 |
| Australia | 16 |
| Indonesia | 16 |
| New Zealand | 16 |
| Thailand | 16 |
| Croatia | 17 |
| Serbia and Montenegro | 17 |
| Singapore | 17 |
| Switzerland | 17 |
| United States | 17 |
| Austria | 18 |
| Canada | 18 |
| Japan | 21 |
| Bulgaria | 22 |
| **Global percentage** | **22** |
| Czech Republic | 24 |
| Portugal | 24 |
| France | 25 |
| Italy | 26 |
| South Africa | 26 |
| Sweden | 26 |
| Belgium | 28 |
| Chile | 30 |
| Netherlands | 31 |
| Finland | 36 |
| Vietnam | 36 |
| Iceland | 39 |
| Norway | 41 |
| Denmark | 46 |
| Turkey | 58 |

SOURCE: Durex (2006).

affairs had a greater incidence of substance abuse and expressed more sexual dissatisfaction in their marriages than men who were faithful in their marriages. More permissive sexual attitudes and higher interest in sex were also correlated with increased extramarital sex. When men and women were matched for sexual attitudes and interest, women were as likely as men to engage in extramarital sex. This finding was contrary to other studies, which showed greater likelihood for men to have affairs, but in those studies, the sexual attitudes and interest variables were not controlled (Atkins et al., 2005; Treas & Giesen, 2000).

Work and living circumstances play a role, too. People are more likely to be unfaithful if they have greater access to potential partners at work, through out-of-town travel, or simply by living among many people in the relative anonymity of a large city. The increased number of women in the workforce may account in large part for the increased number of women having affairs. Also, when individuals have weak ties to their spouse's friends, family, and activities and are not involved in a religious community, the chances are greater of having an affair (Ali & Miller, 2004).

A study of couples in marital therapy found several differences between couples in which infidelity was occurring and couples in which it was not. Couples in which it was occurring had more marital instability, dishonesty, arguments about trust, self-centeredness, and time spent apart (Atkins et al., 2005). The important question to ask about these negative marital characteristics is which came first—the dissatisfaction or the infidelity? It is just as possible for the dissatisfaction to have increased because of the infidelity as for the dissatisfaction to have motivated the infidelity. The person having the affair may treat his or her spouse differently due to feelings of guilt or to comparing the marriage with the excitement of the new relationship.

## The Internet's Role in Affairs

With access to the Internet and Web sites specifically for those interested in extramarital affairs, the opportunity for an individual to develop intimate, secret relationships outside his or her committed relationship has taken on new dimensions (Paul, 2004). Even a secret e-mail relationship can become emotionally charged and easily cross the line from confiding in someone to loving someone romantically (Teich, 2006). Although a survey found that 41% of adults (more men than women) do not consider relationships limited to the Internet as cheating on a partner, most marital therapists have seen a significant increase in couples coming to therapy in crisis following a spouse's discovery of an Internet-initiated affair (Cooper, 2004; Ross, 2005; Tangeman, 2006). While the Internet makes it very easy to find people for extramarital sexual relationships, this means of communication makes it almost as easy for a spouse (or an employer) to discover such relationships.

## The Impact of Extramarital Sex on Individuals and Marriage

Involvement in an extramarital affair can have serious consequences for the participants, including loss of self-respect, severe guilt, stress associated with leading a secret life, damage to reputation, loss of love, and complications of sexually transmitted diseases. The dynamics of the secrecy typically have damaging effects on the quality of the couple's relationship. The secrecy and lying (even by omission) erode the connection between spouses and amplify the illusion of closeness to the affair partner. A sex therapist elaborated, "Infidelity . . . consists of taking sexual energy of any sort—thoughts, feelings, and behaviors—outside of a committed sexual relationship in such a way that it damages the relationship, and then pretending that this drain of energy will affect neither partner nor the relationship, as long as it remains undiscovered. Hiding [these feelings] devitalizes the relationship, compromises integrity, and co-opts the other partner's choices to be responsible and responsive" (J. Shaw, 1997, p. 27).

Marital therapists hold differing opinions about whether unfaithful spouses should disclose an affair to their wife or husband. However, research suggests that couples in marital therapy because of disclosure or discovery of an affair benefit even more than couples who have come to marital therapy for other concerns. In contrast, when one of the spouses in marital therapy is keeping an affair secret from the other spouse (but has disclosed the affair confidentially to researchers), the couple is unlikely to make any progress in the counseling. Research also finds that marriages usually fare better when an unfaithful spouse proactively discloses an affair to the other spouse than when the other spouse discovers it on his or her own (Aaronson, 2005).

Regardless of how a betrayed spouse finds out about infidelity, he or she often feels devastated. The betrayed spouse can experience a variety of emotions, including feelings of inadequacy and rejection, extreme anger, resentment, shame, and jealousy. Divorced individuals often mention extramarital relationships as a cause of their breakup. However, the discovery of infidelity does not necessarily end a marriage or ultimately erode the quality of a marriage. In some cases such a crisis is beneficial, in that it motivates a couple to search for, and attempt to resolve, sources of discord in the relationship—a process that can ultimately lead to an improved marriage (Kalb, 2006; Wiviott, 2001).

# ❯ Divorce

Almost 96% of adults in the United States today have married during their lifetime, but 43% of first marriages are predicted to end within 15 years (Bergman, 2006; Kalb, 2006). Research confirms that the proportion of all marriages—first, second, or more—ending in divorce has increased dramatically since the 1950s, when one in four marriages ended in divorce. By 1977 the ratio was one divorce to every two marriages. Since 1977 the ratio of divorces to marriages has tended to level off and has held relatively steady. Most divorced people remarry. In fact, about half of all marriages involve at least one person who has been divorced one or more times (Straus, 2006).

"No heroic measures."

## Explaining the High Divorce Rate

A number of investigators have speculated on the causes of the high divorce rate in the United States. One frequently mentioned cause is increased expectations for marital and sexual fulfillment, which have caused people to be less willing to persist in unsatisfying marriages. Another cause is the comparative ease of obtaining no-fault divorces since the liberalization of divorce laws in the 1970s. Obtaining a divorce has become a simpler, less expensive legal process, and as divorces have occurred more often, the social stigma of divorce has lessened. In an attempt to lower divorce rates, Louisiana, Arkansas, and Arizona have established the option of "covenant marriage," which, like divorce laws before no-fault divorce, allows only a few grounds, such as infidelity, for divorce. Apparently, few people are interested in stricter divorce criteria, since less than 2% of engaged couples opt for covenant marriage in these states (Pollitt, 2005).

Because divorce has become more common, more children have been raised by divorced parents. Research shows that people raised by divorced parents are themselves more likely to divorce than people raised by parents who remained married (Amato, 2001). However, parents who stay together in unhappy marriages may not help prevent their children from divorcing a future spouse. Young adults who believe that their parents should end their marriage are more likely to have positive views of divorce, even when their parents have negative views (Kapinus, 2005).

The increased economic independence of women (one-third of married women earn more than their husbands) increases the importance of relationship satisfaction over financial dependence in women's decisions to divorce (Goad, 2006). Research has revealed another variable associated with marriages ending in divorce: age at marriage. People who marry in their teen years are more than twice as likely to divorce as those who wed in their 20s. Individuals who marry after age 30 have even lower

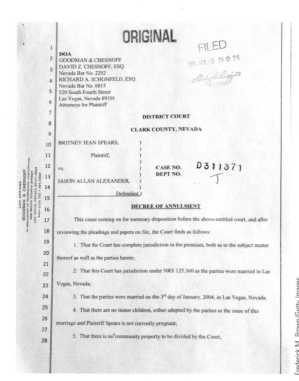

ORIGINAL

FILED

DOA
GOODMAN & CHESNOFF
DAVID Z. CHESNOFF, ESQ.
Nevada Bar No. 2292
RICHARD A. SCHONFELD, ESQ.
Nevada Bar No. 6815
520 South Fourth Street
Las Vegas, Nevada 89101
Attorneys for Plaintiff

DISTRICT COURT

CLARK COUNTY, NEVADA

BRITNEY JEAN SPEARS,

    Plaintiff,

vs.                          CASE NO.   D311371
                             DEPT NO.

JASON ALLAN ALEXANDER,

    Defendant.

DECREE OF ANNULMENT

This cause coming on for summary disposition before the above-entitled court, and after reviewing the pleadings and papers on file, the Court finds as follows:

1. That the Court has complete jurisdiction in the premises, both as to the subject matter thereof as well as the parties hereto;

2. That this Court has jurisdiction under NRS 125.360 as the parties were married in Las Vegas, Nevada;

3. That the parties were married on the 3rd day of January, 2004, in Las Vegas, Nevada;

4. That there are no minor children, either adopted by the parties or the issue of this marriage and Plaintiff Spears is not currently pregnant;

5. That there is no community property to be divided by the Court;

Cavalier celebrity marriages such as Britney Spears and Jason Alexander's 55-hour marriage trivialize the meaning of commitment in marriage.

Frederick M. Brown/Getty Images

divorce rates. The correlation between age at marriage and divorce rate is of particular interest in light of a clear upward trend in the median age at first marriage. Before 1900 most couples in the United States married while they were still in their teens. In 1950 the median marriage age was 22 for men and 20 for women; currently the average age of first marriage in the United States is 25.8 for women and 27.1 for men (Bergman, 2006). The leveling off and even slight decline in the U.S. divorce rate reflects, in part, the influence of older age at first marriage.

There also appears to be an inverse relationship between level of education and divorce rate; that is, the lower the educational level, the higher the divorce rate (Schoen & Cheng, 2006). The one exception is a disproportionately high divorce rate among women who have achieved graduate degrees. Perhaps the increased economic and social independence of professional women with advanced degrees contributes to this exception in divorce rate patterns (Amato & Previti, 2003; Martin & Bumpass, 1989).

## Reasons People Give for Divorce

A study has provided some much-needed empirical evidence of what divorced people say is the cause of their divorce (Amato & Previti, 2003). The researchers readily admit that the study cannot identify whether people's perceptions of their divorces represent actual causes or are after-the-fact reconstructions. In the randomly selected national sample of divorced individuals, the respondents gave infidelity as the most commonly reported cause of divorce. Poor general quality of the relationship—lack of communication, incompatibility, personality clashes, and growing apart—are other factors people reported. Serious problems, such as drinking, drug use, and mental and physical abuse, were further reasons for divorce.

Men and women tended to give different reasons for divorce. Women were more likely to report that their husbands' problematic behavior led to divorce, whereas men were more likely to say that they did not know what caused the divorce. Socioeconomic status (SES) was another variable resulting in differences. High-SES divorced individuals were more likely to attribute their divorces to lack of love and communication, incompatibility, and their spouses' self-centeredness, but low-SES divorced individuals described financial problems, abuse, and drinking as major factors. In terms of positive emotional adjustment following a divorce, people who perceived that they initiated the divorce did better than those who said their partner initiated the divorce (Amato & Previti, 2003).

? Critical Thinking Question

In the research on the reasons people give for their divorce, men are likely to say that they do not know why their marriage ended and women are likely to attribute their husbands' problematic behavior to the divorce. How do you explain this difference?

## Adjusting to Divorce or Breakup of Long-Term Relationships

Although the chain of events leading to marriage is unique for each individual, most people marry with the hope that the relationship will last. Divorce often represents loss of this hope as well as loss of one's spouse, lifestyle, the security of familiarity, and part of one's identity; divorce also often represents changes in parenting time and circumstances (DeGarmo & Kitson, 1996). In the following discussion, we refer to a breakup as divorce, but people who end nonmarital intimate relationships also can experience these losses (Sbarra, 2006).

The loss a person feels during a divorce or a breakup of a meaningful relationship is often comparable to the loss experienced when a loved one dies (Napolitane, 1997). In both cases one undergoes a grieving process, but no recognized grief rituals are provided by society to help one ending a relationship. Initially, a person may experience shock: "This cannot be happening to me." What might follow is a feeling of disorientation—a sense that one's entire world has turned upside down. Volatile emotions may unexpectedly surface. Feelings of guilt may become strong. Loneliness is common. Learning to reach out to others for emotional support can help diminish feelings of aloneness. Finally (usually not for several months or a year), a sense of relief and acceptance may come. After several months of separation a person who is not developing a sense of acceptance may benefit from professional help.

Although many of the feelings that accompany ending a relationship are uncomfortable and painful, a potential exists for personal growth in the adjustment process. Many people come to experience an exciting sense of autonomy. Others find that being single presents opportunities to experience more fully dimensions of themselves that had been submerged in the marriage. The end of an important relationship or marriage can offer an opportunity to reassess oneself and one's past, a process that may lead to a new life.

Despite the challenges of divorce, a majority of divorced individuals become sexually active within the first year following the breakup of their marriage (Stack & Gundlach, 1992). Furthermore, approximately four out of five divorced people remarry, most within 3 years of the divorce (Lown & Dolan, 1988).

# Sexuality and Aging

In the later years of life, most people begin to note certain changes taking place in their sexual response patterns, as described in Chapter 6. Some women and men who understand the nature of these changes accept them with equanimity. Others observe them with concern. An important source of the confusion and frustration that many aging people feel is the prevailing notion that old age is a sexless time (Kellett, 2000).

Why has aging in our society and in other societies often been associated with sexlessness? (See **Figure 13.4** for a global comparison.) Part of the answer is that U.S. culture is still influenced by a philosophy that equates sexuality with procreation and makes it seem not quite acceptable for older people to have and express sexual needs. Moreover, the media usually link love, sex, and romance to the young. However, as the percentage of seniors in the population continues to increase, the consumer goods market more frequently presents vibrant, sensual ads featuring older women and men (Jarrell, 2000). In addition, as the generation that reached adulthood during the so-called "sexual revolution" era moves into senior citizenship, the notion of a sexless old age may become obsolete (Kingsberg, 2002; Zilbergeld, 2001).

## The Double Standard and Aging

In previous chapters we have discussed the double standard as it relates to male and female sexual expression during adolescence and adulthood. The assumptions and prejudices implicit in the sexual double standard continue into old age, imposing a

**Figure 13.4** The percentage of respondents in each country who agreed with the statement "Older people no longer have sex."

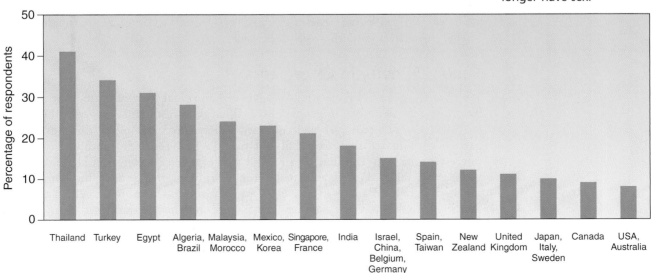

SOURCE: Adapted from *Global Study of Sexual Attitudes and Behavior* (2002).

A great deal of media attention has been given to Demi Moore and Ashton Kutcher's romance because Moore is 15 years older than Kutcher. In contrast, the 25-year age difference between Michael Douglas and Catherine Zeta-Jones has received less attention.

particular burden on women (Scott, 2003). Although a woman's sexual capabilities can continue throughout her lifetime, the cultural image of an erotically appealing woman is commonly one of youth. Popular media typically represent older women as either nurturing caretakers or vindictive manipulators—rarely as sexual. In fact, older women in these media are scarce: Female actors over 40 account for only 9% of movie roles, whereas male actors in the same age group account for 30% of movie roles (Jeffery, 2006).

In contrast, the sexual attractiveness of men is often considered enhanced by aging. Gray hair and facial wrinkles are often thought to look distinguished on men—signs of accumulated life experience and wisdom. Likewise, it is relatively common for a man's achievements and social status—both of which usually increase with age—to be closely associated with his sexual appeal. However, the professional achievements of women may be perceived as threatening to some potential male partners.

The pairing of powerful older men and young beautiful women reflects this double standard of aging. The marriage of a 55-year-old man and a 25-year-old woman generates a much smaller reaction than that of a 55-year-old woman and a 25-year-old man. And as you might expect, pairings of older men and young women occur much more commonly than the reverse. However, a survey found that 34% of women over age 40 were dating younger men, and more women marry younger men now than in the past (Coontz, 2006; Mahoney, 2003).

In response to the double standard of aging, the writer Susan Sontag presented an alternative view:

> Women have another option. They can aspire to be wise, not merely nice; to be competent, not merely helpful; to be strong, not merely graceful; to be ambitious for themselves, not merely themselves in relation to men and children. They can let themselves age naturally and without embarrassment, actively protesting and disobeying the conventions that stem from this society's double standard about aging. Instead of being girls, girls as long as possible, who then age humiliatingly into middle aged women and then obscenely into old women, they can become women much earlier—and remain active adults, enjoying the long, erotic career of which women are capable, for longer (Sontag, 1972, p. 38).

## Sexual Activity in Later Years

We have seen that our society tends to perceive the older years as a time when sexuality no longer has a place in people's lives. What does research show about the reality of sexuality among older people in our own society? For many older adults sexuality is part of what makes their lives full and rich. In fact, research indicates that sexual interest and activity continue as a natural part of aging (Beckman et al., 2006; Nusbaum et al., 2005). For some, sexuality can actually improve in later life. Of a representative sample of adults over age 60, 61% of those who were sexually active said that their sex life today was either the same as or more physically satisfying than in their 40s (Dunn & Cutler, 2000). As a 76-year-old woman said:

*When I was married 47 years ago, my husband and I were both 29, and both virgins. I was taught that sex was for procreation only, so the adjustment to each other was not easy. The years of having babies, raising children, and, for my husband (a workaholic), getting established in his profession took much time and energy, and sex was an unimportant part of our lives. Now we are 76 years old and with the gift of time, good health, and financial security, our sex life is wonderful and very much a part of our fulfilling lives—truly, the best years of our lives. (Authors' files)*

The need for affection and sexual intimacy extends into the older years, which can be a time of sharing and closeness.

Research on married women age 50 and older found that their sexual satisfaction correlated with (in descending order of importance) overall marital satisfaction, greater frequency of orgasm for themselves and their spouses, and greater frequency of sexual intercourse and noncoital sexual activity (Young et al., 2000).

A nationally representative survey of men and women age 60 and older found that about half are sexually active. "Sexually active" was defined as engaging in vaginal intercourse, oral sex, anal intercourse, or masturbation at least once a month (Dunn & Cutler, 2000). Many people remain sexually active well into their 80s and even later, adjusting successfully to the physical changes described in Chapter 6 (Budd, 1999). However, the number of people who engage in sexual activity does decline with each decade, as shown in ❍ **Table 13.4**. Furthermore, people who continue to be sexually active are less frequently so over time.

New sexual relationships may also develop in later adulthood (Vasconcellos et al., 2006). A 67-year-old woman explained:

❍ **T A B L E 13.4** **Percentage of Sexually Active Adults**

|  | Men (%) | Women (%) |
| --- | --- | --- |
| Sexually active in their 60s | 71 | 51 |
| Sexually active in their 70s | 57 | 30 |
| Sexually active in their 80s | 25 | 20 |

SOURCE: Dunn & Cutler (2000).

*Eight years after my husband died, I met a widower on a tour of New Orleans. The physical attraction was intense for both of us. Neither of us had had sex for many years, but two days after discovering each other we were in bed with clothes strewn all over the floor. The sex (which neither of us was sure we'd be able to achieve) was sensational. We're very much in love but have decided not to marry because we both love our homes, need "space," and are financially independent. Our children accept our lifestyle and are very happy with our respective "significant other." (Authors' files)*

Many older adults are dating, and one survey found that 22% of men and 14% of women said that finding someone to marry or live with was their most important reason for dating (Kantrowitz, 2006). Nonsexual friendships with people of either sex can offer affectionate physical contact, emotional closeness, intellectual stimulation, and opportunities for socializing (Jacoby, 1999). A supportive network of close friends helps to minimize loneliness and maintain enthusiasm for life (Potts, 1997). In fact, research reveals that people who have contact with close friends—a "family of choice"—live longer than people who rely only on a spouse and children (Tyre, 2006).

Sexual activity of older adults is, unfortunately, evidenced by the rising incidence of HIV/AIDS in this group (Yared, 2004). About 61% of sexually active older singles say they have unprotected sex (Kantrowitz, 2006), and 10% of people older than 50 have one or more risk factors but are unlikely to request testing. Many health-care professionals do not routinely screen for sexually transmitted diseases in seniors, but some public health agencies offer safe-sex seminars to seniors (Levy, 2001; McGinn & Skipp, 2002).

**?** **Critical Thinking Question**

Why are more older men than women highly interested in finding someone to live with or marry?

## Factors in Maintaining Sexual Activity

Kinsey and colleagues' studies (1948, 1953) revealed a close correlation between the level of a person's sexual activity in early adulthood and his or her sexual activity in later years. Other research has also reported a correlation for both sexes between level of sexual activity before middle age and in later years (Bretschneider & McCoy, 1988; Leiblum & Bachmann, 1988). Lifelong consistent sexual activity may reflect an overall higher sex drive and positive attitudes towards sexuality, since both are significant influences on sexual desire and response (DeLamater & Sill, 2005).

Typically the most crucial factor influencing sexual activity in older adulthood is health. Poor health and illness have a greater effect on sexual functioning than age itself. In long-term relationships the poor health of one person is likely to limit the partner's sexual expression as well (Vasconcellos et al., 2006). Besides contributing to general and sexual health, regular physical exercise, a healthy diet and weight, and light or no alcohol use help maintain sexual desire and response (Harvard Health Publications, 2006).

Older adults often find new techniques for maintaining or enhancing their enjoyment of sex despite progressive physiological changes. Oral sex, viewing sexually explicit materials, fantasy, manual stimulation, and use of a vibrator are some of the variations older couples may integrate into their sexual experiences. When genital contact becomes less frequent, interest, pleasure and frequency of nongenital activities, such as kissing, caressing, and embracing, may remain stable or increase (Kellett, 2000). Openness to experimenting and developing new sexual strategies with a supportive partner are instrumental in continuing sexual satisfaction (Bachmann, 1991).

## Homosexual Relationships in Later Years

Most of the challenges and rewards of aging are experienced by adults regardless of sexual orientation. Gay men and lesbians experience some unique aspects to aging. Some gay men and lesbians are better prepared for coping with the adjustments of aging than are many heterosexual men and women, because having faced the adversities of belonging to a stigmatized group throughout their lives may help prepare them to deal with the losses that come with aging (Altman, 1999). In addition, many have created a more extensive network of supportive friends than most heterosexual individuals (Alonzo, 2003; Nystrom & Jones, 2003).

Overall, studies find that older gays and lesbians match or exceed comparable groups in the general population on a measure of life satisfaction (Woolf, 2001). In a study of gay men there was a change over time toward fewer sexual partners, but frequency of sexual activity remained quite stable, and 75% were satisfied with their current sex lives. Most of these men reported that they socialized primarily with same-age peers. Socializing and partnering with same-age peers is likely an important aspect of life satisfaction for older gay men, because the sexual marketplace setting of bars and bathhouses, where youth and physical appearance define desirability, is often inhospitable to older gay men (Berger, 1996).

As a group, older lesbians have some advantages over older heterosexual women (Koch, 2001). Research shows that most older lesbians prefer women of similar age as partners (Daniluk, 1998). Therefore, an older lesbian is less likely to be widowed than is a heterosexual woman, because women tend to live longer than men. If her partner does die, she does not face the limited pool of potentially eligible male partners. Furthermore, women are less likely than men to base attraction on a physical ideal, so the double standard of aging is less of an issue for lesbians than for straight women (Berger, 1996).

Sexual relationships can improve in later years when individuals redefine their sexual and affectional relationships.

## Last Love

People who continue to grow in age can develop a wholeness of self that transcends the limited roles and life experience of youth. Intimacy can then involve a sharing of that integrated multidimensional self (Friedan, 1994; Wales & Todd, 2001). A sex and marital therapist further explains:

The essence of sexual intimacy lies not in mastering specific sexual skills . . . but in the ability to allow oneself to deeply know and to be deeply known by one's partner. So simple to articulate, so difficult to achieve, this ability of couples to really see each other, to see inside each other during sex, requires the courage, integrity, and maturity to face oneself and, even more frightening, convey that self—all that one is capable of feeling and expressing— to the partner. . . . Adult eroticism is more a function of emotional maturation than of physiological responsiveness. (Schnarch, 1993, p. 43)

The real treasure of the "last love" of partners who have experienced enough life to deeply know themselves and each other can make the "first love" of new partners pale by comparison (Schnarch, 1993). As a Turkish proverb comments, "Young love is from the earth, and late love is from heaven" (Koch-Straube, 1982).

## Widowhood

Although a spouse can die during the early or middle-adult years, widowhood usually occurs later in life. In most heterosexual couples the man dies first, a tendency that became more pronounced during the 20th century. There are more than four widows for every widower (U.S. Bureau of the Census, 2002). Older men without partners often seek young female companions, which reduces the pool of potential partners for older heterosexual women.

The postmarital adjustment of widowhood is different in some ways from that of divorce. Widowed people typically do not have the sense of having failed at marriage. The grief may be more intense, and the quality of the emotional bond to the deceased mate is often quite high. For some people this emotional tie remains so strong that other potential relationships appear dim by comparison. However, many people who have lost a spouse through death do remarry—about half of widowed men and one-fourth of widowed women (Lown & Dolan, 1988).

The transition period following the death of a spouse can be very traumatic, but after a period of mourning, many people remarry.

# SUMMARY

## Single Living

- Although single living is often seen as a transition period before, in between, or after marriage, many people choose it as a long-term lifestyle.

- The proportion of individuals who have never married has increased dramatically since 1970 for men and women in their 20s.

## Cohabitation

- Almost 5.5 million couples were cohabiting (living together without marriage) in 2000.
- Cohabitation is most common among people in their 20s.
- Although people who live together before marriage seem to have a higher risk of marital discord and divorce than couples who have not lived together before marriage, the exact effects of cohabitation before marriage remain to be explained.

## Marriage

- Many governments across the globe see marriage in crisis and are attempting to influence its role in shaping society.
- In a unique matriarchal culture in China, women and men live their entire lives in their mothers' homes. A woman chooses the man she is interested in, and he comes to her room in the evening and leaves in the morning for as long as they both feel love and attraction.
- As recently as 1967, interracial marriage was banned in more than a dozen states. Young adults are most accepting of interracial dating and marriage.
- The expectations of marriage to fulfill many needs and the reduced support networks for couples and their children are part of what makes marriage a challenge.
- Research can predict with a high degree of success the probability that a couple will experience marital happiness.
- Married couples are engaging in a wider variety of sexual behaviors than in the past.
- The conflict about legal marriage for same-sex partners centers around questions of discrimination and separation of church and state.

## Extramarital Relationships

- Consensual extramarital relationships occur with a spouse's knowledge and agreement.
- Swinging is a practice in which couples have sexual relations with other couples simultaneously and in the same location.
- The sexually open marriage and polyamory can include emotional, social, and sexual components in an extramarital relationship.
- Nonconsensual extramarital relationships occur without the partner's consent.
- The NHSLS study found that 25% of married men and 15% of married women have had an extramarital involvement at some time during their marriages.
- It is not clear whether problems in a marriage are a cause or a result of a nonconsensual extramarital affair.
- The Internet has made it easier for people to get involved in extramarital affairs, and for spouses to discover the affairs.

## Divorce

- Forty-three percent of first marriages end in divorce within 15 years.
- Divorces increased dramatically from the 1950s to the late 1970s. Since the 1970s there has been about one divorce for every two marriages.
- Some of the causes of the high divorce rate are the liberalization of divorce laws, a reduction in the social stigma attached to divorce, unrealistic expectations for marital and sexual fulfillment, and increased economic independence of women.
- Women tend to report that their husband's problematic behavior led to divorce, and men are more likely to say that they do not know what caused the divorce.
- Divorce typically involves many emotional, sexual, interpersonal, and lifestyle changes and adjustments.

## Sexuality and Aging

- The options for sexual expression change in the older years, and many individuals continue to enjoy their sexual relationships.
- Good physical health is often the most important variable in maintaining sexual functioning and satisfaction.
- Gay men and lesbians may be better prepared to cope with aging, given the adversity they have already learned to face and the extensive network of friendships they have often established.
- Since men tend to die earlier, there are more than four widows for every widower.

## ❿ Suggested Readings

**Coontz, Stephanie** (2005). *Marriage: A History*. New York: Penguin Group. The award-winning author provides a definitive history of the evolution of marriage, from unions arranged by family or politics to acquire wealth, power, and property to the 19th century's ideal of marriage for the fulfillment of love and intimacy.

**Glass, Shirley** (2002). *Not Just Friends*. New York: Free Press. A discussion by an expert on infidelity of the increasingly common relationship that starts as friendship and evolves into a passionate love affair, even when the current marriage is good.

**Gottman, John, and Nan Silver** (2000). *The Seven Principles for Making Marriage Work*. New York: Crown Publishers. A book that combines science and romance and that uses research findings to help couples strengthen their marriages. Includes exercises and checklists from couples' workshops.

**Hetherington, Mavis** (2002). *For Better or for Worse: Divorce Reconsidered*. New York: Norton. A book that presents the results of 40 years of research on 1,400 families and 2,500 children and that concludes that most children and adults do well, or thrive, years following divorce.

**Strauss, Jillian** (2006). *Unhooked Generation: The Truth About Why We're Still Single*. New York: Hyperion. Interviews with 100 single men and women in their 20s and 30s and the commitment-averse by-product of the wireless generation's sense of endless options.

# ▶ Web Resources

**CengageNOW Web Site**
Go to **academic.cengage.com** to link to practice quiz questions, interactive activities, Internet links, critical thinking exercises, discussion forums, and more. You can also access sites from the Wadsworth Psychology Study Center (**academic.cengage.com/psychology**) or you can connect directly to the following sites:

**The Couples Place**
Free information on building and improving relationships is accessible to public visitors of this Web site, and additional resources are available to those who sign up as members.

**DivorceSource**
This Web site provides information on various aspects of divorce, including child support and custody, alimony, and counseling. In addition, there is a divorce dictionary, access to related articles and publications, and live chat rooms.

**Aging and Sexuality Resource Guide**
Recent literature and resources related to issues of aging and sexuality have been compiled on this Web site by the American Psychological Association. Resource directories include books, publications, journals, and organizations.

**Web MD**
Search *sex* and *aging* for numerous articles on various aspects of aging.

*Our Sexuality* **Book Companion Web Site academic.cengage.com/psychology/ crooks** Visit your book companion Web site where you will find flash cards, practice quizzes, Internet links, and more to help you study.

**Just what you need to know NOW!**
Spend time on what you need to master rather than on information you already have learned. Take a pretest for this chapter, and CengageNOW will generate a personalized study plan based on your results. The study plan will identify the topics you need to review and direct you to online resources to help you master those topics. You can then take a post-test to help you determine the concepts you have mastered and what you will still need to work on. Try it out! Go to **academic.cengage.com/login** to sign in with an access code or to purchase access to this product.

**InfoTrac College Edition Online Library**
Sign in to **academic.cengage.com/login** or visit your free book companion Web site at **academic.cengage.com/psychology/crooks** to access InfoTrac College Edition, an online searchable library that includes a multitude of journals, many specific to human sexuality. These journals include *Archives of Sexual Behavior; Archives of Sexual Health Behavior; Canadian Journal of Human Sexuality; Hispanic Journal of the Behavioral Sciences; Journal of Cross-Cultural Psychology; Journal of Physical Education, Recreation, and Dance; Journal of Sex Research;* and *Sex Roles.*

# Sexual Difficulties and Solutions

Ray Kachatorian/Getty Images

*I wish my first time had been better. I would have had sex with someone I at least liked, instead of just with someone who would do it with me. We were both pretty drunk, but not drunk enough to forget how fast I came. Word got around about it, and I avoided sex for a long time. My first girlfriend after that was cool about it, and after a while I could relax and last longer. (Authors' files)*

Sexual health, "a state of physical, emotional, mental, and sexual well-being related to sexuality," goes beyond identifying and treating sexual problems (Sadovsky & Nussbaum, 2006, p. 3). This definition of sexual health by the World Health Organization is what guides us in this chapter's discussion about a number of relatively common sexual problems, the factors that frequently contribute to them, and self-help and sex therapy approaches to help resolve sexual difficulties. Research indicates that sexual problems are quite common. The prevalence of sexual problems in the sample of the National Health and Social Life Survey (NHSLS) is shown in ◗ **Table 14.1**. However, individuals who say they are having a sexual problem may not always feel distressed and sexually dissatisfied. For example, the NHSLS found that 43% of women stated that they experienced some type of sexual dysfunction. However, a subsequent random phone survey (less rigorous than the NHSLS) by the Kinsey Institute also asked women subjects whether they considered their lack of interest, arousal, or orgasm to be a problem. Slightly over 24% of the subjects reported distress about their sexual dysfunction (Bancroft et al., 2003b). The Kinsey Institute study found that women were most likely to report distress about sex when they reported poor personal emotional well-being and a negative emotional relationship with their partners. Research does indicate that sexual problems can have an impact on overall well-being. People with sexual problems report lower satisfaction with overall life than those without sexual difficulties (Hellstrom et al., 2006; Mallis et al., 2006).

◗ **TABLE 14.1** | **Prevalence of Sexual Problems by Selected Demographic Characteristics**

| | Lack Interest in Sex Women (%) | Men (%) | Cannot Achieve Orgasm Women (%) | Men (%) | Erectile Dysfunction (Men) (%) | Pain During Sex (Women) (%) | Climax Too Early (Men) (%) |
|---|---|---|---|---|---|---|---|
| **Age[a]** | | | | | | | |
| 18–29 | 32 | 14 | 26 | 7 | 7 | 21 | 30 |
| 30–39 | 32 | 13 | 28 | 7 | 9 | 15 | 32 |
| 40–49 | 30 | 15 | 22 | 9 | 11 | 13 | 28 |
| 50–59 | 27 | 17 | 23 | 9 | 18 | 8 | 31 |
| **Education** | | | | | | | |
| Less than high school | 42 | 19 | 34 | 11 | 13 | 18 | 38 |
| High-school graduate | 33 | 12 | 29 | 7 | 9 | 17 | 35 |
| College graduate | 24 | 14 | 18 | 7 | 10 | 10 | 27 |

[a]Sexual problems are most common among younger women and older men.
SOURCE: Laumann et al. (1999).

As you read this chapter, it is important to remember that sexual satisfaction is a subjective perception and an important component in defining a sexual problem (Gierhart, 2006; Shabsigh, 2006). A person or couple could experience sexual problems and yet be satisfied with their sex lives, or they could experience no problems and be very dissatisfied with their sexual experiences (Basson et al., 2003; Smith, 2003). ◗ **Figure 14.1** on the following page shows how men and women around the world rate the pleasure of sexual interaction. For readers currently in a sexual relationship, the self-assessment inventory in the Your Sexual Health box will give you an indication of your level of satisfaction.

## Index of Sexual Satisfaction

For readers who are sexually involved, this questionnaire is designed to measure the degree of satisfaction you have in the sexual relationship with your partner. It is not a test, so there are no right or wrong answers. Answer each item as carefully and accurately as you can by placing a number beside each one according to the following scale:

1 Rarely or none of the time
2 A little of the time
3 Some of the time
4 A good part of the time
5 Most or all of the time

1. I feel that my partner enjoys our sex life. _____
2. My sex life is very exciting. _____
3. Sex is fun for my partner and me. _____
4. I feel that my partner sees little in me except for the sex I can give. _____
5. I feel that sex is dirty and disgusting. _____
6. My sex life is monotonous. _____
7. When we have sex, it is too rushed and hurriedly completed. _____
8. I feel that my sex life is lacking in quality. _____
9. My partner is sexually very exciting. _____
10. I enjoy the sex techniques that my partner likes or uses. _____
11. I feel that my partner wants too much sex from me. _____
12. I think sex is wonderful. _____
13. My partner dwells on sex too much. _____
14. I try to avoid sexual contact with my partner. _____

15. My partner is too rough or brutal when we have sex. _____
16. My partner is a wonderful sex mate. _____
17. I feel that sex is a normal function of our relationship. _____
18. My partner does not want sex when I do. _____
19. I feel that our sex life really adds a lot to our relationship. _____
20. My partner seems to avoid sexual contact with me. _____
21. It is easy for me to get sexually excited by my partner. _____
22. I feel that my partner is sexually pleased with me. _____
23. My partner is very sensitive to my sexual needs and desires. _____
24. My partner does not satisfy me sexually. _____
25. I feel that my sex life is boring. _____

**Scoring:** Items 1, 2, 3, 9, 10, 12, 16, 17, 19, 21, 22, and 23 must be reverse-scored. (For example, if you answered 5 on one of these items, you would change that score to 1.) After these positively worded items have been reverse-scored, if there are no omitted items, the score is computed by summing the individual item scores and subtracting 25. This assessment has been shown to be valid and reliable.

**Interpretation:** Scores can range from 0 to 100, with a high score indicative of sexual dissatisfaction. A score of 30 or above is indicative of dissatisfaction in one's sexual relationship.

SOURCE: Adapted from Hudson et al. (1992).

○ **Figure 14.1** Men and women worldwide were asked, "How physically pleasurable is your relationship?" The Pfizer Global Study of Sexual Attitudes and Behaviors, the first worldwide study of its kind, surveyed more than 26,000 men and women in 29 countries around the globe.

SOURCE: From Global Study of Sexual Attitudes and Behaviors funded by Pfizer Inc. Copyright 2002 Pfizer Inc.

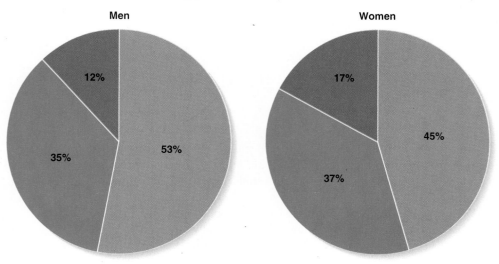

How physically pleasurable is your relationship?

■ Extremely or very     ■ Moderately     ■ Slightly or not at all

# Specific Sexual Difficulties

In this section, we consider some of the specific problems that people encounter with desire, excitement, orgasm, and pain during intercourse. In reality, there is considerable overlap: Problems with desire and arousal also affect orgasm, and orgasm difficulties can easily affect a person's interest and ability to become aroused. For example, about 44% of men who have problems with experiencing erections also frequently ejaculate rapidly (Fisher et al., 2006). In addition, the line between "normal" and a "disorder" remains unclearly defined in clinical practice (Althof et al., 2005). For example, how many times would a man need to have difficulty with his erections to have erectile disorder? In what context would not being able to become erect be normal?

The sexual problems that we will discuss also vary in duration and focus from one person to another. A specific difficulty can occur throughout life (*lifelong sexual disorder*) or be acquired at a specific time (*acquired sexual disorder*). A person can experience the problem in all situations with all partners (*generalized type*) or only in specific situations or with specific partners (*situational type*) (American Psychiatric Association, 2000). The categories and labels for the problems that we discuss come from the *Second International Consultation on Sexual Medicine: Sexual Dysfunctions in Men and Women* (Lue et al., 2004a) and the American Psychiatric Association's *Diagnostic and Statistical Manual* (DSM-IV); we have added a few categories and labels of our own.

To be accurately considered a sexual disorder, a difficulty must occur in the context of adequate physical and psychological sexual stimulation. Research findings that highlight the importance of physical stimulation report that women who routinely experience orgasm engage in a relatively greater repertoire of sexual techniques than women who do not reliably experience orgasm (Fugl-Meyer et al., 2006). On the other side of the coin, a man who ejaculates quickly after his partner demands, "Hurry up and get it over with!" is not receiving adequate physical and psychological stimulation and cannot be considered to have a problem with premature ejaculation from that situation alone. In another example, a diagnosis of lack of sexual desire would be inappropriate for a woman whose partner continually pressures her to be sexual in ways that he likes but that she does not enjoy or find arousing.

**? Critical Thinking Question**

In what situations would you consider it normal for a man to lose his erection? In what context would you consider his difficulty with erections to be a disorder?

**Hypoactive sexual desire disorder (HSDD)** Lack of interest prior to and during sexual activity.

## Desire-Phase Difficulties

In this section, we discuss inhibited sexual desire, dissatisfaction with frequency of sexual activity, and sexual aversion.

### Hypoactive Sexual Desire Disorder

**Hypoactive sexual desire disorder (HSDD)** is the absence or minimal experience of sexual thoughts, fantasies, and interest *prior to* sexual activity, as well as a lack of sexual desire *during* the sexual experience (Basson et al., 2004). Many men and women who do not experience a "sexual appetite" do enjoy and become aroused by and desirous of a sexual experience after it has begun. Until recently, HSDD was defined exclusively by lack of sexual interest, thoughts, and fantasies outside of sexual activity. In those terms, it is a common sexual difficulty experienced by both men and women and is the most frequent problem that brings people to seek sex therapy (Giargiari et al., 2005; McCarthy, 2006). Although desire difficulties are the most common sexual difficulty experienced by women (Hayes et al., 2006) (see Table 14.1), by the late 1990s some sex therapy clinics saw equal numbers of men and women with low sexual desire (Pridal & LoPiccolo, 2000).

### Dissatisfaction With Frequency of Sexual Activity

Sexual partners usually have discrepancies in their preferences for amount, type, and timing of sexual activities. Male/female differences stand out when it comes to frequency: The 2005 Global Sex Survey found that 41% of men and 29%

Hypoactive sexual desire frequently reflects relationship problems.

of women want sex more frequently (Durex, 2006). Sometimes the relationship can accommodate these individual differences. However, when sexual differences are a source of significant conflict or dissatisfaction, a couple can experience considerable distress. Instead of moving toward some compromise, the couple polarizes, and each individual believes that his or her partner either "never" or "always" wants to be sexual.

## Sexual Aversion Disorder

A fear of sex and a compelling desire to avoid sexual situations are considered a **sexual aversion disorder**. Sexual aversion can range from feelings of discomfort, repulsion, and disgust to an extreme irrational fear of sexual activity. Even the thought of sexual contact can result in intense anxiety and panic. A person who experiences sexual aversion exhibits physiological symptoms such as sweating, increased heart rate, nausea, dizziness, trembling, or diarrhea as a consequence of fear.

## Excitement-Phase Difficulties

Inhibited sexual excitement occurs when physiological arousal, erotic sensation, or the subjective feeling of being turned on is chronically diminished or absent. Excitement-phase disorders among women take the form of lack of vaginal lubrication or lack of subjective awareness of physical arousal (Basson, 2002), whereas in men an inability to achieve or maintain erection is typical.

## Female Sexual Arousal Disorder

As we saw in Chapters 4 and 6, vaginal lubrication is a woman's first physiological response to sexual arousal. The persistent inability to attain or maintain the lubrication-swelling response indicates **female genital sexual arousal disorder**. In contrast, **female subjective sexual arousal disorder** is indicated when physical signs of arousal are present but feelings of sexual excitement and pleasure are absent or markedly diminished. **Combined genital and subjective sexual arousal disorder** is a combination of both disorders (Basson et al., 2004).

## Persistent Sexual Arousal Disorder

**Persistent sexual arousal disorder** is spontaneous, intrusive, and unwanted genital arousal—tingling, throbbing, pulsating—in the absence of sexual interest. One or more orgasms do not relieve the uncomfortable feelings of arousal, and the arousal can persist for hours or days (Basson, 2004). This disorder was first identified in 2001, and health-care practitioners have diagnosed about 400 women since then. The women who are evaluated for this disorder have normal findings from physiological and psychiatric evaluations. The causes and treatment for this disorder are unknown and appear to be unique to each individual (Lieblum & Nathan, 2002).

## Male Erectile Disorder

**Erectile disorder (ED)** is defined as the consistent or recurrent inability over at least 3 months to have or maintain an erection sufficient for sexual activity (Lue et al., 2004b). An estimated one in five men older than 20 years experience ED, and ED is a frequent reason that men seek sex therapy (Saigal et al., 2006). The incidence of ED increases with age, as shown in ● **Figure 14.2**. A man in his 50s is over two times more likely to experience erection problems than a man in his 20s.

Special procedures have been developed to evaluate physical factors in erection problems. Some techniques involve recording erection patterns during sleep, because erections normally occur during this time. Other instruments measure penile blood pressure and flow to determine whether erectile difficulties are caused by vascular problems. Injections of medications that produce erections can also be used to detect possible

**Sexual aversion disorder** Extreme and irrational fear of sexual activity.

**Female genital sexual arousal disorder** Persistent inability to attain or maintain the lubrication-swelling response.

**Female subjective sexual arousal disorder** Absent or diminished awareness of physical arousal.

**Combined genital and subjective sexual arousal disorder** Absent or diminished subjective and physical sexual arousal.

**Persistent sexual arousal disorder** Spontaneous, intrusive, and unwanted genital arousal.

**Erectile dysfunction (ED)** Consistent or recurring lack of an erection sufficiently rigid for penetrative sex, for a period of at least 3 months.

○ **Figure 14.2** The incidence of erectile disorder related to age (Kim & Lipshultz, 1997).

difficulties: If no erection occurs following an injection, then vascular impairment is likely (Lue et al., 2004b).

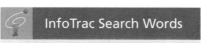

## Orgasm-Phase Difficulties

Other sexual difficulties specifically affect orgasmic response, and both men and women report a variety of such difficulties. Some of these difficulties involve total absence or infrequency of orgasms. Others involve reaching orgasm too rapidly or too slowly. We also consider faking orgasm to be problematic.

## Female Orgasmic Disorder

**Female orgasmic disorder** means the absence, marked delay, or diminished intensity of orgasm, despite high subjective arousal from any type of stimulation (Basson et al., 2004). About 5–10% of adult women in the United States have never experienced orgasm by any means of self- or partner stimulation, but data indicate that the number of women who have never experienced orgasm has decreased (LoPiccolo, 2000). This apparent decrease may be due to excellent self-help books and videos that are now available for women who want to learn to experience orgasm.

A woman who has *situational female orgasmic disorder* is orgasmic when masturbating but not when stimulated by a partner. Women who have experienced orgasm sometimes have difficulty doing so: About 25% of women reported having problems with orgasm within the last year (Laumann et al., 1994). Women most likely to experience difficulty with orgasm are unmarried and younger and have less education than women without problems with orgasm (Laumann et al., 1999). For many women, experiencing orgasm is something they learn to do: One survey found that almost 62% of women were 18 years old or older when they first experienced orgasm (Ellison, 2000). ◗ **Table 14.2** shows the incidence of orgasm in college students.

**Female orgasmic disorder** The absence, marked delay, or diminished intensity of orgasm.

◗ **TABLE 14.2** College Students Answer the Question "Have You Ever Had an Orgasm?"

|  | Female (%) | Male (%) |
| --- | --- | --- |
| Yes | 87 | 94 |
| No | 13 | 6 |

SOURCE: Elliott & Brantley (1997).

## Female Orgasm During Intercourse

Most sex therapists believe that women who enjoy intercourse and experience orgasm in some way other than during coitus do not have a sexual problem (Hamilton, 2002; LoPiccolo, 2000). Many more women experience orgasm from masturbation, manual stimulation by a partner, and oral sex than women who experience it during intercourse (Fugl-Meyer et al., 2006). For many women the stimulation that occurs during coitus is simply less effective than direct manual or oral stimulation of the clitoral area (Bancroft, 2002). As sex therapist pioneer Helen Kaplan stated, "There are millions of women who are sexually responsive, and often multiply orgasmic, but who cannot have an orgasm during intercourse unless they receive simultaneous clitoral stimulation" (1974, p. 397). Unfortunately, women and men may not always understand this: A Canadian study found that 23% of the women in the study identified infrequent orgasm during intercourse as a problem (Gruszecki et al., 2005).

## Male Orgasmic Disorder

The term **male orgasmic disorder** generally refers to the inability of a man to ejaculate during sexual activity. Eight percent of men experience this difficulty (Laumann et al., 1994). *Male coital anorgasmia* (difficulty with orgasm only during intercourse) and *partner anorgasmia* (difficulty with orgasm by partner manual and oral stimulation) are more-descriptive terms than the more general term *male orgasmic disorder* (Apfelbaum, 2000).

**Male orgasmic disorder** The inability of a man to ejaculate during sexual stimulation from his partner.

## Premature Ejaculation

The most common male sexual difficulty is **premature ejaculation (PE)** (Hellstrom et al., 2006). Premature ejaculation is a pattern of quick ejaculations (under two minutes) combined with a man's inability to consistently control, to his or his partner's satisfaction, when he has an orgasm (Sharlip, 2006; Waldinger & Schweitzer, 2006).

**Premature ejaculation (PE)** A pattern of ejaculations within 2 minutes and an inability to delay ejaculation, resulting in a man's impairing his or his partner's pleasure.

Almost all men ejaculate quickly in their first intercourse experience, which may be disappointing but should not be seen as a sexual problem unless it continues. In general, approximately 20–30% of men worldwide aged 18 to 59 repeatedly experience PE (Broderick, 2006), and about 30% of those men ejaculate early without a full erection (Lue et al., 2004). Research indicates that men with PE underestimate the intensity of their physical arousal, experience rapid high arousal to penile stimulation, ejaculate before reaching full sexual arousal, and report less enjoyment of orgasm than men who do not have problems with rapid ejaculation. These factors indicate some degree of physiological involvement (Rowland et al., 2000).

## Faking Orgasms

A final orgasmic difficulty we discuss is faking orgasms—pretending to experience orgasm without actually doing so. Some men fake orgasm, but it is typically discussed in reference to women, and it happens quite often, as shown in ⊙ **Table 14.3**. The most common reason given by women for pretending orgasm is to avoid disappointing or hurting their partners (Ellison, 2000). Some additional factors related to faking orgasm include a desire to get sex over with, poor communication or limited knowledge of sexual techniques, a need for partner approval, and an attempt to hide a deteriorating relationship (Ellison, 2000; Lauersen & Graves, 1984).

Faking orgasm often leads to a vicious cycle. The person's partner is likely not to know that his or her partner has pretended to climax. Consequently, the deceived partner continues to do what he or she has been led to believe is effective, and the other partner continues to fake to prevent discovery of the deception. Once established, a pattern of deception can be difficult to break. Although some women and men find faking orgasm to be an acceptable solution in their individual situations, others find that faking itself becomes troublesome. At the least, faking orgasms creates emotional distance at a time of potential closeness and satisfaction (Ellison, 2000; Masters & Johnson, 1976).

⊙ **TABLE 14.3** College Students Answer the Question "Have You Ever Faked an Orgasm?"

| | Female Heterosexual (%) | Lesbian or Bisexual Female (%) | Male Heterosexual (%) | Gay or Bisexual Male (%) |
|---|---|---|---|---|
| Yes | 60 | 71 | 17 | 27 |
| No | 40 | 29 | 83 | 73 |

SOURCE: Elliott & Brantley (1997).

# Dyspareunia

**Dyspareunia** Pain or discomfort during sexual intercourse.

The medical term for painful intercourse is **dyspareunia** (dis-puh-ROO-nee-uh). Both men and women can experience coital pain, although it is more common for women to have this problem.

## Dyspareunia in Men

**Peyronie's disease** Abnormal fibrous tissue and calcium deposits in the penis.

Painful intercourse in men is unusual but does occur. If the foreskin of an uncircumcised male is too tight, he can experience pain during an erection. Under such circumstances minor surgery may be indicated. Inadequate hygiene of an uncircumcised penis can result in the accumulation of smegma or infections beneath the foreskin, causing irritation of the glans during sexual stimulation. This problem can be prevented by routinely pulling back the foreskin and washing the glans area with soap and water. Problems and infections of the urethra, bladder, prostate gland, or seminal vesicles can induce burning, itching, or pain during or after ejaculation (Davis & Noble, 1991). Proper medical attention can generally alleviate this source of discomfort during coitus.

Another possible source of pain or discomfort for men is **Peyronie's disease** (PAY-run-eez), in which fibrous tissue and calcium deposits develop in the space above and between the cavernous bodies of the penis. This fibrosis results in pain and curvature of the penis upon erection that can interfere with erection and even intercourse. Peyronie's disease is usually caused by traumatic bending of the penis during intercourse or by medical procedures involving the urethra (Gholami et al., 2003; Johnson et al., 2002). There are medical treatments that can sometimes be effective in addressing this condition (Castro et al., 2003).

# Dyspareunia in Women

Experiencing pain with partial vaginal entry and/or intercourse is common among women. At least 60% of women experience dyspareunia at some point in their lives (Jones et al., 1997). If it is severe and ongoing, it is likely to create severe distress in a woman's sexual experiences (Petersen et al., 2006). Discomfort at the vaginal entrance or inside the vaginal walls is commonly caused by inadequate arousal and lubrication. Physiological conditions such as insufficient hormones can reduce lubrication. Using a lubricating jelly can provide a temporary solution so that intercourse can take place comfortably, but this may bring only short-term relief. A permanent solution is more likely if a woman discovers the cause of her discomfort and takes steps to remedy the situation.

A variety of other factors can cause vaginal discomfort during intercourse. Yeast, bacterial, and trichomoniasis infections cause inflammations of the vaginal walls and can result in painful intercourse. Foam, contraceptive cream or jelly, condoms, and diaphragms can irritate the vaginas of some women. Pain at the opening of the vagina can also be attributed to an intact or inadequately ruptured hymen, a Bartholin's gland infection, or scar tissue at the opening (Kellog-Spadt, 2006). If smegma collects under the clitoral hood it can irritate the clitoris when the hood is moved during sexual stimulation. Gentle washing of the clitoris and hood can help prevent this.

About 10% of women experience severe pain at the entrance of the vagina known as **vulvar vestibulitis syndrome**, and this may be the most common cause of painful intercourse (Connor & Robinson, 2006; Pukall, 2005; Zolnoun et al., 2006). Typically, a small reddened area is painfully sensitive, even to light pressure, but the area may be so small that it is difficult for even a health-care practitioner to see. Treatment options include topical medicines and surgery to excise the hypersensitive area (Goldstein et al., 2006).

**Vulvar vestibulitis syndrome** A small area at the entrance of the vagina that causes severe pain.

Pain deep in the pelvis during coital thrusting can be due to jarring of the ovaries or stretching of the uterine ligaments. A woman may experience this type of discomfort only in certain positions or at certain times in her menstrual cycle, usually during ovulation or menstruation. If the woman controls positions and pelvic movements during coitus, she can avoid what is painful. Another source of deep pelvic pain is endometriosis, a condition in which tissue that normally grows on the walls of the uterus implants on various parts of the abdominal cavity. This extra tissue can prevent internal organs from moving freely, resulting in pain during coitus. Birth control pills are sometimes prescribed to control the buildup of tissue during the monthly cycle (Reiter & Milburn, 1994).

Gynecological surgeries for uterine and ovarian cancer can also cause dyspareunia. Infections in the uterus, such as those from gonorrhea, can also result in painful intercourse. In fact, pelvic pain is often the first physical symptom noticed by a woman who has gonorrhea. If the infection has caused considerable scar tissue to develop, surgery may be necessary. Childbirth and rape can tear the ligaments that hold the uterus in the pelvic cavity, and such damage can result in pain during coitus. Surgery can relieve this difficulty partially or completely.

# Vaginismus

**Vaginismus** (vah-juh-NIZ-mus) is characterized by strong involuntary contractions of the muscles in the outer third of the vagina. These contractions make attempts to insert a penis into the vagina extremely uncomfortable or painful for a woman. The painful contractions of vaginismus are a conditioned, involuntary response, usually preceded by a history of painful intercourse (van Lankveld et al., 2006). A woman with vaginismus usually experiences the same contracting spasms during a pelvic exam (Weiss, 2001). Even the insertion of a finger into her vagina can cause great discomfort. It is important for women and their partners to know that intercourse, tampon use, and pelvic exams should not be uncomfortable. If they are uncomfortable, it is essential to investigate the cause of the discomfort.

**Vaginismus** Involuntary spasmodic contractions of the muscles of the outer third of the vagina.

It is important to note that although a woman who experiences vaginismus can learn to prevent the contractions, she does not consciously will them to occur. In fact, the deliberate effort to overcome the problem by having intercourse despite the pain can have just the opposite effect, contributing to a vicious cycle that makes the vaginismus worse.

Some women who experience vaginismus are sexually responsive and orgasmic with manual and oral stimulation, but others are unable to experience desire and arousal (Leiblum, 2000). Because many heterosexual couples regard coitus as a highly important component of their sexual relationship, vaginismus typically causes great concern, even if the couple is sexually involved in other ways.

# Origins of Sexual Difficulties

In the following paragraphs, we examine some of the physiological, cultural, individual, and relational factors that can contribute to sexual difficulties. Significant interaction among these factors also occurs. For example, any degree of physiological impairment can make a person's sexual response and functioning more vulnerable to disruption by negative emotions or situations. Thus a man with moderate diabetes may have no difficulty achieving an erection when he is rested and feeling comfortable with his partner, but he may be unable to do so when he is under stress—after a hard day at work or after an argument with his partner. It is also important to keep in mind that it is usually difficult to identify a consistent cause of a specific sexual difficulty because one factor may cause a problem for one person but not for another (LoPiccolo, 1989).

## Physiological Factors

Physiological factors often play a role in sexual problems, so it is often desirable to have a general physical and a gynecological or urological exam to help rule out such causes. Hormonal, vascular, and neurological problems can contribute to sexual disorders (Beckman et al., 2006). Recent research suggests that individual variations, such as sensitivity to touch, can contribute to sexual disorders. For example, some men with a rapid ejaculation problem may have an innate biological hypersensitivity that causes them to ejaculate quickly (Metz & McCarthy, 2004; Salonia et al., 2006; Waldinger & Schweitzer, 2006). Evidence also suggests that some women with difficulty becoming sexually aroused have lower levels of general sensitivity to touch (Frohlich & Meston, 2005). Research on sexual function continues to increase knowledge about the physiological aspects of sexual problems. At this time, more is known about the effects of illnesses, medications, and disabilities on male sexuality than on female sexuality because of the greater amount of research that has been conducted on male sexual function (Bancroft, 2002).

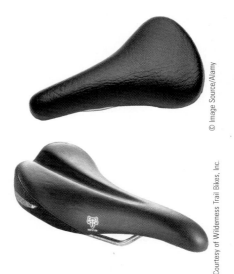

Unfortunately, the aerobic and strength-building benefits of bicycle riding can come at a cost to sexual functioning. Pressure on the genitals from the seat can damage nerves and impair blood flow, resulting in sexual problems. Active cyclists can get genital-friendly bike seats to prevent problems (Carr, 2006).

*© Image Source/Alamy*

*Courtesy of Wilderness Trail Bikes, Inc.*

### Good Health Habits = Good Sexual Functioning

Good health is closely tied to sexual health. A healthy diet and exercise that result in a normal weight form the foundation of sex drive and functioning. For example, body fat, especially around the abdomen, reduces testosterone levels (the sex drive hormone) in men. A study of over 22,000 healthy men over 14 years found that men who were obese were 90% more likely to develop erectile disorder. In contrast, men with the highest exercise levels were 30% less likely than other men to develop ED (Bacon et al., 2006).

Avoiding the use of recreational drugs is another health habit that can contribute to sexual functioning. For example, women who do not smoke, who have a history of moderate or less alcohol use, and who are a healthy weight are much less likely to have sexual dissatisfaction and disorders than those with the opposite characteristics (Addis et al., 2006). Tobacco use can have a dramatic negative effect on male sexual functioning: Men who smoke are five times more likely to have erectile difficulties than men who do not smoke (Manecke & Mulhall, 1999). ○ **Table 14.4** lists other recreational drugs that can impair sexual functioning.

### Chronic Illness

Many of us will confront chronic illness in ourselves or our partners at some point in our lives. The illness may impair the nerves, hormones, or blood flow essential to sex-

**⊙ TABLE 14.4** Sexual Effects of Some Abused and Illicit Drugs

| Drug | Effects |
| --- | --- |
| Alcohol | Chronic alcohol abuse causes hormonal alterations (reduces size of testes and suppresses hormonal function) and permanently damages the circulatory and nervous systems. |
| Marijuana | Reduces testosterone levels in men and decreases sexual desire in both sexes. |
| Tobacco | Adversely affects small blood vessels in the penis and decreases the frequency and duration of erections (Mannino et al., 1994). |
| Cocaine | Causes erectile disorder and inhibits orgasm in both sexes. |
| Amphetamines | High doses and chronic use result in inhibition of orgasm and decrease in erection and lubrication. |
| Barbiturates | Cause decreased desire, erectile disorders, and delayed orgasm. |

SOURCE: Finger et al. (1997).

A limp cigarette makes a graphic statement about the detrimental effects of smoking on sexual functioning.

ual functioning. Some medications for the illness can also negatively affect sexual interest and response. Any accompanying pain and fatigue can distract from erotic thoughts and sensations or limit specific sexual activities (Schover, 2000). For example, erectile dysfunction is often associated with diabetes, high blood pressure, and cardiovascular problems. In fact, when men are unable to experience erections, health-care practitioners often see the sexual problem as a predictor of these serious medical problems (Jackson et al., 2006; Montorsi et al., 2006; Strachan-Bennett, 2006). In contrast, research indicates that men who experience erections but have difficulty maintaining them are more likely to have a psychological cause behind the problem (Corona et al., 2006).

The following paragraphs describe the sexual effects of specific illnesses:

**Diabetes** Diabetes is a disease of the endocrine system that results when the pancreas fails to secrete adequate amounts of insulin. Nerve damage and circulatory problems from diabetes cause about 50% of diabetic men to have a reduction in or loss of capacity for erection. Some diabetic men experience retrograde ejaculation (ejaculating into the bladder) (Manecke & Mulhall, 1999). Heavy alcohol use and poor blood sugar control increase the chances of erectile problems in diabetic men (Romeo et al., 2000). Women with diabetes are likely to have problems with sexual desire, lubrication, and orgasm (Herter, 1998).

**Cancer** Cancer and its treatment can be particularly devastating to sexuality because they can impair hormonal, vascular, and neurological functions necessary for normal sexual interest and response. Chemotherapy and radiation therapy can cause hair loss, skin changes, nausea, and fatigue—all of which can negatively affect sexual feelings (Incrocci, 2006). Some cancer surgeries result in permanent scars, loss of body parts, or an ostomy (a surgically created opening for evacuation of body wastes after removal of the colon or bladder)—all of which can result in a negative body image (Burt, 1995). Pain from the cancer or its treatments can also greatly interfere with sexual interest and arousal (Fleming & Pace, 2001).

Although all forms of cancer can affect sexual functioning, cancers of the reproductive organs often have the worst impact. For example, men who have had prostate cancer experience the absence or significant reduction of ejaculation and are 10 to 15 times more likely to experience sexual problems because of treatment (Glina, 2006; Harvard Health Publications, 2006).

**Multiple Sclerosis** Multiple sclerosis (MS) is a neurological disease of the brain and spinal cord in which damage occurs to the myelin sheath that covers nerve fibers. Vision, sensation, and voluntary movement are affected. Studies have found that most MS patients experience changes in their sexual functioning and that at least half have sexual problems (Stenager et al., 1990). A person with MS can experience either a reduction or a loss of sexual interest, genital sensation, arousal, or orgasm; he or she can also experience uncomfortable hypersensitivity to genital stimulation (Smeltzer & Kelley, 1997).

**Strokes** Strokes, or cerebrovascular accidents, occur when brain tissue is destroyed as a result of either blockage of the blood supply to the brain or hemorrhage (breakage of a vessel, causing internal bleeding). Strokes often result in limited mobility, altered or lost sensation, impairment of verbal communication, and depression. Stroke survivors frequently report a decline in their frequency of sexual interest, arousal, and activity (Giaquinto et al., 2003).

## Medication Effects on Sexual Functioning

At least 200 prescription and nonprescription medications have negative effects on sexuality (Finger et al., 2000). As much as 25% of cases of ED are related to medication side effects (T. Miller, 2000). Health-care practitioners do not always discuss potential sexual side effects of medications, so you may need to ask about the possible effects of any prescribed medicines on sexuality. Often another medication can be substituted that will have fewer or milder negative effects on sexual interest, arousal, and orgasm (Kennedy et al., 2000; Segraves & Kavoussi, 2000).

**Psychiatric Medications** Antidepressants commonly cause reduced sexual interest and arousal and delayed or absent orgasm in up to 60% of users (Kantrowitz & Wingert, 2005). The use of the antidepressant Wellbutrin (bupropion) or of Viagra or ginkgo biloba (240–900 mg a day) can sometimes reverse sexual side effects from antidepressants (Holman, 2003). Antipsychotic medications frequently cause lack of desire and erection and delay or absence of ejaculation and orgasm, and tranquilizers such as Valium and Xanax can interfere with orgasmic response.

**Antihypertensive Medications** Medications prescribed for high blood pressure can cause problems with desire, arousal, and orgasm. Some hypertension medications are more likely than others to have negative sexual effects (Meston et al., 1997).

**Miscellaneous Medications** Prescription gastrointestinal and antihistamine medications can interfere with desire and arousal function. Methadone can cause decreased desire, arousal disorder, lack of orgasm, and delayed ejaculation. Some over-the-counter antihistamines, motion sickness remedies, and gastrointestinal medications have been associated with desire and erection problems.

## Disabilities

Major disabilities, such as spinal cord injury, cerebral palsy, blindness, and deafness, have widely varying effects on sexual responsiveness. Some people with these disabilities can maintain or restore satisfying sex lives; others find that their sexual expression is permanently reduced or impaired by their difficulties (Welner, 1997). In the following sections, we look at some of these problems and discuss sexual adjustments that people with disabilities can make.

**Spinal Cord Injury** People with spinal cord injuries (SCIs) have reduced motor control and sensation because the damage to the spinal cord obstructs the neural pathways between body and brain. Although the SCI does not necessarily impair sexual desire and psychological arousal, a person with a SCI may have impaired physical ability for arousal and orgasm; this impairment varies greatly according to the specific injury. In the documentary *Murderball* quadriplegic rugby players express enthusiasm about their sex lives and talk openly about how they work around their limitations. According to recent research, 86% of men and women with SCIs feel sexual desire, more than half experience arousal from physical stimulation, about 30% become aroused from psychological stimulation, and 33% experience orgasm or ejaculation (Matieu et al., 2005). Research has found that Viagra can increase arousal and erection for men with SCIs (De Forge et al., 2005).

Cutting-edge research on women with complete spinal cord injuries has found that vaginal/cervical self-stimulation can cause orgasm. Brain imaging techniques that have identified brain activity occurring during orgasm in uninjured women have identified similar activity from vaginal/cervical self-stimulation in women with complete spinal injuries. The physiological data indicate that the vagus nerve provides an alternate pathway from the vagina/cervix to the brain, bypassing the spinal cord (Whipple & Komisaruk, 2005).

Much of the sex counseling for individuals and couples faced with SCIs consists of redefining and expanding sexual expression. Thus, *sensory amplification*—developing heightened sexual responsiveness in the inner arm, breasts, neck, or some other area that has retained some feeling—can enhance pleasure and arousal.

**Cerebral Palsy** Cerebral palsy (CP) is caused by damage to the brain that can occur before or during birth or during early childhood. It is characterized by mild to severe lack of muscular control. Involuntary muscle movements can disrupt speech, facial expressions, balance, and body movement. Severe involuntary muscle contractions can cause limbs to jerk or assume awkward positions. A person's intelligence may or may not be affected. Unfortunately, it is often mistakenly assumed that people with CP have low intelligence because of their physical difficulty in communicating.

Genital sensation is unaffected by CP. However, spasticity and deformity of arms and hands can make masturbation difficult or impossible without assistance, and the same problems in the hips and knees can make certain intercourse positions painful or difficult (Joseph, 1991). For women with CP, chronic contraction of the muscles surrounding the vaginal opening can create pain during intercourse (Renshaw, 1987). Options that can help individuals with CP include trying different positions, propping legs up on pillows to ease spasms, and exploring nongenital lovemaking. Partners can help with positions, and focusing on genital pleasure can help to distract from pain. The sexual adjustment of a person with CP depends not only on what is physically possible but also on environmental support for social contacts and privacy. People with CP and SCIs may require the help of someone who can assist in preparation and positioning for sexual relations.

**Blindness and Deafness** The sensory losses of blindness and deafness can affect a person's sexuality primarily when the visual or hearing deficits interfere with learning the subtleties of social interaction skills and with a person's independence (Mona & Gardos, 2000). Sexually, other senses can play an expanded role, as a man who was born blind explained:

> During lovemaking, my other senses—touch, smell, hearing, and taste—serve as the primary way I become aroused. The caress of my partner, and the way she touches me, is tremendously exciting, perhaps even more so than for a sighted person. The feel of her breasts on my face, the hardness of her nipples pressing into my palms, the brush of her hair across my chest . . . these are just some of the ways I experience the incredible pleasures of sex. (Kroll & Klein, 1992, p. 136)

## Enhancement Strategies for People With Chronic Illnesses and Disabilities

Individuals and couples can best cope with the sexual limitations of illness or disability by accepting those limitations and developing the options that remain. For example, couples can minimize the effects of pain by planning sexual activity at optimal times of the day, using methods of pain control such as moist heat or pain medication, finding comfortable positions, and focusing on genital pleasure or arousing erotic images to distract from pain (Schover & Jensen, 1988). As we emphasize in the "Basics of Sexual Enhancement and Sex Therapy" section of this chapter, expanding the definition of sexuality beyond genital arousal and intercourse to include dimensions such as erotic thoughts and sensual touch, and developing flexibility in sexual roles and innovation in sexual technique can be helpful. As a woman with CP explained:

© Chuck Savage/CORBIS

Good communication and creative exploration can help individuals and couples minimize the sexual effects of disabilities and illnesses.

My disability kind of makes things more interesting. We have to try harder, and I think we get more out of it because we do. We both have to be very conscious of each other—we have to take time. That makes us less selfish and more considerate of each other, which helps the relationship in other areas beside sexuality. (Shaul et al., 1978, p. 5)

## Cultural Influences

Culture strongly influences both the way we feel about our sexuality and the way we express it. In this section, we examine some influences in Western society—particularly in the United States—that affect our sexuality and can contribute to sexual problems.

### Negative Childhood Learning

The way others react to childhood genital exploration can affect how children learn to feel about their sexual anatomy.

We learn many of our basic, important attitudes about sexuality during childhood (Barone & Wiederman, 1998). While growing up, we observe and integrate the models of human relationships from our families. We notice how our parents use touch and how they feel about one another (Bartlik & Goldberg, 2000). For example, one researcher found that women with low sexual desire perceived their parents' attitudes toward sex and their affectionate interaction with each other to be significantly more negative than did women with normal sexual desire (Stuart et al., 1998). A variety of therapist researchers have reported that severe religious orthodoxy equating sex with sin is common to the backgrounds of many sexually troubled people (Fox et al., 2006; Richardson et al., 2006).

### The Sexual Double Standard

Global research on sexuality indicates that equality of gender roles is associated with men's and women's sexual satisfaction. In the male-dominated cultures in Asia, Africa, and the Middle East, significantly fewer people report that they have satisfying sexual lives than do the two-thirds of the people in the Western world, where greater gender equality has developed over time (Lauman et al., 2006). With more equality between men and women, the sexual double standard has diminished in the United States.

However, opposing sexual expectations for women and men are still prevalent in U.S. society and can negatively affect sexuality (Greaves, 2001). Women may learn to be sexually restrained to avoid acquiring the reputation of being a "slut," while men frequently learn that sexual conquest is a measure of "manliness":

Erotic materials portray men as always wanting and always ready to have sex, the only problem being how to get enough of it. We have accepted this rule for ourselves and most of us believe that we should always be capable of responding sexually, regardless of the time and place, our feelings about ourselves and our partners, or any other factors. (Zilbergeld, 1978, p. 41)

As a result of these expectations, men tend to see sexual interaction as a performance, in which their highest priority is to "act like a man" to confirm their male gender role in every sexual experience. Acting like a man first mandates exhibiting no "feminine" characteristics, such as tenderness or receptivity. The requirements of masculine self-reliance and dominance can make asking for guidance from a sexual partner untenable (Kilmartin, 1999; Tiefer, 1999). The restrictions of gender-role expectations can lead to anxiety, frustration, and resentment for both women and men (Bonierbale et al., 2006; Sanchez, 2006a).

In contrast, sexual intimacy that transcends gender-role stereotypes—when both individuals are active and receptive, wild and tender, playful and serious—moves beyond caricatures of men and women and expresses the richness of humanness (Kasl, 1999; McCarthy, 2001). Same-sex couples may not have to struggle with opposing gender-role expectations in their sexual expression. They tend to have a more varied sexual repertoire than heterosexuals, in part because of the lack of rigid gender-role scripts and of a concept of how sex "should" happen (Nichols, 2000).

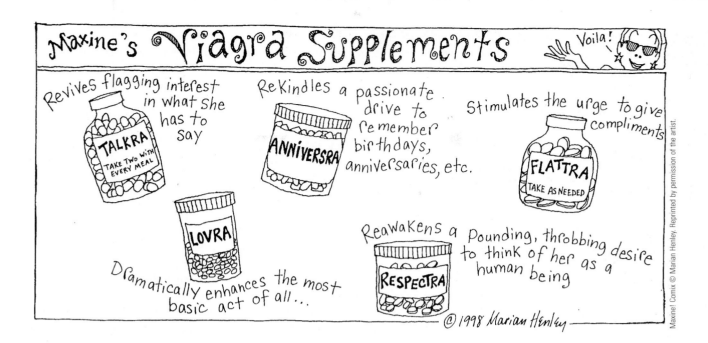

Maxine! Comix © Marian Henley. Reprinted by permission of the artist.

## A Narrow Definition of Sexuality

As we have seen repeatedly in this textbook, the notion that sex equals penile–vaginal intercourse can contribute to inadequate stimulation for women and place burdensome and anxiety-provoking expectations on intercourse. Sex therapist Leonore Tiefer observes that the current emphasis on medical treatments that enhance erection, such as Viagra, reinforces the overemphasis on intercourse. "For every dollar devoted to perfecting the phallus, I would like to insist that a dollar be devoted to assisting women with their complaints about partner impairments in kissing, tenderness, talk, hygiene, and general eroticism. Too many men still can't dance, write love poems, erotically massage the clitoris, or diaper the baby and let Mom get some rest" (Tiefer, 1995, p. 170).

## Performance Anxiety

Performance anxiety can block natural sexual arousal and release by diminishing the pleasurable sensations that would produce them. One study found that men were more likely to be distracted during sexual experiences by performance concerns than women (Meana & Nunnick, 2006). A transitory sexual problem, such as an inability to achieve an orgasm or erection because of fatigue or just not being in the mood, can produce enough anxiety to cause the problem in the next sexual encounter as well (Benson, 2003). Problems with erectile dysfunction frequently begin with the worry that follows a first-time incident, as the following account illustrates:

> When I was 20, my girlfriend and I were in her room at home and decided to have sex. She told me to be quiet because her mom was in the next room. After having sex for a couple of minutes I lost my hard-on. I completely freaked out. After my girlfriend showed me her book from a human sexuality class she'd taken I mellowed out about the whole ordeal and chalked my problem up to a bad situation. (Authors' files)

Inhibited orgasm in both men and women can result from extreme performance pressure and an inability to be "selfish" and pursue one's own heightened arousal instead of focusing on the partner's pleasure (Apfelbaum, 2000).

## Individual Factors

Beyond the cultural influences on sexual feelings and expression, sexual difficulties can stem from psychological factors that are usually unique to each individual.

## Sexual Knowledge and Attitudes

Our knowledge and attitudes about sex have a direct influence on our sexual expression. When difficulties are based on ignorance or misunderstanding, accurate information can sometimes alleviate sexual dissatisfaction. For example, if a woman knows about the function of her clitoris in sexual arousal, she will most likely have experiences different from a woman who lacks this knowledge. That women have fewer sexual problems as they get older and have more self-knowledge supports the idea that sexuality develops throughout our lives (Leland, 2000a).

## Self-Concept

The term *self-concept* refers to the feelings and beliefs we have about ourselves. Our self-concept can influence our relationships and sexuality (Foley, 2003). Research has found that self-esteem and self-confidence correlate with higher sexual satisfaction and lack of sexual problems (Apt et al., 1993; Hally & Pollack, 1993). For example, a woman who feels comfortable with her body, believes she is entitled to sexual pleasure, and takes an active role in attaining sexual fulfillment is likely to have a more satisfying sexual relationship than a woman who lacks those feelings about herself (Nobre & Pinto-Gouveia, 2006; Sanchez et al., 2006). Conversely, a sexual problem can negatively affect self-concept (Althof et al., 2006). For example, in a study about Viagra use, prior to treatment, men with erectile disorder had lower scores on self-esteem tests than men without ED. After 10 weeks of taking Viagra, the men's scores increased to equal the scores of the men without ED (Cappellen et al., 2006).

Body image is an aspect of self-concept that can strongly affect sexuality. The more one is distracted by negative thoughts about one's body, the less one will be able to go with physical and emotional pleasures during sexual activity. In Western cultures women's bodies are looked at, evaluated, and sexualized more than men's bodies, and thinness and beauty are often equated with sexual desirability. Women's concerns about weight begin earlier than men's do. Even when boys and girls have the same percentage of body fat, girls express greater dissatisfaction with their body weight and body image than boys do (Rierdan et al., 1998; Wood et al., 1996). Eve Ensler, author of *The Vagina Monologues*, clarifies: "We Americans like to tell ourselves we are free, but we are imprisoned. We are controlled by a corporate media that decrees what we should look like and then determines what we have to buy in order to get and keep that look" (2006, p. 47).

That media images of women have gotten further and further from the average size of women may have contributed to the perceived importance of thinness. In the early 1980s the average model weighed 8% less than the average American woman; she now weighs 23% less (Jeffery, 2006). In an unprecedented action in 2006 the internationally prominent Madrid Fashion Week imposed minimum weight criteria on models. The show banned too-thin models who did not meet the World Health Organization's guidelines for healthy height-to-weight ratios. Over 30% of the models who had participated in the previous year's show were disqualified, including top models such as Britain's Kate Moss. Other countries are considering establishing similar guidelines, hoping to help promote a healthier body image for women (Terzieff, 2006).

A woman's self-consciousness about her body during physical intimacy with a male partner is quite common (Meana & Nunnick, 2006). One research study of college women in the Midwest found that 35% reported physical self-consciousness during physical intimacy with a male partner, agreeing to statements such as "If a partner were to put a hand on my buttocks, I would think, 'My partner can feel my fat'" and "I would prefer having sex with my partner on top so that my partner is less likely to see my body." The research found patterns linking body image and the experience of being sexual. Women who were less self-conscious about their bodies viewed themselves as good sexual partners, were more assertive with partners, and had more heterosexual experience than women who were more self-conscious—even when their bodies were similar in size (Wiederman, 2000).

Recent trends suggest that media images of men contribute to men's insecurity about their bodies as well, and consequently men compromise their sex lives by concerns about their appearance. For example, college men who spend more time reading men's magazines and watching music videos and prime-time TV are much less com-

Body weight for today's supermodels is super-skinny compared with the voluptuousness of Marilyn Monroe.

China Photos/Getty Images

fortable with their body hair and sweat than men who have less exposure to mass media (Schooler & Ward, 2006). Men in magazines and on television usually have no visible body hair, and *Queer Eye for the Straight Guy* often insists that men wax their back hair as a part of basic grooming. Male body hair is often a subject for jokes, as in the movie *The 40-Year-Old Virgin*, in which the protagonist tries to have his chest hair waxed off to be more appealing to women. Furthermore, men's dissatisfaction with their own bodies was indicated by a study of body preference; most men preferred photos of bodies with 30 pounds more muscle than their own (O'Neill, 2000a). Parts of the gay culture place great emphasis on physical appearance in choosing partners.

Action figure toys, which represent the ideal male to boys, have beefed up over time. The original 1964 G.I. Joe had measurements comparable to the reasonable proportions of actual men. By 1991 Joe's biceps, if he had been full-sized, would have bulged from 12 to 16.2 inches, and G.I. Joe Extreme debuted in the mid-90s with the equivalent of 27-inch biceps (Pope et al., 2000).

Even though most women do not put a priority on penis size, a man's concern about the size of his penis can interfere with his arousal and enjoyment. In a survey of over 52,000 heterosexual men and women, only 55% of men were satisfied with their penis size, but 85% of women were satisfied with their sexual partners' penis size (Lever et al., 2006). Unlike viewing typical-sized penises in classic artwork, such as Michelangelo's nude sculpture *David*, watching pornography can contribute to a man's distorted sense of what is "normal," because male porn stars are selected for their oversized genitals.

A study of over 27,000 men ages 20 to 75 in eight countries (the United States, Britain, Germany, France, Italy, Spain, Mexico, and Brazil) provided a positive sign that men perceive their masculinity differently from the way popular media typically portray it. Men were found to value many qualities more than their physical attractiveness and sexual prowess. Being honorable, self-reliant, and respected by friends and having good health and a positive relationship with their wives were deemed most important to them (Michael et al., 2005).

The Western world does not have an exclusive on concerns about cultural definitions of beauty, as the Sexuality and Diversity box explains.

Hair removal by waxing was once only the province of women.

## SEXUALITY AND DIVERSITY

### Suffering for Beauty

Brazil's 4,700 miles of coastline and Brazilian men's preference for women with large, curvy bottoms have made butt-enhancing cosmetic surgery common in Brazil's cities. One of two methods is used: taking fat from the thighs and injecting it into the buttocks or inserting implants to create a fuller rear. In Asia, the most frequently performed cosmetic surgery, called the "hitch and stitch," creates a fold above each eye to make a woman's eyes look rounder and more "Western." Women in South Africa who consider lighter skin to be the ideal of beauty use bleaching creams

Eyes before and after surgery to make them appear more Caucasian.

and soaps containing a substance that has been banned for causing skin damage and disfigurement (Jones, 2003).

Personal ads in China often specify height—the taller the better. Hundreds of women each year undergo surgeries to increase their leg length so they will be 2 to 4 inches taller. A team of five surgeons spends 3 hours sawing, drilling, and hammering; then a frame is secured around the leg with screws drilled through the leg and into the bone. The frame forces the leg to lengthen while the bone regenerates—a process that takes at least 1 year.

## Emotional Difficulties

Personal emotional difficulties, such as anxiety and depression, have a strong effect on sexuality. The NHSLS found that unhappiness with life correlated with sexual problems. The data do not clarify whether one causes the other, but women and men who were experiencing sexual problems were considerably more likely to be unhappy with their lives in general than were respondents without sexual difficulties (Laumann et al., 1999). Lack of sexual interest and response is a common symptom of depression. Moreover, stressful life problems such as a death in the family, divorce, or extreme family or work difficulties can result in a lack of sexual interest. Severe stress and trauma, as experienced by combat veterans, can also interfere with sexual functioning (Letourneau et al., 1997).

## Sexual Abuse and Assault

The essential conditions for positive sexual interaction—consent, equality, respect, trust, and safety—are absent in sexual abuse. Boys and girls who are sexually abused are robbed of the opportunity to explore and develop their sexuality at their own age-appropriate pace (Braveman & Woodward-Kreitz, 2006; Maltz, 2003). According to the NHSLS, 12% of men and 17% of women were sexually abused before adolescence (Laumann et al., 1999). Lesbian, gay, and bisexual adults are more likely to have experienced sexual abuse in childhood than straight adults (Balsam et al., 2005). It is important to note that not all sexual abuse results in sexual problems in adulthood, but of all childhood experiences, sexual abuse has the greatest negative effect on adult sexual functioning (Courtois, 2000a, 2000b). Research shows that women with a history of childhood sexual abuse are two to four times more likely than other women to have chronic pelvic pain and to experience depression, anxiety, and low self-esteem (Murrey et al., 1993; Reiter & Milburn, 1994). Women survivors of childhood sex abuse have more frequent feelings of anxiety, fear, and disgust during sexual activities than women who have not experienced sex abuse (Meston et al., 2006). Research on male survivors is very limited, but male survivors often have deep-seated concerns about their masculinity from having been a sexual victim (Lew, 2004). In addition, survivors of sexual abuse often experience aversion reactions to sexual behaviors that are similar to what was done to them during the abuse. They may have flashbacks—sudden unwanted memories of the smells, sounds, sights, feelings, or other sensations of past sexual abuse—that dramatically interrupt any positive feelings and sexual pleasure (Courtois, 2000a, 2000b; Koehler et al., 2000).

Even teenage girls who engage in unwanted sex because they fear their boyfriends will be angry if they say no experience subsequent anxiety and depression. One study found that almost 41% of girls between 14 and 17 had been sexual when they did not want to be, and 10% said their boyfriends forced them to have sex. The teen girls who experienced unwanted sex were also more likely to have sexually transmitted diseases and unwanted pregnancies, and their partners were less likely to use condoms (Blythe et al., 2006).

Research has also indicated serious sexual consequences for survivors of sexual assault during adulthood (Lutfey et al., 2006). One study of 372 female survivors of sexual assault found that almost 59% experienced sexual problems after the assault—with about 70% of this group linking these problems to the assault. Fear of sex and lack of desire or arousal were the most frequently mentioned problems (Becker et al., 1986). In addition, the effects of sexual assault can be long-lasting; 60% of rape victims had sexual problems for more than 3 years after the assault (Becker & Kaplan, 1991).

The problems following childhood sexual abuse and adult sexual assault are often difficult for partners of survivors to understand and to cope with effectively (Haansbaek, 2006). Wendy Maltz, a sex therapist, developed *The Sexual Healing Journey* and the DVD or video *Partners in Healing* specifically to help survivors of sexual abuse and their partners resolve problems originating from that abuse.

## Relationship Factors

Besides personal feelings and attitudes, relationship factors strongly influence the satisfaction and quality of a sexual relationship (Real, 2002). These factors often vary according to the couple and their particular circumstances. For example, one couple may find that an argument typically ends with passionate lovemaking, whereas the partners in another couple may move to separate bedrooms for a week after a disagreement. In addition, when one partner is experiencing a sexual disorder—say, lack of interest and erectile difficulty—the other partner's sexual interest and capacity for arousal will likely be negatively affected (Fisher et al., 2006; Samraj et al., 2005).

Unresolved resentments, lack of trust or respect, or dislike of a partner can easily lead to sexual disinterest and problems with arousal and orgasm. One partner can even use his or her lack of sexual interest, consciously or subconsciously, to hurt or punish the other. A person who is frequently pressured to engage in sex or who feels guilty about saying no can feel less and less desire. In addition, someone who experiences a lack of power and control in his or her relationship can lose sexual desire or responsiveness, thereby gaining some sense of control in the sexual aspect of the relationship (Marzucco, 2005; LoPiccolo, 2000). Sexual difficulties can also occur when partners are too dependent on each other; partners need a balance of togetherness and separateness (DeVita-Raeburn, 2006).

When hypoactive sexual desire is not due to hormonal deficits, it often reflects unresolved relationship problems. One study found that women with HSDD reported more dissatisfaction with relationship issues than women with other sexual problems, such as painful intercourse or difficulty reaching orgasm (Stuart et al., 1998). In this study, diminished desire was associated with a few specific relationship characteristics:

- The woman's partner did not behave affectionately except before intercourse.
- Communication and conflict resolution were unsatisfactory.
- The couple did not maintain love, romance, and emotional closeness.

*"Don't be too upset. If we were meant to have good sex, we probably would have married other people."*

## Ineffective Communication

Without effective verbal and nonverbal communication, couples must base their sexual encounters on assumptions, past experiences, and wishful thinking—all of which can make a sexual experience feel routine and unsatisfying. A frequent source of communication problems is stereotyped gender roles—in particular, the myth that "sex is exclusively the man's responsibility and that sexual assertiveness in a woman is 'unfeminine'" (Kaplan, 1974, p. 350). For example, women who do not experience orgasm have more difficulty communicating their desire for direct clitoral stimulation to a partner than women who do experience orgasm (Kelly et al., 1990).

## Fears About Pregnancy or Sexually Transmitted Diseases

The fear of an unwanted pregnancy can interfere with coital enjoyment in a heterosexual relationship, especially when couples do not use an effective method of contraception (Sanders et al., 2003). On the other hand, many couples who want to conceive and have difficulties doing so often find that their sexual relationship becomes anxiety ridden, especially if they have to modify and regulate the timing and pattern of sexual interaction to enhance the possibility of conception.

Anxiety about contracting a sexually transmitted disease, particularly AIDS, can interfere with sexual arousal in both homosexual and heterosexual relationships. For people who are not in a monogamous, disease-free relationship, some risk exists. Guidelines for safer sex are outlined in Chapter 15.

## Sexual Orientation

Another reason that a woman or man experiences sexual dissatisfaction or has sexual problems in a heterosexual relationship can be a desire to be involved with individuals of the same sex (Althof, 2000). Although much progress has been made in establishing gay rights, following one's homosexual orientation still involves facing significant societal disapproval, if not outright discrimination. To avoid these repercussions, some homosexual people attempt to live in heterosexual relationships despite their lack of sexual desire in such relationships.

Sexual difficulties can also occur in homosexual men or women who are in same-sex relationships but have not yet been able to rid themselves of internalized negative beliefs about homosexuality (Nichols, 1989), as this woman explained:

> It had been a 10-year struggle for me to accept myself as a lesbian. I tried dating men, but always found that a special, meaningful feeling was missing. I had several relationships with women that didn't work out. Then I met Carol. I liked her, respected her, and was very attracted to her. I was looking for a long-term relationship, and the compatibilities and feelings were right. Sex was great until she told me she loved me. A switch went off, and I stopped feeling interested. In therapy, I was able to realize that the lingering feelings of my mother's disapproval had stopped me cold from allowing myself to be fully happy and complete in a "queer" relationship. I worked through those feelings and am now enjoying my sexuality in a loving, committed relationship for the first time in my life. (Authors' files)

# ◗ Basics of Sexual Enhancement and Sex Therapy

The various self-help and sex therapy suggestions offered in the following sections have proved helpful to many people in enhancing sexual relationships or resolving sexual problems. However, the same techniques do not work for everyone, and exercises often need to be individually modified. Furthermore, professional help may be called for when individual efforts, couple efforts, or both do not produce the desired results. Recognizing that therapy is sometimes necessary to promote change, we have included guidelines for seeking sex therapy in the last section of this chapter.

Increased self-knowledge is often an important step in sexual enhancement. With this in mind, we briefly outline procedures for improving awareness and acceptance of your body and present activities that provide the most pleasurable stimulation.

## Self-Awareness

Physical and emotional self-awareness and self-expression are crucial elements in satisfying sexual experiences (Morehouse, 2001; Schwartz, 2003). A good way to increase self-awareness and comfort with our sexuality is to become well acquainted with our sexual anatomy, as described in Chapters 4 and 5. Experimenting with masturbation is also an effective way for both men and women to learn about and expand sexual response, as we explained in Chapter 8. Self-stimulation and exploration is frequently an important part of women's learning how to experience orgasm and men's learning to delay ejaculation.

People may have a style of masturbation that interferes with their ability to be aroused by a partner. For example, 65% of men who sought help for ejaculatory inhibition had patterns of intensity, pressure, and speed of self-stimulation that were impossible to reproduce during intercourse. Some of the men rubbed against specific surfaces, used very heavy manual pressure, or exceptionally fast strokes (Helien et al., 2005). Women can also have patterns of masturbation, such as crossing their legs and rocking, that are not possible for a partner to replicate. Modifying masturbation techniques to resemble partner stimulation and intercourse more closely is one step toward experiencing orgasm from partner stimulation.

## Communication

One of the primary benefits of sex therapy—whether the immediate goal is learning to have orgasms with partners, how to overcome premature ejaculation, or solve almost any other problem—is that partners participating together in the treatment often develop more effective communication skills. This quotation from our files illustrates how important communication can be in solving sexual difficulties:

> He would say he was sorry he was so fast, and that maybe it would get better with time. Finally, I asked him to come to class with me the day you showed the film demonstrating the technique. Once we really talked openly things began to work well. He showed me how he liked to be stimulated, things he had never told me before. He became much more aware of my needs and what I needed to be satisfied. We really started getting into a lot of variety in our lovemaking, instead of just kissing and intercourse. By the way, the technique did work in slowing him down, but I think the biggest benefit has been breaking down the communication barriers. (Authors' files)

We encourage you to review the communication strategies in Chapter 7 to help improve your communication.

It can be particularly valuable for partners to communicate with each other about what kind of touching they find arousing by showing each other how they masturbate. This activity is often a part of sex therapy for women learning to experience orgasm with a partner and for resolving premature ejaculation and erectile difficulties. Masturbation is also a way to accommodate a potentially problematic difference in sex drive in a couple. The partner who wants sexual release more often than the other can masturbate while the other partner kisses and caresses him or her without needing to become aroused or experience orgasm.

**InfoTrac Search Words**

• Sensate focus

## Sensate Focus

One of the most useful couple-oriented activities for enhancing mutual sexual enjoyment is a series of touching exercises called **sensate focus** (● **Figure 14.3**, on the following page). Masters and Johnson developed the technique of sensate focus to use as a

**Sensate focus** A process of touching and communication used to enhance sexual pleasure and to reduce performance pressure.

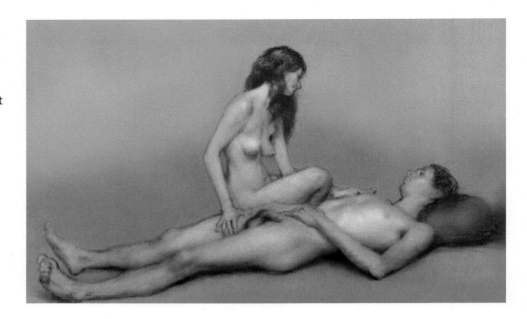

○ **Figure 14.3** The process of sensate focus, in which partners sensually explore each other's body, can contribute to the mutual enhancement of a couple's sexual enjoyment.

basic step in treating sexual problems. Sensate focus can help to reduce anxiety caused by goal orientation and to increase communication, pleasure, and closeness (De Villers & Turgeon, 2005). This technique is also useful for any couple to enhance their sexual relationship.

In the sensate focus touching exercises, partners take turns touching each other while following some essential guidelines. Both same-sex and straight couples can benefit from sensate focus. In the following descriptions, we assume that the one doing the touching is a woman and the one being touched is a man. To start, the person who will be doing the touching takes some time to "set the scene" so that the environment will be comfortable and pleasant for her; for example, she might unplug the phone and arrange a warm, cozy place with relaxing music and lighting. The two people then undress, and the toucher begins to explore her partner's body, following this important guideline: She is to touch not to please or arouse her partner but to please herself. The goal is for the toucher to focus on her perception of textures, shapes, and temperatures. The person being touched notices how the touching feels, and he remains quiet except when any touch is uncomfortable. In that case, he describes the uncomfortable feeling and what the toucher could do to make it more comfortable. For example: "That tickles. Please touch the other side of my arm." This guideline helps the toucher attend fully to her own sensations without worrying about whether something she is doing is unpleasant for her partner. The nondemanding quality of this kind of touching helps reduce or eliminate performance anxiety and allows the couple to expand touch beyond goal-directed stimulation.

In the next sensate focus exercise, the two people switch roles, following the same guidelines as before. In these initial sensate focus experiences, intercourse and touching the breasts and genitals are prohibited. Only after the partners have focused on touch and on communicating uncomfortable feelings do they include breasts and genitals as part of the exercise. Again, the toucher focuses on his or her own interest and pleasure, not the partner's. After the inclusion of breasts and genitals, the partners progress to a simultaneous sensate focus experience. Now they touch one another at the same time and experience feelings from both touching and being touched. ■

Modern Western sex therapy is based on the assumption that the values of open communication, emotional intimacy, and physical pleasure for both partners guide treatment and are its goals. However, these principles are antithetical to many cultures' norms (D. Goodman, 2001), as we explain in the following Sexuality and Diversity discussion.

## How Modern Sex Therapy Can Clash With Cultural Values

Cultural beliefs influence sexual practices, the perception of sexual problems, and modes of treatment. A study conducted in Saudi Arabia, where the marital sexual relationship is based primarily on the two dimensions of male sexual potency and couple fertility, found that the most common problem leading a couple to sex therapy was erectile disorder. Women in Saudi Arabia, who are raised to inhibit their sexual desires, came to sex therapy only with problems of painful intercourse. Unlike their counterparts in Western countries, the women did not seek help for lack of desire, arousal, or orgasm. For both men and women, only when intercourse itself was impaired—not interest or pleasure—did couples seek treatment (Osman & Al-Sawaf, 1995).

Many cultural traditions allow for little or no education or communication about sexual matters. In Pakistan the lack of formal sex education leads to misinformation. For example, men who experience premature ejaculation usually believe that masturbation and ejaculation during sleep have damaged muscles and blood vessels in the penis, causing their sexual problem (Bhatti, 2005). Asians consider it shameful to discuss sex, especially with someone outside the family. In cultures in which women are expected to be innocent about sex, the sex-education component of therapy conflicts with the prevailing values. Muslims are often taught to avoid talking about sexuality with people of the other sex (including their spouses). Taking a sex history can be distressing for clients with these beliefs, especially when the husband and wife are interviewed together.

Specific sex therapy techniques also often contradict cultural values (Rosenau et al., 2001; Timmerman, 2001). For example, masturbation exercises to treat anorgasmia, erectile difficulties, or premature ejaculation conflict with religious prohibitions of Orthodox Jews and some fundamentalist Christians. The gender equality inherent in sensate focus exercises and the avoidance of intercourse in such exercises are also often objectionable to many religious and ethnic groups.

Sex therapy needs to take into account the clients' cultural values and the implications they have for intimate behavior. Therapists should attempt to adjust therapy to their clients' well-integrated ethnic and religious perspectives (Richardson et al., 2006; Shtarkshall, 2005). This is likely to be more helpful than attempting to impose the cultural norms inherent in Western sex therapy (Hodge, 2004).

In the remainder of this chapter, we look at some strategies and sex therapy approaches that are used to deal with female and male sexual problems and sexual desire disorder.

## Specific Suggestions for Women

In this section, we describe procedures that may help women learn to increase sexual arousal and reach orgasm by themselves or with a partner. We also include suggestions for dealing with vaginismus.

### Becoming Orgasmic

Therapy programs for learning to experience orgasm are based on progressive self-awareness activities that a woman does at home between therapy sessions. At the beginning of treatment, body exploration, genital self-exam, and Kegel exercises (see Chapter 4) are emphasized; then therapy and home exercises move progressively to self-stimulation exercises similar to those described in Chapter 8 (see "Self-Pleasuring Techniques"). One advantage of self-stimulation is that a woman who does not have a partner can learn to become orgasmic.

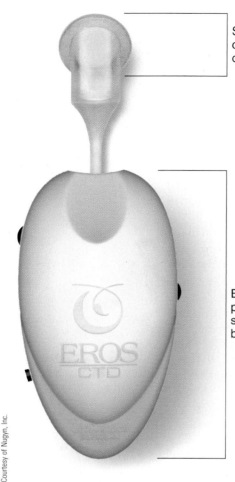

Small, soft plastic cup that is placed on clitoris

Battery-operated pump that creates suction to increase blood flow to clitoris

Courtesy of Nugyn, Inc.

**● Figure 14.4** The Eros Clitoral Therapy Device, approved by the FDA in 2000, works by increasing vasocongestion of the clitoris.

A vibrator is sometimes used to help a woman experience orgasm for the first time so she knows that she can have this response. (A vibrator is often less tiring to use than the fingers and supplies more intense stimulation.) After she has experienced a few orgasms with the vibrator, it is helpful for her to return to manual stimulation. This step is important because it is easier for a partner to replicate a woman's own touch than the stimulation of a vibrator. Another method, involving the Eros Clitoral Therapy Device (shown in **● Figure 14.4**) is designed to increase blood flow to, and thereby arousal of, the clitoris (Munarriz et al., 2003). The hormones and products discussed in the last section on treating low sexual desire may also be useful for increasing arousal.

## Experiencing Orgasm With a Partner

Once a woman has learned to experience orgasm through self-stimulation, sharing her discoveries with her partner can help her partner know what forms of stimulation are most pleasing to her. Each partner takes turns visually exploring the other's genitals, locating all the parts discussed in Chapters 4 and 5. After looking thoroughly, they experiment with touch, noticing and sharing what different areas feel like. The next step is for the woman to stimulate herself in her partner's presence, and her partner can be holding and kissing her or lying beside her, as shown in **● Figure 14.5**. This step is often a difficult one. One woman described how she dealt with her discomfort:

*When I wanted to share with my partner what I had learned about myself through masturbation, I felt anxious about how to do it. Finally, we decided that to begin with, I would be in the bedroom, and he would be in the living room, knowing I was masturbating. Then he would sit on the bed, not looking at me. The next step was for him to hold and kiss me while I was touching myself. Then I could be comfortable showing him how I touch myself. (Authors' files)*

**● Figure 14.5** Masturbating in the presence of a partner can be an effective way for an individual to indicate what kind of touching she or he finds arousing.

Next the partner begins nondemanding manual genital pleasuring. The couple can do this in any position that suits them. The woman places her hand over her partner's hand on her genitals to guide the partner's touch. They can use lubricants to increase pleasure of the sensations. The purpose of the initial sessions is for the woman to teach her partner what feels good rather than to produce orgasm. Once the woman thinks she is ready to experience orgasm, she indicates to her partner to continue the stimulation until she experiences climax. Orgasm will probably not occur until the couple has had several sessions.

Couples can use several specific techniques to increase a woman's arousal and the possibility of orgasm during intercourse. The first has to do with when to begin intercourse. Rather than beginning intercourse after a certain number of minutes of foreplay or when there is sufficient lubrication, a woman can be guided by her feeling of what might be called "readiness." Readiness is a vaginal sensation of wanting intercourse. Not all women experience this feeling of readiness, but for those who do, beginning intercourse at this time (and not before) can enhance the ensuing erotic sensations. Of course, the woman's partner will have to cooperate by waiting for her to indicate when she is ready and by not attempting to begin intercourse before then.

A woman who wants increased stimulation during coitus might benefit from initiating the kinds of movements and pressure she finds most arousing. A woman can also stimulate her clitoris manually or with a vibrator during intercourse, as shown in ◗ **Figure 14.6**. Her partner's manual stimulation of her clitoris during intercourse will likely also enhance arousal. ◗ **Table 14.5** highlights how women who are routinely orgasmic during intercourse facilitate experiencing orgasm (Ellison, 2000).

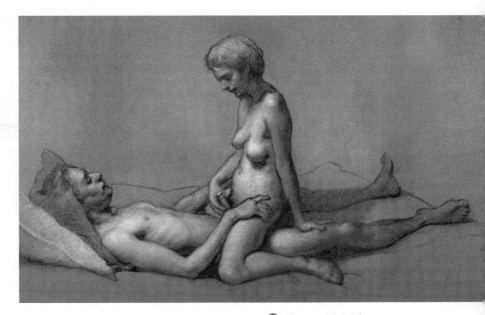

◗ **Figure 14.6** The use of a vibrator for clitoral stimulation during coitus.

◗ **T A B L E 14.5** **Facilitating Orgasm**

2,371 women completed the sentence "In addition to getting specific physical stimulation, I often have done the following to help me reach orgasm during sex with a partner"

| Activity | Percentage |
| --- | --- |
| Positioned my body to get the stimulation I needed | 90 |
| Paid attention to my physical sensations | 83 |
| Tightened and released my pelvic muscles | 75 |
| Synchronized the rhythm of my movements to my partner's | 75 |
| Asked or encouraged my partner to do what I needed | 74 |
| Got myself in a sexy mood beforehand | 71 |
| Focused on my partner's pleasure | 68 |
| Felt/thought how much I love my partner | 65 |

SOURCE: Ellison (2000, p. 244).

## Dealing With Vaginismus

Treatment for vaginismus usually begins during a pelvic exam, in which the healthcare practitioner demonstrates the vaginal spasm reaction to the woman or couple. Subsequent therapy starts with relaxation and self-awareness exercises, including a soothing bath, general body exploration, and manual external genital pleasuring. Next the woman learns to insert first a fingertip, then a finger, and eventually three fingers into her vagina without experiencing muscle contractions. At each stage the woman practices relaxing and contracting the vaginal muscles, as with Kegel exercises (see Chapter 4). Dilators, which are cylindrical rods of graduated sizes, are also sometimes used to accustom the vaginal walls to relaxing (Leiblum, 2000). Biofeedback and physical therapy treatments might also be included (Koehler, 2002).

Once the woman has completed the preceding steps, her partner can begin to participate by following the same steps that she completed by herself. After the man can insert three fingers without inducing a muscle spasm, the woman controls a slow insertion of her partner's penis, with many motionless pauses that allow the woman to become familiar with vaginal containment of the penis. Pelvic movements and pleasure focusing are added later, only when both partners are comfortable with penetration.

## Specific Suggestions for Men

In the following paragraphs, we outline methods for dealing with the common difficulties of premature ejaculation and erectile disorder. We also discuss a way to treat the less common condition of orgasmic disorder.

### Lasting Longer

Some self-help and sex therapy approaches to learning ejaculatory control are easy to implement—in many cases, without professional guidance.

**Strategies for Delaying Ejaculation** In some cases, men can gain considerable control over ejaculation by practicing a few simple strategies. Men for whom premature ejaculation is not a problem and women readers may find the following discussion valuable simply because they would sometimes like sexual intercourse to last longer.

- *Ejaculate more frequently.* Men with premature ejaculation problems sometimes find that they can delay ejaculation when they are having more frequent orgasms, by masturbation or partner sex.
- *Come again!* A couple can experiment with continuing sexual interaction after the man's first ejaculation, then resume intercourse when his erection returns. This strategy is most useful for younger men, who experience erections again soon after ejaculation.
- *Change positions.* If a man wants to delay ejaculation, he may gain some control by lying on his back and increasing physical relaxation (Blais et al., 2005). (See page 229 for variations of the woman-above position.) However, if a man attempts energetic pelvic movements in this position it will be counterproductive because he will be increasing muscle tension by moving both his own weight and his partner's.
- *Talk with each other.* To delay climax, the man often finds it essential to slow down or completely cease movements. He needs to tell his partner when to reduce or stop stimulation.
- *Consider alternatives.* To minimize performance anxiety about rapid ejaculation (and most of the other problems discussed here), it is often useful to think of intercourse as just one of several options for sexual sharing. ■

**Stop-start technique**
A treatment technique for premature ejaculation, consisting of stimulating the penis to the point of impending orgasm and then stopping until the pre-ejaculatory sensations subside.

**The Stop-Start Technique** James Semans, a urologist, developed the **stop-start technique**, which enables the man to become acquainted with and ultimately control his ejaculatory reflex. The partner is instructed to stimulate the man's penis, either manually or orally, to the point of impending orgasm—at which time stimulation is stopped until the pre-ejaculatory sensations subside (Semans, 1956). (A man can also practice this technique on himself during solo masturbation sessions [Zilbergeld, 1992].) These sessions generally last 15 to 30 minutes and occur as often as once a day for several days or weeks. During each session, the couple repeats the stimulation and the stop-start procedure several times and then allows ejaculation to occur on the last cycle. The couple should reach an agreement about sexual stimulation and orgasm for the man's partner. If the partner desires these, the couple can engage in nonintercourse sexual activity.

As the man's ejaculatory control improves, the couple progresses to intercourse. For heterosexual couples, the best position is the woman above, sitting up. The first step is for the man to guide his penis in the woman's vagina and lie quietly for several moments before beginning slow movements. When he begins to feel close to orgasm, they lie quietly again. This stop-start intercourse technique is continued as the man experiences progressively better ejaculatory control.

**Medical Treatments** Small doses of certain medications usually prescribed for depression can help men to delay ejaculation. One of the side effects of these medications is suppressed orgasm in men and women, which is often helpful in treating rapid ejaculation (Kim & Seo, 1998; Polonsky, 2000). Other medications to treat premature ejaculation are under study, including dapoxetine, which has been developed specifically for such treatment (Broderick, 2006; McVary et al., 2006).

## Dealing With Erectile Dysfunction

Besides physically caused erection difficulties, performance anxiety is a major source of erectile dysfunction. Therefore, most sex therapy concentrates on reducing or eliminating anxiety. Initially, a couple uses the sensate focus exercises, understanding that at this point the touching is intended not to result in erection, ejaculation, or intercourse, but to focus on and enjoy the touch without a further goal. The following account shows a common reaction to the exercise:

> When the therapist told us that intercourse was off limits, at least for the time being, I couldn't believe how relieved I felt. If I couldn't get hard, so what? After all, I was told not to use it even if I did. Those first few times touching and getting touched by my wife were the first really worry-free pleasurable times I had experienced in years. (Authors' files)

If a couple wants to, they can agree in advance for the partner to have an orgasm at the close of a session by whatever mode of stimulation other than intercourse seems comfortable to both (self-stimulation, being touched by the partner, oral stimulation, etc.). When the couple has progressed to a point where both partners feel comfortable with sensate focus, the couple explores what kinds of genital stimulation other than intercourse are particularly pleasurable for the man. When the man experiences a full erection, his partner should stop doing what has aroused him. It is crucial that they allow his erection to subside at this point to alter the man's belief that once his erection is lost it will not return. The couple spends this time holding each other close or exchanging nongenital caresses. Once the penis is completely flaccid, the man's partner resumes genital pleasuring.

The final phase of treatment for heterosexual couples who desire intercourse involves penetration and coitus. With the man on his back and the woman astride, the couple begins with sensate focus and then moves to genital stimulation. When the man has an erection, his partner lowers herself onto his penis, maintaining stimulation with gentle pelvic movements. It is important to allow the man to be "selfish," concentrating exclusively on his own pleasure (Kaplan, 1974). Occasionally a man loses his erection after penetration. If this happens, his partner returns to the oral or manual stimulation that originally produced his erection. If his response continues to be blocked, it is wise to stop genital contact and return to the original nondemand pleasuring of sensate focus before moving forward again.

**Medical Treatments** Some men who have impaired erectile functioning as the result of physiological problems make a satisfactory sexual adjustment to the absence of erection by emphasizing and enjoying other ways of sexual sharing. For other men with erection difficulties, several types of medical treatments are available. Viagra, a pill for erectile problems, became available in 1998. Originally developed for cardiovascular disease, it became the fastest selling prescription drug in history. Almost 40,000 prescriptions were dispensed in the first 2 weeks on the market (Holmes, 2003). In 2003 and 2004 the FDA approved two additional Viagra-like drugs, Levitra and Cialis.

Viagra, Levitra, and Cialis have similar side effects; the most common are flushing, headaches, and nasal congestion (Gotthardt, 2003). Erectile dysfunction drugs can also cause priapism, in which an erection does not subside and can result in permanent damage to penile tissue unless medical treatment is obtained (Adams, 2003). A small number of men have died after taking Viagra (49 men per 1 million prescriptions), but most of the deaths were attributed to the men's preexisting high mortality risk from cardiovascular disease (Mitka, 2000).

Viagra ads initially focused on older men with erectile dysfunction. Ads now tend to appeal to a wider variety of ages, including younger men and even women who use Viagra for sexual enhancement rather than treatment.

For unknown reasons, half of all Viagra prescriptions are never refilled (Duenwald, 2003). We hope that some men do not refill them because Viagra helped them and their partners overcome obstacles to sexual interaction. For many couples erection-enhancing drugs can be wonder drugs that restore the intimacy of intercourse. Studies do show significant improvement in the partners' feelings of sexual desirability and sexual functioning and satisfaction when the men use erection-enhancing medications (Eardley et al., 2006; Fisher et al., 2006; McCullough et al., 2006). However, many men may have found that firm erections are secondary to a good relationship. In a troubled relationship the use of such a medication can clarify for the couple that they have other relationship problems, which may lead the couple to work toward resolving them (Cooper, 2006).

Viagra has greatly increased general conversation and awareness about erectile problems. In fact, men who do not have erectile dysfunction are using erection-enhancing drugs for firmer and longer-lasting erections. The appeal to men to be able to extend intercourse beyond one or more ejaculations contributes to the recreational use of such drugs (Naughton, 2004). Reports also indicate that Viagra has emerged among college students and others as a party drug for recreational and casual sex. Mixing Viagra and recreational drugs combines enduring erections with an altered mental state in which straight and gay people often engage in high-risk sexual behaviors that they otherwise would avoid (Adams, 2003).

Prior to Viagra, a common treatment for ED was an injection of a vasoactive medication. Because vascular impairment can be a factor in erectile difficulty, the same vasoactive medications used to diagnose vascular impairment in erectile disorder can be used for treatment (Lewis & Heaton, 2000). These medications relax smooth muscle tissue in the spongy body of the penis, causing increased blood flow, which in turn results in engorgement and erection. A physician teaches the man to inject the medication into the cavernous bodies of the penis; erection typically occurs 4–10 minutes after the almost painless injection and lasts from 1 to 4 hours. Complications include transitory numbness of the glans, infection, tissue damage at the injection site, and prolonged erection. Long-term effects of these injections are not yet known. Medication inserted into the urethra in a suppository is also available (Simon, 2003).

**Mechanical Devices** Devices that suction blood into the penis and hold it there during intercourse have been available since the mid-1980s (Korenman & Viosca, 1992). External vacuum constriction devices, which are available by prescription, consist of a vacuum chamber, pump, and penile constriction bands. The vacuum chamber is placed over the flaccid penis. The pump creates a negative pressure inside the chamber and draws blood into the penis. The elastic band is then placed around the base of the penis to trap the blood, and the chamber is removed (Levy et al., 2000).

A newer, nonprescription product, Rejoyn, is a penile support sleeve made from soft, medical-quality rubber that fits over a flaccid or erect penis to provide the support necessary for intercourse. A lubricated, open-ended condom-like cover fits over the sleeve.

**Surgical Treatments** A surgically implanted penile prosthesis is an option for men who are not helped by Viagra or other methods (Carson, 2003). The surgery is expensive and involves risks, including infection, and men should evaluate this option carefully and include their partner in pre- and postsurgical counseling. There are two basic types of penile implants. One type consists of a pair of semirigid rods made of metal wires or coils inside a silicone covering; the rods are placed inside the cavernous bodies of the penis. Although this type is easier to implant than the second type, a potential disadvantage is that the penis is always semierect. The second type of prosthesis is an inflatable device that enables the penis to change from flaccid to erect (◗ **Figure 14.7**). Two inflatable cylinders are implanted into the cavernous bodies of the penile shaft. They are connected to a fluid-filled reservoir located near the bladder and to a pump in the scrotal sac. To become erect, a man squeezes the pump several times, and the fluid fills the collapsed cylinders, producing an erection. When an erection is no longer desired, a release valve causes the fluid to go back into the reservoir.

Neither of these devices can restore sensation or the ability to ejaculate if it has been lost as a result of medical problems. Furthermore, the surgery to implant the devices may diminish sensation. They do, however, provide an alternative for men who want to mechanically restore their ability to have erections, and most men who have them report improved sexual activity (Richter et al., 2006).

Revascularization is another surgical solution for erectile difficulties; it involves microsurgical vascular repairs. Revascularization surgery is done only at a few centers for carefully selected patients, but it can restore sexual functioning for some men (Nash, 1997).

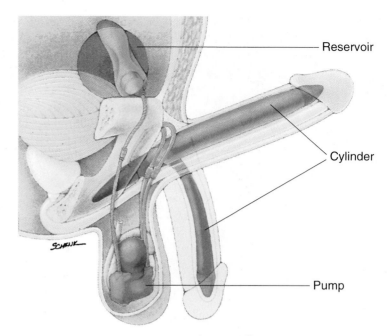

**Figure 14.7** An inflatable penile prosthesis.

## Reducing Male Orgasmic Disorder

Sex therapy usually begins with a few days of sensate focus, when the man should not have an ejaculation by masturbation or partner interaction. If his partner desires orgasm, this can be accomplished in whatever fashion is comfortable for both partners. The next step is for the man to stimulate himself to orgasm with his partner present. Once both partners feel comfortable with the man masturbating, the couple can move on to the next phase, where the partner attempts to bring him to orgasm with whatever stimulation is most arousing. It may take several days before the partner's stimulation produces an ejaculation, and it is important for the man not to ejaculate by masturbation during this period. Most therapists agree that once he can reach orgasm by his partner's touch, an important step has been accomplished.

When the man is ejaculating consistently in response to partner stimulation, the couple can move on to the final phase of treatment, in which ejaculation takes place during penetration. After building arousal by other means, the couple tries penetration. If he does not ejaculate shortly after penetration, he should withdraw and resume other stimulation until he is about to ejaculate, at which point the couple resumes penetration. Once the man experiences a few ejaculations during penetration, the mental block that is usually associated with ejaculatory disorder often disappears. In addition, psychotherapy to understand and resolve deeper personal or couple problems may be necessary to resolve male orgasmic disorder.

## Treating Hypoactive Sexual Desire Disorder

Many aspects of the treatment for hypoactive sexual desire disorder are similar to specific suggestions for resolving other sexual problems. These include

- Encouraging erotic responses through self-stimulation and arousing fantasies
- Reducing anxiety with appropriate information and sensate focus exercises
- Enhancing sexual experiences through improved communication and increased skills—both in initiating desired sexual activity and in refusing undesired sexual activity
- Expanding the repertoire of affectionate and sexual activities

Most therapists combine suggestions for specific activities with insight therapy, which can help a person understand and resolve any subconscious conflicts about sexual pleasure and intimacy. When low sexual desire is a symptom of unresolved relationship problems, therapy focuses on the interactions between partners that contribute to the lack of sexual desire (Alperstein, 2001).

## Medical Treatments

Men with low levels of testosterone often use testosterone supplementation—usually a transdermal gel—to increase their sex drive (Tomlinson et al., 2006). The number of testosterone prescriptions has tripled in recent years as a growing number of men are taking testosterone to offset the normal age-related decline of the hormone (Harvard Health Publications, 2006).

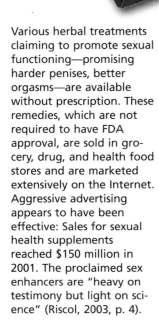

A review of controlled studies on estrogen and testosterone and post-menopausal women's sexual functioning found that both estrogen and testosterone therapies are associated with increased sexual interest, arousal, and satisfaction with masturbation and partner sexual activity (Leventhal-Alexander, 2005). Testosterone can also increase sexual interest for premenopausal women with below-normal levels of testosterone (Reinberg 2006; Berga & McCord, 2005). In 2004 the FDA turned down an application for Intrinsa, a testosterone patch for women, in spite of studies showing improvement in desire and pleasure (Dennerstein & Goldstein, 2005; Pollitt, 2005). Therefore, testosterone is available to women only by prescription for off-label use (Garcia-Banigan, 2005). Research about side effects, especially cancer and heart disease, from testosterone therapy for both men and women continues in order to clarify risks and benefits (Reinberg, 2006; Striecher, 2006; Tamimi et al., 2006).

Various herbal treatments claiming to promote sexual functioning—promising harder penises, better orgasms—are available without prescription. These remedies, which are not required to have FDA approval, are sold in grocery, drug, and health food stores and are marketed extensively on the Internet. Aggressive advertising appears to have been effective: Sales for sexual health supplements reached $150 million in 2001. The proclaimed sex enhancers are "heavy on testimony but light on science" (Riscol, 2003, p. 4).

Since the instant financial success of Viagra, commercial interests and scientists have searched for a pill to spark female sexual interest and response. Most of the research that tests whether Viagra works for women has had disappointing results. Viagra may be helpful to some women, but for which women and to what extent are not clear (Johnson, 2003). Part of the difficulty in finding a medicine for women comparable to Viagra for men is that scientific knowledge about the physiological process of female sexual functioning is rather limited (Bechara et al., 2003).

Two nonprescription products that have been researched in accordance with FDA standards and published in peer-reviewed journals are Zestra, an oil applied to the clitoris and vulva, and ArginMax, a nutritional supplement. Zestra was found to increase sexual response, and study participants using ArginMax reported increased clitoral sensation, sexual desire, vaginal lubrication, frequency of orgasm, and sexual satisfaction (Ferguson et al., 2003; Ito et al., 2001).

Initial placebo-controlled studies of bremelanotide, a fast-acting inhalant that acts on neural pathways in the brain, have shown significant increases in sexual desire, genital arousal, and reports of sexual satisfaction (Diamond et al., 2006). Future research will include giving women the option of using bremelanotide at their own homes rather than at a research site. Creams containing alprostadil, prostaglandins, or L-arginine amino acid have been shown to encourage blood flow to the genitals, and they may enhance arousal, orgasm, and satisfaction (Gearson, 2003; Gittelman et al., 2006).

## Seeking Professional Assistance

Although some people with sexual problems improve over time without professional help, sometimes therapy is necessary (De Amicis et al., 1984). Seeking therapy is often a difficult step. A community medical practice found that, when asked, 33% of men reported problems with premature ejaculation, 10% reported erectile difficulty, and 10% stated low sexual interest, but none had sought professional help (Rosenberg et al., 2006).

## What Happens in Therapy?

Many people are apprehensive about going to see a sex therapist, and it can be helpful to have some idea about what to expect. Each therapist works differently, but most therapists follow certain steps. During the first appointment, the therapist will help the client (or clients, if a couple) clarify the problem and his or her feelings about it and to identify the client's goals for the therapy. The therapist will usually ask questions about when the problem began, how it has developed over time, what the client thinks caused it, and how she or he has already tried to resolve it. The client may only need the therapist to provide specific information he or she lacks or to reassure the client that his or her thoughts, feelings, fantasies, desires, and behaviors that enhance personal satisfaction are normal and do not have potentially negative consequences. At the same time, some people may benefit from permission not to engage in certain sexual activities they dislike.

Over the next few sessions (most therapy occurs in 1-hour weekly sessions), the therapist may gather more extensive sexual, personal, and relationship histories. The therapist will likely obtain information about medical history and current physical functioning to make any necessary referrals for further physical screenings. During these sessions, the therapist will also explore whether the client has a lifestyle conducive to a good emotional and sexual relationship and determine whether she or he has problems with substance abuse or domestic violence.

Once the therapist and the individual (or couple) more fully realize the nature of the difficulty and have defined the therapy goals, the therapist helps the client understand and overcome obstacles to meeting the goals as the sessions continue. The therapist often provides psychoeducational information and gives assignments, such as masturbation or sensate focus exercises, for the client to do between therapy sessions (Althof, 2006). Successes and difficulties with the assignments are discussed at subsequent meetings. In some cases personal emotional difficulties or relationship problems are causing the sexual issue, and various forms of intensive therapy are necessary.

Therapy is terminated when the client reaches his or her goals. The therapist and client may also plan one or more follow-up sessions. It is often helpful for a client to leave with a plan for continuing and maintaining progress.

## Selecting a Therapist

To select a therapist, you might ask your sexuality course instructor or health-care practitioner for referrals or contact either the American Association of Sex Educators, Therapists, and Counselors or the American Board of Sexology (see the Web Resources section at the end of this chapter for links to these organizations' Web sites). After consulting some of these sources, you should have several potential therapists from which to choose. A professional who has specialized in sex therapy should have a minimum of a master's degree and credentials as a licensed psychiatrist, psychologist, social worker, or counselor. To do sex therapy, he or she should also have participated in sex therapy training, supervision, and workshops. It is very appropriate for you to inquire about the specific training and certification of a prospective therapist.

To help determine whether a specific therapist will meet your needs, pay attention to how you feel about talking with the therapist. Therapy is not intended to be a light social interaction, and it can be quite uncomfortable to discuss personal sexual concerns. However, for therapy to be useful, you need to have the sense that the therapist is open and willing to understand you.

After the initial interview, you can decide to continue with that particular therapist or ask for a referral to another therapist more appropriate to your personality or needs. If you become dissatisfied once you begin therapy, discuss your concerns with your therapist. Decide jointly, if possible, whether to continue therapy or to seek another therapist. It is usually best to continue for several sessions before making a decision to change. Occasionally, clients expect magic cures rather than the difficult but rewarding work that therapy often demands. ■

## Unethical Relationships: Sex Between Therapist and Client

It is highly unethical for professional therapists to engage in sexual relationships with clients they treat—both during therapy and after it has ended (Lamb et al., 2003; Reamer, 2003). It is the professional's responsibility to set boundaries that ensure the integrity of the therapeutic relationship (Norris et al., 2003). Psychiatry, psychology, social work, and counseling professional associations have codes of ethics against sexual relations between psychotherapists and their clients. In addition, some states have

! Sexual Health

! Sexual Health

criminalized sexual behavior with patients. However, research has found that up to 3% of female therapists and 12% of male therapists admit to having sexual contact with a current client (Berkman et al., 2000).

Sexual involvement between client and therapist can have negative effects on the client (Plaut, 1996). Research has indicated that women who experienced sexual contact with their therapists (including psychotherapists in general, not just sex therapists) felt greater mistrust of and anger toward men and therapists than did a control group of women. They also experienced more psychological and psychosomatic symptoms, including anger, shame, anxiety, and depression (Finger, 2000; Regehr & Glancy, 1995). If at any time a therapist makes verbal or physical sexual advances toward you, you have every right to leave immediately and terminate therapy. Furthermore, it would be helpful to others who might become victims of this abuse of professional power if you reported the incident to the state licensing board for the therapist's profession (Schoener, 1995). ■

# SUMMARY

- Sexual health is a state of physical, emotion, mental, and sexual well-being.
- The National Health and Social Life Survey (NHSLS) found that many people reported problems in their sex lives.
- Sexual problems can contribute to lower satisfaction with overall life.

## Specific Sexual Difficulties

- A sexual problem must occur within the context of adequate physical and psychological stimulation to be considered a disorder.
- Hypoactive sexual desire disorder (HSDD) is characterized by the absence or minimal experience of sexual interest prior to and during the sexual experience.
- Dissatisfaction with frequency of sexual activity occurs when individual differences in sexual interest result in relationship distress.
- Sexual aversion disorder is an extreme irrational fear or dislike of sexual activity.
- Female genital sexual arousal disorder is an inhibition of the vasocongestive response; female subjective sexual arousal disorder is a lack of subjective feelings of arousal when physical signs of arousal are present; combined genital and subjective sexual arousal disorder combines both.
- Persistent sexual arousal disorder is spontaneous and unwanted genital arousal that is not relieved by orgasm.
- Male erectile dysfunction is the consistent or recurring inability over at least 3 months to have or maintain an erection.
- Female orgasmic disorder is the absence, marked delay, or diminished intensity of orgasm despite high subjective arousal.
- Situational female orgasmic disorder is when a woman can experience orgasm during masturbation but not with a partner.

- Coitus provides mostly indirect clitoral stimulation, and for many women it does not provide sufficient stimulation to result in orgasm.
- Male orgasmic disorder is the inability of a man to ejaculate during sexual activity with a partner.
- Premature ejaculation occurs when a man consistently ejaculates quickly and is unable to control the timing of his ejaculation.
- Both men and women fake orgasm, although women do so more often. Pretending usually perpetuates ineffective patterns of relating and reduces the intimacy of the sexual experience.
- Dyspareunia, or pain during coitus, is disruptive to sexual interest and arousal in both women and men. Numerous physical problems can cause painful intercourse. Vulvar vestibulitis syndrome may be the most common cause of painful intercourse for women.
- Peyronie's disease, in which fibrous tissue and calcium deposits develop in the penis, can cause pain and curvature of the penis during erection.
- Vaginismus is an involuntary contraction of the outer vaginal muscles that makes penetration of the vagina difficult and painful. Many women who have vaginismus are interested in and enjoy sexual activity.

## Origins of Sexual Difficulties

- Physiological conditions can be the primary causes of sexual problems or can combine with psychological factors to result in sexual dysfunction. It is important to identify or rule out physiological causes of sexual problems through medical examinations.
- Good sexual functioning correlates with good health habits, including a healthy diet, exercise, moderate or no alcohol use, and not smoking.
- Chronic illnesses and their treatments can greatly affect sexuality. Diseases of the neurological, vascular, and endocrine systems can impair sexual functioning.

- Diabetes causes damage to nerves and the circulatory system, impairing sexual arousal.
- Cancer and its therapies can impair the hormonal, vascular, and neurological functions necessary for normal sexual activity. Cancer of the reproductive organs often has the worst impact.
- Multiple sclerosis is a neurological disease of the brain and spinal cord that can affect sexual interest, genital sensation, arousal, or capacity for orgasm.
- Cerebrovascular accidents, or strokes, can reduce a person's frequency of interest, arousal, and sexual activity.
- Most people with spinal cord injuries remain interested in sex, and more than half experience some degree of sexual arousal.
- People with cerebral palsy, which is characterized by mild to severe lack of muscular control, may need help with preparation and positioning for sexual relations.
- Blind and deaf individuals can enhance sexual interaction by developing increased sensitivity with their other senses.
- Medications that can impair sexual functioning include drugs used to treat high blood pressure, psychiatric disorders, depression, and cancer. Use of recreational drugs (including barbiturates, narcotics, and marijuana), alcohol, and tobacco can interfere with sexual interest, arousal, and orgasm.
- Equality of gender roles is associated with greater sexual satisfaction for men and women.
- An emphasis on intercourse can increase performance anxiety and reduce pleasurable options in lovemaking.
- Sexual difficulties can be related to personal factors such as limited or inaccurate sexual knowledge, problems of self-concept and body image, or emotional difficulties.
- Experiencing sexual abuse as a child or sexual assault as an adult often leads to sexual problems. As a result of the abuse experiences, a survivor often associates sexual activity with negative, traumatic feelings.
- Relationship problems, ineffective communication, and fear of pregnancy or sexually transmitted diseases can often inhibit sexual satisfaction.
- A woman or man whose sexual orientation is homosexual will often have difficulty with sexual interest, arousal, and orgasm in a heterosexual sexual relationship.

## Basics of Sexual Enhancement and Sex Therapy

- Exploring one's own body, sharing knowledge with a partner, and good communication between partners are important elements of therapy.
- Sensate focus is a part of therapy for many different sexual problems.
- Masturbating in each other's presence can be an excellent way for partners to indicate to each other what kind of touching they find arousing.
- Therapy programs for women to learn to experience orgasm are based on progressive self-awareness activities.
- Women who wish to become orgasmic with a partner can benefit from programs that start with sensate focus, mutual genital exploration, and nondemand genital pleasuring by the partner.
- Treatment for vaginismus generally involves promoting increased self-awareness and relaxation. Insertion of a lubricated finger (first one's own and later the partner's) into the vagina is an important next step in overcoming this condition. Penile insertion is the final phase of treatment for vaginismus.

- A variety of approaches can help a man learn to delay his ejaculation, and a couple can use the stop-start technique. Certain antidepressant medications can also help delay ejaculation.
- A behavioral approach designed to reduce performance anxiety is used to treat psychologically based erectile disorder.
- Medications to stimulate blood flow to the penis are in widespread use, and vascular surgery, surgically implanted penile prostheses, external vacuum constriction, and vasoactive injections are available if medication does not help.
- A behavioral approach to male orgasmic disorder combines self-stimulation, sensate focus, and partner manual stimulation, ultimately leading to ejaculation by the partner's stimulation.
- Many of the basic sex therapy techniques are used to help with hypoactive sexual desire disorder, and therapists also often include insight therapy and couples counseling.
- Testosterone can be helpful for men and women with low sexual desire, but because of its possible links to cancer and heart disease, its safety is not well established.
- Two nonprescription products have been shown in research to be helpful with low desire and arousal in women, and other products are being studied.
- Professional counseling is often helpful and sometimes necessary in overcoming sexual difficulties, but few people with problems seek help.
- A skilled therapist can provide useful information, problem-solving strategies, and sex therapy techniques.
- It is unethical for a therapist to have sexual relations with a client, either during or after treatment.

## ◗ Suggested Readings

**Berman, Jennifer, and Laura Berman** (2001). *For Women Only: A Revolutionary Guide to Overcoming Sexual Dysfunction and Reclaiming Your Sex Life*. New York: Henry Holt. A comprehensive handbook about female sexual arousal and treatments for sexual problems.

**Leiblum, Sandra, and Raymond Rosen** (Eds.) (2000). *Principles and Practice of Sex Therapy*. New York: Guilford Press. An up-to-date, comprehensive, authoritative book with contributions by leading clinical authorities in the field of sex therapy.

**McCarthy, Barry, and Emily McCarthy** (2003). *Rekindling Desire: A Step-by-Step Program to Help Low-Sex and No-Sex Marriages*. New York: Brunner-Routledge. A 10-step program to help couples revitalize the sexual and emotional intimacy in their relationships.

**Zilbergeld, Bernie** (1992). *The New Male Sexuality: A Guide to Sexual Fulfillment*. New York: Bantam. An exceptionally well-written and informative treatment of male sexuality, including such topics as gender issues, sexual functioning, self-awareness, and overcoming difficulties.

## ◗ Resources

**Impotence Anonymous**
This is a self-help group for men and their partners. For information about the 100-plus chapters in the United States, call 1-800-669-1603, or send a stamped, self-addressed envelope to P.O. Box 410, Bowie, MD 20718.

# ❯ Resources

**Impotence Anonymous**

This is a self-help group for men and their partners. For information about the 100-plus chapters in the United States, call 1-800-669-1603, or send a stamped, self-addressed envelope to P.O. Box 410, Bowie, MD 20718.

# ❯ Web Resources

**CengageNOW Web Site**

Go to **academic.cengage.com** to link to practice quiz questions, interactive activities, Internet links, critical thinking exercises, discussion forums, and more. You can also access sites from the Wadsworth Psychology Study Center (**academic.cengage.com/psychology**) or you can connect directly to the following sites:

**American Association of Sex Educators, Therapists, and Counselors**

This Web site has listings of sex therapists throughout the country that the association has certified.

**American Board of Sexology**

This Web site has listings of sex therapists throughout the country that the board has certified.

**Pelvic Pain**

Details about pain during intercourse or menstruation are offered on this Web site.

**Sex Therapy Advice**

This self-help site has information and advice about sexual problems.

**Go Ask Alice!**

This is a refreshingly frank and lively Web site sponsored by Columbia University. It answers questions about common and uncommon sexual concerns with sensitivity and wit. Look for Go Ask Alice's forum on sexual health as well.

**Dr. Ruth**

Dr. Ruth Westheimer offers a frank discussion of sexual issues in a fun and informative format. This Web page includes posted answers to visitors' questions.

**Viagra Information**

On this site the U.S. Food and Drug Administration provides consumers with basic information on Viagra, including precautions about who should not take this medication.

*Our Sexuality* **Book Companion Web Site** academic.cengage.com/psychology/crooks Visit your book companion Web site where you will find flash cards, practice quizzes, Internet links, and more to help you study.

## Just what you need to know NOW!

Spend time on what you need to master rather than on information you already have learned. Take a pretest for this chapter, and CengageNOW will generate a personalized study plan based on your results. The study plan will identify the topics you need to review and direct you to online resources to help you master those topics. You can then take a post-test to help you determine the concepts you have mastered and what you will still need to work on. Try it out! Go to academic.cengage.com/login to sign in with an access code or to purchase access to this product.

## InfoTrac College Edition Online Library

Sign in to academic.cengage.com/login or visit your free book companion Web site at academic.cengage.com/psychology/crooks to access InfoTrac College Edition, an online searchable library that includes a multitude of journals, many specific to human sexuality. These journals include *Archives of Sexual Behavior; Archives of Sexual Health Behavior; Canadian Journal of Human Sexuality; Hispanic Journal of the Behavioral Sciences; Journal of Cross-Cultural Psychology; Journal of Physical Education, Recreation, and Dance; Journal of Sex Research;* and *Sex Roles.*

# Sexually Transmitted Diseases

## THERE'S A WORD SOME FIND HARDER TO SAY THAN AIDS: CONDOM.

*Mary Chapin Carpenter*

COUNTRY AIDS AWARENESS

Using latex condoms does help prevent the spread of HIV, the virus that causes AIDS. But you have to use them properly... and that means every time you have sex, from start to finish. So even if you find it hard to say "condoms," you'll find they are easy to use. They could save your life.

BREAK THE SILENCE

For more information, call your local AIDS service organization or the CDC National AIDS Hotline at

**1 - 8 0 0 - 3 4 2 - A I D S**

David Young-Wolff/Photo Edit

**Bacterial Infections**

Why do health authorities now consider chlamydia infections a major health problem?

What kinds of complications can accompany gonorrhea?

Why are health authorities concerned about syphilis in the United States?

**Viral Infections**

Can the herpes virus be transmitted if an open sore is not present?

Why do health practitioners consider genital warts a serious problem?

Can both hepatitis A and hepatitis B be transmitted sexually? What symptoms are associated with hepatitis?

**Common Vaginal Infections**

What is a male partner's role in transmitting bacterial vaginosis?

What factors are associated with the development of candidiasis, and how is this infection treated?

How common is trichomoniasis, and what possible complications are associated with this infection?

**Ectoparasitic Infections**

Can pubic lice be transmitted by ways other than sexual interaction?

How contagious is scabies, what are its symptoms, and how is it treated?

**Acquired Immunodeficiency Syndrome (AIDS)**

How is HIV transmitted, and what behaviors put one at risk for becoming infected with HIV?

Among what portions of the population is AIDS increasing most rapidly? Has there been significant progress in the search for either an effective treatment or a cure for this disease?

**Preventing Sexually Transmitted Diseases**

What are some effective methods of preventing STDs or reducing the likelihood of contracting one?

*The possibility of getting a sexually transmitted disease has caused me to be extremely cautious and selective about whom I choose to be sexual with. It also makes every decision in a sexual relationship so critical and has made me much more careful in the choices I make. (Authors' files)*

**Sexually transmitted diseases (STDs)** Diseases that are transmitted by sexual contact.

In this chapter, we discuss a variety of **sexually transmitted diseases (STDs)***—that is, diseases that can be transmitted through sexual interaction. ⊙ **Table 15.1** summarizes the STDs described in this chapter. Some of these diseases are curable; others are not. As we will see, the consequences of STDs—such as compromised health, pain and discomfort, infertility, and even death—can adversely affect the quality of our lives. It is estimated that almost 19 million new cases of STDs occur each year in the United States and that, globally, annual new cases of STDs probably exceed 400 million (Koumans et al., 2005; Miller, 2006).

Our purpose in including a chapter on STDs is not to discourage you from exploring the joys of sexuality. Rather, we wish to help you make good decisions by presenting a realistic picture of what STDs are, how to recognize them, what should be done to treat them, and what measures can be taken to avoid contracting or transmitting them. We believe that this information is especially relevant to our college-age readers for the following reasons:

- A large percentage of all STDs in the United States occur among 15- to 24-year-olds. It is estimated that about half of the STDs diagnosed annually in the United States occur among people under the age of 25 (Adam & Rust, 2006; Lonergan & Hern, 2006).
- Approximately 3 million teenagers (1 in 4 sexually experienced adolescents) are infected with one or more STDs each year (Adams & Rust, 2006; Miller et al., 2005).
- Teenage women age 15 to 19 have the highest rates of chlamydia and gonorrhea infections (both potentially highly damaging STDs) of any age group in the United States (Einwalter et al., 2005; Lonergan & Hern, 2006). More than half of all reported cases of chlamydia and gonorrhea occur among 15- to 24-year-olds (Koumans et al., 2005).
- The highest incidence of genital warts, an extremely common STD in North America, occurs among young adults age 15 to 28 (Kahn & Hillard, 2006; McPartland et al., 2005).
- The largest proportion of AIDS cases in the United States occurs among people in their 20s and 30s who were infected with the AIDS virus (HIV) in their teens or 20s (Centers for Disease Control, 2006a). Half of new HIV infections occur among people younger than 25 (Adams and Rust, 2006; Nguyen et al., 2006).

You may wonder why we postpone our discussion of HIV/AIDS until later in this chapter. Certainly AIDS has received far more attention in the media than any of the other diseases discussed in this chapter. This emphasis on AIDS, although understandable in view of the continuing worldwide spread of this deadly disease, tends to obscure the fact that many other STDs are substantially more prevalent. Furthermore, many of these commonly occurring STDs, such as chlamydia and genital warts, pose major health risks that are escalating in proportion to the increasing incidence of these diseases.

Many factors contribute to the epidemic of STDs in the United States. Engaging in risky sexual behavior, such as having multiple sexual partners and unprotected (condomless) sex, is a prime reason for the high incidence of STDs. Such behavior is especially prevalent during adolescence and early adulthood, when the incidence of STDs is the highest. It is also believed that increased use of oral contraceptives has contributed

---

*Some health professionals prefer to call these conditions sexually transmitted infections, or STIs. The terms *STD* and *STI* are essentially interchangeable, but *STD* is the preferred term in the United States and *STI* is the preferred term internationally.

| STD | Transmission | Symptoms | Treatment(s) |
|---|---|---|---|
| Chlamydia | • The *Chlamydia trachomatis* bacterium is passed through sexual contact.<br><br>• Infection can spread from one body site to another via fingers. | • **Women:** Pelvic inflammatory disease, disrupted menstruation, pelvic pain, raised temperature, nausea, vomiting, headache, infertility, and ectopic pregnancy.<br><br>• **Men:** Urethra infection discharge and burning during urination; with epididymitis, heaviness in and painful swelling at bottom of affected testis, inflammation of scrotum. | • Doxycycline for 7 days, or one dose of azithromycin. |
| Gonorrhea | • The *Neisseria gonorrhoeae* bacterium is passed through penile–vaginal, oral–genital, oral–anal, or genital–anal contact. | • **Women:** Green or yellowish discharge (usually remains undetected); pelvic inflammatory disease may develop.<br><br>• **Men:** Cloudy discharge from penis and burning during urination; complications include painful swelling at bottom of affected testis and inflammation of scrotum. | • Dual therapy of one dose of ceftriaxone, cefixime, ciprofloxacin, levofloxacin, or ofloxacin plus one dose of azithromycin (or doxycycline for 7 days) |
| Nongonococcal urethritis (NGU) | • Primarily caused by various bacteria transmitted through coitus.<br><br>• Some NGU results from allergic reactions or from *Trichomonas* infection. | • **Women:** Mild discharge of pus from vagina (often remains undetected).<br><br>• **Men:** Discharge from penis and irritation during urination. | • One dose of azithromycin, or doxycycline for 7 days. |
| Syphilis | • The *Treponema pallidum* bacterium is passed from open lesions during penile–vaginal, oral–genital, oral–anal, or genital–anal contact. | • **Primary Stage:** Painless chancre at site where bacterium entered body.<br><br>• **Secondary Stage:** Chancre disappears, and generalized skin rash appears.<br><br>• **Latent Stage:** There may be no visible symptoms.<br><br>• **Tertiary Stage:** Heart failure, blindness, mental disturbance, and more; death may result. | • Benzathine penicillin G, doxycycline, erythromycin, or ceftriaxone. |
| Herpes | • HSV-2 (genital herpes virus) passed primarily through penile–vaginal, oral–genital, oral–anal, or genital–anal contact.<br><br>• HSV-1 (oral herpes) passed by kissing or oral–genital contact. | • Small painful red bumps appear in the genital region or mouth.<br><br>• Bumps become painful blisters and eventually rupture to form wet, open sores. | • No known cure.<br><br>• A variety of treatments can reduce symptoms.<br><br>• Oral acyclovir, valacyclovir, or famciclovir promote healing and suppress recurrent outbreaks. |
| Genital warts | • Human papillomavirus (HPV) is passed primarily through penile–vaginal, oral–genital, oral–anal, or genital–anal contact. | • Hard and yellow-gray growths on dry skin areas.<br><br>• Soft, pinkish-red, and cauliflowerlike growths on moist areas. | • Freezing, application of topical agents, cauterization, surgical removal, or vaporization by carbon dioxide laser. |

*continued*

○ **TABLE 15.1**    **Common Sexually Transmitted Diseases: Transmission, Symptoms, and Treatment,** *continued*

| STD | Transmission | Symptoms | Treatment(s) |
|---|---|---|---|
| Viral hepatitis | • Hepatitis B virus can be passed through blood, semen, vaginal secretions, and saliva.<br>• Manual, oral, or penile stimulation of anus is strongly associated with spread of hepatitis B.<br>• Hepatitis A is spread by means of oral–anal contact, especially when the mouth encounters fecal matter.<br>• Hepatitis C is spread through intravenous drug use and less frequently through contaminated blood products, sexual contact, or mother-to-fetus or mother-to-infant contact. | • Varies from no symptoms to mild, flulike symptoms to an incapacitating illness characterized by high fever, vomiting, and severe abdominal pain. | • No specific treatment for hepatitis A and B.<br>• Bed rest and adequate fluid intake.<br>• Combination therapy with pegylated interferon and ribavirin may be effective against hepatitis C. |
| Bacterial vaginosis | • Different types of bacterial microorganisms are passed through coitus. | • **Women:** Fishy- or musty-smelling, light-gray thin discharge (consistency of flour paste).<br>• **Men:** Usually asymptomatic. | • Metronidazole (Flagyl) by mouth.<br>• Intravaginal applications of topical metronidazole gel or clindamycin cream. |
| Candidiasis (yeast infection) | • The fungus *Candida albicans* accelerates growth when normal chemical balance of the vagina is disturbed.<br>• Can be passed through sexual interaction. | • **Women:** White "cheesy" discharge, irritation of vaginal and vulval tissues.<br>• **Men:** Usually asymptomatic but may have itching or reddening of the penis and burning during urination. | • Vaginal suppositories or topical cream, such as clotrimazole and miconazole.<br>• Oral fluconazole. |
| Trichomoniasis | • The protozoan parasite *Trichomonas vaginalis* is usually passed through sexual contact. | • **Women:** White or yellow vaginal discharge with unpleasant odor; vulva is sore and irritated.<br>• **Men:** Usually asymptomatic but may have urethral discharge, urge to urinate frequently, or painful urination. | • One dose of metronidazole (Flagyl) for women and men. |
| Pubic lice ("crabs") | • Pubic louse is spread through body contact or through shared clothing or bedding. | • Persistent itching.<br>• Lice are visible and can be located in pubic or other body hair. | • 1% permethrin or pyrethrin lotion or cream applied to all affected areas. |
| Scabies | • Highly contagious.<br>• Can be passed by close physical contact (sexual and nonsexual). | • Small bumps and a red rash that itch intensely (especially at night). | • Topical scabicide applied from neck down to toes. |
| Acquired immunodeficiency syndrome (AIDS) | • Blood, semen, and vaginal fluids are the major vehicles for transmitting HIV (which attacks the immune system).<br>• Passed primarily through penile–vaginal, oral–genital, oral–anal, or genital–anal contact or by needle sharing among injection drug users. | • Varies with the types of opportunistic infections or cancers that can afflict an infected person.<br>• Common symptoms include fever, night sweats, weight loss, chronic fatigue, swollen lymph nodes, diarrhea and/or bloody stool, atypical bruising or bleeding, skin rashes, headache, chronic cough, and a whitish coating on the tongue or throat. | • Commence treatment with a combination of three or more antiretroviral drugs (HAART) when CD4 count is significantly low.<br>• Specific treatments may be necessary to treat opportunistic infections and tumors. |

to the epidemic of STDs—both by increasing susceptibility of women to some STDs and by reducing the use of condoms, a contraceptive method known to offer protection against many infections. Lack of adequate public health measures and limited access to effective systems for prevention and treatment of STDs also contribute to this ongoing epidemic. In addition, many health-care providers in the United States are reluctant to ask questions about their patients' sexual behaviors, thus missing opportunities for STD-related counseling, diagnosis, and treatment.

The spread of STDs is facilitated by the unfortunate fact that many of these diseases do not produce obvious symptoms. In some cases, particularly among women, there may be no outward signs at all. Under these circumstances, people may unknowingly infect others. In addition, feelings of guilt and embarrassment that often accompany having an STD may prevent people from seeking adequate treatment or from informing their sexual partners. In the boxed discussion "Telling a Partner" on the following page, we explore why informing sexual partners is important and suggest ways to do so more easily.

In the following sections, we focus on the most common STDs. We also provide an expanded discussion of AIDS and the progress being made in treating this dreadful disease. The Centers for Disease Control and Prevention (CDC) periodically provides updated guidelines for treating STDs. The most recent guidelines, available online (Centers for Disease Control, 2006a), are the basis for most of the treatment information provided for the diseases discussed in this chapter.

If you want more information, we recommend that you contact your county health service or STD clinic, or that you call the National STD Hotline.* These services can answer questions, send free literature, and most importantly, give you the name and phone number of a local physician or public clinic that will treat STDs for free or at minimal cost. ■

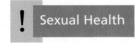

# Bacterial Infections

A variety of STDs are caused by bacterial agents. We begin this section with a discussion of chlamydia, one of the most prevalent and damaging of all STDs. The other bacterial infections we describe are gonorrhea, nongonococcal urethritis, and syphilis. We discuss bacterial vaginosis, a common vaginal infection, in a later section of this chapter.

## Chlamydia Infection

**Chlamydia** (cluh-MID-ee-uh) is caused by *Chlamydia trachomatis*, a bacterial microorganism that grows in body cells. This organism is now recognized as the cause of a diverse group of genital infections and is a common cause of preventable blindness.

**Chlamydia** Urogenital infection caused by the bacterium *Chlamydia trachomatis*.

### Incidence and Transmission

Chlamydia is the most common bacterial STD in the United States (Centers for Disease Control, 2006b). An estimated 3 to 4 million Americans develop a chlamyhdia infection each year (Lonergan & Hern, 2006). Sexually active teenagers, especially females, have higher infection rates than any other age group (Einwalter et al., 2005; Lonergan & Hern, 2006).

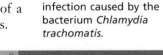

**InfoTrac Search Words**

- Chlamydia

Chlamydia disease is transmitted primarily through vaginal, anal, or oral sexual contact (Centers for Disease Control, 2006b). It can also be spread by fingers from one body site to another, such as from the genitals to the eyes.

### Symptoms and Complications

Two general types of genital chlamydia infections affect females. The first of these, infection of the mucosa of the lower reproductive tract, commonly takes the form of an inflammation of the urethral tube or an infection of the cervix. In both cases women experience few or no symptoms (Centers for Disease Control, 2006b; Einwalter et al., 2005). When symptoms do occur, they include a mild irritation or itching of the genital tissues, a burning sensation during urination, and a slight vaginal discharge.

---

*The National Sexually Transmitted Disease Hotline can be dialed toll-free from 8:00 A.M. to 8:00 P.M. on weekdays and from 10:00 A.M. to 6:00 P.M. on weekends, Pacific time. The number is (800) 227-8922.

## Telling a Partner

Most of us would find it difficult to discuss with our lover(s) the possibility that we have transmitted a disease to her or him during sexual activity. Because of the stigma often associated with STDs, it can be bad enough admitting to yourself that you have one of these diseases. The need to tell others that they might have "caught" something from you may seem like a formidable task. You might fear that such a revelation will jeopardize a valued relationship, or you might worry that you will be considered "dirty." In relationships presumed to be monogamous, you might fear that telling your partner about an STD will threaten mutual trust. At the same time, however, concealing a sex-related illness places a good deal more at risk in the long run.

Most important, not disclosing the existence of an STD risks the health of your partner(s). Many people may not have symptoms and thus may not become aware that they have contracted a disease until they discover it for themselves, perhaps only after they have developed serious complications. Furthermore, if a lover remains untreated, she or he may reinfect you even after you have been cured. Unlike some diseases (such as measles and chicken pox), STDs do not provide immunity against future infections. You can get one, give it to your lover, be cured, and then get it back again if he or she remains untreated.

The following suggestions provide some guidelines for telling a partner about your STD. Remember, these are only suggestions that have worked for some people; they may need to be modified to fit your particular circumstances. This sensitive issue requires thoughtful consideration and planning.

1. Be honest. There is nothing to be gained by downplaying the potential risks associated with STDs. If you tell a partner, "I have this little drip, but it probably means nothing," you may regret it. Be sure your partner understands the importance of obtaining a medical evaluation.

2. Even if you suspect that your partner may have been the source of your infection, there is little to be gained by blaming him or her. Instead, you may wish simply to acknowledge that you have the disease and are concerned that your partner gets proper medical attention.

3. Your attitude may have a considerable effect on how your partner receives the news. If you display high levels of anxiety, guilt, fear, or disgust, your partner may reflect these feelings in her or his response. Try to present the facts in as clear and calm a fashion as you can manage.

4. Be sensitive to your partner's feelings. Be prepared for reactions of anger or resentment. These are understandable initial responses. Being supportive and demonstrating a willingness to listen without becoming defensive may be the best tactics for diffusing negative responses.

5. Engaging in sexual intimacies after you become aware of your condition and before you obtain medical assurances that you are no longer contagious is clearly inappropriate. Discuss with your partner that abstinence from sexual intercourse is crucial for persons who are being treated for an STD or whose partners are undergoing treatment.

6. Medical examinations and treatments for STDs, when necessary, can be a financial burden. Offering to pay for some or all of these expenses may help to maintain (or reestablish) goodwill in your relationship.

---

**Pelvic inflammatory disease (PID)** An infection in the uterus and pelvic cavity.

**InfoTrac Search Words**

- Pelvic inflammatory disease

The second type of genital chlamydia infection in women is invasive infection of the upper reproductive tract, expressed as **pelvic inflammatory disease (PID)**. PID typically occurs when bacteria that cause chlamydia or gonorrhea spread from the cervix upward, infecting the lining of the uterus (*endometritis*), the fallopian tubes (*salpingitis*), and possibly the ovaries and other adjacent abdominal structures (Crossman, 2006; Miller, 2006). Chlamydia accounts for most of the 1.5 million recognized cases of PID that occur annually in the United States (Crossman, 2006). An estimated 40% of women with untreated chlamydia will develop PID (Centers for Disease Control, 2006b). Adolescents and women in their early 20s have the highest PID rates in the United States (Feroli & Burstein, 2003; Messner, 2003).

PID resulting from chlamydia infection often produces a variety of symptoms, which can include disrupted menstrual periods, chronic pelvic pain, lower back pain, fever, nausea, vomiting, and headache. Salpingitis caused by chlamydia infection is the primary preventable cause of female infertility and ectopic pregnancy (Bakken et al., 2006; Miller, 2005). Even after PID has been effectively treated, residual scar tissue in the fallopian tubes can leave some women sterile.

A woman who has had PID should be cautioned about the use of the IUD as a method of contraception. An IUD does not prevent fertilization (see Chapter 10 for an explanation of how the IUD prevents pregnancy); thus a tiny sperm cell could negotiate a partially blocked area of a scarred fallopian tube and fertilize an ovum that, because of its larger size, subsequently becomes lodged in the scarred tube. The result is an *ectopic pregnancy*, a serious hazard to the woman. The incidence of ectopic pregnancies in the United States has increased dramatically in the last 2 decades, largely because of an escalation in the occurrence of chlamydia infections.

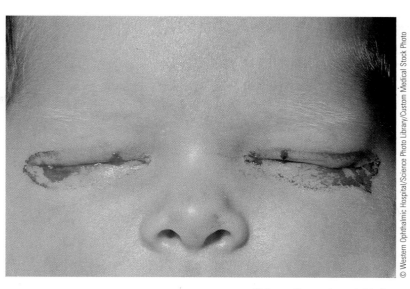

Chlamydia conjunctivitis in a newborn, acquired from an infected mother during birth.

In men untreated chlamydia may result in *epididymitis* (infection of the epididymis) or *nongonococcal urethritis* (NGU; infection of the urethral tube not caused by gonorrhea) (Centers for Disease Control, 2006b; Donovan, 2004). The symptoms of epididymitis include a sensation of heaviness in the affected testis, inflammation of the scrotal skin, and the formation of a small area of hard, painful swelling at the bottom of the testis. Symptoms of NGU include a discharge from the penis and a burning sensation during urination (more details are provided in a later section on NGU).

One of the most disheartening aspects of chlamydia is that symptoms are either minimal or nonexistent in a majority of infected women and about half of infected men (Centers for Disease Control, 2006b). Most women and men with rectal chlamydia infections also manifest few or no symptoms (Kent et al., 2005).

Another complication associated with *Chlamydia trachomatis* is **trachoma** (truh-KOHmuh), a chronic, contagious form of **conjunctivitis** (kun-junk-ti-VIE-tus) (inflammation of the mucous membrane that lines the inner surface of the eyelid and the exposed surface of the eyeball). Trachoma is the world's leading cause of preventable blindness; it is particularly prevalent in Asia and Africa. *Chlamydia trachomatis* is a common cause of eye infections (conjunctivitis) in newborns, who can become infected as they pass through the birth canal (Centers for Disease Control, 2006b; Einwalter et al., 2005). In addition, many babies of infected mothers will develop pneumonia caused by chlamydia infection (Centers for Disease Control, 2006b). Chlamydia infection in pregnant women can also lead to premature delivery (Centers for Disease Control, 2006b). The CDC recommends that pregnant women be tested for chlamydia during their first prenatal visit.

**Trachoma** A chronic, contagious form of conjunctivitis caused by chlamydia infections.

**Conjunctivitis** Inflammation of the mucous membrane that lines the inner surface of the eyelid and the exposed surface of the eyeball.

## Treatment

CDC guidelines suggest treating uncomplicated chlamydia infections with a 7-day regimen of doxycycline taken by mouth or a single 1-gram dose of azithromycin. All sexual partners exposed to chlamydia should be examined for STDs and treated if necessary (Centers for Disease Control, 2006b; Ebell, 2005).

To reduce the risk of an infant developing chlamydia conjunctivitis after passing through the birth canal of an infected mother, either erythromycin or tetracycline ointment is put into the eyes of exposed newborns as soon as possible after birth.

InfoTrac Search Words

- Gonorrhea

## Gonorrhea

**Gonorrhea** (gah-nuh-REE-uh), known in street language as "the clap," is an STD caused by the bacterium *Neisseria gonorrhoeae* (also called *gonococcus*).

**Gonorrhea** An sexually transmitted disease that initially causes inflammation of mucous membranes.

## Incidence and Transmission

Gonorrhea is the second most reported infectious disease in the United States (Lonergan & Hern, 2006). The CDC estimates that there are about 700,000 new cases of gonorrhea each year (Centers for Disease Control, 2006c). The late 1970s witnessed the beginning of an intensified public health effort to curtail gonorrhea infections in the United States. These efforts resulted in a downward trend in the overall incidence of gonorrhea in the U.S. population. In 2004 the gonorrhea rate in the United States fell to the lowest level since federal health officials started tracking cases in 1941 (Strobbe, 2005). Nevertheless, gonorrhea rates remain exceptionally high among teenagers and young adults, especially in lower socioeconomic ethnic minority communities (Calvert, 2003; Kuehn, 2005). In contrast to the general decline in U.S. gonorrhea rates that has occurred over most of the last 2 decades, the world's most populous nation, China, has experienced a marked resurgence of gonorrhea and other STDs in recent years, as described in the following Sexuality and Diversity discussion.

## SEXUALITY AND DIVERSITY

### STDs in China: A Reemerging Epidemic

The overall incidence of STDs in China, a nation of more than 1.3 billion people, is considerably lower than in many other developing countries in Africa and Asia. However, this situation is changing as the prevalence of STDs in China rapidly escalates. Before the founding of the People's Republic of China in 1949, syphilis, gonorrhea, and other STDs were prevalent (X. Chen et al., 2000; M. Cohen et al., 2000). The spread of STDs in prerevolutionary China was fueled by drug use, widespread commercial sex work, and poverty (M. Cohen et al., 2000). When Mao Zedong came to power, his government implemented a massive campaign to wipe out STDs. Mao's approach was heavy-handed but successful. By 1964 STDs were virtually eradicated from China (X. Chen et al., 2000; M. Cohen et al., 2000). However, this situation changed rapidly after China implemented its open-door policy in the 1980s, which encouraged contact with the Western world, promoted rapid migration of people from rural to urban areas, and led to changes in the economic and sociocultural environments of China.

In the last 2 decades commercial sex work has reemerged, and findings from a number of studies have demonstrated that STDs (including HIV/AIDS) and the behaviors that spread them are rapidly increasing in China (Beyrer, 2003; Liu et al., 2006; Wang et al., 2005). The first case of AIDS in China was reported in 1985 (Ammann, 2000). Over the next few years HIV infection was sporadically reported in a small number of people who were either primarily foreigners granted access to China or returning "overseas Chinese" (Ammann, 2000). Rapid spread of HIV began in 1995, and an estimated 800,000 to 1,500,000 cumulative cases of HIV infection had occurred in China by the end of 2001 (Choi et al., 2003b). The Chinese Ministry of Health (2006) estimates that 70,000 new HIV infections occur every year in the Chinese population.

The critical issue for HIV/AIDS in China involves China's vulnerability to a widespread heterosexual HIV epidemic. Recent data demonstrating an overall escalation in STD rates—especially a high incidence of chlamydia infection and the increased activity of commercial sex workers in China—suggest that risky sexual behaviors are on the rise. A recent nationally representative study revealed that 9.3% of surveyed men reported inconsistent condom use in sexual relations with sex workers (Parish et al., 2003). This pattern of sexual risk taking has been documented in Thailand and Cambodia, where Asia's worst HIV epidemics have occurred (Rojanapithayakorn & Hannenberg, 1996; Ryan et al., 1998). In both these countries large numbers of men having sex with both primary partners and sex workers, without condom protection, drove explosive heterosexual epidemics throughout the 1990s.

National government-supported public health campaigns to encourage sex workers and their clients to use condoms have had a major effect on reducing HIV infection rates in Thailand and Cambodia (Beyrer, 2003). Unfortunately, open publicity and education about condom use by sex workers in China is difficult because prostitution remains illegal in this nation and police and security agencies continue to harass and arrest sex workers instead of educating them about condom use (Beyrer,

2003). We can only hope that government officials will change their tactics as the wisdom of education versus harassment becomes increasingly clear. China could mobilize an effective national campaign against HIV/AIDS similar to the successful effort in Thailand. Currently, the Chinese government controls the media, and every village has a government official who monitors menstrual cycles as part of China's one-child policy. If government officials would commit to preventing HIV infections with the same level of zealousness that they apply to preventing unauthorized births, they could curtail the spread of this disease and thus aid immeasurably in averting major expansion of the global HIV pandemic.

On a more positive note, a comprehensive, community-based sex education program targeting unmarried 15- to 24-year-olds was recently implemented in a suburb of Shanghai. Participation in this program, which included information on safer sexual behaviors and contraception, was associated with an increase in healthy sexual behavior, including use of condoms (Wang et al., 2005). We hope that the positive results of this pilot project will encourage the development of more widespread sex education in China.

The *gonococcus* bacterium thrives in the warm mucous membrane tissues of the genitals, anus, and throat. Its mode of transmission is by sexual contact—penile–vaginal, oral–genital, oral–anal, or genital–anal.

## Symptoms and Complications

Early symptoms of gonorrhea infection are more likely to be evident in men than in women (Centers for Disease Control, 2006c). Most men who experience gonococcal urethritis have some symptoms, ranging from mild to pronounced. However, it is not uncommon for men with this type of infection to have no symptoms and yet be potentially infectious.

**Early Symptoms in the Male** In men early symptoms typically appear 1–5 days after sexual contact with an infected person. However, symptoms can show up as late as 30 days after contact or, in a small number of cases, may not appear at all. The two most common signs of infection are a bad-smelling, cloudy discharge from the penis (see ● **Figure 15.1**) and a burning sensation during urination. Some infected men also have swollen and tender lymph glands in the groin. These early symptoms sometimes clear up on their own without treatment. However, this is no guarantee that the disease has been eradicated by the body's immune system. The bacteria may still be present, and a man may still be able to infect a partner.

**Complications in the Male** If the infection continues without treatment for 2 to 3 weeks, it can spread up the genitourinary tract. Here, it can involve the prostate, bladder, kidneys, and testes. Most men who continue to harbor *gonococcus* have only periodic flare-ups of the minor symptoms of discharge and a burning sensation during urination. In a small number of men, however, abscesses form in the prostate. These can result in fever, painful bowel movement, difficulty urinating, and general discomfort. In approximately 1 out of 5 men who remain untreated for longer than a month, the bacteria move down the vas deferens to infect one or both of the epididymal structures that lie along the back of each testis. In general, only one side is infected initially, usually the left. (Symptoms of epididymitis were described in the discussion of chlamydia infection.) Even after successful treatment, gonococcal epididymitis leaves scar tissue, which can block the flow of sperm from the affected testis. Sterility does not usually result, because this complication typically affects only one testis. However, if treatment is still not carried out after epididymitis has occurred on one side, the infection can spread to the other testis, causing permanent sterility.

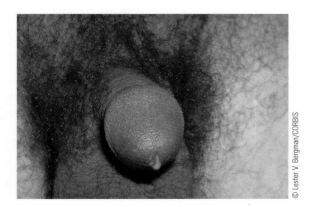

© Lester V. Bergman/CORBIS

● **Figure 15.1** A cloudy discharge symptomatic of gonorrhea infection.

**Early Symptoms in the Female** Most women infected with gonorrhea are unaware of the early symptoms of this disease. The primary site of infection, the cervix, can become inflamed without producing any observable symptoms. Symptoms that may occur include a painful or burning sensation when urinating and/or increased vaginal discharge. However, because this discharge is rarely heavy, it commonly goes unnoticed. A woman who is aware of her vaginal secretions is more likely to note the infection during these early stages. Sometimes the discharge is irritating to the vulval tissues. However, when a woman seeks medical attention for an irritating discharge, her physician may fail to consider gonorrhea because many other infectious organisms produce this symptom. Also, many women who have gonorrhea also have trichomoniasis (discussed later in this chapter), and this condition can mask the presence of gonorrhea. Consequently, it is essential for any woman who thinks she may have gonorrhea to make certain that she is tested for the disease when she is examined. (A Pap smear is *not* a test for gonorrhea.)

**Complications in the Female** Serious complications result from the spread of this disease to the upper reproductive tract, where it often causes PID (Centers for Disease Control, 2006c). The symptoms of PID, discussed in the section on chlamydia infection, are often more severe when the infecting organism is *gonococcus* rather than *Chlamydia trachomatis*. Sterility and ectopic pregnancy are serious consequences occasionally associated with gonococcal PID. Another serious complication that can result from PID is the development of tough bands of scar-tissue adhesions that may link several pelvic cavity structures (fallopian tubes, ovaries, uterus, etc.) to each other, to the abdominal walls, or to both. These adhesions can cause severe pain during coitus or when a woman is standing or walking.

**Other Complications in Both Sexes** In about 2% of adult men and women with gonorrhea, the bacteria enter the bloodstream and spread throughout the body to produce a variety of symptoms, including chills, fever, loss of appetite, skin lesions, and arthritic pain in the joints (Calvert, 2003). If arthritic symptoms develop, quick treatment is essential to avoid permanent joint damage. In rare cases the *gonococcus* organism can invade the heart, liver, spinal cord, and brain.

An infant can develop a gonococcal eye infection, which may cause blindness, after passing through the birth canal of an infected woman (Meyers, 2005). The use of silver nitrate eyedrops or antibiotic ophthalmic ointment immediately after birth averts this potential complication. In a few rare cases, adults have transmitted the bacteria to their own eyes by touching this region immediately after handling their genitals—one reason why it is important to wash with soap and water immediately after self-examination. ∎

Oral contact with infected genitals can result in infection of the throat (Centers for Disease Control, 2006c). Although this form of gonorrhea can cause a sore throat, most people experience no symptoms. Rectal gonorrhea can be caused by anal intercourse or, in a woman, by transmission of the bacteria from the vagina to the anal opening by means of menstrual blood or vaginal discharge. Rectal gonorrhea is often asymptomatic, particularly in females, but it might be accompanied by itching, bleeding, rectal discharge, and painful bowel movements.

## Treatment

Because gonorrhea is often confused with other ailments, it is important to make the correct diagnosis. Because coexisting chlamydia infections often accompany gonorrhea, health practitioners often use a treatment strategy that is effective against both (Centers for Disease Control, 2006c). Before 1976 gonorrhea could be effectively treated with penicillin or tetracycline. Since 1976, however, penicillin- and tetracycline-resistant strains of gonococcal bacteria have emerged (Bauer et al., 2005). Consequently, treatment guidelines suggest the use of drugs effective against both resistant and nonresistant strains. The current treatment regimen recommended by the CDC includes the dual therapy of a single dose of ceftriaxone, cefixime, ciprofloxacin, levofloxacin, or ofloxacin plus a single dose of azithromycin (or doxycycline for 7 days).

In recent years there has been an alarming worldwide increase in strains of gonorrhea resistant to fluoroquinolone antibiotics (ciprofloxacin, levofloxacine, and ofloxacin) (Bauer et al., 2005). A disproportionate number of these fluoroquinolone-resistant cases in the United States have occurred in California, Hawaii, and among men who have sex with men (MSM) (Kuehn, 2005). Consequently, the CDC has recommended that this class of antibiotics should no longer be used to treat gonorrhea cases occurring in MSM or in California or Hawaii.

It is quite common for sexual partners of infected individuals to have also contracted gonorrhea. Consequently, all sexual partners exposed to a person with diagnosed gonorrhea should be examined, cultured, and, if necessary, treated with a drug regimen that covers both gonococcal and chlamydia infections (Centers for Disease Control, 2006c).

## Nongonococcal Urethritis

Any inflammation of the urethra that is not caused by gonorrhea is called **nongonococcal urethritis (NGU)**. It is believed that two microscopic bacterial organisms, *Chlamydia trachomatis* and *Mycoplasma genitalium* are primary causes of NGU (Bradshaw et al., 2006; Handsfield, 2006). NGU can also result from invasion by other infectious agents, allergic reactions to vaginal secretions, or irritation from soaps, vaginal contraceptives, or deodorant sprays.

**Nongonococcal urethritis (NGU)** An inflammation of the urethral tube caused by organisms other than *gonococcus*.

### Incidence and Transmission

NGU is quite common among men: In the United States NGU occurs much more frequently than gonorrhea. Although NGU generally produces urinary tract symptoms only in men, there is evidence that women harbor the organisms that can cause NGU. The most common forms of NGU are generally transmitted through coitus. That NGU rarely occurs in men who are not involved in sexual interaction supports this contention.

### Symptoms and Complications

Men who contract NGU often manifest symptoms similar to those of gonorrhea infection, including discharge from the penis and a mild burning sensation during urination. Often the discharge is less pronounced than with gonorrhea; it may be evident only in the morning before urinating.

Women with NGU are generally unaware of the disease until they are informed that it has been diagnosed in a male partner. They frequently show no symptoms, although there may be some itching, a burning sensation during urination, and a mild discharge of pus from the vagina. A woman may unknowingly have the infection for a long time, during which she may pass it to sexual partners.

The symptoms of NGU generally disappear after 2 to 3 months without treatment. However, the disease may still be present. If left untreated in women, it can result in cervical inflammation or PID; in men it can spread to the prostate, epididymis, or both. In rare cases NGU can produce a form of arthritis.

### Treatment

A single dose of azithromycin or a regimen of doxycyline for 7 days usually clears up NGU. All sexual partners of individuals diagnosed with NGU should be examined for the presence of an STD and treated if necessary.

## Syphilis

**Syphilis** (SIH-fuh-lus) is an STD caused by a thin, corkscrewlike bacterium called *Treponema pallidum* (also commonly called a spirochete).

**Syphilis** A sexually transmitted disease caused by a bacterium called *Treponema pallidum*.

### Incidence and Transmission

Syphilis rates declined steadily in the United States throughout the 1990s (Rosen, 2006). In fact, by the end of the 20th century the incidence of syphilis was so low that the CDC announced a bold plan to eliminate this disease in the United States by 2005. Unfortunately, syphilis rates have recently risen. The reported rate of primary or early-stage syphilis rose by 29% between 2000 and 2004 (Stobbe, 2005). This overall increased incidence of syphilis was largely attributable to an increase among MSM (Centers for Disease Control, 2006d; Rosen, 2006). Syphilis outbreaks among MSM have been reported in several large urban areas, such as Chicago, Seattle, San Francisco, New York, and Miami. For example, health officials in Chicago recently reported a fourfold increase in syphilis cases occurring among MSM (Worcester, 2004). Almost 15% of these Chicago cases were attributable to oral sex (Worcester, 2004). Even though the risk of HIV transmission via oral sex is considerably lower than through vaginal or anal sex, many people who operate under the mistaken assumption that oral sex is a safe replacement for higher-risk sexual behavior may never use a condom during oral sex.

*Treponema pallidum* requires a warm, moist environment for survival. It is transmitted almost exclusively from open lesions of infected individuals to the mucous membranes or skin abrasions of sexual partners through penile–vaginal, oral–genital, oral–anal, or genital–anal contacts. An infected pregnant woman can also transmit *Treponema pallidum* to her unborn child through the placental blood system. The resulting infection can cause miscarriage, stillbirth, or *congenital syphilis*, which can result in death or extreme damage to infected newborns (Centers for Disease Control, 2006d; Donovan, 2004). If syphilis is successfully treated before the 4th month of pregnancy, the fetus will not be affected. Therefore pregnant women should be tested for syphilis sometime during their first 3 months of pregnancy. The CDC recommends that all pregnant women be tested for syphilis at the first prenatal visit.

## Symptoms and Complications

If untreated, syphilis can progress through the primary, secondary, latent, and tertiary phases of development. We provide a brief description of each phase in the following paragraphs.

**Chancre** A raised red painless sore that is symptomatic of the primary phase of syphilis.

**Primary Syphilis** In its initial or primary phase syphilis is generally manifested in the form of a single, painless sore called a **chancre** (SHANG-kur), which usually appears about 3 weeks after initial infection at the site where the spirochete organism entered the body (see ○ **Figure 15.2**). In women this sore most commonly appears on the inner vaginal walls or cervix. It can also appear on the external genitals, particularly the labia. In men the chancre most often occurs on the glans of the penis, but it can also show up on the penile shaft or on the scrotum. Although most chancres are genital, the sores can occur in the mouth or rectum or on the anus or breast. People who have had oral sex with an infected individual might develop a sore on the lips or tongue. Anal intercourse can result in chancres appearing in the rectum or around the anus.

○ **Figure 15.2** The first stage of syphilis. A syphilitic chancre as it appears on (a) the penis and (b) the labia.

(a)

(b)

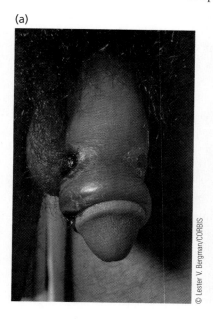
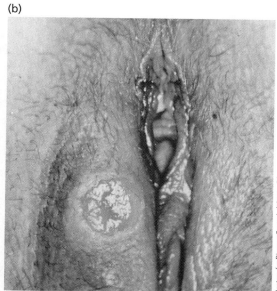

© Lester V. Bergman/CORBIS

Centers for Disease Control, Atlanta, GA

Since the chancre is typically painless, it often goes undiscovered when it occurs on internal structures, such as the rectum, vagina, or cervix. (Occasionally, chancres may be painful, and they may occur in multiple sites.) Even when the chancre is noticed, some people do not seek treatment. Unfortunately (from the long-term perspective), the chancre generally heals without treatment 1 to 6 weeks after it first appears. For the next few weeks, the infected person usually has no symptoms but can infect an unsuspecting partner. After about 6 weeks (although sometimes after as little as 2 weeks or as many as 6 months), the disease progresses to the secondary stage in about 50% of the people with untreated primary syphilis (Goens et al., 1994).

**Secondary Syphilis** In the secondary phase, which usually emerges 2 to 8 weeks after exposure, a skin rash appears on the body, often on the palms of the hands and soles of the feet (see **○Figure 15.3**). The rash can vary from barely noticeable to severe, with raised bumps that have a rubbery, hard consistency. Although the rash may look terrible, it typically does not hurt or itch. Besides a generalized rash, a person may experience flulike symptoms, such as fever, swollen lymph glands, fatigue, weight loss, and joint or bone pain. Even when not treated, these symptoms usually subside within a few weeks. Rather than being eliminated, however, the disease can then enter the potentially more dangerous latent phase (Centers for Disease Control, 2006d).

**Latent Syphilis** The latent stage can last for several years, during which time there may be no observable symptoms (Centers for Disease Control, 2006d). Nevertheless, the infecting organisms continue to multiply, preparing for the final stage of syphilitic infection. After 1 year of the latent stage, the infected individual is no longer contagious to sexual partners. However, a pregnant woman with syphilis in any stage can pass the infection to her fetus.

**Tertiary Syphilis** Approximately 30% of individuals who do not obtain effective treatment during the first three stages of syphilis enter the tertiary stage later in life (Augenbraun, 2000). The final manifestations of syphilis can be severe, often resulting in death. They usually occur anywhere from 5 to 25 years after initial infection and include such conditions as heart failure, blindness, ruptured blood vessels, paralysis, skin ulcers, liver damage, and severe mental disturbance (Centers for Disease Control, 2006d; Osterbauer, 2005). Depending on the extent of the damage, treatment even at this late stage can be beneficial (Osterbauer, 2005).

(b)

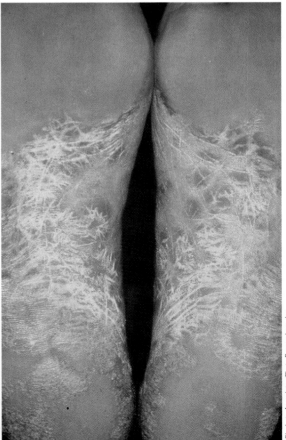

○ **Figure 15.3** In the secondary phase of syphilis a skin rash appears on the body, often on (a) the palms and (b) the feet.

(a)

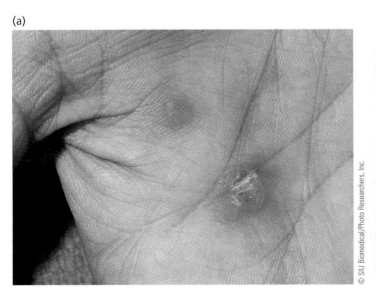

### Treatment

Primary, secondary, or latent syphilis of less than 1 year's duration can be effectively treated with intramuscular injections of benzathine penicillin G (Centers for Disease Control, 2006d). People who are allergic to penicillin can be treated with doxycycline, erythromycin, or ceftriaxone. Syphilis of more than 1 year's duration is treated with intramuscular injections of benzathine penicillin G once a week for 3 successive weeks.

All sex partners who have been exposed to a person with infectious syphilis should be treated. *All* individuals who have been treated for this disease should have several diagnostic blood tests at 3-month intervals after treatment is completed to make certain that they are completely free of the *Treponema pallidum* organism (Mossad, 2003). ■

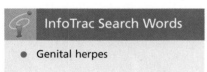

Sexual Health

## ◗ Viral Infections

Viruses are the cause of several common STDs. A virus is an organism that invades, reproduces, and lives within a cell, thereby disrupting normal cellular activity. Most viruses are transmitted through direct contact with infectious blood or other body fluids. We begin our discussion with herpes, the most common viral STD. Next, we describe genital warts caused by several varieties of viruses that have reached epidemic proportions in the U.S. population. We conclude with some information about viral hepatitis. AIDS, caused by HIV infection, is described in detail later in this chapter.

## Herpes

**Herpes** A disease characterized by blisters on the skin in the regions of the genitals or mouth. It is caused by the *Herpes simplex* virus and is easily transmitted through sexual contact.

**Herpes** is caused by the *Herpes simplex* virus (HSV). Eight different herpes viruses infect humans, the most common being the varicella-zoster virus (VZV) that causes chicken pox, followed in frequency by *Herpes simplex* virus type 1 (HSV-1) and *Herpes simplex* virus type 2 (HSV-2). In the following discussion we confine our attention to HSV-1 and HSV-2 because these are the two herpes viruses that are widely transmitted through sexual contact. HSV-1 typically manifests itself as lesions or sores—called cold sores or fever blisters—in the mouth or on the lips (oral herpes). HSV-2 generally causes lesions on and around the genital areas (genital herpes).

InfoTrac Search Words

● Genital herpes

Although genital and oral herpes are usually associated with different herpes viruses, oral–genital transmission is possible. HSV-1 can affect the genital area, and, conversely, HSV-2 can produce a sore in the mouth (Engelberg et al., 2003). However, most infections of the genitals are of the HSV-2 variety, and most mouth infections are HSV-1 (Singh et al., 2005).

### Incidence and Transmission

Current estimates indicate that more than 100 million Americans have oral herpes, and at least 45 million (1 in 5 people over age 12) have genital herpes (Centers for Disease Control, 2006e; Rosen, 2006). Genital herpes infections in the United States are more common in women than in men, which may indicate that male-to-female transmission is more likely than female-to-male transmission (Centers for Disease Control, 2006e).

Genital herpes appears to be transmitted primarily by penile–vaginal, oral–genital, genital–anal, or oral–anal contact. Oral herpes can be transmitted by kissing or through oral–genital contact. A person who receives oral sex from a partner who has herpes in the mouth region can develop either type 1 or type 2 genital herpes.

When any herpes sores are present, the infected person is highly contagious. It is extremely important to avoid bringing the lesions into contact with someone else's body through touching, sexual interaction, or kissing.

Although it was once believed that herpes could be transmitted only when lesions were present, we now know that HSV can be transmitted even when there are no symptoms (Centers for Disease Control, 2006e). In fact, research strongly indicates that asymptomatic "viral shedding" (the emission of viable HSV onto body surfaces) is likely to occur at least some of the time in many people infected with HSV. This asymptomatic viral shedding can result in transmission of the virus despite the absence of symptoms that suggest active infection.

Research has shown that herpes viruses do not pass through latex condoms. Thus condoms are effective in preventing transmission from a male whose only lesions occur on the glans or shaft of the penis. Condoms are helpful but less effective in preventing transmission from a female to a male, because vaginal secretions containing the virus can wash over the male's scrotal area. Nevertheless, using condoms consistently and correctly can minimize the risk of either acquiring or transmitting genital herpes (London, 2006).

What can infected people do to reduce the risk that they will transmit the virus to a sexual partner? Clearly, when lesions are present, they should avoid any kind of intimate or sexual activity that will expose a partner's body to viral shedding of HSV. However, as previously described, even when no sores or other symptoms are present, infected individuals are at risk for shedding the virus. Consequently, "unprotected sex is like Russian roulette—they can never be certain regarding when they are contagious" (Stanberry, 2000, p. 268). The best strategy for people who are either infected themselves or involved with an infected partner is to consistently and correctly use condoms even when they or their partners are asymptomatic.

People can also spread the virus from one part of their bodies to another part by touching a sore and then scratching or rubbing somewhere else. However, self-infection appears to be possible only immediately after the initial appearance of infection. Soon the body produces antibodies that ward off infection at other sites. Nevertheless, it is good practice for people with herpes to wash their hands thoroughly with soap and water after touching a sore. It is better to avoid touching sores, if possible. ∎

! Sexual Health

## Symptoms and Complications

The symptoms associated with HSV-1 and HSV-2 infections are quite similar.

**Genital Herpes (Type 2) Symptoms** The incubation period of genital herpes is 2 to 14 days, and the symptoms usually last 2 to 4 weeks (Centers for Disease Control, 2006e). However, many individuals with genital herpes experience minimal or no recognizable symptoms (Centers for Disease Control, 2006e). When symptoms are present, they consist of one or more small painful red bumps, called *papules*, that usually appear in the genital region. In women the areas most commonly infected are the labia. The mons veneris, clitoris, vaginal opening, inner vaginal walls, and cervix can also be affected. In men the infected site is typically the glans or shaft of the penis. Men and women who have engaged in anal intercourse can develop eruptions in and around the anus.

Soon after their initial appearance, papules rapidly develop into tiny painful blisters filled with a clear fluid containing highly infectious virus particles. The body then attacks the virus with white blood cells, causing the blisters to fill with pus (see ◗ **Figure 15.4** on the following page). Soon the blisters rupture to form wet painful open sores surrounded by a red ring (health practitioners refer to this as the period of viral shedding). A person is highly contagious during this time. About 10 days after the first appearance of a papule, the open sore forms a crust and begins to heal—a process that can take as long as 10 more days. Sores on the cervix can continue to produce infectious material for as long as 10 days after labial sores have completely healed. Consequently, it is wise to avoid coitus for a 10-day period after all external sores have healed.

Other symptoms can accompany genital herpes, including swollen lymph nodes in the groin, fever, muscle aches, and headaches. In addition, urination may be accompanied by a burning sensation, and women may experience increased vaginal discharge.

**Oral Herpes (Type 1) Symptoms** Oral herpes is characterized by the formation of papules on the lips and sometimes on the inside of the mouth, on the tongue, and on the throat. These blisters tend to crust over and heal in 10 to 16 days. Other symptoms include fever, general muscle aches, swollen lymph nodes in the neck, flulike symptoms, increased salivation, and sometimes bleeding in the mouth.

> **? Critical Thinking Question**
>
> Many individuals with genital herpes who have rare outbreaks of the disease worry about being rejected by prospective sexual partners if they disclose their condition. Do you believe that people who carefully monitor their health and take reasonable precautions can ethically enter into sexual relationships without revealing that they have genital herpes? Why or why not?

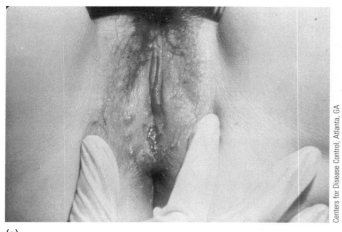

(a)

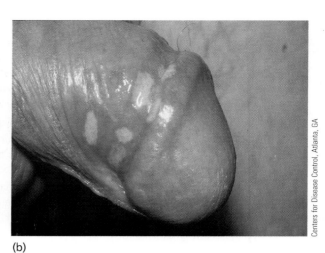

(b)

Centers for Disease Control, Atlanta, GA

Centers for Disease Control, Atlanta, GA

⊙ **Figure 15.4** Genital herpes blisters as they appear on (a) the labia and (b) the penis.

**Prodromal symptoms** Symptoms that warn of an impending herpes eruption.

**Recurrence** Even after complete healing, lesions can recur. Unfortunately, the herpes virus does not typically go away; instead, it retreats up the nerve fibers leading from the infected site (Colgan et al., 2003). Ultimately, the genital herpes virus finds a resting place in nerve cells adjacent to the lower spinal column, whereas the oral herpes virus becomes lodged in nerve cells in the back of the neck. The virus can remain dormant in these cells, without causing any apparent damage, perhaps for a person's entire lifetime. However, in many cases there will be periodic flare-ups as the virus retraces its path back down the nerve fibers leading to the genitals or lips.

Although some people never experience a recurrence of herpes following the initial or primary infection, research suggests that most people who have undergone a primary episode of genital herpes infection experience at least one recurrence. Individuals who experience recurrences may do so frequently or only occasionally. Symptoms associated with recurrent attacks tend to be milder than primary episodes, and the disease tends to run its course more quickly (Centers for Disease Control, 2006e). The recurrence rates for genital herpes caused by HSV-1 are lower than recurrence rates for genital HSV-2 infections (Engelberg et al., 2003).

Most people prone to recurrent herpes outbreaks experience some type of **prodromal symptoms** that warn of an impending eruption. These indications include itching, burning, throbbing, or "pins-and-needles" tingling at the sites commonly infected by herpes blisters, and sometimes pain in the legs, thighs, groin, or buttocks. Many health authorities believe that a person's degree of infectiousness increases during this stage and that it further escalates when the lesions appear. Research indicates that viral shedding is much more common on days when prodromal symptoms are present than on days when such symptoms are absent (Krone et al., 2000). Consequently, a person should be particularly careful to avoid direct contact from the time he or she first experiences prodromal symptoms until the sores have completely healed. Even during an outbreak, it is possible to continue sexual intimacies with a partner, as long as infected skin does not come into contact with healthy skin. During this time, partners may wish to experiment with other kinds of sensual pleasuring, such as sensate focus (see Chapter 14), hugging, or manual stimulation.

A variety of factors can trigger reactivation of the herpes virus, including emotional stress, anxiety, depression, acidic food, ultraviolet light, fever, menstruation, poor nutrition, being overtired or run-down, and trauma to the affected skin region (Emmert, 2000; Kirchner & Emmert, 2000). Because triggering factors vary so widely, it is often difficult to associate a specific event with a recurrent herpes outbreak.

Some people may not experience a relapse of genital herpes until several years after the initial infection. Therefore, if you have been in what you believe is a sexually exclusive relationship and your partner shows symptoms or transmits the virus to you, it does not necessarily mean that she or he contracted the disease from someone else during the course of your relationship. Furthermore, as stated earlier, many people with genital herpes infections are asymptomatic or have such mild symptoms that they are often unrecognizable. Thus a first episode of symptomatic genital herpes may not be due to recent sexual contact with an infected person.

**Other Complications** Although the sores are painful and bothersome, it is unlikely that men will experience major physical complications of herpes. Women, however, face two serious, although quite uncommon, complications: cancer of the cervix and infection of a newborn. Evidence suggests that the risk of developing cervical cancer is somewhat higher among women who have had genital herpes (Centers for Disease Control, 2006e). However, the role of genital herpes in cervical cancer is at most that of a cofactor, not that of a direct causative agent (Centers for Disease Control, 2006e). Fortunately, the great majority of women infected with herpes will never develop cancer of the cervix. Nonetheless, it is advisable for all women, particularly those who have had genital herpes, to obtain an annual cervical Pap smear. Some authorities recommend that women with genital herpes should have this test every 6 months.

A newborn can be infected with genital herpes while passing through the birth canal, and such an infection can cause severe damage or death (Centers for Disease Control, 2006e; Donoval et al., 2006). It is believed that viral shedding from the cervix, vagina, or vulva plays the primary role in transmitting the disease perinatally from mother to infant. Most infected newborns develop typical skin sores (papules), which should be cultured to confirm a herpes diagnosis. The presence of genital herpes sores when delivery is imminent poses a significant risk for transmission of HSV from an infected mother to her baby. To avert this possibility, a cesarean delivery may be performed, and the CDC recommends cesarean delivery for women in labor who have symptomatic disease, especially if it is the initial outbreak of herpes lesions. Cesarean delivery has been the standard of care for more than 30 years for women who have genital herpes lesions present at the time of delivery (Brown et al., 2003). A recent large-scale study of 58,362 pregnant women clearly demonstrated that cesarean delivery reduces the risk of transmission of genital HSV-1 or HSV-2 from mother to child during delivery (Brown et al., 2003).

One additional serious complication can occur when a person transfers the virus to an eye after touching a virus-shedding sore. This can lead to a severe eye infection known as ocular herpes. The best way to prevent this complication is to avoid touching herpes sores. If you cannot avoid contact, thoroughly wash your hands with hot water and soap immediately after touching the lesions. There are effective treatments for ocular herpes, but they must be started quickly to avoid eye damage. ■

**! Sexual Health**

Many people who have recurrent herpes outbreaks are troubled with mild to severe psychological distress (Centers for Disease Control, 2006e; Mills & Mindel, 2003). In view of the physical discomfort associated with the disease, the unpredictability of recurrent outbreaks, and the lack of an effective cure (see next section), it is no small wonder that people who have herpes undergo considerable stress. We believe that becoming better informed about herpes may help to alleviate some of these emotional difficulties. In addition, talking with supportive partners might ease a person's psychological adjustment to recurrent genital herpes infections. Certainly, herpes is not the dread disease that some people believe it to be. In fact, many individuals have learned to cope effectively with it, as did the person in the following account:

*When I first discovered I had herpes several years ago, my first reaction was, "Oh no, my sex life is destroyed!" I was really depressed and angry with the person who gave me the disease. However, with time I learned I could live with it, and I even began to gain some control over it. Now, on those infrequent occasions when I have an outbreak, I know what to do to hurry up the healing process. (Authors' files)*

## Treatment

At the time of this writing, no medical treatment has been proven effective in curing either oral or genital herpes. However, medical researchers are pursuing an effective treatment on many fronts, with mounting optimism. Current treatment strategies are designed to prevent outbreaks or to reduce discomfort and to speed healing during an outbreak.

Three separate antiviral drugs are often highly effective in the management of herpes. Acyclovir, sold under the trade name Zovirax, is the cheapest and most commonly used medication. It is available in three forms: topical (ointment), oral, and injectable. Although the ointment has not proven to be particularly helpful, a number of studies have shown that acyclovir administered orally or intravenously (by injection) significantly reduces viral shedding and the duration and severity of herpes outbreaks (Colgan et al., 2003). Oral acyclovir taken several times daily is a common drug treatment for genital herpes. Intravenous acyclovir is generally used only with severe infections. Two new antiviral agents, valacyclovir (Valtrex) and famciclovir (Famvir), taken orally, have proven effective for management of genital herpes (Mills & Mindel, 2003; Romanowski et al., 2003b).

Two antiviral treatment strategies are used to manage recurrent genital herpes infections. In *suppressive therapy* medication is taken daily to prevent recurrent outbreaks. *Episodic treatment* involves treating herpes outbreaks when they occur with an antiviral agent (Romanowski et al., 2003b). Episodic treatment has been shown to reduce the duration and severity of lesion pain and the time needed for total healing (Romanowski et al., 2003a). Suppressive therapy often prevents HSV reactivation and development of herpes lesions (Mills & Mindel, 2003; Romanowski et al., 2003a). A recent study compared the responses and preferences of 225 individuals with a history of recurrent genital herpes outbreaks. The participants were randomly assigned to receive 24 weeks of suppressive therapy with valacyclovir, followed by 24 weeks of episodic treatment with the same drug, or vice versa. Both treatment strategies were effective. Suppressive therapy reduced the frequency of recurrences by 80%, and episodic treatment reduced the severity and duration of outbreaks. Suppressive therapy was preferred to episodic treatment by 72% of the subjects, and "overall treatment satisfaction and quality of life were significantly greater during suppressive therapy" (Romanowski et al., 2003a, p. 226).

Suppressive antiviral therapy reduces but does not eliminate asymptomatic viral shedding between outbreaks, and therefore potentially decreases the risk of sexual transmission of HSV infections (Romanowski et al., 2003b). Reduced transmission rates related to suppressive therapy have yet to be conclusively confirmed. However, a recent study reported that suppression with valacyclovir reduced the risk of transmission of genital herpes from an infected person to his or her disease-free partner by 48% over an 8-month period (Corey et al., 2004).

Long-term suppressive therapy with one of the three available antiviral medications is generally recommended for people who experience six or more outbreaks of genital herpes per year or for those with exceptionally severe recurrences (Colgan et al., 2003).

A number of other measures can provide relief from the discomfort associated with herpes. The following suggestions can be helpful. Because the effectiveness of these measures varies from person to person, we encourage people to experiment to find an approach that best meets their needs.

1. Keeping herpes blisters clean and dry will lessen the possibility of secondary infections, significantly shorten the period of viral shedding, and reduce the total time of lesion healing. Washing the area with warm water and soap two to three times daily is adequate for cleaning. After bathing, dry the area thoroughly by patting it gently with a soft cotton towel or by blowing it with a hair dryer set on cool. Because the moisture that occurs naturally in the genital area can slow the healing process, sprinkling the dried area liberally with cornstarch or baby powder can help. It is desirable to wear loose cotton clothing that does not trap moisture (cotton underwear absorbs moisture, but nylon traps it).

2. Two aspirin every 3 to 4 hours might help to reduce the pain and itching. Application of a local anesthetic, such as lidocaine jelly, can also help to reduce soreness. Ice packs applied directly to the lesions can also provide temporary relief (but avoid wetting the lesions as the ice melts). Keeping the area liberally powdered can also alleviate itching.

3. Some people have an intense burning sensation when they urinate if the urine comes into contact with herpes lesions. This discomfort can be reduced by pouring water over the genitals while voiding or by urinating in a bathtub filled with water. It might help to dilute the acid in the urine by drinking lots of fluids (but avoid liquids that make the urine more acidic, such as cranberry juice).

4. Because stress has been implicated as a triggering event in recurrent herpes (Cohen et al., 1999), it is a good idea to try to reduce this negative influence.

A variety of approaches may help reduce stress. These include relaxation techniques, yoga or meditation, and counseling about ways to cope with daily pressures.

5. If you are prone to repeated relapses of herpes, try recording events that occur immediately before an outbreak (either after the fact or as part of an ongoing journal). You may be able to recognize common precipitating events, such as fatigue, stress, or excessive sunlight, which you can then avoid in the future. ■

Researchers are working on vaccines to protect people from herpes infections. In one recent study, the effectiveness of a vaccine against genital herpes in humans was demonstrated for the first time. However, this vaccine had a beneficial effect for only a small subgroup of women in the total study population of almost 3,000 men and women, and the vaccine was not significantly effective for any men in the study population (Stanberry et al., 2002). Recent research also suggests that a vaginal microbicide to reduce the risk of HSV infection may be available in the future (Johnson, 2006). (See the On the Edge box later in the chapter for a discussion of vaginal microbicides.)

## Genital Warts

**Genital warts** are caused by a virus called the *human papillomavirus* (HPV). Application of recently developed technology has led to the identification of more than 100 types of HPV, about half of which cause genital infections (Centers for Disease Control, 2006f).

> **Genital warts** Viral warts that appear on the genitals and are primarily transmitted sexually.

InfoTrac Search Words

● Genital warts

### Incidence and Transmission

The incidence of HPV infections has been increasing so rapidly in both sexes that this disease has reached epidemic proportions in recent years. HPV is now one of the most common STDs in North America (Steinbrook, 2006; Kahn & Hillard, 2006). It is estimated that at least 15% of people in the United States are infected with HPV and that more than 6 million new cases occur each year (Centers for Disease Control, 2006f; Steinbrook, 2006). HPV is primarily transmitted through vaginal, anal, oral, or oral–genital sexual interaction (Bailey & Cymet, 2006). Even condoms, which significantly reduce transmission of many bacterial and viral infections, are far from an ideal preventive measure for HPV because the virus is often present on skin not covered by a condom (Gilbert et al., 2003). Although condoms do provide some protection, they do not prevent transmission of viral infections on the vulva, the base of the penis, the scrotum, and any other genital area not covered by the condom (Choma, 2003).

Subclinical or asymptomatic infections with HPV are common, and viral shedding and transmission of the virus can occur during asymptomatic periods of infection (Centers for Disease Control, 2006f; Richardson et al., 2000). In fact, HPV is most commonly transmitted by asymptomatic individuals (Strand et al., 1997).

### Symptoms and Complications

Most people who have genital HPV infections do not develop visible symptoms and thus are unaware that they are infected (Centers for Disease Control, 2006f). Visible warts, which have an average incubation period of about 3 months, may appear 3 to 8 months after contact with an infected person.

In women genital warts most commonly appear on the bottom part of the vaginal opening. They can also occur on the perineum, the labia, the inner walls of the vagina, and the cervix. In men genital warts commonly occur on the glans, foreskin, or shaft of the penis (see ● **Figure 15.5** on the following page). Genital warts can also occur in the anus of either sex. In moist areas (such as the vaginal opening and under the foreskin), genital warts are pink or red and soft, with a cauliflowerlike appearance. On dry skin areas they are generally hard and yellow-gray.

A healthy immune system often suppresses the virus, and most infected people with an effective immune response will become HPV-negative in 6–24 months after the initial positive test for the virus. However, it is unclear whether the virus is eradicated or merely suppressed to undetectable levels (Choma, 2003; Wright & Schiffman, 2003).

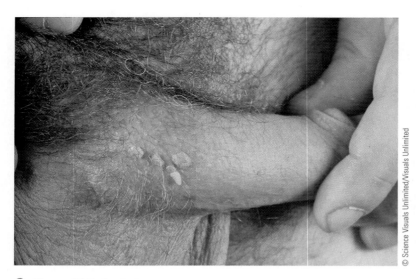

⊕ **Figure 15.5** Genital warts on the penis.

Genital warts are sometimes associated with serious complications. They can invade the urethra, causing urinary obstruction and bleeding. Research has also revealed an association between HPV infection and cancers of the cervix, vagina, vulva, urethra, penis, and anus (Brown et al., 2005; Centers for Disease Control, 2006f). HPV types 6 and 11 are linked to cancers of the genitals and anus, whereas HPV types 16 and 18 are most often associated with the development of cervical cancer (Bailey & Cymet, 2006; Kahn & Hillard, 2006). Recent evidence indicates that HPV infections account for 85–90% of the attributable risk for the development of cervical cancer, which is the second most common cancer diagnosed in women worldwide and the leading cause of death from cancer among women in developing nations (Kahn & Hillard, 2006). It is not known whether HPV acts alone to cause these cancers of the cervix and genitalia or in conjunction with cofactors, such as other infections, smoking, immunosuppression, pregnancy, the use of oral contraceptives, and poor nutrition (Donovan, 2004; Gilbert et al., 2003). There is actually little risk that a woman infected with HPV will develop cervical cancer unless the virus remains undetected and untreated (Centers for Disease Control, 2006f). This is the reason that regular Pap testing and appropriate follow-up treatment for precancerous lesions are essential to prevent most women from getting cervical cancer (Choma, 2003; Kahn & Hillard, 2006).

Another rare but serious complication of HPV is that pregnant women infected with the virus can transmit it to their babies during birth (Rintala et al., 2005). Infected infants can develop a condition known as *respiratory papillomatosis*, which results from HPV infection of their upper respiratory tracts. Respiratory papillomatosis can have serious health consequences that produce lifelong distress and require multiple surgeries.

## Treatment

No single treatment has been shown to be uniformly effective in removing warts or in preventing them from recurring (American College of Obstetricians and Gynecologists, 2005). Current CDC guidelines suggest several fairly conservative approaches to HPV management that focus on the removal of visible warts. The most widely used treatments include cryotherapy (freezing) with liquid nitrogen or cryoprobe and topical applications of podofilox, imiquimod cream, or trichloroacetic acid. For large or persistent warts, cauterization by electric needle, vaporization by carbon dioxide laser, or surgical removal may be necessary. However, these more radical treatments can cause severe side effects. Even though there is no "cure" for HPV infections, genital warts often disappear on their own without treatment (Centers for Disease Control, 2006f). Consequently, some people elect to adopt a "wait and see" approach in lieu of immediate treatment.

Recent studies have demonstrated the effectiveness of newly developed vaccines against several types of HPV (Harper et al., 2004; Mao et al., 2006; Villa et al., 2005). The availability of effective HPV vaccines will provide a major advance in efforts to reduce adverse health consequences of this disease in the United States and worldwide.

In June 2006 Merck & Co., developer of a vaccine against 4 HPV types responsible for the majority of genital warts and cancers associated with HPV, obtained Food and Drug Administration (FDA) approval for their product Gardasil. In the same month, the Advisory Committee of Immunization Practices, appointed by the U.S. Department of Health and Human Services, voted unanimously that females ages 11–26 should be vaccinated with Gardasil (women older than 26 were not included in clinical trials) and that the vaccine should be available to girls as young as 9 (Tran, 2006).

Unfortunately, misguided resistance from vocal political and religious organizations that oppose providing an STD preventive vaccine to teenagers and preteens may impede efforts to make this vaccine available to young females in the United States (Guyan, 2006; Noller, 2006; Pollitt, 2006). This is yet another example of how activist groups politicize public health issues related to sexual behavior, regardless of the harmful consequences of their actions, in seeking to exert control over our sexuality. Apparently, people who seek to block young American females' access to an HPV vaccine believe that "sex today is worse than cancer tomorrow" (Pollitt, 2006, p. 1). The opposition to an HPV vaccine is mounted by the same groups that oppose over-the-counter sale of emergency contraception and comprehensive sex education in public schools because of the erroneous assumption that denying young people access to sexuality information, health protection, and birth control will prevent them from experiencing sexual intercourse before marriage. ■

**Sex and Politics**

**? Critical Thinking Question**

Should government agencies have the option of denying teenage women access to an HPV vaccine? Why or why not? What are the implications for society of politicizing and possibly blocking a chance to prevent cervical cancer?

## Viral Hepatitis

**Viral hepatitis** (heh-puh-TIE-tus) is a disease in which liver function is impaired by a viral infection. There are three major types of viral hepatitis: hepatitis A, hepatitis B, and hepatitis C. Each of these forms of viral hepatitis is caused by a different virus.

**Viral hepatitis** A disease in which liver function is impaired by a viral infection.

### Incidence and Transmission

Hepatitis A is the most common form of viral hepatitis in the United States, followed in order of frequency by hepatitis B and hepatitis C (Centers for Disease Control, 2006g). Although all three types of hepatitis can be transmitted through sexual contact, types A and B are more likely to be transmitted sexually than type C. Hepatitis B is transmitted more often through sexual activity than is hepatitis A. Sexual transmission among adults accounts for most hepatitis B infections in the United States (Centers for Disease Control, 2006g). Hepatitis A is a relatively common infection of young homosexual men, especially those who have multiple sex partners and those who engage in anal intercourse (Des Jarlais et al., 2003). Furthermore, both hepatitis A and hepatitis B are often transmitted by means of needle sharing among injection drug users (Centers for Disease Control, 2006g; Des Jarlais et al., 2003).

Hepatitis B can be transmitted through blood or blood products, semen, vaginal secretions, and saliva. Perinatal transmission from infected mothers to untreated infants can be as high as 90% (Centers for Disease Control, 2005b). The CDC recommends that pregnant women should be tested for hepatitis B (Centers for Disease Control, 2002g). Manual, oral, or penile stimulation of the anus is strongly associated with the spread of this viral agent. Hepatitis A seems to be spread primarily through the fecal–oral route. Consequently, epidemics often occur when infected handlers of food do not wash their hands properly after using the bathroom. Oral–anal sexual contact seems to be a primary mode for sexual transmission of hepatitis A (Donovan, 2004).

Recently, health officials in the United States have focused considerable attention on the most health-threatening of the hepatitis viruses, hepatitis C, which is an emerging communicable disease of epidemic proportions (Bacon et al., 2005; Romanowski et al., 2003a). Over the last few years, hepatitis C has become a major global health problem, and it is now one of the most common chronic viral infections in North America (Edlin & Carden, 2006). It is estimated that more than 170 million people in the world have chronic hepatitis C infections—5 million of whom are in the United States (Edlin & Carden, 2006). People whose immune systems are deficient are especially vulnerable to hepatitis C infection. An estimated 15–30% of HIV-infected individuals in the United States are also infected with hepatitis C—representing 150,000 to 300,000 people (Manns & Wedemeyer, 2004).

**InfoTrac Search Words**

• Hepatitis C

Hepatitis C is transmitted most commonly through blood-contaminated needles shared by injection drug users (Edlin & Carden, 2006; Hagen et al., 2006). Other modes of transmission include transfusion of contaminated blood products, sexual contact, and perinatal transmission from an infected mother to her fetus or infant (Murray et al., 2003; Steininger et al., 2003). Whether transmission of hepatitis C through unprotected sexual intercourse is a significant factor in the spread of hepatitis C is debatable, but evidence indicates that some hepatitis C infections are sexually transmitted (Centers for Disease Control, 2006; Murray et al., 2003).

### Symptoms and Complications

Symptoms of viral hepatitis vary from nonexistent to mild flulike symptoms (poor appetite, upset stomach, diarrhea, sore muscles, fatigue, headache) to an incapacitating illness characterized by high fever, vomiting, and severe abdominal pain. One of the most notable signs of viral hepatitis is a yellowing of the whites of the eyes; the skin of light-complexioned people can also take on a yellow, or jaundiced, look. Hospitalization is required only in severe cases. Chronic infections with hepatitis B or C are a major risk factor for developing cancer of the liver, one of the most common cancers in the world (Bacon et al., 2005; Centers for Disease Control, 2006g). About 20–25% of people infected with hepatitis C manifest progressive disease associated with severe complications, including liver cancer, cirrhosis, and end-stage liver disease culminating in liver failure (Bacon et al., 2005; Colgan et al., 2003).

### Treatment

No specific therapy is known to be effective against hepatitis A. Treatment generally consists of bed rest and adequate fluid intake to prevent dehydration. The disease generally runs its course in a few weeks, although complete recovery can take several months in cases of severe infection. Infection with hepatitis B is typically treated in the same manner as hepatitis A, and it also generally runs its course in a few weeks. However, sometimes hepatitis B infections become chronic and persist for more than 6 months. These chronic infections can be treated effectively with several antiviral drugs, including interferon, lamivudine, entecavir, and adefovir dipivoxil (Hoofnagle, 2006).

Hepatitis C presents a more serious treatment problem. About 75–80% of infected people become chronic carriers who have relatively mild disease that is stable over several decades and does not significantly erode their health. However, for the 20–25% with progressive disease, active treatment is essential to avert severe complications and/or death (Manns & Wedemeyer, 2004; Romanowski et al., 2003b). A combination therapy with the antiviral drugs interferon and ribavirin has been shown to be relatively effective in controlling hepatitis C (Han et al., 2004; Manns & Wedemeyer, 2004).

An effective and safe vaccine to prevent hepatitis B infection has been available since 1982, and in 1995 the U.S. Food and Drug Administration approved an effective and safe hepatitis A vaccine. Unfortunately, no effective vaccine for hepatitis C exists, although efforts are under way to develop this prevention tool (Pancholi et al., 2003). Persons at high risk for contracting hepatitis A or hepatitis B should seriously consider getting immunized. These high-risk people include health-care workers who are exposed to blood, injection drug users and their sex partners, homosexual and bisexual men, heterosexually active persons with multiple sexual partners, sexual partners or housemates of people infected with the hepatitis A or B virus, people with chronic liver disease, and military personnel working in field conditions (Centers for Disease Control, 2002g; Miller & Graves, 2000). In addition, the CDC recommends that all children be immunized for hepatitis B.

## ◗ Common Vaginal Infections

Several kinds of vaginal infections can be transmitted through sexual interaction. The infections we discuss in this section are also frequently contracted through nonsexual means. *Vaginitis* and *leukorrhea* are general terms applied to a variety of vaginal infections characterized by a whitish discharge. The secretion can also be yellow or green because of the presence of pus cells, and it often has a disagreeable odor. Additional symptoms of vaginitis include irritation and itching of the genital tissue, burning sensation during urination, and pain around the vaginal opening during intercourse.

Vaginal infections are common. Practically every woman experiences one or more of these infections during her lifetime. In fact, vaginitis is one of the most common reasons women consult health-care providers (Calvert, 2003; Karasz & Anderson,

2003). Under typical circumstances many of the organisms that cause vaginal infections are relatively harmless. In fact, some routinely live in the vagina and cause no trouble unless something alters the normal vaginal environment and allows them to overgrow. The vagina normally houses bacteria (*lactobacilli*) that help maintain a healthy vaginal environment (Jeavons, 2003). The pH of the vagina is usually sufficiently acidic to ward off most infections. However, certain conditions can alter the pH toward the alkaline side, which can leave a woman vulnerable to infection. Some factors that increase the likelihood of vaginal infection include antibiotic therapy, use of contraceptive pills, menstruation, pregnancy, wearing pantyhose and nylon underwear, and lowered resistance from stress or lack of sleep (Jeavons, 2003; Priestly et al., 1997). Douching also increases the risk of vaginal infections, especially bacterial vaginosis (Centers for Disease Control, 2006h; Ness et al., 2003). Research also suggests that the alkalinity of seminal fluid may be a factor in altering vaginal pH, thus increasing susceptibility to infections (Priestly et al., 1997).

Most women with vaginitis have an infection diagnosed as bacterial vaginosis, candidiasis, or trichomoniasis. Bacterial vaginosis is the most common of these infections.

## Bacterial Vaginosis

**Bacterial vaginosis (BV)** is a vaginal infection caused by a replacement of the normal vaginal *lactobacilli* by an overgrowth of microorganisms, which can include anaerobic bacteria, *Mycoplasma* bacteria, and a bacterium known as *Gardnerella vaginalis*.

**Bacterial vaginosis**
A vaginal infection caused by bacterial microorganisms; it is the most common form of vaginitis among U.S. women.

### Incidence and Transmission

The presence of moderate levels of bacterial microorganisms in the vaginal environment is normal. However, under conditions of decreased levels of beneficial *lactobacilli*, an overgrowth of other vaginal microorganisms occurs. This can result in high concentrations of one or more of the bacterial microorganisms associated with BV (Hudson & Kochan, 2005; Watts et al., 2005). BV is the most common vaginal infection in U.S. women (Centers for Disease Control, 2006h). Both male and female sex partners of women with BV can also harbor the infectious microorganisms without clinical symptoms (Centers for Disease Control, 2006h). Although the role of sexual transmission in BV is not fully understood, it is believed that coitus often provides a mode of transmission for the infection. BV occurs more frequently among sexually active women than among sexually inactive women (Doskoch, 2005; Feroli & Burstein, 2003). However, BV is not necessarily sexually transmitted, because this infection has been diagnosed in teenagers and women who have not experienced sexual intercourse (Coco & Vandenbosche, 2000).

### Symptoms and Complications

The most prominent symptom of bacterial vaginosis in women is a foul-smelling thin discharge that resembles flour paste in consistency. The discharge is usually gray, but it can also be white, yellow, or green. The disagreeable odor, often noticed first by an infected woman's sexual partner, is typically described as fishy or musty. This smell may be particularly noticeable after coitus because the alkaline seminal fluid reacts with the bacteria, causing the release of the chemicals that produce the smell. A small number of infected women experience irritation of the genital tissues and a mild burning sensation during urination. Recent evidence suggests a link between bacterial vaginosis and both PID and adverse pregnancy outcomes, including premature rupture of the amniotic sac and preterm labor (Doskoch, 2005; Hampton, 2006). As mentioned earlier, most men are asymptomatic. However, some infected males develop inflammation of the foreskin and glans of the penis, **urethritis** (inflammation of the urethral tube), and **cystitis** (bladder infection).

**Urethritis** An inflammation of the urethral tube.

**Cystitis** An infection of the bladder.

### Treatment

For many years the treatment of choice for bacterial vaginosis has been metronidazole (Flagyl) taken by mouth for 7 days. However, recent research indicates that intravaginal application of topical metronidazole gel or clindamycin cream is as effective as oral metronidazole (Burstein & Murray, 2003; Feroli & Burstein, 2003). Studies indicate that there is little or no proven benefit in treating male sex partners of women diagnosed with BV (Centers for Disease Control, 2006h). Female sex partners should be evaluated and treated if necessary.

## Candidiasis

**Candidiasis** An inflammatory infection of the vaginal tissues caused by the yeast-like fungus *Candida albicans*.

**Candidiasis** (kan-duh-DIE-uh-sus), also commonly referred to as a yeast infection, is primarily caused by a yeastlike fungus called *Candida albicans*.

### Incidence and Transmission

Candidiasis is the second most common vaginal infection in North America (Bauters et al., 2002). An estimated 75% of women will have at least one genital candidiasis infection in their lifetime (Centers for Disease Control, 2006i). The microscopic *Candida albicans* organism is normally present in the vagina of many women; it also inhabits the mouth and large intestine of a large number of women and men. A disease state results only when certain conditions allow the yeast to overgrow in the vagina. This accelerated growth can result from pregnancy, use of oral contraceptives, or diabetes—conditions that increase the amount of sugar stored in vaginal cells (*Candida albicans* thrives in the presence of sugar) (Centers for Disease Control, 2006i; Fink, 2006). Another factor is the use of oral antibiotics or spermicidal jellies or creams, which reduce the number of *lactobacilli* (mentioned earlier as important for a healthy vaginal environment) (Jeavons, 2003). This reduction permits *Candida albicans* to multiply rapidly.

If the yeast organism is not already present in the woman's vagina, it can be transmitted to this area in a variety of ways. It can be conveyed from the anus by wiping back to front or on the surface of a menstrual pad, or it can be transmitted through sexual interaction, because the organism can be harbored in various reservoirs in the male body, especially under the foreskin of an uncircumcised man (Ringdahl, 2000). The organism can also be passed from a partner's mouth to a woman's vagina during oral sex (Greer, 1998).

### Symptoms

A woman with a yeast infection may notice that she has a white, clumpy discharge that looks something like cottage cheese. In addition, candidiasis is often associated with intense itching and soreness of the vaginal and vulval tissues, which typically become red and dry (Coco & Vandenbosche, 2000).

### Treatment

A variety of treatments have proved effective in combating yeast infections. Traditional treatment strategies consist of vaginal suppositories or topical creams, such as clotrimazole, miconazole, butoconazole, or terconazole. Over-the-counter intravaginal preparations of clotrimazole and miconazole are now available for treatment of candidiasis; however, these medications are recommended only for women who have previously been medically diagnosed and treated and who have a recurrence of symptoms (Coco & Vandenbosche, 2000). Research indicates that many women incorrectly diagnose themselves as having vaginal candidiasis and thus begin a course of self-treatment with over-the-counter antifungal medications (Centers for Disease Control, 2006i; Jeavons, 2003). Even though women who self-treat conditions mistaken for candidiasis may eventually realize their error and seek medical attention, this delay in treatment can have serious consequences, especially because other infections may be present that require different treatments (Ringdahl, 2000).

A drug taken by mouth, fluconazole, has also proven effective in treating candidiasis (Burstein & Murray, 2003). Because *Candida albicans* is a hardy organism, treatment should be continued for the prescribed length of time (usually several days to 2 weeks), even though the symptoms may disappear in 2 days.

Practical tips to help women reduce the risk of a yeast infection include decreasing sugar intake, adding yogurt or a daily *lactobacillus acidophilus* supplement to their diet, and avoiding glycerin-based lubricants that can fuel a yeast infection (Fink, 2006).

# Trichomoniasis

**Trichomoniasis** (trih-kuh-muh-NIE-uh-sus) is caused by a one-celled protozoan parasite called *Trichomonas vaginalis*.

**Trichomoniasis** A form of vaginitis caused by the one-celled protozoan *Trichomonas vaginalis*.

## Incidence and Transmission

Trichomoniasis is a common STD in both women and men. Between 7 and 8 million new cases of trichomoniasis occur each year in the United States (Centers for Disease Control, 2006j). The primary mode of transmission of this infection is through sexual contact. Women can acquire the disease from infected men via penile–vaginal intercourse and from infected women via vulva-to-vulva contact; however men usually contact trichomoniasis only from infected women via coitus (Centers for Disease Control, 2006j).

## Symptoms and Complications

The most common symptom of trichomoniasis infection in women is an abundant, frothy, white or yellow-green vaginal discharge with an unpleasant odor. The discharge can irritate the tissues of the vagina and vulva, causing them to become inflamed, itchy, and sore (Centers for Disease Control, 2006j). The infection is usually limited to the vagina and sometimes the cervix, but occasionally the organism invades the urethra, bladder, or Bartholin's glands. Inflammation of genital tissues caused by trichomoniasis can increase a women's susceptibility to HIV infection (Centers for Disease Control, 2006j; Huppert, 2006). Some health specialists also believe that long-term trichomonal infection can damage the cells of the cervix and increase susceptibility to cervical cancer. However, prompt, effective treatment prevents permanent cervical damage. Untreated trichomoniasis infection in pregnant women is associated with premature rupture of the amniotic sac and preterm delivery (Centers for Disease Control, 2006j; Huppert, 2006). Trichomoniasis infections in men, usually asymptomatic, may be associated with an urge to urinate frequently, painful urination, or a slight urethral discharge.

## Treatment

To avoid passing the protozoan back and forth, it is important that the sex partner(s) of an infected woman be treated, even if they are asymptomatic. If a male partner is not treated, the couple should use condoms to prevent reinfection. The recommended drug regimen for both sexes is a single 2-gram dose of metronidazole (Flagyl) taken by mouth. ■

! Sexual Health

# ▶ Ectoparasitic Infections

**Ectoparasites** are parasitic organisms that live on the outer skin surfaces of humans and other animals (*ecto* means "outer"). Two relatively common STDs are caused by ectoparasites: pubic lice and scabies.

**Ectoparasites** Parasitic organisms that live on the outer skin surfaces.

## Pubic Lice

**Pubic lice**, more commonly called crabs, belong to a group of parasitic insects called biting lice. They are known technically as *Phthirus pubis*. Although tiny, adult lice are visible to the naked eye. They are yellowish-gray and under magnification resemble crabs, as ▶**Figure 15.6** on the following page shows. A pubic louse generally grips a pubic hair with its claws and sticks its head into the skin, where it feeds on blood from tiny blood vessels.

**Pubic lice** Lice that primarily infest the pubic hair and are transmitted by sexual contact.

## Incidence and Transmission

Pubic lice are quite common and are seen frequently in public health clinics and by private physicians. Pubic lice are especially prevalent among young (15- to 25-year-old) single people and are frequently associated with the presence of other sexually transmitted infections (Varela et al., 2003). Pubic lice are often transmitted during

**Figure 15.6** A pubic louse, or "crab."

sexual contact when two people bring their pubic areas together (Heukelbach & Feldmeier, 2004). The lice can live away from the body for as long as 1 day, particularly if their stomachs are full of blood. They may drop off onto underclothes, bedsheets, sleeping bags, and so forth. Eggs deposited by the female louse on clothing or bed sheets can survive for several days. Thus it is possible to get pubic lice by sleeping in someone else's bed or by wearing his or her clothes. Furthermore, a successfully treated person can be reinfected by being exposed to her or his own unwashed sheets or underclothes. Pubic lice do not necessarily limit themselves to the genital areas. They can be transmitted, usually by the fingers, to the armpits or scalp.

### Symptoms

Most people begin to suspect something is amiss when they start itching. Suspicions become stronger when scratching brings no relief. However, a few people seem to have great tolerance for the bite of a louse, experiencing little if any discomfort. Self-diagnosis is possible simply by locating a louse on a pubic hair.

### Treatment

The recommended regimen for treatment of pubic lice is 1% permethrin or pyrethrin lotion or cream applied to all affected areas and washed off after 10 minutes. It is advisable to apply the lotion to all areas where there are concentrations of body hair—the genitals, armpits, scalp, and even eyebrows. These treatments should be repeated 7 to 10 days later if lice are still present. Be sure to wash all clothes and sheets that were used before treatment.

## Scabies

**Scabies** An ectoparasitic infestation of tiny mites.

**Scabies** is caused by a tortoise-shaped parasitic mite with four stubby legs called *Sarcoptes scabiei*. Unlike pubic lice, mites are too tiny to be seen by the naked eye. Scabies infestations are initiated by the female mite; after mating, she burrows beneath the skin to lay her eggs, which hatch shortly thereafter. Each hatched egg becomes a full-grown adult in 10 to 20 days. The adult mite forages for nourishment in the host's skin that is adjacent to the site of the original burrow. The average person with scabies is infested with 5 to 15 live adult female mites (Chosidow, 2006).

### Incidence and Transmission

Although scabies is not among the infectious diseases reported to health organizations in the United States and elsewhere, the worldwide prevalence of this disease is estimated at about 300 million annual cases (Chosidow, 2006). Scabies is a highly contagious condition that can be transmitted by close physical contact, both sexual and nonsexual. The mites can also be transferred on clothing or bedding, where they can remain viable for up to 72 hours (Centers for Disease Control, 2006k). In addition to sexually active people, schoolchildren, nursing home residents, and indigent people are especially at risk for scabies infestations.

### Symptoms

Small vesicles or pimplelike bumps occur in the area where the female mite tunnels into the skin. A red rash around the primary lesion indicates the area where hatched adult mites are feeding. Areas of infestation itch intensely, especially at night. Favorite sites of infestation typically include the webs and sides of fingers, wrists, abdomen, genitals, buttocks, and female breasts.

### Treatment

Scabies is treated with a topical scabicide that is applied from the neck down to the toes. Several lotions, both prescription and nonprescription, are available; they are applied at bedtime and left on for 8 hours, then washed off with soap and water. A single application is usually effective, although some physicians advocate a second application 7–10 days later. It is recommended that all household members and close contacts of an infested person, including asymptomatic ones, be treated simultaneously. In addition, all clothing and bedding used by treated people should be washed in hot water or dry cleaned.

# Acquired Immunodeficiency Syndrome (AIDS)

The **acquired immunodeficiency syndrome (AIDS)** epidemic, which constitutes a worldwide public health threat of rapidly increasing magnitude, is now recognized as the most serious disease pandemic of our time. An all-out research assault on this deadly disease, unprecedented in scope and extent, is being conducted throughout the world, and new findings are surfacing with startling rapidity.

AIDS results from infection with the **human immunodeficiency virus (HIV)**. HIV falls into a special category of viruses called *retroviruses*, so named because they reverse the usual order of reproduction within cells they infect, a process called *reverse transcription*.

Two forms of HIV have been linked with the development of AIDS: HIV-1 and HIV-2. HIV-1 was the first human immunodeficiency virus to be identified and is the one that causes the greatest number of AIDS cases in the United States and throughout the world. HIV-2 occurs in some African countries along with HIV-1. HIV-1, the more virulent of the two forms, is a formidable enemy because it is constantly mutating and is present in multiple strains or subtypes. To simplify our discussion of AIDS, we refer to the infective agent simply as HIV.

A great deal of speculation about the origin of AIDS has occurred since the emergence of the global pandemic. It has been variously proposed that HIV came from residents of Africa or Haiti, mosquitoes, monkeys, pigs, or even from early testing of a polio vaccine in Africa in the 1950s. Recently published research appears to have solved the riddle of the origin of HIV/AIDS. Persuasive evidence that HIV was introduced to humans from chimpanzees was obtained by two international teams of scientists who traced the roots of HIV to a related virus in a subspecies of chimpanzees that reside in central and southwestern Africa (Gao et al., 1999; Keele et al., 2006). Genetic analysis revealed that this subspecies, *Pan troglodytes troglodytes*, harbors a simian immunodeficiency virus (SIV) that is the origin of HIV-1. Scientists believe that SIV genetically converted to HIV either while it was still in a chimpanzee or after a human contracted SIV, perhaps through exposure to chimpanzee blood from hunting or handling the meat during food preparation.

Armed with evidence implicating a specific subspecies of chimpanzees in the origin of HIV, another research team conducted tests that allowed them to estimate that HIV first evolved from the SIV carried by these chimpanzees sometime between 1915 and 1941, with 1931 being the most likely year (Korber et al., 2000). With such an early date of origin, why was HIV not identified as the AIDS-causing virus until 1983? Scientists believe that when SIV turned into a human killer, probably in the early 1930s, it likely remained confined to a small population in an isolated area, such as a village, until migration into large cities and jet travel spread the virus worldwide. Evidence that HIV existed well before its identification in 1983 was provided by discovery of HIV in a frozen blood sample collected in 1959 from an adult African male (Zhu et al., 1998). Thus it now appears likely that HIV originated early in the 20th century by means of cross-species transmission from a subspecies of chimpanzees to humans, and then was spread worldwide much later, when Africa became less isolated.

HIV specifically targets and destroys the body's CD4 lymphocytes, also called T-helper cells or helper T-4 cells. In healthy people these cells coordinate the immune system's response to disease. The impairment of the immune system resulting from HIV infections leaves the body vulnerable to a variety of cancers and opportunistic infections (infections that take hold because of the reduced effectiveness of the immune system). Initially, HIV infection was diagnosed as AIDS only when the

**Acquired immunodeficiency syndrome (AIDS)** A catastrophic illness in which a virus (HIV) invades and destroys the ability of the immune system to fight disease.

**Human immunodeficiency virus (HIV)** The immune-system-destroying virus that causes AIDS.

InfoTrac Search Words
- AIDS
- HIV

immune system became so seriously impaired that the person developed one or more severe, debilitating diseases, such as cancer or an unusual form of pneumonia caused by the protozoan *Pneumocystis carinii*. However, effective January 1, 1993, the CDC broadened this definition of AIDS to include any HIV infection in which the immune system is severely impaired. Now anyone who is infected with HIV and has a CD4 count of 200 cells or less per microliter of blood is considered to have full-blown AIDS, regardless of other symptoms. (Normal CD4 counts in healthy people not infected with HIV range from 600 to 1,200 cells per microliter of blood.)

## Incidence

By January 2006 over 1 million cumulative cases of AIDS had been reported in the United States, and more than 525,000 people had died of the disease since it was first diagnosed in 1981. The number of persons in the United States living with HIV continues to increase. An estimated 1.2 million Americans are currently infected with HIV (Stall & Mills, 2006). The CDC estimates that about 25% of the infected people are unaware of their HIV-positive status (Centers for Disease Control, 2006l). Some health experts suggest that as many as half of HIV-infected Americans are unaware of their status (Rosen, 2006).

Each year about 5 million new HIV infections occur globally (almost 600 every hour), and by the end of 2005 an estimated 40.3 million people worldwide were infected (Stall & Mills, 2006; UNAIDS, 2006). This disease claims more than 3 million lives in the world community each year (UNAIDS, 2006). At the end of 2005 sub-Saharan Africa was estimated to be home to two-thirds (25.8 million) of all people living with HIV (UNAIDS, 2006). ◗ Figure 15.7 provides a global overview of the number of adults and children estimated to be living with HIV at the end of 2005.

In November 2006, researchers affiliated with the World Health Organization (WHO) estimated that nearly 120 million people could die from AIDS in the next 25 years (Mathers & Loncar, 2006). According to this grim forcast, AIDS will join heart disease and stroke as the top three causes of death worldwide.

The number of new AIDS cases reported annually in the United States grew rapidly throughout the early 1980s, increasing by about 85% each year, and reached a peak rate in the middle of the decade. The rate of new AIDS diagnoses slowed in the late 1980s. Since the early 1990s approximately 40,000 new HIV infections have occurred annually in the United States (Centers for Disease Control, 2006l). Although the overall incidence of new HIV infections in the U.S. population has been stable for several years, the number of new cases among teenagers, women, and racial and ethnic minorities continues to rise.

Many people with AIDS were infected during their adolescent years (Aronowitz et al., 2006). The growing problem of HIV infection among adolescents has been attributed to a number of factors, including the following:

- Many teenagers have multiple sexual partners, increasing their exposure to infection.
- Many adolescents engage in sexual activity without using condoms.
- Access to condoms is generally more difficult for adolescents than for other age groups.

**Eastern Europe and Central Asia**
1.6 million
(990,000–2.3 million)

**Western and Central Europe**
720,000
(570,000–890,000)

**East Asia**
870,000
(440,000–1.4 million)

**North America**
1.2 million
(650,000–1.8 million)

**North Africa and Middle East**
510,000
(230,000–1.4 million)

**South and South-East Asia**
7.4 million
(4.5–11.0 million)

**Caribbean**
300,000
(200,000–510,000)

**Latin America**
1.8 million
(1.4–2.4 million)

**Sub-Saharan Africa**
25.8 million
(23.8–28.9 million)

**Oceania**
74,000
(45,000–120,000)

**TOTAL: 40.3 (36.7–45.3) million**

◗ **Figure 15.7** Global estimates of number of adults and children living with HIV, end of 2005.

- Teenagers have high rates of other STDs, which are often associated with HIV infection.
- Substance abuse, which often increases risky behavior, is relatively widespread among adolescents.
- Teenagers tend to be especially likely as a group to have feelings of invulnerability (see Chapter 12).

Ethnic and racial minority groups in the United States account for a majority of the total number of AIDS cases reported since 1981 (Centers for Disease Control, 2005c, Robinson et al., 2005; Rosen, 2006). The higher AIDS rates among ethnic and racial minority groups might reflect, among other factors, (1) reduced access to health care, associated with disadvantaged socioeconomic status, (2) cultural or language barriers that limit access to information about strategies for preventing STDs, and (3) differences in HIV risk behaviors, especially higher rates of injection drug use.

Since AIDS first appeared in the United States, most cases have been directly or indirectly related to two risk-exposure categories: men who have sex with men (MSM) and injection drug users. However, some significant shifting trends in exposure-risk categories have begun to emerge. Even though the prevalence of HIV infection in the United States and the rest of the Western world remains highest among MSM, in the United States the proportion of reported AIDS cases among MSM declined sharply and then leveled off in the period between the mid-1980s and the late 1990s (Adam et al., 2005; Centers for Disease Control, 2005c). Unfortunately, in the early years of this century the incidence rates of HIV infection among MSM are again moving upward (Adam et al., 2005; Brewer et al., 2006; Stolte et al., 2006). This resurgence of the HIV epidemic among MSM is especially prevalent among young MSM and among MSM of color.

In the United States, AIDS cases attributable to heterosexual transmission are accelerating (Centers for Disease Control, 2006a). Heterosexual contact has always been the primary form of HIV transmission worldwide, especially in Africa and Asia (UNAIDS, 2006).

Over the last few years the number of women infected with HIV has steadily increased in the United States and worldwide (Centers for Disease Control, 2006l; UNAIDS, 2006). Women account for the fastest growing population infected with HIV in the United States (Lonergan & Hern, 2006; Rosen, 2006). In sub-Saharan Africa, women ages 15 to 24 are three times more likely to be infected with HIV than young men their age (Lamptey et al., 2006).

Research indicates that HIV is not as easily transmitted from women to men as it is from men to women (Betts, 2001; Eschenbach et al., 2001; Ray & Quinn, 2000). Thus the risk of becoming infected through heterosexual intercourse appears to be much greater for a female with an HIV-infected male partner than for a male with an infected female partner. One explanation for women's greater risk during heterosexual intercourse is that semen contains a higher concentration of HIV than vaginal fluids do, and the female mucosal surface is exposed to HIV in the ejaculate for a considerably longer time than a male's penis is exposed to HIV in vaginal secretions (Lamptey et al., 2006; Ray & Quinn, 2000). In addition, a larger area of mucosal surface is exposed on the vulva and in the vagina than on the penis, and the female mucosal surface is subjected to greater potential trauma than is typically the case with the penis (Lamptey et al., 2006; Ray & Quinn, 2000). Furthermore, some women experience unprotected anal intercourse, a high-risk behavior because HIV transmission from an infected man to an uninfected woman is thought to be 10 times as likely with anal intercourse as with vaginal intercourse (Abner et al., 2005). In fact, receptive unprotected anal intercourse has been shown to be associated with the highest risk of HIV infection through sexual activity for both men and women (Abner et al., 2005). Finally, adolescent women are especially biologically vulnerable to HIV infection because their immature reproductive tracts, especially the cervix, are highly susceptible to infection by STDs (Lamptey et al., 2006; Wiesenfeld et al., 2003).

The global proportionate incidence of HIV/AIDS among women is considerably greater in Africa, Asia, and the Caribbean than in the United States. In sub-Saharan Africa—the epicenter of HIV/AIDS—more women than men are HIV infected (UNAIDS, 2006). About 75% of HIV infections among African youth are of females

(Vickerman et al., 2006). There has also been a dramatic rise in the number of pregnant African women infected with HIV, with rates of 20% or more found among tested populations of women in six southern African countries (UNAIDS, 2006). The terrible plight of Africa during these plague years is described in the following Sexuality and Diversity discussion.

## SEXUALITY AND DIVERSITY

### AIDS in Africa: Death and Hope on a Dying Continent

To date, more than 80% of AIDS deaths have occurred in Africa, primarily in sub-Saharan nations, which collectively contain the largest concentration of people living with HIV/AIDS worldwide (Lamptey et al., 2006; UNAIDS, 2006). Even though countries such as India, China, and Russia have rapidly escalating HIV/AIDS epidemics, African countries are still the hardest hit by this horrific pandemic. Of the more than 12 million AIDS orphans—children who have lost their parents to the disease—over 90% live in sub-Saharan African nations (Summers et al., 2002). By 2010, 18 million children are expected to be orphaned by HIV/AIDS (Lamptey et al., 2006).

In a tragedy whose scope defies comprehension, HIV/AIDS is devastating a continent already ravaged by wars and poverty. Unless action against this disease is significantly escalated in scope and improved in focus, the damage already done will seem minor compared with what lies ahead. AIDS is poised to wipe out large portions of a generation of African people. Families are being destroyed, and skilled workers—the essence of a nation's wealth—are dying at an unprecedented rate.

In many sub-Saharan African nations it is estimated that more than 15% of all adults are infected with HIV (Summers et al., 2002; UNAIDS, 2006). Botswana, which has a population of 1.6 million, has one of the highest HIV infection rates in the world, with more than 1 in 3 adults being HIV-positive (Paz-Bailey et al., 2006). A Botswana 15-year-old now has an estimated 80% chance of dying of AIDS, given the current infection rates in this nation and the lack of either a cure or an effective vaccine (Summers et al., 2002). South Africa now has the fastest growing AIDS epidemic in the world and the largest number of people living with HIV—6 million (Lamptey et al., 2006). A recent survey of pregnant women attending South African clinics revealed that more than 22% were infected with HIV, as compared with less than 1% 9 years earlier (Sherfer et al., 2002). Approximately one in five South African youths age 15 to 24 is infected with HIV (Hartwell, 2005).

Many factors account for the widespread dissemination of the AIDS plague in Africa, where HIV is transmitted primarily through heterosexual sex. Widespread poverty and lack of general medical care are clearly important contributors to the African HIV/AIDS pandemic. Another important factor is that STDs that cause genital ulcers are endemic in Africa. Genital ulcers can increase the susceptibility of uninfected persons to HIV and can heighten the infectivity of people who are already HIV-positive (Celum et al., 2005; Todd et al., 2006). Furthermore, despite growing awareness of HIV/AIDS throughout Africa and in developing nations around the world, there is also widespread ignorance (especially among young people) about how to reduce one's vulnerability to HIV infection (Hartwell, 2005; UNAIDS, 2001a).

Cultural factors may play an even greater role in perpetuating the African AIDS plague. African nations are home to male-dominated societies in which most women find themselves in relationships of economic dependency and sociocultural subordination to men. These relationship inequities result in elevated vulnerability to HIV infection due to these women's lack of rights within relationships and to their difficulties in negotiating safer sex with partners who dislike using condoms and who typically refuse to acknowledge and discuss their other unsafe sexual relationships (Lamptey et al., 2006; Hoffman et al., 2006; Sinding, 2005). Social conventions in these countries generally require that men promise material support but not sexual fidelity to their partners. Regular use of condoms is low within marriages in cultures where fertility is often central to one's identity. Condoms are also rarely used by men who engage in extramarital liaisons with sex workers or "girlfriends" (Ezzell, 2000; Kesby, 2000). Several studies have revealed an alarmingly high rate of HIV infection among sex workers in Africa (Ghani & Aral, 2005).

Another cultural contributor to the spread of HIV in Africa is the so-called sugar daddy syndrome, in which older men with money, many of whom are HIV-positive, look to young teenage women for sex. This cultural trend is also aided by the superstitious belief in some African societies that an HIV-infected man can be cured by having sex with a virgin (Bartholet, 2000). Finally, it is fairly common for women in some southern African nations to swab their vaginal walls with cloth, paper, or cotton immediately before and during intercourse, a practice referred to as "dry sex," which is favored by many men (Ezzell, 2000). Dry sex increases the risk of HIV transmission to women by disrupting the normal balance of healthy vaginal *lactobacilli*, by increasing the likelihood of condom breakage, and by causing tiny tears in the vaginal walls that allow HIV to enter the bloodstream.

Many African nations ravaged by HIV/AIDS are gripped by a pervasive sense of hopelessness that often erodes individual initiative to engage in safer sexual behavior. African people are often influenced by a societal narrative that poses a likely life course including early marriage, unprotected sex, multiple births, HIV infection, early death, and children left without means of support (Mill & Anarfi, 2002). Individuals held hostage by this life expectation are often immobilized or unmotivated to effect positive behavioral changes. Furthermore, many of the HIV prevention programs implemented in African nations thus far have had only limited success. These programs have sought to persuade individuals to make rational decisions to change their behavior based solely on the power of words, usually emanating from the mouths of "experts."

Against such a grim background, can there be any hope for Africa's future? The answer is a cautious yes. There have been a few success stories. In recent years a number of programs have been designed and implemented both to combat the crippling effects of hopelessness and to move beyond more traditional information-based prevention approaches. These innovative intervention methods use trained community members as *peer educators* to reach out to their peers in a grassroots educational effort that includes providing information and resources, a format for talking openly about sexual issues, and a supportive context for positive behavior changes. A major advantage of peer education over the more traditional information-based expert-purveyor model is that peer education places health-related knowledge in the hands of ordinary people, who act not only as peer educators but also as role models for positive behavior change. A number of studies have demonstrated that such grassroots programs increase the likelihood that people will engage in health-promoting behaviors (Campbell & Mzaidume, 2001; Crooks & Tucker, 2006; Galavotti et al., 2001; Wheeler, 2003).

A peer-educator-based HIV/AIDS intervention program was recently established in the Makindu region of southeastern Kenya, with planning and guidance provided by Bob Crooks and his wife, Sami Tucker, in collaboration with a number of Kenyan citizens and with the assistance of a German NGO. This program, which employs more than 40 Kenyans, has been partially funded by royalty revenues from this textbook. The involvement of Crooks and Tucker includes developing a research strategy to evaluate the impact of this grassroots program, designing and implementing a peer-educator-based educational strategy, and conducting 2-week training sessions for peer educator staff. In addition to providing free treatment of STDs and centers where individuals can receive voluntary and confidential counseling and testing for HIV, the Makindu program provides community education using peer educators drawn from the local population.

Peer educators meet with groups of 12 to 18 people twice weekly over a 6-week period in various locations throughout the Makindu region. Content covered in these sessions includes risk behaviors for HIV infection and how HIV infection is transmitted, strategies for avoiding infection, communication skills (such as assertiveness training and condom negotiation skills), gender issues, and other topics pertinent to behavior change and safer sexual behavior. Group sessions use small and large group discussions, role-playing, theater, games and group activities, and participatory instruction (e.g., practicing proper condom application by using wood penis models). To date, several thousand adults and youth have participated in these community educational workshops, including members of workers' cooperatives, sport teams, women support groups, religious organizations, and commercial sex workers. Recently the program was expanded to include elementary schools in which children ages 9 to 18 and their parents and teachers participate in training workshops led by peer educators. Research evidence obtained via administration of anonymous pre- and post-workshop questionnaires has revealed improved awareness of HIV/AIDS risk behaviors and prevention strategies and significant increases in safer sexual behaviors among all categories of participants as a direct result of the educational program (Crooks & Tucker, 2006).

Perhaps the best hope for Africa lies in the development of the ultimate weapon against any virus—an effective preventive vaccine. However, as discussed elsewhere in this chapter, progress on this front has been slow, and the likelihood of having such a vaccine soon is slight at best.

## Transmission

HIV has been found in the semen, blood, vaginal secretions, saliva, urine, and breast milk of infected individuals. It also can occur in any other bodily fluids that contain blood, including cerebrospinal fluid and amniotic fluid. Blood, semen, and vaginal secretions are the three bodily fluids that most consistently contain high concentrations of the virus in infected people. Most commonly, HIV enters the body when bodily fluids are exchanged during unprotected vaginal or anal intercourse or oral–genital contact with an infected person. Transmission of HIV through sexual contact is estimated to be the cause of about 80% of worldwide HIV infections. HIV is also readily transmitted by means of blood-contaminated needles shared by injection drug users.

The virus can also be passed perinatally from an infected woman to her fetus before birth, to her infant during birth, or to her baby after birth through breast-feeding (Richardson et al., 2003a; Rousseau et al., 2003). Mother-to-child transmission (MTCT) is the primary way that children are infected with HIV (Lamptey et al., 2006).

**Viral load** The amount of HIV present in an infected person's blood.

The likelihood of transmitting HIV during sexual contact depends on both the viral dose and the route of HIV exposure. Viral dose is a direct effect of the **viral load**—how much virus is present in an infected person's blood. The viral load measurement widely used is the number of individual viruses in a milliliter of blood. In general, the greater the viral load, the higher the chance of transmitting the infection. As common sense would suggest, when a person is in a late stage of HIV/AIDS disease, with more advanced infection and thus greater viral load, he or she is highly infectious. However, many of our readers might be surprised to learn that evidence strongly indicates that in the initial period between exposure to HIV and the appearance of HIV antibodies in the blood—a period called *primary infection*, which usually lasts a few months—viral load can be extremely high, creating a state of heightened infectiousness (Pilcher et al., 2004; Wawer et al., 2005). This relatively brief peak in the transmissibility of HIV soon after a person is infected is especially troubling because most infected people are likely to remain unaware during these few months that they have been invaded by HIV. Some experts believe that transmission during primary infection accounts for a large portion of HIV infections worldwide (Cohen & Pilcher, 2005; Wawer et al., 2005).

The likelihood of infection during sexual activity is greater when HIV is transmitted directly into the blood (e.g., through small tears in the rectal tissues or vaginal walls) rather than onto a mucous membrane. Researchers have become increasingly aware that circumcision status affects a man's risk for contracting HIV. The foreskin of the uncircumcised penis is soft and prone to tiny lacerations that may allow HIV to enter the bloodstream more easily. In addition, the foreskin has high concentrations of CD4 and Langerhans cells, the immune cells typically targeted by HIV (Reynolds et al., 2004; Seppa 2004, 2005). While health-care providers continue to debate the practice of circumcision on medical and ethical grounds, the case for circumcision as a means for reducing HIV transmission is building. Evidence supporting this position is discussed in the box titled "Circumcision as a Strategy for Preventing HIV Infection," on the following page.

! Sexual Health

Research also suggests that HIV can be transmitted during oral sex when the virus present in semen or vaginal secretions comes into contact with mucous membrane tissues in the mouth (X. Liu et al., 2003). Unfortunately, many people mistakenly consider oral sex to be a safe practice. Current CDC recommendations for preventing HIV transmission call for using a condom during mouth-to-penis contact. However, it is extremely rare for people to use condoms during oral sex (Torassa, 2000). If you engage in unprotected oral sex with partners whose HIV status is unknown, it would be wise to take certain precautions: Make sure that your gums are in good shape (oral sores or breaks in gum tissue provide HIV easier access to blood), avoid flossing immediately before or after sex (flossing can damage oral tissue and cause bleeding), and avoid taking ejaculated semen into your mouth. Furthermore, in light of the often substantial concentration of HIV in vaginal fluids (Money et al., 2003), you might also be cautious about engaging in cunnilingus with a female partner who has not tested negative for HIV. ■

In the early 1980s, before the U.S. government required screening of donated blood for HIV, contaminated blood and blood products infected an estimated 25,000 transfusion recipients and people with blood-clotting disorders (such as hemophilia) in the United States (Graham, 1997). However, since early 1985, donated blood and blood products have been screened with extensive laboratory testing for the presence of HIV antibodies. The transition from paid to primarily volunteer donors has further enhanced the integrity of the U.S. blood supply by eliminating persons who would donate primarily for monetary gain (Williams et al., 1997). (Health officials believe that blood donors might be less candid about their histories when offered incentives to give blood.) In addition, U.S. blood centers now use behavioral-history-based screening procedures in a format of face-to-face oral interviews by trained staff. These developments have reduced the risk of transfusion-transmitted HIV to an estimated level of approximately two infections per 1 million blood units. This minuscule number of infections is due almost entirely to donations made in the early stage of primary infection, before antibodies are present in the blood (Williams et al., 1997).

However, precautions designed to safeguard the nation's blood supply, although admirably effective, are not foolproof. One problem is that the blood test detects antibodies to HIV rather than the virus itself. And because HIV antibodies can take months or even years to show up in the blood, contaminated units of blood have on rare occasions slipped by. There is, however, no danger of being infected as a result of donating blood. Blood banks, the Red Cross, and other blood-collection centers use sterile equipment and a new disposable needle for each donor. Unfortunately, U.S. procedures for safeguarding the blood supply are not widely practiced globally. This problem is especially acute in some of the world's poorest nations, which also have high rates of blood-transmitted diseases, such as HIV and viral hepatitis (Lamptey et al., 2006).

Research indicates that a small percentage of people appear to be resistant to HIV infection (Misrahi et al., 1998; Royce et al., 1997). There are documented cases of sex workers and homosexual men who remain uninfected despite repeatedly engaging in unprotected sexual intercourse with HIV-infected partners (Cohen, 1998; Dean et al., 1996; Fowke et al., 1996). We can hope that research will someday unlock these mysteries of immunity and perhaps pave the way to development of better prevention and treatment strategies.

It is believed that the risk of transmitting HIV through saliva, tears, and urine is extremely low. Furthermore, no evidence indicates that the virus can be transmitted by casual contact, such as hugging, shaking hands, cooking or eating together, or other forms of casual contact with an infected person (Courville et al., 1998). All the research to date confirms that it is sexual contact with an infected person or sharing contaminated needles that places an individual at risk for HIV infection. Furthermore, certain high-risk behaviors increase the chance of infection. These behaviors include

© Bettmann/CORBIS

The late tennis great Arthur Ashe at a news conference announcing that he had AIDS as a result of receiving an HIV-tainted blood transfusion.

# Circumcision as a Strategy for Preventing HIV Infection

A number of health professionals and researchers have suggested that circumcision may significantly reduce the risk of HIV infection by removing an entry point for the virus—the thin foreskin with its high concentrations of cells that are easily infected by HIV. This contention received strong support from a recent study in South Africa. The study was conducted by an international team of researchers headed by Bertran Auvert, a French physician scientist.

These investigators recruited 3,274 uncircumcised heterosexual men ages 18–24 from an area where about 20% of males are circumcised. All participants expressed a desire to be circumcised and agreed to have the procedure performed at either the beginning or the end of a planned 21-month study. Participants were randomly divided into two groups. The 50% in the early-procedure group were circumcised at the onset of the clinical trial and instructed to abstain from sex for 6 weeks to allow complete healing. Men in both early and late circumcision groups were counseled on safer sex practices and tested for HIV infection several times during the course of the study.

The project was halted after 18 months, when it became clear that circumcision significantly reduced the risk of HIV infection. During this 18-month period 49 of the uncircumcised men and only 20 of the circumcised men contracted an HIV infection. Thus while circumcision reduced the risk of HIV infection by 60%, it certainly did not provide full protection. The differences in infection rates between the uncircumcised men and the circumcised men were not attributable to different levels of sexual activity. In fact, during the study period, the level of sexual activity in the circumcised group was 18% higher than in the uncircumcised group (Auvert et al., 2005). Other studies indicate the preventive potential of circumcision against HIV infection. One study of 2,298 men in India found that circumcised men were six times *less* likely to contract HIV than uncircumcised men (Reynolds et al., 2004). A study of Kenyan men found that uncircumcised men's risk of contracting HIV per act of sexual intercourse with an infected partner was more than double circumcised men's risk (Baeten et al., 2005).

It is prudent to wait for results of other clinical trials before concluding with absolute certainty that circumcision is an effective tool to add to the arsenal of HIV prevention strategies. The South African study conducted by Auvert and his associates is the first of three clinical trials designed to assess the preventive potential of circumcision against HIV infection. Two other trials are now under way in Uganda and Kenya. As we await further data, it is noteworthy that African countries where male circumcision is common, such as Senegal, Nigeria, and Gabon, have markedly lower numbers of HIV-infected men than countries like Botswana, Zimbabwe, and South Africa, where a majority of men are uncircumcised (AIDS Alert, 2005; Seppa, 2004).

having multiple sexual partners, engaging in unprotected sex, sexual contact with people known to be at high risk (such as injection drug users, sex workers, and people with multiple sexual partners), sharing drug injection equipment, and using noninjected drugs such as cocaine, marijuana, and alcohol, which can impair good decision making.

## Symptoms and Complications

As with many other viruses, HIV often causes a brief flulike illness within a few weeks of initial infection. Symptoms include fevers, muscle aches, skin rashes, loss of appetite, diarrhea, fatigue, and swollen lymph glands (Lamptey et al., 2006). These initial reactions, which represent the body's defenses at work, tend to fade fairly rapidly. However, as the virus continues to deplete the immune system, other symptoms can occur, such as persistent or periodically repeating fevers, night sweats, weight loss, chronic fatigue, persistent diarrhea or bloody stools, easy bruising, persistent headaches, a chronic dry cough, and oral candidiasis. Candidiasis of the mouth and throat is the most common infection in HIV-infected people. Many of these physical manifestations also indicate common, everyday ailments that are by no means life threatening. However, observing that you have one or more of these symptoms that are persistent can alert you to seek a medical diagnosis of your ailment.

## HIV Antibody Tests

Within a few months of being infected with HIV, most people develop antibodies to the virus, in a process called *seroconversion*. Seroconversion typically occurs sometime between 25 days and 6 months after initial infection. HIV infection can be detected by standard blood tests for blood serum antibodies to HIV. Most HIV tests are now performed with a simplified diagnostic test kit that uses a finger-stick sample of blood and provides results that are 99.6% accurate in as little as 20 minutes. HIV antibodies can also be detected with a high degree of accuracy in urine and saliva samples (Strauss et al., 2003; Wright & Katz, 2006). For more information about HIV tests and test sites, contact the CDC National Hotline at 1-800-342-2437 (English), 1-800-344-7432 (Spanish), or 1-800-243-7889 (TTY), or go online to the Web site of the American Social Health Association.

Although quite uncommon, "silent" HIV infections can be present in some individuals for 3 years or more before being detected by standard serum antibody tests. More costly and more labor-intensive tests for the virus itself can be performed to detect a silent or latent infection. Once infected with HIV, a person should be considered contagious and capable of infecting others indefinitely, regardless of whether clinical signs of disease are present.

The development of better treatment strategies offers compelling reasons for people at risk to discover their HIV status as soon as possible. Presumably, once people become aware of their HIV-positive status, they will be much less likely to pass the infection on to others. This assumption was supported by a study that found that, of 615 men and women diagnosed with HIV infection, most adopted safer sexual behaviors after diagnosis, including regular use of condoms, less frequent or no sex, or engaging only in oral sex (Centers for Disease Control, 2000a). Another recent study found that a substantial majority of 1,363 HIV-infected men and women were using condoms during vaginal or anal intercourse with partners known to be HIV-negative and with partners of unknown HIV status (Centers for Disease Control, 2003a).

Efforts to encourage testing have focused most on people at higher than normal risk for HIV infection, including MSM, injection drug users, clients at STD clinics, people who have unprotected vaginal and/or anal intercourse with multiple partners, and health-care workers exposed to patients' blood. Unfortunately, despite the potential benefits of early antibody testing and the availability of treatment and counseling for infected persons, many at-risk individuals, especially sexually active young people (gay, bisexual, and heterosexual), are not being tested for HIV. For example, in one study that targeted a large sample of young MSM, researchers found that of the 573 study participants who turned out to be HIV-positive, 77% had been unaware that they were infected (Mackellar et al., 2002). A survey conducted by the Centers for Disease Control (2005d) found that of 450 MSM participants infected with HIV, 48% were unaware of their infection.

Most HIV-infected people in the United States are not tested for HIV until they develop symptoms of disease, and most HIV infections are transmitted by people who are unaware of their status (Koo et al., 2006; Wright & Katz, 2006). These alarming facts prompted the CDC to recommend expanding HIV testing in the United States by including HIV screening in routine health-care services and testing all pregnant women unless they specifically opt out (Wright & Katz, 2006).

As discussed near the end of this chapter, we believe that all couples poised on the brink of a new sexual relationship should seriously consider undergoing medical examinations and laboratory testing designed to rule out HIV and other STDs before beginning any sexual activity that might put them at risk for infection. The following account expresses one man's experience in this matter:

> ? Critical Thinking Question
>
> It has been suggested that all adolescents and adults should be required to undergo screening for the presence of HIV. Do you agree with this recommendation? How might the results of such testing be effectively used to reduce the transmission of HIV? What problems might occur as a result of compulsory screening? Do you believe that mandatory testing would be an unjustifiable violation of privacy rights?

*In the early stages of dating and getting to know one another, my future wife and I candidly discussed our prior relationship histories. Neither of us had been sexual with another for over a year, and we were both confident that we were free of diseases transmitted during sex. But since we were aware that the AIDS virus in an infected person's body may go undetected for years, we decided to be tested for the virus. We had our blood samples drawn at the same time, in the same room, and later shared our respective lab reports. Thankfully, as expected, we both tested negative. This process, while clearly reassuring, was also helpful in contributing to a sense of mutual trust and respect that has continued into our married years. (Authors' files)*

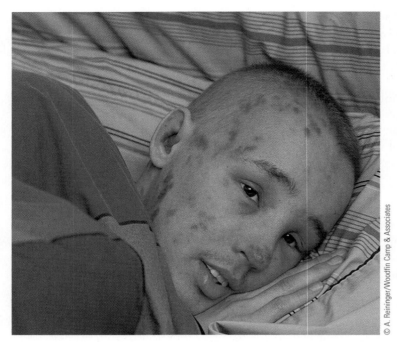

Kaposi's sarcoma, shown here with its distinctive skin lesions, is the most common cancer afflicting men with AIDS.

## Development of AIDS

As HIV continues to proliferate and invade healthy cells in an infected person's body, the immune system loses its capacity to defend the body against opportunistic infections. The incubation period for AIDS (i.e., the time between HIV infection and the onset of one or more severe, debilitating diseases associated with extreme impairment of the immune system) typically ranges from 8 to 11 years in adults, with a median duration of about 10 years. However, a small percentage of people infected with HIV remain symptom-free for much longer periods. Furthermore, as we will see, powerful new treatment strategies can also dramatically slow the progress of HIV/AIDS in individuals who have access to these costly treatments.

People who experience progression to full-blown AIDS can develop a range of life-threatening complications. The most common severe disease among HIV-infected people, and one that accounts for many AIDS deaths, is pneumonia caused by overgrowth of the protozoan *Pneumocystis carinii*, which normally inhabits the lungs of healthy people. Other opportunistic infections associated with HIV include tuberculosis, encephalitis (viral infection of the brain), severe fungal infections that cause a type of meningitis, salmonella illnesses (bacterial diseases), and toxoplasmosis (caused by a protozoan). The body is also vulnerable to cancers, such as lymphomas (cancers of the lymph system), cervical cancer, and Kaposi's sarcoma, the most common cancer in male AIDS patients, which affects the skin and can also involve internal organs.

Before the advent of much-improved antiretroviral treatments, once people living with AIDS developed life-threatening illnesses, such as pneumonia or cancer, the disease tended to run a fairly rapid course. Death usually occurred within 2 years for both men and women (Suligoi, 1997). Furthermore, most people who have developed AIDS since the beginning of the epidemic in the United States have already died. However, a significant decline in the rate of AIDS deaths began in 1996 (the first year that the death rate declined since the onset of the epidemic) and has continued to the present time. This reversal in death trends was largely due to improvement in combination drug therapies, which we discuss in the next section.

A reduction in AIDS deaths is also occurring in other developed nations that have the resources to implement the more effective drug therapies. Unfortunately, this reversal in AIDS deaths is not occurring in developing nations, especially those located in Africa, Asia, and the Caribbean, where HIV/AIDS is continuing to escalate both in number of infections and number of deaths. The high cost and difficulty of administering new and better therapies are barriers to the effective use of these treatments in poor, undeveloped nations. In sub-Saharan Africa only about 11% of those in need of antiretroviral treatment are receiving it (Lamptey et al., 2006).

## Treatment

At the time of this writing, there is still no cure for HIV/AIDS. However, thousands of scientists are involved in an unprecedented worldwide effort to ultimately cure and/or prevent this horrific disease. This war is being waged on several fronts, including attempts to develop effective antiretroviral drugs that will kill or at least neutralize HIV and efforts to create a vaccine effective against HIV.

As we described earlier, HIV is classified as a retrovirus because, after invading a living cell, it works backward, using an enzyme called *reverse transcriptase*. This enzyme transcribes the viral RNA into DNA, which then acts to direct further synthesis of the lethal HIV RNA. HIV also encodes another enzyme, called a *protease* (protein digesting), that is equally critical to its reproduction. Once HIV invades a host CD4 cell, it eventually takes over the host cell's genetic material and manufacturing capacity, producing additional viruses to infect other cells. During this process, HIV kills the host cell and injects copies of its own lethal RNA into the blood to invade other healthy cells.

To date, treatment strategies have focused on drug interventions designed to block the proliferation and seeding of HIV throughout the immune system and other bodily tissues and organs. Up to the mid-1990s the main class of drugs used to combat HIV comprised products that inhibited the action of the reverse transcriptase enzyme. These reverse transcriptase (RT) inhibitors were designed to prevent the virus from copying its own genetic material and making more viruses. A major breakthrough in drug therapy took place in 1996 with the emergence of a new class of drugs that inhibit HIV's protease enzyme, which the virus uses to assemble new copies of itself. When a protease inhibitor (PI) drug was combined with two RT inhibitor drugs in early clinical trials, the combination was shown to dramatically reduce viral load in blood to minimal or undetectable levels in most patients (Louis et al., 1997; Wong et al., 1997).

## Highly Active Antiretroviral Therapy

The use of a combination of three or more drugs to combat HIV, which initially was commonly referred to as combination or triple-drug therapy (or in the popular media, as the "AIDS cocktail"), has come to be known as **highly active antiretroviral therapy (HAART)**. Most clinicians commence treatment of HIV/AIDS with either a combination of three RTs or a combination of two RTs and one PI, according to the latest guidelines from the National Institutes of Health and the CDC.

It is generally agreed that HAART should be administered to any HIV-infected person whose CD4 count is below 200 or to anyone who manifests symptomatic disease (i.e., infections or cancers associated with HIV/AIDS). However, deciding the optimal stage of HIV infection at which to initiate HAART among people with CD4 counts above 200 who are asymptomatic is a complex issue that is still being debated (Ahdieh-Grant et al., 2003; Khalsa, 2006). The potential benefits and risks of early or delayed therapy need to be carefully evaluated by both the treating clinician and the patient. ● **Table 15.2** provides a summary of these potential benefits and risks.

In the United States and other developed nations HAART has proven to be an effective treatment regimen for many HIV/AIDS patients. Various studies have demonstrated that, when properly administered, HAART can inhibit HIV replication

**Highly active antiretroviral therapy (HAART)** A strategy for treating HIV-infected people with three or more antiretroviral drugs.

InfoTrac Search Words

- HAART

| ● TABLE 15.2 | Potential Benefits and Risks of Early or Delayed HAART Initiation for Asymptomatic HIV-Infected Persons | | | |
|---|---|---|---|---|
| Potential Benefits of Early Treatment | Potential Risks of Early Treatment | Potential Benefits of Delayed Treatment | Potential Risks of Delayed Treatment |
| • Earlier suppression of viral replication.<br>• Preservation of immune function.<br>• Prolongation of disease-free survival.<br>• Decrease in the risk of transmitting HIV to others. | • Adverse effects of HAART on quality of life.<br>• Reduced adherence over time due to inconvenient and complicated drug regimens.<br>• Development of drug resistance due to suboptimal adherence to HAART.<br>• Limitation of future treatment options as a result of premature cycling of a patient through the available drugs.<br>• Development of drug-resistant HIV strains.<br>• Development of serious drug side effects. | • Minimization of adverse drug side effects and treatment-related negative effects on quality of life.<br>• Delayed development of viral drug resistance.<br>• Preservation of treatment options (i.e., reserving the limited number of available drugs until later in the course of HIV disease). | • Possibility of irreversible damage to the immune system, which might have been averted by earlier treatment.<br>• Possibility that suppression of viral replication might be more difficult at a later stage of disease.<br>• Increased risk of HIV transmission to others during a longer untreated period. |

SOURCES: Ahdieh-Grant et al. (2003) and Centers for Disease Control (2002a).

In 1991 Earvin (Magic) Johnson, Los Angeles Lakers basketball All-Star, announced that he had been infected with HIV through heterosexual contact. By April 1997, HAART had reduced HIV to undetectable levels in his body.

and frequently can reduce viral load to an undetectable level, improve immune function, and delay progression of the disease (Centers for Disease Control, 2006l; Gallant et al., 2006; Gandhi et al., 2006).

The excellent clinical results produced by HAART in the early years after it was implemented led to a surge of optimism that this advance in antiretroviral therapy might not only delay HIV/AIDS progression but also ultimately eradicate the virus. Unfortunately, as we will see, these early projections were overly optimistic.

The success of HAART depends directly on people's ability to consistently and correctly adhere to complicated medication dosing schedules for long time periods. Unfortunately, patient adherence to the HAART regimen is often not very good (Starace et al., 2006).

A significant drawback of HAART that influences adherence is drug toxicity. Low compliance is often associated with adverse drug side effects, including anemia, insomnia, mouth ulcers, diarrhea, inflammation of the pancreas, respiratory difficulties, metabolic disturbances, increased cholesterol and triglyceride levels (major risk factors for cardiovascular diseases), gastrointestinal discomfort, liver damage, excess fat accumulation in areas such as the abdomen, upper back, and breasts, fat atrophy in the face, legs, and arms, and skin rashes (Chesney, 2003; Hawkins, 2006). Some of these side effects can be so severe that affected people are unable to tolerate HAART.

Lack of adherence to HAART because of dosing complexities and/or drug toxicity side effects can lead to less than optimal therapy, outright treatment failure, and the development of drug-resistant strains of HIV (Novak et al., 2005; Starace et al., 2006). Recent improvements in medication dosing schedules (e.g., once or twice a day versus three times a day) and reductions in pill quantity (e.g., combining two or three drugs in one pill) have resulted in better adherence to HAART. In July 2006, the FDA approved the world's first single-pill, once-a-day HAART medication. This new combination pill, called Atripla, represents a medical milestone in the treatment of HIV/AIDS.

Treatment failure, defined as HAART drugs that no longer suppress viral loads, can occur even in people who correctly adhere to the treatment regimen (Centers for Disease Control, 2000a; Kaufmann et al., 2000). When treatment failures occur, patients are generally switched to another three-drug combination in established HAART regimens, which might reestablish effective viral load suppression.

Another problem with HAART that surfaced in recent years further dampened the optimism and excitement associated with the early years of this treatment protocol. It is now clear that HAART does not eradicate HIV from latent or silent reservoirs in the brain, lymph nodes, intestines, and other tissues, cells, and organs where the virus may reside undetected and intact, even though blood plasma viral loads drop to minimal or undetectable levels (Chesney, 2003). Once treatment with the HAART regimen stops or is seriously compromised because a patient is too sick with toxic side effects or too confused by the complexity of dosing regimens, the virus sequestered in these lethal reservoirs typically comes roaring back, or it mutates, resulting in new strains of HIV that are less susceptible to the HAART drugs.

On a more positive note, the drastically reduced and sustained low viral loads that result from successful HAART treatment "substantially [reduce] the likelihood of HIV transmission" (Centers for Disease Control, 2002a). However, despite a strong association between reduced risk for HIV transmission and sustained low viral loads, a person can transmit the virus at any time after becoming infected, even while undergoing successful HAART (Centers for Disease Control, 2002a). Consequently, HAART is no substitute for safer sexual behavior or abstinence.

Has the availability of HAART influenced HIV-negative people to change their sexual behaviors? Do people undergoing this treatment regimen change their sexual behaviors after beginning treatment? Evidence collected in the early years of HAART indicated that at least some HIV-negative gay and bisexual men increased their involvement in risky sex, perhaps because of the availability of this treatment regimen (Dilley et al., 1997; Kelly et al., 1998). More-recent studies have confirmed a continuation of this trend toward increased sexual risk taking among gay and bisexual men as a result, at least in part, of improved treatment for HIV/AIDS (Brewer et al., 2006; Peterson & Bakeman, 2006; Stolte et al., 2006).

Many persons who are aware that they are infected with HIV do refrain from engaging in risky sexual behavior. Two recent studies—one a 16-state sample of HIV-infected MSM and the other a representative sample of the adult U.S. population in care for HIV/AIDS—found that 31% of the MSM and 32% of the adult respondents in the broader study were engaging in "deliberate abstinence" by refraining from vaginal, anal, or oral intercourse over the previous 6 months to a year (Bogart et al., 2006). However, some HIV-positive individuals do continue to behave in a sexually reckless manner, as evidenced by research conducted in several large urban areas in the United States that indicates that "the overall rate of continued unprotected intercourse among persons living with HIV disease is 33%" (Heckman et al., 2003, p. 134).

Patients undergoing HAART must strictly adhere to a rigid and complex regimen that often involves taking large daily doses of drugs at different time intervals.

## Drug Therapy to Prevent Mother-to-Child Transmission of HIV

In 1994, research demonstrated that zidovudine, an RT inhibitor drug administered to both HIV-infected mothers and their newborns, reduced perinatal mother-to-child-transmission (MTCT) by two-thirds (Connor et al., 1994). In August 1994 the U.S. Public Health Service recommended zidovudine to reduce perinatal MTCT of HIV. The standard treatment protocol involves administering zidovudine orally to pregnant women (starting between 14 and 34 weeks of gestation), intravenously during labor, and orally to the newborn for the first 6 weeks of life (Thaker & Snow, 2003). Since 1994 the number of infants infected through MTCT has declined dramatically in the United States, largely because of the widespread use of the zidovudine treatment regimen, which prevents MTCT in most instances (Minkoff, 2003).

The success of this relatively long and complex regimen of zidovudine for reducing MTCT has stimulated a search for a less costly, more practical and effective short-course antiretroviral regimen. Recent studies in South Africa and Uganda found that infants who were provided with either (1) a single dose of the RT inhibitor drug nevirapine within 24 hours of birth or (2) a short-course regimen with this drug experienced excellent protection from HIV infection (Altman, 2002; Centers for Disease Control, 2005f; D. Moodley et al, 2003). Because single-dose or short-course nevirapine therapy is dramatically less costly than the longer and more complex zidovudine regimen, many countries with limited resources are now utilizing this drug to reduce MTCT of HIV. Recently, another antiretroviral drug, cotrimoxizole, has also been shown to effectively prevent MTCT of HIV (Lamptey et al., 2006).

Preventing perinatal MTCT does not eliminate the possibility of later transmission of the virus from a mother to a child through breast-feeding. Global data indicate that one-third to one-half of all HIV infections in infants occur through breast-feeding (Rousseau et al., 2003). Unfortunately, there is no therapeutic regimen that significantly reduces MTCT through breast-feeding (Rousseau et al., 2003). Health authorities are hopeful that presenting alternatives to breast-feeding, such as breast-milk substitutes or early weaning, will help reduce transmission of HIV through breast milk. Unfortunately, alternatives to breast milk are often unaffordable or are undesirable because of contaminated water in resource-poor developing countries where breast-feeding (regardless of maternal HIV status) continues to be the most prevalent form of infant feeding (Rousseau et al., 2003).

## The Search for a Vaccine

We close this section on treatment with an update on efforts to develop an effective vaccine for HIV. Development of a safe, effective, and affordable vaccine is a global public health priority and remains the best long-term hope for bringing the worldwide HIV/AIDS pandemic under control.

There are two broad categories of vaccines: (1) those that prevent initial infection by HIV (prophylactic vaccines) and (2) those that delay or prevent progression of disease in people already infected (therapeutic vaccines). Despite extensive efforts, researchers have failed to develop vaccines from either category that are broadly effective against HIV.

However, recent developments in HIV vaccine research have been favorable. For example, an increasing number of vaccine candidates are entering the development pipeline (more than 30 as of 2005), and several major efficacy trials of vaccine candidates do provide a basis for some guarded hope for future successes in this critical research area (Lamptey et al., 2006). A number of problems confront vaccine researchers, including the absence of an ideal animal model for research and the combined facts that HIV is extremely complicated, is present in multiple strains, and can change rapidly through genetic mutation (Hu et al., 2003; Prabu-Jeyabalan et al., 2003).

To date, several therapeutic HIV vaccines have been tested in small-scale human studies and found to be largely ineffective. We hope that continuing efforts in this area will yield more positive results. Prophylactic vaccines are being tested in several countries (AIDS Vaccine Advocacy Coalition, 2006).

For the sake of the world's population, especially in developing countries where minuscule per-capita health expenditures limit the use of costly drug therapies, we can only hope that effective, low-cost vaccines are available soon. Unfortunately, the timeline for finding an effective HIV vaccine appears to stretch years into the future and the "reality is that we are on a long-term mission" (AIDS Vaccine Advocacy Coalition, 2006, p. 1).

## Prevention

!  Sexual Health

The only certain way to avoid contracting HIV *sexually* is either to avoid all varieties of interpersonal sexual contact that place one at risk for infection or to be involved in a monogamous, mutually faithful relationship with one noninfected partner. If neither of these conditions is applicable, a wise person will act in a way that significantly reduces his or her risk of becoming infected with HIV.

Safer-sex practices that reduce the risk of contracting HIV/AIDS and other STDs are described in some detail in the last section of this chapter. Most of these preventive methods are directly applicable to HIV/AIDS. However, it is important to note that any strategies that reduce your risk of developing the other STDs previously discussed will also reduce your risk of HIV infection because of the known association between HIV/AIDS and other STDs. Research throughout the world has shown that the risk of contracting HIV is elevated in people who have other STDs, such as genital herpes, gonorrhea, syphilis, chlamydia, and trichomoniasis (Celum et al. 2005; Todd et al., 2006). STDs that cause genital ulcers, such as herpes and syphilis, have shown the highest association with HIV infection in North America and Africa, because genital ulcers allow HIV easy access to the bloodstream. Herpes infections are the predominant cause of genital ulcers in Africa (Paz-Bailey et al., 2006) and the most significant risk factor for HIV infection (Todd et al., 2006).

Beyond the obvious safer-sex strategies of consistently and correctly using latex condoms and avoiding sex with multiple partners or with individuals at high risk for HIV, the following list provides suggestions particularly relevant to avoiding HIV infection. Note that several of these suggestions, such as avoiding oral contact with semen and vaginal fluids, are less significant for two healthy people in a monogamous relationship who apply common sense in evaluating what is most likely to be risky for them.

1. If you use injected drugs, do not share needles or syringes (boiling does not guarantee sterility). If needle sharing continues, use bleach to sterilize your needles and syringes. However, be aware that research has shown that bleach has only limited effectiveness for the disinfection of injection equipment (Lurie & Drucker, 1997).

2. Injection drug users may wish to check with local health departments to see if a needle- or syringe-exchange program exists. These programs, which provide clean syringes or needles in exchange for used syringes or needles, have been shown to reduce the spread of HIV and other blood-borne infections among high-risk injection drug users (Centers for Disease Control, 2005e).

3. Avoid oral, vaginal, or anal contact with semen.

4. Avoid anal intercourse, because this is one of the riskiest of all sexual behaviors associated with HIV transmission (Abner et al., 2005; Calzavara et al., 2003).

5. Do not engage in insertion of fingers or fists ("fisting") into the anus as an active or receptive partner. Fingernails can easily cause tears in the rectal tissues, thereby creating a route for HIV to penetrate the blood.

6. Avoid oral contact with the anus (a practice commonly referred to as rimming).

7. Avoid oral contact with vaginal fluids.

8. Do not allow a partner's urine to enter your mouth, anus, vagina, eyes, or open cuts or sores.

9. Avoid sexual intercourse during menstruation. HIV-infected women are at increased risk for transmitting their infection through intercourse while menstruating (Royce et al., 1997).

10. Do not share razor blades, toothbrushes, or other implements that could become contaminated with blood (Khalsa, 2006).

11. In view of the remote possibility that HIV may be transmitted by means of prolonged open-mouth wet kissing, it might be wise to avoid this activity. There is no risk of HIV transmission through closed-mouth kissing.

12. Avoid sexual contact with sex workers (male or female). Research indicates that sex workers have unusually high rates of HIV infection (Lamptey et al., 2006). ■

All of these methods for preventing HIV infection focus on preventing exposure to the virus. Recently the U.S. Department of Health and Human Services issued guidelines for using antiretroviral drugs to prevent HIV infection after unanticipated sexual or injection-drug-use exposure. These guidelines indicate that a 28-day course of HAART commenced as soon as possible after exposure can significantly reduce the risk of infection (Centers for Disease Control, 2005f). A number of health departments, clinics, and individual physicians in the United States are now providing post-exposure prophylaxis (PEP) via HAART after unanticipated exposure to HIV. Some scientists believe that pre-exposure prophylaxis (PREP) via a pill a day may also be a viable option for preventing HIV infection. This possibility is discussed in the box "A Daily Pill to Prevent HIV Infection" on the following page.

At present, the best hope for curtailing the spread of HIV/AIDS is through education and behavior change. Because neither an effective vaccine nor a drug-based cure seems likely to be available soon, the only viable strategy for significantly curtailing this pandemic is preventing exposure through education about effective prevention and risk-reduction strategies (Hoxworth et al., 2003). A wide range of published studies of a variety of prevention strategies, directed at a broad range of target populations, has provided promising findings, indicating that intensive educational and behavioral interventions are often effective in reducing risky behaviors that increase vulnerability to HIV infection (Albarracin et al., 2003; DiClemente & Wingwood, 2003; Johnson et al., 2003).

A recent meta-analysis (a complex statistical procedure that collectively analyzes data from many studies) of 46 studies that assessed the effectiveness of persuasive communication in HIV prevention found that a number of communication strategies lead to an increase in safer sexual behavior, especially condom use (Albarracin et al., 2003). Two of the most effective strategies were (1) messages designed to teach people successful condom use strategies, such as how to negotiate with partners who refuse to use condoms, and (2) attitudinal messages that clearly described the preventive outcomes of condom use. Another recent meta-analysis of 44 studies of HIV prevention

## A Daily Pill to Prevent HIV Infection

Is it possible that uninfected people could take a pill once daily to prevent HIV infection? A number of HIV/AIDS experts believe that pre-exposure prophylaxis (PREP) with a once-daily ingestion of tenofovir (a reverse transcriptase inhibitor) may accomplish this goal (AIDS Vaccine Advocacy Coalition, 2006; Lamptey et al., 2006). Research has shown that tenofovir may reduce the risk of SIV (simian immunodeficiency virus) infection in monkeys if taken prior to exposure to the virus (Koen et al., 2001, 2002). Research on HIV-infected people has shown that tenofovir taken once daily has few side effects (Lamptey et al., 2006). However, the long-term effects of daily doses of this drug are unknown (AIDS Vaccine Advocacy Coalition, 2006).

Some health professionals have suggested that PREP may prove especially advantageous for uninfected people whose primary partners are infected, for people who feel unable to insist on condom use, and for commercial sex workers who often experience unprotected exposure to HIV. Behavioral researchers have also expressed concern that people utilizing PREP may become less concerned about HIV infection and thus less vigilant about protecting themselves via safer sexual behaviors. If a PREP drug provides less than 100% protection (a near certainty) or is taken inconsistently, PREP could result in an increased rather than a decreased risk of infection. These and other concerns resulted in the early termination of clinical trials of tenofovir-based PREP being conducted in Cambodia, Nigeria, and Cameroon. However, new clinical trials to determine if tenofovir can protect people from HIV infection were recently initiated in seven countries (AIDS Advocacy Coalition, 2006; Lamptey et al., 2006). Researchers are also investigating the PREP potential of tenofovir administered with another antiretroviral drug, emtricitabine (Marchione, 2006).

strategies applied to adolescents found that a variety of intensive behavioral interventions reduces HIV risk by accomplishing one or more of the following goals: (1) increasing condom use, (2) improving sexual communication between partners, (3) delaying sexual debut (i.e., first intercourse experience), (4) decreasing the number of sexual partners, and (5) increasing both overall knowledge of and skills in applying prevention tactics (Johnson et al., 2003).

The findings of these two meta-analyses demonstrate that HIV prevention interventions can result in safer sexual behaviors. In the absence of a cure or an effective vaccine, these educational efforts provide the best weapons in the current worldwide war being waged against this devastating disease.

## ◗ Preventing Sexually Transmitted Diseases

Many approaches to curtailing the spread of STDs have been advocated. These range from attempting to discourage sexual activity among young people to providing easy public access to information about the symptoms of STDs, along with free medical treatment. Unfortunately, the efforts of public health agencies have not been very successful in curbing the rapid spread of STDs. For this reason, it is doubly important to stress a variety of specific preventive measures that can be taken by an individual or a couple.

Clearly, abstinence from partner sex is one virtually surefire way to avoid an STD infection. Being disease-free and monogamous yourself and having a partner who is also disease-free and monogamous is another way to prevent contracting an STD. However, it is often difficult for people to assess the disease-risk status of prospective or current partners and, for that matter, to assess how committed their partners are to being monogamous.

Having a frank and open discussion before initial sexual interaction may seem difficult and embarrassing. However, in this era of epidemic health-damaging and life-threatening STDs, such discussions are essential to making sound judgments that may have profound ramifications for your physical and psychological well-being. Consequently, we address this issue early in our outline of prevention guidelines.

### Prevention Guidelines

We discuss several methods of prevention—steps that can be taken before, during, or shortly after sexual contact to reduce the likelihood of contracting an STD. Many of these methods are effective against the transmission of a variety of diseases. Several are applicable to oral–genital and anal–genital contacts in addition to genital–genital interaction. None of the methods is 100% effective, but each method acts to significantly reduce the chances of infection. Furthermore—and this cannot be overemphasized—the use of preventive measures may help to curtail the booming spread of STDs. Because many infected people have sexual contact with one or more partners before realizing that they have a disease and seeking treatment, improved prevention rather than better treatment seems to hold the key to reducing these unpleasant effects of sexual expression.

## Assess Your Risk Status and Your Partner's Risk Status

As a result of informed concern about acquiring an STD, you may understandably focus on assessing the risk status of a prospective sexual partner. However, in doing so, you may overlook the equally important need to evaluate your own risk status. If you previously engaged in sexual activity with others, is there any possibility that you may have contracted an STD from them? Have you been tested for STDs in general, not just for one specific infectious agent? Remember, many of the STDs discussed in this chapter produce little or no noticeable symptoms in an infected person. If you care enough to be sexually intimate with a new partner, is it not reasonable that you should also be open and willing to share information about your own sexual health?

Some experts maintain that one of the most important STD prevention messages to convey to people is to spend time, ideally several months or more, getting to know prospective sexual partners before engaging in genital sex. Unfortunately, research indicates that effective communication about risk factors and safer sexual behavior seems to be "more the exception than the rule in dating couples" (Buysse & Ickes, 1999, p. 121). We strongly encourage you to take time to develop a warm, caring relationship in which mutual empathy and trust are key ingredients. Use this time to convey to the other person any relevant information from your sexual history regarding your risk status—and to inquire about your partner's present or past behavior in the areas of sex and injection drug use. As discussed in Chapter 7, self-disclosure can be an effective strategy for getting a partner to open up. Thus you might begin your dialogue about these matters by discussing why you think that such an information exchange is vitally important in the AIDS era, and then share information about your own sexual history.

Getting to know someone well enough to trust his or her answers to these important questions means taking the time to assess a person's honesty and integrity in a variety of situations. If you observe your prospective partner lying to friends, family members, or you about other matters, you may rightfully question the truthfulness of her or his responses to your risk-assessment queries.

Research suggests that we cannot always assume that potential sexual partners will accurately disclose their risk for STDs. One study found that a sizable percentage of both men and women said that they would not be fully honest when questioned about their past sexual and drug-use histories. Of more than 400 sexually experienced Southern California college students surveyed, 35% of the men and 10% of the women said that they had lied about such things as pregnancy risk and other sexual involvements in order to have sex. In addition, 47% of the men and 42% of the women said that they would report fewer previous sexual partners than they really had. Finally, 20% of the men and 4% of the women indicated that they would falsely claim that they had tested negative for HIV (Cochran & Mays, 1990). In another survey of 169 students at a large Midwestern university, approximately 30% of the male respondents and 6% of the female respondents admitted to lying in order to have sex (Stebleton & Rothenberger, 1993). In still another study, researchers found that 40% of 203 HIV-infected men and women had not disclosed their HIV status to all their sexual partners in the prior 6 months. Of the nondisclosers, half had not disclosed to their one and only partner. Furthermore, among those who had not disclosed, only 42% used condoms consistently (Stein et al., 1998).

## Obtain Prior Medical Examinations

Even when people are entirely candid about their own sexual histories, there is no way to ensure that their previous sexual partners were honest with them—or, for that matter, that they even asked previous partners about STD risk status. In view of these concerns, we strongly encourage couples who want to begin a sexual relationship to abstain from any activity that puts them at risk for STDs until both partners have had medical examinations and laboratory testing designed to rule out all STDs, including HIV. Taking this step not only reduces one's chance of contracting a disease but also contributes immeasurably to a sense of mutual trust and comfort with developing intimacy. If cost is an issue, contact your campus health service or a public health clinic in your area; both of these venues can provide examinations and laboratory testing free of charge or on a sliding fee scale commensurate with your financial status.

Health departments often provide screening and treatment for STDs.

Ryan McVay/Getty Images

## Use Condoms

It has been known for decades that condoms, when consistently and correctly used, help to prevent the transmission of many STDs. The condom is one of the great underrated aids to sexual interaction. Male latex condoms, when used correctly and consistently, are effective in preventing the sexual transmission of HIV, and they reduce the risk of transmission of other STDs, such as chlamydia, gonorrhea, NGU, bacterial vaginosis, and trichomoniasis, that are also transmitted by fluids from mucosal surfaces. Condoms are less effective in preventing infections that are transmitted by skin-to-skin contact, such as syphilis, HSV, and HPV, and they have no value in combating pubic lice and scabies. Condoms made from sheep's membrane (also known as "natural skin" or "natural membrane") contain small pores that may permit passage of some STDs, including HIV, HSV, and hepatitis viruses.

Unfortunately, the proven value of condoms in reducing the spread of HIV/AIDS in Africa has recently been undermined by a change in U.S. policy during George W. Bush's administration. This is discussed in the box titled "U.S. Policy Reduces Condom Promotion in Africa."

Correctly used condoms help prevent the transmission of many STDs, including HIV.

© Michael Newman/PhotoEdit

Laboratory studies indicate that the female condom (see Chapter 10) is an effective barrier to viruses, including HIV. If used correctly and consistently, the female condom can substantially reduce the risk of transmission of some STDs, and when the use of male condoms is not an option, we strongly encourage our readers to consider using a female condom. The female condom can be especially valuable to sexually active women who are at substantial risk for acquiring STDs from male partners who are unwilling to use male condoms consistently or at all.

Evidence indicates that widely used vaginal spermicides containing nonoxynol-9 (N-9) are not effective in preventing transmission of chlamydia, gonorrhea, or HIV (Roddy et al., 2002). In fact, frequent use of N-9 has been associated with genital lesions in the vagina, which can increase vulnerability to HIV infection transmitted during vaginal intercourse (van Damme, 2000). Furthermore, animal research has shown that N-9 can damage the cells lining the rectum, thus providing a portal of entry for HIV and other STD pathogens (Phillips et al., 2000). The CDC recommends against use of condoms lubricated with N-9 spermicide.

## U.S. Policy Reduces Condom Promotion in Africa

In the last two decades, the ABC model of HIV/AIDS prevention has been widely promoted by health professionals in sub-Saharan Africa countries. Certainly all three components of this model, Abstinence for youth, Be faithful in relationships, and Condom promotion, have a place in efforts to reduce the spread of HIV/AIDS. However, many health officials believe that condom promotion is the essential ingredient in prevention efforts in African societies where males traditionally have multiple wives and/or sex partners and where high levels of sexual activity among youth are the norm. Unfortunately, policy changes implemented by the U.S. government have made ABC controversial and represent a serious setback in efforts to bring this disease pandemic under control. "Conservative U.S. government officials have made clear the Bush administration's preference for abstinence-only approaches and have registered strong misgivings about the moral and ethical advisability of providing condoms as part of AIDS prevention programs, arguing—incorrectly—that condoms may encourage early sex and sexual promiscuity. In addition, U.S. officials have removed scientifically accurate information about condom use effectiveness from the Web sites of several federal agencies and have questioned whether or not condoms provide protection against STIs, including HIV" (Sinding, 2005, p. 39).

To date, there is absolutely no evidence that abstinence-only programs have reduced HIV transmission anywhere in the world (Sinding, 2005). Nevertheless, this unproven approach is being exported to many sub-Saharan nations, especially Uganda, as part of President Bush's Emergency Plan for AIDS Relief (PEPFAR) (Cohen et al., 2005; Human Rights Watch, 2006). Recent investigations have revealed that U.S. contractors discourage teachers in Uganda from discussing condoms with students because the new policy is "abstinence-only," and that a curriculum for secondary schools in Uganda (funded by PEPFAR) incorrectly states that condoms have small pores that allow passage of HIV (Cohen et al., 2005; Human Rights Watch, 2006).

A recent report by the U.S. Government Accountability Office revealed that the requirement to allocate a sizable portion of PEPFAR's funds to promote abstinence and fidelity has significantly eroded other preventive efforts, including MTCT, prevention services for couples in which one person is HIV infected and the other is not infected, and promotion of comprehensive programs focused on high-risk groups such as sexually active youth (Brown, 2006).

The abstinence-only emphasis in U.S.-funded HIV/AIDS prevention efforts is especially damaging to African women, many of whom contract HIV from their husbands (Sinding, 2005). These women, who have little or no power in male-dominated cultures, are generally unable to "abstain" from being sexually coerced by unfaithful husbands or to insist on their spouse's fidelity (Cohen et al., 2005; Human Rights Watch, 2006). Furthermore, in an atmosphere in which prevention programs de-emphasize condom use, it is unlikely that women can successfully insist on condom use during sexual relations.

Two leading HIV/AIDS researchers, Deborah Cohen and Thomas Farley (2004), stated that the greatest obstacle to prevention of HIV transmission worldwide is a lack of condom availability. Unfortunately, this problem is magnified by a U.S. government-funded approach to HIV/AIDS prevention that is redirecting efforts away from the effective strategy of condom promotion to unproven and ideologically driven programs that focus primarily on promoting sexual abstinence (LaFranchi, 2006).

---

Available barrier methods for preventing STD transmission are often disadvantageous to women because they are either male controlled (the male condom) or require male cooperation (the female condom). Consequently, researchers are actively pursuing methods for STD prevention that can be controlled solely by women. These efforts are described in the boxed discussion "New Hope for Preventing STDs: The Search for Effective Vaginal Microbicides" on page 454.

We review the proper use of condoms in the following list:

- Store condoms in a cool, dry place out of direct sunlight.
- Throw away condoms in damaged packages and any condoms that are beyond the expiration date; are brittle, sticky, or discolored; or show any other signs of age.
- Handle condoms with care so that they are not punctured.
- Put on a condom before any genital contact, to prevent exposure to fluids that may contain infectious agents.
- Be sure that the condom is adequately lubricated. If you need to add a lubricant, be sure to use only water-based products, such as K-Y Jelly, Astroglide, AquaLube, or glycerin. Latex is weakened by petroleum- or oil-based lubricants (such as Vaseline, baby oil, cooking oils, shortening, massage oils, and many body lotions).
- Do not blow up a condom like a balloon or fill it with water before using it to test for leaks. Such stretching weakens the latex and makes the condom more likely to break during use.

## New Hope for Preventing STDs: The Search for Effective Vaginal Microbicides

The currently available barrier methods for preventing STD transmission are often disadvantageous to women. Latex condoms provide excellent protection against many STDs, but they are frequently used inconsistently and/or incorrectly and are a male-controlled method. Even use of the female condom—which is a promising device for preventing pregnancy and STD transmission—depends on cooperation and acceptance by male partners. In many resource-poor nations HIV and other STDs are epidemic, and women are often subjected to unprotected intercourse with men unwilling to use condoms.

Because women are often disadvantaged by gender inequity in relationships in which they lack the power to negotiate condom use or say no to sex with their male partners, and by the limited options for disease prevention, the development of methods for preventing STDs that can be totally controlled by women is a high priority (Koo et al., 2005; Lamptey et al., 2006; Mantell et al., 2006). Simply advising women to insist that their partners use condoms is often unrealistic in situations where women lack either the power or the assertive skills necessary to ensure correct and consistent use of condoms.

Research efforts are currently under way to develop safe and effective topical gel or cream products or suppositories, called **microbicides,** that can be inserted into the vagina or rectum to prevent or minimize the risk of being infected with HIV and other STDs. These products would be applied before sexual intercourse, but they would not be a substitute for condoms. Rather, they would provide extra protection at low cost. In the developing world, where financial resources are limited and women are often unable to depend on male cooperation, microbicides would offer an especially beneficial option for STD prevention. Ideally, such products will eventually be widely available at minimal cost, will be broadly effective in preventing transmission of a wide range of STDs, will not result in vaginal or rectal irritation or damage, and will have no adverse effect on vaginal *lactobacilli* that help to maintain a healthy vaginal environment.

Technically, the term *microbicide* means "a product that kills microbes." However, there are several ways that microbicide products could function to prevent STDs. Some microbicides would kill or destroy disease-causing organisms present in semen or vaginal secretions. Other microbicides under development would work not by destroying a disease-causing pathogen but by blocking its entry or fusion with target cells or by stopping its replication once inside target cells (Lamptey et al., 2006).

More than 30 microbicide candidates are being studied in clinical trials with large study populations in developing countries who are at high risk for infection by HIV and other STDs (Dhawan & Mayer, 2006; Keller et al., 2006).

Some of the products currently under investigation have both spermicidal and antimicrobial capabilities. Health officials hope to eventually have effective products from both categories, because some users will want protection against both unwanted pregnancies and STDs, whereas others will seek only disease protection. We hope that one or more of these much-needed products will be available soon.

**Microbicide** A topical gel or cream product that women can use vaginally to prevent or minimize the risk of being infected with HIV or other STDs.

- If a penis is uncircumcised, pull back the foreskin before putting on the condom.
- Do not unroll the condom first and then pull it on like a sock; this also tends to weaken the latex, making it more likely that the condom will break during use. The proper way to put on a condom is to unroll it directly onto the erect penis (either while pinching the reservoir tip or while holding a twisted end to create a reservoir area).
- If a condom does break, replace it immediately.
- After ejaculation, take care that the condom does not slip off. Withdraw the condom-clad penis while the penis is still erect, holding the base of the condom firmly to prevent slippage.
- Never reuse a condom.

Various surveys have indicated that rates of condom slippage and breakage are considerably higher during anal intercourse than during vaginal intercourse (Silverman & Gross, 1997). We urge readers who engage in anal intercourse to be especially cautious in their use of condoms during this variety of sexual interaction (e.g., avoid vigorous thrusting, use adequate lubrication, and take special care to avoid slippage). To be effective as STD prophylactics, condoms must be used correctly *every time* a person has sex. Consistent, correct use may be difficult, particularly because logic has a tendency to shut down in the heat of passion (Strong et al., 2005). Thus we strongly encourage you to incorporate into your sex life knowledge about the benefits of condoms and how they can be used most effectively to prevent both disease transmission and conception.

## Avoid Sexual Activity With Multiple Partners

You may wish to reevaluate the importance of sex with multiple partners in light of the clear and extensive evidence that having many sexual partners is one of the strongest predictors of becoming infected with HIV, HSV, chlamydia, HPV, and numerous other sexually transmitted infections. You might also elect not to have sex with individuals who you know or suspect have had multiple partners. People with multiple partners probably know each partner less well and thus may be less successful in avoiding people who engage in high-risk behaviors. Research indicates that in spite of the demonstrable risks associated with multiple-partner involvement, a substantial majority of American college students, both men and women, report sexual activity with multiple partners while using condoms inconsistently (LaBrie et al., 2005).

## Inspect Your Partner's Genitals

Examining your partner's genitals before coital, oral, or anal contact might reveal the symptoms of an STD. Herpes blisters, vaginal and urethral discharges, chancres and rashes associated with syphilis, genital warts, and gonorrhea may be seen. In most cases symptoms are more evident on a man. (If he is uncircumcised, be sure to retract the foreskin.) The presence of a discharge, an unpleasant odor, sores, blisters, a rash, warts, or anything else out of the ordinary should be viewed with some concern. "Milking" the penis is a particularly effective way to detect a suspicious discharge. This technique, sometimes called the "short-arm inspection," involves grasping the penis firmly and pulling the loose skin up and down the shaft several times, applying pressure on the base-to-head stroke. Then part the urinary opening to see if any cloudy discharge is present.

People frequently find it difficult to openly conduct such an inspection before sexual involvement. Sometimes the simple request "Let me undress you" can provide some opportunity to examine your partner's genitals. Sensate focus pleasuring, discussed in Chapter 14, could provide the opportunity for more-detailed visual exploration. Some people suggest a shower before sex, with an eye toward examining a partner. This may be helpful for noting visible sores, blisters, and so forth, but soap and water can also remove the visual and olfactory cues associated with a discharge.

If you note signs of infection, you may justifiably and wisely elect not to have sexual relations. Your intended partner may or may not be aware of his or her symptoms. Therefore it is important that you explain your concerns. Some people may decide to continue their sexual interaction after discovering possible symptoms of an STD; they would be wise, though, to restrict their activities to kissing, hugging, touching, and manual genital stimulation.

## Wash Your—and Your Partner's—Genitals Before and After Sexual Contact

Opinions differ about how beneficial soap-and-water washing of the genitals before sexual interaction is. However, there can be little doubt that washing has some benefits. Washing the man's penis is generally more effective as a prophylactic measure, although washing the woman's vulva can also be helpful.

You may find it difficult to suggest that your partner wash (or allow you to wash) his or her genitals before having sex. However, you may accomplish this unobtrusively by including washing of the genitals in the sex play that occurs in the shower or bathtub. Or you may frankly announce that you are cleansing your partner's and your own genitals for your mutual protection.

After sexual contact, thorough washing of the genitals and surrounding areas with soap and water is highly recommended as a preventive procedure when the transmission of an infection is a possibility. We are not, however, suggesting that this procedure should always follow sexual activity. Many lovers in long-term monogamous relationships would find this unnecessary and possibly even offensive, implying that a person is somehow unclean after sex.

Promptness is probably as important as thoroughness in postsex washing. However, some people might object to jumping out of bed immediately to wash, as this may break the relaxed and intimate mood. For those who are uncomfortable letting their partners know that they are taking this precaution, perhaps simply announcing that you need to go to the bathroom (a not uncommon need after sex) will suffice. Both women and men can wash their genitals while sitting over the sink. First fill the sink with warm, soapy water, then turn your back to it and boost yourself up so that you are sitting over the sink or straddling it. In this position it is relatively easy to thoroughly wash your exposed genitals with a soapy washcloth.

Urinating after coitus may have some limited prophylactic benefits, particularly for men. Many infectious organisms do not survive in the urethra in the acidic environment created by urine. Urinating can also help to flush out disease-causing organisms.

## Obtain Routine Medical Evaluations

Many authorities recommend that sexually active people with more than one partner routinely visit their health practitioner or local STD clinic for periodic checkups, even when no symptoms of disease are evident. In view of the number of people, both women and men, who are symptomless carriers of STDs, this seems like good advice. How often to have such examinations is a matter of opinion. Our advice to people who are sexually active with several partners is that they should have checkups every 3 months and certainly no less often than twice a year.

## Inform Your Partner(s) if You Have an STD

The high frequency of infections without symptoms makes it imperative for infected individuals to inform their sexual partner(s) once they are diagnosed with an STD (Hoxworth et al., 2003; Potterat, 2003). Partner notification, which is beneficial in reducing the spread of all STDs, is an especially imperative prevention tactic for curtailing the spread of HIV infections. Partner notification can be conducted by the infected person, by health-care providers, or by specially trained city, state, and federal employees called disease intervention specialists (DISs) (Kissinger et al., 2003). The discussion box titled "Telling a Partner," which appeared earlier in this chapter, offers suggestions that may be helpful to a person who elects to notify a partner about an STD infection. A potential benefit of partner notification conducted by a health-care provider or DIS is that informed people typically receive counseling about how to reduce the risk of exposure to STDs and are often provided with options for health-care services, including testing and treatment (Hoxworth et al., 2003).

A new approach to partner notification has recently become available through Web sites launched in San Francisco and Los Angeles. These two sites, www.inspot.org and www.inspotla.org, provide people with a way to inform casual sex partners of possible STD risk while avoiding awkward face-to-face disclosure. Users of these sites can choose from several free e-cards to send to sexual contacts, either unsigned or with a personal message. In view of the escalating number of people who use the Internet to meet partners, the use of cyberspace to help slow the spread of STDs is a welcome new tool in the prevention arsenal.

A number of studies have found that partner notification often facilitates several desirable behavior changes, including increased condom use, reduction in number of sexual partners, and reduction in the incidence of STDs following notification (Kissinger et al., 2003; Niccolai et al., 2006; Semaan et al., 2004). Even though partner notification can be a powerful STD prevention strategy, we cannot assume that a sexual partner will be forthcoming about a diagnosed STD. For example, a study of 92 people diagnosed with HPV found that, although most had disclosed their infection to primary partners at the time of diagnosis, of the 60% of the participants who had new sexual partners 6 months after diagnosis, less than one-third disclosed their HPV to their new partners before engaging in sexual relations (Keller et al., 2000).

A recent survey of a national sample of 1,421 people receiving medical care for HIV infection found that 42% of gay or bisexual men, 19% of heterosexual men, and 17% of women participants reported engaging in sexual interaction without disclosing their HIV-positive status to their sex partners. This nondisclosure occurred primarily within nonexclusive partnerships (Ciccarone et al., 2003). In general, research indicates that even when people diagnosed with an STD inform a primary partner, other sexual contacts are likely to be left uninformed (Niccolai et al., 2006).

The U.S. legal system has witnessed the emergence of a new kind of legal action based on sexual fraud. Perhaps the most noteworthy and visible cases are those in which people who have tested positive for HIV engage in unprotected sexual contact with partners who are uninformed about the HIV status. Such actions typically result in severe legal sanctions. Several such legal proceedings have occurred in our home state of Oregon, including one involving the first man in the United States convicted and sentenced to prison for attempted murder based on evidence that he had unprotected sexual relations with three women despite his knowledge that he was HIV-positive.

In addition to cases involving criminal prosecution, sexual-deceit civil lawsuits increasingly provide the basis for successful civil litigation in U.S. courts. In these civil proceedings it is alleged that a person has lied about an STD—either through failure to disclose the condition to a partner or by engaging in outright deception. In many states, most notably California, state appeals courts have given a green light for such legal actions, thus providing an impetus for monetary judgments and out-of-court settlements ranging well into six figures.

# SUMMARY

- In the United States the incidence of sexually transmitted diseases (STDs) is increasing, especially among young people ages 15 to 25.
- A number of factors probably contribute to the high incidence of STDs, including more people having unprotected (condomless) sex with multiple partners, the increased use of birth control pills, limited access to effective systems for prevention and treatment of STDs, inaccurate diagnosis and treatment, and the fact that many of these diseases do not produce obvious symptoms, which results in people unknowingly infecting others.

## Bacterial Infections

- Chlamydia infections are among the most prevalent and the most damaging of all STDs. Chlamydia is transmitted primarily through sexual contact. It can also be spread by fingers from one body site to another—for example, from the genitals to the eyes.
- There are two general types of genital chlamydia infections in females: infections of the lower reproductive tract, commonly manifested as urethritis or cervicitis; and invasive infections of the upper reproductive tract, expressed as PID (pelvic inflammatory disease).
- Most women with lower reproductive tract chlamydia infections have few or no symptoms. Symptoms of PID caused by chlamydia infection include disrupted menstrual periods, pelvic pain, elevated temperature, nausea, vomiting, and headache.
- Chlamydia salpingitis (infection of the fallopian tubes) is a major cause of infertility and ectopic pregnancy.
- In men chlamydia infections are a common cause of epididymitis and nongonococcal urethritis.
- Chlamydia infection also causes trachoma, the world's leading cause of preventable blindness.
- Recommended drugs for treating chlamydia infections include doxycycline and azithromycin.
- Gonorrhea, a common communicable disease in the United States, is a bacterial infection transmitted through

sexual contact. The infecting organism is a *gonococcus* bacterium.
- Early symptoms of gonorrhea infection are more likely to be manifested by men, who will probably experience a discharge from the penis and a burning sensation during urination. The early sign in women, often not detectable, is a mild vaginal discharge that may be irritating to vulval tissues.
- Complications of gonorrhea infection in men include prostate, bladder, and kidney involvement and, infrequently, gonococcal epididymitis, which can lead to sterility. In women gonorrhea can lead to PID, sterility, and abdominal adhesions.
- Recommended treatment for gonorrhea is the dual therapy of a single dose of ceftriaxone, cefixime, cipofloxacin, levofloxacin, or ofloxacin plus a single dose of azithromycin (or doxycycline for 7 days).
- Nongonococcal urethritis (NGU) is a common infection of the urethral passage, typically seen in men. It is primarily caused by infectious organisms transmitted during coitus.
- Symptoms of NGU most apparent in men include penile discharge and a slight burning sensation during urination. Women may have a minor vaginal discharge and are thought to harbor the infecting organisms.
- Doxycycline or azithromycin therapy usually clears up NGU.
- Syphilis is less common but potentially more damaging than gonorrhea. It is almost always transmitted through sexual contact.
- If untreated, syphilis can progress through four phases: primary, characterized by the appearance of chancre sores; secondary, distinguished by the occurrence of a generalized skin rash; latent, a several-year period of no overt symptoms; and tertiary, during which the disease can produce cardiovascular disease, blindness, paralysis, skin ulcers, liver damage, and severe mental pathological conditions.
- Syphilis can be treated with benzathine penicillin G at any stage of its development. People allergic to penicillin can be treated with doxycycline, erythromycin, or ceftriaxone.

## Viral Infections

- Some of the most common herpes viruses are type 1, which generally produces sores on or in the mouth, and type 2, which generally infects the genital area. Type 1 can be found in the genital area, and type 2 can be found in the mouth area. Type 2 is transmitted primarily through sexual contact; type 1 can be passed by sexual contact or kissing.
- It has been estimated that more than 100 million Americans are afflicted with oral herpes and that 45 million people in the United States have genital herpes.
- The presence of painful sores is the primary symptom of herpes. A person is highly contagious during a herpes eruption, but evidence indicates that herpes can also be transmitted during asymptomatic periods.
- Genital herpes can predispose a woman to cervical cancer. It can also infect her newborn child, resulting in severe damage to or death of the child.
- Herpes has no known cure. Treatment is aimed at reducing pain and speeding the healing process. Acyclovir, valacyclovir, or famciclovir administered orally is effective in promoting healing during first episodes and, if taken continuously, in suppressing recurrent outbreaks.
- Genital and anal warts are an extremely common viral STD in the United States.
- Genital warts are primarily transmitted through vaginal, anal, or oral–genital sexual interaction.
- Research has revealed a strong association between genital warts and cancers of the cervix, vagina, vulva, urethra, penis, and anus.
- Genital warts are treated by freezing, applications of topical agents, cauterization, surgical removal, or vaporization by a carbon dioxide laser.
- A vaccine effective against 4 HPV types responsible for the majority of genital warts and cancers associated with HPV was recently developed and approved by the FDA.
- Hepatitis A, hepatitis B, and hepatitis C are three major types of viral infections of the liver. All three types can be sexually transmitted.
- Hepatitis B can be transmitted through blood or blood products, semen, vaginal secretions, and saliva. Manual, oral, and/or penile stimulation of the anus are practices strongly associated with the spread of this viral agent.
- Oral–anal contact seems to be the primary mode of sexual transmission of hepatitis A.
- Hepatitis C is transmitted most commonly by means of injection drug use or less frequently through contaminated blood products and sexual contact; perinatal mother-to-fetus or mother-to-infant transmission is also possible.
- The symptoms of viral hepatitis vary from mild to incapacitating illness. No specific therapy is available to treat Hepatitis A. Chronic hepatitis B infections can be effectively treated with a variety of antiviral drugs. Most people infected with A and B types recover in a few weeks with adequate bed rest.
- The most health-threatening of the hepatitis viruses, hepatitis C, is an emerging communicable disease of epidemic proportions.
- Hepatitis C accounts for the majority of deaths from complications of viral hepatitis. Combination therapy with two antiviral drugs is relatively effective in controlling the severe complications associated with hepatitis C.

## Common Vaginal Infections

- Bacterial vaginosis—typically caused by an overgrowth of anaerobic bacteria, *Mycoplasma* bacteria, or a bacterium known as *Gardnerella vaginalis*—is the most common cause of vaginitis (vaginal infection) in U.S. women. Male partners of infected women also harbor the infectious microorganisms, usually without clinical symptoms. Coitus often provides a mode of transmission for this infection.
- The most prominent symptom of bacterial vaginosis in women is a fishy- or musty-smelling, thin discharge that is like flour paste in consistency. Women can also experience irritation of the genital tissues. A small number of men develop inflammation of the foreskin and glans, urethritis, or cystitis.
- The treatment for bacterial vaginosis is metronidazole (Flagyl) taken by mouth or intravaginal applications of topical metronidazole gel or clindamycin cream.
- Candidiasis is a yeast infection that affects many women. The *Candida albicans* organism is commonly present in the vagina but causes problems only when overgrowth occurs. Pregnancy, diabetes, and the use of birth control pills or oral antibiotics are often associated with yeast infections. The organism can be transmitted through sexual or nonsexual means.
- Symptoms of yeast infections include a white clumpy discharge and intense itching of the vaginal and vulval tissues.
- Traditional treatment for candidiasis infection consists of vaginal suppositories or topical creams, such as clotrimazole, miconazole, or butoconazole.
- Trichomoniasis is a common STD that results in 7 to 8 million new cases each year. Male partners of infected women are thought to carry the *Trichomonas vaginalis* organism in the urethra and under the foreskin if they are uncircumcised. The primary mode of transmission of this infection is through sexual contact.
- Women infected with trichomoniasis and their male sexual partners can be successfully treated with metronidazole.

## Ectoparasitic Infections

- Ectoparasites are parasitic organisms that live on the outer skin of humans and other animals. Pubic lice and scabies are two relatively common STDs caused by ectoparasites.
- Pubic lice ("crabs") are tiny biting insects that feed on blood from small vessels in the pubic region. They can be transmitted through sexual contact or by using bedding or clothing contaminated by an infested individual.
- The primary symptom of a pubic lice infestation is severe itching that is not relieved by scratching. Sometimes pubic lice can be seen.
- Pubic lice are treated by application of 1% permethrin or pyrethrin lotion or cream to affected body areas
- Scabies is caused by a tiny parasitic mite that forages for nourishment in its host's skin. Scabies is a highly contagious condition that can be transmitted by close sexual or nonsexual physical contact between people.
- The primary symptoms of scabies are small bumps and a red rash that itches intensely, especially at night. The bumps and rash indicate areas of infestation.
- A single application of a topical scabicide applied from the neck to the toes, is usually an effective treatment.

## Acquired Immunodeficiency Syndrome (AIDS)

- AIDS is caused by infection with a virus (HIV) that destroys the immune system, leaving the body vulnerable to a variety of opportunistic infections and cancers.
- It now appears likely that HIV originated early in the 20th century by means of cross-species transmission from a subspecies of African chimpanzees to humans. The

virus then spread worldwide much later, when Africa became less isolated.

- An estimated 1.2 million people in the United States and 40.3 million people worldwide are infected with HIV.
- The number of new AIDS cases reported annually in the United States grew rapidly through the early 1980s and moderated in the late 1980s. This more moderate rate has continued to the present time.
- Even though the overall incidence of new HIV infections in the United States has remained relatively stable in recent years, the number of new cases among teenagers, women, and racial and ethnic minorities continues to rise. Furthermore, there is evidence of a recent escalation in the incidence of new HIV infections occurring among both heterosexuals and men who have sex with men (MSM).
- Although most AIDS cases that have occurred in the United States since the beginning of the epidemic have involved MSM and injection drug users, cases attributable to heterosexual transmission have risen steadily.
- Even though the prevalence of HIV infection in the United States and the rest of the Western world remains highest among MSM, the proportion of reported AIDS cases among MSM declined sharply and then leveled off in the period from the mid-1980s to the late 1990s. In recent years the incidence of HIV infections among MSM has been increasing.
- In the United States, AIDS cases attributable to heterosexual transmission are accelerating, and heterosexual contact has always been the primary form of HIV transmission worldwide.
- HIV has been found in semen, blood, vaginal secretions, saliva, tears, urine, breast milk, and any other bodily fluids that can contain blood.
- Blood, semen, and vaginal fluids are the major vehicles for transmitting HIV, which appears to be passed primarily through sexual contact and through needle sharing among injection drug users.
- HIV can also be passed perinatally from an infected woman to her fetus or infant before or during birth, or by breast-feeding.
- *Viral load* refers to how much virus is present in an infected person's blood. In general, the greater the viral load, the higher the chance of transmitting the infection.
- HIV can be transmitted to the receptive partner during oral sex, when HIV comes into contact with mucous membrane tissues in the mouth.
- The present possibility of being infected with HIV by means of transfusion of contaminated blood is remote. Furthermore, there is no danger of being infected as a result of donating blood.
- A small percentage of people appear to be resistant to HIV infection.
- The risk of transmitting HIV through saliva, tears, and urine appears to be low. There is no evidence that HIV can be transmitted by casual contact.
- High-risk behaviors that increase one's chances of becoming infected with HIV include engaging in unprotected (condomless) sex, having multiple sexual partners, having sexual contact with people known to be at high risk, and sharing injection equipment for drug use.
- HIV is not as easily transmitted from women to men as it is from men to women.
- HIV often causes a brief, flulike illness within a few weeks of initial infection. The initial illness tends to fade fairly rapidly. However, as the virus continues to deplete the immune system, other symptoms occur.
- Most people develop antibodies to HIV within months of being infected, but some silent infections can go undetected for 3 years or more.

- HIV infection can be detected by blood tests for blood serum antibodies to HIV.
- The incubation time for AIDS—defined as the time between infection with HIV and the onset of one or more severe, debilitating diseases—is estimated to range between 8 and 11 years.
- The symptoms of HIV/AIDS disease are many and varied, depending on the degree to which the immune system is compromised and the particular type of cancer or opportunistic infection that afflicts an infected person.
- A significant decline in the rate of AIDS deaths began in 1996. This reversal in death trends was due to improvement in combination drug therapies.
- There is still no cure for HIV/AIDS. However, when properly used, a combination of three or more antiretroviral drugs—a treatment approach known as highly active antiretroviral therapy (HAART)—can dramatically reduce viral load, improve immune function, and delay progression of the disease.
- HAART involves a complex protocol of drug dosing that is difficult to adhere to. Furthermore, drug toxicity can result in adverse side effects that induce low compliance with the HAART protocol.
- HAART does not eradicate HIV from latent or silent reservoirs in various bodily tissues or organs.
- The availability of HAART has apparently influenced some people to increase their involvement in risky sex.
- The administration of the RT inhibitor drugs zidovudine, nevirapine, or cotrimoxizole to newborns significantly reduces the incidence of mother-to-child transmission of HIV.
- Although progress has been made in developing HIV vaccines, many health officials believe that we may be years away from having an effective vaccine available.
- The best hope for curtailing the HIV/AIDS epidemic is through education and behavioral change.
- A person can significantly reduce her or his risk of becoming infected with HIV by following safer-sex strategies, which include using condoms and avoiding sex with multiple partners or with individuals who are at high risk for HIV infection.

## Preventing Sexually Transmitted Diseases

- Taking the time to carefully assess your risk status and your partner's risk status for transmitting STDs is perhaps the most important preventive strategy.
- Because it is often difficult to accurately assess risk status from conversations alone, couples are encouraged to undergo medical examinations and laboratory testing to rule out STDs before engaging in any sexual activity that puts them at risk for STDs.
- Condoms, when used correctly, offer good but not foolproof protection against the transmission of many STDs.
- Avoid sex with multiple partners or with individuals who likely have had multiple partners.
- Inspecting a partner's genitals before sexual contact may be a way to detect symptoms of an STD.
- Washing the genitals with soap and water both before and after sexual interaction offers additional protection against being infected with an STD.
- Sexually active people with multiple partners should routinely visit their health-care practitioner or local STD clinic for periodic checkups, even when no symptoms of disease are present.
- It is imperative for infected individuals to tell their sexual partner(s) once they are diagnosed as having an STD.

## Suggested Readings

*AIDS Education and Prevention.* An interdisciplinary journal, published by the International Society for AIDS Education, that is available in many major library systems. It contains excellent information regarding the prevention of AIDS and is one of the best sources of material on AIDS education.

*The MMWR (Morbidity and Mortality Weekly Report).* A publication of the Centers for Disease Control and Prevention available in many major library systems and on the Internet. The *MMWR* frequently contains valuable information about the nature, transmission, prevention, and treatment of STDs. It is perhaps the single best source for keeping abreast of the latest developments regarding AIDS and other STDs.

Shilts, Randy (1987). *And the Band Played On: Politics, People, and the AIDS Epidemic.* New York: St. Martin's Press. A compelling book, written by an investigative reporter, that provides shocking information about how government incompetence and infighting among research groups in the scientific and medical communities hindered efforts to mobilize an effective campaign against the AIDS epidemic. This book also humanizes the AIDS crisis by telling personal stories of people who have lived with and died from AIDS.

## Resources

**CDC National HIV/AIDS Hotline:** (800) 342-AIDS (English), (800) 344-7432 (Spanish), (800) 243-7889 (TTY service for hearing impaired). An informative recording with current information. Those who have specific questions not answered by the recording can call (800) 447-AIDS. Many cities have a local AIDS information hotline; check your local white pages for listings.

**The Herpes Resource Center,** a program of the American Social Health Association, provides excellent services, including a quarterly journal complete with up-to-date information about herpes, access to local chapters (support groups), and a private telephone information, counseling, and referral service. For information about these services, call (800) 230-6039, or send $1 (postage and handling) to Herpes Resource Center, ASHA, Dept. PR46, P.O. Box 13827, Research Triangle Park, NC 27709. (No self-addressed, stamped envelope is required.)

**Herpes Anonymous,** P.O. Box 278, Westbury, NY 11590; (516) 334- 5718. A nonprofit social organization composed of people with herpes who wish to help others overcome the difficulties associated with this disease. Herpes Anonymous assists in developing companionable associations among people who have herpes. The organization also distributes a free newsletter containing up-to-date information about this disease.

## Web Resources

**CengageNOW Web Site**
Go to **academic.cengage.com** to link to practice quiz questions, interactive activities, Internet links, critical thinking exercises, discussion forums, and more. You can also access sites from the Wadsworth Psychology Study Center (**academic.cengage.com/psychology**) or you can connect directly to the following sites:

**American Social Health Association**
This Web site contains STD resources, including a sexual health glossary, educational brochures, hotline numbers,

links to support groups, a Herpes Resource Center, and an STD news bulletin.

**JAMA HIV/AIDS Information Center**
The *Journal of the American Medical Association* maintains this Web site with updates on the latest treatment strategies for people with HIV/AIDS. It includes a reference library and a resource center for patient and support group information.

**An Introduction to Sexually Transmitted Diseases**
This fact sheet from the National Institute of Allergy and Infectious Diseases (a division of the National Institutes of Health) provides basic statistics and prevention information on sexually transmitted diseases. In addition, an index gives detailed information on specific STDs.

**SaferSex.org**
A comprehensive resource providing detailed information about how to have safer sex, including explicit and practical information: how to use a condom, how to talk to your kids about AIDS, how to talk to your partner about safer sex.

**AIDSinfo**
A comprehensive Web site that provides excellent up-to-date information about HIV/AIDS, including links to treatment guidelines and vaccine research progress.

**National Herpes Resource Center**
This Web site provides accurate, up-to-date information about all aspects of herpes (causes, transmission, treatment, etc.) and information about local support groups.

**Centers for Disease Control and Prevention**
This government Web site provides information about STDs.

---

***Our Sexuality* Book Companion Web Site academic.cengage.com/psychology/crooks** Visit your book companion Web site where you will find flash cards, practice quizzes, Internet links, and more to help you study.

### Just what you need to know NOW!
Spend time on what you need to master rather than on information you already have learned. Take a pretest for this chapter, and CengageNOW will generate a personalized study plan based on your results. The study plan will identify the topics you need to review and direct you to online resources to help you master those topics. You can then take a post-test to help you determine the concepts you have mastered and what you will still need to work on. Try it out! Go to **academic.cengage.com/login** to sign in with an access code or to purchase access to this product.

### InfoTrac College Edition Online Library
Sign in to **academic.cengage.com/login** or visit your free book companion Web site at **academic.cengage.com/psychology/crooks** to access InfoTrac College Edition, an online searchable library that includes a multitude of journals, many specific to human sexuality. These journals include *Archives of Sexual Behavior; Archives of Sexual Health Behavior; Canadian Journal of Human Sexuality; Hispanic Journal of the Behavioral Sciences; Journal of Cross-Cultural Psychology; Journal of Physical Education, Recreation, and Dance; Journal of Sex Research;* and *Sex Roles.*

# Atypical Sexual Behavior

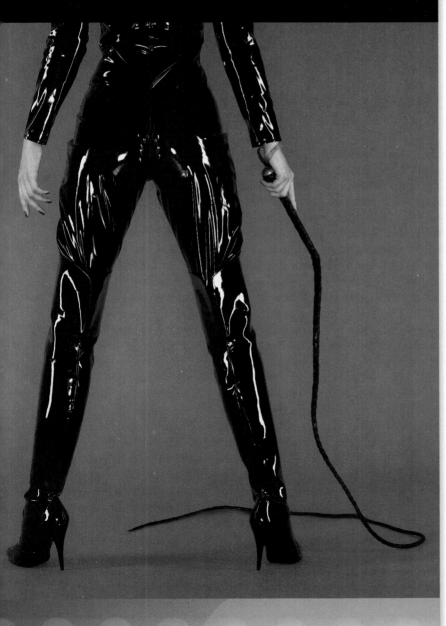

© Mike Diver/Getty Images

*My last sexual partner was very much into golden showers. Having spent a little of my time watching G. G. Allen movies, I was well acquainted with the existence of water-sports, but somehow it never occurred to me that I would like to partake in them. When my partner revealed his desire to drink my urine, I was taken off guard. I have been known to try some things I would deem a little atypical, so I gave it a shot. I was very nervous about the actual art of the procedure, though. Thoughts such as "What if he was joking—he would think I'm nuts" and "What if I completely miss" entered my head. It was nerve-racking and made it especially hard to pee. Eventually, my anxiety subsided and I was able to participate. His reaction was amazing to me. He began to masturbate feverishly and lapped up my urine ecstatically. I had never seen him so turned on. More surprising, though, was how much I enjoyed it. Although I cannot imagine being on the other end, it was really an empowering and enjoyable experience. (Authors' files)*

This description of a rather unusual sexual experience, provided by a student in a sexuality class, may strike our readers as reflecting an abnormal or perhaps even deviant form of sexual behavior. However, we believe it is more realistic to consider this anecdote an account of uncommon or atypical sexual behavior. One note of caution: Because HIV has been found in the urine of infected persons, it is prudent to avoid contact with a partner's urine unless he or she is known to be HIV-negative and not infected with any other STDs. Now let us consider for a moment what constitutes atypical sexual behavior.

## What Constitutes Atypical Sexual Behavior?

**Paraphilia** A term used to describe uncommon types of sexual expression.

In this chapter, we focus on a number of sexual behaviors that have been variously labeled as deviant, perverted, aberrant, or abnormal. More recently, the less judgmental term **paraphilia** (pair-uh-FILL-ee-uh) has been used to describe these somewhat uncommon types of sexual expression. Literally meaning "beyond usual or typical love," this term stresses that such behaviors are usually not based on an affectionate or loving relationship but rather are expressions of behavior in which sexual arousal and/or response depends on some unusual, extraordinary, or even bizarre activity (American Psychiatric Association, 2000). The term *paraphilia* is used in much of the psychological and psychiatric literature. However, in our own experience in dealing with and discussing variant sexual behaviors, the one common characteristic that stands out is that each behavior in its fully developed form is not typically expressed by most people in our society. Therefore we also categorize the behaviors discussed in this chapter as **atypical sexual behaviors.**

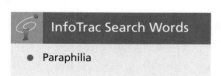

InfoTrac Search Words

- Paraphilia

**Atypical sexual behaviors** Behaviors not typically expressed by most people in our society.

Several points should be noted about atypical sexual expression in general before we discuss specific behaviors. First, as with many other sexual expressions discussed in this book, the behaviors singled out in this chapter represent extreme points on a continuum. Atypical sexual behaviors exist in many gradations, ranging from mild, infrequently expressed tendencies to full-blown, regularly manifested behaviors. Although these behaviors are *atypical,* many of us may recognize some degree of such behaviors or feelings in ourselves—perhaps manifested at some point in our lives, or mostly repressed, or emerging only in private fantasies.

A second point has to do with the state of our knowledge about these behaviors. In most of the discussions that follow, the person who manifests the atypical behavior is assumed to be male, and evidence strongly indicates that in most reported cases of atypical or paraphilic behaviors, the agents of such acts are male (American Psychiatric Association, 2000; Seligman & Hardenburg, 2000). However, the tendency to assume that males are predominantly involved may be influenced by the somewhat biased nature of differential reporting and prosecution. Female exhibitionism, for example, is far less likely to be reported than is similar behavior in a male. John Money (1981) suggested that atypical sexual behavior is decidedly more prevalent among males than females because male *erotosexual differentiation* (the development of sexual arousal in response to various kinds of images or stimuli) is more complex and subject to more errors than that of the female.

A third noteworthy point is that atypical behaviors often occur in clusters. That is, the occurrence of one paraphilia appears to increase the probability that others will also be manifested, simultaneously or sequentially (Bradford et al., 1992; Durand & Barlow, 2000). Research on men whose paraphilias resulted in medical or legal attention revealed that over half of the men reported engaging in more than one paraphilia and almost one in five reported experience with four or more paraphilias (Abel & Osborn, 2000). One hypothesis offered to account for this cluster effect is that engaging in one atypical behavior, such as exhibitionism, reduces the participant's inhibitions to the point that engaging in another paraphilia, such as voyeurism, becomes more likely (Stanley, 1993).

A final consideration is the effect of atypical behaviors both on the person who exhibits them and on the people to whom they may be directed. People who manifest atypical sexual behaviors often depend on these acts for sexual satisfaction. The behavior is frequently an end in itself. It is also possible that the unconventional behavior will alienate others. Consequently, these people often find it difficult to establish satisfying sexual and intimate relationships with partners. Instead, their sexual expression can assume a solitary, driven, even compulsive quality. Some of these behaviors do involve other people whose personal space is violated in a coercive, invasive fashion. In the following section, we consider the distinction between coercive and noncoercive paraphilias.

**?** **Critical Thinking Question**

Do you think that social and cultural conditioning contributes to the much higher incidence of atypical sexual behavior among men than among women? Explain.

## Noncoercive Versus Coercive Paraphilias

A key distinguishing characteristic of paraphilias is whether they involve an element of coercion. Several of the paraphilias are strictly solo activities or involve the participation of consensual adults who agree to engage in, observe, or just put up with the particular variant behavior. Because coercion is not involved and a person's basic rights are not violated, such so-called noncoercive atypical behaviors are considered relatively benign or harmless by many. Clearly, the chapter opening account falls into this category. However, as we will see, these noncoercive behaviors occasionally engender potentially adverse consequences for people drawn into their sphere of influence.

Some paraphilias, such as voyeurism or exhibitionism, are definitely coercive or invasive, in that they involve unwilling recipients of the behavior. Furthermore, research suggests that such coercive acts can harm their targets, who may be psychologically traumatized by the experience. Such recipients may feel that they have been violated or that they are vulnerable to physical abuse, and they may develop fears that such unpleasant episodes will recur. This is one reason that many of these coercive paraphilias are illegal. On the other hand, many people who encounter such acts are not adversely affected. Because of this fact, and because many of these coercive behaviors do not involve physical or sexual contact with another person, many authorities view them as minor sex offenses (sometimes called nuisance offenses). However, evidence that some people progress from nuisance offenses to more serious forms of sexual abuse may lead to a reconsideration of whether these offenses are "minor" (Bradford et al., 1992; Fedora et al., 1992). We examine this issue in more detail later in this chapter.

In our discussion of both coercive and noncoercive paraphilias, we examine how each of these behaviors is expressed, common characteristics of people who exhibit the paraphilia, and various factors thought to contribute to the development of the behavior. More severe forms of sexual coercion, such as rape, incest, and child abuse, are discussed in Chapter 17.

## ● Noncoercive Paraphilias

In this section, we first discuss four fairly common types of noncoercive paraphilias: fetishism, transvestic fetishism, sexual sadism, and sexual masochism. We will also describe four less common varieties of noncoercive paraphilias.

# Fetishism

**Fetishism** A sexual behavior in which a person obtains sexual excitement primarily or exclusively from an inanimate object or a particular part of the body.

**Fetishism** (FET-ish-iz-um) refers to sexual behavior in which an individual becomes sexually aroused by focusing on an inanimate object or a part of the human body. As with many other atypical behaviors, it is often difficult to draw the line between normal activities that might have fetishistic overtones and activities that are genuinely paraphilic. Many people are erotically aroused by the sight of undergarments and certain specific body parts, such as feet, legs, buttocks, thighs, and breasts. Many men and some women use articles of clothing and other paraphernalia as an accompaniment to masturbation or sexual activity with a partner. Only when a person becomes focused on these objects or body parts to the exclusion of everything else is the term *fetishism* truly applicable (Lowenstein, 2002). In some instances, a person cannot experience sexual arousal and orgasm in the absence of the fetish object. In other situations where the attachment is not so strong, sexual response can occur in the absence of the object but often with diminished intensity. For some people fetish objects serve as substitutes for human contact and are dispensed with if a partner becomes available. Some common fetish objects include women's lingerie, shoes (particularly those with high heels), boots (often affiliated with themes of domination), hair, stockings (especially black mesh hose), and a variety of leather, silk, and rubber goods (American Psychiatric Association, 2000; Davison & Neale, 1993).

© Thomas Hoeffgen/Getty Images

Inanimate objects or a part of the human body, such as feet, can be sources of sexual arousal for some people.

How does fetishism develop? One way is through incorporating the object or body part, often through fantasy, in a masturbation sequence in which the reinforcement of orgasm strengthens the fetishistic association (Juninger, 1997). Another possible explanation for the origins of some cases of fetishism looks to childhood. Some children learn to associate sexual arousal with objects (such as panties or shoes) that belong to an emotionally significant person, such as their mothers or older sisters (Freund & Blanchard, 1993). The process by which this occurs is sometimes called *symbolic transformation*. In this process, the object of the fetish becomes endowed with the power or essence of its owner, so that the child (usually a male) responds to this object as he might react to the actual person (Gebhard et al., 1965). If such a behavior pattern becomes sufficiently ingrained, the person will engage in little or no sexual interaction with other people during the developmental years and even as an adult may continue to substitute fetish objects for sexual contact with other humans.

Only rarely does fetishism develop into an offense that might harm someone. Occasionally, an individual may commit burglary to supply a fetish object, as in the following account:

> Some years ago we had a bra stealer loose in the neighborhood. You couldn't hang your brassiere outside on the clothesline without fear of losing it. He also took panties, but bras seemed to be his major thing. I talked to other women in the neighborhood who were having the same problem. This guy must have had a roomful. I never heard that he was caught. He must have decided to move on because the thefts suddenly stopped. (Authors' files)

Burglary is the most frequent serious offense associated with fetishism (Lowenstein, 2002). Uncommonly, a person may do something bizarre, such as cut hair from an unwilling person. In extremely rare cases a man may murder and mutilate his victim, preserving certain body parts for fantasy masturbation activities.

**InfoTrac Search Words**

• Fetishism

Common fetish items include women's lingerie and shoes. People involved in fetishism can become aroused by these common inanimate objects.

## Transvestic Fetishism

Until recently, nontranssexual cross-dressers were generally labeled *transvestites*. This term is now considered appropriately applied only to people who put on the clothes of the other sex to achieve sexual arousal (Langstrom & Zucker, 2005). The sexual component of cross-dressing for these individuals distinguishes them from female impersonators who cross-dress to entertain, gay men who occasionally "go in drag" to attract men or as a kind of "camp" acting out, and transsexuals who, as we discussed in Chapter 3, cross-dress to obtain a partial sense of physical and emotional completeness rather than to achieve sexual arousal.

**Transvestic fetishism**
A sexual behavior in which a person derives sexual arousal from wearing clothing of the other sex.

Transvestism comprises a range of behaviors. Some people prefer to don the entire garb of the other sex. This is often a solitary activity, occurring privately in their homes. Occasionally, a person may go out on the town while so attired, but this is unusual. In general, the cross-dressing is a momentary activity, producing sexual excitement that often culminates in gratification through masturbation or sex with a partner. In many cases of transvestism a person becomes aroused by wearing only one garment, perhaps a pair of panties or a brassiere. Because this behavior has a strong element of fetishism (Freund et al., 1996), the American Psychiatric Association (2000) formalized the link between transvestism and fetishism by placing both conditions in the diagnostic category **transvestic fetishism**. A distinguishing feature of transvestic fetishism is that the clothing article is actually worn instead of just being viewed or fondled, as is the case with fetishism.

According to the American Psychiatric Association (2000), a diagnosis of transvestic fetishism is appropriately applied to heterosexual males who experience significant psychological distress or impaired functioning as a result of recurrent sexual fantasies, urges, or behavior involving cross-dressing that persist for at least 6 months.

Many people who engage in transvestic fetishism feel that cross-dressing is an appropriate and legitimate source of arousal and expression, rather than a disorder or impairment.

Today, many members of the transgendered community (see Chapter 3), who are increasingly gaining a voice in both the professional literature and the popular media, contend that cross-dressing is often an appropriate and legitimate source of sexual arousal and expression rather than an indicator of disordered behavior or psychological impairment. Consequently, they reject the label of transvestic fetishism and its implication of abnormality.

The diagnostic criteria previously outlined specify that transvestic fetishism is the sole province of heterosexual males. Apparently, it is usually men who are attracted to transvestic fetishism. This seems true of all contemporary societies for which we have data. However, a few isolated cases of women cross-dressing for sexual pleasure also appear in the clinical literature (Bullough & Bullough, 1993; Stoller, 1982).

Several studies of both clinical and nonclinical populations suggest that transvestic fetishism occurs primarily among married men with predominantly heterosexual orientations (Brown, 1990; Bullough & Bullough, 1997; Doctor & Prince, 1997).

As with fetishism and some other atypical behaviors, the development of transvestic fetishism often reveals a pattern of conditioning. Reinforcement, in the form of arousal and orgasm, may accompany cross-dressing activities at an early point in the development of sexual interest, as illustrated in the following anecdote:

> When I was a kid, about 11 or 12, I was fascinated and excited by magazine pictures of women modeling undergarments. Masturbating while looking at these pictures was great. Later, I began to incorporate my mother's underthings in my little masturbation rituals, at first just touching them with my free hand, and later putting them on and parading before the mirror while I did my handjob. Now, as an adult, I have numerous sexual encounters with women that are quite satisfying without the dress-up part. But I still occasionally do the dress-up when I'm alone, and I still find it quite exciting. (Authors' files)

## Sexual Sadism and Sexual Masochism

**Sadomasochistic (SM) behavior** The association of sexual expression with pain.

Sadism and masochism are often discussed under the common category **sadomasochistic** (SAY-doh-ma-suh-kis-tik) **(SM) behavior** because they are two variations of the same phenomenon: the association of sexual expression with pain. Furthermore, the dynamics of the two behaviors are similar and overlapping. Thus in the discussion that follows we will often refer to SM behavior or activities. However, a person who engages in one of these behaviors does not necessarily engage in the other, and thus sadism and masochism are actually distinct behaviors. The American Psychiatric Association (2000) underlines this distinction by listing these paraphilias as separate categories: **sexual sadism** and **sexual masochism**. Sexual masochism is the only paraphilia that is expressed by women with some frequency (American Psychiatric Association, 2000). (People who engage in SM often label these activities as bondage-domination-sadism-masochism, or BDSM [Gross, 2006].)

**Sexual sadism** The act of obtaining sexual arousal through giving physical or psychological pain.

**Sexual masochism** The act of obtaining sexual arousal through receiving physical or psychological pain.

Labeling behavior as sexual sadism or sexual masochism is complicated because many people enjoy some form of aggressive interaction during sex play (such as "love bites") for which the label *sadomasochistic* seems inappropriate. Alfred Kinsey and his colleagues found that 22% of the males and 12% of the females in their sample responded erotically to stories with SM themes. In another study, approximately 25% of both sexes reported erotic response to receiving love bites during sexual interaction (Gross, 2006). Hunt (1974) found that 10% of males and 8% of females in his sample (subjects younger than age 35) reported obtaining sexual pleasure from SM activities during interaction with a partner.

InfoTrac Search Words

- Sadomasochism

Another survey of 975 men and women found that 25% reported occasionally engaging in a form of SM activity with a partner (Rubin, 1990). There are indications that ease of access to people with SM inclinations, facilitated by the Internet, has resulted in an increased number of people who are exploring their SM interests (Gross, 2006; Kleinplatz & Moser, 2004).

Although SM practices have the potential for being physically dangerous, most participants generally stay within mutually agreed-on limits, often confining their activities to mild or even symbolic SM acts with a trusted partner. In mild forms of sexual sadism the pain inflicted is often more symbolic than real. For example, a willing partner may be "beaten" with a feather or a soft object designed to resemble a club. Under these conditions the receiving partner's mere feigning of suffering is sufficient to induce sexual arousal in the individual inflicting the symbolic pain.

People with masochistic inclinations are aroused by such things as being whipped, cut, pierced with needles, bound, or spanked. The degree of pain that the person must experience to achieve sexual arousal varies from symbolic or very mild to, rarely, severe beatings or mutilations. Sexual masochism is also reflected in individuals who achieve sexual arousal as a result of "being held in contempt, humiliated, and forced to do menial, filthy, or degrading service" (Money, 1981, p. 83). The common notion that any kind of pain, physical or mental, will sexually arouse a person with masochistic inclinations is a misconception. The pain must be associated with a staged encounter whose express purpose is sexual gratification.

In yet another version of masochism, some individuals derive sexual pleasure from being bound, tied up, or otherwise restricted. This behavior, called **bondage**, usually takes place with a cooperative partner who binds or restrains the individual and sometimes administers *discipline*, such as spankings or whippings (Santilla et al., 2002). One survey of 975 heterosexual women and men revealed that bondage is a fairly common practice: One-fourth of respondents reported engaging in some form of bondage during some of their sexual encounters (Rubin, 1990).

**Bondage** A sexual behavior in which a person derives sexual pleasure from being bound, tied up, or otherwise restricted.

Many individuals who engage in SM activities do not confine their participation to exclusively sadistic or masochistic behaviors. Some alternate between the two roles, often out of necessity, because it may be difficult to find a partner who prefers only to inflict or to receive pain. Most of these people seem to prefer one or the other role, but some are equally comfortable in either role (Mosher & Levitt, 1987; Taylor & Ussher, 2001).

Research has indicated that individuals with sexual sadistic tendencies are less common than their masochistic counterparts (Sandnabba et al., 1999). This imbalance might reflect a general social script—certainly it is more virtuous to be punished than to carry out physical or mental aggression toward another. A person who needs severe pain as a prerequisite for sexual response may have difficulty finding a cooperative partner. Consequently, such individuals may resort to causing their own pain by burning or mutilation. Likewise, a person who needs to inflict intense pain to achieve sexual arousal may find it difficult to find a willing partner, even for a price. We occasionally read of sadistic assaults against unwilling victims: The classic lust murder is often of this nature (Money, 1990). In such instances orgasmic release may be achieved by the homicidal violence itself.

Many people in contemporary Western societies view sadomasochism in a highly negative light. This attitude is certainly understandable, particularly in people who regard sexual sharing as a loving, tender interaction between partners who wish to exchange pleasure. However, much of this negativity stems from a generalized perception of SM activities as perverse forms of sexual expression that involve severe pain, suffering, and degradation. It is commonly assumed that individuals caught up in such activities are often victims rather than willing participants.

One group of researchers disputed these assumptions, suggesting that the traditional medical model of sadomasochism as a pathological condition is based on a limited sample of individuals who come to clinicians' attention because of personality disorders or severe personality problems. As with some other atypical behaviors

Some individuals derive sexual pleasure from the restrictions created by bondage attire and role-playing.

discussed in this chapter, these researchers argued that it is misleading to draw conclusions from such a sample. They conducted their own extensive fieldwork in nonclinical environments, interviewing a variety of sadomasochism participants and observing their behaviors in many different settings. Although some subjects' behaviors fit traditional perceptions, the researchers found that, for most participants, sadomasochism was simply a form of sexual enhancement involving elements of dominance and submission, role-playing, and consensuality, "which they voluntarily and mutually chose to explore" (Weinberg et al., 1984, p. 388). Another study of 164 men who were members of sadomasochism-oriented clubs revealed that these individuals were socially well adjusted and that "sadomasochistic behavior was mainly a facilitative aspect of their sexual lives" (Sandnabba et al., 1999, p. 273).

Many people who engage in SM activities are motivated by a desire to experience dominance and/or submission rather than pain (Weinberg, 1987, 1995). This desire is reflected in the following account, provided by a student in a sexuality class:

*I fantasize about sadomasochism sometimes. I want to have wild animalistic sex under the control of my husband. I want him to "force" me to do things. Domination and mild pain would seem to fulfill the moment. I have read books and talked to people about the subject, and I am terrified at some of the things, but in the bounds of my trusting relationship I would not be afraid. It seems like a silly game, but it is so damned exciting to think about. Maybe someday it will happen. (Authors' files)*

Studies of sexual behavior in other species reveal that many nonhuman animals engage in what might be labeled combative or pain-inflicting behavior before coitus (Gross, 2006). Some theorists have suggested that such activity has definite neurophysiological value, heightening accompaniments of sexual arousal such as blood pressure, muscle tension, and hyperventilation (Gebhard et al., 1965). For a variety of reasons (such as guilt, anxiety, or apathy), some people may need additional nonsexual stimuli to achieve sufficient arousal. It has also been suggested that resistance or tension between partners enhances sex and that sadomasochism is just a more extreme version of this common principle (Tripp, 1975).

Sadomasochism might also provide participants with an escape from the rigidly controlled, restrictive role they must play in their everyday public lives. This possibility helps explain why men who engage in SM activity are much more likely to play masochistic roles than are women (Baumeister, 1997). A related theory sees sexual masochism as an attempt to escape from high levels of self-awareness. Similar to some other behaviors (such as getting drunk) in which a person may attempt to lose him- or herself, masochistic activity blocks out unwanted thoughts and feelings, particularly those that induce anxiety, guilt, or feelings of inadequacy or insecurity (Baumeister, 1988).

Clinical case studies of people who engage in sadomasochism sometimes reveal early experiences that may have established a connection between sex and pain. For example, being punished for engaging in sexual activities (such as masturbation) might lead a child or an adolescent to associate sex with pain. A child might even experience sexual arousal while being punished—for example, getting an erection or lubricating when his or her pants are pulled down and a spanking is administered (spanking is a common SM activity).

Many people, perhaps the majority, who participate in SM behaviors do not depend on these activities to achieve sexual arousal and orgasm. SM interests often exist concurrently with more conventional sexual desires (Kleinplatz & Moser, 2004). Those who practice sadomasochism only occasionally find that at least some of its excitement and erotic allure stem from its being a marked departure from more conventional sexual practices. Other people who indulge in SM acts may have acquired strong negative feelings about sex, often believing it is sinful and immoral. For such people masochistic behavior provides a guilt-relieving mechanism: Either they get their pleasure simultaneously with punishment, or they first endure the punishment to entitle them to the pleasure. Similarly, people who indulge in sadism may be punishing partners for engaging in anything so evil. Furthermore, people who have strong feelings of personal or sexual inadequacy may resort to sadistic acts of domination over their partners to temporarily alleviate these feelings.

## Other Noncoercive Paraphilias

In this section, we consider four additional varieties of noncoercive paraphilias that are generally uncommon or even rare. We begin our discussion by describing autoerotic asphyxia, a dangerous form of variant sexual behavior. We then offer a few brief comments about three other uncommon noncoercive paraphilias: klismaphilia, coprophilia, and urophilia.

### Autoerotic Asphyxia

**Autoerotic asphyxia** (also called *hypoxyphilia* or *asphyxiophilia*) is a rare and life-threatening paraphilia in which an individual, almost always a male, seeks to reduce the supply of oxygen to the brain during a heightened state of sexual arousal (American Psychiatric Association, 2000; Stanley, 1993). The oxygen deprivation is usually

**Autoerotic asphyxia**
The enhancement of sexual excitement and orgasm by pressure-induced oxygen deprivation.

accomplished by applying pressure to the neck with a chain, leather belt, ligature, or rope noose (by means of hanging). Occasionally, a plastic bag or chest compression is used as the asphyxiating device. A person might engage in these oxygen-depriving activities while alone or with a partner.

InfoTrac Search Words
● Autoerotic asphyxia

We can only theorize from limited data about what motivates such behavior. People who practice autoerotic asphyxia rarely disclose this activity to relatives, friends, or therapists, let alone discuss why they engage in such behavior (Garza-Leal & Landron, 1991; Saunders, 1989). For some the goal seems to be to increase sexual arousal and to enhance the intensity of orgasm. In this situation the item used to induce oxygen deprivation (such as a rope) is typically tightened around the neck to produce heightened arousal during masturbation and is then released at the time of orgasm. Individuals often devise elaborate techniques that enable them to free themselves from the strangling device before losing consciousness.

The enhancement of sexual excitement by pressure-induced oxygen deprivation may bear some relationship to reports that orgasm is intensified by inhaling amyl nitrate ("poppers"), a drug used to treat heart pain. This substance is known to temporarily reduce brain oxygenation through peripheral dilation of the arteries that supply blood to the brain.

It has also been suggested that autoerotic asphyxia is a highly unusual variant of sexual masochism in which participants act out ritualized bondage themes (American Psychiatric Association, 2000; Cosgray et al., 1991). People who engage in this practice sometimes keep diaries of elaborate bondage fantasies and, in some cases, describe fantasies of being asphyxiated or harmed by others as they engage in this rare paraphilia.

One important fact about this seldom-seen paraphilia is quite clear: This is an extremely dangerous activity that often results in death (Cooper, 1996; Cosgray et al., 1991; Garos, 1994). Accidental deaths sometimes occur because of equipment malfunction or mistakes, such as errors in the placement of the noose or ligature. Data from the United States, England, Australia, and Canada indicate that 1 to 2 deaths per 1 million people are caused by autoerotic asphyxiation each year (American Psychiatric Association, 2000). The Federal Bureau of Investigation estimates that deaths in the United States resulting from this activity may run as high as 1,000 per year.

## Klismaphilia

**Klismaphilia** (kliz-muh-FILL-ee-uh) is an unusual variant of sexual expression in which an individual obtains sexual pleasure from receiving enemas (Agnew, 2000). Less commonly, the erotic arousal is associated with giving enemas. The case histories of many individuals who express klismaphilia reveal that as infants or young children they were frequently given enemas by concerned and affectionate mothers. This association of loving attention with anal stimulation may eroticize the experience for some people so that as adults they may manifest a need to receive an enema as a substitute or prerequisite for genital intercourse.

**Klismaphilia** An unusual variant of sexual expression in which an individual obtains sexual pleasure from receiving enemas.

## Coprophilia and Urophilia

**Coprophilia** (kah-pruh-FILL-ee-uh) and **urophilia** (yoo-roh-FILL-ee-uh) refer to activities in which people obtain sexual arousal from contact with feces and urine, respectively. Individuals who exhibit coprophilia achieve high levels of sexual excitement from watching someone defecate or by defecating on someone. In rare instances, they achieve arousal when someone defecates on them. Urophilia is expressed by urinating on someone or being urinated on. This activity, reflected in the chapter opening anecdote, has been referred to as "water sports" and "golden showers." There is no consensus of opinion about the origins of these highly unusual paraphilias.

**Coprophilia** A sexual paraphilia in which a person obtains sexual arousal from contact with feces.

**Urophilia** A sexual paraphilia in which a person obtains sexual arousal from contact with urine.

## ❍ Coercive Paraphilias

In this section, we first discuss three common forms of coercive paraphilic behaviors: exhibitionism, obscene phone calls, and voyeurism. Three other varieties of coercive paraphilias—frotteurism, zoophilia, and necrophilia—are also discussed.

# Exhibitionism

**Exhibitionism**, often called indecent exposure, refers to behavior in which an individual (almost always male) exposes his genitals to an involuntary observer (usually an adult woman or a girl) (American Psychiatric Association, 2000; Marshall et al., 1991). Typically, a man who has exposed himself obtains sexual gratification by masturbating shortly thereafter, using mental images of the observer's reaction to increase his arousal. Some men, while having sex with a willing partner, fantasize about exposing themselves or replay mental images from previous episodes. Still others have orgasm triggered by the act of exposure, and some masturbate while exhibiting themselves (American Psychiatric Association, 2000; Freund et al., 1988). The reinforcement of associating sexual arousal and orgasm with the actual act of exhibitionism or with mental fantasies of exposing oneself contributes significantly to the maintenance of exhibitionistic behavior (Blair & Lanyon, 1981). Exposure can occur in a variety of locations, most of which allow for easy escape. Subways, relatively deserted streets, parks, and cars with a door left open are common places for exhibitionism to occur. However, sometimes a private dwelling is the scene of an exposure, as revealed in the following account:

> One evening I was shocked to open the door of my apartment to a naked man. I looked long enough to see that he was underdressed for the occasion and then slammed the door in his face. He didn't come back. I'm sure my look of total horror was what he was after. But it is difficult to keep your composure when you open your door to a naked man. (Authors' files)

Certainly, many of us have exhibitionistic tendencies: We may go to nude beaches, parade before admiring lovers, or wear provocative clothes or scanty swimwear. However, such behavior is considered appropriate by a society that in many ways exploits and celebrates the erotically portrayed human body. That legally defined exhibitionistic behavior involves generally unwilling observers sets it apart from these more acceptable variations of exhibitionism.

**InfoTrac Search Words**

- Exhibitionism

Our knowledge of who displays this behavior is based largely on studies of arrested offenders—a sample that may be unrepresentative. This sampling problem is common to many forms of atypical behavior that are defined as criminal. From the available data, however limited, it appears that most people who exhibit themselves are men in their 20s or 30s, and over half are married or have been married (Murphy, 1997). They are often shy, nonassertive people who feel inadequate and insecure and suffer from problems with intimacy (Arndt, 1991; Marshall et al., 1991). Their sexual relationships are likely to have been unsatisfactory. Many were reared in atmospheres characterized by puritanical and shame-inducing attitudes toward sexuality.

**? Critical Thinking Question**

People are typically much less concerned about female exhibitionism than they are about male exhibitionism. For example, if a woman observed a man undressing in front of a window, the man might be accused of being an exhibitionist. However, if the roles were reversed and the woman was undressing, the man would likely be labeled a voyeur. What do you think of this sex-based inconsistency in labeling these behaviors?

A number of factors influence the development of exhibitionistic behavior. Many individuals have such powerful feelings of personal inadequacy that they are afraid to reach out to another person out of fear of rejection (Minor & Dwyer, 1997). Their exhibitionism is thus a limited attempt to somehow involve others, however fleetingly, in their sexual expression. Limiting contact to briefly opening a raincoat before dashing off minimizes the possibility of overt rejection. Some men who expose themselves may be looking for affirmation of their masculinity. Others, feeling isolated and unappreciated, may simply be seeking attention, which they desperately crave. A few feel anger and hostility toward people, particularly women, who have failed to notice them or who they believe have caused them emotional pain. Under these circumstances exposure can be a form of reprisal, designed to shock or frighten the people they see as the source of their discomfort. In addition, exhibitionism is not uncommon in emotionally disturbed, intellectually disabled, or mentally disoriented individuals. In these cases the behavior reflects a limited awareness of what society defines as appropriate actions, a breakdown in personal ethical controls, or both.

In contrast to the public image of an exhibitionist as a person who lurks about in the shadows, ready to grab hapless victims and drag them off to ravish them, most men who engage in exhibitionism limit this activity to exposing themselves (American Psychiatric Association, 2000). Yet the word *victim* is not entirely inappropriate, in that observers of such exhibitionistic episodes may be emotionally traumatized by the experience (Cox, 1988; Marshall et al., 1991). Some feel that they are in danger of being raped or otherwise harmed. A few, particularly young children, can develop negative feelings about genital anatomy from such an experience.

Investigators have noted that some people who expose themselves, probably a small minority, actually physically assault their victims (R. Brown, 2000). Furthermore, it seems probable that some men who engage in exhibitionism progress from exposing themselves to more serious offenses, such as rape and child molestation (Abel, 1981; Bradford et al., 1992).

What is an appropriate response if someone exposes himself to you? It is important to keep in mind that most people who express exhibitionist behavior want to elicit reactions of excitement, shock, fear, or terror. Although it may be difficult not to react in any of these ways, a better response is to calmly ignore the exhibitionist act and go about your business. Of course, it is also important to immediately distance yourself from the offender and to report such acts to the police or campus security as soon as possible. ■

! Sexual Health

## Obscene Phone Calls

People who make obscene phone calls share characteristics with exhibitionists. Thus obscene phone calling (sometimes called *telephone scatologia*) is viewed by some professionals as a subtype of exhibitionism. People who make obscene phone calls typically experience sexual arousal when their victims react in a horrified or shocked manner, and many masturbate during or immediately after a "successful" phone exchange. These callers are typically male, and they often suffer from pervasive feelings of inadequacy and insecurity (Matek, 1988; Nadler, 1968). Obscene phone calls are frequently the only way they can find to have sexual exchanges. However, when relating to the other sex, they frequently show greater anxiety and hostility than do people inclined toward exhibitionism, as revealed in the following account:

© Jutta Klee/CORBIS

*One night I received a phone call from a man who sounded quite normal until he started his barrage of filth. Just as I was about to slam the phone down, he announced, "Don't hang up. I know where you live (address followed) and that you have two little girls. If you don't want to find them all mangled up, you will hear what I have to say. Furthermore, I expect you to be available for calls every night at this time." It was a nightmare. He called night after night. Sometimes he made me listen while he masturbated. Finally I couldn't take it any longer, and I contacted the police. They were unable to catch him, but they sure scared him off in short order, thank heaven. I was about to go crazy. (Authors' files)*

Exhibitionists often want to elicit reactions of excitement, shock, fear, or terror. The best response is to calmly ignore the act and casually go about your business.

Fortunately, a caller rarely follows up his verbal assault with a physical attack on his victim.

What is the best way to handle obscene phone calls? Information about how to deal with such calls is available from most local phone company offices. Because these offices are commonly besieged by such queries, you may need to be persistent in your request. A few tips are worth knowing; they may even make it unnecessary to seek outside help.

! Sexual Health

First, quite often the caller has picked your name at random from a phone book or perhaps knows you from some other source and is just trying you out to see what kind of reaction he can get. Your initial response may be critical in determining his subsequent actions. He wants you to be horrified, shocked, or disgusted; thus the best response is usually not to react overtly. Slamming down the phone may reveal your

Although your initial reaction to an obscene phone call may be horror, shock, or disgust, it is usually best not to respond emotionally. A caller who doesn't receive the desired response from you is less likely to call again.

**Voyeurism** The act of obtaining sexual gratification by observing undressed or sexually interacting people without their consent.

? **Critical Thinking Question**

Are strippers and dancers who perform partially or totally nude engaging in a genuine form of exhibitionism? Why or why not? What about people who observe these performances? Are they voyeurs? What, if anything, differentiates diagnosed exhibitionists and voyeurs from exotic dancers and people in the audience?

**InfoTrac Search Words**

• Voyeurism

emotional state and provide reinforcement to the caller. Simply set it down gently and go about your business. If the phone rings again immediately, ignore it. Chances are that he will seek out other, more responsive victims.

Other tactics may also be helpful. One, used successfully by a former student, is to feign deafness. "What is that you said? You must speak up. I'm hard of hearing, you know!" Setting down the phone with the explanation that you are going to another extension (which you never pick up) may be another practical solution. Finally, screening calls with an answering machine or caller ID might also prove helpful. The caller is likely to hang up in the absence of an emotionally responding person.

If you are persistently bothered by obscene phone calls, you may need to take additional steps. Your telephone company should cooperate in changing your number to an unlisted one at no charge. It is probably not a good idea to heed the common advice to blow a police whistle into the mouthpiece of the phone (which may be quite painful and even harmful to the caller's ear) because you may end up receiving the same treatment from your caller.

Call tracing, a service offered by many telephone companies, may assist you in dealing with repetitive obscene or threatening phone calls. After breaking connection with the caller, you enter a designated code, such as *star 57*. The telephone company then automatically traces the call. After a certain number of successful traces to the same number, a warning letter is sent to the offender indicating that he or she has been identified as engaging in unlawful behavior that must stop. The offender is warned that police intervention or civil legal action is an option if the behavior continues. Call tracing is clearly not effective when calls are placed from a public pay phone, and calls made from cellular phones cannot be traced. ■

## Voyeurism

**Voyeurism** (voi-yur-IH-zum) refers to deriving sexual pleasure from looking at the naked bodies or sexual activities of others, usually strangers, without their consent (American Psychiatric Association, 2000). Because a degree of voyeurism is socially acceptable (witness the popularity of R- and NC-17-rated movies and sex sites on the Internet), it is sometimes difficult to determine when voyeuristic behavior becomes a problem (Arndt, 1991; Forsyth, 1996). To qualify as atypical sexual behavior, voyeurism must be preferred to sexual relations with another person or indulged in with some risk (or both). People who engage in this behavior are often most sexually aroused when the risk of discovery is high—which may explain why most are not attracted to such places as nudist camps and nude beaches, where looking is acceptable (Tollison & Adams, 1979).

As the common term *peeping Tom* implies, voyeurism is typically, although not exclusively, expressed by males (Davison & Neale, 1993). This behavior includes peering into bedroom windows, stationing oneself by the entrance to women's bathrooms, and boring holes in the walls of public dressing rooms. Some men travel elaborate routes several nights a week for the occasional reward of a glimpse, through a window, of bare anatomy or, rarely, a scene of sexual interaction. A new form of voyeurism has emerged in which small, technologically advanced video cameras are used to surreptitiously invade the personal privacy of many unaware victims. This troubling trend is described in the boxed discussion titled "Video Voyeurism."

Again, people inclined toward voyeurism often share characteristics with people who expose themselves (Arndt, 1991; Langevin et al., 1979). They may have poorly developed sociosexual skills, with strong feelings of inferiority and inadequacy, particularly as directed toward potential sexual partners (Kaplan & Krueger, 1997). They tend to be young men, usually in their early 20s (Davison & Neale, 1993; Dwyer, 1988). They rarely "peep" at someone they know, preferring strangers instead. Most individuals who engage in such activity are content merely to look, keeping their distance. However, in some instances such individuals go on to more serious offenses, such as burglary, arson, assault, and even rape (Abel & Osborn, 2000; Langevin, 2003).

## Video Voyeurism

Technological advances have added a new dimension to voyeurism, perhaps best described as *video voyeurism*. Small, affordable video cameras are increasingly being used to invade and record some of our most private moments. These images might then be displayed on the Internet or on someone's VCR or DVD player. High-tech video devices—hidden in such locations as smoke detectors, exit signs, ceiling fixtures, and gym bags—make it easy for unscrupulous individuals with either a penchant for peeping or an eye for a quick buck to victimize people by secretly recording them.

Video voyeurism was first brought to our attention several years ago when the media in our hometown reported that women patrons of a tanning salon had been victimized by secret video recordings while they were disrobing. A more recent instance of video voyeurism, reported by the media, involved the owners of a public marina on a lake in New York. They had installed hidden video cameras in the restroom and shower facilities of their establishment and subsequently played edited versions of these videotapes to amuse patrons of a local bar they owned and operated (Hamblett, 1999). Such accounts have become all too familiar as both local and national media report on a proliferation of various forms of video voyeurism, which include hidden cameras in such places as bathrooms ("bathroomcams"), shower facilities ("shower-cams"), locker rooms ("lockerroomcams"), and bedrooms ("bedroomcams") and under working women's desks ("upskirt-cams"). Cell phones with video and still photography features have added another disconcerting dimension to the proliferation of video voyeurism

People who use "voyeurcams" do so either for their own sexual gratification or for financial gain. Technological advances in video equipment, together with the Internet, have allowed the emergence of a disturbing new financial market in which unethical entrepreneurs sell secret video invasions of privacy either for home VCR/DVD viewing or for viewing at pay-per-view Web sites. The number of both unauthorized and authorized occurrences of voyeuristic Internet video displays has exploded. Try this exercise. Call up your favorite Web search engine and type in *voyeur*. This action will produce hits numbering in the thousands. The multiplicity of Web sites that appeal to video voyeurs are set up on a pay-per-view or subscription basis, and a person can log on to watch the activities of people, often attractive women, who may not know that they are being watched.

Unfortunately, many embarrassed and angry victims of video voyeurism have discovered that they have little legal recourse when secret videos are marketed by unscrupulous entrepreneurs based in foreign countries where the legal codes allow them to function without fear of legal reprisals. Currently 44 states have some kind of statute that makes video voyeurism a crime (Williams, 2005). Unfortunately, vague legal wording and the dramatic increase in legal video surveillance since 9/11 have rendered these state laws difficult to interpret and enforce. A recently passed federal law may help sort out these problems. The new law, titled the Video Voyeurism Protection Act 2004, makes it a federal crime to secretly video people on federal property in situations where the people have reasonable expectations of privacy. While this law will only protect federal workers or soldiers, it is an important first step in reducing this onerous form of privacy invasion. We hope that state lawmakers across the country will copy the clear and enforceable language of this welcome new law.

We also hope that more states will enact laws that prosecute high-tech video voyeurism, and that the general public will become more aware of this serious form of personal privacy invasion. Furthermore, as we become more knowledgeable about the potential for this invasive process, we can be more aware and careful in situations where we might be victimized in this fashion. For example, when changing in a gym or health club, be on the lookout for clothes bags positioned so that they might allow secret video recording. Clearly, some small, technologically advanced cameras can be hidden in ways that make detection difficult. Nevertheless, an aware person is less likely to be victimized than an uninformed individual who assumes that being alone ensures his or her personal privacy.

---

It is difficult to isolate specific influences that trigger voyeuristic behavior, particularly because so many of us demonstrate voyeuristic tendencies in a somewhat more controlled fashion. The adolescent or young adult male who displays this behavior often feels great curiosity about sexual activity (as many of us do) but at the same time feels inadequate or insecure. His voyeurism, either while physically present or by means of hidden video cameras, becomes a vicarious fulfillment because he may be unable to consummate sexual relationships without experiencing a great deal of anxiety. In some instances voyeuristic behavior is also reinforced by feelings of power and superiority over those who are secretly observed.

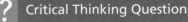

**? Critical Thinking Question**

Is it ethically acceptable to visit Web sites that offer video feeds from hidden cameras or unauthorized videos of people's private lives? Why or why not?

## Other Coercive Paraphilias

We conclude our discussion of coercive paraphilias with a few brief comments about three additional varieties of these coercive or invasive forms of paraphilia. The first two, frotteurism and zoophilia, are actually fairly common. The third variant form, necrophilia, is a rare and extremely aberrant form of sexual expression.

## Frotteurism

**Frotteurism** A fairly common paraphilia in which a person obtains sexual pleasure by pressing or rubbing against another person in a crowded public place.

**Frotteurism** (frah-toor-IH-zum) is a fairly common coercive paraphilia that goes largely unnoticed. It involves an individual, usually a male, who obtains sexual pleasure by pressing or rubbing against a fully clothed female in a crowded public place, such as an elevator, a bus, a subway, a large sporting event, or an outdoor concert. The most common form of contact is between the man's clothed penis and a woman's buttocks or legs. Less commonly, he may use his hands to touch a woman's thighs, pubic region, breasts, or buttocks. This form of contact, called "toucherism," may seem to be inadvertent, and the woman who is touched may not notice or may pay little heed to the seemingly casual contact. On the other hand, she may feel victimized and angry (Freund et al., 1997).

A man who engages in frotteurism may achieve arousal and orgasm during the act. More commonly, he incorporates the mental images of his actions into masturbation fantasies at a later time. Men who engage in this activity have many of the characteristics manifested by those who practice exhibitionism. They are frequently plagued by feelings of social and sexual inadequacy. Their brief, furtive contacts with strangers in crowded places allow them to include others in their sexual expression in a safe, nonthreatening manner.

Frotteurism is a fairly common paraphilia practiced in crowded public places, such as buses, subways, and outdoor concerts.

As with other paraphilias, it is difficult to estimate just how common this variety of coercive paraphilia is. One study of reportedly typical or normal college men found that 21% of the respondents had engaged in one or more frotteuristic acts (Templeman & Sinnett, 1991).

## Zoophilia

**Zoophilia** A paraphilia in which a person has sexual contact with animals.

**Zoophilia** (zoh-oh-FILL-ee-uh), sometimes called *bestiality*, involves sexual contact between humans and animals (American Psychiatric Association, 2000). You may wonder why we classify this as a coercive paraphilia, because such behavior does not involve coercing other people into acts that they would normally avoid. In many instances of zoophilia it is reasonable to presume that the animals involved are also unwilling participants, and the acts performed are often both coercive and invasive. Consequently, assigning this paraphilia to the coercive category seems appropriate.

In Kinsey's sample populations 8% of the males and almost 4% of the females reported having had sexual experience with animals at some point in their lives. The frequency of such behavior among males was highest for those raised on farms (17% of these men reported experiencing orgasm as a result of animal contact). The animals most frequently involved in sex with humans are sheep, goats, donkeys, large fowl (ducks and geese), dogs, and cats. Males are most likely to have contact with farm animals and to engage in penile–vaginal intercourse or to have their genitals orally stimulated by the animals (Hunt, 1974; Kinsey et al., 1948; Miletski, 2002). Women are more likely to have contact with household pets, involving an animal in licking their genitals or masturbating a male dog. Less commonly, some women have trained a dog to mount them and engage in coitus (Gendel & Bonner, 1988; Kinsey et al., 1953).

Sexual contact with animals is commonly only a transitory experience of young people to whom a human sexual partner is inaccessible or forbidden (Money, 1981). Most adolescent males and females who experiment with zoophilia make a transition to adult sexual relations with human partners. True, or nontransitory, zoophilia exists only when sexual contact with animals is preferred, regardless of what other forms of sexual expression are available. Such behavior, which is rare, may be expressed only by people with deep-rooted psychological problems or distorted images of the other sex. For example, a man who has a pathological hatred of women may be attempting to express his contempt for them by choosing animals in preference to women as sexual partners. However, some men who engage in zoophilia do not appear to fit this profile. A recent anonymous Internet questionnaire study of 114 self-defined "zoophile" men found that while the majority of respondents indicated preferring animal sex to human sex, a desire for affection and pleasurable sex, and not hatred of women, were presented as the major reasons for sexual interest in animals (Williams & Weinberg, 2003).

## Necrophilia

**Necrophilia** (ne-kruh-FILL-ee-uh) is an extremely rare sexual variation in which a person obtains sexual gratification by viewing or having intercourse with a corpse. This paraphilia appears to occur exclusively among males, who may be driven to remove freshly buried bodies from cemeteries or to seek employment in morgues or funeral homes (Tollison & Adams, 1979). However, the vast majority of people who work in these settings do not have tendencies toward necrophilia.

There are a few cases on record of men with necrophilic preferences who kill someone to gain access to a corpse (Milner & Dopke, 1997). The notorious Jeffrey Dahmer, the Milwaukee man who murdered and mutilated his young male victims, is believed by some experts in criminal pathology to have been motivated by uncontrollable necrophilic urges. More commonly, the difficulties associated with gaining access to dead bodies lead some men with necrophilic preferences to limit their deviant behavior to contact with simulated corpses. Some prostitutes cater to this desire by powdering themselves to mimic the pallor of death, dressing in a shroud, and lying very still during intercourse. Any movement on their part may inhibit their customers' sexual arousal.

Men who engage in necrophilia almost always manifest severe emotional disorders (Goldman, 1992). They may see themselves as sexually and socially inept and may both hate and fear women. Consequently, the only "safe" woman may be one whose lifelessness epitomizes a nonthreatening, totally subjugated sexual partner (Rosman & Resnick, 1989; Stoller, 1977).

**Necrophilia** A rare sexual paraphilia in which a person obtains sexual gratification by viewing or having intercourse with a corpse.

# ◗ Sexual Addiction: Fact, Fiction, or Misnomer?

Both the professional literature and the popular media have directed considerable attention to a condition commonly referred to as sexual addiction. The idea that people can become dominated by insatiable sexual needs has been around for a long time, as exemplified by the terms *nymphomania*, applied to women, and *satyriasis* or *Don Juanism*, applied to men. Many professionals have traditionally reacted negatively to these labels, suggesting that they are disparaging terms likely to induce unnecessary guilt in individuals who enjoy an active sex life. Furthermore, it has been argued that one cannot assign a label implying excessive sexual activity when no clear criteria establish what constitutes "normal" levels of sexual involvement. The criteria often used to establish alleged subconditions of *hypersexuality*—nymphomania and satyriasis—are subjective and value laden. Therefore these terms are typically defined moralistically rather than scientifically, a fact that has generated harsh criticism from a number of professionals (Klein, 1991, 2003; Levine & Troiden, 1988). Psychotherapist Marty Klein (2003) is especially critical of the sex addiction movement, which in his view both exploits people's fear of their own sexuality and pathologizes sexual behavior and impulses that are not unhealthy. Nevertheless, the concept of sexual addiction achieved a heightened legitimacy with the publication of Patrick Carnes's book *Sexual Addiction* (1983), later retitled *Out of the Shadows: Understanding Sexual Addiction* (2001, 3rd ed.).

According to Carnes, many people who engage in some of the atypical or paraphilic behaviors described in this chapter (as well as extreme coercive behaviors, such as child molestation) are manifesting the outward symptoms of a psychological addiction in which feelings of depression, anxiety, loneliness, and worthlessness are temporarily relieved through a sexual high not unlike the high achieved by mood-altering chemicals such as alcohol and cocaine.

The concept of sexual addiction has generated considerable attention in the professional community. While Carnes and his supporters argue for acceptance of sexual addiction as a legitimate diagnostic category, detractors point to a continuing "tradition in the sex addiction literature of forgoing empirical research and presenting conjectures as fact" (Chivers, 2005, p. 476). Many sexologists do not believe that sexual addiction should be a distinct diagnostic category, because it is rare and lacking in distinction from other compulsive disorders, such as gambling and eating disorders, and because this label negates individual responsibility for "uncontrollable" sexual compulsions that victimize others (Levine & Troiden, 1988; Satel, 1993). This position is reflected in a decision not to include a category encompassing hypersexuality in the most recent version of the *Diagnostic and Statistical Manual (DSM-IV-TR)* of the American Psychiatric Association (2000) (the most widely accepted system for classifying psychological disorders).

A number of professionals acknowledge the validity of such arguments against the addiction concept but nevertheless recognize that some people become involved in patterns of excessive sexual activity. Noteworthy in this group is sexologist Eli Coleman (1990, 1991, 2003), who prefers to describe these behaviors as symptomatic of sexual compulsion rather than addiction. According to Coleman, a person manifesting excessive sexual behaviors often suffers from feelings of shame, unworthiness, inadequacy, and loneliness. These negative feelings cause great psychological pain, and this pain then causes the person to search for a "fix," or an agent that has pain-numbing qualities, such as alcohol, certain foods, gambling, or, in this instance, sex. Indulging oneself in this fix produces only a brief respite from the psychological pain, which returns in full force, thus triggering a greater need to engage in such behaviors to obtain further temporary relief. Unfortunately, these repetitive compulsive acts soon tend to be self-defeating; that is, they compound feelings of shame and lead to intimacy dysfunction by interrupting the development of normal, healthy interpersonal functioning.

Other sexologists, notably John Bancroft and Zoran Vukudinovic (2004), believe that because of a lack of empirical research, the currently fashionable concepts of sexual addiction and compulsive sexual behavior are of uncertain scientific value. These authors suggest that until we have more data to evaluate the scientific validity of these concepts, it is preferable to use the more general descriptive term "out of control" to describe such problematic sexual behavior.

Because sex has become a highly sought-out topic among users of the Internet, some professionals have suggested that a new variety of sexual addiction or sexual compulsivity has emerged. The boxed discussion titled "Cybersex Addiction and Compulsivity: Harmless Sexual Outlet or Problematic Sexual Behavior?" examines this emerging phenomenon.

We can expect that professionals in the field of sexuality will continue to debate for some time how to diagnose, describe, and explain problems of excessive or uncontrolled sexuality. Even as this discussion continues, professional treatment programs for compulsive or addictive sexual behaviors have emerged throughout the United States (more than 2,000 programs at last count), most modeled after the 12-step program of Alcoholics Anonymous (National Council on Sexual Addiction and Compulsivity, 2002). Data pertaining to treatment outcomes for these programs are still too limited to allow evaluation of therapeutic effectiveness. Besides formal treatment programs, a number of community-based self-help organizations have surfaced throughout the United States. These groups include Sex Addicts Anonymous, Sexaholics Anonymous, Sexual Compulsives Anonymous, and Sex and Love Addicts Anonymous.

**? Critical Thinking Question**

Which of the atypical sexual behaviors discussed in this chapter do you find the most unacceptable? Why?

# Cybersex Addiction and Compulsivity: Harmless Sexual Outlet or Problematic Sexual Behavior?

A prominent physician in our home state recently lost his position and staff privileges at a local hospital when it was discovered that he was using a hospital computer to visit sexually explicit Internet sites that specialize in child pornography. An investigation revealed that this individual spent an inordinate amount of time, both on the job and at home, compulsively surfing sexually oriented Web sites, especially those with explicit sexual content dealing with children. This case illustrates a variety of behavior, spawned by the Internet, that has raised the concern of a number of mental health specialists.

Sexually oriented Internet sites are among the most widely visited topical areas of the World Wide Web. At the time of this writing, there are more than 100,000 Web sites featuring all kinds of sexual content, and visits to these sites have increased dramatically, with some sites reporting as many as 50 million cumulative hits (Philaretou, 2005). Research indicates that at least one-third of Internet users visit some type of sexually oriented Web site (Cooper, 2002, 2003). Does this widespread incidence of "surfing for sex" indicate problematic behavior and warrant societal concern? Some suggest the opposite—that pursuing cybersex is a harmless recreational pursuit offering anonymous access to sexually oriented material that provides sexual outlets (such as chat room sex or masturbating to sexual images) that are safe from the dangers of STDs and other relationship risks (Waskul, 2004). In addition, the Internet can also be useful to people who wish to explore sexual fantasies online in the safety and privacy of their homes (Quittner, 2003).

A less benign view of Internet sex emerges from a growing awareness that for a small but ever-increasing number of individuals who surf the Internet primarily for erotic stimulation and sexual outlets, the affordability, accessibility, and anonymity of the Internet are creating a new breed of sexual compulsives addicted to cybersex. Many of these individuals are using cybersex to the exclusion of personal relationships (Cooper, 2002, 2003; Dew & Chaney, 2004; Philaretou, 2005).

It is difficult to accurately estimate what percentage of the approximately 150 million Internet users in the United States experience problems associated with visiting Web sex sites (Dew & Chaney, 2004). A large majority of people who access the Internet for sexual purposes do not appear to experience adverse consequences (Waskul, 2004). However, some research indicates that 6–10% of Internet users do report being concerned about the possible negative consequences of their online sexual activities (Dew & Chaney, 2004). Furthermore, studies indicate that 1% of sex site surfers are so hooked on or addicted to cybersex that their capacity to function effectively in their everyday lives is severely damaged (Carnes, 2000; Cooper et al., 2000). Such individuals are likely to spend endless hours each day surfing sex sites, masturbating to sexually explicit images, or engaging in mutual online sex with someone contacted through a chat room.

The sexual excitement, stimulation, and orgasmic outlets provided by a virtually infinite variety of Internet sexual opportunities may lead to a compulsive pursuit of cyberspace sex that can have a devastating effect on a cybersex addict's life and family (Cooper, 2002; Woodward, 2003). Partners of these individuals report feeling ignored, abandoned, devalued, or betrayed as a result of their mate's compulsive pursuit of cybersex (Brody, 2000; Cooper, 2002). Some people devote so much time to forays into cybersex that they end up neglecting family members and/or job responsibilities (Philaretou, 2005).

An additional hazard faced by some cybersex addicts and compulsives who pursue online sexual relationships is that they may progress to arranging off-line meetings that can have seriously adverse consequences, including exposure to STDs and sexual assault (Cooper, 2002; Genius & Genius, 2005).

Mental health professionals have expressed concern about teenage addiction to cybersex (Fleming & Rickwood, 2004; Jancin, 2005). Teenagers in the United States are heavier users of the Internet than adults (Feming & Rickwood, 2004). Research into teenagers' Web surfing behavior is relatively limited and thus it is difficult to assess how many are engaging in problematic Internet behavior, including cybersex addiction. Nevertheless, some clinicians believe that teenagers, especially males, are becoming addicted to sex on the Internet. According to psychotherapist Ann Freeman, it is common to encounter youths who are addicted to masturbating to Web sex sites 3 or 4 times daily (in Jancin, 2005). Such excessive Internet-based sexual behavior may lead to social isolation, unhealthy sexual attitudes, loneliness, depression, and possible "stranger-danger" in the form of being tracked and lured by cybersex pedophile predators (Fleming & Rickwood, 2004; Jancin, 2005). (See Chapter 17 for a discussion of pedophiles in cyberspace.)

We hope that future studies of cybersex will provide a clearer answer to the question "Is compulsive exploration of online sex a relatively harmless sexual outlet or a potentially harmful variety of problematic sexual behavior?" For the present, a number of professionals have raised our awareness of the potentially adverse consequences of getting hooked on cybersex.

## What Constitutes Atypical Sexual Behavior?

- Atypical, paraphilic sexual behavior involves a variety of sexual activities that, in their fully developed form, are statistically uncommon in the general population.
- Such behaviors exist in many gradations, ranging from mild, infrequently expressed tendencies to full-blown, regularly manifested behaviors.
- Paraphilias are usually expressed by males, are sometimes harmful to others, may be preludes to more-serious sexual offenses, and tend to occur in clusters.

## Noncoercive Paraphilias

- Noncoercive paraphilias are often solo activities or behaviors that involve the participation of adults who agree to engage in, observe, or just put up with the particular variant behavior.
- Fetishism, transvestic fetishism, sexual sadism, sexual masochism, autoerotic asphyxia, klismaphilia, coprophilia, and urophilia are all varieties of noncoercive paraphilias.
- Fetishism is a form of atypical sexual behavior in which an individual obtains arousal by focusing on an inanimate object or a part of the human body.
- Fetishism is often a product of conditioning, in which the fetish object becomes associated with sexual arousal through the reinforcement of masturbation-produced orgasm.
- Transvestic fetishism involves obtaining sexual excitement by cross-dressing. It is usually a solitary activity, expressed by a heterosexual male in the privacy of his own home.
- Sadomasochism can be defined as obtaining sexual arousal through receiving or giving physical and/or mental pain.
- Most participants in sadomasochism view it as a form of sexual enhancement that they voluntarily and mutually choose to explore.
- People who engage in sadomasochistic behavior may be seeking additional nonsexual stimuli to achieve sufficient arousal. They may also be acting out of deeply rooted beliefs that sexual activity is sinful and immoral.
- For some participants, sadomasochism acts as an escape valve that allows them temporarily to step out of the rigid, restrictive roles they play in their everyday lives.
- Individuals who engage in sadomasochism sometimes describe early experiences that may have established a connection between sex and pain.
- Autoerotic asphyxia is a rare and life-threatening paraphilia in which an individual, almost always a male, seeks to enhance sexual excitement and orgasm by pressure-induced oxygen deprivation.
- Klismaphilia is a paraphilia that involves achieving sexual pleasure from receiving enemas.
- Coprophilia and urophilia are paraphilias in which a person obtains sexual arousal from contact with feces or urine, respectively.

## Coercive Paraphilias

- Coercive paraphilias are invasive, in that they involve unwilling recipients of behavior such as voyeurism or exhibitionism. Coercive acts may harm their targets, who may be psychologically traumatized by the experience.
- Exhibitionism, obscene phone calls, voyeurism, frotteurism, zoophilia, and necrophilia are all varieties of coercive paraphilias.
- Exhibitionism is behavior in which an individual, almost always a male, exposes his genitals to an involuntary observer.
- People who exhibit themselves are usually young adult males who have strong feelings of inadequacy and insecurity. Sexual relationships, either past or present, are likely to be unsatisfactory.
- Gratification is usually obtained when the reaction to exhibitionism is shock, disgust, or fear. Physical assault is generally not associated with exhibitionism.
- The characteristics of individuals who make obscene phone calls are similar to those of exhibitionists.
- Although there may be an element of hostility in obscene phone calls, the caller rarely follows up his verbal assault with a physical attack on his victim.
- Voyeurism is obtaining sexual pleasure from looking at the exposed bodies or sexual activities of others, usually strangers.
- People inclined toward voyeurism, typically males, are often sociosexually underdeveloped, with strong feelings of inferiority and inadequacy.
- Frotteurism involves a person obtaining sexual pleasure by pressing or rubbing against another person in a crowded public place.
- Zoophilia involves sexual contact between humans and animals; it occurs most commonly as a transitory experience of young people to whom a sexual partner is inaccessible or forbidden.
- Necrophilia involves obtaining sexual gratification by viewing or having intercourse with a corpse.

## Sexual Addiction: Fact, Fiction, or Misnomer?

- The concept of sexual addiction suggests that some people who engage in excessive sexual activity are manifesting symptoms of a psychological addiction, in which feelings of depression, anxiety, loneliness, and worthlessness are temporarily relieved through a sexual high.
- Many sexologists do not believe that sexual addiction should be a distinct diagnostic category, because it is rare and lacking in distinction from other compulsive disorders, such as gambling and eating disorders, and because this label negates individual responsibility for "uncontrollable" sexual compulsions that victimize others.

# ❯ Suggested Readings

**Boyd, Helen** (2003). *My Husband Betty.* New York: Thunder Mouth Press. A frank, empathetic, engaging, and informative discussion of cross-dressing from an insider's perspective.

**Cooper, Al** (Ed.) (2002). *Sex and the Internet: A Guide Book for Clinicians.* A compilation of articles by international experts on the emerging phenomenon of cybersex.

**Easton, Dossie, and Catherine Liszt** (2000). *When Someone You Love is Kinky.* San Francisco: Greenery Press. A practical, informative guide designed to help SM participants explain their sexual interests to partners, friends, and families.

**Money, John, and Margaret Lamacz** (1989). *Vandalized Lovemaps.* New York: Prometheus. An intriguing theory about how the erotosexual experiences we have in childhood establish patterns in the brain, called "lovemaps," that determine the kinds of stimuli and activities that become sexually arousing to each of us. The primary thesis of the book is that when these lovemaps become distorted or vandalized by traumatic childhood experiences, various paraphilias result.

**Weinberg, Thomas** (Ed.) (1995). *Studies in Dominance and Submission.* New York: Prometheus Books. A collection of articles that provide much thought-provoking information about sadomasochism.

# ❯ Web Resources

### CengageNOW Web Site
Go to **academic.cengage.com** to link to practice quiz questions, interactive activities, Internet links, critical thinking exercises, discussion forums, and more. You can also access sites from the Wadsworth Psychology Study Center (**academic.cengage.com/psychology**) or you can connect directly to the following sites:

### Paraphilias and Fetishes
Visitors to this Web site, part of the Human Sexuality Web site provided by the University of Missouri, Kansas City, can gain a better understanding of various paraphilias and fetishes.

### Paraphilias
This Web site describes criteria, treatment, and prognosis information for different paraphilias. It is part of a larger directory of psychiatric disorders.

### Tri-ESS
This Web site describes a support organization for heterosexual transvestic fetishists (cross-dressers).

### National Council on Sexual Addiction and Compulsivity (NCSAC)
This Web site, maintained by the private nonprofit NCSAC, provides information designed to promote awareness and understanding of sexual addiction and sexual compulsivity. Educational material and referral sources are provided.

### *Our Sexuality* Book Companion Web Site
**academic.cengage.com/psychology/crooks** Visit your book companion Web site where you will find flash cards, practice quizzes, Internet links, and more to help you study.

### Just what you need to know NOW!
Spend time on what you need to master rather than on information you already have learned. Take a pretest for this chapter, and CengageNOW will generate a personalized study plan based on your results. The study plan will identify the topics you need to review and direct you to online resources to help you master those topics. You can then take a post-test to help you determine the concepts you have mastered and what you will still need to work on. Try it out! Go to **academic.cengage.com/login** to sign in with an access code or to purchase access to this product.

### InfoTrac College Edition Online Library
Sign in to **academic.cengage.com/login** or visit your free book companion Web site at **academic.cengage.com/psychology/crooks** to access InfoTrac College Edition, an online searchable library that includes a multitude of journals, many specific to human sexuality. These journals include *Archives of Sexual Behavior; Archives of Sexual Health Behavior; Canadian Journal of Human Sexuality; Hispanic Journal of the Behavioral Sciences; Journal of Cross-Cultural Psychology; Journal of Physical Education, Recreation, and Dance; Journal of Sex Research;* and *Sex Roles.*

# Sexual Coercion

AP

*I was sexually abused by my stepbrother throughout a great part of my childhood. The abuse started the summer I was ten. He is three and a half years older than me, and he was my designated baby-sitter all summer. He usually wasn't violent. It was more coaxing and coercion, and threats of what would happen if I told. The strongest memories I have are of times when it was particularly physically painful. I put myself out of my body, and would just watch the ceiling fan go around and around. When I was 13 I saw a talk show on incest and then told a woman at my church what was happening to me, and it kind of all fell apart from there. As much as the thought of the whole experience is repulsive, what hurt the most is my parents calling it child's play in discussion with CPS [Child Protection Services]. My parents even had me believing at one point that I really had wanted it and was telling them about it for attention. Because of this reaction, I believed for a while that it was my fault and that I was dirty because of it. My stepbrother plea-bargained his case, and he was put on probation. I was taken out of the home and put in foster and group homes. I attempted suicide numerous times and was in four different psychiatric hospitals over about four years. I no longer have any contact with the "family." I am blessed to have been adopted into another loving family. My new dad is the one who saved me from hating all men forever. But I still have problems regarding sex. My boyfriend can't even hold me romantically. I have only stopped having flashbacks and nightmares fairly recently. I am in therapy for the umpteenth time, but this time it is really working. (Authors' files)*

A person has been sexually victimized when she or he is deprived of free choice and is coerced or forced to comply with sexual acts under duress. Victims of coercive sexual acts often suffer grievous consequences, as revealed in the preceding account, provided by a 19-year-old college student. In this chapter, we focus on three particularly abusive and exploitative forms of sexual coercion: rape, the sexual abuse of children, and sexual harassment. All these behaviors involve strong elements of coercion, sometimes even violence.

# ❿ Rape

Although the legal definition of **rape** varies from state to state, most state laws define rape as sexual intercourse occurring under actual or threatened forcible compulsion that overcomes the earnest resistance of the victim. This coercive act can range from violent assault by a stranger, an acquaintance, or a family member to a planned romantic date that degrades into an episode of coerced sex. What these acts have in common is a lack of empathy for the feelings of victims and a willingness to take advantage of and often harm them. Most writers and researchers on this topic distinguish at least three different types of rape. **Stranger rape** is rape by an unknown assailant. **Acquaintance rape,** or **date rape,** is committed by someone known to the victim. **Statutory rape** is intercourse with a person under the age of consent. (The age of consent varies by state and ranges from 14 to 18.) Statutory rape is considered to have occurred regardless of the apparent willingness of the underage partner.

## Prevalence of Rape

Despite the fact that rape is a significant problem in our society, it has been difficult to obtain accurate statistics on its frequency. One reason is that many individuals do not report this crime. Estimates of the percentage of rapes that women victims report to police or other public agencies range from 11.9% (Hanson et al., 1999) to 28% (U.S. Department of Justice, 2001). This low percentage of reporting has led some writers to suggest that rape is the most underreported crime in the United States (Lonsway & Fitzgerald, 1994; Romeo, 2004). According to the Federal Bureau of Investigation (2006), 94,635 females nationwide reported being raped in 2004. Based on the estimates of underreporting of rape we just stated, it is likely that the actual number of rapes occurring in 2004 ranged from 338,000 to 795,000.

**Rape** Sexual intercourse that occurs without consent as a result of actual or threatened force.

**Stranger rape** Rape of a person by an unknown assailant.

**Acquaintance rape** Sexual assault by a friend, acquaintance, or date—that is, someone known to the victim.

**Date rape** Sexual assault by an acquaintance when on a date.

**Statutory rape** Intercourse with a person under the age of consent.

**InfoTrac Search Words**

- Rape
- Acquaintance rape
- Date rape

| TABLE 17.1 | Lifetime Incidence of Rape by Sex of Victim | |
| --- | --- | --- |
| Rape Incident | Women (n = 8,000) | Men (n = 8,000) |
| Completed | 14.8% | 2.1% |
| Attempted only | 2.8% | 0.9% |
| Total | 17.6% | 3.0% |

SOURCE: Adapted from Tjaden & Thoennes (1998).

Previous estimates of the number of women who have experienced actual or attempted rape have varied widely and have been beset by a number of methodological problems. In an effort to overcome these problems, the National Institutes of Justice (NIJ) and the Centers for Disease Control and Prevention (CDC) commissioned a large-scale telephone survey of 8,000 women and 8,000 men (Tjaden & Thoennes, 1998). The investigators reported that more than 1 out of 6 women indicated that they had been raped or had been the victim of an attempted rape, as did 3% of men (see ⊙ **Table 17.1**). More recently, a national survey conducted by the NIJ found that over the course of time spent in college, 20–25% of college women experience a completed or attempted rape (Fisher et al., 2000). Other research has confirmed that approximately 1 out of 4 college women have experienced rape or attempted rape (Foubert et al., 2002).

Victims of rape do not report the crime for a number of reasons, including self-blame ("I shouldn't have had so much to drink"), fear of being blamed by others, concern for the rapist, fear of retaliation, and an attempt to block their recall of a traumatic experience (Parrot, 1991; Romeo, 2004; Simonson & Subich, 1999). A person who has been raped may feel vulnerable and frightened, and reliving the experience by telling about it can be understandably difficult. Also, mistrust of the police or legal system, fear of reprisal by the offender or his family, and concern about unwanted publicity may deter individuals from reporting rapes. And, as we discuss later in this chapter, a large proportion of rapes are committed by an acquaintance of the victim. Under these circumstances a woman's preconception of a "real" rape as a violent attack by a stranger may not match her experience of an acquaintance rape, and therefore she may not consider it reportable criminal behavior (Cowan, 2000; Rickert & Wiemann, 1998).

In the following pages, we look at a number of aspects of the act of rape, including the cultural context in which it occurs, the characteristics of perpetrators, and the characteristics of victims.

## False Beliefs About Rape

An important factor in explaining the high incidence of rape in our society is the prevalence of misconceptions about this crime. False beliefs concerning rape, rapists, and rape victims abound (Cowan, 2000; O'Donohue et al., 2003). Many people believe that roughing up a woman is acceptable, that many women are sexually aroused by such activity, and that it is impossible to rape a healthy woman against her will (Gilbert et al., 1991; Malamuth et al., 1980). Research indicates that acceptance and endorsement of rape myths increase men's proclivity to commit rape (Bohner et al., 2006). The effect of such rape myths is often "to deny and justify male sexual aggression against women" (Lonsway & Fitzgerald, 1994, p. 133). Another frequent effect is to place the blame on the victim. Many victims believe that the rape was basically their fault. Even when they were simply in the wrong place at the wrong time, a pervasive sense of personal guilt often remains. The following are some of the most common false beliefs about rape:

1. *False belief: "Women can't be raped if they really don't want to be."* The belief that women can always resist a rape attempt is false, for several reasons. First, men are usually physically larger and stronger than women. Second, female gender-role conditioning often trains a woman to be compliant and submissive. Such conditioning can limit the options a woman believes she has in resisting rape. Third, in many rapes, the rapist chooses the time and place. He has the element of surprise on his side. The fear and intimidation a woman usually experiences when attacked work to the assailant's advantage. His use of weapons, threats, or physical force further coerces her compliance.

2. *False belief: "Women say no when they mean yes."* Some rapists have distorted perceptions of their interactions with the women they rape—before, during, and even after the assault. They believe that women want to be coerced into sexual

activity, even to the extent of being sexually abused (Muehlenhard & Rodgers, 1998). These distorted beliefs help the rapist justify his behavior: His act is not rape but rather "normal" sex play. Afterward, he may feel little or no guilt about his behavior because, in his own mind, it was not rape.

3. *False belief: "Many women 'cry rape.'"* False accusations of rape are quite uncommon, and they are even less frequently carried as far as prosecution. Given the difficulties that exist in reporting and prosecuting a rape, few women (or men) could successfully proceed with an unfounded rape case. As mentioned earlier, "Women are much more likely to suffer rape victimization and not report the crime to any authorities" (Lonsway & Fitzgerald, 1994, p. 136).

4. *False belief: "All women want to be raped."* That some women have rape fantasies is sometimes used to support the idea that women want to be sexually assaulted. However, it is important to understand the distinction between an erotic fantasy and a conscious desire to be harmed. In a fantasy a person retains control. A fantasy carries no threat of physical harm or death; a rape does.

5. *False belief: "Rapists are 'obviously' mentally ill."* The mistaken idea that a potential rapist somehow "looks the part" is also prevalent. "This rape myth is particularly dangerous because potential victims may feel that they can identify a rapist (the crazed stranger) or that they are safe with someone they know" (Cowan, 2000, p. 809). As we discuss later, most rapes are committed by people who are not mentally ill and who are known to the victim.

6. *False belief: "The male sex drive is so high that men often cannot control their sexual urges."* The problem with this myth is that it shifts the responsibility from the perpetrator to the victim (Cowan, 2000). Women are seen as either the precipitator of the rape ("She should not have worn that dress") or as having been careless or naive ("What did she think would happen if she went back to his apartment with him?").

Women in Austin, Texas, protest against sexual assault. These women and others like them have helped challenge societal assumptions about rape.

**? Critical Thinking Question**

Which of these false beliefs about rape do you think is most dangerous and why?

## Factors Associated With Rape

In an effort to understand the underlying causes of rape, researchers have looked at a number of factors associated with rape.

### Psychosocial Basis of Rape

Many researchers and clinicians view rape more as a product of socialization processes that occur within the fabric of "normal" society than as a product of the individual rapist's pathological condition (Hill & Fischer, 2001; Simonson & Subich, 1999). Strong support for the view that rape is in many ways a cultural phenomenon was provided by the research of Peggy Reeves Sanday (1981), an anthropologist who compared the incidences of rape in 95 societies.

Sanday's research indicated that the frequency of rape in a given society is influenced by several factors. Foremost among these were the nature of the relations between the sexes, the status of women, and the attitudes that boys acquire during their developmental years. Sanday found that "rape-prone" societies tolerate and even glorify masculine violence, encouraging boys to be aggressive and competitive, and they view physical force as natural and exemplary. In these societies, men tend to have greater economic and political power than women, remaining aloof from "women's work," such as child rearing and household duties.

In contrast, relations between the sexes are quite different in societies where there is virtually no rape. Women and men in "rape-free" societies share power and authority and contribute equally to the community welfare. In addition, children of both

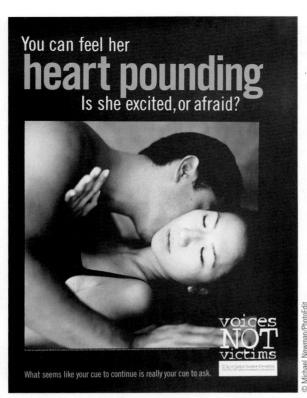

You can feel her **heart pounding** Is she excited, or afraid?

voices NOT victims

What seems like your cue to continue is really your cue to ask.

© Michael Newman/PhotoEdit

Advertisements like this one are intended to educate men and women about rape.

sexes in these societies are raised to value nurturance and to avoid aggression and violence. With this cultural framework in mind, let us take a closer look at some of the aspects of male socialization in our own culture that contribute to the occurrence of rape and other forms of sexual coercion.

The United States has the highest incidence of rape of all Western nations (*Contemporary Sexuality*, 1996). One important reason for this fact may have to do with stereotypical gender roles. Males in our society are often taught that power, aggressiveness, and getting what one wants—by force, if necessary—are all part of the proper male role. Furthermore, they frequently learn that they should seek sex and expect to be successful—often with few qualms about using unethical means to achieve their goal.

It is not surprising, therefore, that many U.S. men view aggression as a legitimate means to obtain sexual access to women. "Sexual assault is a logical extension of a system in which men are taught to fight for what they want, whereas women are taught to be passive and yielding and to put men's needs above their own" (Muehlenhard et al., 1991, p. 161). Men whose peer groups openly legitimize and support these attitudes and behaviors are particularly likely to victimize women sexually (Sanday, 1996).

## Impact of the Media

The media play a powerful role in transmitting cultural values and norms. Some novels, films, videos, and computer games perpetuate the notion that women want to be raped. Often, fictionalized rape scenes begin with a woman resisting her attacker, only to melt into passionate acceptance. In the rare cases where male-to-male rape is shown, as in the films *Deliverance* and *The Shawshank Redemption*, the violation and humiliation of rape are more likely to be realistically portrayed.

A number of social scientists have suggested that sexually violent films, books, magazines, videos, and computer games contribute to some rapists' assaultive behaviors (Boeringer, 1994; Hall, 1996; Linz et al., 1992). Other evidence suggests that exposure to degrading but nonviolent pornography might also have deleterious effects on men's attitudes toward sex and women and might increase their inclinations to engage in coercive sex (Check & Guloien, 1989; Zillmann, 1989).

Boeringer (1994) found that, although exposure to nonviolent pornography was not predictive of any form of sexual coercion or rape, viewing pornography that depicted violent rape was strongly associated with judging oneself capable of sexual coercion and aggression and engaging in such coercive acts. Other research suggests that "exposure to media that combine arousing sexual images with violence may promote the development of deviant patterns of physiological sexual arousal" (Hall & Barongan, 1997, p. 5).

Is rape, then, a sexualization of violence? The evidence is equivocal. In two studies, the erectile responses of matched groups of rapists and nonrapists were measured as the men listened to audiotape descriptions of rape and of mutually consenting sexual activity. In both studies, rapists were more aroused by the sexual assault description than were nonrapists (Abel et al., 1977; Bernat et al., 1999). However, other research has failed to support this conclusion, finding little difference in the erectile responses of rapists and nonrapists in similar research designs (Eccles et al., 1994; Proulx et al., 1994). More research is needed to clarify these findings.

## Characteristics of Rapists

Are rapists characterized by a single personality or behavioral pattern? Until recently, efforts to answer this question have been hindered by both a narrow conceptualization of rape and inadequate research methods. This was because our knowledge of the characteristics and motivations of rapists was based primarily on studies of men convicted of the crime—a sample group that probably represents less than 1% of rapists. Because convicted rapists are less educated, more inclined to commit other antisocial or criminal acts, and more alienated from society than are rapists who do not pass through the criminal justice system, we cannot say with certainty that men who rape without being prosecuted and convicted match the profile of convicted rapists (Smithyman, 1979).

We can say that many of the men incarcerated for rape have a strong proclivity toward violence, one that is often reflected in their acts of rape. This fact, along with certain assumptions about male/female relationships, has led a number of writers to argue that rape is not sexually motivated but is rather an act of power and domination (Brownmiller, 1975). This viewpoint prevailed for a number of years, during which the sexual component of rape and other assaults was de-emphasized. However, more recent research suggests that, although power and domination are often involved in sexual coercion, such coercion is also frequently motivated by a desire for sexual gratification. This view has been supported by several studies of the incidence and nature of sexual coercion among nonincarcerated males (Hickman & Muehlenhard, 1999; Senn et al., 1999).

It appears that a wide range of personality characteristics and motivations underlie sexual assault and how that assault is committed. Men who embrace traditional gender roles, particularly that of male dominance, are more likely to commit rape than men who do not embrace traditional gender stereotypes (Ben-David & Schneider, 2005; Murnen et al., 2002; Robinson et al., 2004). Anger toward women is a prominent attitude among some men who sexually assault women (Anderson et al., 1997; Hall & Barongan, 1997). Alcohol can also contribute to rapists' behavior; rapists often had been drinking just before assaulting their victims (Abbey et al., 1998, 2003; Muehlenhard & Linton, 1987). Furthermore, alcohol-involved rapes are often associated with a high level of violence (Abbey et al., 2003).

Many rapists have self-centered personalities, which may render them insensitive to others' feelings (Dean & Malamuth, 1997; Marshall, 1993; Pithers, 1993). Research has provided strong evidence that men with a narcissistic personality trait may be especially inclined to commit rape and other acts of sexual coercion (Baumeister et al., 2002; Bushman et al., 2003). The *Diagnostic and Statistical Manual of Mental Disorders* (American Psychiatric Association, 2000) describes *narcissism* as being characterized by an inflated sense of self-importance, an unreasonable sense of entitlement, deficient empathy for others, and exploitative tendencies toward others. Research indicates that narcissists are also inclined to engage in aggressive retaliation against others for real or imagined slights (Baumeister et al., 2002; Bushman & Baumeister, 1998). In addition to these aggressive tendencies, narcissists' unreasonable sense of entitlement may influence them to view women as owing them sexual favors. Their lack of empathy for others would negate the impact of their victims' discomfort or suffering. Finally, their exaggerated sense of self-importance may facilitate their ability to rationalize their behavior and "convince themselves that their coercion victims had really desired sex or had expressed some form of consent" (Bushman et al., 2003, p. 1028).

Anger, power, and sexual gratification all play varying roles in rape. However, anger and a need to express power appear to predominate in stranger rape, whereas a desire for sexual gratification seems to predominate in acquaintance or date rape.

## Characteristics of Female Rape Victims

Although females of all ages are raped, more than 50% of U.S. female rape victims reported that their first rape occurred before they were 18 years old, and 22% reported that their first rape occurred before they were 12 (see ● **Figure 17.1**). Women age 16 to 24 are the most frequent victims of reported rape in the United States. (U.S. Department of Justice, 2003). Being raped before the age of 18 greatly increases the chances

● **Figure 17.1** Age breakdown of women rape victims at time of first rape.

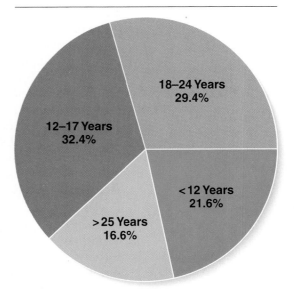

**Women Victims' Age at Time of First Rape**
(*n* = 1,323 women victims)

12–17 Years 32.4%

18–24 Years 29.4%

<12 Years 21.6%

>25 Years 16.6%

SOURCE: Tjaden & Thoennes (1998).

> **Critical Thinking Question**

Some people perceive a woman who wears "suggestive clothing" and is then raped as somehow responsible for her own rape. In contrast, a man who dons an expensive suit, carries a lot of cash, and wears a Rolex watch is seldom, if ever, held responsible for being robbed on the street. What are your thoughts about this inconsistency in assigning the label *victim precipitation* to these two events? Is it ever appropriate to label a victim responsible for her or his own victimization?

that a woman will be raped again (Nishith et al., 2000; Tjaden & Thoennes, 1998). The younger the age of the rape victim, the more likely it is that the perpetrator is a relative or an acquaintance (U.S. Department of Justice, 2003). Research also indicates that women who were victims of childhood sexual abuse are at increased risk for adult sexual revictimization by rapists (Miner et al., 2006).

As noted earlier, the frequency of reported rape varies by culture. Asian and Pacific Islander women report being raped significantly less often than do white and African American women, Hispanic women report being raped less often than non-Hispanic women, and Native American and Native Alaskan women report a much higher frequency of rape than any other group (Tjaden & Thoennes, 1998). Koss and colleagues (1987), however, reported similar incidences of rape across various ethnic groups when socioeconomic status (SES) was controlled for. They found that the lower women's SES was, the more often the women were victims of sexual assault. This finding is not surprising, because people who live in poverty are more frequent victims of all types of crimes. Given these divergent findings, however, more research is needed to ascertain whether there are ethnic and socioeconomic variables that influence the frequency of rape in our society—and if so, why.

## Acquaintance Rape and Sexual Coercion

Most rapes are committed by someone who is known to the victim—by an acquaintance or a friend—not (as popularly thought) by a stranger (Ben-David & Schneider, 2005; Fisher et al., 2000; Howard et al., 2003). Research indicates that in approximately 3 out of 4 sexual assaults against women, the perpetrator is known by the victimized person (Romeo, 2004). A significant number of these acquaintance rapes occur in dating situations—hence the term *date rape*.

Considerable research has focused on the prevalence of sexual coercion in dating situations (Jenkins & Aube, 2002; Oswald & Russell, 2006; Shook et al., 2000). Until recently, much of this research examined women as victims and men as perpetrators of sexual coercion. Various studies have reported that 20–35% of teenage and adult women have been victims of coerced sexual activity, most commonly in dating situations (Rhynard et al., 1997; Shrier et al., 1998; Small & Kerns, 1993). However, women are not the only ones to experience sexual coercion. A number of studies have revealed that high school and college men also report experiencing some form of coercive sexual activity (Archer, 2000; Russell & Oswald, 2001, 2002; Struckman-Johnson et al., 2003). For example, a survey of several hundred Canadian college students found that about 25% of the men and more than 40% of the women participants reported being pressured or forced into sexual activity during a dating experience in the past year (O'Sullivan et al., 1998). In another study, 10% of about 4,000 teenage males reported being pressured to have sexual intercourse (Shrier et al., 1998).

While sexual coercion in dating situations can be either verbal or physical, the verbal variety (e.g., threats to end a relationship or insistent arguing) is considerably more common. A study of college students found that 82% of participants reported using verbal sexual coercion and 21% acknowledged using physical sexual coercion against a dating partner in the past year (Shook et al., 2000). However, it is important to note that although many of the women in the studies previously cited were physically forced to engage in unwanted sex acts, physical force is considerably less likely to be used in the sexual coercion of men (Krahe et al., 2003; Struckman-Johnson et al., 2003).

## Acquaintance Rape: The Role of Perceptions and Communication

Earlier in this chapter, we examined the relationship between sexual coercion and cultural expectations for males in our society. The socializing process that encourages men to be aggressive to get what they want is undoubtedly an important factor in rape and sexual coercion. As many have pointed out, in our society many males and females learn **sexual scripts** that encourage men to be aggressive and women to be passive (Byers & O'Sullivan, 1996; Carpenter, 1998; Dworkin & O'Sullivan, 2005). Yet some experts argue that in at least some cases of acquaintance rape, the picture is more complicated.

**Sexual scripts** Culturally learned ways of behaving in sexual situations.

Consider the issue of men's misinterpretation of women's signals. Men often consider women's actions such as cuddling or kissing as indicating a desire to engage in intercourse (Muehlenhard, 1988; Muehlenhard & Linton, 1987). However, a woman who feels like cuddling does not necessarily want to have sex, and she may express this to her date. Even if a woman clearly expresses her desire not to have sex, her date may read her actions as "token resistance," concluding that she really wants to have sex but does not want to appear "too easy" (Krahe et al., 2000; Muehlenhard & Hollabaugh, 1989).

In some cases this "reading" is entirely motivated by exploitative self-interest. But some women do say no when they mean yes. One study of 610 female undergraduates revealed that 39.3% had engaged in token resistance to sex at least once. Reasons for saying no when they really meant yes included not wanting to appear promiscuous, uncertainty about a partner's feelings, undesirable surroundings, game playing (wanting a partner to be more physically aggressive, to persuade her to have sex, etc.), and desiring to be in control (Muehlenhard & Hollabaugh, 1989). This kind of double message may actually promote rape by providing men with a rationale for ignoring sincere refusals. The researchers in this study concluded that if a man has had the experience of ignoring a woman's protests only to find that she actually did want to have sex, then "his belief that women's refusals are not to be taken seriously will be strengthened" (Muehlenhard & Hollabaugh, 1989, p. 878). He may thus proceed with his sexual advances despite further protests and genuine resistance from his date. Such a man may not even define his actions as rape.

The concept of token resistance underscores the fact that many sexual interactions are beset with problems of poor communication. The ambiguity and miscommunication that often characterize sexual encounters underscore the importance of building a foundation of clear communication, a topic addressed in Chapter 7.

Even men who believe their female partner when she says no may think that it is defensible to use force to obtain sex if they feel that they have been "led on." A number of studies have found that many men regard rape as justifiable, or at least hold the woman more responsible than themselves, if she leads a man on by such actions as dressing "suggestively" or going to his apartment (Muehlenhard & Linton, 1987; Muehlenhard et al., 1991; Workman & Freeburg, 1999). The implications of these findings for acquaintance rape prevention are discussed in the box titled "Dealing With Rape and Attempted Rape" on the following page.

> **? Critical Thinking Question**
>
> Why might people engage in unwanted sexual activity when force is not used? Do you think there are reasons that are common to both sexes? What explanations might apply to only one sex?

## Date Rape Drugs

In the early 1990s reports began to circulate about the increasing use of Rohypnol (roh-HIPnol) to facilitate sexual conquest or to incapacitate victims who are then sexually molested or raped (O'Neill, 1997; Staten, 1997). Rohypnol, commonly known on the street as "roofies," is the brand name for flunitrazepam, a powerful tranquilizer that has a sedative effect 7 to 10 times more potent than that of Valium. In addition to producing a sedative effect in 20 to 30 minutes that can last for several hours, Rohypnol causes muscle relaxation and mild to pronounced amnesia (Romeo, 2004). Rohypnol is odorless and is excreted from the victim's system in a relatively short time, making discovery and prosecution of rapists who use this drug difficult. Many cases have emerged in which women were raped after their dates had given them the drug surreptitiously—hence the term *date rape drug*. When combined with alcohol, the drug's effects are greatly enhanced and can result in a dramatic "high," markedly reduced inhibitions, unconsciousness, and total amnesia concerning events that occur while a person is under its influence. Rohypnol has also led to death. In March 2000, four men were sentenced to prison for involuntary manslaughter in the death of a 15-year-old girl in Michigan (Bradsher, 2000). This is one of the many deaths reportedly caused by Rohypnol.

In an effort to counter the negative image of Rohypnol as a date rape drug, the manufacturer, Roche Pharmaceuticals, has changed the color and formulation of this drug. The result is a pill that is more difficult to dissolve and that produces a blue solution when dissolved (Olsen et al., 2005). In addition, recently developed laboratory procedures have made it easy to detect this reformulated drug in drinks spiked to accomplish date rape (Olsen et al., 2005).

## Dealing With Rape and Attempted Rape

Although rape is a society-wide problem, it is the rape victim who experiences the direct, personal violation. The suggestions offered in the following lists present strategies for reducing the risk of acquaintance rape and for avoiding stranger rape. However, following these suggestions offers no guarantee of avoiding rape. Even a woman who leads an extremely cautious and restricted life can be assaulted. Rape prevention consists primarily of making it as difficult as possible for a rapist to victimize you. Many of the following suggestions are commonsense measures against other crimes besides rape.

### Reducing the Risk of Acquaintance Rape

1. The less you know about a person before meeting, the more important it is to be cautious. Thus, when dating someone for the first time, seriously consider doing so in a group situation or meeting your date at a public place. This will allow you to assess your date's behavior in a relatively safe environment.
2. Watch for indications that your date may be a dominating person who may try to control your behavior. A man who plans all activities and makes all decisions during a date may also be inclined to dominate in a private setting.
3. If the man drives and pays for all expenses, he may think he is justified in using force to get "what he paid for." If you cover some of the expenses, he may be less inclined to use this rationale to justify acting in a sexually coercive manner (Muehlenhard & Schrag, 1991; Muehlenhard et al., 1991).
4. Avoid using alcohol or other drugs when you definitely do not wish to be sexually intimate with your date. Consumption of alcohol or other drugs, by both victim and perpetrator, is commonly associated with acquaintance rape (Mohler-Kuo et al., 2004; Thompson & Kingree, 2006). Drug intoxication can both diminish your capacity to escape from an assault and reduce your date's reluctance to engage in assaultive behavior.
5. Avoid behavior that may be interpreted as "teasing." Clearly state what you do and do not wish to do in regard to sexual contact. For example, you might say, "I hope you do not misinterpret my inviting you back to my apartment. I definitely do not want to do anything more than relax, listen to some music, and talk." If you are interested in initiating an exploration of some kind of early physical contact, you might say, "Tonight I would like to hold you and kiss, but I would not be comfortable with anything else at this point in our relationship." Such direct communication can markedly reduce a man's inclinations to force unwanted sexual activity or to feel "led on" (Muehlenhard & Andrews, 1985; Muehlenhard et al., 1985).

Many women take self-defense training to protect themselves from assault.

6. If, despite direct communication about your intentions, your date behaves in a sexually coercive manner, you may use a "strategy of escalating forcefulness—direct refusal, vehement verbal refusal, and, if necessary, physical force" (Muehlenhard & Linton, 1987, p. 193). One study found that college students were most likely to label a scenario of date sex as rape if such activity was preceded by a clearly stated *no* (Sawyer et al., 1998). In another study, the response rated by men as most likely to get men to stop unwanted advances was for the woman to vehemently say, "This is rape, and I'm calling the cops" (Beal & Muehlenhard, 1987). If verbal protests are ineffective, reinforce your refusal with physical force, such as pushing, slapping, biting, kicking, or clawing your assailant. Men are more likely to perceive their actions as at least inappropriate, if not rape, when a woman protests not only verbally but also physically (Beal & Muehlenhard, 1987; Muehlenhard & Linton, 1987).

### Reducing the Risk of Stranger Rape

1. Do not advertise that you are a woman living alone. Use initials on your mailbox and in the phone book; even add a fictitious name.
2. Install and use secure locks on doors and windows, changing door locks after losing keys or moving into a new residence. A peephole in your front door can be particularly helpful.
3. Do not open your door to strangers. If a repairman or public official is at your door, ask him to identify himself and call his office to verify that he is a reputable person on legitimate business.

Other drugs, such as gamma hydroxybutyrate (GHB) and ketamine hydrochloride (Special K) have also been implicated in date rapes (Elliott & Burgess, 2005; Romeo, 2004). GHB was developed more than 40 years ago and was initially used as an anesthetic. Its mind-altering effects soon became well known, and it has become increasingly popular as a recreational drug—often with devastating results. GHB is a central

4. When you are in situations in which strangers may be encountered, demonstrate self-confidence through your body language and speech to communicate that you will not be intimidated. Research reveals that rapists often tend to select as victims women who exhibit passivity and submissiveness (Richards et al., 1991).
5. Take a cell phone with you when you are out alone.
6. Lock your car when it is parked and while you are driving.
7. Avoid dark and deserted areas and be aware of your surroundings when you are walking. Such precautions can help if you need an opportunity to escape. Should a driver ask for directions when you are a pedestrian, avoid approaching his car. Instead, call out your reply from a safe distance.
8. Have house or car keys in hand before going to your door, and check the backseat before getting into your car.
9. Should your car break down, attach a white cloth to the antenna and lock yourself in. If someone other than a uniformed officer in an official car stops to offer help, ask this person to call the police or a garage but do not open your locked car door.
10. Never hitchhike or provide rides to hitchhikers or get into a car with a stranger.
11. Wherever you go, it can be helpful to carry a device for making a loud noise, such as a whistle or, even better, a pint-sized compressed-air horn (available in many sporting goods and boat supply stores). Sound the noise alarm at the first sign of danger.

Many cities have crime-prevention bureaus that provide further suggestions and home-safety inspections.

### What to Do in Threatening Situations Involving Strangers

If you are approached by a man or men who may intend to rape you, you will have to decide what to do. *Each situation, assailant, and woman is unique. There are no absolute rules.*

1. Run away if you can.
2. Resist if you cannot run. Make it difficult for the rapist. On locating a potential victim, many men test her to see if she is easily intimidated. Resistance by the woman is often responsible for thwarting rape attempts (Heyden et al., 1999; Page, 1997). Active and vociferous resistance—shouting, being rude, causing a scene, running away, fighting back—may deter the attack. This was the finding of a study of 150 rapes or attempted rapes: Women who used forceful verbal or physical resistance (screaming, hitting, kicking, biting, running, and the like) were more likely to avoid being raped than women who tried pleading, crying, or offering no resistance (Zoucha-Jensen & Coyne, 1993).
3. Ordinary rules of behavior do not apply. Vomiting, screaming, or acting crazy—whatever you are willing to try—can be appropriate responses to an attempted rape.
4. Talking can be a way to stall and can give you a chance to devise an escape plan or another strategy. It can be helpful to get the attacker to start talking ("What has happened to make you so angry?"), to express some empathy ("It is really discouraging to lose a job"), or to negotiate ("Let's take time to talk about this"). Even when talking does not prevent an assault, it may reduce the degree of violence (Prentky et al., 1986).
5. Remain alert for an opportunity to escape. In some situations, it may be impossible to fight or elude an attacker initially. However, later on, you may have a chance to deter the attack and escape—for example, if the rapist becomes distracted or a passerby comes on the scene.

Self-defense classes are a resource for learning techniques of physical resistance that can injure the attacker(s) or distract him long enough for you to escape.

### What to Do if You Have Been Raped

If someone has raped you or tried to rape you, you will have to decide whether to report the attack to the police.

1. It is advisable to report a rape or even an unsuccessful rape attempt. The information you provide may prevent another woman from being raped.
2. When you report such an attack, any details you can remember about it may be helpful—the assaulter's physical characteristics, voice, clothes, car, even an unusual smell.
3. If you have been raped, you should call the police as soon as possible; do not bathe or change your clothes. Semen, hair, and material under fingernails or on your clothing may be useful in identifying the rapist.
4. It may be helpful to contact a rape crisis center, where qualified staff members can assist you in dealing with your trauma. Most large urban communities in the United States have such programs. If you cannot make the contact yourself, have a friend, family member, or the police make the call.
5. In addition to general counseling, there are effective treatment programs for women who have been raped. If your symptoms do not subside after a period of time, consider entering a treatment program. You do not have to continue to suffer.
6. Finally, it is important to remember that many women mistakenly blame themselves for the rape. However, being raped is not a crime; the crime has been committed by the man who raped you.

nervous system depressant that can be especially lethal when combined with alcohol (Elliott & Burgess, 2005). Since 1990, emergency rooms have reported thousands of cases of GHB overdoses, some of which have resulted in death (Elliott & Burgess, 2005; Smalley, 2003). GHB is odorless and tasteless, which makes it easy to administer to unsuspecting victims. GHB exits the body in 6 to 12 hours, which makes it an especially ideal drug for sexual predators, because a lack of toxicological evidence makes prosecution difficult.

It is important to be alert for potential victimization by means of a date rape drug. Do not accept a drink (alcohol, coffee, soda, etc.), especially an open-container beverage, from someone other than a trusted friend. Never leave your drink unattended. If you experience one or more of the following symptoms after ingesting a beverage, it is possible that your drink was tainted: nausea, dizziness, slurred speech, movement impairment, or euphoria. If you find yourself in such a circumstance, call 911 or ask someone other than your date or companion to help you seek medical attention and, if possible, retain a sample of the beverage. ■

As a result of abuse and deaths associated with date rape drugs, the U.S. Congress has passed laws that strengthen the penalties for possessing Rohypnol, GHB, and other similar drugs and that significantly increase the prison sentences for rapists who use drugs to incapacitate victims.

## Wartime Rape

Although rape is most often a coercive interaction between two individuals, it has also been a strategy of war throughout history. Records abound of the mass rape of women during war, from the time of ancient Greece to the more recent atrocities in Rwanda, Darfur, and the former Yugoslavia. In the 20th century hundreds of thousands of women have been victimized by wartime rape (Bergoffen, 2006; Polgreen, 2005; Van Zeijl, 2006). In the 1990s reports of mass rapes perpetrated by Serbian soldiers on thousands of Bosnian and Croatian women and girls increased the public's support for measures to label rape a war crime. Awareness was further heightened by reports that thousands of women and girls were raped during the 1994 war in Rwanda (Flanders, 1998). More recently rape has been employed as a weapon in the conflict in the Darfur region of Sudan (Polgreen, 2005).

U.S. soldiers have also been guilty of wartime rape. Cases of gang rape of Vietnamese women appear in the records of courts-martial for American troops in Vietnam (Brownmiller, 1993). American soldiers have also been prosecuted for raping Iraqi women during the invasion of Iraq. In 1996 the United Nations International Criminal Tribunal for the Former Yugoslavia ruled that wartime rape is a crime punishable by severe criminal sanctions (marking the first time that sexual assault was treated separately as a war crime). In 2001 this U.N. tribunal established "sexual enslavement" as a war crime and convicted several Bosnian Serbs for the multiple rapes of Muslim women enslaved in so-called rape camps. Convicted rapists received sentences ranging from 12 to 28 years (Comiteau, 2001).

Why is rape so common during war? Wartime rape, in addition to being used as a means to dominate, humiliate, and control women, "can also be intended to disable an enemy by destroying the bonds of family and society" (Swiss & Giller, 1993, pp. 612–613). In wars instigated by ethnic conflict, as in the former Yugoslavia, Rwanda, and Darfur, mass rape is used as a military strategy to terrorize and demoralize a whole population, to destroy its cultural integrity, and sometimes to force entire communities to flee their houses, thereby achieving the goal of "ethnic cleansing" (Carlson, 1997; Eaton, 2004; Hargreaves, 2004; Shanks et al., 2001). Thus rape is an act of war that assaults not only the individual woman but also her family and her community.

The Sexuality and Diversity discussion on punishing women who have been raped provides insights into how societal reaction to rape, whether during wartime or otherwise, can add to the suffering of rape victims.

## SEXUALITY AND DIVERSITY

### Punishing Women Who Have Been Raped

How would it feel to be raped by your enemies and then rejected by your family and friends for being sexually violated? Shortly after the war in Kosovo ended in 1999, reports surfaced in the press of the difficulties that Kosovar women who had been raped were having as they returned to their homes and families.

Despite the tremendous suffering they had already endured from being sexually assaulted, if these women admitted that they had been raped, they risked being disowned by their families and friends. Instead of getting the support and compassion that they deserved, which have been shown to be helpful in healing the wounds caused by trauma, they had to keep their painful memories, thoughts, and feelings locked away from others or risk being shunned by their families and communities (Lorch & Mendenhall, 2000).

During the recent 5-year war in the Congo, an estimated 1 in 3 Congolese women were subjected to gang rape so violent that thousands suffer from vaginal fistula (rupture of the vaginal wall, which can cause urine and feces to leak uncontrollably). Many of these victimized women, instead of receiving health care, have been abandoned by their husbands and ostracized by their communities (*Reproductive Health Matters*, 2004).

Unfortunately, these attitudes are not confined to Kosovo or the Congo. Research has shown that in the United States some men also tend to blame the victim of sexual abuse. In a study conducted among multiethnic groups in New York City, Cuban American men evaluated the teenage female *victim* of sexual abuse negatively (Rodriguez-Stednicki & Twaite, 1999). Another study found that Hispanic men in the United States tended to hold women more responsible for their rapes than did Caucasian men (Cowan, 2000).

Most of us find this blaming of the victim deplorable, but others argue that we need to accept that other cultures are different from ours and have a right to their own values. A recent investigation suggests, however, that these cultural attitudes and behaviors have a profoundly negative effect on the victims of rape and sexual assault. In a study that evaluated 157 victims of violent crime, researchers found that shame and anger play an important role in determining whether victims will develop posttraumatic stress disorder and that shame especially plays a role in the severity of the victim's subsequent symptoms (Andrews et al., 2000). Thus it would appear that cultural values that blame women who have been raped (and those who uphold and apply them) can be a major contributing factor to these victims' continued suffering.

## The Aftermath of Rape

Whether a person is raped by a stranger, an acquaintance, or a partner, the experience can be traumatic and can have long-term repercussions. Given the characteristics of rape—the physical violation and psychological trauma that it inflicts and our societal attitudes about it—it is understandable that many rape survivors suffer long-lasting emotional effects.

Feelings of shame, anger, fear, guilt, depression, and powerlessness are common (Draucker & Stern, 2000; Koss et al., 2002; Vandeusen & Carr, 2003). One of the reasons that some women feel guilt and shame is that they are often seen, and see themselves, as being responsible—no matter what the circumstances—for not preventing unwanted sexual activity from taking place. Another reason for these uncomfortable feelings is that women who have been raped may have experienced arousal, even to the point of orgasm, during the assault (Sarrel & Masters, 1982). Sexual response during an assault, particularly if orgasm occurs, can be a source of great distress to rape survivors, and in some instances they may find their sexual response to be more upsetting than the physical and psychological trauma produced by the assault. However, as sex researcher Alfred Kinsey and his associates noted, "The physiologic mechanism of any emotional response (anger, fright, pain, etc.) may be the mechanism of sexual response" (Kinsey et al., 1948, p. 165). Thus, responding sexually during an intense experience may be a normal physiological reaction for some.

In addition to the psychological impact of rape, physical symptoms such as nausea, headaches, gastrointestinal problems, genital injuries, and sleep disorders also frequently occur (Hilden et al., 2005; Krakow et al., 2000; Ullman & Brecklin, 2003). Approximately 32% of women and 16% of men who were raped after age 18 reported being physically injured during the assault (Tjaden & Thoennes, 1998). Rape survivors may associate sexual activity with the trauma of their assault. As a result, sexual activity may induce anxiety rather than desire or arousal (Koss et al., 2002, 2003). In one long-term study of rape survivors, 40% refrained from sexual contact for 6 months to 1 year after the assault, and almost 75% reported decreased sexual activity for as long as 6 years (Burgess & Holmstrom, 1979).

**Posttraumatic stress disorder (PTSD)** A psychological disorder caused by exposure to overwhelmingly painful events.

When the emotional and physical reactions women experience following rape or attempted rape are severe, victims may be classified as suffering from **posttraumatic stress disorder (PTSD)**. PTSD, an official diagnostic category of the American Psychiatric Association (2000), refers to the long-term psychological distress that can develop after a person is subjected to a physically or psychologically traumatic event (or events). People who experience a profoundly disturbing incident, such as sexual assault, wartime combat, or a horrendous accident, often exhibit a range of distressing symptoms as an aftermath of the occurrence. These reactions include disturbing dreams, nightmares, depression, anxiety, and feelings of extreme vulnerability. In addition, just as combat veterans may have flashbacks of traumatic war experiences, so too might a rape survivor have vivid flashbacks of the attack in which she re-experiences all the terror of the assault. Research indicates that rape produces one of the highest rates of PTSD among nonwartime traumatic events (Koss et al., 2002; Ullman et al., 2005).

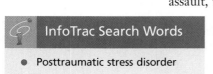

InfoTrac Search Words

- Posttraumatic stress disorder

Victims often find that supportive counseling, either individually or in groups, can help ease the trauma caused by rape (Romeo, 2004; Symes, 2000; Vandeusen & Carr, 2003). Research has shown that women who receive help soon after an assault experience less severe emotional repercussions than women whose treatment is delayed (Campbell, 2006; Duddle, 1991). Most rape survivors find that it helps to talk about their assault and the emotional upheaval they are experiencing. Often the process of reviewing the event allows them to gain control over their painful feelings and to begin the process of healing. The box titled "Helping a Partner or Friend Recover From Rape" suggests ways to communicate and interact with a rape victim.

## Rape and Sexual Assault of Males

Health professionals who work with rape survivors know that men are raped. Although the vast majority of rape victims are women, men are also targets of sexual aggression, including rape (Davies et al, 2006; Kassing et al., 2005; Krahe et al., 2003). The survey conducted by Tjaden and Thoennes (1998), described earlier, found that 3% of male respondents had experienced completed or attempted rape. An exhaustive review of 120 studies of sexual victimization that collectively analyzed data from more than 100,000 respondents found incidence rates for completed and attempted male rape by female perpetrators of 3.3% and 5.5%, respectively (Spitzberg, 1999). More recently, two German surveys of several hundred heterosexual men reported incidence rates for attempted and completed female-perpetrated rape of 2.8% and 4.0% (study 1) and 5.2% and 2.6% (study 2), respectively (Krahe et al., 2003).

Statistics on the frequency of male sexual victimization have been difficult to obtain for a variety of reasons, not the least of which is that men are even less likely than women to report that they have been raped (Davies et al., 2006; Kassing et al, 2005; Mitchell et al., 1999). It is estimated that only 1 in 10 male rapes are reported to the police (Kassing et al., 2005). One reason for this failure to report may be that men fear they will be judged harshly if they report abuse. At least one study supports this concern (Spencer & Tan, 1999). The investigators found that men who reported being sexually abused were viewed negatively, especially by other men. Victimized men may also anticipate that law enforcement personnel may not believe that a crime occurred or may believe that they somehow instigated or asked for the rape (Kassing et al., 2005; Walker et al., 2005). In addition, men who are socialized to be physically strong and able to protect themselves may believe that reporting their victimization will reflect weakness or personal blame (Kassing et al., 2005).

The sexual assault of men is rarely reported in the media or in the psychological and medical literature (Stermac et al., 1996). The result is that little research has been conducted on the issue of sexual aggression against men (Krahe et al., 2000, 2003). In fact, only in the last decade or so have many states revised their criminal codes to include adult males as victims in the definition of rape (Isely & Gehrenbeck-Shim, 1997).

# Helping a Partner or Friend Recover From Rape

The rape of a partner or friend can be a difficult experience for both partners and friends of rape survivors. To some degree, partners and close friends are also victimized by the assault. They may feel a range of emotions, including rage, disgust, and helplessness. They may also be confused and unsure about how to react to a lover's or friend's victimization. This confusion can prove painful for all concerned because reactions of partners and friends can profoundly affect a rape survivor's recovery. In the following list, we suggest ways to communicate and interact with a rape victim to help her recover from this traumatic experience. Some of these suggestions are adapted from two excellent books: *Sexual Solutions* (1980), by Michael Castleman, and *"Friends" Raping Friends: Could It Happen to You?* (1987), by Jean Hughes and Bernice Sandler. Although we will frequently refer to the victim as female, our recommendations are equally applicable to male rape survivors.

1. *Listen.* Probably the most important thing a person can do to help a rape victim begin recovering is to listen to her. A person comforting a rape survivor might understandably try to divert her attention from the terrible event. However, professionals who work with survivors of sexual assault have found that many victims need to talk repeatedly about the assault to come to terms with it. A partner or friend can help by encouraging her to discuss the rape as often as she can, in any way that she can.

2. *Let her know you believe her account of what happened.* A rape survivor needs to be believed by people she loves or feels close to. Consequently, it is essential to accept her version of the assault without questioning any of the facts. A simple statement, such as "What you describe is an intolerable violation, and I am so sorry that you had to endure such a dreadful experience," will convey both your acceptance of her account and your empathy with her pain.

3. *Let her know that it was not her fault and that she is not to blame.* Many victims of rape believe that they were somehow responsible for the attack ("I should not have invited him to my home," "I should have tried to fight him," or the like). Such impressions can lead to profound feelings of guilt. Try to head off these damaging self-recriminations by stating clearly and calmly, "I know that you are not to blame for what happened," or "You are the victim here and not responsible for what happened to you."

4. *Control your own emotions.* The last thing a rape survivor needs is the response of the partner who gets sidetracked by focusing attention on his or her own anger or imagined shortcomings ("I should have been along to protect you"). She has just been victimized by a violent man (or men), and being confronted with her own partner's or friends' outbursts will not help her regain control.

5. *Give comfort.* A rape victim is urgently in need of comfort, especially from someone she loves or cares about. She may want to be held, and the nurturing comfort of being encircled by the arms of someone she trusts may provide a powerful beginning to the process of healing. On the other hand, she also may not want to be touched at all. Respect that wish. Words can also be quite nurturing. Simply being told, "I love you very much and will be here for you in any way that is right for you" may offer a great deal of welcome comfort.

6. *Allow the victim to make decisions.* A rape survivor may recover more quickly when she is able to decide for herself how to deal with the assault. Making her own decisions about what should be done after a rape is an important step in regaining control over her life after having been stripped of control by her attacker(s). Asking some open-ended questions (see Chapter 7) may help her regain control. Questions might include, "What kind of living arrangements for the next few days or weeks would you be comfortable with?" or "What can I do for you now?" Sometimes suggesting alternatives can be helpful. For example, while encouraging her to take some type of positive action, you might ask, "Would you like to call the police, go to a hospital, or call a rape hotline?" Remember, the decision is hers and one that needs to be respected and not questioned even if you do not agree with it.

7. *Offer shelter.* If she does not already live with you, offer to stay with her at her home, have her stay with you, or assist her in securing other living arrangements with which she is comfortable. Again, this is her choice to make.

8. *Continue to provide support.* In the days, weeks, and even months following the rape, partners and friends can continue to offer empathy, support, and reassurance to a rape survivor. They can encourage her to resume a normal life and be there for her when she feels particularly vulnerable, fearful, or angry. They can take time to listen, even if it means hearing the same things over and over again. If her assailant is prosecuted, she is likely to need support and understanding throughout the often arduous legal proceedings.

9. *Be patient about resuming sexual activity.* Resuming sexual activity after a rape may present problems for both the victim and her partner. Rape may precipitate sexual difficulties for the woman; she may not want to be sexually intimate for quite a while. However, some women may desire relations very soon after the attack, perhaps for assurance that their lovers still care for them and do not consider them "tainted."

    Open-ended questions may help to fuel dialogue about resuming sexual sharing. Possibly helpful queries include "What are your thoughts and feelings about being sexual with me?" or "What kinds of concerns do you have about resuming our sexual activity?"

    Some women may prefer not to have intercourse for a while, opting instead for just closeness and affection. Deciding when and how to engage in intimate sharing is best left up to the woman. Her partner's support in this matter is important. Even when sexual intimacy resumes, it may be some time before she is able to relax and respond the way she did before the rape. A patient, sensitive partner can help her reach the point where she is again able to experience satisfying sexual intimacy.

10. *Consider counseling.* Sometimes a rape victim needs more help than lovers, friends, and families are able to provide, no matter how supportive they are. People close to her may recognize these needs and encourage her to seek professional help. Short- or long-term therapy may help a victim recover from the emotional trauma and reconstruct her life. Similarly, partners of sexually assaulted women may also need help coping with severe conflicts and deep feelings of rage and guilt.

Rapes of males may be perpetrated by heterosexual men, who often commit their crime with one or more cohorts (Frazier, 1993; Isely & Gehrenbeck-Shim, 1997). As in rape of women, violence and power are often associated with the sexual assault of men. The possibility of being raped is a serious issue among male homosexuals because they are often the victims of such attacks. Although homosexual men are frequently raped by heterosexual men, the rapist is often a homosexual man who is a current or former sexual partner (Hickson et al., 1994; Walker et al., 2005).

Rape of inmates in penal institutions is a serious problem (Bell, 2006; Hensley et al., 2003). One comprehensive survey of almost 2,000 male inmates in 7 prisons found that 21% had been sexually threatened or assaulted and 7% acknowledged being raped (Struckman-Johnson & Struckman-Johnson, 2000). Men who do the raping typically consider themselves heterosexual. When released, they usually resume sexual relations with women. The men who are raped often experience brutal gang assaults. Such a man may become the sexual partner of one particular dominant inmate for protection from others (Braen, 1980).

If a man is forced to penetrate someone's vagina, anus, or mouth with his penis, this is also classified as rape (McCabe & Wauchope, 2005). Accounts of men being sexually coerced by women who use threats of bodily harm have been reported with increasing frequency (Kassing et al., 2005). The idea that mature males can be raped by women has been widely rejected because it has been assumed that a man cannot function sexually in a state of extreme anxiety or fear. However, this common impression is not accurate. Alfred Kinsey and his associates were perhaps the earliest sex researchers to note that both sexes can function sexually in a variety of severe emotional states. Sexual response during sexual assault, particularly if orgasm occurs, may be a source of great confusion and anxiety for both female and male rape survivors.

Philip Sarrel and William Masters (1982) reported on 11 men who had been raped by women. None of the victims had reported the assault, and none could talk about it until he became involved in therapy several years later. All of these men experienced emotional distress, sexual performance anxieties, feelings of inadequacy, and impaired sexual functioning. Other studies have also reported that, like women, men who are sexually assaulted often experience long-term emotional and sexual consequences (Kassing et al., 2005; Walker et al., 2005).

Sexual assault of males also occurs during war. However, men as victims of wartime rape and sexual assault have received only scant media coverage and limited research attention. Among the few studies in this area are investigations of male sexual assault during wars in Greece (Lindholm et al., 1980), El Salvador (Agger & Jensen, 1994), and Croatia (Medical Center for Human Rights, 1995). The widespread belief that only females can be victimized by sexual assault has led many national legal systems to bury the issue of wartime male sexual assault under the more generalized categories of torture or abuse (Carlson, 1997). However, awareness that men also can be victimized was expanded when the International Criminal Tribunal for the Former Yugoslavia reported that many men were raped or otherwise sexually assaulted during the conflict in that region (Carlson, 1997).

## Sexual Abuse of Children

The sexual (and physical and emotional) abuse of children in U.S. society and throughout the world is a problem of staggering proportions. Child sexual abuse can have long-lasting, painful effects. Consider the following:

> *When I was ten, my mother remarried, and we moved into my stepfather's house. When I was eleven he started coming upstairs to say goodnight to me. The touching began soon after and lasted for years. I used to just lie there and pray that he would go away, but he never did. For a long time I thought it was my fault. I had trouble being in a sexual relationship because I felt so guilty, so dirty. I thought that if I didn't exist this never would have happened. I think my mother may have known, but she never did anything. She didn't want to upset things, because she was afraid of being alone again, of being poor. (Authors' files)*

In this section, we look at the prevalence of child sexual abuse, the effects it has on many of its victims, what can be done to reduce the incidence of such abuse, and how to help those who have been abused. **Child sexual abuse** is defined as engagement by an adult in sexual contact of any kind with a child (inappropriate touching, oral–genital stimulation, coitus, etc.). Even if no overt violence or threats of violence occur, such interaction is considered coercive and illegal because a child is not considered mature enough to provide informed consent to sexual involvement. Informed consent implies the possession of adequate intellectual and emotional maturity to understand fully both the meaning and possible consequences of a particular action. Adults' exploitation of the naiveté of unsuspecting victims has become a serious problem for children who use the Internet, as discussed later in this chapter.

Most researchers distinguish between nonrelative child sexual abuse, referred to as **pedophilia** or **child molestation**, and **incest**, which is sexual contact between two people who are related (one of whom is often a child). Incest includes sexual contact between siblings as well as sexual contact between children and their parents, grandparents, uncles, or aunts. Incest can occur between related adults, but more commonly it involves a child and an adult relative (or an older sibling) perpetrator. Although its definition varies slightly from culture to culture, incest is one of the world's most widely prohibited sexual behaviors.

Each state has its own legal codes that determine whether sexual interaction between an adult and a younger person is considered child molestation (usually if the younger person is under age 12), statutory rape (usually age 12 to 16 or 17), or a consenting sexual act. The age of consent in the United States tends to range from 16 to 18, but it can be as low as 14 or 15 (Findholt & Robrecht, 2002). The legal codes may appear ludicrous at times, particularly in cases of teenage interactions in which one partner is technically an adult and the other technically a minor, although only one or two years separate their ages.

Incest occurs at all socioeconomic levels and is illegal regardless of the ages of the participants. However, an incestuous relationship between consenting adult relatives is considerably less likely to precipitate legal action than one between an adult and a child.

Although it has been commonly assumed that father-daughter incest is most prevalent, studies have shown that brother-sister and first-cousin contacts are more common (Canavan et al., 1992; Finkelhor, 1979). Sexual relations between brothers and sisters are seldom discovered, and when they are, they do not typically elicit the extreme reactions that father-daughter sexual contacts usually do. However, coercive sexual abuse by a sibling or a parent often has a devastating effect on the child victim.

The incestuous involvement of a father (or stepfather) with his daughter often begins without the child understanding its significance. It may start as playful activities involving wrestling, tickling, kissing, and touching. Over time the activities may expand to include touching of the breasts and genitals, perhaps followed by oral or manual stimulation and intercourse. In most cases, the father relies on his position of authority or on the pair's emotional closeness rather than on physical force to fulfill his desires. He may pressure his daughter into sexual activity by reassuring her that he is "teaching" her something important, by offering rewards, or by exploiting her need for love. Later, when she realizes that the behavior is not appropriate or when she finds her father's demands to be unpleasant and traumatizing, it may be difficult for her to escape. Occasionally, a daughter may value the relationship for the special recognition or privileges it brings her. The incestuous involvement may come to public attention when she gets angry with her father, often for nonsexual reasons, and "tells on him." Sometimes a mother may discover, to her horror, what has been transpiring between her husband and daughter. Other times, the mother may have been aware of the incest but allowed it to continue for reasons of her own. These may include shame, fear of reprisals, concern about having her family disrupted, or the fact that the incestuous activity allows her to avoid her husband's demands for sex.

Father-daughter sexual abuse is more likely to be reported to authorities than other varieties of incest. However, a child often does not report being victimized because of fear that the family may be disrupted—through imprisonment for the father, economic difficulties for the mother, and perhaps placement in foster homes

**Child sexual abuse** An adult's engaging in sexual contact of any kind with a child, including inappropriate touching, oral–genital stimulation, and coitus.

**Pedophilia, or child molestation** Sexual contact between an adult and a child who are not related.

**Incest** Sexual contact between two people who are related (one of whom is often a child), other than husband and wife.

> **InfoTrac Search Words**
>
> - Child sexual abuse
> - Pedophilia

for the victim and other siblings. Separation or divorce may result. Sometimes the victim herself is blamed. These potential consequences of revealing an incestuous relationship place tremendous pressures on the child to keep quiet. For these and other reasons, she may be extremely reluctant to tell anyone else in her family, let alone another adult such as a teacher or neighbor.

## Characteristics of People Who Sexually Abuse Children

No classic profile of the pedophile offender has been identified, other than that most pedophiles are heterosexual males and are known to the victim (Murray, 2000; Salter et al., 2003). Child molesters cover the spectrum of social class, educational achievement, intelligence, occupation, religion, and ethnicity. Evidence suggests that many pedophile offenders, especially those who are prosecuted, are shy, lonely, poorly informed about sexuality, and moralistic or religious (Bauman et al., 1984). Many are likely to have poor interpersonal and sexual relations with other adults and may feel socially inadequate and inferior (Dreznick, 2003; Minor & Dwyer, 1997). However, it is not uncommon to encounter pedophiles outside the legal system who are well educated, socially adept, civic-minded, and financially successful (Baur, 1995). They often pick their victims from among family friends, neighbors, or acquaintances (Murray, 2000). Relating to these children sexually may be a way of coping with powerful feelings of inadequacy that are likely to emerge in sociosexual relationships with other adults.

Other characteristics of some child molesters include alcoholism, severe marital problems, sexual difficulties, and poor emotional adjustment (Johnston, 1987; McKibben et al., 1994). Many of these offenders were sexually victimized themselves during their own childhood (Bouvier, 2003; Putnam, 2003).

Like pedophiles, perpetrators of incest are primarily males who cannot be easily identified or categorized by a classic profile. Rather, "they are a complex, heterogeneous group of individuals who look like everyone else" (Scheela & Stern, 1994, p. 91). However, the incest offender does tend to share some of the traits of many pedophiles. He tends to be economically disadvantaged, heavy drinking, unemployed, devoutly religious, and emotionally immature (Rosenberg, 1988; Valliant et al., 2000). His behavior might result from general tendencies toward pedophilia, severe feelings of inadequacy in adult sexual relations, or rejection by a hostile spouse; his actions can also be an accompaniment to alcoholism or other psychological disturbances (Rosenberg, 1988). He also tends to have certain distorted ideas about adult-child sex. For example, he may think that a child who does not resist him desires sexual contact, that adult-child sex is an effective way for children to learn about sex, that a father's relationship with his daughter is enhanced by having sexual contact with her, and that a child does not report such contact because she enjoys it (Abel et al., 1984).

## Prevalence of Child Sexual Abuse

How high is the incidence of child sexual abuse in the United States? It is difficult to estimate the incidence of either incest or pedophilia. For reasons previously mentioned, child victims of incest frequently do not reveal what is occurring at the time and may not utter a word about it until they reach adulthood, if then. Acts of child molestation are unlikely to be reported at the time they occur for several reasons. For example, a child may be unable to distinguish between expressions of affection and illicit sexual contact. Often, when a child does inform his or her parents of improper sexual advances, the parents may not believe the child or may be reluctant to expose the child, themselves, or a spouse to prosecution, with its resultant stress on the family. That the offender is often a family friend, an acquaintance, or perhaps a community or religious leader can further complicate the issue.

Because child sexual abuse often goes unreported at the time it occurs, researchers have relied heavily on reports provided by adults regarding their childhood experiences of sexual abuse. The estimates of child abuse in U.S. society are startling. Various surveys indicate that the proportion of girls victimized ranges from 20% to 33%, whereas comparable figures for boys range from 9% to 16% (Finkelhor, 1993, 1994; Gorey & Leslie, 1997; Guidry, 1995). To date, the most comprehensive effort to estimate the prevalence of child sexual abuse was a 1997 meta-analysis in which data from 16 separate studies were combined and analyzed. Each of the investigations— 14 U.S. and 2 Canadian studies—surveyed adult subjects who were asked to recall experiences of sexual abuse inflicted on them before they reached age 18. Combining these diverse samples yielded an aggregate sample of about 14,000 respondents. A summarization of all the studies indicated that approximately 22% of the women and 9% of the men reported being sexually abused as children (Gorey & Leslie, 1997).

We should also realize that, although the clinical literature has indicated that more girls than boys are victims of sexual abuse, the number of young boys who are sexually molested in the United States may be substantially higher than previously estimated (Denov, 2003a, 2003b). In fact, two recent surveys found that almost one-fourth of male participants reported having experienced some form of sexual abuse by age 13 (Dilorio et al., 2002; Stander et al., 2002).

Mental health professionals have become increasingly aware that, although most sexual abusers of children are male, some children, both female and male, are sexually abused by women, often their mothers (Denov, 2003b; Goldman & Padayachi, 2000; Guidry, 1995). The belief that women sometimes sexually victimize children has been slow to emerge, both because of the prevailing notion that such abuse is a male activity and because "this subject is more of a taboo because female sexual abuse is more threatening—it undermines feelings about how women should relate to children" (Elliott, 1992, p. 12).

The statistics on the prevalence of sexual abuse of children have aroused significant controversy. Some people claim that the statistics underestimate the problem, and others claim that they overestimate it. One of the most controversial types of reports has concerned the case of adults reporting so-called recovered memories of sexual abuse that they endured as children.

## Recovered Memories of Childhood Sexual Abuse

The media have reported numerous cases in which alleged perpetrators of sexual abuse have been accused and convicted based on the testimony of adult women who "recover" memories of their childhood sexual abuse. This "recovery" has usually occurred during psychotherapy. But can a person repress memories of sexual abuse that may have occurred years or decades earlier and then suddenly or gradually "recover" them after exposure to certain triggering stimuli? Or can a "memory" of an event that never happened in childhood be suggested to an adult and then "remembered" as true? These questions lie at the heart of a debate among clinicians, researchers, and lawyers.

Skeptics of recovered memories claim that thousands of families and individuals have been devastated by the widespread inclination to accept claims of recovered memories at face value, in the absence of validating evidence. These skeptics offer as proof of their concern cases in which falsely accused and convicted individuals were later exonerated, either by the legal system or by victim recantation (Frazier, 2006; Gardner, 2006; Hoover, 1997).

The possibility of being falsely accused of such a heinous crime is the substance of nightmares. But just how often are the accusations false; that is, what is the probability that recovered memories are imagined? To gain some perspective on this issue, let us briefly consider some of the evidence.

Support for the legitimacy of recovered memories has been provided by several studies. In one investigation 129 adult women who had experienced childhood sexual abuse in the 1970s were identified and interviewed in the 1990s. Of this group, 38% did not recall the abuse that had been reported and documented 17 years earlier. The author of this investigation concluded that, if having no recall of child sexual abuse is a common occurrence for adult women, as indicated by the study's results, then "later recovery of child sexual abuse by some women should not be surprising" (Williams, 1994, p. 1174). In another study, 56% of 45 adult women survivors of childhood sexual abuse indicated that they had been amnesic about their abuse for varied lengths of time, and 16% reported remembering their abuse while receiving psychotherapy (Rodriguez et al., 1997). A survey of several hundred university students found that

20% of 111 victims of childhood sexual abuse reported that they had recovered memories of abuse (Melchert & Parker, 1997). Finally, a national survey of a sample of psychologists found that about 25% of the respondents reported being sexually abused in their childhood and that 40% of these victimized individuals stated that they had forgotten the abuse for various lengths of time (Feldman-Summers & Pope, 1994).

On the other hand, several researchers have expressed skepticism about recovered memories of childhood sexual abuse. Some have argued that "repressed memories" are inadvertently planted in suggestible clients by overzealous or poorly trained psychotherapists who believe that most psychological problems stem from childhood sexual abuse (Gardner, 2006; Gross, 2004; Yapko, 1994). Numerous studies have demonstrated the relative ease with which "memories" of events that never occurred can be created in the research laboratory (Brainerd & Reyna, 1998; Loftus et al., 1994; Porter et al., 1999). In one 11-week study, for instance, young children were asked at weekly intervals whether they had ever experienced five distinct events. Four of the events were real, and one—getting treated in the hospital for an injured finger—was fictitious. The children readily recognized the real events. However, more than one-third also became gradually convinced over the course of the 11 weeks that one of their fingers had been injured. In some cases, they even "remembered" elaborate details about their injuries. Many continued to insist that these false memories were true even after being told otherwise (Ceci et al., 1994).

Clearly, the concept of client suggestibility has become central to the arguments offered by skeptics of recovered memories. Research has demonstrated that both children and adults are vulnerable to suggestibility (Gross, 2004). However, the results of one investigation challenge the suggestibility rationale for dismissing reports of recovered memories of childhood sexual abuse. In this study, suggestibility was measured in 44 women who had reported recovered memories of childhood sexual abuse and in a comparison group of 31 women without a history of sexual abuse. The subjects without a history of abuse were more inclined to alter memory to suggestive prompts than were the recovered-memory subjects (Leavitt, 1997). In contrast, a different study reported that women who claimed to have recovered memories of childhood sexual abuse were more likely to make memory errors than those who were sexually abused as children and always remembered it (Clancy et al., 2000).

So where are we now on this controversial issue? The American Psychological Association, the American Psychiatric Association, and the American Medical Association have all issued statements supporting the belief that memories can be recovered later in life. These professional organizations also acknowledge that a "memory" may be suggested and then remembered as true. As the controversy continues, it is important to remember that, despite the media spotlight on defendants who claim they have been falsely accused, sexual abuse of children is a fact, not a question. The recovered-memories debate must not turn back the clock to a time when victims of sexual abuse did not report their traumatic experiences out of fear of not being believed. In the same spirit, we must act responsibly to protect the innocent from wrongful accusations that stem from false memories.

## Pedophiles in Cyberspace

Before the emergence of the Internet, pedophiles were largely isolated. Now, with several pedophile support groups online, child molesters can exchange child pornography, discuss their molestation experiences, validate each other's abusive acts, and secure reinforcement for the shared belief that sexual interaction between adults and children is acceptable (Burke et al., 2002; Malesky & Ennis, 2004). The Internet has also facilitated victimization of children by pedophiles, who, "hiding behind a veil of anonymity, roam cyberspace relatively undetected, posing all sorts of pretenses in their efforts to lure unsuspecting victims" (Philaretou, 2005, p. 181). These cyberspace predators can explore the bulletin boards on the Internet and cruise chat rooms designed for children and teenagers. These chat rooms provide rich hunting grounds for adults seeking unsuspecting kids in need of attention and kids with confused notions of sexuality.

Typically, pedophiles first gain a child's trust by appearing to be genuinely empathic and interested in the child's problems and concerns. Then they may try to get their intended victim to agree to e-mail, postal mail, or phone contacts. Next they may send the child pornographic materials suggesting that adult-child sexual interaction is normal and appropriate. The final step is to arrange a meeting. One case in which this strategy was used involved a 32-year-old Seattle engineer, who used the Internet to lure a 13-year-old girl, whom he then repeatedly raped. He was sentenced in 2000 to a 23-year prison term. In New York State a 15-year-old boy's statement led police to a number of prominent local men who had been systematically abusing local boys, some as young as 13 (West, 2000).

In one of the most shocking cases of cyberspace pedophilia, a 10-year-old girl was invited to a slumber party at the home of a friend in Greenfield, California, in April 1996. During the night, images of her being molested by her friend's father were broadcast to other members of a sex club, who watched the event live on their computer monitors. This instance of pedophiles using the Internet for real-life and real-time abuse of a child resulted in indictments of 16 members of the club. By May 1997, 14 of the 16 had pled guilty, and the club leader was sentenced to life in prison (Mintz, 1997).

For many these stories bring up images of drooling, disheveled men in trench coats lurking at their computer terminals instead of around school playgrounds. However, such an easy stereotype does not reflect every cyberspace pedophile. Many offenders are upper-middle-class white males from a variety of professions who use the perceived anonymity of the Internet to explore their pedophilic fantasies, and sometimes, unfortunately, to act them out (Curry, 2000). What can be done to combat pedophiles in cyberspace? In September 1996 the U.S. Congress passed the Communications Decency Act (CDA), which prohibited the distribution of indecent materials to minors by computer. In July 1997 the Supreme Court overruled this legislation on constitutional grounds, concluding that the CDA would seriously erode the right of free speech (Levy, 1997). In 2002 the Supreme Court, in further defense of this right, struck down a section of the federal child pornography law that made it a crime to own or sell computer-created images of children engaged in sex ("virtual" child pornography). According to Justice Anthony Kennedy, making it a crime to show sexual images that only appear to be children would damage legitimate filmmakers, photographers, and advertisers (Savage, 2002). As a result of this decision, it is legal to display on the Internet both computer-generated images of children in sexual situations and depictions of minors by adult actors in sexual situations, provided that no real children are shown or "composited" into a sex scene.

The congressional page scandal of 2006, in which Florida Republican Congressman Mark Foley resigned after being accused of sending sexually explicit e-mail messages to male teenage pages, has prompted several states to pursue tougher penalties against adults who use the Internet to solicit minors for sex. While most states do have laws prohibiting adults from soliciting sex from minors via the Internet, interpretation of these laws is flawed. "It's unfortunate that it takes media attention on a case like this to bring to light these flaws in state child-protection laws" (Atwell-Davis in Bakst, 2006). In the authors' home state of Oregon, the 2007 legislature will consider a bill that will establish stiff penalties for adults who engage in sexually explicit conversations with minors via e-mail or chat rooms. Immediately after the page scandal surfaced, public officials in Texas proposed severe penalties for such offenses. New Hampshire governor John Lynch has called for stiffer sentences for Internet predators. California recently passed a law that facilitates prosecution of Internet predators. We hope that these state-by-state trends indicate that the congressional page scandal will expose weaknesses in online predator laws and result in more-stringent measures to protect youth from Internet predators throughout the United States.

Florida Republican Congressman Mark Foley resigned in September 2006 after being accused of sending sexually explicit e-mail messages to male teenage pages.

Some of the gateways to the Internet, such as America Online (AOL), have attempted to protect children from cyberspace predators by using "guards" to monitor kids-only chat rooms for inappropriate or suspicious dialogue. Unfortunately, these efforts are only minimally effective, because private messages cannot be screened. Knowledgeable cyberspace pedophiles are most likely to make conversations private before making inappropriate overtures. A recent announcement by MySpace.com that it will develop technologies to block access of convicted sex offenders to this popular online hangout is an encouraging development in efforts to protect youth from cyberspace predators.

Even if widely applied and effective laws or in-house procedures existed to curb cyberspace pedophilia, the responsibility for protecting children resides with parents. Just as most of us would not allow our children to play unsupervised in dangerous places, we should not allow them to cruise cyberspace or spend time in chat rooms without supervision. One potentially helpful strategy is to keep computers in a central location where children can be monitored more easily when they go online. It would be especially beneficial for parents to go online with a child to instruct him or her in how to identify inappropriate requests. Parents should instruct their children never to give out personal information, such as a phone number or home address, without parental approval. Parents should also be clear that a child should never meet a cyberspace acquaintance in person without a parent or another responsible adult present. Finally, parents concerned about cyberspace pornography may wish to purchase Internet filtering software designed to block children's access to Web sites with obscene pictures or words. Screening software may help to curtail children's surfing of pornographic sites, but unfortunately it offers little protection to children exposed to pedophiles in chat rooms. Parents who want to learn more about Internet safety can explore three Web sites, listed at the end of this chapter, that deal with this issue.

## Effects of Child Sexual Abuse

Much research suggests that child sexual abuse can be a severely traumatizing and emotionally damaging experience, with long-term negative consequences for many of the victims (Dong et al., 2003; Miner et al., 2006; Noll et al., 2003). Clinical contact with adult survivors of child sexual abuse often reveals memories of a childhood filled with distress and confusion. Survivors speak of their loss of childhood innocence, the contamination and interruption of normal sexual development, and a profound sense of betrayal by a relative, family friend, priest or clergy person, or a community leader.

A number of factors influence the severity of a child victim's response to sexual abuse. The longer the molestation goes on, the worse the prognosis is for recovery from the trauma of the abuse (McLean & Gallop, 2003; Vandeusen & Carr, 2003). Feelings of powerlessness and betrayal may be especially pronounced when physical force is used to perpetrate an act of child sexual abuse or when the victim has a close relationship to the offender. These two factors—physical force and victim-offender relationship—probably correlate strongest with subsequent negative consequences for survivors of child sexual abuse (Hanson et al., 2001; Rind & Tromovitch, 1997).

Many victims of child sexual abuse have difficulty forming intimate adult relationships (Rumstein-McKean & Hunsley, 2001; Vandeusen & Carr, 2003). When relationships are established, they often lack emotional and sexual fulfillment (Jackson et al., 1990; Rumstein-McKean & Hunsley, 2001). For both sexes, a strong link exists between sexual abuse in childhood and sexual difficulties in adulthood (Najman et al., 2005; Vandeusen & Carr, 2003). Other common symptoms of sexual abuse survivors include low self-esteem, guilt, shame, depression, alienation, a lack of trust in others, revulsion at being touched, drug and alcohol abuse, obesity, elevated suicide rates, a predisposition to being repeatedly victimized in a variety of ways, and long-term medical problems, such as chronic pelvic pain and gastrointestinal disorders (Miner et al., 2006; Saewyc et al., 2004; Thomas, 2005; Vandeusen & Carr, 2003).

Research indicates that males and females may differ from each other in some of the ways child sexual abuse affects them. Two meta-analyses of studies using college samples (Rind et al., 1998) and national probability samples (Rind & Tromovitch, 1997) found that males tend to be less adversely affected by child sexual abuse than females. However, not all research supports this conclusion. For example, one investigation of about 1,500 12- to 19-year-olds found that sexually abused males had more emotional and behavioral problems than their female counterparts (Garnefski & Diekstra, 1997).

A variety of treatment approaches have emerged to help survivors of child sexual abuse resolve issues regarding these experiences and their emotional aftermath (Putnam, 2003; Vandeusen & Carr, 2003; Wolfsdorf & Zlotnick, 2001). These treatment strategies range from individual therapy to group and couple-oriented approaches. Most metropolitan areas in the United States also have self-help support organizations for survivors of sexual abuse. (If you want more information about how to seek professional therapeutic assistance, we suggest reviewing the guidelines in Chapter 14.)

## Preventing Child Sexual Abuse

Efforts to reduce the sexual victimization of children have focused on punishing those who have perpetrated the abuse, protecting children from them, and educating children to protect themselves. As of this writing, despite much research, treatment programs have not demonstrated much long-term effectiveness in preventing recidivism among sexual offenders (Dewhurst & Nielsen, 1999). Some critics of existing legal sanctions have advocated increasing the penalties for those convicted (Vachss, 1999), and several states have passed laws requiring community notification and registration of convicted pedophiles when they are released from prison. This registration and notification requirement is often referred to as Megan's law—named for Megan Kanka, a 7-year-old New Jersey girl who was raped and murdered in 1994 by a convicted sex offender who had moved into a home across the street from her. Although some people have expressed concern over the constitutionality of such laws (M. Johnson, 1998), others have argued that these laws represent a fundamental shift in the way we view these criminals. This shift is from trying to "cure" perpetrators to protecting the community from their behaviors (Simon, 1998).

Elementary school students light the "Candle of Hope," in recognition of National Child Abuse Prevention Month.

Most child sexual abuse is perpetrated by someone known to the victim. Thus some health professionals suggest that many children can avoid being victimized if they are taught about their right to say no, the difference between "okay" and "not okay" touches, and strategies for coping with an adult's attempt to coerce them into inappropriate intimate contact.

As indicated in Chapter 12, parents often avoid discussing sex with their children. Therefore it is probably unrealistic to expect better parent-child communication to significantly protect children. Furthermore, parents themselves are often the abusers. The following list, drawn from the writings of a number of child abuse specialists, offers suggestions for preventing child sexual abuse. They may be helpful to parents, educators, and other caregivers of children.

1. It is important to present prevention-oriented material to young children, because as many as 25% of child sexual abuse victims are younger than age 7 (Finkelhor, 1984a). Be sure to include boys, because they too can be abused.
2. Educators and parents will be more effective if they keep things simple, translating "the notions of sexual abuse into concepts that make sense within the world of the child" (Finkelhor, 1984b, p. 3).
3. Avoid making a discussion of child sexual abuse unduly frightening. It is important that children be sufficiently concerned so that they will be on the lookout for potentially abusive adult behavior. However, they should also be confident in their ability to avoid such a situation.
4. Take time to carefully explain the differences between okay touches (pats, snuggles, and hugs) and not-okay touches that make a child feel uncomfortable or confused. Not-okay touches can be explained as touching under the panties or underpants or touching areas that bathing suits cover. Be sure to indicate that a child should not have to touch an adult in these areas even if the adult says it is all right. It is also a good idea to explain not-okay kisses (prolonged lip contact or tongue in mouth).
5. Encourage children to believe that they have rights—the right to control their bodies and the right to say no when they are being touched in a way that makes them uncomfortable.

A child abuse specialist uses puppets to teach children about child abuse.

6. Encourage children to tell someone right away if an adult has touched them in a way that is inappropriate or if an adult has made them do something with which they are uncomfortable. Emphasize that you will not be angry with them and that they will be okay when they tell, even if someone else has told them that they will get in trouble. Stress that no matter what happened, it was not their fault and they will not be blamed. Also, warn them that not all adults will believe them. Tell them to keep telling people until they find someone like you who will believe them.

7. Discuss with children some of the strategies that adults might use to get children to participate in sexual activities. For example, tell them to trust their own feelings when they think something is wrong, even if an adult who is a friend or relative says that it is okay and that he or she is "teaching" them something helpful. Given that many adults use the "this is our secret" strategy, it can be particularly helpful to explain the difference between a secret (something one is never to tell—a bad idea) and a surprise (a good idea because it is something one tells later to make someone happy).

8. Discuss strategies for getting away from uncomfortable or dangerous situations. Let children know that it is okay to scream, yell, run away, or get assistance from a friend or trusted adult.

9. Encourage children to state clearly to an adult who touches them inappropriately that they will tell a particular responsible adult about what went on. Interviews with perpetrators of child sexual abuse have revealed that many of them would be deterred from their abusive actions if a child said that she or he would tell a specific adult about the assault (Budin & Johnson, 1989; Daro, 1991).

10. Perhaps one of the most important things to incorporate in this prevention discussion, particularly for parents, is the message that private touching can be a loving and pleasurable experience, as they will discover when they grow older and meet someone they care for or love. Without some discussion of the positive aspects of sexuality, there is a risk that a child will develop a negative view of any kind of sexual contact between people, regardless of the nature of their relationship.

## When the Child Tells

Research demonstrates that children who have been sexually abused often either delay disclosure of the abuse to a parent or another adult or do not tell at all (Goodman-Brown et al., 2003). In fact, many children do not disclose their abuse until adulthood, if then (Berliner & Conte, 1995; Goodman-Brown et al., 2003). "Fears of retribution and abandonment, and feelings of complicity, embarrassment, guilt, and shame all conspire to silence children and inhibit their disclosures of abuse" (Goodman-Brown et al., 2003, p. 526). A recent study of 218 sexually abused children found that several factors are associated with a child's decision to delay disclosure, including (1) fear of negative consequences to self and others, (2) perceptions of responsibility for the abuse, (3) relationship to the abuser (children whose abuser was a family member took longer to disclose than children abused by someone outside the family), and (4) the child's age (older children, more fearful of negative consequences of disclosure, were slower to disclose) (Goodman-Brown et al., 2003).

As described previously, children suffer many adverse effects of sexual abuse. Their fears about potential consequences of revealing their victimization and their resultant hesitancy to reveal it further magnify their misery. Furthermore, the emotional trauma that a child experiences as a result of a sexual encounter with an adult may be intensified by excessive parental reactions (Davies, 1995). When telling a parent what happened, children may merely be relaying a sense of discomfort over something they do not fully understand. If parents react with extreme agitation, children are likely to respond with increased emotional negativity, developing a sense of being implicated in something terrible and often feeling extremely guilty about having participated in such an event. Children may feel guilty about such experiences even without parental displays of distress, because they sense the guilt of the person who molested them.

It is important that parents respond appropriately to instances of child abuse involving their child. Such acts should not be ignored! While remaining calm in the face of their child's revelation, parents should take great precautions to see that the child is not alone with the offender again. In many instances children are repeatedly molested by the same person, and they may come to feel a sense of obligation and guilt. It is essential to ensure that the child is protected from further experiences of this kind. Because it is also likely that the child will not have been the offender's only victim, it is essential to report the offender to the police to protect other children.

**? Critical Thinking Question**

When children have been sexually abused, what steps should be taken to reduce the potentially adverse effects of the abuse?

# Sexual Harassment

Whether in industry, the military, or academia, **sexual harassment** is widespread in U.S. society. Sexual harassment is more than just a demand for sexual favors. Sexual harassment can also occur when people's actions create a hostile or offensive working environment. One woman offered her experience:

> I was the first woman they hired at that level. I was proud of what I had accomplished and looked forward to the challenges, but it has been much harder than I expected. I have been amazed and disgusted by the jokes and the unbelievable crude remarks that some men have made. People have sent me the most disgusting e-mails, and every day I get obscene messages on my voice mail. I spoke to my boss about this and told him how upsetting it was to me, but he told me that I needed to be a "team player" and that this was just the guys' way of welcoming me to the group. Maybe it shouldn't bother me as much as it does, but it is hurting my work. I'm having trouble concentrating, and I cringe every time I listen to my messages. (Authors' files)

**Sexual harassment**
Unwelcome sexual advances, requests for sexual favors, and other verbal or physical conduct of a sexual nature in the workplace or academic setting.

Sexual harassment gained unprecedented public attention in the early 1990s as a result of two incidents that received national media coverage: law professor Anita Hill's allegations that she had been sexually harassed by Supreme Court nominee Clarence Thomas and the U.S. Navy's Tailhook scandal, in which Pentagon investigators concluded that many women had been sexually harassed or assaulted by drunken aviators. In this section, we define and discuss sexual harassment, especially its occurrence on the job and in educational environments.

Sexual harassment in the workplace is prohibited by Title VII of the 1964 Civil Rights Act. In 1980 the Equal Employment Opportunity Commission (EEOC) issued guidelines on sexual harassment. These guidelines made it clear that both verbal and physical harassment are illegal:

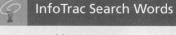

**InfoTrac Search Words**

● Sexual harassment

> Unwelcome sexual advances, requests for sexual favors, and other verbal or physical conduct of a sexual nature constitute sexual harassment when (1) submission to such conduct is made either explicitly or implicitly a term or condition of an individual's employment, (2) submission to or rejection of such conduct by an individual is used as a basis for employment decisions affecting such individual, or (3) such conduct has the purpose or effect of unreasonably interfering with an individual's work performance or creating an intimidating, hostile, or offensive working environment. (Equal Employment Opportunity Commission, 1980, pp. 74676–74677)

The EEOC guidelines describe two kinds of sexual harassment. One form, commonly labeled *quid pro quo*, is reflected in the first two situations described in the guidelines. Here, compliance with unwanted sexual advances is made a condition for securing a job or education benefits or for favorable treatment in employment or

Law professor Anita Hill, who testified during the confirmation hearings of Supreme Court Justice Clarence Thomas, triggered a national debate about sexual harassment in the workplace.

academic settings (such as receiving a promotion or high grades) (Pierce, 1994). Harassment is often evident in reprisals that follow refusals to comply (Charney & Russell, 1994).

A second form of sexual harassment, often referred to as a "hostile or offensive environment," is described in the third situation in the EEOC guidelines. This kind of sexual harassment is less clear but probably more common than the *quid pro quo* variety. Here, one or more supervisors, coworkers, teachers, or students engage in persistent, inappropriate behaviors that make the workplace or academic environment hostile, abusive, and generally unbearable. Unlike *quid pro quo* harassment, this second form does not necessarily involve power or authority differences. It may, however, involve attempts to defend status and position, because men often view the entrance of women into formerly male bastions of power and privilege as threatening (Dall'Ara & Maass, 1999).

Cases involving hostile or offensive environments have been the subject of considerable debate over what constitutes such an environment. Essentially, a hostile environment is seen as one in which a reasonable person in the same or similar circumstances would find the conduct of the harasser(s) to be intimidating, hostile, or abusive.

The reasonable-person interpretation is illustrated by a decision in which the U.S. Supremer Court ruled unanimously that a Tennessee woman was subjected to sexual harassment in the form of a hostile environment "that would seriously affect a reasonable person's psychological well-being" (Justice Sandra Day O'Connor, writing for the Court in *Harris* v. *Forklift Systems*, 92 U.S. 1168 [1993]). In this case the victim's male boss (the company president) (1) urged her to retrieve coins from his front pants pocket, (2) ridiculed the size of her buttocks, (3) described her as a "dumb-ass woman" in the presence of others, and (4) insinuated that she had won a large sales contract by providing sexual favors. The defendant's attorney unsuccessfully tried to pass off these behaviors as merely joking without any hostile intent. This case is noteworthy because it involved neither sexual blackmail nor unwanted touching. Nevertheless, the Supreme Court ruled that a reasonable person would find the offensive sexual speech intimidating and abusive.

## Varieties and Incidence of Sexual Harassment on the Job

Sexual harassment on the job can take many forms. It can start with such things as remarks of a sexual nature; sexist comments; unwelcome attention; violations of personal space; repeated unwelcome requests for a date; inappropriate, derogatory put-downs; leering and/or whistling; offensive and crude language; and displaying sexually oriented objects, materials, or pictures that create a hostile or offensive environment. Some of these behaviors occupy a gray area because not all people would view them as genuine sexual harassment. However, they clearly become sexual harassment if they persist after the target of such acts has asked the offending person to stop.

At an intermediate level of severity, sexual harassment in the workplace can include inappropriate, graphic comments about a person's body or sexual competence, sexual propositions not directly linked to employment, verbal abuse of a sexual nature, and unwanted physical contact of a nonsexual nature. In its most severe manifestations sexual harassment on the job can involve a boss or supervisor requiring sexual services from an employee as a condition for keeping a job or getting a promotion, unwanted physical contact or conduct of a sexual nature, and, less commonly, sexual assault.

Sexual harassment creates anxiety and tension in the workplace.

© Willie Hill, Jr./The Images Works

### Prevalence of Sexual Harassment in the Workplace

The annual number of sexual harassment complaints filed with the EEOC more than doubled from 5,623 in 1989 to 13,136 in 2004. The percentage of total claims filed by males has steadily increased from 9.1% in 1992 to 15.1% in 2004 (Equal Employment Opportunity Commission, 2006). A number of surveys have revealed that sexual harassment is all too common in the workplace (Birdeau et al., 2005; Sev'er, 1999; Welsh, 1999).

Perhaps the most reliable available data come from a national survey of more than 24,000 federal employees. This survey, which adhered closely to the EEOC definition of sexual harassment, had an 85% response rate. Of the more than 20,000 respondents, 42% of women and 15% of men reported experiencing sexual harassment (U.S. Merit Systems Protection Board, 1981). In the years since this survey, these rates have increased slightly, with 44% of women and 19% of men reporting being sexually harassed (U.S. Merit Systems Protection Board, 1996). Other surveys have found sexual harassment rates among working women ranging from 50% (Gutek, 1985; Loy & Stewart, 1984) to 66% (MacKinnon, 1979). A 1995 survey of 90,000 women service members on active duty found that at least half of the respondents in each branch of the military believed that they had been sexually harassed (Firestone & Harris, 1999; Vistica, 1996).

Sexual harassment is not limited to low-paying jobs or indeed to any particular segment of the employment force. It occurs in all professions and at every level. For example, recently the army's highest-ranking woman (a general) filed a complaint of sexual harassment that was substantiated by army investigators (Myers, 2000; Ricks & Suro, 2000). Although some people think of sexual harassment as something that occurred most frequently in the old economy, with its more traditional values, complaints of harassment of women working for Internet companies are increasing (Ligos, 2000). Several studies have revealed high incidences of sexual harassment in medical settings as well. In one survey of 133 physicians, 73% of the female respondents and 22% of the men reported experiencing sexual harassment during their residency training (Komaromy et al., 1993). Other studies have revealed that 69% to 85% of nurses experience sexual harassment on the job (Valente & Bullough, 2004).

## Same-Sex Sexual Harassment in the Workplace

Sexual harassment involving members of the same sex has become more and more of an issue, both in the workplace and in the U.S. courts. People who are victims of same-sex sexual harassment have generally found it difficult to obtain satisfactory legal judgments, regardless of their own sexual orientation. This unfortunate situation is due both to the absence of a federal law specifically prohibiting same-sex sexual harassment and to many courts' narrow interpretation of Title VII as prohibiting sex discrimination only between men and women (Bible, 2006; Landau, 1997). The courts have found the issue of same-sex harassment difficult, and many conflicting decisions have been issued. In March 1998, however, the U.S. Supreme Court reversed an earlier decision and ruled that workplace sexual harassment involving an offender and a victim of the same sex is prohibited by Title VII. Attorneys representing victims of same-sex harassment frequently find themselves needing to prove that the accused acted out of "sexual interest." Proving this can be extremely difficult, because most defendants in these cases claim to be heterosexual. Furthermore, gay or lesbian plaintiffs may fear being "outted" or exposed, and plaintiffs who are not gay or lesbian may fear being thought of as such (Gover, 1996). Nevertheless, same-sex sexual harassment claims are increasing. The EEOC has reported a significant increase in the proportion of sexual harassment claims that involve same-sex harassment (Bible, 2006; Hunsberger, 2003).

## Effects of Workplace Sexual Harassment on the Victim

On-the-job sexual harassment can seriously erode a victim's financial status, job performance, career opportunities, psychological and physical health, and personal relationships (Rhode, 1997; Woodzicka & LaFrance, 2005). The financial ramifications of refusing to endure sexual harassment may be severe, especially for people in lower-level positions. Many victims, particularly if they are supporting families, cannot afford to be unemployed. Many find it exceedingly difficult to look for other jobs while maintaining their present job. If they are fired for resisting harassment, they may be unable to obtain unemployment compensation; and even if they do obtain compensation, it will probably provide only a fraction of their former income.

Various surveys report that the great majority of harassed workers (between 75% and 90%) report adverse psychological effects, including eating disorders, crying spells, loss of self-esteem, and feelings of anger, humiliation, shame, embarrassment, nervousness, irritability, alienation, vulnerability, helplessness, and lack of motivation (Harned & Fitzgerald, 2002; Jorgenson & Wahl, 2000; Sev'er, 1999).

## Dealing With Sexual Harassment on the Job

If you face sexual harassment at work, you have a number of options. The suggestions in the following list provide guidelines for dealing with this abuse:

1. If the harassment includes actual or attempted rape or assault, you can file criminal charges against the perpetrator.

2. If the harassment has stopped short of attempted rape or assault, consider confronting the person who is harassing you. State in clear terms that what he or she is doing is clearly sexual harassment, that you will not tolerate it, and that if it continues, you will file charges through appropriate channels. You may prefer to document what has occurred and your response to it in a letter directed to the harasser (keep a copy). In such a letter, you should include specific details of previous incidents of harassment, your unequivocal rejection of such inappropriate overtures, and your intent to take more serious action if they do not stop immediately.

3. If the offender does not stop the harassment after direct verbal and/or written confrontation, it may be helpful to discuss your situation with your supervisor and/or the supervisor of the offender.

4. If neither the harasser nor the supervisor responds appropriately to your concern, you may want to gather support from your coworkers. You may discover that you are not the only victim in your company. Discussing the offense with sympathetic women and men in your workplace may produce sufficient pressure to terminate the harassment. Be very sure of your facts, though, because such actions could result in a slander lawsuit.

5. If your attempts to deal with this problem within your company are unsuccessful or if you are fired, demoted, or refused promotion because of your efforts to end harassment, you can file an official complaint with your city or state Human Rights Commission or with the Fair Employment Practices Agency (the names may vary locally). You can also ask the local office of the federally funded EEOC to investigate the situation.

6. Finally, you may wish to pursue legal action to resolve your problem with sexual harassment. Lawsuits can be filed in federal courts under the Civil Rights Act. They can also be filed under city or state laws prohibiting employment discrimination. Moreover, a single lawsuit can be filed in a number of jurisdictions. A person who has been a victim of such harassment is most likely to receive a favorable court judgment if she or he has first tried to resolve the problem within the company before going to court. A number of legal decisions, including one made by the U.S. Supreme Court in 2004, have revealed that an employer may successfully defend against liability if a plaintiff does not seek relief from harassment by pursuing the employer's established sexual harassment grievance procedure (Mink, 2005). ■

U.S. businesses are becoming increasingly sensitive to the issue of sexual harassment in the workplace, in part because of the damage to morale and productivity caused by such behaviors but also because of court decisions that have awarded large sums of money to victims. In 1998 Mitsubishi Motor Company agreed to pay $34 million in compensation to 350 women who were allegedly sexually harassed. Because Title VII imposes liability on companies for sexual harassment perpetrated by their employees, many corporations have implemented programs designed to educate employees about sexual harassment.

Nevertheless, despite these programs in business and in the military services, many women still keep silent when they have been harassed (Bruns & Bruns, 2005). They do so for many reasons, including a desire to protect their career (Becker, 2000) and the fear that formal reporting will not be helpful and will lead to their being negatively evaluated by others (Marin & Guadagno, 1999).

## Sexual Harassment in Academic Settings

Sexual harassment also occurs in educational settings. College students often find themselves in the unpleasant situation of experiencing unwanted sexual advances from their professors. Both sexes are vulnerable to this form of harassment. However, it is most commonly male professors or instructors who harass female students (Bingham, & Battey, 2005; Kelley & Parsons, 2000).

Academic sexual harassment differs somewhat from harassment that occurs in the workplace. For one thing, a student who encounters unwanted sexual advances often has the option of selecting a different instructor or adviser. In contrast, workers in an employment setting tend to have fewer alternatives for avoiding or escaping the harassment while still keeping their jobs. However, students can experience coercive pressures associated with the need to obtain a good grade, a letter of recommendation, or a desirable work or research opportunity. Furthermore, sexual harassment of students can result in poor school performance, altered or derailed academic careers, and a variety of psychological and physical symptoms comparable to those experienced by people harassed on the job (Bingham & Battey, 2005; Bruns & Bruns, 2005).

Students also tend to be more naive than workers about the implications of becoming sexually involved with someone who may be important to their successful pursuit of an education or a career. There is a real potential for inappropriate exploitation of youthful naiveté and awe regarding prestige and power. Furthermore, evidence has suggested that a student victim "might wonder whether her academic success has been due to her ability or her professor's sexual interest in her" (Satterfield & Muehlenhard, 1990, p. 1).

An increasing number of colleges and universities have policies prohibiting faculty from dating their students (Bruns & Bruns, 2005). The growing debate over professor–student romances, together with decisions to ban such relationships, is fueled largely by the belief that many relationships between faculty and students may seem consensual on the surface but actually are not. Rather, the power of professors and/or advisers to determine students' futures through grades and recommendations often creates pressure for students to comply to protect their class standing or future prospects (Begley, 1993).

Sexual harassment also occurs in high schools and even middle schools. In 1992 the U.S. Supreme Court ruled that school districts are liable for hostile sexual environments created by school employees and can be sued for damages. However, the Supreme Court has yet to extend this liability to sexual harassment perpetrated by peers. Nevertheless, many district courts have allowed students to litigate cases of peer harassment under Title IX, a 1972 civil rights law that prohibits federally funded schools from denying students opportunities based on their sex (Scher, 1997). Furthermore, the U.S. Department of Education has published a manual of peer sexual harassment guidelines in which it is clearly stated that schools that do not take measures to remedy this form of harassment could lose federal funds (Scher, 1997).

## Prevalence of Sexual Harassment in Academic Settings

Just how common is sexual harassment in educational settings? A survey of California high schools found that approximately 50% of the female respondents reported experiencing sexual harassment (Roscoe et al., 1994). Another survey of over 1,000 Canadian adolescent females in grades 7 through 12 found that more than 23% had experienced at least one event of sexual harassment in the previous 6 months (Bagley et al., 1997). A review of research suggests that the incidence of sexual harassment in American high schools, especially harassment by peers, is quite high—ranging in various studies from 37% to 87% (Terrance et al., 2004). Sexual harassment in high schools and colleges is receiving considerable attention from school officials fueled in part by two recent Supreme Court decisions that found educational institutions liable for negligence in dealing with sexual harassment complaints (Terrance et al., 2004; Ramson, 2006).

In surveys of college and university populations, 20–40% of undergraduate women and 30–50% of graduate women report having been the target in one or more incidents of sexual harassment in their academic settings (Birdeau et al., 2005; Bruns & Bruns, 2005; Ramson, 2006). Because most studies of college populations have included only female students, we have less information about harassment of male students. However, research has revealed that between 9% and 29% of male undergraduates report having been sexually harassed (Kalof et al., 2001; Sundt, 1994). The number of male victims of sexual harassment in academic settings may be even higher, as indicated by a recent Internet survey of over 2,000 college students ages 18–24, in which almost two-thirds of both male and female respondents reported being sexually harassed on campus (Cohen, 2006).

### Dealing With Sexual Harassment on Campus

What can you do if you experience sexual harassment on campus? Some students avoid or escape the harassment by dropping a class, finding another faculty adviser, or even leaving school. However, we advise someone who feels that she or he is being harassed to report it in order to curtail these inappropriate actions and to reduce the likelihood that other students will be victimized by the same person (it is common for people who harass students to have several targets). You may wish to speak to the offending individual's chairperson or dean. If you are not satisfied with that person's response, contact the campus officer or department that handles matters of civil rights or affirmative action. Although you may be concerned about grade discrimination or loss of position, federal affirmative action guidelines forbid discrimination against people who, in good conscience, file legitimate claims of sexual harassment. Furthermore, a professor guilty of such action will usually be closely monitored and will be less likely to continue to harass. ∎

# SUMMARY

## Rape

- The legal definition of rape varies from state to state, but most laws define rape as sexual intercourse that occurs under actual or threatened forcible compulsion that overcomes the earnest resistance of the victim.
- Although evidence strongly suggests that rape is widespread, it is difficult to obtain accurate statistics on the actual number of rapes and rape victims in the United States.
- Many false beliefs about rape tend to hold the victim responsible for the crime and excuse the attacker.
- Rape is often partly a product of socialization processes that occur in certain rape-prone societies. These processes glorify masculine violence, teach boys to be aggressive, and demean the role of women in the economic and political aspects of life.
- Males in U.S. society often acquire callous attitudes toward women that, when combined with a belief that "might makes right," provide a cultural foundation for rape and other acts of sexual coercion.
- Exposure to sexually violent media can contribute to more-accepting attitudes toward rape, decrease one's sensitivity to the tragedy of rape, and perhaps even increase men's inclinations to be sexually aggressive toward women.
- No single personality or behavioral pattern characterizes rapists, and a wide range of individual differences exist among rapists.
- Incarcerated rapists have a strong proclivity toward violence. Men who embrace traditional gender roles are more likely to commit rape than men who do not support such roles.
- Anger toward women is a prominent attitude among some rapists. Some rapists have self-centered, or narcis-

sistic, personalities that may render them insensitive to the feelings of the people they victimize.
- More than 50% of U.S. female rape victims reported that their first rape occurred before they were 18 years old.
- Most rapes are acquaintance rapes, in which the perpetrator is known to the victim.
- Sexual coercion in dating situations is prevalent. Both sexes experience sexual coercion, but women are more likely than men to be physically forced into sexual activity they do not want.
- A variety of "date rape" drugs are widely used by unscrupulous individuals to facilitate sexual conquest or to incapacitate date partners.
- Rape has been a strategy of war throughout history. In addition to being used as a means to humiliate and control women, wartime rape is also intended to destroy the bonds of family and society.
- Rape survivors often suffer severe emotional and physical difficulties that can lead to a diagnosis of posttraumatic stress disorder (PTSD).
- Rape victims often find that supportive counseling, either individually or in groups, can help ease the trauma caused by rape.
- Although the vast majority of rape victims are women, research indicates that as many as 3% of U.S. men have been raped.
- Males who are sexually assaulted often experience long-term adverse consequences similar to those reported by females who are sexually victimized.

## Sexual Abuse of Children

- Child sexual abuse is sexual contact between an adult and a child. A distinction is generally made between nonrelative child sexual abuse, called pedophilia or child molestation, and incest, which involves sexual contact between an adult and a child relative.

- Most child sexual abusers are male relatives, friends, or neighbors of their victims.
- No classic profile of a pedophile exists, other than that most pedophiles are heterosexual males and known to the victim. Prosecuted offenders tend to be shy, lonely, conservative, and often moralistic or religious. They frequently have difficulty relating to other adults and tend to feel inadequate and inferior.
- Some pedophiles were sexually victimized themselves during childhood.
- It is difficult to estimate the frequency of incest and pedophilia in U.S. society. Estimates of the number of girls sexually victimized range from 20% to 33%, whereas comparable estimates for boys range from 9% to 16%.
- Research suggests that the number of boys who are sexually molested in the United States may be substantially higher than was previously reported.
- Considerable controversy exists over whether a person can repress memories of sexual abuse and then suddenly or gradually recover them after exposure to certain triggering stimuli.
- Cyberspace pedophilia is widespread, and the responsibility for protecting children, in the absence of other effective safeguards, resides primarily with parents.
- Child sexual abuse can be a traumatic and emotionally damaging experience, with long-term negative consequences for the victim.
- Survivors often experience a loss of childhood innocence, a disruption of their normal sexual development, and a profound sense of betrayal. Other damaging consequences include low self-esteem and difficulty establishing satisfying sexual and emotional relationships as adults.
- There are a number of treatment programs for survivors of child sexual abuse, ranging from individual therapy to group and couple-oriented approaches.
- It is important to talk to children about protecting themselves from sexual abuse. Children need to know the difference between okay and not-okay touching, the fact that they have rights, the fact that they can report abuse without fear of blame, and strategies for escaping uncomfortable situations.

## Sexual Harassment

- Sexual harassment in the workplace or in an academic setting is any unwanted sexual attention from someone on the job or in academia that creates discomfort and/or interferes with the victim's job or education.
- Guidelines provided by the Equal Employment Opportunity Commission essentially describe two kinds of sexual harassment. In the *quid pro quo* variety, a worker or student believes that failure to comply with sexual advances will be detrimental to his or her professional or academic standing. In the second form, the actions of supervisors, coworkers, professors, or students make the workplace or academic setting a "hostile or offensive environment."
- Title VII of the 1964 Civil Rights Act prohibits sexual harassment. A company can be liable for such coercive actions by its employees.
- Estimates of the percentage of women sexually harassed on the job range from 44% to 88%. A comparable estimate for men is approximately 19%.

- Despite increased attention to the issue of same-sex sexual harassment, victims of this form of harassment have generally found it difficult to obtain legal satisfaction in U.S. courts.
- Victims of sexual harassment may experience a variety of negative financial, emotional, and physical effects.
- Sexual harassment also occurs in educational settings. Most commonly, perpetrators are male professors or instructors who harass female students.
- Surveys indicate that 20–40% of undergraduate women, 30–50% of graduate women, and 9–29% of male undergraduates report having been sexually harassed.

## ❯ Suggested Readings

**Francis, Leslie Pickering** (2000). *Sexual Harassment as an Ethical Issue in Academic Life*. Walnut Creek, CA: Rowman & Littlefield. A discussion on a range of topics related to sexual harassment in academic settings, including philosophical, legal, and ethical issues associated with efforts to regulate and minimize campus sexual harassment.

**Francke, Linda Bird** (1997). *Ground Zero: The Gender Wars in the Military*. New York: Simon & Schuster. A sobering account of the extent to which women in the military are consistently subjected to demeaning and disparaging treatment, including sexual harassment and sexual assault.

**Gold, Jodi, and Susan Villari** (Eds.) (2000). *Just Sex: Students Rewrite the Rules on Sex, Violence, Equality, and Activism*. Walnut Creek, CA: Rowman & Littlefield. An informative collection of the writings of student activists and young scholars who are part of a student movement aimed at ending sexual violence and altering the sexual landscape of America's campuses.

**Maltz, Wendy** (2001). *The Sexual Healing Journey*. New York: HarperCollins. An excellent book that helps survivors of sexual abuse and their partners understand and recover from its effects.

**Parrot, Andrea, and Laurie Bechhofer** (Eds.) (1991). *Acquaintance Rape: The Hidden Crime*. New York: Wiley. A fine book that provides in-depth analysis of the nature and extent of acquaintance rape, along with excellent suggestions for its treatment and prevention.

**Sanday, Peggy Reeves** (1996). *A Woman Scorned: Acquaintance Rape on Trial*. New York: Doubleday. A first-rate text written by an eminent anthropologist who has conducted extensive cross-cultural research on rape. It analyzes several rape trials (including that of boxer Mike Tyson) and describes the cultural traditions that have made the United States a "rape-prone" society.

**Salter, Anna** (2003). *Predators: Pedophiles, Rapists & Other Sex Offenders: Who They Are, How They Operate, and How We Can Protect Ourselves and Our Children*. New York: Basic Books. A well-written, well-researched, and very informative book by a noted psychotherapist and researcher. It provides a wealth of information about sexual predators, much of it based on her extensive interviews with sex offenders.

**Scarce, Michael** (1997). *Male on Male Rape: The Hidden Toll of Stigma and Shame*. New York: Insight Books. A compelling book by a rape-prevention educator and a survivor of such violence himself. It examines the impact of same-sex rape on both the victim and society at large.

## Resources

**Rape crisis centers** are listed in the phone books of many cities. Victims of sexual assault can also call the Rape, Abuse, and Incest National Network (RAINN) (1-800-656-HOPE), a Washington, D.C., organization that helps connect callers to local rape crisis centers.

## Web Resources

**CengageNOW Web Site**
Go to **academic.cengage.com** to link to practice quiz questions, interactive activities, Internet links, critical thinking exercises, discussion forums, and more. You can also access sites from the Wadsworth Psychology Study Center (**academic .cengage.com/psychology**) or you can connect directly to the following sites:

**Rape Abuse and Incest National Network**
A nonprofit organization, the Rape Abuse and Incest National Network provides news, hotlines, a list of local crisis centers, and statistics on the incidence of rape and incest.

**Sexual Assault Information Page**
This Web site contains information on and links related to sexual assault, including acquaintance rape, child sexual abuse, incest, and rape. Also included is information for crisis centers and counseling and support groups, as well as university resources from across the country. Among the topics covered is Rohypnol—one of the so-called date rape drugs.

**National Clearinghouse on Child Abuse and Neglect Information**
This Web page is a large resource on child welfare, including issues of child sexual abuse. It includes statistics, state laws, fact sheets, and searchable databases.

**Information on Sexual Harassment**
An interactive exploration of the topic of sexual harassment is included on this Web site, which invites visitors not only to learn definitions of harassment but also to apply these definitions to everyday situations as they consider case studies and are given the opportunity to evaluate their own behavior. State and federal laws are provided, and groundbreaking legal battles are presented.

**Sexual Harassment Hotline Resource List of the Feminist Majority Foundation**
This Web site provides advice and other resources, including links to state hotlines, for people victimized by sexual harassment.

*Three Internet Sites That Deal With Web Safety:*

**A Parent's Guide to Internet Safety**
This Web site provides valuable information to families who want to learn more about Internet safety.

**American Academy of Pediatrics**
Locate the "Internet and Your Family" link for important information about Web safety for children.

**Get Net Wise**
This Web site, a joint effort of several public-interest organizations and Internet corporations, offers Internet safety strategies for different age levels and activities.

*Our Sexuality* **Book Companion Web Site academic.cengage.com/psychology/ crooks** Visit your book companion Web site where you will find flash cards, practice quizzes, Internet links, and more to help you study.

**Just what you need to know NOW!**
Spend time on what you need to master rather than on information you already have learned. Take a pretest for this chapter, and CengageNOW will generate a personalized study plan based on your results. The study plan will identify the topics you need to review and direct you to online resources to help you master those topics. You can then take a post-test to help you determine the concepts you have mastered and what you will still need to work on. Try it out! Go to **academic.cengage.com/login** to sign in with an access code or to purchase access to this product.

**InfoTrac College Edition Online Library**
Sign in to **academic.cengage.com/login** or visit your free book companion Web site at **academic.cengage.com/psychology/crooks** to access InfoTrac College Edition, an online searchable library that includes a multitude of journals, many specific to human sexuality. These journals include *Archives of Sexual Behavior; Archives of Sexual Health Behavior; Canadian Journal of Human Sexuality; Hispanic Journal of the Behavioral Sciences; Journal of Cross-Cultural Psychology; Journal of Physical Education, Recreation, and Dance; Journal of Sex Research;* and *Sex Roles.*

# Sex for Sale

Laurence Dutton/Getty Images

▶ **Pornography**

How is pornography defined, and what are different types of pornography?

Since the Middle Ages, what technological developments have made pornography more accessible to the general population?

How has pornography been used for social criticism?

How are obscenity and indecency determined?

What is the current focus of the censorship/free speech controversy?

What arguments can be made as to whether pornography is helpful or harmful to individuals and couples?

What are the indications of the "pornification" of mainstream culture?

▶ **Prostitution and Sex Work**

What are the different types of male and female prostitutes and sex workers?

To what kinds of locations do female sex tourists travel?

What percentage of sex workers enter the business before age 18?

What is the primary reason that people become sex workers?

What are the symptoms of PTSD?

Has the United States been a leader in the international effort against trafficking women and children?

What are the pros and cons for decriminalization, legalization, and depenalization of prostitution?

*I view porn as dirty smut magazines and movies that old perverted men look at. I really don't appreciate pornography, it does nothing for me. I love naked women in person and in bed, but seeing magazines or movies is a pointless turn-on. Pornography is really degrading toward women, and it gives young people the wrong ideas about women. (Authors' files)*

*I have found that when my partner and I watch pornos I get extremely aroused and let myself go wild with my sexuality. One time I got so turned on that I took control of the evening by making him do everything I wanted, like being rough, domineering, or sensitive. We also tried different areas in the room, like the coffee table, recliner, and couch. It wore us out so bad that we fell asleep naked in the middle of the floor tangled in each other's embrace. I feel that my partner and I have really benefited from including pornos in our sex. We have become so comfortable, close, and in love knowing that sex is a good thing. (Authors' files)*

Throughout this text, we have explored many aspects of sexuality—from biology and behavior to sexual problems and their treatment. One topic we have not yet investigated is sex as business—the exchange of money for sexual stimulation. As we will see in this chapter, a great deal of controversy surrounds sex in the marketplace. In the following pages, we examine pornography and sex work in depth. We explore some of the social and legal issues surrounding these activities. We look first at pornography.

## ◑ Pornography

**Pornography** Sexually explicit material (e.g., images or text) intended to cause sexual arousal.

**InfoTrac Search Words**

• Pornography

The term **pornography** refers to any written, visual, or spoken material depicting sexual activity or genital exposure that is intended to be sexually arousing. Pornography is usually considered hard-core when explicit images of genitals are shown, whereas soft-core stops short of revealing genitals. We can separate pornography into two additional categories. *Degrading pornography* objectifies and denigrates its subjects. Racial stereotypes presented in interracial pornography are one form of degradation (Cowan & Campbell, 1994). *Violent pornography* involves aggression and brutality; the violence might take the form of rape, beatings, dismemberment, and even murder. Violent and abusive fantasies are common in chat rooms; titles such as "Torture Females" or "Daughter Blows Dad" can easily be found (Michaels, 1997). In fact, a study comparing pornographic magazines, videos, and Internet newsgroups found that newsgroups had considerably more sexual violence than the other two forms of media (Barron & Kimmel, 2000).

### Erotica

**Erotica** Respectful, affectionate depictions of sexuality.

**InfoTrac Search Words**

• Erotica

A subtype of sexually explicit materials is **erotica**. Erotica can be either soft- or hard-core, but it is a distinct kind of pornography, regardless of how explicit the material is. *Erotica* is rooted in *eros,* or "passionate love" (Steinem, 1998). Erotica consists of "depictions of sexuality which display mutuality, respect, affection, and a balance of power" (Stock, 1985, p. 13). As more women have become involved in the production of sexually explicit materials, equality between the sexes has become more common (Klinger, 2003; Milne, 2005). For example, Femme Productions' hard-core adult films emphasize sensuality and women's pleasure and assertiveness. Films such as *Nina Hartley's Guide to Better Cunnilingus* and *The Sluts and Goddesses Video Workshop* promote the development and expression of women's desire and arousal.

Is erotica appealing only to women? Not according to research on college students. The subjects, who were at least 21 years old, watched four video segments, each of which represented different combinations of high versus low expressions of love and affection in conjunction with high versus moderate sexual explicitness (hard-core versus soft-core X-rated material). The study found that both male and female subjects rated most arousing the video that was both highly romantic, displaying love and affection, *and* highly sexually explicit. The researchers speculated that these results indicate that college-educated men and women have integrated love and affection with sexual arousal (Quackenbush et al., 1995). Another study of interviews with 150 men in the United States, Canada, and Europe found that men enjoyed pornography the most when men and women were equal participants or when men were recipients of female sexual assertion. For the men to enjoy watching the material, they consistently emphasized the importance of the women appearing to experience genuine pleasure (Loftus, 2002).

In keeping with this perspective, Constance Penley, a university professor who teaches a course on pornography, believes that the pervasive theme of popular pornography is men's "utopian desire for a world where women aren't socially required to say and believe that they don't like sex as much as men do" (1996, p. 18). The author of *Sex, Time, and Power*, Leonard Shlain, goes even further when he states, "Pornography would disappear tomorrow if women were as eager to have sex and behaved sexually as indiscriminately as men" (Shlain, 2003, p. 352).

Candida Royalle began producing porn videos designed for women and couples in the 1980s. *Stud Hunters* is a lighthearted look at the adult entertainment industry.

## Variations in Straight, Gay, and Lesbian Pornographic Films

Sexually explicit films developed for heterosexual, gay, or lesbian consumers differ in some of their general characteristics. Much of straight porn is based on a formula of close-up views of various positions of intercourse and oral and anal sex. Two women having sex, threesomes, and group sex are often part of the formula. Women are usually portrayed as eager sexual participants, and their bodies are the primary focus of the film. Most of the female porn stars have stereotypical underweight bodies with implant-enhanced large breasts. Eroticism of the male body is rare, and the male actors are often, sometimes at best, ordinary looking. The "money shot," a close-up of the man ejaculating outside of the woman's vagina or mouth, is a marker of straight male porn (Paul, 2006).

The gay porn industry is comparable in size to the straight porn industry and shows the same range of low-cost to well-made films. Most of today's gay porn is made with well-groomed, muscular, good-looking men. Gay porn emphasizes eroticism of the male body and unfettered lust that ranges from aggressive to tender. Subgenres include more variation in body type. For example, bear porn features large men with extensive body hair (Blue, 2003).

Far fewer lesbian porn films are made, and they tend to be low-budget and unpolished compared with straight and gay porn. Most lesbian porn films feature real-life lovers. They realistically portray diverse and powerful lesbian sexual interaction instead of a performance for the viewer. A different style of beauty and sex is evident: A great variety of body types and a range of butch and femme styles pervade the films. Role-playing, talking, costuming, and sex toys take precedence over plot. Safer-sex practices are often included in the sexual activity (Blue, 2003).

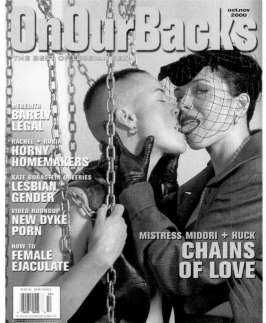

## To Each His or Her Own

Straight, gay, and lesbian porn are broad categories that do not begin to include the enormous variety of sexually explicit topics. Specialty pornography "is a mighty testament to the infinite variety of human imagination" (Hanus, 2006, p. 59). It caters to the wide range of interests in bondage and discipline, sadomasochism fetishes, transgender, pregnant, old/mature, interracial, orgies, pubic shaving, pornographic Japanese animation, and almost any other imaginable topic (Blue, 2003; Hongo, 2006).

The lesbian magazine *On Our Backs* broke new ground in sexual explicitness and "kinkiness" in 1984, when it first hit newsstands.

The various categories of pornography previously described are useful as a working model to conceptualize different types of sexually explicit material, but we should stress that in real life, individual reactions to pornography have more variations than any specific category. "One person's pornography is another person's erotica, and one person's erotica can cause someone else to lose her lunch" (Kipnis, 1996, p. 64). And what may be harmless in one context (for instance, a couple using an erotic video to explore different ways of making love) may be potentially damaging in another context (such as a young child finding the video and watching it).

## Child Pornography

The production, sale, and distribution of sexual images of children under the age of 18 are illegal under numerous federal and state laws. Federal law also prohibits the sale or distribution of images of adult women pretending to be under age 18. Child pornography has been targeted for prosecution by the Attorney General's office and is excluded from the First Amendment protection of free speech.

The Internet provides child pornographers with greatly increased access to illegal materials. Internet child pornography is a $20 billion-per-year industry that continues to expand throughout the world. Sexual predators prey on children as young as 18 months old, and they use children in real-time sexual exploitation (Brockman, 2006). Internet sting operations can be very successful and have resulted in many arrests of child pornographers. Prevention is most important, and the Technology Coalition, composed of online companies, is developing and implementing technological solutions to disrupt the ability of predators to use the Internet for child pornography.

In the last few years, especially since inexpensive webcams became available, minors have sold sexually explicit images of themselves for money. A huge Internet porn case began in 2005 when a teenager, Justin Berry, a self-described "camwhore," decided to cooperate with authorities. At age 13 he began his business on the Internet, providing pictures and real-time webcam shows of himself undressing, showering, masturbating, and having sex. He was 19 when he gave the FBI and Department of Justice the names and credit card numbers of over 1,500 customers, all of whom are liable for criminal charges. A majority of Berry's customers were doctors, lawyers, businessmen, and teachers—many of whom worked with children every day. Marketing sites for adolescent webcam connections also face criminal charges for marketing and distributing child pornography, and they shut down after this case became public (Eichenwald, 2005).

The Internet has exponentially expanded access to sexually explicit material. However, as we see in the following section, throughout history, advances in technology have both expanded access to and reduced control of sexual materials by the governing church or state.

> The public can report child pornography to the National Center for Missing and Exploited Children at www.cybertipline.com or 1-800-843-5678.

## Historical Overview

Pictorial and written representations of sexuality are not modern inventions; even prehistoric cave drawings depict sexual activity. The ancient Indian love manual *Kama Sutra*, dating from about 400 CE, summarized philosophies of sexuality and spirituality in its descriptions of specific sexual techniques. Graphic representations of coitus in Japanese *schunga* paintings and woodcuts from the 1600s and 1700s are regarded as art masterpieces. Ancient Greek and Roman societies extensively used sexual themes to decorate housewares and public architecture.

With the emergence of Christianity and the fall of the Roman Empire, the Roman Catholic Church became the most significant central authority in the West. During the Middle Ages, it controlled the production of the printed word and fine art to reflect its restrictive attitudes toward sexuality. Monks handwrote the books of that era, and the wealth of the Church enabled it to commission the majority of artworks. Johannes Gutenberg's introduction of movable metal

This Greek tomb painting of male lovers dates back to 480 BCE.

© Mimmo Jodice/CORBIS

type in Europe in 1450 ended the Church's monopoly on the written word (Lane, 2000). After the initial printings of the Bible, some presses became busy producing pornographic stories, which are credited with helping bring literacy to the masses. By the 1550s, books had veered so far from the Church's influence that Pope Paul IV established the Church's first list of prohibited books (Lane, 2000).

The next technology to expand pornography was photography, developed before the Civil War. With the advent of photography, erotic photographs proliferated so extensively that Congress passed the first U.S. law prohibiting the mailing of obscenity (P. Johnson, 1998). By the mid-1800s sexually explicit "advice literature," the burgeoning production of inexpensive pornographic novels, and the U.S. publication of the notorious English novel *Fanny Hill* prompted civic leaders to establish laws against publishing and selling pornographic materials. The champion of this cause was Anthony Comstock, who was appointed to the Society for the Suppression of Vice and as a special agent for the U.S. Post Office. Comstock claimed to have convicted more than 3,600 individuals and to have destroyed more than 160 tons of obscene literature. By the 1890s public sentiment changed from support for Comstock's moral outrage about pornography to dismissal of him as old-fashioned and provincial. More importantly, the postal service's monopoly on the country's shipping was eliminated by the development of the railroad and automobile, private shipping companies, and the subsequent emergence of the airplane—all of which made the distribution of pornography much more difficult to control (Lane, 2000).

The transition of the pornography business from an underground enterprise to a multibillion-dollar industry began in 1953, with the publication of the first issue of *Playboy* magazine. The World War II generation bought 50,000 copies of the first issue, and the magazine's growing readership throughout the next decade made its publisher, Hugh Hefner, a multimillionaire. Another change involved sexually explicit movies. These films had been distributed only in the underground stag-film market until the 1973 film *Deep Throat*, which was the first adult film that drew mainstream audiences, including women, to X-rated movie houses. It generated $600 million in theater and video revenues. The success of *Deep Throat* launched the modern pornography industry and expanded the boundaries of sexual content in mainstream films. The increase in sexual explicitness also led to increased opposition by conservative political and religious groups that believed pornography was immoral, had a negative effect on adults, and increased crime around porn shops and adult movie theaters. Supreme Court decisions and government commissions attempted to determine legal questions regarding sexually explicit materials.

An erotic color lithograph created sometime between 1830 and 1848.

© Stapleton Collection/CORBIS

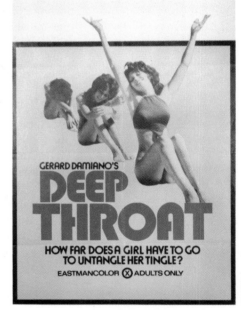

Photofest

In 1973, *Deep Throat* was the first mainstream adult film to attract both men and women viewers.

## Freedom of Speech Versus Censorship

The U.S. Constitution's First Amendment guarantees freedom of speech and freedom of the press. Do these constitutional protections apply to sexually explicit materials? A 1957 Supreme Court decision declared that First Amendment guarantees of free speech did not apply categorically to "obscene" materials. This ruling has remained controversial to this day, beginning with the difficulty of clearly defining **obscenity**. Those who oppose limits on free speech believe that any such laws violate the First Amendment and infringe on freedom of personal expression and choice. Furthermore, they argue, censorship is then at the discretion of those with the most political power, who have the authority to interpret and rule on a wide variety of sexual images (Hudson & Graham, 2004). In fact, those outside of mainstream political power have employed

**Obscenity** A term that implies a personal or societal judgment that something is offensive.

pornography to challenge social norms and the hypocrisy of religion, politics, and the middle and upper classes (Beck, 1999; Kipnes, 1996; Penley, 1996).

The On the Edge box titled "Pornography as Social Criticism" discusses how sexually explicit materials have at times been used for a greater purpose than sexual arousal.

**? Critical Thinking Question**

What examples have you seen of present-day pornography that challenge social and political hypocrisy?

## What Constitutes Obscenity?

The 1957 Supreme Court decision defined *obscenity* in order to implement censorship. It established the following three criteria for evaluating obscenity:

1. The dominant theme of the work as a whole must appeal to prurient interest in sex.
2. The work must be patently offensive to contemporary community standards.
3. The work must be without serious literary, artistic, political, or scientific value (*Roth* v. *United States*, 354 U.S. 476 [1957]).

Determining what materials are "obscene" and qualify for censorship has been plagued by ambiguity because the criteria are still highly subjective. The subjectivity of these criteria is perhaps best reflected in Supreme Court Justice Potter Stewart's comment regarding obscenity: It is difficult to define intelligently, "but I know it when I see it" (*Jacobelis* v. *Ohio*, 379 U.S. 197 [1965]).

In addition, community standards for obscenity vary dramatically from one location to another. In small, rural communities, magazines such as *Playboy* have been banned, and the books *The Color Purple* and *Our Bodies, Ourselves* and *Ms.* magazine have been deemed obscene and have consequently been banned from high school libraries (Klein, 1999). Furthermore, the advent of cable TV, VCRs, and the Internet and other wireless technologies has made "community standards" even more nebulous because people use these technologies in the privacy of their homes. In fact, some highly conservative communities have the highest rates of Internet use for access to pornography. For example, according to the FBI, Salt Lake City, Utah ranks number one for Internet searches for adult-related content (Knox, 2006). With community standards in many cases essentially irrelevant, it becomes questionable whether government should spend taxpayers' resources to attempt to control the use of sexually explicit materials in the home (Calvert & Richards, 2006).

## The Commissions on Obscenity and Pornography

In addition to Supreme Court rulings regarding sexually explicit materials, since the late 1960s two presidential commissions have been appointed to study pornography. They came to very different conclusions. President Lyndon Johnson appointed the Commission on Obscenity and Pornography to study the effects of sexually explicit materials, and its report was published in 1970. It analyzed the effects of legalizing pornography in Denmark (which had occurred in 1967) and the findings of various studies done in the United States. The commission found that the increased availability of pornography after legalization did *not* result in an increase in sex offenses. Furthermore, no significant, long-lasting changes in behavior were evident in college-student volunteer research subjects in the United States after they were exposed to pornography. On that basis, this commission recommended repealing all laws prohibiting access to pornography for adults. However, both President Nixon and the U.S. Senate rejected these recommendations.

In 1986, President Ronald Reagan appointed another commission to study pornography, the U.S. Attorney General's Commission on Pornography (sometimes called the Meese Commission, after then-attorney general Edwin Meese). It reached different conclusions and made radically different recommendations from those of the earlier commission. It claimed that violent or degrading pornography caused sexually aggressive behavior toward women and that all pornography promoted promiscuity. It recommended prosecuting pornography vigorously and prohibiting "dial-a-porn" telephone services and sexual cable TV programs. However, leading researchers criticized the Meese Commission report for basing its recommendations on politics instead of science, because it did not produce adequate scientific evidence to support its conclusions (D'Amato, 2006). The recommendations were not implemented, except for one making possession of child pornography a felony (U.S. Attorney General's Commission on Pornography, 1986).

## Pornography as Social Criticism

Over the course of history pornography has sometimes played the role of social critic. During the French Revolution, pornography like the example shown in this box helped incite the poor to rebel against the king and queen. Hundreds of pamphlets were printed and circulated that linked "degenerate" sexual activity with the material excesses and political corruption of royalty (Beck, 1999). In 18th-century Great Britain virtuous women were supposed to be repelled by sex, and female characters in novels who transgressed the established social order always met with eventual disaster. John Cleland's novel *Fanny Hill*, first published in Great Britain in 1748, was notorious because of the happy ending in the main character's life of sexual adventure.

The role of present-day pornography in social and political criticism is also evident. *Hustler* magazine fuses nudity and vulgarity with attacks on political power, organized religion, and class privilege. For example, stark social and political criticism is evident in a 1989 photomontage titled "Farewell to Reagan: Ronnie's Last Bash." The faces of the political elite of that era are superimposed on top of naked bodies doing "obscene" things to one another. The accompanying text declares, "It's been eight great years—for the power elite, that is.... A radical tax plan that more than halved taxes for the rich while doubling the working man's load; ... more than 100 appointees who resigned in disgrace over ethics or outright criminal

From *Porn 101: Eroticism, Pornography, and the First Amendment* edited by James Elias, Veronica Diehl Elias, Gwen Brewer, Vern L. Bullough, Jeffrey J. Douglas, and Will Jarvis (Amherst, NY: Prometheus Books). Copyright © 1999 by James Elias, Veronica Diehl Elias, Gwen Brewer, Vern L. Bullough, Jefferey J. Douglas, and Will Jarvis.

Pornography can be a form of political subversion, linking "degenerate" sexual activities to political corruption. This illustration shows a man of the lower classes servicing Queen Marie Antoinette's sexual appetites, implying that the king could not control his wife's sexual adventures or be certain of the paternity of his children. If he could not keep his own house in order, his ability to rule a country and its people could be challenged (Beck, 1999).

charges ... and we'll still get ... sexual intimidation policies for years to come, particularly with conservative whores posing as Supreme Court justices" (Kipnis, 1996, pp. 152–153).

Another form of social criticism found in some pornography is the violation of conventional norms regarding what is "sexy." Geriatric sexually explicit materials, such as "Promiscuous Granny," defy common views that older adults are asexual. Transgender pornography wreaks havoc with standard concepts of gender or sexual orientation in its portrayals of transsexuals with breasts and penises engaging in sexual interaction with same-sex and other-sex partners. Perhaps the most dramatic example of pornography's defiance of contemporary social norms is the subgenre of fat pornography. Large (between 200- and 500-pound) naked women in sexual situations are featured in an array of magazines and videos with titles such as *Life in the Fat Lane* and *Jumbo Jezebel*. Disbelief by many people that fat, fleshy bodies could be a turn-on shows how completely cultural conformity seems universally "normal." Actually, the amount of body fat considered most sexually appealing is historically and culturally relative. The 20th century's preference for thinness contrasted with the previous 400 years' preference for hefty, rotund body types. Thinness was not sexually attractive during those years, because it connoted lower-class poverty and ill-health (Kipnis, 1996).

What if pornography use actually reduces sexual violence? A recent study leads to that conclusion. The incidence of rape in the United States has declined by 85% since 1973, although the Internet has dramatically increased the availability of pornography. Furthermore, the research found that between 1980 and 2000, states with the *greatest access* to the Internet also had the *greatest decrease* in incidence of rape, per capita. The four states with the highest rate of Internet access (Alaska, Colorado, New Jersey, and Washington) had a 27% decrease in rape. In contrast, the four states with the lowest rate of Internet access (Arkansas, Kentucky, Minnesota, and West Virginia) had an increase in rape of 53%. The large increase in rape in these states is especially remarkable given the 85% overall national decrease (D'Amato, 2006). As we know, correlation is not the same as causation, but the statistics are compelling. However, research indicating that pornography does not increase sex crimes has not deterred attempts at censorship, as discussed in the Sex and Politics box on the next page.

**? Critical Thinking Question**

What are other possible reasons that the incidence of rape is lowest in states where Internet access is highest, and vice versa?

# Contemporary Censorship and Free Speech Controversies

During the George W. Bush administration, Attorney General John Ashcroft and his successor, Alberto Gonzales, reinvigorated prosecutions of people who make and distribute pornography. Court cases have been pursued, won, thrown out, overturned, and reinstated. The Supreme Court continues to address issues of censorship, especially in response to technological developments. For example, in 1997 in *Reno v. American Civil Liberties Union et al.* the Court gave free speech protection to material on the Internet (except for child pornography). The decision was based on the Court's opinion that the Internet is the most participatory form of communication ever developed and therefore it is entitled to the "highest protection from governmental intrusion" (Beck, 1999, p. 83).

### From Obscenity to Indecency

Television and radio broadcasters have a huge profit motive for putting sexual content on the air because that is what most often raises ratings. Fighting to slow the loss of their market share to cable, Internet, and movies also leads them to push the envelope of sexual content. The Federal Communications Commission (FCC) licenses the publicly held airwaves that radio and TV broadcasters use, and it establishes and enforces rules for "indecency." The FCC defines *indecency* as "material that, in context, depicts or describes sexual or excretory activities or organs in terms patently offensive as measured by contemporary community standards for the broadcast medium" and "material that panders, titillates, or shocks the audience is treated quite differently than material that is primarily used to educate or inform the audience" (Ranii, 2006).

The difficulty in finding a consistent, clear definition of "decency" is apparent in many of the FCC censorship decisions. For example, at the 2003 Golden Globe Awards presentation, Bono of the band U2 exclaimed that it was "fucking brilliant" for his band to win the award. Afterward, the FCC

The "Spirit of Justice", a 12-foot-tall statue created by a WPA sculptor in 1936, stands in the Great Hall of the Justice Department where officials give press conferences. Former U.S. Attorney General John Ashcroft had $8,000 drapes placed to cover the statue so he would not be photographed with the statue's breast behind him.

ruled that his language was not indecent because Bono was not describing a sex act. Five months later the FCC reversed its decision, but it did not fine the network. The FCC also said the word *fuck* was not indecent in the film *Saving Private Ryan*, but after receiving one viewer complaint, it enforced a fine for the same word in a public television broadcast of Martin Scorsese's documentary *The Blues* (McCollum, 2006).

"For far too long, the discussion of 'decency' or 'moral values' has been dominated by censorious concerns about what people read, what they watch, what they listen to, or even what they say. . . . The debate over decency at a national and state level, however, should be about how the citizens of this country treat each other and how this nation behaves in the global community" (Lane, 2006, p. 280).

While the FCC's rulings are inconsistent, the general public appears to be hypocritical about its stated beliefs and

## The Marriage of Technology and Sexually Explicit Materials

Although fines on broadcast TV and radio have increased, new technologies have made pornography more difficult to regulate and censure as well as enormously more lucrative. Technological advances and the direct-to-the-consumer market have turned sexually explicit media into an estimated $10 to $14 billion-a-year industry—more than the combined revenues of professional football, basketball, and baseball (Williams, 2004). The ease of access and privacy afforded by the advent of cable television and the VCR, followed closely by the Internet, has extended access to pornography to people who previously would not have gone to an adult movie theater or bookstore. Rentals of X-rated videos and DVDs in the United States increased from 79 million in 1985 to 759 million in 2001, an increase of more than 850% (Kloer, 2003). Currently nearly one in five DVD and VCR rentals is X-rated. The pornography industry produces about 11,000 films per year, whereas Hollywood makes 400 feature films each year (Paul, 2004). A new group of adult television networks has been developed exclusively for video-on-demand technology. Porn's appearance on cell phones, iPods, PDAs, and PSP game handhelds provides portable access to sexually explicit materials.

**FCC Fines**

| Company | Fine | Reason |
|---|---|---|
| Young Broadcasting | $27,500 | A morning news segment about a play called *Puppetry of the Penis* that unexpectedly turned explicit on San Francisco's KRON-TV. |
| Clear Channel Radio | $495,000 | Discussion of sexual activity, including fake product "Sphincterine," on the Howard Stern Show. |
| CBS | $550,000 | Janet Jackson's sexually explicit performance and "wardrobe malfunction" during the Super Bowl XXXVIII half-time show. |
| Clear Channel Radio | $755,000 | A single individual's complaints about radio talk-show host Bubba "The Love Sponge" Clem's discussion of sex among cartoon characters. |
| Fox | $1,183,000 | Scenes of bachelor and bachelorette parties, including partygoers licking whipped cream off strippers' bodies on reality-TV show *Married By America*. |

Getty Images

⚪ **Figure 18.1** In the past few years, the FCC has been aggressive in fining television and radio broadcasters, such as Howard Stern, for airing material it considers indecent.

actual behavior when it comes to indecency. In a *Time* magazine poll, more than half of the respondents said that there was too much sex, profanity, and violence on TV and believed that the FCC should be stricter. However, programs that are the most popular are also often the most sexually explicit. For example, in conservative Atlanta, where nearly 58% of voters cast their ballots for Bush in 2004, that city's top TV show, *Desperate Housewives*, features sexual escapades, including that of a married woman who sleeps with her teenage gardener (Levy, 2005).

The Bush administration has significantly increased funding and personnel to investigate and prosecute indecency. In 2002 the FCC began aggressively fining broadcast networks and radio (CBS, Fox, NBC, and Clear Channel Radio) for sexual material and swear words. ⚪ **Figure 18.1** shows some examples of fines. Total yearly fines increased from $440,000 in 2002 to $7.7 million in 2003. In 2006, fines *per infraction* (for each indecent swear word) were raised from $32,500 to $325,000 (Triplett, 2006). Some political analysts believe that the goal of the Bush administration's censorship efforts was to motivate far-right voters to get to the polls and help elect Republicans in close state election battles (Lane, 2006; Piccionelli, 2006).

Decency advocates are working to further increase the dollar amount of fines that the FCC can levy against TV and radio broadcasters. They also hope to bring cable and satellite radio and TV under FCC jurisdiction. The FCC currently does not have jurisdiction over cable and satellite because private industry, not the government, pays for cable and satellite TV and radio equipment and transmissions. This is why words that are bleeped out by TV broadcasters are not censored by cable and satellite TV companies, such as HBO, ESPN, and FX. The censorship of broadcast media also explains why some programs move from broadcast programs. For example, in early 2005 Howard Stern left his broadcast radio program for a satellite radio program, to be outside the FCC's jurisdiction.

Adult content on mobile devices became a multinational billion-dollar business in less than one year following its inception (Piccionelli, 2006).

Because the pornography business generates such high earnings, major corporations, including mainstream entertainment companies, have close ties to the industry. For example, TV viewers in the United States spent $465 million in 2001 watching adult pay-per-view movies in their homes, and most of the money goes to media companies such as Time Warner and AT&T.

## Sexually Explicit Materials: Helpful or Harmful?

Graphic sexual images have become so ubiquitous in our culture that many university literature, film, anthropology, law, and women's studies departments offer "porn curriculum" courses that delve into pornography issues (Cullen, 2006). One important issue is the impact of pornography on those who use it. Arguments are made on both sides of the question of whether and how pornography is helpful or harmful. Pornography can be helpful by providing sexual stimulation without the potential of being rejected, criticized by a partner, becoming pregnant, or contracting an STD. "Nobody fails to get an erection, the woman doesn't have trouble achieving orgasm,

**? Critical Thinking Question**

Do you think that far-right religious groups will be successful in deterring pornography? Why or why not?

© 2006 STAHLER—COLUMBUS DISPATCH

nobody fears their gut looks too big. . . . Nobody gets pregnant or wants to get married or tries to pin down a date for the next weekend" (Paul, 2005, p. 41). Pornography can also provide an endless variety of sexual fantasy material. In a relationship, sexually explicit materials can even out differences in frequency of interest between partners by facilitating sexual arousal during masturbation when one partner is not in the mood or is out of town.

Some individuals and couples find that mainstream pornography or erotica have helped improve their sexual experiences. One study found that 37% of men and 28% of women said they had expanded what they found erotic by looking at Internet sex sites. Individuals may also increase their communication about sex after revealing their sexual interests anonymously online: After doing so, about 50% of women and 44% of men told their partners about sexual desires they had previously concealed (Gowen, 2005). Sexually explicit adult sex educational videos can help enhance a couple's sexual communication and experimentation.

On the other hand, many observers have expressed concern about the influence of pornography on intimate relationships. One study found that after repeated exposure to pornography, both men and women research subjects became less satisfied with the physical appeal and sexual performance of their partners (Zillmann & Bryant, 1988). Marriage therapists and divorce attorneys have seen a great increase in couples in which Internet pornography played a significant part in what brought them to counseling or divorce (Greenfield, 2005; Hanus, 2006). Porn use can lead men and women to become numb to the pleasures of conventional sex and to prefer the company of computer porn to involvement in a face-to-face relationship. Individuals may also pressure their partners to engage in typical pornographic behaviors that the partners dislike (including, perhaps, ejaculating on a woman's face or body, having sex with other partners, or having anal sex) (Paul, 2006). Such influences of Internet pornography may help cause a relationship to deteriorate, as reflected in the following account:

*During my early and mid-twenties I spent a lot of time (and a fair bit of change) paying women with Web cam businesses to role-play sexual scenarios I liked to masturbate to. I considered it a healthy, safe, simple way to take care of my needs instead of counting on dating for sex. Then I met Jennifer and fell for her. After several months I started getting bored with our vanilla sex and asked her to do the "schoolgirl" roleplay I'd liked via Web cam. She tried her best, but I was kind of pissed that she didn't do it "right," and I made her feel like she wasn't sexy enough for me. I hadn't figured out that I couldn't expect her to pull off a fantasy like the Web cam professionals. It's a trade off, but I'd rather have sex with a woman who really cares about me than one who's a good actor (Authors' files).*

Common themes in pornography are usually poor "sex education." Pornography often stresses male performance, rushed and nonsensual interactions, and conquest rather than pleasure (Cook, 2006). It restricts male sexuality to oversized penises and penile performance. It perpetuates the myths that a real man should always be ready for sex and that he should "get it" whenever possible, without regard for the other person or his own complex nature (Zilbergeld, 1978). In addition, women are usually portrayed as wildly responsive to just about any stimulation from men. When women do not react in such a manner in real life, men may feel inadequate or cheated, and men and women may doubt the normality of their own sexuality (Castleman, 2005). The superficial portrayal of sexuality in commercial sex has become ubiquitous in the United States, as discussed in the On the Edge box titled "The 'Pornification' of U.S. Culture."

## The "Pornification" of U.S. Culture

The mainstreaming of aspects of pornography and sex work into U.S. culture is so prevalent that author Ariel Levy has defined this era as "raunch culture" (Levy, 2005). For example, porn stars host programs on cable TV, including the reality show *Can You Be a Porn Star?* Eminem, Kid Rock, and Metallica feature porn stars in their music videos, and pre-adolescent girls wear T-shirts with "PORN STAR" in rhinestones on the front (Paul, 2005). Hundreds of young women cheerfully strip and mimic pornographic poses for *Girls Gone Wild* videos.

Women can take classes to learn the skills of red-light entertainment. On her talk show, Oprah Winfrey featured a stripper instructor whose program has taught over 12,000 women how to strip and pole dance. Other classes teach women how to give oral sex to men, and TV programs instruct and demonstrate how to "lap dance" a man to orgasm. The book *How to Make Love Like a Porn Star* continues the pornography/sex work education.

Is the recent trend of imitating sex workers and learning their skills good fun? Are sex workers' behaviors a positive model for women? Does such a model signify greater sexual freedom for women or a new emphasis on serving men while overlooking their own sexual pleasure? The president of the

The "reality TV" show *Can You Be a Porn Star?* with hosts Tabitha Stevens and Mary Carey began airing on pay-per-view in early 2004, illustrating a trend toward mainstreaming of the porn industry.

Institute for the Advanced Study of Human Sexuality, Ted McIlvenna, believes that it is empowering for women to enhance their sexual confidence by taking charge of obtaining more skills and options. On the other hand, it is ironic to see sex workers as role models of female empowerment when, in reality, many of these workers feel trapped in their situations, as we discuss in the next section on prostitution. The author of *Female Chauvinist Pigs: Women and the Rise of Raunch Culture* questions the value as erotic role models of women who act sexy and have sex for money regardless of whether they are in the mood. The best erotic role models would "be the women who get the most pleasure out of sex, not the women who get the most money for it," if sex is most valued for pleasure or as an expression of love (Levy, 2005, p. 179).

In contrast, women in most of the amateur pornography on the Internet are sexually excited, rather than pretending to be aroused. The women enjoy their bodies and are not inhibited by lack of youth or "perfect" figures. Amateur porn is enormously popular on the Internet. Watching real people instead of actors may more strongly validate the viewers' desire for normalizing erotic and lustful sexual expression (Klein, 2006).

## ▶ Prostitution and Sex Work

**Prostitution** is the exchange of sexual services for money. Prostitution is typically thought of in terms of a woman selling sexual services to a man, although transactions between two males are also common. Payment for a man's services to a woman is less common. *Sex worker* is a term for a person involved in prostitution and related activities, such as phone sex, nude dancing, erotic massage, Internet sex, and acting in porn movies. Most people who are sex workers for more than a few months often move from one type of commercial sex work to another (Farley, 2004).

Relationships that involve exchanging sex for money also occur outside of sex work. Advertising frequently portrays the "trade goods for sex" theme, and in 2000, one of the first reality TV shows, *Who Wants to Marry a Multimillionaire?* highlighted the prostitutionlike aspects sometimes present in common male/female relationships (Peyser, 2000b). A case could be made that a woman who marries a good provider instead of her heartthrob, the wife who is especially sexually pleasing before asking for extra money from her husband, or the woman who wants out of her marriage but stays for economic security all play out the dynamics of prostitution (Ridgeway, 1996).

**Prostitution** The exchange of sexual services for money.

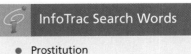

InfoTrac Search Words

● Prostitution

## History of Prostitution and Sex Work

Prostitution has existed throughout history and has been called the oldest profession. Evidence shows that men sold sexual services to other men as far back as the ancient Sumerian and ancient Greek civilizations. However, the importance and meaning of prostitution have varied in different times and societies. During some periods of ancient Greek history certain types of prostitutes were valued for their intellectual, social, and sexual companionship. Female prostitution was part of revered religious rituals in other ancient societies. Sexual relations between prostitutes and men often took place within temples and were seen as sacred acts. In medieval Europe prostitution was tolerated, and public baths provided opportunities for contact between customers and prostitutes. In Victorian Great Britain, prostitution was viewed as a scandalous but necessary sexual and social outlet for men: It was a lesser evil for a middle-class man to have sexual relations with a prostitute than with another middle-class man's wife or daughter (Taylor, 1970).

## Customers of Sex Workers

Sex workers exist because there is a demand for their services. Sex in exchange for money gives a customer sexual contact without any expectation of intimacy or future commitment; it eliminates the risk of rejection and offers an opportunity to engage in sexual techniques the customer would not use with a partner (Califia, 2002). A study of a representative sample of men around the world found that about 10% of them had exchanged money for sex in the last 12 months (Carael et al., 2006). In a study of men in the United States who used prostitutes, 93% of the men had contact with a prostitute at least once a month (Freund et al., 1991).

Women are far less likely than men to pay for sex. However, female sex tourism has greatly increased. Single, divorced, and married white women, primarily from Europe and North America, travel to third-world locales such as Mombassa, Kenya, for liaisons with "beach boys," who provide flattery, companionship, and sex for money or gifts. African American women are most likely to travel as sex tourists to Jamaica, and Japanese women usually go to Bali (Hari, 2006). One female sex tourist stated, "In England, men our age aren't remotely interested. . . . Here, the men make us feel like gorgeous, sexy women again" (Knight, 2006, p.2).

The female sex tourists and the men they hire often hold a benign view of their commercial relationship. One researcher found that the men often imagine they receive gifts of appreciation for helping these women, and female sex tourists believe they are helping the men and the local economy by giving them money and gifts (Hari, 2006). Female sex tourism is the theme of a French film, *Heading South*, in which three U.S. women travel to Haiti to sample the young islanders' sexual talents. A 2006 London play, *Sugar Mummies*, bluntly shows how female sex tourists objectify the black male body, talking about how "big" one beach boy is compared with another. (Burr, 2006).

## Adult Male and Female Prostitutes

Adult prostitutes vary from one another in characteristics such as public visibility, the amount of money they make, and social class. Some sex workers work part-time and otherwise pursue conventional school, work, or social lifestyles. People who work as prostitutes on a temporary, part-time basis and have other occupational skills can leave sex work more easily than other prostitutes. Many of these women and men have not identified themselves as "profes-

Advertisements often demonstrate prostitution's sex-for-sale basis of relationships.

Courtesy of The Advertising Archives

Jamaica is one of the countries where women "sex tourists" travel for their vacations to find local men for companionship and sex.

© Peter Dench/CORBIS

sionals." In contrast, the full-time sex worker who has identified herself or himself as part of the prostitute subculture (being arrested facilitates this identification), typically has little education and few marketable skills. One study found that 89% of sex workers wanted to leave "the profession" (○ **Table 18.1**), but without other resources, many find it difficult to become successfully independent of prostitution (Butcher, 2003; Farley, 2004).

Female *streetwalkers* and male *hustlers* solicit straight and gay male customers, respectively, on the street or in bars. Hustlers extend their search for business into gay bathhouses, public parks, and restrooms (Friedman 2003; Parsons, 2005).

**○ TABLE 18.1** | **Responses of Sex Workers to "What Do You Need?" (in Descending Order of Importance)**

| What women say they need in order to leave prostitution |
| --- |
| Job training |
| Home or safe place |
| Health care |
| Individual counseling |
| Legal assistance |
| Peer support |
| Drug/alcohol treatment |
| Self-defense training |
| Child care |
| Legalization of prostitution |
| Physical protection from pimp |

SOURCE: Farley (2004).

Streetwalkers and hustlers charge the least of all sex workers for their services. Hustlers rarely work for pimps, but streetwalkers usually do and must share a large portion of their earnings with them. Hustlers and streetwalkers are most likely to be victims of abuse and robbery by customers or pimps (Valera et al., 2001). News stories all too frequently describe the discovery of a murdered prostitute or a hunt for a serial killer of sex workers (Green, 2000). In addition, due to their visibility, streetwalkers and hustlers are easily subject to arrest. Most repeat the cycle of arrest, short jail sentences, and release many times throughout their careers.

A **brothel** is a house in which a group of female prostitutes work. Brothels were common in the United States during much of its history and are legal in some areas of Nevada today. A "madam" usually acts as the hostess and is usually the business manager of the brothel. Prostitutes who work in brothels where prostitution is illegal are somewhat more protected from arrest than are streetwalkers, because they are less visible to the police. However, prostitutes in Nevada brothels are often completely under the control of the owner and are not allowed to leave the brothel for 8 consecutive days. One study found that women working in legal Nevada brothels actually felt safer in street prostitution because they could refuse dangerous-appearing or intoxicated customers, whereas brothel managers did not permit them to reject any customers. The researcher did find more physical violence in street prostitution than in brothel prostitution, but the prostitutes' incidence and severity of mental distress from their work was the same in both situations (Farley, 2004).

Massage parlors are often seen as a modern "quick service" version of brothels. Manual stimulation (a "local" or "hand finishing") or oral stimulation to orgasm is often arranged for a fee once the customer is in the massage room. In addition, the customer can often dictate in what state of dress or undress he would like his masseuse to be. Intercourse may occur as part of the "massage."

*Call girls* and *call boys*, who provide services for men, and *gigolos*, who service women, earn more than other kinds of prostitutes. They often come from middle-class backgrounds and frequently provide social companionship as well as sexual services for their typically wealthy, middle-aged and older customers. Contacts with such prostitutes are usually made by personal referral or through "escort services," and these prostitutes commonly have several regular customers (Blackmun, 1996a). There is often a pretense, on the sex worker's part, of romantic interest in the customer. Regular customers are likely to give such prostitutes goods, such as clothing, jewelry, and living accommodations.

**Brothel** A house in which a group of prostitutes work.

Streetwalkers are at high risk for abuse by customers, pimps, and police.

Public visibility for these prostitutes is minimal, and their risk of arrest is much lower than that for the sex worker on the street.

One study found that call boys working through an escort agency had an average of six clients a month, client calls lasted about an hour, and oral sex was the most common sexual service they provided. Most of the escorts avoided anal sex. About 80% of the escorts disliked having sex with clients; the escorts preferred clients who were seeking nonsexual companionship for conversation, entertainment, or travel (Hagen, 2006).

## Teenage Prostitution

A nine-country research study found that 47% of sex workers are younger than 18 when they enter the sex industry (Farley, 2004). Statistics from the National Incident-Based Reporting System indicate that in the United States, male juvenile prostitutes outnumber female juvenile prostitutes by 61% to 39% (Finkelhor & Ormrod, 2004). Teenagers often become prostitutes as a means of survival after they have run away from home (Ring, 2001). Approximately 95% have been victims of sexual abuse, and most have been rejected by their families, often after parents found out their children are gay, lesbian, bisexual, or transgendered (Mok, 2006). However, teens from middle- and upper-class homes are increasingly involved in sex work and appear to sell themselves for excitement and the quick money to spend as they wish, without parental interference. After school some girls even invite customers to their homes while their parents are at work (Smalley, 2003).

## The Internet and Sex Work

The Internet is transforming the world's oldest profession. Web sites offer "escorts" with a great variety of physical, intellectual, and sexual specialties (bondage, sado-masochism, fantasy enactment). One Web male escort site has 36,000 escorts in 121 cities worldwide (Hagen, 2006). Male and female sex workers are increasingly operating through individual Web sites. The prostitute and customer negotiate through e-mail, which eliminates the need for part of the prostitute's fees to go to Web site companies, pimps, or brothels (Reynolds, 2006). Live models on video-conferencing sites earn $25 to $50 per hour but receive only a fraction of the money they generate. Their company makes at least $300 per hour from each sex worker. Whether working through a company or an individual Web site, sex workers on the Internet have far safer and less oppressive working conditions than other sex workers. While arrests of Internet sex workers are uncommon, the Internet does provide easy leads for arrest by police posing as customers (Linskey, 2006).

## Why Women and Men Become Sex Workers

A combination of psychological, social, environmental, and economic factors is involved in becoming a sex worker. One study found that some people go into prostitution as a matter of free personal choice or the right to sexual liberation (Lim, 1998). Sex work may bring a feeling of power, especially in having control over negotiations for the service and fee (Deshotels & Forsyth, 2006). Desire for the attention received from customers can give sex work appeal (Andreas, 2005). Young gay men may find sexual affirmation from client appreciation and flattery, in significant contrast to the hostile anti-gay sentiment that surrounded them when they were younger (Steele, 2006).

Economic incentive and necessity are usually the primary motivations to enter and continue sex work (Carter, 2003; Kempner, 2005). Melissa Farley's comprehensive research on sex workers in nine countries (Canada, Colombia, Germany, Mexico, South Africa, Thailand, Turkey, the United States, and Zambia) found that the most common and compelling reason that individuals from both developed and developing countries enter sex work is to earn money. Most are in dire need of resources for survival needs: 75% were homeless when they became prostitutes (Farley, 2004). In the United States a majority of individuals became involved in sex work because they were unable to find work that paid a living wage. Many had previously held babysitting, food service, and cleaning jobs (Thukral, 2005).

A traumatic childhood may also contribute to a person's becoming a sex worker. Farley's research found that when the sex workers were children, their caregivers had beaten 59% of them to the point of physical injury. Furthermore, a majority of women in the sex industry had experienced child sexual abuse, and 63% were sexually abused by an average of four different perpetrators per child.

According to Farley, it is a misconception that sex workers enter the business to support their drug habits. Various studies have reported that prostitution precedes drug and alcohol abuse for 39% to 60% of individuals. Sex workers often began to abuse drugs and alcohol to try to cope with overwhelming negative feelings while working (Farley, 2004).

## The High Personal Costs of Sex Work

Sex workers have many physical and mental health problems as a direct result of violence, chronic stress, and exposure to sexually transmitted diseases (Ward & Day, 2006; Wong et al., 2006). Two-thirds of the sex workers in Farley's nine-country study met diagnostic criteria for posttraumatic stress disorder (PTSD), which develops when an individual experiences overwhelming trauma. Some of the symptoms include recurrent nightmares, emotional numbness or fear, difficulty sleeping and concentrating, and flashbacks (feelings of reliving the original traumatic experience). Sex workers experienced two times the percentage of PTSD as Vietnam vets did, and the rate and severity was the same in all countries, whether developed or developing. Details about sex workers' experiences clarify the source of PTSD. The following experiences occurred to a woman who prostituted mainly in strip clubs:

> The job required her to tolerate verbal abuse (with a coerced smile), being grabbed and pinched on the legs, buttocks, breasts, and crotch. . . . Her breasts were squeezed until she was in severe pain. She was humiliated by customers ejaculating on her face . . . [and] her hair was pulled as a means of control and torture. She was severely bruised from beatings and frequently had black eyes. She was repeatedly beaten on the head with closed fists, sometimes causing concussions and unconsciousness. From these beatings, her jaw was dislocated and her eardrum was damaged. Many years later her jaw is still dislocated. She was cut with knives. She was burned with cigarettes by customers who smoked while raping her. She was gang raped. . . . Rapes by johns and pimps sometimes resulted in internal bleeding. (Farley, 2004, p. 64)

## Prostitution and HIV/AIDS

HIV/AIDS is another danger prostitutes face. The sex workers who are the most desperate for money, are in the United States illegally, or are poor, older, and drug addicted face the greatest pressures to practice unsafe sex (Chapkis, 1997). A study in Mexico found that prostitutes receive a premium of between 23% and 46% for unprotected sex—an increase from over $14,000 to $51,000 in income per year (Gertler, P., et al., 2006). Hoping to make safer sex financially beneficial to sex workers, a pilot project in India sponsored by the Bill and Melinda Gates Foundation provides prostitutes with a "smart card," which gives them discounts at grocery and clothing stores for having a medical check-up every three months (Beary, 2006).

While most individuals are pressured into sex work because of dire economic conditions, others are forced through deception and violence, as described in the following Sexuality and Diversity box, titled "Worldwide Exploitation of Women and Children in Prostitution."

## SEXUALITY AND DIVERSITY

### *Worldwide Exploitation of Women and Children in Prostitution*

The 50-year history of modern sex trafficking began with the U.S. military occupation of South Korea. Currently, "camp towns" adjacent to the 100 U.S. military

Courtesy of the U.S. Dept. of Health & Human Services, Administration for Children & Families

One of the posters developed by the Campaign to Rescue and Restore Victims of Human Trafficking to promote public awareness, identification, and assistance of victims of trafficking.

bases are filled with more than 1 million sex workers, primarily women trafficked from eastern Europe and the Philippines. Traffickers are criminals who entice women and children from underdeveloped and socially, economically, or politically unstable nations by promising employment. Instead of giving these people legitimate employment, traffickers sell them to others who force them into sex work, primarily in wealthier, more stable nations or in locales known for sex tourism (Farr, 2003). For example, after the fall of communism in Europe during the 1990s, traffickers would falsely promise legitimate employment in western Europe to eastern European women facing poverty in their home countries. Some women are also lured into prostitution by promises of marriage in a foreign country. Girls from tribal minority ethnic groups are most easily led into trafficking because they have such limited economic options, given their low social status in their countries of origin.

Traffickers also buy children from parents when the children are more of a financial burden than the family can manage. Orphans whose parents died of AIDS or were killed in the ethnic and tribal wars of Africa and eastern Europe are highly vulnerable to exploitation (Rios, 1996). There has been a notable increase in young boy prostitutes to meet the demands of sex tourism (Lim, 1998). Younger and younger children are sought for prostitution because customers regard them as more likely to be free of HIV. Traffickers also rely on kidnapping. Due to the chaos caused by the U.S. occupation of Iraq, by 2006, criminal trafficking gangs had abducted an estimated 2,000 girls (Bennett, 2006). It is impossible to know how many women and children are trafficked across the world, but a CIA–State Department report estimated that within the United States alone, 50,000 women and children are essentially slaves in the sex industry (Leuchtag, 2003).

Traffickers range from mom-and-pop operations to networks of highly sophisticated multinational crime groups. Corrupt individuals in legitimate positions of trust are also involved: police officers, border guards, immigration officials, travel agents, and bankers. That one trafficked sex worker can make between $75,000 to $250,000 a year for her "employer" provides enormous financial incentives to all involved (Farr, 2004). The worldwide exploitation of children and women through sex trafficking is estimated to generate a $7 billion to $10 billion profit each year (Cwikel & Hoban, 2005).

A sex tourist is an adult who travels to have sexual relations in return for money or presents. The growing sex tourism industry, whose clients come from industrialized countries, profits from trafficked women and children and the economic desperation of the local urban and rural poor people. The men who work as "beach boys" in female sex tourism often do so because it is the only way they can support their families. Many of the countries where female sex tourism occurs are former slave colonies that have not recovered economically from past colonialism (Hoggard, 2006).

Sex tourism for men is most prevalent in the Asian countries of Thailand, the Philippines, India, Sri Lanka, Vietnam, and Cambodia and in the South American

**Acquaintance rape** Sexual assault by a friend, acquaintance, or date—that is, someone known to the victim.

**Acquired immunodeficiency syndrome (AIDS)** A catastrophic illness in which a virus (HIV) invades and destroys the ability of the immune system to fight disease.

**Afterbirth** The placenta and amniotic sac following their expulsion through the vagina after childbirth.

**Amenorrhea** The absence of menstruation.

**Anaphrodisiac** A substance that inhibits sexual desire and behavior.

**Androgen insensitivity syndrome (AIS)** A condition resulting from a genetic defect that causes chromosomally normal males to be insensitive to the action of testosterone and other androgens. These individuals develop female external genitals of normal appearance.

**Androgens** A class of hormones that promote the development of male genitals and secondary sex characteristics and influence sexual motivation in both sexes. These hormones are produced by the adrenal glands in males and females and by the testes in males.

**Androgyny** A blending of typical male and female behaviors in one individual.

**Anilingus** Oral stimulation of the anus.

**Aphrodisiac** A substance that allegedly arouses sexual desire and increases the capacity for sexual activity.

**Artificial insemination** A medical procedure in which semen is placed in a woman's vagina, cervix, or uterus.

**Assisted reproductive technology (ART)** The techniques of extrauterine conception.

**Attachment** Intense emotional tie between two individuals, such as an infant and a parent or adult lovers.

**Atypical sexual behaviors** Behaviors not typically expressed by most people in our society.

**Autoerotic asphyxia** The enhancement of sexual excitement and orgasm by pressure-induced oxygen deprivation.

**Autosomes** The 22 pairs of human chromosomes that do not significantly influence sex differentiation.

**Backup methods** Contraceptive methods used simultaneously with another method to support it.

**Bacterial vaginosis** A vaginal infection caused by bacterial microorganisms; it is the most common form of vaginitis among U.S. women.

**Bartholin's glands** Two small glands slightly inside the vaginal opening that secrete a few drops of fluid during sexual arousal.

**Basal body temperature method** Birth control method based on body temperature changes before and after ovulation.

**Bisexuality** Sexual attraction to both men and women.

**Blastocyst** Multicellular descendant of the united sperm and ovum that implants on the wall of the uterus.

**Bondage** A sexual behavior in which a person derives sexual pleasure from being bound, tied up, or otherwise restricted.

**Brothel** A house in which a group of prostitutes work.

**Calendar method** A birth control method based on abstinence from intercourse during calendar-estimated fertile days.

**Candidiasis** An inflammatory infection of the vaginal tissues caused by the yeastlike fungus *Candida albicans*.

**Case study** A nonexperimental research method that examines either a single subject or a small group of subjects individually and in depth.

**Castration** Surgical removal of the testes.

**Cavernous bodies** The structures in the shaft of the clitoris or penis that engorge with blood during sexual arousal.

**Celibacy** Historically defined as the state of being unmarried; currently defined as not engaging in sexual behavior.

**Cerebral cortex** The outer layer of the brain's cerebrum that controls higher mental processes.

**Cerebral hemispheres** The two sides (right and left) of the cerebrum.

**Cerebrum** The largest part of the brain, consisting of two cerebral hemispheres.

**Cervix** The small end of the uterus, located at the back of the vagina.

**Cesarean section** A childbirth procedure in which the infant is removed through an incision in the abdomen and uterus.

**Chancre** A raised red painless sore that is symptomatic of the primary phase of syphilis.

**Child sexual abuse** An adult's engaging in sexual contact of any kind with a child, including inappropriate touching, oral–genital stimulation, and coitus.

**Chlamydia** Urogenital infection caused by the bacterium *Chlamydia trachomatis*.

**Circumcision** Surgical removal of the foreskin of the penis.

**Climacteric** Physiological changes that occur during the transition period from fertility to infertility in both sexes.

**Clitoris** A highly sensitive structure of the female external genitals, the only function of which is sexual pleasure.

**Cohabitation** Living together and having a sexual relationship without being married.

**Colostrum** A thin fluid secreted by the breasts during later stages of pregnancy and the first few days after delivery.

**Combined genital and subjective sexual arousal disorder** Absent or diminished subjective and physical sexual arousal.

**Coming out** The process of becoming aware of and disclosing one's homosexual identity.

**Commitment** The thinking component of Sternberg's triangular love theory.

**Companionate love** A type of love characterized by friendly affection and deep attachment based on extensive familiarity with the loved one.

**Complete celibacy** An expression of sexuality in which an individual does not engage in either masturbation or interpersonal sexual contact.

**Condom** A sheath that fits over the penis and is used for protection against unwanted pregnancy and sexually transmitted diseases.

**Conjunctivitis** Inflammation of the mucous membrane that lines the inner surface of the eyelid and the exposed surface of the eyeball.

**Consensual extramarital relationship** A sexual relationship that occurs outside the marriage bond with the consent of one's spouse.

**Constant-dose combination pills** Birth control pills that contain a constant daily dose of estrogen and progestin.

**Conversion therapy/sexual reorientation therapy** Therapy to help homosexual men and women change their sexual orientation.

**Coprophilia** A sexual paraphilia in which a person obtains sexual arousal from contact with feces.

**Corona** The rim of the penile glans.

**Corpus callosum** The broad band of nerve fibers that connects the left and right cerebral hemispheres.

**Corpus luteum** A yellowish body that forms on the ovary at the site of the ruptured follicle and secretes progesterone.

**Cowper's glands** Two pea-sized glands located alongside the base of the urethra in the male that secrete an alkaline fluid during sexual arousal.

**Crura** The innermost tips of the cavernous bodies that connect to the pubic bones.

**Cryptorchidism** A condition in which the testes fail to descend from the abdominal cavity to the scrotal sac.

**Cunnilingus** Oral stimulation of the vulva.

**Cystitis** An infection of the bladder.

**Date rape** Sexual assault by an acquaintance when on a date.

**Demographic bias** A kind of sampling bias in which certain segments of society (such as white, middle-class, white-collar workers) are disproportionately represented in a study population.

**Dependent variable** In an experimental research design, an outcome or a resulting behavior that the experimenter observes and records but does not control.

**DHT-deficient male** A chromosomally normal (XY) male who develops external genitalia resembling those of a female as a result of a genetic defect that prevents the prenatal conversion of testosterone into dihydrotestosterone (DHT).

**Dilation and evacuation (D and E)** An abortion procedure in which a curette and suction equipment are used.

**Direct observation** A method of research in which subjects are observed as they go about their activities.

**Domestic partnership** An unmarried couple living in the same household in a committed relationship.

**Dopamine** A neurotransmitter that facilitates sexual arousal and activity.

**Douching** Rinsing out the vagina with plain water or a variety of solutions. It is usually unnecessary for hygiene, and douching too often can result in vaginal irritation.

**Dysmenorrhea** Pain or discomfort before or during menstruation.

**Dyspareunia** Pain or discomfort during sexual intercourse.

**Ectoparasites** Parasitic organisms that live on the outer skin surfaces.

**Ectopic pregnancy** A pregnancy that occurs when a fertilized ovum implants outside the uterus, most commonly in a fallopian tube.

**Effacement** Flattening and thinning of the cervix that occurs before and during childbirth.

**Either/or question** A question that allows statement of a preference.

**Ejaculation** The process by which semen is expelled from the body through the penis.

**Ejaculatory ducts** Two short ducts located within the prostate gland.

**Elective abortion** Medical procedure performed to terminate pregnancy.

**Emission phase** The first stage of male orgasm, in which the seminal fluid is gathered in the urethral bulb.

**Endometriosis** A condition in which uterine tissue grows on various parts of the abdominal cavity.

**Endometrium** The tissue that lines the inside of the uterine wall.

**Epididymis** The structure along the back of each testis in which sperm maturation occurs.

**Episiotomy** An incision in the perineum that is sometimes made during childbirth.

**Erectile dysfunction (ED)** Consistent or recurring lack of an erection sufficiently rigid for enetrative sex, for a period of at least 3 months.

**Erection** The process by which the penis or clitoris engorges with blood and increases in size.

**Erogenous zones** Areas of the body that are particularly responsive to sexual stimulation.

**Erotica** Respectful, affectionate depictions of sexuality.

**Estrogens** A class of hormones that produce female secondary sex characteristics and affect the menstrual cycle.

**Excitement phase** Masters and Johnson's term for the first phase of the sexual response cycle, in which engorgement of the sexual organs and increases in muscle tension, heart rate, and blood pressure occur.

**Exhibitionism** The act of exposing one's genitals to an unwilling observer.

**Experimental research** Research conducted in precisely controlled laboratory conditions so that subjects' reactions can be reliably measured.

**Expulsion phase** The second stage of male orgasm, during which the semen is expelled from the penis by muscular contractions.

**Extramarital relationship** Sexual interaction by a married person with someone other than his or her spouse.

**Failure rate** The number of women out of 100 who become pregnant by the end of 1 year of using a particular contraceptive.

**Fallopian tubes** Two tubes, extending from the sides of the uterus, in which the egg and sperm travel.

**Fellatio** Oral stimulation of the penis.

**Female genital sexual arousal disorder** Persistent inability to attain or maintain the lubrication-swelling response.

**Female orgasmic disorder** The absence, marked delay, or diminished intensity of orgasm.

**Female subjective sexual arousal disorder** Absent or diminished awareness of physical arousal.

**Fertility awareness methods** Birth control methods that use the signs of cyclic fertility to prevent or plan conception.

**Fetal alcohol syndrome (FAS)** Syndrome in infants caused by heavy maternal prenatal alcohol use; characterized by congenital heart defects, damage to the brain and nervous system, numerous physical malformations of the fetus, and below-normal IQ.

**Fetally androgenized female** A chromosomally normal (XX) female who, as a result of excessive exposure to androgens during prenatal sex differentiation, develops external genitalia resembling those of a male.

**Fetishism** A sexual behavior in which a person obtains sexual excitement primarily or exclusively from an inanimate object or a particular part of the body.

**Fimbriae** Fringelike ends of the fallopian tubes, into which the released ovum enters.

**First-stage labor** The initial stage of childbirth in which regular contractions begin and the cervix dilates.

**Follicle-stimulating hormone (FSH)** A pituitary hormone secreted by a female during the secretory phase of the menstrual cycle. FSH stimulates the development of ovarian follicles. In males it stimulates sperm production.

**Foreskin** A covering of skin over the penile glans.

**Frenulum** A highly sensitive thin strip of skin that connects the glans to the shaft on the underside of the penis.

**"Friends with benefits" relationships (FWBRs)** Sexual interaction between friends who do not define their relationship as romantic.

**Frotteurism** A fairly common paraphilia in which a person obtains sexual pleasure by pressing or rubbing against another person in a crowded public place.

**Gamete intrafallopian transfer (GIFT)** Procedure in which the sperm and ovum are placed directly in a fallopian tube.

**Gay** A homosexual person, typically a homosexual male.

**Gay-affirmative therapy** Therapy to help homosexual clients cope with negative societal attitudes.

**Gender** The psychological and sociocultural characteristics associated with our biological sex.

**Gender assumptions** Assumptions about how people are likely to behave based on their maleness or femaleness.

**Gender dysphoria** Unhappiness with one's biological sex or gender role.

**Gender identity** How one psychologically perceives oneself as either male or female.

**Gender nonconformity** A lack of conformity to stereotypical masculine and feminine behaviors.

**Gender role** A collection of attitudes and behaviors that a specific culture considers normal and appropriate for people of a particular sex.

**Genital warts** Viral warts that appear on the genitals and are primarily transmitted sexually.

**Giving permission** Providing reassurance to one's partner that it is okay to talk about specific feelings or needs.

**Glans** The head of the clitoris or penis, which is richly endowed with nerve endings.

**Gonadotropins** Pituitary hormones that stimulate activity in the gonads (testes and ovaries).

**Gonads** The male and female sex glands: ovaries and testes.

**Gonorrhea** A sexually transmitted disease that initially causes inflammation of mucous membranes.

**Grafenberg spot** Glands and ducts in the anterior wall of the vagina. Some women experience sexual pleasure, arousal, orgasm, and an ejaculation of fluids from stimulation of the Grafenberg spot.

**Gynecology** The medical practice specializing in women's health and in diseases of the female reproductive and sexual organs.

**Herpes** A disease characterized by blisters on the skin in the regions of the genitals or mouth. It is caused by the *Herpes simplex* virus and is easily transmitted through sexual contact.

**Highly active antiretroviral therapy (HAART)** A strategy for treating HIV-infected people with three or more antiretroviral drugs.

**Homophobia** Irrational fears of homosexuality, the fear of the possibility of homosexuality in oneself, or loathing toward one's own homosexuality.

**Homosexual** A person whose primary erotic, psychological, emotional, and social orientation is toward members of the same sex.

**Hook-ups** Short-term, loveless sexual liaisons that occur during a brief interval.

**Hormone therapy (HT)** The use of supplemental hormones during and after menopause or following surgical removal of the ovaries.

**Human chorionic gonadotropin (HCG)** A hormone that is detectable in the urine of a pregnant woman within 1 month of conception.

**Human immunodeficiency virus (HIV)** The immune-system-destroying virus that causes AIDS.

**Hymen** Tissue that partially covers the vaginal opening.

**Hypoactive sexual desire disorder (HSDD)** Lack of interest prior to and during sexual activity.

**Hypogonadism** Impaired hormone production in the testes that results in testosterone deficiency.

**Hypothalamus** A small structure in the central core of the brain that controls the pituitary gland and regulates motivated behavior and emotional expression.

**Hysterectomy** Surgical removal of the uterus.

**In vitro fertilization (IVF)** Procedure in which mature eggs are removed from a woman's ovary and fertilized by sperm in a laboratory dish.

**Incest** Sexual contact between two people who are related (one of whom is often a child), other than husband and wife.

**Independent variable** In an experimental research design, a condition or component that is under the control of the researcher, who manipulates or determines its value.

**Intersexed** A term applied to people who possess biological attributes of both sexes.

**Interstitial cells** Cells located between the seminiferous tubules that are the major source of androgen in males.

**Intimacy** The emotional component of Sternberg's triangular love theory.

**Intracytoplasmic sperm injection (ICSI)** Procedure in which a single sperm is injected into an egg.

**Intrauterine device (IUD)** A small, plastic device that is inserted into the uterus for contraception.

**Introitus** The opening to the vagina.

**Intromission** Insertion of the penis into the vagina.

**Kegel exercises** A series of exercises that strengthen the muscles underlying the external female or male genitals.

**Klinefelter's syndrome** A condition characterized by the presence of two X chromosomes and one Y chromosome (XXY) in which affected individuals have undersized external male genitals.

**Klismaphilia** An unusual variant of sexual expression in which an individual obtains sexual pleasure from receiving enemas.

**Labia majora** The outer lips of the vulva.

**Labia minora** The inner lips of the vulva, one on each side of the vaginal opening.

**Lamaze** A method of childbirth preparation using breathing and relaxation.

**Lesbian** A homosexual female.

**Limbic system** A subcortical brain system composed of several interrelated structures that influences the sexual behavior of humans and other animals.

**Lochia** A reddish uterine discharge that occurs after childbirth.

**Luteinizing hormone (LH)** The hormone secreted by the pituitary gland that stimulates ovulation in the female. In males it is called the interstitial cell hormone (ISCH) and stimulates production of androgens by the testes.

**Male orgasmic disorder** The inability of a man to ejaculate during sexual stimulation from his partner.

**Mammary glands** Glands in the female breast that produce milk.

**Mammography** A highly sensitive X-ray test for the detection of breast cancer.

**Mastectomy** Surgical removal of the breast(s).

**Masturbation** Stimulation of one's own genitals to create sexual pleasure.

**Matriarchal society** A society in which women carry the family name through the generations, and women govern the economic and social affairs of the community.

**Medical abortion** The use of medications to end a pregnancy of 7 weeks or less.

**Menarche** The initial onset of menstrual periods in a young woman.

**Menopause** Cessation of menstruation as a result of the aging process or surgical removal of the ovaries.

**Menstrual synchrony** Simultaneous menstrual cycles that sometimes occur among women who live in close proximity.

**Menstruation** The sloughing off of the built-up uterine lining that takes place if conception has not occurred.

**Mere exposure effect** A phenomenon in which repeated exposure to novel stimuli tends to increase an individual's liking for such stimuli.

**Microbicide** A topical gel or cream product that women can use vaginally to prevent or minimize the risk of being infected with HIV or other STDs.

**Mons veneris** A triangular mound over the pubic bone above the vulva.

**Mucosa** Collective term for the mucous membranes; moist tissue that lines certain body areas such as the penile urethra, vagina, and mouth.

**Mucus method** A birth control method based on determining the time of ovulation by means of the cyclical changes of the cervical mucus.

**Multiple orgasms** More than one orgasm experienced within a short time period.

**Mutual empathy** The underlying knowledge that each partner in a relationship cares for the other and knows that the care is reciprocated.

**Myometrium** The smooth muscle layer of the uterine wall.

**Myotonia** Muscle tension.

**Necrophilia** A rare sexual paraphilia in which a person obtains sexual gratification by viewing or having intercourse with a corpse.

**Neuropeptide hormones** Chemicals produced in the brain that influence sexuality and other behavioral functions.

**Nocturnal emission** Involuntary ejaculation during sleep; also known as a wet dream.

**Nocturnal orgasm** Involuntary orgasm during sleep.

**Noncoital sex** Physical contact, including kissing, touching, and manual or oral–genital stimulation —but excluding coitus.

**Nonconsensual extramarital sex** Sexual interaction in which a married person engages in an outside sexual relationship without the consent (or presumably, the knowledge) of his or her spouse.

**Nongonococcal urethritis (NGU)** An inflammation of the urethral tube caused by organisms other than *gonococcus*.

**Nonresponse** The refusal to participate in a research study.

**Obscenity** A term that implies a personal or societal judgment that something is offensive.

**Oophorectomy** Surgical removal of the ovaries.

**Open marriage** A marriage in which spouses, with each other's permission, have intimate relationships with other people as well as with the marital partner.

**Open-ended question** A question that allows a respondent to share any feelings or information she or he thinks is relevant.

**Orchidectomy** The surgical procedure for removing the testes.

**Orgasm** A series of muscular contractions of the pelvic floor muscles occurring at the peak of sexual arousal.

**Os** The opening in the cervix that leads to the interior of the uterus.

**Outercourse** Noncoital forms of sexual intimacy.

**Ovaries** Female gonads that produce ova and sex hormones.

**Ovulation** The release of a mature ovum from the ovary.

**Ovum** The female reproductive cell.

**Oxytocin** A neuropeptide produced in the hypothalamus that influences sexual response and interpersonal attraction.

**Pap smear** A screening test for cancer of the cervix.

**Paraphilia** A term used to describe uncommon types of sexual expression.

**Partial celibacy** An expression of sexuality in which an individual does not engage in interpersonal sexual contact but continues to engage in masturbation.

**Passing** Presenting a false image of being heterosexual.

**Passion** The motivational component of Sternberg's triangular love theory.

**Passionate love** State of extreme absorption in another person. Also known as romantic love.

**Pedophilia, or child molestation** Sexual contact between an adult and a child who are not related.

**Pelvic inflammatory disease (PID)** An infection in the uterus and pelvic cavity.

**Penis** A male sexual organ consisting of the internal root and the external shaft and glans.

**Perimenopause** The time period before menopause when estrogen is decreasing.

**Perimetrium** The thin membrane covering the outside of the uterus.

**Perineum** The area between the vagina and anus of the female and the scrotum and anus of the male.

**Persistent sexual arousal disorder** Spontaneous, intrusive, and unwanted genital arousal.

**Peyronie's disease** Abnormal fibrous tissue and calcium deposits in the penis.

**Pheromones** Certain odors produced by the body that relate to reproductive functions.

**Phimosis** A condition characterized by an extremely tight penile foreskin.

**Physical attractiveness** Physical beauty, which is a powerful factor in attracting lovers to each other.

**Placenta** A disk-shaped organ attached to the uterine wall and connected to the fetus by the umbilical cord. Nutrients, oxygen, and waste products pass between mother and fetus through the cell walls of the placenta.

**Placenta previa** A birth complication in which the placenta is between the cervical opening and the infant.

**Plateau phase** Masters and Johnson's term for the second phase of the sexual response cycle, in which muscle tension, heart rate, blood pressure, and vasocongestion increase.

**Pornography** Sexually explicit material (e.g., images or text) intended to cause sexual arousal.

**Postpartum depression (PPD)** Symptoms of depression and obsessive thoughts of hurting the baby.

**Postpartum period** The first several weeks after childbirth.

**Posttraumatic stress disorder (PTSD)** A psychological disorder caused by exposure to overwhelmingly painful events.

**Premature ejaculation (PE)** A pattern of ejaculations within 2 minutes and an inability to delay ejaculation, resulting in a man's impairing his or his partner's pleasure.

**Premenstrual dysphoric disorder (PMDD)** Premenstrual symptoms severe enough to significantly disrupt a woman's functioning.

**Premenstrual syndrome (PMS)** Symptoms of physical discomfort and emotional irritability that occur 2 to 12 days before menstruation.

**Prepared childbirth** Birth following an education process that can involve information, exercises, breathing, and working with a labor coach.

**Prepuce** The foreskin or fold of skin over the clitoris.

**Primary erogenous zones** Areas of the body that contain dense concentrations of nerve endings.

**Prodromal symptoms** Symptoms that warn of an impending herpes eruption.

**Progestational compounds** A class of hormones, including progesterone, that are produced by the ovaries.

**Progestin-only pills** Contraceptive pills that contain a small dose of progestin and no estrogen.

**Prostaglandins** Hormones that induce uterine contractions. They are sometimes used to induce contractions and fetal expulsion for second-trimester abortions.

**Prostate gland** A gland located at the base of the bladder that produces about 30% of the seminal fluid released during ejaculation.

**Prostitution** The exchange of sexual services for money.

**Proximity** The geographic nearness of one person to another, which is an important factor in interpersonal attraction.

**Pseudohermaphrodites** Individuals whose gonads match their chromosomal sex but whose internal and external reproductive anatomy has a mixture of male and female structures or structures that are incompletely male or female.

**Psychosocial** Refers to a combination of psychological and social factors.

**Puberty** A period of rapid physical changes in early adolescence during which the reproductive organs mature.

**Pubic lice** Lice that primarily infest the pubic hair and are transmitted by sexual contact; also known as "crabs."

**Random sample** A randomly chosen subset of a population.

**Rape** Sexual intercourse that occurs without consent as a result of actual or threatened force.

**Reciprocity** The principle that when we are recipients of expressions of liking or loving, we tend to respond in kind.

**Refractory period** The period of time following orgasm in the male, during which he cannot experience another orgasm.

**Representative sample** A type of limited research sample that provides an accurate representation of a larger target population of interest.

**Resolution phase** The fourth phase of the sexual response cycle, as outlined by Masters and Johnson, in which the sexual systems return to their nonexcited state.

**Retrograde ejaculation** The process by which semen is expelled into the bladder instead of out of the penis.

**Root** The portion of the penis that extends internally into the pelvic cavity.

**Rugae** The folds of tissue in the vagina.

**Sadomasochistic (SM) behavior** The association of sexual expression with pain.

**Scabies** An ectoparasitic infestation of tiny mites.

**Scrotum** The pouch of skin of the external male genitals that encloses the testes.

**Seasonale** Birth control pills that reduce menstrual periods to four times a year.

**Secondary erogenous zones** Areas of the body that have become erotically sensitive through learning and experience.

**Secondary sex characteristics** The physical characteristics other than genitals that indicate sexual maturity, such as body hair, breasts, and deepened voice.

**Second-stage labor** The middle stage of labor, in which the infant descends through the vaginal canal.

**Self-selection** The bias introduced into research study results because of participants' willingness to respond.

**Semen, or seminal fluid** A viscous fluid ejaculated through the penis that contains sperm and fluids from the prostate, seminal vesicles, and Cowper's glands.

**Seminal vesicles** Small glands adjacent to the terminals of the vas deferens that secrete an alkaline fluid (conducive to sperm motility) that constitutes the greatest portion of the volume of seminal fluid released during ejaculation.

**Seminiferous tubules** Thin, coiled structures in the testes in which sperm are produced.

**Sensate focus** A process of touching and communication used to enhance sexual pleasure and to reduce performance pressure.

**Serotonin** A neurotransmitter that inhibits sexual arousal and activity.

**Sex** Biological maleness and femaleness.

**Sex chromosomes** A single set of chromosomes that influences biological sex determination.

**Sex flush** A pink or red rash that can appear on the chest or breasts during sexual arousal.

**Sexology** The study of sexuality.

**Sexual aversion disorder** Extreme and irrational fear of sexual activity.

**Sexual harassment** Unwelcome sexual advances, requests for sexual favors, and other verbal or physical conduct of a sexual nature in the workplace or academic setting.

**Sexual intelligence** Sexual intelligence involves self-understanding, interpersonal sexual skills, scientific knowledge, and consideration of the cultural context of sexuality.

**Sexual masochism** The act of obtaining sexual arousal through receiving physical or psychological pain.

**Sexual orientation** Sexual attraction to one's own sex (homosexual), to the other sex (heterosexual), to both sexes (bisexual), or lack of sexual interest to either sex (asexual).

**Sexual sadism** The act of obtaining sexual arousal through giving physical or psychological pain.

**Sexual scripts** Culturally learned ways of behaving in sexual situations.

**Sexually transmitted diseases (STDs)** Diseases that are transmitted by sexual contact.

**Shaft** The length of the clitoris or penis between the glans and the body.

**Similarity** The similarity of beliefs, interests, and values, which is a factor in attracting people to one another.

**Smegma** A cheesy substance of glandular secretions and skin cells that sometimes accumulates under the foreskin of the penis or hood of the clitoris.

**Socialization** The process by which our society conveys behavioral expectations to the individual.

**Speculum** An instrument used to open the vaginal walls during a gynecological exam. The speculum opens the walls of the vaginal canal.

**Sperm** The male reproductive cell.

**Spermatic cord** A cord attached to the testis that contains the vas deferens, blood vessels, nerves, and cremasteric muscle fibers.

**Spongy body** A cylinder that forms a bulb at the base of the penis, extends up into the penile shaft, and forms the penile glans.

**Spontaneous abortion (miscarriage)** The spontaneous expulsion of the fetus from the uterus early in pregnancy, before it can survive on its own.

**Standard days method** A birth control method that requires couples to avoid unprotected intercourse for a 12-day period in the middle of the menstrual cycle.

**Statutory rape** Intercourse with a person under the age of consent.

**Stereotype** A generalized notion of what a person is like based only on that person's sex, race, religion, ethnic background, or similar criteria.

**Steroid hormones** The sex hormones and the hormones of the adrenal cortex.

**Stop-start technique** A treatment technique for premature ejaculation, consisting of stimulating the penis to the point of impending orgasm and then stopping until the pre-ejaculatory sensations subside.

**Stranger rape** Rape of a person by an unknown assailant.

**Suction curettage** A procedure in which the cervical os is dilated by using graduated metal dilators or a laminaria; then a small plastic tube, attached to a vacuum aspirator, is inserted into the uterus, drawing the fetal tissue, placenta, and built-up uterine lining out of the uterus.

**Surrogate mother** A woman who is artificially inseminated by the male partner in a childless couple, carries the pregnancy to term, delivers the child, and gives it to the couple for adoption.

**Survey** A research method in which a sample of people are questioned about their behaviors and/or attitudes.

**Swinging** The exchange of marital partners for sexual interaction.

**Syphilis** A sexually transmitted disease caused by a bacterium called *Treponema pallidum*.

**Testes** Male gonads inside the scrotum that produce sperm and sex hormones.

**Third-stage labor** The last stage of childbirth, in which the placenta separates from the uterine wall and comes out of the vagina.

**Toxemia** A dangerous condition during pregnancy in which high blood pressure occurs.

**Toxic shock syndrome (TSS)** A disease that occurs most commonly in menstruating women and that can cause a person to go into shock.

**Trachoma** A chronic, contagious form of conjunctivitis caused by chlamydia infections.

**Transcervical sterilization** A method of female sterilization using a tiny coil that is inserted through the vagina, cervix, and uterus into the fallopian tubes.

**Transgendered** A term applied to people whose appearance and/or behaviors do not conform to traditional gender roles.

**Transsexual** A person whose gender identity is opposite to his or her biological sex.

**Transvestic fetishism** A sexual behavior in which a person derives sexual arousal from wearing clothing of the other sex.

**Tribadism** Rubbing one's genitals against another's body or genitals.

**Trichomoniasis** A form of vaginitis caused by the one-celled protozoan *Trichomonas vaginalis*.

**Triphasic pills** Birth control pills that vary the dosages of estrogen and progestin during the menstrual cycle.

**True hermaphrodites** Exceedingly rare individuals who have both ovarian and testicular tissue in their bodies; their external genitals are often a mixture of male and female structures.

**Tubal sterilization** Female sterilization accomplished by severing or tying the fallopian tubes.

**Turner's syndrome** A rare condition, characterized by the presence of one unmatched X chromosome (XO), in which affected individuals have normal female external genitals but their internal reproductive structures do not develop fully.

**Urethra** The tube through which urine passes from the bladder to the outside of the body.

**Urethritis** An inflammation of the urethral tube.

**Urology** The medical specialty dealing with reproductive health and genital diseases of the male and urinary tract diseases in both sexes.

**Urophilia** A sexual paraphilia in which a person obtains sexual arousal from contact with urine.

**Uterus** A pear-shaped organ inside the female pelvis, within which the fetus develops.

**Vagina** A stretchable canal in the female that opens at the vulva and extends about 4 inches into the pelvis.

**Vaginal spermicides** Foam, cream, jelly, suppositories, and film that contain a chemical that kills sperm.

**Vaginismus** Involuntary spasmodic contractions of the muscles of the outer third of the vagina.

**Vaginitis** Inflammation of the vaginal walls caused by a variety of vaginal infections.

**Varicocele** A damaged or enlarged vein in the testis or vas deferens.

**Vas deferens** A sperm-carrying tube that begins at the testis and ends at the urethra.

**Vasectomy** Male sterilization accomplished by cutting and closing each vas deferens.

**Vasocongestion** The engorgement of blood vessels in particular body parts in response to sexual arousal.

**Vasovasostomy** Surgical reconstruction of the vas deferens to reverse a vasectomy.

**Vernix caseosa** A waxy, protective substance on the fetus's skin.

**Vestibular bulbs** Two bulbs, one on each side of the vaginal opening, that engorge with blood during sexual arousal.

**Vestibule** The area of the vulva inside the labia minora.

**Viral hepatitis** A disease in which liver function is impaired by a viral infection.

**Viral load** The amount of HIV present in an infected person's blood.

**Voyeurism** The act of obtaining sexual gratification by observing undressed or sexually interacting people without their consent.

**Vulva** The external genitals of the female, including the pubic hair, mons veneris, labia majora, labia minora, clitoris, and urinary and vaginal openings.

**Vulvar vestibulitis syndrome** A small area at the entrance of the vagina that causes severe pain.

**Yes/no question** A question that asks for a one-word answer (yes or no) and thus provides little opportunity for discussing an issue.

**Zoophilia** A paraphilia in which a person has sexual contact with animals.

**Zygote** The single cell resulting from the union of sperm and egg cells.

**Zygote intrafallopian transfer (ZIFT)** Procedure in which an egg is fertilized in the laboratory and then placed in a fallopian tube.

Aaronson, L. (2005). The mend of the affair. *Psychology Today*, September/October, 48.

Aaronson, L. (2006). An upside to infertility? *Psychology Today*, March/April, 38.

AAUW (American Association of University Women) (1992). *Shortchanging Girls, Shortchanging America*. Washington, DC: American Association of University Women.

Abbey, A., Clinton-Sherrod, A., McAuslan, P., Zawacki, T., & Buck, P. (2003). The relationship between the quantity of alcohol consumed and the severity of sexual assaults committed by college men. *Journal of Interpersonal Violence*, 18, 813–833.

Abbey, A., McAuslan, P., & Ross, L. (1998). Sexual assault perpetuation by college men: The role of alcohol, misperception of sexual intent, and sexual beliefs and experiences. *Journal of Social and Clinical Psychology*, 17, 167–195.

Abbott, E. (2000). A History of Celibacy. New York: Scribner.

Abel, G. (1981). *The Evaluation and Treatment of Sexual Offenders and Their Victims*. Paper presented at St. Vincent Hospital and Medical Center, Portland, Oregon, October 15.

Abel, G., & Osborn, C. (2000). The paraphilias. In M. Gelder, J. Lopez-Ibor, & N. Andreasen (Eds.), *New Oxford Textbook of Psychiatry*. Oxford: Oxford University Press.

Abel, G., Barlow, D., Blanchard, E., & Guild, D. (1977). The components of rapists' sexual arousal. *Archives of General Psychiatry*, 34, 895–903.

Abel, G., Becker, J., & Cunningham-Ratder, J. (1984). Complications, consent, and cognitions in sex between children and adults. *International Journal of Law and Psychiatry*, 7, 89–103.

Abner, S., Guenthner, P., Guarner, J., Hancock, K., Cummins, J., et al. (2005). A human colorectal explant culture to evaluate topical microbicides for the prevention of HIV infection. *Journal of Infectious Diseases*, 192, 1545-1556.

Abrahams, J. (1982). Azoospermia before puberty. *Medical Aspects of Human Sexuality*, 1, 13.

Absi-Semaan, N., Crombie, G., & Freeman, C. (1993). Masculinity and femininity in middle childhood: Developmental and factor analysis. *Sex Roles*, 28, 187–202.

Ackard, D., & Neumark-Sztainer, D. (2001). Health care information sources for adolescents: Age and gender differences on use, concerns, and needs. *Journal of Adolescent Health*, 29, 170–176.

Acker, M., & Davis, M. (1992). Intimacy, passion, and commitment in adult romantic relationships: A test of the triangular theory of love. *Journal of Social and Personal Relationships*, 9, 21–50.

Ackerman, M., Montague, D., & Morganstern, S. (1994). Impotence: Help for erectile dysfunction. *Patient Care*, March, 22–56.

ACLU (2006). Sex toys: Therapy for some, symbols of indecency to others. Retrieved April 3, 2006, from aclu.org/privacy/gen/15353prs20001127.html.

Acosta-Belen, E., & Bose, C. (2003). U.S. Latinas: Active at the intersections of gender, nationality, race, and class. In R. Morgan (Ed.), *Sisterhood Is Forever*. New York: Washington Square Press.

Adam, B., Sears, A., & Schellenberg, E. (2000). Accounting for unsafe sex: Interviews with men who have sex with men. *Journal of Sex Research*, 37, 24–36.

Adams, B. (2003). Keeping it up. *The Advocate*, November 11, 38–40.

Adams, T., & Rust, D. (2006). "Normative gaps" in sexual behaviors among a national sample of college students. *American Journal of Health Education*, 37, 27–33.

Adamson, A. (2003). *Scents to Raise Your . . . Blood Pressure*. Retrieved April 5, 2003, from http://www.philly.com/mld/philly/living/food/5161648.htm.

Addiego, F., Belzer, E., Comolli, J., Moger, W., Perry, J., & Whipple, B. (1981). Female ejaculation: A case study. *Journal of Sex Research*, 17, 13–21.

Addis, I., Van Den Eeden, S., Wassel-Fyr, C., & Vittinghoff, E. (2006). Sexual activity and function in middle-aged and older women. *Obstetrics & Gynecology*, 107, 755–764.

Adducci, C., & Ross, L. (1991). Common urethral injuries in men. *Medical Aspects of Human Sexuality*, October, 32–44.

Adelman, W., & Joffe, A. (2000). Revisiting the adolescent male genital examination. *Patient Care*, February 29, 83–98.

Adler, N., Hendrick, S., & Hendrick, C. (1989). Male sexual preference and attitudes toward love and sexuality. *Journal of Sex Education and Therapy*, 12, 27–30.

Adler, N., Ozer, E., & Tschann, J. (2003). Abortion among adolescents. *American Psychologist*, 58, 211–217.

Afifi, W., & Faulkner, S. (2000). On being "just friends": The frequency and impact of sexual activity in cross-sex friendships. *Journal of Social and Personal Relationships*, 17, 205–222.

Agbayani-Siewert, P. (2004). Assumptions of Asian American similarity: The case of Filipino and Chinese students. *Social Work*, 49, 39–51.

Agger, I., & Jensen, S. (1994). Sexuality as a tool of political repression. In H. Riguelme (Ed.), *Era in Twilight: Psychocultural Situation Under State Terrorism in Latin America*. Bilbao, Spain: Instituto Horizonte.

Agnew, J. (2000). Klismaphilia. *Venereology*, 13, 75–79.

Ahdieh-Grant, L., Yamashita, T., Phair, J., Detels, R., Wolinsky, S., Margolick, J., Rinaldo, C., & Jacobson, L. (2003). When to initiate highly active antiretroviral therapy: A cohort approach. *American Journal of Epidemiology*, 157, 738–746.

AIDS Alert (2005). International AIDS Society Conference update: Male circumcision as a prevention. Author, September 1.

AIDS Vaccine Advocacy Coalition (2006a). *AIDS Vaccine Trials—Getting the Global House in Order*. Retrieved January 18, 2006, from http://www.avac.org/pdf/reports/2004.

AIDS Vaccine Advocacy Coalition (2006b). *Will a Pill a Day Prevent HIV?* Retrieved May 17, 2006, from http://www.avac.org/pdf/tenofovir.pdf.

Ainsworth, M. (1979). Infant–mother attachment. *American Psychologist*, 34, 932–937.

Ainsworth, M. (1989). Attachments beyond infancy. *American Psychologist*, 44, 709–716.

Ainsworth, M., Blehar, M., Waters, E., & Walls, S. (1978). *Patterns of Attachment: A Psychological Study of the Strange Situation*. Hillsdale, NJ: Erlbaum.

Akert, J. (2003). A new generation of contraceptives. *RN*, 66, 54–61.

Alan Guttmacher Institute (2002). *Facts in Brief: Contraceptive Use*. Retrieved June 20, 2003, from http://www.agi-usa.org/pubs/fb_contr/use.html.

Alan Guttmacher Institute (2006). *Top 10 Ways Sexual and Reproductive Health Suffered in 2004*. Retrieved February 2, 2006, from http://www.guttmacher.org.

Albarracin, D., McNatt, P., Klein, C., Ho, R., Mitchell, A., & Kumkale, G. (2003). Persuasive communications to change actions: An analysis of behavioral and cognitive impact in HIV prevention. *Health Psychology*, 22, 166–177.

Aldridge, L., Daniels, J., & Jukic, A. (2006). Mammograms and healthcare access among US Hispanic and non-Hispanic women 40 years and older. *Family and Community Health*, 29, 80–89.

Alexander, B. (2006, August 17). Will technology revolutionize boinking? Retrieved August 21, 2006, from http://www.msnbc.msn.com/id/14292504/print/1/displaymode/1098/.

Alexander, C., Sipski, M., & Findley, T. (1994). Sexual activities, desire, and satisfaction in males pre- and post-spinal cord injury. *Archives of Sexual Behavior*, 22, 217–228.

Alexander, G. (2003). An evolutionary perspective of sex-typed toy preferences: Pink, blue, and the brain. *Archives of Sexual Behavior*, 32, 7–14.

Alexander, J. (2005). Evidence from randomised double-blind clinical trials. Paper presented at the World Congress of Sexology, Montreal, Canada, July 10–15.

Alexander, N. (2003). No pill, but other male birth control likely in not-too-distant future. *Contemporary Sexuality*, January, 8.

Alfano, P. (2006). The shadowy world of sex tours: Critics say businesses like the one run by a Fort Worth man promote prostitution. He says he is merely taking men to "night-life areas." *Fort Worth Star-Telegram*, August 6, pNA.

Ali, A. (2006). *The Caged Virgin: An Emancipation Proclamation for Women and Islam*. New York: Free Press.

Ali, L. & Miller, L. (2004). The secret lives of wives. *Newsweek*, July 12, 47–54.

Al-Krenawi, A., & Wiesel-Lev, R. (1999). Attitudes toward and perceived psychosocial impact of female circumcision as practiced among the Bedouin-Arabs of the Negev. *Family Process*, 38, 431–443.

Allen, L. & Gorski, R. (1990). Sex difference in the bed nucleus of the stria terminalis of the human brain. *Journal of Comparative Neurology*, 302, 697–706.

Allen, L., Hines, M., Shryne, J., & Gorski, R. (1989). Two sexually dimorphic cell groups. *Journal of Neurosciences*, 9, 497–506.

Allgeier, E. (1981). The influence of androgynous identification on heterosexual relations. *Sex Roles*, 7, 321–330.

Alonzo, D. (2003). *Dancing in the Autumn Light: Gay Men, Sexuality, and the Mid-Life Transition*. Paper presented at the Western Region Annual Conference Society for the Scientific Study of Sexuality, Los Angeles, April.

Alperstein, L. (2001). *For Two: Some Basic Perspectives and Skills for Couples Therapy*. Paper presented at the 33rd Annual Conference of the American Association of Sex Educators, Counselors, and Therapists, San Francisco, May 2–6.

Althaus, F. (1994). Age at which young men initiate intercourse is tied to sex education and mother's presence in the home. *Family Planning Perspectives*, 26, 141–143.

Althof, S., Dean, J., Derogatis, L., & Rosen, R. (2005). Current perspectives on the clinical assessment and diagnosis of female sexual dysfunction and clinical studies of potential therapies: A statement of concern. *The Journal of Sexual Medicine*, 2, 146–153.

Althof, S., Rowland, D., McNulty, P., & Rothman, M. (2006). Evaluation of the impact of premature ejaculation on a man's self-esteem, confidence, and overall relationship. Paper presented at the Sexual Medicine Society of North America Fall Meeting, New York, November.

Altman, C. (1999). Gay and lesbian seniors: Unique challenges of coming out in later life. *SIECUS Report*, 27, 14–17.

Altman, L. (2002). Inexpensive drug prevents HIV in newborns, study shows. *The Oregonian*, July 14, AJO.

Alzate, H. (1990). Vaginal erogeneity, the "G spot," and female ejaculation. *Journal of Sex Education and Therapy*, 16, 137–140.

Amato, P. (2001). What children learn from divorce. *Population Today*, 29, 1.

Amato, P., & Previti, D. (2003). People's reasons for divorcing: Gender, social class, the life course, and adjustment. *Journal of Family Issues*, 24, 602–626.

Amato, P., Johnson, D., Booth, A., & Rogers, S. (2003). Continuity and change in marital quality between 1980 and 2000. *Journal of Marriage and the Family*, 65, 1–22.

American Academy of Pediatrics (2001a). Adolescents and human immunodeficiency virus infection: The role of the pediatrician in prevention and intervention. *Pediatrics*, 107, 188–190.

American Academy of Pediatrics. (2001b). *Sexuality, Contraception, and the Media*. Retrieved January 29, 2001, from http://www.aap.org/policy/re0038.html.

American Academy of Pediatrics (2006). *Adolescent Pregnancy: Current Trends and Issues*. Retrieved February 2, 2006, from http://www.Pediatrics.org.

American College of Obstetricians and Gynecologists (2005). ACOG guidelines on the management of human papillomavirus infection. *American Family Physician*, 72, 178.

American Fertility Association (2006, June 20). Survey of 17,500 women in 10 countries shows global lack of awareness of basic facts about fertility. Retrieved June 26, 2006, from http://www.prnewswire.com/cgi-bin/stories.pl?ACCT=104&STORY=/www/story/06-20-2006/0004383938&EDATE.

American Life League (2006). About all policy. Retrieved July 18, 2006 from http://www.all.org/about_policy.php.

American Psychiatric Association (2000). *Diagnostic and Statistical Manual of Mental Disorders* (4th ed., Text Revision). Washington, DC: American Psychiatric Association.

Ammann, A. (2000). HIV in China: An opportunity to halt an emerging epidemic. *AIDS Patient Care and STDs*, 14, 109–112.

Amodio, D., & Showers, C. (2005). "Similarity breeds liking" revisited: The moderating role of commitment. *Journal of Social and Personal Relationships*, 22, 817–836.

Anand, M. (1991). *The Art of Sexual Ecstasy*. Los Angeles: Tarcher.

Anderson, K., Cooper, H., & Okamura, L. (1997). Individual differences and attitudes toward rape: A meta-analytic review. *Personality and Social Psychology Bulletin*, 23, 295–315.

Anderson, S., Dallal, G., & Must, A. (2003). Relative weight and race influence average age at menarche: Results from two nationally representative surveys of U.S. girls studied 25 years apart. *Pediatrics*, 111, 844–850.

Anderson-Hunt, M., & Dennerstein, L. (1994). Increased female sexual response after oxytocin. *British Medical Journal*, 309, 929.

Andreas, P. (2005). Female exotic dancing: An exploratory investigation of intrapersonal and interpersonal dynamics. Paper presented at the World Congress of Sexology, Montreal, Canada, July 10–15.

Andrews, A., & Patterson, E. (1995). Searching for solutions to alcohol and other drug abuse during pregnancy: Ethics, values, and constitutional principles. *Journal of the National Association of Social Workers*, 40, 55–63.

Andrews, B., Brewin, C. Rose, S., & Kirk, M. (2000). Predicting PTSD symptoms in victims of violent crime: The role of shame, anger, and childhood abuse. *Journal of Abnormal Psychology*, 109, 69–73.

Andrews, G. (2006). Treating menopausal women. *Practice Nurse*, February 10, 1.

Andrews, L., & Elster, N. (2000). Regulating reproductive technologies. *Journal of Legal Medicine*, 21, 35–65.

Angier, N. (1999). *Woman: An Intimate Geography*. Boston: Houghton Mifflin.

Apfelbaum, B. (2000). Retarded ejaculation: A much misunderstood syndrome. In S. Leiblum & R. Rosen (Eds.), *Principles and Practice of Sex Therapy*. New York: Guilford Press.

Aponte, R. & Machado, M. (2006). Marital aspects associated with sexual satisfaction. *The Journal of Sexual Medicine*, 3, 382–452.

Apperloo, M., Van Der Stege, J., Hoek, A., & Schultz, W. (2003). In the mood for sex: The value of androgens. *Journal of Sex and Marital Therapy*, 29, 87–102.

Apt, C., Hurlbert, D., & Powell, D. (1993). Men with hypoactive sexual desire disorder: The role of interpersonal dependency and assertiveness. *Journal of Sex Education and Therapy*, 19(2, 108–116.

Archer, J. (2000). Sex differences in aggression between heterosexual partners: A meta-analytic review. *Psychological Bulletin*, 126, 651–680.

Ards, A. (2000). Dating and mating. *Ms.*, June–July, 10.

Arevalo, M., Jenning, V., & Sinai, I. (2002). Efficacy of a new method of family planning: The standard days method. *Contraception*, 65, 333–338.

Argiolas, A. (1999). Neuropeptides and sexual behavior. *Neuroscience Biobehavioral Review*, 23, 1127–1142.

Armstrong, K., Eisen, A., & Weber, B. (2000). Assessing the risk of breast cancer. *New England Journal of Medicine*, 342, 564–571.

Arndt, W. (1991). *Gender Disorders and the Paraphilias*. Madison, CT: International Universities Press.

Arnold, A. (2003). The gender of the voice within; the neural origin of sex differences in the brain. *Current Opinion in Neurobiology*, 13, 759–764.

Arnold, A. (2004). Sex chromosomes and brain gender. *Nature Reviews Neuroscience*, 5, 701–708.

Arnow, B., Desmond, J., Banner, L., Glover, G., et al. (2002). Brain activation and sexual arousal in healthy, heterosexual males. *Brain*, 125, 1014–1023.

Aronowitz, T., Rennells, R., & Todd, E. (2006). Ecological influences of sexuality on early adolescent African American females. *Journal of Community Health Nursing*, 23, 113–122.

Ashby, S., Arcari, C., & Edmonson, M. (2006). Television viewing and risk of sexual initiation by young adolescents. *Archives of Pediatric Adolescent Medicine*, 160, 375–380.

Aspelmeier, J., & Kerns, K. (2003). Love and school: Attachment/exploration dynamics in college. *Journal of Social and Personal Relationships*, 20, 5–30.

Athanasiou, R., Shaver, P., & Tavris, C. (1970). Sex. *Psychology Today*, July, 39–52.

Atkins, D., Yi, J., Baucom, D., & Christensen, A. (2005). Infidelity in couples seeking marital therapy. *Journal of Family Psychology*, 19, 470–473.

Atwood, J., & Seifer, M. (1997). Extramarital affairs and constructed meanings: A social constructionist therapeutic approach. *American Journal of Family Therapy*, 25, 55–75.

Augenbraun, M. (2000). Treatment of latent and tertiary syphilis. *Hospital Practice*, April 15, 89–95.

Austoni, E., & Guarneri, G. (1999). Penile elongation and thickening: A myth? Is there a cosmetic or medical indication? *Andrologia*, 31(suppl. 1), 45–51.

Auvert, B. Taljaard, D., et al. (2005). Impact of male circumcision on the female-to-male transmission of HIV: Results of the intervention trial: ANRS 1265. Paper presented at the IAS Conference on HIV Pathogenesis and Treatment, Rio de Janeiro, Brazil, July.

Avis, N., Stellato, R., & Crawford, S. (2001). Is there a menopausal syndrome? Menopausal status and symptoms across racial/ethnic groups. *Social Science and Medicine*, 52, 345–356.

Babcock, B. (2006). Law changed for adult items. *The Kansas City Star*, March 8, pNA.

Bachmann, G. (1991). Sexual dysfunction in the older woman. *Medical Aspects of Human Sexuality*, February, 42–45.

Bacon, C., Mittleman, M., Kawachi, I., & Giovannucci, E. (2006). A prospective study of risk factors for erectile dysfunction. *The Journal of Urology*, 176, 217–221.

Baeten, J., Richardson, B., Lavreys, L., Rakwar, J., Kishorchandra, M., et al. (2005). Female-to-male infectivity of HIV-1 among circumcised and uncircumcised Kenyan men. *Journal of Infectious Diseases*, 191, 546–553.

Bagley, C., Bolitho, F., & Bertrand, L. (1997). Sexual assault in school, mental health and suicidal behaviors in adolescent women in Canada. *Adolescence*, 32, 361–366.

Bailey, J., Gaulin, S., Agyei, Y., & Gladue, B. (1994). Effects of gender and sexual orientation on evolutionarily relevant aspects of human mating psychology. *Journal of Personality and Social Psychology*, 66, 1081–1093.

Bailey, T., & Cymet, T. (2006). Planning for the HPV vaccine and its impact on cervical cancer prevention. *Comprehensive Therapy*, 32, 102–105.

Baill, I., Cullins, V., & Pati, S. (2003). Counseling issues in tubal sterilization. *American Family Physician*, 67, 1287–1294.

Bain, J. (2001). Andropause: Testosterone replacement therapy for aging men. *Canadian Family Physician*, 47, 91–97.

Bakken, I., Nordbo, S., & Skjeldestad, F. (2006). *Chlamydia trachomatis* testing patterns and prevalence of genital chlamydial infection among young men and women in Central Norway 1990–2003: A population-based registry study. *Sexually Transmitted Diseases*, 33, 26–30.

Bakst, B. (2006). Page scandal brings calls for adult-child e-mail laws. *Oregonian*, October 15, A6.

Baldwin, J., & Baldwin, J. (2000). Heterosexual anal intercourse. *Archives of Sexual Behavior*, 29, 357–373.

Ball, H. (2005). Extensive genital cutting elevates risk of infertility among Sudanese women. *International Family Planning Perspectives*, 31, 154–156.

Balsam, K., Rothblum, E., & Beauchaine, T. (2005). Victimization over the life span: A comparison of lesbian, gay, bisexual, and heterosexual siblings. *Journal of Consulting and Clinical Psychology*, 73, 477–487.

Bancroft, J. (2002a). Biological factors in human sexuality. *Journal of Sex Research*, 39, 15–21.

Bancroft, J. (2002b). The medicalization of female sexual dysfunction: The need for caution. *Archives of Sexual Behavior*, 31, 451–455.

Bancroft, J. (Ed.) (2003). *Sexual Development in Childhood*. Bloomington: Indiana University Press.

Bancroft, J., & Vukadinovic, Z. (2004). Sexual addiction, sexual compulsivity, sexual impulsivity, or what? Toward a theoretical model. *Journal of Sex Research*, 41, 225–234.

Bancroft, J., Herbenick. D., & Reynolds, M. (2003a). Masturbation as a marker of sexual development. In J. Bancroft (Ed.), *Sexual Development in Childhood*. Bloomington: Indiana University Press.

Bancroft, J., Loftus, J., & Long, J. (2003b). Distress about sex: A national survey of women in heterosexual relationships. *Archives of Sexual Behavior*, 32, 193–209.

Banerjee, N. (2006). Episcopal Church picks woman as leader. *Oregonian*, June 19, A1 & A6.

Barbach, L. (1975). *For Yourself: The Fulfillment of Female Sexuality*. Garden City, NY: Doubleday.

Barbach, L. (1982). *For Each Other: Sharing Intimacy*. New York: Anchor Press/Doubleday.

Barbaree, H., Marshall, W., & Lanthier, R. (1979). Deviant sexual arousal in rapists. *Behavior Research and Therapy*, 17, 215–222.

Bardoni, B., Zanaria, E., Guioli, S., Floridia, G., Worley, K., Tonini, G., Ferrante, E., Chiumello, G., McCabe, E., Fraccaro, M., Zuffardi, O., & Camerino, G. (1994). A dosage sensitive locus at chromosome Xp21 is involved in male to female sex reversal. *Nature Genetics*, 7, 497–501.

Barfield, R., Wilson, C., & Mcdonald, P. (1975). Sexual behavior: Extreme reduction of postejaculatory refractory period by midbrain lesions in male rats. *Science*, 189, 147–149.

Barker, R. (1987). *The Green-Eyed Marriage: Surviving Jealous Relationships*. New York: Free Press.

Barkley, B., & Mosher, E. (1995). Sexuality and Hispanic culture: Counseling with children and their parents. *Journal of Sex Education and Therapy*, 21, 255–267.

Barnhart, K., Furman, I., & Devoto, L. (1995). Attitudes and practice of couples regarding sexual relations during the menses and spotting. *Contraception*, 51, 93–98.

Baron, R., Markman, G., & Bollinger, M. (2006). Exporting social psychology: Effects of attractiveness on perceptions of entrepreneurs, their ideas for new products, and their financial success. *Journal of Applied Social Psychology*, 36, 467–492.

Barone, N., & Wiederman, M. (1998). Young women's sexuality as a function of perceptions of maternal sexual communication during childhood. *Journal of Sex Education and Therapy*, 22(3, 33–38.

Barrett, G., Pendry, E., & Peacock, J. (2000). Women's sexual health after childbirth. *British Journal of Gynecology*, 107, 186–195.

Barroso, C. (2006). Reproductive repercussions. *The Baltimore Sun*, January 2, pNA.

Bartels, A., & Zeki, S. (2004). The neural correlates of maternal and romantic love. *Neuroimage*, 21, 1155–1166.

Bartholet, J. (2000). The plague years. *Newsweek*, January 17, 32–38.

Bartlik, B., & Goldberg, J. (2000). Female sexual arousal disorder. In S. Leiblum & R. Rosen (Eds.), *Principles and Practice of Sex Therapy*. New York: Guilford Press.

Bartlik, B., Kaplan, P., Kaminetsky, J., Roentsch, G., & Goldberg, J. (1999). Medications with the potential to enhance sexual responsivity in women. *Psychiatric Annals*, 29, 46–52.

Basoff, E., & Glass, G. (1982). The relationship between sex roles and mental health: A meta-analysis of twenty-six studies. *Counseling Psychologist*, 10, 105–112.

Basow, S. (1992). *Gender: Stereotypes and Roles* (3rd ed.). Pacific Grove, CA: Brooks/Cole.

Basow, S., & Rubenfeld, K. (2003). Troubles talk: Effects of gender and gender-typing. *Sex Roles*, 48, 183–187.

Basson, R. (2002). A model of women's sexual arousal. *Journal of Sex and Marital Therapy*, 28, 1–10.

Basson, R., Leiblum, S., Brotto, L., & Derogatis, L. (2004). Revised definitions of women's sexual dysfunction. *The Journal of Sexual Medicine*, 1, 40–48.

Basson, R., Leiblum, S., Brotto, L., Derogatis, L., Fourcroy, J., Fugl-Meyer, K., Graziottin, A., Heiman, J., Laan, E., Meston, C., Schover, L., van Lankveld, J., & Schultz W. (2003). Definitions of women's sexual dysfunction reconsidered: Advocating expansion and revision. *Journal of Psychsomatic Obstetrics and Gynecology*, 24, 221–229.

Bastian, L., Smith, C., & Nanda, K. (2003). Is this woman perimenopausal? *Journal of the American Medical Association*, 289, 895–901.

Bauer, H., Mark, K., Samuel, M., Wang, S., Weismuller, P., et al. (2005). Prevalence of and associated risk factors for Fluoroquinolone-resistant Neisseria gonorrhoeae in California, 2000–2003. *Clinical Infectious Diseases*, 41, 795–803.

Baumeister, R. (1988). Masochism as escape from self. *Journal of Sex Research*, 25, 28–59.

Baumeister, R. (1997). The enigmatic appeal of sexual masochism: Why people desire pain, bondage, and humiliation in sex. *Journal of Social and Clinical Psychology*, 16, 133–150.

Baumeister, R., & Leary, M. (1995). The need to belong: Desire for interpersonal attachments as a fundamental human motivation. *Psychological Bulletin*, 11, 497–529.

Baumeister, R., Catanese, K., & Wallace, H. (2002). Conquest by force: A narcissistic reactance theory of rape and sexual coercion. *Review of General Psychology*, 6, 92–135.

Baur, K. (1995). Socioeconomic and personality traits of nonadjudicated child sex offenders in a clinical practice. Unpublished.

Bauters, T., Dhont, M., Temmerman, M., & Nelis, H. (2002). Prevalence of vulvovaginal candidiasis and susceptibility to fluconazole in women. *American Journal of Obstetrics and Gynecology*, 187, 569–574.

Beach, F. (Ed.) (1978). *Human Sexuality in Four Perspectives*. Baltimore: Johns Hopkins University Press.

Beal, G., & Muehlenhard, C. (1987). *Getting Sexually Aggressive Men to Stop Their Advances: Information for Rape Prevention Programs*. Paper presented at the Annual Meeting of the Association for Advancement of Behavior Therapy, Boston, November.

Beary, H. (2006). Discounts for India sex workers. Retrieved July 10, 2006, from http://newsvote.bbc.co .uk/mpapps/pagetools/print/news.bbc.co.uk/2/hi/ south_asia.

Bechara, A., Bertolino, M., Casabe, A., Munarriz, R., Goldstein, I., Morin, A., Secin, F., Literat, B., Pesaresi, M., & Fredatovich, N. (2003). Duplex Doppler ultrasound assessment of clitoral hemodynamics after topical administration of Alprostadil in women with arousal and orgasmic disorders. *Journal of Sex and Marital Therapy*, 29(suppl.), 1–10.

Beck, C. (2006). Postpartum depression: It isn't just the blues. *American Journal of Nursing*, 106, 40–49.

Beck, M. (1999). The pornographic tradition: Formative influences in sixteenth- to nineteenth-century European literature. In J. Elias, V. Elias, V. Bullough, G. Brewer, J. Douglas, & W. Jarvis (Eds.), *Porn 101: Eroticism, Pornography, and the First Amendment*. Amherst, NY: Prometheus Books.

Beck, M., Wickelgren, I., Quade, V., & Wingert, P. (1988). Miscarriages. *Newsweek*, August 15, 46–49.

Becker, E. (2000). Women in military say silence on harassment protects careers. *New York Times*, May 12, AI.

Becker, J., & Kaplan, M. (1991). Rape victims: Issues, theories, and treatment. *Annual Review of Sex Research*, 2, 267–272.

Becker, J., Skinner, L., Abel, G., & Axelrod, R. (1986). Level of postassault sexual functioning in rape and incest victims. *Archives of Sexual Behavior*, 15, 37–49.

Beckman, N., Waern, M., & Skoog, I. (2006). Determinants of sexuality in 70-year-olds. *Journal of Sex Research*, 43, 876.

Beech, H. (2005). Sex, please—We're young and Chinese. *Time*, December, 61.

Begley, S. (1993). Hands off Mr. Chips! *Newsweek*, May 3, 58.

Begley, S. (1998). Designer babies. *Newsweek*, November 9, 61–62.

Begley, S. (1999). From both sides now. *Newsweek*, June 14, 52–53.

Begley, S. (2001). Brave new monkey. *Newsweek*, January 22, 50–52.

Beji, N. (2003). The effect of pelvic floor training on sexual function. *Nursing Standard*, 16, 33–36.

Bell, A., & Weinberg, M. (1978). *Homosexualities: A Study of Diversity Among Men and Women*. New York: Simon & Schuster.

Bell, A., Weinberg, M., & Hammersmith, S. (1981). *Sexual Preference: Its Development in Men and Women*. Bloomington: Indiana University Press.

Bell, D. (2006). "They deserve it." *The Nation*, July 10, 18–24.

Beller, M., & Gafni, N. (2000). Can item format (multiple choice vs. open-ended) account for gender differences in mathematics achievement? *Sex Roles*, 42, 1–21.

Bellizzi, K. & Blank, T. (2006). Predicting posttraumatic growth in breast cancer survivors. *Health Psychology*, 25, 47–56.

Belluck, P., & Zezima, K. (2004). Gays to cross wedding threshold. *The Oregonian*, May 16, A2.

Belzer, E., Whipple, B., & Moger, W. (1984). A female ejaculation. *Journal of Sex Research*, 20, 403–406.

Bem, S. (1975). Sex role adaptability: One consequence of psychological androgyny. *Journal of Personality and Social Psychology*, 31, 634–643.

Bem, S. (1993). *The Lenses of Gender*. New Haven, CT: Yale University Press.

Benagiano, G., & Cottingham, J. (1997). Contraceptive methods: Potential for abuse. *International Journal of Gynecology and Obstetrics*, 56, 39–46.

Ben-David, S., & Schneider, O. (2005). Rape perceptions, gender role attitudes, and victim-perpetrator acquaintance. *Sex Roles: A Journal of Research*, 53, 385–399.

Bennett, B. (2006). Stolen away: As criminal gangs run amuck in Iraq, hundreds of girls have gone missing. Are they being sold for sex? *Time*, May 1, 37–38.

Bennett, W. (1996). Leave marriage alone. *Newsweek*, June 3, 27.

Bennion, J. (2005, July 19). Rough cut: The women's kingdom. Retrieved June 28, 2006, from http://www.pbs.org/frontlineworld/rough/2005/07/introduction_togen.html.

Benotsch, E., Kalichman, S., & Cage, M. (2002). Men who have sex partners via the Internet: Prevalence, predictors, and implications for HIV prevention. *Archives of Sexual Behavior*, 31, 177–183.

Benson, E. (2003). The science of sexual arousal. *Monitor on Psychology*, 34, 50–52.

Benson, J., Clark, K., Gerhardt, A., & Randall, L. (2003). Early abortion services in the United States: A provider survey. *Contraception*, 67, 287–294.

Benson, R. (1985). Vacuum cleaner injury to penis: A common urologic problem? *Urology*, 25, 41–44.

Ben-Ze'ev, A. (2003). Privacy, emotional closeness, and openness in cyberspace. *Computers in Human Behavior*, 19, 451–467.

Berger, R. (1996). *Gay and Gray: The Older Homosexual Man*. New York: Haworth Press.

Bergoffen, D. (2006). From genocide to justice: Women's bodies as a legal writing pad. *Feminist Studies*, 32, 11–37.

Berkman, C., Turner, S., & Cooper, M. (2000). Sexual contact with clients: Assessment of social workers' attitudes and educational preparation. *Social Work*, 45, 223–235.

Berkowitz, B. (2006). How to sell to men. Retrieved May 4, 2006, from http://www.womensbiz.us/archives/histurn1105.asp.

Berkowitz, J. (2000). Personal view: Two boys and a girl please and hold the mustard. *Public Health*, 114, 5–7.

Berman, J., & Berman, L. (2001). *For Women Only: A Revolutionary Guide to Overcoming Sexual Dysfunction and Reclaiming Your Sex Life*. New York: Henry Holt and Company.

Berman, L. (2004). *The Health Benefits of Sexual Aids and Devices*. Evanston, IL: Northwestern University.

Berman, L., & Berman, J. (2000). Viagra and beyond: Where sex educators and therapists fit in from a multidisciplinary perspective. *Journal of Sex Education and Therapy*, 25, 17–24.

Bernat, J., Calhoun, K., & Adams, H. (1999). Sexually aggressive and nonaggressive men: Sexual arousal and judgments in response to acquaintance rape and consensual analogues. *Journal of Abnormal Psychology*, 108, 662–673.

Bernstein, E. & Schaffner, L. (2005). *Regulating Sex: The Politics of Intimacy & Identity*. New York: Routledge.

Bernstein, W., Stephenson, B., Snyder, M., & Wicklund, R. (1983). Causal ambiguity and heterosexual affiliation. *Journal of Experimental Social Psychology*, 19, 78–92.

Best, D., & Davis, S. (1997). Testicular cancer education: Differences in approaches. *American Journal of Health Behavior*, 21, 83–87.

Betts, A. (2001). Role of semen in female-to-male transmission of HIV. *Annals of Epidemiology*, 11, 154–155.

Beyrer, C. (2003). Hidden epidemic of sexually transmitted diseases in China: Crises and opportunity. *Journal of the American Medical Association*, 289, 1303–1305.

Bhatnagar, V., & Kaplan, R. (2005). Treatment options for prostate cancer: Evaluating the evidence. *American Family Physician*, 71, 1915–1922, 1929–1930.

Bhatti, F. (2005). The role of non availability of sex education on the prevalence of sexual dysfunction in conservative Muslim society like Pakistan. Paper presented at the World Congress of Sexology, Montreal, Canada, July 10–15.

Bible, J. (2006). Disorder in the courts: Proving same-sex sex discrimination in Title VII cases via "gender stereotyping." *Employee Relations Law Journal*, 31, 42–72.

Bierce, A. (1943). *The Devil's Dictionary*. New York: World.

Bingham, S., & Battey, K. (2005). Communication of social support to sexual harassment victims: Professors' responses to a student's narrative of unwanted sexual attention. *Communication Studies*, 56, 131–155.

Bingham, S., Luben, R., Welch, A., & Wareham, N. (2003). Are imprecise methods obscuring a relation between fat and breast cancer? *The Lancet*, 362, 212–214.

Binik, Y., Mah, K., & Kiesler, S. (1999). Ethical issues in conducting sex research on the Internet. *Journal of Sex Research*, 36, 82–90.

Birdeau, D., Somers, C., & Lenihan, G. (2005). Effects of educational strategies on college students' identification of sexual harassment. *Education*, 125, 496–510.

Bjorklund, D., & Pellegrini, A. (2000). Child development and evolutionary psychology. *Child Development*, 71, 1687–1708.

Black, M. (2006). Anti choice legislation: The South Dakota case as a national warning. *Network for Reproductive Options*, 2, 4.

Blackburn, R., Cunkelman, J., & Zlidar, V. (2000). Oral contraceptives: An update. *Population Reports*, 28, 1–39.

Blackless, M., Charuvastra, A., Derryck, A., Fausto-Sterling, A., Lauzanne, K., & Lee, E. (2000). How sexually dimorphic are we? Review and synthesis. *American Journal of Human Biology*, 12, 151–166.

Blackmun, M. (1996a). Escort services: Look all you want but don't touch. *The Oregonian*, June 16, D1, D4.

Blackwell, D., & Lichter, D. (2000). Mate selection among married and cohabiting couples. *Journal of Family Issues*, 21, 275–302.

Blaicher, W., Gruber, D., Bieglmayer, C., Blaicher, A., Knogler, W., & Huber, J. (1999). The role of oxytocin in relation to female sexual arousal. *Gynecology and Obstetrics Investigations*, 47, 125–126.

Blair, C., & Lanyon, R. (1981). Exhibitionism: Etiology and treatment. *Psychological Bulletin*, 89, 439–463.

Blais, M., Chaffai, I., & Desjardins, J. (2005). Body-related factors associated with male sexual dysfunction and skills promoting sexual health. Paper presented at the World Congress of Sexology, Montreal, Canada, July 10–15.

Blake, A., Ledsky, R., Goodenow, C., Sawyer, R., Lohrman, D., & Windsor, R. (2003). Condom availability programs in Massachusetts high schools: Relationships with condom use and sexual behavior. *American Journal of Public Health*, 93, 955–962.

Blank, J. (2000). *Good Vibrations: The New Complete Guide to Vibrators*. San Francisco: Down There Press.

Blee, K., & Tickamyer, A. (1995). Racial differences in men's attitudes about women's gender roles. *Journal of Marriage and the Family*, 57, 21–30.

Bloche, M. (2004). Health care disparities: Science, politics, and race. *New England Journal of Medicine*, 350, 1568–1570.

Block, J. (1983). Differential premises arising from differential socialization of the sexes: Some conjectures. *Child Development*, 54, 1335–1354.

Blue, V. (2003). *The Ultimate Guide to Adult Videos: How to Watch Adult Videos and Make Your Sex Life Sizzle*. San Francisco: Cleis Press.

Blythe, M., Fortenberry, D., Temkit, M., & Tu, W. (2006). Incidence and correlates of unwanted sex in relationships of middle and late adolescent women. *Archives of Pediatric & Adolescent Medicine*, 160, 591–595.

Bockting, W. (2005). Biological reductionism meets gender diversity in human sexuality. *Journal of Sex Research*, 42, 267–270.

Boekhout, B., Hendrick, S., & Hendrick, C. (1999). Relationship infidelity: A loss of perspective. *Journal of Personal and Interpersonal Loss*, 4, 97–124.

Boen, J. (2006). Pap test changes with the times. *The News-Sentinel*, February 6, pNA.

Boeringer, S. (1994). Pornography and sexual aggression: Association of violent and nonviolent depictions with rape and rape proclivity. *Deviant Behavior: An Interdisciplinary Journal*, 15, 289–304.

Bogart, L., Collins, R., Kanovse, D., et al. (2006). Patterns and correlates of deliberate abstinence among men and women with HIV/AIDS. *American Journal of Public Health*, 96, 1078–1084.

Bogren, L. (1991). Changes in sexuality in women and men during pregnancy. *Archives of Sexual Behavior*, 20, 35–46.

Bohner, G., Siebler, F., & Schmelcher, J. (2006). Social norms and the likelihood of raping: Perceived rape myth acceptance of others affects men's rape proclivity. *Personality and Social Psychology Bulletin*, 32, 286–297.

Bolin, A. (1997). Transforming transvestism and transsexualism: Polarity, politics, and gender. In B. Bullough, V. Bullough, and J. Elias (Eds.), *Gender Blending*. New York: Prometheus Books.

Bolus, J. (1994). Teaching teens about condoms. *Registered Nurse*, March, 44–47.

Bonierbale, M., Clement, A., Loundou, A., & Simeoni, M. (2006). A new evaluation of concept and its measurement: "Male sexual anticipating cognitions." *The Journal of Sexual Medicine*, 3, 96–103.

Boonstra, H., & Sonfield, A. (2000). Rights without access: Revisiting public funding of abortion for poor women. *Guttmacher Report*, 3, 1–5.

Boonstra, H., Gold, R., Richards, C., & Finer, L. (2006). *Abortion in Women's Lives*. New York: Guttmacher Institute.

Bornstein, R. (1989). Exposure and effect: Overview and meta-analysis of research, 1968–1987. *Psychological Bulletin*, 106, 265–289.

Boschert, S. (2004). Majority of circumcisions are performed without analgesia. *Family Practice News*, 34, 63.

Boss, S., & Maltz, W. (2001). *Private Thoughts: Exploring the Power of Women's Sexual Fantasies*. Novato, CA: New World Library.

Boston Women's Health Collective (1971). *Our Bodies, Ourselves*. New York: Simon & Schuster.

Boswell, J. (1980). *Christianity, Social Tolerance, and Homosexuality*. Chicago: University of Chicago Press.

Botros, S., Abramov, Y., Miller, J., & Sand, P. (2006). Effect of parity on sexual function. *Obstetrics & Gynecology*, 107, 765–770.

Bouvier, P. (2003). Child sexual abuse: Vicious circles of fate or paths to resilience? *Lancet*, 361, 446.

Bowen, A. (2005). Internet sexuality research with rural men who have sex with men: Can we recruit and retain them? *Journal of Sex Research*, 42, 317–323.

Boyd, A. & Wilmoth, M. (2006). An innovative community-based intervention for African American women with breast cancer: The witness project. *Health and Social Work*, 31, 77–80.

Boyer, D., & Fine, D. (1992). Sexual abuse as a factor in adolescent pregnancy and child maltreatment. *Family Planning Perspectives*, 24, 4–11.

Boynton, P. (2003). "I'm just a girl who can't say no"? Women, consent, and sex research. *Journal of Sex and Marital Therapy*, 29(suppl.), 23–32.

Brackett, N., Bloch, W., & Abae, M. (1994). Neurological anatomy and physiology of sexual function. In C. Singer & W. Weiner (Eds.), *Sexual Dysfunction: A Neuromedical Approach*. New York: Futura.

Bradford, J. (1998). Treatment of men with paraphilia. *New England Journal of Medicine*, 338, 464–465.

Bradford, J., Boulet, J., & Pawlak, A. (1992). The paraphilias: A multiplicity of deviant behaviors. *Canadian Journal of Psychiatry*, 37, 104–107.

Bradley, S., & Zucker, K. (1997). Gender identity disorder: A review of the past 10 years. *Journal of the American Academy of Child and Adolescent Psychology*, 36, 872–880.

Bradley, S., Oliver, G., Chernick, A., & Zucker, K. (1998). Experiment of nurture: Ablatio penis at 2 months, sex reassignment at 7 months, and a psychosexual follow-up in young adulthood. *Pediatrics*, 102, E91–E95.

Bradshaw, C. (1994). Asia and Asian American women: Historical and political considerations in psychotherapy. In L. Comas-Diaz & B. Greene (Eds.), *Women of Color*. New York: Guilford Press.

Bradshaw, C., Tabrizi, S., Read, T., Garland, S., et al. (2006). Etiologies of nongonococcal urethritis: bacteria, viruses, and the association with orogenital exposure. *Journal of Infectious Diseases*, 193, 333–345.

Bradsher, K. (2000). Four get prison time in death of girl from date rape drug. *New York Times*, March 31, A15.

Braen, G. (1980). Examination of the accused: The heterosexual and homosexual rapist. In C. Warner (Ed.), *Rape and Sexual Assault*. Germantown, MD: Aspen Systems.

Brainerd, C., & Reyna, V. (1998). When things that were never experienced are easier to "remember" than things that were. *Psychological Science*, 9, 484–489.

Brandon, K. (2001). Nursing mothers hit office obstacles. *The Sunday Oregonian*, April 15, L11.

Braveman, S. & Woodward-Kreitz, M. (2006). Male sexual abuse and victimization: Innovative ways to treat adult male survivors of childhood abuse. Paper presented at the Gumbo Sexualite Upriver: Spicing Up Education & Therapy (AASECT 38th Annual Conference), St. Louis, June/July.

Braverman, P., & Strasburger, V. (1993b). Contraception. *Clinical Pediatrics*, 33, 100–109.

Brehm, S., Miller, R., Perlman, D., & Campbell, S. (2002). *Intimate Relationships*. Boston: McGraw-Hill.

Bremer, J. (1959). *Asexualization*. New York: Macmillan.

Bretschneider, J., & McCoy, N. (1988). Sexual interest and behavior in healthy 80- to 102-year-olds. *Archives of Sexual Behavior*, 17, 109.

Brewer, D., Golden, M., & Handsfield, H. (2006). Unsafe sexual behavior and correlates of risk in a probability sample of men who have sex with men in the era of highly active antiretroviral therapy. *Sexually Transmitted Diseases*, 33, 250–255.

Brewster, W., DiSaia, P., & Grosen, E. (1999). An experience with estrogen replacement therapy in breast cancer survivors. *International Journal of Fertility*, 44, 186–192.

Briddell, D., & Wilson, G. (1976). Effects of alcohol and expectancy set on male sexual arousal. *Journal of Abnormal Psychology*, 85, 225–234.

Bridges, A. (2006). FDA approves contraceptive implant. *The Oregonian*, July 19, A4.

Bringle, R., & Buunk, B. (1991). Extradyadic relationships and sexual jealousy. In K. McKinney & S. Sprecher (Eds.), *Sexuality in Close Relationships*. Hillsdale, NJ: Erlbaum.

Britton, G., & Lumpkin, M. (1984). Battle to imprint for the 21st century. *Reading Teacher*, 37, 724–733.

Brockman, J. (2006). Child sex as Internet fare, through eyes of a victim. *The New York Times*, April 5, A20.

Broderick, G. (2006). Premature ejaculation. Retrieved September 4, 2006, from http://www.medscape.com/viewarticle/507262.

Brody, J. (2000). Cybersex gives birth to a psychological disorder. *The New York Times*, May 16, F7, F12.

Brook, C. (1999a). Mechanism of puberty. *Hormone Research*, 51(suppl.), 52–54.

Brooks, J., & Watkins, M. (1989). Recognition memory and the mere exposure effect. *Journal of Experimental Psychology: Learning, Memory, and Cognition*, 15, 968–976.

Brooks, T. (2002). Association of adolescent risk behaviors with mental health symptoms in high school students. *Journal of Adolescent Health*, 31, 240–246.

Brotto, L., Chik, H., Ryder, A., & Gorzalka, B. (2005). Acculturation and sexual function in Asian women. *Archive of Sexual Behavior*, 34, 613–627.

Brown, D. (2006). GAO faults Bush's AIDS-abstinence emphasis. *Oregonian*, April 5, A2.

Brown, D., Shew, M., Qadadri, B., Neptune, N., Vargas, M., et al. (2005). A longitudinal study of genital human papillomavirus infection in a cohort of closely followed adolescent women. *Journal of Infectious Diseases*, 191, 182–192.

Brown, E. (1988). Affairs: The hidden meanings have major impact on therapeutic approach. *Behavior Today*, October 24, 3–4.

Brown, G. (1990). The transvestite husband. *Medical Aspects of Human Sexuality*, June, 35–42.

Brown, J. (2002, February). *Mass Media Influences on Sexuality*. Retrieved April 11, 2003, from http://www.findarticles.com/cf_0/m2372/1_39/87080439/print.jhtml.

Brown, M., Perry, A., Cheesman, A., & Pring, T. (2000). Pitch change in male-to-female transsexuals: Has phonosurgery a role to play? *International Journal of Language and Communications Disorders*, 35, 129–136.

Brown, R. (2000). Understanding the disorders of sexual preference. *The Practitioner*, 244, 438–442.

Brown, S. (2003). Relationship quality dynamics of cohabiting unions. *Journal of Family Issues*, 24, 583–601.

Brown, T., & Fee, E. (2003). Alfred Kinsey: A pioneer of sex research. *American Journal of Public Health*, 93, 896–897.

Brown, Z., Wald, A., Morrow, R., Selke, S., Zeh, J., & Corey, L. (2003). Effect of serologic status and cesarean delivery on transmission rates of herpes simplex virus from mother to infant. *Journal of the American Medical Association*, 289, 203–209.

Brownmiller, S. (1975). *Against Our Will: Men, Women, and Rape*. New York: Simon & Schuster.

Brownmiller, S. (1993). Making female bodies the battlefield. *Newsweek*, January 4, 37.

Bruns, D., & Bruns, J. (2005). Sexual harassment in higher education. *Academic Exchange Quarterly*, 9, 201–204.

Bryjak, G., & Soroka, M. (1994). *Sociology: Cultural Diversity in a Changing World* (2nd ed.). Boston: Allyn and Bacon.

Budd, K. (1999). The facts of life: Everything you wanted to know about sex (after 50). *Modern Maturity*, September–October, 86–87.

Budhos, M. (1997). Putting the heat on sex tourism.

*Ms.*, March–April, 12–16.

Budin, L., & Johnson, C. (1989). Sex abuse prevention programs: Offenders' attitudes about their efficacy. *Child Abuse and Neglect*, 13, 77–87.

Bulcroft, R., Carmady, D., & Bulcroft, K. (1996). Patterns of parental independence giving to adolescents: Variations by race, age, and gender of child. *Journal of Marriage and the Family*, 58, 866–883.

Bullock, K., & McGraw, S. (2006). A community capacity-enhancement approach to breast and cervical cancer screening among older women of color. *Health & Social Work*, 31, 16–25.

Bullough, B., & Bullough, V. (1997). Are transvestites necessarily heterosexual? *Archives of Sexual Behavior*, 26, 1–12.

Bullough, V. (2001). Religion, sex, and science: Some historical quandaries. *Journal of Sex Education and Therapy*, 26, 254–258.

Bullough, V., & Bullough, B. (1993). *Cross Dressing, Sex and Gender*. Philadelphia: University of Pennsylvania Press.

Bureau of Labor Statistics (2006). *Labor Force Statistics from the Current Population Survey*. Retrieved January 4, 2006, from http://www.stats.bls.gov.

Burgess, A., & Holmstrom, L. (1979). Rape: Sexual disruption and recovery. *American Journal of Orthopsychiatry*, 49, 648–657.

Burke, A., Sowerbutts, S., Blundell, B., & Sherry, M. (2002). Child pornography and the Internet: Policing and treatment issues. *Psychiatry, Psychology and Law*, 9, 79–84.

Burke, W., Daly, M., Garber, J., Botkin, J., Kahn, M., Lynch, P., McTiernan, A., Offit, K., Perlman, J., Petersen, G., Thomson, E., & Varricchio, C. (1997). Recommendations for follow-up care of individuals with an inherited predisposition to cancer. *Journal of the American Medical Association*, 277(12, 997–1003.

Burkett, A. & Hewitt, G. (2005). Progestin only contraceptives and their use in adolescents: Clinical options and medical indications. *Adolescent Medicine*, 16, 553–567.

Burn, S., O'Neil, A., & Nederend, S. (1996). Childhood tomboyism and adult androgyny. *Sex Roles*, 34, 419–428.

Burr, T. (2006). "Heading South" sheds some light on sexual tourism. *Chicago Sun-Times*, August 18, B1.

Burstein, G., & Murray, P. (2003). Diagnosis and management of sexually transmitted disease pathogens among adolescents. *Pediatrics in Review*, 24, 75–81.

Burt, K. (1995). The effects of cancer on the body image and sexuality. *Nursing Times*, 91(7, 36–37.

Bush, C., Bush, J., & Jennings, J. (1988). Effects of jealousy threats on relationship perceptions and emotions. *Journal of Social and Personal Relationships*, 5, 285–303.

Bushman, B., & Baumeister, R. (1998). Threatened egoism, narcissism, self-esteem, and direct and displaced aggression: Does self-love or self-hate lead to violence? *Journal of Personality and Social Psychology*, 43, 372–384.

Bushman, B., & Bonacci, A. (2002). Violence and sex impair memory for television ads. *Journal of Applied Psychology*, 87, 27–32.

Bushman, B., Bonacci, A., Dijk, M., & Baumeister, R. (2003). Narcissism, sexual refusal, and aggression: Testing a narcissistic reactance model of sexual aggression. *Journal of Personality and Social Psychology*, 84, 1027–1040.

Buss, D. (1994). *The Evolution of Desire: Strategies of Human Mating*. New York: Basic Books.

Buss, D. (1999). *Evolutionary Psychology: The New Science of the Mind*. Boston: Allyn and Bacon.

Buss, D. (2000). *The Dangerous Passion: Why Jealousy Is as Necessary as Love and Sex*. New York: Free Press.

Buss, D., & Schmitt, D. (1993). Sexual strategies theory: An evolutionary perspective on human mating. *Psychological Review*, 100, 204–232.

Butcher, K. (2003). Confusion between prostitution and sex trafficking. *The Lancet*, 361, 1983.

Butts, J. (1981). Adolescent sexuality and teenage pregnancy from a black perspective. In T. Ooms (Ed.), *Teenage Pregnancy in a Family Context*. Philadelphia: Temple University Press.

Byers, E. (2005). Relationship satisfaction and sexual satisfaction: A longitudinal study of individuals in long-term relationships. *Journal of Sex Research*, 42, 113–118.

Byers, E., & Demmons, S. (1999). Sexual satisfaction and sexual self-disclosure within dating relationships. *Journal of Sex Research*, 36, 180–189.

Byers, S., & O'Sullivan, L. (1996). *Sexual Coercion in Dating Relationships*. New York: Haworth Press.

Byrd, J., Hyde, J., DeLamater, J., & Plant, E. (1998). Sexuality during pregnancy and the year postpartum. *Journal of Family Practice*, 47, 305–308.

Byrne, D. (1997). An overview (and underview) and research and theory within the attraction paradigm. *Journal of Social and Personal Relationships*, 14, 417–431.

Byrne, D., & Murnen, S. (1988). Maintaining loving relationships. In R. Sternberg & M. Barnes (Eds.), *The Psychology of Loving*. New Haven, CT: Yale University Press.

Cado, S., & Leitenberg, H. (1990). Guilt reactions to sexual fantasies during intercourse. *Archives of Sexual Behavior*, 19, 49–71.

Cain, S. (2000). Breast cancer genetics and the role of tamoxifen in prevention. *Journal of the American Academy of Nurse Practitioners*, 12, 21–28.

Calderoni, M. & Coupey, S. (2005). Combined hormonal contraception. *Adolescent Medicine*, 16, 517–537.

Caldwell, J. (2005). Sheath that scalpel: the only way to be sure of an intersex baby's gender is to wait until you can ask them, researchers say. *The Advocate*, April 12, 44.

Califia, P. (2002). Whoring in utopia. In A. Soble (Ed.), *The Philosophy of Sex: Contemporary Readings*. Lanham, MD: Rowman & Littlefield.

Callahan, S. (2002). Abortion and the sexual agenda: A case for prolife feminism. In A. Soble (Ed.), *The Philosophy of Sex: Contemporary Readings*. Lanham, MD: Rowman & Littlefield.

Calvert, C., & Richards, R. (2006). Pointless prosecution. *New Jersey Law Journal*, August 14, 7.

Calvert, H. (2003). Sexually transmitted diseases other than human immunodeficiency virus infection in older adults. *Clinical Infectious Diseases*, 36, 609–614.

Calzavara, L., Burchell, A., Remis, R., Major, C., Corey, P., Myers, T., Millson, M., Wallace, E., and the Polaris Study Team (2003). Delayed application of condoms is a risk factor for human immunodeficiency virus infection among homosexual and bisexual men. *American Journal of Epidemiology*, 157, 210–217.

Camp, A. (2006). We deserve some answers. *Ms.*, Spring, 17.

Campbell, C., & Mzaidume, Z. (2001). Grassroots participation, peer education, and HIV prevention by sex workers in South Africa. *American Journal of Public Health*, 91, 1978–1986.

Campbell, D., Lake, M., Falk, M., & Backstrand, J. (2006). A randomized control trial of continuous support in labor by a lay doula. *Journal of Obstetric, Gynecologic, & Neonatal Nursing*, 35, 456.

Campbell, R. (2006). Rape survivors' experiences with the legal and medical systems: Do rape victim advocates make a difference? *Violence Against Women*, 12, 30–45.

Campo, J., Nijman, H., Merckelbach, H., & Evers, C. (2003). Psychiatric comorbidity of gender identity disorders: A survey among Dutch psychiatrists. *American Journal of Psychiatry*, 160, 1332–1336.

Campo-Flores, A. (2006). Mississippi churning. *Newsweek*, March 20, 29.

Canary, D., & Dindia, K. (Eds.) (1998). *Sex Differences and Similarities in Communication.* Mahwah, NJ: Erlbaum.

Canavan, M., Meyer, W., & Higgs, D. (1992). The female experience of sibling incest. *Journal of Marital and Family Therapy*, 18, 129–142.

Capellen, J., Bell, S., & Althof, S. (2006). Comparison between sildenafil-treated subjects with erectile dysfunction and control subjects on the self-esteem and relationship questionnaire. *The Journal of Sexual Medicine*, 3, 274–282.

Caplan, L., May, D., & Richardson, L. (2000). Time to diagnosis and treatment of breast cancer: Results from the National Breast and Cervical Cancer Early Detection Program, 1991–1995. *American Journal of Public Health*, 90, 130–134.

Carael, M., Slaymaker, E., Lyerla, R., & Sarkar, S. (2006). Clients of sex workers in different regions of the world: Hard to count. *Sexually Transmitted Infections*, 82(suppl. 3), iii26–iii33.

Cardenas, K., & Frisch, K. (2003). Comprehensive breast cancer screening. *Postgraduate Medicine*, 113, 34–46.

Carlson, E. (1997). Sexual assault on men in war. *The Lancet*, 349, 129.

Carmichael, M. (2002). How to make a baby. *Newsweek*, July 15, 9.

Carnes, P. (1983). *Out of the Shadows: Understanding Sexual Addiction.* Minneapolis: Compcare Publications.

Carnes, P. (2000). Cybersex: The scope of the problem. *The Carnes Update*, Summer, 11.

Carpenter, L. (1998). From girls into women: Scripts for sexuality and romance in *Seventeen* magazine. *Journal of Sex Research*, 35, 158–168.

Carroll, L. (2000). *Families of Two: Interviews with Happily Married Couples Without Children by Choice.* Philadelphia: Xlibris.

Carroll, R. (1999). Outcomes of treatment for gender dysphoria. *Journal of Sex Education and Therapy*, 24, 128–136.

Carson, C. (2003). Penile prostheses: Are they still relevant? *British Journal of Urology International*, 91, 176–177.

Carson, C. (2003). To circumcise or not to circumcise? Not a simple question. *Contemporary Urology*, 15, 11.

Carter, C. (1998). Neuroendocrine perspectives on social attachment and love. *Psychoneuroendocrinology*, 13, 779–818.

Carter, J. (2005). *Our Endangered Values: America's Moral Crisis.* Waterville, Maine: Thorndike Press.

Carter, S. (2000). Math skill, confidence multiplying for girls. *The Oregonian*, March 4, A1, A11.

Carter, V. (2003). Prostitution = slavery. In R. Morgan (Ed.), *Sisterhood Is Forever.* New York: Washington Square Press.

Cassel, E. (2006). Underlying these laws are themes of religious fundamentalism. Retrieved July 31, 2006, from http://writ.news.findlaw.com/cassel/20060314.html.

Cassell, C. (2002). Let it shine: Promoting school success, life aspirations to prevent school-age parenthood. *SIECUS Report*, 30, 7–16.

Castleman, M. (1980). *Sexual Solutions.* New York: Simon & Schuster.

Castleman, M. (1997). Recipes for lust. *Psychology Today*, July–August, 50–56.

Castleman, M. (2005). XXX Harmful: How pornography misleads men about women's sexuality and their own and contributes to sex problems. Paper presented at the What's New and What Works: Pioneering Solutions for Today's Sexual Issues (AASECT 37th Annual Conference), Portland, OR, May.

Castro, P., Vallejo, L., Lopez, R., & Curado, A. (2003). Combined treatment with vitamin E and colchicines in the early stages of Peyronie's disease. *British Journal of Urology International*, 91, 522–524.

Catalona, W., Loeb, S., & Han, M. (2006). Viewpoint: Expanding prostate cancer screening. *Annals of Internal Medicine*, 144, 441–443.

Catania, J. (1999b). A framework for conceptualizing reporting bias and its antecedents in interviews assessing human sexuality. *Journal of Sex Research*, 36, 25–38.

Caufriez, A. (1997). The pubertal spurt: Effects of sex steroid on growth hormone and insulin-like growth factor I. *European Journal of Obstetrics and Gynecology and Biology*, 71, 215–217.

CBS News & N.Y. Times Poll (2004). *Pharmacists and Birth Control.* November. Retrieved from http://prochoiceamerica.org/assets/files/Birth-Control-Pharmacy-Access/pdf.

Ceci, S., Loftus, E., Leichtman, M., & Bruck, M. (1994). The role of source misattributions in the creation of false beliefs among preschoolers. *International Journal of Clinical and Experimental Hypnosis*, 42, 304–320.

Celum, C., Robinson, N., & Cohen, M. (2005). Potential effect of HIV type 1 antiretroviral and herpes simplex virus type 2 antiviral therapy on transmission and acquisition of HIV type 1 infection. *Journal of Infectious Diseases*, 191, S107–S114.

Centers for Disease Control (1998b). Trends in sexual risk behaviors among high school students: United

States, 1991–1997. *Morbidity and Mortality Weekly Report, 47,* 749–752.

Centers for Disease Control (2000a). Adoption of protective behavior among persons with recent HIV infection and diagnosis: Alabama, New Jersey, and Tennessee, 1997–1998. *Morbidity and Mortality Weekly Report, 49,* 512–515.

Centers for Disease Control (2000b). Alcohol policy and sexually transmitted disease rates: United States, 1981–1995. *Morbidity and Mortality Weekly Report, 49,* 346–349.

Centers for Disease Control (2000b). Youth risk behavior surveillance: United States, 1999. *Morbidity and Mortality Weekly Report, 49,* 1–79.

Centers for Disease Control (2000c). HIV/AIDS among racial/ethnic minority men who have sex with men: United States, 1989–1998. *Morbidity and Mortality Weekly Report, 49,* 4–11.

Centers for Disease Control (2002a). Guidelines for using antiretroviral agents among HIV-infected adults and adolescents: Recommendations of the Panel on Clinical Practices for Treatment of HIV. *Morbidity and Mortality Weekly Report, 51*(RR-7), 1–55.

Centers for Disease Control (2002c). Youth risk behavior surveillance: United States, 2001. *Morbidity and Mortality Weekly Report, 51,* 1–62.

Centers for Disease Control (2002e). Primary and secondary syphilis among men who have sex with men: New York City, 2001. *Morbidity and Mortality Weekly Report, 51,* 853–856.

Centers for Disease Control (2002g). Sexually transmitted diseases treatment guidelines, 2002. *Morbidity and Mortality Weekly Report, 51,* 36–82.

Centers for Disease Control (2003a). Advancing HIV prevention: New strategies for a changing epidemic—United States, 2003. *Morbidity and Mortality Weekly Report, 52,* 329–332.

Centers for Disease Control (2004). *HIV/AIDS Surveillance Report.* Retrieved February 15, 2004, from http:// www.cdc.gov/hiv/stats/hasr1302/commentary.htm.

Centers for Disease Control (2005b). A comprehensive immunization strategy to eliminate transmission of hepatitis B virus infection in the United States. *Morbidity and Mortality Weekly Report, 50,* 1–30.

Centers for Disease Control (2005c). Trends in HIV/AIDS diagnoses—33 states, 2001–2004. *Morbidity and Mortality Weekly Report, 54,* 1149–1156.

Centers for Disease Control (2005d). HIV prevalence, unrecognized infection, and HIV testing among men who have sex with men—five U.S. cities, June 2004–April 2005. *Morbidity and Mortality Weekly Report, 54,* 597–601.

Centers for Disease Control (2005e). Update: Syringe exchange programs—United States, 2002. *Morbidity and Mortality Weekly Report, 54,* 673–676.

Centers for Disease Control (2005f). Antiretroviral postexposure prophylaxis after sexual, injection-drug use, or other nonoccupational exposure to HIV in the United States: Recommendations from the U.S. Department of Health and Human Services. *Morbidity and Mortality Weekly Report, 54,* (RR-2), 1–20.

Centers for Disease Control (2006). Youth risk behavior surveillance: United States, 2005. *Morbidity and Mortality Weekly Report, 55,* 1–108.

Centers for Disease Control (2006a). *Sexually Transmitted Diseases.* Retrieved January 17, 2006, from http://www.cdc.gov/std.

Centers for Disease Control (2006b). *Chlamydia—CDC Fact Sheet.* Retrieved January 17, 2006, from http://www.cdc.gov/std/chlamydia/STDFact-Chlamydia.htm.

Centers for Disease Control (2006c). *Gonorrhea—CDC Fact Sheet.* Retrieved January 17, 2006, from http://www.cdc.gov/std/Gonorrhea/STDFact-gonorrhea.htm.

Centers for Disease Control (2006d). *Syphilis—CDC Fact Sheet.* Retrieved January 17, 2006, from http://www.cdc.gov/std/syphilis/STDFact-Syphilis .htm.

Centers for Disease Control (2006e). *Genital Herpes—CDC Fact Sheet.* Retrieved January 17, 2006, from http://www.cdc.gov/std/Herpes/STDFact-Herpes .htm.

Centers for Disease Control (2006f). *Genital HPV Infection—CDC Fact Sheet.* Retrieved January 17, 2006, from http://www.cdc.gov/std/HPVSTDFact-HPV.htm.

Centers for Disease Control (2006g). *Hepatitis Surveillance Report No. 60.* Retrieved January 17, 2006, from http://cdc.gov/hepatitis.

Centers for Disease Control (2006h). *Bacterial Vaginosis—CDC Fact Sheet.* Retrieved January 17, 2006, from http://www.cdc.gov/std/bv/STDFact-Bacterial-Vaginosis.htm.

Centers for Disease Control (2006i). *Genital Candidiasis—CDC Fact Sheet.* Retrieved January 17, 2006, from http://www.cdc.gov/ncidod/dbmd/diseaseinfo/candidiasis_gen_g.

Centers for Disease Control (2006j). *Trichomoniasis—CDC Fact Sheet.* Retrieved January 17, 2006, from http://www.cdc.gov/std/trichomoniasis/STDFact-Trichomoniasis.

Centers for Disease Control (2006k). *Fact Sheet Scabies.* Retrieved January 18, 2006, from http://www .cdc.gov/ncidod/dpd/parasites/scabies/factsht_ scabies.htm.

Centers for Disease Control (2006l). *HIV/AIDS Prevention in the United States: Basic Statistics Overview.* Retrieved January 18, 2006, from http://www.cdc/ hiv/.

Chang, H., & Holt, G. (1991). The concept of *yuan* and Chinese interpersonal relationships. In S. Ting-Toomey & F. Korzenny (Eds.), *Cross- Cultural Interpersonal Communication.* Newbury Park, CA: Sage.

Chapkis, W. (1997). *Live Sex Acts: Women Performing Erotic Labor.* New York: Routledge.

Chappell, K., & Davis, K. (1998). Attachment, partner choice, and perception of romantic partners: An experimental test of the attachment–security hypothesis. *Personal Relationships, 5,* 327–342.

Charney, D., & Russell, R. (1994). An overview of sexual harassment. *American Journal of Psychiatry, 151,* 10–17.

Check, J., & Guloien, T. (1989). Reported proclivity for coercive sex following repeated exposure to sexually violent pornography, nonviolent dehumanizing pornography, and erotica. In D. Zillman & J. Bryant (Eds.), *Pornography: Research Advances and Policy Considerations.* Hillsdale, NJ: Erlbaum.

Chen, W. (2006). Unopposed estrogen therapy and the risk of invasive breast cancer. *Archives of Internal Medicine*, 166, 1027-1032.

Chen, X., Gong, X., Liang, G., & Zhang, G. (2000). Epidemiologic trends of sexually transmitted diseases in China. *Sexually Transmitted Diseases*, 27, 138–142.

Chesney, M. (2003). Adherence to HAART regimens. *AIDS Patient Care and STDs*, 17, 169–177.

Cheung, A. (2006). Assisted reproductive technology: Both sides now. *The Journal of Reproductive Medicine*, 51, 283–292.

Chiasson, M., Hirshfield, S., & Humberstone, M. (2003). The Internet and high-risk sex among men who have sex with men. Paper presented at the 10th Conference on Retroviruses and Opportunistic Infection. Boston, February.

Chigbo, M. (2003). The fight for her life. *Ms.*, Summer, 26.

Chinese Ministry of Health (2006). 2005 update on the HIV/AIDS epidemic and response in China. Retrieved May 14, 2006, from http://www.unchina.org/unaids/2005-China%20HIV-AIDS%Estimation-English.pdf.

Chivers, M. (2005). Clinical management of sex addiction (book review). *Archives of Sexual Behavior*, 34, 476–478.

Chocano, C. (2003). Sharper image: Bravo's *Queer Eye* gives the makeover-show genre an edge. *Entertainment Weekly*, August 8, 62.

Choi, K., Gregorich, S., Anderson, K., & Grinstead, O. (2003a). Patterns and predictors of female condom use among ethnically diverse women attending family planning clinics. *Sexually Transmitted Diseases*, January, 91–97.

Choi, K., Liu, H., Guo, Y., Ran, L., Mandel, J., & Rutherford, G. (2003b). Emerging HIV-I epidemic in China in men who have sex with men. *The Lancet*, 361, 2125–2126.

Choma, K. (2003). ASC-US HPV testing. *American Journal of Nursing*, 103, 42–50.

Chosidow, D. (2006). Scabies. *New England Journal of Medicine*, 354, 1718-1727.

Chretien, F. (2003). Involvement of the glycoproteic meshwork of cervical mucus in the mechanism of sperm orientation. *Acta Obstetricia et Gynecologica Scandinavica*, 82, 449–461.

Chrisler, J., & Levy, K. (1990). The media construct a menstrual monster: A content analysis of PMS articles in the popular press. *Women and Health*, 16(2, 89–104.

Chrisler, J., Johnston, I., Champagne, N., & Preston, K. (1994). Menstrual joy. *Psychology of Women Quarterly*, 18, 375–387.

Chumlea, W., Schubert, M., Roche, A., Kulin, H., Lee, P., Himes, J., & Sun, S. (2003). Age at menarche and racial comparisons in U.S. girls. *Pediatrics*, 111, 110–113.

Chung, P. (2006, July 14). Government to expand childbirth incentives. Retrieved July 24, 2006, from http://times.hankooki.com/service/print/Print.php?po=times.hankooki.com/lpage/nation/20. . . .

Chung, W., & Choi, H. (1990). Erotic erection versus nocturnal erection. *Journal of Urology*, 143, 294–297.

Chung, W., De Vries, G., & Schaab, D. (2002). Sexual differentiation of the bed nucleus of the stria terminalis in humans may extend into adulthood. *Journal of Neurosciences*, 22, 1027–1033.

Ciccarone, D., Kanouse, D., Collins, R., Miu, A., Chen, J., Morton, S., & Stall, R. (2003). Sex without disclosure of positive HIV serostatus in a U.S. probability sample of persons receiving medical care for HIV infection. *American Journal of Public Health*, 93, 949–954.

Clancy, S., Schacter, D., McNally, R., & Pitman, R. (2000). False recognition in women reporting recovered memories of sexual abuse. *Psychological Science*, 11, 26–31.

Clanton, G., & Smith, L. (1977). *Jealousy*. Englewood Cliffs, NJ: Prentice Hall.

Clark, J. (2003). Furor erupts over NIH "hit list." *British Medical Journal*, 327, 1065.

Clark, J. (2005). The big turnoff: Stymied by politics and Viagra, sex research goes limp. *Psychology Today*, January/February, 17–18.

Clark, J., Smith, E., & Davidson, J. (1984). Enhancement of sexual motivation in male rats by yohimbine. *Science*, 225, 847–849.

Clark, K. (2000). The new midlife. *U.S. News and World Report*, March 20, 70–83.

Clark, S., Bruce, J., & Dude, A. (2006). Protecting young women from HIV/AIDS: The case against child and adolescent marriage. *International Family Planning Perspectives*, 32, 79–88.

Clarnette, T., Sugita, Y., & Hutson, J. (1997). Genital anomalies in human and animal models reveal the mechanisms and hormones governing testicular descent. *British Journal of Urology*, 79, 99–112.

Clements, M. (1994). Sex in America today. *Parade*, August 7, 4–6.

Clementson, L. (2000b). A search for God's welcome. *Newsweek*, March 20, 60–61.

Cobb, N., Larson, J., & Watson, W. (2003). Development of the attitudes about romance and mate selection scale. *Family Relations*, 52, 222–231.

Cochran, S., & Mays, V. (1990). Sex, lies, and HIV. *New England Journal of Medicine*, 322, 774.

Cochran, S., Mays, V., & Leung, L. (1991). Sexual practices of heterosexual Asian American young adults: Implications for risk of HIV infection. *Archives of Sexual Behavior*, 20, 381–392.

Cockey, C. (2003). Breast cancer risk from HRT confirmed. *AWHONN Lifelines*, 7, 16–23.

Coco, A., & Vandenbosche, M. (2000). Infectious vaginitis. *Postgraduate Medicine*, 107, 63–74.

Cocores, J., & Gold, M. (1989). Substance abuse and sexual dysfunction. *Medical Aspects of Human Sexuality*, February, 22–31.

Coe, C., Lulbach, G., & Schneider, M. (2002). Prenatal disturbance alters the size of the corpus callosum in young monkeys. *Developmental Psychobiology*, 41, 178–185.

Cohen, E. (2001). *New Treatments Hold Out Hope for Breast Cancer Patients*. Retrieved January 26, 2001, from http://www.cnn.com/2001/HEALTH/cancer/01/26/breast.cancer/index.html.

Cohen, F., Kemeny, M., Kearney, K., Zegans, L., Neuhaus, J., & Conant, M. (1999). Persistent stress as a predictor of genital herpes recurrence. *Archives of Internal Medicine*, 159, 2430–2436.

Cohen, J. (1998). Uninfectable. *The New Yorker*, July 6, 34–39.

Cohen, J., Schleifer, R., & Tate, T. (2005). AIDS in Uganda: The human-rights dimension. *Lancet*, 365, 2075–2076.

Cohen, L., Soares, C., Vitonis, A., & Otto, M. (2006). Risk for new onset of depression during the menopausal transition. *Archives of General Psychiatry*, 63, 385–390.

Cohen, M., & Pilcher, C. (2005). Amplified HIV transmission and new approaches to HIV prevention. *Journal of Infectious Diseases*, 191, 1391–1393.

Cohen, M., Ping, G., Fox, K., & Henderson, G. (2000). Sexually transmitted diseases in the People's Republic of China in Y2K. *Sexually Transmitted Diseases*, 27, 143–145.

Cohen, R. (2006). Sex harassment high at colleges. *Bangor Daily News*, January 27, NA.

Cohen, S. (2006). The global contraceptive shortfall: U.S. Contributions and U.S. hindrances. *Guttmacher Institute*, 9, 1–2.

Cohen-Kettenis, P. (2005). Gender change in 46, XY persons with 5[alpha]-reductase-2 deficiency and 17[beta]-hydroxysteroid dehydrogenase-3 deficiency. *Archives of Sexual Behavior*, 34, 399–410.

Cohen-Kettenis, P., & Gooren, L. (1999). Transsexualism: A review of etiology, diagnosis, and treatment. *Journal of Psychosomatic Research*, 46, 315–333.

Colapinto, J. (2000). *As Nature Made Him: The Boy Who Was Raised as a Girl*. New York: HarperCollins.

Cole, C., & Cole, A. (1999). Marriage enrichment and prevention really works: Interpersonal competence training to maintain and enhance relationships. *Family Relations: Interdisciplinary Journal of Applied Family Studies*, 48, 273–275.

Cole, C., O'Boyle, M., Emory, L., & Meyer, W. (1997). Comorbidity of gender dysphoria and other major psychiatric diagnoses. *Archives of Sexual Behavior*, 26, 13–26.

Cole, D. (1987). It might have been: Mourning the unborn. *Psychology Today*, July, 64–65.

Cole, J. (1992). Commonalities and differences. In M. Andersen & P. Collins (Eds.), *Race, Class, and Gender*. Belmont, CA: Wadsworth.

Coleman, E. (1990). The obsessive-compulsive model for describing compulsive sexual behavior. *American Journal of Preventive Psychiatry and Neurology*, 2, 9–14.

Coleman, E. (1991). Compulsive sexual behavior: New concepts and treatments. *Journal of Psychology and Human Sexuality*, 4, 37–51.

Coleman, E. (2000). A new sexual revolution in health, diversity, and rights. *SIECUS Report*, 28, 4–5.

Coleman, E. (2003). Compulsive sexual behavior: What to call it, how to treat it? *SIECUS Report*, 31, 12–16.

Coleman, M., & Ganong, L. (1985). Love and sex role stereotypes: Do macho men and feminine women make better lovers? *Journal of Personality and Social Psychology*, 49, 170–176.

Coles, R., & Stokes, G. (1985). *Sex and the American Teenager*. New York: Harper & Row.

Coley, R., & Chase-Lansdale, P. (1998). Adolescent pregnancy and parenthood. *American Psychologist*, 53, 152–166.

Colgan, R., Michocki, R., Greisman, L., & Moore, T. (2003). Antiviral drugs in the immunocompetent host. Part I. Treatment of hepatitis, cytomegalovirus, and herpes infections. *American Family Physician*, 67, 757–762.

Colino, S. (1991). Sex and the expectant mother. *Parenting*, February, 111.

Colino, S. (2006). Your period: What's normal, what's not; Changes in your cycle can be nothing—or signal a serious health problem. Here's how to tell the difference. *Shape*, March, 88–92.

Collier, M. (1991). Conflict competence within African, Mexican, and Anglo American friendships. In S. Ting-Toomey & F. Korzenny (Eds.), *Cross-Cultural Interpersonal Communication*. Newbury Park, CA: Sage.

Collins, D. (2002). Scarring after penile augmentation. *Contemporary Urology*, 14, 12.

Collins, N., Ford, M., Guichard, A., & Allard, L. (2006). Working models of attachment and attribution processes in intimate relationships. *Personality and Social Psychology Bulletin*, 32, 201–219.

Collins, R., Elliott, M., Berry, S., Kanouse, D., Kunkel, D., et al. (2005). Watching sex on television predicts adolescent initiation of sexual behavior. *Journal of the Academy of Child and Adolescent Psychiatry*, 44, 427.

Colucci, J. (2006). Eight years of great laughs. *The Advocate*, May 9, 57.

Comas-Diaz, L., & Greene, B. (Eds.) (1994). *Women of Color*. New York: Guilford Press.

Comfort, A. (1972). *The Joy of Sex*. New York: Crown.

Comiteau, L. (2001). "Sexual enslavement" established as a war crime. *USA Today*, February 23, A10.

Conde-Agudelo, A., Rosas-Bermudex, A., & Kafury-Goeta, A. (2006). Birth spacing and risk of adverse perinatal outcomes. *Journal of the American Medical Association*, 295, 1809–1823.

Connell, J. (1992). Seeking common ground. *The Oregonian*, April 5, B1–B4.

Connor, E., Sperling, R., & Gelber, R. (1994). Reduction of maternal-infant transmission of human immunodeficiency virus type 1 with zidovudine treatment. *New England Journal of Medicine*, 331, 1173–1180.

Contemporary Sexuality (1996). U.S. has most rapes in the Western world. *Contemporary Sexuality*, 30, 5.

Contemporary Sexuality (1998). Children and healthy sexuality. *Contemporary Sexuality*, 32, 1–2.

Contemporary Sexuality (1999b). Japanese hardly swallow the pill. *Contemporary Sexuality*, 33, 8.

Contemporary Sexuality (1999d). Playful language. *Contemporary Sexuality*, 33, 1–2.

Cook, I. (2006). Western heterosexual masculinity, anxiety, and web porn. *The Journal of Men's Studies*, 14, 47–64.

Cook, L., Kamb, M., & Weiss, N. (1997). Perineal powder exposure and the risk of ovarian cancer. *American Journal of Epidemiology*, 145, 459–465.

Cooksey, E., Mott, F., & Neubauer, S. (2002). Friendships and early relationships: Links to sexual initiation among American adolescents born to young mothers. *Perspectives on Sexual and Reproductive Health*, 34, 118–126.

Coontz, S. (2005). The heterosexual revolution. *The New York Times*, July 5, A17.

Coontz, S. (2006). Three "rules" that don't apply. *Newsweek*, June 5, 49.

Cooper, A. (1996). Autoerotic asphyxiation: Three case reports. *Journal of Sex and Marital Therapy*, 22, 47–53.

Cooper, A. (2003). *Cybersex Addictions: How to Identify and Treat the Affects of Aberrant Online Sexual Pursuits.* Paper presented at the American Society of Professional Education, Portland, Oregon, December.

Cooper, A. (2004). Online sexual activity in the new millennium. *Contemporary Sexuality*, 38, i–vii.

Cooper, A (Ed.) (2002). *Sex and the Internet.* Philadelphia: Brunner-Routledge.

Cooper, A., & Sportolari, L. (1997). Romance in cyberspace: Understanding online attraction. *Journal of Sex Education and Therapy*, 22, 7–14.

Cooper, A., Scherer, C., Boies, S., & Gordon, B. (1999). Sexuality on the Internet: From sexual exploration to pathological expression. *Professional Psychology: Research and Practice*, 30, 154–164.

Cooper, C. (2000). Abortion: Take back the right. *Ms.*, June–July, 17–21.

Cooper, G. (2006). Viagra's false promise. *Psychotherapy Networker*, March/April, 21.

Corey, L., Wald, A., & Patel, R. (2004). Once-daily valacyclovir to reduce the risk of transmission of genital herpes. New England Journal of Medicine, 350, 11-20.

Corliss, R., & Steptoe, S. (2004). *Time Special Issue*, January 19, 117–122.

Corona, G., Petrone, L., Mannucci, E., & Forti, G. (2006). Difficulties in achieving versus maintaining erection: Organic, psychogenic and relational determinants. *The Journal of Sexual Medicine*, 3(suppl. 3), 224–286.

Cose, E. (2003). The black gender gap. *Newsweek*, March 3, 46–51.

Cosgray, R., Hanna, V., Fawley, R., & Money, M. (1991). Death from auto-erotic asphyxiation in long-term psychiatric setting. *Perspectives in Psychiatric Care*, 27, 21–24.

Cottrell, B. (2003). Vaginal douching. *Journal of Obstetrical, Gynecological, and Neonatal Nursing*, 32, 12–18.

Couper, M., & Stinson, L. (1999). Completion of self-administered questionnaires in a sex survey. *Journal of Sex Research*, 36, 321–330.

Couper, M., Singer, E., & Tourangeau, R. (2003). Understanding the effects of audio-CASI on self-reports of sensitive behavior. *Public Opinion Quarterly*, 67, 385–395.

Courtois, C. (2000a). The aftermath of child sexual abuse: The treatment of complex posttraumatic stress reactions. In L. Szuchman & F. Muscarella (Eds.), *Psychological Perspectives on Human Sexuality.* New York: Wiley.

Courville, T., Caldwell, B., & Brunell, P. (1998). Lack of evidence of transmission of HIV-1 to family contacts of HIV-1 infected children. *Clinical Pediatrics*, 37, 175–178.

Coventry, M. (2000). Making the cut. *Ms.*, October–November, 52–60.

Cowan, G. (2000). Beliefs about the causes of four types of rape. *Sex Roles*, 42, 807–823.

Cowan, G., & Campbell, R. (1994). Racism and sexism in interracial pornography. *Psychology of Women Quarterly*, 18, 323–338.

Cowan, P., & Cowan C. (1992). *When Partners Become Parents.* New York: HarperCollins.

Cowley, G. (2003). Ratings: Not Mother's Day. *Newsweek*, May 12, 8.

Cox, D. (1988). Incidence and nature of male genital exposure behavior as reported by college women. *Journal of Sex Research*, 24, 227–234.

Crawford, M., & Popp, D. (2003). Sexual double standards: A review and methodological critique of two decades of research. *Journal of Sex Research*, 40, 13–26.

Crawford, P. & Kaufmann, L. (2006). How safe is vaginal birth after cesarean section for the mother & fetus? *Clinical Inquiries*, 55, 149-152.

Crenshaw, T. (1996). *The Alchemy of Love and Lust.* New York: Putnam.

Crenshaw, T., & Goldberg, J. (1996). *Sexual Pharmacology: Drugs That Affect Sexual Function.* New York: Norton.

Crohan, S. (1996). Marital quality and conflict across the transition to parenthood in African American and white couples. *Journal of Marriage and the Family*, 58, 933–944.

Crooks, R., & Tucker, S. (2006). A peer-educator based HIV/AIDS prevention program in Kenya. Unpublished.

Crosby, R., & Lawrence, J. (2000). Adolescents' use of school-based health clinics for reproductive health services: Data from the National Longitudinal Study of Adolescent Health. *Journal of School Health*, 70, 22–27.

Crosby, R., Sanders, S., Yarber, W., Graham, C., & Dodge, B. (2002). Condom use errors and problems in college men. *Sexually Transmitted Diseases*, 29, 552–557.

Crossman, S. (2006). The challenge of pelvic inflammatory disease. *American Family Physician*, 73, 859–863.

Crowe, D. (2005). Adult content projected to drive video podcasting, cellular sales. *Los Angeles Business Journal*, 27, 14–15.

Cui, J. (2006). China's cracked closet. *Foreign Policy*, May–June, 90–92.

Cullen, L. (2006). Sex in the syllabus. *Time*, April 3, 80–81.

Curry, L. (2000). Net provides new expression for sexual offenders. *APA Monitor*, April, 21.

Curtis, K. & Mohllajee, A. (2004). World health organization updates guidance on how to use contraceptives. *INFO Reports*, April, 1–7.

Curtis, R., & Miller, K. (1997). Believing another likes or dislikes you: Behavior making the beliefs come true. *Journal of Personality and Social Psychology*, 51, 284–290.

Cutler, W. (1999). Human sex-attractant pheromones: Discovery, research, development, and application in sex therapy. *Psychiatric Annals*, 29, 54–59.

Cutler, W., Preti, G., Krieger, A., Huggins, G., Garcia, C., & Lawley, H. (1986). Human axillary secretions influence women's menstrual cycles: The role of donor extract from men. *Hormones and Behavior*, 20, 463–473.

Cwikel, J., & Hoban, E. (2005). Contentious issues in research on trafficked women working in the sex industry: Study design, ethics, and methodology. *The Journal of Sex Research*, 42, 306–317.

Czuczka, D. (2000). The twentieth century: An American sexual history. *SIECUS Report*, 28, 15–18.

D'Amato, A. (2006). *Porn Up, Rape Down.* Chicago: Northwestern Law School.

D'Emilio, J., & Freedman, E. (1988). *Intimate Matters.* New York: Harper & Row.

D'Epiro, P. (1997). Complicated UTI. *Patient Care,* April 15, 196–208.

Dabbs, J. (2000). *Heroes, Rogues, and Lovers: Testosterone and Behavior.* New York: McGraw-Hill.

Dailard, C. (2006). The public health promise and potential pitfalls of the world's first cervical cancer vaccine. *Guttmacher Policy Review,* 9, 6–9.

Dall'Ara, E., & Maass, A. (1999). Studying sexual harassment in the laboratory: Are egalitarian women at higher risk? *Sex Roles,* 41, 681–704.

Daly, M., Wilson, M., & Weghorst, S. (1982). Male sexual jealousy. *Ethology and Sociobiology,* 3, 11–27.

Daniluk, J. (1998). *Women's Sexuality Across the Life Span: Challenging Myths, Creating Meanings.* New York: Guilford Press.

Darling, C., Davidson, J., & Conway-Welch, C. (1990). Female ejaculation: Perceived origins, the Grafenberg spot/area, and sexual responsiveness. *Archives of Sexual Behavior,* 19, 29–47.

Daro, D. (1991). Child sexual abuse prevention: Separating fact from fiction. *Child Abuse and Neglect,* 15, 1–4.

David, H., & Russo, N. (2003). Psychology, population, and reproductive behavior. *American Psychologist,* 58, 193–196.

Davidson, J. (2006). South Carolina: Yes to Uzis, No to Vibrators. Retrieved April 25, 2006, from www.joybloggl.com.

Davies, M. (1995). Parental distress and ability to cope following disclosure of extra-familial sexual abuse. *Child Abuse and Neglect,* 19, 399–408.

Davies, M., Pollard, P., & Archer, J. (2006). Effects of perpetrator gender and victim sexuality on blame toward male victims of sexual assault. *Journal of Social Psychology,* 146, 275–291.

Davis, A. (2002). Don't let nobody bother yo' principle: The sexual economy of American slavery. In S. Harley & the Black Women and Work Collective (Eds.), *Sister Circle: Black Women and Work.* New Brunswick, NJ: Rutgers University Press.

Davis, B., & Noble, M. (1991). Putting an end to chronic testicular pain. *Medical Aspects of Human Sexuality,* April, 26–34.

Davis, D. (2000). Most cancer is made, not born. *San Francisco Chronicle,* August 10, 1–3.

Davis, K., & Latty-Mann, H. (1987). Love styles and relationship quality: A contribution to validation. *Journal of Social and Personal Relationships,* 4, 409–428.

Davis, S. (1999). The therapeutic use of androgens in women. *Journal of Steroid Biochemistry and Molecular Biology,* 69, 177–184.

Davis, S. (2000). Testosterone and sexual desire in women. *Journal of Sex Education and Therapy,* 25, 25–32.

Davison, G., & Neale, J. (1993). *Abnormal Psychology* (6th ed.). New York: Wiley.

Davtyan, C. (2000). Contraception for adolescents. *Western Journal of Medicine,* 172, 166–171.

De Bro, S., Campbell, S., & Peplau, L. (1994). Influencing a partner to use a condom. *Psychology of Women Quarterly,* 18, 165–182.

De Cuypere, G., T'sjoen, G., Beerten, R., Selvaggi, G., De Sutter, P., et al. (2005). Sexual and physical health after sex reassignment surgery. *Archives of Sexual Behavior,* 34, 679–690.

De Lacoste, M., Adesanya, T., & Woodward, D. (1990). Measures of gender differences in the human brain and their relationship to brain weight. *Biological Psychiatry,* 28, 931–942.

Dean, K., & Malamuth, N. (1997). Characteristics of men who aggress sexually and men who imagine aggressing: Risk and moderating variables. *Journal of Personality and Social Psychology,* 72, 449–455.

Dean, M., Carrington, M., & Winkler, C. (1996). Genetic restriction of HIV-1 infection and progression to AIDS by a deletion allele of the CKR5 structural gene. *Science,* 273, 1856–1862.

Deckers, P., & Ricci, A., Jr. (1992). Pain and lumps in the female breast. *Hospital Practice,* February 28, 67–94.

DeForge, D., & Blackmer, J. (2005). Male sexuality following spinal cord injury. A systematic review. Paper presented at the World Congress of Sexology, Montreal, Canada, July 10–15.

DeGarmo, D., & Kitson, G. (1996). Identity relevance and disruption as predictors of psychological distress for widowed and divorced women. *Journal of Marriage and the Family,* 58, 983–997.

Degler, C. (1980). *At Odds: Women and the Family in America from the Revolution to the Present.* Oxford: Oxford University Press.

Deitch, C. (1983). Ideology and opposition to abortion: Trends in public opinion, 1972–1980. *Alternative Lifestyles,* 6, 6–26.

Dekker, J., Everaerd, W., & Verhelst, N. (1985). Attending to stimuli or to images of sexual feelings: Effects on sexual arousal. *Behavior Research and Therapy,* 23, 139–149.

Del Carmen, R. (1990). Assessment of Asian-Americans for family therapy. In F. Serafica, A. Schwebel, R. Russell, P. Isaac, & L. Myers (Eds.), *Mental Health of Ethnic Minorities.* New York: Praeger.

DeLaMar, R. (2003). And babies make six. *The Advocate,* June 24, 73–74.

DeLamater, J., & Friedrich, W. (2002). Human sexual development. *Journal of Sex Research,* 39, 10–14.

DeLamater, J., & Sill, M. (2005). Sexual desire in later life. *The Journal of Sex Research,* 42, 138–150.

Delaney, J., Lupton, M., & Toth, E. (1976). *The Curse: A Cultural History of Menstruation.* New York: Dutton.

Deliganis, A., Maravilla, K., Heiman, J., Carter, W., Garland, P., & Weisskoff, R. (2000). Dynamic MR imaging of the female genitalia using Angiomark: Initial experience evaluating the female sexual response [abstract]. *Radiology,* 214, 611. Originally presented as an RSNA Hot Topic presentation, Chicago, November 1999.

Delzell, J., & Lefevre, M. (2000). Urinary tract infections during pregnancy. *American Family Physician,* 61, 713–721.

Démare, D., Briere, J., & Lips, H. (1988). Violent pornography and self-reported likelihood of sexual aggression. *Journal of Research in Personality,* 22, 140–153.

DeMartino, M. (1970). How women want men to make love. *Sexology,* October, 4–7.

Dempsey, C. (1994). Health and social issues of gay, lesbian, and bisexual adolescents. *Families in Society*, March, 160–167.

Dennerstein, L., & Goldstein, I. (2005). Post-menopausal female sexual dysfunction: At a cross-roads. Retrieved April 15, 2006, from http://www.blackwell-synergy.com/doi/full/10.1111/j.1743-6109.2005.00127.x.

Dennerstein, L., Burrows, G., Wood, C., & Hyman, G. (1980). Hormones and sexuality: The effects of estrogen and progestogen. *Obstetrics and Gynecology*, 56, 316–322.

Dennis, C. (2004). The most important sexual organ. *Nature*, 427, 390–392.

Denov, M. (2003a). *Perspectives on Female Sexual Offending: A Culture of Denial.* Brookfield, VT: Ashgate Publishing.

Denov, M. (2003b). To a safer place: Victims of sexual abuse by females and their disclosures to professionals. *Child Abuse and Neglect*, 27, 47–61.

Derlego, V., Metts, S., Petronia, S., & Margulis, S. (1993). *Self-Disclosure.* Newbury Park, CA: Sage.

Des Jarlais, D., Diaz, T., Perlis, T., Vlahov, D., Maslow, C., Latka, M., Rockwell, R., Edwards, V., Friedman, S., Monterroso, E., Williams, I., & Garfein, R. (2003). Variability in the incidence of human immunodeficiency virus, hepatitis B virus, and hepatitis C virus infection among young injecting drug users in New York City. *American Journal of Epidemiology*, 157, 467–471.

Deshotels, T., & Forsyth, C. (2006). Strategic flirting and the emotional tab of exotic dancing. *Deviant Behavior*, 27, 223–241.

Dessens, A., Cohen-Kettenis, P., Mellenbergh, G., Poll, N., Kopper, J., & Boer, K. (1999). Prenatal exposure to anticonvulsants and psychosexual development. *Archives of Sexual Behavior*, 28, 31–44.

Dessens, A., Slijper, F., & Drop, S. (2005). Gender dysphoria and gender change in chromosomal females with congenital hyperplasia. *Archives of Sexual Behavior*, 34, 389–397.

Deveny, K. (2003). We're not in the mood. *Newsweek*, June 30, 40–46.

Devi, K. (1977). *The Eastern Way of Love: Tantric Sex and Erotic Mysticism.* New York: Simon & Schuster.

De Villers, L. & Turgeon, H. (2005). The uses and benefits of "sensate focus" exercises. *Contemporary Sexuality*, 39, i–vii.

DeVita-Raeburn, E. (2006). Lust for the long haul. *Psychology Today*, Jan/Feb, 1–5.

Dewhurst, A., & Nielsen, K. (1999). A resiliency-based approach to working with sexual offenders. *Sexual Addiction and Compulsivity*, 6, 271–279.

Dhawan, D. & Mayer, K. (2006). Microbicides to prevent HIV transmission: Overcoming obstacles to chemical barrier protection. *Journal of Infectious Diseases*, 193, 36–45.

Diamond, L., Earle, D., Garcia, W., & Spana, C. (2005). Co-administration of low doses of intranasal PT-141, a melanocortin receptor antaganist, and sildenafil to men with erectile dysfunction results in an enhanced erectile response. *Urology*, 65, 755–759.

Diamond, L., Earle, D., Heiman, J., & Rosen, R. (2006). An effect on the subjective sexual response in premenopausal women with sexual arousal disorder by Bremelanotide (PT-141), a Melanocortin receptor agonist. *The Journal of Sexual Medicine*, 3, 628–638.

Diamond, L., Earle, D., Rosen, R., Willet, M., & Molinoff, P. (2004). Double-blind, placebo-controlled evaluation of the safety, pharmacokinetic properties and pharmacodynamic effects of intranasal PT-141, a melanocortin receptor agonist, in healthy males and patients with mild-to-moderate erectile dysfunction. *International Journal of Impotence Research*, 16, 51–59.

Diamond, M. (1991b). Hormonal effects on the development of cerebral lateralization. *Psychoneuroendocrinology*, 16, 121–129.

Diamond, M. (1997). Sexual identity and sexual orientation in children with traumatized or ambiguous genitalia. *Journal of Sex Research*, 34, 199–211.

Diamond, M. (1998). Intersexuality: Recommendations for management. *Archives of Sexual Behavior*, 27, 634–641.

Diamond, M., & Sigmundson, H. (1997). Sex reassignment at birth: Long-term review and clinical implications. *Archives of Pediatric and Adolescent Medicine*, 151, 298–304.

Diamond, R., Kezur, D., Meyers, M., Scharf, C., & Weinshel, M. (1999). *Couple Therapy for Infertility.* New York: Guilford Press.

Diaz-Parker, C., & Bratslavsky, G. (2005). Male genitourinary disease: Urethritis, epididymitis, and prostatitis. *Clinician Reviews*, 15, 39–46.

Dibbell, J. (2005). Is the world ready for libido in a nasal spray? *New York Magazine*, November, 1–15.

Dickey, R. (2003). It has really been 15 years of inaction on high-order multiple pregnancies due to ovulation induction. *Fertility and Sterility*, 79, 28–29.

Dickinson, T. (2006). The politics of fear. *Rolling Stone*, June 29, 43–45.

DiClemente, R., & Wingood, G. (2003). Human immunodeficiency virus prevention for adolescents. *Archives of Adolescent and Pediatric Medicine*, 157, 319–320.

Dietz, P. (1999). Unintended pregnancy among adult women exposed to abuse or household dysfunction during their childhood. *Journal of the American Medical Association*, 282, 1359–1364.

Dilley, J., Woods, W., & McFarland, W. (1997). Are advances in treatment changing views about high-risk sex? *New England Journal of Medicine*, 337, 501–502.

Dilorio, C., Hartwell, T., & Hanson, N. (2002). Childhood sexual abuse and risk behaviors among men at high risk for HIV infection. *American Journal of Public Health*, 92, 214–219.

Dirks, T. (2006). Timeline of influential milestones and turning points in film history. Retrieved October 13, 2006 from http://www.filmsite.org/milestonespre1900s.html.

Dittman, M. (2003). Sex: Worth the risk? *Monitor on Psychology*, 34, 58–60.

Dittus, P., & Jaccard, J. (2000). Adolescents' perceptions of maternal disapproval of sex: Relationships to sexual outcomes. *Journal of Adolescent Health*, 26, 268–278.

Doctor, R., & Prince, V. (1997). Transvestism: A survey of 1,032 cross-dressers. *Archives of Sexual Behavior*, 26, 589–605.

Dodson, B. (1974). *Liberating Masturbation*. New York: Betty Dodson.

Doheny, K. (2006). A new cure for serious PMS. *Shape*, February, 84.

Donenberg, G., Bryant, F., Emerson, E., Wilson, H., & Pasch, K. (2003). Tracing the roots of early sexual debut among adolescents in psychiatric care. *Journal of the American Academy of Child and Adolescent Psychiatry*, 42, 594–608.

Dong, M., Anda, R., Dube, S., Giles, W., & Felitti, V. (2003). The relationship of exposure to childhood sexual abuse to other forms of abuse, neglect, and household dysfunction during childhood. *Child Abuse and Neglect*, 27, 625–639.

Donnelly, P., & White, C. (2000). Testicular dysfunction in men with primary hypothyroidism: Reversal of hypogonadotrophic hypogonadism with replacement thyroxine. *Clinical Endocrinology*, 52, 197–201.

Donnerstein, E., & Linz, D. (1984). Sexual violence in the media: A warning. *Psychology Today*, January, 14–15.

Donoval, B., Passaro, D., & Klausner, J. (2006). The public health imperative for a neonatal herpes simplex virus infection surveillance system. *Sexually Transmitted Diseases*, 33, 170–174.

Donovan, B. (2004). Sexually transmissible infections other than HIV. *Lancet*, 363, 545–556.

Doskoch, P. (2005). Evidence supporting the notion that bacterial vaginosis can be transmitted sexually continues to accumulate. *Perspectives on Sexual and Reproductive Health*, 37, 206.

Douglas, C., Verna, P., Goktepe, K., & Nixon, L. (2005). United States: Men coerce women into vaginal cosmetic surgery. *Off Our Backs*, 35, 9.

Douglas, K. (1999). *Sexuality and the Black Church: A Womanist Perspective*. Maryknoll, NY: Orbis Books.

Douglas, T. (2006). The new world is on the ascent. *Education News*, August 14, 27.

Dow, M., Hart, D., & Forrest, C. (1983). Hormonal treatments of unresponsiveness in post-menopausal women: A comparative study. *British Journal of Obstetrics and Gynecology*, 90, 361–366.

Doyle, J., & Paludi, M. (1991). *Sex and Gender* (2nd ed.). Dubuque, IA: Brown and Benchmark.

Draucker, C., & Stern, P. (2000). Women's responses to sexual violence by male intimates. *Western Journal of Nursing Research*, 22, 385–406.

Dreger, A. (2003). *Notes on the Treatment of Intersex*. Retrieved February 19, 2003, from http://www.isna.org

Dreznick, M. (2003). Heterosocial competence of rapists and child molesters: A meta-analysis. *Journal of Sex Research*, 40, 170–178.

Drigotas, S., Rusbult, C., & Verette, J. (1999). Level of commitment, mutuality of commitment, and couple well-being. *Personal Relationships*, 6, 389–409.

Duddle, M. (1991). Emotional sequelae of sexual assault. *Journal of the Royal Society of Medicine*, 84, 26–28.

Duenwald, M. (2003). Effort to make sex drug for women challenges experts. *New York Times*, March 25, D5.

Duffy, J., Warren, K., & Walsh, M. (2001). Classroom interactions: Gender of teacher, gender of student and classroom subject. *Sex Roles*, 45, 579–593.

Dunleavey, R. (2006). Strategies for treating and managing testicular cancer. *Nursing Times*, 102, 28–30.

Dunn, M., & Cutler, N. (2000). Sexual issues in older adults. *AIDS Patient Care and STDs*, 14, 67–69.

Dunn, M., & Trost, J. (1989). Male multiple orgasms: A descriptive study. *Archives of Sexual Behavior*, 18, 377–388.

Dunn, M., Bartee, R., & Perko, M. (2003). Self-reported alcohol use and sexual behaviors of adolescents. *Psychological Reports*, 92, 339–348.

Durand, V., & Barlow, D. (2000). *Abnormal Psychology: An Introduction*. Belmont, CA: Wadsworth/Thomson Learning.

Durex (2006). 2005 global sex survey results. Retrieved July 3, 2006, from www.durex.com/gss.

Duty, S., Silva, M., Barr, D., & Brock, J. (2003). Phthalate exposure and human semen parameters. *Epidemiology*, 14, 269–277.

Dworkin, S., & O'Sullivan, L. (2005). Actual versus desired initiation patterns among a sample of college men: Tapping disjunctures within traditional male sexual scripts. *Journal of Sex Research*, 42, 150–158.

Dwyer, M. (1988). Exhibitionism/voyeurism. *Journal of Social Work and Human Sexuality*, 7, 101–112.

Eardley, I., Collins, O., Hackett, G., & Edwards, D. (2006). Partners of heterosexual men with erectile dysfunction, treated with vardenafil, feel themselves to be sexually more desirable. *The Journal of Sexual Medicine*, 3(suppl. 3), 224–286.

Eastham, J., & Kattan, M. (2000). Disease recurrence in black and white men undergoing radical prostatectomy for clinical stage T1-T2 prostate cancer. *Journal of Urology*, 163, 143–145.

Eaton, S. (2004). Sierra Leone: The proving ground for prosecuting rape as a war crime. *Georgetown Journal of International Law*, 35, 873–919.

Ebell, M. (2005). Treating partners immediately reduces recurrence of STDs. *American Family Physician*, 72, 325.

Eccles, A., Marshall, W., & Barbaree, H. (1994). Differentiating rapists and non-rapists using the rape index. *Behaviour Research and Therapy*, 32, 539–546.

Eccles, J., Barber, E., & Jozefowicz, D. (1999). Linking gender to educational, occupational, and recreational choices: Applying the Eccles et al. model of achievement-related choices. In W. Swann & J. Langlois (Eds.), *Sexism and Stereotypes in Modern Society: The Gender Science of Janet Taylor Spence*. Washington, DC: American Psychological Association.

Ecker, N. (1993). Culture and sexual scripts out of Africa. *SIECUS Report*, 22, 16.

Edelman, A., Koontz, S., Nichols, M., & Jensen, J. (2006). Continuous oral contraceptives: Are bleeding patterns dependent on the hormones given? *Obstetrics & Gynecology*, 107, 657–665.

Editorial Board (2006). Choosing women's health over sexual politics. *The Oregonian*, May 30, B4.

Edlin, B., & Carden, M. (2006). Injection drug users: the overlooked core of the hepatitis C epidemic. *Clinical Infectious Diseases*, 42, 673–676.

Edwards, T. (2000). Flying solo. *Time*, August 28, 47–53.

Eheman, C., Peipins, L., Wynn, M., & Ryerson, B. (2006). Development of a public health research program for ovarian cancer. *Journal of Women's Health*, 15, 339-345.

Ehrenfeld, T. (2002). Infertility: A guy thing. *Newsweek*, March 25, 60–61.

Eichenwald, K. (2005). Child Pornography sites face new obstacles. *The New York Times*, December 30, A23.

Eichenwald, K. (2005). Through his webcam, a boy joins a sordid online world. *The New York Times*, December 19, A1.

Einwalter, L., Ritchie, J., Ault, K., & Smith, E. (2005). Gonorrhea and chlamydia infection among women visiting family planning clinics: Racial variation in prevalence and predictors. *Perspectives on Sexual and Reproductive Health*, 37, 135–140.

Eisner, T., Conner, J., & Carrel, J. (1990). Systemic retention of ingested cantharidin by frogs. *Chemoecology*, 1, 57–62.

Eitzen, D., & Zinn, M. (2000). *Social Problems* (8th ed.). Boston: Allyn and Bacon.

Eke, N. & Nkanginieme, K. (2006). Female genital mutilation and obstetric outcome. *The Lancet*, 367, 1799-1800.

Elder, S. (2005). The lock box. *Psychology Today*, March/April, 42-46.

Elias, J., & Gebbard, P. (1969). Sexuality and sexual learning in childhood. *Phi Delta Kappan*, 50, 401-405.

Eliasson, R., & Lindholmer, C. (1976). Functions of male accessory genital organs. In E. Hafez (Ed.), *Human Semen and Fertility Regulations in Men*. St. Louis: Mosby.

Elkind, D. (1967). Egocentrism in adolescence. *Child Development*, 38, 1025–1034.

Elliott, L., & Brantley, C. (1997). *Sex on Campus*. New York: Random House.

Elliott, M. (1992). Tip of the iceberg? *Social Work Today*, March, 12–13.

Elliott, S., & Burgess, V. (2005). The presence of gamma-hydroxybutyric acid (GHB) and gamma-butyrolactone (GBL) in alcoholic and nonalcoholic beverages. *Forensic Science International*, 151, 289–292.

Ellison, C. (2000). *Women's Sexualities*. Oakland, CA.: New Harbinger Publications.

El-Noshokaty, A. (2006). Sex and the city. Retrieved September 26, 2006 from http://weekly.ahram.org.eg/print/2006/813/lil.htm.

Elwood, A. (2005). Female genital cutting, "circumcision" and mutilation: Physical, psychological and cultural perspectives. *Contemporary Sexuality*, 39, i–v.

El-Zanaty, F. & Way, A. (2006). *Egypt Demographic and Health Survey* 2005. Cairo, Egypt: Ministry of Health and Population, National Population Council, El-Zanaty and Associates, and ORC Macro.

Emmert, D. (2000). Treatment of common cutaneous herpes simplex virus infections. *American Family Physician*, 61, 1697–1704.

Engelberg, R., Carrell, D., Krantz, E., Corey, L., & Wald, A. (2003). Natural history of genital herpes simplex virus type 1 infection. *Sexually Transmitted Diseases*, 30, 174–177.

Ensler, E. (2006). Belly, dancing. *O: The Oprah Magazine*, June, 47.

Epp, S. (1997). The diagnosis and treatment of athletic amenorrhea. *Physician Assistant*, March, 129–144.

Equal Employment Opportunity Commission (1980). Guidelines on discrimination because of sex. *Federal Register*, 45, 74,676–74,677.

Equal Employment Opportunity Commission (2003). *Sexual Harassment Charges EEOC and FEPHS Combined: FYI992–FY2002*. Retrieved September 28, 2003, from http://www.eeoc.gov/stats/harass.html.

Ernst, E., & Pittler, M. (1998). Yohimbine for erectile dysfunction: A systematic review and meta-analysis of randomized clinical trials. *Journal of Urology*, 159, 433–436.

Eschenbach, D., Patton, D., Hooton, T., Meier, A., Stapleton, A., Aura, J., & Agnew, K. (2001). Effects of vaginal intercourse with and without a condom on vaginal flora and vaginal epithelium. *Journal of Infectious Diseases*, 183, 913–918.

Escobar-Chaves, S., Tortolero, S., Markham, C., & Low, B. (2005). Impact of the media on adolescent sexual attitudes and behaviors. *Pediatrics*, 116, 303–326.

Eskeland, B., Thom, E., & Svendsen, K. (1997). Sexual desire in men: Effects of oral ingestion of a product derived from fertilized eggs. *Journal of International Medical Research*, 25, 62–70.

Eskridge, W., & Spedale, D. (2006). *Gay Marriage: For Better or For Worse?: What We've Learned From the Evidence*. New York: Oxford University Press.

Espinoza, G. (2003). There goes the bride. *AARP*, July–August, 11.

Ethics Committee, American Society for Reproductive Medicine (1997). Ethical considerations of assisted reproductive medicine. *International Journal of Gynecology and Obstetrics*, 67(5), 15–95.

Evans, N. (2006). *State of Evidence*. San Francisco: Breast Cancer Fund.

Ezzell, C. (2000). Care for a dying continent. *Scientific American*, May, 96–105.

Faerman, M., Kahila, G., & Smith, P. (1997). DNA analysis reveals the sex of infanticide victims. *Nature*, 385, 212.

Fagot, B. (1995). Psychosocial and cognitive determinants of early gender-role development. *Annual Review of Sex Research*, 6, 1–31.

Fair, W., Fuks, Z., & Scher, H. (1993). Cancer of the urethra and penis. In V. DeVita, S. Hellman, & S. Rosenberg (Eds.), *Cancer: Principles and Practice of Oncology*, v. 1 (4th ed.). Philadelphia: Lippincott.

Fallon, B., Miller, R., & Gerber, W. (1981). Nonmicroscopic vasovasostomy. *Journal of Urology*, 126, 361–365.

Falwell, J. (2001). Perspectives 2001. *Newsweek*, December 24, 61.

Fan, M. (2006, September 20). On China's airwaves, a discourse on sex ed: Radio show caters to young audience. Retrieved September 26, 2006 from http://www.boston.com/news/world/asia/articles/2006/09/20/on_chinas_airwaves_a_discourse_on_sex_ed.

Farley, M. (2004). *Prostitution, Trafficking, and Traumatic Stress*. New York: Haworth Maltreatment and Trauma Press.

Farr, K. (2004). *Sex Trafficking: The Global Market in Women and Children*. New York: W. H. Freedman.

Farr, L. (2000). The danger zone. *W*, June, 100–104.

Fauntleroy, G. (2005). Whose decision is it? The long-term legal implications of informed consent. *Mothering*, September–October, 58–61.

Fausto-Sterling, A. (1993). The five sexes: Why male and female are not enough. *The Sciences*, 33, 20–24.

Fausto-Sterling, A. (2000). *Sexing the Body: Gender Politics and the Construction of Sexuality*. New York: Basic Books.

Fazleabas, A., & Kim J. (2003). What makes an embryo stick? *Science*, 299, 355–356.

Federal Bureau of Investigation (2006). *Uniform Crime Reports, 2004*. Retrieved May 13, 2006, from http://www.fbi.gov/ucr/cius_04/offenses_reported/violent_crime/forcible_rape.html.

Federman, D. (2006). The biology of human sex differences. *The New England Journal of Medicine*, 354, 1507–1514.

Fedora, O., Reddon, J., Morrison, J., & Fedora, S. (1992). Sadism and other paraphilias in normal controls and aggressive and nonaggressive sex offenders. *Archives of Sexual Behavior*, 21, 1–15.

Feeney, J., & Noller, P. (1996). *Adult Attachment*. Thousand Oaks, CA: Sage.

Fehring, R. (2004). The future of professional education in natural family planning. *Journal of Obstetric, Gynecologic, and Neonatal Nursing*, 33, 34–43.

Feingold, A. (1992). Good-looking people are not what we think. *Psychological Bulletin*, 111, 304–341.

Feldmann, L. (2006). A scorecard on curtailing unwanted pregnancy. *The Christian Science Monitor*, March 1, 2.

Feldman-Summers, S., & Pope, K. (1994). The experience of "forgetting" childhood abuse: A national survey of psychologists. *Journal of Consulting and Clinical Psychology*, 62, 636–639.

Felix, J. (2003). The science behind the effectiveness of in vivo screening. *American Journal of Obstetrics and Gynecology*, 188, S8–S12.

Fennell, R. (2006). "The emperor has no clothes": Emergency contraception should be available over-the-counter. *Journal of American College Health*, 54, 257–260.

Fentiman, I., Fourquet, F., & Hortobagyi, G. (2006). Male breast cancer. *The Lancet*, 367, 595–605.

Ferguson, D., Steidle, C., Singh, G., & Alexander, S. (2003). Randomized, placebo-controlled, double blind, crossover design trial of the efficacy and safety of Zestra for women in women with and without female sexual arousal disorder. *Journal of Sex and Marital Therapy*, 29, 33–44.

Feroli, K., & Burstein, G. (2003). Adolescent sexually transmitted diseases. *American Journal of Maternal/Child Nursing*, 28, 113–118.

Ferrer, F., & McKenna, P. (2000). Current approaches to the undescended testicle. *Contemporary Pediatrics*, 17, 106–112.

Ferroni, P., & Jaffee, J. (1997). Women's emotional well-being: The importance of communicating sexual needs. *Sexual and Marital Therapy*, 12, 127–138.

Fields, J., & Casper, L. (2001). *America's Families and Living Arrangements: March 2000*. Washington, DC: U.S. Census Bureau.

Filicori, M. (2003). Use of luteinizing hormone in the treatment of infertility: Time for reassessment? *Fertility and Sterility*, 79, 253–255.

Fillion, K. (1996). This is the sexual revolution? *Saturday Night*, February, 36–41.

Findholt, N., & Robrecht, L. (2002). Legal and ethical considerations in research with sexually active adolescents: The requirement to report statutory rape. *Perspectives on Sexual and Reproductive Health*, 34, 259–264.

Finer, L., Frohwirth, L., Dauphinee, L., & Singh, S. (2005). Reasons U.S. women have abortions: Quantitative and qualitative perspectives. *Perspectives on Sexual and Reproductive Health*, 37, 110–118.

Finger, W. (2000). Avoiding sexual exploitation: Guidelines for therapists. *SIECUS Report*, 28, 12–13.

Finger, W., Lund, M., & Slagle, M. (1997). Medications that may contribute to sexual disorders. *Journal of Family Practice*, 44, 33–43.

Finger, W., Quillen, J., & Slagle, M. (2000). *They Can't All Be Viagra: Medications Causing Sexual Dysfunctions*. Paper presented at the 32nd Annual Conference of the American Association of Sex Educators, Counselors, and Therapists, Atlanta, Georgia, May 10–14.

Fink, J. (2006). Practical tips for women who suffer from yeast infections. *RN*, 69, 52.

Finkelhor, D. (1979). *Sexually Victimized Children*. New York: Free Press.

Finkelhor, D. (1984a). *Child Sexual Abuse: Theory and Research*. New York: Free Press.

Finkelhor, D. (1984b). The prevention of child sexual abuse: An overview of needs and problems. *SIECUS Report*, 13, 1–5.

Finkelhor, D. (1993). Epidemiological factors in the clinical identification of child sexual abuse. *Child Abuse and Neglect*, 17, 67–70.

Finkelhor, D. (1994). The international epidemiology of child sexual abuse. *Child Abuse and Neglect*, 18, 409–417.

Finkelhor, D., & Ormrod, R. (2004). Prostitution of juveniles: Patterns from NIBRS. *Juvenile Justice Bulletin*, June, 1–2.

Firestone, J., & Harris, R. (1999). Changes in patterns of sexual harassment in the U.S. military: A comparison of the 1988 and 1995 DoD surveys. *Armed Forces and Society: An Interdisciplinary Journal*, 25, 613.

Fischer, J., & Heesacker, M. (1995). Men's and women's preferences regarding sex-related and nurturing traits in dating partners. *Journal of College Student Development*, 36, 260–269.

Fischman, J. (2001). New-style mammograms detect cancer. *U.S. News & World Report*, February 5, 58–59.

Fisher, B., Cullen, F., & Turner, G. (2000). *The Sexual Victimization of College Women*. Washington, DC: National Institutes of Justice, Bureau of Justice Statistics.

Fisher, H. (1999). *The First Sex: The Natural Talents of Women and How They Will Change the World*. New York: Random House.

Fisher, T. (1987). Family communication and the sexual behavior and attitudes of college students. *Journal of Youth and Adolescence*, 16, 481–495.

Fisher, W., & Gray, J. (1988). Erotophobia, erotophilia, and sexual behavior during pregnancy and postpartum. *Journal of Sex Research*, 25, 379–396.

Fisher, W., Branscombe, N., & Lemery, C. (1983). The bigger the better? Arousal and attributional responses to erotic stimuli that depict different size penises. *Journal of Sex Research*, 19, 377–396.

Fisher, W., Rosen, R., Eardley, I., & Niederberger, C. (2006). Female experience of men's attitudes to sexuality and life events: The FEMALES study. *Journal of Sex Research*, 43, 16.

Fisher, W., Rosen, R., Sand, M., & Eardley, I. (2006). Prevalence of premature ejaculation among men with erectile dysfunction in the men's attitudes to life events and sexuality (MALES) study. *The Journal of Sexual Medicine*, 3 (suppl. 3), 176–198.

Fisher, W., Rosen, R., Wood, R., & Mollen, M. (2006). Female partners of men with erectile dysfunction receiving Vardenafil have improved sexual function: Results from a randomized double-blind placebo-controlled trial. *The Journal of Sex Research*, 32, 17–18.

Fisher-Thompson, D. (1990). Adult sex typing of children's toys. *Sex Roles*, 23, 291–303.

Flanders, L. (1998). Rwanda's living casualties. *Ms.*, March–April, 27–30.

Flannery, D., Ellingson, L., Votaw, K., & Schaefer, E. (2003). Anal intercourse and sexual risk factors among college women, 1993–2000. *American Journal of Health Behavior*, 27, 228–234.

Fleming, M., & Kleinbart, E. (2001). Breast cancer and sexuality. *Journal of Sex Education and Therapy*, 26, 215–224.

Fleming, M., & Pace, J. (2001). Sexuality and chronic pain. *Journal of Sex Education and Therapy*, 26, 204–214.

Fleming, M., & Rickwood, D. (2004). Teens in cyberspace: Do they encounter friend or foe? *Youth Studies Australia*, 23, 46–52.

Flobbe, K., Bosch, A., Kessels, A., & Beets, G. (2003). The additional diagnostic value of ultrasonography in the diagnosis of breast cancer. *Archives of Internal Medicine*, 163, 1194–1199.

Flory, N., Bissonnette, F., Amsel, R., & Binik, Y. (2006). The psychosocial outcomes of total and subtotal hysterectomy: A randomized controlled trial. *The Journal of Sexual Medicine*, 3, 483–491.

Foa, U., Anderson, B., Converse, J., & Urbanski, W. (1987). Gender-related sexual attitudes: Some cross-cultural similarities and differences. *Sex Roles*, 16, 511–519.

Folb, K. (2000). "Don't touch that dial!" TV as a—what!—positive influence. *SIECUS Report*, 28, 16–18.

Foley, D. (2006). Spice up your love life. *Prevention*, 58, 172.

Foley, D., & Nechas, L. (1995). *Before You Hit the Pillow, Talk*. New York: Bantam Books.

Foley, S. (2003). Women in sex therapy: Developing a sexual identity. *Contemporary Sexuality*, 37, 7–13.

Folkes, V. (1982). Forming relationships and the matching hypothesis. *Personality and Social Psychology Bulletin*, 9, 631–636.

Food and Drug Administration (1997). *FDA Statement on Generic Premarin*. Retrieved May 5, 2003, from

http://www.fda.gov/cder/cepressrelease.htm.

Forbes, G. (1992). Body size and composition of perimenarchal girls. *American Journal of Diseases in Children*, 146, 63–66.

Forbes, G., Adams-Curtis, L., White, K., & Holmgren, K. (2003). The role of hostile and benevolent sexism in women's and men's perceptions of the menstruating women. *Psychology of Women Quarterly*, 27, 58–63.

Ford, C., & Beach, F. (1951). *Patterns of Sexual Behavior*. New York: Harper & Row.

Ford, K., Sohn, W., & Lepowski, J. (2002). American adolescents: Sexual mixing patterns, bridge partners, and concurrency. *Sexually Transmitted Diseases*, 29, 13–19.

Forsyth, C. (1996). The structuring of vicarious sex. *Deviant Behavior: An Interdisciplinary Journal*, 17, 279–295.

Fosas, N., Marina, F., Torres, P., & Jove, I. (2003). The births of five Spanish babies from cryopreserved donated oocytes. *Human Reproduction*, 18, 1417–1421.

Foubert, J., Garner, D., & Thaxter, P. (2006). An exploration of fraternity culture: implications for programs to address alcohol-related sexual assault. *College Student Journal*, 40, 361–373.

Fowke, K., Nagelkerke, N., Kiman, J., Simonsen, J., Anzala, A., Bwayo, J., MacDonald, K., Nguigi, E., & Plummer, F. (1996). Resistance to HIV-1 infection among persistently seronegative prostitutes in Nairobi, Kenya. *The Lancet*, 348, 1347–1351.

Fox, M. (2006, November 17). *Government Censured on Family Planning Policies*. Retrieved November 29, 2006, from http://news.yahoo.com/s/nm/20061117/pl_nm/contraception_dc_1.

Fox, R., Burton, D., & Lawson, D. (2006). The effect of spiritual attitudes on hypoactive sexual desire disorder. Paper presented at the Gumbo Sexualite Upriver: Spicing Up Education & Therapy (AASECT 38th Annual Conference), St. Louis, June/July.

Fox, T. (1995). *Sexuality and Catholicism*. New York: George Braziller.

Frankowski, B. (2004). Sexual orientation and adolescents. *Pediatrics*, 113, 1827–1832.

Fraser, L. (1999). Why more men are going under the knife. *The Ottawa Citizen*, September 6, A10.

Fraunfelder, F. (2000). Treating your patients with breast cancer. *British Medical Journal*, 320, 457–459.

Frayser, S. (1994). Defining normal childhood sexuality: An anthropological approach. *Annual Review of Sex Research*, 5, 173–217.

Frazier, K. (2006). Memory wars and monster stories. *Skeptical Inquirer*, 30, 4.

Frazier, P. (1993). A comparative study of male and female victims seen at hospital-based rape crises programs. *Journal of Interpersonal Violence*, 8, 65–79.

Freeman, E., Bloom, D., & McGuire, E. (2001). A brief history of testosterone. *Journal of Urology*, 165, 371–373.

Freeman, E., Sammel, M., Lin, H., & Nelson, D. (2006). Associations of hormones and menopausal status with depressed mood in women with no history of depression. *Archives of General Psychiatry*, 63, 375–382.

French, D., & Dishion, T. (2003). Predictors of early

initiation of sexual intercourse among high-risk adolescents. *Journal of Early Adolescence*, 23, 295–315.

Freund, K., & Blanchard, R. (1993). Erotic target location errors in male gender dysphorics, paedophiles, and fetishists. *British Journal of Psychiatry*, 162, 558–563.

Freund, K., Seto, M., & Kuban, M. (1996). Two types of fetishism. *Behaviour Research and Therapy*, 34, 687–694.

Freund, K., Seto, M., & Kuban, M. (1997). Frotteurism and the theory of courtship disorder. In D. Laws & W. O'Donohue (Eds.), *Sexual Deviance: Theory, Assessment, and Treatment*. New York: Guilford Press.

Freund, K., Watson, R., & Rienzo, D. (1988). The value of self-reports in the study of voyeurism and exhibitionism. *Annals of Sex Research*, 1, 243–262.

Freund, M., Lee, N., & Leonard, T. (1991). Sexual behavior of clients with street prostitutes in Camden, N.J. *Journal of Sex Research*, 28, 579–591.

Friday, N. (1980). *Men in Love*. New York: Delacorte.

Friedan, B. (1994). *The Fountain of Age*. New York: Simon & Schuster.

Friedman, M. (2003). *Strapped for Cash: A History of American Hustler Culture*. Los Angeles: Aylson Publications.

Friedman, S. (1994). *Secret Lives: Women with Two Lives*. New York: Crown.

Friedrich, W., Fisher, J., Broughton, D., Houston, M., & Shafran, C. (1998). Normative sexual behavior in children: A contemporary sample. *Pediatrics*, 101, 1–13. Retrieved May 30, 2000, from http://www.pediatrics.org/cgi/content/full/101/4/e9.

Friedrich, W., Grambsch, P., Broughton, D., Kuiper, J., & Beilke, R. (1991). Normative sexual behavior in children. *Pediatrics*, 88, 456–464.

Frohlich, P., & Meston, C. (2005). Tactile sensitivity in women with sexual arousal disorder. *Archives of Sexual Behavior*, 34, 207–218.

Fromm, E. (1965). *The Ability to Love*. New York: Farrar, Straus & Giroux.

Fu, H., Darroch, J., Hass, T., & Ranjit, N. (1999). Contraceptive failure rates: New estimates from the 1995 National Survey of Family Growth. *Family Planning Perspectives*, 31, 56–63.

Fugl-Meyer, K., Oberg, K., Lundberg, P., & Lewin, B. (2006). On orgasm, sexual techniques, and erotic perceptions in 18- to 74-year-old Swedish women. *The Journal of Sexual Medicine*, 3, 56–68.

Furnham, A., & Mak, T. (1999). Sex-role stereotyping in television commercials: A review and comparison of fourteen studies done on five continents over 25 years. *Sex Roles*, 41, 413–437.

Gaboury, J. (2005). A personal perspective: Saying "I don't." *SIECUS Report*, 33, 29.

Gaby, A. (2005). Vitamin E relieves menstrual pain. *Townsend Letter for Doctors and Patients*, December, 46.

Gacci, M., Bartoletti, R., Figlioli, S., Sarti, E., Eisner, B., Boddi, V., & Rizzo, M. (2003). Urinary symptoms, quality of life, and sexual function in patients with benign prostatic hypertrophy before and after prostatectomy: A prospective study. *British Journal of Urology International*, 91, 196–200.

Gager, C., & Sanchez, L. (2003). Two as one? *Journal of Family Issues*, 24, 21–50.

Galewitz, P. (2000). *New Birth Control Method Approved*. Retrieved October 6, 2000, from http://www.salon.com/mwt/wire/2000/10/06/birth_control/index.html.

Gallant, J., DeJesus, E., Arribas, J., et al. (2006). Tenofovir DF, emtricitabine, and efavirenz vs. zidovudine, lamivudine, and efavirenz for HIV. *New England Journal of Medicine*, 354, 251–260.

Gallo, L., & Smith, T. (2001). Attachment style in marriage: Adjustment and responses to interaction. *Journal of Social and Personal Relationships*, 18, 263–289.

Gallup Poll (2006). Constitutional amendment defining marriage as only between a man and a woman. Retrieved from http://www.gallup.com/poll/1651/Homosexual-Relations.aspx.?

Gandhi, T., Wei, W., Amin, K., & Kazanjian, P. (2006). Effect of maintaining highly active antiretroviral therapy on AIDS events among patients with late-stage HIV infection and inadequate response to therapy. *Clinical Infectious Diseases*, 42, 878–884.

Gange, S. (1999). *When Is Adult Circumcision Necessary?* Retrieved September 20, 1999, from http://www.cnn.com/HEALTH/men/circumcision.adult/index.html.

Gangestad, S., & Buss, D. (1993). Pathogen prevalence and human mate preferences. *Ethology and Sociobiology*, 14, 89–96.

Gangestad, S., & Simpson, J. (2000). The evolution of human mating: Trade-offs and strategic pluralism. *Behavioral and Brain Sciences*, 23, 573–587.

Ganong, L., & Coleman, M. (1987). Sex, sex roles, and family love. *Journal of Genetic Psychology*, 148, 45–52.

Gao, F., Bailes, E., Robertson, D., Chen, Y., Rodenburg, C., Michael, S., Cummings, L., Arthur, L., Peeters, M., Shaw, G., Sharp, P., & Hahn, B. (1999). Origin of HIV-1 in chimpanzee *Pan troglodytes troglodytes*. *Nature*, 397, 436–441.

Garcia, L. (1982). Sex-role orientation and stereotypes about male female sexuality. *Sex Roles*, 8, 863–876.

Garcia-Banigan, D., & Guay, A. (2005). Testosterone treatment in women. *Contemporary Sexuality*, 39, i–vii.

Gardner, M. (2006). The memory wars: Part I. *Skeptical Inquirer*, 30, 28–31.

Gardner, R., Blackburn, M., & Ushma, D. (1999). Closing the condom gap. *Population Reports*, 27, 1–35.

Garnefski, N., & Diekstra, R. (1997). Child sexual abuse and emotional and behavioral problems in adolescence: Gender differences. *Journal of the Academy of Child and Adolescent Psychiatry*, 36, 323–329.

Garos, S. (1994). Autoerotic asphyxiation: A challenge to death educators and counselors. *Omega: Journal of Death and Dying*, 28, 85–99.

Garza-Leal, J., & Landron, F. (1991). Autoerotic asphyxial death initially misinterpreted as suicide and review of the literature. *Journal of Forensic Science*, 36, 1753–1759.

Gaynor, M. (2003). Isoflavones and the prevention and treatment of prostate disease: Is there a role? *Cleveland Clinic Journal of Medicine*, 70, 203–214.

Gearhart, P., & Robboy, A. (2005). Sex and sexuality in pregnancy. Paper presented at What's New and What Works: Pioneering Solutions for Today's Sexual Issues (AASECT 37th Annual Conference), Portland, OR, May.

Gearson, C. (2003). *The Search for a Female Viagra*. Retrieved August 3, 2003, from http://health .discovery.com/centers/womens/viagra/viagra_print .html.

Geary, S., & Moon, Y. (2006). The human embryo in vitro: Recent progress. *The Journal of Reproductive Medicine*, 51, 293–302.

Gebhard, P. (1971). Human sexual behavior: A summary statement. In D. Marshall & R. Suggs (Eds.), *Human Sexual Behavior: Variations in the Ethnographic Spectrum*. Englewood Cliffs, NJ: Prentice Hall.

Gebhard, P., Gagnon, J., Pomery, W., & Christenson, C. (1965). *Sex Offenders: An Analysis of Types*. New York: Harper & Row.

Geer, J., & Manguno-Mire, G. (1997). Gender differences in cognitive processes in sexuality. *Annual Review of Sex Research*, 7, 90–124.

Gelfand, M. (2000). The role of androgen replacement therapy for postmenopausal women. *Contemporary Obstetrics and Gynecology*, February, 107–116.

Gelperin, N. (2005). Oral sex and teens: The new third base? Paper presented at What's New and What Works: Pioneering Solutions for Today's Sexual Issues (AASECT 37th Annual Conference), Portland, OR, May.

Gendel, E., & Bonner, E. (1988). Gender identity disorders and paraphilias. In H. Goldman (Ed.), *Review of General Psychiatry*. Norwalk, CT: Appleton & Lange.

Genevie, L., & Margolies, E. (1987). *The Motherhood Report: How Women Feel About Being Mothers*. New York: Macmillan.

Genuis, S., & Genuis, S. (2005). Implications of cyberspace communication. *Southern Medical Journal*, 98, 451–455.

George, A., Waxman, A., Scott, C., & Kimmel, S. (2006). "Hooking up" and its clinical implications. Paper presented at the American College of Obstetricians and Gynecologists 54th Annual Clinical Meeting, May.

Gertler, P., Shah, M., & Bertozzi, S. (2005). Risky business: The market for unprotected commercial sex. *Journal of Political Economy*, 113, 518–551.

Getahun, D., Oyelese, Y., Slihu, H., & Ananth, C. (2006). Previous cesarean delivery and risks of placenta previa and placental abruption. *Obstetrics & Gynecology*, 107, 771–778.

Ghani, J., & Aral, S. (2005). Patterns of sex worker–client contacts and their implications for the persistence of sexually transmitted infections. *Journal of Infectious Diseases*, 191, 534–541.

Ghizzani, A., & Montomoli, M. (2000). Anorexia nervosa and sexual behavior in women: A review. *Journal of Sex Education and Therapy*, 25, 80–88.

Gholami, S., Gonzalez-Cadavid, N., Lin, C., & Rajfer, J. (2003). Peyronie's disease: A review. *Journal of Urology*, 169, 1234–1241.

Giaquinto, S., Buzzelli, S., Di Francesco, L., & Nolfe, G. (2003). Evaluation of sexual changes after stroke. *Journal of Clinical Psychiatry*, 64, 302–307.

Giargiari, T., Mahaffey, A., Craighead, W., & Hutchison, K. (2005). Appetitive responses to sexual stimuli are attenuated in individuals with low levels of sexual desire. *Archives of Sexual Behavior*, 34, 547–557.

Gibbons, A. (1991). The brain as a "sexual organ." *Science*, 253, 957–959.

Gibbs, N. (2001). Renegade scientists say they are ready to start applying the technology of cloning to human beings. *Time*, February 19, 47–57.

Gibbs, N. (2002). Making time for a baby. *Time*, April 15, 48–54.

Gilbert, B., Heesacker, M., & Gannon, L. (1991). Changing the sexual aggression-supportive attitudes of men: A psychoeducational intervention. *Journal of Counseling Psychology*, 38, 197–203.

Gilbert, L., Alexander, L., Grosshans, J., & Jolley, L. (2003). Answering frequently asked questions about HPV. *Sexually Transmitted Diseases*, 30, 193–194.

Ginsburg, K., Wolf, N., & Fidel, P. (1997). Potential effects of midcycle cervical mucus on mediators of immune reactivity. *Fertility and Sterility*, 67, 46–56.

Girman, A., Lee, R., & Kligler, B. (2003). An integrative medicine approach to premenstrual syndrome. *American Journal of Obstetrics and Gynecology*, 188, . S56–S63.

Gittelman, M., Liao, Q., Song, X., & Geng, L. (2006). A placebo-controlled, double-blind study of the efficacy and safety of an alprostadil topical cream in patients with female sexual arousal disorder. *The Journal of Sexual Medicine*, 3(suppl. 3), 224–286.

Glaser, G. (2006). Oregon births a boom in surrogate babies. *The Oregonian*, July 9, A1.

Glei, D. (1999). Measuring contraceptive use patterns among teenage and adult women. *Family Planning Perspectives*, 31, 73–80.

Glennon, L. (1999). *The 20th Century: An Illustrated History of Our Lives and Times*. North Dighton, MA: JG Press.

Glick, P., & Fiske, S. (2001). An ambivalent alliance: Hostile and benevolent sexism as complementary justifications for gender inequality. *American Psychologist*, February, 109–118.

Glina, S. (2006). What to say to the couple regarding their future sex life at the time of working out the treatment strategy? *The Journal of Sexual Medicine*, 3(suppl. 2), 85.

Global Agenda. (2003). Sex for sale, legally: Prostitution, the oldest profession, goes legit. *Global Agenda*, July 11.

Global Study of Sexual Attitudes and Behaviors (2002). *Global Study of Sexual Attitudes and Behaviors*. Retrieved December 11, 2003, from http://www .pfizerglobalstudy.com/study-results.asp.

Glover, D., Amonkar, M., Rybeck, B., & Tracy, T. (2003). Prescription, over-the-counter, and herbal medicine use in a rural obstetric population. *American Journal of Obstetrics and Gynecology*, 188, 1039–1045.

Goad, K. (2006). Big-earning wives, and the men who love them. Retrieved August 12, 2006 from http:// lifestyle.msn.com/Relationships/CouplesandMarriage.

Godow, A (1999). Playful sexuality. *Contemporary Sexuality*, 33, 1–2.

Goens, J., Janniger, C., & De Wolf, K. (1994a). Dermatologic and systematic manifestations of syphilis. *American Family Physician*, 50, 1013–1020.

Gold, D., Balzano, B., & Stamey, R. (1991). Two studies of females' sexual force fantasies. *Journal of Sex Education and Therapy*, 17, 15–26.

Goldberg, M. (2006). *Kingdom Coming: The Rise of Christian Nationalism*. New York: W. W. Norton & Company.

Golden, N., Seigel, W., & Fisher, M. (2001). Emergency contraception: Pediatricians' knowledge, attitudes, and opinions. *Pediatrics*, 107, 287–292.

Goldman, H. (1992). *Review of General Psychiatry*. Norwalk, CT: Appleton & Lange.

Goldman, J., & Padayachi, U. (2000). Some methodological problems in estimating incidence and prevalence in child sexual abuse research. *Journal of Sex Research*, 37, 305–315.

Goldman, R., & Goldman, J. (1982). *Children's Sexual Thinking: A Comparative Study of Children Aged 5 to 15 Years in Australia, North America, Britain, and Sweden*. London: Routledge & Kegan Paul.

Goldstein, A., Klingman, D., Christopher, K., & Johnson, C. (2006). Surgical treatment of vulvar vestibulitis syndrome: Outcome assessment derived from a postoperative questionnaire. *The Journal of Sexual Medicine*, 3, 923–931.

Goldstein, I., & Alexander, J. (2005). Practical aspects in the management of vaginal atrophy and sexual dysfunction in perimenopausal and post-menopausal women. *The Journal of Sexual Medicine*, 2, 154–165.

Golombok, S., & Fivush, R. (1995). Gender is determined biologically and socially. In D. Bender & B. Leone (Eds.), *Human Sexuality: Opposing Viewpoints*. San Diego: Greenhaven Press.

Goodheart, A. (2004). Change of heart. *AARP Bulletin*, May, 45–47.

Goodman, D. (2001). *Communicating with Strangers . . . or How to Become More Culturally Competent Sex Educators and Counselors*. Paper presented at the 33rd Annual Conference of the American Association of Sex Educators, Counselors, and Therapists, San Francisco, May 2–6.

Goodman-Brown, T., Edelstein, R., Goodman, G., Jones, D., & Gordon, D. (2003). Why children tell: A model of children's disclosure of sexual abuse. *Child Abuse and Neglect*, 27, 525–540.

Goodrum, J. (2000). *A Transgender Primer*. Retrieved February 16, 2000, from http://www.ntac.org/tg101.html.

Goodson, P., Suther, S., Pruitt, B., & Wilson, K. (2003). Defining abstinence: Views of directors, instructors, and participants in abstinence-only-until-marriage programs in Texas. *Journal of School Health*, 73, 91–96.

Goodyear, R., Newcomb, M., & Allison, R. (2000). Predictors of Latino men's paternity in teen pregnancy: A test of a mediational model of childhood experiences, gender role attitudes, and behaviors. *Journal of Counseling Psychology*, 47, 116–128.

Gordon, S., & Gordon, J. (1989). *Raising a Child Conservatively in a Sexually Permissive World*. New York: Simon & Schuster.

Gordon, S., Brenden, J., Wyble, J., & Ivey, C. (1997). When the Dx is penile cancer. *RN*, March, 41–44.

Gorey, K., & Leslie, D. (1997). The prevalence of child sexual abuse: Integrative review adjustment for potential response and measurement biases. *Child Abuse and Neglect*, 21, 391–398.

Gorman, C. (2002). The limits of science. *Time*, April 15, 52.

Gorski, E. (2002). New Bible: Revised gender version. *The Oregonian*, February 9, C7.

Gotthardt, M. (2003). Lust and found. *AARP*, November–December, 28–31.

Gottman, J. (1993). *What Predicts Divorce*. Hillsdale, NJ: Lawrence Erlbaum.

Gottman, J. (1994). *Why Marriages Succeed or Fail*. New York: Simon & Schuster.

Gottman, J., & Silver, N. (2000). *The Seven Principles for Making Marriage Work*. New York: Crown Publishers.

Gottman, J., Coan, J., Carrere, S., & Swanson, C. (1998). Predicting marital happiness and stability from newlywed interactions. *Journal of Marriage and the Family*, 60, 5–22.

Gottman, J., Murray, J., Swanson, C., Tyson, R., & Swanson, K. (2003). *The Mathematics of Marriage: Dynamic Linear Models*. Cambridge, MA: MIT Press.

Gover, T. (1996). Occupational hazards. *The Advocate*, November 26, 36–38.

Gowen, L. (2005). Normative use of online sexual activities. *The Oregon Psychologist*, November/December, 5–6.

Grady, D. (2000). New test for cervical cancer beats Pap smear, studies find. *San Francisco Chronicle*, January 5, C1.

Graham, J. (2006). Doctors push "morning-after pill": Campaign urges prescriptions that are written ahead. *Chicago Tribune*, May 9, NA.

Graham, N. (1997). Epidemiology of acquired immunodeficiency syndrome: Advancing to an endemic era. *American Journal of Medicine*, 102(suppl. 4A), 2–8.

Gravholt, C., Juul, S., Naeraa, R., & Hansen, J. (1998). Morbidity in Turner syndrome. *Journal of Clinical Epidemiology*, 51, 147–158.

Greaves, K. (2001). *The Social Construction of Sexual Activity in Heterosexual Relationships: A Qualitative Analysis*. Paper presented at the 33rd Annual Conference of the American Association of Sex Educators, Counselors, and Therapists, San Francisco, May 2–6.

Green, B., DeBacker, T., Ravindron, B., & Krows, A. (1999). Goals, values, and beliefs as predictors of achievement and effort in high-school mathematics classes. *Sex Roles*, 40, 421–458.

Green, J. (2000). A killer on land and sea? *Newsweek*, April 24, 65.

Green, L., Fein, D., Modahl, C., Feinstein, C., Waterhouse, L., & Morris, M. (2001). Oxytocin and autistic disorder: Alterations in peptide forms. *Biological Psychiatry*, 50, 609–613.

Green, R. (1974). *Sexual Identity Conflict in Children and Adults*. New York: Basic Books.

Greenberg, B., & Woods, M. (1999). The soaps: Their sex, gratifications, and outcomes. *Journal of Sex Research*, 36, 150–157.

Greene, B. (1994). African-American woman. In L. Comas-Diaz & B. Greene (Eds.), *Women of Color*. New York: Guilford Press.

Greene, K., & Faulkner, S. (2005). Gender, belief in the sexual double standard, and sexual talk in heterosexual dating relationships. *Sex Roles: A Journal of Research*, 53, 239–251.

Greenfield, D. (2005). The net effect: Internet addiction and compulsive Internet use. *The Oregon Psychologist*, November/December, 15–17.

Greenstein, A., Plymate, S., & Katz, G. (1995). Visually stimulated erection in castrated men. *Journal of Urology*, 153, 650–652.

Greenwald, E., & Leitenberg, H. (1989). Long-term effects of sexual experiences with siblings and nonsiblings during childhood. *Archives of Sexual Behavior*, 18, 389–400.

Greer, P. (1998). Vaginal thrush: Diagnosis and treatment options. *Nursing Times*, 94, 50–52.

Gregersen, E. (1996). *The World of Human Sexuality: Behaviors, Customs, and Beliefs*. New York: Irvington.

Gregorian, R., Golden, K., Bahce, A., Goodman, C., Kwong, W., & Khan, Z. (2002). Antidepressant-induced sexual dysfunction. *Annals of Pharmacotherapy*, 36, 1577–1589.

Gribble, J., Miller, H., Rogers, S., & Turner, C. (1999). Interview mode and measurement of sexual behaviors: Methodological issues. *Journal of Sex Research*, 36, 16–24.

Grisell, T. (1988). Brief report. *Indiana Medical Journal*, 81, 252.

Grodstein, F., Manson, J., & Stampfer, M. (2006). Hormone therapy and coronary heart disease: The role of time since menopause and age at hormone initiation. *Journal of Women's Health*, 15, 35–44.

Gron, G., Wunderlich, A., Spitzer, M., Tomczak, R., & Riepe, M. (2000). Brain activation during human navigation: Gender-different neural networks as substrate of performance. *Nature Neuroscience*, 3, 404–408.

Gross, B. (2004). Sleeping dogs—dreams and repressed memories. *Annals of the American Psychotherapy Association*, 7, 43–44.

Gross, B. (2006). The pleasure of pain. *The Forensic Examiner*, 15, 56–61.

Gross, L. (2001). *Up from Invisibility: Lesbians, Gay Men, and the Media in America*. New York: Columbia University Press.

Gross, M. (2003a). The second wave will drown us. *American Journal of Public Health*, 93, 872–881.

Gruszecki, L., Forchuk, C., & Fisher, W. (2005). Factors associated with common sexual concerns in women: New findings from the Canadian contraception study. *The Canadian Journal of Human Sexuality*, 14, 1–14.

Gu, G., Cornea, A., & Simerly, R. (2003). Sexual differentiation of projections from the principal nucleus of the bed nuclei of the stria terminalis. *Journal of Comparative Neurology*, 460, 542–562.

Gudykunst, W., Matsumoto, Y., Ting-Toomey, S., Nishida, T., Kim, K., & Keyman, S. (1996). The influence of cultural individualism-collectivism, self construals, and individual values on communication styles across cultures. *Human Communication Research*, 22, 510–543.

Guerrero-Pavich, E. (1986). A Chicano perspective on Mexican culture and sexuality. In L. Lister (Ed.), *Human Sexuality, Ethnoculture, and Social Work*. New York: Haworth Press.

Guidry, H. (1995). Childhood sexual abuse: Role of the family physician. *American Family Physician*, 51, 407–414.

Gupta, P., & Subramoney, S. (2006). Smokeless tobacco use and risk of stillbirth: A cohort study in Mumbai, India. *Epidemiology*, 17, 47–51.

Gur, R., Mozley, L., Mozley, P., Resnick, S., Karp, J., Alavi, A., Arnold, S., & Gur, R. (1995). Sex differences in regional cerebral glucose metabolism during a resting state. *Science*, 267, 528–531.

Gutek, B. (1985). *Sex and the Workplace*. San Francisco: Jossey-Bass.

Guttmacher, S., Lieberman, L., Ward, D., Freudenberg, N., Radosh, A., & Des Jarlais, D. (1997). Condom availability in New York City public high schools: Relationships to condom use and sexual behavior. *American Journal of Public Health*, 87, 1427–1433.

Guy-Sheftall, B. (2003). African American women: The legacy of black feminism. In R. Morgan (Ed.), *Sisterhood Is Forever*. New York: Washington Square Press.

Haansbaek, T. (2006). Partner to a rape victim: How is he doing? *The Journal of Sex Research*, 43, 18–19.

Hack, M. (2002). Outcomes in young adulthood for very-low-birth-weight infants. *New England Journal of Medicine*, 346, 149–157.

Haffner, D. (1993). Toward a new paradigm of adolescent sexual health. *SIECUS Report*, 21, 26–30.

Haffner, D. (2004). Sexuality and scripture. *Contemporary Sexuality*, 38, 7–13.

Haffner, D., & Wagoner, J. (1999). Vast majority of Americans support sexuality education. *SIECUS Report*, 27, 22–23.

Hagan, P., & Knott, P. (1998). Diagnosing and treating polycystic ovary syndrome. *The Practitioner*, 242, 98–106.

Hagen, H., Latka, M., Campbell, J., Golub, E., Garfein, R., et al. (2006). Eligibility for treatment of hepatitis C virus infection among drug users in 3 U.S. cities. *Clinical Infectious Diseases*, 42, 669–673.

Hagen, R. (2006). At your service. *The Advocate*, August 15, 26.

Hahn, J., & Blass, T. (1997). Dating partner preferences: A function of similarity of love styles. *Journal of Social Behavior and Personality*, 12, 595–610.

Halberstadt, A. (1985). Race, socioeconomic status, and nonverbal behavior. In A. Siegman & S. Feldstein (Eds.), *Multichannel Integration of Nonverbal Behavior*. Hillsdale, NJ: Erlbaum.

Hall, B. (2006, January 17). Pro-Bush, pro-equality. Retrieved May 24, 2006, from http://www.advocate.com/exclusive_detail_ektid24536.asp.

Hall, G. (1996). *Theory-Based Assessment, Treatment, and Prevention of Sexual Aggression*. New York: Oxford University Press.

Hally, C., & Pollack, R. (1993). The effects of self-esteem, variety of sexual experience, and erotophilia on sexual satisfaction in sexually active heterosexuals. *Journal of Sex Education and Therapy*, 19(3, 183–192.

Halpern, D., & LaMay, M. (2000). The smarter sex: A critical review of sex differences in intelligence. *Educational Psychology Review*, 12, 229–246.

Halpern-Felsher, B., Cornell, J., Kropp, R., & Tschann, J. (2006). Oral versus vaginal sex among adolescents: Perceptions, attitudes, and behavior. *Pediatrics*, 44, 115, 845–851, 1023–1024.

Halpern-Felsher, B., Kropp, B., Boyer, C., Tschann, J., & Ellen, J. (2004). Adolescents' self-efficacy to communicate about sex: its role in condom attitudes, commitment, and use. *Adolescence*, 39, 443–456.

Hamblett, M. (1999). No insurance for "video voyeurism." *New York Law Journal*. Retrieved December 28, 1999, from http://www.law.com.

Hamilton, E. (1978). *Sex, with Love*. Boston: Beacon Press.

Hamilton, E., Wallis, M., Barlow, J., & Cullen, L. (2003). Women's views of a breast screening service. *Health Care for Women International*, 24, 40–48.

Hamilton, T. (2002). *Skin Flutes and Velvet Gloves*. New York: St. Martin's Press.

Hammond, C. (2006). Time to change. *Obstetrics & Gynecology*, 107, 549.

Hampton, T. (2005). Researchers discover a range of factors undermine sperm quality, male fertility. *Journal of the American Medical Association*, 294, 2829–2830.

Hampton, T. (2006). High prevalence of lesser-known STDs. *Journal of the American Medical Association*, 295, 2467.

Han, J., Wrablewski, G., Xu, Z., Silverman, R., & Barton, D. (2004). Sensitivity of hepatitis C virus RNA to the antiviral enzyme ribonuclease L is determined by a subset of efficient cleavage sites. *Journal of Interferone & Cytokine Research*, 24, 664–676.

Handsfield, H. (2006). Nongonococcal urethritis: A few answers but mostly questions. *Journal of Infectious Diseases*, 193, 333–335.

Haney, D. (1994). Study strongly ties environment to birth defects. *San Francisco Examiner*, July 7, A7.

Hanrahan, S. (1994). Historical review of menstrual toxic shock syndrome. *Women and Health*, 21, 141–157.

Hanson, R., Resnick, H., Saunders, B., Kilpatrick, D., & Best, C. (1999). Factors related to the reporting of childhood rape. *Child Abuse and Neglect*, 23, 559–569.

Hanson, R., Saunders, B., Kilpatrick, D., Resnick, H., Crouch, J., & Duncan, R. (2001). Impact of childhood rape and aggravated assault on mental health. *American Journal of Orthopsychiatry*, 71, 108–118.

Hanus, J. (2006). Monomaniacal monogamy. *Utne*, March–April, 55.

Hanus, J. (2006). The culture of pornography is shaping our lives, for better and for worse. *Utne*, September–October, 58–60.

Harer, W. (2001). A look back at women's health and ACOG, a look forward to the challenges of the future. *Obstetrics and Gynecology*, 97, 1–4.

Hargreaves, D., & Plail, R. (1994). Fracture of the penis causing a corporo-urethral fistula. *British Journal of Urology*, 73, 97.

Hargreaves, S. (2004). Recognizing rape as torture: Legal and therapeutic challenges. *Lancet*, 363, 1916.

Hari, J. (2006). What we can learn from female sex tourists. *The Independent* (London), July 13, C 7.

Harley, V., Jackson, D., Hextall, P., Hawkins, J., Berkovitz, G., Sockanathan, S., Lovell-Badge, R., & Goodfellow, P. (1992). DNA binding activity of recombinant *SRY* from normal males and XY females. *Science*, 255, 453–456.

Harlow, H., & Harlow, M. (1962). The effects of rearing conditions on behavior. *Bulletin of the Menninger Clinic*, 26, 13–24.

Harned, M., & Fitzgerald, L. (2002). Understanding a link between sexual harassment and eating disorder symptoms: A mediational analysis. *Journal of Consulting and Clinical Psychology*, 70, 1170–1181.

Harper, C. (2005). The effect of increased access to emergency contraception among young adolescents. *Obstetrics & Gynecology*, 106, 483–491.

Harper, D., Franco, E., Wheeler, C., et al. (2004). Efficacy of a bivalent L1 virus-like particle vaccine in prevention of infection with human papillomavirus types 16 & 18 in young women: A randomized, controlled trial. *Lancet*, 364, 1757–1765.

Harris Poll (2006). Large majority support more access to birth control information. Retrieved February 2, 2006, from www.harrisinteractive.com/news/NewsID=1064.

Harris, A. (2005). The state as the "Top": The government's control of sex. Retrieved April 15, 2006, from http://www.findarticles.com/p/articles/mi_m2372/is_4_42/ai_n15929185/print.

Harris, C. (2002). Sexual and romantic jealousy in heterosexual and homosexual adults. *Psychological Science*, 13, 7–12.

Harris, C. (2003). A review of sex differences in sexual jealousy, including self-report data, psychophysiological responses, interpersonal violence, and morbid jealousy. *Personality and Social Psychology Review*, 7, 102–128.

Harrison, T. (2003). Adolescent homosexuality and concerns regarding disclosure. *Journal of School Health*, 73, 107–112.

Hartmann, J., Albrecht, C., Schmoll, H., Kuczyk, M., Kollmannsberger, C., & Bokemeyer, C. (1999). Long-term effects on sexual function and fertility after treatment of testicular cancer. *British Journal of Cancer*, 80, 801–807.

Hartwell, C. (2005). HIV/AIDS in South Africa: A review of sexual behavior among adolescents. *Adolescence*, 40, 171–181.

Harvard Health Publications (2006, March). Life after 50: A Harvard study of male sexuality. Retrieved August 9, 2006, from http://health.msn.com/centers/mensexualhealth/articlepage.aspx?cp-documentid=100127818.

Hass, A. (1979). *Teenage Sexuality*. New York: Macmillan.

Hatcher, R., & Guillebaud, J. (1998). The pill: Combined oral contraceptives. In R. Hatcher, J. Trussell, F. Stewart, W. Cates, G. Stewart, F. Guest, & D. Kowal (Eds.), *Contraceptive Technology*. New York: Ardent Media.

Hatfield, E., & Sprecher, S. (1986a). Measuring passionate love in intimate relationships. *Journal of Adolescence*, 9, 383–410.

**Hatfield, R.** (1994). Touch and sexuality. In V. Bullough & B. Bullough (Eds.), *Human Sexuality: An Encyclopedia*. New York: Garland.

**Hausknecht, R.** (2003). Mifepristone and misoprostol for early medical abortion: 18 months experience in the United States. *Contraception*, 67, 463–465.

**Hawkins, T.** (2006). Appearance-related side effects of HIV-1 treatment. *AIDS Patient Care*, 20, 6–13.

**Hayes, R., Bennett, C., Fairley, C., & Dennerstein, L.** (2006). What can prevalence studies tell us about female sexual difficulty and dysfunction? *The Journal of Sexual Medicine*, 3, 589–595.

**Haynes, J., & Miller, J.** (2003). Introduction. In J. Haynes & J. Miller (Eds.), *Inconceivable Conceptions: Psychological Aspects of Infertility and Reproductive Technology*. Hove, United Kingdom: Brunner–Routledge.

**Hays, M.** (2004). Unveiling Islam. *The Advocate*, March 2, 27.

**Hazan, C., & Shaver, P.** (1987). Love conceptualized as attachment process. *Journal of Personality and Social Psychology*, 52, 511–524.

**Hazan, C., & Zeifman, D.** (1999). Pair bonds as attachment: Evaluating the evidence. In J. Cassidy & P. Shaver (Eds.), *Handbook of Attachment: Theory, Research, and Clinical Applications*. New York: Guilford Press.

**Healy, B.** (2003). Whose breasts, anyway? *U.S. News & World Report*, August 11, 50.

**Heath, D.** (1984). An investigation into the origins of a copious vaginal discharge during intercourse "enough to wet the bed" that is not urine. *Journal of Sex Research*, 20, 194–215.

**Heavey, S.** (2006). Plan B decision made before data review: FDA staff. Retrieved August 4, 2006, from http://news.yahoo.com/s/nm/20060804/hl_nm/contraceptive_dc&printer=1.

**Hecht, M., Ribeau, S., & Collier, M.** (1993). *African American Communication: Ethnic Identity and Cultural Interpretation*. Thousand Oaks, CA: Sage.

**Hecht, M., Ribeau, S., & Sedano, M.** (1990). A Mexican American perspective on interethnic communication. *International Journal of Intercultural Relations*, 14, 31–55.

**Heck, J., Sell, R., & Gorin S.** (2006). Health care access among individuals involved in same-sex relationships. *American Journal of Public Health*, 96, 1111–1118.

**Heckman, T., Silverthorn, M., Waltje, A., Meyers, M., & Yarber, W.** (2003). HIV transmission risk practices in rural persons living with HIV disease. *Sexually Transmitted Diseases*, 30, 134–136.

**Heim, N.** (1981). Sexual behavior of castrated sex offenders. *Archives of Sexual Behavior*, 10, 11–19.

**Heinlein, R.** (1961). *Stranger in a Strange Land*. New York: Putnam.

**Hellstrom, W., Nehra, A., Shabsigh, R., & Sharlip, I.** (2006). Premature ejaculation: The most common male sexual dysfunction. Paper presented at the Sexual Medicine Society of North America Fall Meeting, New York, November.

**Helstrom, L., Sorbom, D., & Backstrom, T.** (1995). Influence of partner relationship on sexuality after subtotal hysterectomy. *Acta Obstetricia et Gynecologica Scandinavica*, 74, 142–146.

**Hendrick, C., & Hendrick, S.** (1986). A theory and method of love. *Journal of Personality and Social Psychology*, 50, 392–402.

**Hendrick, C., & Hendrick, S.** (2003). Romantic love: Measuring cupid's arrow. In S. Lopez and C. Snyder (Eds.), *Positive Psychological Assessment: A Handbook of Models and Measures*. Washington, DC: American Psychological Association.

**Hendrick, C., Hendrick, S., & Adler, N.** (1988). Romantic relationships: Love, satisfaction, and staying together. *Journal of Personality and Social Psychology*, 54, 980–988.

**Hendrick, S., & Hendrick, C.** (1992). *Liking, Loving, and Relating*, 2nd ed. Pacific Grove, CA: Brooks/ Cole.

**Hendrick, S., & Hendrick, C.** (1995). Gender differences and similarities in sex and love. *Personal Relationships*, 2, 5–65.

**Henshaw, S., & Finer, L.** (2003). The accessibility of abortion services in the United States, 2001. *Perspectives on Sexual and Reproductive Health*, 35, 16–24.

**Hensley, C., Tewksbury, R., & Castle, T.** (2003). Characteristics of prison sexual assault targets in male Oklahoma's correctional facilities. *Journal of Interpersonal Violence*, 18, 595–606.

**Henson, H.** (2002). Breast cancer and sexuality. *Sexuality and Disability*, 20, 261–273.

**Herter, C.** (1998). Sexual dysfunction in patients with diabetes. *Journal of the American Board of Family Practice*, 11, 327–330.

**Hesketh, R., & Xing, A.** (2006). Abnormal sex ratios in human populations: Causes and consequences. *Proceedings of the National Academy of Sciences*, 103, 13271–13275.

**Heukelbach, J., & Feldmeier, H.** (2004). Ectoparasites: The underestimated realm. *Lancet*, 363, 889–891.

**Heyden, M., Anger, B., Tiel, T., & Ellner, T.** (1999). Fighting back works: The case for advocating and teaching self-defense against rape. *Journal of Physical Education, Recreation, and Dance*, 70, 31–34.

**Heyl, P.** (1997). Multiplying the risks. *Newsweek*, December 1, 66.

**Hickman, S., & Muehlenhard, C.** (1999). "By the semi-mystical appearance of a condom": How young women and men communicate sexual consent in heterosexual situations. *Journal of Sex Research*, 36, 258–272.

**Hickson, F., Davies, P., Hunt, A., Weatherburn, P., McManus, T., & Coxon, A.** (1994). Gay men as victims of nonconsensual sex. *Archives of Sexual Behavior*, 23, 281–294.

**Higa, G.** (2000). Altering the estrogenic milieu of breast cancer with a focus on the new aromatase inhibitors. *Pharmacotherapy*, 20, 280–291.

**Hilden, M., Schei, B., & Sidenius, K.** (2005). Genitoanal injury in adult female victims of sexual assault. *Forensic Science International*, 154, 200–205.

**Hill, M., & Fischer, A.** (2001). Does entitlement mediate the link between masculinity and rape-related variables? *Journal of Counseling Psychology*, 48, 39–50.

**Hillard, P.** (2005). Overview of contraception. *Adolescent Medicine*, 16, 485–493.

**Hillis, S.** (1994). PID prevention: Clinical and societal stakes. *Hospital Practice*, 29, 121–130.

**Hines, M.** (2004). *Brain Gender*. New York: Oxford

University Press.

Hines, M., Ahmed, S., & Hughes, I. (2003). Psychological outcomes and gender-related development in complete androgen insensitivity syndrome. *Archives of Sexual Behavior*, 32, 93–101.

Hingson, R., Heeren, T., Winter, M., & Wechsler, H. (2003). Early age of first drunkenness as a factor in college students' unplanned and unprotected sex attributable to drinking. *Pediatrics*, 111, 34–41.

Hiort, O., & Holterhus, P. (2000). The molecular basis of male sexual differentiation. *European Journal of Endocrinology*, 142, 101–110.

Hirokawa, K., Yagi, A., & Miyata, Y. (2004). An experimental examination of the effects of sex and masculinity/femininity on psychological, physiological, and behavioral responses during communication situations. *Sex Roles: A Journal of Research*, 51, 91–99.

Hite, S. (1976). *The Hite Report: A Nationwide Study of Female Sexuality*. New York: Dell Books.

Hitt, J., Hendericks, S., Ginsberg, S., & Lewis, J. (1970). Disruption of male but not female sexual behavior in rats by medial forebrain bundle lesions. *Journal of Comparative and Physiological Psychology*, 73, 377–384.

Hobbs, M. (2006). Adult entertainment lawyer wins battle over Georgia obscenity law. *New Jersey Law Journal*, March 27, pNA.

Hocht, S., & Hinkelbein, W. (2005). Postoperative radiotherapy for prostate cancer. *Lancet*, 366, 524–525.

Hodge, D. (2004). Working with Hindu clients in a spiritually sensitive manner. *Social Work*, 49, 27–38.

Hodge, D. (2005). Social work and the house of Islam: Orienting practitioners to the beliefs and values of Muslims in the United States. *Social Work*, 50, 162–173.

Hodson, J. (2006). Clinical: Put HRT risks in perspective. *GP*, February 17, 29.

Hoffman, R. (2003). An argument against routine prostate cancer screening. *Archives of Internal Medicine*, 163, 663–664.

Hoffman, R. (2006). Viewpoint: Limiting prostate cancer screening. *Annals of Internal Medicine*, 144, 438–440.

Hoffman, S., O'Sullivan, L., Harrison, A., Dolezal, C., & Monroe-Wise, A. (2006). HIV risk behaviors and the context of sexual coercion in young adults' sexual interactions: Results from a diary study in rural South Africa. *Sexually Transmitted Diseases*, 33, 52–58.

Hoggard, L. (2006). Women who travel for sun and sex. *The Sunday Independent*, July 16, A5.

Holden, S. (2000). Look! It's the Smiths from Elm Street. *The New York Times*, March 16, C13.

Holder, D., Durant, R., Harris, T., Daniel, J., Obeidallah, D., & Goodman, E. (2000). The association between adolescent spirituality and voluntary sexual activity. *Society for Adolescent Medicine*, 26, 295–302.

Hollander, D. (2006). Skills-oriented counseling holds promise for increasing women's use of barrier methods. *Perspectives on Sexual and Reproductive Health*, 38, 58–59.

Holman, M. (2003). *Reclaiming Your Lost Libido*. Retrieved August 3, 2003, from http://health.discovery.com/centers/womens/sexualhealth/healthysex_print.html.

Holmes, S. (2003). Tadalafil: A new treatment for erectile dysfunction. *British Journal of Urology International*, 92, 466–468.

Holstege, G., Georgiadis, J., Paans, A., Meiners, L., et al. (2003). Brain activation during human male ejaculation. *Journal of Neuroscience*, 23, 9185–9193.

Hoofnagle, J. (2006). Hepatitis B—Preventable and now treatable. *New England Journal of Medicine*, 354, 1074–1076.

Hoover, E. (1997). Memory therapy turns woman's life into nightmare. *The Oregonian*, April 13, A1, A12.

Horton, M. (2005). Circumcision shouldn't hurt. *Fit Pregnancy*, 12, 25.

Horwitz, A., White, H., & Howell-White, S. (1996). Becoming married and mental health: A longitudinal study of a cohort of young adults. *Journal of Marriage and the Family*, 58, 895–907.

Howard, A., Riger, S., Campbell, R., & Wasco, S. (2003). Counseling services for battered women: A comparison of outcomes for physical and sexual assault survivors. *Journal of Interpersonal Violence*, 18, 717–734.

Howard, C., Howard, F., Garfunkel, L., de Blieck, E., & Weitzman, M. (1998). Neonatal circumcision and pain relief: Current training practices. *Pediatrics*, 101, 423–428.

Howard, M., & McCabe, J. (1990). Helping teenagers postpone sexual involvement. *Family Planning Perspectives*, 22, 929–932.

Hoxworth, T., Spencer, N., Peterman, T., Craig, T., Johnson, S., & Maher, J. (2003). Changes in partnerships and HIV risk behavior after partner notification. *Sexually Transmitted Diseases*, 30, 83–88.

Hoyert, D., Danel, I., & Tully, P. (2000). Maternal mortality, United States and Canada, 1982–1997. *Birth*, 27, 4–11.

Hu, D., Vitek, C., Bartholow, B., & Mastro, T. (2003). Key issues for a potential human immunodeficiency virus vaccine. *Clinical Infectious Diseases*, 36, 638–644.

Hudson, T. (2006). Bio-identical hormones: One clinician's perspective. *Townsend Letter for Doctors and Patients*, April, 113–116.

Hudson, T., & Kochan, L. (2005). Vaginitis: Two common causes, bacterial vaginosis and atrophic vaginitis. *Townsend Letter for Doctors and Patients*, August–September, 116–119.

Hughes, J., & Sandler, B. (1987). *"Friends" Raping Friends: Could It Happen to You?* Washington, DC: Association of American Colleges.

Hughes, M., Morrison, K., & Asada, K. (2005). What's love got to do with it? Exploring the impact of maintenance rules, love attitudes, and network support on friends with benefits relationships. *Journal of Sex Research*, 42, 113–118.

Hull, E., Lorrain, D., Du, J., Matuszewich, L., Lumley, L., Putnam, S., & Moses, J. (1999). Hormone– neurotransmitter interactions in the control of sexual behavior. *Behavioral Brain Research*, 105, 105–116.

Human Rights Campaign (2006). Marriage/relationship recognition laws: International. Retrieved August 7, 2006 from http://hrc.org/PrinterTemplate.cfm?Section=Center&CONTENTID=26546.

**Human Rights Watch** (2006). The less they know, the better: Abstinence-only HIV/AIDS programs in Uganda. Retrieved July 18, 2006, from http://hrw.org/reports/2005/uganda 0305/.

**Humphries, K., & Gill, S.** (2003). Risks and benefits of hormone replacement therapy: The evidence speaks. *Canadian Medical Association Journal*, 168, 1001–1010.

**Hunsberger, B.** (2003). Same-sex harassment catches firms off guard. *The Oregonian*, April 6, Cl, C5.

**Hunt, M.** (1974). *Sexual Behavior in the 1970s*. Chicago: Playboy Press.

**Hunter, J.** (1990). Violence against lesbian and gay male youths. *Journal of Interpersonal Violence*, 5, 295–300.

**Huppert, J.** (2006). New detection methods for trichomoniasis may help curb more serious STIs. *Patient Care*, May, 32–36.

**Hurlbert, D., & Whittaker, K.** (1991). The role of masturbation in marital and sexual satisfaction: A comparative study of female masturbators and non-masturbators. *Journal of Sex Education and Therapy*, 17, 272–282.

**Hutchinson, M., & Cooney, T.** (1998). Patterns of parent-teen sexual risk communication: Implications for intervention. *Family Relations*, 47, 185–194.

**Hutti, M.** (2003). New and emerging contraceptive methods. *Association of Women's Health, Obstetric, and Neonatal Nurses Lifelines*, 7, 32–39.

**Huyghe, P.** (2003). *Suo Yang (Koro: The Genital Retraction Syndrome*. Retrieved March 13, 2003, from http://www.omnimag.com/antimater/new/penis.html.

**Hyde, J.** (2004). *Half the Human Experience: The Psychology of Women* (6th edition). Boston, MA: Houghton Mifflin.

**Iervolino, A., Hines, M., Golombok, S., Rust, J., & Plomin, R.** (2005). Genetic and environmental influences on sex-typed behavior during preschool years. *Child Development*, 76, 826–840.

**Illingworth, B.** (2006). Birth control in developing nations. Retrieved June 7, 2006, from http://www.plannedparenthood.org/pp2/portal/files/portal/webzine/globaldispatch.

**Imam, N.** (2006, June 28). Country tops world maternal mortality rating, says NGO. Retrieved July 5, 2006, from http://allafrica.com/stories/printable/200606280407.html.

**Imperato-McGinley, J., Peterson, R., Gautier, T., & Sturla, E.** (1979). Androgens and the evolution of male-gender identity among male pseudohermaphrodites with 5-alpha-reductase deficiency. *New England Journal of Medicine*, 300, 1233–1237.

**Incrocci, L.** (2006). The effect of cancer on sexual function. *The Journal of Sexual Medicine*, 3(suppl. 2), 73.

**Internet World Stats** (2006). World Internet Usage and Population Statistics. Retrieved October 12, 2006 from http://www.InternetWorldStats.com.

**Intersex Society of North America** (2006). *Frequency: How Common Are Intersex Conditions?* Retrieved Jan. 4, 2006, from http://www.isna.org/faq/frequency.html.

**Iovine, V.** (1997a). *The Girlfriends' Guide to Pregnancy*. New York: Perigee.

**Iovine, V.** (1997b). *The Girlfriends' Guide to Surviving the First Year of Motherhood*. New York: Perigee.

**Ireland, D.** (2006). Iraqi exile. *The Advocate*, May 9, 12.

**Ireland, D.** (2006). Iran's solution for gays. *The Advocate*, May 23, 31.

**Isaacs, J.** (2006). Ask the pro/infertility. *Newsweek*, March 13, 66.

**Isely, P., & Gehrenbeck-Shim, D.** (1997). Sexual assault of men in the community. *Journal of Community Psychology*, 25, 159–166.

**Ishii-Kuntz, M.** (1997a). Chinese American families. In M. DeGenova (Ed.), *Families in Cultural Context: Strengths and Challenges in Diversity*. Mountain View, CA: Mayfield.

**Ishii-Kuntz, M.** (1997b). Japanese American families. In M. DeGenova (Ed.), *Families in Cultural Context: Strengths and Challenges in Diversity*. Mountain View, CA: Mayfield.

**Ito, T., Trant, A., & Polan, M.** (2001). A double-blind placebo-controlled study of ArginMax, a nutritional supplement for enhancement of female sexual function. *Journal of Sex and Marital Therapy*, 27, 541–549.

**Iuliano, A., Speizer, I., Santelli, J., & Kendall, C.** (2006). Reasons for contraceptive nonuse at first sex and unintended pregnancy. *American Journal of Health Behavior*, 30, 92–102.

**Jaccard, J., Dittus, P., & Gordon, V.** (1996). Maternal correlates of adolescent sexual and contraceptive behavior. *Family Planning Perspectives*, 28, 159–165.

**Jaccard, J., Dittus, P., & Gordon, V.** (2000). Parent–teen communication about premarital sex. *Journal of Adolescent Research*, 15, 187–208.

**Jack, G., & Zeitlin, S.** (2005). Treatment strategies for a patient with chronic prostatitis. *Patient Care*, 39, 18–24.

**Jackson, G., Rosen, R., Kloner, R., & Kostis, J.** (2006). The second Princeton consensus on sexual dysfunction and cardiac risk: New guidelines for sexual medicine. *The Journal of Sexual Medicine*, 3, 28–36.

**Jacoby, S.** (1999). Great sex: What's age got to do with it? *Modern Maturity*, September–October, 43–45.

**Jain, J., Dutton, C., Harwood, B., & Meckstroth, K.** (2002). A prospective randomized, double-blinded, placebo-controlled trial comparing mifepristone and vaginal misoprostol to vaginal misoprostol alone for elective termination of early pregnancy. *Human Reproduction*, 17, 1477–1482.

**Jakobsen, J., & Pellegrini, A.** (2003). *Love the Sin: Sexual Regulation and the Limits of Religious Tolerance (Sexual Cultures*. New York: New York University Press.

**James, T., & Cinelli. B.** (2003). Exploring gender-based communication styles. *Journal of School Health*, 73, 41–42.

**Jamison, P., & Gebhard, P.** (1988). Penis size increase between flaccid and erect states: An analysis of the Kinsey data. *Journal of Sex Research*, 24, 177–183.

**Jancin, B.** (2005). Teen addiction to cybersex called pervasive. *Family Practice News*, 35, 36–37.

**Jani, A., & Hellman, S.** (2003). Early prostate cancer: Clinical decision-making. *The Lancet*, 361, 1045–1053.

**Janssen, N., & Genta, M.** (2000). The effects of immunosuppressive and anti-inflammatory medications on fertility, pregnancy, and lactation. *Archives of Internal Medicine*, 160, 610–619.

**Janus, S., & Janus, C.** (1993). *The Janus Report on Sexual Behavior*. New York: Wiley.

**Jarrell, A.** (2000). Model maturity. *The Sunday Oregonian*, April 16, L13.

**Jeavons, H.** (2003). Prevention and treatment of vulvo-vaginal candidiasis using exogenous lactobacillus. *Journal of Obstetrical, Gynecological, and Neonatal Nursing*, 32, 287–296.

**Jeffery, C.** (2006). Why women can't win for trying. *Mother Jones*, January/February, 22–23.

**Jegalian, K., & Lahn, B.** (2001a). New answers for men: Y am I infertile? *Scientific American*, February, 61.

**Jegalian, K., & Lahn, B.** (2001b). Why the Y is so weird. *Scientific American*, February, 56–61.

**Jehl, D.** (1998). Western masterpieces locked away from Iranian view. *The Oregonian*, October 4, A7.

**Jenkens, S., & Aube, J.** (2002). Gender differences and gender-related constructs in dating aggression. *Personality and Social Psychology Bulletin*, 28, 1106–1118.

**Jennings, V., Lamprecht, V., & Kowal, D.** (1998). Fertility awareness methods. In R. Hatcher, J. Trussell, F. Stewart, W. Cates, G. Stewart, F. Guest, & D. Kowal (Eds.), *Contraceptive Technology*. New York: Ardent Media.

**Joannides, P.** (1996). *The Guide to Getting It On!* Walport, OR: Goofy Foot Press.

**Johnsen, M.** (2005). Bill targets right to refuse/right to fill debate. *Drug Store News*, 27, 21–22.

**Johnson, B., Carey, M., Marsh, K., Levin, K., & Scott-Sheldon, L.** (2003). Interventions to reduce sexual risk for human immunodeficiency virus in adolescents, 1985–2000. *Archives of Pediatric and Adolescent Medicine*, 157, 381–388.

**Johnson, D.** (2006). Silencing herpes simplex virus with a vaginal microbicide. *New England Journal of Medicine*, 354, 970–971.

**Johnson, H., Weerakoon, P., & Stricker, P.** (2002). The incidence, aetiology, and presentation of Peyronie's disease in Sydney, Australia. *Sexuality and Disability*, 20, 109–113.

**Johnson, K.** (2002). Time, patience needed to find right testosterone level with HRT. *Family Practice News*, 32, 31.

**Johnson, K.** (2003). Viagra may ease women's sexual arousal disorder. *Internal Medicine News*, 36, 29.

**Johnson, M.** (1998). Notification dilemmas: Megan's law spawned flurry of state acts, but implementation proves problematic for all. *The Quill*, 86, 9.

**Johnson, P.** (1998). Pornography drives technology: Why not censor the Internet? In R. Baird & S. Rosenbaum (Eds.), *Pornography: Private Right or Public Menace?* Amherst, NY: Prometheus Books.

**Johnston, S.** (1987). The mind of the molester. *Psychology Today*, February, 60–63.

**Jones, H., & Crocklin, S.** (2000). On assisted reproduction, religion, and civil law. *Fertility and Sterility*, 73, 447–452.

**Jones, K., Lehr, S., & Hewell, S.** (1997). Dyspareunia: Three case reports. *Journal of Obstetrical, Gynecological, and Neonatal Nursing*, 26, 19–23.

**Jones, R.** (2003). The height of vanity: in China, height equals more than beauty. It can land you a job, and even a husband. Richard Jones investigates the growth of a painful beauty trend—and its often tragic consequences. *Marie Claire*, 10, 92–98.

**Jones, R., & Henshaw, S.** (2002). Mifepristone for early medical abortion: Experiences in France, Great Britain, and Sweden. *Perspectives on Sexual and Reproductive Health*, 34, 154–161.

**Jones, R., Darroch, J., & Henshaw, S.** (2002a). Contraceptive use among U.S. women having abortions in 2000–2001. *Perspectives on Sexual and Reproductive Health*, 34, 294–303.

**Jones, R., Darroch, J., & Henshaw, S.** (2002b). Patterns in the socioeconomic characteristics of women obtaining abortions in 2000–2001. *Perspectives on Sexual and Reproductive Health*, 34, 226–235.

**Jones, R., Purcell, A., & Singh, S.** (2005). Adolescents' reports of parental knowledge of adolescents' use of sexual health services and their reactions to mandated parental notification for prescription contraception. *Journal of the American Medical Association*, 93, 340–348.

**Jones, W., Chernovetz, M., & Hansson, R.** (1978). The enigma of androgyny: Differential implications for males and females. *Journal of Consulting and Clinical Psychology*, 46, 298–313.

**Jong, E.** (2003). The zipless fallacy. *Newsweek*, June 30, 48.

**Jorgenson, L., & Wahl, K.** (2000). Psychiatrists as expert witnesses in sexual harassment cases under Daubert and Kumho. *Psychiatric Annals*, 30, 390–396.

**Joyce, T., Kaestner, R., & Colman, S.** (2006). Changes in abortions and births and the Texas parental notification law. *The New England Journal of Medicine*, 354, 1031–1038.

**Juarez, V.** (2006). www.findlovehere.com. *Newsweek*, February 20, 60.

**Juninger, J.** (1997). Fetishism: Assessment and treatment. In D. Laws & W. O'Donohue (Eds.), *Sexual Deviance: Theory, Assessment, and Treatment*. New York: Guilford Press.

**Kabir, A.** (2005). Racial differences in cesareans: An analysis of U.S. 2001 national inpatient sample data. *Obstetrics & Gynecology*, 105, 710-718.

**Kaelin, C., Fuller, A., & Coltrera, F.** (2006). New hopes, longer life. *Newsweek*, April 24, 65.

**Kaestle, C., Morisky, D., & Wiley, D.** (2002). Sexual intercourse and age difference between adolescent females and their romantic partners. *Perspectives on Sexual and Reproductive Health*, 34, 304–309.

**Kagan-Krieger, S.** (1998). Women with Turner syndrome: A maturational and developmental perspective. *Journal of Adult Development*, 5, 125–135.

**Kahn, J., & Hillard, P.** (2006). Progress in preventing cervical cancer and other HPV-related diseases. *Contemporary Pediatrics*, 23, 56–63.

**Kaiser Family Foundation** (2002). *Abortion in the U.S.* Fact sheet. Menlo Park, CA: Henry J. Kaiser Family Foundation.

**Kaiser Family Foundation** (2003a, February). *Seventeen Magazine and Kaiser Family Foundation Release New Survey of Teens About Gender Roles*. Retrieved June 12, 2003, from http://www.kff.org/content/2003/3301.

Kaiser Family Foundation (2003b). *Sex on Television. 3. Content and Context.* Retrieved from http://www.kff .org/content/2003/20030204a/.

Kaiser Family Foundation (2006). Sex on TV 4. Retrieved February 15, 2006, from http://www.kff .org/entmedia/entmedia/0905nr.cfm .

Kaiser, C. (2003). Throwing the backlash off balance. *The Advocate*, October 14, 96.

Kaiser, C. (2004). Civil marriage, civil rights. *The Advocate*, March 30, 72.

Kalb, C. (2003a). Farewell to "Aunt Flo." *Newsweek*, February 3, 48.

Kalb, C. (2006). Marriage: Act II. *Newsweek*, February 20, 62–63.

Kalb, C., & Springen, K. (2006). The war on HPV. *Newsweek*, April 24, 61–64.

Kalick, M., Zebowitz, L., Langlois, J., & Johnson, R. (1998). Does human facial attractiveness honestly advertise health? Longitudinal data on an evolutionary question. *Psychological Science*, 9, 8–13.

Kalof, L., Eby, K., Matheson, J., & Kroska, R. (2001). The influence of race and gender on student self-reports of sexual harassment by college professors. *Gender and Society*, 15, 282–302.

Kane, E. (2006). "No way my boys are going to be like that!" Parents' responses to children's gender noncomformity. *Gender and Society*, 20, 149–176.

Kann, I., Brener, N., & Allensworth, D. (2001). Results from the School Health Policies and Programs Study 2000. *Journal of School Health*, 71, 266–278.

Kantrowitz, B. (1992). Sexism in the schoolhouse. *Newsweek*, February 24, 62–70.

Kantrowitz, B. (2006). Sex & love: The new world. *Newsweek*, February 20, 51–60.

Kantrowitz, B. (2006). The quest for rest. *Newsweek*, April 24, 51–56.

Kapinus, C. (2005). The effect of parental marital quality on young adults' attitudes toward divorce. *Sociological Perspectives*, 48, 319–335.

Kaplan, E. (2004). With God on their side: How Christian fundamentalists trampled science, policy, and democracy in George W. Bush's White House. *SIECUS Report*, 32, 4–8.

Kaplan, H. (1974). *The New Sex Therapy: Active Treatment of Sexual Dysfunction.* New York: Brunner/Mazel.

Kaplan, H. (1979). *Disorders of Sexual Desire.* New York: Brunner/Mazel.

Kaplan, M., & Krueger, R. (1997). Voyeurism: Psychopathology and theory. In D. Laws & W. O'Donohue (Eds.), *Sexual Deviance: Theory, Assessment, and Treatment.* New York: Guilford Press.

Kapoor, D., & Jones, T. (2005). Smoking and hormones in health and endocrine disorders. *European Journal of Endocrinology*, 152, 491–499.

Karama, S., Lecours, A., Leroux, J., Blurgovin, P., et al. (2002). Areas of brain activation in males and females during viewing of erotic film excerpts. *Human Brain Mapping*, 16, 1–13.

Karasz, A., & Anderson, M. (2003). The vaginitis monologues: Women's experiences of vaginal complaints in a primary care setting. *Social Science and Medicine*, 56, 1013–1021.

Karney, B., & Bradbury, T. (1995). The longitudinal course of marital quality and stability: A review of theory, method, and research. *Psychological Review*, 118, 3–34.

Karofsky, P., Zeng, L., & Kosorok, M. (2000). Relationship between adolescent-parental communication and initiation of first intercourse by adolescents. *Journal of Adolescent Health*, 28, 41–45.

Kasl, C. (1999). *If the Buddha Dated: Handbook for Finding Love on a Spiritual Path.* New York: Penguin/ Arkana.

Kassabian, V. (2003). Sexual function in patients treated for benign prostatic hyperplasia. *The Lancet*, 361, 60–62.

Kassing, L., Beesley, D., & Frey, L. (2005). Gender role conflict, homophobia, age, and education as predictors of male rape myth acceptance. *Journal of Mental Health Counseling*, 27, 311–328.

Katz, E. (2003). *I Can't Believe I'm Buying This Book.* Berkeley, CA: Ten Speed Press.

Katz, P., & Ksansnak, K. (1994). Developmental aspects of gender role flexibility and traditionality in middle childhood and adolescence. *Developmental Psychology*, 30, 272–282.

Kaufman, G., Bloch, M., Zaunders, J., Smith, D., & Cooper, D. (2000). Long-term immunological response in HIV-1 infected subjects receiving potent antiretroviral therapy. *AIDS 2000*, 14, 959–969.

Kaunitz, A. (1994). Long-acting injectable contraception with depot medroxyprogesterone acetate. *American Journal of Obstetrics and Gynecology*, 170, 1543–1549.

Keele, B., Van Heuverswyn, F., Li, Y., et al. (2006). Chimpanzee reservoirs of pandemic and nonpandemic HIV-1. Retrieved June 22, 2006, from http://www.sciencexpress.org.

Keller, J. (2002). Blatant stereotype threat and women's math performance. *Sex Roles*, 47, 193–198.

Keller, M., Sadovszky, V., Pankratz, B., & Hermsen, J. (2000). Self-disclosure of HPV infection to sexual partners. *Western Journal of Nursing Research*, 22, 285–302.

Kellett, J. (2000). Older adult sexuality. In L. Szuchman & F. Muscarella (Eds.), *Psychological Perspectives on Human Sexuality.* New York: Wiley.

Kelley, M., & Parsons, B. (2000). Sexual harassment in the 1990s. *Journal of Higher Education*, 71, 548.

Kelley, R. (2005). Going straight for IVF. *Newsweek*, July 4, 55.

Kellogg-Spadt, S. (2006). Innovative treatments for vulvar and sexual pain. Paper presented at the Gumbo Sexualite Upriver: Spicing Up Education & Therapy (AASECT 38th Annual Conference), St. Louis, June/July.

Kelly, J., Hoffman, R., Rompa, D., & Gray, M. (1998). Protease inhibitor combination therapies and perceptions of gay men regarding AIDS severity and the need to maintain safer sex. *AIDS*, 12, F91–F95.

Kelly, M., & McGee, M. (1999). Teen sexuality education in the Netherlands, France, and Germany. *SIECUS Reports*, 27, 11–14.

Kelly, M., Strassberg, D., & Kircher, J. (1990). Attitudinal and experiential correlates of anorgasmia. *Archives of Sexual Behavior*, 19, 165–181.

Kelsberg, G., Bishop, R., & Morton, J. (2006). When should a child with an undescended testis be referred to a urologist? *Journal of Family Practice*, 55, 336–337.

Kempner, M. (2001). Fewer debates about sexuality education as abstinence-only programs take foothold *SIECUS Report, 29,* 4–16.

Kempner, M. (2005). Sex workers: A glimpse into public health perspectives. *SIECUS Report, 33,* 2.

Kennedy, K., & Trussell, J. (1998). Postpartum contraception and lactation. In R. Hatcher, J. Trussell, F. Stewart, W. Cates, G. Stewart, F. Guest, & D. Kowal (Eds.), *Contraceptive Technology.* New York: Ardent Media.

Kennedy, S., Eisfeld, B., & Dickens, S. (2000). Antidepressant-induced sexual dysfunction during treatment with moclobemide, paroxetine, sertraline, and venlafaxine. *Journal of Clinical Psychiatry, 61,* 276–281.

Kent, C., Chaw, J., Wong, W., Liska, S., Gibson, S., et al. (2005). Prevalence of rectal, urethral, and pharyngeal chlamydia and gonorrhea detected in 2 clinical settings among men who have sex with men. *Clinical Infectious Diseases, 41,* 67–74.

Kerin, J., Copper, J., Price, T., & Van Herendael, B. (2003). Hysteroscopic sterilization using a micro-insert device: Results of a multicenter Phase II study. *Human Reproduction, 18,* 1223–1230.

Kerr, K. (2006, May 12). FDA chief's secret "Plan B" meeting. Retrieved June 18, 2006, from http://www .newsday.com/business/ny-bzplan124738768may12, 0,5663803,print.story.

Kesby, M. (2000). Participatory diagramming as a means to improve communication about sex in rural Zimbabwe: A pilot study. *Social Science and Medicine, 50,* 1723–1741.

Kessler, S. (1998). *Lessons from the Intersexed.* New Brunswick, NJ: Rutgers University Press.

Khalsa, A. (2006). Preventive counseling, screening, and therapy for the patient with newly diagnosed HIV infection. *American Family Physician, 73,* 271–272.

Kiel, R., & Nashelsky, J. (2003). Does cranberry juice prevent or treat urinary tract infection? *Journal of Family Practice, 52,* 154–155.

Kilbourn, C., & Richards, C. (2001). Abnormal uterine bleeding. *Postgraduate Medicine, 109,* 137–150.

Kilmartin, C. (1999). Pleasure and performance: Male sexuality. In K. Lebacqz & D. Sinacore-Guinn (Eds.), *Sexuality: A Reader.* Cleveland: Pilgrim Press.

Kim, S., & Seo, K. (1998). Efficacy and safety of fluoxetine, sertraline, and clomipramine in patients with premature ejaculation: A double-blind, placebo controlled study. *Journal of Urology, 159,* 425–427.

Kimlicka, T., Cross, H., & Tarnai, J. (1983). A comparison of androgynous, feminine, masculine, and undifferentiated women on self-esteem, body satisfaction, and sexual satisfaction. *Psychology of Women Quarterly, 1,* 291–294.

Kimura, D. (1992). Sex differences in the brain. *Scientific American, 267,* 118–125.

King, W. (2006). Success rates climb as "test-tube" technology improves. *The Seattle Times,* March 10, pNA.

Kingsberg, S. (2002). The impact of aging on sexual function in women and their partners. *Archives of Sexual Behavior, 31,* 431–437.

Kingsberg, S., Applegarth, L., & Janata, J. (2000). Embryo donation programs and policies in North America: Survey results and implications for health and mental health professionals. *Fertility and Sterility, 73,* 215–220.

Kinkade, S., Meadows, S., & Garcia-Trujillo, J. (2005). Does neonatal circumcision decrease morbidity? *Journal of Family Practice, 54,* 81–82.

Kinsey, A., Pomeroy, W., & Martin, C. (1948). *Sexual Behavior in the Human Male.* Philadelphia: Saunders.

Kinsey, A., Pomeroy, W., Martin, C., & Gebhard, P. (1953). *Sexual Behavior in the Human Female.* Philadelphia: Saunders.

Kipnis, L. (1996). *Bound and Gagged: Pornography and the Politics of Fantasy in America.* New York: Grove Press.

Kirby, D. (2000). Making condoms available in schools. *Western Journal of Medicine, 172,* 149–151.

Kirby, D. (2001). *Emerging Answers: Research Findings on Programs to Reduce Teenage Pregnancy.* Washington, DC: National Campaign to Prevent Teenage Pregnancy.

Kirby, D. (2002). The impact of schools and school programs upon adolescent sexual behavior. *Journal of Sex Research, 39,* 27–33.

Kirchmeyer, C. (1996). Gender roles in decision-making in demographically diverse groups: A case for reviving androgyny. *Sex Roles, 34,* 649–663.

Kirchner, J., & Emmert, D. (2000). Sexually transmitted diseases in women: *Chlamydia trachomatis* and herpes simplex infections. *Postgraduate Medicine, 107,* 55–65.

Kirkpatrick, L., & Davis, K. (1994). Attachment style, gender, and relationship stability: A longitudinal analysis. *Journal of Personality and Social Psychology, 66,* 502–512.

Kissinger, P., Niccolai, L., Magnus, M., Farley, T., Maher, J., Richardson-Alston, G., Dorst, D., Myers, L., & Peterman, T. (2003). Partner notification for HIV and syphilis. *Sexually Transmitted Diseases, 30,* 75–82.

Kissinger, P., Trim, S., Williams, E., Mielke, E., Koporc, K., & Brown, R. (1997). An evaluation of initiatives to improve family planning use by African-American adolescents. *Journal of the National Medical Association, 89,* 110–114.

Kissling, E. (2002, January). *On the Rag on Screen: Menarche in Film and Television.* Retrieved May 25, 2003, from http://www.findarticles.com/cf_0/m2294/ 2002_Jan/90333581/p1/article.jhtml.

Kissling, F. (2003). *The Vatican: Out of Touch with Catholics.* Retrieved June 22, 2003, from http://www .cath4choice.org/spanish/lowbandwidth/youthvatican .htm.

Kitch, M. (2006). Perceptions of gays undergoing an evolution. *The Sunday Oregonian,* August 13, F2.

Klein, J. (2005). Adolescent pregnancy: Current trends and issues. *Pediatrics, 116,* 281–286.

Klein, M. (1991). Why there's no such thing as sexual addiction and why it really matters. In R. Francoeur (Ed.), *Taking Sides: Clashing Views of Controversial Issues in Human Sexuality* (3rd ed.). Guilford, CT: Dushkin.

Klein, M. (1999). Censorship and the fear of sexuality. In J. Elias, V. Elias, V. Bullough, G. Brewer, J. Douglas, & W. Jarvis (Eds.), *Porn 101: Eroticism, Pornography, and the First Amendment.* Amherst, NY: Prometheus Books.

Klein, M. (2000). Sexual intelligence: An electronic newsletter. Retrieved May 3, 2006, from www.sexed .org/newsletters/issue09.html.

Klein, M. (2003). Sex addiction: A dangerous clinical concept. *SIECUS Report*, 31, 8–11.

Klein, M. (2006). *America's War on Sex: The Attack on Law, Lust, and Liberty.* Westport, CT: Praeger.

Kleinplatz, P., & Moser, C. (2004). Toward clinical guidelines for working with BDSM clients. *Contemporary Sexuality*, 38, 1 & 4.

Klinger, K. (2003). Prostitution, humanism, and a woman's choice. *The Humanist*, January–February, 16–19.

Kloer, P. (2003). Upscale vendors cash in on pornography. *Knight Ridder/Tribune Business News*, August 17, E2.

Kluger, J. (2004). The power of love. *Time*, January 19, 62–65.

Knafo, D., & Jaffe, Y. (1984). Sexual fantasizing in males and females. *Journal of Research in Personality*, 19, 451–462.

Knight, K. (2006). Men for sale? Retrieved August 16, 2006, from http://www.dailymail.co.uk/pages/test/print.hrml?in_article_id=400187&in_page_id=1879.

Kobrin, S. (2006, April 15). More women seek vaginal plastic surgery. Retrieved April 15, 2006, from http://www.womensenews.org/article.cfm/dyn/aid/2067/context/archive.

Koch-Straube, U. (1982). Attitude toward sexuality in old age. *Zeitschrift für Gerontologie*, 15, 220–227.

Koehler, J. (2002). Vaginismus: Diagnosis, etiology, and intervention. *Contemporary Sexuality*, 36, i–viii.

Koehler, J., Zangwill, W., & Lotz, L. (2000). *Integrating the Power of EMDR into Sex Therapy.* Paper presented at the 32nd Annual Conference of the American Association of Sex Educators, Counselors, and Therapists, Atlanta, Georgia, May 10–14.

Koen, K., Rompay, V., McChesney, N., Schmidt, K., et al. (2001). Two low doses of tenofovir protect newborn macaques against oral simian immunodeficiency virus infection. *Journal of Infectious Diseases*, 184, 429–438.

Koen, K., Rompay, V., Schmidt, K., Lawson, J., et al. (2002). Topical administration of low-dose tenofovir disoproxil fumarate to protect infant macaques against multiple oral exposure of low doses of simian immunodeficiency virus. *Journal of Infectious Diseases*, 186, 1508–1513.

Kohl, J. (2002). *The Scent of Eros: Mysteries of Odor in Human Sexuality.* Lincoln, NE: iUniverse Inc.

Kolodny, R. (1980). *Adolescent Sexuality.* Paper presented at the Michigan Personnel and Guidance Association Annual Convention, Detroit, November.

Komaromy, M., Bindman, A., Haber, R., & Sande, M. (1993). Sexual harassment in medical training. *New England Journal of Medicine*, 328, 322–326.

Koo, D., Begier, E., Henn, M., Sepkowitz, K., & Kellerman, S. (2006). HIV counseling and testing: Less targeting, more testing. *American Journal of Public Health*, 96, 962–963.

Koo, H., Woodsong, C., Dalberth, B., Viswanathan, M., & Simons-Rudolph, A. (2005). Context of acceptability of topical microbicides: Sexual relationships. *Journal of Social Issues*, 61, 67–93.

Korber, B., Muldoon, M., Theiler, J., Gao, F., Gupta, R., Lapedes, A., Hahn, B., Wolinsky, S., & Bhattacharya, T. (2000). Timing the ancestor of the HIV-1 pandemic strains. *Science*, 288, 1789–1796.

Korenman, S., & Viosca, S. (1992). Use of a vacuum tumescence device in the management of impotence in men with a history of penile implant or severe pelvic disease. *Journal of the American Geriatric Society*, 40, 61–64.

Kort, M. (2006). Denial by delay. *Ms.*, Winter, 12–13.

Koss, L., Gidycz, C., & Wisniewski, N. (1987). The scope of rape: Incidence and prevalence of sexual aggression and victimization in a national sample of higher education students. *Journal of Consulting and Clinical Psychology*, 55, 162–170.

Koss, M., Bailey, J., Yuan, N., Herrera, V., & Lichter, E. (2003). Depression and PTSD in survivors of male violence: Research and training initiatives to facilitate recovery. *Psychology of Women Quarterly*, 27, 130–142.

Koss, M., Figueredo, A., & Prince, R. (2002). Cognitive mediation of rape's mental, physical, and social health impact: Tests of four models in cross-sectional data. *Journal of Consulting and Clinical Psychology*, 70, 926–941.

Koukounas, E., & McCabe, M. (1997). Sexual and emotional variables influencing sexual response to erotica. *Behavior Research and Therapy*, 35, 221–231.

Koumans, E., Sternberg, M., Motamed, C., Kohl, K., Schillinger, J., & Markowitz, L. (2005). Sexually transmitted disease services at U.S. colleges and universities. *Journal of College Health*, 53, 211–217.

Kovacs, A., & Osvath, P. (2006). Genital retraction syndrome in Korean woman: A case of Koro in Hungary. Retrieved January 7, 2006, from http://www .Medscape/abstract/9697166.

Krahe, B., Scheinberger-Olwig, R., & Bieneck, S. (2003). Men's reports of nonconsensual sexual interactions with women: Prevalence and impact. *Archives of Sexual Behavior*, 32, 165–175.

Krahe, B., Waizenhofer, E., & Moller, I. (2003). Women's sexual aggression against men: Prevalence and predictors. *Sex Roles*, 49, 219–232.

Krakow, B., Germain, A., Tandberg, D., Koss, M., Schrader, R., Hollifield, M., Cheng, D., & Edmond, T. (2000). Sleep breathing and sleep movement disorders masquerading as insomnia in sexual-assault survivors. *Comprehensive Psychiatry*, 41, 49–56.

Kreahling, L. (2005). The perils of needles to the body. *The New York Times*, February 1, F5.

Kreinin, T. (2002a). Critical issues about pregnancy and parenting. *SIECUS Report*, 30, 5–6.

Kreinin, T., Rodriquez, M., & Edwards, M. (2001). Adolescents would prefer parents as primary sexuality educators. *SIECUS Report Supplement*, December–January, 1.

Kripke, C. (2006). Cyclic vs. continuous or extended-cycle combined contraceptives. *American Family Physician*, 73, 803.

Krist, A. (2001). Obstetric care in patients with HIV disease. *American Family Physician*, 63, 107–122.

Kristof, N. (2006). Beyond chastity belts. *The New York Times*, May 2, A25.

Kroll, K., & Klein E. (1992). *Enabling Romance*. New York: Harmony Books.

Krone, M., Wald, A., Tabet, S., Paradise, M., Corey, L., & Celum, C. (2000). Herpes simplex virus type 2 shedding in human immunodeficiency virus-negative men who have sex with men: Frequency, patterns, and risk factors. *Clinical Infectious Diseases*, 30, 261–267.

Krujiver, F., Zhou, J., Pool, C., Hoffman, N., Gooren, L., & Swaab, D. (2000). Male-to-female transsexuals have female neuron member in a limbic nucleus. *Journal of Clinical Endocrinology*, 85, 2034–2040.

Ku, L., Sonenstein, F., & Pleck, J. (1993). Young men's risk behaviors for HIV infection and sexually transmitted diseases, 1988 through 1991. *American Journal of Public Health*, 83, 1609–1615.

Kuehn, B. (2005). Syphilis rates rise among men: Trends for other STDs mixed. *Journal of the American Medical Association*, 294, 3072–3073.

Kuipers. H. (1998). Anabolic steroids: Side effects. *Encyclopedia of Sports Medicine and Science*, March 7, pNA.

Kulin, H., Frontera, M., Deuers, L., Bartholomew, M., & Lloyd, T. (1989). The onset of sperm production in pubertal boys. *American Journal of Diseases of Children*, 143, 190–193.

Kunzle, R., Mueller, M., Hanggi, W., & Birkhauser, M. (2003). Semen quality of male smokers and non-smokers in infertile couples. *Fertility and Sterility*, 79, 287–291.

Kurdek, L. (1995a). Developmental changes in relationship quality in gay and lesbian cohabiting couples. *Developmental Psychology*, 31, 86–94.

Kurdek, L. (1995b). Lesbian and gay couples. In A. D'Augelli & C. Patterson (Eds.), *Lesbian, Gay, and Bisexual Identities over the Lifespan*. New York: Oxford University Press.

Kuriansky, J. (1996). Sexuality and television advertising: An historical perspective. *SIECUS Report*, 24, 13–15.

Kuriansky, J., & Simonson, H. (2005). What is tantra? Paper presented at What's New and What Works: Pioneering Solutions for Today's Sexual Issues (AASECT 37th Annual Conference), Portland, OR, May.

Kuzma, C. (2004, October 11). A brief history of marriage. Retrieved June 2, 2006, from http://www .plannedparenthood.org/pp2/portal/files/portal/ webzine/newspoliticsactivism/fea. . . .

Laan, E., & Everaerd, W. (1996). Determinants of female sexual arousal: Psychophysiological theory and data. *Annual Review of Sex Research*, 6, 32–76.

LaBrie, J., Earleywine, M., Schiffman, J., Pedersen, E., & Marriot, C. (2005). Effects of alcohol, expectancies, and partner type on condom use in college males: Event-level analyses. *Journal of Sex Research*, 42, 259–266.

Lacey, R., Reifman, A., Scott, J., Harris, S., & Fitzpatrick, J. (2004). Sexual-moral attitudes, love styles, and mate selection. *Journal of Sex Research*, 41, 121–128.

LaFranchi, H. (2006). AIDS after 25 years. *Oregonian*, May 31, A7.

Lagana, L. (1999). Psychological correlates of contraceptive practices during late adolescence. *Adolescence*, 34, 463–482.

Lain, K., Luppi, P., McGonigal, S., & Roberts, J. (2006). Intracellular adhesion molecule concentrations in women who smoke during pregnancy. *Obstetrics & Gynecology*, 107, 588–594.

Lam, J., Shvarts, O., & Belldegrun, A. (2004). A new era for cryotherapy of prostate cancer? *Contemporary Urology*, 16, 46–56.

Lamb, D., Catanzaro, S., & Moorman, A. (2003). Psychologists reflect on their sexual relationships with clients, supervisees, and students: Occurrence, impact, rationales, and collegial intervention. *Professional Psychology: Research and Practice*, 34, 102–107.

Lambe, E. (1999). Dyslexia, gender, and brain imaging. *Neuropsychologia*, 37, 521–536.

Lambert, T., Kahn, A., & Apple, K. (2003). Pluralistic ignorance and hooking up. *Journal of Sex Research*, 40, 129–133.

Lammers, C., Ireland, M., Resnick, M., & Blum, R. (2000). Influences on adolescents' decisions to postpone onset of sexual intercourse: A survival analysis of virginity among youths ages 13 to 18 years. *Journal of Adolescent Health*, 26, 42–48.

Lamptey, P., Johnson, J., & Khan, M. (2006). The global challenge of HIV and AIDS. *Population Bulletin*, 61, 3–24.

Lance, L. (2004). Attitudes of college students toward contraceptives: A consideration of gender differences. *College Student Journal*, 38, 579–586.

Landau, J. (1997). Out of order: How same-sex harassers beat the rap. *New Republic*, 216, 9–10.

Landen, M., Walinder, J., & Lundstrom, B. (1998). Clinical characteristics of a total cohort of female and male applicants for sex reassignment: A descriptive study. *Acta Psychiatrica Scandinavica*, 97, 189–194.

Landler, M. (2006). World cup brings little pleasure to German brothels. *The New York Times*, July 3, A3.

Landry, D., Kaeser, L., & Richards, C. (1999). Abstinence promotion and the provision of information about contraception in public school district sexuality education policies. *Family Planning Perspectives*, 31, 280–286.

Landry, E. (2002). *Contraceptive Sterilization: Global Issues and Trends*. New York: EngerderHealth.

Lane, F. (2000). *Obscene Profits: The Entrepreneurs of Pornography in the Cyber Age*. New York: Routledge.

Lane, F. (2006). *The Decency Wars: The Campaign to Cleanse American Culture*. New York: Prometheus Books.

Langevin, R. (2003). A study of the psychosexual characteristics of sex killers: Can we identify them before it is too late? *International Journal of Offender Therapy & Comparative Criminology*, 47, 366–382.

Langevin, R., Paitich, D., & Ramsay, G. (1979). Experimental studies of the etiology of genital exhibitionism. *Archives of Sexual Behavior*, 8, 307–331.

Langstrom, N., & Zucker, K. (2005). Transvestic fetishism in the general population: Prevalence and correlates. *Journal of Sex & Marital Therapy*, 31, 87–95.

Lapham, L. (1997). In the garden of tabloid delight. *Harper's Magazine*, August, 35–39, 42, 43.

Larimore, W. (1995). Family-centered birthing: History, philosophy, and need. *Family Medicine*, 27(2), 132–137.

Larimore, W., & Stanford, J. (2000). Postfertilization effects of oral contraceptives and their relationship to informed consent. *Archives of Family Medicine*, 9, 126–133.

Larson, C. (2006). The hormone dilemma. *U.S. News & World Report*, March 6, 66.

Larsson, I., & Svedin, C. (2002). Sexual experiences in childhood: Young adults' recollections. *Archives of Sexual Behavior*, 31, 263–273.

Latty-Mann, H., & Davis, K. (1996). Attachment theory and partner choice: Preference and actuality. *Journal of Social and Personal Relationships*, 13, 5–23.

Lauer, J., & Lauer, R. (1985). Marriages made to last. *Psychology Today*, June, 22–26.

Lauersen, N., & Graves, Z. (1984). Pretended orgasm. *Medical Aspects of Human Sexuality*, 18, 74–81.

Laumann, E., Gagnon, J., Michael, R., & Michaels, S. (1994). *The Social Organization of Sexuality: Sexual Practices in the United States*. Chicago: University of Chicago Press.

Laumann, E., Masi, C., & Zuckerman, E. (1997). Circumcision in the United States: Prevalence, prophylactic effects, and sexual practice. *Journal of the American Medical Association*, 277, 1052–1057.

Laumann, E., Paik, A., & Rosen, R. (1999). Sexual dysfunction in the United States. *Journal of the American Medical Association*, 281, 537–544.

Laumann, E., Paik, A., Glasser, D., & Kang, J. (2006). A cross-national study of subjective sexual well-being among older women and men: Findings from the global study of sexual attitudes and behaviors. *Archives of Sexual Behavior*, 35, 143–159.

Laurent, B. (1995). Intersexuality: A plea for honesty and emotional support. *AHP Perspective*, November–December, 8–9, 28.

Lavee, Y., Sharlin, S., & Katz, R. (1996). The effect of parenting stress on marital quality. *Journal of Family Issues*, 17, 114–135.

Lawless, L. (2006). Healthy vs. unhealthy sex. Retrieved September 30, 2006, from http://www.holisticwisdom.com/newsletter-9-28-06.htm.

Lawrence, A. (2003). Factors associated with satisfaction or regret following male-to-female sex reassignment surgery. *Archives of Sexual Behavior*, 32, 299–316.

Lawrence, A. (2005). Sexuality before and after male-to-female sex reassignment surgery. *Archives of Sexual Behavior*, 34, 147–166.

Leadbeater, B., & Way, N. (1995). *Urban Adolescent Girls: Resisting Stereotypes*. New York: University Press.

Leaper, C., Anderson, K., & Sanders, P. (1998). Moderators of gender effects on parents' talk to their children: A meta-analysis. *Developmental Psychology*, 34, 3–27.

Leavitt, F. (1997). False attribution of suggestibility to explain recovered memory of childhood sexual abuse following extended amnesia. *Child Abuse and Neglect*, 21, 265–272.

Lee, A., & Scheurer, V. (1983). Psychological androgyny and aspects of self-image in women and men. *Sex Roles*, 9, 289–306.

Lee, J. (1974). The styles of loving. *Psychology Today*, 8, 43–51.

Lee, J. (1988). Love-styles. In R. Sternberg & M. Barnes (Eds.), *The Psychology of Love*. New Haven, CT: Yale University Press.

Lee, J. (1998). Ideologies of lovestyle and sexstyle. In V. de Munck (Ed.), *Romantic Love and Sexual Behavior*. Westport, CT: Praeger.

Lee, M., Donahoe, P., Silverman, B., Hasegawa, T., Hasegawa, Y., Gustafson, M., Chang, Y., & MacLaughlin, D. (1997). Measurements of serum Mullerian inhibitory substance in the evaluation of children with nonpalpable gonads. *New England Journal of Medicine*, 336, 1480–1486.

Lehr, S., Demi, A., Dilorio, C., & Facteau, J. (2005). Predictors of father-son communication about sexuality. *Journal of Sex Research*, 42, 119–129.

Leibenluft, E. (1996). Sex is complex. *American Journal of Psychiatry*, 15, 969–972.

Leiblum, S. (2000). Vaginismus: A most perplexing problem. In S. Leiblum & R. Rosen (Eds.), *Principles and Practice of Sex Therapy*. New York: Guilford Press.

Leiblum, S., & Nathan, S. (2002). Persistent sexual arousal syndrome in women: A not uncommon but little recognized complaint. *Sexual & Relationship Therapy*, 17, 191-198.

Leibowitz, D., & Hoffman, J. (2000). Fertility drug therapies: Past, present, and future. *Journal of Obstetrical, Gynecological, and Neonatal Nursing*, 29, 201–210.

Leigh, B. (1989). Reasons for having and avoiding sex: Gender, sexual orientation, and relationship to sexual behavior. *Journal of Sex Research*, 26, 199–208.

Leiner, S. (1997). Urinary tract infections in otherwise healthy nonpregnant adult women. *Physician Assistant*, May, 36–68.

Leitenberg, H., & Henning, K. (1995). Sexual fantasy. *Psychological Bulletin*, 117(3, 469–496.

Leitenberg, H., Detzer, M., & Srebnik, D. (1993). Gender differences in masturbation and the relation of masturbation experience in preadolescence and/or early adolescence to sexual behavior and sexual adjustment in young adulthood. *Archives of Sexual Behavior*, 22, 87–98.

Leland, J. (2000a). The science of women and sex. *Newsweek*, May 29, 46–53.

Leland, J., & Beals, G. (1997). In living color. *Newsweek*, May 5, 58–60.

Lemonick, M. (2000). Teens before their time. *Time*, October 30, 65–74.

Lepowsky, M. (1994). *Fruit of the Motherland: Gender in an Egalitarian Society*. New York: Columbia University Press.

Lerman, S., McAleer, I., & Kaplan, G. (2000). Sex assignment in cases of ambiguous genitalia and its outcome. *Urology*, 55, 8–12.

Leshner, A. (2003). Don't let ideology trump science. *Science*, 302, 1479.

Letourneau, E., Schewe, P., & Frueh, B. (1997). Preliminary evaluation of sexual problems in combat veterans with PTSD. *Journal of Traumatic Stress*, 10, 125–132.

Leuchtag, A. (2003). Human rights, sex trafficking, and prostitution. *The Humanist*, January–February, 10–15.

Levant, R. (1997). *Men and Emotions: A Psychoeducational Approach*. New York: Newbridge Communications.

Lever, J. (1994). Sexual revelations. *The Advocate*, August 23, 17–24.

Lever, J., Frederick, D., & Peplau, L. (2006). Does size matter? Men's and women's views on penis size across the lifespan. *Psychology of Men & Masculinity*, 7, 127.

Levin, R. (2002). The physiology of sexual arousal in the human female: A recreational and procreational synthesis. *Archives of Sexual Behavior*, 31, 405–411.

Levin, R. (2003). Do women gain anything from coitus apart from pregnancy? Changes in the human female genital tract activated by coitus. *Journal of Sex and Marital Therapy*, 29(suppl.), 59–69.

Levin, R. (2003). Is prolactin the biological "off switch" for human sexual arousal? *Sexual and Relationship Therapy*, 18, 237–243.

Levin, R. & Meston, C. (2006). Nipple/breast stimulation and sexual arousal in young men and women. *Journal of Sexual Medicine*. 3, 450-454.

Levine, M., & Troiden, R. (1988). The myth of sexual compulsivity. *Journal of Sex Research*, 25, 347–363.

Levine, R., Sato, S., Hashomoto, T., & Verman, J. (1995). Love and marriage in eleven cultures. *Journal of Cross-Cultural Psychology*, 26, 554–571.

Leventhal-Alexander, J. (2005). Female sexual dysfunction and menopause. Paper presented at the XVII World Congress of Sexology, Montreal, July 10-15.

Levy, A., Crowley, T., & Gingell, C. (2000). Nonsurgical management of erectile dysfunction. *Clinical Endocrinology*, 52, 253–260.

Levy, J. (2001). HIV and AIDS in people over 50. *SIECUS Report*, 30, 10–15.

Levy, S. (1997). On the Net, anything goes. *Newsweek*, July 7, 28–30.

Lew, M. (2004). Adult male survivors of sexual abuse: Sexual issues in treatment and recovery. *Contemporary Sexuality*, 38, i–v.

Lewis, R., & Heaton, J. (2000). A novel strategy for individualizing erectile dysfunction treatment. *Patient Care*, January 30, 91–99.

Leye, E., Powell, R., Nienhuis, G., & Claeys, P. (2006). Health care in Europe for women with genital mutilation. *Health Care for Women International*, 27, 362–378.

Li, D., Liu, L., & Odouli, R. (2003). Exposure to non-steroidal anti-inflammatory drugs during pregnancy and risk of miscarriage: Population based cohort study. *British Medical Journal*, 327, 368–374.

Liang, L. (2000). Most popular birth control? Sterilization. *The Sunday Oregonian*, September 24, L13.

Lidster, C., & Horsburgh, M. (1994). Masturbation: Beyond myth and taboo. *Nursing Forum*, 29(3), 18–26.

Liebowitz, M. (1983). *The Chemistry of Love*. Boston: Little, Brown.

Lief, H., & Hubschman, L. (1993). Orgasm in the postoperative transsexual. *Archives of Sexual Behavior*, 22, 145–155.

Ligos, M. (2000). Harassment suits hit the dot-coms. *New York Times*, April 12, G1.

Lim, L. (1998). *The Sex Sector*. Geneva: International Labour Office.

Lindberg, L., Frost, J., Sten, C., & Dailard, C. (2006). The provision and funding of contraceptive services at publicly funded family planning agencies: 1995–2003. *Perspectives on Sexual and Reproductive Health*, 38, 37–46.

Lindholm, J., Lunde, I., Rasmussen, O., & Wagner, G. (1980). Gonadal and sexual functions in tortured Greek men. *Danish Medical Bulletin*, 27, 243–245.

Linskey, A. (2006). Police target Internet-advertised prostitution. *Baltimore Sun*, August 9, pNA.

Linz, D., Wilson, B., & Donnerstein, E. (1992). Sexual violence in the mass media: Legal solutions, warnings, and mitigation through education. *Journal of Social Issues*, 48, 145–171.

Lips, H. (1997). *Sex and Gender* (2nd ed.). Mountain View, CA: Mayfield.

Lisotta, C. (2006). Radical Islam in your backyard. *The Advocate*, May 23, 30–32.

Liu, C. (2003). Does quality of marital sex decline with duration? *Archives of Sexual Behavior*, 32, 55–60.

Liu, P., Swerdloff, R., Christenson, P., & Gandelsman, D. (2006). Rate, extent, and modifiers of spermatogenic recovery after hormonal male contraception: An integrated analysis. *The Lancet*, 367, 1412–1421.

Liu, X., Zha, J., Chen, H., Nishitani, J., Camargo, P., Cole, S., & Zack, J. (2003). Human immunodeficiency virus type I infection and replication in normal human oral keratinocytes. *Journal of Virology*, 77, 3470–3476.

Lively, V., & Lively, E. (1991). *Sexual Development of Young Children*. Albany, NY: Delmar.

Loftus, E., Polonsky, S., & Fullilove, M. (1994). Memories of childhood sexual abuse: Remembering and repressing. *Psychology of Women Quarterly*, 18, 67–84.

London, S. (2004). Risk of pregnancy-related death is sharply elevated for women 35 and older. *Perspectives on Sexual and Reproductive Health*, 36, 87–88.

London, S. (2006). Consistent condom use reduces the risk of type 2 herpes virus. *Perspectives on Sexual and Reproductive Health*, 38, 54–55.

Lonergan, S., & Hern, G. (2006). Refresher course on sexually transmitted diseases. *Emergency Medicine*, January, 33–46.

Long, V. (2002). Contraceptives choices: New options in the U.S. market. *SIECUS Report*, 31, 13–18.

Lonsway, K., & Fitzgerald, L. (1994). Rape myths. *Psychology of Women Quarterly*, 18, 133–164.

Looy, H., & Bouma, H. (2005). The nature of gender: Gender identity in persons who are intersexed or transgendered. *Journal of Psychology and Theology*, 33, 166–178.

LoPiccolo, J. (1989). *Sexual Dysfunctions: Advances in Diagnosis and Treatment*. Workshop for the Oregon Division of the American Association for Marriage and Family Therapy, Portland, Oregon, April.

LoPiccolo, J. (2000). *Post-Modern Sex Therapy: An Integrated Approach*. Paper presented at the 32nd Annual Conference of the American Association of Sex Educators, Counselors, and Therapists, Atlanta, Georgia, May 10–14.

Lorch, D., & Mendenhall, P. (2000). A war's hidden tragedy. *Newsweek*, August, 35–36.

Loughlin, K. (2005). Penile carcinoma: New answers to 6 controversial questions. *Contemporary Urology*, 17, 26–32.

Louis, M., Wasserheit, J., & Gayle, H. (1997). Janus considers the HIV pandemic: Harnessing recent advances to enhance AIDS prevention [editorial]. *American Journal of Public Health*, 87, 10–12.

Loulan, J. (1984). *Lesbian Sex*. San Francisco: Spinsters Ink.

Love, P. (2001). *The Truth About Love*. New York: Simon & Schuster.

Love, S., & Rochman, S. (2006). Going natural: Are "bio-identical" hormones better than synthetics for menopausal relief? *Ms.*, Spring, 63–64.

Lowenstein, L. (2002). Fetishes and their associated behavior. *Sexuality and Disability*, 20, 135–147.

Lown, J., & Dolan, E. (1988). Financial challenges in remarriage. *Lifestyles: Family and Economic Issues*, 9, 73–88.

Loy, P., & Stewart, L. (1984). The extent and effects of the sexual harassment of working women. *Sociological Focus*, 17, 31–43.

Lucentini, J. (2005). Love is like an addiction: Looking for correlates in human and animal attraction. *The Scientist*, 19, 20–21.

Lue, T., Basson, R., Rosen, R., & Giuliano, F. (2004). *Second International Consultation on Sexual Medicine: Sexual Dysfunctions in Men and Women.* Paris: Health Publications.

Lue, T., Giuliano, F., Montorsi, F., & Rosen, R. (2004). Summary of the recommendations on sexual dysfunctions in men. *The Journal of Sexual Medicine*, 1, 6–23.

Lukwago, S., Kreuter, M., Holt, C., & Steger-May, K. (2003). Sociocultural correlates of breast cancer knowledge and screening in urban African American women. *American Journal of Public Health*, 93, 1271–1274.

Lurie, P., & Drucker, E. (1997). An opportunity lost: HIV infections associated with lack of a national needle-exchange programme in the U.S.A. *The Lancet*, 349, 604–608.

Lutfey, K., Link, C., & McKinlay, F. (2006). Prevalence and predictors of female sexual dysfunction: Results from the Boston Area Community Health (Back) Survey. Paper presented at the Sexual Medicine Society of North America Fall Meeting, New York, November.

Lyman, F. (2006). The geography of breast cancer. *Ms.*, Fall, 47–51.

Lynch, C., Sinnott, J., Holt, D., & Herold, A. (1991). Use of antibiotics during pregnancy. *American Family Physician*, 43, 1365–1368.

Lynch, D., Krantz, S., Russell, J., Hornberger, L., & Van Ness, C. (2000). HIV infection: A retrospective analysis of adolescent high-risk behaviors. *Journal of Pediatric Health Care*, 14, 20–25.

Lynxwiler, J., & Gay, D. (1994). Reconsidering race differences in abortion attitudes. *Social Science Quarterly*, 75, 67–84.

Lytton, H., & Romney, D. (1991). Parents' differential socialization of boys and girls: A meta-analysis. *Psychological Bulletin*, 109, 267–296.

Maccoby, E. (1988). Gender as a social category. *Developmental Psychology*, 26, 755–765.

Maccoby, E. (1990). Gender and relationships: A developmental account. *American Psychologist*, 45, 513–520.

Maccoby, E. (1998). *The Two Sexes: Growing Up Apart, Coming Together.* Cambridge: Harvard University Press.

Maccoby, E., & Jacklin, C. (1987). Gender segregation in childhood. *Advances in Child Development and Behavior*, 20, 239–287.

MacDonald, T., MacDonald, G., Zanna, M., & Fong, G. (2000). Alcohol, sexual arousal, and intentions to use condoms in young men: Applying alcohol myopia theory to risky sexual behavior. *Health Psychology*, 19, 290–298.

MacGeorge, E., Graves, A., Feng, B., & Gillihan, S. (2004). The myth of gender cultures: Similarities outweigh differences in men's and women's provision of and responses to supportive communication. *Sex Roles: A Journal of Research*, 50, 143–175.

MacKay, A., Berg, C., King, J., & Duran, C. (2006). Pregnancy-related mortality among women with multifetal pregnancies. *Obstetrics & Gynecology*, 107, 563–568.

Mackellar, D., Valleroy, L., Secura, G., & Behel, S. (2002). *Unrecognized HIV Infection, Risk Behaviors, and Misperceptions of Risk Among Young Men Who Have Sex with Men: 6 United States Cities, 1994–2000.* Paper presented at the 14th International AIDS Conference, Barcelona, Spain, July 5–12.

MacKinnon, C. (1979). *Sexual Harassment of Working Women.* New Haven, CT: Yale University Press.

Macklon, N., & Fauser, B. (1999). Aspects of ovarian follicle development throughout life. *Hormone Research*, 52, 161–170.

MacLean, R. (2005). Odds of penile HPV are reduced for circumcised men and condom users. *International Family Planning Perspectives*, 31, 42.

Mah, K., & Binik, Y. (2002). Do all orgasms feel alike? Evaluating a two-dimensional model of orgasm experience across gender and sexual context. *Journal of Sex Research*, 39, 104–113.

Mahoney, S. (2003). Seeking love: The 50-plus dating game has never been hotter. *AARP*, November–December, 57–66.

Majewska, M. (1996). Sex differences in brain morphology and pharmacodynamics. In M. Jensvold & U. Halbreich (Eds.), *Psychopharmacology and Women: Sex, Gender, and Hormones.* Washington, DC: American Psychiatric Press.

Makadon, H. (2006). Improving health care for the lesbian and gay communities. *New England Journal of Medicine*, 354, 895–897.

Malamuth, N., & Check, J. (1981). The effects of mass media exposure on acceptance of violence against women: A field experiment. *Journal of Research in Personality*, 15, 436–446.

Malamuth, N., Haber, S., & Feshback, S. (1980). Testing hypotheses regarding rape: Exposure to sexual violence, sex differences, and the normality of rapists. *Journal of Research in Personality*, 14, 121–137.

Malesky, L., & Ennis, L. (2004). Supportive distortions: An analysis of posts on a pedophile Internet message board. *Journal of Addictions & Offender Counseling*, 24, 92–100.

Mallis, D., Moisidis, K., Kirana, P., & Papaharitou, S. (2006). Moderate and severe erectile dysfunction equally affects life satisfaction. *The Journal of Sexual*

*Medicine*, 3, 442–449.

**Malloy, K., & Patterson, M.** (1992). *Birth or Abortion? Private Struggles in a Political World.* New York: Plenum Press.

**Maltz, W.** (2001c). *The Sexual Healing Journey: A Guide for Survivors of Sexual Abuse.* New York: Quill.

**Maltz, W.** (2003). Treating the sexual intimacy concerns of sexual abuse. *Contemporary Sexuality*, 37, I–vii.

**Maltz, W., & Boss, S.** (1997). *In the Garden of Desire.* New York: Broadway Books.

**Mandoki, M., Sumner, G., Hoffman, R., & Riconda, D.** (1991). A review of Klinefelter's syndrome in children and adolescents. *Journal of the American Academy of Child and Adolescence Psychiatry*, 30, 167–172.

**Manecke, R., & Mulhall, J.** (1999). Medical treatment of erectile dysfunction. *Annals of Medicine*, 31, 388–398.

**Manji, I.** (2006). My Islam. *The Advocate*, May 23, 33.

**Manlove, J., Ryan, S., & Franzetta, K.** (2004). Contraceptive use and consistency in U.S. teenagers' most recent sexual relationships. *Perspectives on Sexual and Reproductive Health*, 36, 265–275.

**Mannino, D., Klevens, R., & Flanders, W.** (1994). Cigarette smoking: An independent risk factor for impotence? *American Journal of Epidemiology*, 140, 1003–1008.

**Manns, M., & Wedemeyer, H.** (2004). Treatment of hepatitis C in HIV-infected patients. *Journal of the American Medical Association*, 292, 2909–2913.

**Mansfield, P., Voda, A., & Koch, P.** (1995). Predictors of sexual response changes in heterosexual midlife women. *Health Values: The Journal of Health Behavior, Education, and Promotion*, 19, 10–20.

**Manson, J., & Bassuk, S.** (2006). Is estrogen for you? *Newsweek*, April 24, 72–73.

**Mantell, J., Morar, N., Myer, L., & Ramjee, G.** (2006). "We have our protector": misperceptions of protection against HIV among participants in a microbicide efficacy trial. *American Journal of Public Health*, 96, 1073–1077.

**Mao, C., Koutsky, L., Ault, K., Wheeler, C., et al.** (2006). Efficacy of human papillomavirus-16 vaccine to prevent cervical intraepithelial neoplasia. *Obstetrics & Gynecology*, 107, 18–27.

**Maravilla, K., Cao, Y., Garland, P., Echelard, D., Heiman, J., Hart, L., Peterson, B., & Weisskoff, R.** (2000). Reproducibility of serial MR measurement of female sexual arousal response. RSNA Hot Topic presentation, Chicago, November 2000. Abstract available in *Radiology*, 218, 610 (2000).

**Maravilla, K., Heiman, J., Garland, P., Cao, Y., Carter, W., Peterson, B., & Weisskoff, R.** (2003). Dynamic MR imaging of the sexual arousal response in women. *Journal of Sex and Marital Therapy*, 29(suppl.), 71–76.

**Marchione, M.** (2003). Breast cancer risk falls with aspirin, ibuprofen use. *The Oregonian*, April 10, A15.

**Marchione, M.** (2006). Studies test AIDS abstinence emphasis. *Oregonian*, March 28, A2.

**Marcus, D., & Miller, R.** (2003). Sex differences in judgments of physical attractiveness: A social relations analysis. *Personality and Social Psychology Bulletin*, 29, 325-335.

**Margolis, L.** (2000). Ethical principles for analyzing

dilemmas in sex research. *Health Education and Behavior*, 27, 24–27.

**Marin, A., & Guadagno, R.** (1999). Perceptions of sexual harassment as a function of labeling and reporting. *Sex Roles*, 41, 921–940.

**Marin, B., Kirby, D., Hudes, E., Coyle, K., & Gomez, C.** (2006). Boyfriends, girlfriends and teenagers' risk of sexual involvement. *Perspectives on Sexual and Reproductive Health*, 38, 76–83.

**Marin, R., & Miller, S.** (1997). Ellen steps out. *Newsweek*, April 14, 65–67.

**Markowitz, J., Donovan, J., DeVane, C., & Ruan, R.** (2003). Effect of St. John's wort on drug metabolism by induction of cytochrome P450 3A4 enzyme. *Journal of the American Medical Association*, 290, 1500–1504.

**Marshall, D.** (1971). Sexual behavior on Mangaia. In D. Marshall & R. Suggs (Eds.), *Human Sexual Behavior: Variations in the Ethnographic Spectrum.* Englewood Cliffs, NJ: Prentice Hall.

**Marshall, W.** (1988). The use of sexually explicit stimuli by rapists, child molesters, and nonoffenders. *Journal of Sex Research*, 25, 267–288.

**Marshall, W.** (1993). A revised approach to the treatment of men who sexually assault adult females. In G. Hall, R. Hirschman, J. Graham, & M. Zaragoza (Eds.), *Sexual Aggression: Issues in Etiology, Assessment, and Treatment.* Washington, DC: Taylor & Francis.

**Marshall, W., Eccles, A., & Barbaree, H.** (1991). The treatment of exhibitionists: A focus on sexual deviance versus cognitive and relationship features. *Behaviour Research and Therapy*, 29, 129–135.

**Marson, C.** (2005). Impact on contraceptive practice of making emergency hormonal contraception available over the counter in Great Britain: Repeated cross sectional surveys. *British Medical Journal*, July 11.

**Martin, T., & Bumpass, L.** (1989). Recent friends in marital disruption. *Demography*, 26, 37–51.

**Martinez, G., Chandra, A., Abma, J., Jones, J., Mosher, W.** (2006). Fertility, contraception, and fatherhood: Data on men and women from Cycle 6 (2002) of the National Survey of Family Growth. *National Center for Health Statistics. Vital Health Stat* 23(26).

**Martinson, F.** (1994). *The Sexual Life of Children.* Westport, CT: Bergin & Garvey.

**Marvan, M., Cortes-Iniestra, S., & Gonzalez, R.** (2005). Beliefs about and attitudes toward menstruation among young and middle-aged Mexicans. *Sex Roles: A Journal of Research*, 53, 273–280.

**Marvan, M., Ramirez-Esparza, D., Cortes-Iniestra, S., & Chrisler, J.** (2006). Development of a new scale to measure beliefs about and attitudes toward menstruation (BATM): Data from Mexico and the United States. *Health Care for Women International*, 27, 453–473.

**Marx, J., & Hopper, F.** (2005). Faith-based versus fact-based social policy: The case of teenage pregnancy prevention. *Social Work*, 50, 280–282.

**Marx, T., & Mehta, A.** (2003). Polycystic ovary syndrome: Pathogenesis and treatment over the short and long term. *Cleveland Clinic Journal of Medicine*, 70, 31–41.

Marzucco, J. (2005). Premature ejaculation: Medical and mental health working together. Paper presented at the XVII World Congress of Sexology, Montreal, July 10-15.

Masters, W., & Johnson, V. (1961). Orgasm, anatomy of the female. In A. Ellis & A. Abarbonel (Eds.), *Encyclopedia of Sexual Behavior*, v. 2. New York: Hawthorn.

Masters, W., & Johnson, V. (1966). *Human Sexual Response*. Boston: Little, Brown.

Masters, W., & Johnson, V. (1970). *Human Sexual Inadequacy*. Boston: Little, Brown.

Masters, W., & Johnson, V. (1976). *The Pleasure Bond*. New York: Bantam Books.

Matek, O. (1988). Obscene phone callers. *Journal of Social Work and Human Sexuality*, 7, 113–130.

Mathers, C., & Loncar, D. (2006). Projections of global mortality and burden of disease from 2002 to 2030. Retrieved November 29, 2006, from http://dx.doi.org/10.1371/journal.pmed.0030442.

Mathes, E., & Verstrate, C. (1993). Jealous aggression: Who is the target, the beloved or the rival? *Psychological Reports*, 72, 1071–1074.

Mathieu, C., Courtois, F., & Noreau, L. (2005). Sexual activities, desire and sensations in 227 paraplegic and tetraplegic men and women. Paper presented at the World Congress of Sexology, Montreal, Canada, July 10–15.

Matteo, S., & Rissman, E. (1984). Increased sexual activity during the midcycle portion of the human menstrual cycle. *Hormones and Behavior*, 18, 249–255.

Matthews, G., McGee, K., & Goldstein, M. (1997). Microsurgical reconstruction following failed vasectomy reversal. *Journal of Urology*, 157, 844–846.

May, R. (1969). *Love and Will*. New York: Norton.

Mayo Clinic Health Oasis (1999). *Urinary Tract Infections*. Retrieved November 23, 1999, from http://cnn.com/HEALTH/mayo/9911/23/uti/.

Mazur, T. (2005). Gender dysphoria and gender change in androgen insensitivity or micropenis. *Archives of Sexual Behavior*, 34, 411–421.

McBride, C., Paikoff, R., & Holmbeck, G. (2003). Individual and familial influences on the onset of sexual intercourse among urban African American adolescents. *Journal of Consulting* and *Clinical Psychology*, 71, 159–167.

McCabe M., & Wauchope, M. (2005). Behavioral characteristics of men accused of rape: Evidence for different types of rapists. *Archives of Sexual Behavior*, 34, 241–253.

McCabe, M. (1999). The interrelationship between intimacy, relationship functioning, and sexuality among men and women in committed relationships. *Canadian Journal of Human Sexuality*, 8, 31–39.

McCarthy, B. (2001). *Primary and Secondary Prevention of Sexual Problems and Dysfunction*. Paper presented at the 33rd Annual Conference of the American Association of Sex Educators, Counselors, and Therapists, San Francisco, May 2–6.

McCarthy, B. (2006). Male inhibited sexual desire. Paper presented at the Gumbo Sexualite Upriver: Spicing Up Education & Therapy (AASECT 38th Annual Conference), St. Louis, June/July.

McCollum, C. (2006). New PBS chief earns reporters' respect with frank talk about FCC, indecency. *San Jose Mercury News*, July 31, pNA.

McCormick, S. (2002). Breast cancer activism: Moving beyond the mammography debate. *Ms.*, Summer, 4–5.

McCoy, N., & Pitino, L. (2002). Pheromonal influences on sociosexual behavior in young women. *Physiology and Behavior*, 75, 367–375.

McCullough, A., Tsend, L., & Seigel, R. (2006). Women's satisfaction with sexual intercourse is associated with their partner's improved erectile function and satisfaction after treatment of erectile dysfunction with Viagra (sildenafil citrate). *The Journal of Sexual Medicine*, 3 (suppl. 3), 224–286.

McElroy, W. (1995). *A Woman's Right to Pornography*. New York: St. Martin's Press.

McEwen, B. (1997). Meeting report: Is there a neurobiology of love? *Molecular Psychiatry*, 2, 15–16.

McEwen, B. (2001). Estrogen effects on the brain: Multiple sites and molecular mechanisms. *Journal of Applied Physiology*, 91, 2785–2801.

McFarlane, J., Martin, C., & Williams, T. (1988). Mood fluctuations: Women versus men and menstrual versus other cycles. *Psychology of Women Quarterly*, 12, 201–224.

McFarlane, M., Bull, S., & Reitmeijer, C. (2002). Young adults on the Internet: Risk behaviors for sexually transmitted diseases and HIV. *Journal of Adolescent Health*, 31, 11–16.

McGinn, D. (2006). Marriage by the numbers. *Newsweek*, June 5, 40–48.

McGinn, S., & Skipp, C. (2002). Does Gran get it on? *Newsweek*, June 3, 10.

McGinnis, M. (2005). Kinder cut. *Prevention*, 57, 127.

McKay, A. (2005). Sexuality and substance use: The impact of tobacco, alcohol, and selected recreational drugs on sexual function. *Canadian Journal of Human Sexuality*, 14, 47–56.

McKibben, A., Proulx, J., & Lusignan, R. (1994). Relationships between conflict, affect, and deviant sexual behaviors in rapists and pedophiles. *Behavior Research and Therapy*, 32, 571–575.

McLaren, A. (1990). *A History of Contraception: From Antiquity to the Present Day*. Cambridge, MA: Basil Blackwell.

McLaren, C., & Ringe, A. (2006). Curious mental illnesses around the world. Retrieved January 7, 2006, from http://www.stayfreemagazine.org/archives/21/mental_illness.html.

McLean, L., & Gallop, R. (2003). Implications of childhood sexual abuse for adult borderline personality disorder and complex posttraumatic stress disorder. *American Journal of Psychiatry*, 160, 369–371.

McNaught, J., & Jamieson, M. (2005). Barrier and spermicidal contraceptives in adolescence. *Adolescent Medicine*, 16, 495–515.

McNeil, E., & Rubin, Z. (1977). *The Psychology of Being Human*. San Francisco: Canfield Press.

McNeill, B., Prieto, L., Niemann, Y., Pizarro, M., Vera, E., & Gomez, S. (2001). Current directions in Chicana/o psychology. *Counseling Psychologist*, 29, 5–17.

McNicholas, T., Dean, J., Mulder, H., Carnegie, C., & Jones, N. (2003). Andrology. *British Journal of Urology International*, 91, 69–74.

McNiven, P., Hodnett, E., & O'Brien-Pallas, L. (1992). Supporting women in labor: A work sampling study of the activities of labor and delivery nurses. *Birth*, 19, 3–8.

McPartland, T., Weaver, B., Lee, S., & Koutsky, L. (2005). Men's perceptions and knowledge of human papillomavirus (HPV) infection and cervical cancer. *Journal of American College Health*, 53, 225–230.

McVary, K., Rosen, R., Ho, K., & Kell, S. (2006). Effect of Dapoxetine on intravaginal ejaculatory latency time in men with lifelong or acquired premature ejaculation. Paper presented at the Sexual Medicine Society of North America Fall Meeting, New York, November.

Meana, M., & Nunnink, S. (2006). Gender differences in the content of cognitive distraction during sex. *The Journal of Sex Research*, 43, 59–68.

Medical Center for Human Rights (1995). *Characteristics of Sexual Abuse of Men During War in the Republic of Croatia and Bosnia*. Zagreb, Croatia: Medical Center for Human Rights.

Meeks, B., Hendrick, S., & Hendrick, C. (1998). Communication, love, and relationship satisfaction. *Journal of Social and Personal Relationships*, 15, 755–773.

Mehta, S., Rothman, R., Kelen, G., Quinn, T., & Zenilman, J. (2001). Clinical aspects of diagnosis of gonorrhea and chlamydia infection in an acute care setting. *Clinical Infectious Diseases*, 32, 655–659.

Meier, E. (2000). RU-486 and implications for use among adolescents seeking an abortion. *Pediatric Nursing*, 26, 93–94.

Meiselman, K. (1978). *Incest*. San Francisco: Jossey-Bass.

Melby, T. (2002a). Intersex interrupted. *Contemporary Sexuality*, 36, 1–6.

Melby, T. (2002b). Pain and (possibly) a loss of pleasure. *Contemporary Sexuality*, 36, 1–6.

Melby, T. (2004). Spotlight on a hidden crime. *Contemporary Sexuality*, 38, 1–4.

Melchert, T., & Parker, R. (1997). Different forms of childhood abuse and memory. *Child Abuse and Neglect*, 21, 125–135.

Meldrum, K., & Rink, R. (2005). Nonspecific penile anomalies: Practical management in infants and children. *Contemporary Urology*, 17, 13–20.

Meltzer, D. (2005). Complications of body piercing. *American Family Physician*, 72, 2029.

Menvielle, E. (2004). Parents struggling with their child's gender issues. *The Brown University Child and Adolescent Behavior Letter*, 20, 1–3.

Merkin, D. (2006). Our vaginas, ourselves. *The New York Times Magazine*, January 1, 13.

Meschke, L., Bartholomae, S., & Zentall, S. (2000). Adolescent sexuality and parent–adolescent processes: Promoting healthy teen choices. *Family Relations*, 49, 143–154.

Messenger, J. (1971). Sex and repression in an Irish folk community. In D. Marshall & R. Suggs (Eds.), *Human Sexual Behavior: Variations in the Ethnographic Spectrum*. Englewood Cliffs, NJ: Prentice Hall.

Meston, C. (2000). The psychophysiological assessment of female sexual function. *Journal of Sex Education and Therapy*, 25, 6–16.

Meston, C., & Worcel, M. (2002). The effects of yohimbine plus L-arginine glutamate on sexual arousal in postmenopausal women with sexual arousal disorder. *Archives of Sexual Behavior*, 31, 323–332.

Meston, C., Gorzalka, B., & Wright, J. (1997). Inhibition of subjective and physiological sexual arousal in women by clonidine. *Psychosomatic Medicine*, 59, 399–407.

Meston, C., Rellini, A., & Heiman, J. (2006). Women's history of sexual abuse, their sexuality, and sexual self-schemas. *Journal of Consulting Clinical Psychology*, 74, 229–236.

Metz, M., & McCarthy, B. (2004). A biopsychosocial approach to evaluating and treating premature ejaculation. *Contemporary Sexuality*, 38, i–vii.

Meyer, P. (2006). Former sex worker hopes for fresh start back in Korea. *Dallas Morning News*, May 15, pNA.

Meyer, W., Webb, A., Stuart, C., Finkelstein, J., Lawrence, B., & Walker, P. (1986). Physical and hormonal evaluation of transsexual patients: A longitudinal study. *Archives of Sexual Behavior*, 15, 121–138.

Meyer-Bahlburg, H. (2005). Introduction: Gender dysphoria and gender change in persons with intersexuality. *Archives of Sexual Behavior*, 34, 371–373.

Meyer-Bahlburg, H., Gruen, R., New, M., Bell, J., Morishima, A., Shimski, M., Bueno, Y., Vargas, I., & Baker, S. (1996). Gender change from female to male in classical congenital adrenal hyperplasia. *Hormones and Behavior*, 30, 319–322.

Meyerhoff, M. (2004). An androgynous generation? *Pediatrics for Parents*, 21, 8–9.

Meyers, D. (2005). Screening for gonorrhea. *American Family Physician*, 72, 1799–1802.

Mezin, Z. (2006). France's birth rate booms but marriage loses favor. *The Oregonian*, January 29, A17.

Michael, R., Gagnon, J., Laumann, E., & Kolata, G. (1994). *Sex in America*. Boston: Little, Brown.

Michaels, D. (1997). Cyber-rape: How virtual is it? *Ms.*, March–April, 68–72.

Michelson, D., Kociban, K., Tamura, R., & Morrison, M. (2002). Mirtazapine, yohimbine, or olanzapine augmentation therapy for serotonin reuptake-associated female sexual dysfunction: A randomized, placebo controlled study. *Journal of Psychiatric Research*, 36, 147–152.

Midyett, L., Moore, W., & Jacobson, J. (2003). Are pubertal changes in girls before age 8 benign? *Pediatrics*, 111, 47–51.

Migeon, C., Wisniewski, A., Gearhart, J., Meyer-Bahlburg, H., Rock, J., Brown, T., Casella, S., Maret, A., Ngai, K., & Money, J. (2002). Ambiguous genitalia with perineoscrotal hypospadias in 46,XY individuals: Long-term medical, surgical, and psychosexual outcome. *Pediatrics*, 110, 616–621.

Milbourn, T. (2006). Great-grandma, 62, has baby; she says, "Age is a number." *The Sacramento Bee*, February 19, pNA.

Miletski, H. (2002). *Understanding Bestiality and Zoophilia*. Bethesda, MD: East-West Publishing.

Milhausen, R., & Herold, E. (1999). Does the sexual double standard still exist? Perceptions of university women. *Journal of Sex Research*, 36, 361–368.

Mill, J., & Anarfi, J. (2002). HIV risk environment for Ghanaian women: Challenges to prevention. *Social Science and Medicine*, 54, 325–337.

Miller, J., & Haynes, J. (Eds.) (2003). *Inconceivable Conceptions: Psychotherapy, Fertility, and the New Reproductive Technologies*. London: Brunner-Routledge.

Miller, K. (2006). Correct and consistent use of condoms in preventing STDs. *American Family Physician*, 73, 703–706.

Miller, K., & Graves, J. (2000). Update on the prevention and treatment of sexually transmitted diseases. *American Family Physician*, 61, 379–386.

Miller, K., Farrell, M., Barnes, G., Melnick, M., & Sabo, D. (2005). Gender/racial differences in jock identity, dating, and adolescent sexual risk. *Journal of Youth and Adolescence*, 34, 123–136.

Miller, K., Forehand, R., & Kotchik, B. (1999). Adolescent sexual behavior in two ethnic minority samples: The role of family variables. *Journal of Marriage and the Family*, 61, 85–98.

Miller, L. (2001). Continuous administration of 100 µg levonorgestrel and 20 µg ethinyl estradiol for elimination of menses: A randomized trial. *Obstetrics and Gynecology*, 97, 16S.

Miller, L., & Dickey, C. (2005). Catholics celebrate a legacy, and contemplate many difficult choices ahead. *Newsweek*, April 18, 31–38.

Miller, L., & Underwood, A. (2006). Not always "the Happiest Time." *Newsweek*, April 24, 80–82.

Miller, P. (2005). The last resort: Abortion providers in Kansas and Mississippi hold ground despite states' attacks. *Ms.*, Fall, 16–17.

Miller, P. (2006). Our bodies under siege. *Ms.*, Spring, 12–13.

Miller, T. (2000). Diagnostic evaluation of erectile dysfunction. *American Family Physician*, 61, 95–104.

Miller, T. (2006, June 14). Hypocrisy on the hill: Anti-choice lawmakers vote "No" on measures to help pregnant women. Retrieved June 18, 2006, from http://www.prochoiceamerica.org/news/press-releases/2006/hypocrisy-on-the-hill.html.

Miller, T. (2006, June 19). NARAL pro-choice America calls Supreme Court decision to review federal abortion ban ominous. Retrieved July 3, 2006, from http://www.naral.org/news/press-releases/2006/pr06192006_scotus_ban.hrml?print=t.

Miller, W. (2005). Screening for chlamydial infection: Are we doing enough? *Lancet*, 365, 456–457.

Mills, A., & Barclay, L. (2006). None of them were satisfactory: Women's experiences with contraception. *Health Care for Women International*, 27, 379–398.

Mills, J., & Mindel, A. (2003). Genital herpes simplex infections: Some therapeutic dilemmas. *Sexually Transmitted Diseases*, 30, 232–233.

Milner, J., & Dopke, C. (1997). Paraphilia not otherwise specified: Psychopathology and theory. In D. Laws & W. O'Donohue (Eds.), *Sexual Deviance: Theory, Assessment, and Treatment*. New York: Guilford Press.

Milow, V. (1983). Menstrual education: Past, present, and future. In S. Golub (Ed.), *Menarche*. Lexington, MA: Lexington Books.

Miner, M., Flitter, J., & Robinson, B. (2006). Association of sexual revictimization with sexuality and psychological function. *Journal of Interpersonal Violence*, 21, 503–524.

Mink, G. (2005). Stop sexual harassment now! *Ms*, Fall, 36–37.

Minkoff, H. (2003). Human immunodeficiency virus infection in pregnancy. *Obstetrics and Gynecology*, 101, 797–810.

Minnis, A., & Padian, N. (2001). Choice of female-controlled barrier methods among young women and their male sexual partners. *Family Planning Perspectives*, 33, 28–34.

Minor, M., & Dwyer, S. (1997). The psychosocial development of sex offenders: Differences between exhibitionists, child molesters, and incest offenders. *International Journal of Offenders Therapy and Comparative Criminology*, 41, 36–44.

Mintz, H. (1997). Most alleged members of Internet child pornography ring plead guilty. *Knight-Ridder/Tribune News Service*, May 12.

Misrahi, M., Teglas, J., N'Go, N., Burgard, M., Mayaux, M., Rouzioux, C., Delfraissy, J., & Blanche, S. (1998). CCR5 chemokine receptor variant in HIV-1 mother-to-child transmission and disease progression in children. *Journal of the American Medical Association*, 279, 277–280.

Mitchell, D., Hirschman, R., & Hall, G. (1999). Attributions of victim responsibility, pleasure, and trauma in male rape. *Journal of Sex Research*, 36, 369–373.

Mitka, M. (2000). Some men who take Viagra die: Why? *Journal of the American Medical Association*, 283, 590–593.

Mitka, M. (2003a). CDC resource focuses on DES exposure. *Journal of the American Medical Association*, 289, 1624–1627.

Mitka, M. (2003b). Researchers seek mammography alternatives. *Journal of the American Medical Association*, 290, 450–451.

Moats, D. (2004). The tipping point. *The Advocate*, May 11, 29–35.

Mohler-Kuo, M., Dowdall, G., Koss, M., & Wechsler, H. (2004). Correlates of rape while intoxicated in a national sample of college women. *Journal of Studies on Alcohol*, 65, 37–45.

Mok, F. (2006). A haven for homeless youths. *The Advocate*, August 29, 26–27.

Moller, L., Hymel, S., & Rubin, K. (1992). Sex typing in play and popularity in middle childhood. *Sex Roles*, 26, 331–335.

Mona, L., & Gardos, P. (2000). Disabled sexual partners. In L. Szuchman & F. Muscarella (Eds.), *Psychological Perspectives on Human Sexuality*. New York: Wiley.

Money, D., Arikan, Y., Remple, V., Sherlock, C., Craib, K., Birch, P., & Burdge, D. (2003). Genital tract and plasma human immunodeficiency virus viral load throughout the menstrual cycle in women who are infected with ovulatory human immunodeficiency virus. *American Journal of Obstetrics and Gynecology*, 188, 122–128.

Money, J. (1961). Sex hormones and other variables in human eroticism. In W. Young (Ed.), *Sex and Internal Secretions* (3rd ed.). Baltimore: Williams & Wilkins.

Money, J. (1963). Cytogenetic and psychosexual incongruities with a note on space-form blindness. *Ameri-*

can *Journal of Psychiatry*, 119, 820–827.

**Money, J.** (1965). Psychosocial differentiation. In J. Money (Ed.), *Sex Research: New Developments*. New York: Holt, Rinehart & Winston.

**Money, J.** (1968). *Sex Errors of the Body: Dilemmas, Education, Counseling*. Baltimore: Johns Hopkins University Press.

**Money, J.** (1981). Paraphilias: Phyletic origins of erotosexual dysfunction. *International Journal of Mental Health*, 10, 75–109.

**Money, J.** (1990). Forensic sexology: Paraphilic serial rape (biastophilia) and lust murder (erotophono- philia). *American Journal of Psychotherapy*, 44, 26–37.

**Money, J.** (1994a). The concept of gender identity disorder in childhood and adolescence after 39 years. *Journal of Sex and Marital Therapy*, 20, 163–177.

**Money, J.** (1994b). *Sex Errors of the Body and Related Syndromes: A Guide to Counseling Children, Adolescents, and Their Families* (2nd ed.). Baltimore: Brookes.

**Money, J., & Ehrhardt, A.** (1972). Prenatal hormonal exposure: Possible effects on behavior in man. In R. Michael (Ed.), *Endocrinology and Human Behavior*. London: Oxford University Press.

**Money, J., Lehne, G., & Pierre-Jerome, F.** (1984). Micropenis: Adult follow-up and comparison of size against new norms. *Journal of Sex and Marital Therapy*, 10, 105–116.

**Mongeau, P., Ramirez, A., & Vorrell, M.** (2003). Friends with benefits: Initial exploration of sexual, non-romantic relationships. Paper presented at the annual meeting of the Western Communication Association, Salt Lake City, Utah, February.

**Montagu, A., & Matson, F.** (1979). *The Human Connection*. New York: McGraw-Hill.

**Montgomery, M., & Sorell, G.** (1997). Differences in love attitudes across family life stages. *Family Relations*, 46, 55–61.

**Montorsi, P., Ravagnani, P., Galli, S., & Briganti, A.** (2006). Erectile dysfunction predicts extension of coronary artery disease in acute coronary syndromes. *The Journal of Sexual Medicine*, 3(suppl. 3), 176–198.

**Moodley, P., Sturm, P., Vanmali, T., Wilkinson, D., Connolly, C., & Sturm, A.** (2003). Association between HIV-1 infection, the etiology of genital ulcer disease, and response to syndromic management. *Sexually Transmitted Diseases*, 30, 241–248.

**Moore, D.** (2006). Cervical cancer. *Obstetrics & Gynecology*, 107, 1152–1161.

**Morales, A.** (2003). The andropause: Bare facts for urologists. *British Journal of Urology International*, 91, 311–313.

**Moran, R.** (2001). *Interracial Intimacy: The Regulation of Race and Romance*. Chicago: University of Chicago Press.

**Morehouse, R.** (2001). *Using the Crucible Approach to Enhance Women's Sexual Potential*. Paper presented at the 33rd Annual Conference of the American Association of Sex Educators, Counselors, and Therapists, San Francisco, May 2–6.

**Morgan, R.** (2003). Saving the world. *Ms.*, Summer, 95.

**Morgan, R.** (2006). The burning time. *Ms.*, Spring, 67–70.

**Morin, J.** (1981). *Anal Pleasure and Health*. Burlingame, CA: Down There Press.

**Morrell, M., Dixen, J., Carter, C., & Davidson, J.** (1984). The influence of age and cycling status on sexual arousability in women. *American Journal of Obstetrics and Gynecology*, 148, 66–71.

**Morris, G.** (2003). Is it a boy or a girl? *Just Out*, January 17, 22–25.

**Mosher, C., & Levitt, E.** (1987). An exploratory-descriptive study of a sadomasochistically oriented sample. *Journal of Sex Research*, 23, 322–337.

**Mosher, C., & Tomkins, S.** (1988). Scripting the macho man: Hypermasculine socialization and enculturation. *Journal of Sex Research*, 25, 60–84.

**Mosher, D., & MacIan, P.** (1994). College men and women respond to X-rated videos intended for male or female audiences: Gender and sexual scripts. *Journal of Sex Research*, 31, 99–113.

**Mosher, W.** (2005). Sexual behavior and selected health measures: Men and women 15–44 years of age, United States, 2002. *Vital and Health Statistics* 2005, 362.

**Mossad, S.** (2003). How do you manage a healthy, asymptomatic 24-year-old with positive RPR on a premarital blood test? *Cleveland Clinic Journal of Medicine*, 70, 101–102.

**Muehlenhard, C.** (1988). Misinterpreting dating behaviors and the risk of date rape. *Journal of Social and Clinical Psychology*, 6, 20–37.

**Muehlenhard, C., & Andrews, S.** (1985). *Open Communication About Sex: Will It Reduce Risk Factors Related to Rape?* Paper presented at the Annual Meeting of the Association for Advancement of Behavior Therapy, Houston, November.

**Muehlenhard, C., & Hollabaugh, L.** (1989). Do women sometimes say no when they mean yes? The prevalence and correlates of women's token resistance to sex. *Journal of Personality and Social Psychology*, 54, 872–879.

**Muehlenhard, C., & Linton, M.** (1987). Date rape and sexual aggression in dating situations: Incidence and risk factors. *Journal of Consulting Psychology*, 34, 186–196.

**Muehlenhard, C., & Schrag, J.** (1991). Nonviolent sexual coercion. In A. Parrot & L. Bechhofer (Eds.), *Acquaintance Rape: The Hidden Crime*. New York: Wiley.

**Muehlenhard, C., Felts, A., & Andrews, S.** (1985). *Men's Attitudes Toward the Justifiability of Date Rape: Intervening Variables and Possible Solutions*. Paper presented at the Midcontinent Meeting of the Society for the Scientific Study of Sex, Chicago, June.

**Muehlenhard, C., Goggins, M., Jones, J., & Satterfield, A.** (1991). Sexual violence and coercion in close relationships. In K. McKinney & S. Sprecher (Eds.), *Sexuality in Close Relationships*. Hillsdale, NJ: Erlbaum.

**Muehlenhard, C., Peterson, Z., Karwoski, L., Bryan, T., & Lee, R.** (2003). Gender and sexuality: An introduction to the Special Issue. *Journal of Sex Research*, 40, 1–3.

**Mulchahey, K.** (2005). Practical approaches to prescribing contraception in the office setting. *Adolescent Medicine*, 16, 665–674.

Munarriz, R., Maitland, S., Garcia, S., Talkakoub, L., & Goldstein, I. (2003). A prospective duplex Doppler ultrasonographic study in women with sexual arousal disorder to objectively assess genital engorgement induced by EROS therapy. *Journal of Sex and Marital Therapy*, 29, 85–94.

Murnen, S., & Stockton, M. (1997). Gender and self-reported sexual arousal in response to sexual stimuli: A meta-analytic review. *Sex Roles*, 37, 135–154.

Murphy, D., Sarr, M., Durako, S., Mosciki, A., Wilson, C., & Muenz, L. (2003). Barriers to HAART adherence among human immunodeficiency virus-infected adolescents. *Archives of Pediatric and Adolescent Medicine*, 157, 249–255.

Murphy, E. (2003). Being born female is dangerous for your health. *American Psychologist*, 58, 205–209.

Murphy, P. (2003). New methods of hormonal contraception. *Nurse Practitioner*, 28, 11–21.

Murphy, W. (1997). Exhibitionism: Psychopathology and theory. In D. Laws & W. O'Donohue (Eds.), *Sexual Deviance: Theory, Assessment, and Treatment*. New York: Guilford Press.

Murray, J., (2000). Psychological profile of pedophiles and child molesters. *Journal of Psychology*, 134, 211–224.

Murray, K., Richardson, L., Morishima, C., Owens, J., & Gretch, D. (2003). Prevalence of hepatitis C virus infection and risk factors in an incarcerated juvenile population: A pilot study. *Pediatrics*, 111, 153–157.

Murray, L. (1992). Love and longevity. *Longevity*, August, 64.

Murrey, G., Bolen, J., Miller, N., Simensted, K., Robbins, M., & Truskowski, F. (1993). History of childhood sexual abuse in women with depressive and anxiety disorders: A comparative study. *Journal of Sex Education and Therapy*, 19(1), 13–19.

Murry, V. (1996). An ecological analysis of coital timing among middle-class African American adolescent females. *Journal of Adolescent Research*, 11, 261–279.

Murstein, B., & Mercy, T. (1994). Sex, drugs, relationships, contraception, and fears of disease on a college campus over 17 years. *Adolescence*, 29, 303–22.

Murstein, B., & Tuerkheim, A. (1998). Gender differences in love, sex, and motivation for sex. *Psychological Reports*, 82, 425–450.

Mustanski, B. (2001). Getting wired: Exploiting the Internet for the collection of valid sexuality data. *Journal of Sex Research*, 38, 292–302.

Mwai, E. (2006). Health workers performing FGM secretly, says report. Retrieved July 31, 2006 from http://www.eastandard.net/print/news.php?articleid=1143955619.

Myers, S. (2000). Female general in army alleges sex harassment. *New York Times*, March 31, A1.

Nadler, R. (1968). Approach to psychodynamics of obscene telephone calls. *New York Journal of Medicine*, 68, 521–526.

Najman, J., Dunne, M., Purdie, D., Boyle, F., & Coxeter, P. (2005). Sexual abuse in childhood and sexual dysfunction in adulthood: An Australian population-based study. *Archives of Sexual Behavior*, 34, 517–526.

Napolitane, C. (1997). *Living and Loving After Divorce*. New York: Signet.

Nash, J. (1997). Personal communication.

Nass, S., & Strauss, F. (2004). *New Frontiers in Contraceptive Research: A Blueprint for Action*. Washington, DC: National Academy Press.

National Council on Sexual Addiction and Compulsivity (2002). Information statement: Women sex addicts. *Sexual Addiction and Compulsivity*, 9, 293–295.

National Pro-Life Alliance (2006). Abortion stops a beating heart. Retrieved July 8, 2006 from http://www.prolifealliance.com/default.htm.

National Survey of Family Growth (2006). *Fertility, contraception, and fatherhood: Data on men and women from the National Survey of Family Growth*. Hyattsville, MD: U.S. Department of Health and Human Services.

Nattinger, A. (2000). Older women, mammography, and mortality from breast cancer. *American Journal of Medicine*, 108, 174–175.

Naughton, K. (2004). The soft sell. *Newsweek*, February 2, 46–47.

Navarro, M. (2004). The most private of makeovers. *The New York Times*, November 28, 1–2.

Nedrow, A., Miller, J., Walker, M., & Nygren, P. (2006). Complementary and alternative therapies for the management of menopause-related symptoms. *Archives of Internal Medicine*, 166, 1453–1465.

Nelson, A. (2006). Extended-regimen contraception: Effects on menstrual symptoms and quality of life. *Journal of Family Practice*, 55, S1–S9.

Ness, C. (2000a). *Gay-Straight School "Alliances" Thriving*. Retrieved September 6, 2000, from http://www.examiner.com/alliances.html.

Ness, R., Hillier, S., Richter, R., Soper, D., Stamm, C., Bass, D., Sweet, R., Rice, P., Downs, J., & Aral, S. (2003). Why women douche and why they may or may not stop. *Sexually Transmitted Diseases*, 30, 71–74.

Neto, F. (2001). Love styles of three generations of women. *Marriage and Family Review*, 33, 19–30.

Nevid, J. (1984). Sex differences in factors of romantic attraction. *Sex Roles*, 11, 401–411.

Nguyen, T., Ford, C., Kaufman, J., Leone, P., Suchidran, C., & Miller, W. (2006). HIV testing among young adults in the United States: Association with financial resources and geography. *American Journal of Public Health*, 96, 1031–1034.

Niccolai, L., King, E., D'Entremont, D., & Pritchett, N. (2006). Disclosure of HIV serostatus to sex partners: A new approach to measurement. *Sexually Transmitted Diseases*, 33, 102–105.

Nichols, M. (1989). Sex therapy with lesbians, gay men, and bisexuals. In S. Leiblum & R. Rosen (Eds.), *Principles and Practice of Sex Therapy*. New York: Guilford Press.

Nichols, M. (2000). Therapy with sexual minorities. In S. Leiblum & R. Rosen (Eds.), *Principles and Practice of Sex Therapy*. New York: Guilford Press.

Niedowski, E. (2006, August 6). From Russia with love. Retrieved August 7, 2006, from http://baltimoresun.com/news/opinion/ideas/bal-id.births06aug06,1,4659161,print.stor. . . .

Nielson, J., & Wohlert, M. (1991). Chromosome abnormalities found among 34,910 newborn children: Results from a 13-year incidence study in Arhus, Denmark. *Human Genetics*, 87, 81–83.

Nieschlag, E., & Henke, A. (2005). Hopes for male contraception. *The Lancet*, 365, 554.

Nilsson, L., Bergh, C., Bryman, I., & Thorburn, J. (1994). How do we treat unexplained infertility? *Acta Obstetricia et Gynecologica Scandinavia*, 73, 174–175.

Nishith, P., Mechanic, M., & Resnick, P. (2000). Prior interpersonal trauma: The contribution to current PTSD symptoms in female rape victims. *Journal of Abnormal Psychology*, 109, 20–25.

Nixin, D. (2003). *Are Penises Going the Way of the Dodo?* Retrieved March 13, 2003, from http://www.mamimonline.com/grit/articles/article_3715.html.

Nobre, P., & Pinto-Gouveia, J. (2006). Dysfunctional sexual beliefs as vulnerability factors for sexual dysfunction. *The Journal of Sex Research*, 43, 68–76.

Noll, J., Trickett, P., & Putnam, F. (2003). A prospective investigation of the impact of childhood sexual abuse on the development of sexuality. *Journal of Consulting and Clinical Psychology*, 71, 575–586.

Noller, K. (2006). HPV vaccination: More questions than answers. *Obstetrics & Gynecology*, 107, 4–5.

Norris, D., Gutheil, T., & Strasburger, L. (2003). This couldn't happen to me: Boundary problems and sexual misconduct in the psychotherapy relationship. *Psychiatric Services*, 54, 517–522.

Nour, N. (2000). Female circumcision and genital mutilation: A practical and sensitive approach. *Contemporary OB/GYN*, March, 50–55.

Nour, N. (2006). Female genital cutting. *Internal Medicine News*, 39, 16.

Novak, R., Chen, L., MacArthur, R., Baxter, J., Hullsiek, K., et al. (2005). Prevalence of antiretroviral drug resistant mutations in chronically HIV-infected, treatment-naïve patients: Implications for routine resistance screening before initiation of antiretroviral therapy. *Clinical Infectious Diseases*, 40, 468–474.

Nusbaum, M., Lenahan, P., & Sadovsky, R. (2005). Sexual health in aging men and women: Addressing the physiologic and psychological sexual changes that occur with age. *Geriatrics*, 60, 18–28.

Nussbaum, E. (2000). A question of gender. *Discover*, January, 92–99.

Nuttin, J. (1987). Affective consequences of mere ownership: The name letter effect in twelve European languages. *European Journal of Social Psychology*, 17, 381–402.

Nystrom, N., & Jones, T. (2003). Community building with aging and old lesbians. *American Journal of Community Psychology*, 31, 293–299.

O'Brien, P., Wyatt, K., & Dimmock, P. (2000). Premenstrual syndrome is real and treatable. *The Practitioner*, 244, 185–189.

O'Connor, A. (1998). Marriages that cross racial line increase in U.S. *The Oregonian*, May 3, A20.

O'Donnell, L., Myint-U, A., O'Donnell, C., & Stueve, A. (2003). Long-term influence of sexual norms and attitudes on timing of sexual initiation among urban minority youth. *Journal of School Health*, 73, 68–75.

O'Neill, P. (1997). Date-rape drug may be in Oregon. *The Oregonian*, February 26, B1, B7.

O'Neill, P. (2000a). The Adonis complex. *The Sunday Oregonian*, July 9, L11.

O'Sullivan, L., Byers, E., & Finkelman, L. (1998). A comparison of male and female college students' experiences of sexual coercion. *Psychology of Women Quarterly*, 22, 177–195.

Ochs, E., & Binik, Y. (1999). The use of couple data to determine the reliability of self-reported sexual behavior. *Journal of Sex Research*, 36, 374–384.

Ofman, U. (2000). Guest editor's note. *Journal of Sex Education and Therapy*, 25, 3–5.

Ogden, J. (1989). Visuospatial and other "right-hemispheric" functions after long recovery periods in left-hemispherectomized subjects. *Neuropsychologia*, 27, 765–776.

Okazaki, S. (2002). Influences of culture on Asian Americans' sexuality. *Journal of Sex Research*, 39, 34–41.

Olds, D., Henderson, C., & Tatelbaum, R. (1994). Intellectual impairment in children of women who smoke cigarettes during pregnancy. *Pediatrics*, 93(2), 221–227.

Olivera, A. (1994). Sexual dysfunction due to Clomipramine and Sertraline: Nonpharmacological resolution. *Journal of Sex Education and Therapy*, 20(2), 119–122.

Oliwenstein, L. (2005). On fertile ground. *Psychology Today*, November/December, 62–66.

Olsen, V., Gustavsen, I., Bramness, J., Hasvold, I., Karinen R., et al. (2005). The concentrations, appearance and taste of nine sedating drugs dissolved in four different beverages. *Forensic Science International*, 151, 171–174.

Olsson, S., & Moller, A. (2003). On the incidence and sex ratio of transsexualism in Sweden. *Archives of Sexual Behavior*, 32, 381–386.

Osman, A., & Al-Sawaf, M. (1995). Cross-cultural aspects of sexual anxieties and the associated dysfunction. *Journal of Sex Education and Therapy*, 21, 174–181.

Osterbauer, P. (2005). Sex on the brain: Remembering neurosyphilis. *Southern Medical Journal*, 97, 526.

Ostling, R. (2000). Schism threatens Southern Baptists. *The Sunday Oregonian*, October 29, A3.

Oswald, D., & Russell, B. (2006). Perceptions of sexual coercion in heterosexual dating relationships: The role of aggressor gender and tactics. *Journal of Sex Research*, 43, 87–96.

Ott, M., Adler, N., Millstein, S., Tschann, J., & Ellen, J. (2002). The trade-off between hormonal contraceptives and condoms among adolescents. *Perspectives on Sexual and Reproductive Health*, 34, 6–14.

Otto, H. (1999). A short history of sex toys with an extrapolation for the new century. In J. Elias, V. Elias, V. Bullough, G. Brewer, J. Douglas, & W. Jarvis (Eds.), *Porn 101: Eroticism, Pornography, and the First Amendment*. Amherst, NY: Prometheus Books.

Overbeck, G., Vollebergh, W., Engels, R., & Meeus, W. (2003). Parental attachment and romantic relationships: Associations with emotional disturbance during late adolescence. *Journal of Counseling Psychology*, 50, 28–39.

Owen, L. (1993). *Her Blood Is Gold.* San Francisco: HarperCollins.

Pace, B. (2000). Urinary tract infections. Journal of the American Medical Association, 283, 1646.

Pace, B. (2001). Screening for breast cancer. *Journal of the American Medical Association*, 285, 246.

Padawer, J., Fagan, C., Janoff-Bulman, R., Strickland, B., & Chorowski, M. (1988). Women's psychological adjustment following emergency cesarean versus vaginal delivery. *Psychology of Women Quarterly*, 12, 25–34.

Page, D., Mosher, R., Simpson, E., Fisher, E., Mardon, G., Pollack, J., McGillivray, B., Chapelle, A., & Brown, L. (1987). The sex-determining region of the human Y chromosome encodes a finger protein. *Cell*, 51, 1091–1104.

Palmer, J., Rao, R., Adams-Campbell, L., & Rosenberg, L. (1999). Correlates of hysterectomy among African-American women. *American Journal of Epidemiology*, 150, 1309–1315.

Palmer, J., Rosenberg, L., Wise, L., & Horton, N. (2003). Onset of natural menopause in African American women. *American Journal of Public Health*, 93, 299–306.

Palmer, L. (2000). RU-486: Changing the debate. *The Oregonian*, January 7, A16.

Pan, E. (2000). Why Asian guys are on a roll. *Newsweek*, February 21, 48–51.

Pancholi, P., Perkus, M., Tricoche, N., Liu, Q., & Prince, A. (2003). DNA immunization with hepatitis C virus (HCV) polycistronic genes or immunization by HCV DNA primary-recombinant canarypox virus boosting induces immune responses and protection from recombinant HCV-Vaccinia virus infection in HLA-A2 l-transgenic mice. *Journal of Virology*, 77, 382–390.

Panzer, C., Guay, A., & Goldstein, I. (2006). Do oral contraceptives produce irreversible effects on women's sexuality? A reply. *The Journal of Sexual Medicine*, 3, 568–570.

Paredes, R., & Baum, M. (1997). Role of the medial preoptic area/anterior hypothalamus in the control of masculine sexual behavior. *Annual Review of Sex Research*, 8, 68–101.

Parham, T., White, J., & Ajamu, A. (1999). *The Psychology of Blacks: An African-Centered Perspective* (3rd ed.). Upper Saddle, NY: Prentice Hall.

Parish, W., Laumann, E., Cohen, M., Pan, S., Zheng, H., Hoffman, I., Wang, T., & Ng, K. (2003). Population-based study of chlamydial infection in China. *Journal of the American Medical Association*, 289, 1265–1273.

Parker, C., & Dearnaley, D. (2003). Hormonal therapy as an adjuvant to radical radiotherapy for locally advanced prostate cancer. *British Journal of Urology International*, 91, 6–8.

Parker, L. (1998). Ambiguous genitalia: Etiology, treatment, and nursing implications. *Journal of Obstetrical, Gynecological, and Neonatal Nursing*, 27, 15–22.

Parks, C., & Vu, A. (1994). Social dilemma behavior of individuals from highly individualist and collectivist cultures. *Journal of Conflict Resolution*, 38, 708–718.

Parks, K., Pardi, A., & Bradizza, C. (2006). Collecting data on alcohol use and alcohol-related victimization: A comparison of telephone and Web-based survey methods. *Journal of Studies on Alcohol*, 67, 318–324.

Parrot, A. (1991). Institutionalized response: How can acquaintance rape be prevented? In A. Parrot & L. Bechhofer (Eds.), *Acquaintance Rape: The Hidden Crime.* New York: Wiley.

Parry, J. (2006). Controversial new vaccine to prevent cervical cancer. *Bulletin of the World Health Organization*, 84, 86–88.

Parsons, J. (1983). Sexual socialization and gender roles in childhood. In E. Allgeier & N. McCormick (Eds.), *Changing Boundaries: Gender Roles and Sexual Behavior.* Palo Alto, CA: Mayfield.

Passariello, C. (2002). A new approach to the oldest profession: More countries are trying to regulate—and tax—brothels. *Business Week*, October 7, 34.

Pathfinder International (2006). Creating partnerships to prevent early marriage in the Amhara region. *Pathfinder International*, July, pNA.

Patz, A. (2000). Will your marriage last? *Psychology Today*, January–February, 58–65.

Paukku, M., Kilpikari, R., Puolakkainen, M., Oksanen, H., Apter, D., & Paavonen, J. (2003a). Criteria for selective screening for chlamydia trachomatis. *Sexually Transmitted Diseases*, 30, 120–123.

Paul, L., & Galloway, J. (1994). Sexual jealousy: Gender differences in response to partner and rival. *Aggressive Behavior*, 20, 203–211.

Paul, P. (2004). The porn factor. *Time*, Special Issue, January 19, 99–100.

Paul, P. (2005). Pornified: *How Pornography is Transforming Our Lives, Our Relationships, and Our Families.* New York: Times Books.

Pauls, R., Mutema, G., Segal, J., Silva, A., Kleeman, S., Dryfhout, V., & Karram, M. (2006). A prospective study examining the anatomic distribution of nerve density in the human vagina. *The Journal of Sexual Medicine*, 3, 979–987.

Paulson, R. (2000). Should we help women over 50 conceive with donor eggs? *Contemporary OB/GYN*, January, 36–46.

Pawson, M. (2003). The battle with mortality and the urge to procreate. In J. Haynes & J. Miller (Eds.), *Inconceivable Conceptions: Psychological Aspects of Infertility and Reproductive Technology.* Hove, United Kingdom: Brunner-Routledge.

Paz-Baily, G., Rahman, M., Chen, C., et al. (2006). Changes in the etiology of sexually transmitted diseases in Botswana between 1993 and 2002: Implications for the clinical management of genital ulcer disease. *Clinical Infectious Diseases*, 41, 1304–1312.

Pealer, L., & Weiler, R. (2000). Web-based health survey research: A primer. *American Journal of Health Behavior*, 24, 69–72.

Pearlstein, T., Halbreich, U., & Batzar, E. (2000). Psychosocial functioning in women with premenstrual dysphoric disorder before and after treatment with Sertraline or placebo. *Journal of Clinical Psychiatry*, 61, 101–109.

**Pearson, H.** (2000). So that's why you can't fit into your jeans. . . . *New Scientist*, April 8, 6.

**Pedersen, C.** (1992). *Oxytocin in Maternal, Sexual, and Social Behavior*. New York: New York Academy of Sciences.

**Penley, C.** (1996). From NASA to the 700 Club (with a detour through Hollywood): Cultural studies in the public sphere. In C. Nelson & D. Gaonkar (Eds.), *Disciplinarity and Dissent in Cultural Studies*. New York: Routledge.

**Perel, E.** (2003). Erotic intelligence. *Psychotherapy Networker*, May–June, 24–31.

**Perez, A., Labbok, M., & Queenan, J.** (1992). Clinical study of the lactational amenorrhoea method for family planning. *The Lancet*, 339, 968–970.

**Perleman, M.** (2001). Integrating Sildenafil and sex therapy: Unconsummated marriage secondary to erectile dysfunction and retarded ejaculation. *Journal of Sex Education and Therapy*, 26, 13–21.

**Perris, A.** (2000). *At the Pharmacy: OTC*. Retrieved December 1, 2000, from http://www.fertilitext .org/p3_pharmacy/OTCproducts.html.

**Perry, J., & Whipple, B.** (1981). Pelvic muscle strength of female ejaculators: Evidence in support of a new theory of orgasm. *Journal of Sex Research*, 17, 22–39.

**Peterson, C., Kristensen, E., Giraldi, A., & Lundvall, L.** (2006). Sexual dysfunction among women with vulvar vestibulitis. *The Journal of Sexual Medicine*, 3 (suppl. 3), 176–198.

**Peterson, J., & Bakeman, R.** (2006). Impact of beliefs about HIV treatment and peer condom norms on risky sexual behavior among gay and bisexual men. *Journal of Community Psychology*, 34, 37–46.

**Petitti, D., & Reingold, A.** (1988). Tampon characteristics and menstrual toxic shock syndrome. *Journal of the American Medical Association*, 259, 686–687.

**Pew Research Center** (2006, March 14). Guess who's coming to dinner: 22% of Americans have a relative in a mixed-race marriage. Retrieved August 7, 2006, from http://pewresearch.org/social/pack.php?PackID=4.

**Peyser, M.** (2000b). Prime time "I do's." *Newsweek*, February 28, 48.

**Peyser, M.** (2006). The spouses of "Big Love." *Newsweek*, December 26, 2005/January 2, 2006, 91.

**Philaretou, A.** (2005). Sexuality and the Internet. *Journal of Sex Research*, 42, 180–181.

**Philliber, S., Kaye, J., Herrling, S., & West, E.** (2002). Preventing pregnancy and improving health care access among teenagers: An evaluation of the Children's Aid Society–Carrera Program. *Perspectives on Sexual and Reproductive Health*, 34, 244–251.

**Phillips, D., Taylor, C., Zacharopoulos, U., & Maguire, R.** (2000). Nonoxynol-9 causes rapid exfoliation of sheets of rectal epithelium. *Contraception*, 62, 149–154.

**Phillips, K.** (2006). *American Theocracy: The Peril and Politics of Radical Religion, Oil, and Borrowed Money in the 21st Century*. New York: Viking Press.

**Piccionelli, G.** (2006). Adult mobile and the law: 1. Retrieved September 17, 2006, from http://xbiz .com/article_print.php?cat=40&id=15504.

**Piccionelli, G.** (2006). Midterm porn politics: 1. Retrieved September 17, 2006, from http://xbiz .com/article_print.php?cat=40&id=16336.

**Picker, L.** (2005). And now, the hard part. *Newsweek*, April 25, 46–50.

**Pickett, M., Bruner, D., Joseph, A., & Burggraf, V.** (2000). Prostate cancer elder alert: Living with treatment choices and outcomes. *Journal of Gerontological Nursing*, February, 22–34.

**Pierce, P.** (1994). Sexual harassment: Frankly, what is it? *Journal of Intergroup Relations*, 20, 3–12.

**Pike, J., & Jennings, N.** (2005). The effects of commercials on children's perceptions of gender appropriate toy use. *Sex Roles: A Journal of Research*, 52, 83–91.

**Pilcher, C., Tien, H., Eron, J., et al.** (2004). Brief but efficient: Acute HIV infection and the sexual transmission of HIV. *Journal of Infectious Diseases*, 189, 1785–1792.

**Pinhas, V.** (1985). Personal communication.

**Pinkerton, J., & Zion, A.** (2006). Vasomotor symptoms in menopause: Where we've been and where we're going. *Journal of Women's Health*, 15, 135–143.

**Pirie, P., Lando, H., & Curry, S.** (2000). Tobacco, alcohol, and caffeine use and cessation in early pregnancy. *American Journal of Preventive Medicine*, 18, 54–61.

**Pithers, W.** (1993). Treatment of rapists: Reinterpretation of early outcome date and exploratory constructs to enhance therapeutic efficacy. In G. Hall, R. Hirschman, J. Graham, & M. Zaragoza (Eds.), *Sexual Aggression: Issues in Etiology, Assessment, and Treatment*. Washington, DC: Taylor & Francis.

**Planned Parenthood Federation of America** (2002). *Masturbation: From Stigma to Sexual Health*. White Paper. New York: Katherine Dexter McCormick Library.

**Planned Parenthood Federation of America** (2003a). Masturbation: From myth to sexual health. *Contemporary Sexuality*, 37, i–vii.

**Plant, E., Hyde, J., Keltner, D., & Devine, P.** (2000). The gender stereotyping of emotions. *Psychology of Women Quarterly*, 24, 81–92.

**Platner, J.** (2005). Bush and birth control. Retrieved May 10, 2006, from http://www.plannedparenthood.org/ pp2/portal/files/portla/webzine/newspoliticsactivism.

**Plaud, J., Gaither, G., Hegstad, H., & Rowan, L.** (1999). Volunteer bias in human psychophysiological sexual arousal research: To whom do our research results apply? *Journal of Sex Research*, 36, 171–179.

**Plaut, S.** (1996). *Sexual Exploitation by Health Professionals: The Victim's Perspective*. Paper presented at the 21st Annual Meeting of the Society of Sex Therapy and Research, Miami, March.

**Polgreen, L.** (2005). Casualities of Sudan's war: Rape is a weapon in the fight over land and ethnicity in Darfur. *Oregonian*, February 18, A19.

**Polinsky, M.** (1995). Functional status of long-term breast cancer survivors: Demonstrating chronicity. *Health and Social Work*, 19(3), 165–173.

**Pollitt, K.** (2005). Practice what you preach. *The Nation*, May 16, 84.

**Pollitt, K.** (2005, June 13). Stiffed. Retrieved June 4, 2006, from http://www.thenation.com/docprint .mhtml?i=20050613&s=pollitt.

Pollitt, K. (2006). Virginity or death. Retrieved June 4, 2006, from http://www.thenation.com/doc/20050530/pollitt.

Polonsky, D. (2000). Premature ejaculation. In S. Leiblum & R. Rosen (Eds.), *Principles and Practice of Sex Therapy*. New York: Guilford Press.

Pomerantz, M., & Kantoff, P. (2006). Genetics and inherited prostate cancer risk. *Contemporary Urology*, 18, 18–25.

Pope, H., Phillips, K., & Olivardia, R. (2000). *The Adonis Complex: The Secret Crisis of Male Body Obsession*. New York: Free Press.

Population Council, New York (2005). Emergency contraception's mode of action clarified. *SIECUS Report*, 33, 20–22.

Porter, S., Yuille, J., & Lehman, D. (1999). The nature of real, implanted, and fabricated childhood emotion events: Implications for the recovered memory debate. *Law and Human Behavior*, 23, 517–537.

Potdar, R., & Koenig, M. (2005). Does audio-CASI improve reports of risky behavior? Evidence from a randomized field trial among young urban men in India. *Studies in Family Planning*, 36, 107–116.

Potter, J., & Ship, A. (2001). Survivors of breast cancer. *New England Journal of Medicine*, 344, 309–314.

Potter, L., Oakley, D., & de Leon-Wong, E. (1996). Measuring compliance among oral contraceptive users. *Family Planning Perspectives*, 28, 154–158.

Potterat, J. (2003). Partner notification for HIV: Running out of excuses. *Sexually Transmitted Diseases*, 30, 89–90.

Potts, M. (1997). Social support and depression among older adults living alone: The importance of friends within and outside of a retirement community. *Journal of the National Association of Social Workers*, 42(3), 348–362.

Power, C. (1998a). The new Islam. *Newsweek*, March 16, 35–38.

Power, C. (2006). A generation of women wiped out? *Glamour*, August, 172–175.

Powlishta, K., Serbin, L., & Moller, L. (1993). The stability of individual differences in gender typing: Implication for understanding gender segregation. *Sex Roles*, 29, 723–737.

Prabu-Jeyabalan, M., Nalivaika, E., King, N., & Schiffer, C. (2003). Viability of a drug-resistant human immunodeficiency virus type 1 protease variant: Structural insights for better antiviral therapy. *Journal of Virology*, 77, 1306–1315.

Prentice, R. (2003). Breast-cancer prevention: Is the risk-benefit ratio in favour of tamoxifen? *The Lancet*, 362, 183.

Prentky, R., Burgess, A., & Carter, D. (1986). Victim responses by rapist type: An empirical and clinical analysis. *Journal of Interpersonal Violence*, 1, 73–98.

Prescott, J. (1975). Body pleasure and the origins of violence. *The Futurist*, April, 64–74.

Prescott, J. (1989). Affectional bonding for the prevention of violent behaviors: Neurological, psychological, and religious/spiritual determinants. In L. Hertzberg (Ed.), *Violent Behavior*, v. 1, *Assessment and Intervention*. New York: PMA Publishing.

Preston, P. (2005). Nonverbal communication: Do you really say what you mean? *Journal of Healthcare Management*, 50, 83–86.

Price, J., Dake, J., Kirchofer, G., & Telljohann, S. (2003). Elementary school teacher's techniques of responding to student questions regarding sexuality issues. *Journal of School Health*, 73, 9–14.

Pridal, C., & LoPiccolo, J. (2000). Multielement treatment of desire disorders: Integration of cognitive, behavioral, and systemic therapy. In S. Leiblum & R. Rosen (Eds.), *Principles and Practice of Sex Therapy*. New York: Guilford Press.

Priestly, C., Jones, B., Dhar, J., & Goodwin, L. (1997). What is normal vaginal flora? *Genitourinary Medicine*, 73, 23–28.

Prince-Gibson, E. (2000). Success story, *Ms.*, April–May, 22–23.

Prior, P., & Hayes B. (2003). The relationship between marital status and health. *Journal of Family Issues*, 24, 124–148.

Proctor, F., Wagner, N., & Butler, J. (1974). The differentiation of male and female orgasm: An experimental study. In N. Wagner (Ed.), *Perspectives on Human Sexuality*. New York: Behavioral Publications.

Propst, A., & Laufer, M. (1999). Diagnosing and treating adolescent endometriosis. *Contemporary OB/GYN*, December, 52–59.

Proulx, J., Aubut, J., McKibben, A., & Cote, M. (1994). Penile responses of rapists and nonrapists to rape stimuli involving physical violence or humiliation. *Archives of Sexual Behavior*, 23, 295–310.

Puente, S., & Cohen, D. (2003). Jealousy and the meaning (or nonmeaning) of violence. *Personality and Social Psychology Bulletin*, 29, 449–460.

Putnam, F. (2003). Ten-year research update review: Child sexual abuse. *Journal of the American Academy of Child and Adolescent Psychiatry*, 42, 269–278.

Pyke, K., & Johnson, D. (2003). Asian American women and racialized femininities: "Doing" gender across cultural worlds. *Gender and Society*, 17, 33–53.

Quackenbush, D., Strassberg, D., & Turner, C. (1995). Gender effects of romantic themes in erotica. *Archives of Sexual Behavior*, 24, 21–35.

Quindlen, A. (2003a). Getting rid of the sex police. *Newsweek*, January 13, 72.

Quindlen, A. (2003b). Out of the time warp. *Newsweek*, January 27, 26.

Quittner, J. (2003). Addicted to dot.com sex. *The Advocate*, February 4, 34–36.

Rabock, J., Mellon, J., & Starka, L. (1979). Klinefelter's syndrome: Sexual development and activity. *Archives of Sexual Behavior*, 8, 333–340.

Radar, B. (2001). *American Ways: A Brief History of American Cultures*. Sydney, Australia: Thomson Wadsworth.

Radar, B. (2003). Personal communication.

Radlove, S. (1983). Sexual response and gender roles. In E. Allgeier & N. McCormick (Eds.), *Changing Boundaries: Gender Roles and Sexual Behavior*. Mountain View, CA: Mayfield.

Raffaelli, M., & Ontai, L. (2004). Gender socialization in Latino families: Results from two retrospective studies. *Sex Roles, 50,* 287–300.

Rako, S. (1996). *The Hormone of Desire.* New York: Harmony Books.

Rako, S. (1999). Testosterone deficiency and supplementation for women: Matters of sexuality and health. *Psychiatric Annals, 29,* 23–26.

Rako, S., & Friebely, J. (2004). Pheromonal influences on sociosexual behavior in postmenopausal women. *Journal of Sex Research, 41,* 372–380.

Ramakrishnan, K., & Scheid, D. (2006). Ectopic pregnancy: Forget the "classic presentation" if you want to catch it sooner. *The Journal of Family Practice, 55,* 388–395.

Ramson, A. (2006). Sexual harassment education on campus: Communication using media. *Community College Review, 33,* 38–54.

Ranii, D. (2006). Broadcasters wonder: What's indecent to the FCC? *News & Observer* (Raleigh, NC), July 22, pNA.

Ranjit, N., Bankole, A., & Darroch, J. (2001). Contraceptive failure in the first two years of use: Differences across socioeconomic subgroups. *Family Planning Perspectives, 33,* 19–27.

Rannestad, T., Eikeland, O., & Helland, H. (2001). The quality of life in women suffering from gynecological disorders is improved by means of hysterectomy. *Acta Obstetricia et Gynecologica Scandinavica, 80,* 46–51.

Rapp, D., & Gerber, G. (2005). A "slightly high" PSA: When should you call the urologist? *Consultant, 45,* 437–442.

Rasch, V. (2003). Cigarette, alcohol, and caffeine consumption: Risk factors for spontaneous abortion. *Acta Obstetricia et Gynecologica Scandinavica, 82,* 182–188.

Rasheed, A., White, C., & Shaikh, N. (1997). The incidence of post-vasectomy chronic testicular pain and the role of nerve stripping (denervation) of the spermatic cord in its management. *British Journal of Urology, 79,* 269–270.

Ray, A., & Gold, S. (1996). Gender roles, aggression, and alcohol use in dating relationships. *Journal of Sex Research, 33,* 47–55.

Ray, S., & Quinn, T. (2000). Sex and the genetic diversity of HIV-1. *Nature Medicine, 6,* 23–25.

Raz, R., Gennesin, Y., & Wasser, J. (2000). Recurrent urinary tract infections in postmenopausal women. *Clinical Infectious Diseases, 30,* 152–156.

Real, T. (2002). *How Can I Get Through to You? Reconnecting Men and Women.* New York: Screbuer.

Reape, K. (2005). Current contraceptive research and development. *Adolescent Medicine, 16,* 617–633.

Rebar, R. (2004). Assisted reproductive technology in the United States. *New England Journal of Medicine, 350,* 1603–1604.

Reddy, S., Warner, H., Guttuso, T., & Messing, S. (2006). Gabapentin, estrogen, and placebo for treating hot flashes. *Obstetrics & Gynecology, 108,* 4–48.

Redmond, G. (1999). Hormones and sexual function. *International Journal of Fertility, 44,* 193–197.

Reeder, H. (1996). The subjective experience of love through adult life. *International Journal of Aging and Human Development, 43,* 325–340.

Regan, P. (1998). Of lust and love: Beliefs about the role of sexual desire in romantic relationships. *Personal Relationships, 5,* 139–157.

Regan, P., & Berscheid, E. (1995). Gender differences about the causes of male and female sexual desire. *Personal Relationships, 2,* 345–358.

Regehr, C., & Glancy, G. (1995). Sexual exploitation of patients: Issues for colleagues. *American Journal of Orthopsychiatry, 65*(2), 194–202.

Regnerus, M., & Luchies, L. (2006). The parent-child relationship and opportunities for adolescents' first sex. *Journal of Family Issues, 27,* 159–183.

Reid, B. (2003). Truth, stretched. *Men's Health, 20,* 58.

Reid, P., & Bing, V. (2000). Sexual roles of girls and women: An ethnocultural lifespan perspective. In C. Travis & J. White (Eds.), *Sexuality, Society, and Feminism.* Washington, DC: American Psychological Association.

Reinberg, S. (2006). Testosterone offers women benefits, risks: Higher levels may boost sexual function, but increase heart trouble, studies find. Retrieved July 10, 2006, from http://health.msn.com/healthnews/articlepage.aspx?cp-documentid=100138390.

Reiner, W. (1997a). Sex assignment in the neonate with intersex or inadequate genitalia. *Archives of Pediatric and Adolescent Medicine, 151,* 1044–1045.

Reiner, W. (1997b). To be male or female: That is the question. *Archives of Pediatric and Adolescent Medicine, 151,* 224–225.

Reiner, W. (2000). *Gender and "Sex Reassignment."* Paper presented at the Lawson Wilkins Pediatric Endocrine Society meeting, Boston, May 12. Retrieved August 19, 2000, from http://mayohealth.org/mayo/headline/htm/hw000516.htm.

Reinisch, J., & Beasley, R. (1990). *The Kinsey Institute's New Report on Sex.* New York: St. Martin's Press.

Reiter, R., & Milburn, A. (1994). Exploring effective treatment for chronic pelvic pain. *Contemporary OB/GYN,* March, 84–103.

Rempel, J., & Baumgartner, B. (2003). The relationship between attitudes towards menstruation and sexual attitudes, desires, and behavior in women. *Archives of Sexual Behavior, 32,* 155–163.

Renaud, C., & Byers, S. (2001). *Positive and Negative Sexual Cognitions: Subjective Experience and Relationships to Sexual Adjustment.* Retrieved September 2, 2003, from http://infotrac-college.thomsonlearning.com/itw/infomark/684/939/38133136w6/5!xrn_1_0. . . .

Renshaw, D. (1987). Painful intercourse associated with cerebral palsy. *Journal of the American Medical Association, 257,* 2086.

Renzetti, C., & Curran, D. (1992). *Women, Men, and Society* (2nd ed.). Boston: Allyn & Bacon.

Reproductive Health Matters (2004). Destruction of the vagina in violent rape a war crime in Congo. Author, 12, 181–182.

Resnick, M., Bearman, P., Blum, R., Bauman, K., Harris, K., Jones, J., Tabor, J., Beuhring, T., Sieving, R., Shew, M., Ireland, M., Bearinger, L., & Udry, J. (1997). Protecting adolescents from harm: Findings from the National Longitudinal Study on Adolescent Health. *Journal of the American Medical Association, 278,* 823–832.

Resnik, R. (2006). Can a 29% cesarean delivery rate possibly be justified? *Obstetrics & Gynecology*, 107, 752–753.

Reuters (2003). *Penis Extensions Top the List in Britain*. Retrieved February 18, 2003, from http://www.reuters.com/newsArticle.jhtml.

Reynolds, J. (2006). Sex, secrets and cyberspace: Area prostitution flourishes via Web. *Monterey County Herald*, July 9, pNA.

Reynolds, S., Shepherd, M., Risbud, A., Gangakhedkar, R., Brookmeyer, R., Divekar, A., Mehendale, S., & Bollinger, R. (2004). Male circumcision and risk of HIV-1 and other sexually transmitted infections in India. *Lancet*, 363, 1039–1040.

Rhode, D. (1997). Harassment is alive and well and living at the water cooler. *Ms.*, November–December, 28–29.

Rhodes, S., Bowie, D., & Hergenrather, K. (2003). Collecting behavioral data using the World Wide Web: Considerations for researchers. *Journal of Epidemiology and Community Health*, 57, 68–73.

Rhodes, S., DiClemente, R., Yee, I., & Hergenrather, K. (2001a). Correlates of hepatitis B vaccination in a high-risk population: An Internet sample. *American Journal of Medicine*, 110, 628–632.

Rhodes, S., DiClemente, R., Yee, I., & Hergenrather, K. (2001b). Factors associated with testing hepatitis C in an Internet-recruited sample of men who have sex with men. *Sexually Transmitted Diseases*, 28, 515–520.

Rholes, W., Simpson, J., & Friedman, M. (2006). Avoidant attachment and the experience of parenting. *Personality and Social Psychology Bulletin*, 32, 275–285.

Rhynard, J., Krebs, M., & Glover, J. (1997). Sexual assault in dating relationships. *Journal of School Health*, 67, 89–93.

Ribadeneira, D. (1998). More women step up to pulpit, but they still take a back pew. *The Oregonian*, April 19, G3.

Richard, D. (2002). Tantra 101. *Contemporary Sexuality*, 36, 1 & 4–7.

Richard, D. (2002a). Senior sexuality. *Contemporary Sexuality*, 36, 1–6.

Richards, L., Rollerson, B., & Phillips, J. (1991). Perceptions of submissiveness: Implications for victimization. *Journal of Psychology*, 125, 407–411.

Richards, M., Rubinow, D., Daly, R., & Schmidt, P. (2006). Premenstrual symptoms and perimenopausal depression. *American Journal of Psychiatry*, 163, 133–137.

Richardson, B., John-Stewart, G., Hughes, J., Nduati, R., Mbori-Ngacha, D., Overbaugh, J., & Kreiss, J. (2003a). Breast-milk infectivity in human immunodeficiency virus type I–infected mothers. *Journal of Infectious Diseases*, 187, 736–740.

Richardson, D., Wood, K., & Goldmeier, D. (2006). A qualitative pilot study of Islamic men with lifelong premature (rapid) ejaculation. *The Journal of Sexual Medicine*, 3, 337–343.

Richardson, H., Franco, E., Pintos, J., Bergeron, J., Arella, M., & Tellier, P. (2000). Determinants of low-risk and high-risk cervical human papillomavirus infections in Montreal university students. *Sexually Transmitted Diseases*, 27, 79–86.

Richter, S., Leibovitch, I., & Alkalay, R. (2006). Anejaculation and orgasmic disorders in men after penile implant surgery. *The Journal of Sexual Medicine*, 3 (suppl. 3), 224–286.

Rickert, V., & Wiemann, C. (1998). Date rape: Office-based solutions. *Contemporary OB/GYN*, 43, 133–153.

Rickert, V., Sanghvi, R., & Wiemann, C. (2002). Is lack of sexual assertiveness among adolescent and young adult women a cause for concern? *Perspectives on Sexual and Reproductive Health*, 34, 178–183.

Ricks, T., & Suro, R. (2000). Army confirms harassment charge by top woman general. *The Oregonian*, May 11, A8.

Rider, E. (2000). *Our Voices: Psychology of Women*. Belmont, CA: Wadsworth/Thomson Learning.

Ridgeway, J. (1996). *Inside the Sex Industry*. New York: Powerhouse Books.

Rienzo, B., Button, J., Sheu, J., & Li, Y. (2006). The politics of sexual orientation issues in American schools. *Journal of School Health*, 76, 93–97.

Rierdan, J., Koff, E., & Stubbs, M. (1998). Gender, depression and body image in early adolescents. *Journal of Early Adolescence*, 8, 109–117.

Riley, A., & Riley, E. (2000). Controlled studies on women presenting with sexual drive disorder. I. Endocrine status. *Journal of Sex and Marital Therapy*, 26, 269–283.

Rind, B., & Tromovitch, P. (1997). A meta-analytic review of findings from national samples on psychological correlates of child sexual abuse. *Journal of Sex Research*, 34, 237–255.

Rind, B., Tromovitch, P., & Bauserman, R. (1998). A meta-analytic examination of assumed properties of child sexual abuse using college samples. *Psychological Bulletin*, 124, 22–53.

Ring, W. (2001). *Vermont Teens Drawn to Prostitution*. Retrieved February 9, 2001, from http://www.salon.com/mwt/wire/2001/02/09/prostitution//index.html.

Ringdahl, E. (2000). Treatment of recurrent vulvovaginal candidiasis. *American Family Physician*, 61, 3306–3312.

Rintala, M., Grenman, S., Jarvenkyla, M., Syrjanen, K., & Syrjanen, S. (2005). High-risk types of human papillomavirus (HPV) DNA in oral and genital mucosa of infants during their first 3 years of life: Experience from the Finnish HPV family study. *Clinical Infectious Diseases*, 41, 1728–1733.

Rios, D. (1996). The gone girls. *The Oregonian*, November 17, E1–E3.

Riscol, L. (2003). Bigger, harder, better: Natural sex enhancers or Viagra-era snake oil? *Contemporary Sexuality*, 37, 1.

Ritter, J. (2003). *More Choices Available for Birth Control*. Retrieved April 11, 2003, from http://www.suntimes.com/output/news/cst-nws-birth06.html.

Ritter, T. (1919). The people's home medical book. In R. Barnum (Ed.), *The People's Home Library*. Cleveland: Barnum.

Ritts, V. (2003). *Infusing Culture into Psychopathology*. Retrieved March 13, 2003, from http://www.stlcc.cc.mo.us/mc/users/vritts/psypath.htm.

Robinson, B., Scheltema, K., & Cherry, T. (2005). Risky sexual behavior in low-income African American women: The impact of sexual health variables. *Journal of Sex Research*, 42, 224–237.

Robinson, D., Gibson-Beverly, G., & Schwartz, J. (2004). Sorority and fraternity membership and religious behaviors: Relation to gender attitudes. *Sex Roles: A Journal of Research*, 50, 871–877.

Robinson, G. (1999). China: Surfeit of bachelors predicted in China. *World Press Review*, March, 18.

Robinson, J., & Godbey, G. (1998). No sex, please. We're college graduates. *American Demographics*, 20(2), 18–23.

Roddy, R., Zekeng, K., Ryan, A., Tamoufe, U., & Tweedy, K. (2002). Effect of nonoxynol-9 gel on urogenital gonorrhea and chlamydial infection: A randomized controlled trial. *Journal of the American Medical Association*, March 6, 1117–1122.

Rodriguez, N., Ryan, S., Vande Kemp, H., & Foy, D. (1997). Posttraumatic stress disorder in adult female survivors of childhood sexual abuse: A comparison study. *Journal of Consulting and Clinical Psychology*, 65, 53–59.

Rodriguez-Stednicki, O., & Twaite, J. (1999). Attitudes toward victims of child abuse among adults from four ethnic/cultural groups. *Journal of Child Sexual Abuse*, 8, 1–24.

Roffman, D. (2005). Lakoff for sexuality educators: The power and magic of "framing." *SIECUS Report*, 33, 20–25.

Rogers, C. (1951). *Client-Centered Therapy: Its Current Practice, Implications, and Theory.* Boston: Houghton Mifflin.

Rojanapithayakorn, W., & Hannenberg, R. (1996). The 100% condom program in Thailand. *AIDS*, 10, 1–7.

Romano, A. (2006). Walking a new beat. *Newsweek*, April 24, 48.

Romanowski, B., Preiksaitis, J., Campbell, P., & Fenton, J. (2003a). Hepatitis C seroprevalence and risk behaviors in patients attending sexually transmitted disease clinics. *Sexually Transmitted Diseases*, 30, 33–38.

Romanowski, B., Valtrex HS230017 Study Group, Marina, R., & Roberts, J. (2003b). Patients' preference for valacyclovir once-daily suppressive therapy versus twice-daily episodic therapy for recurrent genital herpes: A randomized study. *Sexually Transmitted Diseases*, 30, 226–231.

Romeo, F. (2004). Acquaintance rape on college and university campuses. *College Student Journal*, 38, 61–65.

Romeo, J., Seftel, A., Madhun, Z., & Aron, D. (2000). Sexual function in men with diabetes type 2: Association with glycemic control. *Journal of Urology*, 163, 788–791.

Ronsman, C., Holtz, S., & Stanton, C. (2006). Socioeconomic differentials in caesarean rates in developing countries: A retrospective analysis. *The Lancet*, 368, 1516–23.

Roots, K. (2006). A better pill to swallow? Retrieved June 22, 2006 from http://www.science-spirit.org/new_detail.php?news_id=545.

Roscoe, B., Strouse, J., & Goodwin, M. (1994). Sexual harassment: Early adolescents' self-reports of experiences and acceptance. *Adolescence*, 115, 515–523.

Rosen, R., & Ashton, A. (1993). Prosexual drugs: Empirical status of the "new aphrodisiacs." *Archives of Sexual Behavior*, 22, 521–541.

Rosen, R., & Beck, J. (1988). *Patterns of Sexual Arousal.* New York: Guilford Press.

Rosen, R., Diamond, L., Earle, D., Shadiack, A., & Molinoff, P. (2004). Evaluation of the safety, pharmacokinetics, and pharmacodynamic effects of subcutaneously administered PT-141, a melanocortin receptor agonist, in healthy male subjects and in patients with inadequate response to Viagra. *International Journal of Impotence Research*, 16, 135–142.

Rosen, T. (2006). Sexually transmitted diseases 2006: A dermatologist's view. *Cleveland Clinic Journal of Medicine*, 73, 537–550.

Rosenau, D., Taylor, D., Sytsma, M., & McClusky, C. (2001). *Conducting Sex Therapy with Conservative Christian Couples.* Paper presented at the 33rd Annual Conference of the American Association of Sex Educators, Counselors, and Therapists, San Francisco, May 2–6.

Rosenberg, D. (2003a). Chipping away at Roe. *Newsweek*, March 17, 40–41.

Rosenberg, M. (1988). Adult behaviors that reflect childhood incest. *Medical Aspects of Human Sexuality*, May, 114–124.

Rosengard, C., Adler, N., Gurvey, J., & Ellen, J. (2005). Adolescent partner-type experience: Psychosocial and behavioral differences. *Perspectives on Sexual and Reproductive Health*, 37, 141-146.

Rosenthal, D., Smith, A., & de Visser, R. (1999). Personal and social factors influencing age at first intercourse. *Archives of Sexual Behavior*, 28, 319–333.

Rosenthal, E. (2006). Study finds genital cutting can be deadly. *The New York Times*, June 2, F4.

Rosenzweig, J., & Daily, D. (1989). Dyadic adjustment/sexual satisfaction in women and men as a function of psychological sex role self-perception. *Journal of Sex and Marital Therapy*, 15, 42–56.

Rosler, A., & Witztum, E. (1998). Treatment of men with paraphilia with a long-acting analogue of gonadotropin releasing hormone. *New England Journal of Medicine*, 338, 416–422.

Rosman, J., & Resnick, P. (1989). Sexual attraction to corpses: A psychiatric review of necrophilia. *Bulletin of the American Academy of Psychiatry and the Law*, 17, 153–163.

Ross, H., Godeau, E., Dias, S., Vignes, C., & Gross, L. (2004). Setting politics aide to collect cross-national data on sexual health of adolescents. *SIECUS Report*, 32, 28–34.

Ross, M. (2005). Typing, doing, and being: Sexuality and the Internet. *Journal of Sex Research*, 42, 342–353.

Rothbaum, B., & Jackson, J. (1990). Religious influence on menstrual attitudes and symptoms. *Women & Health*, 16(1), 63–77.

Rotheram, M., & Weiner, N. (1983). Androgyny, stress, and satisfaction. *Sex Roles*, 9, 151–158.

Rousseau, C., Nduati, R., Richardson, B., Steele, M., John-Stewart, G., Mbori-Ngacha, D., Kreiss, J., & Overbaugh, J. (2003). Longitudinal analysis of human immunodeficiency virus type I RNA in breast milk and its relationship to infant infection and maternal diseases. *Journal of Infectious Diseases*, 187, 741–747.

Routh, L. (2000). *Inside the Mind of a Woman: Neuropsychiatric Disorders and the Impact of Hormones Throughout the Female Lifecycle.* Paper presented at a workshop given by the Amen Clinic for Behavioral Medicine Inc., Fairfield, California, May 26.

Rowland, D., Strassberg, D., de Gouveia Brazao, C., & Slob, A. (2000). Ejaculatory latency and control in men with premature ejaculation: An analysis across sexual activities using multiple sources of information. *Journal of Psychosomatic Research,* 48, 69–77.

Royce, R., Sena, A., Cates, W., & Cohen, M. (1997). Sexual transmission of HIV. *New England Journal of Medicine,* 336, 1072–1078.

Rubin, J., Provenzano, F., & Luria, Z. (1974). The eye of the beholder: Parents' views on sex of newborns. *American Journal of Orthopsychiatry,* 44, 512–519.

Rubin, L. (1990). *Erotic Wars.* New York: Farrar, Straus & Giroux.

Rubin, Z. (1970). Measurement of romantic love. *Journal of Personality and Social Psychology,* 16, 265–273.

Rubinsky, H., Eckerman, D., Rubinsky, E., & Hoover, C. (1987). Early-phase physiological response patterns to psychosexual stimuli: Comparisons of male and female patterns. *Archives of Sexual Behavior,* 16, 45–55.

Rumstein-McKean, O., & Hunsley, J. (2001). Interpersonal and family functioning of female survivors of childhood sexual abuse. *Clinical Psychology Review,* 21, 471–490.

Ruowei, L. (2002). Prevalence of exclusive breastfeeding among U.S. infants. *American Journal of Public Health,* 92, 1107–1110.

Russell, B., & Oswald, D. (2001). Strategies and dispositional correlates of sexual coercion perpetrated by women: An exploratory investigation. *Sex Roles,* 45, 103–115.

Russell, B., & Oswald, D. (2002). Sexual coercion and victimization of college men: The role of love styles. *Journal of Interpersonal Violence,* 17, 273–285.

Ryan, C., Vathing, O., & Gorbach, P. (1998). Explosive spread of HIV-1 and sexually transmitted diseases in Cambodia. *The Lancet,* 351, 1175–1180.

Ryan, G. (2000). Childhood sexuality: A decade of study. Part I. Research and curriculum development. *Child Abuse and Neglect,* 24, 33–48.

Ryan, G. Miyoshi, T., & Krugman, R. (1988). *Early Childhood Experience of Professionals Working in Child Abuse.* Paper presented at the 17th Annual Symposium on Child Sexual Abuse and Neglect, Keystone, Colorado.

Saad, L. (2006, January 20). Abortion views reviewed as Alito vote nears. Retrieved July 8, 2006, from http://poll.gallup.com/content/default.aspx?ci=20983&pg=1.

Saario, T., Jacklin, C., & Tittle, C. (1973). Sex role stereotyping in public schools. *Harvard Educational Review,* 43, 386–416.

Sadker, M., & Sadker, D. (1994). *Failing at Fairness: How America's Schools Cheat Girls.* New York: Scribners.

Sadovsky, R. (2005). Androgen therapy for effects of aging in older men. *American Family Physician,* 72, 170–171.

Sadovsky, R., & Nusbaum, M. (2006). Sexual health inquiry and support is a primary care priority. *The Journal of Sexual Medicine,* 3, 3–11.

Saewyc, E., Magee, L., & Pettingell, S. (2004). Teenage pregnancy and associated risk behaviors among sexually abused adolescents. *Perspectives on Sexual and Reproductive Health,* 36, 98–105.

Safren, S., & Heimberg, R. (1999). Depression, hopelessness, suicidality, and related factors in sexual minority and heterosexual adolescents. *Journal of Consulting and Clinical Psychology,* 67, 859–866.

Saigal, C., Wessells, H., Pace, J., & Schonlau, M. (2006). Predictors and prevalence of erectile dysfunction in a racially diverse population. *Archives of Internal Medicine,* 166, 207–212.

Salem, R. (2006). New attention to the IUD. *Population Reports,* Series B, No. 7. Baltimore: Johns Hopkins Bloomberg School of Public Health, The INFO Project, February, 47–56.

Salisbury, N. (1991). Personal communication.

Salonia, A., Zanni, G., Fantini, G., & Deho, F. (2006). Psychometric parameters of sexual health in infertile couples due to a male factor. Preliminary results of a multivariate analysis. *The Journal of Sexual Medicine,* 3(suppl. 3), 193.

Salovey, P., & Rodin, J. (1985). The heart of jealousy. *Psychology Today,* September, 22–29.

Salter, D., McMillan, D., Richards, M., Talbot, T., Hodges, J., Bentovim, A., Hastings, R, Stevenson, J., & Skuse, D. (2003). Development of sexually abusive behavior in sexually victimized males: A longitudinal study. *The Lancet,* 361, 471–476.

Sampson, E. (1985). The decentralization of identity: Toward a revised concept of personal and social order. *American Psychologist,* 40, 1203–1211.

Samraj, G., Kuritzky, L., & Seftel, A. (2005). Current and future strategies for premature ejaculation. *Contemporary Urology,* 17, 12–18.

Samuels, H. (1997). The relationships among selected demographics and conventional and unconventional sexual behaviors among black and white heterosexual men. *Journal of Sex Research,* 34, 85–92.

Sanchez, D., Kiefer, A., & Ybarra, O. (2006). Sexual submissiveness in women: Costs for sexual autonomy and arousal. *Personality and Social Psychology Bulletin,* 32, 512–524.

Sanchez, Y. (1997). Families of Mexican origin. In M. DeGenova (Ed.), *Families in Cultural Context: Strengths and Challenges in Diversity.* Mountain View, CA: Mayfield.

Sanday, P. (1981). The sociocultural context of rape: A cross-cultural study. *Journal of Social Issues,* 37, 5–27.

Sanday, P. (1996). *A Woman Scorned: Acquaintance Rape on Trial.* New York: Doubleday.

Sandelowski, M. (2000). "This most dangerous instrument": Propriety, power, and the vaginal speculum. *Journal of Obstetrical, Gynecological, and Neonatal Nursing,* 29, 73–82.

Sanders, G. (2000). Men together: Working with gay couples in contemporary times. In P. Papp (Ed.), *Couples on the Fault Line.* New York: Guilford Press.

Sanders, S., & Reinisch, J. (1999). Would you say you "had sex" if . . . ? *Journal of the American Medical Association,* 281, 275–277.

Sanders, S., Graham, C., & Janssen, E. (2003). *Factors Affecting Sexual Arousal in Women.* Retrieved March

8, 2003, from http://www.kinseyinstitute.org/research/focus_group.html.

**Sandlow, J.** (2000). Shattering the myths about male infertility. *Postgraduate Medicine, 107,* 235–242.

**Sandnabba, N., Santtila, P., & Nordling, N.** (1999). Sexual behavior and social adaptation among sadomasochistically oriented males. *Journal of Sex Research, 36,* 273–282.

**Sangrador, J., & Yela, C.** (2000). What is beautiful is loved: Physical attractiveness in love relationships in a representative sample. *Social Behavior and Personality, 28,* 207–218.

**Santelli, J., Morrow, B., Anderson, J., & Lindberg, L.** (2006). Contraceptive use and pregnancy risk among U.S. high school students, 1991–2003. *Perspectives on Sexual and Reproductive Health, 38,* 106–111.

**Santilla, P., Sandnabba, K., Alison, L., & Nordling, N.** (2002). Investigating the underlying structure in sadomasochistically oriented behavior. *Archives of Sexual Behavior, 31,* 185–196.

**Sarrel, P.** (1988). *Sex and Menopause.* Paper presented at the 21st Annual Meeting of the American Association of Sex Educators, Counselors, and Therapists, San Francisco, April.

**Sarrel, P., & Masters, W.** (1982). Sexual molestation of men by women. *Archives of Sexual Behavior, 11,* 117–131.

**Satel, S.** (1993). The diagnostic limits of addiction. *Journal of Clinical Psychiatry, 54,* 237.

**Satterfield, A., & Muehlenhard, C.** (1990). *Flirtation in the Classroom: Negative Consequences on Women's Perceptions of Their Ability.* Paper presented at the annual meeting of the Society for the Scientific Study of Sex, Minneapolis, November.

**Saunders, E.** (1989). Life-threatening autoerotic behavior: A challenge for sex educators and therapists. *Journal of Sex Education and Therapy, 15,* 77–81.

**Savage, D.** (2002). Justices void law on child sex images. *The Oregonian,* April 17, A1, A7.

**Savic, I., Berglund, H., & Lindstrom, P.** (2005). Brain responses to putative pheromones in homosexual men. *Proceedings of the National Academy of Sciences, 102,* 7356–7361.

**Sawyer, R., Pinciaro, P., & Jessell, J.** (1998). Effects of coercion and verbal consent on university students' perception of date rape. *American Journal of Health Behavior, 22,* 46–53.

**Sbarra, D.** (2006). Predicting the onset of emotional recovery following nonmarital relationship dissolution: Survival analyses of sadness and anger. *Personality and Social Psychology Bulletin, 32,* 298–312.

**Schaalma, H., Abraham, C., Gillmore, R., & Kok, G.** (2004). Sex education as health promotion: What does it take? *Archives of Sexual Behavior, 33,* 259–269.

**Schaffir, J.** (2006). Sexual intercourse at term and onset of labor. *Obstetrics & Gynecology, 107,* 1310–1314.

**Scharf, C., & Weinshel, M.** (2000). Infertility and late-life pregnancies. In P. Papp (Ed.), *Couples on the Fault Line.* New York: Guilford Press.

**Scharfe, E., & Bartholomew, K.** (1995). Accommodation and attachment representations in young couples. *Journal of Social and Personal Relationships, 12,* 389–401.

**Schatz, C., & Robb-Nicholson, C.** (2006). Anatomy of a hot flash. *Newsweek,* April 24, 73.

**Scheela, R., & Stern, P.** (1994). Falling apart: A process integral to the remodeling of male incest offenders. *Archives of Psychiatric Nursing, 8,* 91–100.

**Scheidler, A.** (2006). The deception of contraception: League takes the lead exposing the abortion-birth control link. Retrieved July 8, 2006, from http://www.prolifeaction.org/news/2006v25n2/contraception.htm.

**Scher, H.** (1997). The drive to stop harassment in schools. *Ms.,* March–April, 22.

**Schmidt, L.** (2006). Psychosocial burden of infertility and assisted reproduction. *The Lancet, 367,* 379–381.

**Schmitt, D.** (2003). Universal sex differences in the desire for sexual variety: Tests from 52 nations, 6 continents, and 13 islands. *Journal of Personality and Social Psychology, 85,* 85–104.

**Schmitt, D., Shackelford, T., Duntley, J., Tooke, W., & Buss, D.** (2001). The desire for sexual variety as a key to understanding basic human mating strategies. *Personal Relationships, 8,* 425–455.

**Schnarch, D.** (1991). *Constructing the Sexual Crucible.* New York: Norton.

**Schnarch, D.** (1993). Inside the sexual crucible. *Networker,* March–April, 40–48.

**Schoen, E., Anderson, G., Bohon, C., Hinman, F., Poland, R., & Wakeman, E.** (1989). Report of the Task Force on Circumcision. *Pediatrics, 84,* 388–391.

**Schoen, J.** (2006). *Choice and Coercion: Birth Control, Sterilization and Abortion in Public Health and Welfare.* North Carolina: University of North Carolina Press.

**Schoen, R., & Cheng, Y.** (2006). Partner choice and the differential retreat from marriage. *Journal of Marriage and Family, 68,* 1–10.

**Schoener, G.** (1995). Assessment of professionals who have engaged in boundary violations. *Psychiatric Annals, 25*(2), 95–99.

**Schooler, D., & Ward, M.** (2006). Average Joes: Men's relationships with media, real bodies, and sexuality. *Psychology of Men & Masculinity, 7,* 27–41.

**Schooler, D., Ward, L., Merriweather, A., & Caruthers, A.** (2005). Cycles of shame: Menstrual shame, body shame, and sexual decision-making. *The Journal of Sex Research, 42,* 324–335.

**Schover, L.** (2000). Sexual problems in chronic illness. In S. Leiblum & R. Rosen (Eds.), *Principles and Practice of Sex Therapy.* New York: Guilford Press.

**Schover, L., & Jensen, S.** (1988). *Sexuality and Chronic Illness.* New York: Guilford Press.

**Schredl, M., Ciric, P., Gotz, S., & Wittmann, L.** (2004). Typical dreams: Stability and gender differences. *The Journal of Psychology, 138,* 485–495.

**Schrinsky, D.** (1998, January). Personal communication.

**Schroder, M., & Carroll, R.** (1999). New women: Sexological outcomes of male-to-female gender reassignment surgery. *Journal of Sex Education and Therapy, 24,* 137–146.

**Schroedel, J.** (2000). *Is the Fetus a Person: A Comparison of Policies Across the Fifty States.* Ithaca, NY: Cornell University Press.

**Schroeder, J.** (1995). Offensive attack. *The Advocate,* August 22, 34–38.

Schubach, G. (1996). *Urethral Expulsions During Sensual Arousal and Bladder Catherization in Seven Human Females*. Ed.D. thesis, Institute for Advanced Study of Human Sexuality, San Francisco.

Schwartz, J., & Gabelnick, H. (2002). Current contraceptive research. *Perspectives on Sexual and Reproductive Health*, 34, 310–315.

Schwartz, K., Deschere, B., & Xu, J. (2005). Screening for prostate cancer: Who and how often? *Journal of Family Practice*, 54, 586–596.

Schwartz, P. (2006). Revitalizing sexuality for mental and physical health. Paper presented at the Women's Health Conference, Portland, OR, April.

Scott, L. (2006). An alternative to surgery in treating ectopic pregnancy. *Nursing Times*, 102, 24–26.

Seal, B., Brotto, L., & Gorzalka, B. (2005). Oral contraceptive use and female genital arousal: Methodological considerations. *Journal of Sex Research*, 42, 249–258.

Seal, D., Bloom, F., & Somlai, A. (2000). Dilemmas in conducting qualitative sex research in applied field settings. *Health Education and Behavior*, 27, 10–23.

Seaman, B., & Seaman, G. (1978). *Women and the Crisis in Sex Hormones*. New York: Bantam Books.

Segraves, R., & Kavoussi, R. (2000). Evaluation of sexual functioning in depressed outpatients: A double-blind comparison of sustained-release bupropion and sertraline treatment. *Journal of Clinical Psychopharmacology*, 20, 122–128.

Segraves, R., & Segraves, K. (1995). Human sexuality and aging. *Journal of Sex Education and Therapy*, 21, 88–102.

Seibert, C., Barbouche, E., Fagan, J., & Myint, E. (2003). Prescribing oral contraceptives for women older than 35 years of age. *Annals of Internal Medicine*, 138, 54–64.

Seidman, S., & Rieder, R. (1994). A review of sexual behavior in the United States. *American Journal of Psychiatry*, 151, 330–341.

Seligman, L., & Hardenburg, S. (2000). Assessment and treatment of paraphilias. *Journal of Counseling and Development*, 78, 107–113.

Semaan, S., Klovdahl, A., & Aral, S. (2004). Protecting the privacy, confidentiality, relationships, and medical safety of sex partners in partner notification and management studies. *Journal of Research Administration*, 35, 39–53.

Semans, J. (1956). Premature ejaculation: A new approach. *Southern Medical Journal*, 49, 353–358.

Sem-Jacobsen, C. (1968). *Depth-Electrographic Stimulation of the Human Brain and Behavior*. Springfield, IL: Thomas.

Senn, C., Desmarais, S., Verberg, N., & Wood, E. (1999). Predicting coercive sexual behavior across the lifespan in a random sample of Canadian men. *Journal of Social and Personal Relationships*, 17, 95–113.

Seppa, N. (2004). Foreskin may permit HIV entry, infection. *Science News*, 165, 212–213.

Seppa, N. (2005). Defense mechanism: Circumcision averts some HIV infections. *Science News*, 168, 275.

Sev'er, A. (1999). Sexual harassment: Where we are and prospects for the new millennium. *Canadian Review of Sociology and Anthropology*, 36, 469–482.

Shackelford, T., Buss, D., & Bennett, K. (2002). Forgiveness or breakup: Sex differences in responses to a partner's infidelity. *Cognition and Emotion*, 16.

Shah, J., & Fisch, H. (2006). Managing the vasectomy patient: From preoperative counseling through postoperative follow-up. *Contemporary Urology*, 18, 40–45.

Shah, P., Aliwalas, L., & Shah V. (2006). Breastfeeding or breast milk for procedural pain in neonates. *Cockrane Database of Systematic Reviews* 2006, Issue 3. Art. No.: CD004950. DOI: 101002/14651858. CD004950.pub2.

Shahinian, V., Kuo, Y., Freeman, J., & Goodwin, J. (2006). Risk of the "androgen deprivation syndrome" in men receiving androgen deprivation for prostate cancer. *Archives of Internal Medicine*, 166, 465–471.

Shanks, L., Ford, N., Schull, M., & de Jong, K. (2001). Responding to rape. *The Lancet*, 357, 304.

Shapiro, J. (1987). The expectant father. *Psychology Today*, January, 36–42.

Sharlip, I. (2006). Guidelines for the diagnosis and management of premature ejaculation. *The Journal of Sexual Medicine*, 3, 309–317.

Sharpsteen, D. (1995). *Sex, Attachment, and Infidelity: The Context of Jealousy*. Paper presented at the annual meeting of the Southwestern Psychological Association, Austin, Texas, April.

Sharpsteen, D., & Kirkpatrick, L. (1997). Romantic jealousy and adult romantic attachment. *Journal of Personality and Social Psychology*, 72, 627–640.

Shaul, S., Bogle, J., Hale-Harbaugh, J., & Norman, A. (1978). *Toward Intimacy: Family Planning and Sexuality Concerns of Physically Disabled Women*. New York: Human Sciences Press.

Shaver, P., Hazan, C., & Bradshaw, D. (1988). Love as attachment: The integration of three behavioral systems. In R. Sternberg & M. Barnes (Eds.), *The Psychology of Love*. New Haven, CT: Yale University Press.

Shaw, C. (1997). The perimenopausal hot flash: Epidemiology, physiology, and treatment. *Nurse Practitioner*, 22(3), 55–66.

Shaw, J. (1997). Treatment rationale for Internet infidelity. *Journal of Sex Education and Therapy*, 22(1), 21–28.

Shearer, B., Mulvihill, B., Klerman, L., Wallander, J., Hovinga, M., & Redden, D. (2002). Association of early childbearing and low cognitive ability. *Perspectives on Sexual and Reproductive Health*, 34, 236–243.

Sheeran, P. (1987). *Women, Society, the State, and Abortion: A Structuralist Analysis*. New York: Praeger.

Sheets, V., Fredendall, L., & Claypool, H. (1997). Jealousy evocation, partner reassurance, and relationship stability: An exploration of the potential benefits of jealousy. *Evolution and Human Behavior*, 18, 387–402.

Sherfer, T., Strebel, A., Wilson, T., Shabalala, N., Simbayi, L., Ratele, K., Potgieter, C., & Andipatin, M. (2002). The social construction of sexually transmitted infections (STIs) in South African communities. *Qualitative Health Research*, 12, 1373–1390.

Sherfey, M. (1972). *The Nature and Evolution of Female Sexuality*. New York: Random House.

Sherman, R., & Jones, J. (1994). A response to the article on "The validity of the Myers-Briggs Type Indicator for predicting marital problems." *Family Relations*, 43, 94–95.

Shernoff, M. (2006). The heart of a virtual hunter. *The Gay & Lesbian Review Worldwide*, 13, 20–23.

Shifen, J., Braunstein, G., Simon, J., Casson, P., Buster, J., Redmond, G., Burki, R., Ginsburg, E., Rosen, R., Leiblum, S., Carmelli, K., & Mazer, N. (2000). Transdermal testosterone treatment in women with impaired sexual function after oophorectomy. *New England Journal of Medicine*, 34, 682–688.

Shimonaka, Y., Nakazato, K., Kawaai, C., & Sato, S. (1997). Androgyny and successful adaptation across the life span among Japanese adults. *Journal of Genetic Psychology*, 158, 389–400.

Shlain, L. (2003). *Sex, Time, and Power: How Women's Sexuality Changed the Course of Human Evolution*. New York: Penguin.

Shook, N., Gerrity, D., Jurich, J., & Segrist, A. (2000). Courtship violence among college students: A comparison of verbally and physically abusive couples. *Journal of Family Violence*, 15, 1–22.

Shorto, R. (2006). Is the president for or against birth control? Retrieved June 14, 2006, from http://birthcontrolwatch.org/nytimes.htm.

Shrier, L., Pierce, J., Emans, S., & DuRant, R. (1998). Gender differences in risk behaviors associated with forced or pressured sex. *Archives of Pediatric and Adolescent Medicine*, 152, 57–63.

Shtarkshall, R. (2005). Conducting sex therapy in a cross-cultural environment: When the paradigm of the therapy and the worldview of the clients mismatch. Paper presented at the World Congress of Sexology, Montreal, Canada, July 10–15.

Shuit, D. (1996). Penile enlargement patients sue, say they were disfigured. *Los Angeles Times*, March 4, B1, B3.

SIECUS (2003). *SIECUS Fact Sheet: The Truth About STDs*. New York: SIECUS.

Siegel, K., Krauss, B., & Karus, D. (1994). Reporting recent sexual practices: Gay men's disclosure of HIV risk by questionnaire and interview. *Archives of Sexual Behavior*, 23, 217–230.

Sieving, R., Eisenberg, M., Pettingell, S., & Skay, C. (2006). Friends' influence on adolescents' first sexual intercourse. *Perspectives on Sexual and Reproductive Health*, 38, 13–19.

Silver, R., Landon, M., Rouse, D., & Leveno, K. (2006). Maternal morbidity associated with multiple repeat cesarean deliveries. *Obstetrics & Gynecology*, 107, 1226–1232.

Silverman, B., & Gross, T. (1997). Use and effectiveness of condoms during anal intercourse. *Sexually Transmitted Diseases*, 24, 11–17.

Silvertsen, C. (2000). *Court: Discard Embryos*. Retrieved June 2, 2000, from http://abcnews.go.com/sections/us/DailyNews/embryos000602.html.

Simon, C. (2006). Breast cancer screening: Cultural beliefs and diverse populations. *Health and Social Work*, 31, 36–44.

Simon, H. (2003). Alternatives to Viagra. *Newsweek*, June 16, 63.

Simon, J. (1998). Managing the monstrous: Sex offenders and the new penology. *Psychology, Public Policy, and Law*, 4, 452–467.

Simon, W., & Gagnon, J. (1998). Psychosexual devel-opment. *Society*, 35, 60–67.

Simonson, K., & Subich, L. (1999). Rape perceptions as a function of gender-role traditionality and victim-perpetrator association. *Sex Roles*, 40, 617–633.

Sinclair, D., & Kligman, E. (2005). Do antiaging approaches promote longevity? *Patient Care*, 39, 10-17.

Sinderbrand, R. (2005). A shameful little secret: North Carolina confronts its history of forced sterilization. *Newsweek*, March 28, 33.

Sinding, S. (2005). Does 'CNN' (condoms, needles and negotiation) work better than 'ABC' (abstinence, being faithful and condom use) in attacking the AIDS epidemic? *International Family Planning Perspectives*, 31, 38-40.

Singer, L. (2002). Cognitive and motor outcomes of cocaine-exposed infants. *Journal of the American Medical Association*, 287, 1952–1960.

Singer, N. (2005). The revised birthday suit. *The New York Times*, September 1, E3.

Singh, A., Romanowski, B., Wong, T., et al. (2005). Herpes simplex virus seroprevalence and risk factors in 2 Canadian sexually transmitted disease clinics. *Sexually Transmitted Diseases*, 32, 95–100.

Singh, S., & Darroch, J. (2000). Adolescent pregnancy and childbearing levels and trends in developed countries. *Family Planning Perspectives*, 32, 14–23.

Sinnott, J. (1986). *Sex Roles and Aging: Theory and Research from a Systems Perspective*. Basel, Switzerland: Karger.

Sipe, A. (1990). *A Secret World: Sexuality and the Search for Celibacy*. New York: Brunner/Mazel.

Skolnick, A. (1992). *The Intimate Environment: Exploring Marriage and the Family*. New York: HarperCollins.

Slijper, F., Drop, S., Molenaar, J., & Keizer-Schrama, S. (1998). Long-term psychological evaluation of intersex children. *Archives of Sexual Behavior*, 27, 125–143.

Sluzki, C. (1982). The Latin lover revisited. In M. McGoldrick & J. Giordano (Eds.), *Ethnicity and Family Therapy*. New York: Guilford Press.

Small, C., Manatunga, A., Klein, M., & Feigelson, H. (2006). Menstrual cycle characteristics: Associations with fertility and spontaneous abortion. *Epidemiology*, 17, 52–60.

Small, M. (1999). Nosing out a mate. *Scientific American Presents*, 10, 52–55.

Small, S., & Kerns, D. (1993). Unwanted sexual activity among peers during early and middle adolescence: Incidence and risk factors. *Journal of Marriage and the Family*, 55, 941–952.

Smalley, S. (2003a). The perfect crime. *Newsweek*, February 3, 52.

Smalley, S. (2003b). "This could be your kid." *Newsweek*, August 18, 44–47.

Smeltzer, S., & Kelley, C. (1997). Multiple sclerosis. In M. Sipski & C. Alexander (Eds.), *Sexual Function in People with Disability and Chronic Illness*. Gaithersburg, MD: Aspen Publishers.

Smith, D. (2003). Women and sex: What is "dysfunctional"? *Monitor on Psychology*, 34, 54–56.

Smith, D., & Over, R. (1987). Correlates of fantasy-induced and film-induced male sexual arousal. *Archives of Sexual Behavior*, 16, 395–409.

Smith, P., White, J., & Holland, L. (2003). A longitudinal perspective on dating violence among adolescent and college-age women. *American Journal of Public Health*, 93, 1104–1109.

Smith, R. (1985). Abortion, right and wrong. *Newsweek*, March 25, 16.

Smith, R., Aboitiz, F., Schroter, C., Barton, R., Denenberg, V., et al. (2005). Relative size versus controlling for size: Interpretation of ratios in research on sexual dimorphism in the human corpus callosum. *Current Anthropology*, 46, 249–273.

Smith, W. (2005). Reducing teen pregnancy. *Issues in Science and Technology*, 21, 18–19.

Smithyman, S. (1979). Characteristics of undetected rapists. In W. Parsonage (Ed.), *Perspectives on Victimology*. Beverly Hills, CA: Sage.

Solinger, R. (2005). *Pregnancy and Power: A Short History of Reproductive Politics in America*. New York: New York University Press.

Solomini, C. (1991). Cures for yeast infections. *New Woman*, May, 129.

Solomon, R. (1981). The love lost in cliches. *Psychology Today*, October, 83–94.

Solomonese, J., (2006). Quietly to victory: Congress passed and President Bush signed into law new 401(k) benefits for same-sex couples. *The Advocate*, September 26, 4

Somers, C., & Surmann, A. (2004). Adolescents' preferences for source of sex education. *Child Study Journal*, 34, 47–59.

Sonfield, A., (2004). New refusal clause shatters balance between provider "conscience", patient needs. *The Guttmacher Report*, 2, 47–50.

Sonfield, A., Gold, R., Frost, J., & Darroch, J. (2004). U.S. insurance coverage of contraceptive coverage mandates, 2002. *Perspectives on Sexual and Reproductive Health*, 36, 72–77.

Sontag, D. (1997). Partial birth abortions. *The Oregonian*, March 22, A8.

Sontag, S. (1972). The double standard of aging. *Saturday Review*, September 23, 29–38.

Soukup, E. (2006). Polygamists unite. *Newsweek*, March 20, 52.

Soukup, E. (2006). We are here to stay. *Newsweek*, June 26, 8.

South-Paul, J. (2003). Cross-cultural issues concerning sexuality, fertility, and childbirth. *Journal of the American Board of Family Practice*, 16, 180–181.

Speer, R. (2005). The fuzz that was. *Willamette Week*, December 14, 12–18.

Spence, J., & Helmreich, R. (1978). *Masculinity and Femininity*. Austin: University of Texas Press.

Spencer, T., & Tan, J. (1999). Undergraduate students' reactions to analogue male disclosure of sexual abuse. *Journal of Child Sexual Abuse*, 8, 73–90.

Speroff, L. & Ritz, M. (2005). *Clinical Gynecologic Endocrinology and Infertility* (7th Ed.). Philadelphia: Lippincott Williams & Wilkins.

Spitzberg, B. (1999). An analysis of empirical estimates of sexual aggression, victimization, and perpetration. *Violence and Victims*, 14, 241–260.

Sprauve, M., Lindsay, M., Herbert, S., & Graves, W. (1997). Adverse perinatal outcome in parturients who use crack cocaine. *Obstetrics and Gynecology*, 89, 674–678.

Sprecher, S. (2002). Sexual satisfaction in premarital relationships: Associations with satisfaction, love, commitment, and stability. *Journal of Sex Research*, 39, 190–196.

Sprecher, S., & McKinney, K. (1993). *Sexuality*. Newbury Park, CA: Sage.

Sprecher, S., & Regan, P. (1998). Passionate and companionate love in courting and young married couples. *Sociological Inquiry*, 68, 163–185.

Sprecher, S., Metts, S., Burleson, B., Hatfield, E., & Thompson, A. (1995). Domains of expressive interaction in intimate relationships: Associations with satisfaction and commitment. *Family Relations*, 44, 203–210.

Springen, K. (2003). New year, new breasts? *Newsweek*, January 13, 65–66.

Springen, K. (2005). A more posh vibe. *Newsweek*, July 25, 16.

Springen, K. (2005). The miscarriage maze. *Newsweek*, February 7, 63.

Spring-Mills, E., & Hafez, E. (1980). Male accessory sexual organs. In E. Hafez (Ed.), *Human Reproduction*. New York: Harper & Row.

Spruyt, A., Steiner, M., Joanis, C., Glover, L., Piedrahita, C., Alvarado, G., Ramos, R., Maglaya, C., & Cordero, M. (1998). Identifying condom users at risk for breakage and slippage: Findings from three international sites. *American Journal of Public Health*, 88, 239–244.

Srivastava, A., & Krieger, N. (2000). Relation of physical activity to risk of testicular cancer. *American Journal of Epidemiology*, 151, 78–87.

Sroufe, L. (1985). Attachment classification from the perspective of infant–caregiver relationships and infant temperament. *Child Development*, 56, 1–14.

Stack, S., & Gundlach, J. (1992). Divorce and sex. *Archives of Sexual Behavior*, 21, 359–368.

Stall, R., & Mills, T. (2006). A quarter century of AIDS. *American Journal of Public Health*, 96, 959–961.

Stanberry, L. (2000). Asymptomatic herpes simplex virus shedding and Russian roulette. *Clinical Infectious Diseases*, 30, 268–269.

Stanberry, L., Spruance, S., & Cunningham, A. (2002). Glycoprotein-D-adjuvant vaccine to prevent genital herpes. *New England Journal of Medicine*, 347, 1652–1661.

Stander, V., Olson, C., & Merrill, L. (2002). Self-definition as a survivor of childhood sexual abuse among navy recruits. *Journal of Consulting and Clinical Psychology*, 70, 369–377.

Stanford, J., Lemaire, J., & Thurman, P. (1998). Women's interest in natural family planning. *Journal of Family Practice*, 46, 65–71.

Stanley, D. (1993). To what extent is the practice of autoerotic asphyxia related to other paraphilias? In K. Haas & A. Haas (Eds.), *Understanding Sexuality*. St. Louis: Mosby.

Starce, F., Massa, A., Amico, K., & Fisher, J. (2006). Adherence to antiretroviral therapy: An empirical test of the information-motivation-behavioral skills model. *Health Psychology*, 25, 153–162.

Stark, C. (2005). Behavioral effects of stimulation of the medial amygdala in the male rat are modified by prior experience. *Journal of General Psychology, 132,* 207–224.

Staropoli, C., Flaws, J., Bush, T., & Moulton, A. (1997). *Cigarette Smoking and Frequency of Menopausal Hot Flashes.* Abstract for the 30th Annual Meeting of the Society for Epidemiologic Research, Edmonton, Alberta, Canada, 71.

Starr, B., & Weiner, M. (1981). *The Starr Weiner Report on Sex and Sexuality in the Mature Years.* New York: Stein & Day.

Starr, C. (1997). Beyond the birds and the bees: Talking to teens about sex. *Patient Care,* April 15, 103–129.

Staten, C. (1997). "Roofies": The new "date rape" drug of choice. *Emergency Net News,* October 21.

Stearns, S. (2001). PMS and PMDD in the domain of mental health nursing. *Journal of Psychosocial Nursing, 39,* 16–27.

Stebleton, M., & Rothenberger, J. (1993). Truth or consequences: Dishonesty in dating and HIV/AIDS-related issues in a college-age population. *Journal of American College Health, 42,* 51–54.

Steele, B., & Kennedy, S. (2006). Hustle and grow. *The Advocate,* April 11, 53–60.

Steele, J. (1999). Teenage sexuality and media practice: Factoring in the influences of family, friends, and school. *Journal of Sex Research, 36,* 331–341.

Stein, J., & Reiser, L. (1994). A study of white middle-class adolescent boys' responses to "semenarche" (the first ejaculation). *Journal of Youth and Adolescence, 23,* 373–384.

Stein, M., Freedberg, K., Sullivan, L., Savetsky, J., Levenson, S., Hingson, R., & Samet, J. (1998). Disclosure of HIV-positive status to partners. *Archives of Internal Medicine, 158,* 253–257.

Steinbrook, R. (2006). The potential of human papillomavirus vaccines. *New England Journal of Medicine, 354,* 1109–1112.

Steinem, G. (1998). Erotic and pornography: A clear and present difference. In R. Baird & S. Rosenbaum (Eds.), *Pornography: Private Right or Public Menace?* Amherst, NY: Prometheus Books.

Steininger, C., Kundi, M., Jatzko, G., Kiss, H., Lischka, A., & Holzman, H. (2003). Increased risk of mother-to-infant transmission of hepatitis C virus by intrapartum infantile exposure to maternal blood. *Journal of Infectious Diseases, 187,* 345–351.

Stener-Victorin, E., Waldenstrom, U., & Tagnfors, U. (2000). Effects of electro-acupuncture on anovulation in women with polycystic ovary syndrome. *Acta Obstetricia et Gynecologica Scandinavica, 79,* 180–188.

Stephen, T., & Harrison, T. (1985). A longitudinal comparison of couples with sex-typical and non-sex-typical orientation to intimacy. *Sex Roles, 12,* 195–206.

Stephenson, J. (2003b). Male infertility: Little help from varicocele repair. *Journal of the American Medical Association, 289,* 2929.

Stermac, L., Sheridan, P., Davidson, A., & Dunn, S. (1996). Sexual assault of adult males. *Journal of Interpersonal Violence, 11,* 52–64.

Stern, E. (1987). Sex during pregnancy. *American Baby,* March, 71–79.

Stewart, F. (1998c). Vaginal barriers. In R. Hatcher, J. Trussell, F. Stewart, W. Cates, G. Stewart, F. Guest, & D. Kowal (Eds.), *Contraceptive Technology.* New York: Ardent Media.

Stewart, G. (1998). Intrauterine devices (IUDs). In R. Hatcher, J. Trussell, F. Stewart, W. Cates, G. Stewart, F. Guest, & D. Kowal (Eds.), *Contraceptive Technology.* New York: Ardent Media.

Stewart, G., & Carignan, C. (1998). Female and male sterilization. In R. Hatcher, J. Trussell, F. Stewart, W. Cates, G. Stewart, F. Guest, & D. Kowal (Eds.), *Contraceptive Technology.* New York: Ardent Media.

Stier, D., Leventhal, J., Berg, A., Johnson, L., & Mezger, J. (1993). Are children born to young mothers at increased risk of maltreatment? *Pediatrics, 91,* 642–648.

Stobbe, M. (2005). C-section rate hits record high in '04 despite efforts to curb use. *The Oregonian,* November 16, B13.

Stobbe, M. (2005). Gonorrhea rate falls in the U.S. *Oregonian,* November 9, A4.

Stolberg, S. (1999). Racial health gap widest at childbirth. *The Sunday Oregonian,* August 8, A3.

Stolberg, S. (2001). Couple offer embryos for adoption. *The Sunday Oregonian,* February 25, A9.

Stoller, R. (1977). Sexual deviations. In F. Beach (Ed.), *Human Sexuality in Four Perspectives.* Baltimore: Johns Hopkins University Press.

Stoller, R. (1982). Transvestism in women. *Archives of Sexual Behavior, 11,* 99–115.

Stolte, I., De Wit, J., Kolader, M., et al. (2006). Association between "safer sex fatigue" and rectal gonorrhea is mediated by unsafe sex with casual partners among HIV-positive homosexual men. *Sexually Transmitted Diseases, 33,* 201–208.

Stone, N., & Ingham, R. (2002). Factors affecting British teenager's contraceptive use at first intercourse: The importance of partner communication. *Perspectives on Sexual and Reproductive Health, 34,* 191–197.

Stone, R., & Waszak, C. (1992). Adolescent knowledge and attitudes about abortion. *Family Planning Perspectives, 24,* 52–58.

Stoparic, B. (2006). Anti-poverty efforts face child marriage hurdle. Retrieved September 12, 2006, from http://www.womensenews.org/article.cfm/dyn/aid/2831/context/archive.

Stotland, N. (1998). *Abortion Facts and Feelings.* Washington, DC: American Psychiatric Press.

Strachan-Bennett, S. (2006). Erectile dysfunction could predict CHD. *Archives of Internal Medicine, 166,* 201–219.

Strassberg, D., & Mahoney, J. (1988). Correlates of contraceptive behavior of adolescents/young adults. *Journal of Sex Research, 25,* 531–536.

Straus, J. (2006). *Unhooked Generation: The Truth About Why We're Still Single.* New York: Hyperion.

Strauss, S., Des Jarlais, D., Astone, J., & Vassilev, Z. (2003). On-site HIV testing in residential drug treatment units: Results of a nationwide survey. *Public Health Reports, 118,* 37–43.

Streicher, L. (2005). No relief in sight for women's lagging libidos. Retrieved April 15, 2006, from http://www.findarticles.com/p/articles/mi_qn4155/is_20051202/ai_n15907736/print.

Streisand, B. (2005). Doing it in prime time. *U.S. News & World Report*, October 17, 50–51.

Striar, S., & Bartlik, B. (2000). Stimulation of the libido: The use of erotica in sex therapy. *Psychiatric Annals*, 29, 60–62.

Strong, D., Bancroft, J., Carnes, L., Davis, L., & Kennedy, J. (2005). The impact of sexual arousal on sexual risk-taking: A qualitative study. *Journal of Sex Research*, 42, 185–191.

Struckman-Johnson, C., & Struckman-Johnson, D. (2000). Sexual coercion rates in seven midwestern prison facilities for men. *Prison Journal*, 80, 379–390.

Struckman-Johnson, C., Struckman-Johnson, D., & Anderson, P. (2003). Tactics of sexual coercion: When men and women won't take no for an answer. *Journal of Sex Research*, 40, 76–86.

Stuart, F., Hammond, C., & Pett, M. (1998). Inhibited sexual desire in women. *Archives of Sexual Behavior*, 16, 91–106.

Stubbs, K. (1992). *Sacred Orgasms*. Berkeley, CA: Secret Garden.

Sugar, N., & Graham, E. (2006). Common gynecologic problems in prepubertal girls. *Pediatrics in Review*, 27, 213–222.

Suggs, R. (1962). *The Hidden Worlds of Polynesia*. New York: Harcourt, Brace & World.

Suligoi, B. (1997). The natural history of human immunodeficiency virus infection among women as compared with men. *Sexually Transmitted Diseases*, 24, 77–83.

Sullivan, A. (1996). Let gays marry. *Newsweek*, June 3, 26.

Sullivan, A. (1997). Winning the religious war. *The Advocate*, October 14, 91–93.

Sullivan, A. (2006). The Vatican's new stereotype. *Time*, December 12, 92.

Sullivan, M. (2005). Abstinence pledges don't protect against STDs. *Family Practice*, 35, 24.

Summers, N. (2005). Podcasting: Talking dirty on your iPod. *Newsweek*, August 1, 10.

Summers, T., Kates, J., & Murphy, G. (2002). The global impact of HIV/AIDS on young people. *SIECUS Report*, 31, 14–23.

Sundt, M. (1994). *Identifying the Attitudes and Beliefs That Accompany Sexual Harassment*. Ph.D. dissertation, University of California, Los Angeles.

Superville, D. (1996). Genital mutilation ruled persecution. *The Oregonian*, June 15, A8.

Swaab, D., Gooren, L., & Hoffman, M. (1995). Brain research, gender, and sexual orientation. *Journal of Homosexuality*, 28, 283–301.

Swiss, S., & Giller, J. (1993). Rape as a crime of war. *Journal of the American Medical Association*, 270, 612–615.

Symes, L. (2000). Arriving at readiness to recover emotionally after sexual assault. *Archives of Psychiatric Nursing*, 14, 30–38.

Taddio, A., Katz, J., Ilevsich, A., & Koren, G. (1997a). Effects of neonatal circumcision on pain response during subsequent routine vaccination. *The Lancet*, 349, 599–603.

Taddio, A., Stevens, B., Craig, K., Rastogi, P., Ben-David, S., Shennan, A., Mulligan, P., & Koren, G. (1997b). Efficacy and safety of lidocaine-prilocaine cream for pain during circumcision. *New England Journal of Medicine*, 336, 1197–1201.

Tamimi, R., Hankinson, S., Chen, W., & Rosner, B. (2006). Combined estrogen and testosterone use and risk of breast cancer in postmenopausal women. *Archives of Internal Medicine*, 166, 1483–1489.

Tanenbaum, L. (1997). Can sperm affect fetal health? *Ms.*, March–April, 31.

Tangeman, R. (2003). Personal communication.

Tannen, D. (1990). *You Just Don't Understand: Women and Men in Conversation*. New York: Ballantine Books (paperback edition, 1991).

Tannen, D. (1994). *Gender and Discourse*. New York: Oxford University Press.

Tannen, D. (2001). *You Just Don't Understand: Women and Men in Conversation*. New York: Quill.

Task Force on Circumcision (1999). Circumcision policy statement. *Pediatrics*, 103, 686–693.

Tauber, M., Smith, K., & Fields-Meyer, T. (2005). Abstinence: can sex wait? Funded by big federal dollars, abstinence-only programs encourage teens to hold off. Do they work? *People Weekly*, 63, 94–95.

Tavris, C. (2005). Brains, biology, science, and skepticism: On thinking about sex differences (again). *Skeptical Inquirer*, 29, 11–12.

Taylor, E., & Sharkey, L. (2003). *The Big Bang*. New York: Plume.

Taylor, G., & Ussher, J. (2001). Making sense of S & M: A discourse analytic account. *Sexualities*, 4, 293–314.

Taylor, J. (1971). Introduction. In R. Haber & C. Eden (Eds.), *Holy Living* (rev. ed.). New York: Adler.

Taylor, J. (1995). The long, hard days of Dr. Dick. *Esquire*, September, 120–123.

Taylor, L. (2005). All for him: Articles about sex in American lad magazines. *Sex Roles: A Journal of Research*, 52, 153–164.

Taylor, P. (2006, July 26). Wedge issues on the ballot. Retrieved July 26, 2006, from http://pewresearch.org/obdeck/?ObDeckID=40.

Taylor, R. (1970). *Sex in History*. New York: Harper & Row.

Teachman, J. (2003). Premarital sex, premarital cohabitation, and the risk of subsequent marital dissolution among women. *Journal of Marriage and the Family*, 65, 444–455.

Teich, M. (2006). Love at the margins. *Psychology Today*, September/October, 88–95.

Teich, M. (2006). Love but don't touch. *Psychology Today*, March/April, 81–86.

Templeman, T., & Sinnett, R. (1991). Patterns of sexual arousal and history in a "normal" sample of young men. *Archives of Sexual Behavior*, 20, 137–150.

Terrance, C., Logan, A., & Peters, D. (2004). Perceptions of peer sexual harassment among high school students. *Sex Roles: A Journal of Research*, 51, 479–490.

Terzieff, J. (2006). Fashion world says too thin is too hazardous. Retrieved September 24, 2006 from http://www.womensenews.org.

Thaker, H., & Snow, M. (2003). HIV viral suppression

in the era of antiretroviral therapy. *Postgraduate Medicine*, 79, 36–42.

**Thanasiu, P.** (2004). Childhood sexuality: Discerning healthy from abnormal sexual behaviors. *Journal of Mental Health Counseling*, 26, 309–319.

**Tharaux-Deneux, C., Bouyer, J., Job-Spira, N., Coste, J., & Spira, A.** (1998). Risk of ectopic pregnancy and previous induced abortion. *American Journal of Public Health*, 88(3), 401–405.fe abortion and poverty. Retrieved February 19, 2006, from http://www.ippf .org/ContentController .aspx?ID=13100.

**Thomas, J.** (2005). Young women victimized in adolescence are at risk of further sexual violence. *Perspectives on Sexual and Reproductive Health*, 37, 50–51.

**Thompson, J.** (2003a). Preconceptual care, Part 2. *Community Practitioner*, 76, 143–144.

**Thompson, M., & Kingree, J.** (2006). The roles of victim and perpetrator alcohol use in intimate partner violence outcomes. *Journal of Interpersonal Violence*, 21, 163–177.

**Thorne, S., & Murray, C.** (2000). Social constructions of breast cancer. *Health Care for Women International*, 21, 141–159.

**Tiefer, L.** (1995). *Sex Is Not a Natural Act and Other Essays*. Boulder, CO: Westview Press.

**Tiefer, L.** (1999). In pursuit of the perfect penis: The medicalization of male sexuality. In K. Lebacqz & D. Sinacore-Guinn (Eds.), *Sexuality: A Reader*. Cleveland: Pilgrim Press.

**Tierney, J.** (2005). The doofus dad. Retrieved May 4, 2006, from http://www.nytimes.com/2005/06/ opinion/18tierney.html.

**Timmerman, J.** (2001). When religion is its own worst enemy: How therapists can help people shed hurtful notions that masquerade as good theology. *Journal of Sex Education and Therapy*, 26, 259–266.

**Ting-Toomey, S., & Korzenny, F.** (Eds.) (1991). *Cross-Cultural Interpersonal Communication*. Newbury Park, CA: Sage.

**Tingulstad, S., Skjeldestad, F., Halvorsen, T., & Hagen, B.** (2003). Survival and prognostic factors in patients with ovarian cancer. *Obstetrics and Gynecology*, 101, 885–891.

**Tjaden, P., & Thoennes, N.** (1998). *Prevalence, Incidence, and Consequences of Violence Against Women: Findings from the National Violence Against Women Survey*. Washington, DC: National Institutes of Justice.

**Todd, J., Grosskurth, H., Changaluncha, J., et al.** (2006). Risk factors influencing HIV infection incidence in a rural African population: A nested case-control study. *Journal of Infectious Diseases*, 193, 458–466.

**Tollison, C., & Adams, H.** (1979). *Sexual Disorders: Treatment, Theory, Research*. New York: Gardner.

**Tomlinson, F., Raphael, H., & Mehta, R.** (2006). Is androgen replacement therapy for hypogonadal men in the form of a transdermal gel (Tesogel) acceptable to patients attending a men's sexual health clinic, compared with older applications? *The Journal of Sexual Medicine*, 3(suppl. 3), 199–223.

**Tone, A.** (2002). The contraceptive conundrum. *SIECUS Report*, 31, 4–8.

**Toner, J.** (2002). Progress we can be proud of: U.S. trends in assisted reproduction over the first 20 years. *Fertility and Sterility*, 78, 943–950.

**Torassa, U.** (2000). *S.F. Study: HIV Spread Through Oral Sex*. Retrieved February 1, 2000, from http://www .examiner.com/oral.html.

**Torpy, J.** (2003). Perimenopause: Beginning of menopause. *Journal of the American Medical Association*, 289, 940.

**Torres, J.** (1998). Masculinity and gender roles among Puerto Rican men: Machismo on the U.S. mainland. *American Journal of Orthopsychiatry*, 68, 16–26.

**Toufexis, A.** (1993). The right chemistry. *Time*, February 15, 49–51.

**Townsend, J.** (1995). Sex without emotional involvement: An evolutionary interpretation of sex differences. *Archives of Sexual Behavior*, 24, 173–182.

**Townsend, J., & Wasserman, T.** (1998). Sexual attractiveness: Sex differences in assessment and criteria. *Evolution and Human Behavior*, 19, 171–191.

**Trafimow, D., Triandis, H., & Goto, S.** (1991). Some tests of the distinction between the private self and the collective self. *Journal of Personality and Social Psychology*, 60, 649–655.

**Traish, A., Kim, K., Munarriz, R., & Goldstein, I.** (2002a). Role of androgens in female genital sexual arousal: Receptor expression, structure, and function. *Fertility and Sterility*, 77(suppl. 4), 511–518.

**Tran, M.** (2006). Panel pushes cancer shield for pre-teens. *Oregonian*, June 30, A1 & A7.

**Treas, J., & Giesen, D.** (2000). Sexual infidelity among married and cohabiting Americans. *Journal of Marriage and the Family*, 62, 48–60.

**Trevor, C.** (2002). Number of controversies decline as schools adopt conservative policies. *SIECUS Report*, 30, 4–17.

**Triplett, W.** (2006). Pols drawing a fine line. *Variety*, 403, 3–4.

**Tripp, C.** (1975). *The Homosexual Matrix*. New York: McGraw-Hill.

**Troiden, R.** (1988). *Gay and Lesbian Identity: A Sociological Analysis*. New York: General Hall.

**Troy, A., Lewis-Smith, J., & Laurenceau, J.** (2006). Interracial and intraracial romantic relationships: The search for differences in satisfaction, conflict, and attachment style. *Journal of Social and Personal Relationships*, 23, 65–80.

**Truitt, W., & Coolen, L.** (2002). Identification of a potential ejaculation generator in the spinal cord. *Science*, 297, 1566–1599.

**Trull, D.** (2003). *Invasion of the Penis Snatchers*. Retrieved March 13, 2003, from http://www .noveltynat.org/paranormal/www.pariscope.com/ articles7196/penis.htm.

**Trussell, J., Vaughan, B., & Stanford, J.** (1999). Are all contraceptive failures unintended pregnancies? Evidence from the 1995 National Survey of Family Growth. *Family Planning Perspectives*, 31, 246–247.

**Tucker, M.** (2004). Sexual desire, activity up with testosterone patch. *Family Practice News*, 34, 44.

**Tudge, C.** (1991). Can we end rhino poaching? *New Scientist*, 132, 34–35.

Tuiten, A., Van Honk, J., Koppeschaar, H., Bernaards, C., Thijssen, J., & Verbaten, R. (2000). Time course of effects of testosterone administration on sexual arousal in women. *Archives of General Psychiatry*, 57, 149–153.

Tummino, A. (2006). FDA's plan B ruling doesn't end battle for access. Women's eNews, October 25.

Turner, H. (1999). Participation bias in AIDS-related telephone surveys: Results from the National AIDS Behavior Study (NABS) nonresponse study. *Journal of Sex Research*, 52–58.

Tyre, P. (2004). A new generation gap. *Newsweek*, January 19, 68–75.

Tyre, P. (2006). Poker buddies for life. *Newsweek*, February 20, 61.

U.S. Attorney General's Commission on Pornography (1986). *Final Report of the Attorney General's Commission on Pornography.* Washington, DC: U.S. Justice Department.

U.S. Bureau of the Census (2002). *Statistical Abstract of the United States: 2002.* Washington, DC: U.S. Government Printing Office.

U.S. Census Bureau (2006). The Population Profile of the United States: A Dynamic Version. Retrieved December 11, 2006, from http://census.gov/population/www/pop-profile/profiledynamic.html.

U.S. Census Bureau (2006, May 25). Americans marrying older, living alone more, see households shrinking, census bureau reports. Retrieved August 10, 2006 from http://www.census.gov/Press-Release/www/releases/archives/families_households.

U.S. Department of Justice (2001). *Criminal Victimization in the United States: 1999 Statistical Tables.* NCJ 184938. Washington, DC: U.S. Government Printing Office.

U.S. Department of Justice (2003). *Bureau of Justice Statistics, Criminal Victimization, 2002.* Washington, DC: U.S. Department of Justice.

U.S. Merit Systems Protection Board (1981). *Sexual Harassment in the Federal Workplace: Is It a Problem?* Washington, DC: U.S. Government Printing Office.

U.S. Merit Systems Protection Board (1996). *Sexual Harassment in the Federal Workplace: Trends, Progress, Continuing Challenges.* Washington, DC: U.S. Government Printing Office.

U.S. Preventive Services Task Force (2003a). Chemoprevention of breast cancer: Recommendations and rationale. *American Family Physician*, 67, 1309–1314.

U.S. Preventive Services Task Force (2003b). Screening for prostate cancer: Recommendation and rationale. *American Family Physician*, 67, 787–792.

Ubell, E. (1984). Sex in America today. *Parade*, October 28, 11–13.

Ullman, S., & Brecklin, L. (2003). Sexual assault history and health-related outcomes in a national sample of women. *Psychology of Women Quarterly*, 27, 46–57.

Ullman, S., Filipas, H., Townsend, S., & Starzynski, L. (2005). Trauma exposure, posttraumatic stress disorder and problem drinking in sexual assault survivors. *Journal of Studies on Alcohol*, 66, 610–619.

Umberson, D., Williams, K., Powers, D., & Liu, H. (2006). You make me sick: Marital quality and health over the life course. *Journal of Health and Social Behavior*, 47, 1–16.

Umstead, R. (2005). Sexing up technology: Adult channels lead the charge into new media opportunities. *Multichannel News*, 26, 28–30.

UN Office for the Coordination of Humanitarian Affairs (2006, July 24). Swaziland: Facing the culture shock of monogamy. Retrieved July 24, 2006, from http://www.irinnews.org/print.asp?ReportID=54737.

UN Office for the Coordination of Humanitarian Affairs (2006, July 31). Pakistan: Over a thousand women freed under change in law. Retrieved July 31, 2006 from http://www.irinnews.org/print.asp?ReportID=54498.

UNAIDS (2001a). *Children and Young People in a World of AIDS.* New York: United Nations.

UNAIDS (2006). *AIDS Epidemic Update: December* 2005. Retrieved January 16, 2006, from http://www.unaids.org/Epi2005/doc/EPIupdate2005_html_en/epi05_03.

Unger, J., & Molina, G. (2000). Acculturation and attitudes about contraceptive use among Latina women. *Health Care for Women International*, 21, 235–249.

Unger, R., & Crawford, M. (1992). *Women and Gender: A Feminist Psychology.* New York: McGraw-Hill.

United Nations Development Program (2006). Polygamous husbands behind rise in HIV/AIDS in women: UN study. Retrieved August 16, 2006 from http://www.hindu.com/thehindu/holnus/001200607301110.htm.

Upadhyay, U. (2005). New contraceptive choices. *Population Reports*, 32, 1–2.

Urman, B., & Yakin, K. (2006). Ovulatory disorders and infertility. *The Journal of Reproductive Medicine*, 51, 267–282.

Vachss, A. (1999). If we really want to keep our children safe. *Parade*, May 2, 6–7.

Valente, S., & Bullough, V. (2004). Sexual harassment of nurses in the workplace. *Journal of Nursing Care Quality*, 19, 234–241.

Valera, R., Sawyer, R., & Schiraldi, G. (2001). Perceived health needs of inner-city street prostitutes: A preliminary study. *American Journal of Health and Behavior*, 25, 50–59.

Valliant, P., Gauthier, T., Pottier, D., & Kosmyna, R. (2000). Moral reasoning, interpersonal skills, and cognitions of rapists, child molesters, and incest offenders. *Psychological Reports*, 86, 67–75.

Van Damme, L. (2000). *Advances in Topical Microbicides.* Paper presented at the 13th International AIDS Conference, Durban, South Africa, July 9–14.

Van den Bossche, F., & Rubinson, L. (1997). Contraceptive self-efficacy in adolescents: A comparative study of male and female contraceptive practices. *Journal of Sex Education and Therapy*, 22(2), 23–29.

Van Griensven, F., Naorat, S., Kilmarx, P., Jeeyapant, S., et al. (2006). Palmtop-assisted self-interviewing for the collection of sensitive behavioral data: Randomized trial with drug use urine testing. *American Journal of Epidemiology*, 163, 271–278.

Van Hook, M., Gjermeni, E., & Haxhiymeri, E. (2006). Sexual trafficking of women. *International*

*Social Work, 49*, 29–40.

**Van Howe, R.** (1998). Circumcision and infectious diseases revisited. *Pediatric Infectious Diseases Journal, 17*, 1–6.

**Van Lankveld, J., ter Kuile, M., de Groot, H., & Melles, R.** (2006). Cognitive-behavioral therapy for women with lifelong vaginismus: A randomized waiting-list controlled trial of efficacy. *Journal of Consulting and Clinical Psychology, 74*, 168–178.

**Van Oss Marin, B., & Gomez, C.** (1994). Latinos, HIV disease, and culture: Strategies for HIV prevention. In P. Cohen, M. Sande, & P. Volberding (Eds.), *The AIDS Knowledge Base.* New York: Little Brown.

**Van Wyk, P.** (1984). Psychosocial development of heterosexual, bisexual, and homosexual behavior. *Archives of Sexual Behavior, 13*, 505–544.

**Van Zeijl** (2006). The agony of Darfur. *Ms.*, Winter, 24–26.

**Vandello, J., & Cohen, D.** (2003). Male honor and female fidelity: Implicit cultural scripts that perpetuate domestic violence. *Journal of Personality and Social Psychology, 84*, 997–1010.

**Vandeusen, K., & Carr, J.** (2003). Recovery from sexual assault: An innovative two-stage group therapy model. *International Journal of Group Psychotherapy, 53*, 201–223.

**Varela, J., Otero, L., Espinoza, E., Sanchez, C., Junquera, M., & Vazquez, F.** (2003). Phthirus pubis in a sexually transmitted diseases unit. *Sexually Transmitted Diseases, 30*, 292–296.

**Vasconcellos, D., VionDury, K., & Kuntz, D.** (2006). Sexuality and well-being among older women: A cross-cultural approach. *The Journal of Sex Research, 43*, 9–11.

**Vason, E.** (2003). Medical abortion with mifepristone: An update. *Official Journal of the American Academy of Physician Assistants, 16*, 49–54.

**Vasquez, M.** (1994). Latinas. In L. Comas-Diaz & B. Greene (Eds.), *Women of Color.* New York: Guilford Press.

**Vaughn, G.** (2003). *Koro: A Natural History of Penis Panics.* Retrieved March 13, 2003, from http://www.koro5hin.org/story.

**Vejar, C., Madison-Colmore, O., & Ter Maat, M.** (2006). Understanding the transition from career to fulltime motherhood: A qualitative study. *The American Journal of Family Therapy, 34*, 17–31.

**Verloop, J., Rookus, M., van der Kooy, K., & van Leeuwen, F.** (2000). Physical activity and breast cancer risk in women aged 20–54 years. *Journal of the National Cancer Institute, 92*, 128–135.

**Vermani, M., Milosevic, I., Smith, F., & Katzman, M.** (2005). Herbs for mental illness: Effectiveness and interaction with conventional medicines: Some herbs do work as claimed; all have the potential for downside activity as well. *Journal of Family Practice, 54*, 789–800.

**Vickerman, P., Watts, C., Delany, S., et al.** (2006). The importance of context: Model projections on how microbicide impact could be affected by the underlying epidemiologic and behavioral situation in 2 African settings. *Sexually Transmitted Diseases, 33*, 397–405.

**Victory, J., & Nilsson, S.** (2006, May 8). Gynecologists fed up with morning-after pill roadblocks. Retrieved June 22, 2006, from http://abcnews.go.com/Health/print?id=1936328.

**Vilain, E.** (2001). Genetics of sexual development. *Annual Review of Sex Research, 11*, 1–25.

**Villa, L., Costa, R., Petta, C., Andrade, R., Ault, K., et al.** (2005). Prophylactic quadrivalent human papillomavirus (types 6, 11, 16, and 18) L1 virus-like particle vaccine in young women: A randomized double-blind placebo-controlled multicentre phase II efficacy trial. *Lancet Oncology, 6*, 271–278.

**Villanueva-Diaz, C., Flores-Reyes, G., & Beltran-Zuniga, M.** (1999). Bacteriospermia and male infertility: A method for increasing the sensitivity of semen culture. *International Journal of Fertility, 44*, 198–203.

**Vinardi, S., Magro, P., Manenti, M., Lala, R., Costantino, S., Cortese, M., & Canarese, F.** (2001). Testicular function in men treated in childhood for undescended testes. *Journal of Pediatric Surgery, 36*, 385–388.

**Vistica, G.** (1996). Rape in the ranks. *Newsweek*, November 25, 28–32.

**Voelker, R.** (2000). Breast cancer vaccine. *Journal of the American Medical Association, 284*, 430.

**Volm, L.** (1997). Personal communication.

**Wade, J., Pletsch, P., Morgan, S., & Menting, S.** (2000). Hysterectomy: What do women need and want to know? *Journal of Obstetrical, Gynecological, and Neonatal Nursing, 29*, 33–42.

**Waite, L., & Joyner, K.** (2001). Emotional satisfaction and physical pleasure in sexual unions: Time horizon, sexual behavior, and sexual exclusivity. *Journal of Marriage and the Family, 63*, 247–264.

**Waldinger, M., & Schweitzer, D.** (2006). Changing paradigms from a historical DSM-III and DSM-IV view toward an evidence-based definition of premature ejaculation. Part II—Proposals for DSM-V and ICD-11. *The Journal of Sexual Medicine, 3*, 693–705.

**Wales, S., & Todd, K.** (2001). *Sexuality and Intimacy Across the Lifespan.* Paper presented at the 33rd Annual Conference of the American Association of Sex Educators, Counselors, and Therapists, San Francisco, May 2–6.

**Walfish, S., & Myerson, M.** (1980). Sex role identity and attitudes toward sexuality. *Archives of Sexual Behavior, 9*, 199–203.

**Walker, J., Archer, J., & Davies, M.** (2005). Effects of rape on men: A descriptive analysis. *Archives of Sexual Behavior, 34*, 69–80.

**Wallace, M.** (2004). Prostate cancer update: When to screen, how to treat. *Clinician Reviews, 14*, 45–52.

**Walling, A.** (2005). Prevention and diagnosis of fetal alcohol syndrome. *American Family Physician, 73*, 1837.

**Wallis, M., Daneback, K., Mansson, S., Tikkahen, R., & Cooper, A.** (2003). Characteristics of men and women who complete or exit from an on-line Internet sexuality questionnaire: A study of instrument dropout bias. *Journal of Sex Research, 40*, 396–402.

**Walsh, A.** (1991). *The Science of Love: Understanding Love and Its Effects on Mind and Body.* Buffalo, NY: Prometheus.

Walsh, T., Frezieres, R., & Peacock, K. (2004). Contraceptive effectiveness of male condoms high. *Reproductive Health Matters*, 13, 184–185.

Wang, B., Hertog, S., Meier, A., Lou, C., & Gao, E. (2005). The potential of comprehensive sex education in China: Findings from suburban Shanghai. *International Family Planning Perspectives*, 31, 63–72.

Ward, H., & Day, S. (2006). What happens to women who sell sex? Report of a unique occupational cohort. Retrieved June 26, 2006, from http://sti.bmjjournals.com/cgi/content/abstract/sti.2006.020982v1.

Waskul, D. (Ed.) (2004). *Net. SeXXX: Readings on Sex, Pornography, and the Internet*. New York: Peter Lang.

Watt, P., Hughes, R., Rettew, L., & Adams, R. (2003). A holistic programmatic approach to natural hormone replacement. *Family and Community Health*, 26, 53–63.

Wawer, M., Gray, R., Sewankambo, N., et al. (2005). Rates of HIV-1 transmission per coital act, by stage of HIV-1 infection, Rakai, Uganda. *Journal of Infectious Diseases*, 191, 1403–1409.

Waxman, J., & Mazhar, D. (2003). How are we looking after prostate cancer? *QJM: An International Journal of Medicine*, 96, 75–79.

Weber, A. (1998). Losing, leaving, and letting go: Coping with nonmarital breakups. In B. Spitzberg & W. Cupah (eds.), *The Dark Side of Close Relationships*. Mahwah, NJ: Erlbaum.

Wegner, D., Lane, J., & Dimitri, S. (1994). The allure of secret relationships. *Journal of Personality and Social Psychology*, 66, 287–300.

Wehrfritz, G. (1996). Joining the party. *Newsweek*, April 1, 46, 48.

Weinberg, M., Williams, C., & Moser, C. (1984). The social constituents of sadomasochism. *Social Problems*, 31, 379–389.

Weinberg, T. (1987). Sadomasochism in the United States: A review of recent sociological literature. *Journal of Sex Research*, 23, 50–69.

Weiner, A. (1996). Understanding the social needs of streetwalking prostitutes. *Journal of the National Association of Social Workers*, 41, 97–105.

Weiss, J. (2001). Treating vaginismus: Patient without partner. *Journal of Sex Education and Therapy*, 26, 28–33.

Wells, B. (1983). Nocturnal orgasms: Females' perceptions of a "normal" sexual experience. *Journal of Sex Education and Therapy*, 9, 32–38.

Welner, S. (1997). Gynecologic care and sexuality issues for women with disabilities. *Sexuality and Disability*, 15, 33–39.

Welsh, S. (1999). Gender and sexual harassment. *Annual Review of Sociology*, 25, 169–190.

Werness, B., & Eltabbakh, G. (2001). Familial ovarian cancer and early ovarian cancer: Biologic, pathologic, and clinical features. *International Journal of Gynecological Pathology*, 20, 48–63.

Wessells, H., Lue, T., & McAninch, J. (1996). Complications of penile lengthening and augmentation seen at one referral center. *Journal of Urology*, 155, 1617–1620.

West, D. (2000). Aftermath of incest pedophilia case: Guilt and a new awareness danger. *New York Times*, July 12, B5.

Westhoff, C., Picardo, L., & Morrow, E. (2003). Quality of life following early medical or surgical abortion. *Contraception*, 67, 41–47.

Westoff, C. (2006). Recent trends in abortion and contraception in 12 countries. Retrieved January 10, 2006 from http://www.measuredhs.com/pubs/pdf/AS8/AS8.pdf.

Wheeler, M. (1991). Physical changes of puberty. *Endocrinology and Metabolism Clinics of North America*, 20, 1–14.

Wheeler, M. (2003). *AIDS Education Through Imams* (2003. Retrieved January 2, 2003, from http://www.unaids.org/publications/documents/sectors/religion/imamscse.pdf.

Whipple, B. (2000). Beyond the G spot. *Scandinavian Journal of Sexology*, 3, 35–42.

Whipple, B., & Komisaruk, B. (1999). Beyond the G spot: Recent research on female sexuality. *Psychiatric Annals*, 29, 34–37.

Whipple, B., & Komisaruk, B. (2006). Where in the brain is a woman's sexual response? Laboratory studies including brain imaging during orgasm. *The Journal of Sex Research*, 43, 29–30.

Whipple, B., Ogden, G., & Komisaruk, B. (1992). Physiological correlates of imagery-induced orgasm in women. *Archives of Sexual Behavior*, 21, 121–133.

Whitaker, D., & Miller, K. (2000). Parent-adolescent discussions about sex and condoms: Impact on peer influence of sexual risk behavior. *Journal of Adolescent Research*, 15, 251–273.

Whitaker, D., Miller, K., May, D., & Levin, M. (1999). Teenage partners' communication about sexual risk and condom use: The importance of parent-teenagers discussions. *Family Planning Perspectives*, 31, 117–121.

White, G., & Helbick, R. (1988). Understanding and treating jealousy. In R. Brown & J. Fields (Eds.), *Treatment of Sexual Problems in Individuals and Couples Therapy*. Boston: PMA Publishing.

White, M. (2006). *Religion Gone Bad: The Hidden Danger of the Christian Right*. New York: Penguin Group.

Whiteford, A., & Wordley, J. (2003). Raising awareness and detection of testicular cancer in young men. *Nursing Times*, 99, 34–36.

Wiederman, M. (2000). Women's body image self-consciousness during physical intimacy with a partner. *Journal of Sex Research*, 37, 60–68.

Wiederman, M. (2001). *Understanding Sexuality Research*. Belmont, CA: Wadsworth.

Wiederman, M., Maynard, C., & Fretz, A. (1996). Ethnicity in 25 years of published sexuality research: 1971–1995. *Journal of Sex Research*, 33, 339–343.

Wiesenfeld, H., Hillier, S., Krohn, M., Landers, D., & Sweet, R. (2003). Bacterial vaginosis is a strong predictor of *Neisseria gonorrhoeae* and *Chlamydia trachomatis* infections. *Clinical Infectious Diseases*, 36, 663–668.

Wiesner-Hanks, M. (2000). *Christianity and Sexuality in the Early Modern World*. London: Routledge.

Wiest, W. (1977). Semantic differential profiles of orgasm and other experiences among men and women. *Sex Roles*, 3, 399–403.

Wilcox, A., Weinberg, C., & Baird, D. (1995). Timing of sexual intercourse in relation to ovulation. Effects on the probability of conception, survival of the pregnancy, and sex of the baby. *New England*

*Journal of Medicine*, 333, 1517–1521.

**Wildman, S.** (2001). Continental divide. *The Advocate*, January 16, 47–48.

**Wilkes, D.** (2006). Clinical: GP involvement in fertility treatment. *GP*, January 20, 30.

**Willetts, M.** (2006). Union quality comparisons between long-term heterosexual cohabitation and legal marriage. *Journal of Family Issues*, 27, 110–127.

**Willford, J., Leech, S., & Day, N.** (2006). Moderate prenatal alcohol exposure and cognitive status of children at age 10. *Alcoholism: Clinical and Experimental Research*, 30, 1051–1059.

**Williams, A., Thomson, R., Schreiber, G., Watanabe, K., Bethel, J., Lo, A., Kleinman, S., Hollingsworth, C., & Nemo, G.** (1997). Estimates of infectious disease risk factors in U.S. blood donors. *Journal of the American Medical Association*, 277, 967–972.

**Williams, C., & Weinberg, M.** (2003). Zoophilia in men: A study of sexual interest in animals. *Archives of Sexual Behavior*, 32, 523–535.

**Williams, D., & D'Alessandro, J.** (1994). A comparison of three measures of androgyny and their relationship to psychological adjustment. *Journal of Social Behavior and Personality*, 9, 469–480.

**Williams, K.** (2005). Policing video voyeurs: The feds join the battle against perverts with cameras. *Newsweek*, February 14, 35.

**Williams, L.** (1994). Recall of childhood trauma: A prospective study of women's memories of child sexual abuse. *Journal of Consulting and Clinical Psychology*, 62, 1167–1176.

**Williams, L.** (1999). *Hard Core*. Berkeley: University of California Press.

**Williams, S.** (2000). A new smoking peril. *Newsweek*, April 24, 78.

**Williams, T., Connolly, J., Pepler, D., & Craig, W.** (2005). Peer victimization, social support, and psychosocial adjustment of sexual minority adolescents. *Journal of Youth and Adolescence*, 34, 471–482.

**Williams, Z., Litscher, E., Darie, C., & Wassarman, P.** (2006). Rational design of pregnancy vaccine. *Obstetrics & Gynecology* (Supplement), 107, 14S–15S.

**Willis, B., & Levy, B.** (2003). Child prostitution: Global health burden, research needs, and interventions. *The Lancet*, 359, 1417–1422.

**Willis, E.** (2002). Abortion: Is a woman a person? In A. Soble (Ed.), *The Philosophy of Sex: Contemporary Readings*. Lanham, MD: Rowman & Littlefield.

**Wilson, B., & Lawson, D.** (1976). Effects of alcohol on sexual arousal in women. *Journal of Abnormal Psychology*, 85, 489–497.

**Wilson, J.** (2003). *Biological Foundations of Human Behavior*. Belmont, CA: Wadsworth/Thomson Learning.

**Wilson, M., Kastrinakis, M., D'Angelo, L., & Getson, P.** (1994). Attitudes, knowledge, and behavior regarding condom use in urban black adolescents males. *Adolescence*, 29, 13–26.

**Wind, R.** (2006, May 4). A tale of two Americas for women. Retrieved May 10, 2006, from http://www.guttmacher.org/media/mr/2006/05/05/index.html.

**Winer, R., Hughes, J., Feng, Q., & O'Reilly, S.** (2006). Condom use and the risk of genital human papillomavirus infection in young women. *The New England Journal of Medicine*, 354, 2645–2654.

**Winters, S.** (1999). Current status of testosterone replacement therapy in men. *Archives of Family Medicine*, 8, 257–263.

**Wise, N.** (2006). Polyamory and other forms of negotiated non-monogamy: A crash course for the curious. Paper presented at the Gumbo Sexualite Upriver: Spicing Up Education & Therapy (AASECT 38th Annual Conference), St. Louis, June/July.

**Wisniewski, A., Prendeville, M., & Dobs, A.** (2005). Handedness, functional cerebral hemispheric lateralization, and cognition in male-to-female transsexuals receiving cross-sex hormone treatment. *Archives of Sexual Behavior*, 34, 167–172.

**Witt, S.** (1997). Parental influence on children's socialization to gender roles. *Adolescence*, 32, 253–258.

**Wiviott, G.** (2001). *An Existential Approach to Marital Therapy in Cases of Marital Infidelity*. Paper presented at the 33rd Annual Conference of the American Association of Sex Educators, Counselors, and Therapists, San Francisco, May 2–6.

**Wolfsdorf, B., & Zlotnick, C.** (2001). Affect management in group therapy for women with posttraumatic stress disorder and histories of childhood sexual abuse. *Journal of Clinical Psychology*, 57, 169–181.

**Wolfson, E.** (2005). Ending marriage discrimination: America in a civil rights moment. *SIECUS Report*, 33, 13–18.

**Women on Words and Images** (1972). *Dick and Jane as Victims*. Princeton, NJ: Women on Words and Images.

**Women's Health Initiative** (2002). Risks and benefits of estrogen plus progestin in healthy postmenopausal women: Principal results from the Women's Health Initiative randomized controlled trial. *Journal of the American Medical Association*, 288, 321–333.

**Wong, C., & So-kum Tang, C.** (2004). Coming out experiences and psychological distress of Chinese homosexual men in Hong Kong. *Archives of Sexual Behavior*, 33, 149–158.

**Wong, J., Gunthard, H., Havlir, D., Haase, A., Zhang, Z., & Kwok, S.** (1997). *Reduction of HIV in Blood and Lymph Nodes After Potent Antiretroviral Therapy*. Paper presented at the 4th Conference on Retroviruses and Other Opportunistic Infections, Washington, D.C., January.

**Wong, W., Holroyd, E., Gray, A., & Ling, D.** (2006). Female street sex workers in Hong Kong: Moving beyond sexual health. *Journal of Women's Health*, 15, 390–399.

**Wood, G., & Ruddock, E.** (1918). *Vitalogy*. Chicago: Vitalogy Association.

**Wood, K., Becker, J., & Thompson, K.** (1996). Body image dissatisfaction in preadolescent children. *Journal of Applied Developmental Psychology*, 17, 85–100.

**Woodrum, D., Brawer, M., Partin, A., Catalona, W., & Southwick, P.** (1998). Interpretation of free prostate specific antigen clinical research studies for the detection of prostate cancer. *Journal of Urology*, 159, 5–12.

**Woodward, S.** (2003). Him, her—and the Internet. *The Oregonian*, September 7, L1, L8.

Woodzicka, J., & LaFrance, M. (2005). The effects of subtle sexual harassment on women's performance in job interview. *Sex Roles: A Journal of Research*, 53, 67–77.

Woolf, L. (2001). Gay and lesbian aging. *SIECUS Report*, 30, 16–21.

Worcester, S. (2004). Syphilis and oral sex. *Internal Medicine News*, 37, 57.

Worden, M., & Worden, B. (1998). *The Gender Dance in Couples Therapy*. Pacific Grove, CA: Brooks/Cole.

Workman, J., & Freeburg, E. (1999). An examination of date rape, victim dress, and perceiver variables within the context of attribution theory. *Sex Roles*, 41, 261–277.

Worthman, C. (1999). Faster, farther, higher: Biology and the discourses on human sexuality. In D. Suggs & A. Miracle (Eds.), *Culture, Biology, and Sexuality*. Athens: University of Georgia Press.

Wright, A., & Katz, I. (2006). Home testing for HIV. *New England Journal of Medicine*, 354, 437–440.

Wright, K. (2004). On-line relational maintenance strategies and perceptions of partners within exclusively Internet-based and primarily Internet-based relationships. *Communication Skills*, 55, 239–253.

Wright, T., & Schiffman, M. (2003). Adding a test for human papillomavirus DNA to cervical cancer screening. *New England Journal of Medicine*, 348, 489–500.

Wyand, F., & Arrindell, D. (2005). Understanding human papillomavirus and cervical cancer. *SIECUS Report*, 33, 13–15.

Wyatt, G. (1997). *Stolen Women: Reclaiming Our Sexuality, Taking Back Our Lives*. New York: Wiley.

Wyatt, T. (2003) *Pheromones and Animal Behavior: Communication by Smell and Taste*. New York: Cambridge University Press.

Yakush, J. (2005). Emergency contraception: The science and politics driving the debate. *SIECUS Report*, 33, 16–19.

Yang, M., Fullwood, E., Goldstein, J., & Mink, J. (2005). Masturbation in infancy and early childhood presenting as a movement disorder: 12 cases and a review of the literature. *Pediatrics*, 116, 1427–1452.

Yapko, M. (1994). *Suggestions of Abuse: True and False Memories of Childhood Sexual Trauma*. New York: Simon & Schuster.

Yarab, P., & Allgeier, E. (1998). Don't even think about it: The role of sexual fantasies as perceived unfaithfulness in heterosexual dating relationships. *Journal of Sex Education and Therapy*, 23, 246–254.

Yared, R. (2004). AIDS rate surges in people 50+. *AARP Bulletin*, May, 2.

Yarian, D., & Anders, S. (2006). Tantra and sex therapy: Convergence of ancient wisdom and modern sexology, a didactic and experiential workshop. Paper presented at the Gumbo Sexualite Upriver: Spicing Up Education & Therapy (AASECT 38th Annual Conference), St. Louis, June/July.

Yassin, A., Kliniken, S., & Saad, F. (2005). Modulation of erectile function with long-acting testosterone injection i.m. in hypogonadal patients. Paper presented at the 17th World Congress of Sexology, Montreal, Canada, July 12.

Yates, A., & Wolman, W. (1991). Aphrodisiacs: Myth and reality. *Medical Aspects of Human Sexuality*, December, 58–64.

Young, M., Denny, G., & Young, T. (2000). Sexual satisfaction among married women age 50 and older. *Psychological Reports*, 86, 1107–1122.

Yuan, W., Basso, O., & Sorensen, H. (2001). Maternal prenatal lifestyle factors and infectious disease in early childhood: A follow-up study of hospitalization within a Danish birth cohort. *Pediatrics*, 107, 357–362.

Yuan, W., Steffensen, F., & Nielsen, G. (2000). A population-based cohort study of birth and neonatal outcome in older primipara. *International Journal of Gynecology and Obstetrics*, 68, 113–118.

Zabin, L., Hirsch, M., Smith, E., & Hardy, J. (1984). Adolescent sexual attitudes and behavior: Are they consistent? *Family Planning Perspectives*, 16, 181–185.

Zak, A., & McDonald, C. (1997). Satisfaction and trust in intimate relationships: Do lesbians and heterosexual women differ? *Psychological Reports*, 80, 904–906.

Zambrana, R., & Scrimshaw, S. (1997). Maternal psychosocial factors associated with substance use in Mexican-origin and African American low-income pregnant women. *Pediatric Nursing*, 23(3), 253–254.

Zapka, J., Pbert, L., & Stoddard, A. (2000). Smoking cessation counseling with pregnant and postpartum women: A survey of community health center providers. *American Journal of Public Health*, 90, 78–84.

Zaviacic, M., & Whipple, B. (1993). Update on the female prostate and the phenomenon of female ejaculation. *Journal of Sex Research*, 30, 148–151.

Zaviacic, M., Albin, R., Ruzickova, M., Stvrtina, S., et al. (2000). Immunohistochemical study of prostate-specific antigen in normal and pathological human tissues: Special reference to the male and female prostate and breast. *Journal of Histotechnology*, 23, 105–111.

Zenilman, J. (2006). The state of condom use education in a Texas community: Is this the future? *Sexually Transmitted Diseases*, 33, 5.

Zepf, B. (2005). Prostate cancer screening: What is enough or too much? *American Family Physician*, 71, 1191–1192.

Zhou, J., Hofman, M., Gooren, L., & Swaab, D. (1995). A sex difference in the human brain and its relation to transsexuality. *Nature*, 378, 68–70.

Zhu, T., Korber, B., Nahmias, A., Hooper, E., Sharp, P., & Ho, D. (1998). An African HIV-1 sequence from 1959 and implications for the origin of the epidemic. *Nature*, 391, 594–597.

Zia, H. (2003). Reclaiming the past, redefining the future: Asian American and Pacific Islander women. In R. Morgan (Ed.), *Sisterhood Is Forever*. New York: Washington Square Press.

Zielinski, L. (2006). Jane Doe's choice. *Ms.*, Winter, 69–71.

Zilbergeld, B. (1978). *Male Sexuality: A Guide to Sexual Fulfillment*. Boston: Little, Brown.

Zilbergeld, B. (1992). *The New Male Sexuality*. New York: Bantam Books.

**Zilbergeld, B.** (2001). *Sexuality at Midlife and Beyond.* Paper presented at the 33rd Annual Conference of the American Association of Sex Educators, Counselors, and Therapists, San Francisco, May 2–6.

**Zilbergeld, B., & Kilmann, P.** (1984). The scope and effectiveness of sex therapy. *Psychotherapy,* 21, 319–326.

**Zillmann, D.** (1989). Effects of prolonged consumption of pornography. In D. Zillman & J. Bryant (Eds.), *Pornography: Research Advances and Policy Considerations.* Hillsdale, NJ: Erlbaum.

**Zillmann, D., & Bryant, J.** (1988). Pornography's impact on sexual satisfaction. *Journal of Applied Social Psychology,* 18, 438–453.

**Zimmerman, C., Yun, K., Shvab, I., & Watts, C.** (2003). *The Health Risks and Consequences of Trafficking in Women and Adolescents: Findings From a European Study.* London: London School of Hygiene & Tropical Medicine (LSHTM).

**Zlidar, V.** (2000). Helping women use the pill. *Population Reports,* 28, 1–28.

**Zoldbrod, A.** (1993). *Men, Women, and Infertility.* New York: Norton.

**Zolnoun, D., Harmann, K., Lamvu, G., & As-Sanie, S.** (2006). A conceptual model for the pathophysiology of vulvar vestibulitis syndrome. *Obstetrical and Gynecological Survey,* 61, 395.

**Zoucha-Jensen, J., & Coyne, A.** (1993). The effects of resistance strategies on rape. *American Journal of Public Health,* 83, 1633–1634.

Ensuring Access to Contraceptives Act of 2006, 265
far-right and, 265
Federal Communications Commission (FCC), 518–19
Food and Drug Administration (FDA), 274, 284
gender role stereotypes and, 67–71, 75
gender roles and, 4, 75
herpes and, 422, 458
HIV/AIDS and, 436, 437, 459
Holocaust Memorial Museum, 256
homosexuality and, 242, 258
infertility statistics, 296, 319
interracial marriage, 356–57, 357f
intrauterine insemination statistics, 298
marriage and, 355, 362
maternal and infant mortality rates, 313
and menarche, age at, 329, 330t
military policies and, 258, 525–26, 527
multiracial populations in, 4
National Institute of Allergy and Infectious Diseases, 276
National Institute of Health, 276
Navy Tailhook scandal, 503
oral herpes statistics and, 458
and orgasms, female, 139
paid parental leave and, 319
penile augmentation and, 123
Pension Protection Act, 363
"pornification" of culture and, 521
and pregnancies, adolescence, 339, 341
Preventive Services Task Force, U.S. (USPSTF), 130
prostitution and, 525–26, 527
rape and, 481–82, 482t, 491, 508
same-sex marriage and, 362–64
school-based sex education for adolescence, 345, 346
and sex, importance of, 6f
sex for procreation and, 8
sexual abuse of children and, 494, 497
sexuality, and diversity within, 4–5, 23
single living lifestyle, 350, 373
surrogate mothers and, 298
Trafficking Victims Protection Act of 2000, 527
trafficking women and children for prostitution, 525–26

Urethera
described, 83, 108, 118, 119f
and opening, urethral, 78f, 83, 108, 112f, 119f
sphincters, ejaculation and urethral, 121

urethral bulb, and ejaculation, 121f, 131
urethritis, 431, 457
and urethritis (NGU), nongonoccal, 411t, 415, 419, 457
urinary opening, 86f
urinary tract infection, 99, 108, 131
urology, 127
urophilia behavior, 469, 478
USAID (U.S. Agency for International Development), 265
USPSTF (U.S. Preventive Services Task Force), 130
Uterus. See also Fetal development
anatomy of, 86f, 89, 108
anteflexed, 89
endometrium layer, 86f, 89, 311f
hysterectomy and, 100–101, 108
internal reproductive structures and, 108
intrauterine insemination and, 298, 320
myometrium layer, 89
perimetrium layer, 89
position of, 89
retroflexed, 89
surgery, and removal of, 100–101

Vagina. See also Vaginal lubrication
anatomy of, 85–87, 86f, 108
and arousal, sexual, 83, 87, 145, 163
bacterial vaginosis and, 412t, 431–32, 458
chemical balance of, 88
contraceptives, and vaginal ring (NuvaRing), 274, 274f, 290
devices for measuring sexual arousal in, 39, 39f, 43
douching practices and, 88
dyspareunia and, 383
Grafenberg spot (G spot) and, 87–88, 108, 155, 156f, 163
health issues and, 88
hymen and, 83, 108
and infections, vaginal, 430–33, 458
and introitus, vaginal, 78f, 84, 108
intromission and, 230
mucosa and, 87
and myograph, vaginal, 39, 39f
and opening, vaginal, 86f
and orgasms, vaginal, 26, 28, 36–37, 154, 163
penile-vaginal intercourse, 123, 124, 126, 128, 131
pH levels and, 87
and photoplethysmography, vaginal, 39, 39f
rugae and, 87
and secretions, vaginal, 88, 145
self-exam of, 86
sex-reassignment procedures and, 65
speculum and, 89

and spermicides, vaginal, 278–79, 279f, 290, 291
stimulation during intercourse and, 83
vaginismus, 383–84, 399–400, 406, 407
vaginitis and, 99–100, 108, 430–31
vasocongestion and, 87, 93, 150–51
The Vagina Monologues (Ensler), 88, 390
Vaginal lubrication. See also Vagina
aging and, 157, 158t, 163
dry sex practices and, 139, 439
dyspareunia and, 383
estrogens and, 135
purposes of, 87, 109
remedies for insufficient, 87
Van de Velde, Theodore, 15
Vanatinai Island, and gender-appropriate behavior, 46
Vanity Fair (magazine), 309
Variant gender identity, and sexual orientation, 62–63
Varicocele, and male infertility, 297
Variety, love and sexual, 185–86, 187, 209
Vas deferens, 115, 115f, 117, 118f, 119f, 131
Vasectomies, and contraception, 117, 287–88, 288f
Vasoactive injections, and erectile dysfunction (ED), 402, 407
Vasocongestion, 87, 93, 150–51
Vernix caseosa, and fetal development, 312
Vestibular bulbs, 84, 108
Vestibule, and vulva, 78f, 83
Viagra, 20, 148, 355, 402, 404
Vibrators, 219, 398, 398f
Victorian era, 12–13, 23, 522
Videos, 19–20, 473, 518. See also specific films
The Vindication of the Rights of Women (Wollstone-craft), 12
Violence, 17, 35, 37. See also Rape
Viral hepatitis, 412t, 429–30, 458
Viral infections, 411–12t, 422–30, 458
Viral load, and HIV, 440, 459
Virgin Mary, and traditions of sexuality, 11, 12–13; 23
Virginity, 83, 108, 332
Virtually Normal: An Argument About Homosexuality (Sullivan), 362
Vision, and sexual arousal, 143–44, 162
VMO (vomeronsal organ), 144
Vomeronsal organ (VMO), 144
Vulva. See also Clitoris
anatomy of, 78–84, 78f, 82f, 108
artwork, and vulva shapes, 79
Bartholin's glands, 84–85
clitoral hood (prepuce), 78f, 80
flowers, and vulva-like shapes, 79
labia majora, 78f, 79, 108
labia minora, 78f, 80–81, 83, 108

labiaplasty and, 81
mons veneris, 49, 78f, 108
pelvic floor muscles and, 85, 85f, 108
perineum, 78f, 84
pubic hair and, 108, 328, 329f
self-exam of, 78, 80, 108
underlying structures of, 84–85
urethral opening, 78f, 83, 108
vaginal introitus, 78f, 84, 108
vestibular bulbs, 84, 108
vestibule, 78f, 83
vulvar vestibulitis syndrone, 383, 406

Wartime rape, 490–91, 494, 508
Waxman, Henry, 33
Western societies. See also specific countries
abortion and, 301–2, 302f
adolescence pregnancies and, 339, 341–42
adolescence sexual experiences and, 323, 334–35, 335t
breastfeeding and, 318–19
contraceptives and, 264–65
extramarital sex relationships statistics, 364
foreplay and, 140
individualist cultures, and marriage, 353–54
kissing on the mouth and, 140
marriage and, 356
maternal and infant mortality rates, 313
oral sex and, 140
same-sex marriage, and partnership benefits, 363, 363t
sexual orientation and, 243–44, 243t, 260
variations in sexual arousal and, 139
Wet dreams, 122
WHI (Women's Health Initiative), 98
White Americans
adolescence sexual experiences and, 334t
breast cancer and, 105
communication and, 188–89
douching practices and, 88
interracial marriage, 357, 357f
and menarche, age at, 330t
oral-genital stimulation statistics, 227t
and orgasms, female, 139
partner choices and, 171, 171t
rape statistics and, 486
reproduction and, 264f
sexual behavior and, 4, 33, 35, 35t
Who Wants to Marry a Multimillionaire? (television program), 363, 521
WHO (World Health Organization), 318, 334, 377, 390, 436
Whore/Madonna dichotomy, and traditions of sexuality, 12–13
Why Marriages Succeed or Fail (Gottman), 358

## TO THE OWNER OF THIS BOOK:

I hope that you have found *Our Sexuality, 10th Edition*, useful. So that this book can be improved in a future edition, would you take the time to complete this sheet and return it? Thank you.

School and address: _____

_____

Department: _____

Instructor's name: _____

1. What I like most about this book is: _____

_____

_____

2. What I like least about this book is: _____

_____

_____

3. My general reaction to this book is: _____

_____

_____

4. What is your reaction to the accompanying CD-ROM? Did you find it useful?_____

_____

_____

5. Did you use your InfoTrac account to help you with assignments or studying for this course?_____

6. In the space below, or on a separate sheet of paper, please write specific suggestions for improving

   this book and anything else you'd care to share about your experience in using this book.

_____

_____

_____

_____

_____

_____

## BUSINESS REPLY MAIL

FIRST-CLASS MAIL      PERMIT NO. 34      Belmont CA

POSTAGE WILL BE PAID BY ADDRESSEE

Attn: *Rachel Guzman, Psychology*

Wadsworth

10 Davis Drive

Belmont, CA 94002

OPTIONAL:

Your name: _____    Date: _____

May we quote you, either in promotion for *Our Sexuality, 10th Edition,* or in future publishing ventures?

Yes: _____    No: _____

Sincerely yours,

*Bob Crooks*
*Karla Baur*